Index to the Catalogue of a Portion of the Public Library of the City of Boston,

Arranged in the Lower hall

Unknown

Alpha Editions

This edition published in 2020

ISBN : 9789354027765

Design and Setting By
Alpha Editions
email - alphaedis@gmail.com

PREFATORY NOTICE.

THE first Catalogue of the Public Library was printed in 1854, and contained the titles of about twelve thousand volumes. Of these, less than one half could be regarded as well fitted for general circulation. But the rest, most of which were donations, were often of great value, and all of them were desirable for fulfilling the wide purposes of such an institution.

The present Catalogue, or rather Index, contains the titles of about fifteen thousand volumes, all placed for the convenience of easy use in the lower hall of the Library Building, and all believed to be well fitted for free and general circulation. As a popular circulating Library, therefore, the collection now offered to the public contains probably three times as many desirable books as the one offered four or five years ago.

About fourteen thousand of the volumes embraced in it are in the English language, and the remaining thousand consists of books of general interest and a popular character, in French, German and Italian. It is not, however, even for its especial purpose, supposed to be a perfect collection. Far from it. But it is believed to be a collection begun and well advanced on the true principle of a Free Public Library; — that of providing, first, by interesting, wholesome and useful reading, for the intellectual, moral, and religious progress of those portions of our community that are not so able as they may desire to be, to provide such reading for themselves and for their families. Time, however, as the Trustees believe, is alone needed to make this part of the Library all that can be desired. A very large proportion of the books contained in it has been purchased by the Trustees with careful reference to the widest and freest circulation. They have been bought, in a large degree, from funds or from the income of funds given by the benefactors of the Library, but also from funds furnished annually by the liberality of the City Government. It has been the desire of the Trustees to make this part of the Library as ample, as attractive and as useful as possible.

The remainder, which is in the large upper hall, consists of above fifty thousand volumes, and has come to us almost entirely by donation, but chiefly from the munificence of our great benefactor, Mr. Bates, who — over and above his original gift of fifty thousand dollars, the income of which for the last five years has been devoted, as he required it should be, to the purchase of "books of permanent value and authority," — has more recently given the city between twenty and thirty thousand volumes of other valuable and often very costly books, selected on the same wise principle. Nor does he stop with such beneficence, but from month to month continues to afford us fresh proofs of his desire to promote the welfare of an institution for which he first laid a sure and sufficient foundation, and to which he first gave a guiding and decisive impulse. Many of the books in this large and important portion of the Library are more or less fitted for circulation, and destined to it, like those in the lower hall. The preparation of a catalogue of all of them is far advanced, and the index to it will be published without unnecessary delay. But it has been thought advisable by the Trustees not to postpone the circulation of the books in the lower hall until the catalogue of the books in the upper hall can be completed, and its index carried with the needful care through the press. They are quite aware that the institution has become too important to large masses of our citizens and their families, to permit any of its resources to remain inaccessible for a day after it has become possible to open them for use.

It will be observed that the catalogue now published is entitled "An Index." The larger one, when published, will probably offer a title-page of no higher pretensions. The main catalogue, as the annual reports have heretofore explained, is much more ample and important, and is to be found in manuscript, alphabetically arranged on separate cards, indicating the contents of the Library with as much minuteness of detail, both by subjects and by authors, as the means at the disposition of the Trustees have permitted them to make it. Any person enjoying the privileges of the Library can have access to this catalogue, and, by the aid of the Superintendent or one of his assistants, can readily learn from it whatever the Library contains on any subject concerning which he may desire to make especial researches. Next to the collection of its books, the Trustees look upon this catalogue as the most important part of the Library, for it is the part by which the whole mass of its resources is opened for easy use; — the key by which all its treasures are unlocked to the many who, in this community, are now asking for them so often and so earnestly. A large Library without good catalogues has sometimes

been compared to a Polyphemus without an eye, and more frequently to a chaos, which it certainly too much resembles. This reproach the Trustees hope to avoid for the Public Library, which they desire, above everything else, to render useful.

The index now published has been prepared by the Superintendent of the Library, Charles C. Jewett, Esq., and by competent and faithful persons under his direction. It is the result of much patient labor and much practical knowledge and skill. The Trustees believe it to be well fitted to its purpose, which is that of rendering the portion of the Library represented by it, intelligible and accessible to all; — to those who are little in the habit of using books, as well as to those who make reading and study the main business of their lives. Its arrangement and details they conceive can hardly be made plainer. It is alphabetical throughout. It is, therefore, as simple in its construction as an English dictionary, and as easily used. At the same time, they have no doubt that it is sufficiently ample and minute. For not only does it give the title of each book once with considerable fulness under the *name of its author*, if known, or, if not known, under its first leading word, but the same book will be found more briefly indicated again under its *subject:* and, if need be, yet again under one or more of the principal words in its *title*. Those who may wish to examine any *subject* will therefore turn to the subject itself in its alphabetical order and place, and will see, at once, what the Library offers for their especial purpose; — those who know only the *title* of the book they need, will seek it under one of its prominent words; — and those who wish to find a given *author*, will simply look for his name. It is, in fact, an unpretending piece of practical bibliography adapted to the wants, not of scholars, but of the mass of the people, and intended as much as possible to render the use of the Library pleasant and profitable. At the same time, it will serve to direct students whose pursuits may demand researches either more minute, or more comprehensive, to the ampler catalogue on the cards, where they will, with equal ease, find a notice of every thing the Library can give them.

The Trustees feel under no small obligations to Mr. Jewett for the excellent manner in which this index and the catalogue on which it is founded have been prepared, and for the great amount of labor, both in season and out of season, which he has most faithfully bestowed on both of them. The system adopted is substantially the system explained by him in a pamphlet which he published several years ago; but when the catalogue of the Public Library was originally undertaken, there was no thought that the institution would ever be indebted to his services, and no reason whatever existed for selecting Mr. Jewett's system in preference to any other, except that it was believed to be the best and the most practical for the purposes to which it was here to be applied.

But while the Trustees offer this statement of the condition of the Library, and of the catalogues by which its use is to be made easy and agreeable to the public, they do not wish to be understood as claiming the institution itself to be all they would gladly have it. Private munificence has, indeed, in a comparatively short time, made the collection of its books large and respectable, and its catalogues, by the zeal and fidelity of those employed to make them, have been prepared — so far as they are yet prepared — with extraordinary rapidity and success. Taken together it is hoped they may prove to be the foundation of a good Library, with a good apparatus to promote or ensure its usefulness. But the Trustees do not suppose that the institution as yet is anything more or anything better than this statement implies. Many important books will be sought for in vain on its shelves and in its catalogues by those who examine them with intelligence and with care. These books will, no doubt, be purchased as fast as the funds at the disposal of the Trustees will permit, so that, in time, the whole Library may become in every department of human knowledge such a Library as the City of Boston ought to have, and such as its citizens not only ask for, but will faithfully use for their own benefit and for the advancement of the city's character and prosperity. To reach this most desirable end, and to reach it at no distant day, the Trustees rely confidently on the beneficence of the patrons and friends of the Library, who have already done so much for it; on the interest felt in it by our citizens generally, who, with their families, daily enjoy its great privileges; and on the City Government, which never ceases to feel the paramount duty of protecting and fostering whatever promotes the education and the moral advancement of the whole community.

EDWARD EVERETT,
GEO. TICKNOR,
JOHN P. BIGELOW,
NATH. B. SHURTLEFF,
W. W. GREENOUGH,
GEORGE DENNIE,
HENRY W. HAYNES.

PUBLIC LIBRARY, 19 Oct., 1858.

INDEX.

ABADDON: a poem. Fairfield, S. L. 349.2
ABBEOKUTA: the Yoruba mission. Tucker, Miss. 699.14
ABBOT, A. Letters in Cuba. Boston, 1829. 8° . 635.1
ABBOT, The: a novel. Scott, Sir W. 460.55-59
ABBOTSFORD. *See* Irving, W.
ABBOTT, J. The corner stone. Boston, 1855. 12° 1087.16
— [Franconia stories.] New York, n.d. 10v. 16° 738.4
    Contents. — Vol. I. Malleville. II. Wallace. III.
    Mary Erskine. IV. Mary Bell. V. Beechnut. VI.
    Rodolphus. VII. Ellen Linn. VIII. Stuyvesant.
    IX. Caroline. X. Agnes.
— General course of history to [1789.] New
    York, 1856. 8° 948.1
— Harper's story books. N. Y., n.d. 27v. in 9. 16° 739.1
    Contents. — Vol. I. Bruno; Willie and the Mortgage;
    The strait gate. II. Virginia; Timboo and Joliba;
    Timboo and Fanny. III. The little Louvre; Prank;
    Emma. IV. Harper establishment; Franklin; The
    studio. V. Ancient history; English history;
    American history. VI. John True; Elfred; The mu-
    seum. VII. The engineer; Rambles among the Alps;
    Three gold dollars. VIII. The Gibraltar gallery; The
    alcove; Dialogues. IX. The great elm; Aunt Marga-
    ret; Vernon.
— Harper establishment. N. Y., n.d. 16° . . . 739.2
— History of Alexander the G. N. Y., n.d. 16° 549.1-4
— - Alfred of England. N. Y., 1849. 16° . . 559.1-5
— - Charles I. of England. N. Y., n.d. 16° . 559.18-21
— - Charles II. of England. N. Y., 1852. 16° . 559.22-24
— - Cleopatra. New York, n.d. 16° 549.5-10
— - Cyrus the Great. New York, 1852. 16° . 549.11-13
— - Darius the Great. New York, n.d. 16° . 549.15-16
— - Q. Elizabeth. New York, 1854. 16° . . . 559.1-6
— - Hannibal. New York, n.d. 16° 549.14
— - Julius Cæsar. New York, 1852. 16° . . 549.17-18
— - Mary Q. of Scots. New York, 1854. 16°. 559.7-12
— - Nero. New York, 1853. 16° 549.19
— - Pyrrhus. New York, 1854. 16° 549.20-24
— - Richard I. of England. N. Y., 1857. 16°. 559.8-12
— - Richard II. of England. N. Y., 1858. 16° 579.8-12
— - Richard III. of England. N. Y., 1858. 16° 579.13-17
— - Romulus. New York, 1852. 16° 549.27-28
— - William the Conq. N. Y., n.d. 16° . . . 559.6-7
— - Xerxes the Great. N. Y., 1852. 16° . . 549.25-26
— Rollo on the Atlantic. Boston, n.d. 16° . . 659.1-4
— - in London. Boston, 1858. 16° 659.5-7
— - in Paris. Boston, 1854. 16° 659.8
— - in Switzerland. Boston, 1854. 16° . . . 659.9-11
— - in Geneva. Boston, 1857. 16° 659.12-16
— - in Holland. Boston, 1857. 16° 659.17-21
— - on the Rhine. Boston, 1857. 16° 659.22-24
— Springfield Armory. n.p., n.d. 16° 738.5-7
— Summer in Scotland. New York, 1848. 12° 647.18-21
— Way to do good. New York, [1852.] 12° . 1087.6
— Young Christian. New York, [1851.] 12° . . 1087.7
ABBOTT, J. S. C. Child at home. N. Y., n.d. 16° 1109.14
— History of Henry IV. of Fr. N. Y., 1856. 16° 559.13-17
— - Hernando Cortez. N. Y., 1855. 16° . . . 579.1-5
— - Josephine. New York, 1854. 16° . . . 539.17-22
— - King Philip. New York, 1857. 16° . . . 579.7
— - Maria Antoinette. New York, 1854. 16°. 569.13-16
— - Mme. Roland. New York, 1853. 16°. . 569.23-27
— Mother at home. New York, n.d. 16° . . . 119.12
— Napoleon at St. Helena. New York, 1855. 8° 602.2-4
— Napoleon Bonaparte. N. Y., 1855-6. 2v. 8°. 601.1-8
ABDUL MEDJID. *See* Gilson, A. Czar and sultan. 918.16
ABDY, E. S. Journal in the United States, 1833-4.
    London, 1835. 3v. 8° 629.7

ABEL, F. A. and Bloxham, C. L. Handbook of
    chemistry. Pref. by Dr. Hofmann. Philad.,
    1854. 8° 156.3
ABELL, L. G. The skillful housewife's book. N.
    York, 1855. 12° 188.29
ABERCROMBIE, J. Intellectual powers, rev. ed.
    with add. by J. Abbott. N. Y., 1853. 12° . 124.20-21
— Intellectual powers. New York, n.d. 18° . 810.46
— The moral feelings. New York, 1848. 18° . . 810.57
ABERNETHY, J. Memoirs of. Macilwain, G. . . 588.8
ABIPONES of Paraguay, Acc't of. Dobrizhoffer, M. 266.2
ABOLITION. *See* Slavery.
ABORIGINES of Am., Manners of. Nuttall, T. . . 624.8
— of the U. S., Acc't of. Sanford, E. 305.1
— of N. Eng., Hist. of. Thacher, J. 227.11
ABORTION, Causes and treatm't of. Whitehead, J. 153 3
ABOUT, E. Germaine. Paris, 1857. 12° 1078.15
— La Grèce contemporaine. 2d ed. Paris, 1855. 12° 1078.54
— Greece and the Greeks, transl. N. Y., 1857. 12° 918.15
— Tolla: a tale of mod. Rome. Boston, 1856. 16° 478.13
ABRADATES and Panthea: a poem. Atherstone,
    E. 349.9-10
ABRANTES, Duchesse d'. *See* Junot, Mme. L. P.
ABUSE, School of. Gosson, S. 342.2
ABYSSINIA. Gobat, S. Three years in 697.7
— Johnston, C. Travels in Southern 697.1
— Parkyns, M. Life in 697.5-6
— Russell, M. History, etc., of 810.61
ACADIAN geology. Dawson, J. W. 163.23
ACCUM, F. Chemical tests. 3d ed. Lond., 1820. 12° 156.24
ACCOUNT of pilgrim celebration, Plymouth, Aug.
    1, 1853. Boston, 1853. 8° 224.17
ACHILLES Tatius, Romances of. Tr. by Smith, R. 844.10
ACKERMANN, Charlotte. Roman. Müller, O. . . 1013.12
ACLAND, C. Manners and customs of India.
    London, 1847. p.8° 889.2
ACTON, E. English bread-book. Lond., 1857. 12° 188.33
ACTON, W. Diseases of urinary and generative
    organs. Fr. 2d Lond. ed. N. Y., 1852. 8° 151.21
ACTON, Mass., A history of. Shattuck, L. . . . 224.20
ACTORS in the plays of Shakespeare, Memoirs
    of. Collier, J. P. 342.31
ACTORS, An apology for. Heyward, T. 342.2
ACTS of the Apostles. Barnes, A. Notes 1097.9
— Hackett, H. B. Commentary. 1093.2
    See also: Bible.
ADAIR, R. Mission to the court of Vienna, 1806.
    London, 1844. 8° 667.3
ADALBERT, Pr. of Prussia. Travels in South of
    Europe and in Brazil. Transl. by Sir R. H.
    Schomburgk and J. E. Taylor. Introd. by
    Bar. von Humboldt. Lond., 1849. 2v. 8°. 633 11
ADAM, A. Roman antiquities. Notes by J. Boyd
    7th N. Y. ed. by L. L. Da Ponte. New York,
    1836. 8° 954.7
ADAM Blair, Passages in life of. Lockhart, J. G. 769.9
ADAM Brown, the merchant. Smith, H. 802.21
ADAM Græme of Mossgray. Oliphant, Mrs. . . 753.13
ADAMS, Mrs. A. Journal and corresp. 1786. Ed.
    by [C. A. DeWindt.] N. Y., 1841. 2v. 12° 217.18
— Letters, with memoir by C. F. Adams. 4th ed.
    Boston, 1848. 16° 537.2
ADAMS, H. History of the Jews. Boston, 1812.
    2v. 12° 949.6
— Memoir, by herself. Boston, 1832. 12° . . . 599.3
— View of religious, in 2 parts, 2d ed. Boston,
    n.d. 8° 1099.5

ADAMS, H. G. Cyclopædia of poetical quotations. London, n.d. 16° 344.21

ADAMS, J. Letters to his wife. Ed. by C. F. Adams. Boston, 1841. 2v. 16° 507.3

— Works, with life and notes, by C. F. Adams. Boston, 1850–56. 10v. 8° 283.1

Contents. —Vol. I. Life. II. Diary; Notes of debates in congress, 1775–6; Autobiography; App. III. Autobiography, continued; Diary; Notes of debate in the senate of the U. S.; Essays; Disputation on the canon and the feudal law; Instructions of Braintree to its representatives, 1765; Instructions of Boston to their representatives, 1768–9; On the independence of the judiciary; controversy between W. Brattle and J. Adams; App. IV. Novanglus, or a history of the dispute with America from 1754; Thoughts on government, 1776; Report of a constitution for Massachusetts, 1779; Defence of the Constitutions of the U. S. 1778, vol. I. V. Defence, vols. 2 and 3. VI. Defence, vol. 3, continued; Discourses on Davila; Four letters on government; Three letters on the Constitution; Letters to Jno. Taylor of Caroline, in reply to strictures on the Defence; Review of Mr. Hillhouse's propositions for amending the Constitution. VII.–IX. Offici.ll.tters, messages, and public papers. IX., X. General correspondence; Indexes.

— Administration of. Gibbs, G. 285.5

— Diplomatic hist. of the administration of. Trescot, W. H. 297.5

— Suppressed history of the administration of. Wood, J. 309.7

ADAMS, J. Q. Dermot Mac Morrogh, in 4 cantos. Boston, 1832. 8° 314.10

— Letters on the Bible. Auburn, 1850. 32° . . 129.36

— Letters on the masonic institution. Boston, 1847. 8° 134.6

— Letters on the study of the Bible, with letters of Mrs. A. Adams 507.2

— Life of. Quincy, J. 512.1

— Life and Public Services. Seward, W. H . . 517.25

ADAMS, Nath'l. Annals of Portsmouth, [N. H.] Portsmouth, 1825. 8° 224.26

ADAMS, *Rev.* Nch. Christ a friend, 13 discourses. Boston, 1855. 8° 1106.3

— South side view of slavery. 127.21

— The communion Sabbath. Boston, 1855. 12° 1106.3

— The friends of Christ in the N. T. 3d ed. Boston, 1853. 8° 1083.19

ADAMS, R. Narrative of an Am. sailor wrecked on W. coast of Africa, 1810. Boston, 1817. 8° 692.7

ADAMS, *Rev.* W., *M.A.* Sacred allegories. Philadelphia, 1858. sm. 4° 1094.9

ADAMS, W., *D. D.* The three gardens, Eden, Gethsemane, and Paradise. N. York, 1854. 12° 1086.27

ADAMS, W. T. All aboard, or life on the lake. Boston, 1856. 16° 729.3

— The boat club; a tale for boys. Boston, 1855. 12° 729.7–8

— Now or never. A story for young folks. Boston, 1857. 12° 729.4–6

ADAPTATION of external nature to man. Chalmers, T. 826.6

ADCOCK, H. Rules and data for the steam engine. London, 1839. 12° 198.20

ADDISON, J. Poetical works, with life. London, [1796?] 24° 369.19

— The spectator; complete. London, 1827. 8° 873.12

— – With the lives of the authors. Phila. 1851. 12v. in 4. 12° 968.8–9

— – Selections from the. N. Y., 1840. 2v. 18° 830.2

— Sir Roger de Coverley, notes by W. H. Wills. London, 1852. p. 8° 409.1

— Life of. Aikin, L. 584.2

— – and writings of. Macaulay, T. B. 409.17

ADÈLE. A tale. Kavanagh, J. 454.1–3

ADÈLE et Théodore: ou lettres sur l' éducation. Genlis, Mme. de. 1068.6

ADIRONDACK, The: or, life in the woods. Headley, J. T. 636.29

ADOLPHE; [roman.] Constant, B. 1066.8

ADOLPHUS, J. Hist. of England, [reign of Geo. III.] London, 1840–45. 7v. 8° 964.1

ADOLPHUS, J. L. Letters to R. Heber on the [Waverley] novels. Boston, 1822. 8° . . . 868.16

ADONIS; poëme. La Fontaine, J. de 1069.7

ADOPTED child, Hist. of an. Jewsbury, G. E. . . 469.2

ADRIATIC, Highl'ds and islands. Paton, A. A. . 667.4

ADSHEAD, J. Prisons and prisoners. London, 1845. 8° 135.12

ADULTERATIONS, in food and med. Hassall, A. H. 156.12

— in drugs, chemicals, etc. Peirce, C. H. . . . 156.13

ADVENTURE. *See* American A. by land and sea. 820.68

ADVENTURER, The. Hawkesworth, J. 850.26

— *See* British essayists, v. 23–25 . . . . . . 850.24

— *See* Johnson, S. Works, I. 901.6

ADVENTURES of British seamen in the So. Ocean. Edinburgh, 1827. 18° 830.26

ADVICE to his grandchildren. Hale, M. 139.6

ÆGEAN, Letters from the. Emerson, J. 683.4

ÆSCHYLUS. Popular Eng. specimens of the Greek dramat. poets, with essays and notes. London, 1831. 24° 359.6

— Tragedies; transl. by T. A. Buckley. London, 1849. p. 8° 814.6–7

ÆSOPUS. [Fables, translated.] 16° 728.10

ÆSTHETIC papers. Peabody, E. P. 873.6

ÆSTHETIC works. Schlegel, F. von 838.8

AFFLICTED, An offering to the. Parkman, F. . . 1089.25

AFFLICTED man's companion. Willison, J. . . . 1109.5

AFGHANISTAN. Ferrier, J. P. Caravan journeys . 694.3

— Fraser, J. B. Description of. 810.68

— Gleig, G. R. Sale's brigade in 899.11

— Sale, Lady. Disasters in. 1841,2 . . . . . 987.6

AFLOAT and ashore. Cooper, J. F. 760.1–5

AFRICA. Adams, R. Western coast of, in 1810 . 692.7

— Andersson, C. J. Four years in So. Western . 697.4

— Backhouse, J. Narrative of a visit to South. 692.13

— Barrow, *Sir* J. Travels into Southern . . . 692.1

— Barth, H. Travels in North and Central . . 691.12

— Burton, R. F. First footsteps in East 692.5–6

— Caillié, R. Travels through Central 693.10

— Campbell, J. Travels in South 692.12

— Carnes, J. A. Voyage to the W. coast of . 698.16–17

— Clarke, E. D. Travels in. 682.1

— Denham, D. and Clapperton, H. Travels in N. and Central 693.6

— Foote, A. H. Afr. and the American flag . . 698.13

— Frost, J. Travels in 608.20

— Hamilton, J. Wanderings in North 697.2

— Huntley, *Sir* H. Service on the slave coast of. 698.15

— Hutchinson, T. J. Impressions of Western. 697.3

— Laing, A. G. Travels in Western 692.4

— Leonard, P. Journal on the Western coast . 699.10

— Livingstone, D. Missionary travels in South. 691.1–11

— Murray, H. Discoveries and travels in . . . 692.10–11

— – Discovery and adventure in 810.18

— Napier, E. E. Excursions in Southern . . . 692.15

— Owen, W. F. W. Voyages to explore . . 702.8

— Park, M. Voyages 820.11

— Philip, J. Native tribes of South 692.8

— Taylor, J. B. A journey to Central 699.4–9

— Wilson, J. L. History and prospects of W. . 938.1

NOTE. — See also the names of the several parts of Africa.

AFRICAN hist., Lights and shadows of. Goodrich, S. G. 939.1

AFRICAN question, The. Livingstone, D. 894.4

AFRICAN wanderings. Werne, F. 409.29

AFTER the ball. A tale. Opie, A. 469.45

AGASSIZ, L., *R.N.* Journey to Switzerland. London, 1833. 8° 663.8

AGASSIZ, *Prof.* L. Contributions to the natural history of the U. S. Boston, 1857. 2v. 4° 170.2

Contents. — Vol. I. Part I. Essay on classification. Part 2. N. A. testudinata. II. Part 3. Embryology of the turtle.

— Lake Superior: its phys. char., etc.: with a nar. of tour, by J. E. Cabot. Boston, 1850. 8° 624.1

— and Gould, A. A. Principles of zoology. Part I. Comp. physiology. Rev. ed. Boston, 1853. 12° 177.6–7

— – Comparative physiology. Edited by T. Wright. From rev. ed. London, 1851. p. 8° 816.12

AGATHA's husband. A novel. Muloch, D. M. v.II. 762.1–2

AGE, The: a colloquial satire. Bailey, P. J. . . . 339.5
AGE of gold, The: and other poems. Lunt, G. . 349.14
AGNES de Mansfeldt: a tale. Grattan, T. C. . . . 798.4
AGNES: a Franconia story. v.10. Abbott, J. . . 738.4
AGNES: a novel. Pike, M. H. 427.2-4
AGRICOLA, Cn. J. Life of, transl. Tacitus, C. C. 872.11
AGRICULTURAL chemistry. Liebig, J. von. . . . 155.24
— Nash, J. A. 168.4
    See also: Agriculture.
AGRICULTURAL engineering. Andrews, G. H. . 829.2
AGRICULTURAL essays. Taylor, Col. J. 169.12
AGRICULTURAL instructor. Murphy, E. . . v. II of 169.15
AGRICULTURE. Allen, J. F. Culture of the grape.165.19-21
— Banfield, T. C. Agriculture of the Rhine. . . 810.1
— Chorlton, W. Grape grower's guide. 165.25
— Colman, H. European. 165.9
— Dana, S. L. Muck manual. 169.31
— Dumas, J. B. Manures, nutrit. of plants . v.II of 165.4
— Eastwood, B. Cultivation of the cranberry. 165.24
— Fownes, G. Application of chemistry to. . . 819.1
— Harris, T. W. Insects injurious to vegetation 165.1
— Johnston, J. F. W. Chemistry and geology
    applied to 164.14
— - Relations between science and 164.15
— Kenrick, W. New American orchardist . . . 169.7
— Liebig, J. v. Chemistry in its application to 164.6
— Massachusetts. Manual of the mulberry tree 169.10
— Olcott, H. S. Sorgho and imphee, the sugar
    canes. 166.12
— Pardee, R. G. Cultivation of the strawberry 165.26
— Russell, R. A. of North America 623.4
— Stöckhardt, J. A. Chemistry of. 836.1
— Ysabeau, A. Plantes fourragères 1075.6
— - Arbres fruitiers 1075.5
— - Engrais et amendements 1075.4
— - Operations agricoles 1075.1
    See also: Farming, Gardening, Husbandry,
    Rural and domestic economy.
AGUILAR, G. Days of Bruce. N. Y., 1853. 2v. 12°.765.1-10
— Home Influence: a tale. New ed. N.Y., 1854. 12° 764.2-4
— - Same. New ed. Boston, 1854. 12° . . . 764.1&5
— Mother's recompense. New York, 1853. 12°. 764.6-8
— Vale of Cedars, [with biogr. sketch.] New
    York, 1854. 12° 764.16-22
— Woman's friendship. A story. New York,
    1850. 12° 764.9-15
— Women of Israel. N. Y., 1853. 2v. 12° . .765.11-15
AGUIRRE, The crimes of. Southey, R. 266.9
AHMED Ibn Hemdem. Turkish evening enter-
    tainments. Transl. by J. P. Brown. New
    York, 1850. 12° 737.10-11
AIKIN, A. Illustr. of arts and manufactures.
    London, 1841. 16° 199.17
AIKIN, J. Select works of the Br. poets, fr. Ben
    Jonson to Croly; with biog. & crit. notices.
    Philadelphia, 1850. 3v. 8° 312.1
— The juvenile budget opened: with life, by
    Mrs. S. J. Hale. Boston, 1840. 18° . . . 499.10-11
— The juvenile budget re-opened: with notes.
    Boston, 1840. 18° 499.12-13
— Critical essay on the "Chase," and life of
    Falconer. 359.5
— Memoir: with selection of pieces. Aikin, L.. 575.6
— and Barbauld, A. L. Evenings at home. Re-
    vised by C. Hartley. London, 1853. 16° . 719.11-12
— - Miscel. pieces in prose. 3d ed. London,
    1792. 8° 349.6
AIKIN, L. Life of Joseph Addison. Philadelphia,
    1846. p. 8° 584.2
— Mem. of J. Aikin: with selections from his
    pieces. Philadelphia, 1824. 8° 575.6
— Court of Charles I. Philadelphia, 1833. 2v. 8° 976.6
— - Q. Elizabeth. 6th ed. Lond., 1826. 2v. 8° 554.3
— - James I. 3d ed. London, 1823. 2v. 8° . 552.8
AINSLIE, W. Hist. of Br. India. See Murray, H. 810.51
AINSWORTH, W. F. Travels in the track of the
    ten thousand Greeks. London, 1844. 12°. 687.12
AINSWORTH, W. H. James II. An historical ro-
    mance. New York, 1848. 8° 802.7
AIR, Change of: or, the pursuit of health. John-
    son, J. 153.4

AIR, Uses and abuses of. Griscom, J. H 207.14
AIRS of Palestine: a poem. Pierpont, J. 369.17
AIRY, G. B. Gravitation. London, 1834. 12° . 146.24
— Lect. on astronomy. 2d ed. Lond., [1849.] 8° 147.8
AKENSIDE, M. Poetical works: with life. Lon-
    don, 1805. 24° 369.27
— - Same. London, 1845. p.8° 319.1
— Pleasures of the imagination. New ed., with
    essay by Mrs. Barbauld. London, 1825. 16° 258.25
— - Same. See "Poems of established repu-
    tation" 258.24
— Life, writings and genius of. Bucke, C. . . 586.16
ALADDIN: a poem. Oehlenschläger, A. G. 354.23
ALBERT et Isabelle, Histoire d' 1075.14
ALBIGENSES, Hist. of the crusades against. Sis-
    mondi, J. C. L. S. de 949.5
    See also: Waldenses.
ALBINUS. Introduction to Plato. Works IV. . . 814.3
ALBUM österreichischer Dichter. Wien, 1850. 8° 1013.3
    *Containing biograph. notices and selections from
    Nikolaus Lenau [pseud. for Niembsch von Strehlenau,
    Nicol]; Anastasius Grün [pseud. for Auersperg, Ant.
    Al. M. Graf von]; Franz Grillparzer; Friedrich Halm,
    [ps. for Münch-Bellinghausen, Elig. Franz Josef,
    Freiherr von]; Edward von Bauernfeld; J. F. Cas-
    telli; Ludwig Aug. Frankl; Ad. von Tschabuschnigg;
    Joh. Gab-. Seidl; C. F. Draxler-Manfred; Johann N.
    Vogl; Heinrich von Levitschnigg.*
ALCAN, M. Manuel du tisserand. Bruxelles,
    1851. 12° 1075.33
ALCHEMY and the alchemists. Hitchcock, E. A.. 197.4
ALCINOUS. Introduction to Plato. Works IV. . 814.3
ALCOHOLIC drinks, Effects of. Forbes, J. . . . 127.19
ALCOHOLIC liquors, Use and abuse of. Carpenter,
    W. B. 157.17
ALCOTT, L. M. Flower fables. Boston, 1855. 12° 729.2
ALCOTT, W. A. Moral philosophy of courtship
    and marriage. Boston, 1857. 12°. 127.5
— Young woman's guide. Boston, 1840. 16°. . 139.16
ALCOVE, The. Abbott, J. Harper's st. bks., VIII. 739.1
ALDA Grey: a tale of N. Jersey. 801.1
ALEPPO to Jerusalem. Journey. Maundrell, H. 684.9
ALEXANDER the Great, Essay on. Schlegel, K.
    W. F. v. 848.1
— History of. Abbott, J. 549.1-4
— Life and actions of. Williams, J. 810.8
ALEXANDER VI. Pope. Life of. Gordon, A. . . 544.2
ALEXANDER I. of Russia, Last days of. Lee, R. 547.16
ALEXANDER, A. Authenticity, etc. of the Scrip-
    tures. 5th ed. Philadelphia, n.d. 12° . . 118.4
— Founder and alumni of the Log College.
    Princeton, 1845. 12° 1089.8
ALEXANDER, J. E. L'Acadie: or seven years in
    Brit. America. London, 1849. 2v. 12°. . 626.8
ALEXANDER, W., Earl of Stirling. Life of.
    Duer, W. A. 513.8
ALFIERI, V. Commedie. Londra, 1804. 2v. in 1. 16° 1045.4
    Contents.—Vol. I. L'Uno; I Pochi; I Troppi. II.
    L'Antidoto; La Finestrina; Il Divorzio.
— Tragedie. Firenze, 1855. 2v. 12°. 1046.3
    Contents.—Vol. I. Filippo; Polinice; Antigone; Vir-
    ginia; Agamennone; Oreste; Rosmunda; Ottavia;
    Timoleone; Merope; Maria Stuarda; La congiura
    de' Pazzi; Don Garzia. II. Saul; Agide; Sofonisba;
    Bruto primo; Mirra; Bruto secundo; Antonio e
    Cleopatra; Abele; Alceste secunda; Sull'arte comica
    in Italia; Lettera di Ranieri de' Calsabigi; Riposta;
    Lettere dell' abate Cesarotti; — di G. M. Lampredi;—
    di M. Cesarotti; Risposte, ec.
— Tragedies, transl. by C. Lloyd. London, 1815.
    3v. 16° 358.26
    Contents. — Vol. I. Philip; Polinices; Antigone;
    Virginia; Agamemnon; Orestes. II. Rosmunda; Oc-
    tavia; Timoleon; Merope; Mary Stuart; Conspiracy
    of the Pazzi. III. Don Garcia; Saul; Agis; Sophon-
    isba; The first Brutus; Myrrha; The second Brutus.
— Vita, scritta da esso. Ed. arrich. di giunte.
    Firenze, 1853. 12° 1045.2
— Autobiography. Transl. with an essay, by C.
    E. Lester. 2d ed. New York, 1845. 12°. 544.6-7
— Life and adventures of. Copping, E. 544.5
ALFORD, H. Poetical works. Boston, 1853. 16° 324.10
ALFRED the Great, History of. Abbott, J. 559.1-5

ALFRED the Great, Asser's life of 846.4
— Life and times of. Giles, J. A. 552.1
— Life of; and version of Orosius. Paull, R. . 853.4
— ou l'Angleterre sous les Anglo-Saxons. Gui-
zot, F. P. G. 1078.14
— Poems of. Tupper, M. F. Works, IV. . . . 887.3
ALGEBRA. A. and arithmetic 365.17
— De Morgan. Double algebra. 147.14
— - Elements of 147.15
— Haddon, J. Elements of. 829.21
— Kirkman, T. P. Mnemonic lessons in 829.35
— Lund, T. A short course of 149.27
— Peirce, B. Elementary treatise on. 148.4
ALGEBRAIC geometry. Waud, S. W. 365.17
ALGEBRAICAL equations, Theory of. Murphy, R. 365.15
ALGER, W. R. Hist. of the cross of Christ. Bos-
ton, 1858. 16°. 1089.9
— Poetry of the East. Boston, 1856. 16° . . . 315.12-13
ALGERIA in 1845. St. Marie, Count. 698.23
ALGIC researches. Schoolcraft, H. R. 489.9
ALGIERS. Bowen, A. War with. 215.11
— Campbell, T. Letters from. 698.25
— Davies, E. W. L. Its climate and resources . 918.3
— Lamping, C. & France A. de. The French in. 889.18
— Shaler, W. Sketches of. 915.4
ALHAMBRA, The. See Irving, W.
ALI Pasha, Life of. Davenport, R. A. 379.15
ALICE: or, the mysteries. Lytton, E. Bulwer . . 465.16
ALISON, Rev. A. Essays on taste. With correc-
tions by A. Mills. New York, 1850. 12°. . 129.12
ALISON, Sir A. History of Europe from 1789 to
1815. New York, 1848–50. 4v. 8°. 943.1
— Epitome of the hist. of Europe, from 1789 to
1815. London, 1852. 8° 947.7
— History of Europe, 1815–52. New York, 1855-
58. 3v. 8° 943.2
— Miscellaneous essays. Philadelphia, 1850. 8° 863.5
ALKALIMETRY, New methods of. Fresenius, C.
R. and Will, H. 156.21
ALL aboard: or, life on the lake. Adams, W. T. 729.3
ALL is not gold that glitters. Opie, A. 469.28-29
ALLAN, G. Life of Sir W. Scott. Edin., 1834. 8°. 585.1
ALLEGHANY mountains, Letters from the. Lan-
man, C. 628.11
ALLEGORIES, Sacred. Adams, W. 1094.9
ALLEINE, R. Heaven opened. New York, n.d. 12° 1107.5
ALLEN, C. B. Cottage building. 2d ed. London,
1854. 16°. 819.29
ALLEN, D. O. India, anc. & mod. Boston, 1856. 8° 934.1-2
ALLEN, E. Narrative of his captivity. Walpole,
N. H., 1807. 12° 528.18
— - Same. 4th ed. Burlington, 1846. 12°. . . 528.17
— and the Green mount. heroes. De Puy, H. W. 528.16
— Life of. Sparks, J. Lives of em. indiv. II. 518.5
— - Same 528.22
— - Same. Amer. biog., v. I 529.1
— Life of. Moore, H. 528.19
ALLEN, J. Battles of the British navy. New ed.
London, 1852. 2v. p. 8° 825.1
ALLEN, J. F. Culture of the grape vine. 3d ed.
New York, 1853. 12° 165.19-21
ALLEN, P. Expedition of Lewis and Clarke. New
York, 1845–47. 2v. 8° 820.52
ALLEN, W., D.D. Memoir of John Codman. Bos-
ton, 1853. 8° 534.8
— Wunnissoo: a poem. Boston, 1856. 12°. . . 338.8
ALLEN, W. and Thompson, T. R. H. Expedition
to the Niger, 1841. London, 1848. 2v. 8°. 693.9
ALLEN, W., F.R.S. Memoir of Sherman, J. . 568.6
ALLEYN, E. Memoirs of. Collier, J. P. 342.1
ALLEYN papers. Collier, J. P. 342.17
ALLSTON, W. Lectures on art, and poems, ed. by
R. H. Dana, jr. N. Y., 1850. 12° 208.10
— Monaldi: a tale. Boston, 1856. 16°. 755.1
— On the works and genius of. Ware, W. . . 208.11
ALMACKS revisited. A novel. London, 1828. 3v. 12° 769.4
— - Same. New York, 1828. 2v. 12°. 769.5
ALNWICK castle and other poems. Halleck, F. G. 345.10
ALONE: a novel. Hawes, V. 805.23-25
ALPHONSO and Dalinda: a tale. Genlis, Mme. de. 449.21

ALPS. Abbott, J. Rambles among the. Harper's
story books. VII. 739.1
— Brockedon, W. Excursions in the. 663.13
— Forbes, J. D. Travels through A. of Savoy. 663.2
— Headley, J. T. A. and the Rhine. 676.18
— Hinchliff, T. W. Summer months among the 667.14
— Murray, J. Handbook of Savoy and Piedmont 649.18
— Muston, A. The Israel of the 879.13
ALTAMONT: or the charity sister. Norton, Mrs. 802.2
ALTAR, Companion for the. Hobart, J. H. 118.10
— at home. Prayers, etc. Miles, H. A. 118.16
ALTON Locke, tailor and poet. Kingsley, C. . . . 484.13-14
AMABEL, a family history. Wormeley, M. E. . . . 416.2
AMADIS of Gaul. Lobeira, V. de. 779.2
AMALIE von Sachsen. Original Beiträge zur deut-
schen Schaubühne. Dresden. 1836–44. 7v. 12° 1025.2
    Contents. — Vol. I. Lüge und Wahrheit; Die Braut
    aus der Residenz; Der Oheim. II. Die Fürstenbraut;
    Der Landwirth; Der Verlobungsring. III. Der Zög-
    ling; Vetter Heinrich; Der Unentschlossene. IV.
    Der Majoratserbe; Der Pflegevater; Das Fräulein vom
    Lande. V. Die Unbelesene; Die Stieftochter; Pflicht
    und Liebe. VI. Capitän Firnewald; Die Heimkehr
    des Sohnes; Folgen einer Gartenbeleuchtung. VII.
    Der Siegelring; Der alte Herr; Regine.
— Dramas. Tr. etc., by Mrs. Jameson. London,
1840. 2v. 12° 876.15
    Contents. — Vol. I. Introductory sketch; Falsehood
    and truth; The uncle. II. The young ward; The
    princely bride; The country cousin.
AMARANTH, The. Philadelphia, n.d. 18° 850.28
AMARI, M. La guerra del vespro Siciliano. 5ta
ed. Torino, 1852. sm. 8° 1046.7
— War of the Sicilian vespers. Tr. and ed. by
the earl of Ellesmere. London, 1850. 3v. 12° 915.6
AMAZON river. Prince Adalbert. Voyage up the 633.11
— Edwards, W. H. Voyage up the 635.15
— Maw, H. L. Passage by the, to the Atlantic. 633.13
— Warren, J. E. Scenes and adventures on the. 636.30-31
AMAZON steamship. Loss of the 989.9
AMBER witch, The. Meinhold, J. W. 889.34
AMBLY, P. B. d'. Les cartes à jouer. Paris, 1854. 12° 1078.28
AMENITIES of literature. D'Israeli, I. 897.7-8
AMERICA. Alexander, J. E. Seven years in British. 626.8
— Baily, J. Description of Central. 266.4
— Baird, R. Religion in 113.2
— Baxter, W. E. A. and the Americans. . . . 629.30
— Beltrami, J. C. Pilgrimage in 625.18
— Biggs, J. Miranda's attempt in South. . . . 266.7
— Birkbeck, M. Journey in 625.17
— Bogen, F. W. The German in 629.33
— Brackenridge, H. M. Voyage to South . . . 633.19
— Bremer, F. Impressions of 627.2
— Buckingham, J. S. A. historical, statist., etc. 624.4
— Carver, J. Travels through North 639.8
— Chambers, W. Things in 627.22
— Columbus, C. First voyage to 214.1
— Crowe, F. The gospel in Central 1087.4
— Darusmont, F. W. Society and manners in . 624.9
— Esquemeling, J. Buccaneers of 254.3
— Everett, A. H. Political situation of 297.3
— Fearon, H. B. Sketches of 624.15
— Frost, J. Remarkable events in hist. of . . . 304.7
— Gass, P. Travels through North. 625.6
— Godley, J. R. Letters from 629.6
— Goodrich, S. G. Contes de Pierre Parley . . 1069.8
— Gordon, T. F. Span. discov. previous to 1520 259.9
— Grant, A. Manners and scenery in 878.7
— Graves, A. J. Woman in 820.61
— Griswold, R. W. Poets and poetry of . . . 314.4&6
— Gurowski, A. G. de. A. and Europe 134.19
— Hamilton, T. Men and manners in 626.1
— Holmes, A. Annals of, 1492–1826 . . . . . . 304.9
— Humboldt, A. von. Anc. inhabitants of . . . 256.2
— Jobson, F. J. A. and Am. Methodism 625.22
— Jones, G. History of ancient 254.1
— Johnston, J. F. W. Notes on North 624.16-17
— Lanman, C. Adventures in North 409.16
— Lieber, F. The stranger in. 628.19
— Long. G. Geography of 365.3
— Lossing, B. J. Anglo Americans, 1763–1788. 213.8-9
— Lucas, S. Charters of the Eng. colonies in . 305.3

AMERICA. M'Intosh, M. J. Woman in 888.23
— Macgillivray, W. Humboldt's journeys in . 810.54
— Mackenzie, A. Voyages through North . . . 625.19
— Marryat, Capt. F. Diary in 628.7
— Martineau, H. Society in 628.17
— Murat, A. A. and the Americans 297.20
— Murray, C. A. Travels in North 639.3
— Murray, H. Discoveries and travels in North 625.14
— — Account of British 820.8
— Neff, J. K. Army and navy of 215.10
— Parkinson, R. Tour in, 1798–1800 . . . . . 624.13
— Powell, T. Living authors of, 1850 . . . . . 518.15
— Pritts, J. Early history of 245.2
— Rafinesque, C. S. Trav. and researches in N. 629.11
— Raumer, F. von. A. and the Amer. people . 297.1
— Roberts, O. W. Excursions in Central . . . 830.35
— Robertson, W. History of 830.5
— Robinson, C. Voyages along the coast of
     North, 1520–1573 . . . . 625.1
— Russell, R. Agriculture and climate of N. . 623.4
— Saxe-Weimar, Duke of. Travels through No. 623.11
— Schaff, P. Lectures on 1088.10
— Scherzer, C. Travels in Central 638.2
— Shireff, P. Tour through North 621.10
— Simpson, T. Discov's on coast of N., 1836–39 625.2
— Smith, J. T. Discovery of, by the Northmen 309.6
— Squier, E. G. Notes on Central 263.1
— Stansbury, P. Pedestr. tour in North . . . 624.10
— Stephens, J. L. Incidents of trav. in Central 621.5–9
— Stuart, J. Three years in North 639.6
— Sutcliff, R. Travels in North 628.29
— Trumbull, H. Discovery of 245.7
— Tudor, H. Tour in North 638.1
— Tytler, P. F. The northern coasts of . . . 627.18
— Wakefield, E. G. Social and political state of
     England and 645.1
— Warner, H. W. The liberties of 297.15
— Waterton, C. Wanderings in South 633.16
— Weld, I. Travels through North 625.15
— Wells, W. V. War in Central 266.8
— — Travels in Central 621.2
— Whately, R. Historic certainties respecting. 868.15
     *See also the various divisions under their several names,
     as United States, Brazil, etc.*

AMERICAN adventure by land and sea. New
     York, [1847.] 2v. 18° 820.68
AMERICAN anecdotes, original and select. Bos-
     ton, 1830. 2v. 12° 216.13
— Am. anec. added to the Percy anecdotes . . . 892.3
AMERICAN Anti-slavery Soc. Slavery and the in-
     ternal S. trade in the U. S. London, 1841. 8° 127.1
AMERICAN antiquities in the west. Priest, J . . . 256.1
AMERICAN biographical dictionary. Rogers, T. J. 518.14
AMERICAN biography. Belknap, J. 820.58
— Sparks, J. 529.1
— Medical. Thacher, J. 523.11
— Medical. Williams, S. W. 523.12
     See also : Biography.
AMERICAN citizen: his rights and duties. Hop-
     kins, J. H. 134.17
AMERICAN colonies, Introd. hist. to the revolt of.
     Chalmers, G. 304.8
— Memoirs of a missionary in the North. Mus-
     grave, P. 889.1
AMERICAN criminal trials. Chandler, P. W. . . . 297.17
AMERICAN eloquence, speeches, etc. Moore, F. . 861.1
AMERICAN frugal housewife. Child, L. M. . . . 188.27
AMERICAN gentleman's guide to politeness and
     fashion. New York, 1857. 12°. 127.33
AMERICAN government, History of. Benton, T. H. 282.1–4
AMERICAN history, to 1787. Abbott, J. Harper's
     story books. V. 739.1
— Banvard, J. Romance of 228.15
— Schoolcraft, H. R. Contributions to 244.6
— Willard, E. Last leaves of 309.11
     See also : America.
AMERICAN housewife. Philadelphia, 1851. 24°. 189.13
AMERICAN institute of homœopathy. Topograph-
     ical anatomy. Report, 1850. [Boston, n.d.] 16° 158.13
AMERICAN inst. of instruc. Lect. at Manchester,
     N.H. 1857, incl. Jour., [etc.] Bost., 1858. 12° 138.3

AMERICAN liberty and government questioned.
     Ryle, T. 134.15
AMERICAN literature. Chambers, W. and R.
     Hand-book of 404.13
— Cleveland, C. D. Compendium of 404.3
— Duyckinck, E. A. and G. L. Cyclopædia of 392.2
— Griswold, R. W. A survey of literature. . . 872.12
— — Curiosities of 402.5
— Knapp, S. L. Lectures on 402.3
AMERICAN merchant in Europe, Asia and Aus-
     tralia. Train, G. F. 705.18
AMERICAN naval officers, Lives of. Cooper, J. F. 527.3
AMERICAN notes. Dickens, C. . . . . 471.16&17
— Change for. By an American lady . . . . 471.16&18
AMERICAN oratory, Golden age of. Parker, E. G. 866.3
AMERICAN painters, Sketches of. Tuckerman,
     H. T. 526.8
AMERICAN poetry, Specimens of. Kettell, S. . . 339.4
AMERICAN poets, Selections from. Bryant, W. C. 820.24
AMERICAN poultry yard. Browne, D. J. 168.6
AMERICAN privateers, 1812. Coggeshall, G. . . . 215.8
AMERICAN pulpit. Fowler, H. 534.9
AMERICAN rejected addresses. Bigelow, J. . . . 325.4–5
AMERICAN revolution, The. Bancroft, G. 212.3–5
— Botta, C. G. G. War of independence . . . 213.11–12
— Campbell, W. W. Border warfare of New
     York 217.11
— Ellet, E. F. Domestic hist. of 217.8–10
— — Women of 538.13
— Fox, E. Adventures in 219.5
— Frothingham, R., jr. Siege of Boston, etc. 214.2–8
— Garden, A. Anecdotes of 213.14
— Gordon, W. Account of 214.11
— Graydon, A. Reminiscences of 213.5
— Hinman, R. R. Connecticut in 213.7
— History of 219.3
— Lamb, R. Journal during 213.13
— Magoon, E. L. Orators of 528.1
— Marshall, C. Diary kept during 217.13
— Moore, F. Songs and ballads of 314.2
— Morse, J. Annals of 213.15
— Nell, W. C. Colored patriots of 216.8
— Onderdonk, H., jr. Incidents in Queen's co.. 217.17
— Ramsay, D. History of 214.12
— Saffell, W. T. R. Records of 216.12
— Sears, R. Pictorial history of 305.2
— Simcoe, J. G. Journal of the "Queen's
     rangers". 212.2
— Sparks, J. Correspondence of 213.2
— — Diplomatic correspondence of 216.1
— Stone, W. L. Border wars of 820.62
— Sullivan, W. Public men of 213.3
— Thacher, J. Military journal during 214.9
— Trescot, W. H. Diplomacy of 217.16
— Warren, M. Hist. of, with biog. observ. . . 214.10
— Wilkinson, E. Occupation of Charleston,
     S. C. 216.10
— Wilson, S. F. History of 216.9
     See also : America and United States.
AMERICAN slavery and colour. Chambers, W. . . 297.8
AMERICAN theatre, History of the. Dunlap, W. . 353.5–6
AMERICAN Tract Soc. Anecdotes for the family.
     New York, n.d. 16° 119.21
AMERICAN travel, Appleton's hand book of. Rich-
     ards, T. A. 639.17
AMERICAN women, Noble deeds of. Clement, J. . 538.2–3
AMERICAN Union, Guide to understanding the.
     Johnson, A. B. 297.16
AMERICAN'S guide : compr. the decl. of independ-
     ence, etc. Philadelphia, n.d. 12° 299.7
AMERICANS. Cooper, J. F. Notions of the . . . 629.12
— Lossing, B. J. Hist. of the Anglo- 213.8–9
— — Memoirs of eminent 518.11
AMERIKA-Müde (Der). Roman. Kürnberger, F. 1013.9
AMES, F. Works, ed. [with life] by his son. Bos-
     ton, 1854. 2v. 8° 524.8
AMI des enfants et des adolescents. Berquin, A. de 1067.2
AMINTA. Favola boschereccia. Tasso, T. 1047.9
AMMER, Die Familie. Sittenroman. Willkomm, E. 1013.5
AMPÈRE, J. J. La Grèce, Rome et Dante. Paris,
     1854. 12° 1066.1

AMPHIBIANS, Natural history of. Swainson, W. .   408.1
AMUSEMENTS, Plea for. Sawyer, F. W. 129.14
— Festivals, games and. Smith, H. 810.31
AMY Herbert. A novel. Sewell, E. M. 425.1-2
AMYAS Leigh, Sir: a novel. Kingsley, C. . . . 484.9-10
AMYOT, T. Old taming of a shrew. Repr. fr. ed.
  of 1594. *Also :* A merry jest of a shrewd
  and curst wife. London, 1844. 8° 342.24
ANA, Selections from the 830.30
ANABASIS: or, expedition of Cyrus. Xenophon.   844.4
ANACREON. Transl. by Th. Bourne. New York,
  1852. 18° 830.23
— Odes, transl. with notes, by T. Moore. Phila-
  delphia, 1804. 12° 335.9
ANALOGY of religion to nature. Butler, J. . .   858.6
ANAM, Some account of 825.8
ANATOMIST's vade mecum. Wilson, E. 157.34
ANATOMY. Carpenter, W. B. Physiological. . .   149.23
— Cutter, C. Anat. and physiology 158.6
— Fau, J. Anat. for artists 144.9
— Flagg, J. F. Topographical 158.13
— Schwann, T. A. du corps humain 1065.49
— Wilson, E. Human 151.4
— - Practical and surgical 153.7
ANATOMY, Comparative. Beneden, P. J. von . .   1065.5
— Owen, R. Invertebrate animals 172.15
— - Vertebrate animals 172.16
— - Forms of skeleton and teeth 177.5
— Siebold, C. Th. von. Comparative 175.1
ANATOMY of melancholy. Burton, R. 872.7-9
ANCÉLOT, J. F. A. Fiesque. Trag. 3d ed. Paris,
  1826. 8° 1078.8
ANCIENT cities, Ruins of. Bucke, C. 379.6
ANCIENT and Honorable Artill. Company. Hist.
  of. Whitman, Z. G. 294.6
ANCIENT régime, The: a tale. James, G. P. R. .   464.7
ANCIENT times. A drama. Strutt, J. 499.6
ANCIENT world, The. Ansted, D. T. 167.14
ANCRE, Assassinat d'. Marillac, M. de 1078.33
ANDERSEN, H. C. Märchen. 6te. Aufl. Leipzig,
  n.d. 16° 1035.11
— Only a fiddler ! and O. T. Lond., 1845. 3v. 12°   766.8
— Story book: with memoir. N. Y., 1852. 16°.   719.9
— True story of my life. London, 1847. 12° . .   546.23
— The two baronesses. London, 1848. 2v. 12°   766.9
— Wonderful tales. New York, 1852. 12° . . .   719.8
ANDERSON, J. Course of creation. Cincin., 1851. 8°   167.23
ANDERSON, R. Life of T. Smollett. Edin., 1803. 8°   584.9
ANDERSON, W. Mercantile correspondence. New
  York, 1851. 12° 136.21
ANDERSSON, C. J. Lake Ngami. 2d ed. London,
  1856. 8° 692.2
— - Same. New York, 1856. 12° 697.4
ANDES, Journeys among the. Head, Sir F. B. . .   889.22
— Twenty months in the. Holton, I. F. 633.2
ANDRÉ. A tragedy. Lord, W. W. 338.3
ANDRÉ, Maj. J. Causes of the death of. Smith,
  J. H. 565.3
ANDREINI, G. B. Adam. A drama. Cowper, W.
  Works X. 337.1
ANDREWS, A. The eighteenth century. London,
  1856. . . . .   988.2
ANDREWS, C. Dartmoor prison. N. Y., 1815. 12°   219.2
ANDREWS, C. C. Minnesota and Dacotah. 2d ed.
  Washington, 1857. 12° 237.10
ANDREWS, G. H. Agricultural engineering. Lon-
  don, 1852-53. 3v. 16° 829.2
ANDREWS, W. W. Eulogy on J. C. Smith 898.6
ANDROMEDA. A poem. Kingsley, C. 324.18
ANDRYANE, A. Memoirs of a prisoner of state.
  London, 1842. 2v. 12° 544.10
ANECDOTES, Original and select. *See* American
  anecdotes 216.13
— anciennes et modernes. *See* Choix 1079.14
— Dictionnaire d'. *See* Dictionnaire 1068.5
— for the family. *See* American Tract Soc. . .   119.21
— historiques et littéraires. Paris, 1853. 12° .   1078.48
— moral and religious. Arvine, K. 892.2
— of foreign courts. *See* Private anecdotes . .   1005.5
— of his own time. King, Dr. W. 588.15

ANGELA. A novel. Marsh, Mrs. A. 795.9
ANGLER, The complete. Walton, I. 177.2
ANGLER's guide. Brown, J. J. 177.1
ANGLING literature of all nations 177.29
ANGLO Amer. literature and manners. Chasles, P.   404.11
ANGLO Saxon chronicle. Bede 846.1
ANGLO Saxon grammar and literature. Klipstein,
  L. F. 404.4
ANGLO Saxons. Miller, T. History of the . . .   835.6
— Palgrave, F. History of the 389.17
— Turner, S. History of the 965.1
ANIMAL kingdom. Goodrich, S. G. Anecdotes of   169.14
— Jones, T. R. Organization of 172.16
ANIMAL life, Sketches of. Wood, J. G. 178.24
ANIMAL magnetism. Deleuze, J. P. F. Instruct. in   157.16
— Gregory, W. Letters on 124.11
ANIMAL mechanics. Bell, Sir C. 365.12
ANIMAL mechanism. Edwards, M. and Comte, A.   177.23
— Griscom, J. H. 810.78
ANIMAL products. Owen, R. Lectures on 199.16
ANIMALI parlanti. Poema. Casti, G. 1049.4
ANIMALS. Jones, T. R. Natural history of . . .   177.16
— Marcet, Mrs. Lessons on 178.36
— Swainson, W. Geog. and classification of . .   398.17
— - Habits and instincts of 408.4
— - A. in menageries 398.19
— Trimmer, Mrs. Treatment of 129.4
— Webster, N., jr. History of 177.31
ANIMATED nature. Goldsmith, O. 172.14
ANNALS of England. Oxford, 1855-57. 3v. 16°.   979.7
ANNE Boleyn. A tragedy. Boker, Geo. H. . . .   335.2
ANNE of Geierstein. Scott, Sir W., XXII. 480.27-30
ANNE, Court of Queen A. Thomson, Mrs. A. T. .   594.1
ANNUAL of scientific discov., 1850-58. Wells, D. A.   159.1
ANSPACH-Bayreuth, Margravine of. Memoirs by
  herself. London, 1826. 2v. 8° 542.5
ANSTED, D. T. The anc't world. Phila., 1847. 12°   167.14
— Element. geology, mineralogy, and physical
  geography. 2d ed. London, 1856. 12° . .   163.24
— Scenery, science and art. London, 1854. 8° .   208.2
ANSTER fair. A poem. Tennant, W. 369.11
ANTAR ; a Bedoueen romance. Asmai. 418.4
ANTARCTIC regions, Voyage in the. Ross, Sir J. C.   702.14
ANTHON, C. Manual of Greek literature. New
  York, 1853. 12° 403.5
ANTHON, C. E. Pilgrimage to Treves. New
  York, 1845. 12° 667.12
ANTHON, J. The law student. New York, 1850. 8°.   133.4
ANTHROPOLOGY, Neurological system of. Bu-
  chanan, J. R. 124.5
ANTIGNOSTIKUS, or the spirit of Tertullian. Ne-
  ander, J. A. W. 848.9
ANTILLES, Wanderings in the. Waterton, C. . .   633.16
ANTIQUARY, The. Scott, Sir W., III 460.13, 15-16
ANTIQUITIES in the British Museum. London,
  1848. 18° 209.15
— Böckh, A. Public economy of Athens 953.1
— Brand, J. Popular, of Great Britain 846.8
— Napier, J. Ancient workers in metal 199.4
ANTISELL, T. Handbook of the useful arts. New
  York, 1852. 8° 197.2
ANTISLAVERY recollections. Stephen, Sir G. . . 1089.17
ANTOLOGIA Italiana. Genova, 1846. 12° 1046.1
ANTOMMARCHI, F. Last days of Napoleon. 2d
  ed. London, 1826. 8° 602.7
ANVERS, Marquisat d'. Huydens, G. 1075.18
ANXIOUS enquirer after salvation. James, J. A.   1109.25
APENNINES, Travels in. Spallanzani, L. 676.4
APES, W. Indian nullification. Boston, 1835. 16°   249.3
APHORISMS. Bartlett, J. 878.12
APHRA Behn. Roman. Mundt, K. 1016.7
APOCALYPSE revealed. Swedenborg, E. 1084.3
APOSTLES. *See* Constitutions and canons of the   1083.1
APPARITIONS. Brierre de Boismont, A. Rational
  history of. 122.1
— Ferriar, J. Theory of. 118.13
  See also : Supernaturalism.
APPEARANCE is against her. Opie, Mrs. A. . . . 469.38-39
APPERLEY, C. J. The chace, turf and road. Lon-
  don, 1852. 8° 177.14

APPLETON'S cyclopædia of drawing. Worthen, W. E. 201.5
APPLETON'S guide book. Williams, W. 639.11
APPLETON'S hand bk. of Am. trav. Richards, T.A. 639.17
APULEIUS. Works, with Mrs. Tighe's Psyche. London, 1853. p. 8°. 834.15
— Doctrines of Plato by 814.3
AQUARIAN naturalist. Jones, T. R. 175.10
AQUARIUM. Hand book. Gosse, P. H. 178.14
— Marine and fresh. Somerby, G. B. 178.18
ARABELLA Stuart. A romance. James, G. P. R. 463.2 & 18–21
ARABIA. Crichton, A. History of 810.67
— Wellsted, J. R. Voyage to 693.3
ARABIA Petræa. Laborde, L. de. Journey . . . 685.8
— Robinson, E. Biblical researches 684.4
— Stephens, J. L. Incidents of travel. 699.1–2
ARABIAN nights' entertainments 733.2
— - Same, translated by E. W. Lane. New ed. Boston, 1853. 18°. 733.1
ARABIAN tales and anecdotes. Lane, E. W. . . . 840.30
ARABS in Spain, History of the. Condé, J. A. . . 827.3
ARAGO, D. F. J. Biographies of scientific men. Transl. London, 1857. 8° 541.3
— Éloge of Jas. Watt. Transl. by J. P. Muirhead London, 1839. 8°. 573.6
— History of my youth. Transl. by B. Powell. London, 1855. 16°. 548.20
— Meteorological essays. Introduced by Humboldt. Tr. by Col. Sabine. Lond., 1855. 8° 145.17
— Popular astronomy. Transl. by W. K. Kelly. 6th ed. by L. Tomlinson. London, 1856. 16° 149.34
ARATOR. Agricultural essays. Taylor, J. . . 169.12
ARAUCANIANS. Indians of So. Chili. Smith, E. R. 635.9
ARC, Joan of. See Joan of Arc.
ARCHÆOLOGY, biblical. Jahn, J. 1103.5
ARCHITECT, The American. Ritch, J. W. 201.1–2
ARCHITECTURAL criticism. Gwilt, J. 202.2
ARCHITECTURE. Allen, C. B. Cottage building 819.29
— Andrews, G. H. Agricultural buildings . . 829.2
— Bardwell, W. Healthy homes 203.7
— Barnard, H. School 203.3
— Bartholomew, A. Specifications for 202.7
— Bottari, G. Lettere 1049.1
— Brown, R. A. of temples and churches . . . 201.3
— Bullock, J. American cottage builder 207.7
— - History and rudiments of 207.6
— Burnell, G. R. Treatise on limes, mortars, etc. 199.19
— Bury, T. T. Rudimentary 819.12
— Dobson, E. Art of building 819.15
— - Brick making 819.16
— - Foundations 819.31
— Downing, A. J. A. of country houses . . . 203.11–14
— - Rural 203.8–10
— Fergusson, J. Illustrated hand book of . . . 203.21
— Field, M. Rural 203.16
— Fowler, O. S. Gravel wall, and octagon . . . 207.10
— Garbett, E. L. Design in 819.13
— Gwilt, J. Encyclopædia of 202.6
— - Rudiments of 202.4
— Hibbard, S. Rustic adornments 207.11
— Hosking, W. Regulation of build's in towns 207.13
— - Treatise on, from Encyclopædia Brit. . . . 201.4
— Jarves, J. J. Art hints 208.16
— Law, H. Manuel de construction 1075.32
— Leeds, W. H. Orders of 819.12
— Memes, J. S. History of 830.48
— Moseley, H. Mechanical principles of 203.20
— Nicholson, P. Principles of 202.5
— - Student's instructor in 203.22
— Ruskin, J. Lectures on 206.2
— - Seven lamps 208.24
— Scott, G. G. Secular and domestic 203.17
— Schayes, A. G. B. A. en Belgique 1065.47
— Turnbull, W. Strength of timber 196.10
— Vaux, C. Cottage 203.15
— Weale, J. Dictionary of 819.26
— Wheeler, G. Homes for the people 207.8
— - Rural homes 207.9
— Wilds, W. Earthen walls 207.4
See also: Carpentry, Chimneys, Masonry, Naval architecture, Timber, Ventilation, Warming.

ARCHITECTURE of birds. Rennie, J. 839.2
ARCHITECTS, Lives of British. Cunningham, A. 379.9
ARCHITECTS, Lives of the most eminent. Vasari, G. 848.6
ARCO, S. d'. Corrispondenze 1058.12
ARCTIC adventure. Sargent, E. 704.70–56
ARCTIC expedition. 1833–35. Back, G. 703.12
ARCTIC explorations. Smucker, S. M. 704.17
ARCTIC journal. Stray leaves. Osborn, S. . . . 709.7–8
ARCTIC regions, The. Barrow, J. Hist. of voyages 702.16
— - Discovery, from 1818 . . . . 709.13
— Scoresby, W. jr. An account of 702.10
ARCTIC ocean, Journey to the. King, R. 704.18
ARCTIC searching expedition. Richardson, Sir J. 704.8–9
ARCULF, Narrative of. Wright, T. 846.7
ARFWEDSON, C. D. U. S. and Canada, in 1832–34. 624.12
ARGENTINE provinces, Jour. in, 1849. Strain, I. G. 635.13
ARGENTINE republic, Twenty-four years in. King, J. A. 263.8
ARIOSTO, L. Commedie e Satire. Firenze, 1856. 8° 1049.5
    Contents. — La Cassaria; I Suppositi; La Lena; Il Negromante; La Scolastica; Commedie in versi; La Cassaria; I Suppositi; Commedie in prosa; Satire.
— Orlando Furioso. Preceduto da pensieri di Gioberti. 3a ed. Firenze, 1854. 2v. 12°. . . 1046.6
— Orlando Furioso. Tr. by W. S. Rose. London, 1823–31. 8v. 8° 345.2
ARISTOCRACY, Trials connect. with the. Burke, P. 133.8
ARISTOPHANES. The birds, with notes, etc.; by C. C. Felton, Cambridge, 1849. 12°. 357.3
— Comedies. Tr. by W. J. Hickie. Lond., 1853. p.8° 834.13
ARISTOTELES. Metaphysics. Tr. by J. H. McMahon. Lond., 1857. p.8°. 854.4
— Ethics. Transl. by R. W. Browne. London, 1853. p.8°. 824.1
— Organon: with the introd. of Porphyry. Tr. by O. F. Owen. Lond., 1853. 2v. p.8°. . 834.12
— Politics and Economics. Tr. by E. Walford. Introd. essay and life by J. Gillies. Lond., 1853. p.8° 834.9
— Rhetoric, also poetic. Tr. by T. A. Buckley. New ed. Lond., 1851. p.8° 814.8
ARITHMETIC. Cours élémentaire 1075.39
— Hipsley, W. A. applied to interest, annuities, etc. 829.20
— Lardner, D. Treatise on 398.6
— Mailly, E. Science du calcul 1065.37
— Meulder, L. de. Calcul mental et chiffré . . 1065.39
— Waud, S. W. Treatise on 365.17
— Young, J. R. Treatise on 829.18
— - Key to treatise 829.19
ARKANSAS territory in 1819, Travels. Nuttall, T. 624.8
ARMADA, The: a fragment. Macaulay, T. B. . 324.13
ARMENIA. Curzon, R. A year at Erzeroom, etc. 687.5
— Hamilton, W. J. Researches in 694.14
— Morier, J. Journey through, 1808–9. . . . . 694.15
— Southgate, H. Tour through 687.3
ARMIN, R. Fools and jesters. Nest of ninnies. 1608. With notes, [and introd. by J. P. Collier.] London, 1842. 8° 342.9
ARMITAGE, J. History of Brazil, 1808–31. London, 1836. 2v. 8°. 263.6
ARMSTRONG, J., *M.D.* Miscellanies [chiefly in verse.] London, 1770. 2v. 8° 348.17
    Contents. — Vol. I. Art of preserving health; Benevolence; Taste; Imitations of Shakespear and Spenser; Universal almanac. II. Forced marriage, a tragedy; Sketches or essays by Launcelot Temple.
— The art of preserving health 358.34
ARMSTRONG, Gen. J. War of 1812. New York, 1840. 2v. 12° 217.4
— Lives of Anthony Wayne, and Richard Montgomery. Lives of eminent men III. 518.5
— - Same. See Sparks' Am. biogr.
ARMSTRONG, L. Temperance ref. New York, 1853. 12° 127.22
ARMSTRONG, R. Treatise on steam-boilers. London, 1850. 16° 819.41
ARMSTRONG, R. G. Memoir of Hannah Hobbie. N. York, n.d. 16° 119.11
ARMY and navy of America. Neff, J. K. 215.10
ARMY on the Rio Grande. Thorpe, T. B. 259.6
ARNALDO da Brescia. Tragedia. Niccolini, G. B. 1056.8

ARNOULT, E. Pronouncing reading book of the French language. Boston, 1857. 8° 392.3

ARNDT, E. M. Gedichte. Neue Ausg. Leipzig, 1843. 12° 1034.16

ARNIM, E. von. Bettina. Goethe's Briefwechsel mit einem Kinde. Berlin, 1835. 3v. 16°. .   1034.20

ARNIM, L. A. v. Ausgewählte Novellen. Berlin, 1853. 3v. 16° 1029.1

Contents. — Vol. I. Die drei liebreichen Schwestern und der glückliche Färber; Die Ehenschmiede; Die Verkleidungen des französischen Hofmeisters und seines deutschen Zöglings; Angelika die Genueserin. II. Holländische Liebhabereien; Philander; Wunder über Wunder; Fürst Ganzgott und der Sänger Halbgott; Eurial und Lukrezia; Liebesgeschichte des Kanzlers Schlik und der schönen Sienerin; Seltsames Begegnen und Wiedersehen; Frau von Savern. III. Raphael und seine Nachbarinnen; Die Abenteuer des Prinzen Carl Stuart; Die Majoratsherren; Martin Marter; Die zerbrochene Postkutsche.

ARNOLD, B. Life of. Sparks, J. Am. biogr. III.   529.1

ARNOLD, M. Poems. New ed. Boston, 1853. 16°   325.11

ARNOLD, T. Introd. lectures on mod. history. Ed. by H. Reid. Fr. 2d Lond. ed. N.Y., 1852. 12°   947.11

— History of Rome. Fr. last London ed. New York, 1846. 2v. 8° 953.2

— - Same. New York, 1853. 8° 953.3

— Later Rom. commonwealth. N. Y., 1846. 8°   956.3

— Miscel. works. 1st Am. ed., with additional essays. New York, 1845. 8° 1083.14

Contents. — The church; Oxford malignants and Dr. Hampden; Christian duty of conceding the Roman Catholic claims; Church of England; Tracts for the times; Divisions and mutual relation of knowledge; Social progress of states; Rugby school; Use of the classics; Discipline of the public schools; Early Roman history; Social condition of the operative classes; Christian politics; National church establishments.

— Sermons in Rugby school. N. Y., 1846. 12°.   137.32

— Life and correspondence. Stanley, A. P.   574.2-3

ARNOLD, W. D. Oakfield. A novel. 2d ed. London, 1854. 2v. p.8° 418.6

— - Same. Boston, 1855. 12° 418.7

ARNOT, W. Race for riches. Pref. and notes by S. Colwell. Philadelphia, 1853. 12° 127.7

ARNOTT, N. Elements of physics. 2d Am. ed. by I. Hays. Philadelphia, 1831. 8° 145.10

— - Same. New ed. Philadelphia, 1848. 8° .   146.1

ARRAH Neil. A romance. James, G. P. R. 463.3-4

ARRINGTON, A. W. Rangers and regulators of the Tanaha. New York, n.d. 12° 488.4

ART. Allston, W. Lectures on 208.10

— Brande, W. T. Dictionary 135.1

— Deleutre, C. Précis de l'histoire de l' 1065.13

— Dwight, M. A. Introduction to the study of   208.18

— Greeley, H. A. at the Crystal Palace. New York, 1853-54 . . . .   198.9

— Harris, J. Treatise on 209.4

— Hazlitt, W. Criticisms on 207.19

— Howitt, A. M. A. student in Munich 207.16-17

— Jameson, Mrs. A. Essays on 876.14

— - Hand book to galleries, London 208.9

— Jarves, J. J. Art hints 208.16

— Ruskin, J. Political economy of 208.25

— Wallace, H. B. Art in Europe 208.3

— Winckelmann, J. History of ancient 205.7

See also: Arts, Fine arts, and Artist.

ART, Application of, to manufact's. Mason, G. C.   197.1

ART: a dramatic tale. Reade, C. 415.6

ART of dining. 2d ed. London, 1853. 16° 189.12

ART dramatique, Histoire de l'. Baron, A. 1065.4

ART militaire, Précis de l'. Brialmont, A. 1065.9

ARTHUR Arundel. A novel. Smith, H. 802.20

ARTHUR Mervyn. A novel. Brown, C. B. 757.3

ARTHUR, Prince. History of P. Arthur and his knights of the round table, red. into Eng. by T. Malory. London, 1816. 3v. 24° . . .   850.29

ARTHUR, T. S. The hand but not the heart. New York, 1858. 12° 416.17

— Insubordination. Baltimore, 1841. 12° 449.11

— Steps towards heaven. New York, 1858. 12°   1105.17

ARTHUR, T. S. *See* Carpenter, W. H. Hist. of Vt.   228.13

— Successful merchant. Life of S. Budgett. New York, 1853. 12° 526.21

ARTIST, Leisure moments of an. Brackett, E. A.   348.19

ARTIST life. Sketches of Amer. painters. Tuckerman, H. T. 526.8

ARTIST wife: and other tales. Howitt, M. 459.3-7

ARTIST's [Dürer's] married life. Schefer, L. . . .   416.16

ARTISTS of America. Biog. sketches. Lester, C. E.   524.14

ARTISTS of Spain. Stirling, W. 543.4

ARTS. Aikin, A. Illustrations of the 199.17

— Antisell, T. Handbook of useful. 197.2

— Ewbank, T. Ancient South American 633.1

— Fosbroke, T. D. Of the Greeks and Romans   378.3

— Guillery, E. Arts céramiques 1065.18

— Joyce, J. Introduction to the 859.4

— Manual of the. 197.19

— Novelties, inventions, etc., in 199.26

— Potter, A. Science applied to the 197.5

— Ure, A. Dictionary of 146.2

ARTS of design in the U. S. Dunlap, W. 202.1

See also: Art, Fine arts, Useful arts, Recreative arts.

ARVINE, K. Anecdotes of literature and the fine arts. Boston, 1853. 8° 802.1

— Moral and religious anecdotes. N.Y., 1852. 1.8°   802.2

ASHBURNHAM, J. Charles I. Lond., 1830. 2v. 8°   975.10

ASHMUN, J. Memoir of Rev. S. Bacon. Washington, 1822. 8° 534.13

— Life of. Gurley, R. R. 524.16

ASHWELL, S. Diseases peculiar to women: with notes by P. B. Goddard. 2d American ed. Philadelphia, 1848. 8° 151.16

ASIA. Chandler, R. Travels in A. Minor 683.5

— Clarke, E. D. Travels in. 682.1

— Fellows, Sir C. Travels in A. Minor 687.6

— Hamilton, W. J. Researches in A. Minor. .   694.14

— Malcom, H. Travels in South Eastern . . .   709.3-4

— Morier, J. Journey through. 694.15

NOTE.—For the various divisions, see their several names.

ASMAI. Antar, a Bedoueen romance. Translated by T. Hamilton. 418.4

ASSASSINS, Hist. of the. Hammer-Purgstall, J.v.   937.4

ASSASSINS of the east. 849.5

See Secret societies.

ASSAYING. Mitchell, J. Manual of 144.10

— Overman, F. A. and mining 197.16

ASSER's life of Alfred. Giles, J. A. 846.4

ASSURANCE, Life. Babbage, C. 147.10

See also: Insurance.

ASSYRIA and Mesopotamia. Fraser, J. B. 820.54

ASSYRIANS, Manners and arts of ancient. Layard, A. H. 685.14-16

ASTIÉ, J. F. Louis XIV. and the writers of his age. Transl. by E. N. Kirk. Boston, 1855. 12°. .   1008.10

ASTORIA. Irving, W. VIII. 367.2-3

ASTRONOMER, The practical. Dick, T. 149.14

ASTRONOMY. Airy, G. B. Lectures on 147.8

— Arago, D. F. Popular. 149.34

— Bouvier, H. M. Familiar 146.3

— Brewster, Sir D. More worlds than one. . .   146.28

— Carey, G. G. A. at the present day. 147.11

— Carpenter, W. B. 836.7

— Ferguson, J. A. explained 146.9

— - Lectures on. 146.8

— Grant, R. Hist. of physical 146.10

— Hall, T. G. Outlines of 149.40

— Herschel, Sir J. F. W. Outlines of 146.5

— - Treatise on 398.10

— Hind, J. R. The illustrated London 147.12

— - The solar system. 146.26

— Jeans, H. W. Nautical. 829.30

— Lardner, D. Hand book 147.18-19

— Loomis, E. Progress of 146.22

— Main, R. Rudimentary 829.27

— Malkin, B. H. 365.14

— Mitchell, O. M. Discov. and theories in. .   879.11

— - Planetary and stellar worlds. 146.27

— Moseley, H. Lectures on 147.13

— Nichol, J. P. Architecture of the heavens. .   144.5

INDEX

TO THE

CATALOGUE OF A PORTION

OF THE

PUBLIC LIBRARY

OF THE

CITY OF BOSTON,

ARRANGED IN THE LOWER HALL.

BOSTON:
PRESS OF GEO. C. RAND AND AVERY,
PRINTERS TO THE CITY.
1858.

ASTRONOMY. Nichol, J. P. Solar system 147.22
— - System of the world 146.12
— Olmsted, D. Compendium of 149.8-9
— - An introduction to 146.4
— - Letters on 149.11-12
— Quetelet, A. Astronomie 1065.46
— Rothman, R. W. Hist. of. Lib. Us. Kn. III. 365.14
— Somerville. Mechanism of the heavens. . . 149.38
— Universe no desert 149.6
— Whewell, W. A. with ref. to nat. theology . 826.4
— - Plurality of worlds. 146.18-21
See also : Navigation.
ATHANASIA : or fore-gleams of immortality. Sears,
E. H. 118.18
ATHEISM. Buchanan, J. Modern 1096.8
— Godwin, B. Philosophy of 1088.34
— Parker, T. Sermons of. 1086.19
See also : Theology.
ATHELINGS, The : a novel. Oliphant, M. 753.5
ATHENÆUS. Deipnosophists. Tr. by C. D. Yonge.
London, 1853. 4v. 8° 844.1
ATHENIA of Damascus. A poem. Dawes, R. . . 358.8
ATHENIANS, Public economy of the. Böckh, A. . 953.1
ATHENS. Lytton, E. Bulwer. Rise and fall of . 957.7
— Stuart, J. Antiquities of. 835.17
— Wright, F. A few days in 868.5
ATHENS and Attica. Müller, K. O. 955.7
— Wordsworth, C. Residence in 683.6
ATHERN, A. Here and hereafter : or, the two
altars. Boston, 1858. 12° 478.5
ATHERSTONE, E. Last days of Herculaneum ;
Abradates, and Panthea. London, 1821. 16° 349.9-10
ATHERTON, and other tales. Mitford, M. R. . . . 794.13
At home and abroad. Ossoli, M. F. d' 654.5-6
ATKINSON, E. W. Memoirs of the queens of Prus-
sia. London, 1858. 8° 546.1
ATKINSON, H. G. Man's nature and development.
Boston, 1851. 8° 137.18
ATKINSON, T. W. Oriental and western Siberia.
London, 1858. 8° 701.1
ATLANTIC, Rollo on the. Abbott, J. 659.1-4
ATLANTIC and trans-A. sketches. Mackinnon, Capt. 628.9
ATLANTIS, The new. Bacon, Lord 888.14
ATOMIC theory, Introduction to the. Daubeny, C. 149.30
See also : Chemistry.
ATTACHÉ, The. Haliburton, T. C. 801.1
ATTIC philosopher in Paris. Souvestre, E. 767.10
ATTICA and Athens. Müller, K. O. 955.7
ATTICA, Residence in. Wordsworth, C. 683.6
ATTILA. A romance. James, G. P. R. 464.6
ATTLEBOROUGH, Mass. Hist. of. Daggett, J. . . 224.11
ATTORNIES, Duties of. Warren, S. 134.25
ATTUCKS, C. Trial of British soldiers for murder
of, Boston, March 5, 1770 . . . . 219.1
AUBIGNÉ, J. H. Merle d'. See Merle d' Aubigné.
AUDUBON, J. J. Adventures and discoveries. St.
John, Mrs. H. 529.2
AUERBACH, B. Dichter u. Kaufmann. Mannheim,
1855. 16° 1037.4
— Schwarzwälder Dorfgeschichten. Mannheim,
1855. 4v. 8° . . . . .1037.1&3
— Spinoza, ein Denkerleben. Mannheim, 1855.
sm. 8° 1037.2
— The professor's lady. Translated by M. How-
itt. New York, n.d. 8° 802.18
AUGER, E. Voyage en Californie. Paris, 1851. 12° 1078.53
AUGUSTINUS, St. Schaff, P. 544.17
AUGUSTUS, Reign of. Arnold, T. 956.3
AULDJO, J. Visit to Constantinople and the
Greek Islands. London, 1835. 8° 685.4
AULICUS Coquinariæ. Secret history of court of
James I, vol. II 552.6
AULNOY, Ctesse d'. Cabinet des Fées. II. Contes
des fées. III.—V. Fées à la mode. VI.
Les chevaliers errans et la génie fa-
milier. 1077.1
AUNT Margaret. Abbott, J. 739.1
AURELIAN, or Rome in the third century. Ware,W. 808.10
AURICULAR confession, History of. Lasteyrie,
C. P. de. 1098.10
AUSCULTATION, Student's aid to. Bowditch, H. I. 153.10

AUSTEN, J. Novels. London, 1853. 5v. 16° . . 758.3
Contents — Vol. I. Sense and sensibility. II. Pride
and prejudice. III. Emma. IV. Mansfield park.
V. Northanger abbey, and Persuasion.
— Mansfield park. A novel. London, 1847. 16° 758.5-6
— Pride and prejudice. A novel. London, 1853. 16° 758.7
— Sense and sensibility. A novel. London,
1846. 16° 758.4
— - Same. New York, 1856. 12° 758.2
AUSTIN, B. jr. Constitutional republicanism. Bos-
ton, 1803. 8° 297.11
AUSTIN, J. T. Life of E. Gerry. Boston, 1828-29.
2v. 8° 513.11
AUSTIN, S. Germany, 1760 to 1814. Lond., 1854. 12° 667.15
— Girls' schools and the training of working
women. London, 1857. 12° 137.23
— Goethe and his contemporaries. 2d ed. Lon-
don, 1836. 12° 897.9
AUSTIN, Wm. Letters from London, 1802 & 1803.
Boston, 1804. 8° 647.2
AUSTRALASIAN colonies, Residence in the. Mun-
dy, G. C. 705.1
AUSTRALIA. Grey, G. Expeditions in. 705.4
— Hargraves, E. H. A. and its gold fields . . . 958.7
— Haygarth, H. W. Bush life in. 889.21
— Meredith, Mrs. C. Nine years in. 707.10
— Rise and progress of 705.15
— Sidney, S. Three colonies of 705.2
AUSTRALIAN backwoods, Sixteen years in. . . . 850.10
AUSTRALIAN colonies. Hughes, W. Origin and
condition of the. 409.11
AUSTRALIAN Crusoes. Rowcroft, C. 737.7
AUSTRALIAN gold discoveries. Stirling, P. J. . . 136.12
AUSTRALIAN gold fields. Wathen, G. H. Geology 707.15
AUSTRIA. Coxe, W. History of the house of . . 828.2
— Kohl, J. G. Vienna, Prague, Hungary, etc. . 667.2
— Murray, J. Handbook for So. Germany . . 649.5
— Stiles, W. H. A. in 1848-49 . . . . 924.2
— Sutton, R. Lexington papers. Courts of Lon-
don and Vienna. 17th century 975.11
— Turnbull, P. E. Austria 667.1
— Vehse, E. Court of 927.10
— Wilde, W. R. Scientific institutions of . . . 667.17
AUSTRIAN dungeons in Italy. Orsini, F. 919.7
AUSTRIAN empire. Russell, J. Tour in 663.5
AUSTRIAN poets. Album österreichischer Dichter 1013.3
AUTHENTIC details of the Valdenses. London,
1827. 8° 1096.1
AUTHORS, Calamities of. D'Israeli, I. 897.5-6
AUTOBIOGRAPHY. See Biography.
AUTOGRAPHS for freedom. Stowe, H. B. 899.23
AUTUMNAL leaves. Tales and sketches. Child,
L. M. 488.12
AUVERGNE, Pilgrimage to. Costello, L. S. 654.1
AVA and the Burmese, Account of 825.8
AVA, Embassy to. Symes, M. 696.6
AVILLION and other tales. Muloch, D. M. 762.1-2
AVON, The. Rambles by rivers. Thorne, J. H. . 850.18
AVVENTUROSO Ciciliano. Romanzo storico. Bu-
sone da Gubbio. 1059.8
AWFUL disclosures of the Hotel Dieu nunnery,
Montreal. Monk, M. 1098.24
AXEL and Anna : a tale. Bremer, F. 817.5-6
AYDER Ali Khan. See Hyder Ali Khan.
AYESHA, the maid of Kars : a novel. Morier, J. . 418.3
AYRSHIRE legatees : a novel. Galt, J. 788.8
AYTOUN, W. E. Ballads of Scotland. Edinburgh,
1858. 2v. p.8° 375.1
— Bothwell : a poem. Boston, 1856. 12° 334.2-5
— Life and times of Richard I. Lond., 1840. 16° 379.1
AZEGLIO, M d'. Ettore fieramosca ossia la disfida
di Barletta. Firenze, 1850. 12° 1056.19
— Florence betrayed. Boston, 1854. 12° 478.9
— Niccolò de' Lapi. Firenze, 1850. 12° 1056.21

BABBAGE, C. Economy of machinery and manu-
factures. 4th ed. London, 1846. 12° . . . 198.30
— Institutions for the assurance of lives. Lon-
don, 1826. 8° 147.10
BABYLON. Layard, A. H. Discoveries in . . . 685.12-13
— Rich, C. J. Journey to, in 1811 . . . . 694.8

BACHE, F. *See* Wood, G. B. Dispensatory . . . 151.12
BACHELOR of the Albany. A novel. Savage, M. W. 438.1–3
BACHELORS, The, and other tales. Knapp, S. L. . 498.12
BACK, G. Arctic land expedition, 1833–35. London, 1836. 8° 703.12
BACKHOUSE, J. Visit to the Mauritius and South Africa. London, 1844. 8° 692.13
BACON, D. Philosophy of the plays of Shakspere unfolded. Pref. by N. Hawthorne. Boston, 1857. 8° 353.3
BACON, E. A. Memoir of Rev. Henry Bacon. Boston, 1857. 12° 535.13
BACON, F. Essays. Also, conduct of the understanding, by J. Locke. N. Y., n.d. 18° . . 820.65
— Essays and wisdom of the ancients. Ed. by B. Montagu. London, [1845.] 16° 868.20
— Essays: with annot. by R. Whately. N. Y., 1857. 8° 901.3
— Moral and hist. works, with introd. and notes, by J. Devey. London, 1852. p.8° 858.9
— Works. New ed. with life, by B. Montagu. Phil., 1852. 3 v. roy. 8° 901.2
   Contents. — Vol. I. Life of Bacon; Essays; Meditationes Sacræ; Colours of good and evil; Miscel. tracts upon human philos.; Apophthegms; Ornamenta rationalia; Collec. of sentences; Notes for conversation; Essay on death; Advanc. of learning; New Atlantis; Wisdom of the ancients; Civil hist.; Biog.; Mis. tracts. II. Sylva Sylvarum; Tracts relat. to Scotland, Ireland, Spain, England; Speeches; Charges; Papers relat. to Earl of Essex; Theological tracts; Miscellaneous; Judicial charges and tracts; Misc. tracts, [tr. from the Latin.] III. Letters; Law tracts; The great instauration of Lord Bacon; Misc. tracts; Index.
— Works. Phys. and metaphysics. Ed. by J. Devey. London, 1853. p.8° 826.7
   Contents. — The great instauration. I. Dignity and advancement of learning. II. Novum Organum.
— Brougham, H. Acc't of the novum organon. 365.11
— Campbell, J. Life of 586.26
— Craik, G. L. Writings and philosophy . . . 840.13
— Macaulay, T. B. Life and writings of . . . 409.17
— New Atlantis. See More, T. 888.14
BACON, H. Memoir of. Bacon, E. A. 535.13
BACON, J. Life and times of Francis I. of France. London, 1830. 2 v. 8° 616.1
BACON, J. F. Six years in Biscay, 1831–1837. London, 1838. 8° 673.2
BACON, L. Slavery discussed. N. Y., 1846. 12° 127.10
— Life of Baxter 1094.8
BACON, N. Life, by Ware, W. Sparks's American biography. XIII. 529.1
BACON, O. N. Hist. of Natick. Boston, 1856. 8°. 224.8
BACON, S. Memoir of. Ashmun, J. 534.13
BAFFIN'S Bay. Voyage of discovery. Ross, J. . 703.11
BAGE, R. Man as he is not . . . . . v. XLVIII. of 779.1
BAGEHOT, W. Estimates of some Englishmen and Scotchmen. London, 1858. 8° 563.9
BAILEY, J. Life of. Bartlet, W. S. 534.5
BAILEY, P. J. The age: a satire. Boston, 1858. 16° 349.5
— Festus: a poem. 17th Am. ed. Bost., 1855. 12° 344.10–12
— - Same. Illustrated by Billings. From 3d Lond. ed. Boston, 1853. 8° 322.6
— The mystic: and other poems. Boston, 1856. 16° 344.9
BAILEY, S. Essays on the pursuit of truth, etc. Philadelphia, 1831. 12° 878.14
— Formation of opinions. Fr. last Lond. edition. Philadelphia, 1831. 12° 137.33
— - Same. New edition. Boston, 1854. 12°. 125.18
BAILLIE, J. Life-studies. New York, 1857. 16°. 548.12
BAILLIERE, H. Library of standard scientific works. London, 1847–54. 16 v. 8° *As follow:*
— Fau's anatomy of man. Plates, 4° 144.9
— Graham's elements of chemistry 144.7
— Hogg, J. The microscope 144.2
— Knapp's technology. 3 v. 144.3–4
— Mitchell's assaying 144.10
— Müller's physics and meteorology 144.11
— Nichol's architecture of the heavens 144.5
— Quekett's use of the microscope . . . . . . 144.1&6
— Weisbach's mechanics of machinery. 2 v. . . 144.8
BAILLY, J. S. Révolution Française 1079.14

BAILY, J. Central America. London, 1850. 8°. . 266.4
BAINBRIDGE, W., Life and services of. Harris, T. 527.1
BAIRD, H. M. Modern Greece. N. Y., 1856. 12° 918.11
BAIRD, R. H. Am. cotton spinner. Philadelphia, 1852. 12° 199.5
BAIRD, R. W. Indies and North America in 1849. Philadelphia, 1850. 12° 628.6
— Protestantism in Italy. Boston, 1845. 12° . . 1096.13
— Religion in America. New York. 1856. 8° . . 113.2
BAKER, A. R. School history of the U. S. See Hall, S. R. 309.10
BAKER, G. E. Life of W. H. Seward, with select. fr. his works. New York, 1855. 12° 526.3
BAKER, H. N., Mrs. First and second marriages. Boston, 1856. 12° 476.1–2
— Household angel in disguise. Boston, 1857. 12° 476.3
BAKER, J. L. Men and things. Boston, 1858. 12° 136.16
BAKER, S. W. The rifle and the hound in Ceylon. London, 1854. 8° 695.8
BAKER, T. Elements of mechanism. London, 1852. 16° 829.29
— Statics and dynamics. London, 1851. 16° . . 829.28
— Treatise on mensuration. London, 1850. 16° 829.25
BAKING. Donovan, M. Domestic economy, I. . . 408.8
BALANCE of organic nature. Dumas, J. 156.34
BALBO, C. Della storia d' Italia. Firenze, 1856. ed. 10a. sm. 8° 1046.9
— Life and times of Dante. Transl. by Bunbury. London, 1852. 2 v. 12° 544.8
— Novelle [e frammenti.] Per cura di Stefani. Firenze. 1854. 12° 1046.8
   Contents.— Di Cesare Balbo e della letteratura civile odierna; Quattro novelle narrate da un maestro di scuola; Imilda, Novella quinta; I due spagnuoli; Nov. sesta; Nuove novelle; Tre novelle volgarizzate da De Maistre, W. Irving, Mérimée; Frammenti sul Piemonte; Altri frammenti.
BALBOA, Vasco Nuñez de. Life of 539.21–22
BALCH, W. S. Lectures on language. Providence, 1838. 12° 406.25
BALDWIN, J. G. Party leaders; sketches of Jefferson, Hamilton, Jackson, Clay, Randolph. New York, 1855. 12° 518.7
BALFOUR, J. H. Manual of botany. London, 1851. 2d ed. 8° 166.17
BALIOL, M. B. *Pseud.* Diary, 1753–54. Lond., 1853. p.8° 596.4
BALL, B. L. Rambles in Eastern Asia. Boston, 1855. 12° 708.6–7
BALL, S. Cultiv. of tea in China. London, 1848. 8° 136.5
BALLADS. Aytoun, W. A. B. of Scotland 375.1
— Evans, T. Old 316.4
— Finlay, J. Scottish 316.10
— Hayes, E. B. of Ireland 316.5
— Howitt, M. B. and other poems 345.12
— Moore, F. B. of the American revolution . . 314.2
— Thackeray, W. M. Ballads 325.6
— Tupper, M. F. B. for the times. Works III. 887.3
   See also: Poetry.
BALLANTYNE, R. M. Snow-flakes and sunbeams. New York, 1856. 12° 728.12–16
BALLANTYNE, T. Biograph. mem. of T. Carlyle. 885.12
BALLOU, A. Memoir of A. A. Ballou. Hopedale, 1853. 16° 539.9
— Pract. Christian socialism. Hopedale, 1854. 8° 134.2
BALLOU, A. A. Memoir of. Ballou, A. 539.9
BALLOU, H. Nine sermons. Philadelphia, 1835. 12° 1089.4
— Sermons on doct. subjects. Boston, 1832. 16° 1089.19
— Biography of. Ballou, M. M. 535.11
BALLOU, H. 2d. Anc. hist. of Universalism. 2d ed. Providence, 1842. 12° 1099.12
BALLOU, M. M. Biog. of Rev. H. Ballou. Boston, 1852. 12° 535.11
— History of Cuba. Boston, 1854. 12° 266.5
BALMES, I. Protestantism and Catholicity compared. 2d ed. Baltimore, 1851. 8° 1083.3
BALTIC. Hill, S. S. Shores of the 687.20
— Letters from the shores of 889.29
BALZAC, H. de. Lettre et étude littéraire, sur H. Beyle 1067.28
BANCROFT, A. The life of George Washington. Boston, 1839. 2 v. 18° 519.2

BANCROFT, G. American Revolution. Boston, 1858. V. I. 8° 212.3-5
— History of the U. S. Boston, 1858. 7v. 8° . 301.1-3
— Literary and hist. misc. New York, 1855. 8° 873.1
BANDITTI of the prairies. A tale. Bonney, E. . 735.13
BANDITTI, Lives and exploits of. MacFarlane, C. 379.16
BANFIELD, T. C. Industry of the Rhine. London, 1846-48. 2v. 24° 840.1
BANIM, J. Crohoore of the bill-hook. A tale. London, n.d. 16° 469.13
— The croppy. A tale. Boston, 1839. 12° . . . 807.9
— The fetches. A tale. London, 1852. 16° . . 469.14
— Ghost hunter and his family. Lond., 1833. 12° 807.10
— Murray, P. J. Life of 586.21
BANK of England, History of. Francis, J. . . . 136.13
BANK of N. Amer. History of. Clarke, M. St. C. 296.1
BANK of the United States. Clarke, M. St. C. . . 296.1
BANKER'S common place book. Boston, 1851. 12° 136.17

Contents.— Art. I. On banking. By A. B. Johnson. II. On keeping a banker. By J. W. Gilbart. III. Byles on bills of exchange. IV. On bills of exchange. By J. R. M'Culloch. V. Forms of bills of exchange, in eight European languages. VI. Forms of notices of protest, with remarks. VII. Synopsis of the bank laws of Mass. now in force. VIII. Decisions of the Supr. Jud. Court of Mass.

BANKER'S wife, The. Gore, Mrs. C. G. 776.1
BANKING. Gilbart, J. W. Treatise on 135.5
— Wilson, J. Banking 136.8
BANKS. Hildreth, R. Banks, etc. 136.23
— McCulloch, J. R. Essay on 135.4
See also : Political economy.
BANKS, J. Life of Peter the Great. Trenton, 1813. 12° 516.21
BANVARD, J. Illust. of the life and character of D. Webster. Boston, 1853. 16° 526.24
— Plymouth and the pilgrims. Bost., 1853. 18° 228.14
— Romance of American history. Bost., 1853. 18° 228.15
BAPTISM. Chase, I. Design of 1089.11
— Noel, B. W. Essay on Christian 1099.25
BAPTIST churches, Principles and practices of. Wayland, F. 1088.8
BAPTIST missions, Hist. of Amer. Gammell, W. 1106.10
BARBADOS. History of. Schomburgk, R. H. . . 264.1
BARBARY. Chateaubriand, F. A. de. Travels. . 665.7
— Hay, J. H. D. Wild tribes, etc., of Western. 889.20
— Russell, M. Hist. and present condition of . 810.70
BARBAULD, A. L. Works. Mem. by L. Aikin. Boston, 1826. 2v. 12° 888.5
— Poems. New ed. London, 1792. 8° 349.6
— A legacy for young ladies. Boston, 1826. 12° 137.31
— Aikin, J. and Barbauld, A. L. Evenings at home 719.11-12
— - Misc. pieces in prose. London, 1792. 12° 349.6
— British novelists. London, 1810. 50v. 12° . 778 & 779

Contents.—Vols. I.—VIII. Clarissa. Richardson, S. IX.—XV. Sir Charles Grandison. Richardson, S. XVI.—XVII. Robinson Crusoe. De Foe, D. XVIII. Joseph Andrews. Fielding, H. XIX.—XXI. Tom Jones, a foundling. Fielding, H. XXII. Old English baron. Reeve, Mrs. C.; Castle of Otranto. Walpole, H. XXIII. Pompey the little. Coventry, F.; Vicar of Wakefield. Goldsmith, O. XXIV.—V. Female Quixote. Lennox, Mrs. C. XXVI. Rasselas. Johnson, S.; Almoran and Hamet. Hawkesworth, J. XXVII. Julia Mandeville. Brooke, Mrs. F. M.; Nature and art. Inchbald, Mrs. E. S. XXVIII. A simple story. Inchbald, Mrs. E. S. XXIX. The man of feeling. Mackenzie, H.; Julia de Roubigné, Mackenzie, H. XXX.—I. Humphrey Clinker. Smollett, T. XXXII.—III. The spiritual Quixote. Graves, R. XXXIV.—V. Zeluco. Moore, Dr. J. XXXVI.—VII. The old manor-house. Smith, Mrs. C. XXXVIII.—IX. Evelina. Burney, F. XL.—II. Cecilia. Burney, F. XLIII.—IV. Romance of the Forest. Radcliffe, Mrs. A. XLV.—VII. Mysteries of Udolpho. Radcliffe, A. XLVIII. Man as he is not. Bage, R. XLIX.—L. Belinda. Edgeworth, M.; Modern Griselda. Edgeworth, M.

— Correspondence of S. Richardson, with biography and observations 599.2
BARBER, J. Grammar of Elocution. N. Haven, 1830, 12° 405.12

BARBER, J. W. History and antiquities of New Eng., N. Y., N. J., and Penn. 3d ed. Hartford, 1847. 8° 237.5
— Historical collections relating to every town in Mass. Worcester, 1848. 8° 223.8
BARCA. See Calderon de la Barca 638.4
BARCLAY, J. T. City of the great king. Philadelphia, 1858. l. 8° 684.3
BARCLAY, R. Apology for the true Christ. divinity. Providence, 1847. 8° 1095.4
BARCLAYS of Boston. A novel. Otis, Mrs. H. G. 417.2-7
BARD, S. A. Waikna, or adventures on the Mosquito shore. New York, 1855. 12° 623.21
BARDS of the Bible. Gilfillan, G. 118.2
BARDWELL, W. Healthy homes, and how to make them. London, n.d. 8° 203.7
BARHAM, R. H. Ingoldsby legends. Fr. 10th Eng. ed. Philadelphia, 1856. 2v. 12° . . . 345.6
BARKER, E. H. Lit. anecdotes of Porson and others. London, 1852. 2v. 8° 584.8
BARKER, W. B. Cilicia and its governors. Ed. by W. F. Ainsworth. London, 1853. 8° . . 694.2
— Short historical account of the Crimea. Hartford, 1855. 16° 929.1
BARLETTA, La Disfida di. Azeglio, M. d' 1056.19
BARLOW, John. Connection between physiology and intellectual philosophy. 2d ed. Philadelphia, 1846. 16° . . . . v.I. of 850.25
— Man's power over himself to prevent insanity. Philadelphia, 1846. 16° . . . . . . v.I. of 850.25
BARLOW, Joel. Vision of Columbus. A poem. Hartford, 1787. 8° 314.1
BARNABY Rudge. Dickens, C. 471.1-6, 11
BARNARD, H. Education in Europe. 2d ed. N. York, 1854. 8° 137.1
— School architecture. 3d ed. New York, 1849 203.23
BARNES, A. Notes on the gospels 1097.3
— - Acts of the apostles 1097.9
— - the Romans 1097.10
— - 1st Corinthians 1097.11
— - 2d Corinthians and Galatians. 1097.12
— - Hebrews 1097.15
— - Ephesians, Philippians, and Colossians . 1097.13
— - Thessalonians, Timothy, Titus, and Philemon, ... 1097.14
— - James, John, Peter, and Jude 1097.16
— - the Revelation 1097.17
— - on Job 1097.18
— - on Isaiah 1097.19
BARNEY, J. Biogr. memoir. Ed. by M. Barney. Boston, 1832. 8° 513.7
BARNUM, P. T. Life, by himself. N. Y., 1855. 12° 526.6-7
BARNWELL, R. G. Life and times of J. De Witt. New York, 1856. 12° 545.16
BARON, A. Histoire de l' art dramatique. Bruxelles, n.d. 12° 1065.4
— Manuel abrégé de rhétorique. Brux., n.d. 12° 1065.3
BARON, J. Life of Jenner. London, 1838. 2v. 8° 573.1
BARRETT, B. F. The golden reed or true measure of a true church. New York, 1855. 12° . . 1088.15
BARRINGTON, Sir J. Personal sketches of his own times. New York, 1853. 12° 884.16
— Rise and fall of the Irish nation. New York, n.d. 12° 987.8
— Rise and fall of the Irish nation. London, 1844. 8° 986.6
BARROW, Geo. Ceylon, past and present. London, 1857. 8° 695.11
BARROW, Sir J. Autobiographical memoir. London, 1847. 8° 564.6
— Life of Peter the Great. 3d ed. London, 1839. 16° 389.16
— Life of Peter the Great. New York, 1848. 18° 810.66
— Life of Richard, earl Howe. Lond., 1838. 8° 564.7
— Mutiny of H. M. S. Bounty. 3d ed. London, 1839. 16° 389.1
— Pitcairn's island, with mutiny of the Bounty. New York, n.d. 18° 810.42
— Travels into South Africa. 2d ed. Lond., 1806. 2v. 4° 692.1
— Voyages into the Arctic reg. Lond., 1818. 8° 702.16

BARROW, *Sir J.* Voyages within the Arctic regions from 1818. New York, 1846. 12°.. 709.13
BARROW, J. Life and correspondence of Admiral Sir W. S. Smith. London, 1848. 2v. 8°.. 564.3
— Life, voyages, etc., of Sir F. Drake. London, 2d ed., abr. 1844. p.8°................ 889.13
— Naval worthies of Q. Elizabeth's reign. London, 1845. 8°.................... 564.8
— Tour on the continent, 1852. Lond., 1853. 8° 409.26
— Tour round Ireland, 1835. London, 1836. 12° 646.17
— Excursion in the North of Europe, 1830-33. London, 1834. 12°................ 668.6
BARRY Cornwall, *pseud. for* Procter, B. W. Poems 345.11
BARRY, J., Opie, J., and Fuseli, H. Lectures on painting. Ed. by R. N. Wornum. London, 1848. p.8°...................... 816.2
BARRY, J. S. History of Hanover, Mass. Boston, 1853. 8°.................. 224.13
— History of Massachusetts. Bost., 1855-7. 3v. 8° 223.3
BARRY, W. History of Framingham, Mass., 1640-1847. Boston, 1847. 8°............ 224.7
BARSTOW, G. History of New Hampshire. Concord, N. H., 1842. 8°............ 234.3
BARTH, H. Travels and discoveries in North and Central Africa, 1849-55. London, 1857-58. 5v. 8°.................... 691.12
BARTHOLOMEW, A. Specifications for architecture. London, 1840. 8°.............. 202.7
BARTLET, W. S. Memoir of J. Bailey, with pref. by G. Burgess. Boston, 1853. 8°...... 534.5
BARTLETT, E. Fevers of the United States. Philadelphia, 1852. 3d ed. 8°.......... 152.12
BARTLETT, John. Familiar quotations. Cam., 1855 344.20
— Familiar quotations. 3d ed., with supplem't. Cambridge, 1858. 12°.............. 344.19
BARTLETT, J. R. Personal narrative, connected with the U. S. and Mexican commission. New York, 1854. 2v. 8°.......... 624.2
BARTLETT, Jos. Aphorisms, physiognomy, etc. Boston, 1823. 12°................ 878.12
BARTLETT, W. H. Pilgrim fathers. Lond., 1853. 8° 223.1
— The Nile boat: or, glimpses of Egypt. New York, 1851. Imp. 8°............ 684.1
BARTOL, C. A. Church and congregation. Boston, 1858. 12°................ 1086.30
— Pictures of Europe. Boston, 1855. 12°... 648.10-11
BARTON, B. Memoir, letters and poems. Ed. by his daughter. Philadelphia, 1850. 12°... 584.19
BARTON, W. Memoirs of David Rittenhouse, with philos. and other papers. Phila., 1813. 8°. 524.12
BARTON, *Gen.* W. Life of. Williams, Mrs. C. R. 528.12
BASQUE provinces, State of the. Herbert, H. J. G. 889.8
BASS rock, The: geology and history of. Miller, H..................... 167.27
BASS's straits, Visit to islands in. Nixon, F. R.. 707.9
BASSNETT, T. Mechanical theory of storms. New York, 1854. 12°.............. 145.25
BASTARD, Der: Roman. Spindler, C........ 1026.6
BASTILE, History of the. Davenport, R. A.... 379.12
BASTILLE, Deux années à la. Staal, Mme. de... 1078.26
BATCHELDER, E. Romance of the fashionable world. Boston, 1857. 16°.......... 339.6
BATES, D. B. Four years on the Pacific coast. Boston, 1857. 12°.............. 708.12
BATES, J. Reminiscences of John Codman... 534.8
BATHURST, C. Lectures. London, 1854. 16°... 878.20
BATTLE fields, Pictures from.......... 988.5-6
BATTLE of life: a christmas story. Dickens, C.. 481.12-16
BATTLE of the books, etc. Swift, J....... 738.2
BATTLE of the frogs and mice. Tr. by T. A. Buckley. Homerus.................. 824.5
BATTLE summer, The, 1848. Mitchell, D. G.. 884.11
BATTLES of the British navy. Allen, J..... 825.1
BATTLES of the world, 15 decisive. Creasy, E. S. 948.3
BAUCHER, F. Horsemanship. 3d ed. Phila.,1856. 12° 164.7
BAUERNFÜRST, Der: Roman. Schücking, C. B. L. 1017.1
BAUERN-SPIEGEL, Der: Novelle. Bitzius, A.... 1016.3
BAUSSET, L. F. J. de. Private memoirs of the court of Napoleon, 1805-14. Phila., 1828. 8° 603.5
BAVARIA, A glance at. Inglis, H. D....... 663.15

BAXTER, R. Call to the unconverted, with introd. essay, by T. Chalmers. Hartford, 1851. 12° 1087.3
— Practical writings, with life, by L. Bacon. N. Haven. 1831. 2v. 8°.......... 1094.8
Contents. — Vol. I. Life: Spiritual peace and comfort; Making light of Christ, (Sermon); Passages of the life of Mrs. Baker. II. Character of a sound confirmed Christian; Dying thoughts; Sermon of repentance; Sermon on right rejoicing; How to do good to many; God's goodness vindicated; Reasons for ministers using plainness with their people; Extracts from the poor man's family book.
— Saint's everlasting rest. Abr. by B. Fawcett. Essay by T. Erskine. Hartford, 1851. 12° 1087.3
BAXTER, W. E. America and the Americans. London, 1855. 18°.............. 629.30
BAYARD, Chevalier. P. Du Terrail. *See* Du Terrail, P.
BAYLIES, F. Histor. mem. of New Plymouth, 1620-41. Boston, 1830. 2v. in 3...... 223.11
BAYNE, P. Christian life. Boston, 1855. 12°... 1086.12-13
— Essays in biography and criticism. 1st and 2d series. Boston, 1857-8. 12°...... 885.1-2
BAY-PATH, The: a tale. Holland, J. G...... 415.1-2
BEARD, J. R. Life of Toussaint l' Ouverture. London, 1853. 8°.............. 539.2
BÉARN and the Pyrenees. Costello. L. S.... 604.2
BEASLEY, H. Pocket formulary. 1st American edition. Philadelphia, 1852. 12°...... 153.6
BEATRICE: or the unknown relatives. Sinclair, C. 456.3-7
BEATTIE, J. Evidences of the Christian religion. 4th ed. London, 1795. 2v. 16°...... 1089.26
— Poetical works. London, 1831. p.8°.... 319.2
— The minstrel: or, progress of genius..... 358.24
BEATTIE, W. Life and letters of Thomas Campbell..................... 584.14
BEAUCHAMP: or, the error. James, G. P. R... 463.1&26
BEAUCHAMPE: or, the Kentucky tragedy. Simms, W. G................... 790.35-39
BEAUCHAMPS, P. F. G. de. Funestine. Cabinet des Feés. XXXI............... 1077.1
BEAUCHESNE, A. de. Louis XVII. Tr. by W. Hazlitt. N. Y., 1853. 2v. 12°...... 615.5-6
BEAUMARCHAIS, P. A. C. de, and his times. Loménie, L. de.............. 615.4
BEAUMONT, F. and Fletcher, J. Works, with notes and a memoir, by A. Dyce. London, 1843-46. 11v. 8°................... 351.2
Contents. — Vol. I. Biographical memoir; Dedication, etc.; Commendatory poems; The woman hater; Thierry and Theodoret; Philaster; The maid's tragedy. II. The faithful shepherdess; The knight of the burning pestle; King and no king; Cupid's revenge; Masque of the Inner-Temple and Gray's Inn; Four plays in one. III. The scornful lady; The coxcomb; The captain; The honest man's fortune; The little French lawyer. IV. Wit at several weapons; Wit without money; The faithful friends; The widow; The custom of the country. V. Bonduca; The knight of Malta; Valentinian; The laws of Candy; The Queen of Corinth. VI. The loyal subject; The mad lover; The false one; The double marriage; The humorous lieutenant. VII. Women pleased; The woman's prize; The chances; Monsieur Thomas; The island princess. VIII. The pilgrim; The wild-goose chase; The prophetess; The sea voyage; The Spanish curate. IX. Beggar's bush; Love's cure; The maid in the mill; A wife for a month; Rule a wife and have a wife. X. The fair maid of the inn; The noble gentleman; The elder brother; The nice valor, or, the passionate madman; The bloody brother, or, Rollo, Duke of Normandy. XI. The lover's progress; The night-walker, or, the little thief; Love's pilgrimage; The two noble kinsmen; Poems by Beaumont; Poems by Fletcher; Index to the notes.
— Beauties of, selected, etc., by Leigh Hunt. London. 1855. p.8°............. 837.1
— Don John, a musical drama, founded on B. and F.'s comedy of "The chances"...... 355.11
BEAUTIFUL, The, Philosophy of. Cousin, Victor. 125.21
BEAUTY. Hay, D. R. First principles of symmetrical.................. 208.20
— Walker, A. Analysis and classification of, in woman................ 128.4

BECHSTEIN, J. M. Cage and chamber birds, incl. Sweet's warblers. Tr. with additions by H. G. Adams. London, 1853. p.8°. . . . 825.6

BECHSTEIN, L. Der Dunkelgraf. [Roman.] Frankfurt a.M., 1854. 8° 1013.7

— Der Sagenschatz des Thüringerlandes. Meiningen, 1835–38. 4 thle. in 2v. 16°. . . . 1025.3

BECHER, A. B. Landfall of Columbus. London, 1856. 8°. 625.13

BECK, L. C. Botany of the U. S. North of Virginia. 2d ed. New York, 1848. 12° 166.7

BECKER, Prof. W. A. Charicles. Private life of the ancient Greeks, transl., new ed. London, 1854. 12° 957.1

— Gallus: or, Roman scenes in the time of Augustus. Tr. London, 1849. 12° 957.2

BECKET, Thomas à. Life and letters of. Giles, J. A. 575.4

BECKETT, G. A. à. Comic history of Rome. London, n.d. 8° 956.9

BECKFORD, Wm. Italy, Spain and Portugal. N. York, 1845. 2 parts in 1 v. 12°. 675.18

— Italy: with sketches of Spain and Portugal. Philadelphia, 1834. 2v. 12° 679.6

— Vathek: an Arabian tale, with mem. of the author. Philadelphia, 1854. 12° 799.14

— Vathek: 2d Am. from last Lond. ed. Philadelphia, 1834. 12°. 799.15

BECKMANN, J. Hist. of inventions, etc., transl. by W. Johnston. Rev. by W. Francis and J. W. Griffith. London, 1846. 2v. p.8°. . 818.8–9

BECKWOURTH, J. P. Life written from dictation, by T. D. Bonner. N. Y., 1856. 12°. 526.5

BEDE. Eccles. hist. of Eng. Also: the Anglo-Saxon chronicle. Ed. by J. A. Giles. London, 1849. p.8°. 846.1

BEDFORD, Mass. History of. Shattuck, L. . . . 224.20

BEECHCROFT, a novel. Yonge, C. M. 786.8–9

BEECHER, C. E. Domestic economy. New York, [var. ster. eds. 1842 to 1852.] 12° 188.17–19

— Domestic receipt-book. N. Y., [var. ster. eds., 1852–5.] 12° 188.13 16

— On health and happiness. N. Y., 1855. 12° . 158.11

— The Bible and the people. N. Y., 1857. 12°. . 1086.4

— True remedy for the wrongs of woman. Boston, 1851. 12°. 868.13

BEECHER, E. Conflict of ages. 5th ed. Boston, 1854. 12° 1106.20–21

— The papal conspiracy exposed. Bost., 1855. 12° 1098.9

BEECHER, H. W. Star papers. N. Y., 1855. 12°. 885.4–5

— Life thoughts. Boston, 1858. 12°. 1086.16

BEECHEY, F. W., Capt. Voyage to the Pacific and Beering's St. in 1825–28. Lond., 1831. 2v. 8° 702.13

BEECHNUT, a Franconia story. V. Abbott, J. . . 738.4

BEE-KEEPER's manual. Langstroth, L. L. . . . 165.23

BEES, Natural history of. Huber, F. 165.22

BEETHOVEN, L. von. Life of. Schindler, A. . . . 545.3

BEHAVIOUR book, The. Leslie, Miss E. 127.12–17

BEITZKE, H. Geschichte der deutschen Freiheitskriege, 1813 u. 1814. Berlin, 1854–55. 3v. 8°. 1013.1

BELCHER, E. Voyage round the world, 1836–42. London, 1843. 2v. 8° 702.9

BELFORD Regis: a novel. Mitford, M. R. 804.4

BELGIUM. Bell, R. Wayside pictures through. . 675.5

— Coomans ainé. Les communes belges 1075.22

— Deby, J. Histoire naturelle de la Belgique . 1075.25

— Dobson, E. Railways of 194.3

— Dufau, J. B. Hagiographie belge 1075.24

— Gens, E. Ruines et paysages 1075.23

— Hannon, J. D. Flore belge 1075.26

— Hasselt, A. v. Les belges aux croisades . . . 1075.21

— Histoire d' Albert et Isabelle. 1075.14

— Lenaerts, J. Organisation provinciale 1065.33

— Leutre, C. de. Révolution de, 1830 . . . . . 1065.34

— Moke. Mœurs, usages, etc., des belges . . . 1075.11

— Murray, J. Handbook 649.19

— Saint-Genois, J. de. Voyageurs belges . . . 1075.10

— Schayes, A. G. B. Architecture en 1065.47

— Siborne, Capt. W. Hist. of the war in 1815 . 1005.2

— Tarlier, J. Description géographique 1065.55

BELIEF, The restoration of 1086.28

BELISARIUS, Life of. Stanhope, P. H., Earl S. . . 546.13

BELKNAP, J. American biog. N. Y., 1851. 3v. 18° 820.58

— Life, with selections from his corresp. New York, 1847. 16° 539.15

BELL, Acton, Currer and Ellis. Pseudonyms. See Brontë, Miss.

BELL, Sir C. Animal mechanics in Lib. Us. Kn. . 365.12

— Illustrative notes to Paley's natural theology. Paley, W. 820.4

— The hand, its mechanism and vital endowments. Philadelphia, 1835. 12° 139.3

BELL, H. G. Life of Mary Queen of Scots. Edinburgh, 1828. 2v. 18° 830.40

— - Same. New York, 1855. 2v. 18° 810.21–28

— Late operations in the Birmese Empire. See Symes, M. 830.29

— Selections of the most remarkable phenomena of nature. Edinburgh, 1827. 18°. . . . 830.32

BELL, J. Observations on Italy. Bost., 1826. 12° 679.3

— On regimen and longevity. Phila., 1842. 12° 157.21

— Chemical and pharmac. processes. Lectures on the Exhibition 199.16

BELL, Mrs. M. Julia Howard. Romance. New York, 1850. 8° 802.13

BELL, R. [Lives of] English poets. London, 1839. 2v. 16°. 398.2

— History of Russia. London, [1836–38.] 3v. 16° 378.7

— Life of Canning. London, 1846. p.8° 566.12

— - Same. New York, 1846. 12° 566.13

— Lives of the Brit. admirals. See Southey, R. 388.5

— History of England. See Mackintosh, Sir J. 368.3

— Wayside pictures thro' France, Holland, Belgium, and up the Rhine. Lond., 1858. 12°. 675.5

BELL, Th. British quadrupeds, incl. the cetacea. London, 1837. 8° 172.18

BELLE Brittan on a tour at Newport. Fuller, H. . 635.22

BELLOT, J. R. Memoirs, with journal to Polar sea. London, 1855. 2v. p.8° 617.13

BELOOCHISTAN, Description of. Fraser, J. B. . . 810.68

BELSHAM, Wm. Reign of George III., 1802–20. London, 1824. 2v. 8° 553.9

BELTRAMI, J. C. Pilgrimage in Europe and America. London, 1828. 2v. 8° 625.18

BELZONI, G. Discoveries in Egypt and Nubia. 3d ed. London, 1822. 2v. 8° 693.12

BEMENT, C. N. American poulterer's companion. New ed. New York, 1856. sq. 12° 168.8

BEMIS, G. Report of the case of John W. Webster. Boston, 1850. 8° 133.3

BENAULY, pseud. See Cone cut corners. 428.12

BENEDEN, P. J. van. Anatomie comparée. Bruxelles, n.d. 12° 1065.5

BENEDICT, J. Life of Felix Mendelssohn Bartholdy. 2d ed. London, 1853. 8° 545.4

BENEFICENCE, The divine law of. Cooke, P. . . . 119.13

BENGAL, A year in, before the mutinies. Wallace-Dunlop, (M. & R.) 695.10

BENGER, E. O. Memoirs of Anne Boleyn. 3d ed. London, 1827. 8° 594.14

— - Same. Philadelphia, 1822. 8° 554.1

— — - Same, with a memoir of the author, by Miss Aikin. 2d Am. ed. Phil., 1851. 12° 594.15–16

— Memoirs of Mary Q. of Scots. London, 1823. 2v. 8° 594.9

— - Same. Philadelphia, 1851. 2v. 12° . . . 594.2–8

— Memoirs of Mrs. E. Hamilton, with sel. from her correspond. Lond., 1818. 2v. 8° . . . 599.6

BENYOWSKY, M. A. Memoirs and travels by himself. Transl. Dublin, 1790. 2v. 8°. . . 546.6

BENJAMIN of Tudela. Early travels in Palestine. Wright, Thos. 846.7

BENNETT, E. T. Gardens, etc., of the zoological society. Birds. Chiswick, 1831. 8° 172.20

— - Same. Quadrupeds. Chiswick, 1830. 8° . 172.19

BENNETT, J. C. The poultry book. Bost., 1852. 12° 168.7

BENNISON, Mrs. D. M. Poems. Boston, 1847. 16° 348.21

BENTHAM, G. Handbook of British Flora. London, 1858. 8° 166.18

BENTHAM, J. Benthamiana, extracts from the works of. Edinburgh, 1843. 12° 134.23

BENTLEY ballads. Doran, Dr. 316.13

BENTON, T. H. Thirty years' view, Am. governm't, 1820–50. New York, 1854–56. 8° 282.1-4
BÉRANGER, P. J. de. Œuvres complètes. Paris, 1854–55. 2v. 12° 1066.2
— Chansons. Notice sur l' auteur par P. F. Tissot. Paris, 1829. 4v. 12° 1068.9
— Chansons nouvelles et dernières. Paris, 1833. 12° 1068.10
— Two hundred lyrical poems, transl. by W. Young. New ed. New York, 1857. 12° . . 324.8
— Memoirs by himself. London, 1858. 8° . . . 613.8
BERGER, E. Charles Auchester: a memorial. New York, 1853. 8° 802.39
BERINGTON, J. Literary history of the middle ages. London, 1846. p.8° 404.9
BERKELEY, G. F. A month in the forests of France. London, 1857. 12° 654.4
BERKELEY the banker: a tale. Martineau, H. XIV. 749.2-3
BERKSHIRE county, Mass., History of 227.9
BERLIOZ, H. Essays on industrial subjects . . . 147.21
BERLYN, P. and Fowler, C. The crystal palace: its architectural history. London, 1851. 8° 205.6
BERNADOTTE, Marshal, afterwards king of Sweden. See Carl XIV. Johann.
BERNAN, W. History and art of warming and ventilating buildings. London, 1845. 2v. 12° 207.15
BERNARD. See Wright, T. Early travels in Palestine 846.7
BERNARD Lile: an hist. romance. Clemens, J. . 496.7
BERNARDO del Carpio. Translated by J. G. Marvin. Montgomery, Don J. 802.5
BERNECK, K. G. v., Die Schlachten bei Leipzig. Leipzig, 1855. 16° 1029.2
BERQUIN, A. de. L'ami des enfants et des adolescents. Nouv. ed. Paris, 1851. 2v. 8° . 1067.2
— Le livre de famille. Bibliothèque des villages. Choix de lectures. Nouv. ed. Paris, 1851. 8° 1067.3
— Children's friend. New tr. Bost., 1846. 2v. 16° 729.20
— The child's friend. Boston, 1840. 18° 729.21
BERRY, Miss M. Social life of England and France. London, 1828–31. 2v. in 1. 8° 986.4
BERRY, Miss F. M. See Wicher, Mrs. F. M. Widow Bedott papers 428.16
BERSOT, E. Mesmer et le magnétisme animal. 2de ed. Paris, 1854. 12° 1078.41
BERTRAM Noel: a story for youth. May, E. J. . 805.27
BERTRANDON de la Brocquière. See Wright, T. Early travels in Palestine 846.7
BERZELIUS, J. J. The use of the blowpipe. Tr. by J. D. Whitney. Boston, 1845. 12° . . 155.22
BESSÉ, A. de. The Turkish empire. Transl., revised and enlarged from the 4th German ed. with memoir of the sultan, etc., by E. J. Morris. Philadelphia, 1854. 12° 680.12
BÉTAIL, L'élève et l'engraissement du. Ysabeau, A. 1075.2
BETHLEM, Conn. History of. Cothren, W. . . 225.2
BETHUNE, G. W. Orations and occasional discourses. New York, 1850. 12° 865.5
BETHUNE, M. de, Duke of Sully. Memoirs. Tr. 5th ed. London, 1763–78. 6v. 12° 609.3
— Memoirs. Translated. New ed. London, 1856. 4v. p.8° 857.5
BETROTHAL, The: a play. Boker, G. H. II. . . 335.2
BETROTHED, The: a novel. Manzoni, A. 488.2
BETROTHED, The: a novel. Scott, Sir W. . . . 480.8-13
BETSEY, Cruise of the. Miller, H. 167.6
BETTINA. See Arnim, E. von.
BEVAN, E. The honey bee; its natural history, etc. Philadelphia, 1843. 8° 165.8
BEVERLY, Mass., History of. Stone, E. M. . . . 227.3
BEWEGTES Leben. Geschichten. Hoefer, E. . . 1037.9
BEYLE, H. Chroniques italiennes. Paris, 1855. 12° 1067.16
— Correspondance inédite. Introd. par P. Mérimée. Paris, 1855. 2v. 12° 1067.19
— De l' amour. Paris, 1856. 12° 1067.25
— Histoire de la peinture en Italie. Paris, 1854. 12° 1067.24
— La chartreuse de Parme. Nouv. ed. Étude sur Beyle par Balzac. Paris, 1854. 12° . . . 1067.28
— Le Rouge et le Noir. Paris, 1854. 12° 1067.17
— Mémoires d' un touriste. Nouv. ed. Paris, 1854. 2v. 12° 1067.21

BEYLE, H. Nouvelles inédites. Paris, 1855. 12°. 1067.29
— Promenades dans Rome. Paris, 1853. 2v. 12° 1067.20
— Racine et Shakspeare, études sur le romantisme. Nouv. ed. Paris, 1854. 12° 1067.23
— Romans et nouvelles. Notice biographique par R. Colomb. Paris, 1854. 12° 1067.22
    Contents. — Armance; Mina de Wangel; San Francesco à Ripa; Philibert Leseale; Souvenirs d'un gentilhomme italien.
— Rome, Naples et Florence. Paris, 1854. 12° 1067.27
— Vie de Rossini. Nouv. ed. Paris, 1854. 12°. 1067.26
— Vies de Haydn, de Mozart et de Metastase. Nouv. ed. Paris, 1854. 12° 1067.18
BIANCA Cappello: an historical romance. Lytton, Lady R. L. B. 466.18
BIBLE. Texts with and without comments :—
— The Holy Bible. London, 1848. 8° 1092.1
— The Holy Bible. Translated, with Canne's notes, [apocrypha; J. Brown's concord.; and psalms in metre.] Hartford, Andrus, 1855. 8° 1092.2
— The Holy Bible, with explanatory notes by T. Scott. Ster. ed. from the 5th London ed. Boston, 1855. 6v. 8° 1091.1
— The cottage Bible, and family expositor, with expositions and explanatory notes by T. Williams. Chronological index, etc., etc., by W. Patton. Hartford, 1857. 2v. 8°. . . 1091.2
— La Sainte Bible: revue sur les orig. par D. Martin. N. York, Soc. bibl. Am. 1856. 8°. 1064.1
— La Sacra Bibbia, tradotta in lingua italiana da G. Diodati. Londra, 1850. 8° 1055.1
— La Biblia Sagrada, trad. en español. N. York, ed. esteriotip. 1852. 8° 1092.3
— Die Bibel. N. Y., Amerik. Bibel-Gesellschaft. 1856. 8° 1023.1
— Sacred history from the scripture. By Mrs. Trimmer. 7th ed. London, 1817. 6v. 12°. 129.1
— Abridg. of scripture hist. from the Old Test. By Mrs. Trimmer. London, 1811. 12°. . 129.3
— Heavenly arcana. [Comm. on] Genesis, Exodus. By E. von Swedenborg. Boston, 1837–48. 13v. 8° 1084.6
— Notes on the book of Job. By A. Barnes. 3d ed. New York, 1845. 2v. 12° 1097.18
— New transl. of the book of Job: introd. and notes by G. R. Noyes. 2d ed. Boston, 1858. 12° 1097.20
— New transl. of the Psalms: introd. and notes by G. R. Noyes. 2d ed. Boston, 1846, 12°. 1097.22
— New transl. of the Prov., Eccl. and the Canticles: with notes by G. R. Noyes. Boston, 1846. 12° 1097.21
— Commen. on Proverbs, by M. Stuart. New York, 1852. 12° 1097.23
— Commen. on Ecclesiastes, by M. Stuart. New York, 1851. 12° 1097.25
— New transl. of the Hebrew Prophets, by G. R. Noyes. Boston, 1833–37. 3v. 12° . . . 118.7
— Notes on the book of Isaiah, by A. Barnes. New impr. ed. New York, 1853. 2v. 12°. 1097.19
— Abridg. of the N. Testament, by Mrs. Trimmer. London, n.d. 12° 129.2
— New Test. transl. from the Syriac, Peshito version. By J. Murdock. N. York, 1852. 8° 1093.7
— New Testament. Commen. and notes by A. Clarke. New York, 1825. 2v. roy. 8°. . 1093.1
— Notes on the Gospels, by A. Barnes. N. Y. [Var. ster. eds. 1852–58.] 2v. 12° 1097.3-8
— The Gospels: with moral reflections, by P. Quesnel, with introd. essay, by D. Wilson. Rev. by H. A. Boardman. Philadelphia, 1855. 2v. 8° 1093.3
— The Gospels: transl. by A. Norton, with notes. Boston, 1855. 2v. 8° 1093.5
— Notes and illustr. of the parables, by T. Whittemore. Boston, 1832. 18° 1089.15
— Notes on the Acts of the Apostles, by A. Barnes. 10th ed. New York, 1852. 12° . 1097.9
— Notes on the epistle to the Romans, by A. Barnes. 9th ed. New York, 1852. 12° . . 1097.10

BIBLE. Epistles to the Corinthians: with notes by
A. P. Stanley. London, 1855. 2v. 8° . . . 1093.15
— Epistles to the Thessalonians, Galatians, Ro-
mans: notes by B. Jowett, 1855. 2v.8° 1093.14
— Notes on I. epistle to the Corinthians, by A.
Barnes. 3d ed. New York, 1849. 12° . . . 1097.11
— Notes on II. Corinth. and the epist. to the Ga-
latians, by A. Barnes. New York, 1851. 12° 1097.12
— Notes on the epistles to the Ephesians, Phil-
ippians and Colossians, by A. Barnes. New
York, 1852. 12° 1097.13
— Notes on epistles of Paul to the Thess., Tim.,
Titus and Philemon, by A. Barnes. New
York, 1853. 12° 1097.14
— Notes on the epistle to the Hebrews, by A.
Barnes. New York, 1852. 12° 1097.15
— Notes on the epistles of James, Peter, John
and Jude. New York, 1852. 12° 1097.16
— Notes on the book of Revelation, by A.
Barnes. New York, 1852. 12° 1097.17
Apocryphal New Testament. Transl., with
notes. New York, n.d. 8° 1097.2
Works on the Bible, including commentaries without the text.
— Adams, J. Q. Letters to his son on the study
of the Bible. With letters of Mrs. Adams 537.2
— - The Bible and its teachings. 129.36
— Alexander, A. Authenticity, inspira. etc., of 118.4
— Beecher, C. E. Bible and the people. 1086.4
— Boardman, H. A. The Bible in the counting-
house. 1103.19
— Bogue, D. Divine authority of the New Test. 119.8
— Book, The, and its story 1094.12
— Conybeare, W. J. Life and epistles of St.
Paul 113.9
— Crofton, D. Genesis and geology 118.20
— Cumming, J. Scripture readings. Genesis. 116.9
— - Sabbath morning readings. Leviticus . . 116.18
— - Lectures on the book of Daniel. 116.10
— - Lectures on the book of Revelation . . . 116.6-7
— - Sabbath evening readings. Matthew . . 116.8
— - Sabbath evening readings. Mark 116.15
— - Sabbath evening readings. Luke 116.16
— - Lectures on our Lord's miracles 116.4
— - Lectures on our Lord's parables 116.5
— De Wette, W. M. L. Introduction to the Old
Testament 1093.6
— - Introd. to the New Testament 1093.10
— Gilfillan, G. Bards of the 118.2
— Gleig, G. R. History of the 810.14
— Goodrich, C. A. Geography of the 1089.28
— Greenleaf, S. Exam. of the testimony of the
evangelists 1093.16
— Hackett, H. B. Commen. on the Acts of the
Apostles 1093.2
— Hall, J. Scripture history 1107.9
— Halsey, Le Roy J. Literary attractions of the 1087.11
— Hamilton, J. Lectures on Ecclesiastes . . . 1088.31
— Herder, J. G. v. Spirit of Hebrew poetry . . 1087.17
— Higginson, E. Spirit of the 1103.4
— Hopkins, E. Exposition of the ten com-
mandments 1107.19
— Horne, T. H. Introduction to the study of the 1088.28
— Kitto, J. Cyclopædia of biblical literature . 1083.8
— - Scripture lands 815.7
— Literary history of the New Testament . . . 1085.5
— McClure, A. W. Mem. of the translators of 548.10
— Melvill, H. B. thoughts 119.17
— Noble, S. Plenary inspiration asserted . . . 1086.26
— Norton, A. Evidence of the genuineness of
the Gospels 1093.11-13
— Paley, W. Horæ Paulinæ 1099.37
— Prideaux, H. Old and New Testament con-
nected with the history of the Jews . . . 1093.12
— Robinson, E. Biblical researches in Palestine 1103.7
— Sears, R. History of the 1085.4
— Spring, G. B. not of man 1107.14
— Stuart, M. Commentary on book of Daniel 1093.4
— - Comment. on the epistle to the Romans . 1097.1
— - Critical history and defence of the Old
Testament canon 1097.24

BIBLE. Sharpe, S. Notes on Eng. version of New
Testament 1089.18
— Swedenborg, E. v. Apocalypse revealed 1084.3
— Trimmer, Mrs. S. B. explained in a familiar
way 129.6
— Trench, R. C. On the authorized version of
the New Testament 128.6
— - Notes on the miracles 1093.8
— - Notes on the parables 1093.9
— Wilson D. Lectures on the epistle to the Col-
ossians 1097.26
See also: Theology.
BIBLICAL archæology. Jahn, J. 1103.5
BIBLICAL geography, Travels in the year 1838, un-
dertaken with reference to. Robinson, E.. 684.4
BIBLICAL literature, Cyclopædia of. Kitto, J.. 1083.8
BIBLICAL trinity. By Theophilus. Hartf., 1850. 12° 1096.20
BIBLIOTHÈQUE industrielle instituée par le gouv.
belge. 1re ser. Bruxelles, 1850-53. 10v. 12°.
Containing:
1. Géométrie pratique 1075.30
2. Tomlinson, Ch. Physique générale. Trad.
de l'angl. 1075.31
3. Law, H. Manuel de construction. Trad.
de l'angl. 1075.32
4. Alcan, M. Manuel du tisserand 1075.33
5. Connaissance des métaux 1075.34
6. Girardin, J. Manuel de chimie appliquée . 1075.35
7. De la charpente 1075.36
8. Connaissance des bois. 1075.37
9. Manuel du Serrurier. 1075.38
10. Cours d'arithmétique élémentaire 1075.39
BIBLIOTHÈQUE nationale, publ. sous le patronage
du gouv. belge. 43v. 12°. *Containing:*
1. Borgnet, J. Histoire du comté de Namur. 1075.12
2. Coomans ainé. Les communes belges . . 1075.22
3. Histoire d'Albert et Isabelle 1075.14
4. Deby, J. Hist. naturelle de la Belgique. 2v. 1075.25
5. Dufau, J. B. Hagiographie belge 1075.24
6. Fétis, E. Les musiciens belges. 2v. . . . 1075.29
7. Gens, E. Histoire du comté de Flandre . 1075.7
8. Gens, E. Ruines et paysages en Belgique 1075.23
9. Hannon, J. D. Flore belge. 3v. 1075.26
10. Hasselt, A. v. Histoire des Belges. 2v. . 1075.17
11. Hasselt, A. v. Les Belges aux croisades. 2v 1075.21
12. Huydens, G. Histoire du marquisat d'
Anvers. 1075.18
13. Juste, T. Précis de l'histoire du moyen
age. 5v. 1075.15
14. Juste, T. Précis de l'histoire moderne. 2v. 1075.16
15. Juste, T. Charlemagne. 1075.9
16. Laveleye, E. de. Histoire des rois francs.
2v. 1075.13
17. Lagarde, M. Histoire du duché de Limbourg 1075.8
18. Lagarde, M. Histoire du duché de Luxembourg. 2v. 1075.20
19. Moke. Mœurs, usages, fêtes et solennités
des Belges. 2° 1075.11
20. Moke, H. G. Histoire de la littérature
française. 4v. 1075.27
21. Reiffenberg, F. A. F. T. de. Histoire du
comté de Hainaut. 3v. 1075.19
22. Saint Génois, J. de. Les voyageurs belges
du XIII—XIX siècle. 2v. 1075.10
23. Snellaert, A. Hist. de la littér. flamande. 1075.28
BI-CENTENNIAL book of Malden. Boston, 1850. 16° 227.18
BICKFORD, Mrs. J. T. Scandal. Boston, 1857.
12° 416.12
BIDDLES, H. P. A few poems. Cincinnati, 1858. 12° 349.5
BIDPAŸ. Contes et fables indiennes. Cabinet des
Fées. XVII. 1077.1
BIERNATZKI, J. C. The hallig. Translated by
Mrs. G. P. Marsh. Boston, 1856. 12° . . . 884.1
BIGELOW, A. Rambles in N. Britain and Ireland
in 1817. Boston, 1821. 12° 648.16
— Travels in Malta and Sicily, with sketches of
Gibraltar. Boston, 1831. 8° 676.2
BIGELOW, J. Eolopoesis. Am. rejected addresses.
New York, n.d. 12° 325.4-5

BIGELOW, J. Nature in disease. Miscellaneous writings. Boston, 1854. 16° 157.25–26
— The useful arts, with the applications of science. New York, 1851. 2v. 12° 198.7–8
BIGGS, J. History of Miranda's attempt in South America. Boston, 1808. 18° 266.7
BIGLOW papers, The. Lowell, J. R. 896.13–14
BIGLOW, W. History of Natick, Mass. Boston, 1830. 8° 224.12
BILLOW and the rock: a tale. Martineau, H. . . 840.42
BINGHAM, H. Residence in the Sandwich islands. Hartford, 1847. 8° 934.4
BINNEY, T. Is it possible to make the best of both worlds? New York, 1854. 16° 118.22
— Sir T. F. Buxton. A study for young men. London, 1853. p.8° 588.10
BINNING, R. B. M. Two years' travel in Persia, Ceylon, etc. London, 1857. 2v. 8° 685.1
BINNS, W. Orthographic projection. Lon., 1857. 8° 206.8
BIOGRAPHIES of eminent men from the 13th century. London, n.d. 4v. 12° 839.6
BIOGRAPHY. Hood, E. P. Uses of 878.24
BIOGRAPHY — Collections :
— Arago, F. Scientific men 511.3
— Atkinson, E. W. Queens of Prussia. 546.1
— Bagehot, W. Estimates of some Englishmen and Scotchmen 563.9
— Baillie, J. Life studies 548.12
— Baldwin, J. G. Party leaders 518.7
— Barker, E. H. Porson and others 584.8
— Barrow, J. Naval worthies of Q. Elizabeth's reign 564.8
— Bayne, P. Essays in biography 885.1–2
— Belknap, J. American biography 820.58
— Bell, R. English poets 398.2
— Biographies of eminent men in literature, etc. 839.6
— Bossuet, J. B. Oraisons funèbres 1066.5
— Bradford, A. Distinguished men in N. E. . . 518.6
— Brewster, Sir D. Martyrs of science 548.15
— British cabinet, 1853 . . . . 599.9
— Brougham, H., Lord. Men of letters of the time of Geo. III. 548.7
— - Philosophers of the time of Geo. III. . . . 548.7
— - Statesmen in the time of Geo. III. 840.5
— Bush, Mrs. F. Queens of France 606.8–13
— Butler, A Fathers, martyrs and prin. saints. 541.5
— Cabinet portrait gallery of British worthies.840.10–11
— Campbell, J., L'd. Chief justices of England 568.2
— - Lord chancellors and keepers of the seal. 568.1
— Caro, E. St. Dominique et les Dominicains . 1078.35
— Child, L. M. Good wives 548.8–9
— Clarke, A. Wesley family 535.12
— Clement, J. Noble deeds of Am. women . . 538.2–3
— Coleridge, H. Northern worthies 589.10
— Cooper, J. F. Distinguished Am. naval officers 527.3–5
— Cormenin, L. M. de La H. Orators of France 617.9
— Costello, L. S. Mem's of em. English women 595.1
— Creasy, E. S. Eminent Etonians 582.2
— Crowe, E. E. Eminent foreign statesmen . . 388.7
— Cunningham, A. British painters, sculptors and architects 379.9
— Davenport, R. A. Individuals who raised themselves from poverty 379.13
— De Quincey, T. The Cæsars 895.9
— - Biographical essays 895.7
— Distinguished men of modern times 820.29
— Doran, Dr. J. Queens of England 593.3
— Dufau, J. B. Hagiographie belge 1075.24
— Dunham, S. A. Literary and scientific men of Great Britain 398.3
— Düntzer, H. Frauenbilder aus Goethe's Jugendzeit 1034.8
— Eddy, D. C. Heroines of the missionary enterprise 539.13
— Edwards, B. B. Self-taught men 548.18–19
— Ellet, E. F. Women of the Amer. revol. . . 538.13
— Ellis, G. A., L'd Dover. Eminent sovereigns of modern Europe 548.28
— Elton, C. A. Roman emperors. 28 B. C.—A. D. 1453 . . . . 548.11
— Emerson, R. W. Representative men . . . 876.5

BIOGRAPHY — Collections, continued.
— Eminent men in literature, etc., from the 13th century 839.6
— Fénélon. Ancient philosophers 820.42
— Flanders, H. Chief justices of the U. States. 523.3
— Forster, J. Historical and biographical essays 894.3
— - Statesmen of the commonwealth 562.3
— Fowler, H. American pulpit 534.9
— Fuller, T. Worthies of England 574.5
— George, A. Queens of Spain 544.4
— Gleig, G. R. British military commanders . 388.3
— Godwin, W. Lives of the necromancers . . . 125.1
— Gorrie, P. D. Eminent methodist ministers . 535.14
— Great men's boyhood 548.13
— Green, M. A. E. Letters of royal and illustrious ladies of Great Britain 596.5
— - Lives of the princesses of England 594.13
— Griswold, R. W. Biographical annual 518.12–13
— Hale, S. J. Distinguished women 541.1
— Hall, M. Queens before the conquest 594.12
— Hardwicke, R. Annual for 1856 . . . . . . 548.27
— Headley, J. T. Napoleon and his marshals . 605.1–2
— - Washington and his generals 516.1–5
— Herbert, H. W. Henry VIII. and his queens 558.1–3
— Howitt, W. Homes and haunts of Br. poets . 896.1–2
— Hunter, H. Sacred biography 541.4
— Huntington, Lady, and her friends 1107.7
— Irving, D. Lives of Scottish writers 586.13
— Jameson, Mrs. A. Celebrated female sover. 810.44
— - Early Italian painters 840.23
— Jervis-White-Jervis, Mary, Lady. Great painters' boyhood 548.14
— Jesse, J. H. Geo. Selwyn and contempora. . 563.2
— - Pretenders and their adherents 553.5
— Johnson, S. Lives of the English poets . . . 586.20
— Kirby, R. S. Remarkable characters 894.1
— Knapp, S. L. Emin. lawyers, statesmen, etc. .524.10–11
— Lamartine, A. de. Celebrated characters . . 547.4
— Lancelott, Thomas. Queens of England . . 593.2
— Larrabee, W. C. Wesley and his coadjutors . 578.9
— Lawrence, E. Lives of the Brit. historians.586.11–12
— Lester, C. E. Artists of America 524.14
— Lewes, G. H. Biog. history of philosophy . 547.1
— Lives of eminent individuals celebrated in American history 518.5
— Lodge, E. Illustr. personages of Gt. Britain 815.1
— Lossing, B. J. Our countrymen 518.11
— - Signers of the declaration of independence 518.10
— Macaulay, T. B. Biogr. and histor. sketches. 884.19
— Macaulay, T. B. and others. Illustrious men 547.7
— McDonald, J. Biographical sketches 518.8
— Mackintosh, J. Eminent British statesmen . 388.6
— McClure, A. W. Authors of Eng. version of Bible 548.10
— Madden, R. R. United Irishmen 598.1–3
— Magoon, E. L. Living orators in America. . 518.16
— - Orators of the American revolution 528.1
— Maury, S. M. Statesmen of America 525.1
— Men of the time 518.1–2
— Merz, H. Christliche frauenbilder 1014.3
— Plutarchus. Select lives 850.1
— Powell, T. Living authors of America . . . 518.15
— - Living authors of England 586.9–10
— Pratt, A. Lives of some eminent men of the last century 548.26
— Prescott, W. H. Biogr. and crit. miscellanies 872.2
— Robertson, I. L. Public characters 518.9
— Rogers, T. J. Biographical dictionary . . . 518.14
— Roscoe, H. British lawyers 388.4
— St. Hilaire, E. M. de. Napoléon et la grande armée 1008.16
— St. John, J. A. Celebrated travellers 810.47
— Schloenbach, A. Frauenbilder aus der Goethe Schiller Epoche 1024.1
— Scott, W. Novelists 586.19
— Shell, R. L. Sketches of the Irish bar 598.5
— Shelley, Mrs. M. W. Literary and scientific men of Italy, Spain and Portugal 398.1
— - Literary and scientific men of France . . 388.8
— Sketches of eminent surgeons and physicians of Paris 609.1

BIOGRAPHY — *Collections, continued.*
— Southey, R. British admirals 388.5
— Sparks, J. American biography 529.1
— Stirling, W. Artists of Spain 543.4
— Strickland, A. Queens of England 592.1-4
— - Queens of Scotland 593.4-5
— Swainson, W. Zoölogists 408.5
— Thacher, J. American medical biography . . 523.11
— Thatcher, B. B. Indian biography 249.6
— Thackeray, W. M. English humorists of the
     18th century 586.1-4
— Thomson, A. S. Jacobites of 1715 and 1745 . 562.2
— Timbs, J. School days of eminent men . . . 589.3
— Tuckerman, H. T. Artist life : or, sketches
     of American painters 526.8
— - Biographical essays 547.2
— Tytler, P. F. Scottish worthies 399.9-10
— Updike, W. Mem. of the Rhode Island bar . 518.1-2
— Van Santvoord, G. Chief justices of the
     United States 523.4
— Varnhagen von Ense, K. A. Biographische
     Deukmale 1026.3
— Vasari, G. Eminent painters, sculptors and
     architects 848.6
— Vicars, J. England's worthies 588.13
— Warburton, E. Pr. Rupert and the cavaliers 553.6
— Watson, E. Men of the revolution 513.9
— Whitman, Z. G. Distin. men of colony, etc.,
     of Massachusetts 294.6
— Williams, E. Twelve stars of our republic . 513.13
— Williams, S. W. American medical biog . . . 523.12
— Willmott, R. A. Jeremy Taylor, his prede-
     cessors, contemporaries and successors . . 578.6
— Wilson, T. American heroes 527.8
— Wynne, J. Literary and scientific men of
     America 518.3-4

BIOGRAPHY *and correspondence of individuals,
    under their several names, viz.:*

Abernethy, J.
Adams, A.
Adams, H.
Adams, J.
Adams, J. Q.
Addison, J.
Agrippa v. Nettesheim.
    See Cornelius.
Aikin, J.
Akenside, M.
Alexander the Great
Alexander I. of Russia
Alexander VI., Pope
Alexander, W., Earl of
    Stirling
Alfieri, V.
Alfred of Eng.
Ali Pasha
Allen, E.
Allen, Wm.
Allston, W.
Ancre, Maréchal D'
Andersen, II. C.
Anspach Bayreuth,
    Margravine of
Arago, F.
Arnold, T.
Ashmun, J.
Audubon, J. J.
Bacon, F., L'd
Bacon, II.
Bacon, S.
Bailey, J.
Bainbridge, W.
Balboa, V. N. do
Baliol, M. B., *pseud.*
Ballou, A. A.
Ballou, II.
Banim, J.
Barney, J.
Barnum, P. T.
Barrow, Sir J.
Barton, B.
Barton, W.
Bayard, Chev.
Beaumarchais, P. A.
    C. de
Becket, T. à
Beckwourth, J. P.
Beethoven, L. v.

Belisarius
Belknap, J.
Bellot, J. R.
Benyowsky, M. A.
Béranger, P. J. de
Bernadotte
Béthune, M. de, Duke
    of Sully
Black Hawk
Blair, H.
Blennerhassett, H.
Blessington, Countess
Boleyn, A.
Bolivar
Borgia, Cæsar
Boswell, J.
Bowditch, N.
Brainerd, D.
Brant, J.
Brenton, Sir J.
Brock, Sir I.
Bronté, C.
Bruce, J.
Brummell, G.
Buchanan, C.
Buchanan, J.
Buckingham, J. T.
Buckminster, J.
Buckminster, J. S.
Budgett, S.
Bunyan, J.
Buonarroti, M. Angelo
Burke, E.
Burns, R.
Burr, A.
Buxton, Sir T. F.
Byron, L'd
Cabot, S.
Cæsar, C. J.
Cagliostro
Calderon de la Barca
Caldwell, C.
Calhoun, J. C.
Calvin, J.
Campan, Mad.
Campbell, I.
Campbell, T.
Canning, G.
Cappe, C.
Cardan

Carleton, G.
Carl XIV., Johann of
    Sweden
Carpenter, L.
Carter, E.
Cartwright, P.
Cary, II. F.
Cary, R., Earl of Mon-
    mouth
Cass, L.
Castriot, King of Alba-
    nia (Scanderbeg)
Catharine II. of Russia.
Caulfield, J., Earl of
    Charlemont
Cavendish, T.
Cellini, B.
Chalmers, T.
Channing, W. E.
Charlemagne
Charles I. of Eng.
Charles II. of Eng.
Charles V. of Germ'y
Chatterton, T.
Cheverus, Cardinal
Chrysostom, St.
Churchill, J., Duke of
    Marlborough
Churchill, S., Duchess
    of Marlborough
Cicero, M. T.
Clapp, T.
Clarke, E. D.
Clay, II.
Cleopatra
Clinton, D.
Clive, R., Lord
Cockburn, II., Lord
Codman, J.
Coiburn, Z.
Cole, T.
Coleridge, S. T.
Columbus
Colquhoun, Lady
Combe, A.
Conder, J.
Congar, O.
Cooke, G. F.
Cooper, J. F.
Copleston, Bishop E.

BIOGRAPHY *and correspon. of individuals, continued.*
Copway, G.
Cortez, H.
Cotton, II.
Craig, Sir T.
Cranmer, Archbishop
Crichton, Adm. J.
Cromwell, O.
Croswell, W.
Cumberland, R.
Curran, J. P.
Currie, J.
Curtis, J.
Cyrus
Dampier, W.
Dante
D'Arblay, Mme. F.
Darius
Darwin, E.
Davidson, M. M.
Davidson, L. M.
Davy, Sir II.
Decatur, S.
Defoe, D.
De Quincey, T.
De Veaux, J.
De Witt, J.
Dexter, S.
Dibdin, T.
Disraeli, B.
Doddridge, P.
Dolcino, Fra
Dolgorookov, Nathalia,
    Princess
Donne, J.
Dongiass, F.
Dow, L.
Drake, Sir F.
Duncan, M. L.
Dunton, J.
Du Guesclin, B.
Eaton, W.
Edgeworth, Abbé
Edgeworth, R. L.
Edward, the black
    prince
Edwards, J.
Edwards, M.
Eldon, Earl of
Elizabeth of Eng.
Elizabeth of Hungary
Elliott, E.
Elliott, J. D.
Elliston, R. W.
Emerson, J. E.
Emmett, R.
Emmett, T. A.
Exmouth, Visc. E. Pel-
    lew
Fairchild, J. H.
Fanshawe, Lady
Félix, Rachel
Fénelon, F. de
Ferdinand I. of Aust'a
Ferguson, J.
Fielding, H.
Fitch, J.
Fitzgerald, Lord E.
Foote, S.
Forbes, D.
Foster, J.
Fouché, J.
Fourier, C.
Fox, C. J.
Fox, G.
Francis I. of France
Franklin, B.
Frederic II. of Prussia
Frémont, J. C.
Fry, E.
Fulton, R.
Fuseli, II.
Galt, J.
Gardiner, Col. J.
Garrick, D.
George III. of Eng.
Gerry, E.
Gibbon, E.
Godolphin, Mrs. M.
Gorgei, A.
Goethe, J. W. v.
Goldoni, C.
Goldsmith, O.
Goodrich, S. G.
Good, J. M.

Graeme, J., Marquis of Jortin, J.
Montrose
Graham, Sir T.
Graham, Mrs. I.
Grant, Mrs. A.
Grattan, II.
Greene, N.
Greenough, H.
Gregory VII., Pope
Gresham, Sir T.
Griffin, E. D.
Grimaldi, J.
Gustavus Adolphus
Guyon, Mme.
Gwyn, Nell
Hale, Sir M.
Hale, N.
Hallock, J.
Hamilton, A.
Hamilton, Mrs. E.
Hamlin, H. A. L.
Hammond, M. M.
Hampden, J.
Handel
Hannibal
Hanson, J.
Harrison, W. H.
Hastings, W.
Hatton, Sir C.
Havelock, Sir H.
Haven, N. A.
Haydn
Haydon, B. R.
Heber, Bishop R.
Hemans, Mrs. F. D.
Henriette d'Angleterre
Henry IV. of France
Henry V. of Eng.
Henry VIII. of Eng.
Henry, M.
Henry, P.
Herbert, E., of Cher-
    bury
Herbert, G.
Hill, R.
Hobbie, H.
Holbrook, S. F.
Holcrott, T.
Holley, H.
Holtei, K. v.
Hook, T. E.
Hooker, R.
Hopper, I. T.
Horner, F.
Houston, S.
Howard, J.
Howe, R., Earl
Howell, J. W.
Howland, J.
Hubbell, M. E.
Huet, P. D.
Hull, W.
Humboldt, A. v.
Humboldt, W. v.
Hume, D.
Hunt, J. N. L.
Huntington, Mrs. S.
Hutchinson, Col.
Hutten, U. von
Hyde, E., Earl of Clar-
    endon
Hyder Ali
Jackson, A.
Jackson, A., jr.
Jackson, W.
James I. of Eng.
James, Duke of Mon-
    mouth
Jay, J.
Jay, W.
Jefferson, T.
Jeffrey, F., L'd
Jennison, M.
Jenner, E.
Jervis, J., Earl of St.
    Vincent
Joan of Arc
Johnson, J.
Johnson, R. M.
Johnson, S.
Jones, D. S.
Jones, J.
Jones, J. P.
Jones, Sir W.

Joseph Bonaparte
Josephine, Empress
Judd, S.
Judson, A.
Judson, A. H.
Judson, E. C.
Judson, S. B.
Julian, Emp.
Ksh-ge-ga-gah-bowh, or
    Geo. Copway
Kane, E. H.
Kelly, M.
Kemble, J. P.
Keppel, A.
Kidd, Capt.
King, W.
Kirkaldy, Sir W.
Knight, F.
Kotzebue, A. von
La Fayette, Marq. de
Lamb, J.
La Rochejaquelein,
    M. L. V. de D.
Lawrence, A.
Lawrence, J.
Lawrence, Sir Thos.
Lawrence, W.
Ledyard, J.
Lee, C.
Lee, R. H.
L'Enclos, Ninon de
Leo Xth.
Lewis, M. G.
Linn, L. F.
Longueville, Mme. de
Lorenzo de' Medici
Louis XIV. of France
Louis XVII., the lost
    prince
Louis Napoleon
Louis, Prince of Condé
Louis Philippe of Fr.
Lovat, Lord
Lumisden, A.
L'Ouverture, Toussaint
Lutfullah
Luther, M.
Mackintosh, J.
Macomb, A.
Mahomet
Maintenon, Mme. de
Ma-ka-tai-me-she-kia-
    kiah, or Black H'k
Malcolm, John
Malibran, Mme.
Mallet-du-Pan, J.
Marble, D.
Marguerite d'Angou-
    lème
Maria Antoinette
Mary Q. of Scots
Marie de' Medici
Marion, F.
Marlborough, Duke of
Marlborough, Duchess
    of
Martyn, II.
Maximilian II. of Aus.
Mayhew, J.
Mazarin, Card.
Melancthon, P.
Mendelssohn, Barthol-
    dy F.
Merriman, Archd.
Metastasio, P.
Michael Angelo
Miller, II.
Milnor, J.
Milton, J.
Mirabeau
Mitford, M. R.
Mohammed
Monk, G., Duke of Al-
    bermarle
Montagu, Mrs. E.
Montagu, M. W.
Montaigne, M. de
Montgomery, J.
Moore, Sir John
Moore, Th.
Mora, A. H. De
More, II.

BIOGRAPHY *and correspon. of individuals, continued.*

More, Sir T.	Putnam, I.	Stiles, Ezra
Morgan, D.	Pyrrhus	Stilling, H.
Morris, Gouv.	Rachel, Mlle.	Story, J.
Mountain, A. S. H.	Raikes, R.	Strange, Sir R.
Mozart	Raleigh, Sir W.	Summerfield, J.
Muffling, F. K. F.	Randolph, J.	Swedenborg, E.
Muhlenberg, P.	Ran'oul, R., jr.	Swift, Jona.
Munro, Sir T.	Raphael	Symonds, W.
Murray, L.	Reed, J.	Tai-Ping-Wang
Napier, Sir C.	Retz, Cardinal de	Talbot, S.
Napoleon I. of France	Reynolds, F.	Talleyrand, Prince
Napoleon III. of Fr.	Reynolds, Sir J.	Taylor, J.
Nathalia Borissovna,	Richard I., Cœur-de-	Taylor, J. B.
Prin. Dolgorookov	Lion	Taylor, Z.
Neander, J. A. W.	Richard II. of Eng.	Tecumseh
Neff, F.	Richard III. of Eng.	Thorburn, G.
Nelson, H. Visc.	Richardson, S.	Thurston, L. G.
Nero	Richelieu, Cardinal de	Titian
Newell, Mrs. H.	Richmond, I.	Tonna, C. E.
Newton, Sir I.	Richter, J. P. F.	Tooke, J. H.
Newton, J.	Ripa, Father	Torrey, J.
Nicholas of Russia	Ritchie, Mrs. A. C. M.	Toussaint, Pierre
Niebuhr, B. G.	Rittenhouse, D.	Trench, Baron
Nolte, V.	Robertson, W.	Trumbull, J.
Northington, Earl of	Robespierre	Turenne, Marshal
Oberkirch, Baroness	Robin Hood	Tuttle, W.
Oberlin, J. F.	Roland, Mme.	Van Buren, M.
Oehlenschläger, A.	Romain, R. D.	Van Campen, M.
Oglethorpe, J.	Romilly, S.	Van Shaack, P.
O'Keeffe, J.	Romulus	Varnhagen von Ense,
Oldfield, Mrs. A.	Rosa, Salvator	R. A. F.
Olin, S.	Roscoe, W.	Vespucius, Americus
Olney, S.	Rossini	Vicars, H. S. J.
Opie, A.	Russell, Rachel, Lady	Vidocq, E. F.
Ossoli, S. M. F. d'	St. Vincent, Earl of	Vinci, Leonardo da
Otis, J.	Salt, H.	Voltaire, F. M. A. de
Page, H.	Sampson, W.	Walker, J.
Paine, T.	Sanderson, R.	Wallace, Sir W.
Paine, R. T.	Schamyl	Walpole, H.
Palissy, B.	Schiller, F. von	Ware, H., jr.
Park, Mungo	Schimmelpenninck,	Ware, M. L.
Parr, S.	M. A.	Warner, S.
Parry, Sir W. E.	Schlatter, M.	Washington, G.
Payson, E.	Schulze, E.	Washington, Martha
Pearce, S.	Scott, J., Earl of Eldon	Washington, Mary
Pellew, E., *Lord Ex-*	Scott, Sir W.	Watson, R.
mouth	Scott, Gen. W.	Watt, J.
Penn, W.	Segur, Count	Watts, I.
Penn, Sir W.	Sevigné, Mme. la Mar-	Webster, D.
Pepperrell, Sir Wm.	quise de	Wellesley, A., Duke
Perez, Antonio	Seward, W. H.	of Wellington
Perkins, J. H.	Shakespeare	Wheaton, R.
Perkins, T. H.	Sharp, Archb'p J.	White, J. B.
Perthes, F.	Shaw, W. S.	White, W.
Perry, Com. O. H.	Shelley, P. B.	Wickliff, J.
Peter the Cruel, of Cas-	Sheridan, R. B.	Wilberforce
tile and Leon	Schopenhauer, J.	Wilkes, J.
Peter the Great, of Rus.	Slater, S.	Wilkie, D.
Peters, A. R.	Smith, A.	Wilkinson, J.
Peters, H.	Smith, E.	Willard, S.
Petrarch, F.	Smith, Jas.	William the Con-
Philip, King	Smith, Jer.	queror
Philip II. of Spain	Smith, Capt. John	William III. of Eng.
Philippe Auguste	Smith, J. E.	Williams, J.
Phillips, S.	Smith, S.	Williams, Roger
Pichler, C.	Smith, Mrs. S. L. H.	Winslow, Mrs. H. L.
Pickard, Mrs. H. M.	Smith, Sir W. S.	Wirt, W.
Pierce, F.	Smollett, T.	Wolsey, Card. T.
Pinkney, W.	Sophia Dorothea	Wordsworth, W.
Pitt, Wm.	Southey, R.	Wotton, Sir H.
Pizarro, F.	Spencer, T.	Wren, Sir C.
Plater, E.	Spinoza	Wright, S.
Poggio Bracciolini	Staël, Mme. de	Xerxes
Popkin, I. S.	Stephenson, G.	Yarran'on, A.
Prentiss, S. S.	Sterling, J.	Zouch, T.

BION, Idylls. Translated by J. Banks and J. M. Chapman 834.6
BIRCH, S. Introduction to Egyptian hieroglyphs   957.8
— History of ancient pottery. London, 1858. 2v. 8°   196.1
BIRCH, T. Court and times of James I. London, 1848. 2v. 8°   552.10
BIRD, G. Electricity and galvanism, in their physiol. and therap. relations. London, 1849. 16°   145.29
— and Brooke, C. Natural philosophy. 4th ed. London, 1854. 12° 149.24
BIRD, J. Gleanings from the history of music. Boston, 1850. 12° 209.3
BIRD, R. M. Calavar: a novel. Philadelphia, 1834. 2v. 12° 726.7
— Sheppard Lee. New York, 1836. 2v. 12° .   498.11
BIRD architecture. Rennie, J. 839.2

BIRD fancier, The American. Browne, D. J. 177.21-22
BIRD-keeper's manual. Mann, J. 177.24
BIRD miscellanies. Rennie, J. 850.8
BIRDS. Bechstein, J. M. Nat. hist. of cage and chamber 825.6
— Bennett, E. T. Gardens of the Zoological Soc.   172.20
— Giraud, J. P. B. of Long Island 172.7
— Gosse, P. H. B. of Jamaica 178.16
— Rennie, J. Domestic habits of 839.11
— - Faculties of 839.10
— - Natural history of 820.5
— Stanley, E. Familiar history of 177.26
— Swainson, W. Nat hist. and classification of   398.20
BIRKBECK, M. Letters from Illinois. Philadelphia, 1818. 12° 629.21
— Notes on America. 2d ed. London, 1818. 8°   625.17
BIRTHRIGHT, The: a novel. Gore, C. G. 776.2
BISCAY, Six years in. Bacon, J. F. 673.2
BISSET, R. Reign of George III. London, 1820. 6v. 8° 976.5
BITZIUS, A. Der Bauern-Spiegel oder Lebensgesch. des J. Gotthelf. 3tte Aufl. Berlin, 1851. 12°   1016.3
— Gotthelf's Schriften. Berlin, 1856. 7v. 16° .   1026.1

   Contents.— Vol. I. Der Bauernspiegel oder Lebensgeschichte des Jeremias Gotthelf. II. Uli, der Knecht. III. Uli, der Pächter. IV. Käthi, die Grossmutter oder der wahre Weg durch jede Noth. V.—VI. Leiden und Freuden eines Schulmeisters. VII. Erzählungen und Bilder aus dem Volksleben der Schweiz.

— Uli, der Knecht. Ein Volksbuch. 3tte Aufl. Berlin, 1854. sm. 8° 1034.13
BLACK dwarf. Scott, W. 460.22-23.25-26
BLACK Hawk. Drake, B. Life and adventures of.   539.7
— Life, dictated by himself 539.6
— Smith, E. H. Black Hawk, etc. A poem . . .   338.11
BLACK prophet: a tale of Irish famine. Carleton, W. 758.10
BLACK sea, Russian shores of the. Oliphant, L. . .   674.2
BLACK velvet pelisse. Opie, A. 460.48
BLACKSTONE, W. Commentaries on the laws of England. Portland, 1807. 4v. 8° 133.6
— The student's Blackstone, by R. M. Kerr. London, 1858. 12° 133.12
BLACKWOOD, F. T. *Lord Dufferin.* Letters from high latitudes. London, 1857. 8° 708.1
BLACKWOOD, Stories from 469.22
BLAIR, H. Life and writings of. Hill, J. 575.10
BLAIR's chronological tables to Apr., 1856, by J. W. Rosse. London, 1856. p.8° 836.2
BLAKE, J. Annals of Dorchester, Mass. 227.16
BLAKE, J. L. The world. New York, 1853. 12° .   947.8
BLAKELY, J. Theology of inventions. New York, 1856. 12° 1087.14
BLAKEY, R. Angling literature. Lond., 1856. 16°   177.29
BLANC, J. J. Louis. History of ten years, 1830–40. London, 1844–45. 2v. 8° 1002.5
BLANCHARD, L. Sketches from life. Edited with memoir, by Sir E. B. Lytton. New York, 1848. 12° 877.18
BLAND, T. jr. Bland papers, with a memoir. Petersburg, 1840–43. 2v. in 1. 8° 216.3
BLAND, W. Hints on the form of ships and boats. London, 1852. 16° 829.16
BLAQUIERE, E. Greek revolution, with remarks on the religion, etc., of the Greeks. 2d ed. London, 1825. 8° 918.1
— Second visit to Greece, incl. last days of Lord Byron. London, 1825. 8° 683.11
BLASTING and quarrying of stone, Treatise on. Burgoyne, J. 819.25
BLAZE de Bury, *Baroness.* Mem. of the princess Palatine, incl. corresp. Lond., 1853. 8° . .   545.15
— Racine, and the French classical drama. London, 1845. 24° 840.4
BLEAK house. Dickens, C. 460.20-21
BLEBY, H. Death struggles of slavery [in Jamaica.] London, 1853. 8° 127.20
BLENNERHASSETT, H. Safford, W. H. Life of. Compris. a narrative of Burr's expedition. 517.12-13
— Robertson, D. Motion to commit 296.6
BLESSINGTON, Countess of. *See* Gardiner, M.

BLEWITT O. Hand-book for Rome. 3d ed. London, 1853. 12°. 649.10
— Hand-book for Southern Italy. 2d ed. Lond., 1855. 12°. 649.3
— Hand-book for Southern Tuscany and the Papal States. 3d ed. London, 1853. 12°. 649.6
BLIND man's offering. Bowen, B. B. 888.6
BLISS, G. Address at the opening of the town hall in Springfield. Springfield, 1828. 8°. . 227.15
BLISS, G. jr. and Wells, D. A. Annual of scientific discovery, 1850-58. . . . . 159.1
BLISS, Mrs. Practical cook-book. Philadelphia, 1857. 12°. 188.12
BLITHEDALE romance. Hawthorne, N. 457.11-13
BLONDEL: a historic fancy. Rice, G. E. 356.22
BLOODY assize, Full account of. Roberts, G. . . 566.5
BLOW-PIPE, The. Berzelius, J. J. Use of 155.22
— Plattner, C. F. and Muspratt, S. Use of . . 155.18
BLUNT, J. Shipmaster's assistant. 5th ed. New York, 1851. 8°. 135.2
BLUNT, I. J. Reformation in England. 5th ed. London, 1840. 16°. 379.2
BOADEN, J. Memoirs of John Philip Kemble. London, 1825. 2v. 8°. 597.5
BOARDMAN, H. A. Bible in the counting-house. Philadelphia, 1853. 12°. 1106.19
BOAT-CLUB, The : a tale for boys. Adams, W. T. 729.7-8
BOCCACCIO, G. Decameron, translated. New ed. London, 1822. 4v. in 2. 24°. 759.14
— Fables transl. from. Dryden, J. 315.17
— Novelle scelte. Lettera a Pino de Rossi, e la Descr. della Pestilenza. Vita. Parma, 1845. 16°. 1059.3
— Notices of. Campbell, T. 543.6
BOCK, A. Die thüringische Eisenbahn. Leipzig, 1856. 16°. 1029.8
BÖCKH, A. Public econ. of the Athenians. Transl. fr. 3d Ger. ed., by A. Lamb. Boston, 1857. 8° 953.1
BOCKSHAMMER, G. F. Freedom of the will. Transl. by A. Kaufman. Andover, 1835. 12° 1099.9
BODENSTEDT, F. Schamyl. See Wagner, F. . . 409.28
BODY, The, in its connection with man. Wilkinson, J. J. G. 157.6
BOGEN, F. W. The German in America. Boston, 1851. 18°. 629.33
BOGUE, D. Divine authority of the New Testament. Rev. ed. New York, n.d. 16°. . . . 119.8
BÖHMERWALDE, Aus dem : Erzählungen. Rank, J. 1036.2
BÖHMISCHEN Bäder, Die. Kapper, S. 1029.11
BOHN, H. G. Hand-book of games. London, 1850. p.8°. 816.5
— Polyglot of for'n proverbs. Lond., 1857. p.8° 856.14
— Pottery, porcelain, the Bernal collection, etc. London, 1857. p.8°. 835.11
BOHN, H. G. Antiquarian library. Lond, 38v. p.8°.
Containing :
1. Bede's ecclesiastical history of England . 846.1
2. Mallet's Northern antiquities 846.2
3. William of Malmesbury's chronicle of kings of England 846.3
4. Six old English chronicles. Ed. by J. A. Giles. 846.4
5. Ellis's early English metrical romances . 846.5
6. Chronicles of the Crusades. 846.6
7. Early trav. in Palestine. Ed. by T. Wright 846.7
8. Brand's antiq's of Eng., Scot. & Irel'd. 3v. 846.8
9. Roger of Wendover's flowers of English hist. [ascrib. to Matthew Paris.] transl. 2v. 846.9
10. Keightley's fairy mythology 846.10
11. Sir T. Browne's wks. Ed. by S. Wilkin. 3v. 846.11
12. Matthew Paris's chronicle. Ed. by J. A. Giles. 3v. 856.1
13. Yule-tide stories. Ed. by B. Thorpe . . 846.12
14. Roger de Hoveden's annals of England . 2v. 856.2
15. Henry of Huntingdon's chron. of Engl'd 856.3
16. Pauli's life of Alfred. Orosius, with English translation 856.4
17. Matthew of Westminster's flowers of hist. Translated. 2v. 856.5
18. Lepsius's letters from Egypt. etc. Transl. 856.6

BOHN, H. G. Antiquarian library, continued.
19. Ordericus Vitalis. Eccl. history of Engl'd and Normandy. 2v. 856.7
20. Ingulph's chronicle of the abbey of Croyland. Transl. 856.8
21. Lamb's specimens of Engl. dramatic poets 856.9
22. Florence of Worcester's chronicle. Tr. . 856.11
23. Ray's hand-book of proverbs : ed. by H. G. Bohn. 856.12
24. Chronicle of the tombs, by Pettigrew. . . 856.13
25. Polyglot of for'n proverbs, by H. G. Bohn 856.14
BOHN, H. G. Classical library. London. 80v. p.8°.
Containing :
1. Herodotus ; new transl. by Rev. H. Cary . 814.1
2, 3. Thucydides : transl. by Rev. H. Dale. 2v 814.2
4, 6, 18, 23, 29, 54. Plato : transl. by H. Cary and others. 6v. 814.3
5, 7, 11, 19. Livy : new transl. by Dr. Spillau and others. 4v. 814.4
8. Sophocles : tragedies, transl. 814.5
9. Æschylus : trag.: transl. by T. A. Buckley 814.6, 7
10. Aristotle's rhetoric and poetic. Transl. by T. A. Buckley. 814.8
12, 14. Euripides : literally transl. according to the text of Dindorf. 2v. 814.9
13. Virgil : literally transl. by Davidson . . . 814.10
15. Horace : lit. transl. by Smart ; new ed. by T. Buckley. 814.11
16. Aristotle's ethics : transl. by R. W. Browne 824.1
17. Cicero's offices, old age, friendship, etc.: transl. by C. R. Edmonds 824.2
20. Cæsar : comment. with the Alexandrian, African, and Spanish wars. 824.3
21. Homer's Iliad, lit. transl. into Eng. prose 824.4
22. Homer's Odyssey ; hymns : battle of the frogs and mice, transl. 824.5
24. Ovid's fasti, tristia, epistles, etc., transl. by H. T. Riley 824.6
25. Ovid's metamorphoses : transl. by H. T. Riley 824.7
26. Lucretius : nature of things : transl. by J. S. Watson 824.9
27, 30, 31, 34. Cicero's orations : transl. by Yonge. 4v. 824.10
28. Pindar : transl. by D. W. Turner. 824.11
32. Ovid : containing the heröides, amours, etc.: transl. by H. T. Riley 824.8
33, 36. Plautus : comedies : transl. by H. T. Riley. 2v. 824.12
35. Juvenal, Persius, Sulpicia and Lucilius : transl. by Rev. L. Evans. 824.13
37. Greek anthology : transl. by G. Burges. . 834.8
38. Demosthenes' Olynthiac and other public orations : transl. 834.1
39. Sallust, Florus, and Velleius Paterculus : transl., with notes, by Rev. J. S. Watson . 834.4
40. Lucan's Pharsalia : transl., with notes, by H. T. Riley 834.5
41. Theocritus, Bion, Moschus, and Tyrtæus : transl. by Rev. J. Banks 834.6
42. Cicero's academics, de finibus, and Tusculan disput. transl. by C. D. Yonge . . . 834.7
43. Aristotle's politics and economics : transl. by E. Walford 834.9
44. Diogenes Laërtius. Lives and opinions of the emin. philosophers : transl. by Yonge. 834.10
45. Terence and Phædrus : tr. by H. T. Riley 834.11
46, 47. Aristotle's organon : transl., with notes, by O. F. Owen. 2v. 834.12
48, 49. Comedies of Aristophanes : transl. by W. J. Hickie. 834.13
50. Cicero on the nature of the gods, divination, fate, etc.: transl. by Yonge. 834.14
51. Apuleius. The golden ass : god of Socrates, etc.: transl. 834.15
52. Justin, Cornelius Nepos, and Eutropius : transl. by J. S. Watson 834.16
53, 58. Tacitus. v.1. contains the annals. H. History ; Germany ; Agricola ; and oratory : transl. 834.17
55. 56. 57. Athenæus : tr. by C. D. Yonge. 3v. 844.1

BOHN, H. G. *Classical library, continued.*
59. Catullus, Tibullus, and the vigil of Venus: transl. by W. H. Kelly 844.2
61, 74, 82. Geography of Strabo: transl. by W. Falconer, and H. C. Hamilton. 844.3
62. Xenophon's anabasis and memorabilia: transl., with notes, by J. S. Watson . . . 844.4
63. Cyropædia and Hellenics: transl. by J. S. Watson and H. Dale. 844.5
64, 67, 69, 72, 78, 81. Pliny's natural history: transl. by J. Bostock and H. T. Riley. 6v. 844.7
65. Suetonius: lives of the twelve Cæsars, etc. transl. by A. Thomson 844.8
66. Demosthenes. Orations on the crown and embassy: transl. by C. R. Kennedy 834.2
68. Cicero on oratory and orators: transl. by J. S. Watson 844.9
70. The Greek romances of Heliodorus, Longus, Achilles Tatius: transl. by R. Smith. 844.10
71, 76. Quintilian's institutes of oratory: tr. by J. S. Watson. 2v. 854.1
73. Hesiod, Callimachus and Theognis: tr. by J. Banks 854.2
75. Dictionary of Latin quotations. Ed. by H. T. Riley 854.3
77. Orations of Demosthenes against Leptines, etc.: transl. by C. R. Kennedy 834.3
79. Xenophon's minor works: transl. by J. S. Watson 844.6
80. Aristotle's metaphysics: transl., with notes, by J. H. M'Mahon 854.4

BOHN, H. G. Ecclesiastical library. London, 8v. p.8°. *Containing:*
1. Eusebius: Eccl. hist.: tr. by C. F. Crusé. 845.1–2
2. Socrates scholasticus: Eccl. hist., transl. 845.3–4
3. Theodoret and Evagrius: History of the Church A. D. 322–427 and 431–594 . . . . 845.5–6
4, 5, 7, 8. Philo Judæus. Works. Transl. by C. D. Yonge 845.7–8
6. Sozomen. Eccl. hist., also eccl. hist. of Philostorgius: transl. by E. Walford . . . 845.9–10

BOHN, H. G. Extra volumes, uniform with Standard library. London, p.8°. *Namely:*
Hamilton, A. Mem. of court of Charles II. . 857.1
— Fairy tales and romances. 857.2
Cervantes, M. de. Exemplary novels. Transl. by W. H. Kelly 857.3
Joyce, J. Introd. to arts and sciences . . . 859.4
Long, G. Cyclopædia of polit. knowledge. 4v. 859.5
Miller's histories philosophically illustrated 859.6

BOHN, H. G. Illustrated library. London. 46v. p.8°. *Namely:*
1–8. Lodge's portraits of illustr. personages of Great Britain 815.1
9. Cruikshank's three courses and a dessert . 815.2
10. Pickering's hist. of the races of man . . . 815.3–6
11. Kitto's scripture lands and biblical atlas . 815.7
12. White's nat. hist. of Selborne. 815.8
13. Didron's Christian iconography. Vol. I. 815.9
14. Redding's hist. and descr. of mod. wines . 815.10
15, 16. Allen's battles of the British navy . . 825.1
17, 18. Rome in the 19th century. Miss C. A. Eaton. 5th ed. 825.2
19. Maxwell's victories of Wellington and the British armies 825.3
20. Life of Wellington 825.4
21. Howitt's, Wm. & M., Stories of English and foreign life 825.5
22. Bechstein's cage and chamber birds . . . 825.6
23. Price, E. Norway and its scenery 825.7
24. China, pictorial, descrip. and histor. . . . 825.8
26. Howitt's, M., pictor. calend. of the seasons 825.10
28, 29. Mudie's British birds 825.12
30. Tasso's Jerusalem delivered. Transl. by J. H. Wiffen 835.1
31. India, pictorial, descrip. and hist., by Miss Corner. 835.2
32. Nicolini's history of the Jesuits 835.3
33. Robinson Crusoe. Defoe, D. 835.4
34. Walker's manly exercises. Revised by "Craven" [Capt. Carleton] 835.5

BOHN, H. G. *Illustrated library, continued.*
35. Miller's history of the Anglo Saxons. . . 835.6
36. Michael Angelo and Raphael. Their lives and works, by Duppa and Quatremère de Quincy. 835.7
37. Walton's and Cotton's complete angler. Ed by E. Jesse 835.8
38. Marryat's Masterman Ready 835.9
39. Tales of the genii, by J. Ridley 835.10
40. Guide to the knowl. of pottery, porcelain, etc., by H. G. Bohn 835.11
41. Life of Alex. Pope, by Robt. Carruthers . 835.12
42. Pope's Homer's Iliad, with Flaxman's designs 835.13
43. Bonomi's Nineveh and its palaces 835.14
44. Pope's Homer's Odyssey, with Flaxman's designs 835.15
45. Pope's poetical works. Ed. by R. Carruthers. Vol. 1 . . . . 835.16
46. Stuart and Revett's antiq. of Athens. . . 835.17

BOHN, H. G. Library of French memoirs. Lond., 1855–56. 6v. p.8°. *Namely:*
1, 2. Commines, P. de. Memoirs. *Also* The Scandal. chronicle, by Jean de Troyes. 2v. 857.4
3–6. Bethune, M. de. *Duke of Sully.* Memoir. Translated. 4v. 857.5

BOHN, H. G. Philological and philosophical library. London. 9v. p.8°. *Containing:*
1. Tennemann, W. A. History of philosophy. Translated by A. Johnson 855.1
2. Herodotus. Analysis and summary, by J. T. Wheeler 855.2
3. Turner, D. W. Notes on Herodotus . . . 855.3
4. Devey, J. Logic. 855.4
5. Kant, I. Critique of pure reason. Translated by J. W. D. Meiklejohn 855.5
6. Thucydides. Analysis and summary, by J. T. Wheeler 855.6
7. Wright, T. Dictionary of obsolete and provincial English. 2v. 855.7
8. Hegel, G. W. F. Philosophy of history. Translated by J. Sibree. 855.8

BOHN, H. G. Scientific library. London. p.8° *Containing:*
1. Staunton, H. Chess player's handbook . 816.1
2. Barry, Opie, and Fuseli. Lectures on painting 816.2
3, 4, 8, 15. Humboldt, A. von. Cosmos . . 816.3
5. Staunton, H. Chess-player's companion . 816.4
6. Handbook of games, ed. by H. G. Bohn . 816.5
7. Humboldt, A. von. Views of Nature . . 816.6–7
9. Richardson, G. F. Introduc. to geology . 816.10
10. Stöckhardt, J. A. Principles of chemistry 816.8–9
11. Mantell, G. A. Petrifactions and their teachings 816.11
12. Agassiz, L. and Gould, A. A. Compar. physiology 816.12
13, 19, 28. Humboldt, A. von. Travels to the equinoctial regions of America 816.13
14. Smith, J. P. Holy script. and geology . . 816.14
16. Oersted, H. C. Soul in nature 816.15
17. Staunton, H. Chess tournament 826.1
18, 20. Kirby, W. Power, etc., of God manifested in the creation of animals 826.2
21. Kidd, J. Adapt. of extern. nature to man 826.3
22. Whewell, W. Astronomy and general physics, with reference to nat. theology . 826.4
23. Schouw, J. F. Earth, plants, and man, and sketches from the mineral kingdom, by F. von Kobell 826.5
24. Chalmers, T. Adaptation of external nature to man 826.6
25. Bacon, F. Physical and metaphysical works 826.7
26, 27. Humphreys, H. N. Coin collector's manual 826.8
29. Lewes, G. H. Comte's philosophy of the sciences 826.9
30. Mantell, G. A. Geological excursions round the Isle of Wight. 826.10
31. Hunt, R. Poetry of science 826.11

BOHN, H. G. *Scientific library, continued.*
32, 33. Ennemoser's history of magic 826.12
34. Hunt, R. Elementary physics. 826.13
35. Handbook of domestic medicine 826.14
36. Stanley, G. Painters of the Dutch and
Flemish schools. 826.15
37. Prout, W. Chemistry, etc., with reference
to natural theology 826.16
38. Joyce, J. Scientific dialogues. 826.17-18
39. Stöckhardt, J. A. Chemical field lectures.
Translated. 836.1
40. Blair's chronological tables, to April, 1856,
by J. W. Rosse 836.2
41. Bolley, P. A. and Paul, B. H. Manual of
technical analysis 836.3
42. Mantell, G. A. Wonders of geology. . . 836.4-5
43, 46. Carpenter, W. B. Zoology. New ed.
by W. S. Dallas. 2v. 836.6
44. Carpenter, W. B. Mechanical philosophy,
horology and astronomy 836.7
BOHN, H. G. Standard library. London. 129v.
p.8°. Containing:
1. Hall, Rev. R. Miscel. works and remains 818.1
2, 3. Roscoe, W. Life and pontificate of Leo
X. 2v. 818.2
4. Schlegel, F. von. Philosophy of history 818.3
5, 6. Sismondi, J. C. L. S. de. Historical
view of the literature of South Europe. 2v. 818.4
7. Roscoe, W. Life of Lorenzo de' Medici . 818.6
8. Schlegel, A. W. v. Lectures on dramatic
art and literature 818.7
9, 11. Beckmann, J. History of inventions,
etc. 2v. 818.8-9
12. Schiller, F. v. Revolt of the Netherlands.
Hist. and dramatic works 818.10
13. Hutchinson, L. Life of Col. Hutchinson 818.13
14. Cellini, B. Memoirs 828.1
15, 18, 22, 85. Coxe, W. History of the House
of Austria, 1218–1792. 3v. 828.2-3
16, 19, 23. Lanzi, A. L. History of painting in
Italy. 3v. 828.4
17. Ockley, S. History of the Saracens . . . 828.5
20. Schiller's historical dramas, Don Carlos,
Mary Stuart, Maid of Orleans, Bride of
Messina 818.11
21, 26, 33. Lamartine's history of the Girondists. Translated 828.6
24. Machiavelli, N. History of Florence . . 828.7
25. Schlegel, F. von. Philosophy of life and
language 828.8-9
27, 32, 36. Ranke, L. History of the Popes.
Translated by E. Foster 838.1
28, 30, 34. Coxe, W. Memoirs of the Duke of
Marlborough. 3v. 838.2
29. Sheridan's dramatic works, with a memoir 828.10
31, 43. Goethe, J. W. von. Autobiography .2v. 838.3-4
35. Wheatly, C. Illustration of the book of
common prayer 838.6
37, 39, 40, 81, 86. Milton, J. Prose works. 5v. 838.7
38, 41, 45. Menzel, W. Hist. of Germany. 3v. 848.2
42. Schlegel, F. von. Æsthetic works 838.8
44. Schiller, F. von. Works. Early dramas
and romances 818.12
46. Schlegel, F. von. Lectures on modern
history 848.1
47. Lamartine, A. de History of the French
revolution of 1848 . . . . 848.3-4
48, 50. Junius. Letters. 2v. 848.5
49, 55, 60, 65, 71. Vasari, G. Lives of painters,
sculptors, and architects. 5v. 848.6
51. Taylor, J. Holy living and dying 848.7
52. Goethe, J. W. von. Dramatic works. Tr.
by A. Swanwick and W. Scott 838.5
53, 56, 58, 61, 66, 67, 75, 82. Neander, A. Hist.
of Christ. relig. and Church. 8v. 858.1
54. Neander, A. Life of Jesus Christ 848.8
59. Gregory, O. Evidences of the Christian
religion 858.2
62, 63. James, G. P. R. Life and times of
Louis XIV. 2v. 858.3
68, 70. Reynolds, Sir J. Literary works. 2v. 858.4

BOHN, H. G. *Standard library, continued.*
69. Fuller, A. Principal works and memoir. 858.5
72. Butler, J. Analogy of religion to nature 858.6
73. Bremer, F. The neighbors, and other
tales 817.1-2
74. Neander, A. Memorials of Christian life. 858.7
76. Bremer, F. President's daughters . . . 817.3
77, 80. Foster, J. Life and correspond. 2v. . 858.8
78. Bacon, F. Moral and historical works . . 858.9
79. Guizot, F. Origin of representative gov't 817.7
83. Bremer, F. The home, Strife and peace.
Translated by Howitt 817.4
84. De Lolme, J. L. Constitution of Eng. . . 817.8
87, 88. Foster, J. Lectures at Broadmead
chapel. 2v. 817.9
89. Bremer, F. A diary, H—family, Axel and
Anna, and other tales 817.5-6
90. Smith, A. Theory of moral sentiments . 817.10
91, 95, 96, 99, 102, 103, 105, 106. Cowper's complete works. Ed. by R. Southey. 8v. . . 817.11
92. Ranke, L. History of Servia. 827.1
94. Reumont, A. von. Carafas of Maddaloni 827.2
97, 109, 112. Condé, J. A. Dominion of the
Arabs in Spain 827.3
98, 104. Locke, J. Philosophical works. 2v. 827.4
100. Hungary and its revolutions, with a memoir of Kossuth 827.5
101, 113. Kelly, W. K. History of Russia. 2v. 827.6
107, 108. James, G. P. R. Life of Richard
Cœur-de-Lion. 2v. 827.7
110, 111. Smyth, W. Lectures on modern history. 2v. 827.8-9
114. Goethe, J. W. v. Wilhelm Meister's apprenticeship 827.10
115. Beaumont and Fletcher. Beauties of. Selections by L. Hunt 837.1
116, 117. Smyth, W. Lectures on the French
revolution. 2v. 837.2
118. Mignet, F. A. History of the French
revolution 837.3
119. Guizot, F. English revolution of 1640.
Translated by W. Hazlitt 837.4
120, 121, 122. Guizot, F. Hist. of civiliza. 3v. 837.5
123, 124. Thierry, A. Conquest of England. 2v. 837.6
125, 126. Foster, J. Critical essays. Ed. by
J. E. Ryland. 837.7
127. Luther, M. Table talk. Translated by W.
Hazlitt. Life of Luther, by Chalmers . . 837.8
128, 129, 130, 131. Lamartine, A. de. Restoration of monarchy in France. 4v. 837.9
132. Carrel, J. B. N. A. Counter revolution in
England. Fox's James II. Lonsdale's
James II. 837.10
133. Sturm, C. C. Morning communings with
God. Translated by W. Johnstone. . . . 837.11
BOIS, V. Les Chemins de fer français. Paris,
1853. 12°. 1078.27
— La télégraphie électrique. Paris, 1855. 12°. 1078.32
BOISMONT, Brierre de. *See* Brierre de Boismont.
BOKER, G. H. Plays and poems. Bost., 1856. 2v. 12° 335.2
Contents.—Vol. I. Calaynos; Anne Boleyn; Leonor
de Guzman; Francesca de Rimini. II. The betrothal;
Widow's marriage; Poems; Songs; Str. lyrics; Sonnets.

BOKHARA. Burnes, A. Travels into. 604.11
— Khanikoff. Its amir and its people. 604.4
— Wolff, J. Narrative of a mission to. 605.2
BOLEYN, Anne, Memoir of. Benger, E. O. 594.14
BOLINGBROKE, Lord. *See* St. John, Henry . . . 891.3
BOLIVAR, S., Memoir of, and of his generals. Hol-
stein, H. L. V. D. 539.1
BOLLEY, P. A. and Paul, B. H. Manual of techni-
cal analysis. London, 1857. p.8° 836.3
BOLTON, W. J. Evidences of Christianity,—apolo-
gists down to Augustine. Boston, 1854. 12° 1094.11
BONAPARTE, Napoleon. *See* Napoleon I.
BONAPARTE, Louis Napoleon. *See* Napoleon III.
BONAPARTE, C. L. American ornithology. *See*
Wilson, A. 830.66
BOND, H. Family memorials. Early settlers of
Watertown. Waltham and Weston, Mass.
Boston, 1855. 2v. in 1. 8° 224.1

BOND, J. W. Minnesota and its resources. Chicago, 1856. 12° 237.8
BONDMAN, The. London, 1833. p.8° 798.10
BONNECHOSE, E. de. Histoire de France. 9th ed. Paris, 1859. 2v. 12° 1066.3
— History of France, translated by W. Robson. London, 1853. p.8° 1007.2-3
— Les réformateurs avant la réforme. 2d ed. Paris, 1846. 2v. 12° 1066.4
— The reformers before the reformation. Translated by C. Mackenzie. N. Y., 1844. 8° . 1085.9
BONNEFOUX, Baron. History of Columbus. See Becher, A. B. 625.13
BONNER, J. Child's history of Greece. New York, 1857. 2v. 16° 959.10
— Child's history of Rome. N. Y., 1856. 2v. 16° 959.11
— Child's history of the U. S. N. Y., 1855. 2v. 18° 309.12
BONNEY, E. The banditti of the prairies. A tale. Chicago, 1856. 8° 735.13
BONNYCASTLE, R. H. Newfoundland in 1842. London, 1842. 2v. 12° 629.8
BONOMI, J. Nineveh and its palaces. Lond., n.d. 8° 685.10
— Nineveh and its palaces. 2d ed. Lond., 1853. 8° 956.8
— Nineveh and its palaces. 3d ed. London, 1857. p.8° 835.14
BONPLAND, A. Travels to the equinoctial regions of America. See Humboldt, A. von 816.13
BOOK, The, and its story; with preface by Rev. T. Phillips. 1st Am. ed. Phila., 1854. 12° . . 1094.12
BOOK, The, of my lady. Boston, 1833. 16° . . . 449.18
BOOK of table-talk. New ed. Lond., 1847. 2v. 24° 840.2
BOOK of trades. 11th ed. London and Glasgow, 1854. sq. 16° 199.37
BOOK. Hunt, L. B. for a corner: or selections in prose and verse 895.15
— Smith, C. W. B. of recitations 356.25
— Thackeray, W. M. B. of snobs 509.4
— Tyler, Mrs. M. W. A book without a title. . 478.10
BOOKS, Method of keeping, by double entry. Comer, G. N. 135.11
BOONE, D. Life of. Peck, J. M. Sparks's Am. biography. XXIII. 529.1
BOOTH, D. The art of brewing. Lib. Us. Kn. . 365.12
— Explan. of scientific terms. Lib. Us. Kn. I. . 365.14
BORDER beagles, a tale of Mississippi. Simms, W. G. 800.3-7
BORDER life. Mirror of olden time. Pritts, J. . . 245.2
BORDER tales and legends. Maxwell, W. H. . . . 807.12
BORDER warfare of New York, during the revolution. Campbell, W. W. 217.11
BORDER wars of the Am. revolution. Stone, W. L. 820.62
BORGHINI, V. Studi sulla divina commedia . . . 1058.5
BORGNET, J. Histoire du comté de Namur. Bruxelles, n.d. 12° 1075.12
BORNEO, The expedition to, for suppression of piracy. Keppel, H. 707.14
BORROW, G. The Bible in Spain. London, 1843. p.8° 889.4
— The Bible in Spain. 13th ed. N. Y., 1851. 8° 673.1
— Lavengro: the scholar, the gipsey, the priest. New York, 1851. 12° 478.2-3
— Romany rye. London, 1857. 2v. 12° 478.4
— Romany rye. New York, 1857. 8° 802.22
— The Zincali: or, gypsies of Spain. 4th ed. London, 1846. p.8° 889.5
BORTHWICK, J. D. Three years in California. Edinburgh, 1857. 8° 624.6
BOSCAVEN, H. Manuel de versification. Bruxelles, n.d. 12° 1065.6
BOSCOBEL tracts. 857.1
BOSNIA, Insurrection in. Ranke, L. 827.1
BOSOM friend, The: a novel. Grey, Mrs. 802.28
BOST, M. Letters and biography of Neff, F. . . . 544.15
BOSSUET, J. B. Oraisons funèbres. Essai par Villemain. Notices, etc., par Dussault. Choix d' oraisons fun. de Fléchier et de Mascaron. Paris, 1854. 12° 1066.5
BOSTON, England. The history and antiquities of. Thompson, P. 962.1
BOSTON (Mass.) memorial of Daniel Webster, ed. by G. S. Hillard. Boston, 1853. 8° 512.6

BOSTON book. The. Boston, 1850. 12° 888.8
BOSTON common. A tale. Boston, 1856. 12°. . . 417.1
BOSTON notions. Dearborn, N. 229.8-9
BOSTON, stage, Records of the. Clapp, W. W. jr. 356.10-11
BOSTON theatre. Spencer, W. V. 355.9
BOSTON, Mass. Drake, S. G. History of, 1630-1770. 222.1
— Frothingham, R. Siege of 214.2-8
— Homans, J. S. Sketches of 229.7
— Local loiterings in the vicinity of 228.9
See also: East B., South B., Brattle st., Copp's Hill, Granary burial grounds, Orators, etc.
BOSTON, T. Human nature in its fourfold state. New York, 1853. 12° 1109.9
— The crook in the lot. New York, 1852. 12°. 1089.29
BOSWORTH, N. Hist. of Montreal. Mont., 1839. 12° 265.4
BOSWELL, J. Essays in favor of the Corsicans. London, 1769. 16° 679.12
— Letters to the Rev. W. J. Temple. London, 1857. 8° 582.5
— Life of Samuel Johnson. New ed. London, n.d. 4v. p.8° 869.2-6
— Life of S. Johnson, incl. journal of a tour to the Hebrides. New York, 1846-50. 2v. 8° 582.4
— Tour to the Hebrides with Samuel Johnson. From London edition. Phila., 1810. 8° . . 646.2
— Tour to the Hebrides with S. Johnson. New ed. London, [1852.] p.8° 869.1
BOTANICAL letters to a friend. Unger, F. 166.14
BOTANICAL text-book. Gray, A. 166.3
BOTANIST, Marine. Gifford, I. 169.21
BOTANY. Balfour, J. H. Manual of 166.17
— Beck, L. C. B. of the U. S., North of Virginia 166.7
— Bentham, G. Handbook of British flora . . 166.18
— Burnett, G. T. Outlines of 166.1
— Darby, J. Manual of, for the Southern states 169.4
— Downing, A. J. Fruits and fruit-trees . . . 165.14
— Flagg, W. Studies in the field and forest . . 166.6
— Flower garden, from Quarterly Review . . . 165.28
— Forests and forest trees 165.10
— Gray, A. B. for young people. How plants grow 166.13
— — Manual of, of the northern U. S. 166.8
— Griffith, R. E. Medical. 152.11
— Hannon, J. D. Flore belge 1075.26
— Henfrey, A. Outlines of structural and physiological 169.17
— — Rudiments of 169.32
— Henslow, J. S. Principles of descriptive and physiological 408.6
— Johns, C. A. Flowers of the field 169.24
— Lincoln, Mrs. A. H. Familiar lectures on . . 169.3
— Lindley, J. Botany. Lib. Us. Kn. 365.15
— — Introd. to the natural system of 164.3
— — School 169.25
— — Ladies' 164.2
— Nuttall, T. Introduction to systematic and physiological 169.1
— Phelps, Mrs. B. for beginners 169.16
— Pratt, A. Field, garden and woodland. . . . 169.33
— Schleiden, M. J. Popular exposition of . . . 166.9-10
— — The plant, a biography 164.5
— Soc. for prom. Christ. knowl. Conservatories of Kew 178.22
— Spring, A. Botanique 1065.54
— Thomson, S. Wanderings among wild flowers 169.22
— Woodland gleanings: Br. forest trees 169.20
See also: Gardening.
BOTHWELL: a poem. Aytoun, W. E. 334.3-5
BOTTA, C. G. G. Storia d'Italia sino al 1789. Capolago, 1832-33. 12v. 16° 1048.2
— Storia d'Italia dal 1789 al 1814. Capolago, 1833. 6v. 16° 1048.1
— Hist. of the war of Am. independence. Tr. by G. A. Otis. 8th ed. N. Haven, 1838. 2v. 8° 213.12
— Same. Tr. by G. A. Otis. 9th ed. Cooperstown, N. Y., 1847-8. 2v. 8° 213.11
BOTTA, P. E. Discoveries of, appl. to the elucidation of Holy Writ. Bonomi, J. 835.14

BOTTARI, G. Dialoghi sopra le tre arti del disegno. Dial. a difesa di Felsina: Discorso sulla nobiltà attrib. al frat. Paggi. Ed. 2da Parma, 1845. 16° 1059.13
— Lettere sulla pittura, scultura, ed architettura. Contin. da S. Ticozzi. Milano, 1822-25. 8v. 16° 1049.1
BOUDON, H. M. de. Life of. Butler, C. 617.14
BOUILLY, J. N. Tales for mothers. From the French. New York, 1824. 12° 498.13
BOUNTY, (ship,) Home of the mutineers of the . . 1109.8
— Barrow, J. Auth. acc't of the mutiny of the. 810.42
— - Eventful hist. of the mutiny 389.1
— Murray, T. B. Short acc't of the mutiny of the 939.6
BOURDALOUE, in the court of Louis XIV. Bungener, L. 1096.4-6
BOURNE, B. F. The captive in Patagonia: or, life among the giants. Boston, 1853. 12° . . .635.16-17
BOURNE, J. Catechism of the steam engine. New ed. New York, 1851. 18° 198.22-28
— Treatise on the screw propeller. 2d ed. London, 1855. 4° 191.3
— Treatise on the steam engine. Lond., 1851. 4° 191.2
BOURRIENNE, L. A. F. de. Life of Napoleon. Philadelphia, 1832. 8° 602.8
— Mem. of Napoleon Bonaparte. Transl. by J. S. Memes. Edinburgh, 1830. 3v. 18° . . . 830.60
BOUSSINGAULT, M. J. B. Balance of organic nature. See Dumas, M. J. 156.34
BOUTMY. Personal history of Louis Philippe, fr. 1773-1848. London, 1848. 12° 616.10
BOUTON, N. History of Concord, N. H. Concord, 1856. 8° 224.3
BOUTERWEK, F. Spanish literature. Transl. by T. Ross, with notes. London, 1847. 16° . . 404.10
BOUVET, F. The Turks in Europe, etc. Gilson, A. 918.16
BOUVIER, H. M. Familiar astronomy. Philadelphia, 1857. 8° 146.3
BOVEE, C. N. Thoughts, feelings and fancies. New York, 1857. sm. 4° 877.2
BOWDITCH, H. I. The young stethoscopist. 2d ed. New York, 1848. 12° 153.10
BOWDITCH, N. Memoir of, prepared for the young. Boston, 1841. 16° 526.10
— The practical navigator, contin. by J. I. Bowditch. 18th ed. New York, 1848. 8° . . . 135.3
BOWDLER, Miss H. Poems and essays. Fr. 16th London ed. Boston, 1827. 12° 888.12
BOWDLER, H. M. Acc't of life and character of Miss E. Smith 599.7
BOWEN, A. Naval monument, 1812-15. Boston, 1816. 8° 215.11
BOWEN, B. B. Blind man's offering. 4th ed. New York, 1854. 12° 888.6
BOWEN, F. Life of J. Otis. Sparks's Am. biog., XII. 529.1
— Life of B. Lincoln. Sparks's Am. biog., XXIII. 529.1
— Life of Sir W. Phips. Sparks's Am. biog., VII. 529.1
— Life of Baron Steuben. Sparks's Amer. biog., IX. 529.1
— Metaphysical and ethical science appl. to the evidences of religion. New ed. Bost.,1855. 12° 125.8
— Principles of political economy. Bost., 1856. 8° 135.7
BOWEN, G. F. Hand-book for Greece. New ed. London, 1854. 12° 649.8-9
BOWMAN, A. The castaways: or, adven. in the wilds of Africa. London, 1857. 12° 719.7
BOWMAN, J. E. Handbook of medical chemistry. Philadelphia, 1850. 12° 157.11
BOWRING, J. Ancient poetry and romances of Spain. London, 1824. 12° 316.9
— Matins and vespers. From 2d London ed. Boston, 1827. 12° 349.18
— Poetry of the Magyars, and sketch of the language and lit. of Hungary. Lond., 1830. 8° 316.2
— Specimens of the Russian poets, with mem'rs and biog. notices. Boston, 1822. 12° 315.14
— Kingdom and people of Siam in 1855. London, 1857. 2v. 8° 696.3
BOXFORD, Mass. History of Rowley, anciently incl. Boxford. Gage, T. 227.6

BOX tunnel, The: a fact. Reade, C. 415.8
BOYD, J. M'N. Manual for naval cadets. London, 1857. 16° 199.3
BOYHOOD of great men. New York, 1853. 16° . . 548.13
— Jervis, M. J. W. B. of great painters 548.14
— Russell, W. B. and early life of extraord. men 879.15
BOY hunters, The: a novel. Reid, M. 718.1
BOY's adventures in Australia. Howitt, W. . . . 719.4-6
BOY's book. Encyclop. of sports. Forrest, G. . . 197.25
BOY's book of industrial information. Noyce, E. . 196.15
BOY's own book. 1st Am. ed. Bost., 1829. sq.16° 199.40
BOZMAN, J. L. History of Maryland from 1633-1660. Baltimore, 1837. 2v. in 1 . . . . . . 235.3
BRACCIOLINI, P. Life of Shepherd, W. 543.8
BRACE, C. L. Home-life in Germany. New York, 1856. 12° 667.7-11
— Hungary in 1851: with an experience of the Austrian police. New York, 1853. 12° . . 667.5-6
— The Norse-folk. New York, 1857. 12° . . 668.9-11
BRACEBRIDGE hall. See Irving, W.
BRACKENRIDGE, H. H. Modern chivalry: adventures of a captain and Teague O'Regan his servant. Pittsburgh, 1819. 2v. 12° . . 498.19
BRACKENRIDGE, H. M. Hist. of the late war between the U. S. and G. B. Phila., 1839. 12° 217.5
— Recollections of persons and places in the West. Philadelphia, n.d. 16° 239.7
— Voyage to South America, 1817-18. Baltimore, 1819. 2v. 8° 633.19
BRACKETT, E. A. Twilight hours of an artist. Boston, 1845. 12° 348.19
BRADDOCK's expedition against Fort Du Quesne. Sargent, W. 244.1
BRADFORD, A. Biographical notices of distinguished men in N. Eng. Boston, 1842. 12° 518.6
— History of Mass. from 1620-1820. Bost., 1835. 8°223.9-10
— Memoir of Rev. J. Mayhew. Boston, 1838. 8° 534.2
BRADFORD, J. Address at 2d centennial anniversary of the settlement of Rowley 227.6
BRADFORD, S. H. History of Peter the Great. New York, 1858. 12° 546.22
— Story of Columbus. New York, 1857. 12° . . 544.19
BRADFORD, T. G. See Encyclopædia Americana.
BRADFORD, W. History of Plymouth colony and dialogue. See Morton, N. Memorial . . . 223.14
— History of Plymouth colony. Journal, dialogue, and memoir of Brewster. Young, A. 223.13
— Hist. of Plymouth planta. Now first printed. Boston, 1856. Mass. hist. col. 4th series, III. 278.4
BRADFORD, Mass. History of Rowley, anciently including Bradford. Gage, T. 227.6
BRADSHAW, J. Biography of. Trials of Charles I., and some of the regicides 309.7
BRADY, W. Kedge-anchor, or young sailor's assistant. 8th ed. enl. New York, 1855. 8° . 194.6
BRAHE, Tycho. Life of. Brewster, Sir D. 820.34
BRAINARD, J. G. C. Literary remains, with a sketch of his life. By J. G. Whittier. Hartford, n.d. 12° 338.16
BRAINERD, D. Life of. Edwards, J. 534.11
— Life of. Abridged. Edwards, J. 119.25
— Life of. Peabody, W. B. O. 518.5
BRAINNE, C. La Nouvelle Calédonie. Paris, 1854. 12° 1078.50
BRAMAN, D. E. E. Information about Texas. Phila., 1857. 12° 239.10
BRAMBLETYE house. Smith, H. 797.1
BRAMIERE, L. Novelle. See Soave, F. 1058.2
BRAND, J. Obs. on the popular antiquities of Gt. Britain. London, 1848-49. 3v. p.8° 846.8
— Obs. on popular antiquities. New ed. London, 1841. 3v. sq.16° 949.8
BRANDE, W. T. Dictionary of science, literature and art. Ed. by W. T. B., assisted by J. Cauvin. New York, 1843. roy.8° 135.1
BRANDENBURG, House of, in the 17th and 18th centuries. Ranke, L. 925.7
BRANDIS, C. A. Essay on the character and influence of B. G. Niebuhr 583.1
BRANDON, or 100 years ago. Tiffany, O. 445.14

BRANSTON, T. F. Hand-book of practical receipts:
a manual for the chemist. 1st Am. ed.
Philadelphia, 1857. 12° 198.1
BRANT, J. Life of. Stone, W. L. 513.12
BRATTLE street church, Boston. A history of.
Lothrop, S. K. 297.22
BRAUN, T. Principes d'éducation. Bruxelles,
n.d. 12° 1065.7
BRAVO, The: a tale. Cooper, J. F. 760.9–13
BRAY, A. E. Courtenay of Walreddon: a romance.
New ed. London, 1846. 16° 448.13
— De Foix; an historical romance. New ed.
London, 1845. 16° 448.11
— Fitz of Fitz-Ford: a legend. New ed. Lon-
don, 1845. 16° 448.15
— Henry de Pomeroy: a legend. Also, The
white rose. New edition. London, 1846.
16° 448.10
— The protestant. A tale of the reign of Q.
Mary. New ed. London, 1845. 16° 448.16
— The Talba: a romance. New ed. London,
1845. 16° 448.14
— Trelawny of Trelawne: a legend. New ed.
London, 1845. 16° 448.9
— Warleigh: a legend. New ed. London, 1845.
16° 448.12
— The White-hoods: an historical romance.
New ed. London, 1845. 16° 448.17
BRAYLEY, E. W. Londiniana. Lond., 1829. 4v. 12° 989.7
BRAZIL. Adalbert, Prince. Travels in 633.11
— Armitage, J. History of. 1808 to 1831 . . . . 263.6
— Ewbank, T. Life in 633.1
— Kidder, D. P. and Fletcher, J. C. B. and the
Brazilians 263.2–5
— Mansfield, C. B. Letters in 1852–53 . . . . . 635.10
— Spix, J. B. von. Travels in 1817–20 . . . . . 633.18
— Stewart, C. S. Record of a cruise 635.14
— Walsh, R. Notices of, in 1828–29 . . . . . . 266.6
BREACH of promise: a novel. Curtis, Miss . . . 802.30
BREAD-BOOK, English. Acton, E. 188.33
BRECK, J. The flower garden. New ed. rev. Bos-
ton, 1856. 12° 166.11
BREEN, H. H. Modern English literature, its
blemishes and defects. London, 1857. 8°. 401.2
BREMER, F. Brothers and sisters: a tale. Tr.
by M. Howitt. N. Y., 1848. 8° 455.1
— The curate. Translated. See Omnibus Mod.
Rom. 801.2
— Diary, the H—family, and other tales. Tr.
by M. Howitt. 4th ed. London, 1853. p.8° 817.5–6
— Hertha. Translated by M. Howitt. New
York, 1856. 12° 455.14–18
— The home. Transl. by M. Howitt. Author's
ed. New York, 1850. 12° 455.10
— The home. Strife and peace. Transl. by M.
Howitt. London, 1853. p.8° 817.4
— Homes of the new world. Transl. by Mary
Howitt. N. Y., 1853–54. 2v. 12° 627.2
— Midnight sun. Transl. by M. Howitt. New
York, n.d. 8° 455.4–5
— Morning watches. Strauss and the Gospels.
The confession of faith of F. R. Transl.
Boston, 1843. 8° 1094.3
— The neighbors: a story. Translated by M.
Howitt. London, 1842. 2v. 12° 455.11
— - Same. Author's edition. N. York. 1850.
12° 455.12
— - Same. Boston, 1843. 2v. in 1. 12° 455.13
— - Same. And other tales. Transl. by M.
Howitt. 4th ed. London, 1852. p.8° . . . 817.1–2
— New sketches of every day life: a diary; with
Strife and peace. Translated by M. Howitt.
New York, 1844. 8° 455.2–3
— President's daughters. Translated. Boston,
1843. 12° 455.8
— - Same. Part 2. Nina. Translated by M.
Howitt. New York, 1843. 8° 455.6
— - Same. Including Nina. Translated by
M. Howitt. London, 1843. 3v. 12° 455.9
— - Same. Including Nina. Translated by
M. Howitt. London, 1852. p.8° 817.3

BRENTANO, Cl. Märchen. Herausg. v. Görres.
Stuttgart, 1846–47. 2v. 8° 1013.8

Contents. — Vol. I. Vorwort zur Erinnerung an den
Dichter dieser Märchen; Von dem Rhein und dem
Müller Radlauf; von dem Hause Staarenberg u. den
Ahnen des Müllers Radlauf; vom Murmelthier; vom
Schneider Siebentodt auf einen Schlag; von dem
Witzenspitzel; von dem Myrthenfräulein. II. Das
Märchen von den Märchen oder Liebseelchen; von
dem Schulmeister Klopfstock u. seinen fünf Söhnen;
von Gockel und Hinkel; von Rosenblättchen; von
dem Baron von Hüpfenstich; von Fanferlieschen
Schönefüsschen; von dem Dilldapp; von Komandit
chen; [fragment;] von Schnärlieschen; [fragment.]

BRENTON, E. P. Naval history of Great Britain,
1783–1836. New ed. London, 1837. 2v. 8° 986.3
BRENTON, Sir J., Memoir of. Raikes, H. 565.7
BRESCIANI, A. Biografie di tre giovinetti 1058.7
BRESLAU und die schlesischen Eisenbahnen. Kur-
nik, M. 1029.9
BREWER, E. C. Scientific knowledge of things
familiar. New York, 1851. 18° 199.31
— Sound and its phenomena. London, 1854. 18° 199.32
BREWING. Booth. The art of 365.12
— Byrn, M. L. The art of 199.8
— Donovan, M. Domestic economy. I. 408.8
BREWSTER, Sir D. Lives of Galileo, Tycho Brahe
and Kepler. 2d ed. London, 1846. 16° . . 548.15
— Same. New York, 1847. 18° 820.34
— Natural magic. London, 1834. 16° 379.10
— Same. 6th ed. London, 1851. 16° 379.3
— Life of Sir I. Newton. New York, n.d. 18° . 810.32
— Same. London, 1831. 16° 379.4
— Memoirs of Sir I. Newton. Edin., 1855. 2v. 8° 573.2
— More worlds than one. London, 1854. sm.8° 146.28
— Same. New York, 1854. 16° 146.29
— Optics. 2d Am. ed. Phila., 1835. 12° . . . 149.35
— Same. New ed. London, 1843. 16° 398.11
— Optics. Double refraction and polarisation of
light. Lib. Us. Kn., I. 365.14
— The stereoscope, its history, etc. London,
1856. 12° 207.18
— Treatise on new philosophical instruments.
Edinburgh, 1813. 8° 144.12
— Lives of eminent men. See Shelley, Mrs. . . 398.1
BREWSTER, M. M. Work: or, plenty to do, etc.
New York, 1855. 12° 1099.20–21
BREWSTER, W. Mem. of, by Bradford, W. . . . 223.12–13
— Life and times of. Steele, A. 223.15
BRIALMONT, A. Life of Arthur, duke of Welling-
ton. London, 1858. 2v. 8° 565.9
— Précis d'art militaire. Bruxelles, n.d. 12°. . 1065.9
BRICKS. Dobson, E. Manufacture of, and tiles . 819.16
— Wilds, W. Manufacture of 207.4
See also: Architecture.
BRIDE of Fort Edward. New York, 1839. 12° . . 358.2
BRIDE of the northern wilds. Curtis, N. M. . . . 802.29
BRIDE of Lammermoor. Scott, Sir W. 460.34–38
BRIDGE-construction. Theory of. Haupt, H. . . 195.1
BRIDGES, Tubular and iron girder. Dempsey, G. D. 819.30
BRIDGES, F. Phrenology made practical. Lond.,
1857. 16° 124.26
BRIDGEWATER, Mass. History of. Mitchell, N. 224.6
BRIDGMAN, T. Epitaphs from Copp's hill burial
ground. Boston, 1851. 12° 229.4
— Inscriptions in Northampton and valley of
the Conn. Northampton, 1850. 12° 228.3
— Pilgrims of Boston and their descendants.
New York, 1856. 8° 223.5
BRIEF analysis of the sects, heresies and writers
of the first three centuries. Cambridge,
1857. 12° 1096.15
BRIEF view of Greek philosophy to the age of Peri-
cles. Phila., 1846. 16°. Sm. books. II. . . 850.25
BRIEF view of Greek philosophy from Socrates to
Christ. Phila., 1846. 16°. Sm. books. II. . 850.25
BRIEFE aus dem Freundeskreise von Goethe, Her-
der, Höpfner u. Merck. Leipzig, 1847.
sm.8° 1034.10
BRIERRE de Boismont, A. Hallucinations: rational
hist. of apparitions, etc. 1st Am. ed. Phila.,
1853. 8° 122.1

BRIGGS, C. F. and Maverick, A. Story of the telegraph, and hist. of the Atlantic cable. New York, 1858. 12° 196.16
BRIGHTWELL, C. L. Memorials of the life of A. Opie. Norwich, 1854. 8°. . . : 595.4
BRIMLEY, G. Essays : ed. by W. G. Clarke. Cambridge, 1858. p.8°. 877.5
BRISSON, M. de, Captivity of 830.31
BRISSOT de Warville, J. P. Travels in the U. S. in 1788, by B. and Claviere. 2d ed. London, 1794. 2v. 8°. 625.16
— New travels in U. S. in 1788. Transl. Boston, 1797. 12°. 629.27
BRISTED, C. A. Five years in an Eng. university. 2d ed. New York, 1852. 12° 884.14
BRITAIN, Great. See Great Britain.
BRITANNIC researches. Poste, B. 985.2
BRITISH admirals, Lives of the. Southey, R. and Bell, R. 388.5
BRITISH army as it is 894.2
BRITISH army, Campaigns of the, at Washington and New Orleans. Gleig, G. R. 889.19
BRITISH cabinet in 1853. London, 1853. 12° . . 599.9
BRITISH coasts, Natural history of the. Harvey, W. H. 178.25
BRITISH commerce, History of. Craik, G. L. . . . 840.14
BRITISH commonwealth. Cox, H. 134.22
BRITISH constitution, Outline of the. Goldsmith, O. 968.6
BRITISH costume, History of. Planché, J. R. . . 840.51
BRITISH drama, The anc. and mod. Scott, Sir W. 331.1-2
BRITISH eloquence, Select. Goodrich, C. A. . . . 861.2
BRITISH empire, Pictorial and literary sketch-book of the 641.1
BRITISH essayists : with prefaces by A. Chalmers. London, 1817. 45v. 18° 850.24
    Contents. — Vol. I.—V. Tatler, Steele, with hist.
    and biog. pref. VI.—XV. Spectator, with prefaces.
    XVI.—XVIII. Guardian, with index. XIX.—XXII.
    Rambler. Johnson, S. XXIII.—V. Adventurer.
    Hawkesworth. XXVI.—IX. The world. Moore, E.
    XXX.—II. Connoisseur. Colman and Thornton, B.
    XXXIII. Idler. Johnson, S. XXXIV.—V. Mirror.
    Mackenzie, H. and oth. XXXVI.—VII. Lounger.
    Mackenzie, H. XXXVIII.—XL. Observer. Cumberland, R. XLI.—IV. Looker-on. Roberts, W.
    XLV. Index.
BRITISH flora, Handbook of. Bentham, G. 166.18
BRITISH historians, Lives of. Lawrence, E. . . . 586.11-12
BRITISH institutions, Character and tendency of. Isham, W. 135.21
BRITISH invasion of North Carolina in 1776. Swain, D. L. 235.6
BRITISH lawyers, Lives of eminent. Roscoe, H. . 388.4
BRITISH manufactures. Dodd, G. 840.20
BRITISH military commanders, Lives of. Gleig, R. 388.3
BRITISH mines, as a means of investment. Murchison, J. H. 136.32
BRITISH museum, Antiquities and marbles in the 209.15
BRITISH navy. Allen, J. Battles of the 825.1
— Giffard, E. Anecdotes of the 989.8
BRITISH novelists. Barbauld, A. L. . . . . 778&779
BRITISH painters, Lives of. Cunningham, A. . . . 810.19
BRITISH poets. Aikin, J. Select works of the. . 312.1
— Campbell, T. Notices of the 889.7
— Campbell, T. Specimens of 343.14
— Dictionary of quotations from 358.5
— Halleck, F. G. Selections from the 820.25
— Howitt, W. Homes and haunts of 896.1-2
— Reed, H. Lectures on the 346.9
— Southey, R. Chaucer to Jonson 312.11
— Specimens of the 369.12
BRITISH satirist, comprising the best satires fr. Pope to Byron. Glasgow, 1826. 24° 309.13
    Contents. — English bards and Scotch reviewers,
    Byron; New morality, Canning; The Lousiad, Epistle to James Boswell, Bozzy and Piozzi, Pindar; An
    heroic epistle to Sir W. Chambers, Knt.; An heroic
    epistle to the public; London, Johnson; The vanity
    of human wishes, Johnson; The Rosciad, Churchill;
    Retaliation, Goldsmith; The state dunces, Whitehead; Advice and reproof, Smollet; Taste, Armstrong; A day, Armstrong; On poetry, Swift; A character of the Legion Club, Swift; Life and character
    of Dr. Swift; The Dunciad, Pope.

BRITISH senate. Grant, J. 898.18
BRITISH spy, Letters of. Wirt, W. 909.5-6
BRITISH statesmen. Mackintosh, Sir J. Lives of eminent. 388.6
— Speeches of. 866.12
BRITISH theatre. Inchbald, E. 354.1
BRITISH worthies. Cabinet portrait gallery of . 840.10-11
BRITTAN, Belle. See Fuller, H.
BRITTANY. Froissart, J. The ancient chronicles of 1001.2
— Hope, I. B. and the Bible. 409.9
— — - B. and the chase 409.9
— Lowell, J. R. A legend of. 346.17
— Souvestre, E. B. and La Vendée. 767.4-8
BROAD grins from China. A novel. Sealy, T. H. 469.16
BROCK, Sir I. Life and corresp. Ed. by F. B. Tupper. London, 1845. 12° 556.10
BROCK, Wm. Biogr. sketch of Sir H. Havelock. London, 1858. 16° 578.11
— Same. New York, 1858. 12° 578.12
BROCKEDON, W. Excursions in the Alps. 3d ed. London, 1845. 12°. 663.13
BROCKHAUS's Reise Bibliothek. Leipzig, 1855-57. 20v. 16°. Containing:
    1. Berneck, K. G. v. Schlachten bei Leipzig 1029.2
    2. Bock, A. Die thüringische Eisenbahn . 1029.8
    3. Buddeus, A. Eisenbahnfahrt u. Wanderungen im süddeutschen Rheinland. . 1029.16
    4. Gottschall, R. Das schlesische Gebirge. 1029.19
    5. Förster, M. Briefe aus Südrussland. . . 1029.13
    6. Häring, W. Reise-Pitaval 1029.10
    7. Hocker, N. Der Rhein 1029.21
    8. — Das Moselthal 1029.3
    9. Horn, J. E. Brüssel nach seiner Vergangenheit und Gegenwart. 1029.7
    10. Kapper, S. Die böhmischen Bäder. . . 1029.11
    11. Müller v. Königswinter, W. Münchener Skizzenbuch 1029.17
    12. Kühne, F. G. Wien in alter u. neuer Zeit 1029.4
    13. Kurnik, M. Breslau u. die schlesischen Eisenbahnen. 1029.9
    14. Müller, E. Das hessische Land u. Volk . 1029.5
    15. Pröhle, H. Harzbilder. 1029.14
    16. Rank, J. Schillerhäuser 1029.12
    17. — Poetisches-Reise-Album 1029.6
    18. Schücking, L. Eine Eisenbahnfahrt durch Westfalen 1029.20
    19. — Von Minden nach Köln 1029.18
    20. Willkomm, E. Von Berlin nach Hamburg 1029.15
BROCKLESBY, J. Elements of meteorology. 3d ed. New York, 1849 . . . . 145.27
BRODERIP, W. J. Leaves from the note-book of a naturalist. London, 1852. p.8°. 178.5
— Zoological recreations. 3d ed. Lond., 1858. p.8° 177.8
BRODIE, Sir B. C. Mind and matter; with notes by the Am. ed. New York, 1857. 12° . . . 125.6
— Psychological inquiries. 2d ed. London, 1855. 16° 129.18
BRODHEAD, J. R. History of the State of New York. 1609-64. N. Y., 1853. 8° 234.10
BROGLIO-Solari, C. H. See: Solari, C. H. B.
BRONTË, A. Tenant of Wildfell hall. New York, 1848. 12° 435.18-19
BRONTË, C. Jane Eyre. New York, 1848. 8°. . 435.2-3
— Jane Eyre. New York, 1856. 12° 435.4-8
— The professor. A tale. N. Y., 1857. 12°. . 435.13-14
— Shirley. A tale. New York, 1856. 12° . . . 435.11
— Villette. New York, 1853. 8° 435.9
— Villette. New York, 1856. 12° 435.10
— Life of. Gaskell, E. C. 596.11-15
BRONTË, E. Wuthering heights. A novel. New York, 1855. 12° 435.12
BROOKE and Brooke farm. A tale. Martineau, H. III 749.2-3
BROOKE, Chr. Ghost of Richard III. A poem, 1614. With introduc. and notes, by J. P. Collier. London, 1844. 8° 342.21
BROOKE, Chs. Elements of nat. philos. See Bird, G. 149.24
BROOKE, H. The fool of quality. New ed. Dublin, 1796. 3v. 16° 799.4
BROOKE, Mrs. F. M. Julia Mandeville. . . v. 27 of 778.1
BROOKS, C. Hist. of Medford, Mass. Bost., 1855. 8° 224.5
BROOKS, C. T. German lyrics. Boston, 1843. 12° 316.8

BROOKS, C. T. Songs and ballads; tr. from German lyric poets. Boston, 1842. 12° 316.6
BROOKS, J. T. Four months among the gold-finders in California. New York, 1849. 8° . . . 623.6
BROOKS, M. Idomen. A story. N. Y., 1843. 16° 469.27
BROOKS, S. Russians of the South. London, 1854. p.8° 409.2
BROTHER and sister: a tale. Opie, A. 469.34-35
BROTHERS, The. A tale of the Fronde. Herbert, H. W. 498.6
BROTHERS and sisters: a tale. Bremer, F. 455.1
BROUCKERE, C. de. La charité et l'assistance publique. Bruxelles, n.d. 12° 1065.11
— Principes d'économie politique. Bruxelles, n.d. 12° 1065.10
BROUGHAM, H., Lord. Acc't of Bacon's organon. pt. 1, 2. 8° 365.11
— Dialogues on instinct, with view of the researches on fossil osteology. Lond., 1844. 24° 840.7
— - Same. Philadelphia, 1845. 24° 840.8
— Discourses of. 1. Science ; II. Political science. London, 1846. 24° 840.6
— Historical sketches of statesmen in the time of Geo. III. 1-3 series, each in 2v. Lond., 1845-48. 6v. 24° 840.5
— Historical sketches of statesmen in the time of Geo. III. London, 1855-56. 3v. 12° . . 568.7
— Hydrostatics. Lib. Us. Kn. I. 365.14
— Letters and speeches. Phila., 1840. 2v. 12° 888.4
— Men of letters and science in the time of Geo. III. London, 1845. 8° 547.3
— Men of letters of the time of Geo. III. London, 1855. sm.8° . . . . v. II. of 548.7
— Philosophers of the time of Geo. III. Lond., 1855. sm.8° 548.7
— Objects, advantages, and pleasures of science. Lib. Us. Kn. I. 365.14
— Opinions on politics, etc. [with a memoir.] London, 1837. 12° 888.2
— Opinions on politics, etc. Paris, 1841. 8° . 888.1
— Sketches of public characters. Philadelphia, 1839. 2v. 12° 888.3
— Speeches; with hist. introductions. Phila., 1841. 2v. 8° 862.1
— Historical dissertations 988.7
— Notes to Paley's natural theology 820.4
— and Routh, E. J. Analytical view of Newton's Principia. London, 1855. 8° 147.6
— Sedgwick, A. and Verplanck, G. C. Discourses on literature and science. N. Y., n.d. 18° . 820.72
BROUGHAM, J. Dramatic works; with memoir by R. S. Mackenzie. v.1. N. Y., n.d. 12° . 356.17

Contents. — Vol. I. Game of life; Love and murder; David Copperfield; Temptation; Game of love; Pocahontas; Dombey and son; Romance and reality.

BROWN, C. B. Arthur Mervyn, or memoirs of the year 1793. Philadelphia, 1857. 2v. 12° 757.3
— Clara Howard: a novel. Phila., 1857. 12° . 757.2
— Edgar Huntley. Philadelphia, 1857. 12° . . 757.5
— Jane Talbot: a novel. Philadelphia, 1857. 12° 757.4
— Ormond. Philadelphia, 1857. 12° 757.2
— Wieland. With memoir of the author. Phila., 1857. 12° 757.1
— Life of, by W. H. Prescott. Sparks's American biography. I. 529.1
BROWN, D. P. The forum: or forty years at the Philadelphia bar. Phila., 1856. 2v. 8° . . 294.4
BROWN, H. S. Lectures to the men of Liverpool. Liverpool, 1858. 8° 885.16
BROWN, J. North-west passage and search for Sir J. Franklin. London, 1858. 8° 701.11
BROWN, J. B. Memoirs of J. Howard, the philanthropist. 2d ed. London, 1823. 8° 575.12
BROWN, J. J. American angler's guide. N. York, 1849. 16° 177.30
— - Same. Part I-II. 4th ed. N. Y., 1857. 12°. 177.1
BROWN, J. W. Life of L. da Vinci, with a critical account of his works. London, 1828. 8° . . 543.9
BROWN, R. Sacred architecture. London, n.d. 4° 201.3
BROWN, T. Account of the Shakers. Troy, 1812. 12° 1089.13

BROWN, Capt. Thomas. The book of butterflies, sphinxes and moths. London, 1832-34. 3v. 18° 830.69-70
— Conchologist's text book. Glasgow, 1833. 12° 178.34
— - Same. 4th ed. Glasgow, 1836. 12° . . 178.33
BROWN, T. N. Life and times of H. Miller, N. Y., 1858. 12° 586.8
BROWN'S letters to a young man about town. Thackeray, W. M. 508.12-14
BROWNE, C. T. Life of R. Southey. London, 1854. 16° 584.6-7
BROWNE, D. J. American poultry yard, with app. by S. Allen. New York, 1850. 12° . . . 168.6
— The American bird-fancier. N. Y., n.d. 12° 177.21-22
BROWNE, F. E. Poems. Boston, 1848. 16° . . . 349.16
BROWNE, J. History of the highlands and the highland clans. New ed. London, 1852-54. 4v. 8° 985.3
BROWNE, Sir R. Correspondence with Sir E. Hyde 977.4
BROWNE, R. W. History of Greek literature. Philadelphia, 1852. 8° 401.3
BROWNE, Sir T. Works, ed. by S. Wilkin. London, 1852. 3v. p.8° 846.11
BROWNING, E. B. Poems. N. York, 1850. 2v. 12° 335.10
— Poems. New ed. with introductory essay by H. T. Tuckerman. Boston, 1854. 2v. 12°. 335.11
BROWNING, R. Men and women. [Poems.] Boston, 1856. 16° 335.4-5
— Poems. New ed. Boston, 1850. 2v. 12° . . 335.9

Contents. — Vol. I. Paracelsus ; Pippa Passes, a drama ; King Victor and King Charles, tragedy ; Columbe's birth day, a play. II. A blot in the 'scutcheon, trag.; The return of the Druses, trag.; Luria, trag.; A soul's tragedy ; Dramatic romances and lyrics.

BROWNSON, O. A. Charles Elwood, or the Infidel converted. Boston, 1840. 12° 1109.6
— The spirit-rapper. Boston, 1854. 12° . . . 125.3
— Theology, politics and socialism. N. York, 1852. 12° 1086.31
BRUCE, J. Life of. Head, Sir F. B. 820.32
BRUCE, M. Poems. Edinburgh, 1782. 12° . . . 355.19
BRUCE, Days of. Story from Scot. hist. Aguilar, G.765.1-10
BRUEN, M. Scenes in Italy, Switzerland and France. Edinburgh, 1823. 12° 679.5
BRUMMELL, Geo., Life of. Jesse, Capt. 892.10
BRUNO ; or fidelity, etc., taught by a dog. Abbott, J. Harper's story books. I. 739.1
BRÜSSEL, nach seiner Vergangenheit und Gegenwart. Horn, J. E. 1029.7
BRUSSELS. A diary of. Legaré, H. S. 872.3
BRYANT, J. D. Immaculate conception of the Virgin Mary. Boston, 1855. 12°. 1008.17
BRYANT, W. C. Letters of a traveller, in Europe and America. 2d ed. N. Y., 1850. 12° . .658.12-13
— Poems. Complete in 1v. Phila., 1851. 12° . 324.7
— Selections from the American poets. N. Y., n.d. 18° 820.24
BRYDONE, P. Tour through Sicily and Malta. N. York, 1813. 12° 679.11
BRYDGES, Sir S. E. Character and political genius of Lord Byron. London, 1824. 8° 585.8
BUCCANEERS of America. History of. Esquemeling, J. 254.3
BUCHANAN, C. Memoir of. Pearson, H. S. . . 1109.22
BUCHANAN, James, Pres. U. S. Life of. Horton, R. G. 517.10
BUCHANAN, James, D.D. Modern atheism. Boston, 1857. 12° 1096.8
BUCHANAN, J. R. Neurological system of anthropology. Cincinnati, 1854. 8° 124.5
BUCKE, C. Beauties, harmonics, and sublimities of nature. New York, 1846. 18° 820.46
— Life of John Churchill, Duke of Marlborough. London, 1839. 16° 379.5
— Life, writings and genius of Akenside. London, 1832. p.8° 586.16
— Ruins of ancient cities. London, 1840. 2v. 16° 379.6
— Ruins of ancient cities. N. Y., 1848. 2v. 18° 820.38

BUCKLE, H. T. Hist. of civilization in England.
Vol. I. London, 1857. 8° 942.1
— - Same. From 2d Lond. ed. Vol. I. New
York, 1858. 8° 942.2
BUCKEYE abroad: or, wanderings in Europe and
in the Orient. Cox, S. S. 658.9
BUCKINGHAM, J. S. America, historical, statistic
and descriptive. New York, 1841. 2v. 8°. 624.4
— Travels in Mesopotamia, with researches on
Nineveh, Babylon, etc. London, 1827. 2v. 8° 694.16
BUCKINGHAM, J. T. Miscellanies, from the public
journals. 2v. in 1. Boston, 1822. 12° . . . 868.4
— Personal memoirs and recollections of edito-
rial life. Boston, 1852. 2v. 16° 525.21
— Specimens of newspaper literature, with anec.
and reminiscences. Boston, 1852. 2v. 12° 868.3
— Annals of Mass. Charitable Mechanic Assoc.
Boston, 1853. 8° 204.5
BUCKINGHAM and Chandos, Duke of. See Gren-
ville, R. P. T.
BUCKMINSTER, J. and J. Stevens, Memoirs of.
Lee, E. B. 535.8
BUCKMINSTER, J. S. Works: with memoirs. [By
Rev. S. C. Thacher.] Boston, 1839. 2v. 12° 117.5
BUDDEUS, A. Eisenbahnfahrt u. Wanderungen
im süddeutschen Rheinland. Leipzig, 1856.
16° 1029.16
BUDGETT, S., Sketches of the life of. Arthur, W. 526.21
BUEL, J. Am. husbandry, with additions by W.
Gaylord and L. Tucker. N. Y., 1840. 2v. 24° 169.29
— Farmer's companion: or, Am. husbandry, with
life, by A. Dean. 2d ed. New York, 1847. 12° 169.8
— Farmer's instructer. New York, 1847. 2v. 18° 169.30
BUENA Vista, Battle of. Carleton, J. H 259.8
BUENOS Ayres, Letters from. Davie, J. P. . . . 633.14
BUFF, H. Physics of the earth. Ed. by A. W.
Hofmann. London, 1851. 12° 149.31
BUFFUM, E. G. Six months in the gold mines of
California, 1847-49. Philadelphia, 1850. 12° 628.12
BUG-JARGAL. [Conte.] Hugo, V. 1066.19
BUILDING. Dobson, E. Rudiments of the art of. 819.15
— Encyclopædia Britannica. Treatises on . . . 201.4
— Fowler, O. S. B. with gravel walls, in octag.
form 207.10
See also : Architecture, Carpentry, Timber.
BUILDINGS in towns, Guide to regulating. Hos-
king, W. 207.13
BUIST, R. Family kitchen gardener. N. Y., 1850. 12° 168.5
BULFINCH, S. G. Holy land and its inhabitants.
Cambridge, 1834. 18° 1089.24
— Poems. Charleston, 1834. 16° 358.20
BULFINCH, T. Age of fable. Boston, 1855. 12°.1087.21-24
BULLOCK, J. Am. cottage builder. N. Y., 1854. 8° 207.7
— History and rudiments of architecture. New
York, 1853. 12° 207.6
BULLOCK, W. Six months' residence and travels
in Mexico. London, 1824. 8° 633.9
BÜLOW, E. von. Das Novellenbuch, mit Vorworte
von L. Tieck. Leipzig, 1834-6. 4v. sm.8°. 1013.16
BULWER, E. See Lytton, Sir E. B.
BUNBURY, C. J. F. Journal at the Cape of Good
Hope. London, 1848. 12° 692.14
BUNGENER, L. The preacher and the king: or,
Bourdaloue in the court of Louis XIV. Tr.
12th ed. Boston, 1853. 12° 1096.4-6
— The priest and the Huguenot. From the
French. Boston, 1854. 2v. 12° 1096.2-3
BUNKER hill. Emmons, R. Battle of: a poem . 358.3
— Frothingham, R., jr. The battle, and acc't of
the monument of 214.2-8
— Hudson, C. Doubts concern. the battle of. . 217.14
— Panoramic view from monument of 235.15
BUNKLEY, J. M. Testimony of an escaped novice.
New York, 1855. 12° 1008.11
BUNN, A. Old England and New England. Phila-
delphia, 1853. 12° 628.10
BUNNER, E. Hist. of Louisiana. N. Y., n.d. 18° 820.69
BUNSEN, C. C. J. Egypt's place in universal his-
tory. Tr. by C. H. Cottrell. London, 1848-
1854. 2v. 8° 954.4

BUNSEN, C. C. J. Signs of the times. Transl. by
S. Winkworth. London, 1856. 8° 113.3
— - Same. New York, 1856. 12° 134.9
— Character and influence of B. G. Niebuhr . . . 583.19
BUNYAN, J. Works: illustr. ed. Philadelphia,
1853. 2v. in 1. roy.8° 1101.4
Contents. — Vol. I. Grace abounding to the chief of
sinners, in life and death of J. B.; Brief acct. of Mr.
Bunyan's imprisonment ; continuation of Mr. B.'s
life, death, and burial ; Brief character ; Dying
sayings; Pilgrim's progress; Christian behaviour; Solomon's temple spiritualized; Jerusalem sinner saved;
Holy war; The life and death of Mr. Badman. II.
Come, and welcome, to Jesus Christ; The barren fig-
tree; Discourse on prayer; Imprisonment of J. B.;
Prison meditations; Doctrine of election and reprobation asserted; The strait gate; The heavenly footman;
Sighs from hell; Confession of my faith; Poetical
pieces; Differ. in judgment about baptism no bar to
communion; Peaceful principles and true, or ans.
about baptism; Nature of the seventh day Sabbath;
First day the true Sabbath; Last sermon; The Trinity
and a Christian; Law and a Christian; Instruction for
the ignorant ; Justification by imputed righteousness.
— Works, with introduc. to each treatise, and a
sketch of his life and times. Ed. by G. Offor.
Glasgow, 1854. 3v. imp.8° 1101.1
Contents. — Vol. I. Grace abounding to the chief of
sinners; Prison meditations; The Jerusalem sinner
saved; The greatness of the soul; The work of Christ
as an advocate; Christ a complete saviour; Come, and
welcome, to Jesus Christ; Justification by an imputed
righteousness; Saved by grace; The strait gate; Light
for them that sit in darkness; The fear of God; Doctr.
of the law and grace unfolded; Israel's hope encour-
aged ; Discourse touching prayer ; The throne of
grace; The acceptable sacrifice; Paul's departure and
crown; The desire of the righteous granted. II. The
saint's knowledge of Christ's love; Of antichrist and
his ruin; The resurrection of the dead, and eternal
judgment; Some gospel truths opened; A vindication
of gospel truths; The Pharisee and the publican; A
defence of the doctrine of justification by faith in
Jesus Christ; Reprobation asserted; Questions about
the nature and perpetuity of the seventh-day Sabbath; Of the trinity and a Christian; Of the law and a
Christian; Scriptural poems; Exposition of the first
ten chapters of Genesis; A holy life the beauty of
Christianity; Christian behaviour; Caution to stir up
to watch against sin; Discourse of the building, nature, excellency, and government of the house of God;
On the terms of communion and fellowship of Christians at the table of the Lord; A confession of my
faith, and a reason of my practice; Differences about
water-baptism no bar to communion; Peaceable principles and true; On the love of Christ, a poem ; A
case of conscience resolved; J. B.'s catechism; Sea-
sonable counsel ; An exhortation to peace and unity ;
Bunyan's last sermon. III. Pilgrim's progress; The
holy war; The heavenly footman; The holy city, or
the New Jerusalem; Solomon's temple spiritualized;
Discourse of the house of the forest of Lebanon; The
water of life; The barren fig-tree; Life and death of
Mr. Badman; Sighs from hell; One thing is needful;
Ebal and Gerizim; A book for boys and girls, or temporal things spiritualized.

— Pilgrim's progress. Notes by W. Mason. Life
of the author by J. Conder. Boston,
1839. 8° 1094.7
— - Same. Life and notes by T. Scott. Lon-
don, 1841. 24° 1099.31-32
— - Same. Edinburgh, 1842. sm.8° 1099.33
— - Same, with life by R. Southey. New York,
1847. 12° 1099.30
— - Same. New ed., with memoir by J. M.
Hare. London, 1853. p.8° 869.9
— The riches of Bunyan, selected by Rev. J.
Chaplin. Introd. by W. R. Williams. New
York, n.d. 12° 1109.1
— Baillie, J. Life of 518.12
— Cheever, G. B. Life and times of 1094.6
— Southey, R. A biography 889.11
BUONARROTI, Michael Angelo. Duppa, R. Life
and works of 835.7
— Harford, J. S. Life of 542.2
BÜRCK, A. Ulrich von Hutten, der Ritter, der
Gelehrte, der Dichter, der Kämpfer. Dres-
den, 1845. 16° 1025.5

BÜRGER, G. A. Sämmtliche Werke. Göttingen, 1844. 4v. 16° 1025.6

Contents.— Vol. I. Gedichte; Varianten; Anmerkungen. II. Homer's Ilias, Vertheidigung und Proben einer Uebersetzung in Iamben; Homer's Ilias, Proben einer Uebersetzung in Hexametern ; Dido, ein episches Gedicht, aus Virgils Aeneis gezogen; Anthia und Abrokomas, aus dem Griechischen des Xenophon von Ephesus. III. Proben einer Uebersetzung von Ossian's Gedichten ; Macbeth, nach Shakspeare; Anfang einer Bearbeitung des Froschmauslers; Bellin; Prosaische Aufsätze; Fragmente und Herzensergiessungen über Poesie und Kunst; Fragmente über Deutsche Sprache und Schreibart; Freimaurer-Reden. IV. Prosaische Aufsätze; Die republik England; Biographie und characteristik Bürgers; Mittheilungen aus Bürgers Briefwechsel ; Bürger, von August Wilhelm von Schlegel; Facsimile.

— Songs and ballads. Brooks, C. T. 316.6
BURGGRAEVE, Dr. Chirurgie. Bruxelles, n.d. 12° 1065.8
BURGH, A. Anecdotes of music. London, 1814. 3v. 12° 209.8
BURGON, J. W. Life and times of Sir T. Gresham. London, 1839. 2v. 8° 573.8
BURGOYNE, Gen. J. Dramatic and poetical works: with mem. London, 1808. 2v. 8° 314.11

Contents.— Vol. I. Maid of the oaks; Lord of the manor. II. The heiress; Richard Cœur de Lion; Poems; Miscellaneous.

BURGOYNE, J. Blasting and quarrying stone. 2d ed. London, 1852. 16° 819.25
BURKE, E. Works and correspondence. New ed. London, 1852. 8v. 8° 862.9

Contents.— Vol. I. Correspondence, 1744–91. II. Correspondence, 1791–97, ed. by Earl Fitzwilliam, and Sir R. Bourke; Vindication of natural society; On the sublime and beautiful. III. Short account of a late short administration; Observations on "the present state of the nation;" Thoughts on the cause of the present discontents; Speech on American taxation; Speeches at Bristol, 1774; Speech on conciliation with the colonies; Letter on American affairs; Two letters on trade of Ireland; Speech on the independence of parliament; Speech at Bristol, 1780; Speech on Fox's East India bill; Representation to his majesty, 1784. IV. Speech on the nabob of Arcot's debts; Appendix; Speech on the army estimates; Reflections on the French Revolution; Letter to a member of the national assembly; Appeal from the new to the old whigs; Letters on the penal laws against Irish Catholics; Hints for a memorial to Monsieur de M. M.; Thoughts on French affairs. V. Considerations on the present state of affairs; On the policy of the allies; On the conduct of the minority; Preface to M. Brissot's address; Letter to W. E. Elliot, Esq.; Thoughts on scarcity; Letter to a noble lord; Letters on peace; A regicide peace; Letter to the empress of Russia; Letter to Sir C. Bingham; Letter to C. J. Fox; Letter to marquis of Rockingham; Address to the king; Address to the British colonists in North America; Letters to Pery, Burgh, and Merlott ; Letters, with reflections, on the execution of the rioters in 1780; Letter to Dundas, with the sketch of a negro code; Letter on the duration of parliaments. VI. On the laws against popery in Ireland; Letters to W. Smith; Langrishe; R. Burke; On the affairs of Ireland; Fragments and notes of speeches; Hints for an essay on the drama; Essay towards an abridgment of the English history; Ninth and eleventh reports from the committee of the house of commons, on the affairs of the East India Company; Articles of charge against Warren Hastings. VII. Articles (continued) ; Speeches on the impeachment of Warren Hastings. VIII. Speeches on impeachment (continued); Report from committee relating to Warren Hastings' trial; General index.

— Sublime and beautiful. Ed. by A. Mills. N. York, 1829. 12° 125.29
— - Same. New York, 1846. 12° 125.28
— Wisdom and genius of. With life, by P. Burke. London, 1845. 12° 874.13
— Croly, G. Political life of 588.14
— Macknight, T. Life and times of 572.4
— Prior, J. Life of 588.17
BURKE, J. W. Life of R. Emmett, with speeches. Charleston, 1852. 12° 598.16
BURKE, P. Trials connected with the upper classes. London, 1851. 8° 133.9
— Trials connected with the aristocracy. London, 1849. 8° 133.8

BURMAN empire. Account of the Burmese. . . . 825.8
— Chamier, F. Account of the Burman war . . 986.2
— Malcom, H. Account of 709.3–4
— Passages of adventure in. 709.10
— Symes, M. Bell's narrative of the military and political operations in the 830.29
BURMEISTER, H. Manual of entomology. London, 1836. 8° 175.4
BURN, R. S. Illustrated London drawing book, architectural, engineering and mechanical. London, 1853. 8° 206.9
— - Same. Sketching, perspective, engraving. 2d ed. London, 1853. 8° 206.10
— Steam engine, its history and mechanism. 2d ed. London, 1857. 8° 195.22
BURNAP, G. W. Life of L. Calvert. Sparks, J. American biography. XIX. 529.1
— Miscellaneous writings. Baltimore, 1845. 12° 1107.11
— Rectitude of human nature. Boston, 1850. 12° 1088.3
BURNELL, G. R. Treatise on limes, cements, etc. London, 1850. 16° 819.32
— - Same. 2d ed. London, 1856. 12° 199.19
— and Law, H. Hydraulic engineering, II. . . 819.11
BURNES, A. Travels into Bokhara, 1831–33. London, 1834. 3v. 8° 694.11
BURNET, G. Exposition of the thirty-nine articles. New York, 1852. 8° 1103.3
BURNET, J. Early settlements of the N. W. territory. New York, 1847. 8° 236.3
BURNETT, G. T. Outlines of botany. London, 1835. 8° 166.1
BURNEY, J. History of North Eastern voyages of discovery, and E. navigations of the Russians. London, 1819. 8° 702.15
BURNEY, Miss. F. See D'Arblay, Mme. Francis.
BURNHAM, E. J. Old elm and fountain on Boston common. Boston, 1853. 12° 349.12
BURNS, J. Cyclopedia of sermons. N. Y., 1856. 8° 1083.15
BURNS, R. Works, with life and a criticism, and observations on the Scottish peasantry, by J. Currie. London, 1820. 4v. 8° 332.12

Contents.— Vol. I. Life and a criticism on his writings; Observ. on the Scot. peasantry. II. General correspondence, etc. III. Poems, with their history, by G. Burns. IV. Corres. with Mr. G. Thompson, including poetry hitherto unpublished.

— Life and works as edited by J. Currie. New ed. New York, 1824. 4v. 24° 369.22

Contents.— Same as preceding.

— Entire works. With life, etc., by J. Currie. London, 1833. 24° 369.21

Contents.— Same as two preceding.

— Life and works. Ed. by R. Chambers. New York, 1852. 4v. 12° 328.1–6

Containing: "The various compositions, strung in strict chronological order upon the memoir."—Pref.

— Poetical works ; with letters and life, by Dr. Currie. New ed. London, 1826. 8° 332.11
— - Same. London, 1839. 3v. 16° 319.3
— Reliques. Ed. by R. H. Cromek. 4th ed. London, 1817. 8° . . . . v. V. of 332.12
— and Clarinda, [Mrs. McLehose.] Correspondence. Edinburgh, 1843. 12° 586.14
— Cunningham, A. Life and land of 586.15
— Lockhart, J. G. Life of 830.39
BURR, A. Parton, J. Life and times of 515.9–11
— Robertson, D. Trial of 296.6
— Safford, W. H. Acc't of the B. expedition . 517.12–13
BURRITT, E. Works. London, n.d. 12° 898.16

Contents.— Sparks from the anvil; Voices from the forge; Peace papers for the people.

— Thoughts and things at home and abroad. With mem. by M. Howitt. Boston, 1854. 12° 898.3
BURTON, E. Antiq. and curios. of Rome. 2d ed. London, 1828. 2v. p.8° 919.3
BURTON, J. H. Life and corresp. of D. Hume. Edinburgh, 1846. 2v. 8° 582.12
— Lives of Lord Lovat and Duncan Forbes. London, 1847. p.8° 566.6

BURTON, J. H. Narratives from criminal trials in Scotland. London, 1852. 2v. 8° 987.4

BURTON, R. Anatomy of melancholy. 7th ed. Philadelphia, 1856. 8° 872.7–9

BURTON, R. F. Pilgrimage to El-Medinah and Meccah. New York, 1856. 12° 689.10

— First footsteps in E. Africa. London, 1856. 8° 692.5–6

BURTON, W. District school as it was, and other writings. Boston, 1852. 12° 449.8–7

BURTON, W. E. Cyclopædia of wit and humor. New York, 1858. 2v. 8° 901.7

BURY, T. T. Rudimentary architecture. 2d ed. London, 1853. 16° 819.12

BUSCAPIÉ, El, or the serpent. Cervantes Saavedra, M. de 857.3

BUSH, Mrs. F. Memoirs of the queens of France. Fr. 2d Lond. ed. Phil., 1851. 2v. 12° 606.8–13

BUSH, G. Life of Mohammed. N. York, 1847. 18° 810.12

BUSH boys. Reid, M. 718.8–12

BUSH life in Australia. Haygarth, H. W. . . . 880.21

BUSHNAN, J. S. Ichthyology. Jardine's nat. lib. XXXV 179.1

BUSHNELL, H. Sermons for the new life. New York, 1858. 12°. 1088.9

BUSINESS, Practical treatise on. Freedley, E. T. . 136.15

— How to do business 136.25

BUSINI, G. B. Dell' assedio di Firenze. Lettere. Milano, 1847. 16° 1058.4

BUSK, M. M. Hist. of Spain and Portugal. B. C., 1000. — A. D., 1814. Lond., 1823. 8° . . . 365.1

BUSONE da Gubblo. Fortunatus Siculus o sia l'avventuroso Ciciliano. Romanzo storico. Milano, 1833. 16° 1059.8

BUTLER, A. Lives of the fathers, martyrs and other saints. Baltimore, 1844–45. 4v. 8° . . 541.5

BUTLER, Caleb. Hist. of Groton, [Mass.] Boston, 1848. 8° 224.14

BUTLER, Charles. Life of Fénélon. 3d ed. Lives of St. Vincent of Paul, and H. M. de Boudon. Letter on music. Hist. minutes of the Society of Jesus. London, 1819. 8° 617.14

— Life and writings of Rev. A. Butler 541.5

— Reminiscences, and a letter on music. 2d American, from 4th London ed. New York, 1825. 868.11

BUTLER, F. A. K. See Kemble.

BUTLER, J. Analogy of religion to the constitution and course of nature. Life by Kippis. Preface by Halifax. New Haven, 1828. 12° 1108.10

— - Same. New ed. London, 1852. p.8°. . . 858.6

— Ethical discourses. Syllabus by Dr. Whewell. Introd. essay by J. C. Passmore. Philadelphia, 1855. 12° 139.1

BUTLER, S. Poetical works. Lond., 1835. 2v. p.8° 319.4

— Hudibras, with Dr. Grey's annot. New ed. London, 1819. 3v. 8° 314.13

— - Same, and other works. By Ramsay. London, 1846. 24° 840.9

— - Same. With life, annot. and index. Hartford, 1853. 18° 359.8

BUTLER, T. B. Philosophy of the weather. New York, 1856. 12°. 145.26

BUTLER, Wm. Allen. Nothing to wear. [A poem.] New York, 1857. 12° 344.22

— Two millions. [A poem.] N. Y., 1858. 12° . 344.27

BUTLER, Wm. Archer. Lectures on the hist. of ancient philosophy. Ed. by W. H. Thompson. Philadelphia, 1857. 2v. 8° 124.7

BUTTERFLIES, The book of. Brown, T. 830.69–70

BUTTONWOODS, The: or, the refugees of the revolution. [And Alda Grey.] Phila., 1849. 8° 801.1

BUXTON, Sir T. F. Memoirs. 3d ed. London, 1849. p.8°. 889.6

— - Same. 4th ed. London, 1850. p.8° . . . 588.9

— Sir T. F. B., a study for young men. Binney, T. 588.10

BYLES, J. B. Law of bills of exchange. 136.17

BYRN, M. L. Complete practical brewer. Phila., 1852. 12° 199.8

BYRNE, O. Practical model calculator. Philadelphia, 1852. 8° 194.4

BYRON, G. G. N., L'd. Works. N. Y., 1820. 4v. 18° **358.29**

Contents. — Vol. I. Childe Harold. II. Bride of Abydos; The corsair; Lara; The giaour. III. The siege of Corinth; Prisoner of Chillon; Parisina; Beppo; English bards and Scotch reviewers; Mazeppa; Ode; Fragment; Don Juan. IV. Hebrew me odies; Ode to Napoleon Buonaparte; Monody on the death of Sheridan; Lament of Tasso; Manfred; Poems.

— Works, with letters, journals and life, by T. Moore. New York, 1836–37. 6v. 8° . . . 323.2–3

Contents. — Vols. I.–II. Life, letters, etc. III. Childe Harold's pilgrimage; The giaour; The bride of Abydos; The corsair; Lara; The siege of Corinth; Parisina; The prisoner of Chillon; Beppo; Mazeppa. IV. Manfred; Hebrew melodies; Ode to Napoleon; Monody on the death of Sheridan; Lament of Tasso; Minor poems; Ode on Venice; The prophecy of Dante; Cain; Marino Faliero; Sardanapalus; The two Foscari. V. Werner; The deformed transformed; Heaven and earth; The island; Hours of idleness; Translations and imitations; Fugitive pieces; English bards and Scotch reviewers; Hints from Horace; The curse of Minerva; The waltz; Age of Bronze; Morgante Maggiore ; The blues; Third act of Manfred; Occasional pieces. VI. Don Juan.

— Poetical works. London, 1851. 10v. 16°. . . 347.1

Contents. — Vol. I. Hours of idleness; Occasional pieces, 1807–8; English bards and Scotch reviewers; Occasional pieces, 1808–10. II. Childe Harold's pilgrimage. III. Occasional pieces, 1811–13; Hints from Horace; The curse of Minerva; The waltz; The giaour; The bride of Abydos; The corsair; Remarks on the mod. Greek language. IV. Ode to Napoleon Buonaparte; Lara; Hebrew melodies; The siege of Corinth; Parisina; Domestic pieces, 1816; Monody on the death of R. B. Sheridan; Prisoner of Chillon; The dream; Occasional pieces. V. Manfred; The lament of Tasso; Beppo; Mazeppa; Ode on Venice; The Morgante Maggiore of Pulci; The prophecy of Dante; Occasional pieces. VI. Francesca of Rimini; Stanzas to the Po; The blues; Marino Faliero; The vision of judgment; Occasional pieces. VII. Heaven and earth; Sardanapalus; The two Foscari; The deformed transformed. VIII. Cain; Werner; The age of bronze; The island. IX. Testimonies of authors; Letter to the editor of " My Grandmother's Review;" Observations upon an article in Blackwood's Edinburgh Magazine, Aug., 1819; Don Juan. X. Continuation of Don Juan.

— Poetical works, complete in 1 vol. with notes by Moore, Jeffrey, etc. New York, 1851. 8° 332.2

— Beauties of Byron. n.d. n.p. 24° 358.28

— Blaquiere, E. Last days of 683.11

— Brydges, S. E. Character and poetical genius of. 585.8

— Dallas, R. C. Recollections of 585.4

— Galt, J. Life of 810.10–11

— Gamba, P. Last journey of, to Greece 585.12

— Kennedy, J. Conversations on religion with 585.6

— Macaulay, T. B. Essay on 409.18

— Medwin, T. Conversations of 898.20

— Moore, T. Life of, with letters and journals. 585.13

— Parry, W. Last days of 585.5

— Trelawny, E. J. Last days of 585.9–11

BYZANTINE empire. Finlay, G. Hist. of, 716–1057 956.7

— History of the B. and Greek empires, 1057–1453 . . . . 955.5

CABANIS. Roman. Häring, W. . . . . . . v. 1. of 1024.4

CABELL, J. and Jefferson, T. Early history of the University of Virginia 294.2

CABIN book. Sealsfield, C. 735.7

CABINET cyclopædia. See Lardner, D.

CABINET des Fées. Contes des fées, et autres contes merveilleux. Genève, 1785–86. 37v. 12° 1077.1

Contents. — Vol. I. Précis de la vie et des ouvr. de Charles Perrault; Les contes des fées. Perrault, C.; Les nouveaux contes des fées. Murat, Mme. II. Contes des fées. D'Aulnoy, Mme. III. [Same, continued]; Les fées à la mode. D'Aulnoy. IV. [Same, continued]. V. La tyrannie des fées détruite. D'Auneuil, Mme.; Les illustres fées, [various authors;] Les contes moins contes que les autres. De Preschac. VI. Les fées; contes des contes. De la Force, M'lle.; Les chevaliers errans et le génie familier. D'Aulnoy, Mme. VII.–XI. Mille et une nuits,

CABINET des Fées, *continued.*
    tr. par Galland, M. XII. La tour ténébreuse et les jours lumineux. L'Héritier, M'lle.; Les aventures d'Abdallah. Contes arabes, tr. XIII. [Same, continued.] XIV.—XV. Les mille et un jours. La Croix, P. de. XVI. L'histoire de la sultane de Perse et des visirs. Trad. par Galland; Les voyages de Zulma dans le pays des fées, tr. XVII.—XVIII. Les contes et fables indiennes de Bidpaï et de Lokman, trad. par Galland et Cardonne ; Fables et contes de Fénélon ; Boca, par Mme. Le Marchand. XIX. Contes chinois, par Gueullette; Florine, ou la belle italienne. Anon. XX. Le belier; Fleur d'épine; Lesquatre facardins. Hamilton, A. XXI. Les mille et un quart d' heures. Contes tartares, par Gueullette. XXII. [Same, cont.] ; Les sultanes de Guzarate. Contes mogols, par Gueullette. XXIII. [Same, continued]. XXIV. Le prince des Aigues-Marines et le prince invisible. L'Evêque, Mme.; Les féeries nouvelles. Caylus, C'te de. XXV. Les nouveaux contes orientaux. Caylus; Cadichon et Jeannette. Caylus, C'te de; Contes. Moncrif. XXVI. La reine fantasque. Rousseau, J.J.; La belle et la bête. Villeneuve, Mme.; Les Veillées de Thessalie. Lussan, Mme. de. XXVII. [Same, continued]; His'oire du prince Titi. St. Hyacinthe. XXVIII. [Same, concluded]. XXIX. Les contes des génies. Contes persans, tr. par Morell, C., [pseud. for Ridley, J.] XXX. [Same continued.] XXXI. Funestine. Beauchamps; Nouveaux contes de fées; Le loup galleux et Bellinette. XXXII. Les soirées Bretonnes. Gueullette; Contes. Lintot, Mme.; Les aventures de Zeloide et d'Amanzarifdine. Moncrif. XXXIII. Lionnette et Coquerico: Le prince glacé et la princesse Étincelante; La princesse Camion. Lubert, M'lle; Nourjahad, histoire orientale. XXXIV. Contes. Pajon, H.; La bibliothèque des fées et des génies. La Porte, A. de. XXXV. Minet-Bleu et Louvette. Fagnan, Mme.; Acajou et Zirphile. Duclos, M.; Aglaë ou Nabotine. Coypel, C.A.; Contes des fées. Le prince de Beaumont; Le prince Desiré. Selis, M.; Contes choisies, [extr. fr. diff. coll.] XXXVI. Les aventures merveilleuses de Don Silvio de Rosalva. D'Ussieux, Mme. tr. XXXVII. La notice des auteurs; La liste complette des ouvrages qui composent le cabinet des fées.

CABINET-MAKER'S companion. Stokes, J. 199.24
CABINET of curiosities. London, n.d. 8°. 806.11
— Portrait gallery of British worthies. London, 1845–1847. 12v. 24° 840.10–11
CABLE, History of the great Atlantic. Briggs, C. F. 196.16
CABOT, J. E. [Tour of Prof. Agassiz to lake Superior.] *See* Agassiz, L. 624.1
CABOT, S. Memoir, with a hist. of maritime discoveries. 2d ed. London, 1832. 8° 564.10
— Hayward, C. jr. Life of. Sparks's Am. biog. IX. 529.1
— Tytler, P. F. Remarks on a late memoir of . 810.53
CÆSAR Borgia, Life of. Gordon, A. 544.2
CÆSAR, C. J. Translated by W. Duncan, [also Hirtius.] New York, 1852. 2v. 18° 830.11
— Commentaries. Transl. London, 1851. p.8° 824.3
— Abbott, J. History of 549.17–18
— Schlegel, K. W. F. von. Essays on 848.1
CÆSARS, The. De Quincey, T. 895.9
— Suetonius. Lives of the twelve. 844.8
CAFFRARIA, and its inhabitants. Kay, S. 698.22
CAGLIOSTRO, Aventures de. Saint-Félix, J. de . 1078.29
CAILLIÉ, R. Travels to Timbuctoo, 1824–8. London, 1830. 2v. 8° 693.10
CAIN, and other poems. Simms, W. G. 369.14
CAIRNES, J. E. Character and logical method of political economy. London, 1857. 12° . . . 136.11
CAIRO, in 1839. Kinnear, J. G. 689.13
CALAMITIES of authors. D'Israeli, I. 897.5–6
CALAVAR, a romance of Mexico. Bird, R. M. . . 726.7
CALAYNOS: a tragedy. Boker, G. H. 355.2
CALCOTT, J. W. Grammar of music. 11th ed. London, n.d. 24° 209.12
CALCULATOR, The practical model. Byrne, O. . . 194.4
CALCULUS, Cox, H. A treatise of integral . . . 829.32
— De Morgan, A. The differential and integral 365.2
— Haddon, J. Examples, etc., in differential . . 829.34
— Hann, J. Examples of integral 829.33
— Woolhouse, W. S. B. Elements of the differ. 829.31
CALDERON de la Barca, Mme. F. E. Attaché in Madrid. New York, 1856. 12° 675.10–11

CALDERON de la Barca, Mme. F. E. Life in Mexico, with preface by W. H. Prescott. Boston, 1843. 2v. 12° 638.4
— - Same. London, 1843. 8° 636.7
CALDERON de la Barca, Pedro de. His life and genius, with specimens of his plays. Trench, R. C. 808.11
— The Spanish drama. Lope de Vega and C. By Lewes, G. H. 840.35
CALDERON, the courtier. A novel. Lytton, E. B. 466.7–9
CALDWELL, C. Autobiography, with notes by H. W. Warner. Philadelphia, 1855. 8° . . . 524.6
— Discourse on the genius and character of Rev. H. Holley. Boston, 1828. 8° 534.1
— Life and campaigns of Nath. Greene. Philadelphia, 1819. 8° 515.7
CALDWELL, H. H. Poems. Boston, 1858. 12° . 338.20
CALDWELL, J. Trial of British soldiers for the murder of J. C. and others in Boston, March 5, 1770. . . . . 219.1
CALDWELL, W. W. Poems, original and translated. Boston and Cambridge, 1857. 12° . . 348.4
CALEF, R. More wonders of the invisible world. Salem, 1796. 12° 229.5
CALENDAR of the seasons. Howitt, M. 825.10
CALHOUN, J. C. Life, with a selection from his speeches. New York, [1843.] 8° 512.11
— Works. Ed. by R. K. Cralle. New York, 1853–55. 6v. 8° 287.1

    Contents. — Vol. I. Disq. on government. II.—IV. Speeches in congress. V.—VI. Reports and public letters.

CÁLIDÁS. Sacontalá, Indian drama. Transl. [by Sir Wm. Jones.] London, 1792. 18° 356.8
CALIFORNIA. Auger, É. Voyage en Californie . 1078.53
— Brooks, J. T. Four months among the gold-finders of 623.6
— Borthwick, J. D. Three years in 624.6
— Buffum, E. G. Three years in 628.12
— Capron, E. S. History, etc. of 237.13
— Colton, W. Three years in 626.20–26
— - Cruise to 626.19
— Farnham, E. W. Cal. in-doors and out . . . 637.7
— Farnham, T. J. Life, etc., in 633.10
— Frémont, J. C. Exploring expedition to . . 628.13–15
— Greenhow, R. History of 235.9
— Johnson, T. T. Sights in the gold region . . 239.8
— Parkman, F. jr. C. and Oregon trail 626.12–13
— - California trail 626.14
— Revere, J. W. A tour of duty in 637.5
— Sage, R. B. Scenes in 639.16
— Seyd, E. C. and its resources 236.9
— Soulé, F. History, etc., of 235.10
— Taylor, J. B. Voyage to 627.12–16
— Wise, H. A. An inside view of 627.24
CALIFORNIAN gold discoveries. Stirling, P. J. . 136.12
CALIPHS. Travels to the city of the. Wellsted, J. R. 693.3
CALL to the unconverted. Baxter, R. 1087.3
CALLERY and Yvan. Hist. of the insurrection in China. Transl. N. Y., 1853. 12° 938.6
CALLIMACHUS. The works of. Translated by J. Banks and N. W. Tytler. 851.2
CALMET, A. The phantom world, from the French by H. Christmas. Phila., 1850. 2v. in 1. 12° 1106.6
CALVERT, G. H. Scenes and thoughts in Europe. [1st series.] New York, 1851. 12° 647.14
— - Same. [First and] second series. New York, 1852. 2v. in 1. 12° 647.15
— Comedies. Boston, 1856. 12° 356.4

    Contents. — The will and the way; Like unto like.

CALVERT, L. Life of. Burnap, G. W. Sparks's American biography. XIX. 529.1
CALVIN, J. Dyer, T. H. Life of Calvin 545.10
— Mackenzie, J. Life and writings of 1108.9
CAMBACÉRÈS, Prince. Evenings with. Lamothe-Langon, É. L. de. 1004.3
CAMBRIDGE, W. G. Henri: or, the web and woof of life. Boston. 1854. 12° 489.7

CAMBRIDGE essays, 1856. London, n.d. 8° . . . 873.13
Contents. — Roman law and legal education, by H. J. S. Maine; English ethnography, by J. W. Donaldson; Old studies and new, by J. Grote; Taste for the picturesque among the Greeks, by E. M. Cope; Apocryphal gospels, by C. A. Ellicott; Protestant church and religious liberty in France, by W. H. Waddington; The fly-fisher and his library, by H. R. Francis; The text of Shakspeare, by C. Badham; Coleridge, by F. J. A. Hort.
CAMBRIDGE, Epitaphs from the old burying ground in. Harris, W. T. 228.2
CAMBUSLANG, The revival at. Macfarlan, D. . . . 118.9
CAMEL hunt: a narrative. Fabens, J. W. 699.12–13
CAMEL, The, his introduction into the United States. Marsh, G. P. 177.17
CAMILLA: a novel. D'Arblay, Mme. F. B. 499.5
CAMILLE: a novel. Transl. Mangin, V. 801.2
CAMOENS, L. de. Poems, with remarks, etc., by Visc't Strangford. New ed. Lond., 1824. 16° 315.16
CAMP, G. S. Democracy. New York, 1845. 18°. 820.40
CAMP and barrack-room; or, the British army as it is. London, 1846. 12° 894.2
CAMP and march. Grafton, H. D. 197.11
CAMP of refuge. MacFarlane, C. 840.40
CAMP fires of the red men. Orton, J. R. 736.12
CAMPAN, Mme. J. L. H. G. Conversations, secret anecdotes of the French court. Ed. by M. Maigne. London, n.d. 8° 613.7
— Memoirs of the court of Marie Antoinette, with a biog. introd., by Lamartine. New ed. Philadelphia, 1851. 2v. 12° 615.3
CAMPBELL, A. Voyage round the world, from 1806 to 1812. 2d Am. ed. N. York, 1819. 12° 709.9
CAMPBELL, D. Adventures and sufferings by shipwreck and imprisonment in India. 2d Am. ed. New York, 1798. 12° 709.18
— Text book of inorganic chemistry. Lond., 1849. 16° 156.30
CAMPBELL, G. Philosophy of rhetoric. New ed. New York, 1857. 12° 405.6
CAMPBELL, H. Self-devotion: or, hist. of Katherine Randolph. Lond., 1844. 3v. p.8. . . . 768.2
CAMPBELL, I. A memoir of. Story, R. 599.14
CAMPBELL, Sir J. Life of Lord Bacon. London, 1853. 16° 586.26
— Lives of the chief justices of England. Phil., 1851. 2v. 8° 568.2
— Lives of the lord chancellors, and keepers of the great seal of Eng. 2d Am. fr. 3d Lond. ed. Phila., 1851. 7v. 12° 568.1
CAMPBELL, Rev. J. Travels in South Africa. 3d ed. London, 1815. 8° 692.12
— Travels in So. Africa. 2d journey. London, 1822. 2v. 8° 692.9
CAMPBELL, J. L. & Hadley, A. M. Teacher's miscellany. Cincinnati, 1856. 8° 137.11
CAMPBELL, T. Complete poetical works, with mem. and essay on his writings. [G. Gilfillan.] New York, 1852. 12° 346.14
Contents. — Pleasures of Hope; Theodric, a domestic tale; Gertrude of Wyoming; Pilgrim of Glencoe.
— Poetical works [with] biographical sketch. 1st comp. Am. edition. Phila., 1821. 12° 369.18
— Poetical works, including Theodric. Philadelphia, 1826. 12° 346.13
— Poetical works, with biog. and notes, by E. Sargent. Boston, 1854. 8° 324.9
— Essay on English poetry. Boston, 1819. 18° 369.7
— Same. London, 1848. p.8° 889.7
— Gertrude, with a biograph. sketch of the author 237.14
— Life and times of Petrarch, with notice of Boccaccio and contemp. 2d ed. Lond., 1843. 2v. 543.6
— Letters from the south, during a journey to Algiers, etc. Philadelphia, 1836. 12° . . . 698.25
— Life and letters. Ed. by W. Beattie. N. Y., 1850. 2v. 12° 581.14
— Specimens of the British poets, with notices, and an essay on English poetry. New ed. Philadelphia, 1853. 8° 311.6

CAMPBELL, T. Specimens of the British poets. 1400–1805. London, 1819. 7v. p.8° 343.14
Contents. — Vol. I. Essay on English poetry. II. Chaucer, 1400, to Beaumont, 1628. III. Drayton, 1631, to Phillips, 1664. IV. Shirley, 1666, to Prior, 1721. V. Sewell, 1726, to Carey, 1763. VI. Churchill, 1764, to Johnson, 1784. VII. Whitehead, 1785, to Anstey, 1805.
— Contributions to the life of Burns 586.15
CAMPBELL, W. W. Border warfare of N. York during the revolution. N. Y., 1849. 12°. . . 217.11
— Robin Hood and Captain Kidd. N. Y., 1853. 12° 589.2
CAMUS, J. P. Palombe ou la femme honorable. [Roman]. Étude sur Camus et le roman Chrétien, au XVII Siècle, par Rigault. Paris, 1853. 12° 1078.12
CANADA. Arfwedson, C. D. C. in 1832–34 . . . 624.12
— De Roos, F. F. Travels in 624.14
— Dixon, J. Tour through 637.8
— Duncan, J. M. Travels in 628.24
— Finch, I. Travels in 624.7
— Howison, J. Sketches of Upper 637.1
— Jameson, A. Sketches in, among the red men 409.12
— – Sketches in 629.24
— – Winter studies and summer rambles in. . 629.10
— Lambert, J. Travels through Lower 625.20
— Lyell, C. Geological observations on 628.1
— Melish, J. Travels through Upper 623.7
— Moodie, S. Life in. 636.3–11
— Murray, A. M. Letters from. 639.18
— Murray, H. Discoveries and travels in . . . 625.14
— Murray, H. A. Travels in 627.4
— Smith, W. H. Past, present and future of C. West 265.1
— Traill, Mrs. C. P. The backwoods of 839.1
— Tremenheere, H. S. Notes on public subjects during a tour in 297.12
— Weld, I. Travels through Upper and Lower C. 625.15
CANADAS. Heriot, G. Travels through the . . . 629.23
— Shirreff, P. Comprehensive view of the . . . 624.10
CANADIAN forest, Stories of the. Traill, Mrs. C. P. 728.17
CANDLES. Kurten, P. Transparent and camphene oil 198.11–12
— Morfit, C. Chemistry applied to the manufacture of 194.5
CANNING, G. Select speeches. Ed. by R. Walsh. Philadelphia, 1850. 8° 862.2
— Life of. Bell, R. 566.12–13
— Memoir of 830.38
CANOE voyage up the Minnay Sotor. Featherstonhaugh, G. W. 623.14
CANOT, T. Twenty years of an African slaver. Ed. by B. Mayer. New York, 1854. 12° . . 609.2
CANTERBURY tales. Chaucer, G. 754.11
— – Same 336.15
— Lee, H. 437.2
— Lee, S. 437.1
CANTICLES, New translation of, by Noyes, G. R. 1097.21
CANTÙ, C. Ezelino da Romano. Storia d' un Ghibellino. Milano, 1854. 12° 1046.15
— Margherita Pusterla, racconto. La Madonna d'Imbevera, racconto. Isotta, novella. Inni sacri. Firenze, 1845. 12° 1046.13
— Racconti e descrizioni. Milano, 1851. 12° . . 1046.14
— Storia di cento anni [1750–1850.] 3a ed. Firenze, 1855. 3v. 12° 1046.10
— Tre discorsi sulla storia universale. [Notizie biogr. e bibliogr. di Carletti.] Firenze, 1855. 12° 1046.12
CANTÙ, Ig. Macario Spacalancia. Avventure d' un uomo di pace, 1525. Milano, 1845. 12° 1046.11
CANTON Chinese, The. Sojourn in the celestial empire. Tiffany, O. jr. 697.8
CANZONIERE of Dante. Italian and English. Tr. by C. Lyell 355.2
CAPE Ann, Landing at. Thornton, J. W. 223.2
CAPE, The, and the Kaffirs. Ward, H. 699.15
CAPE of Good Hope, The. Journal of a residence at. Bunbury, C. J. F. 692.14
— – Same. 698.14

CAPEFIGUE, B. H. R. Hist. de Philippe Auguste. 3e ed. Paris, 1841. 2v. 12°........ 1066.6
CAPITAL punishment. Defence of. Cheever, G. B. 135.23
CAPITAL and labor. Knight, C..... 840.26
CAPITAL, currency and banking. Wilson, J.... 136.8
CAPPE, C. Memoirs, by herself. Boston, 1824. 12° 599.5
CAPRON, E. S. History of California. Boston, 1854. 12°................. 237.13
CAPTAINS of the old world. Herbert, H. W.... 948.8
CAPTAINS of the Roman repub. Herbert, H. W. 948.7
CAPTIVITY among the Indians. Hunter, J. D... 244.9
CARACCAS. Geographical notices of. Biggs, J.. 266.7
CARAFAS, The, of Maddaloni. Naples under Spanish dominion. Transl. Reumont, A. v. 827.2
CARCANO, G. Dodici novelle. Firenze, 1853. 12° 1056.10
　　Contents. — Della letteratura rusticale. Lettera a G. C.; Memorie d'un fanciullo; Una povera tosa; Il giovine sconosciuto; Benedetta; La vecchia della Mezzegra; La madre e il figlio; Un buon galant-uomo; Rachele; Una simpatia; Tecla; Il cappellano della Rovella; L'Ameda.
— Racconti semplici. Milano, 1853. 16°.... 1056.5
　　Contents. — Memorie d'un fanciullo; Una povera tosa; Il giovine sconosciuto; Benedetta; La vecchia della Mezzegra; La madre e il figlio; Un buon galant-uomo.
CARDANO, G. Life of. Morley, H........ 546.16
CARDONNE, D. Dom. *See* Cabinet des Fées XVII.-XVIII. Les contes et fables Indiennes de Bidpaï et de Lokman. Par Galland et C.................. 1077.1
CARDS. Les cartes à jouer et la cartomancie. Ambly, P. B. d'............. 1078.28
CAREY, A. Clovernook. New York, 1852. 12°. 416.15
CAREY, G. G. Astronomy: as known at the present day. London, n.d. 8°........ 147.11
CAREY, H. C. Essay on wages. Phila., 1835. 8° 136.7
— Past, present and future. Phila., 1848. 8°. 130.4
— Slave trade, domestic and foreign. Philadelphia, 1853. 12°............. 1096.23
CARL XIV., *Johan, king of Sweden, marshal Bernadotte.* Memoirs and campaigns of. Philippart, J.................. 542.3
CARLEN, E. F. Gustavus Lindorm. N. Y., 1853. 12° 766.7
— Marie Louise, and Passages in the life of James Leganger. New York, 1854. 8°.. 766.1
— One year: a tale of wedlock. N. Y., 1853. 12° 766.4-5
— Rose of Tistelön: a tale. London, 1844. 2v. p.8°.................. 766.3
— Smugglers of the Swedish coast. N. Y., 1845. 8° 766.2
— Whimsical woman. New York, 1854. 12°. 766.6
CARLETTI, M. Notizie di C. Cantù....... 1046.12
CARLETON, G. Memoirs by himself; including anecdotes of the war in Spain. Edinburgh, 1808. 8°................. 565.2
CARLETON, J. H. Battle of Buena Vista. New York, 1848. 16°............ 259.8
CARLETON, W. The black prophet: a tale. London, 1847. 18°............ 758.10
CARLISLE, Earl of. *See* Howard, G. W. F.
CARLISLE, Mass., History of. Shattuck, L.... 224.20
CARLYLE, T. Critical and miscellaneous essays. 3d ed. London, 1847. 4v. 8°.... 867.1
— - Same. New ed. Philadelphia, 1850. 8°. 863.7
— Genius and writings of Burns........ 586.15
— French revolution: a history. Boston, 1838. 2v. 12°.............. 1007.7
— - Same. New York, 1847. 2v. 12°.... 1008.4
— German romance. Edinburgh, 1827. 4v. 12° 418.1
　　Contents. — Vol. I. Musæus and La Motte Fouqué. II. Tieck and Hoffmann. III. Richter. IV. Goethe.
— Heroes, hero worship and the heroic in hist. New York, 1852. 12°........ 885.13
— Latter day pamphlets. Boston, 1850. 12°.. 885.15
— Life of Schiller. From 2d London ed. N. Y., 1846. 12°.............. 545.12
— Life of John Sterling. 2d ed. Boston, 1852. 12° 584.15
— Passages selected from: with memoir. London, 1855. 12°............ 885.12
— Past and present. 2d ed. N. York, 1843. 12° 878.16
— Sartor Resartus. N. Y., 1844. 12°..... 878.10
— - Same. Fr. last Lond. ed. Bost., 1846. 12° 885.14

CARMELA oder die Wiedertaufe. Rom. Mundt, T. 1034.17
CARNAHAN, J. Discourse del. in Murray St. ch. New York................ 1083.5
CARNARVON, Earl of. *See* Herbert, H. J. G.
CARNE, J. Letters from the East. 2d ed. Lond., 1826. p.8°.............. 687.7
— Travels in the East. London, 1830. p.8... 694.18
CARNES, J. A. Voyage to the West coast of Africa. Boston, 1852. 12°.....698.16-17
CARO, E. St. Dominique et les dominicains. Paris, 1853. 12°............. 1078.35
CAROLINA, Fort. French settlement at. Banvard, J................. 228.15
CAROLINE. A Franconia story. Abbott, J.v.IX. of 738.4
CAROLINE, Queen of George II. Memoir of. Thompson, A. T.......... 554.6
CARPANI, G. Life of Haydn; with life of Mozart. Providence, 1820. 12°........ 545.20
— - Same. Boston, 1839. 16°....... 545.19
CARPENTER, L. Memoirs, ed. by his son. Bristol, 1842. 8°................ 574.6
CARPENTER, M. Juvenile delinquents; their condition and treatment. London, 1853. 8°.. 135.16
CARPENTER, S. C. Memoirs of T. Jefferson. [N. York.] 2v. 8°............. 523.16
CARPENTER, W. B. Manual of physiology. 2d ed. London, 1851. p.8°........ 149.23
— Mechanical philosophy, horology and astronomy. London, 1848. p.8°...... 146.25
— - Same. New ed. London, 1857. p.8°... 836.7
— The microscope and its revelations. London, 1856. 12°.............. 178.21
— Physiology of temperance and total abstinence. London, 1853. 12°....... 130.8
— Principles of human physiology. 4th ed. London, 1853. 8°........... 152.16
— - Same. 5th ed. By F. G. Smith. Philadelphia, 1853. 8°.......... 152.15
— Use and abuse of alcoholic liquors. Boston, 1851. 12°.............. 157.17
— Zoology. New ed. by W. S. Dallas. London, 1857. 2v. p.8°.......... 836.6
CARPENTER, W. H. History of Massachusetts. Philadelphia, 1853. 12°.....228.11-12
— and Arthur, T. S. History of Vermont. Philadelphia, 1853. 12°........ 228.13
CARPENTER, W. W. Travels and adventures in Mexico. New York, 1851. 12°..... 638.8
CARPENTER of Rouen, a dramat. tale. Jones, J. S. 498.8-9
CARPENTRY. De la charpente........ 1075.6
— Treatise on, from the Encyclopædia Brit... 201.4
　　See also: Architecture.
CARR, P. Trial of British soldiers for murder of, in Boston, 5th March, 1770..... 219.1
CARREL, J. B. N. A. Counter revolution in England. London, 1846. p.8°...... 978.4
— - Same. London, 1857. p.8°....... 837.10
CARRICK, J. D. Life of Sir Wm. Wallace of Elderslie. Edinburgh, 1830. 2v. 18°.... 830.58
CARRUTHERS, R. Life of Alexander Pope. 2d ed. London, 1857. p.8°.......... 835.12
CARSTENS, H. W. A Trifolium. Boston, 1855. 16° 878.5
CARTAPHILUS, the wandering Jew. Chronicles of. Hoffman, D............ 901.5
CARTER, Mrs. E. Park, L. J. Memoir of.... 599.10
— Pennington, M. Life of......... 595.5
CARTWRIGHT, P. Autobiography. New York, 1857. 16°.............. 534.17
CARUS, C. G. The king of Saxony's journey through Engl'd and Scotland in 1844. London, 1846. 8°............. 647.3
CARVAJAL. Famille de. Drame. Mérimée, P... 1069.6
CARVALHO, S. N. Travels in the far West; with Col. Frémont's last expedition. New York, 1857. 12°.............. 620.11
CARVER, J. Travels throughout North America, 1766-69. Walpole, N. H. 1813. 8°.... 639.8
CARY, A. F. C. Chow-chow. A journal kept in India, Egypt, etc. London, 1857. 2v. 8°. 696.1
CARY, H. F. Memoir, literary journal and letters. Ed. by H. Cary. London, 1847. 2v. 8°..584.10-11

CARY, R. Earl of Monmouth. Memoirs by himself, and fragmenta regalia, by Sir R. Naunton. Edinburgh, 1808. 8° 563.8

CARY, T. G. Memoir of T. H. Perkins. Boston, 1856. 8° 524.4

CASE of the Seneca Indians. Phil., 1840. 8° . . 244.8

CASPIAN, Sketches on the shores of the. Holmes, W. R. 674.3

CASS, L. France, its king, court and government. 3d ed. New York, 1848. 8° 1004.5
— Life and character of. Schoolcraft, H. R. . . 523.8
— Life and public services of. Young, W. T. . 523.7

CASTAWAYS, The: or, adventures in the wilds of Africa. Bowman, A. 719.7

CASTI, G. Gli animali parlanti. Poema. Palermo, 1848. 2v. 18° 1049.4

CASTLE, H. J. Treatise on land surveying and levelling. London, 1845. 8° 196.6

CASTLE dangerous. Scott, Sir W. . . . . . 480.35&37-39
CASTLE of Ehrenstein. A novel. James, G. P. R.463.2&22-24
CASTLE of fools: a novel. Howitt, M. 469.11
CASTLE builders, The. [A novel]. Yonge, C. M. . 786.7
CASTLES in the air. A novel. Gore, Mrs. C. G. . 776.3

CASTRIOT, G. [Scanderbeg], king of Albania, Life of. Moore, C. C. 547.10

CASWELL, H. Scotland and the Scottish church. Oxford, 1853. 16° 1089.12

CATACOMBS of Rome. Philadelphia, n.d. 12° . . 1088.6
— as illustrating the church of the first three centuries. Kip, W. I. 1088.13

CATEL, C. S. Treatise on harmony, transl. by Mrs. M. C. Clarke. London, 1854. roy.8° 204.1

CATHERINE II. of Russia. Smucker, S. M. Court and reign of 546.10
— Tooke, W. Life of 546.2

CATHOLIC and prot. nations compar. Roussell, N. 1103.6
CATHOLIC church. Courcy, H. de. Cath. church in the United States 1098.6
— Wiseman, Card. Doctrines and practices of the 1098.5

CATHOLIC missions, Hist. of, among the Indian tribes. Shea, J. G. 1098.7

CATHOLICITY and Protestantism comp. Balmes, J. 1083.3

CATLIN, G. Manners, customs and condition of the N. A. Indians. Phila., 1857. 2v. 8° . . . 245.1
— Ojibbeway and Ioway Indians in Europe. 3d ed. London, 1852. 2v. in 1. 8° 645.4

CATLOW, A. Drops of water: their inhabitants displayed by the microscope. London, 1851. sq.12° 178.29
— Popular conchology. London, 1843. 12° . . . 178.32

CATS and dogs: lessons in natural history. Myrtle, Mrs. II. 177.28

CATTLE, Breeds, management, etc. of. Youatt, W. 172.13

CATULLUS, C. V. Works, [also those] of Tibullus and the Vigil of Venus. Transl. [With] metrical version. London, 1854. p.8° . . . 844.2

CAUCASUS. Captivity of two Russian princesses in the. Verderevsky 687.1

CAUDLE's, Mrs., Curtain lectures. Jerrold, D. III. of 906.1

CAULFIELD, J., Earl of Charlemont. Memoirs of. Hardy, F. 563.6

CAULKINS, F. M. Hist. of New London, Conn. New London, 1852. 8° 225.3

CAVALIERS, Memoirs of the. Warburton, E. . . 553.6
CAVALIERS and Roundheads, Songs of. Thornbury, G. W. 316.3

CAVE et Dittmer. Les soirées de Neuilly. Bruxelles, 1828. 2v. 18° 1079.13

CAVENDISH, G. Life of Cardinal Wolsey. Ed. by S. W. Singer. 2d ed. London, 1827. 8° 566.10

CAVENDISH, T. Life and voyages of 810.41

CAXTON, Wm. Biography of. Knight, C. . . . 840.28

CAXTONS, The. A family picture. Lytton, E. B. 465.28-30

CAYLUS, Comte de. Cabinet des Fées. v.XXIV. Les Féeries Nouvelles, v.XXV. Les nouveaux contes orientaux, Cadichon et Jeannette. 1077.1

CECIL, R. Works, sermons, remains, [etc.] N. York, 1850. 3v. 12° 1087.5

CECILIA; or memoirs of an heiress: a novel. D'Arblay, F. B. 499.4

CELEBRATED characters, Memoirs of. Lamartine, A. de 547.4

CELESTIAL scenery, etc., displayed. Dick, T. . . 810.77

CELLINI, B. Memoirs, by himself. Translated by T. Roscoe; with the notes of G. P. Carpani. New York, 1845. 2v. 12° 544.13
— Same. Coll. with the new text of G. Molini, with notes of Carpani. Transl. by Roscoe. London, 1850. p.8° 828.1

CEMENTS. Burnell, G. R. Treatise on mortars, etc. 819.32
CEMENTS, Treatise on 199.19

CENTRAL America. See America.

CENTURY of inventions. Somerset, E. Marq. of Worcester 199.27

CERVANTES SAAVEDRA, M. de. Don Quixote de la Mancha. Translated by C. Jarvis. Philadelphia, 1852. 2v. 8° 789.1
— Don Quixote. Transl. by Motteux. New ed., with notes and essay by J. G. Lockhart. Boston, 1854. 4v. 12° 789.2
— Don Quixote. Transl. by Smollett. Pref'd life of the author. London, n.d. 4v. 18° . . 789.3
— Exemplary novels. Transl. by W. H. Kelly. London, 1855. p.8° 857.3
— Nouvelles. Traduction nouv. Paris, 1809. 4v. 18° 1069.11

Contents. — Vol. 1. Avant-propos; Mems. sur la vie de Cervantes; La Bohémienne; L'amant généreux; Examen de l'amant. II. Rinconnet et Cortadille; Isabelle et Seïnours; Don Manuel; Le Licencié Vidriéra; Leocadie, ou, la force du sang. III. Le Jaloux; Les Rivales; Cornélie. IV. Constance; Le Trompeur trompé; Dialogue des deux chiens de Mahudes.

— Life and writings of, etc. Roscoe, T. 399.1

CESARI, A. Novelle. Nuova ed. Napoli, 1851. 3v. in 1. 16° 1049.5
— Bellezze di Dante 1047.2
— Novelle. See Manzoni, G. 1058.7

CETACEA, Natural history of the. Bell, T. . . . 172.18

CEYLON. Baker, S. W. Rifle and hound in . . 695.8
— Barrow, Sir G. C. past and present 938.8
— Binning, R. B. M. Two years travel in . . . 685.1
— Forbes, Major. Eleven years in 695.4
— Heber, R. Notes on 889.24

CHACE, The, the turf, and the road. Apperley, C. J. 177.14

CHADWICK, J. Home cookery. Boston, 1853. 12° 188.23

CHAINBEARER, The: a novel. Cooper, J. F. . . 760.14-15

CHALDEA. Travels and researches in. Loftus, W. K. 694.1

CHALMERS, A. Prefaces to the British essayists 850.24

CHALMERS, G. Introduction to the history of the revolt of the American colonies. Boston, 1845. 2v. 8° 304.8

CHALMERS, T. Adaptation of external nature to man, [with] a biographical preface by J. Cumming. London, 1853. p.8° 826.6
— Political economy in connection with morals. New York, 1832. 12° 136.29
— Posthumous works. Ed. by W. Hanna. New York, 1848-51. 9v. 12° 1108.6

Contents. — Vols. I.-III. Daily scripture readings. IV.-V. Horæ biblicæ sabbaticæ; Sabbath scripture readings. VI. Sermons, illustrative of his ministry, 1798-1847. VII.-VIII. Institutes of theology. IX. Prelections on Butler's analogy; Paley's evidences of Christianity, and Hill's lectures in divinity, with two introductory lectures, and four addresses.

— Selections from his correspondence. Ed. by Rev. W. Hanna. N.Y., 1853. 12° 1086.25
— Life of. Hanna, W. 576.7
— Life of. Ed. by J. C. Moffat 576.1

CHAMBERS, R. Cyclopædia of English literature. Boston, 1851. 2v. 8° 392.1
— Domestic annals of Scotland. Edinburgh and London, 1858. 2v. 8° 974.3
— Life of king James I. Edinburgh, 1830. 2v. 18° 830.59
— Rebellions in Scotland, 1638-60. Edinburgh, 1828. 2v. 18° 830.44
— Rebellions in Scotland. 1689 and 1715. Edinburgh, 1829. 18° 830.50

CHAMBERS, R. Rebellions in Scotland. 1745–46.
Edinburgh, 1827. 2v. 18° 830.34
— Select writings. Edinburgh, 1847. 4v. 16°.   366.3
CHAMBERS, W. American slavery and colour.
London, 1857. 8° 297.8
— Hand-book of Amer. literature. Phil., n.d. 12°   404.13
— History of the English language and litera-
ture. Edinburgh, 1853. 16° 404.15
— Information for the people. 15th American
ed. Philadelphia, 1851. 2v. roy.8°. . . .   901.4
— Miscellany of useful and entertaining tracts.
Edinburgh, n.d. 10v. 16° . . . .   366&367
— Papers for the people. Edinburgh, 1850–51.
12v. 12° 386.1–2
— Pocket miscellany. Bost., 1852–53. 12v. in 6. 12°   367.1
— Things as they are in America. Philadelphia,
1854. 12° 627.22
— Youth's Companion. London, [1857.] 16°. .   138.9
CHAMIER, F. Life of a sailor: a novel. N. Y.,
1833. 2v. 12° 737.1
CHANCE medley of light matter. Grattan, T. C. .   802.32
CHANDLER, E. L. This, that and the other. Bos-
ton, 1854. 12° 448.1–8
CHANDLER, M. G. Elements of character. 2d ed.
Boston, 1854. 8° 118.11
— Elements of character. Boston, 1854. 16°. .   127.30
— Elements of character. 3d ed. Boston, 1855. 16°   1086.29
CHANDLER, P. W. American criminal trials. Bos-
ton, 1841–44. 2v. 12° 297.17
CHANDLER, R. Travels in Asia Minor and Greece.
New ed., by N. Revett. Oxford, 1825. 2v.
in 1. 8° 683.5
CHANDLESS, Wm. A visit to Salt Lake. London,
1857. 12° 626.3
CHANGE for the American notes [of Dickens]. By
an American lady. New York, 1843. 8° . .471.16–18
CHANNING, B. H. The sisters abroad: or, an Ital-
ian journey. Boston, 1857. 16° 678.17
CHANNING, E. T. Lectures read in Harvard Col-
lege. Boston, 1856. 12° 405.10
— Life of William Ellery. Sparks's American
biography. v. VI. 529.1
— - Same. Lives of eminent indiv., etc. v. III.   518.5
CHANNING, W. A physician's vacation: or, a sum-
mer in Europe. Boston, 1856. 12° . . .   648.1–2
CHANNING, W. E. Works, with introduction.
2d ed. Boston, 1843. 6v. 12° 117.3

Contents. — Vol. I. Introductory remarks; Character and writings of Milton; Life of Napoleon Bonaparte; Character and writings of Fénelon; Moral
argument against Calvinism; National literature; Associations; The union; Education. II. Slavery; The
abolitionists; Annexation of Texas; Catholicism;
Creeds; Address on temperance; Address on self-culture. III.–IV. Discourses; Evidences of Christianity. V. Remarks on the slavery question; Lecture on
war; Lectures on the elevation of the laboring classes;
Death of Rev. Dr. Follen, a discourse; Charges at the
ordinations of F. T. Gray, R. C. Waterston, and J. S.
Dwight; Miscellanies; Appendix. VI. Emancipation, 1840; Discourse on the life of Rev. J. Tuckerman; Address on the present age; The church; Duty
of the free states; Address on the anniversary of
emancipation in the British W. I.

— Œuvres sociales, trad., etc., par É. Laboulaye.
Paris, 1854. 12° 1067.11

Contents. — Essai sur la vie et les ouvrages de Channing, par M. E. Laboulaye; Introduction aux œuvres
sociales de Channing; De l'éducation personnelle; De
l'élevation des classes laborieuses; Discours sur la
tempérance; Ministère pour les pauvres; De l'obliga-
tion pour les municipalités de veiller à la santé morale
de leurs membres.

— Œuvres. De l' esclavage. Préface par É
Laboulaye. Paris, 1855. 12° 1067.10
— Poetical genius of Milton. 359.3
— Memoir of. Channing, W. H. 535.1–2
CHANNING, W. H. Memoirs of Sarah M. F.
D'Ossoli. Prepared by C. and others . .538.9–10
— Memoir of W. E. Channing. 6th ed. Boston,
1851. 3v. 12° 535.1–2
CHAPLIN, J. D. Convent and the manse, by Ilyla,
Boston, 1854. 12° 417.19–20

CHAPMAN, B. History of Gustavus Adolphus, and
of the thirty years' war. London, 1856. 8°   546.5
CHAPMAN, E. J. Practical mineralogy. London,
1843. 8° 163.12
CHAPMAN, J. Cotton and commerce of India.
London, 1851. 8° 135.10
CHARACTER, Elements of. Chandler, M. G. . . .   118.11
CHARACTERISTICS of literature. Tuckerman, H. T.   548.5
CHARACTERS and criticisms. Jones, W. A. . . .   888.11
CHARICLES. Priv. life of the anc. Greeks. Becker,
W. A. 957.1
CHARICLES, a dramatic poem. Quincy, J. P. . .   346.7
CHARITY. Brouckere, C. de. Charité, etc. . . .   1065.11
— Trimmer, Mrs. The economy of. 129.7
CHARLEMAGNE. Hauréau, B. C. et sa cour . . .   1078.40
— James, G. P. R. The history of 810.60
— Juste, T. Histoire de 1075.9
CHARLEMONT: a tale of Kentucky. Simms, W. G.800.23–26
CHARLES I. of England. Abbott, J. History of559.18–21
— Aikin, L. Court of. 976.6
— Ashburnham, J. Vindication of, from the mis-
representations of Lord Clarendon. . . .   975.10
— D'Israeli, I. Commentaries on. 553.2
— Evelyn, J. Private correspondence of Charles
I. with Sir E. Nicholas. 977.4
CHARLES the first. Hist. tragedy. Mitford,
M. R. 804.4
CHARLES II. of England. Abbott, J. History of559.22–24
— Hamilton, A. Personal history, etc. 857.1
— Sidney, H. Diary of the times of 553.4
CHARLES V. Mignet, F. A. A. Son abdication et
sa mort 1065.1
— Robertson, W. History of the reign of. . .   912.4–5
— - Hist. of the reign of. Abridged 830.6
— Stirling, W. Cloister life of 617.6–8
CHARLES VIII. king of France, History of. Com-
mines, P. de 857.4
CHARLES IX. Les temps de. Mérimée, P. . . .   1069.4
CHARLES X. Hist. of the reign of. Crowe, E. E.   1005.3
CHARLES the Bold, duke of Burgundy, Hist. of.
Commines, P. de 857.4
CHARLES Auchester. A memorial. Berger, E. .   802.39
CHARLES Elwood: or, the infidel converted.
Brownson, O. A. 1109.6
CHARLES et Marie. Nouv. Souza, Mme. de. . .   1079.10
CHARLES O'Malley, the Irish dragoon. Lever, C..501.14–15
CHARLES Tyrrel: or, the bitter blood. James,
G. P. R. 463.30
CHARLESTON, S. C., Invasion of. Wilkinson, E..   216.10
CHARLOTTE Elizabeth. See Tonna.
CHARLOTTE Temple. A tale of truth. Rowson,
S. Mrs. 789.10
CHARMED sea: a tale. Martineau, H. .v. XIII. of740.2–3
CHARMS and counter-charms. M'Intosh, M. J. .   437.18
CHASE, H. and Sanborn, C. W. The north and the
south. Statistical view. Boston, 1856. 12°   297.18
CHASE, I. Baptismal tracts for the times. Boston,
1851. 12° 1089.11
CHASE, The, with critical essays by Dr. Aikin.
Somervile, W. 359.5
CHASLES, V. E. P. Anglo-American literature
and manners 404.11
— Notabilities of France and England, with an
autobiography. New York, 1853. 12° . .   868.7
CHATEAU de Génappe. Récit. Saintine, X. B. . .   1078.39
CHATEAUBRIAND, R. F. A. v'te de. Genius of
Christianity. Transl. by C. I. White. Phila-
delphia, 1856. 8° 1095.1
— Selections from "Genius of Christianity."
Transl., with an introduc., by E. B. Stork.
Philadelphia, 1858. 12° 1088.16
— Mélanges historiques. Bruxelles, 1828. 24°.   1069.13
— Les martyrs. Paris, 1853. 12° 1066.7
— Les Natchez. Bruxelles, 1827. 2v. 24° . . .   1069.14
— Portrait of Bonaparte, with an ode by Lord
Byron. New York, 1814. 18° 609.7
— Travels in Greece, Palestine, Egypt and Bar-
bary, 1806–7. Transl. by F. Shoberl. New
York, 1814. 8° 685.7
CHATEAUGAY woods, A tramp in. Hammond,
S. H. 636.2

CHATSWORTH: a romance. Ward, R. P. 787.1
CHATTERTON, T., with notices of his poetical works, life, Rowley controversy and notes. Cambridge, 1842. 2v. 12°. 346.6
— Life of. Dix, J. 589.7
CHAUCER, G. Poetical works, with mem., by Sir H. Nicolas. London, 1845. 6v. 16°. . . . 319.5

Contents. — Vol. I. Memoir of Chaucer, by Sir H. Nicolas; Essay on the language and versification of Chaucer, by T. Tyrwhitt, Esq.: Introductory discourse to the Canterbury tales. II.—III. Canterbury tales. IV. The romaunt of the rose; Troilus and Creseide, b. 1, 2. V. Troilus and Creseide, b. 3—5; Legend of good women; A goodly ballade of Chaucer; The booke of the dutchesse; The assembly of foules. VI. Queen Annelida and false Arcite; The complaint of the black knight; A praise of women; The house of fame; The complaint of Mars and Venus; The cuckow and the nightingale; The court of love; Chaucer's dream; The flower and the leaf; Chaucer's A. B. C.; Ballads, etc.

— Riches of Chaucer; notes and mem., by C. C. Clarke. London, 1835. 2v. 12° 355.4
— Canterbury tales, n.d. 16° 336.15
— Canterbury tales. Notes of T. Tyrwhitt. New ed. New York, 1855. 12° 754.11
— Canterbury tales. Ed. by J. Saunders. London, 1845-47. 2v. 18° 840.12
— - Tales from, in prose. Clarke, C. C. . . . 754.12
— Dryden, J. Fables translated into verse . . . 315.17
— Saunders, J. Pictures of Eng. life fr. Chaucer 850.9
CHEAP repository tracts. Lond., 1836-39. 3v. 12° 1108.13
CHEETHAM, J. Life of T. Paine. N. Y., 1809. 8° 513.14
CHEEVER, G. B. Lectures on the Pilgrim's progress, and on Bunyan. New York, 1844. 8° 1094.6
— Defence of capital punishment and essay on the reason of punishment by T. Lewis. New York, 1846. 12° 135.23
CHEEVER, H. T. The island world of the Pacific. New York, 1851. 12° 705.11
— Life in the Sandwich Islands. N. Y., 1851. 12° 705.20
— The whale and his captors. N. York, 1850. 12° 728.8
CHELIUS, J. M. System of surgery. Transl. by South, J. F. Philadelphia, 1847. 3v. 8°. . 152.8
CHELSEA pensioners, The: a novel. Gleig, G. R. 777.2
CHEMICAL analysis. Fresenius, C. R. System of, qualitative and quantitative 155.10-11
— Normandy, A. Commercial handbook of . . 156.20
— - Introduction to Rose's treatise on 155.13
— Rose, H. Practical treatise of 155.12
— Will, H. Outlines of 156.2
— Wöhler, F. Manual of 156.16
CHEMICAL and pharmaceutical processes. Bell, J. 199.16
CHEMICAL and pharmaceut. manipulat's. Morfit, C. 155.2
CHEMICAL field lectures. Stöckhardt, J. A. . . . 836.1
CHEMICAL manipulation. Faraday, M. 155.17
— Noad, H. M. 155.9
CHEMICAL philosophy, Introd. to. Daniell, J. F. 155.3
CHEMICAL and physiological balance of organic nature. Dumas and Boussingault 156.34
CHEMICAL problems and reactions. Cooke, J. P. . 156.8
CHEMICAL technology. Ronalds, E. 155.20
CHEMICAL tests. Accum, F. Treat. on use, etc., of 156.24
CHEMISTRY. Abel, F. A. and Bloxam, C. L. Handbook of 156.3
— Berzelius, J. J. The use of the blow-pipe . . 155.22
— Bowman, J. E. Handbook of medical 157.11
— Campbell, D. Text book of inorganic 156.30
— Comstock, J. L. Elements of 156.17
— Daubeny, C. Atomic theory 149.30
— Donovan, M. Treatise on 398.13
— Dyer and colour maker's companion 199.13
— Faraday, M. The non-metallic elements. . . 156.33
— Familiar introduction to 149.39
— Fownes, G. Rudimentary 819.1
— Fresenius, C. R. and Will, H. Alkalimetry. 155.21
— Glover, R. M. Manual of elementary 156.25
— Graham, T. Elements of 144.7
— Gregory, W. Elementary treatise on 156.27
— - Inorganic 156.19
— - Organic 156.18
— Griffin, J. J. Radical theory in 158.23

CHEMISTRY. Griffiths, T. C. of the four seasons. 156.6
— Hassall, A. H. Food and its adulterations. . 155.19
— - Adulterations detected 156.12
— Huard, A. Epitome of 155.23
— Introduction to practical organic . . . v. I. of 850.25
— Johnston, J. F. W. C. applied to agriculture 164.14
— - C. of common life 156.15
— Jones, H. B. Animal C. in stomach diseases 155.16
— Kemp, T. L. Discoveries and applications of modern. 156.22
— Knapp, F. C. applied to the arts and manuf. 144.3-4
— Liebig, J. Agricultural 155.24
— - Animal 155.4
— - Applica. of organ. C. to agric. and physiol. 155.25
— - Handbook of organic analysis 156.23
— - C. in relation to physiology 155.21
— - C. of food 155.7
— Löwig, C. Organic and physiological 156.4
— Manuel de chimie 1075.35
— Marcet, Mrs. J. Conversations on 155.26
— Marcet, W. Composition of food 155.15
— Miller, W. A. Organic. 156.5
— Morfit, C. C. applied to the manufacture of soap and candles 194.5
— Mulder, G. J. C. of vegetable and animal physiology 155.8
— - C. of wine 156.26
— Napier, J. C. applied to dyeing 197.3
— Peirce, C. H. Examination of drugs, etc. . . 156.13
— Phillips, J. A. C. of the metals 196.14
— Plattner, C. F. and Muspratt, S. Use of the blow-pipe 155.18
— Prout, W. C. and natural theology 826.16
— Regnault, M. V. Elements of 155.1
— Reid, D. B. Rudiments of 156.35
— Stöckhardt, J. A. Principles of 156.9-10
— Thomson, R. D. Cyclopædia of 156.7
— - School 156.31
— Turner, E. Elements of 155.5-6
— Williams, C. W. Combustion of coal and prevention of smoke 195.14
CHERUBINI, L. Counterpoint and fugue. Transl. by M. C. Clarke. London, 1854. 8°. . . . 204.2
CHESAPEAKE and Shannon, (ships,) Action betw'n 529.5
CHESEBRO', C. Victoria; or, the world overcome. New York, 1856. 12° 775.11
CHESNEY, F. R. Russo-Turkish campaigns of 1828-29. New York, 1854. 12° 918.6-7
— - Same. 3d ed. Lond., 1854. 12° 918.5
CHESS, Introduction to, with Philidor's analysis 197.27
— Montigny. Stratagems of 197.30
— Staunton, H. Chess player's companion . . 816.4
— - Chess player's hand book 816.1
— - Chess tournament 826.1
— Walker, G. Art of chess play 197.26
CHESTER plays. Edited by T. Wright 342.16
CHESTERFIELD, Lord. See Stanhope, P. D.
CHESTERTON, G. L. Revelations of prison life. 3d ed. London, 1857. p.8° 135.14
CHESTNUT wood. A tale. By Liele Linden. New York, 1854. 2v. 12° 416.3
CHETTLE, H., Dekker, T. and Haughton, W. Patient Grissil, a comedy 342.6
CHEVALIER, M. Essays on industrial subjects . 147.21
— Society, manners, and politics in the United States. Transl. from 3d Paris ed. by T. G. Bradford. Boston, 1839. 8° 624.3
CHEVERUS, J. L. A. M. L. de., Life of, by Hammond, J. 617.17-18
CHEVREUL, M. E. Harmony and contrast of colors. Transl. by C. Martel. Lond., 1854. 8° 208.5
CHICORA and other poems. Grayson, W. J. . . . 349.3
CHIEF justices of the supreme court of the U. States, Lives of. Flanders, H. 523.3
— - Same. Van Santvoord, G. 523.4
CHIHUAHUA, Explorations, etc., in. Bartlett, J. R. 624.2
CHILD at home. Abbott, J. S. C. 1109.11
CHILD, F. J. Four old plays. Thersytes; Jack Jugler; and Heywood's Pardoner and Frere; and Jocasta, a trag. by Gascoigne and Kinwelmarsh. Camb., 1848. 12°. . . 356.1

CHILD, L. M. American frugal housewife. 33d ed. New York, 1855. 16° 188.27
— Autumnal leaves. Tales and sketches in prose and rhyme. New York, 1857. 16° . . 488.12
— Biog. of good wives. 5th ed. N. Y., 1850. 12° 548.8-9
— Fact and fiction: a collection of stories. N. York, 1847-49. 12° 488.13-14
— Flowers for children. New York, 1852. 16°. 738.9
— Isaac T. Hopper: a true life. Bost., 1853. 12° 525.10-15
— Little girl's own book. Bost., 1831. sq.16° 199.41
— Mother's book. 6th edition, with additions. New York, 1849. 12° 137.28
— Oasis, The. Boston, 1834. 16° 139.17
— Philothea. A romance. Boston, 1836. 12° . 488.15
— Progress of relig. ideas. N. Y., 1855. 3v. 8° 1095.6
CHILDREN. Condie, D. F. Diseases of 152.6
— Directions for forming the habits of 139.18
CHILDREN of the new forest. Marryat, F. 745.6
CHILDREN of the abbey. Roche, R. M. 789.8
CHILD's friend, The. Berquin, A. de 729.20-21
CHILD's book of nature. Hooker, W. 177.32
CHILE con carne: or camp and field. Smith, S. C. 623.19
CHILI. Davie, J. C. History of 633.14
— Gardiner, A. F. Visit to the Indians of . . . 635.18
— Gerstäcker, F. Travels in 636.1
— Hall, B. Chili in 1820-22 . . . . 639.7
— Smith, E. R. Indian tribes of southern . . . 635.8
— Strain, I. G. Journey in, 1849. . . . . . . 635.13
— Sutcliffe, T. Sixteen years in 633.17
CHIMES, The: a goblin story. Dickens, C. . . . 481.12-16
CHIMNEYS, Practical treatise on. Eckstein, G. F. 207.12
CHINA, with some account of Ava and the Burmese, Siam and Anam. London, 1853. p.8° 825.8
— Ball, B. L. Rambles in 708.6-7
— Callery and Yvan. Hist. of the insurrection in 938.6
— Cochrane, J. D. Pedestrian journey to the frontiers of 830.46
— Davis, J. F. C. during the war and since . . 696.13
— - Empire of C. and its inhabitants 810.75
— - Sketches of 706.8
— Dobell, P. A residence in 666.2
— Ellis, H. Late embassy to 696.10
— Fishbourne, E. G. Impressions of, and the present revolution 709.15
— Forbes, F. E. Five years in, 1842-47 . . . . 696.9
— Fortune, R. Residence among the Chinese . 696.4
— Gutzlaff, C. Two voyages along the coast of. 706.5-6
— - Sketch of Chinese history 934.7
— Huc, M. l' Abbé. Christianity in 113.4
— - The Chinese empire 706.1
— - Travels in, 1844-46 . . . . 706.4
— Kidd, S. Illustr. of the symbols, philosophy, etc., of 696.8
— Jocelyn, Lord. Six months with the Chinese expedition 709.16
— Meares, J. Voyages from, 1788-89 . . . . . 623.13
— Milne, W. C. Life in 697.9
— Smith, G. Consular cities of 696.14-15
— Taylor, B. C. in 1853 . . . . 708.17-19
— Sirr, H. C. China and the Chinese 696.2
— Tiffany, O. jr. Canton Chinese 697.8
— White, J. History of a voyage to China sea . 623.12
— Williams, S. W. Chinese empire and its inhabitants 696.12
CHIPMAN, D. Memoir of Seth Warner. [Also,] the life of E. Allen, by J. Sparks. Middlebury, 1848. 16° 528.22
CHIPPEWAY Indians, Character, customs, etc., of. M'Kenney, T. L. 625.4
CHITTENDEN, W. B. Life of J. B. Ladd 898.7
CHIVALRY and charity illustrated by the lives of Bertrand du Guesclin and John Howard . . 589.14
CHIVALRY. James, G. P. R. History of 810.20
— Mills, C. History of: or, knighthood and its times 945.2
— Stebbing, H. History of C. and the crusades 830.56
CHOIX d' anecdotes. Précis hist. sur la révolution française par M. Bailly. 5e ed. par Mme. Celnart. Paris, 1828. 4v. 16° 1079.14
CHORLEY, H. F. Memorials of Mrs. Hemans. N. York, 1836. 2v. 12° 596.8

CHORLEY, H. F. Modern German music. Lond., 1854. 2v. 8° 209.5
CHORLTON, W. American grape grower's guide. New York, 1856. 12° 165.25
CHOUANNERIE, The war in the little. Hill, G. J. 1008.13
CHOULES, J. O. Cruise of the steam yacht North Star. Boston, 1854. 12° 647.9-12
CHOW-CHOW: journal in India, Egypt, and Syria. Cary, A. F. 696.1
CHRIST a friend. Adams, N. 1106.1
CHRIST knocking at the door. Flavel, J. 1107.4
CHRIST. Furness, W. H. Jesus and his biograph. 1101.5
— Greenleaf, S. Account of the trial of Jesus . 1093.16
— Neander, A. Life of Jesus Christ 848.8
— Turnbull, R. C. in history 1106.18
— Young, J. The C. of history 1087.13
CHRISTIAN art in the middle ages. Didron, M. . . 815.9
CHRISTIAN character, formation of. Ware, H. jr. 1089.31
CHRISTIAN church. See Church and Ecclesiastical history.
CHRISTIAN contemplated, The. Lectures. Jay, W. 119.14
CHRISTIAN days and thoughts. Peabody, E. . . 117.12
CHRISTIAN divinity, Apology for the true. Barclay, R. 1095.4
CHRISTIAN doctrine and practice in the second century. Philadelphia, 1846. 18° 850.25
CHRISTIAN doctrine, Lectures on. Peabody, A. P. 117.13
CHRISTIAN duty, Pastoral addresses on. James, J. A. 1088.30
CHRISTIAN iconography. Didron, M. 815.9
CHRISTIAN life, in the early and middle ages. Neander, A. 858.7
CHRISTIAN life, social and individual. Bayne, P. 1086.12-13
CHRISTIAN missions. See Missions.
CHRISTIAN morals. Browne, Sir T. . . . . v. III. of 846.11
— More, H. 129.26
See also: Ethics, Morals, etc.
CHRISTIAN professor, Counsels and cautions addressed to the. James, J. A. 118.8
CHRISTIAN progress. James, J. A. 119.22
CHRISTIAN religion. See Evidences.
CHRISTIAN sects. Phila., 1846. 16° . . . . v. III. of 850.25
See also: Ecclesiastical history.
CHRISTIAN slave: a drama. Stowe, H. B. 357.11
CHRISTIAN socialism. Ballou, A. 134.2
CHRISTIAN truth, etc., Views of. Priestley, J. . 1099.10
CHRISTIAN year, The. Thoughts in verse for Sundays and holydays. Keble, J. 1083.20
CHRISTIANITY. Chateaubriand, Visc. de. Genius of 1095.1
— - Selections from "Genius of C." 1088.16
— James, H. C. the logic of creation 1088.7
— Mann, Mrs. H. C. in the kitchen 188.24
— Martineau, J. Studies of 1086.14
— Norton, A. Tracts concerning 1095.3
See also: Evidences, Missions, Theology.
CHRISTIAN's manual of faith and devotion. Hobart, J. H. 1099.16
CHRISTIANS, The early. Eliot, S. 134.8
CHRISTIE Johnstone: a novel. Reade, C. 415.7
CHRISTINA and her court: a novel. Velde, F. K. van der 801.1
CHRISTISON, R. Manual of practical toxicology. Notes and additions, by J. T. Ducatel. Baltimore, 1833. 12° 158.5
CHRISTMAS, H. Echoes of the universe. Phila., 1850. 12° 1106.5
— Nicholas I. Brief mem. of his life and reign. London, 1854. 16° 546.20
CHRISTMAS, Customs, ceremonies, etc., of. Hervey, T. K. 989.2
CHRISTMAS books. Dickens, C. 462.16-17
CHRISTMAS carol, A. Dickens, C. 481.12-16
CHRISTMAS fire, New stories by the. Dickens, C. . 491.1-6
CHRISTMAS holydays in Rome. Kip, W. I. . . . 678.18
CHRISTMAS stories. Dickens, C. 481.12-16
CHRISTOFFEL, R. Zwingli: or, the reformation in Switzerland. Transl. by J. Cochran. Edinburgh, 1858. 8° 1085.14
CHRONICLE of the Cid, from the Spanish, by R. Southey. 1st Am. ed. Lowell, 1846. 8°. 913.2
CHRONICLES of the crusades. London, 1848. p.8°. 846.6

CHRONICLES. Froissart, J. C. of Eng., France
    and Spain, etc. 1001.2
— Jerrold, D. C. of Clovernook. . . . . v. VI. of 906.1
— Pettigrew, T. J. C. of the tombs 855.13
— Young, A. C. of the pilgrim fathers. 223.12–13
CHRONOLOGY. Blair, J. Chronological tables. . 836.2
— Munsell, J. Every day book of hist. and C.. 947.1
— Nicolas, Sir N. H. C. of history. 368.2
— C. of hist., art, literature and civilization . . . 829.39
— Tegg, T. Dictionary of 947.2
— – C. from the earliest period to present time 949.7
CHRYSOSTOM, J. Life of, by Perthes, F. M. . . . 547.20
CHURCH. Barrett, B. F. True measure of a true C. 1088.15
— Bartol, C. A. Unity of C. and congregation . 1086.30
— Coleridge, S. T. Church and state . . v. VI. of 886.2
— Cumming, J. C. before the flood 116.11
— Macaulay, T. B. C. and state. Review of
    Gladstone on 409.20
— Noel, B. W. Union of C. and state 128.3
— Spencer, C. C. Explanation, etc., of C. modes 204.5
    See also : Ecclesiastical hist. and Theology.
CHURCHILL, C. Poetical works, with notes and
    life, by W. Tooke. Lond., 1844. 3v. 16°. . 319.6

    Contents. — Vol. I. Life, letters, will, etc.; The Ros-
    ciad; The apology, addressed to the critical reviewers;
    Night; The prophecy of famine; An epistle to Wm.
    Hogarth. II. The duellist; Gotham; The author;
    The conference; The ghost, b. 1–3. III. The ghost,
    b. 4; The candidate; The farewell; The times; Inde-
    pendence; The journey; Fragment of a dedication;
    Lines written in Windsor park; Index.

— Poetical works, with mem., notes, etc., by G.
    Gilfillan. N. Y., 1855. 8° 322.5
— Biography of. Forster, J. . . . . . . v. II. of 894.3
CHURCHILL, F. Diseases of women. New Am.
    ed.; by D. F. Condie. Philadelphia, 1852. 8° 151.11
CHURCHILL, J. Duke of Marlborough. Bucke, C.
    Life of 379.5
— – Coxe, W. Memoirs of 838.2
CHURCHYARDS, Chapters on. Southey, Mrs. C. . 878.10
CHUTE d'un ange ; épisode. Lamartine, A. de . . 1068.12
CIBBER, C. Dramatic works. London, 1760. 4v. 16° 357.13

    Contents. — Vol. I.° Love's last shift, a comedy ;
    Woman's wit, a comedy; Love makes a man, a com-
    edy; She would and she would not, a comedy. II.
    The careless husband, a comedy; The rival fools, a
    comedy; The lady's last stake, a comedy; Richard
    III., a tragedy. III. The double gallant, a comedy;
    Ximena, a tragedy; The comical lovers, a comedy;
    The non-juror, a comedy. IV. The refusal, a com-
    edy; The provoked husband, a comedy; Love in a
    riddle, a pastoral; King John, a tragedy.

CICERO, M. T. Academic questions. De Finibus
    and Tusculan disputations. Transl. by C.
    D. Yonge. London, 1853. p.8° 834.7
— Three books of offices, etc. Transl. by C. R.
    Edmonds. London, 1853. p.8° 824.2
— Orations, etc. Transl. by C. D. Yonge. Lon-
    don, 1851–52. 4v. p.8° 824.10
— Orations, offices, Cato and Laelius. New
    York, 1852. 3v. 18° 830.12
— Orationum XII selectarum liber. Etonæ,
    1785. 18° 868.22
— Oratory. Transl. by J. S. Watson. London,
    1855. p.8° 844.9
— Three dialogues on the orator. Translated by
    W. Guthrie. 2d Am. ed. N. Y., n.d. 18°. 830.24
— Treatises. Transl. by C. D. Yonge. London,
    1853. p.8° 834.14
— Tusculan questions. Transl. by G. A. Otis.
    Boston, 1839. 12° 128.5
— Life by Dr. Middleton. Letters, transl. by
    W. Melmoth and Heberden. Lond., 1845. 8° 541.2
— Life of. Hollings, J. F. 389.7
CID, the, Chronicle of, transl. by R. Southey . . . 913.2
— Dennis, G. A short chronicle of. 840.19
— Lockhart, J. G. Acct., with specimens of . . 316.1
— Monseignat, C. de. Le C. campeador 1078.36
CILICIA. Hist. acct. of. Barker, W. B.. . . . . . 694.2
CINQ-MARS. Conjuration de. Paris, 1853. 12°. 1078.31
— Conjuration sous Louis XIII. Vigny, A. de 1067.12
CIRCASSIA. Spencer, E. 687.21–22

CIRCUMNAVIGATION of the globe. Hist. acct. etc. 810.76
CITIES, Ruins of ancient ; with accts. of their
    rise, fall, etc. Bucke, C. 379.6
CITIZEN of Prague. Translated by M. Howitt.
    N. Y., 1846. 8° 802.25
CITY of the great king. Barclay, J. T. 684.3
CITY poems. Smith, A.. . . . . 324.11
CIVIL liberty and self-government. Lieber, F.. . . 134.13
CIVILIZATION. Buckle, H. T. Hist. of, in England 942.1–2
— Guizot, F. P. G. Hist. of, in Europe. 949.1–2
— Laforet, N. J. Etudes sur la C. européenne . 1065.29
CLAN-ALBIN : a national tale. 2d ed. London,
    1815. 4v. 12° 429.4
CLAPP, T. Autobiographical sketches and recol-
    lections. Boston, 1857. 12° 534.16
CLAPP, W. W., jr. A record of the Boston stage.
    Boston, 1853. 16° 356.10–11
CLAPPERTON, H. and Denham, D. Trav. in Africa 693.6
— – Second expedition to Africa. [With] R.
    Lander's journal. Phila., 1829. 8° 693.8
CLARA Howard : or, the enthusiasm of love.
    Brown, C. B. 757.2
CLARA : or, slave life in Europe. Hacklländer,
    F. W. 796.14
CLARENCE, a tale of our own times. Sedgwick,
    C. M. 436.11–14
CLARENDON, Earl of. See Hyde, E.
CLARINDA, Mrs. M'Lehose. Correspondence with
    Burns. 586.14
CLARK, D. W. Methodist Episcopal pulpit. G.
    Peck, editor. New York, 1850. 12° 1096.16
CLARK, J. A. Memoir of Anzonetta R. Peters.
    New York, n.d. 16° 119.15
CLARK, J. H. Sight and hearing, how preserved
    and how lost. N. Y., 1856. 12° 157.10
CLARK, R. W. Memoir of J. E. Emerson. N. Y.,
    n.d. 16° 119.19
CLARK, W. G. Gazpacho : or, summer months in
    Spain. London, 1850. 12° 675.13
— Literary remains. Ed. by L. G. Clark. 4th ed.
    N. Y., 1851. 8° 873.5
— Spirit of life, [and other poems.] Phila., 1853.
    12° 358.10
CLARKE, A. Commentary on the N. Testament . 1093.1
— Memoirs of the Wesley family. G. Peck, ed.
    N. Y., 1851. 12° 535.12
CLARKE, C. C. Tales from Chaucer, in prose.
    London, 1833. 12° 754.12
CLARKE, E. D. Travels in Europe, Asia, and
    Africa. 4th ed. Lond., 1816–24. 11v. 8°. 682.1
— Travels in Europe, Asia, and Africa. 5th Am
    ed. Hartford. N. Y., 1815–17. 3v. in 2. 12° 680.6
— Travels. Greece, Egypt and the Holy Land.
    New York, 1813. 8° 683.10
— Life and remains of. Otter, W. 583.10
CLARKE, J. F. Christian doctrine of prayer. Bos-
    ton, 1854. 18° 1109.24
— Eleven weeks in Europe. Bost., 1852. 12°.. 669.4
— Memoirs of S. M. F. D'Ossoli 538.9–10
CLARKE, M. C. Girlhood of Shakespeare's hero-
    ines. 2d series. N. Y., 1852. 12° 335.15
— Iron cousin. A novel. New York, 1854. 12° 434.6–7
CLARKE, M. St. C. and Hall, D. A. Hist. of the
    Bank of the U. S. Wash., 1832. 8° 293.1
CLARKE and Lewis' expedition. History of.
    Allen, P. 820.52
CLARKE, S. J. *Grace Greenwood.* See Lippincott,
    S. J. C.
CLARKSON, T. Mem. of the life of William Penn.
    Phila., 1813. 2v. 12° 526.19
CLASSICAL literature. Browne, R. W. Hist. of
    Greek 401.3
— Eschenburg, J. J. Manual of 402.6
CLASSICAL studies. Sears, B., Edwards, B. B. and
    Felton, C. C. 403.16
CLASSICAL tour, through Italy. Eustace, J. C. . . 675.1
CLASSICS, Greek and Latin.
— Corpus poetarum Latinorum. Walker. . . . 353.1
    NOTE. — For translations of the classics into Eng-
    lish, see Bohn's classical library, and Harper's clas-
    sical library.

DUBLIN, N. H. History of. Proceedings at the centennial celebration 225.1
DUBOIS, E. Old Nick: a satirical story. Dublin, 1801. 2v. 16° 799.12
DUBOURG, G. The violin and its most eminent professors. London, 1852. 4th ed. 12° . . 209.2
DUBOURG, J. Huen. Pseud. See Hamond.
DUCLOS, C. P. Acajou et Zirphile. Cabinet des Fées. v.XXXV 1077.1
DUDDON, The. Rambles by rivers. Thorne, J. . 850.18
DUDEVANT, M. A. Consuelo. Translated by F. G. Shaw. Boston, 1846. 2v. 12° 476.6
DUELLING, History of. Millingen, J. G. 985.4
DUELS and duelling. With hist. essay. Sabine, L. 947.14
DUER, W. A. Constitutional jurisprudence of the United States. New York, n.d. 18° 820.57
— Life of William Alexander, earl of Stirling. New York, 1847. 8° 513.8
DUFAU, J. B. Hagiographie belge. Bruxelles, n.d. 12° 1075.24
DUFF, A. Indian rebellion: its causes and results. New York, 1858. 12° 939.4
DU GUESCLIN, Bertrand, and John Howard, Lives of: or, chivalry and charity illustrated . . 589.14
DUHRING, H. The United States with regard to Europe. London, 1833. 12° 297.14
DULCKEN, H. W. German songs; from the 16th to the 19th century. Edited and translated. London, 1856. 12° 316.7
DUMAS, A. Henri III. et sa cour: drame historique. 2d ed. Paris, 1829. 12° 1078.6
— The iron mask. Translated by T. Williams. Philadelphia, 1850. 8° 735.1
— Memoirs of a maitre d'armes. Transl. Lond., 1853. p.8° 409.5
— Memoirs of a physician. Part I. Joseph Balsamo. Transl. London, 1847. 12° . . 499.9
— Pictures of travel in the South of France. Translated. London, n.d. 12° 654.8
— Travels in the South of France. Translated. London, n.d. 12° 869.10
— Trav. sketches in Egypt and Sinai. Translated. London, 1839. 16° 709.20
DUMAS, J. B. and Boussingault, J. B. Chemical and physiological balance of organic nature. Translated. 3d ed. London, 1844. 16° . . 156.34
— Manures: nutrition of plants, etc. Transl. by C. Morfit. New York, 1848. 8° 165.4
DUMAS, M. Memoirs of his own time. Philadelphia, 1839. 2v. 12° 1008.12
DUMONT, P. E. L. Souvenirs sur Mirabeau. Bruxelles, 1832. 12° 1079.1
— Recollections of Mirabeau. Lond., 1832. 8°. 613.3
DUNALLAN, a religious tale. Kennedy, G. . . . 808.15
DUNCAN, H. Sacred philosophy of the seasons, with additions, etc., by F. W. P. Greenwood. Boston, 1839. 4v. 12° 1089.7
DUNCAN, J. British butterflies . . . v.XXIX. of 179.1
— Introduction to entomology . . . . v.XXVIII. of 179.1
DUNCAN, Jona. Hist. of Russia. Lond., n.d. 2v. 12° 869.11
DUNCAN, J. M. Travels in the United States and Canada, 1818-19. New York, 1823. 2v. 12° 628.24
DUNCAN, M. L., Memoir of. Lundie, J. C. . . . 119.7
DUNGLISON, R. Gen. therapeutics and mat. med. 5th ed. Philadelphia, 1853. 2v. 8° . . . 152.4
— Medical lexicon. 10th ed. Phila., 1853. 8° . 151.14
— New remedies, with formulæ. 6th edition, with additions. Philadelphia, 1851. 8° . . 151.15
— Practice of medicine. 3d ed. Phila., 1848. 2v. 8° 152.1
DUNHAM, S. A. History of Europe during the middle ages. London, 1833-34. 4v. 16° . . 378.6
— History of Denmark, Sweden and Norway. London, 1839-40. 3v. 16° 378.10
— History of the Germanic empire. London, 1834-35. 3v. 16° 368.9
— History of Poland. London, 1831. 16° . . . 378.9
— History of Spain and Portugal. London, 1832. 5v. 16° 368.8
— Bell, R. and others. Lives of the most eminent literary and scientific men of Great Britain. London, 1836-38. 3v. 16° 398.3

DUNKELGRAF, Der. Roman. Bechstein, L. . . . 1013.7
DUNLAP, S. F. Vestiges of the spirit-history of man. New York, 1858. 8° 122.16
DUNLAP, W. History of the American theatre. New York, 1832. 8° 353.5-6
— History of the arts of design in the United States. New York, 1834. 2v. 8° 202.1
— Memoirs of a water drinker. 2d edition. New York, 1837. 2v. as 1. 12° 539.26
— Memoirs of G. F. Cooke. N. Y., 1813. 2v. 18°. 597.18
DUNLOP, J. Memoirs of Spain from 1621-1700. Edinburgh, 1834. 2v. 8° 913.3
— History of fiction. From 2d London edition. Philadelphia, 1842. 2v. 12° 405.15
DUNTON, J. Life and errors, by himself. Lond., 1818. 2v. in 1. 8° 583.9
DÜNTZER, J. H. J. Frauenbilder aus Goethe's Jugendzeit. Stuttgart, 1852. 8° 1034.8
— Goethe's Faust erläutert. Leipzig, 1854. 2v. 8° 1034.2
— Goethe's Götz und Egmont. Geschichte, Entwickelung, u. s. w. Braunschweig, 1854. 8° 1034.3
— Goethe's Tasso erläutert. Leipzig, 1854. 8° 1034.7
— Studien zu Göthe's Werken. Elberf'd, 1849. 8° 1034.6
DUPIN, C. Essays on industrial subjects . . . 147.21
DUPPA, R. and Quatremère de Quincy. Lives of Michel Angelo [and] Raffaello. London, 1846. p.8° 543.12
— - Same, London, 1856. p.8° 835.7
DURFEE J. Panidea; or, omnipresent reason the Logos. Boston, 1846. 8° 122.8
DÜRINGSFELD, I. von. Schloss Goczyn, Roman. 2te Aufl. Breslau, 1845. 16° 1034.23
DUTCH and Flemish schools of painting. Stanley, G. 826.15
DUTCH republic, Rise of the. Motley, J. L. . . 923.1-4
DUTCHMAN's fireside. A tale. Paulding, J. K. . 797.9
DU TERRAIL, Pierre. Chevalier Bayard. Life of. Simms, W. G. 547.13
DUTY, Complete, of man. Venn, H. 1107.15
DUVAL, A. Jeunesse de Henri V. Comédie. Paris, 1821. 12° 1078.5
— Sur l' art de la comédie. Paris, 1820. 12° . 1078.4
DUXBURY, Mass. History of. Winsor, J. 224.9
DUYCKINCK, E. A. Wit and wisdom of Sydney Smith 896.5-6
— and G. L. Cyclopædia of American literature. New York, 1855. 2v. 8° 392.2
DWIGHT, M. A. Grecian and Roman mythology. Introductory essay by T. Lewis. 2d ed. N. York, 1849. 8° 1083.10
— Introduction to the study of art. New York, 1856. 12° 208.18
DWIGHT, Theo. Character of Thomas Jefferson. Boston, 1839. 12° 517.16
— History of the Hartford convention. New York, 1833. 8° 305.4
DWIGHT, Theo. jr. History of Connecticut. New York, n.d. 18° 820.37
DWIGHT, Timothy. Travels in New England and New York. New Haven, 1821-22. 4v. 8°. 624.5
— Life of, by W. B. Sprague. Sparks's Amer. biography . . . . v.XIV. of 529.1
DWYER, J. H. Essay on elocution. 6th ed. Albany, 1846. 12° 405.11
DYA-NA-SORE, oder, die Wanderer. Meyern, W. F. von 1037.15
DYEING, Chemistry applied to. Napier, J. . . . 197.3
DYER and color-maker's companion. Philadelphia, 1851. 12° 199.13
DYER, J. Character, etc., of Mary Dyer. Concord, 1819. 12° 1089.14
DYER, S. Songs and ballads. N. Y., 1857. 12° . 338.18
DYER, T. H. Life of John Calvin. N. Y., 1850. 12° 545.10
DYMOND, J. Accordancy of war with Christianity. New York, 1847. 8° 127.2
— Essays on the principles of morality. New York, 1850. 12° 125.9
DYNAMICS, Principles and practice of. Baker, T. 829.28
See also: Mechanics.
DYNEVOR terrace: a tale. Yonge, C. M. 785.1-10
DYSPEPSIA forestalled and resisted. Hitchcock, E. 158.4

EAGER, S. W. History of Orange county, N. Y. Newburgh, 1846–47. 8° 236.12
EAGLES, J. The sketcher. Edinburgh, 1856. 8° . 208.1
EARL, G. W. Native races of the Indian archipelago. Papuans. London, 1853. 12° 176.2
— Voyages in the Indian archipelago. 1832–34. London, 1837. 8° 704.7
EARL's daughter: a novel. Sewell, E. M. 426.1–4
EARLY blossoms. Biographical notices. Styles, J. 878.11
EARTH, The. Buff, H. Physics of. 149.31
— Goldsmith, O. History of. 172.14
— Guyot, A. The earth and man 167.18
— Higgins, W. M. Physical condition of. . . . 810.73
— Mudie, R. General treatise of. 169.18
— Schouw, J. F. The E., plants and man . . . 826.5
EARTHQUAKES and volcanoes. Wittich, W. v.II. of 850.21
EARTHWORM, The, and the common housefly. Samuelson, J. 175.13
EAST, The. Alger, W. R. Poetry of 315.12–13
— Carne, J. Travels in 694.18
— - Letters from 687.7
— Goodell, W. Changes of thirty years in . . . 687.14
— Lamartine, A. de. Travels in 687.15
— MacFarlane, C. Romance of travel in. . . . 840.38–39
EAST Boston, Mass., History of. Sumner, W. H. 233.1
EAST Indian archipel., Glance at the. Gibson, W. M. 707.6–7
EASTBURY : a tale. Drury, A. H. 416.6
EASTERN life, present and past. Martineau, H. . 686.1–4
EASTERN question, Russia and the. Cobden, R. . 928.5
EASTERN states, Letters on the. Tudor, Wm. . . 228.5–6
EASTHAM, Mass, History of. Pratt, E. 224.22
EASTLAKE, C. L. Contributions to the literature of the fine arts. London, 1848. 8° 205.3
— Materials for a history of oil painting. London, 1847. 8° 205.1
EASTWOOD, B. Manual for the cultivation of the cranberry. New York, 1856. 12° 165.24
EASY introduction to the game of chess, including Philidor, etc. New ed. Phil., 1817. 12° . 197.27
EATON, C. Annals of the town of Warren, Me. Hallowell, 1851. 12° 227.7
EATON, C. A. The days of battle : or Quatre Bras and Waterloo. London, 1853. 12° 1008.16
— Rome in the 19th century. 3d ed. London, 1823. 3v. p.8° 678.5
— Rome in the 19th century. 5th ed. London, 1852. 2v. p.8° 825.2
EATON, J. H. Life of Andrew Jackson. 3d ed. Philadelphia, 1828. 12° 517.3
EATON, W., Life of. Brookfield, 1813. 8° 527.2
— Life of. By C. C. Felton. Sparks's Am. biog. . . . . v. IX. of 529.1
EBEN ERSKINE : or the traveller: a novel. Galt, J. 788.9
EBERS, J. Seven years of the King's theatre. Philadelphia, 1828. 12° 353.12
EBRINGTON, Viscount. See Fortescue, Hugh.
ECARTÉ : or the salons of Paris. Richardson, J. . 807.7
ECCLESIASTES. See Bible.
ECCLESIASTICAL history and polity, including history of sects, etc. :
— Baird, R. Protestantism in Italy 1096.13
— - Religion in America 113.2
— Ballou, H., 2d. Anc. hist. of Universalism. 1099.12
— Bartol, C. A. Church and congregation . . . 1086.30
— Bede. Ecclesiastical history of England . . 846.1
— Bonnechose, E. de. Reformers before the reformation 1085.9
— Brown, T. Account of the Shakers 1089.13
— Caswall, H. Scotland and the Scottish church 1089.12
— Christoffel, R. Zwingli : or the reformation in Switzerland 1085.14
— Courcy, H. de. Catholic church in the U. S. . 1098.6
— Dowling, J. History of Romanism 1085.15
— Eusebius Pamphilus. Ecclesiastical history 845.1–2
— Evagrius. Hist. of the church, A. D. 431–594 845.5
— Evans, J. Denominations of the Chr. world 1099.6–7
— Felt, J. B. Eccl. history of New England . 1085.1
— Ferris, B. G. Utah and the Mormons . . . 1095.14
— Fox, J. Acts and monuments of the Church 1101.2
— Goodrich, C. A. Religious ceremonies and customs 1099.4

ECCLESIASTICAL history, polity, etc., continued.
— Gorham, G. C. Gleanings during the reformation in England, 1533–88 . . . . 1085.6
— Gunnison, J. W. The Mormons. 1087.8
— Hetherington, W. M. History of the Westminster assembly of divines 1106.15
— Hungary, Hist. of the Protestant church in . 1095.9
— Kidder, D. P. Mormonism and the Mormons 1099.27
— Kip, W. I. Early conflicts of Christianity . 1088.14
— Macfarlan, D. Revivals of the 18th century. 118.9
— M'Gee, T. D. Protestant refor. in Ireland . 1089.10
— Marshall, T. W. Episcopal polity 118.6
— M'Nemar, R. The Kentucky revival. 1089.20
— Marsden, J. B. History of the later Puritans, 1642–62 . . . . 1085.17
— Merle d' Aubigné, J. H. History of the reformation 1085.13
— Milman, H. H. History of Christianity. . . 1085.3
— Mosheim, J. L. v. Institutes of ecclesiastical history 1085.2
— Neal, D. History of the Puritans 1085.16
— Neander, A. History of the Christian religion and church 1103.1
— - Memorials of Christian life 858.7
— - Planting and training of the church by the apostles 848.9
— Philostorgius. Ecclesiastical history epitomized 845.9
— Punchard, G. History of Congregationalism, A.D. 250–1616 . . . . 1099.13
— Ranke, L. History of the popes 838.1
— - Reformation in Germany . . . . . 1085.12&20
— Reformation in Europe 119.4
— Ritchie, J. E. London pulpit 128.7
— Roussell, N. Catholic and Protestant nations compared 1103.6
— Ryle, J. C. Priest, Puritan and preacher. 1088.32–33
— Sects, heresies and writers of the first three centuries 1096.15
— Sects in the 19th century 850.25
— Sewel, W. History of the Quakers 1085.10
— Smyth, T. History of the Westminster assembly 1096.19
— Sprague, W. B. Annals of the American pulpit 113.1
— Socrates scholasticus. History of the church A.D. 305–445 . . . . 845.3–4
— Southgate, H. Visit to the Syrian church. . 118.15
— Sozomen. Hist. of the church, A.D. 324–440 845.9
— Stebbing, H. Christian church to 1492. . . . 388.1
— Steinmetz, A. History of the Jesuits 1095.7
— Tayler, C. B. Memorials of the English martyrs 1094.10
— Taylor, I. Loyola ; and Jesuitism in its rudiments 1098.8
— - Wesley and Methodism 1108.4
— Theodoretus. History of the church, A.D. 322–427, and 431–594 . . . . 845.5–6
— Trent, Decrees of the council of 1085.18
— Turnbull, R. Christ in history 1106.18
— Valdenses. Authentic details of the 1096.1
— Waddington, G. Church history to the refor. 365.13
— Wagstaff, W. R. Hist. of the soci. of Friends 1085.11
— Wayland, F. Principles and practices of the Baptist churches 1088.8
— Weiss, C. History of the French Protestant refugees 1095.13
— Wilberforce, S. History of the Protestant Episcopal church in America 1099.26
— Wiseman, N. Recollections of the last four popes 1098.1
— - On the principal doctrines and practices of the Catholic church 1098.5
— Young, J. The Christ of history 1087.13
     See also : Theology.
ECHOES of the universe. Christmas, H. 1106.5
ECKERMANN, J. P. Gespräche mit Goethe. Leipzig, 1837–48. 3v. 16° 1034.14
— Conversations with Goethe in the last years of his life. Transl. by S. M. Fuller. Boston, 1839. 12° 874.14

ECKSTEIN, G. F. On chimneys, with remarks on
　　stoves, coal, ventilation, etc. Lond., 1852. 16°　207.12
ECLIPSE of faith. Rogers, H. . . . .　117.11
— Defence of. Rogers, H. . . . .　117.10
ECONOMY, Domestic. *See* Domestic economy.
ECONOMY of machinery. Babbage, C. . . . . . .　198.30
ECONOMY, Political. *See* Political economy.
EDDA, The prose. Transl. by I. A. Blackwell . .　846.2
EDDY, D. C. Heroines of the missionary enter-
　　prise. Boston, 1850. 16° . . . .　539.13
EDGAR, J. G. Footprints of famous men. New
　　York, 1854. 16° . . . .　548.16
EDGAR Huntley: or, memoirs of a sleep-walker,
　　Brown, C. B. . . . .　757.5
EDGARTON, W. P. New York speaker, with intro-
　　duction on declamation by W. Russell. N.
　　York, 1857. 8° . . . .　405.5
EDGEWORTH, C. S. Memoirs of the Abbé Edge-
　　worth, containing narrative of Louis XVI.
　　London, 1815. 8° . . . .　615.8
EDGEWORTH, M. Tales and novels. London,
　　1832-33. 18v. 16° . . . .　468.8
　　Contents. — Vol. I. Castle Rackrent: An essay on
　　Irish bulls: Essay on self justification. II. Forester:
　　The Prussian vase: The good aunt. III. Angelina,
　　or L'amie inconnue: The good French governess;
　　Mlle. Panache: The knapsack. IV. Lame Jervas:
　　The will: The Limerick gloves: Out of debt out of
　　danger: The lottery: Rosanna. V. Murad the un-
　　lucky; The manufacturers: The contrast; The grate-
　　ful negro; To-morrow. VI. Ennui: The dun. VII.
　　Manoeuvring: Almeria. VIII. Vivian. IX. The
　　absentee. X. The absentee, concl.: Mme. de Fleury:
　　Emilie de Coulanges: Modern Griselda. XI.—XII.
　　Belinda. XIII. Leonora: Letters on various subjects.
　　XIV.—XV. Patronage. XVI. Patronage, concluded;
　　Love and Law, a drama; Rose, thistle and shamrock.
　　XVII. Harrington; Thoughts on bores. XVIII. Orm-
　　ond.
— New York, 1855. 20v. in 10. 12° . . . . .　467.1-3
　　Contents. — Same as the preceding. The two addi-
　　tional vols. (19 and 20) contain "Helen."
— Belinda. Barbauld's Br. nov. v.XLIX.—L. of 779.1
— Frank. Boston, n.d. 16° . . . .　468.6
— - Same. New York, 1848. 2v. 12° . . . . .　468.7
— Helen. A tale. London, 1834. 3v. 12° . . . .　468.1
— - Same. London, 1850. 12° . . . .　468.3-4
— Modern Griselda. Barbauld's Br. nov., v.L. of 779.1
— Parent's assistant. Stories for children. Bos-
　　ton, n.d. 16° . . . .　468.10
— - Same. New ed. New York, 1850. 12°. .　468.9
— Rosamond; with other tales. N. Y., 1844. 12°　468.5
— & R. L. Practical education. N. Y., 1849. 12°　137.20
EDGEWORTH, R. L. Mems. by himself, concluded
　　by M. Edgeworth. Bost., 1820-21. 2v. in 1. 8°　583.12
EDITH Allen: a novel. Neville, L. . . . . . .　777.6
EDMOND Dantes: a novel. Noble, G. W. . . . .　735.4
EDMONDS, C. R. Life and times of Washington.
　　London, 1835-36. 2v. 16° . . . .　379.18
EDMONDS, J. W. and Dexter, G. T. Spiritualism.
　　Appendix by N. P. Tallmadge. 8th ed. New
　　York, 1853-55. 2v. 8° . . . .　122.14-15
EDOM, Letters on. Lindsay, *Lord* . . . .　693.16
EDUCATION. Austin, S. Girls' schools, and the
　　training of working women . . . .　137.23
— Barnard, H. Education in Europe . . . . . .　137.1
— Braun, Th. Principes d' éducation . . . . . .　1065.7
— Campbell, J. L. and Hadley, A. M. Teacher's
　　miscellany . . . .　137.11
— Edgeworth, M. and R. L. Practical . . . . .　137.20
— Everett, E. Importance of practical . . . . .　137.21
— Fénélon, F. S. de la M. E. des filles . . . .　1056.13
— Fowle, W. B. The teacher's institute . . . .　137.30
— Genlis, Mme. de. Lettres sur l'éducation . .　1068.6
— Goodrich, S. G. Fireside . . . .　137.26
— Greenwood, C. The child and the man . . .　1096.11
— Grey, M. G. and Shirreff, E. Thoughts on
　　self-culture . . . .　124.12-13
— Grimké, T. S. Relative value of religious and
　　secular . . . .　878.9
— Hall, S. R. Instructor's manual . . . .　129.24
— Hamilton, Sir W. Discussions on . . . . . .　872.1

EDUCATION. Hood, E. P. Self-education . . . .　129.20
— Howard, G. W. F., *Earl of Carlisle.* Lectures
　　in aid of popular . . . .　409.3
— Jefferson, T. Bill for a complete system of .　294.2
— Lessing, G. E. E. of the human race . . . .　138.8
— Macleod, N. Home education . . . .　129.19
— Mann, H. Lectures on . . . .　137.8
— Mansfield, E. D. Principles and elements of
　　American . . . .　137.3
— Martineau, H. Household education . . . . .　137.19
— Mayhew, I. Means and ends of universal. .　137.5
— More, H. Strictures on modern female edu-
　　cation . . . . .v.VI. of 907.2
— Necker de Saussure, Mme. Progressive . . .　137.7
— Northend, C. Teacher and parent . . . . . .　137.17
— Pillans, J. Elementary teaching in Scotland　1099.23
— Potter, A. and Emerson, G. B. School and
　　school-master . . . .　137.14-15
— Self-formation. Hist. of an individual mind　137.22
— Smith, H. I. Hist. of ancient and modern. .　820.53
— Taylor, I. Self-cultivation recommended . .　129.23
— - Home education . . . .　137.6
— Wines, E. C. Popular . . . .　137.10
EDUCATIONAL conference of 1857. Essays read.
　　Ed. by A. Hill. London, 1857. 12° . . . .　137.12
EDWARD the black prince, Hist. of. James, G. P. R.　552.3
EDWARD IV., Histories of. Heywood, T. . . . .　342.12
EDWARD VI. Turner, S. Reign of . . . . . .　965.4
— Tytler, P. F. England under the reign of . .　974.4
EDWARDS, B. B. Biography of self-taught men.
　　Boston, 1832. 12° . . . .　548.18-19
— - Same. Boston, 1850-52. 2v. 18° . . . .　548.22-23
— Writings, with memoir, by E. A. Park. Bos-
　　ton, 1853. 2v. 12° . . . .　1096.12
　　Contents. — Vol. I. Life: Sermons. II. Roman Cath.
　　relig. in Italy: Slavery in ancient Greece, early Chris-
　　tian era, and in the middle ages: Classical studies:
　　Female education: Poetry of Wordsworth: Study of
　　the Hebrew language: Early English versions of the
　　Bible: Authenticity and genuineness of the Penta-
　　teuch: Imprecations in the scriptures: Hebrew po-
　　etry: Importance of theological education; Christians
　　should study the profounder mysteries of their faith;
　　Human depravity; Influence of piety on the intellect.
— Sears, B. and Felton, C. C. Ancient literature
　　and art . . . .　403.16
EDWARDS, F. S. Campaign in New Mexico with
　　Col. Doniphan. Phila., 1847. 12° . . . . .　623.20
EDWARDS, H. B. A year in the Punjab frontier,
　　1848-49. London, 1851. 2v. 8° . . . . . .　695.6
EDWARDS, Jonathan. Works. Reprint of the
　　Worcester edition, with additions. 8th ed.
　　New York, 1851-52. 4v. 8° . . . .　1094.1
　　Contents. — Vol. I. Memoirs of President Edwards:
　　Farewell sermon: Inquiry concerning qualifications
　　for communion: Reply to Rev. Solomon Williams:
　　Hist. of the work of redemption : Distinguishing
　　marks of a work of the spirit of God; Miscellaneous
　　observations on important doctrines: Account of the
　　life of David Brainerd. II. Inquiry into the freedom
　　of the will: Dissertation concerning the end for which
　　God created the world; Dissertation on the nature of
　　true virtue; Doctrine of original sin defended; Mis-
　　cellaneous observations concerning the divine decrees
　　in general and election in particular; Remarks on effi-
　　cacious grace; Observations concerning faith. III.
　　A treatise concerning religious affections: Narrative
　　of surprising conversions; Thoughts on the revival in
　　N. E.; An attempt to promote explicit agreement in
　　extraordinary prayer; Concerning the perseverance
　　of saints; On the notion of the preëxistence of Christ's
　　human soul: Mysteries of scripture; Observations
　　upon particular passages of scripture : Theological
　　questions; Six occasional sermons. IV. Forty ser-
　　mons on various subjects.
— Freedom of the will. [With introductory es-
　　say by I. Taylor.] New ed. Lon., 1831. 8° .　124.6
— Memoirs of the Rev. D. Brainerd, incl. his
　　journal. Ed. by S. E. Dwight. N. Haven,
　　1822. 8° . . . .　534.11
— - Same. Pub. by Am. Tract Soc. New
　　York, n.d. 16° . . . .　119.25
— Life of. By Samuel Miller. Sparks's Am.
　　biog. . . . . .v.VIII. of 529.1

EDWARDS, Rev. Justin, Life and labors of. Hallock, W. A. 535.10
EDWARDS, J. E. Random sketches of European travel in 1856. New York, 1857. 12° 648.3
EDWARDS, H. M. and Comte, A. Physiology and animal mechanism. Transl. by W. S. W. Ruschenberger. Philadelphia, 1841. 12°. 177.23
EDWARDS, Monroe. Life and adventures. New York, 1848. 8° 526.1
EDWARDS, W. H. Voyage up the river Amazon. New York, 1847. 12° 635.15
— Voyage up the Amazon, including a residence at Pará. London, 1847. p.8° 889.15
EDWIN the Fair: drama. Taylor, H. 355.7
EFFINGHAMS, The: or, home as I found it. New York, 1841. 2v. 12° 797.8
EGEDE, H. Description of Greenland, with historical introduction and life of the author. 2d ed. London, 1818. 8° 703.13
EGERTON, F., Earl of Ellesmere. Life of the duke of Wellington. 2d ed. London, 1852. 16° . . 558.11
EGERTON, W. Memoirs of Mrs. Anne Oldfield. London, 1731. 12° 597.6
EGGS of Brit. birds, Popular hist. of. Laishley, R. 177.27
EGMONT. Trauerspiel. Göthe, J W. von . . . 1038.4
— Tragedy. Transl. by A. Swanwick. Göthe, J. W. von 838.5
EGMONT, Lamoral, Count of, Trial of. Schiller, F. von 818.10
EGYPT. Bartlett, W. H. Glimpses of 684.1
— Belzoni, G. Operations and discoveries in . 693.12
— Bunsen, C. C. J. Egypt's place in univ. hist. 954.4
— Chateaubriand, F. A. de. Travels in 685.7
— Clarke, E. D. Travels in . . v.III. and IV. of 682.1
— Dorr, B. Notes of travel in 686.12
— Dumas, A. Travelling sketches in 709.20
— Hahn-Hahn, I. Travels in 687.10
— Hawks, F. L. The monuments of 684.2
— Irby, C. L. and Mangles, J. Travels in . . . 889.25
— Lepsius, K. R. Discoveries in 693.11
— Lindsay, A. W. C., Lord. Letters on 693.16
— Madden, R. R. Travels in 687.9
— Osburn, Wm. Monumental history of . . . 955.1
— Pfeiffer, Ida. Visit to 879.5
— Poole, S. Englishwoman in 850.3
— Prime, S. I. Travels in 647.8
— Prime, W. C. Boat life in 698.8–12
— Russell, M. View of ancient and modern . . 810.29
— Saint John, J. A. Hist. and antiquities of . 683.5
— Seymour, F. G. Romance of ancient history. 959.3
— Sharpe, S. History of, to 640 A. D. 954.3
— Smith, J. V. C. A pilgrimage to 698.18
— Spencer, J. A. Sketches of travel in 686.6
— Stephens, J. L. Incidents of travel in 699.1–2
— Thomas, J. Travels in 699.3
— Thompson, J. P. Photographic views of . . 698.24
— Upham, T. C. Letters from 657.5
— Wilkinson, Sir G. Hand-book for 649.13
— Yates, W. H. Mod. hist. and condition of . . 955.8
EGYPTIAN antiquities in Br. Museum. Long, Geo. 839.7
EGYPTIANS. Lane, E. W. Manners and customs of modern 839.8
— Wilkinson, Sir J. G. Account of ancient . . 959.1
— - Egyptians in the time of the Pharaohs. . 957.8
EICHENDORFF, J. Frhr. v. Werke. Berlin, 1842. 4v. 16° 1027.1

Contents. — Vol. I. Gedichte. II. Ahnung und Gegenwart. III. Dichter und ihre Gesellen; Krieg den Philistern. IV. Kleinere Novellen; Aus dem Leben eines Taugenichts; Das Marmorbild; Viel Lärmen um nichts; Das Schloss Durande; Die Ent führung; Die Glücksritter.

EIGHTEEN Christian centuries, The. White, J. . 1105.1
EIGHTEENTH century, Manners and customs of. Andrews, A. 988.2
EKKEHARD. Geschichte ausd. 10ten Jahrhundert Scheffel, J. V. 1013.11
EL GRINGO: or, New Mexico and her people. Davis, W. W. H. 623.18
ELDER, W. Biography of E. K. Kane. Philadelphia, 1858. 8° 524.9

ELDER sister, The. James, M. 498.15–16
ELDON, Earl of. See Scott, J.
ELECTION, The. Dublin, 1840. 16° 807.11
ELECTRIC telegraph, History and progress of. Highton, E. 819.9
ELECTRICITY. Bird, G. Lectures on 145.29
— Faraday, M. Experimental researches in . . 145.11
— Garvey, M. A. Future effects of 199.23
— Harris, Sir W. S. Principles and purposes of 819.7
— Lardner, D. Manual of 398.14
— La Rive, Aug. de. Treatise of electricity . . 145.7
— Noad, H. M. E., electro-dynamics and E. telegraph 145.12
— Roget, P. M. . . . . v.II. of 365.14
— Reichenbach, K. bar. v. E. in relation to the vital force 145.9
— Wilson. G. E. and the electric telegraph. . . 409.31
ELECTRO-MAGNETIC telegraph. Hist. account of. Turnbull, L. 194.9
ELECTRO-MAGNETISM. Roget, P. M. . . . v.II. of 365.14
ELECTRO-METALLURGY, Elements of. Smee, A. 196.13
ELECTRO-PHYSIOLOGY, Scient. and pract. treatise. Huff, Dr. G. 157.8
ELECTRON: a telegraphic epic. Richards, W. C. . 339.7
ELECTROTYPE manipulation. Walker, C. V. . . 199.33
ELEGANT narratives. Published by the Am. Tract Society. New York, n.d. 12° 1107.8
ELEPHANT, The, in relation to man. Knight, C. . 840.21
— Natural history of the 820.59
ELFRED: or, the blind boy and his pictures. Abbott, J. . . . . v.VI. of 739.1
ELGIN marbles. Ellis, Sir H. 839.9
ELIA, Essays of. Lamb, C. 884.2–3
ELIJAH the Tishbite. Krummacher, F. W. . . . 119.6
ELIOT, J., Life of, by C. Francis. Sparks's Amer. biography . . . . v.V. of 529.1
ELIOT, S. History of liberty. The anc. Romans. New ed. Boston, 1853. 2v. 8° 134.7
— - Same. Part II. The early Christians. Boston, 1853. 2v. 8° 134.8
— Passages from the history of liberty. Boston, 1847. 12° 135.22
— Manual of U. S. history. 1492 to 1850. Boston, 1856. 12° 309.1
ELIOT, S. A. Sketch of the history of Harvard College. Boston, 1848. 16° 297.21
ELIOT, W. G. Discipline of sorrow. Boston, 1855. 18° 1089.22
— Lectures to young men. 3d ed. Boston, 1854. 16° 127.26
— Lectures to young women. 4th ed. Boston, 1854. 16° 127.27
— On the unity of God. Boston, 1854. 12° . . . 1086.23
ELIZA Wharton, the coquette. Foster, H. 807.8
ELIZABETH, Queen of Eng. Abbott, J. Hist. of . 569.1–6
— Aikin, L. Memoirs of the court of 554.3
— Barrow, J. Naval worthies of the reign of . 564.8
— Hazlitt, W. Dramatic lit. of the age of. v.III. of 867.2
— Turner, S. History of the reign of 965.4
— Wright, T. Queen E. and her times 554.2
ELIZABETH, princess of Bohemia, Memoir of, includ. her corresp. Blaze de Bury, Baroness 545.15
ELIZABETH, Saint, of Hungary, Life of. Montalembert, Ct. C. de. 547.15
ELIZABETH, or the exiles of Siberia. Cottin, Mme. M. J. R. 499.14
ELLA of Garveloch. A tale. Martineau, H.v.V. of 749.2–3
ELLEN Linn; a Franconia story. Abbott, J. v.VII.of 738.4
ELLEN Middleton. A tale. Fullerton, Lady G. . 458.4–5
ELLERY, Wm., Life of, by E. T. Channing. . v.III.of 518.5
— - Same. Sparks's American biog. . . v.VI. of 529.1
ELLET, E. F. Characters of Schiller. Boston, 1839. 12° 908.7
— Domestic history of the American revolution. New York, 1851. 12° 217.8–10
— The practical housekeeper. N. Y., 1857. 8°. 187.1
— Women of the American revolution. New York, 1852–53. 3v. 12° 538.13
ELLIOTT, C. W. New England history, 986 to 1776. New York, 1857. 2v. 8° 223.6
ELLIOTT, E., Life and genius of. Searle, J. . . . 599.12

ELLIOTT, E., Life, poetry and lett. of. Watkins, J. 586.18
ELLIOTT, J. D. Biographical notice; reviews of
    the controv. with Perry. Phila., 1835. 12°. 527.10
ELLIS, G. Specimens of early English metrical
    romances. London, 1848. p.8° 846.5
— Specimens of the early English poets, and
    sketch of the progress of English poetry.
    5th ed. London, 1845. 3v. 12° 316.11
ELLIS, G. E. A half-century of the Unitarian con-
    troversy. Boston, 1857. 8° 113.7
— Life of Anne Hutchinson. Sparks's American
    biography . . . . v.XVI. of 529.1
— Life of John Mason. Sparks's American bi-
    ography . . . . v.XIII. of 529.1
— Life of William Penn. Sparks's American
    biography . . . . v.XXII. of 529.1
ELLIS, G. J. W. A., Lord Dover. Character of
    Edward Hyde, earl of Clarendon. London,
    1827. p.8° 566.14
— Life of Frederick II. of Prussia. N. Y., 1848.
    2v. 18° 810.48
— Lives of eminent sovereigns of modern Eu-
    rope. 4th ed. London, [1833.] 12° 548.28
— True history of the iron mask. Lond.,1826. p.8° 615.9
ELLIS, Sir H. Journal of the late embassy to
    China. Philadelphia, 1818. 8° 696.10
— Elgin and Phigaleian marbles. London, 1846.
    2v. 12° 839.9
— Townley gallery of classic sculpture. Lond.,
    n.d. 2v. 16° 849.6
ELLIS, S. S. Daughters of England. London,
    [1842?] 8° 908.4
— Family secrets: a novel. Lond., [1841.] 3v. 8° 804.9
— Home: or the iron rule. New York, 1845.
    2v. in 1. 12° 804.10
— Look to the end: a novel. Lond., n.d. 2v. 12° 804.13
— The morning call. [Self deception.] London,
    n.d. 4v. 8° 804.5
— Mothers of England. London, 1843. 12° . . . 908.3
— Poetry of life. London, 1835. 2v. 12° 908.6
— Prevention better than cure. Lond., 1847. 12° 804.11
— Select works. New York, 1844. [4v. in 1.] 8° 804.7
    Contents.—Women of Eng.; Wives of Eng.; Daugh-
    ters of Eng.; Poetry of life.
— Social distinction: or hearts and homes.
    London, n.d. 3v. 8° 804.8
— Summer and winter in the Pyrenees, 2d ed.
    London, [1841.] 8° 654.16
— Temper and temperament. Novel. London,
    [1846]. 2v. 8° 804.12
— Wives of England. London, n.d. 8° 908.2
— Women of Eng. 13th ed. London, n.d. 12° 908.5
ELLIS, W. Tour through Hawaii. Lond., 1826. 8° 705.5
— History of Madagascar. Lond., [1838?] 2v. 8° 934.5
— Polynesian researches. N. York, 1833. 4v. 12° 707.4
ELLISTON, R. W. Life of, by G. Raymond. . . . 597.16
EL-MEDINAH and Meccah. Pilgrimage to. Bur-
    ton, R. F. 689.10
ELMES, J. Sir Chr. Wren and his times. Lond.,
    1852. 8° 203.18
EL-MUKATTEM. Lands of the Moslem. New
    York, 1851. 8° 684.8
ELOCUTION. Barber, J. Grammar of 405.12
— Dwyer, J. H. Essay on 405.11
— Murdoch, J. E. Vocal culture in 137.16
— Rush, J. Art of 405.1
— Walker, J. Elements of 405.4
ELOQUENCE. Brougham, H., Lord. E. of the
    ancients. 888.3
— Goodrich, C. A. British 861.2
— McQueen, H. E. simplified 405.8
— Maury, J. S. Principles of 830.4
— Moore, F. American 861.1
— Theremin, F. E. a virtue 405.7
ELORA. Seely, J. B. The wonders of Elora . . 695.7
ELPHINSTONE, M. History of India. London,
    1841. 2v. 8° 934.3
ELTON, C. A. Hist of Roman emperors. [B.C. 28
    to A.D. 1453.] London, 1825. 12° 548.11
EMBANKING lands from the sea. Wiggins, J. . . 829.13

EMBASSIES and foreign courts. London, 1855. p.8° 987.5
EMBLEMS, divine and moral. Poems. Quarles, F. 369.24
EMBRYOLOGY of the turtle. Agassiz, L. . . v.II. of 170.2
EMBURY, E. C. Pictures of early life. Boston.
    1839. 18° 878.27
EMERGENCIES, Hints on. South, J. F. 157.7
EMERSON, G. B. The schoolmaster 137.14-15
EMERSON, J. Letters from the Ægean. N. York,
    1829. 8° 683.4
EMERSON, J. E. Memoir. Clark, R. W. 119.19
EMERSON, R. W. English traits. Boston, 1856. 12° 876.8-11
— Essays. 1st and 2d series. (var. eds.) Bost.,
    1852-57. 2v. 16° 876.1-4
— Memoirs of S. M. F. D'Ossoli 538.9-10
— Nature. Addresses and lectures. Boston,
    1849. 16° 876.6-7
— Representative men. Boston, 1850. 12° . . . 876.5
EMIGRANT, The. Head, F. B. 489.14
ÉMILIA Wyndham: a novel. Marsh, A. 795.6
EMILIE et Alphonse. Nouvelle. Souza, Mme. de 1079.8
EMILY, or the Countess of Rosendale: a novel.
    Maberly, K. C. 769.1
EMMA. Abbott, J. Harpers' story books . v.III. of 739.1
EMMA: a novel. Austen, J. . . . . . . v.III. of 758.3
EMMET, R. Burke, J. W. Life of 598.16
— Madden, R. R. Life and times of 598.15
— Appeal at the close of his trial. 862.3-8
EMMET, T. A. Haines, C. G. Memoir of 598.17
— Madden, R. R. Memoir of. 598.15
EMMONS, R. The battle of Bunker hill: a poem.
    2d ed. Boston, 1841. 12°. 358.3
ENAMELLING, The art of. Gessert, M. A. . . . 819.27
ENCYCLOPÆDIA Americana. Ed. by F. Lieber,
    assisted by E. Wigglesworth and T. G.
    Bradford. [v.14] by H. Vethake. Phila.,
    1842-53. 14v. 8° 401.1
    Contents.— Vol. I. A—Bat. II. Bat—Cat. III.
    Cat—Cra. IV. Cra—Eve. V. Eve—Gre. VI. Gre-
    Ind. VII. Ind—Lin. VIII. Lin—Mon. IX. Mon—
    Pen. X. Pen—Rev. XI. Rev—Ste. XII. Ste—Vis.
    XIII. Vis—Zwl. XIV. Supplement.
ENCYCLOPÆDIA of architecture. Gwilt, J. . . . 202.6
ENCYCLOPÆDIA Britannica. 7th ed. Treatises on
    architecture, building, by W. Hosking; ma-
    sonry, joinery, by T. Tredgold; and car-
    pentry by Prof. Robison, with notes by Th.
    Young. Edinburgh, 1846. 4° 201.4
ENCYCLOPÆDIA, The farmer's. Johnson, C. W. . 164.1
ENCYCLOPÆDIA, Female's 187.10
ENCYCLOPÆDIA of geography. Murray, H. . . . 952.4
ENCYCLOPÆDIA of instruction. Johnson, A. B. 127.8
ENCYCLOPÆDIA. See also: Cyclopædia.
ENCYCLOPÉDIE populaire ou répertoire universel
    des connaissances humaines, publiée sous le
    patronage du roi. Bruxelles, n.d. 12°. Con-
    taining:
— Baron, A. Histoire de l' art dramatique . . . 1065.4
— - Manuel abrégé de rhétorique 1065.3
— Beneden, P. J. van. Anatomie comparée. . . 1065.5
— Boscaven, H. Manuel de versification. . . . 1065.6
— Braun, Th. Principes d'éducation. 1065.7
— Brialmont, A. Précis d'art militaire. . . . 1065.9
— Brouckère, C. de. La charité 1065.11
— - Économie politique. 1065.10
— Burggraeve, le Dr. Chirurgie 1065.8
— Closset, A. de. Éléments de droit civil . . 1065.12
— Deleutre, C. Précis de l'histoire de l'art. . . 1065.13
— Fallot, L. Aperçu de la médecine 1065.14
— Fétis, F. I. Traité élém. de musique. 1065.15
— Gendebien, fils, J. Éléments de droit com-
    mercial 1065.16
— Gluge, le Dr. Physiologie 1065.17
— Guillery, E. Arts céramiques 1065.18
— Guillery, H. Technologie 1065.19
— Hannon, le Dr. J. Traité élém. de zoologie . 1065.20
— Hoorebeke, E. v. Instruction criminelle. . . 1065.21
— Houzeau, J. C. Physique du globe. 1065.22
— - Règles de climatologie 1065.23
— Juste, T. Histoire grecque 1065.24
— - Précis de l'histoire romaine 1065.25

ENCYCLOPÉDIE populaire, *continued.*
— Kindt, J. De la vapeur et de ses applications 1065.27
— - Industrie du coton, etc. 1065.28
— - Industrie linière 1065.26
— Laforet, N. J. Études sur la civilisation europ. 1065.29
— Leclerc, J. M. J. Traité de drainage. 1065.30
— Lefrançois, E. Mécanique générale. 1065.31
— Lemaire, Ch. Traité d'horticulture 1065.32
— Leuaerts, J. Organisation provinciale en Belgique 1065.33
— Leutre, C. de. Révolution belge de 1830 . . . 1065.34
— Liagre, J. Géométrie et topographie 1065.35
— - Traité de topographie. 1065.36
— Mailly, E. Science du calcul. 1065.37
— Marton, É. Institutions de prévoyance . . . 1065.38
— Meulder, L. de. Calcul mental et calcul chiffré 1065.39
— Moke, H. G. Précis de l'histoire univ. 3v. . . 1065.40
— Omalius d'Halloy, J. J. d'. Des races humaines 1065.43
— - Géologie 1065.42
—   - Minéralogie 1065.41
— Plateau, J. et Quetelet, A. Physique 1065.44
— Quetelet, Ad. Astronomie. 1065.45
— - Théorie des probabilités 1065.45
— Schayes, A. G. B. Architect. en Belgique. 2v. 1065.47
— Schüermans, H. Précis de droit criminel . . 1065.48
— Schwann, le Dr. Th. Anatomie du corps humain 1065.49
— Simons, C. Droit civil. De la propriéte, etc. 1065.51
— - Droit civil. Des modes d'acquérir, etc. . 1065.50
— Sovet, le Dr. Éduca. physique de l'enfance . 1065.52
— - Hygiène privée et publique. 1065.53
— Spring, A. Botanique 1065.54
— Tarlier, le Dr. J. Description géographique de la Belgique 1065.55
— Thonissen, J. J. Le socialisme dans le passé 1065.57
— - Le socialisme et ses promesses. 1065.56
— Ysabeau, A. Traité des oiseaux de basse-cour 1075.3
— - Des plantes fourragères 1075.6
— - Élève et l'engraissement du bétail 1075.2
— - Traité des arbres fruitiers 1075.5
— - Traité des engrais et amendements 1075.4
— - Traité des opérations agricoles 1075.1
END, The: or, signs of the close of this dispensation. Cumming, J. 116.19
ENERGY. A tale. Hofland, Mrs. B. 878.22
ENFANCE, Education physique de l'. Sovet, le Dr. 1065.52
ENFANS, Les, Contes à l' usage de la jeunesse. Guizot, Mme. 1078.56
ENGINEER, The. Abbott, J. Harpers' story books. v.VII. 739.1
ENGINEERING. Andrews, G. H. Agricultural . 829.2
— Armstrong, R. Steam-boilers 819.41
— Baker, T. Elements of. 829.25
— Evans, O. Mill-wright and miller's guide. . 195.9
— Gillespie, W. M. Road making 195.19
— Haupt, H. Bridge construction 195.1
— Hensman, H. Civil 199.16
— Kindt, J. De la vapeur 1065.27
— Lardner, D. Steam engine 819.24
— Law, H. Civil 819.11
— - and Burnell, G. R. Hydraulic 819.11
— Moseley, H. Mechanical principles of 203.20
— Murray, R. Marine engines 829.12
— Sewell, J. Steam, as applied to general purposes 829.10
— Stephenson, R. M. Railway details 829.1
— Weale, J. Dictionary of terms used in 819.26
— Weisbach, J. Mechanics of 195.2
— Whewell, W. Mechanics of 195.20
    See also : Military art and science.
ENGINEER'S railway guide. Haskoll, W. D. . . . 195.18
ENGINEERS, Handbook for locomotive. Norris, S. 198.17
ENNEMOSER, J. Hist. of magic. Transl. by Wm. Howitt. London, 1854. 2v. p.8° 826.12
ENGLAND, J. Ceremonies of holy-week and Easter Sunday. Rome, 1833. 12° 1098.18
— - The same. Baltimore, n.d. 12° 1098.21
— Construction, furniture, etc., of a church, ceremonies of the mass, etc. Baltimore, n.d. 12° 1098.21

ENGLAND, J. Works. Ed. by I. A. Reynolds. Baltimore, 1849. 5v. 8°. 1095.2

    Contents. — Vol. I. *Dogmatic and polemic theology :* [preceded by biogr. sketch of the author], Infallibility; Judicial office of the Cath. ch.; Ch. authority; Calumnies of Blanco White against the Cath. rel.; Transubstantiation; Doctrine of intention. II. Letters to Dr. Bowen: Misrepresentations of the Cath. rel.; Austerities; Liberality; Definition of faith; *History :* Influence, political and moral of the Roman See; Episcopacy of St. Peter at Rome; Pope's dispensing power; English eccl. laws; Moral character of popes; Papacy and feudalism; Waldenses. III. *History :* Influence, political and moral of the Roman See; Roman chancery; Domestic slavery; Contributions to the eccl. hist. of America; Catholicity in So. Am.; To the propagation soc's of Lyons and Dublin; Hist. of the diocese of Charleston; Mother M. C. Molony; Historical fragments; Denmark, Sweden, etc.; Turkey; *Miscellaneous :* Mass; Holy week at Rome; Miraculous cure of Mrs. Mattingly; Miracles of Prince Hohenlohe; Letters to O'Connell. IV. *Misc. :* Republic in danger; Calumnies against Cath. voters refuted; Vindication of Judge Gaston: Cath. schools; N. Y. school question; Jansenist schism ; Ward and Poinsett; Letters from Rome; Willis' misrepresentations; Imputed superstitions; Cath. tenets; The title "Catholic"; *Discourses, pastoral letters, and orations :* Disc. before Congress ; Ursulines ; On charity ; Pastoral letters; Addresses to conventions; Society of John Baptist; Great fire in Charleston; American Indians, their relig. ; Washington, his character. V. *Discourses,* etc. : On classical education; Pleasures of the scholar ; Epochs of Irish hist. ; Duelling ; Æneas among the Shades; Appendix; Diocese of Charleston; Case of Wm. Hogan; Harold corresp.; Burning of Charlestown convent; Maria Monk's " Disclosures ;" Hotel Dieu, Montreal; Indexes.

ENGLAND. Adolphus, J. E. during the reign of George III 964.1
— Aikin, L. Mems. of the court of Charles I. . 976.6
— - Memoirs of the court of James I. 552.8
— - Memoirs of the court of Queen Elizabeth 554.3
— Ashburnham, J. Attendance on Charles I. . 975.10
— Belsham, W. Reign of George III. 553.9
— Berry, M. Social life of France and 986.4
— Birch, T. Court and times of James I. . . . 552.10
— Bisset, R. Reign of George III. 976.5
— Blunt, J. J. Reformation in 379.2
— Brougham, H., *Lord.* Statesmen of the time of Geo. III. 568.7
— Buckle, H. T. History of civilization in . . . 942.2
— Bunn, A. E. old and new. 628.10
— Carrel, J. B. N. A. History of the counter-revolution 837.10
— Carus, C. G. King of Saxony's journey through 647.3
— Chasles, V. E. P. Notabilities in France and 868.7
— Cooper, J. F. E. with sketches of the metropolis 645.2
— - Gleanings in Europe 646.20
— Copway, G. Sketches of men and places in . 647.16
— Craik, G. L. Pictorial history of 962.2
— - History of literature in 840.15
— Croly, G. Life and times of George IV . . . 810.16-17
— Cunningham, G. G. A history of England in the lives of Englishmen 562.1
— Daniel G. Merrie E. in the olden time . . . 978.1
— De Lolme, J. L. E., its const. and gov't . . . 817.8
— Dickens, C. Child's history of 969.1-2
— Doran, J. Queens of, of the ho. of Hanover . 593.3
— Epitome of the history of 979.7
— Evelyn, J. Diary and corresp., 1641-1705 . . 977.4
— Florence of Worcester. Chronicle. 856.11
— Fonblanque, A. E. under seven administ. . . 979.1
— Froissart, J. The ancient chronicles of . . . 1001.2
— Fuller, T. Worthies of 574.5
— George III., his court and family 976.4
— Goede, C. A. G. A foreigner's opinion of . . 647.4
— Goldsmith, O. Abridg. of the history of. . . 968.6
— - The history of, to 1760 . . . . 968.7
— - Same. Pinnock's ed. 968.5
— Goodman, G. Court of James I. 552.7
— Goodrich, S. G. Outlines of the history of . 960.4

ENGLAND. Grenville, *Duke of Buckingham.* Court
    of E. during the regency, 1811–20 . . . . . 553.10
— - Court and cabinets of George III 976.3
— Guizot, F. P. G. Revolution of 1640 . . . . 978.5
— Hall, A. M. and Foster, J. Stories and stud-
    ies from the chronicles of 979.6
— Hallam, H. The constitut. hist. of, 1509–1760. 975.1
— Halliwell, J. O. Letters of the kings of . . 978.3
— Hamilton, W. D. Constitutional history of. 829.36
— Haskins, G. F. Travels in 658.14
— Headley, J. T. Second war of U. S. with . . 217.2–3
— Henry of Huntingdon. Chronicle of, 55 A. C.
    to A. D. 1154 . . . . 856.3
— Herbert, H. W. Persons and pictures from
    the history of 548.6
— Hervey, J. Reign of George II. 553.7
— Historical pictures 979.10
— Holt. E. Public and domest. life of Geo. III. 553.8
— Howitt, W. Rural life of 986.5
— Hume, D. History of, A. C. 55 to A. D. 1688. 968.1
— Hume, Smollett, and Farr. History of . . . 961.1
— Hyde, E. Rebellion and civil wars in 977.1
— Ingulph's chronicle of the abbey of Croyland. 856.8
— Jesse, J. H. E. dur. the reign of the Stuarts. 976.1
— - Court of, from 1688 to death of George II. 976.2
— Johnston, W. E. in the middle of the 19th
    century 979.4
— Johnstone, Chev. de. Rebellion in 1745 and '46. 976.7
— Keightley, T. History of E. to 1839 . . . . . 820.26
— Knapp, J. F. Country rambles in 177.35
— Kohl, J. G. Ireland, Scotland, and 647.5
— Lancelott, F. The queens of, and their times. 593.2
— Lester, C. E. Condition and fate of 988.9
— - The glory and shame of 646.12
— Lingard, J. History of, to 1689 . . . . . . 964.2
— Lytton, E. B. E. and the English 898.13
— Macaulay, T. B. History of, from 1685 . . . 967.1–3
— Mackenzie, A. S. The American in 658.15
— Mackintosh, Sir J. History of, to 1760 . . . 368.3
— Miller, H. First impressions of 646.7–9
— Montalembert, Comte de. Political future of 988.3
— Old sports of 589.14
— Olmsted, F. L. American farmer in . . . 646.10–11
— Ordericus-Vitalis. Ecclesiastical history of 856.7
— Penrose, E. History of 968.3
— Pepys, S. Diary and correspondence, reigns
    of James II. and Charles II. 977.5
— Pillet, R. M. Views of, during a residence of
    ten years 988.10
— Powell, T. Living authors of 586.9–10
— Raumer, F. L. G. von. England in 1835 . . . 979.2
— - E. in 1841 . . . . 979.3
— Roger de Hoveden. Annals of, 732–1201 . . . 856.2
— Roger of Wendover. Hist. of, A. D. 447–1235 846.9
— Secret history of the court of James I. . . . 552.6
— Sidney, H. Diary of times of Charles II. . . 553.4
— Stanhope, P. H. History of, 1713–63 . . . . 963.2
— Strickland, A. Queens of 592.1–4
— Southey, R. Espriella's letters from 679.13
— - Introductory view of the naval history of 388.5
— Thierry, J. N. A. Conquest of, by the Nor-
    mans 837.6
— Thomson, A. T., George II. of E., Court and
    times 554.6
— Trimmer, S. A concise history of 969.5
— Tuckerman, H. T. A month in 646.15–16
— Turner, S. E. during the middle ages 965.2
— - History of the Anglo-Saxons 965.1
— - Reigns of Edward VI., Mary and Eliza-
    beth 965.4
— - Reign of Henry VIII. 965.3
— Tytler, P. F. Reigns of Edward VI. and
    Mary 974.4
— Vaughan, R. History of, under the house of
    Stuart 365.16
— Wakefield, E. G. Comparison of E. and Am. 645.1
— Wayland, J. Recollections of real life in E. . 899.22
— Wiffen, J. H. Mem. of the house of Russell 975.7
— William of Malmesbury, Chronicle of 846.3
— Wright, T. Literature, history, etc., of, in
    the middle ages 988.13

ENGLAND. Yonge, C. D. History of, to the
    peace of Paris, 1856 . . . . 966.1
— Vicars, J. Worthies of 588.13
— Wade, J. Greatness of, etc 987.9
    See also : Great Britain.
ENGLISH, G. B. Expedition to Dongola and Sen-
    naar. 1st Am. ed. Boston, 1823. 8° . . . 693.4
— Grounds of Christianity examined. Boston,
    1813. 12° 1099.14
ENGLISH battles, etc., in the peninsula. Napier,
    Sir W. F. P. 1007.8
ENGLISH character, Sketches of. Gore, C. G. . . 469.18
ENGLISH comic writers and the English poets.
    Hazlitt, W. . . . . v.IV. of 867.2
ENGLISH commonwealth, Oliver Cromwell and
    the. Guizot, F. P. G. 975.8
ENGLISH constitution. Creasy, E. S. Rise and
    progress of 135.15
— - Howley, E. History of 987.7
ENGLISH dramatic poets. Specimens of the, about
    the time of Shakspeare. Lamb, C. 356.2
ENGLISH family Robinson: a novel. Reid, Capt.
    M. 718.13–14
ENGLISH forests and forest trees. Lond., 1853. 8° 165.10
ENGLISH history. Abbott, J. The story of, to
    1776 . . . . v.V. of 739.1
— Knight, C. Half hours of 975.2
— Paris, M. From 1235–73 . . . . 856.1
— Reed, H. E. history and tragic poetry as
    illustrated by Shakspeare 968.2
ENGLISH humourists of the 18th century. Thack-
    eray, W. M. 586.1–4
ENGLISH language. Chambers, W. and R. His-
    tory of 404.15
— Latham, R. G. Handbook of the 403.12
— Spalding, W. Growth and origin of 404.16
ENGLISH literature. Breen, H. H. Modern . . . 401.2
— Chambers, W. and R. History of 404.15
— Chambers, R. Cyclopædia of 392.1
— Cleveland, C. D. Of the 19th century 404.2
— - Compendium of 404.1
— Reed, H. Lectures on 406.8
— Spalding, W. History of 404.16
ENGLISH metrical romances, Specimens of early.
    Ellis, G. 846.5
ENGLISH of Shakespeare. Craik, G. L. 256.7
ENGLISH, past and present. Trench, R. C. 403.19
ENGLISH poetry. Campbell, T. Essay on 343.14
— Percy, T. Reliques of ancient 332.3
ENGLISH poets, Specimens of the early. Ellis, G. 316.11
ENGLISH princesses, Lives of the. Strickland, A. 593.4–5
ENGLISH reading, Course of. Pycroft, J. . . . 405.19–20
ENGLISH revolution of 1640. Guizot, F. P. G. . . 837.4
ENGLISH songs, Illustrated book of 869.7
— Procter, B. W. 345.11
ENGLISH stage, Some account of, from 1660–1830. 351.1
ENGLISH style of writing. Graham, G. F. . . 406.18
ENGLISH synonymes. Crabb, G. 403.1
    See Synonymes.
ENGLISH tales and sketches. Crosland, N. 808.14
ENGLISH tongue, History of the. Free, J. 338.7
ENGLISH traits. Emerson, R. W. 876.8–11
ENGLISH university, Five years in. Bristed, C. A. 884.14
ENGLISH versification. Everett, Erastus 406.4
ENGLISH women, Mem. of eminent. Costello, L. S. 595.1
ENGLISH writers, Essays on. De Quincey, T. . . 895.15
ENGLISHMEN and Scotchmen, Estimates of some.
    Bagehot, W. 563.9
ENGLISHWOMAN, The, in Russia. N.Y., 1855. 12° 687.24
ENGRAVING, The art of. Fielding, T. H. 202.8
ENRICO Valieri. Racconto. *See* Rusconi, C. . . . 1056.20
ENTAIL, The : a novel. Galt, J. 788.15
ENTERTAINING knowledge, Library of. Society
    for the diffusion of useful knowledge . . . 849.10–21
ENTHUSIASM, Natural history of. Taylor, I. . . . 1108.3
ENTHUSIAST, History of an. Jewsbury, M. J. . . 469.1
ENTOMOLOGISTS' text book. Westwood, J. O. . . 178.35
ENTOMOLOGY. Burmeister, H. Manual of . . . 175.4
— Jardine's (Sir W.) naturalists' lib. 28–34 . . . 179.1
— Newman, E. Grammar of 175.7
    See also : Insects.

EOLINE, or Magnolia vale : a novel. Hentz, C. L. 445.13
EOLOPOESIS : American rejected addresses. Bigelow, J. 325.4-5
EŌTHEN : or traces of travel from the East. Kinglake, A. W. 687.13
EPHESIANS, Epistle to the. See Bible.
EPICUREAN, The : a tale. Moore, T. 759.6
EPIGONEN, Die. Roman. Immermann, K. L. . . 1037.5
EPISCOPAL church in America, History of the. Wilberforce, S. 1099.26
— Illustrations of the book of common prayer of. Wheatly, C. 838.6
   See also : Ecclesiastical Hist. and Theology.
EPISCOPAL polity of the holy Catholic church. Marshall, T. W. 118.6
EPISODES of insect life. By Acheta Domestica. 1st to 3d ser. London, 1849-51. 3v. 8° . . 175.8
EPITAPHS. Bridgman, T. E. from Copp's Hill burial ground. 229.4
— Harris, W.T. E. from the old burying ground in Cambridge 228.2
— Pettigrew, T. J. A select collection of . . . 856.13
EPPS, J. Evidences of Christianity deduced from phrenology. Preface and notes by J. A. Warne. Boston, 1837. 18° 1089.23
EQUATIONAL arithmetic. Hipsley, W. 829.20
EQUATIONS, Algebraical. Murphy, R. Lib. Us. Kn. 365.15
EQUINOCTIAL regions of America, Travels to the. Humboldt, A. von 816.13
ERCOLIANI, L. I valvassori Bresciani. Racconto. 3a ed. Brescia, 1853. 3v. 16° 1058.9
ERICH Randal. Histor. Roman. Mügge, T. . . . 1013.13
ERMAN, A. Travels in Siberia. Translated by W. D. Cooley. Philadelphia, 1850. 2v. 12° . . 709.1
ERNEST Linwood : a novel. Hentz, C. L. 445.1.10
ERNEST Maltravers : a novel. Lytton, E. B. . . . 465.13-14
ERRORS, Popular, explained and illustr. Timbs, J. 197.22
ERSKINE, J. E. Cruise among the islands of the western Pacific. London, 1853. 8° 696.7
ERSKINE, T. Freeness of the gospel. Three essays. 2d ed. Edinburgh, 1828. 16° 1088.25
— On the internal evidence of revealed religion. 5th ed. Edinburgh, 1821. 12° 1087.12
ERUPTIVE fevers, Lectures on. Gregory, G. . . . 152.13
ERWIN von Steinbach. Roman. Melas, T. 1035.2
ERZEROOM, A year at. Curzon, R. 687.5
ESCHENBURG, J. J. Manual of classical literature, with additions by N. W. Fiske. 4th ed. Philadelphia, 1850. 8° 402.6
ESPOUSALS, The : a novel. Patmore, C. K. . . . 334.12-16
ESPRIELLA, Don Manuel Alvarez. Pseud. See Southey, R.
ESQUEMELING, J. History of the Buccaneers of America. New ed. Boston, 1853. 8° . . . 254.3
ESSAYS from " The Times." London, 1852. 16° . 899.13
— - Same. New York, 1852. 16° 899.14
— - Same. 2d ser. New York, 1852. 12° . . 899.15
ESSEX, Cruise and capture of the. 1812-14. Porter, Capt. D. 702.11
ETHEL Churchill : or the two brides. Landon, L. E. 498.18
ETHELWERD'S chronicle. Giles, J. A. Old Engl. chronicles. 846.4
ETHERIZATION, with surgical remarks. Warren, J. C. 157.22
ETHICAL discourses. Butler, J. 139.1
ETHICAL science applied to the evidences of religion. Bowen, F. 125.8
ETHICS. Aristoteles. The E. of 824.1
— De Wette, W. M. L. Human life : or, practical 127.6
— Dymond, J. Accordancy of war with Christianity 127.2
— White, C. Essays in 403.17
   See also : Moral philos. Moral science, etc.
ETHIOPIA. Lepsius, R. Letters from 856.6
— - Discoveries in, in 1842-5 . . . . 693.11
ETHNOGRAPHICAL library. v.I. 176.2
ETHNOGRAPHY. Niebuhr, B. G. Lectures on . . 955.3
— Omalius d' Halloy, J. J. d'. Éléments d' . . 1005.43
ETHNOLOGICAL inquiry, New chapters of. Nott, J. C. 171.2

ETHNOLOGICAL researches. Nott, J. C. 173.1-2
ETHNOLOGY, General. Schoolcraft, H. R. 244.6
ETIQUETTE for gentlemen. 13th ed. London, 1841. 32° 129.35
ETONIAN, The. No. I. — X. 4th ed. London, 1824. 3v. 12° 886.9
ETONIANS, Memoirs of eminent. Creasy, E. S. . 582.2
ETRURIA. Dennis, G. Cities and cemeteries of. 954.2
— Gray, Mrs. H. Tour to the sepulchres of . . 956.12
ETTORE Fieramosca, ossia la disfida di Barletta. Azeglio, M. d' 1056.19
ETTRICK shepherd. See Hogg, J.
ETYMOLOGY, First book of. Lynd, J. 406.3
EUCHARIST, The real presence in the. Wiseman, Cardinal N. 1098.4
EUCLIDES. Elements, notes and essay on logic, by H. Law. London, 1853. 16° 829.40
EUGENE Aram. A tale. Lytton, E. B. 465.19-22
EUGÉNIE et Mathilde. Nouvelle. Souza, Mme. de 1079.9
EULER, L. Letters on different subjects on natural philosophy. With notes and life, by D. Brewster. New York, n.d. 2v. 18° 810.55
EURIPIDES. Transl. by Rev. R. Potter, New York, 1852. 3v. 18° 830.15
— Tragedies. Transl. by T. A. Buckley. London, 1850. 2v. p.8° 814.9
EUROPE. Abbott, J. Rollo's tour in 659.1-4
— Adalbert, Pr. Travels in the south of 633.11
— Alison, A. History of, 1789 to 1815 . . . . . 943.1
— - Same, epitomized. 947.7
— - History of, 1815-52 . . . . 943.2
— Barrow, J. Excursions in North of 668.6
— Bartol, C. A. Pictures of 648.10-11
— Bryant, W. C. Notes of things seen in . . . 658.12-13
— Channing, W. Summer in 648.1-2
— Clarke, E. D. Travels in 682.1
— Clarke, J. F. Eleven weeks in 669.4
— Comyn, R. Hist. of the Western empire . . 1004.7
— Cox, S. S. Wanderings in 658.9
— Dewey, O. Journal in 669.1
— Dunham, S. A. Hist. of, during the mid. ages. 378.6
— Everett, A. H. General survey of 943.6
— Greeley, H. Glances at 647.13
— Griscom, J. A year in 647.7
— Hallam, H. E. during the middle ages . . . 945.1
— - Litera. of, in the 15th, 16th, and 17th cent. 402.4
— Howitt, W. and M. Literature and romance of Northern 404.5
— Kemble, J. M. Social and political state of . 563.1
— Kirkland, C. M. E. from the West 648.14-15
— Lippincott, S. J. C. Haps and mishaps in . . 658.5-7
— Longfellow, H. W. Poets and poetry of . . 322.1
— Murray, J. Handbook for Northern 649.11
— Ossoli, S. M. F. d'. Things and thoughts in. 654.5-6
— Prime, S. I. Travels in 647.8
— Rafinesque-Schmalz, C. S. Travels and researches in Southern 629.11
— Raumer, F. L. G. von. History of 16th and 17th centuries 927.9
— Robertson, W. Progress of society in 830.6
— Russell, W. History of modern 943.5
— - Same. Epitomized 947.6
— Silliman, B. A visit to, in 1851 . . . . 648.6-7
— Sismondi, J. C. L. S. de. Litera. of the So. of. 818.4
— Taylor, B. E. seen with knapsack and staff. 657.15-19
— Ungewitter, F. H. E. past and present . . . 947.13
— Upham, T. C. Letters from 657.5
EUROPEAN acquaintance. De Forest, J. W. . . . 687.18
EUROPEAN capitals, Sketches of. Ware, W. . . . 648.4-5
EUROPEAN celebrities, Visits to. Sprague, W. B. 648.9
EUROPEAN life and manners. Colman, H. . . . 648.12
EUROPEAN literature. Foster, Mrs. 404.6
EUROPEAN travel. Edwards, J. E. 648.3
EUSEBIUS Pamphilus. Eccl. history. Transl. by C. F. Cruse. London, 1851. p.8° 845.1-2
EUSTACE, J. C. Classical tour through Italy, 1802. 6th ed. London, 1821. 4v. 8° . . . 675.1
— - Same. 7th ed. London, 1841. 3v. 16° . 379.19
EUTAW, a tale of the revolution. Simms, W. G. 800.18-22
EUTHANASY. Mountford, W. 1088.19-20
EUTROPIUS, Flavius. Transl. by Watson 834.16

EVAGRIUS. History of the church, A. D. 431 to
   A. D. 594 . . . . 845.5–6
EVANGELISTS, Examination of the testimony of
   the four. Greenleaf, S. 1093.16
EVANS, J. Sketch of the denominations of the
   Christian world. 8th ed. London, 1803. 12° 1099.7
— Sequel to denominations of the Christian
   world. 1st Am. ed. Boston, 1811. 12° . . 1099.6
EVANS, O. Mill-wright and miller's guide. With
   additions, by T. P. Jones. 13th ed. Phila-
   delphia, 1850. 8° 195.9
EVANS, T. Old ballads, with some of mod. date.
   New ed. by R. H. Evans. Lon., 1810. 4v. p.8° 316.4
EVELINA : a novel. D'Arblay, Mme. 499.2
EVELYN, J. Diary and correspondence. Ed. by
   W. Bray. New ed. London, 1850–54. 4v. 8° 977.4
— History of religion. Ed. by R. M. Evanson.
   London, 1850. 2v. 8° 1095.8
— Life of Mrs. Godolphin. Ed. by S. [Wilber-
   force]. New York, 1847. 12° 596.10
EVENINGS at Haddon Hall. Illust. by G. Catter-
   mole. London, 1851. 12° 808.17
EVENINGS at home. Aikin, J. and Barbauld, A. L. 719.11–12
EVERETT, A. H. America, general survey of [its]
   political situation. Philadelphia, 1827. 8° 297.3
— Critical and miscellaneous essays. Boston,
   1845–46. 2v. 12° 877.4
— Europe, or a survey of the situation of the
   principal powers. London, 1822. 8° 943.6
— Life of Gen. Joseph Warren. Sparks's Am.
   biography . . . . v.X. of 529.1
— - Same. Lives of eminent individuals .v.II. of 518.5
— Life of Patrick Henry. Sparks's American
   biography . . . . v.XI. of 529.1
— New ideas on population. London, 1823. 8°. 136.6
EVERETT, Edward. Defence of Christianity. Bos-
   ton, 1814. 12° 1099.15
— Discourse on John Lowell, jr 1083.17
— Dorchester in 1630, 1776 and 1855. An oration.
   Boston, 1855. 8° 224.25
— Importance of practical education. Boston,
   1840. 12° 137.21
— Life of John Stark. Sparks's American biog-
   raphy . . . . v.I. of 529.1
— Life of John Stark. Lives of eminent indi-
   viduals . . . . v.I. of 518.5
— Orations and speeches. 2d ed. Boston, 1850.
   2v. 8° 861.7
EVERETT, Erastus. System of English versifica-
   tion. New York, 1848. 12° 406.4
EVERETT, J. and Holland, J. Memoirs and writ-
   ings of J. Montgomery 584.17
EVERGREENS, Treatise on. Warder, J. A. 166.15
EVERY day book and table book. Hone, W. 892.12
EVIDENCE, Fundamental principle of. Bailey, S. 878.14
EVIDENCES of Christianity. Beattie, J. Evidences
   of the Christian religion 1089.26
— Bolton, W. J. Evidences of Christianity . . 1094.11
— English, G. B. Grounds of Christianity ex-
   amined 1099.14
— Epps, J. Evidences of Christianity from
   phrenology 1089.23
— Erskine, T. Internal evidences of revealed
   religion 1087.12
— Everett, E. Defence of Christianity against
   G. B. English 1099.15
— Greenleaf, S. Examination of the testimony
   of the four Evangelists. 1093.16
— Gregory, O. Evid. of the Christ. religion . . 858.2
— McIlvaine, C. P. Evidences of Christianity . 1107.1
— Morison, J. Evidences of Christianity for
   young men 1109.16
— Norton, A. Internal evidence of the genuine-
   ness of the gospels 1093.11–13
— Paley, W. Evidences of Christianity 1099.34
— Palfrey, J. G. Evidences of Christianity . . 1083.17
— Ware, H. Inquiry into the evidences of relig. 118.12
— Wrangham, F. The pleiad, seven writers on
   the evidences 830.41
   See also : Bible, Theology.

EVIL, Nature of. James, H 1087.18
EWBANK, T. Hydraulic and other machines for
   raising water. 4th ed. New York, 1850. 8° 195.3
— Life in Brazil ; with illustrations of ancient
   South American arts. New York, 1856. 8° 633.1
EXAMPLES from the 18th and 19th centuries.
   Sigourney, L. H. 548.17
EXCHANGE, Essay on. M'Culloch, J. R. 135.4
EXCURSION, The: a poem. Wordsworth, W. . . . 344.3–4
EXCURSIONS in Normandy. Ed. by F. Shoberl.
   London, 1841. 2v. 12° 654.14
EXEMPLARY novels. Cervantes Saavedra, M. de 857.3
EXHIBITION of 1851. Lectures on the results of . 199.16
— Redding, C. Sketch of the great . . . . . . 987.11 .
— Reports by the juries 191.6
— Timbs, J. Origin, progress and details.v.XIV.of 159.2
EXILES, The: a tale. Robinson, T. A. L. v. J . . 449.13
EXMOUTH, Viscount. See Pellew, E.
EXODUS, Book of. See Bible.
EXPECTANT, The: a novel. Pickering, E. . . . 805.10&16
EXPERIENCE of life: a tale. Sewell, E. M. . . . 424.1–2
EXPLORING expedition. Reynolds, J. N. South
   Sea 704.6
— (U. S. 1838–42.) Wilkes, C. Narrative of . 701.6–7
— Four years in. Colvocoresses, G. M. 708.15–16
EXPOSITION of vulgar and common errors, adapt-
   ed to 1845. Philadelphia, 1846. 16° . v.II. of 850.25
EXTRAORDINARY men, their boyhood and early
   life. Russell, W. 879.15
EYES, Economy of the. Kitchiner, W. 158.12
EYRBYGGJA Saga. Abstract of, by Sir W. Scott . 846.2
EZELINO da Romano. Cantù, C. 1046.15

FABENS, J. W. The camel hunt. New ed. New
   York, 1853. 12° 699.12–13
FABLE, The age of. Bulfinch, T. 1087.21–24
FABLE for critics. Lowell, J. R. 346.18
FABLES. Æsopus. Fables, translated 728.10
— Dryden, J. F. from Homer, Ovid, Boccace
   and Chaucer 315.17
— Fiacchi, L. Favole 1049.6
— La Fontaine, J. Fables, various editions.
— Manzoni, G. Favole 1058.7
— Northcote, J. Fables 735.3
— Schefer, L. Fabeln 1018.2
— Vanden Heuvel, Mrs. Mythological 345.8
FABIOLA : or, the church of the catacombs. Wise-
   man, Cardinal N. 809.13
FABULOUS histories on the treatment of animals.
   Trimmer, S. 129.4
FACT and fiction. A collection of stories. Child,
   L. M. 488.13–14
FACTS in a clergyman's life. Tayler, C. B. 449.2
FACULTIES of birds. Rennie, J. 839.10
FAGGOT of French sticks. Head, Sir F. B. . . . 654.18
FAGNAN, Mme. M. A. Minet-Bleu et Louvette.
   Cabinet des Fées . . . . v.XXXV. of 1077.1
FAIR maid of the exchange. Heywood, T. . . . 342.29
FAIR Pauline, The: a story. Genlis, Mme. de . 759.15
FAIRBAIRN, W. Application of iron to building.
   London, 1854. roy.8° 104.1
FAIRBANKS, G. R. History of St. Augustine,
   Florida. New York, 1858. 8° 234.16
FAIRCHILD, J. H. Incidents in the life of. Bost.,
   1855. 12° 534.14
FAIRFIELD, G. G. Irene and other tales. Boston,
   1853. 8° 804.6
FAIRFIELD, S. L. Abaddon and other poems.
   New York, 1830. 8° 349.2
— Last night of Pompeii ; and lays and legends.
   New York, 1832. 8° 338.2
FAIRHOLME, G. Geology of Scripture. Philadel-
   phia, 1833. 16° 169.27
FAIRY mythology. Keightley, T. 846.10
FAIRY queen, The. See Spenser, E.
— Exposition of. Hart, J. S. 324.1
FAIRY tales, Cabinet des Fées 1077.1
— Hamilton, Count A. 857.2
— Hoffmann, E. F. W. 737.14
— Maury, L. F. A. Les Fées du moyen age . . 1078.2

FAIRY tales. Planché, J. R. F. tales from Perrault and others 737.9
— Ségur, Mme. de. Contes des fées 1078.43
— Wolf, J. W. F. tales collected in the Odenwald 719.10
FAITH, The, as unfolded by many prophets. Martineau, H. 1099.29
FAITH, The eclipse of. Rogers, H. 117.11
— Defence of same. Rogers, H. 117.10
FALCONER, W. Poetical works. Lond., 1836. 16° 329.2-3

Contents. — Life of Falconer, by Rev. J. Mitford; The shipwreck; The demagogue; Poem to the memory of the Prince of Wales; Ode on the Duke of York's second departure from England; The fond lover; Scarcity of poetry; Description of a ninety gun ship.

— The shipwreck, and other poems, with life. [Also] The chase, by W. Somervile; with Dr. Aikin's crit. essay and life of author. London, 1838. 16° 359.5
FALK, J. D. Göthe aus näherm persönl. Umgange dargestellt. 3tte Aufl. Leipzig, 1853. 8° 1034.12
— Goethe and his contemporaries. See Austin, S. 897.9
FALKLAND, Viscountess. See Cary, A. F. C.
FALKLAND islands, Cruise off the. Snow, W. P. . 708.9
FALLOT, L. Aperçu de la médecine. Bruxelles, n.d 12° 1065.14
FALSCHE Woldemar, Der: Häring, W. 1024.1
FALSE heir, The: a novel. James, G. P. R. . 463.2&16-17
FALSEHOOD and truth. Tonna, C. E. 469.23
FALSE or true: a tale. Opie, Mrs. A. . v.III. of 801.4-5
FAMILIAR things, Knowledge of. Brewer, E. C. . 199.31
FAMILY at Heatherdale: a tale. Mackay, Mrs. . . 499.7
FAMILY libraries. See Harper and Murray.
FAMILY magazine, The, Miscellaneous pieces from. Trimmer, S. 888.16
FAMILY manual and servant's guide. 7th edition. London, n.d. 12° 188.31
FAMILY memorials of Watertown, Waltham, and Weston. Bond, H. 224.1
FAMILY tour through South Holland, up the Rhine, and to Ostend. London, 1831. 16° 359.2
FAMILY secrets: a novel. Ellis, S. S. 804.9
FAMOUS men, Footprints of. Edgar, J. G. . . . 548.16
FAMOUS persons and places. Willis, N. P. . . 657.7-8
FANATICISM. Taylor, I. 1108.5
FANCIES of a whimsical man. New York, 1852. 16° 449.3
FANCOURT, C. St. J. History of Yucatan. Lond., 1854. 8° 635.6
FANNY: a poem. Halleck, F. G. 328.23
FANNY Mansfield. Philadelphia, n.d. 18°. 499.8
FANNY Fern. See Parton, Mrs. S. P.
FANSHAWE, Lady A. H. Memoirs: [with] the corresp. of Sir R. Fanshawe. Lon., 1829. 8° 595.2
FAR-WEST, Life in the. Ruxton, G. F. 628.22-23
FAR-WEST, Wild sports in the. Gerstäcker, F. . 628.25
FARADAY, M. Chemical manipulation. 3d ed. revised. London, 1842. 8° 155.17
— Experimental researches in electricity. 2d ed. London, 1844-55. 3v. 8° 145.11
— Non-metallic elements. Arranged by J. Scoffern. London, 1853. 12° 155.33
FARCES, Collection of. Inchbald. Mrs. E. . . . 354.2
See also: Dramas.
FARLEY, S. Discourses and essays on theological and speculative topics. Boston, 1851. 12° 117.7
FARM, Book of the. Stephens, H. 165.4
FARM implements. Thomas, J. J. 165.12
FARM. See also: Agriculture.
FARMER, The complete. Fessenden, T. G. 165.13
FARMER, The progressive. Nash, J. A. 168.4
FARMER's companion. Buel, J. 169.8
FARMER's instructor. Buel, J. 169.30
FARMER's encyclopædia. Johnson, C. W. 164.1
FARMING, Productive. Discoveries in vegetable chemistry. Smith, J. A. 169.9
FARMINGDALE: a novel. Thomas, C. 794.10-11
FARNHAM, E. W. California, in doors and out. New York, 1856. 12° 637.7
FARNHAM, T. J. Life, adventures, and travels in California. New York, 1852. 8° 633.10

FAROE islands, Historical and descript. ac't of the. 820.35
FARR, E. Hist. of Eng., 1769-1847. See Hume, D. 961.1
FARRIERY. See Veterinary Art.
FASHION and famine: a novel. Stephens, A. S. . 416.5
FATAL whisper, The: a novel. Galt, J. 801.2
FATHER and daughter: a tale. Opie, A. 469.42
FATHER and son: a tale. Opie, A. 469.43
FATHER Clement: a story. Kennedy, G. 808.16
FATHERS, Lives of the. Butler, A. 541.5
FAU, J. Anatomy of the external forms of man. London, 1849. 8° With atlas in fol. . . . 144.9
FAUGÈRE, A. P., Cousin, V. and Vinet, A. R. Jaqueline Pascal, a glimpse at Port Royal . . 545.8
FAUST. See Göthe, J. W. von.
FAY, T. S. Dreams and reveries of a quiet man. New York, 1832. 2v. 12° 707.14
FEARON, H. B. Journey through the Eastern and Western states of Am. 3d ed. Lon., 1819. 8° 624.15
FEATHERSTONHAUGH, G. W. Canoe voyage up the Minnay Sotor. London, 1847. 2v. 8° . 623.14
FEDERAL constitution. See Const. of the U. S.
FEDERALIST, The: by Hamilton, Madison, and Jay. 285.4
FEHMDE-GERICHT: or, secret tribunals of Westphalia 849.5
FELIX, Mlle. Rachel. Memoirs, by Mme. de B. New York, 1858. 12° 615.12
FELLOWS, C. Travels and researches in Asia Minor. London, 1852. 8° 687.6
FELT, J. B. Annals of Salem. 2d ed. Salem, 1845-49. 2v. 12° 227.13
— Customs of New England. Boston, 1853. 12° 224.21
— Ecclesiastical history of New England. Boston, 1855. 8° 1085.1
— Memorials of W. S. Shaw. Boston, 1852. 12° 537.1
FELTON, A. C. Second festival of the sons of New Hampshire. Report by A.C.F. Boston, 1854. 8° 234.5
FELTON, C. C. Life of Wm. Eaton. Sparks's American biography . . . . v.IX. of 529.1
— Memorial of J. S. Popkin, with biogr. sketch. 534.20
— Sears, B. and Edwards, B. B. Classical studies 403.16
FEMALE's encyclopædia. London, 1830. 8° . . . 187.10
FEMALE poets of America. Griswold, R. W. . . . 314.7
FEMALE poets, Selections from 369.15
FEMALE sovereigns, Memoirs of celebrated. Jameson, A. 810.44
FÉNÉLON, F. de S. de la M. Fables et contes. Cabinet des Fées . . . . v.XVIII. of 1077.1
— Éducation des filles. Dialogues des morts. Opuscules. Vies des anciens philosophes. Paris, 1854. 12° 1066.13
— Life of Plato 898.22
— Lives of ancient philosophers. Translated. New York, n.d. 18° 820.42
— Pious reflections, with life of the author. Cooke's ed. London, n.d. 18° 1089.33
— Selections from, by Mrs. Follen. 6th ed. Boston, 1851. 8° 118.19
— Télémaque. Nouv. ed. Edinb., 1763. 12° . . 1068.3
— Télémaque, suiv. des Fables. Paris, 1854. 12° 1066.12
— Telemachus. From the French, by J. Hawkesworth, with life and remarks on epic poetry. New York, 1853. 18° 759.11-12
— Butler, C. Life of 617.14
— Upham, T. C. Personal history and religious opinions of 617.15-16
FENWICK, T. Four essays on practical mechanics. 2d ed. I. Water wheels; II. Steam engine; III. Mills; IV. Simplification of machinery. Newcastle upon Tyne, 1802. 8° 195.21
FERDINAND I. of Austria. Ranke, L. 409.27
FERDINAND and Isabella, Reign of. Prescott, W. H. 912.1-3
FERGUS, H. Hist. of the Western world. The United States. London, 1830-32. 2v. 16° . 368.10
FERGUSON, A. History of the Roman republic. New ed. Abridged. New York, n.d. 18° . . 830.7
— Progress and termination of the Roman republic. New York, 1849. 8° 956.2

FERGUSON, J. Astronomy explained. With notes, etc., by Sir D. Brewster. 2d ed. Edinburgh, 1821. 2v. 8° 146.9
— Lectures on mechanics, hydrostatics, hydraulics, pneumatics, optics, geography, astronomy and dialling. With notes, etc., by D. Brewster. 3d ed. Edin., 1823. 2v. 8° . . . 146.8
— The shepherd-boy astronomer, Early life of the. Mayhew, H. 589.4
FERGUSON, R. Swiss men and Swiss mountains. London, 1853. p.8 . . . . 409.26
FERGUSSON, J. Illustrated handbook of architecture. London, 1855. 2v. 8° 203.21
— Palaces of Nineveh and Persepolis restored. London, 1851. 8° 694.9
FERGUSSON, W. System of practical surgery. 4th American ed. Philadelphia, 1853. 8° . . . 152.14
FERN, Fanny, pseud. See Parton, S. P.
FERRIAR, J. Theory of apparitions. London, 1813. 12° 118.13
FERRIER, J. P. Caravan journeys in Persia, etc. Transl. by W. Jesse. Edit. by H. D. Seymour. London, 1856. 8° 694.3
FERRIER, Miss S. Destiny: or, the chief's daughter. London, 1852. 16° 777.13
— The inheritance. 2d ed. Lond., 1825. 3v. p.8° 777.12
FERRIS, B. G. Utah and the Mormons. N. York, 1854. 12° 1095.14
FERRIS, Mrs. B. G. The Mormons at home, 1852-53. New York, 1856. 12° 637.6
FERRY, G. Vagabond life in Mexico. New York, 1856. 12° 638.3
FESSENDEN, T. G. The complete farmer and rural economist. 10th ed. New York, 1853. 12°. 165.13
— New Amer. gardener. 5th ed. Bost., 1831. 12° 169.11
— - Same. 30th ed. New York, 1853. 12° . . 165.13
— Terrible tractoration, and other poems. By Chr. Caustic. 4th Am. ed. [Also] Wooden booksellers and miseries of authorship. Boston, 1837. 12° 349.19
FESTIVALS, games and amusements. Smith, H. . 810.31
FESTUS, a poem. Bailey, P. J. 344.10-12
FETCHES, The: a tale. Banim, J. 469.14
FÉTIS, E. Les musiciens belges. Bruxelles, n.d. 2v. 12° 1075.29
FÉTIS, F. I. Music explained to the world. Translated. Boston, 1842. 12° 209.10
— La musique. Exposé succinct. Bruxelles, 1839. 16° 1078.58
— Traité élém. de musique. Bruxelles, n.d. 12° 1065.15
FEUCHTERSLEBEN, E. von. Dietetics of the soul. 7th ed. New York, 1854. 12° 129.15
FEUERBACH, A. R. von. Remarkable criminal trials. Transl. by Lady D. Gordon. London, 1846. 8° 133.7
FIACCHI, L. (Clasio.) Favole. Milano, 1820. 16° 1049.6
FICTION, The history of. Dunlop, J. 405.15
FIELD and forest, Studies in. Flagg, W. 166.6
FIELD artillery, Exercises in. See United States. 194.8
See also: Military art and science.
FIELD book, The: or, sports and pastimes of the British Islands. Maxwell, W. H. 174.1
FIELD, garden and woodland. Pratt, A. 169.33
FIELD operations, Manual of. Jarvis, J. W. . . 197.9
FIELD sports of the United States. Herbert, H. W. 174.4-5
FIELD, B. The true tragedy of Richard III. and the Latin play, Richardus Tertius, by T. Legge, with notes. London, 1844. 8° . . . 342.20
FIELD, G. Rudiments of the painter's art; grammar of coloring. London, 1850. 16° 819.19
FIELD, J. The life of John Howard. London, 1850. 8° 575.13
FIELD, M. Rural architecture: essay on landscape gardening, including a critique on Ruskin. New York, 1857. 8° 203.16
FIELDING, H. Adventures of Joseph Andrews. London, 1810. 16° . . . . v.XVIII. of 778.1
— Hist. of Tom Jones, a foundling. London, 1810. 3v. 16° . . . . v.XIX.-XXI. of 778.1
— Life of. Lawrence, F. 584.3

FIELDING, T. H. The art of engraving. London, 1841. 8° 202.8
FIELDS, J. T. Poems. Cambridge, n.d. 16° . . . 349.25
FIENDS, ghosts and sprites; Origin, and nature of belief in. Radcliffe, J. N. 124.24
FIESQUE, tragédie en cinq actes. Ancelot, M. . . 1078.8
FIGURATIVE language, Characteristics and laws of. Lord, D. N. 406.5
FILIPPO Strozzi. Tragedia. Niccolini, G. B. . . . 1056.9
FINCH, I. Travels in the U. S. and Canada, and essay on the natural boundaries of empires. London, 1833. 8° 624.7
FINE arts, The. General view of 208.22
— Eastlake, C. L. Contributions to 205.3
— Lossing, B. J. Outline history of 820.9
— Ripley, G. Handbook of 406.22
See also: Architecture, Painting, Music, Sculpture, Beauty.
FINLAND, Handbook for. Murray, J. 649.11
FINLAY, G. Byzantine empire, A.D. 716-1057. Edinburgh, 1853. 8° 956.7
— Byzantine and Greek empires. Edinburgh, 1854. 8° 955.5
— Greece under the Romans, B.C. 146 to A.D. 717. Edinburgh, 1844. 8° 956.6
— Greece, A.D. 540-1566, and empire of Trebizond, A.D. 1204-1461. Edinburgh and London, 1851. 8° 956.5
FINLAY, J. Scottish histor. and romantic ballads, chiefly ancient, with notes. Edinburgh, 1808. 2v. in 1. 12° 316.10
FIRE-ARMS, Manufacture of rotating chambered-breech. Colt, Col. S. 195.23
FIRST and second love: a novel. Crawford, H. C. 801.3
FIRST and second marriages: a novel. Baker, H. N. 476.1-2
FIRST things, great facts and moral lessons. Spring, G. 116.1
FISH and fishing in the U. S. Herbert, H. W. . . 174.2-3
See also: Ichthyology.
FISH-BREEDING, Artificial. Fry, W. H. 165.27
FISHBOURNE, E. G. Impressions of China and the present revolution. London, 1855. 12° 709.15
FISHER, R. S. Book of the world. Illustrated. New York, 1849. 2v. 8° 951.4
FISHING tackle, etc. Papers on. Bohn, H. G. . . 835.8
FITCH, G. W. Outlines of physical geography. 5th ed. New York, 1855. 12° 167.8
FITCH, John. Life of. Whittlesey, C. Sparks's American biography. . . . . . . v.XVI. of 529.1
— Life of, by Westcott, T. 525.5
FITCH, S. S. Six lectures on the uses of the lungs, and on longevity. New York, 1848. 12° . . 158.7
FITZ-BOODLE, Confessions of. Thackeray, W. M. 509.8-11
FITZGERALD, Lord E. Life of. Moore, T. 598.13
FITZHUGH, G. Sociology for the South, or the failure of free society. Rich., Va., 1854. 12° 135.19
FITZ of Fitz-Ford: a legend of Devon. Bray, A. E. 448.15
FIVE years of youth. Martineau, H. 749.5
FLAG ship, The, or voyage round the world. Taylor, F. W. 708.8
FLAGG, E. The far West: a tour beyond the mountains. New York, 1838. 2v. 12° . . . 629.18
— Venice, from 1797 to 1849. New York, 1853. 2v. 12° 678.7-8
FLAGG, W. Studies in the field and forest. Boston, 1857. 12° 166.6
FLANDERS. Froissart, J. Ancient chronicles of. 1003.1
— Gens, E. Histoire du comté de Flandre . . . 1075.7
— Snellaert, A. Hist. de la littérature flamande. 1075.28
FLANDERS, H. Lives and times of the chief justices of the supreme court of the U. S. First ser. Philadelphia, 1855. 8° 523.3
FLAVEL, J. Christ knocking at the door of sinners' hearts. New York, n.d. 12° 1107.4
— The fountain of life. New York, n.d. 12°. . 1107.3
— Method of grace. 1st Am. ed. New York, n.d. 12° 1107.6
FLAX, Cultivation of. Ward, J. . . . . . . v.IV. of 169.15
FLÉCHIER, E. Oraisons funèbres 1066.5
FLEETWOOD, or the stain of birth. Sargent, E. . 489.10

FLEMING, W. Vocabulary of philosophy, mental, moral, and metaphysical. London, 1857. 12°ﾠ. 125.30
FLEMISH life, Tales of. Conscience, H.. . . . . . 488.16
FLETCHER, J. History of Poland. New York, n.d. 18°ﾠ. 810.30
FLETCHER, John. Works. See Beaumont, F. . . 351.2
FLETCHER, J. C. and Kidder, D. P. Brazil and the Brazilians 263.2–5
FLEURY de Chaboulon, P. A. E. Private life of Napoleon in 1815. London, 1820. 2v. 8°ﾠ. 604.9
FLINT, T. Francis Berrian, or the Mexican patriot. Boston, 1826. 2v. 12°ﾠ. 769.13
— Indian wars of the West. Cincinnati, 1833. 12° 249.2
— Ten years in the valley of the Mississippi. Boston, 1826. 8°ﾠ. 236.4
FLORA, British, Handbook of. Bentham, G. . . . 166.18
FLORA Lyndsay, or passages in an eventful life. Moodie, S.. . . . . 794.9
FLORENCE. Azeglio, M. d'. F. betrayed. . . . 478.9
— Beyle, H. Rome, Naples et 1067.27
— Busini, G. B. Dell' assedio di Firenze . . . 1058.4
— Dix, J. A. A summer in. 675.8
— Guerrazzi, F. D. L' assedio di Firenze . . . 1057.4
— Machiavelli, N. History of 828.7
— Panzani, A. Misteri di Firenze 1057.7
FLORENCE of Worcester. Chronicle, with continuations. Tr. by T. Forester. Lond., 1854. p.8° 856.11
FLORIAN, J. P. C. de. Claudine: a tale 449.20
— Fables; poëmes; Galatée; Estelle; idées sur nos auteurs comiques; lettres; théatre; Myrtil et Chloé; fables de Lamotte. Paris, 1850. 12°ﾠ. 1066.14
— Galatée. Roman pastoral. Lyon, 1805. 12° 1078.55
— The Moors of Spain, [with] a notice of Islamism. New York, n.d. 18°ﾠ. 820.70
— Numa Pompilius. Paris, 1812. 18°ﾠ. . . . 1079.5
FLORIDA. Irving, T. Conquest of, by de Soto . 237.11
— Giddings, J. R. Exiles of Florida 237.19
— Latour, A. L. War in Florida West 246.1
— Sprague, J. T. The Florida war. 244.7
FLORIDAS, Sketches of the. Forbes, J. G.. . . . 236.8
FLORUS, Lucius Annæus. Transl. by J. S. Watson. 834.4
FLOWER fables. Alcott, L. M. 729.2
FLOWER, fruit, and thorn pieces. Richter, J. P. F. 887.8
FLOWER garden, The. Poetry of gardening. From the Quarterly Review. London, 1852. 16°ﾠ. 165.28
FLOWERS of history. Roger of Wendover . . . 846.9
FLOWERS for children. Stories. Child, L. M.. . 738.9
FLOWERS of the field. Johns, C. A.. . . . . . . 169.24
FLOWERS and their associations. Pratt, A.. . . . 850.4
See also: Botany, Gardening, Horticult., etc.
FLYING islanders, History of the. Wilkins, P. . 799.16
FOLLEN, C. T. C. Works, with a memoir. Boston, 1841–42. 5v. 12°ﾠ. 877.1
    Contents. – Vol. I. Life. II. Sermons. III. Lectures on moral philosophy; Fragment on psychology. IV. Schiller's life and dramas. V. Miscellaneous writings; Future state of man; History; Inaugural discourse; Funeral oration on G. Spurzheim; Address on slavery; Franklin lecture; Religion and the church; Peace and war.
FOLLEN, E. L. Poems. Boston, 1839. 12°ﾠ. . . 358.6
— Sketches of married life. New ed. Boston, 1841. 16°ﾠ. 429.5
— The well-spent hour. New ed. Bost., 1848. 16° 738.8
FOLLOWING the drum. Viélé, E. L.. . . . . . . 626.4
FONBLANQUE, A. England under seven administrations. London, 1837. 3v. 12°ﾠ. . . . 979.1
FONGERAY. Pseudonym. See Cave and Dittmer.
FONTAINE, J. Memoirs of a Huguenot family. Trans. by A. Maury. N. York, 1853. 12°ﾠ. 617.11
FONTENELLE, J. de and Malepeyre, F. The arts of tanning, currying, and leather-dressing; with additions by C. Morfit. Phil., 1852. 8° 194.11
FOOD. Donovan, M. Aliments used by various nations . . . . v. II. of 408.8
— Hassall, A. H. F. and its adulterations . . . 155.19
— Lankester, E. Vegetable substances used for the food of man. 840.32

FOOD. Liebig, J. Chemistry of. 155.7
— Lindley, J. Substances used as. 199.16
— Marcet, W. Composition of 155.15
— Mitchell, J. Falsifications of 156.28
— Pereira, J. Treatise on 157.3
FOOL of quality: a novel. Brooke, H. 799.4
FOOL of the nineteenth century; and other tales. Transl. Zschokke, J. H. D.. . . . . . . 767.13
FOOT-PRINTS of the Creator. Miller, H. . . . 167.15–17
FOOTE, A. H. Africa and the American flag. N. York, 1854. 12°ﾠ. 698.13
FOOTE, H. S. Texas and the Texans. Philadelphia, 1841. 2v. 12°ﾠ. 639.1
FOOTE, Sam'l, Memoirs of. Cooke, W.. . . . . 507.12
FORBES, D., Life of. Burton, J. H. 566.6
FORBES, Prof. E. Literary papers. Lond., 1855. 12° 589.6
— and Spratt, T. A. B. Travels in Lycia, Milyas, and the Cibyratis 683.7
FORBES, F. E. Five years in China, 1842–47. London, 1848. 8°ﾠ. 696.9
FORBES, J. Happiness, in its relations to work and knowledge. London, 1850. 18°ﾠ. . . 1089.30
— Nature and art in the cure of disease. London, 1857. 12°ﾠ. 157.4
— Physician's holiday: or, a month in Switzerland in 1848. 3d ed. London, 1852. 12°ﾠ. . 669.6
— Physiological effects of alcoholic drinks, with documents of the Mass. Temp. Soc. Boston, 1848. 12°ﾠ. 127.19
FORBES, Major Jon. Eleven years in Ceylon. London, 1840. 2v. 8°ﾠ. 695.4
FORBES, J. D. Norway and its glaciers. Edinburgh, 1853. 8°ﾠ. 663.1
— Travels through the Alps of Savoy, with map. Edinburgh, 1843. 8°ﾠ. 663.2
FORBES, J. G. Sketches of the Floridas. N. York, 1821. 8°ﾠ. 236.8
FORBES, R. B. Voyage of the Jamestown. [Report and correspondence.] Boston, 1847. 8° 296.5
FORCES, Elementary treatise on. Peirce, B. . . . 148.2
FORD, J. Dramatic works; with introduction and notes. London, 1831. 2v. 18°ﾠ. 359.7
    Contents. – Vol. I. The lover's melancholy; The broken heart; Perkin Warbeck. II. The lady's trial; The sun's darling; The witch of Edmonton; Love's sacrifice; The fancies, chaste and noble.
— Dramatic works; with notes by W. Gifford. London, 1827. 2v. 8°ﾠ. 353.9
    Contents. – Vol. I. Commendatory verses; Lover's melancholy; 'Tis pity she's a whore; The broken heart; Love's sacrifice. II. Perkin Warbeck; The fancies, chaste and noble; The lady's trial; The sun's darling; The witch of Edmonton; Fame's memorial; Verses to the memory of Jonson; Glossarial index.
FORD, R. Gatherings from Spain. Lond.,1846. p.8° 889.17
— Handbook for Spain. 3d ed. London, 1855. 2v. 12°ﾠ. 649.12
— The Spaniards and their country. New ed. New York, 1850. 12°ﾠ. 675.19
FORD, T. History of Illinois, from 1818 to 1847. Chicago, 1854. 12°ﾠ. 237.6
FORDE, J. Honour triumphant, a line of life. London, 1843. 8°ﾠ. 342.18
For each and for all: a tale. Martineau,H. v.XI. of 749.2–3
FOREFATHERS, Footsteps of our. Miall, J. G.. . 1086.22
FOREIGN reminiscences. Holland, H. R., Lord. . 806.9
FOREIGN travel, Passages in. Jewett, I. A.. . . . 657.4
FOREST and shore: or, legends of the pine-tree state. Ilsley, C. P.. . . . . 428.1
FOREST days; a romance. James, G. P. R.. . . . 463.1
FOREST exiles; a novel. Reid, Capt. M. 718.15
FOREST life and forest trees. Springer, J. S.. . . 628.18
FOREST sanctuary, The: a poem. Hemans, F. v.II.of 324.2
FOREST trees, An account of British. 169.20
FORESTER, Frank. Pseud. See Herbert, H. W.
FORESTER, Th. Norway in 1848 and 1849. Lond., 1850. 8°ﾠ. 668.3
FORESTERS, The: a novel. Wilson, J.. . . . . . 759.8
FORESTS and forest trees, English 165.10
FORESTS of France, A month in. Berkeley, G. F. 654.4
FORGIVENESS of sin. Owen, J. 1100.3

FORMULARY, Pocket. Beasley, H. 153.6
— Universal medical. Griffith, R. E. 152.9
FORREST, G. Every boy's book : complete ency-
    clopædia of sports and amusements. Lon-
    don, 1855. 12° 197.25
FORRESTER, J. J. Prize essay on Portugal. 2d ed.
    London, 1854. 8° 673.3
FORSAKEN, The : a tale. Phila., 1831. 2v. 12°. .   498.2
FORSTER, J. Historical and biographical essays.
    London, 1858. 2v. 16° 894.3

     Contents. — Vol. I. *Historical :* The debates on the
   grand remonstrance, 1641; The Plantagenets and the
   Tudors; The civil wars and Oliver Cromwell. II.
   Biographical : Daniel De Foe; Sir Richard Steele;
   Charles Churchill; Samuel Foote.

— Life and adventures of Oliver Goldsmith.
    London, 1848. 8° 583.13
— Statesmen of the commonwealth of England.
    Edited by J. O. Choules. N. Y., 1846. 8° .   562.3
— Lives of British statesmen . v.II. IV. VI. VII. of 388.6
FÖRSTER, M. Briefe aus Südrussland. Leipzig,
    1856. 16° 1029.13
FORSYTH, W. Captivity of Napoleon at St. Helena.
    London, 1853. 3v. 8° 1005.1
— - Same. New York, 1853. 2v. 12° 605.5
FORTESCUE, H., *Visc. Ebrington.* Two conversa-
    tions with Napoleon. Boston, 1823. 8° v. III. of 603.1
FORTIFICATION, Elements of. Lendy, Capt. A. F.   197.8
FORTUNE by land and by sea : a tragi-comedy. By
    T. Heywood and W. Rowley 342.29
FORTUNE Wildred, a story. Dickens, C. 491.1–6
FORTUNE, R. Residence among the Chinese, 1853–
    1856. London, 1857. 8° 696.4
— Tea countries of China and the Himalaya. 3d
    edition. London, 1853. 2v. 12° 706.7
FORTUNES of Nigel : a novel. Scott, Sir W. . . 470.6–12
FORTY-FIVE, The. Narrative of the insurrection,
    1745. Stanhope, P. H., *Visc. Mahon* . . .   989.6
FORUM, The : or, Forty years' practice at the Phila-
    delphia bar. Brown, D. P. 294.4
FOSBROKE, T. D. Arts, manufactures, manners
    and institutions of the Greeks and Romans.
    London, 1833–35. 2v. 16° 378.3
FOSCARI : a tragedy. Mitford, M. R. 804.4
FOSCOLO, U., Vita ; e delle opere di. Gemelli, C. 1056.11
FOSSILS. *See* Geology.
FOSTER, A. and Lester, C. E. Life of Americus
    Vespucius 544.1
FOSTER, B. F. The merchant's manual. Boston,
    1838. 12° 136.22
FOSTER, H. The coquette : or, the hist. of Eliza
    Wharton. A novel founded on fact. Bos-
    ton, 1855. 12° 807.8
— - Same. 11th ed. Exeter, 1828. 18° . . .   789.11
FOSTER, J. Critical essays. Ed. by J. E. Ryland.
    London, 1857. 2v. p.8° 837.7
— Essays, in a series of letters. N. Y., 1851. 12°   137.13
— - Same. 1st Am. from 18th Lond. ed. New
    York, 1854. 16° 129.17
— - Same. 24th ed. London, 1851. 16° . . .   909.2
— Evils of popular ignorance. 1st Am. edition.
    Boston, 1821. 12° 909.1
— - Same. New ed. London, 1850. 16° . . .   878.19
— Lectures deliv. at Broadmead Chapel. 3d ed.
    London, 1853. 2v. p.8° 817.9
— Life and correspondence. Ed. by J. P. Ryland,
    with notices by J. Sheppard, London, 1852.
    2v. p.8° 858.8
FOSTER, Mrs. J. and Hall, Mrs. A. M. Stories and
    studies from the Chronicles of England . .   979.6
FOSTER, M. E. Handbook of French literature.
    London, n.d. 12° 406.23–24
— Handbook of modern European literature.
    Philadelphia, 1850. 12° 404.6
FOUCHÉ, J., *duke of Otranto,* Memoirs of. Jullian,
    P. L. P. de 613.4
FOUNDATIONS. *See* Architecture.
FOUNTAIN of life, The. Flavel, J. 1107.3
FOUNTAIN of living waters. 3d ed. New York,
    1851. 12° 129.25

FOURIER, F. C. M. Œuvres complètes. 3e éd. 1064.1
    Paris, 1841–48. 6v. 8° . . . .

     Contents. — Vol. I. Préface des éditeurs; Théorie
   des quatre mouvements et destinées générales. II.
   Théorie de l'unité universelle; Sommaires du traité;
   Traité de l'association domestique-agricole. III.
   Théorie de l'unité universelle, en abstrait; Introduction; Prolégomènes. IV. Théorie, etc., *(continued) ;*
   Cis-legomenes; Théorie mixte, ou étude spéculative
   de l'association; Synthèse routinière L. i.; association
   composée. V. Théorie, etc., *(continued) ;* Théorie en
   concret L. ii.; De l'éducation unitaire ou intégrale
   composée L. iii.; Dispositions de haute harmonie L.
   iv. ; De l'équilibre passionnel. VI. Le nouveau
   monde industriel et sociétaire, ou invention du pro-
   cédé d'industrie attrayante et naturelle distribuée en
   séries passionnées.

— Life of. Pellarin, Ch. 545.11
FOWLE, W. B. The teachers' institute. 2d ed.
    Boston, 1847. 12° 137.30
— Parlor dramas. Boston, 1857. 12° 356.9
FOWLER, C. jr. and Berlyn, P. Crystal palace .   265.6
FOWLER, G. Lives of the sovereigns of Russia.
    London, 1858. 2v. p.8° 544.22
FOWLER, H. The American pulpit : sketches biogr.
    and descriptive. New York, 1856. 8° . .   534.9
FOWLER, O. S. A home for all : or, the gravel wall
    and octagon mode of building. New York,
    1854. 12° 207.10
— Physiology, animal and mental. 6th ed. N.
    York, 1853. 12° 157.13
FOWLS, Domestic. *See* Poultry.
FOWNES, G. Rudimentary chemistry ; [with] ap-
    plication to agriculture. London, 1854. 16°   819.1
FOX, C. J. History of the reign of James II. . .   837.10
— Memorials and correspondence, ed. by Lord
    John Russell, Philadelphia, 1853. 2v. 12° .   566.3
— Memoirs of the latter years of. Trotter, J. B.   566.2
FOX, E. Adventures in the revolutionary war.
    Boston, 1848. 18° 219.5
FOX, Geo. Journal of, with notes by W. Armis-
    tead. 7th ed. 2v. in 1. London, 1852. 12° 1095.5
FOX, H. R., *Lord Holland.* Foreign reminiscen-
    ces, ed. by his son. New York, 1851. 12° .   896.9
FOX, J. Acts and monuments of the church.
    [Book of Martyrs.] New ed., with five ap-
    pendices, revised by M. H. Seymour. New
    York, 1855. 8° 1101.2
FRAMINGHAM, Mass. History of. Barry, W. . .   224.7
FRANCE. Astié, J. F. Louis XIV. and the writers
    of his age 1008.10
— Bell, R. Wayside pictures through 675.5
— Berkeley, G. F. A month in the forests of. .   654.4
— Berry, M. Social life of 986.4
— Blanc, J. J. L. History of, 1830–40 . . . . .   1002.5
— Bonnechose, É. de. Histoire de, jusqu'à 1830. 1066.3
— - History of. Transl. by W. Robson . . . 1007.2–3
— Bruen, M. Essays on scenes in 679.5
— Bush, Mrs. A. F. Memoirs of the queens of. 606.8–13
— Cass, L. F. its king, court and government . 1004.4–5
— Chasles, V. E. P. Notabilities in 868.7
— Cockayne, T. O. Outlines of the history of. 989.13
— Colquhoun, J. C. Life in, in the olden time .   915.5
— Cooper, J. F. Gleanings in Europe 659.26–27
— - Residence in 654.9
— Copway, Geo. Running sketches in 647.16
— Corkran, J. F. History of the national con-
    stituent assembly, from May, 1848 . . . . .   1008.3
— Crowe, E. E. History of 1000.11–12
— - History of the reign of Louis XVIII. and
    Charles IX. 1005.3
— Cushing, C. Review of the revolution in 1830 1009.2
— Cushing, Mrs. C. W. Monuments, scenery
    and manners in 888.13
— Donelan, J. P. My trip to 654.13
— Dumas, A. Pictures of travel in the South of.   654.8
— Dumas, M. Memoirs, including the revolu-
    tion, the empire, and the restoration 1008.12
— Froissart, J. Ancient chronicles of 1001.2
— Guizot, F. P. G. Democracy in 134.21
— - Memoirs of my time 1003.5
— Haskins, G. F. Travels in 658.14

FRANCE. Hauréau, B. Charlemagne et sa cour. . 1078.40
— - François I. et sa cour. 1078.20
— Herbert, H. W. Persons and pictures from
     the history of. 548.6
— Hill, G. A. The war in La Vendée and the
     little Chouannerie 1008.13
— History of Napoleon and Fr. to the death of
     Louis Philippe 1009.15
— Inglis, H. D. South of F. and the Pyrenees . 663.14
— Johnson, F. H. The South of 654.7
— Jomini, H. de. History of the campaign of
     Waterloo 987.10
— La Hodde, L. de. Secret societies and repub-
     lican party of, from 1830–1848 . . . . 1004.14
— Laing, S. Social and political state of 409.14
— Lamartine, A. de. Past, present and future
     of the republic 134.11
— - Restoration of the monarchy in 837.9
— Lamothe-Langon, E. L. de. Evenings with
     Cambacérès 1004.3
— Laveleye, E. de. Histoire des rois francs . . 1075.13
— Lemaistre, J. G. F. after the peace of Amiens. 654.3
— Letters on Louis Napoleon and the coup d'
     état 1009.6–7
— Long, G. F. and its revolutions 1001.1
— Marsh, Mrs. A. History of the Protestant
     reformation in 1008.2
— Matthews, H. Tour in. 679.14
— Mérimée, P. Voyage dans le midi de 1069.3
— - Voyage dans l'ouest de 1069.2
— Michelet, J. History of France 1003.2–3
— Moore, J. Society and manners in 657.3
— Morgan, Lady S. F., with appendix by Sir
     T. C. Morgan 1003.4
— Murray, J. Handbook for 649.1
— Napier, W. F. P. War in the South of . . . 1004.1–2
— Napoleon I. F. during the reign of Napoleon. 663.4
— Nodier, C. E. Souvenirs de la révol. 1067.8
— Pardoe, J. Louis XIV. and the court of . . . 616.3–9
— Penrose, Mrs E. A history of. 1007.4
— Phipps, C. H. Paris in 1848 . . . . 1002.4
— Piozzi, H. L. Journey through 676.1
— Ranke, L. Civil wars and monarchy in 16th
     and 17th centuries 1007.6
— Ritchie, L. Romance of history 419.4–5
— Roelker, B. Constitutions of 134.11
— Saint Simon. Louis XIV. et sa cour 1078.18
— Scott, Sir W. Stories of. Tales of a grand-
     father 490.1–6
— Shelley, M. W. Lives of literary and scien-
     tific men of 388.8
— Siborne, Capt. W. History of the war in 1815. 1005.2
— Smedley, Ed. History of, 843–1529. . . . . . 365.5
— Stephen, Sir J. Lectures on the history of . 1002.1–2
— Thierry, A. Formation and progress of the
     "tiers état" in 1008.17
— - Lettres sur l' histoire de 1076.12
— Thiers, A. Révolution française. 1076.16
— Tricolored sketches in Paris, 1851-2-3 . . . . 1008.8
— Vane-Stewart, C. W. F. in 1813–14 . . . . . 1069.3
— Voltaire, F. de. Age of Louis XIV. 1005.7
     See also: French, Paris, etc.
FRANCE, A. de. The prisoners of Abd-el-Kader . 889.18
FRANCESCA da Rimini: a tragedy. Boker, G. H. 335.2
FRANCHERE, G. Voyage to the N. W. coast of
     America, 1811–1814. Transl. and ed. by J.
     V. Huntington. New York, 1854. 12° . . . 626.7
FRANCIA, Dr. J. G. R. de. Reign of, in Paraguay.
     Rengger, J. R. 266.3
— Residence in Paraguay under. Robertson, J.P. 635.11
FRANCIS I. See François I.
FRANCIS Berrian, or the Mexican patriot. Flint, T. 769.13
FRANCIS, C. Historical sketch of Watertown,
     Mass. Cambridge, 1830. 8° 224.2
— Life of John Eliot. Sparks's Am. biogr. v.V. of 529.1
— Life of Sebastian Rale. Sparks's American
     biography . . . . v.XVII. of 529.1
FRANCIS, J. Bank of England. 3d edition. Lon-
     don, n.d. 2v. 8° 136.13
FRANCIS, J. W. Old New York, or the past sixty
     years. New York, 1858. 12° 237.3

FRANCKLIN, W. Tour from Bengal to Persia:
     1786–87. London, 1790. 8° 694.10
FRANÇOIS I. of France. Bacon, J. Life and times. 616.1
— Hauréau, B. François I. et sa cour 1078.20
— Pardoe, J. Court and reign of 616.2
FRANÇOIS d'Assise, St., et les Franciscains. Morin,
     F. 1078.46
FRANCONIA stories. Abbott, J. 738.4
FRANK: a novel. Edgeworth, M. 468.6–7
FRANK Forester. Pseud. See Herbert, H. W.
FRANK Heartwell: a novel. Tiller, B. 801.3
FRANK Mildmay: a novel. Marryat, F. 745.11
FRANK Wildman's adventures. Gerstäcker, F. . . 709.11
FRANKENSTEIN: or, the modern Prometheus.
     Shelley, M. W. 798.9
FRANKLIN, B. Works; with notes, and a life of
     the author by J. Sparks. Bost., n.d. 10v. 8° 286.2

     Contents.— Vol. I. Autobiography : Life contin-
     ued, by Sparks. II. Essays on religious and moral
     subjects, and the economy of life; Essays on politics,
     commerce, and political economy. III. Essays and
     tracts, historical and political, before the American
     revolution; Constitution and government of Penn-
     sylvania. IV. Essays and tracts, continued. V.
     Political papers during and after the American revo-
     lution; Letters and papers on electricity. VI. Letters
     and papers on philosophical subjects. VII. Corres-
     pondence, part 1: Private letters to the time of the
     author's first mission to England, 1725–57; Part 2:
     Letters, private and official, from the time of the au-
     thor's first mission to England to the beginning of the
     American revolution, 1757–75. VIII. Correspond-
     ence, part 2, continued, 1757–75; Part 3: Letters, pri-
     vate and official, from the beginning of the revolution
     to end of the author's mission to France, 1775–85;
     Appendix: Fragment of Polybius, on the Athenian
     government; Memoir of Sir John Dalrymple. IX.
     Correspondence, part 3, continued; Journal of the
     negotiation of the treaty of peace. X. Correspond-
     ence, part 3, continued; Part 4: Private Letters, from
     the termination of the author's mission to France to
     the end of his life, 1785–90; Supplement; Indexes;
     Chronological list of the author's writings.

— Select works. Notes and memoir by E. Sar-
     gent. Boston, 1853. 12° 878.28
— Autobiography ; with a narrative of his pub-
     lic life, by H. H. Weld. New York, n.d. 8° 523.6
— - Familiar letters and miscellaneous papers.
     Boston, 1833. 12° 878.1
— Life, by himself; and essays. N. Y., 1857. 12° 517.21–22
— Memoirs by himself, with miscellaneous writ-
     ings. New York, n.d. 2v. 18° 820.2
— Memoirs by himself and others. Philadelphia,
     1840. 2v. 8° 523.5
— F. the apprentice boy. Abbott, J. . . . . v.IV. of 739.1
— Life. Weems, M. L. 517.23
FRANKLIN, Sir J. Journey to the Polar sea. 1819–
     22. Philadelphia, 1824. 8° 704.5
— Belcher, Sir E. Expedition in search of . . . 702.1
— Bellot, J. R. Voyage in search of 617.13
— Brown, J. N. West passage, and search for . 701.11
— Kane, E. K. Grinnell expedition 702.2–6
— - Second Grinnell expedition in search of . 703.1–9
— Osborn, S. Eighteen months in search of . . 709.7–8
— Richardson, Sir J. Boat voyage in search of. 704.8–9
FRANKLIN, State of, from 1784 to 1788. Ramsey,
     J. G. M. 235.4
FRANKS, History of. Perry, W. C. 925.6
FRARIÈRE, A. de. Les abeilles et l'apiculture.
     Paris, 1855. 12° 1078.11
FRASER, J. B. Historical and descriptive account
     of Persia. New York, n.d. 18° 810.68
— The Kuzzilbash: a tale of Khorasan. Lon-
     don, 1828. 3v. 12° 807.6
— Mesopotamia and Assyria. N. Y., n.d. 18° . . 820.54
— Winter's journey from Constantinople to
     Tehran. London, 1838. 2v. 8° 694.17
FRASERIAN papers. Maginn, W. 884.12
FRED Markham in Russia. Kingston, W. H. G. . 709.14
FREDERIC II. See Friedrich II.
FREE, J. Poems and miscellaneous pieces. Lon-
     don, 1751. 8° 338.7
— Essay towards a history of the English
     tongue. London, 1749. 8° 338.7

FREEDLEY, E. T. Leading pursuits and leading men. Philadelphia, 1856. 8° 296.3
— The legal adviser. Philadelphia, 1857. 12° . . 133.11
— Practical treatise on business. Phila., 1853. 12° 136.15
FREER, M. W. Life of Marguerite d'Angoulême. London, 1854. 2v. 12° 544.12
FREILIGRATH, F. Gedichte. Stuttgart, 1855. 16° 1027.3
FREIMAURER, Die; Roman. Kühne, F. G. 1013.4
FRÉMONT, J. C. Explorations and adventures in Kanzas and California; [with] memoir by S. Smucker. New York, 1856. 12° 517.19
— Exploring expedition to the Rocky mountains, Oregon and California. Auburn, 1854. 12° 628.13-15
— Life of, etc., by C. W. Upham 517.17-18
— and Emory, Maj. Notes of travel in California. New York, 1849. 8° 623.8
FRENCH in Algiers. Lamping, C. and France, A. de. 889.18
FRENCH court. Campan, Mme. J. L. H. G. Secret anecdotes of the 613.7
— Private anecdotes of the 1005.5
FRENCH language, Pronouncing reading-book of the. Arnoult, E. 392.3
FRENCH literature. Foster, M. E. Handbook of. 406.23-24
— Moke, H. G. Histoire de la 1075.27
— Véricour, L. R. de. Modern 404.12
FRENCH, The neutral; or the exiles of Nova Scotia. Williams, Mrs. C. R. 217.12
FRENCH principles and Parisian sights. Jarves, J. J. 654.17
— Same. 2d series 1008.9
FRENCH revolution, [The first.] Brougham, H., Lord. Remarks on . . . . v.V. of 840.5
— Carlyle, T. A history 1007.7
— Croker, J. W. Early period of 1002.3
— Lamartine, A. de. Patriots of the 828.6
— Michelet, J. The women of 1008.6-7
— Mignet, F. A. A. History of 837.3
— Poore, B. P. History of, 1789-1848 . . . . . 1009.1
— Sayous, A. Memoirs of Mallet du Pan. . . . 613.6
— Scott, W. Preliminary memoir on 604.5-6
— Smyth, W. Lectures on. 837.2
— Staël-Holstein, Mme. de. Considerations on 1004.6
— Thiers, L. A. History of 1002.7
— Tocqueville, A. de. The old regime, etc. . . 1008.11
FRENCH revolution [of 1830]. Sarrans, B. Memoirs of Gen. Lafayette. 617.5
FRENCH revolution [of 1848.]. Lamartine, A. de. History of the 848.3-4
FRENCH schools of painting, Hist. of. Head, E. 208.21
FRENCH society in the 18th century. Loménie, L. de 615.4
FRENCH wines and politics: a tale. Martineau, H. . . . . v. XII. of 749.2-3
FRENCH, S. American drama, v. I., with a memoir of E. Forrest. New York, n.d. 12° . 355.10

Contents. — I. Midsummer night's dream. II. Popping the question, by John Baldwin Buckstone. III. La tour de Nesle, from the French of Victor Hugo. IV. Deaf as a post, by T. Poole. V. Theresa, or the orphan of Geneva, transl. and adapted by John Howard Payne. VI. Flying Dutchman, by Edward Fitzball. VII. New Footman, by Charles Selby. VIII. Pleasant neighbor, by Mrs. Eliza Planche.

FRESENIUS, C. R. Quantitative chemical analysis. 2d ed. by J. L. Bullock. London,1854. 8° . 155.11
— Qualitative chemical analysis. 4th ed. by J. L. Bullock. London, 1855. 8° 155.10
— and Will, H. New methods of alkalimetry. Ed. by J. L. Bullock. London, 1843. 12° . . 156.21
FRESH gleanings. Mitchell, D. G. 669.2-3
FRESH leaves, by Fanny Fern. Parton, S. P. . 755.11
FREYTAG, G. Debit and credit, with introduction by C. C. J. Bunsen. N. York, 1858. 12° 434.2-4
— Debit and credit, with preface by C. C. J. Bunsen. Edinburgh, 1857. 2v. 12° . . . 434.5
— Soll und Haben: roman. 4e Auflage. Leipzig, 1855. 3v. 16° 1035.5
FRIEDRICH der Grosse und sein Hof. Roman. Mundt, K. 1039.6

FRIEDRICH II. of Prussia. Ellis, G. A., Lord Dover. Life of 810.48
— Gillies, J. Reign of 546.4
— Raumer, F. L. G. v. F. and his times 546.8
FRIENDS, History of the society of. Wagstaff, W. R. 1085.11
FRIENDS in council. Helps, A. 878.4
FRIGHT, The: a novel. Pickering, E. 805.1
FROISSART, Sir J. Antient chronicles of England, and France, Spain, Port., Scot., Brittany and Flanders. Translated by J. Bourchier. London, 1814. 4v. 8° 1003.1
— - Same. Translated by T. Johnes, with an introductory essay, [etc.] by J. Lord. New York, 1853. 8° 1001.2
FROMBERG, E. O. Painting on glass. London, 1851. 16° 819.28
FRONTIER lands of the Christian and the Turk, in 1850-51. 2d ed. London, 1853. 2v. 8°. . . 685.2
FRONTIER men, Sketches of. Pritts, J. 245.2
FROST, J. Life of Gen. Taylor. N. Y., 1847. 12° 517.8
— Pictorial history of the U. States. Hartford, 1848. 4v. in 2. 8° 304.5-6
— Pictorial life of Andrew Jackson. Hartford, 1853. 8° 517.1
— Remarkable events in the history of America. Embellished. Philadelphia, 1852. 2v. 8°. . 304.7
— Travels in Africa, from the earliest ages. N. York, 1848. 12° 608.20
FROTHINGHAM, N. L. Metrical pieces; translated and original. Boston, 1855. 12° 346.8
— Sermons in the order of a twelvemonth. Boston, 1852. 12° 1105.2
FROTHINGHAM, R. History of the siege of Boston. 2d ed. Boston, 1851. 8° 214.2-8
FRUITS of leisure. Essays. Helps, A. 888.22
FRUITS and fruit trees of Amer. Downing, A.J. 165.14-15
FRY, Elizabeth. Life compiled from her journal, etc. Corder, S. 595.6
— A memoir of. Cresswell, Mrs. F. 595.7
FRY, J. R. Life of Zachary Taylor. Philadelphia, 1847. 12° 517.7
FRY, W. H. Treatise on artificial fish-breeding, translated and edited by Fry. New York, 1854. 12° 165.27
FRYXELL, A. History of Sweden. Translated. Ed. by M. Howitt. London, 1844. 2v. 12° 928.3
FUDGE family in Paris. Moore, T. 358.17
FUEL, Economy of. Prideaux, T. S. 829.9
FULLER, A. Memoir of Rev. Samuel Pearce. N. York, n.d. 16° 1109.18
— Principal works and memoir, by A. G. Fuller. London, 1852. p.8° 858.5
FULLER, H. Belle Brittan on a tour at Newport. New York, 1858. 12° 635.22
FULLER, R. and Wayland, F. Domestic slavery, considered as a scriptural institution. 5th ed. New York, 1847. 16° 1100.23
FULLER, T. History of the worthies of England. New ed. by P. A. Nuttall. Lond., 1840. 3v.8° 574.5
FULLERTON, G., Lady. Ellen Middleton: a tale. From last London ed. New York, 1849. 12° 458.4-5
— Grantley Manor: a tale. New York, 1848. 12° 458.1-3
FULLOM, S. W. Daughter of the night: a story. New York, 1851. 8° 802.10
FULTON, R. Life of. Colden, C. D. 524.7
— Life of, by Renwick, J. . . . . v.I. of 518.5
— - Same. Sparks's Am. biography. . . .v.X. of 529.1
FUN-JOTTINGS. Willis, N. P. 904.11-13
FUNCTIONS, Elementary treatise on. Peirce, B. . 148.2
FUR trade, An account of the. Mackenzie, A. . . 625.19
FURNESS, W. H. Jesus and his biographers. Philadelphia, 1838. 8° 1101.5
— Julius, and other tales from the German. Philadelphia, 1856. 12° 756.10
FURNISS, W. Waraga, or the charms of the Nile. New York, 1850. 12° 698.19
FUSELI, H. Life and writings; ed. by J. Knowles. London, 1831. 3v. 8° 543.5
— Lectures on painting 816.2

FUTURE state, Scripture revelations concerning. Whately, R. 1086.24

GAGE, T. History of Rowley, with address delivered at its 2d cent. anniversary, by Rev. J. Bradford. Boston, 1840. 12°. . . . 227.6
GAIETIES and gravities. Smith, H. 809.17–18
GAJANI, G. The Roman exile. Boston, 1856. 12° 678.2–3
GALATIANS, Epistle to the. *See* Bible.
GALATÉE. Roman pastoral. Florian, J. P. C. de 1078.55
GALBRAITH, J. A. and Haughton, S. Manual of Optics. 2d ed. London, 1855. 16°. 149.33
GALICIA, Portugal and. Herbert, H. J. G. 889.8
GALILEI, G. and Borghini, V. Studi sulla divina commedia. Pubbl. da O. Gigli. Firenze, 1855. 12° 1058.5
— Life of. Brewster, Sir D. 820.34
GALLAGHER, W. D. Poetical literature of the West. Cincinnati, 1841. 8° 338.1
GALLAND, A. Cabinet des Fées, v. VII., VIII., IX., X., XI. "Mille et une nuits." (Tr.) XVI. "L'histoire de la sultane de Perse et des visirs. XVII. XVIII." Les contes et fables indiennes de Bidpaï et de Lokman. Trad. par Galland et Cardonne 1077.1
GALLATIN, A. Memoir on the N. E. boundary . . 297.7
GALLAUDET, T. H. Child's book on the soul. 7th ed. Hartford, 1847. 16° 1109.29
GALLERIES, London, Catalogues of. Jameson, A. 208.9
GALLERY of portraits. 2d–3d ser. Gilfillan, G. . 548.3–4
GALLOWAY, E. History and progress of the steam engine. Appendix by Luke Hebert. London, 1834. 8° 195.17
GALLUS: or, Roman scenes of the time of Augustus. Becker, W. A. 957.2
GALT, J. The Ayrshire legatees. Edinb., 1821. 12° 788.8
— Eben Erskine: or, the traveller. London, 1833. 3v. 12° 788.9
— - Same. Philadelphia, 1833. 2v. 12° . . . 788.10
— The entail, or the lairds of Grippy. N. York, 1823. 2v. 12° 788.15
— The fatal whisper. Omnibus of Romance . . 801.2
— Last of the lairds. New York, 1827. 12° . . 788.12
— Lawrie Todd: or, the settlers in the woods. New York, 1830. 2v. 12° 788.6
— Life of Cardinal Wolsey. 3d ed. London, 1846. p.8° 566.11
— Life of Lord Byron. New York, n.d. 18° . 810.10–11
— Literary life and miscellanies. Edinburgh, 1834. 3v. 12° 584.18
— The provost: a novel. New York, 1822. 12°. 788.14
— Rothelan: a romance of the English histories. New York, 1825. 2v. 12° 788.7
— Southennan. London, 1830. 3v. 12° 788.4
— - Same. New York, 1830. 2v. in 1. 12° . . 788.3
— Stanley Buxton: or, the schoolfellows. London, 1832. 3v. 12° 788.1
— - Same. Philadelphia, 1833. 2v. 12° . . . 788.2
— The steamboat: a novel. N. York, 1823. 12° 788.13
— The stolen child: a tale of the town. London, 1833. 12° 788.11
-- Stories of the study. London, 1833, 3v. 12° 788.5

Contents. — Vol. I. Introduction; Lutherans. II. Lutherans, contin.; Dean of Guild; Black pirate; Greenwich pensioner; Lumberer. III. Jaunt; Craniologists; Horoscope; Heron Glenie; Magos; Stagecoach; Seamstress; English groom; Deluge.

GALTON, F. Art of travel. London, 1855. 12°. 199.25
— - Same. 2d ed. London, 1856. 12° 649.17
GALVANISM. Roget, P. M. . . . . v. II. of 365.14
GAMBA, P. Narrative of Lord Byron's last journey to Greece. Paris, 1825. 12°. 585.12
GAME, American, in its seasons. Herbert, H. W. 174.4
GAME birds, their friends and their foes. Knox, A. E. 177.11
GAMES, festivals, and amusements. Smith, H. . . 810.31
GAMES for all seasons. London, 1858. 16° . . . 197.29
GAMES. Handbook of. Bohn, H. G. 816.5
GAMESTER'S progress: a poetic tale 369.6
GAMMELL, W. History of American Baptist Missions. Boston, 1851. 12° 1106.10

GAMMELL, W. Life of Roger Williams. Sparks's Am. biog. . . . . v. XIV. of 529.1
— Life of Samuel Ward. Sparks's American biog. . . . . v. XIX. of 529.1
GAN-EDEN: or, pictures of Cuba. Hurlbut, W. H. 627.23
GARBETT, E. L. Principles of design in architecture. Parts I.–II. London, 1850. 16° . 819.13
GARDEN. Breck, J. The flower 166-11
— The G., the field, and the woodland 850.5
— Glenny, G. The flower . . . . . . v. IV. of 169.15
— Kemp, E. How to lay out a 175.11
— McIntosh, C. Book of the 165.6
GARDENER. Buist, R. The family kitchen . . . 168.5
— Fessenden, T. G. New American 169.11
GARDENER'S calendar, American. McMahon, B. 165.3
GARDENING. Essay on the poetry of. 165.28
— for ladies. Loudon, Mrs. J. W. 164.9–13
See also: Horticulture, Landscape gardening, Flowers, etc.
GARDENS and menagerie of the Zoölogical Society. Bennett, E. T. 172.19–20
GARDEN, A. Anecdotes of the revolutionary war. Charleston, 1822. 8° 213.14
GARDINER, A. F. Visit to the Indians on the frontiers of Chili. London, 1841. 12° . . 635.18
GARDINER, Col. J., Life of. Doddridge, P. 575.11
GARDINER, M. *Lady Blessington.* Confessions of an elderly lady and gentleman. Philadelphia, 1838. 2v. 12° 498.17
— ∟ Literary life and correspondence of. Madden, R. R. 595.8–9
GARDINER, W. Music and friends. London, 1838. 2v. 8° 204.7
— Music of nature. 3d ed. London, 1849. 8°. 204.6
GARLAND, H. A. Life of John Randolph. New York, 1851. 2v. 12° 525.2
GARRICK, D. Memoirs of. Davies, T. 597.7
GARVEY, M. A. The silent revolution: or, effects of steam and electricity. London, 1852. 16° 199.23
GAS works, Treatise on. Hughes, S. 829.15
GASKELL, E. C. Cranford. New York, 1853. 16° 794.17
— Life of Charlotte Brontë. N. Y., 1857. 2v. 12° 596.11–15
— Mary Barton: a tale. 4th ed. London, 1850. 2v. 12° 794.15
— Ruth: a novel. Boston, 1853. 8° 435.1
GASS, P. Journal of voyages and travels through N. America. 1804–6. London, 1808. 8°. . 625.6
GASTON de Blondeville: a romance. Radcliffe, A. 777.5
GAUDY, F. B. H. W. v. Poetische und prosaische Werke. Neue Ausg. Berlin, 1853–54. 8v. 16° 1029.23

Contents. — Vol. I. Lieder; Romanzen; Terzinen; Aus dem Tagebuche eines wandernden Schneidergesellen. II.–III. Mein Römerzug. IV. Kaiserlieder; Erzählende Dichtungen; Vermischte Gedichte. V. Novellen und Erzählungen. VI. Novellen und Erzählungen; Humoresken. VII. Der Liebe Loos; Portogalli, Reise und Lebensbilder aus Italien. VIII. Venetianische Novellen.

GAUGING, Treatise on. Haswell, C. H. 147.25
GAUT Gurley: a tale of border life. Thompson, D. P. 726.9
GAUTIER, T. Wanderings in Spain. Lond., 1853. 12° 869.12
GAY, S. Celebrated saloons: and Girardin, Mme. D. de. Parisian letters. Translated by L. Willard. Boston, 1851. 18° 609.5
GAYARRÉ, C. History of Louisiana. Spanish domination. New York, 1854. 8° 235.13
— Louisiana. Colonial history and romance. New York, 1851. 8° 235.12
— Romance of the history of Louisiana. New York, 1848. 16° 237.15
GAZETTEER. Hayward, J. Of Massachusetts . . 229.2
— - New Hampshire 229.1
— - Vermont 229.3
— McCulloch, J. R. Universal 951.3
See also: The list of books of reference appended to this Index.
GAZPACHO: or, summer months in Spain. Clark, W. G. 675.13
GAZUL, Clara. *Pseudonym.* See Mérimée, P.

GEARY. *Gov.* J. W. Administration in Kansas. Gihon, J. H. 239.2
GEBEL Teir: a novel. Tudor, W. 799.8-9
GELL, Sir W. Journey in the Morea. London, 1823. 8° 683.3
GEMELLI, C. Della vita e delle opere di Ugo Foscolo. Firenze, 1849. 12° 1056.11
GENDEBIEN, fils, J. Éléments de droit commercial. Bruxelles, n.d. 12° 1065.16
GENEALOGIES of families in Watertown, Waltham and Weston, Mass. Bond, H. 224.1
GENERAL principles of grammar. Philadelphia, 1847. 16° . . . . v. III. of 850.25
GENERAL register of politics and literature in Europe and Amer. for 1827. Edinb., 1828. 18° 830.38
GENERAL view of the fine arts, with introduction by D. Huntington. 4th ed. N. Y., 1851. 12° 208.22
GENERATIVE organs, Diseases of the. Acton, W. 151.21
GENESIS, Book of. *See* Bible.
GENEVIÈVE, conte. Karr, J. B. A. 1067.14
— Histoire d'une servante. Lamartine, A. de . 1066.23
GENII, Tales of the. Ridley, J. 835.10
GENIUS in its relations to culture and society. Giles, H. 875.5
— Infirmities of. Illustrated. Madden, R. R. . 887.7
— Dawnings of. Pratt, A. 548.26
GENLIS, Mme., S. F. D. St. A., *C*tsse de. Adèle et Théodore, ou lettres sur l'éducation. Paris, 1804. 4v. 16° 1068.6
— - Alphonso and Dalinda : a moral tale, translated by T. Holcroft. Fairhaven, 1799. 16°. 449.21
— - Mlle. de Clermont, suivie de nouvelles et notice sur l'auteur par Mme. A. Tastu. Paris, 1844. 12° 1066.17

Contents. — Madame de Genlis, par Madame A. Tastu; Mademoiselle de Clermont; La princesse des Ursins; Le comte de Corke; Trait de la vie de Henri IV.; Les ermites des marais pontins; Le mari instituteur; Les preventions d'une femme; Le jupon vert; Les réunions de famille; Lindane et Valmire; Nourmahal, ou le règne de vingt-quatre heures.

— Mlle. de La Fayette ; suivie de nouvelles. [La jeune pénitente ; Les amants sans amour.] Paris, 1843. 12° 1066.15
— Madame de Maintenon. 4e éd. Paris, 1813-21. 2v. 16°. 1068.4
— Madame de Maintenon ; [suivie de nouvelles : Le bon homme ; Le tulipier.] Paris, 1853. 12° 1066.16
— Les mères rivales, ou la calomnie. Berlin, 1801. 4v. 16°. 1068.7
— New moral tales. New York, 1825. 12° . . . 489.20
— Sainclair and Hortense : [and] Claudine, by M. Florian. Transl. by A. Haralson. New York, 1813. 12° 449.20
— Siége de la Rochelle. Nouv. éd. Bruxelles, 1829. 4v. in 2. 18° 1069.15
— Zuma; the fair Pauline; Zeneida; the reeds of the Tiber; the widow of Luzi. New York, 1818. 18° 759.15
GENOA, Summer tour to. Sewell, E. M. 659.28
GENS, E. Histoire du comté de Flandre. Bruxelles, n.d. 2v. 12° 1075.7
— Ruines et paysages en Belgique. Bruxelles, n.d. 12° 1075.23
GENTILITY. *See* Manners, etc.
GENTLEMAN Jack : a naval story. Neale, W. J. . 737.6
GEOFFREY de Vinsauf. Narrative of the crusade of Richard I. 846.6
GEOFFREY of Monmouth's British history. *See* Giles, J. A. 846.4
GEOGRAPHICAL descr. of the earth. Goldsmith, J. 649.20
GEOGRAPHY. Ferguson, J. Select subjects in . 146.8
— Goodrich, C. A. G. of the Bible 1089.28
— Goodrich, S. G. Pictorial G. of the world . 951.1
— Guy, J. jr. Illustrated London 955.4
— Guyot, A. Comparative physical 167.18
— Kitto, J. Physical G. of the Holy Land . . . 840.25
— - Scripture lands 815.7
— Laurent, P. E. Manual of ancient 954.5
— Lloyd, E. Mathematical . . . . v. III. of 365.14
— Lloyd, H. J. Physical . . . . v. III. of 365.14

GEOGRAPHY. Murray, H. Encyclopædia of . . . 952.4
— Nicolay, C. G. Principles of physical 167.7
— Niebuhr, B. G. Lectures on ancient 955.3
— Robinson, E. Biblical 684.4
— G. of Strabo 844.3
— Swainson, W. G. of animals 398.17
— Vulliet, M. G. of nature 167.13

NOTE. — For the geography of particular regions, see their several names.

GEOLOGICAL excursions around the Isle of Wight. Mantell, G. A. 826.10
GEOLOGICAL knot, Attempt to untie the. Gosse, P. H. 163.17
GEOLOGICAL observations on coral reefs, volcanic islands, and on South America. Darwin, C. 163.15
GEOLOGICAL observer, The. De la Beche, H. T. . 163.13
GEOLOGICAL science and Scriptures. Smith, J. P. 816.14
GEOLOGIST. Ansted, D. T. Extracts from the note-book of a 208.2
— Miller, H. Rambles of a G. over the fossiliferous deposits of Scotland 167.6
GEOLOGY. Anderson, J. Course of creation . . 167.23
— Ansted, D. T. Ancient world 167.14
— - Elementary course of 163.24
— Brougham, H. View of researches on fossil osteology 840.8
— Crofton, D. G. reconciled with Scripture . . 118.20
— Daubeny, C. Description of volcanoes 163.14
— Dawson, J. W. Acadian 163.23
— De la Beche, H. T. How to observe 163.19
— - Researches in theoretical 169.26
— Fairholme, G. G. of scripture 169.27
— Goodrich, S. G. Wonders of 169.13
— Hitchcock, E. G. of Massachusetts 163.10
— - G. of the United States and the globe . . . 163.11
— - Religion of 167.21-22
— Lardner, D. Popular 163.22
— Lee, C. A. Elements of 820.71
— Lesley, J. P. Coal and its topography 197.6
— Lewis, T. Six days of creation 146.17
— Loomis, J. R. Elements of 163.20
— Lyell, C. Elements of 163.16
— - Manual of elementary 163.2-3
— - Principles of 163.5-7
— Mantell, G. A. Wonders of 836.4
— Miller, H. Cruise of the Betsey 167.6
— - Footprints of the Creator 167.15-17
— - Fossiliferous deposits of the Hebrides . . 167.6
— - Bearing of G. on the two theologies . . . 167.2-5
— - G. of the Bass rock 167.27
— - Old red sandstone 167.24-26
— - Testimony of the rocks 167.1
— Omalius d'Halloy, J. J. d' 1065.42
— Owen, R. British fossil mammals and birds . 172.21
— Pattison, S. R. G. for bible students 167.28
— - Fossil botany 169.6
— Phillips, J. Treatise on 408.7
— Phillips, W. Outlines of 163.21
— Portlock, J. E. Rudimentary treatise on . . 819.4
— Richardson, G. F. Introduction to 816.10
— Voices from the rocks — reply to H. Miller . 169.19
GÉOMÉTRIE pratique. Bruxelles, 1850. 12°. . . 1075.30
GEOMETRY. Cresswell, D. Treatise of 147.4
— Hann, J. Rudimentary treatise on analytical. 829.22
— Haswell, C. H. Mensuration and practical . 147.25
— Heather, J. F. Element. treat. on descriptive. 829.8
— Kirkman, T. P. Mnemonical lessons in . . . 829.35
— Lardner, D. Treatise on 398.7
— Liagre, J. Éléments de 1065.35
— Lowell, Mrs. A. C. J. Introduction to 148.1
— Morton, P. Plane, solid and spherical 365.4
— Peirce, B. Elementary treatise on plane and solid 148.5
— Waud, S. W. Treatise on algebraical 365.17
GEORGE II. of England. Hervey, J. Memoirs of the reign of 553.7
— Thomson, A. T. Court and times of 554.6
GEORGE III. His court and family. New edition. London, 1824. 2v. 8° 976.4
— Belsham, W. Reign of 553.9

GEORGE III. Bisset, R. Reign of 976.5
— Brougham, H. Statesmen in the time of. . . 568.7
— Grenville, R. P. T. Court and cabinets of . . 976.3
— Holt, E. Public and domestic life of. . . . 553.8
GEORGE IV., Life and times of. Croly, G. 810.16–17
GEORGE, A. Annals of the Queens of Spain. New York, 1850. 2v. 12° 544.4
GEORGETOWN, Mass., History of. Gage, T. . . . 227.6
GEORGIA. M'Call, H. History of 234.15
— Miller, S. F. Bench and bar of. 294.3
GERALDINE: a poem. Dawes, R. 358.8
GERARD, J. Adventures of the lion killer. New York, 1856. 12° 697.14–18
GERHARD, F. Illinois as it is. Chicago, 1857. 8° 237.7
GERHART, E. V. Introduction to the study of philosophy, with a treatise on logic. Phila., 1858. 12° 403.8
GERMAINE: nouvelle. About, E. 1078.15
GERMAN, The, in America. Bogen, F. W. 629.33
GERMAN literature. Gostick, J. 404.14
GERMAN lyrics. Brooks, C. T. 316.8
GERMAN music, Modern. Recollections and criticisms. Chorley, H. F. 209.5
GERMAN novelists. Roscoe, T. 418.2
GERMAN romance. Carlyle, T. 418.1
GERMAN songs, from the 16th to the 19th century. Ed. and transl. by Dulcken, H. W. 316.7
GERMANIC empire, History of the. Dunham, S. A. 368.9
GERMANY. Amalie, Princess. Social life in . . 876.15
— Austin, S. G. from 1760 to 1814 . . . . 667.15
— Beitzke, H. Freiheitskriege, 1813 u. 1814 . 1013.1
— Brace, C. L. Home life in 667.7–11
— De Pontès, Mme. L. Davésiés. Poets and poetry 355.13
— Hedge, F. H. Prose writers of 545.1
— Howitt, Wm. Student-life of 663.6
— Kohlrausch, F. History of 925.2–3
— Lemaistre, J. G. Travels in 654.3
— Menzel, W. History of 848.2
— Moore, J. Society and manners in. 657.3
— Murray, J. Handbook for Southern. 649.5
— — Handbook for Northern 649.19
— Penrose, Mrs. E. History of. 928.4
— Piozzi, H. L. Observations respecting . . . 676.1
— Ranke, L. Political and religious state of, after the reformation. 409.27
— Russell, J. Tour in 663.5
— Slade, A. Travels in 663.9
— Spencer, E. Sketches of 663.7
— Staël-Holstein, Mme. de. De l' Allemagne . 1069.9
— — Germany. Translated. 667.20
— Tacitus, C. C. Germany. Translated 872.11
— — Germany. Translated . . . . . . v.II. of 834.17
— and France. Vane-Stewart, C. W. War in, 1813 and 1814 . . . . 1009.3
GERRY, E. Life of, by Austin, J. T. 513.11
GERSTÄCKER, F. Frank Wildman's adventures on land and water. Translated by L. Wraxall. London, 1855. 16° 709.11
— Travels in [South America and California.] Translated from the German. London, 1854. 8° 636.1
— Wild sports in the far West, 1854. 12° . . . 628.25
GERTRUDE: a novel. Sewell, E. M. 425.11–15
GERTRUDE of Wyoming: a poem. Campbell, T. . 237.14
GERVINUS, G. G. Introduction to the history of the 19th century. London, 1853. 16° . . . 949.12–13
GESSERT, M. A. Art of painting on glass. Lond., 1851. 16° 819.27
GHIKA, H., C'tesse. Switzerland the pioneer of the reformation. Translated. 1858. 2v. 8° 914.2
GHOSTS. Crowe, C. Night side of nature 124.23
— Radcliffe, S. N. Fiends, ghosts and sprites . 124.24
See also: Supernaturalism.
GHOST-HUNTER and his family: a novel. Banim, J. 807.10
GHOST seer, The: a novel. Schiller, J. C. F. v. . 818.12
GIBBES, R. W. Memoir of James De Veaux. Columbia, S. C., 1846. 8° 524.18
GIBBON, E. Auto-biography. Ed. by Lord Sheffield. New York, 1846. 12° 583.16

GIBBON, E. Decline and fall of the Roman empire. With notes by H. H. Milman. 2d ed. Lond., 1846. 6v. 8° 953.6
— - Same. New ed. Boston, 1850–51. 6v. 12° 957.10
— Life and correspondence. Ed. by H. H. Milman. London, 1839. 8° 583.15
— Student's Gibbon. Decline and fall of the Roman empire. Abr. by W. Smith. London, 1857. 12° 957.5
GIBBONS, D. Law of contracts for services. London, 1849–50. 16° 819.36
GIBBS, G. Mems. of the administrations of Washington and John Adams, from the papers of O. Wolcott. New York, 1846. 2v. 8°. 285.5
GIBRALTAR. Bigelow, A. Sketches of, 1827 . . . 676.2
— Drinkwater, J. Siege of 1779–83. With a history of that garrison 889.14
GIBRALTAR gallery, The. Abbott, J. Harper's story books . . . . v.VIII. of 739.1
GIBSON, W. M. The prison of Weltevreden, and a glance at the E. I. archipelago. New York, 1855. 12° 707.6–7
GIDDINGS, J. R. Exiles of Florida; or crimes committed against the Maroons. Columbus, O., 1858. 12° 237.19
GIFFARD, E. Deeds of naval daring. London, 1852. 16° 989.8
GIFFORD, I. Marine botanist; British sea-weeds. 3d ed. Brighton, 1853. 12° 169.21
GIHON, J. H. Annals of San Francisco. Soulé, F. 235.10
— Gov. Geary's administration, in Kansas. Philadelphia, 1857. 12° 239.2
GILBART, J. W. Advice on keeping a banker . . 136.17
— History and principles of ancient commerce. London, 1847. 12° 136.18
— Treatise on banking. 2d American ed. from 5th London. New York, 1851. 8° 135.5
GIL Blas de Santillane. See Le Sage, A. R.
GILDAS, Works of. See Giles, J. A. 846.4
GILDER's companion 199.11
GILES, H. Christian thought on life. Discourses, 2d ed. Boston, 1851. 16° 1088.27
— Illustrations of genius. Boston, 1854. 16°. 875.5
— Lectures and essays. Boston, 1851. 2v. 16° 875.6–8
GILES, J. A. Life and letters of Thomas à Becket. London, 1846. 2v. 8° 575.4
— Life and times of Alfred the Great. 2d ed. Oxford, 1854. 8° 552.1
— Six old English chronicles. London, 1848. p.8° 846.4
Contents. — Ethelwerd's chronicle ; Asser's life of Alfred ; Geoffrey of Monmouth's British hist. ; Gildas, Nennius, and Richard of Cirencester.
GILFILLAN, G. Bards of the Bible. N. Y., 1851. 12° 118.2
— Modern literature and literary men. Second gallery of portraits. N. York, 1851. 12°. 548.3
— Third gallery of portraits. N. York, 1855. 12° 548.4
GILFORD, N. H., History of. Lancaster, D. . . . 224.24
GILLELAND, J. C. History of the war between the United States and Great Britain, [1812.] 2d ed. Baltimore, 1817. 18° 219.6
GILLESPIE, W. M. Principles and practice of road-making. 3d ed. New York, 1850. 8° . 195.19
GILLIES, J. Reign of Frederick II. of Prussia. London, 1789. 8° 546.4
GILLMAN, J. Life of S. T. Coleridge. London, 1838. 8° 583.5
GILLY, W. S. Shipwrecks of the royal navy. 2d ed. London, 1851. 12° 988.12
GILMAN, C. Recollections of a New England bride and of a Southern matron. New edition. New York, 1852. 12° 437.8–9
— Southern matron. Charleston, 1852. 12°. . 437.10
GILMAN, S. Contributions to literature. Boston, 1856. 12° 887.5
GILMANTON, N. H., History of. Lancaster, D. . . 224.24
GILSON, A. The czar and the sultan, [also] The Turks in Europe. By F. Bouvet. London, 1853. 16° 918.16
GIOBERTI, V. Pensieri di — sull'Orlando Furioso. See Ariosto, L. 1046.6

GIOVANNA d' Angiò. Racconto stor. del quattro-
cento. Maestrazzl, E. 1056.13
GIOVANNI Fiorentino. Novelle scelte. 1a edizione
parmense. Parma. 1843. 16° 1059.4
GIPSEY, The: a tale. James, G. P. R. 464.2-3
GIRARDIN, Mme. É. de. Parisian letters 609.5
— Stories of an old maid, transl. by A. Elwes.
New York, 1856. 12° 478.15
GIRARDIN, J. Manuel de chimie appliquée. Brux-
elles, 1851. 12° 1075.35
GIRAUD, G. Select comedies. Translated 345.3
GIRAUD, J. P., jr. Birds of Long Island. New
York, 1844. 8° 172.7
GIRL's own book. Child, L. M. 199.41
GIRLS' schools, Two letters on. Austin, S. 137.23
GIRONDISTS, History of the. Lamartine, A. de . 828.6
GIURIA, P. Racconti storici e romantici. Voghera,
1854. 12° 1056.7
GLACIERS, Norway and its, in 1851. Forbes, J. D. 663.1
GLADSTONE, T. H. Englishman in Kansas; with
introduc. by F. L. Olmsted. New York.
1857. 12° 239.5
— Kanzas: or, squatter life and border warfare
in the West. London, 1857. 16° 239.4
GLADSTONE, W. E. Essay on church and state,
reviewed. Macaulay, T. B. 409.20
GLAISHER, J. Philosophical instruments. Lect.
on the exhibition 199.16
GLANCES and glimpses. Hunt, H. K. 886.3
GLASS. Fromberg, E. O. Painting on 819.28
— Gessert, M. A. Art of painting on 819.27
— Pellatt, A. Curiosities of glass making . . . 196.11
— Porter, G. R. Manufacture of 408.11
GLAUCUS: or, the wonders of the shore. Kings-
ley, C. 178.27
GLEIG, G. R. British empire in India. London,
1830-35. 4v. 16° 389.3
— Campaigns of the British army at Washing-
ton and N. Orleans, 1814-15. Lond., 1847. p.8° 889.19
— Chelsea pensioners. London, 1829. 3v. 12°. 777.2
— Country curate. London, 1830. 2v. 12° . . 798.2
— History of the Bible. N. Y., n.d. 2v. 18°. . 810.14
— Leipsic campaign. London, 1852. p.8° . . . 409.7
— Life of Robert, first Lord Clive. London,
1848. p.8° 889.9
— Life of Sir T. Munro. New edition. London,
1849. p.8° 899.5
— Light dragoon. London, 1844. 2v. p.8° . . 726.1
— Lives of the most eminent British military
commanders. London, 1832. 3v. 16° . . . 388.3
— Memoirs of Warren Hastings. London, 1841.
3v. 8° 572.1
— Sale's brigade in Afghanistan. London, 1846.
p.8° 899.11
— The subaltern. New ed. Edinb., 1852. 16°. 979.5
GLENNY, G. Flower garden. New ed. London,
n.d. 16° . . . . v.IV.of 169.15
GLIDDON, G. R. and Nott, J. C. Indigenous races
of the earth 171.2
GLORY and shame of England. Lester, C. E. . . 646.12
GLOVER, R. M. Manual of elementary chemistry.
London, 1855. 12° 156.25
GLUGE, le Dr. Physiologie. Bruxelles, n.d. 12° 1065.17
GLYNN, J. Cranes and machinery for raising
heavy bodies. 2d ed. London, 1854. 12° . 199.20
— Power of water to drive mills and other
engines. London, 1853. 16° 829.14
GOADBY, H. Text-book of vegetable and animal
physiology. New York, 1858. 8° 173.5
GOBAT, S. Three years in Abyssinia, translated,
with introduction by S. D. Clark. With
biogr. sketch by R. Baird. N. Y., 1851. 12° 697.7
GOBINEAU, A. de. Diversity of races; with intro-
duction and notes by H. Hotz, [and] an ap-
pendix by J. C. Nott. Phila., 1856. 12° . . 176.3
GOD. Chalmers, T. Power, wisdom and good-
ness of 826.6
— Eliot, W. G. jr. Discourses on the unity of . 1086.23
— Gurney, J. J. Habitual exercise of love to. . 1089.27
— Kirby, W. Power, wisdom, etc., of, as mani-
fested in the creation of animals 826.2
GOD. Osgood, Samuel. God with men: or, Foot-
prints of providential leaders. 117.8
See also: Theology.
GODFREY of Bulloigne; or the recovery of Jeru-
salem. See Tasso, T.
GODIN, Madame, Voyage of, along the river of the
Amazons, 1770 . . . . 830.31
GODLEY, J. R. Letters from America. London,
1844. 2v. 12° 629.6
GODMAN, J. D. American natural history. Part I.
Mastology. Philadelphia, 1826-28. 3v. 8°. 172.12
GODOLPHIN: a novel. Lytton, E. Bulwer. . . . 466.12-14
GODOLPHIN, Mrs. M., Life of. Evelyn, J. . . . 596.10
GODWIN, B. The philosophy of atheism. Lond.,
1853. 16° 1088.34
GODWIN, W. Cloudesley: a tale. N. York, 1830.
2v. 12° 498.1
— Lives of the necromancers. London, 1834. 8° 125.1
— St. Leon: a tale of the 16th century. 2d ed.
London, 1800. 4v. 12° 419.8
GOEDE, C. A. G. A foreigner's opinion of Eng-
land, etc. Translated by T. Horne. Bos-
ton, 1822. 8° 647.4
GOETHE, J. W. von. See Göthe, J. W. v.
GOGUÉ, A. Secrets de la cuisine française. Paris,
1856. 12° 1078.21
GOLD, Use, working and sources of. Hargraves,
E. H. 938.7
GOLD diggings, Sixteen months at the. Woods,
D. B. 637.3
GOLD discoveries, Australian and Californian.
Stirling, P. J. 136.12
GOLD mines, Six months in the. Buffum, E. G. . 628.12
GOLDEN Dagon: or, up and down the Irrawaddi.
New York, 1856. 12° 709.10
GOLDEN legend. Longfellow, H. W. 333.11-13
GOLDONI, C. Commedie scelte. Milano, 1825. 3v. 16° 1047.3

Contents. — Vol. I. Notizie su la vita dell'autore;
Un curioso accidente; Il vero amico; Pamela fanci-
ulla; La bottega del caffè; La locandiera; Il matrimo-
nio per concorso; Il burbero benefico o sia il bisbetico
di buon cuore; Gli innamorati. II. Il cavaliere e la
dama; L'impresario delle Smirne; L'avventuriere
onorato; Terenzio; Gli amori di Zelinda e Lindoro;
Le gelosie di Lindoro; Le inquietudini di Zelinda;
Il Ventaglio. III. La dama prudente; Il Moliere; La
Villeggiatura; Le smanie per la villeggiatura; Le
avventure della villeggiatura; Il ritorno della villeggiatura; Il medico orlandese; Il Torquato Tasso.

GOLDONI, C., Giraud and Nota. Select Italian
comedies, translated. New York, 1849. 12° 345.3

Contents. — Odd mistake, Goldoni; Morose good
man, Goldoni; Jealousy at fault, Giraud; Mad
prophet, Giraud; Projector, Nota; First steps to
folly, Nota.

GOLDONI, C. and Alfieri. Lives and adventures of.
Copping, E. 544.5
GOLDSMITH, J. Manners, customs and curiosities
of nations. Philadelphia, 1810. 2v. 12° . 649.20
GOLDSMITH, L. Secret history of the cabinet of
Bonaparte. New York, 1810. 2v. 16° . . . 1009.14
GOLDSMITH, O. Miscellaneous works, with life,
edited by W. Irving. Phila., 1850. 8° . . . 892.9
— Miscellaneous works, [ed.] by J. Prior. New
York, 1853. 4v. 12° 906.2-3
Contents. — Vol. I. The bee; Essays; An inquiry
into the present state of polite learning in Europe;
Prefaces and introductions. II. Letters from a citizen
of the world to his friend in the East; A familiar intro-
duction to the study of natural history. III. The
vicar of Wakefield; Biographies; Miscellaneous criti-
cism. IV. Poems; Miscellaneous pieces; Dramas;
Criticism relating to poetry and the belles-lettres.
— Poems: a new edition. London, 1800. 12°. . 348.9
— Poetical works. London, 1851. 16° 329.4
— Animated nature: new ed. Liverpool, 1811.
4v. 8° 172.14
— Essays; with the life of the author. London,
n.d. 18° 850.27
— History of England. 6th edition. Perth, 1792.
4v. 16° 968.7
— Same. Pinnock's edition. 15th American
from 24th English ed. Phila., 1838. 12° . . 968.5

GOLDSMITH, O. History of England, abridged. Ed. by Simpson. 19th ed. Edinb., 1850. 12° ... 968.6
— History of Greece to the death of Alexander. London, 1821. 2v. 8° 953.5
— - Same. 7th Am. ed. Philadelphia, 1822. 12° 959.9
— History of Rome. London, 1821. 2v. 8° . . 952.5
— - Same. Pinnock's ed. 1st Am. from the 12th Engl. ed. Philadelphia, 1837. 12° 959.6
— Vicar of Wakefield. Paris, 1800. 12° 759.4
— - Same. Barbauld's Brit. nov. . v.XXIII. of 778.1
— - Same. New York, 1851. 16° 759.3
— - Same, [with] The deserted village. Exeter, 1828. 18° 499.15
— - Same. With ac't of life and writings of the author, by J. Aikin. N. York, 1853. 12° 759.2
— Le ministre de Wakefield, trad. par Hennequin. Boston, 1831. 12° 1078.1
— Life and adventures of. Forster, J. 583.13
— Life, with selections from his writings. See Irving, W.
GOLDSMITH of Paris. Transl. from Hoffmann . . 801.3
GOLOWNIN, W. M. Japan and the Japanese. New ed. London, 1853. 12° 708.14
GONDI, J. F. P. de, Card. de Retz. Memoirs of, [by himself.] Philadelphia, 1817. 3v. 8°. 613.10
GOOD, J. M. Book of nature. N. York, 1827. 8° 172.8
— - Same. From last London edition. Hartford, 1850. 8° 172.9
— Memoirs of. Gregory, O. 578.10
GOODELL, W. Old and new : or the changes of thirty years in the East, with introduction by W. Adams. New York, 1853. 12° . . . 687.11
GOODMAN. G. Court of James I. London, 1839. 2v. 8° 552.7
GOODRICH, Charles A. Geography of the Bible. New York, 1856. 18° 1089.28
— History of the United States. Boston, 1853. 12° 309.9
— Religious ceremonies and customs. Hartford, 1836. 8° 1099.4
GOODRICH, Chauncey A. Select British eloquence. N. York, 1852. 8° 861.3
— - Same. New York, 1853. 8° 861.2
GOODRICH, C. B. Science of government as exhibited in the United States. Bost., 1853. 8° 134.1
GOODRICH, F. B. Man upon the sea : or, history of maritime adventure. Philad., 1858. 8°. 701.10
GOODRICH, S. G. Anecdotes of the animal kingdom. Boston, 1845. 12° 169.14
— Contes de Pierre Parley sur l'Amérique. Boston, 1832. 16° 1069.8
— Early history of the Southern states. Boston, 1854. 16° 239.14
— Fireside education. New York, 1838. 12° . . 137.26
— History of all nations. Boston, 1851. 2v. 8° 951.2
— Lights and shadows of African history. Boston, 1844. 16° 939.1
— Literature, anc. and mod. Boston, 1845. 16° 406.9
— Outlines of the history of England. Boston, 1828. 18° 909.4
— Pictorial geography. New ed. Boston, 1856. 2v. 8° 951.1
— Recollections of a life-time. N.Y., 1856. 2v. 12° 526.4
— Robert Merry's museum. New York, 1849-55. 30v. in 15. 8° 907.1
— The token. Boston, 1828. 18° 899.24
— Wonders of geology. Boston, 1845. 12° . . 169.13
GORDON, A. Lives of Pope Alexander VI. and Cæsar Borgia. Philadelphia, 1844. 8° . . 544.2
GORDON, J. History of Ireland to 1801. London, 1806. 2v. 8° 975.3
GORDON, T. F. Gazetteer of New Jersey. Trenton, 1834. 8° 235.7
— Hist. of America to 1520. Phila., 1831. 2v. 12° 259.9
— History of New Jersey to 1787. Trenton, 1834. 8° 235.7
GORDON, W. History of the independence of the United States. London, 1788. 4v. 8° . . . 214.11
GORDON, W. R. Three-fold test of modern spiritualism. New York, 1856. 12° 1096.18
GORE, C. F. Banker's wife: a novel. New York, 1843. 8° 776.1

GORE, C. F. Birthright : a novel. N. Y., 1843. 8° 776.2
— Castles in the air: a novel. N. York, 1848. 8° 776.3
— Craigallan castle. New York, 1852. 8° . . . 776.10
— Manners of the day. London, 1830. 3v. 12°. 776.9
— Man of capital. London, 1846. 3v. 12° . . . 776.8
— Mrs. Armytage. Philadelphia, 1836. 2v. 12° 489.8
— Peers and parvenus. London, 1846. 3v. 12° 776.5
— - Same. New York, 1846. 8° 805.11
— Percy Ranthorpe. New York, 1848. 8° . . . 776.4
— Polish tales. London, 1833. 3v. 12° 776.6
— Progress and prejudice. New York, n.d. 12° 776.11
— Self. 2d ed. London, 1845. 3v. 12° 776.7
— Sketches of English character. New edition. London, 1852. 16° 469.18
GÖRGEI, A. My life and acts in Hungary in 1848-49. New York, 1852. 12° 547.14
GORHAM, G. C. Gleanings during the reformation in England, 1533-88. London, 1857. 8° 1085.6
GORRIE, P. D. Lives of eminent Methodist ministers. Auburn, 1852. 12° 535.14
GORTON, S., Life of. Mackie, J. M. Sparks's American biography . . . . . . v.XV. of 529.1
GOSPEL, Unconditional freeness of the. Erskine, T. 1088.25
GOSPELS. See Bible, and Theology.
GOSSE, P. H. Aquarium : wonders of the deep sea. London, 1854. 12° 178.13
— Handbook to the marine aquarium. London, 1855. 16° 178.14
— Life in its lower, intermediate and higher forms. 2d ed. London, 1857. 16° 178.15
— Naturalist's rambles on the Devonshire coast. London, 1853. 12° 178.12
— Ocean. London, 1854. 12° 178.11
— - Same. Philadelphia, 1856. 12° 178.10
— Omphalos : an attempt to untie the geological knot. London, 1857. 12° 163.17
— Popular British ornithology. Lond., 1849. 12° 178.17
— and Hill, R. Birds of Jamaica. London, 1847. 12° 178.16
— - Naturalist's sojourn in Jamaica. London, 1851. 12° 178.7
GOSSIP. From Household words. Morley, H. . . 885.17
GOSSON, S. School of abuse. London, 1841. 8° 342.2
GOSTICK, J. German literature. Edinburgh, 1849. 16° 404.14
GÖTHE, J. W. von. Dramatic works, comprising Faust ; Iphigenia in Tauris ; Torquato Tasso ; Egmont, translated by Anna Swanwick, and Goetz von Berlichingen, translated by Sir Walter Scott. Lond., 1850. p.8° 838.5
— Sämmtliche Werke. Stuttgart und Tübingen. 1854. 40v. 16° 1038.1

Contents. — Vol. I. Zueignung; Lieder ; Gesellige Lieder; Aus Wilhelm Meister; Balladen; Antiker Form sich nähernd; Elegien; Episteln; Epigramme; Weissagungen des Bakis; Vier Jahreszeiten; Noten. II. Sonette; Vermischte Gedichte; Kunst; Parabolisch; Epigrammatisch; Politica; Gott und Welt; Chinesisch-Deutsche Jahres-und Tages-Zeiten; Aus fremden Sprachen; Noten. III. Sprüche in Reimen; Sprüche in Prosa; Ethisches. IV. Buch des Sängers, Buch Hafis; Buch der Liebe; Buch der Betrachtungen ; Buch des Unmuths; Buch der Sprüche; Buch des Timur; Buch Suleika; Das Schenkenbuch; Buch der Parabeln ; Buch der Parsen; Buch des Paradieses; Noten und Abhandlungen zu besserem Verständniss des West-östlichen Divans. V. Hermann und Dorothea; Achilleis; Reineke Fuchs. VI. Alles an Personen und zu festlichen Gelegenheiten Gedichtete enthaltend: Loge; Festgedichte; An Personen; Invectiven; Gedichte zu Bildern; Maskenzuge; Im Namen der Bürgerschaft von Carlsbad; Einzelne Scenen zu festlichen Gelegenheiten; Theaterreden; Noten. VII. Die Laune der Verliebten, ein Schäterspiel; Die Mitschuldigen, ein Lustspiel; Das Jahrmarktsfest zu Plundersweilern, ein Schönbartspiel; Das Neueste von Plundersweilern; Ein Fastnachtspiel vom Pater Brey; Satyros oder der vergötterte Waldteufel, Drama; Prolog zu den neuesten Offenbarungen Gottes, verdeutscht durch Carl Friedrich Bahrdt ; Götter, Helden und Wieland; Prometheus, dramatisches fragment ; Künstler's Erdewallen, Drama ; Künstler's Apotheose, Drama ; Der Triumph der Empfindsamkeit, eine dramatische Grille; Die Vögel, nach dem Aristophanes. VIII. Claudine von Villa Bella, ein Singspiel; Erwin und Elmire, ein Singspiel;

GÖTHE, J. W. von, *continued.*

Jery und Bately, ein Singspiel; Lila; Die Fischerin, ein Singspiel; Scherz, List und Rache, ein Singspiel; Die ungleichen Hausgenossen, ein Singspiel; Der Zauberflöte, zweiter Theil, Fragment; Cantaten. IX. Götz von Berlichingen mit der eisernen Hand, Schauspiel; Egmont, Trauerspiel; Clavigo, Trauerspiel; Stella, Trauerspiel; Die Geschwister, Schauspiel. X. Der Gross Cophta, Lustspiel; Der Bürgergeneral, Lustspiel; Die Aufgeregten, politisches Drama; Des Epimenides Erwachen; Pandora, Festspiel. XI.—XII. Faust, Tragödie. XIII. Iphigenie auf Tauris, Schauspiel; Torquato Tasso, Schauspiel; Die natürliche Tochter, Trauerspiel; Elpenor, Trauerspiel. XIV. Leiden des jungen Werthers; Briefe aus der Schweiz; Brief eines Landgeistlichen; Zwo biblische Fragen. XV. Die Wahlverwandschaften, Roman. XVI.—XVII. Wilhelm Meisters Lehrjahre. XVIII. Wilhelm Meisters Wanderjahre oder die Entsagenden, 1 u. 2 Buch. XIX. Wilhelm Meister, Schluss; Reise der Söhne Megaprazon's, Fragment; Unterhaltungen deutscher Ausgewanderten; Die guten Weiber, Novelle. XX.—XXII. Aus meinem Leben; Wahrheit und Dichtung. XXIII. Carlsbad bis auf den Brenner; Vom Brenner bis Verona; Verona bis Venedig; Venedig; Ferrara bis Rom; Rom; Neapel; Sicilien. XXIV. Neapel; Zweiter Aufenthalt in Rom; Ueber Italien, Fragmente. XXV. Campagne in Frankreich, 1792; Belagerung von Mainz, 1793. XXVI. Schweizerreise im Jahre 1797; Reise am Rhein, Main und Neckar in den Jahren, 1814 und 1815; Sanct Rochus Fest zu Bingen; Im Rheingau Herbsttage; Kunst-Schätze am Rhein, Main und Neckar. XXVII. Annalen oder Tag-und Jahres-Hefte von 1749, bis Ende 1822; Reden; Biographische Einzelnheiten. XXVIII. Benvenuto Cellini, 1—3 Buch. XXIX. Benvenuto Cellini, 4tes Buch; Anhang; Rameau's Neffe, ein Dialog von Diderot; Anmerkungen; Nachträgliches zu Rameau's Neffe; Diderots Versuch über die Malerei. XXX. Winckelmann; Philipp Hackert: Einleitung in die Propyläen; Ueber Laokoon; Der Sammler und die Seinigen; Ueber Wahrheit und Wahrscheinlichkeit der Kunstwerke, ein Gespräch; Philostrat's Gemälde und Antik und Modern; Nachträgliches. XXXI. Ferneres über Kunst. XXXII. Deutsche Literatur.—Recensionen in die Frankfurter gelehrten Anzeigen; Recensionen in die Jenaische allgemeine Literaturzeitung; Ferneres über deutsche Literatur. XXXIII. Altgriechische Literatur; Französische Literatur; Englische Literatur; Italianische Literatur; Orientalische Literatur; Volkspoesie. XXXIV. Geschichte Gottfriedens von Berlichingen mit der eisernen Hand, dramatisirt; Iphigenie auf Tauris; Erwin und Elmire, ein Schauspiel; Claudine von Villa Bella, ein Schauspiel; Zwei ältere Scenen aus dem Jahrmarktsfest zu Plunderswellern; Hanswurst's Hochzeit oder der Lauf der Welt, ein mikrokosmisches Drama; Paralipomena zu Faust; Zwei Teufelchen und Amor; Fragmente einer Tragödie; Die natürliche Tochter, Schema der Fortsetzung; Pandora, Schema der Fortsetzung; Nausikaa, ein Trauerspiel. XXXV. Götz von Berlichingen mit der eisernen Hand, Schauspiel; Die Wette, Lustspiel; Mahomet, Trauerspiel, nach Voltaire; Tancred, Trauerspiel, nach Voltaire; Theater und dramatische Poesie. XXXVI. Morphologie, Beiträge zur Optik; I. Bildung und Umbildung organischer Naturen; Die Metamorphose der Pflanzen; Verfolg; Osteologie. 2. Beiträge zur Optik. XXXVII. Zur Farbenlehre, didaktischer Theil. XXXVIII. Der Farbenlehre, polemischer Theil. XXXIX. Geschichte der Farbenlehre. XL. Nachträge zur Farbenlehre; Naturwissenschaftliche Einzelnheiten; Mineralogie, Geologie; Meteorologie; Zur Naturwissenschaft im Allgemeinen; Chronologie der Entstehung Göthescher Schriften.

— Werke. Vollst. Ausg. letzter Hd. Stuttgart und Tübingen, 1837. 5v. 8° 1034.1

Contents.—I. Göthe's Leben; Gedichte: Zueignung; Lieder; Balladen; Elegien; Episteln; Epigramme; Weissagungen des Bakis; Vier Jahreszeiten; Sonette; Cantaten; Vermischte Gedichte; Aus Wilhelm Meister; Antiker Form sich nahernd; An Personen; Kunst; Parabolisch; Gott, Gemüth und Welt; Sprichwörtlich; Epigrammatisch Lyrisches; Paria; Trilogie der Leidenschaft; Loge; Gott und Welt; Kunst; Epigrammatisch; Parabolisch; Aus fremden Sprachen; Zahme Xenien; Inschriften, Denk-und Sende-Blätter; Dramatisches; Zahme Xenien; Jugendgedichte; Lieder für Liebende; Chinesisch-Deutsche Jahres-und Tages-Zeiten; Vermischte Gedichte; Original und Nachbildung; Festgedichte; Gedichte zu Bildern; Zuschriften und Erinnerungs-Blätter; Politica; Der neue Alcinous; West-östlicher Divan; Reineke Fuchs, in 12 Gesängen;

GÖTHE, J. W. von, *continued.*

Hermann und Dorothea; Achilleis; Pandora, Festspiel; Die Laune des Verliebten, Schäferspiel in Versen; Die mitschuldigen, Lustspiel in Versen; Die Geschwister, Schauspiel; Mahomet, Trauerspiel, nach Voltaire; Tancred, Trauerspiel, nach Voltaire; Götz von Berlichingen mit der eisernen Hand, Schauspiel; Egmont, Trauerspiel; Iphigenie auf Tauris, Schauspiel; Torquato Tasso; Die natürliche Tochter. II. Elpenor, Trauerspiel; Clavigo, Trauerspiel; Stella, Trauerspiel; Claudine von Villa Bella, Singspiel; Erwin und Elmire, Singspiel; Jery und Bately, Singspiel; Lila, Singspiel; Die Fischerin, Singspiel; Scherz, List und Rache, Singspiel; Der Zauberflöte, zweiter Theil; Palaeophron und Neoterpe; Vorspiel zur Eröffnung des Weimarischen Theaters; Was wir bringen, Vorspiel; Theaterreden; Faust; Das Jahrmarktsfest zu Plunderswellern, Schönbartspiel; Das Neueste von Plunderswellern; Fastnachtsspiel vom Pater Brey; Satyros, Drama; Prolog zu den neuesten Offenbarungen Gottes; Parabeln; Legende; Hans Sachsens poetische Sendung; Auf Miedings Tod; Künstlers Erdewallen, Drama; Künstlers Apotheose, Drama; Epilog zu Schillers Glocke; Die Geheimnisse, Fragment; Maskenzüge; Im Namen der Bürgerschaft zu Carlsbad; Des Epimenides Erwachen; Der triumph der Empfindsamkeit, dramatische Grille; Die Vögel, nach dem Aristophanes; Der Gross-Cophta, Lustspiel; Der Bürgergeneral, Lustspiel; Die Aufgeregten, politisches Drama; Unterhaltungen deutscher Ausgewanderten; Die guten Weiber; Novelle; Leiden des jungen Werthers; Briefe aus der Schweiz; Die Wahlverwandschaften, ein Roman; Einzelnheiten, Maximen und Reflexionen; Prometheus, Fragment; Götter, Helden und Wieland; Nachspiel zu Tiffands Hagestolzen. III. Wilhelm Meisters Lehrjahre; Wilhelm Meisters Wanderjahre; Aus meinem Leben, Dichtung und Wahrheit; Italiänische Reise. IV. Zweiter Römischer Aufenthalt, 1787, 1788; Campagne in Frankreich, 1792; Aus einer Reise in die Schweiz, 1797; Aus einer Reise am Rhein, Mayn und Neckar 1814, 1815; Benvenuto Cellini; Rameau's Neffe, Dialog von Diderot; Diderot's Versuch über die Malerei; Winckelmann; Philipp Hackert; Propyläen; Bildhauerei; Münzen, Medaillen, geschnittene Steine; Vorbilder für Fabricanten und Handwerker; Altdeutsche Baukunst; Verschiedenes über Kunst aus der nächsten Zeit nach dem Götz von Berlichingen und Werther; Ueber Christus und die zwölf Apostel, nach Raphael, von Marc-Anton gestochen; Christus nebst zwölf-alt-und neutestamentlichen Figuren; Verein der Deutschen Bildhauer; Denkmale; Vorschläge den Künstlern Arbeit zu verschaffen; Rauch's Basrelief am Piedestal von Blücher's Statue; Granitarbeiten in Berlin; Der Markgrafenstein von J. Schoppe; Programm zur Prüfung der Jünglinge der Gewerbeschule; Plastische Anatomie; Verzeichniss der geschnittenen Steine im Museum zu Berlin; Charon, neugriechisches Gedicht; Polygnot's Gemälde; Nachträgliches zu Philostrat's Gemälden; Zahn's Ornamente und Gemälde aus Pompeji, Herculanum und Stabia; Dr. Jacob Roux, über die Farben im technischen Sinne; Pentazonium Vimariense; Architectur in Sicilien; Kirchen, Paläste und Klöster in Italien, gez. von C. E. Ruhl; Das altrömische Denkmal bei Vogel; Der Tänzerin Grab; Homer's Apotheose; Roma sotteranea di Antonio Bosio Romano; Zwei antike weibliche Figuren; Reizmittel in der bildenden Kunst; Tischbein's Zeichnungen; Danae; Beispiele symbolischer Behandlung; Rembrandt der Denker; Georg Friedrich Schmidt; Künstlerische Behandlung landschaftlicher Gegenstände; Aphorismen; Verschiedenes Einzelne; Jungen Künstlern empfohlen; Vortheile eines jungen Malers; Zu malende Gegenstände; Ueber den sogenannten Dilettantismus; Schauspielkunst. V. Literatur; Auswärtige Literatur und Volkspoesie; Zur Naturwissenschaft; Mineralogie und Geologie; Zur Farbenlehre; Zur Pflanzenlehre; Osteologie.

— Auto-biography. Also letters from Switzerland and Travels in Italy; transl. by J. Oxenford and A. J. W. Morrison. London, 1848–49. 2v. p.8° 838.3-4
— Briefwechsel mit einem Kinde. Berlin, 1835. 3v. 12° 1034.20
— Egmont, Trauerspiel. Leipzig, 1788. 16° . . 1038.4
— Faust. Tragödie. London, 1823. 16° 1038.3
— Faust. Transl. into prose by A. Hayward. 1st Am. from 3d Lond. ed. Lowell, 1840. 12° . 327.2
— Same. New ed. Boston, 1852 . . . . . 327.1&3-4
— Faust. Transl. by C. T. Brooks. Bost., 1856. 12° 327.5
— Faust, a tragedy. Pt. II. 2d ed. London, 1842. 12° 327.6

GÖTHE, J. W. von. Göthe und Werther. Briefe. Hrsg. v. A. Kestner. 2te Aufl. Stuttgart, 1855. 12° 1034.11
— Opinions on the world, mankind, literature, science and art. Transl. by O. Wenckstern. London, 1853. 16° 878.25
— Theory of colours. Transl. by C. L. Eastlake. London, 1840. 8° 208.4
— Torquato Tasso, Schauspiel. Neue Aufl. Leipzig, 1816. 16° 1038.2
— Wilhelm Meister. Apprenticeship and travels. [Transl. by T. Carlyle.] New ed. Boston, 1851. 2v. 12° 756.1-2
— Wilhelm Meister's apprenticeship: transl. by R. D. Boylan. London, 1855. p.8° 827.10
— Briefe aus dem Freundeskreise von. 1034.10
— Wilhelm Meister's travels transl. with biogr. Carlyle's German romance . . . . . . v.IV. of 418.1
— Xenien-Manuscript. See Schiller, J. C. F. v. 1013.15
— Götz von Berlichingen. Translated by Sir W. Scott 838.5
— Deycks, F. Andeutungen über G.'s Faust. . 1034.21
— Düntzer, J. H. J. Studien zu Göthe's Werken. 1034.6
— - Frauenbilder aus G.'s Jugendzeit. 1034.8
— - G.'s Faust erläutert 1034.2
— - Götz und Egmont. Geschichte 1034.3
— - Tasso erläutert 1034.7
— Meyer, E. Studien zu G.'s Faust 1034.4
— Austin, S. G. and his contemporaries 897.9
— Eckermann, J. P. Gespräche mit Goethe, in den letzten Jahren seines Lebens 1034.14
— - Conversations with. Translated 874.14
— Falk, J. D. G. aus nährem persönlichen Umgange dargestellt. 1034.12
— Lewes, G. H. Life and works of. 545.5-6
— Rosenkranz, J. K. F. G. und seine Werke. . 1034.5
— Schaefer, J. W. G.'s Leben 1034.9
— Schiller, J. C. F. v. Anecdotes of 876.16
GOTTHELF, J. Pseud. See Bitzius, A.
GOTTSCHALL. R. Das schlesische Gebirge. Leipzig, 1857. 16° 1029.19
GOULD, A. A. Naturalist's library. Bost., 1851. 8° 172.1
— Report on the invertebrata of Massachusetts . 175.2
— and Agassiz, L. Comparative physiology . . 816.12
— - Principles of zoölogy 177.6-7
GOVERNMENT. Eliot, S. History of liberty . . . 134.7-8
— Goodrich, C. B. Science of G. as exhibited in the United States 134.1
— Lieber, F. Civil liberty and self-government 134.13
— O'Brien, W. S. Principles of 135.17
— St. John, J. A. The Nemesis of power . . . 139.14
— Sketches of popular tumults 134.16
    See also: Politics, Political economy.

For works on the institutions of various countries, see the names of those countries.

GOWER. Illustrations of. Todd, H. J. 312.10
GRAAH, W. A. Expedition to the East coast of Greenland. Transl. by G. G. Macdougall. London, 1837. 8° 704.3
GRACE, Method of. Flavel, J. 1107.6
GRACE Greenwood. Pseud. See Lippincott, S. J. C.
GRACE Lee: a tale. Kavanagh, J. 454.12
GRÄFIN Chateaubriant. Roman. Laube, H. . . . 1029.24
GRAFTON, H. D. Treatise on the camp and march. Boston, 1854. 12° 197.11
GRAHAM, G. F. English style: with an historical sketch of the language. London, 1857. 12° 406.18
— English synonymes. Edited by H. Reed. N. York, 1851. 12° 403.9-10
GRAHAM, I. The power of faith, exemplified in the life and writings of Mrs. Graham. New ed. New York, [1843.] 12° 538.23
GRAHAM, J. Life of Gen. D. Morgan. N. York, 1856. 12° 528.3
GRAHAM, M. Three months in the mountains East of Rome. 2d ed. London, 1821. 8° . 676.3
GRAHAM, T. Elements of chemistry. 2d ed. v.I. London, 1850. 8° 144.7

GRAHAME, J. History of the United States till [1776.] 2d ed. Philadelphia, 1850. 2v. 8° . 304.3
GRAMMAR, Comic English 896.18
— General principles of . . . . v.III. of 850.25
GRAMMAR of music. Calcott, Dr. J. W. 209.12
GRAMMARIANS, Lives of the. Suetonius Tranquillus, C. 844.8
GRAMMONT, A., Count de. Memoirs of the court of Charles II. Hamilton, A. 857.1
GRANADA, Conquest of. See Irving, W.
GRANARY burial ground, Inscriptions from. Bridgman, T. 223.5
GRANDFATHER, The: a novel. Pickering, E. . . . 805.6-7
GRANT, A. Letters from the mountains, 1773-1807. 1st Am. from 3d Lond. ed. 2v. in 1. Boston, 1809. 16° 909.3
— Memoir and correspondence, ed. by her son. 2d ed. London, 1845. 3v. 16° 596.6
— Memoirs of an American lady. N. Y., 1809. 16° 878.17
— - Same. New York, 1846. 16° 878.7
GRANT, Dr. A. and the mountain Nestorians. Laurie, T. 686.5
GRANT, J. British senate: or, recollections of the Lords and Commons. Phila., 1838. 2v. 12° 808.18
— Random recollections of the House of Lords. Philadelphia, 1836. 12° 868.9
— Random recollections of the House of Commons. Philadelphia, 1836. 12° 868.10
— Great metropolis. 2d ed. New York, 1837. 2v. in 1. 12° 868.8
— Sketches of London. Phila., 1839. 2v. 12° . 646.13
— Metropolitan pulpit: or, sketches of preachers in London. New York, 1839. 16° . . . 1099.11
— Walks and wanderings in the world of literature. Philadelphia, 1840. 2v. 12° 898.19
— Memoirs of James [Graeme] Marquis of Montrose. London, 1858. 16° 565.8
GRANT, R. History of physical astronomy. London, 1852. 8° 146.10
GRANTLEY manor: a tale. Fullerton, Lady G. . . 458.1-3
GRAPE grower's guide, The American. Chorlton, W. 165.25
GRAPE vine, Culture of. Allen, J. F. 165.19-21
GRATTAN, H., Memoirs of life and times of. New edition. London, 1849. 5v. 8° 563.4
— Speeches of 862.3-8
GRATTAN, T. C. Agnes de Mansfeldt: a tale. London, 1835. 3v. 12° 798.5
— - Same. Philadelphia, 1836. 2v. in 1. 12° . 798.4
— Chance medley of light matter. N.Y., 1845. 8° 802.32
— Heiress of Bruges: a tale of the year 1600. New York, 1831. 2v. 12° 798.8
— High-ways and by-ways. New edition. Boston, 1840. 3v. 12° 798.7
— - Same. 3d series. Phila., 1827. 2v. 12° . 798.6
— - Same. 3d series. London, 1835. 3v. 12° 798.3
— History of the Netherlands. Lond., 1830. 16° 378.8
— - Same. New York, 1843. 18° 919.8
— Traits of travel. Boston, 1829. 2v. 12° . . 798.1
GRAVEL wall mode of building. Fowler, O. S. . . 207.10
GRAVES, A. J. Woman in America. N.Y., n.d. 18° 820.61
GRAVES, R. Spiritual Quixote. 2v. 12°. v.XXXII., XXXIII. of Barbauld's Brit. nov. 779.1
GRAVITATION, An elementary explanation of. Airy, G. B. 146.24
GRAY, A. Botany of the Northern United States. Boston, 1848. 12° 166.8
— Botanical text-book. Parts I.-II. New York. 1842. 12° 166.16
— - Same. 3d edition, enlarged. N.Y., 1850. 8° 166.5
— - Same. 4th edition. New York, 1853. 8° . 166.4
— First lessons in botany and vegetable physiology. New York, 1857. 12° 166.5
— How plants grow. New York, 1858. 12° . . 166.13
GRAY, H. Sepulchres of Etruria in 1839. 2d ed. London, 1841. 12° 956.12
GRAY, J. C. Essays: agricultural and literary. Boston, 1856. 12° 898.1
GRAY, S., Trial of British soldiers for the murder of, in Boston, 1770 . . . . 219.1

GRAY, T. Works. London, 1835–43. 5v. 12° . .   339.2

   Contents. — Vol. I. Life, by J. Mitford; Odes; Progress of poesy; The bard; Elegy; Poemata. II. Essay on the poetry of Gray; Gray's letters. III.—IV. Letters; Criticisms on architecture and painting. V. Letters; Observations on English metre; Remarks on the poems of Lydgate.

GRAY, Dr. T. The Vestal : or, a tale of Pompeii. Boston, 1830. 12° 429.6
GRAYDON, A. Memoirs of his own time and of the revolution. Edited by J. S. Littell. Philadelphia, 1846. 8° 213.5
GRAYSON, W. J. The hireling and the slave, Chicora and other poems. Charleston, 1856. 12° 349.3
GRAZZINI, G. [detto Il Lasca.] Novelle scelte e lezione accademica. Parma, 1843. 16° . . .   1059.5
GREAT Britain. Admiralty. Last of the Arctic voyages. London, 1855. 2v. 8° 702.1
— — Manual of scientific enquiry. Ed. by Sir J. F. W. Herschel. 2d ed. Lond., 1851. 12°   149.3–4
— Exhibition of 1851. Reports by the juries. London, [1852.] 8° 191.6
— Brand, J. Popular antiquities of 846.8
— Brenton, E. P. Naval history of. 986.3
— Dunham, S. A. Literary and scientific men of.   398.3
— Greg, R. P. Mineralogy of 163.8
— Haussez, Baron d'. G. B. in 1833. . . . . .   658.16
— Hazlitt, W. Select poets of 312.9
— Ingersoll, C. J. Sketch of the war of 1812–15.   215.9
— James, William. Naval history of. 986.2
— Long, G. and Porter, G. R. Geography of. .   365.10
— Mills, A. Literature and literary men of G. B.   402.2
— Nicolas, Sir N. H. History of the navy of. .   986.1
— Simond, L. Tour and residence in. 645.3
— Sutton, R. Lexington papers 975.11
— Thomson, R. Illustrations of the history of.   830.37
— Wilson, S. F. Controversies of the colonists with 216.9
— and Ireland. Barrington, Sir J. Union between 986.6
— — Greg, R. P. Mineralogy of 163.8
   See also : England, Scotl'd, Ireland, Wales.
GREAT commission, The. Harris, J. 1088.1
GREAT elm, The. Abbott, J. Harper's story books. . . . . v.IX. of 739.1
GREAT events by great historians. Lieber, F. .   947.12
GREAT Hoggarty diamond. Thackeray, W. M. . 501.12–13
GREAT men, The boyhood of. 548.13
GREAT metropolis, The. Grant, J. 808.8
GREAT secret, The. Judson, Mrs. E. C. 789.7
GREAT teacher, The. Harris, J. 1088.2
GREECE. About, E. G. and the Greeks of the present day. 918.15
— — La Grèce contemporaine 1078.54
— Ampère, J. J. Grèce, Rome et Dante 1066.1
— Baird, H. M. Modern 918.11
— Blaquiere, E. Second visit to 683.11
— Bonner, J. Child's history of 959.10
— Bowen, G. F. Handbook for. 649.8–9
— Chandler, R. Travels in. 683.5
— Chateaubriand, F. A. de. Travels in, 1806–7.   685.7
— Clarke, E. D. Travels in. 689.6
— Dorr, B. Travel in. 686.12
— Dwight, M. A. Grecian mythology 1083.10
— Finlay, G. History of, B.C. 146 to A.D. 717.   956.6
— — History of, 540–1461. . . . .   956.5
— Goldsmith, O. History of 953.5
— Grote, G. History of 958.5
— Hamilton, W. D. and Levien, E. History of.   829.38
— Hervé, F. Residence in 683.8
— Keightley, T. History of 959.7
— — War of independence in 830.61
— Malkin, F. History of. 365.6–7
— Mitford, W. 944.1
— Müller, K. O. Literature of ancient 365.11
— Parry, W. State and prospects of 585.5
— Peter, W. Poets and poetry of 315.1
— Pococke, E. India in 956.10
— Schmitz, L. History of G. to B.C. 146. . . .   958.3
— Smith, W. Hist. of, to the Roman conquest.   952.7

GREECE. Sonnini, C. S. Travels in 683.9
— Stanhope, Col. L. G. in 1823–24 . . . . . .   918.2
— Stephens, J. L. Incidents of travel in 689.1–2
— Thirlwall, C. History of. 366.11
— — History of 952.6
— White, J. History of 959.12
GREEK and Byzantine empires, History of. Finlay, G. 955.5
GREEK anthology. Translated chiefly by G. Burges. London, 1852. p.8° 834.8
GREEK classic poets, Study of. Coleridge, H. N.   466.1
GREEK dramatic poets. Æschylus 359.6
GREEK fairy tales. Kingsley, C. 484.12
GREEK history. Histoire grecque. Juste, T. . .   1065.24
GREEK islands, visit to in 1833. Auldjo, J. . . .   685.4
GREEK literature. Anthon, C. Manual of. . . .   403.5
— Browne, R. W. History of 401.3
— Matthiae, A. Manual of. 466.11
GREEK mission, Narrative of. Wilson, S. S. . .   683.2
GREEK philosophy, Brief view of . . . . . v.II. of 850.25
GREEK revolution. Blaquiere, E. Origin and progress of the 918.1
— Howe, S. G. Historical sketch of the 918.4
GREEK waters, Diary in. Howard, G. W. F. . . 683.12–13
GREEKS. Becker, W. A. Private life of the anc.   957.1
— Fosbroke, T. D. Arts, institutions, etc., of the 378.3
— Hase, H. A. Public and private life of the ancient 959.13
— Winckelmann, J. History of art among the.   205.7
GREELEY, H. Art and industry at the Crystal palace, 1853–54. New York, 1853. 12° . . .   198.9
— Glances at Europe, 1851. New York, 1851. 12°   647.13
— Hints toward reforms. New York, 1850. 12°   877.3
— Introduction to "Woman in the 19th century." Ossoli, S. M. F. d' 885.10
GREEN, M. A. E. Letters of royal and illustrious ladies of Gt. Britain. London, 1846. 3v. 12°   596.5
— Lives of the princesses of England. London, 1850–55. 6v. 8° 594.13
GREEN, S. Life of Mahomet. London, 1840. 16°   389.4
GREEN, T. J. Texian expedition against Mier. New York, 1845. 8° 623.10
GREEN mountain boys. Thompson, D. P. 726.8
GREEN mountain heroes. De Puy, H. W. 528.16
GREENE, G. W. History of the middle ages. New York, 1851. 12° 947.10
— Historical studies. New York, 1850. 12° . .   947.9
— Life of Nathanael Greene. Sparks's American biography . . . . v.XX. of 529.1
GREENE, M. The Kansas region. New York, 1856. 12° 239.6
GREENE, N. Life and campaigns of. Caldwell, C.   515.7
GREENE, R. Dramatic works [and] poems, with account of the author and notes, by A. Dyce. London, 1831. 2v. 12° 355.3

   Contents. — Vol. I. Account of R. Greene; List of Greene's prose works; Orlando Furioso; Looking glass for London and England; Friar Bacon and Friar Bungay; Historie of Fryer Bacon. II. Alphonsus, king of Arragon; James the fourth; George a Greene; Hist. of George a Greene; Ballad of the Jolly Pinder of Wakefield; Poems; Addenda; Index.

GREENHOW, R. History of Oregon and California. 2d ed. Boston, 1845. 8° 235.9
GREENLAND. Egede, H. A description of. . . .   703.13
— Graah, W. A. Expedition to the East coast of.   704.3
— Historical and descriptive account of. 820.35
GREENLEAF, S. Examination of the testimony of the four Evangelists. Trial of Jesus. Boston, 1846. 8° 1093.16
GREENOUGH, H. Memorial of. Tuckerman, H. T.   526.9
GREENWOOD, C. The child and the man. Boston, 1855. 12° 1096.11
GREENWOOD, F. W. P. Miscellaneous writings. Boston, [1846.] 12° 808.2
— Sermons. Boston, 1844. 2v. 12° 117.2
— Sermons of consolation. 3d ed. Boston, 1847. 8°   1088.24
GREENWOOD, *Col.* G. Rain and rivers: or, Hutton and Playfair against Lyell, and all comers. London, 1857. 8° 145.14

GREENWOOD, J. Sailor's sea-book: navigation in two parts. London, 1850. 16° 819.39

GREG, R. P. Mineralogy of Great Britain and Ireland. London, 1858. 8° 163.8

GREGG, J. Commerce of the prairies: or, the journal of a Santa Fé trader. 4th edition. Philadelphia, 1850. 2v. 12° 628.16

— Scenes and incidents in the Western prairies. Philadelphia, 1856. 2v. in 1. 12° 239.12

GREGOROVIUS, F. Corsica, picturesque, histor. and social. Tr. by E. J. Morris. Phila. 1855. 12° 1007.5

GREGORY, G. Eruptive fevers, ed. by H. D. Bulkley. 1st American ed. New York, 1851. 8° 152.13

GREGORY, O. Evidences, etc., of the Christian religion. 9th edition. London, 1851. p.8°. 858.2

— Mathematics for practical men. 2d American from 2d London ed. Philadelphia, 1852. 8° 147.2

— Memoirs of the life, writings and character of J. M. Good. London, 1832. 16° 578.10

— Works of Robert Hall. With a memoir. . . 1089.16

GREGORY, W. Elementary treatise on chemistry. Edinburgh, 1855. 12° 156.27

— Handbook of inorganic chemistry. 3d ed. London, 1853. 12° 156.19

— Handbook of organic chemistry. 3d edition. London, 1852. 12° 156.18

— Letters on animal magnetism. Lond., 1851. 12° 124.11

GREGORY VII., Life and pontificate of. Greisley, Sir R. 543.7

GREISLEY, Sir R. Life and pontificate of Gregory VII. London, 1832. 8° 543.7

GRENVILLE, G. N. T., Lord Nugent. Lands, classical and sacred. London, 1846. 2v. 18° . 840.48

— Legends of the library at Lilies; by Lord and Lady Nugent. London, 1847. 2v. 12° . . . 777.11

— Memorials of John Hampden. London, 1832. 2v. 8° 562.7

GRENVILLE, R. P. T. N. B. C., Duke of Buckingham. Memoir of the court of England during the regency, 1811-20. Lond., 1856. 2v. 8° 553.10

— Memoirs of the court and cabinets of George III. London, 1853-55. 4v. 8° 976.3

GRESHAM, Sir Th. Life. London, 1845. 18°. . . 840.22

— Life, with illustrations. Burgon, J. W. . . . 573.8

GREVILLE, R. K. Hist. of Brit. India. Murray, H. 810.51

GREY, Hon. Mrs. Bosom friend: a novel. New York, 1845. 8° 802.28

— Young prima donna: a romance. Philadelphia, n.d. 8°. 802.26-27

GREY, G. Journals of discovery in Australia, 1837-39. London, 1841. 2v. 8° 705.4

— Polynesian mythology, and history of the New Zealand race. London, 1855. 12° . . 1087.20

GREY, M. G. and Shirreff, E. Thoughts on self-culture. Boston, 1851. 12° 124.12-13

GREYSON letters, The. Rogers, H. 885.6

GRIFFIN, E. D. Remains, compiled by F. Griffin; with a memoir by J. McVickar. N. York, 1831. 2v. 8° 534.10

— Discourse delivered in Murray st. church . . 1083.5

GRIFFIN, F. Junius discovered. Boston, 1854. 16°. 877.12-13

GRIFFIN, G. The invasion; a novel. London, 1832. 4v. 12° 807.1

— The rivals. Tracy's ambition. London, 1830. 3v. 12° 807.2

GRIFFIN, J. J. Radical theory in chemistry. London, 1858. 16° 158.23

GRIFFITH, R. E. Medical botany. Phila., 1847. 8° 152.11

— Universal formulary of medicines. Philadelphia, 1850. 8° 152.9

GRIFFITHS, J. W. On marine and naval architecture. New York, 1851. 4° 191.1

GRIFFITHS, T. Chemistry of the four seasons. London, 1846. 12° 156.6

GRILLPARZER, F. Sappho: a tragedy 489.16

GRIMALDI, J. Memoirs, ed. by Charles Dickens. Philadelphia, 1838. 2v. 12° 507.10

— Memoirs, ed. by Boz. Notes by C. Whitehead. London, 1854. 16° 507.11

GRIMKÉ, T. S. Character and objects of science and literature, and relative excellence of religious and secular education. N. Haven, 1831. 12° 878.9

GRIMM, H. Novellen. Berlin, 1856. 16° 1015.6

Contents. — Die Sängerin; Cajetan; Das Kind; Assly und Kyarem; Armenisches Volkslied; Trost in Einsamkeit; Das Abenteuer; Die Schlange; Eva; Der Landschaftsmaler.

GRIMMELSHAUSEN, C. v. Die Abenteuer des simplicissimus, Roman. Hrsg. v. E. v. Bülow. Leipzig, 1836. 16° 1025.4

GRINNELL expedition in search of Sir J. Franklin. Kane, E. K. 702.2-6

— Second expedition, Kane, E. K. 703.1-9

GRISCOM, J. Year in Europe in 1818-19. New York, 1823. 2v. 8° 647.7

GRISCOM, J. H. Animal mechanism and physiology. New York, n.d. 18° 810.78

— Uses and abuses of air. 2d ed. N. Y., 1850. 12° 207.14

GRISWOLD, C. D. The isthmus of Panama. New York, 1852. 12° 629.16

GRISWOLD, R. W. Biographical annual. New York, 1841. 12° 518.12-13

— Female poets of America. 2d ed. Philadelphia, 1852. 8°. 314.7

— Poets and poetry of America. 10th ed. Philadelphia, 1850. 8° 314.4-6

— Same, with historical introd. Phil., 1842. 8° 314.5

— Poets and poetry of England in the 19th century. 4th ed. Philadelphia, 1852. 8° . . 311-7

— Prose writers of America. Philad., 1847. 8° 872.12

— Sacred poets of England and America. New ed. New York, 1850. 8° 314.8

GROSSI, T. Marco Visconti, storia del trecento. Aggiuntovi Ildegonda, la fuggitiva, Ulrico e Lida. Firenze, 1849. 12° 1056.14

GROSVENOR, B. The mourner. N. York, n.d. 12° 1109.5

GROTE, G. History of Greece. Boston and New York, 1851-56. 12v. 12° 958.5

GROTEFEND, G. F. Attica and Athens, by G. and others. *See* Müller, K. O. 955.7

GROTH, Klaus. Quickborn. Volksleben in plattdeutschen Gedichten ditmarscher Mundart. 6te Aufl. Hamburg, 1856. 16° 1024.2

GROTON, Mass., History of. Butler, C. 224.14

GRUMBLER, The: a novel. Pickering, E. 805.9

GUARD. Histoire de la garde impériale. Saint-Hilaire, E. M. de 1068.17

GUARDIAN, The, and the Tatler; in 1v. 873.11

GUARDIAN spirits. Werner, H. 1084.14

GUATEMALA, Description of. Baily, J. 266.4

— A journey in, 1853-55. Tempsky, G. F. von . 633.8 *See* America.

GUGLIELMUCCI, V. La monaca di Casa; racconto moderno. Firenze, 1846. 12° 1056.1

GUIANA, Discovery of the empire of. Ralegh, Sir W. 266.1

GUILLOTINE, History of the. Croker, J. W. . . 1009.13

GUERRAZZI, F. D. Isabella Orsini. Racconto. 6a impr. Firenze, 1856. 12° 1057.5

— L'assedio di Firenze. Livorno, 1849. 3v. 12° 1057.4

— Scritti. Firenze, 1851. 12° 1057.3

Contents. — Veronica Cybo; La Serpicina; I nuovi Tartufi, racconti; Pensieri; Discorsi; Illustrazioni; Traduzioni; I Bianchi e i Neri, dramma.

GUICCIARDINI, Fr. Istoria d'Italia. Prefaz. di Botta. Milano, 1838. 6v. 16° 1048.3

GUILLERY, E. Arts céramiques. Bruxelles, n.d. 12° 1065.18

GUILLERY, H. Technologie. Bruxelles, n.d. 12° 1065.19

GUIZOT, Mme. E. C. P. de M. Les enfans, contes à l'usage de la jeunesse. Bruxelles, 1837. 2v. 16° 1078.56

— Moral tales. Translated by Mrs. L. Burke. 2d ed. London, 1852. 16° 737.16

— Popular tales. Translated by Mrs. L. Burke. London, 1854. 16° 737.15

— Une famille; conte. Bruxelles, 1837. 2v. 16° 1078.57

GUIZOT, F. P. G. Alfred le grand. Paris, 1856. 16° 1078.14
— Corneille and his times. New York, 1852. 12° 886.8
— Cromwell and the English commonwealth.
Transl. by A. R. Scoble. Lond., 1854. 2v. 8° 975.8
— - Same. Philadelphia, 1854. 2v. 12° . . . 978.2
— Democracy in France. New York, 1849. 12°. 134.21
— Essay on the character and influence of Wash-
ington. Boston, 1851. 16° 518.17
— Étude historique sur Washington. See Witt,
C. de 1067.30
— History of civilization. Transl. by W. Haz-
litt. Lond., 1856. 3v. p.8° 837.5
— - Same. New York, 1850-52. 4v. 12° . . 949.1
— - Same, with notes by C. S. Henry. 7th
American edition. New York, 1848. 12°. . 949.2
— History of the English revolution of 1640.
Translated by W. Hazlitt. Lond., 1851. p.8° 978.5
— - Same. London, 1856. p.8° 837.4
— - Same. New York, 1846. 12° 979.9
— Memoirs to illustrate the history of my time.
v.I. London, 1858. 8° 1003.5
— Monk: or the fall of the republic and the
restoration in 1660. London, 1858. 12° . . 568.11
— Origin of representative government. Lond.,
1852. p.8° 817.7
— Shakespeare and his times. New York, 1852.
12° 357.5
GULLIVER'S travels. Swift, J. 738.2
GUNNISON, J. W. The Mormons: a history of
their rise and progress. Phila., 1853. 12°. 1087.8
GUNPOWDER plot, A narrative of the. Jardine, D. 839.4
GURLEY, R. R. Life of Jehudi Ashmun, with a
sketch of the life of L. Cary. Washington,
1835. 8° 524.16
GURNEY, J. J. Habitual love to God, as a prepara-
tion for heaven. From 5th English edition.
Philadelphia, 1840. 18° 1089.27
— Winter in the W. Indies. 3d ed. Lond, 1841. 8° 635.5
GUROWSKI, A. G. de. America and Europe. New
York, 1857. 12° 134.19
— Russia as it is. New York, 1854. 12° . . . 927.1-2
GUSTAVUS Adolphus. History of. Harte, W. . . 546.3
— Life of. Hollings, J. F. 389.6
GUSTAVUS Lindorm. Carlen, E. F. 766.7
GUTZKOW, K. F. Gesammelte Werke. Frank-
furt a. M. 1845-52. 13v. 16° 1015.5
Contents. — Vol. I. Vorrede; Gedichte; Nero, Tra-
gedie; Hamlet in Wittenberg, dramatische Phanta-
sie; Xenien und Epigramme. II. Offentliche Char-
aktere. III. Aus den Briefen eines Narren an eine
Narrin; Seraphine; Ein Roman; Wiener Eindrucke,
1845. IV. Philosophie der That und des Ereignisses;
Ueber Gothe im Wendepunkte zweier Jahrhunderte.
V. Maha Guru, Geschichte eines Gottes. VI. Bornes
Leben (Aus Bornes ungedrucktem Nachlasse reich
vermehrt); Rosa Maria und J. D. Assing; Friedrich
von Hurter, K. K. Hofrath und Historiograph.
VII.—VIII. Blasedow und seine Sohne, Roman.
IX.—X. Saknlarbilder. XI. Novellenbuch. XII.
Briefe aus Paris 1842; Pariser Eindrucke, 1846. XIII.
Vergangene Tage.
— Die Ritter vom Geiste; Roman. 3te Aufl.
Leipzig, 1854-55. 9v. 16° 1015.4
GÜTZLAFF, K. F. A. Sketch of Chinese history.
London, 1834. 2v. 8° 934.7
— Two voyages along the coast of China, in 1831
and 1832. New York, 1833. 12° 706.5-6
GUY, J. jr. Illustrated London geography. 2d
edition. London, 1853. 8° 955.4
GUEULLETTE, T. S. Cabinet des fées. Contes
Chinois. v.XIX. Contes Tartares. Les
mille et un quart d'heure. v.XXI.-XXII.
Contes Mogols. Les sultanes de Guza-
rate. XXII.-XXIII. Les soirées bretonnes.
XXXII. 1077.1
GUY Mannering: a romance. Scott, Sir W. . . . 460.7-11
GUY rivers. A tale of Georgia. Simms, W. G. . 800.8-11
GUYON, Mme. J. M. B. de la M. Letters, tr. by P.
L. Upham. Boston, n.d. 16° 118.21
— Translations from the French of. Cowper,
Wm. Works, v.IX. 337.1
— Life, religious opinions and experiences of.
Upham, T. C. 617.15-16

GUYOT, A. Earth and man. Translated by C. C.
Felton. Boston, 1849. 12° 167.18
— - Same. 4th ed., revised. Boston, 1851. 12° 167.19-20
GWILT, J. Elements of architectural criticism.
London, 1837. 8° 202.2
— Encyclopædia of architecture. Lond., 1842. 8° 202.6
— Rudiments of architecture. 2d ed. London,
1839. 8° 202.4
— Sciography: or examples of shadows. 3d ed.
London, 1833. 8° 205.4
GWYNN, Nell, Story of. Cunningham, P. 595.10
GYMNASTICS for youth. Salzmann, C. G. . . . 137.2
GYPSIES, Customs, habits, and present state of.
Hoyland, J. 955.6
— of Spain, Account of the. Borrow, George . 889.5

H— family, The: a tale. Bremer, F. 817.5-6
HABERDASHERY and hosiery. A treatise on.
Perkins, E. E. 199.38
HABITS of animals. Swainson, W. 408.4
HACKETT, H. B. Commentary on the Acts of the
apostles. New ed. Boston, 1858. 8° . . . 1093.2
HACKLÄNDER, F. W. Werke. Stuttgart, 1855-56.
20v. 16° 1017.4
Contents. — Vols. I.—II. Namenlose Geschichten.
III. Nam. Gesch. zehn Jahre spater. IV. Das Solda-
tenleben im Frieden. V. Wach/stubenabenteuer. VI.
Kleinere Erzahlungen und humoristische Skizzen.
VII. Handel und Wandel. VIII.—IX. Reise in den
Orient. X.—XII. Eugen Stillfried. XIII. Marchen.
XIV. Der Pilgerzug nach Mekka. XV. Der geheime
Agent, Lustspiel; Magnetische Kuren, Lustspiel;
Schuldig, Scherz. XVI.—XX. Europaisches Skla-
venleben.
— Clara: or slave life in Europe. Prefaced by
Sir A. Alison. New York, 1856. 12° 796.14
HADDON, J. Differential calculus, examples. Lon-
don, 1851. 16° 829.34
— Elements of algebra. London, 1850. 16° . . 829.21
HADJI in Syria. Johnson, S. B. 689.14
HAGEN, E. A. Künstler-Geschichten. Leipzig,
1833-40. 4v. 16° 1025.7
Contents. — Vols. I.—II. Die Chronik seiner Vat-
erstadt vom Florentiner Lorenz Ghiberti, dem be-
rahmtesten Bildgiesser des 15 Jahrhunderts; Nach
dem Italienischen. III. Die Wunder der heil. Kath-
arina von Siena, nacherzahlt. IV. Leonhard da Vinci
in Mailand, nach dem Italienischen.
HAGIOGRAPHIE belge. Dufau, J. B. 1075.24
HAHN-HAHN, I. M. L. L. F. G. von. Countess
Faustina. New York, 1845. 8° 802.12
— Letters of a German countess, during her
travels in Turkey, etc., 1843-44. London,
1845. 3v. 12° 687.10
HAINAUT, Histoire du comté de. Reiffenberg,
Bar. de 1075.19
HAINES, C. G. Memoir of T. A. Emmet. New
York, 1829. 16° 508.17
HAJJI Baba of Ispahan, Adventures of. Morier, J. 808.4
— in England, Adventures of. Morier, J. . . . 808.5
HAKLUYT, R. Vindication of R. Hakluyt. Tyt-
ler, P. F. 810.53
HALE, E. E. Kansas and Nebraska. Boston,
1854. 12° 629.2
— and Miss L. P. Margaret Percival in Amer-
ica: a tale. Boston, 1850. 12° 425.16
HALE, Sir M. Letter of advice to his grandchild-
ren. 2d ed. London, 1823. 12° 139.6
— Memoirs of. Williams, J. B. 558.9
HALE, Capt. N., Life of. Stuart, I. W. 528.21
HALE, S. History of the United States to 1817.
New York, n.d. 2v. 18° 820.27
HALE, S. J. Dictionary of poetical quotations.
Philadelphia, 1852. 8° 312.2
— Keeping house and house-keeping: a story.
New York, 1845. 18° 720.10
— Liberia: or Mr. Peyton's experiments. New
York, 1853. 12° 488.3
— Woman's record: or sketches of distinguished
women. New York, 1853. 8° 541.1
HALEY, W. D. Words for the workers. Boston,
1855. 16° 197.27

HALF century, the, History of, 1800-50. Davis, E.   297.10
HALF hours with the best authors. Knight, C. .   865.3
HALIBURTON, T. C. Sam Slick's wise saws. Philadelphia, 1853. 12° 489.2
— Attaché: or Sam Slick in England. 2d and last series. New York, 1844. 8° 801.1
— Historical and statistical account of Nova Scotia. Halifax, 1829. 2v. 8° 265.2
— Yankee stories. Philadelphia, n.d. 12° . .   489.1
HALIDON hill: a dramatic sketch from Scottish history. Scott, Sir W. 358.21
HALIFAX, S. Character and writings of J. Butler.   1108.10
HALKETT, J. Historical notes respecting the Indians of North America. London, 1825. 8°   245.5
HALL, A. Life of Sylvester Judd. Boston, 1854. 8°   534.21
HALL, Mrs. A. M. Lights and shadows of Irish life. Philadelphia, 1838. 2v. 12° . .   776.12
— Marian: or a young maid's fortune. N. York, 1840. 2v. 12° 776.13
— Midsummer eve. Fairy tale. N. Y., 1848. 8°   804.3
— Sketches of Irish character. Illustrated ed. Philadelphia, 1853. 8° 804.1-2
— Stories of the Irish peasantry. Philadelphia, 1854. 12° 776.16
— Tales of woman's trials. Franklin library ed. New York, 1835. 12° 776.14
— Uncle Horace: a novel. Philadelphia, 1838. 2v. 12° 776.15
— The Whiteboy: a story of Ireland in 1822. New York, 1845. 8° 805.11
— and Mrs. J. Foster. Stories from the history of England. London, 1847. 2v. 12° . . .   979.6
HALL, A. O. The Manhattaner in New Orleans. New York, 1851. 12° 629.15
HALL, B. Journal on the coasts of Chili, Peru, and Mexico, in 1820, 1821-22. Edinburgh, 1826. 18° . . . . v.II. and III. of   830.25
— Same. From the last London ed. Boston, 1824. 2v. in 1. 12° 639.7
— Schloss Hainfeld: or a winter in Lower Styria. Paris, 1836. 12° 667.21
— Voyage of discovery to the W. coast of Corea and the Loo-Choo islands. Philadelphia, 1818. 8° 696.5
— Voyage to Loo-Choo, and other places in the Eastern seas. Edinburgh, 1826. 18°. v.1. of   830.25
HALL, B. H. College words and customs. Cambridge, 1851. 12° 403.15
— Collection of college words and customs. Enlarged. Cambridge, 1856. 12° 403.14
HALL, D. A. History of the bank of the United States. See Clarke, M. St. C. 296.1
HALL, E. B. Memoir of Mary L. Ware. Boston, 1853. 12° 535.3-5
HALL, J. Letters from the West. Lond., 1828. 8°   237.1
— Legends of the West. New York, 1853. 12°   489.5-6
— Same. 2d ed. Philadelphia, 1833. 12° . .   489.19
— Public services of W. H. Harrison. Philadelphia, 1836. 18° 519.1
— Memoir of Thomas Posey. Sparks's American biography . . . . v.XX of   529.1
— Sketches of the West. Phila., 1835. 2v. 12° .   239.13
— The West, its commerce and navigation. Cincinnati, 1848. 12° 239.9
HALL, Rev. J. Scripture history. Abridged by Rev. G. H. Glasse. New York, n.d. 12° . .   1107.9
HALL, M. Prone and postural respiration in drowning. London, 1857. 12° 157.5
HALL, M. Mrs. Queens before the conquest. London, 1854. 2v. 12° 594.12
HALL, Rev. R. Miscellaneous works and remains. London, 1849. p.8° 818.1

Contents. — Memoir, by Dr. Gregory; Observations on Hall as a preacher, by J. Foster; Christianity consistent with a love of freedom; An apology for the freedom of the press; Review of the same; Mr. Hall's reply; Modern infidelity considered; Reflections on war; The sentiments proper to the present crisis; Advantages of knowledge to the lower classes; A sermon on the death of Her Royal Highness the Princess Charlotte of Wales; Reviews; General index.

HALL, Rev. R. Works. [Ed.] with memoir and critical estimate of his character, [by] O. Gregory. London, 1851. 6v. 16° 1089.16

Contents. — Vol. I. Memoir by Dr. Gregory; Estimate of his character and writings, by J. Foster; Letters; Circular letters. II. Sermons and charges; Address to E. Carey, missionary to India; Articles from the Eclectic Review. III. On terms of communion; Difference between Christian baptism and baptism of John. IV. Tracts, political and miscellaneous; Miscellaneous pieces. V. Sermons; Notes of sermons. VI. Sermons; Fragments; Miscellaneous pieces; Index.

HALL, Mrs. S. C. See Hall, Mrs. A. M.
HALL, S. R. Instructor's manual. Revised edition. Boston, 1852. 12° 120.24
— and Baker, A. R. School history of the U. S. Boston, 1836. 12° 309.10
HALL, T. G. Outlines of astronomy. 14th edition. London, 1854. 16° 149.40
HALL, W. W. Consumption. N. York, 1857. 12°   157.12
HALLAM, H. Constitutional history of England. Henry VII. to George II. From 5th Lond. ed. New York, 1853. 8° 975.1
— Europe during the middle ages. From the 6th London ed. New York, 1841. 8° . . .   945.1
— Literary essays and characters. Lond., 1852. 16°   808.19
— Literature of Europe in the XV., XVI. and XVII. centuries. N. York, 1848-51. 2v. 8°   402.4
HALLECK, F. G. Alnwick castle, with other poems. New York, 1845. 12° 345.10
— Fanny, with other poems. N. York, 1839. 12°   338.23
— Selections from the British poets. N. York, n.d. 2v. 18° 820.25
HALLEUR, G. C. H. Art of photography, transl. by S. L. Strauss. London, 1854. 16° 829.11
HALLIDAY, Sir A. The West Indies. London, 1837. 12° 635.19
HALLIG, The: or, the sheepfold in the waters. Biernatzki, J. C. 884.1
HALLIWELL, J. O. Fairy mythology of A midsummer night's dream. London, 1845. 8° .   342.26
— Letters of the kings of England. London, 1848. 2v. 12° 978.3
— Ludus Coventriae. London, 1841. 8° . . .   342.3
— Marriage of wit and wisdom, and illustrations of the early English drama. Lond., 1846. 8°   342.30
HALLOCK, J., Life of. Yale, C. 1107.2
HALLOCK, W. A. Life and labors of J. Edwards. New York, [1855.] 12° 535.10
— Memoir of Harlan Page. N. Y., n.d. 16° . .   1109.15
HALLS, J. J. Life and correspondence of H. Salt. London, 1834. 2v. 8° 563.7
HALLUCINATIONS. See Brierre de Boismont.
HALPIN, N. J. Oberon's vision, illustrated by a comparison with Lylie's Endymion. London, 1843. 8° 342.15
HALSEY, Le R. J. Literary attractions of the Bible. New York, 1858. 12° 1087.11
HALSTED, C. A. Richard III. as duke of Gloucester and king. London, 1844. 2v. 8° 552.5
HAMILTON, A. Works: (exclusive of the Federalist,) civil and military. Edited by J. C. Hamilton. New York, 1851. 7v. 8° 285.1

Contents. — Vol. I. Correspondence (æt. 12–32). II. Political and other papers (æt. 17–32) anterior to the organization of the Fed. gov., including Publius, Continentalist, Phocion, eulogium on Gen. Greene, speeches and papers on the constitution of U. S. III. Reports on public credit, (1790,) manufactures, (1791,) commerce, finance, &c., including a national bank, mint, etc., (æt. 33–37.) IV. Cabinet papers, (May, 1789–Aug., 1794.) V. Cabinet papers, (1791–95); Speech on commercial relations; Acts; Remarks on the treaty with Gt. Brit., (1795) ; Military papers, (1798–1800) ; Correspondence, (æt. 32–38.) VI. Correspondence, (æt. 38–46, and appendix) Letters of H. G.; Address to public creditors; Funding system; Anti-defamer. VII. Political essays, (æt. 35–47) including papers under various signatures; Drafts of papers for Washington; Public conduct of J. Adams; Examination of Jefferson's message, (1801) ; Law briefs; Lansing or Burr.

HAMILTON, A. Official and other papers. v.I.
New York, 1842. 8° 285.2
— History of the United States as traced in the
writings of. Hamilton, J. C. 304.2
— Life of. Renwick, J. 820.33
— Life and times of. Smucker, S. M. 517.9
— Sketch of. Baldwin, J. G. 518.7
HAMILTON, Anthony. Count Grammont's memoirs
of the court of Charles II. Lond., 1853. p.8°. 857.1
— Fairy tales and romances. Transl. London,
1849. p.8° 857.2
— Le belier; fleur d'épine; les quatre facardins.
"Cabinet des Fées." v.XX. 1077.1
HAMILTON, Mrs. E. Memoir of. Benger, E. O. . 509.6
— Cottagers of Glenburnie: a tale. New York,
1808. 18° 789.13
HAMILTON, James. Lectures on Ecclesiastes. New
York, 1853. 16° 1088.31
— Life in earnest. New York, 1854. 18° . . . 1109.26–28
— Memoirs of Lady Colquhoun. N. Y., 1853. 12°. 509.8
HAMILTON, J. Wanderings in North Africa.
London, 1856. 8° 697.2
HAMILTON, J. C. History of the United States,
traced in writings of A. Hamilton and con-
temporaries. New York, 1857–58. 2v. 8°. . 304.2
HAMILTON, R. British fishes. Jardine, W. v.XXV.,
XXVI. and XXXVI. of 179.1
HAMILTON, S. National flag of the United States.
Philadelphia, 1852. 12° 216.7
HAMILTON, T. Annals of the Peninsular cam-
paigns, 1808–14. Philad., 1831. 3v. 12° . 1009.4
— Cyril Thornton: a novel. New ed. New
York, 1831. 2v. 12° 777.14
— Men and manners in America. Phil., 1833. 8°. 626.1
HAMILTON, Sir W. Discussions on philosophy
and literature, education, and university re-
form. New York, 1853. 8° 872.1
— Philosophy. Ed. by O. W. Wight. N. York,
1853. 8° 122.12
HAMILTON, W. D. Outlines of the history of
England. London, 1852–3. 2v. in 1. 16°. . 829.36
— Outlines of the history of Greece. London,
1853–54. 2v. 16° 829.38
HAMILTON, W. G. Parliamentary logic, [and]
two speeches, with appendix, on the corn
laws, by S. Johnson. London, 1808. 12°. 125.22
HAMILTON, W. J. Researches in Asia Minor,
Pontus, and Armenia. London, 1842. 2v. 8°. 694.14
HAMILTON, W. R. Lectures on quaternions.
Dublin, 1853. 8° 147.7
HAMLET, Play of, in a new garb. Rice, G. E. . . 356.22
HAMLEY, E. B. Lady Lee's widowhood. New
York, 1853. 8° 802.37–38
— Story of the campaign in South Russia. Bos-
ton, 1855. 12° 928.7–8
HAMLIN, H. A. L. Memoirs of. Lawrence, M. W. 538.6–8
HAMMER-PURGSTALL, J. v. History of the As-
sassins. Transl. by O. C. Wood. London.
1840. 12° 937.4
HAMMOND, C. Light from the spirit world.
Rochester, N. Y., 1852. 16° 124.25
HAMMOND, J. D. Life and times of Silas Wright.
Syracuse, 1848. 8° 523.9
— History of the political parties of the State of
New York. Albany, 1842. 2v. 8° 234.13
HAMMOND, M. M. Memoir of. N. York, 1858. 12°. 575.17
HAMMOND, S. H. Hills, lakes, and forest streams:
or Chateaugay woods. N. Y., 1854. 12°. . 636.2
— Wild Northern scenes. New York, 1857. 12°. 174.9
HAMOND, —. Life of Card. Cheverus. Transl. by
R. M. Walsh. Philadelphia, 1839. 12°. . 617.17
— - Same. Transl. by E. Stewart. Boston,
1839. 12° 617.18
HAMPDEN, J., Memorials of. Grenville, G. N. T.,
Lord Nugent. 562.7
HAN d'Islande. Hugo, V. 1066.18
HAND, The, but not the heart. Arthur, T. S. . . 416.17
HAND, The, its mechanism, etc. Bell, Sir C. . . . 139.3
HANDBOOK of domestic medicine. Lon., 1855. p.8°. 826.14
HANDEL, G. F., Life of. Schœlcher, V. 545.2

HANDS not hearts: a novel. Wilkinson, J. W. . . 802.9
HANN, J. Examples on integral calculus. Lon-
don, 1850. 16° 829.33
— Plane trigonometry. 2d ed. London, 1854. 16°. 829.23
— Spherical trigonometry. London, 1849. 16°. 829.24
— Treatise on analytic geometry. Lon., 1850. 16°. 829.22
HANNA, W. Life and writings of T. Chalmers.
New York, 1851–52. 4v. 12° 576.7
— - Same. Abridged and edited by J. C. Mof-
fat. Cincinnati, 1853. 12° 576.1
HANNIBAL, History of. Abbott, J. 549.14
HANNO, Voyages of, round the coast of Africa.
See Phenix, The 898.8
HANNON, J. Traité élémentaire de zoologie.
Bruxelles, n.d. 12° 1065.20
HANNON, J. D. Flore belge. Bruxelles, n.d.
3v. 12° 1075.26
HANNOVER, A. Construction and use of the mic-
roscope. Ed. by J. Goodsir. Edinb., 1853. 8° 145.19
HANOVER, Mass., History of. Barry, J. S. 224.13
HANS of Iceland: or the demon dwarf. Hugo, V. 498.14
HANSON, J. H. The lost prince: Ident. of Louis
XVII. and Rev. E. Williams. N. Y., 1854. 12° 615.7
HAPPINESS in its relations to work and knowl-
edge. Forbes, J. 1089.30
HAPPINESS, Treatise concerning. Harris, J. 209.4
HAPPY, The art of being. Droz, J. 139.5
HARBAUGH, H. Life of Rev. M. Schlatter, with
his travels and labors. Phila., 1857. 12°. . 534.18
— The true glory of woman. Phila., 1858. 12°. 896.8
HARD times: a tale. Dickens, C. 481.17–22
HARDENBERG, F. v. Henry of Ofterdingen. Ro-
mance. Cambridge, 1842. 12° 708.13
HARDWICKE, R. Annual biography for 1856. [Ed.]
by E. Walford. London, 1856. 16° 548.27
HARDY, F. Memoirs of the life of Jas. Caulfield,
Earl of Charlemont. 2d ed. London, 1812.
2v. 8° 563.6
HARE, J. C. and A. W. Guesses at truth. 1st ser.
4th ed. London, 1851. 16° 139.10
— - Same. 2d series. 2d ed. London, 1848. 16° 139.11
HARE, J. C. Mission of the comforter. From 2d
London edition, Boston, 1854. 12° 1106.7
— Memoir of J. Sterling 886.1
HARE, J. M. Memoir of J. Bunyan 869.9
HARFORD, J. Life of Michael Angelo Buonarroti.
London, 1857. 2v. 8° 543.2
HARGRAVE, E. H. Australia and its gold fields.
London, 1855. 12° 938.7
HÄRING, W. [W. Alexis, pseud.] Cabanis. [Vater-
länd. Roman.] Berlin, 1856. 6v. in 3. 16° 1024.4
　Contents.—I. Die Knabenwelt; Der Deserteur. II.
Der Marquis; Die Vaterstadt. III. Wintermährchen;
Der Friede.
— Der falsche Woldemar. Vaterl. Roman. Ber-
lin, 1842. 3v. in 1. 16° 1024.7
— - Same. Berlin, 1842. 3v. 16° 1024.8
— Der Roland von Berlin. Berlin, 1840. 3v.in 1. 16° 1024.6
— Der Würwolf. Vaterl. Roman. Berlin, 1848.
3v. 16° 1024.9
　Contents.—II. Hake von Stülpe. II. Die Sandfluth
und der Tempelhofsche Berg. III. Kurfürstin Elisa-
beth und die weisse Frau.
— Dorothe. Roman. Berlin, 1856. 3v. 16°. . 1024.3
— Reise-Pitaval. Leipzig, 1856. 16° 1029.10
— Ruhe ist die erste Bürgerpflicht. Vaterl. Ro-
man. Berlin, 1852. 5v. 16° 1024.5
HARLAND, M. Pseud. See Hawes, V.
HARMONY, Treatise on. Catel, C. S. 204.1
HAROLD and Rosaline: a poem. Perry, A. 369.5
HAROLD, the last of the Saxon kings. [Novel.]
Lytton, E. B. 466.4–5
HARP, The, of Sylva: a poem. Jones, E. C. . . . 338.22
HARPER's classical library. New York. 37v. 18°. 830.8–24
1, 2. Xenophon. Transl. by E. Spelman. 2v. 830.8
3, 4. Demosthenes. Orations. Translated
by T. Leland. 2v. 830.9
5. Sallust, C. C. Translated by W. Rose . . 830.10
6, 7. Cæsar, C. J. Translated by W. Duncan. 2v 830.11

HARPER's classical library, *continued.*

8, 9, 10. Cicero, M. T. Orations, translated by Duncan; Offices by Cockman, and the Cato and Laelius by Melmoth. 3v. 830.12
11, 12. Virgil. The Eclogues, Georgics and Æneid. Translated. 2v. 830.13
14. Sophocles. Translated by T. Francklin. . 830.14
15, 16, 17. Euripides. Translated by Rev. R. Potter. 3v. 830.15
18, 19. Horace. Transl. by Philip Francis. 2v. 830.16
20, 21. Ovid. Translated by Dryden, Pope, Congreve, Addison, etc. 2v. 830.17
22, 23. Thucydides. Peloponnesian war. Tr. by W. Smith. 2v. 830.18
24–28. Livy. Translated by G. Baker. 5v. . 830.19
29–31. Herodotus. Transl. by W. Beloe. 3v. 830.20
32–34. Homer. Transl. by Alex. Pope. 3v. . 830.21
35. Juvenal and Persius. Translated by C. Badham 830.22
36. Pindar and Anacreon. Translated 830.23
37. Cicero on the orator. Translated by W. Guthrie 830.24

HARPER's family library. New York. 187v. 18°
1–3. Milman, H. H. History of the Jews. 3v. 810.1
4, 5. Lockhart, J G Life of Napoleon. 2v. 810.2–3
6. Southey, R. Life of Lord Nelson . . . 810.4–7
7. Williams, J. Alexander the Great 810.8
8, 74. [Rennie, J. and Westwood, J. O.] Nat. history of insects. 2v. 810.9
9. Galt, J. Life of Lord Byron 810.10–11
10. Bush, G. Life of Mohammed 810.12
11. Scott, Sir W. Demonology, etc. 810.13
12, 13. Gleig, Rev. G. R. History of the Bible. 2v. 810.14
14. Murray, H. and others. Polar seas and regions 810.15
15. Croly, G. Life of George IV 810.16–17
16. Murray, H. and others. Discov. in Africa. 810.18
17–19, 66, 67. Cunningham, A. British painters and sculptors. 5v. 810.19
20. James, G. P. R. History of chivalry. . 810.20
21, 22. Bell, H. G. Mary Queen of Scots. 2v. 810.21–28
23. Russell, M. Egypt. 810.29
24. Fletcher, J. History of Poland 810.30
25. Smith, H. Festivals, games, etc. 810.31
26. Brewster, D. Life of Newton 810.32
27. Russell, M. History of Palestine . . . 810.33
28. Memes, J. S. Empress Josephine . . . 810.34–38
29. Court and camp of Bonaparte 810.39–40
30. Lives and voyages of Drake, Cavendish and Dampier 810.41
31. Barrow, Sir J. Pitcairn's island and the mutiny of the Bounty 810.42
32, 72, 84. Turner, S. Sacred history of the world. 3v. 810.43
33, 34. Jameson, Mrs. A. Celebrated female sovereigns. 2v. 810.44
35, 36. Lander, R. and J. Expedition to the Niger. 2v. 810.45
37. Abercrombie, J. Intellectual powers, etc. 810.46
38–40. St. John, J. A. Lives of celebrated travellers. 3v. 810.47
41, 42. Ellis, G. J. W. Agar, *Lord Dover.* Life of Frederick the Great. 2v. 810.48
43, 44. Smedley, Rev. E. Venetian history. 2v. 810.49
45, 46. Thatcher, B. B. Lives of the Indians. 2v. 810.50
47–49. Murray, H. British India. 3v. . . . 810.51
51, 52. Taylor, W. C. History of Ireland. 2v. 810.52
53. Tytler, P. F. Discovery in N. America . 810.53
54. Macgillivray, W. Humboldt's travels . . 810.54
55, 56. Euler, L. Natural philosophy. 2v. . 810.55
57. Mudie, R. Guide to the observation of nature 810.56
58. Abercrombie, J. The moral feelings . . . 810.57
59. Dick, T. Improvement of society 810.58–59
60. James, G. P. R. Charlemagne 810.60
61. Russell, M. Nubia and Abyssinia . . . 810.61
62, 63. — Life of Cromwell. 2v. 810.62–63

HARPER's family library, *continued.*

64. Montgomery, J. Lectures on literature, poetry, etc. 810.64–65
65 Barrow, Sir J. Peter the Great . . . 810.66
68, 69. Crichton, A. History of Arabia. 2v. 810.67
70. Fraser, J. B. Persia 810.68
71. Combe, A. Principles of physiology . . . 810.69
73. Russell, M. The Barbary states 810.70
75, 76. Paulding, J. K. Life of Washington. 2v. 810.71
77. Ticknor, C. Philosophy of living 810.72
78. Higgins, W. M. The earth 810.73
79. Sforzosi, L. History of Italy 810.74
80, 81. Davis, Sir J. F. The Chinese. 2v. . . 810.75
82. Circumnavigation of the globe 810.76
83. Dick, T. Celestial scenery 810.77
85. Griscom, J. H. Animal mechanism . . . 810.78
86–91. Tytler, A. F. Universal history. 6v. 820.1
92, 93. Franklin, B. Life and writings. 2v. 820.2
94, 95. Craik, G. L. Pursuit of knowledge under difficulties. 2v. 820.3
96, 97. Paley, W. Natural theology. 2v. . . 820.4
98. Rennie, J. Natural history of birds . . . 820.5
99. Dick, T. The sidereal heavens 820.6
100. Upham, T. C. Disordered mental action. 820.7
101, 102. Murray, H. British America. 2v. . . 820.8
103. Lossing, B. J. History of the fine arts . 820.9
104. Natural history of quadrupeds 820.10
105. Life and travels of Mungo Park 820.11
106. Dana, R. H. jr. Two years before the mast 820.12–21
107, 108. Parry, Sir W. E. Three voyages. 2v. 820.22
109, 110. Johnson, S. Life and writings. 2v. 820.23
111. Bryant, W. C. Selec. from Amer. poets. 820.24
112, 113. Halleck, F. G. Selections from the British poets. 2v. 820.25
114–118. Keightley, T. History of England. 5v. 820.26
119, 120. Hale, S. Hist. of the U. States. 2v. . 820.27
121, 122. Goldsmith, O. Life, and selections from his writings, by W. Irving. 2v. . . . 820.28
123, 124. Distinguished men of mod. times. 2v. 820.29
125. Renwick, J. Life of Dewitt Clinton . . 820.30
126, 127. Mackenzie, A. S. Life of Com. O. H. Perry. 2v. 820.31
128. Head, Sir F. B. Life of Bruce, the travel'r. 820.32
129. Renwick, H. B. and J. Lives of John Jay and Alexander Hamilton 820.33
130. Brewster, Sir D. Lives of Galileo, Tycho Brahe, and Kepler 820.34
131. Iceland, Greenland, and the Faroe islands. 820.35
132. Manners of the Japanese 820.36
133. Dwight, T. jr. History of Connecticut . 820.37
134, 135. Bucke, C. Ruins of ancient cities. 2v. 820.38
136, 137. Crichton, A. and Wheaton, H. Denmark, Sweden, and Norway. 2v. 820.39
138. Camp, G. S. Democracy 820.40
139. Lanman, J. H. History of Michigan . . . 820.41
140. Fenelon, F. de S. de la M. Lives of ancient philosophers 820.42
141, 142. Ségur, P. P. Cte de. Napoleon's expedition to Russia. 2v. 820.43–44
143, 144. Epitome of the hist. of philosophy. 2v. 820.45
145. Bucke, C. Beauties, etc., of nature . . . 820.46
146. Lieber, F. On property and labour 820.47
147. White, G. Nat. history of Selborne . . . 820.48
148. Wrangell, F. v. Exped. to the Polar Sea. 820.49
149, 150. Hazen, E. Popular technology. 2v. 820.50
151–153. Spalding, W. Italy and the Italian islands. 3v. 820.51
154, 155. Allen, P. Expedition of Lewis and Clarke. 2v. 820.52
156. Smith, H. I. Education 820.53
157. Fraser, J. B. Mesopotamia and Assyria. 820.54
158. Russell, M. Polynesia 820.55
159. Davenport, R. A. Perilous adventures . . 820.56
160. Duer, W. A. Constitutional jurisprudence of the United States 820.57
161–163. Belknap, J. American biography. 3v. 820.58
164. Natural history. The elephant 820.59
165. Potter, A. Handbook for readers and students 820.60

HARPER's family library, *continued*.
166. Graves, Mrs. A. J. Woman in America .   820.61
167, 168. Stone, W. L. Border wars of the
    American revolution. 2v. 820.62
169. Lankester, Dr. E. Vegetable substances
    used for the food of man. 820.63
170. Michelet, J. Modern history 820.64
171. Bacon, F., *Lord*. Essays. Locke, J., on
    the understanding 820.65
172. Kippis, A. Voyages round the world, by
    Cook, with a life. 820.66
173. Polo, M. Travels 820.67
174, 175. American adventure, etc. 2v. . . .   820.68
176. Bunner, E. History of Louisiana . . .   820.69
177. Florian, J. P. C. de. The Moors in Spain.   820.70
178. Lee, C. A. Elements of geology 820.71
179. Brougham, H. and others. Discourses on
    literature and science 820.72
180. Moseley, H. Mechanics 830.1
181, 182. Selections from the Spectator. 2v. .   830.2
183. Potter, A. Political economy 830.3
184. Maury, J. S., *Card*. On eloquence 830.4
185. Robertson, W. History of America, abr.   830.5
186. - Charles V., abridged 830.6
187. Ferguson, A. Hist. of the Rom. repub. ab.   830.7
HARPER's new monthly magazine. Vol. I-XV.,
    June, 1850, to Nov., 1857. New York. 8°. .   880.2
HARPER's story books. *See* Abbott, J.
HARPER establishment, The. Abbott, J. . v.IV. of 739.1
HARRINGTON : [a tale.] Edgeworth, M. v.IX. of 467.1-3
HARRIS, C. A. Dental surgery. 5th ed. Phila-
    delphia, 1853. 8° 151.13
HARRIS, E. Progress of improvement in venti-
    lation. Reid, D. B. 207.1
HARRIS, Jas. Three treatises ; 1st. Art ; 2d. Music,
    painting, and poetry ; 3d. Happiness. Lon-
    don, 1744. 8° 209.4
*HARRIS, John. Great commission, with an intro-
    ductory essay by W. R. Williams. Boston,
    1842. 12° 1088.1
— Great teacher, with introductory essay by H.
    Humphrey. 2d ed. Amherst, 1836. 12°. .   1088.2
— Mammon. New York, n.d. 12° 1109.13
— Man primeval: a contribution to theological
    science. Boston, 1852. 12° 1096.14
HARRIS, T. Life and services of Com. Bainbridge.
    Philadelphia, 1837. 8° 527.1
HARRIS, T. M. Biographical memorials of James
    Oglethorpe. Boston, 1841. 8° 513.10
— Journal of a tour into the territory N. W.
    of the Alleghany mts. in 1803. Bost., 1805. 8°   639.13
HARRIS, T. W. Insects of New England injurious
    to vegetation. 2d ed. Boston, 1852. 8° . .   165.1
HARRIS, W. Life of James I. 2d ed. London,
    1772. 8° 552.9
HARRIS, W. S. Rudimentary electricity. 3d ed.
    London, 1853. 16° 819.7
— Rudiment'y magnetism. Lon., 1850-52. 2v. 16°.   819.8
HARRIS, W. T. Epitaphs from the old burying
    ground in Cambridge. Cambridge, 1845. 12°.   228.2
HARRISON, T. Biography of 309.7
HARRISON, W. H. Life of. 3d ed. Phila, 1840. 18°.   229.6
— Life of. Philadelphia, 1840. 8° 517.4
— Life and services of. Montgomery 517.4
— Memoir of. Hall, J. 519.1
HARRISON almanac, 1841. New York. 8° 517.4
HARRISON melodies. Boston, 1840. 18° 229.6
HART, A. M. History of the valley of the Missis-
    sippi. Cincinnati, 1853. 12° 237.12
HART, J. S. Essay on Edmund Spenser. With
    an exposition of The fairy queen. N. York,
    1847. 8° 324.1
HARTE, W. History of Gustavus Adolphus. 3d
    ed. London, 1807. 2v. 8° 546.3
HARTFORD convention, Hist. of the. Dwight, T.   305.4
HARTIG, E. Genesis of the Austrian revolution,
    1848 . . . .   828.3
HARVARD college, History of. Eliot, S. A. . .   297.21
HARVARD university, History of. Quincy, J. . .   294.1
HARVEY, T. West Indies in 1837. Sturge, J. . .   635.8

HARVEY, W. H. The seaside book. Natural his-
    tory of the British coast. 3d ed. London,
    1854. 12° 178.26
HARZBILDER, Sitten u. Gebräuche. Pröhle, H. .   1029.14
HASE, H. Public and private life of the ancient
    Greeks. Translated. London, 1836. 16°.   959.13
HASHEESH eater. Ludlow, F. 884.10
HASKINS, G. F. Travels in England, France,
    Italy and Ireland. Boston, 1856. 12° . . .   658.14
HASKOLL, W. D. Assistant engineer's railway
    guide. London, 1846-48. 2v. in 1. 8° . . .   195.18
HASSALL, A. H. Adulterations in food and medi-
    cine. London, 1857. 12° 156.12
— Food and its adulterations. London, 1855. 8°   155.19
HASSELT, A. van. Histoire des Belges. Brux-
    elles, n.d. 2v. 12° 1075.17
— Les Belges aux Croisades. Bruxelles, n.d.
    2v. 12° 1075.21
HASTINGS, W. Memoirs of. Gleig, G. R. 572.1
— Essay on. Macaulay, T. B. 409.19
HASWELL, C. H. Mechanics' tables. New York,
    1856. 12° 198.6
— Mensuration and practical geometry. New
    York, 1858. 12° 147.25
HATTON, Sir C. Life and times of. Nicolas, Sir
    N. H. 573.3
HAUENSCHILD, R. G. S. v. Aus der Junkerwelt.
    Hamburg, 1850-51. 2v. 12° 1037.7
— Nach der Natur. 2te Aufl. Hamburg, 1851.
    3v. 16°. 1037.6

     Contents. — Vol. I. In Tyrol. II. In Ober-Schlesien.
     III. In Baden.

HAUFF, W. Sämmtliche Werke. 5te gesammt
    Ausg. Stuttgart, 1853. 5v. 16° 1019.4

     Contents. — Vol. I. Hauff's Leben; Gedichte; Nov-
     ellen, Vertrauliches Schreiben an Spetlich ; Jud
     Süss; Die Bettlerin vom Pont des Arts; Die Sängerin;
     Die letzten Ritter von Marienburg. II. Mittheilungen
     aus den Memoiren des Satan; Das Bild des Kaisers.
     III. Othello; Der Mann im Monde; Controverspredigt
     über H. Clauren und den Mann im Mond: Phan'a-
     sien im Bremer Rathskeller. IV. Mährchen; Skizzen.
     V. Lichtenstein, romantische Sage.

HAUGHTON, S. Manual of optics. *See* Galbraith, I.   149.33
HAUGHTON, W. Patient Grissil : a comedy. *See*
    Dekker, T. 342.6
HAUNTED man, The, and the ghost's bargain.
    Dickens, C. 471.16
HAUPT, H. General theory of bridge construc-
    tion. New York, 1851. 8° 195.1
HAURÉAU, B. Charlemagne et sa cour. Paris,
    1854. 12° 1078.40
— François 1er et sa cour. Paris, 1855. 12° .   1078.20
HAUSSEZ, *Bar.* L. d'. Great Britain in 1833.
    American ed. Philadelphia, 1833. 12° . . .   658.16
HAVELOCK, Sir H. Brock, W. Sketch of 578.12
— Hunt, G. H. Campaign in Persia 938.9
HAVEN, A. B. The coopers : or getting under way.
    New York, 1858. 12° 485.6-11
HAVEN, J. Mental philosophy. Boston, 1857. 8°   124.8
HAVEN, N. A. Remains, with a memoir by Geo.
    Ticknor, 1827. 8° 524.15
HAVERHILL, Mass., History of. Mirick, B. L. . .   227.17
HAWAII, Tour through. Ellis, W. 705.5
HAWAIIAN islands, History of the. Jarves, J. J.   934.6
HAWAIIAN people, Progress of Christianity among
    the. Bingham, H. 934.4
     See also : Sandwich Islands.
HAWES, V. Alone. By Marion Harland. 14th
    ed. Richmond, 1855. 12° 805.23-24
— - Same. New York, 1856. 12° 805.25
— The hidden path. New York, 1855. 12° . . .   805.26
— Moss side. New York, 1857. 12° 805.18-22
HAWKER, P. Instructions to young sportsmen.
    [With] Hunting of N. Am., by W. T. Por-
    ter. 2d Am. ed. Philadelphia, 1853. 8° . .   172.3
HAWKESWORTH, J. The adventurer. London,
    n.d. 2v. 18° 850.26
— Almoran and Hamet: an oriental tale. Lond.,
    1810. 16° . . . . v. XXVI. of 778.1

HAWKS, F. L. Expedition of an American squadron to the China seas and Japan, 1852–54. New York, 1856. 8° 701.2–5
— Monuments of Egypt. 2d ed., revised and enlarged. New York, 1850. 8° 684.2
HAWKSTONE: a tale. Sewell, W. 428.3
HAWTHORNE, N. Blithedale romance. Boston, 1852. 12° 457.11–13
— House of the seven gables. Boston, 1851. 12° 457.3–5
— Life of Franklin Pierce. Boston, 1852. 12° .517.27–28
— Mosses from an old manse. N. York, 1846. 12° 457.2
— - Same. New ed., rev. Bost., 1854. 2v. 16° 457.1
— Scarlet letter: a romance. Boston, 1853. 12° 457.6–9
— Tanglewood tales, for girls and boys. Boston, 1853. 16° 457.10
— Twice-told tales. New ed. Bost., 1851. 2v. 16° 457.14
— Wonder book for girls and boys. Boston, 1853. 16° 737.17
HAXTHAUSEN, Baron von. Russian empire. London, 1856. 2v. 8° 674.1
HAY, D. R. First principles of symmetrical beauty. Edinburgh, 1846. 12° 208.20
— Laws of harmonious colouring. 5th ed. London, 1844. 8° 208.6
HAY, J. H. D. Western Barbary, its wild tribes and savage animals. London, 1844. 12° . . 889.20
HAYDEN, W. B. On modern spiritualism. Boston, 1855. 16° 125.25
HAYDN, J. Beyle, H. Vie de. 1067.18
— Carpani, G. Life of 545.20
HAYDON, B. R. Life. Ed. by Tom Taylor. New York, 1853. 2v. 12° 556.7–9
HAYES, E. The ballads of Ireland. London, 1855. 2v. 12° 355.5
— - Same. Boston, 1856. 2v. 12° 316.5
HAYGARTH, H. W. Bush life in Australia. London, 1848. 12° 889.21
HAYLEY, W. Life of Milton. Dublin, 1797. 8°. 583.8
HAYWARD, C. jr. Life of Sebastian Cabot . v.II. of 518.5
— - Same. Lives of eminent individuals.v.IX. of 529.1
HAYWARD, J. Gazetteer of Massachusetts. Boston, 1849. 12° 229.2
— Gazetteer of N. Hampshire. Boston, 1849. 12° 229.1
— Gazetteer of Vermont. Boston, 1849. 12° . 229.3
HAZEN, E. Popular technology. N. York, 1850. 2v. 18° 820.50
HAZLITT, W. Miscellaneous works. Philadelphia, 1848. 5v. 12° 867.2

Contents.— Vols. I.–II. Table talk. III. Lectures on the dramatic literature of the age of Elizabeth; Characters of Shakspeare's plays. IV. Lectures on the English comic writers: Lectures on the English poets. V. The spirit of the age, or contemporary portraits.

— Characters of Shakspeare's plays. New York, 1845. 12° 356.23
— Criticisms on art, and sketches of the picture-galleries of England. London, 1843. 16° . 207.19
— Dramatic literature of the age of Elizabeth. New York, 1845. 8° 356.24
— Life of Napoleon Buonaparte. 2d ed. London, 1852. 4v. 12° 605.3
— - Same. Philadelphia, 1848. 3v. 12° . . . 605.4
— Men and manners. London, 1852. 16° . . . 886.11
— The round table. Edited by his son. 3d ed. London, 1841. 16° 886.10
— Select poets of Great Britain, [with] critical notices. London, 1825. 8° 312.9
— Spirit of the age. 1st Am. ed. N. Y., 1846. 12° 888.17
— Table talk. New York, 1845–46. 2v. in 1. sq.16° 877.14
— Winterslow: essays written there. London, 1850. 16° 878.26
HAZLITT, W. C. Origin and rise of the republic of Venice. London, 1858. 2v. 8° 915.2
HEAD, Sir E. Spanish and French schools of painting. London, 1848. 12° 208.21
HEAD, Sir F. B. Bubbles from the Brunnen of Nassau. 2d ed. London, 1834. 12° 667.18
— - Same. New York, 1845. 12° 667.19
— Descriptive essays contributed to the Quarterly Review. London, 1857. 2v. 12° 875.1

HEAD, Sir F. B. The emigrant. N. Y., 1847. 12° 489.14
— - Same. 6th ed. London, 1852. 12° 489.15
— Faggot of French sticks: or, Paris in 1851. New York, 1852. 2v. in 1. 12° 654.18
— Life and adventures of Bruce the African traveller. From last Lond. ed. New York, n.d. 18° 820.32
— Rough notes taken during some journeys across the Pampas, and among the Andes. London, 1846. 12° 889.22
— Stokers and pokers: or, the Lond. and North West Railway. London, 1849. 12° 889.23
HEAD of the family. A novel. Muloch, D. M. v.II.of 762.1–2
HEADLEY, J. T. The Adirondack: or, life in the woods. New York, 1851. 12° 636.29
— The Alps and the Rhine. New and revised ed. New York, 1851. 12° 676.18
— Imperial guard of Napoleon. N. Y., 1851. 12° 1008.5
— Letters from Italy. New and revised edition. New York, 1851. 12° 676.18
— Life of George Washington. New York, 1856. 8° 515.1
— Napoleon and his marshals. 22d ed. New York, 1855. 2v. 12° 605.1–2
— Second war with England. N. Y., 1853. 12° . 217.2–3
— Washington and his generals. New York, 1851–55. 2v. 12° 516.1–5
HEADLEY, P. C. Life of Josephine. New York, 1857. 12° 606.7
— Life of Lafayette. Auburn, 1851. 12° 617.3
HEADSMAN, The: a tale. Cooper, J. F. 760.20–24
HEALTH. Beecher, C. E. Letters on 158.11
— Cooke, W. Mind in relation to 137.4
— Hosking, W. Regulation of buildings as a means of 207.13
— Johnson, J. The pursuit of 153.4
— Jones, W. H. for the million 157.33
— Ridge, B. H. and disease 157.35
— Scoffern, J. The science of 157.9
— Smith, S. Philosophy of 850.15
— Solomon, S. A guide to 158.8
— Sovet. Hygiène publ. et priv. 1065.53
— Sunderland, L. Book of 157.30
— Tarbell, J. A. Sources of 158.10
— Warren, J. C. Preservation of 158.19
HEALTHY homes and how to make them. Bardwell, W. 203.7
HEARD, J. A. Life and times of Nathalia Borisovna, princess Dolgoroukov. London, 1857. 12° 546.14
HEART: a social novel. Tupper, M. F. 794.8
HEART-EXPERIENCE: or, the education of the emotions. Jarves, J. J. 766.10
HEART of Mid-Lothian. Scott, Sir W. 460.27–33
HEARTS and homes. Ellis, S. S. 804.8
HEARTSEASE: a novel. Yonge, C. M. 784.1–6
HEARTH-STONE, The. Thoughts upon home life. Osgood, S. 886.4–6
HEAT. Lardner, D. Treatise on 398.12
— Treatise on, by Mr. Ogg. Libr. Us. Kn. v.I. 365.14
HEATHER, J. F. Descriptive geometry, with shadows and perspective. London, 1851. 16° . . 829.8
— Treatise on mathematical instruments. 2d ed. with corrections. London, 1851. 12° . . . 199.21
— - Same. London, 1853. 16° 819.23
HEAVEN and its wonders. Swedenborg, E. von . 1084.11
HEAVEN opened. Alleine, R. 1107.5
HEAVENLY arcana. Swedenborg, E. von. 1084–6
HEAVENS. Nichol, J. P. Architecture of the . . 144.5
— Somerville, M. Mechanism of the 146.7
See also: Astronomy.
HEBER, A. Life of R. Heber, with selections from his private papers, and a history of the Cossaks. New York, 1830. 2v. 8° 574.4
HEBER, R. Journey . through India, 1824–26. London, 1844. 2v. 12° 889.24
— - Same. Philadelphia, 1829. 2v. 12° 708.20
— Poetical works. Philadelphia, 1841. 12° . . 358.16
— Life of. Heber, A. 574.4
HEBERT, L. Appendix to history of the steam engine. See Galloway, E. 195.17

HEBREW commonwealth, Hist. of the. Jahn, J. . 1085.8
HEBREW poetry, The spirit of. Herder, J. G. von. 1087.17
HEBREWS, ancient, Laws of the. Wines, E. C. . 1083.2
HEBREWS, Epistle to the. *See* Bible.
HEBRIDES, Journal of a tour to the. Boswell, J. . 646.2
HEDGE, F. H. Memoirs of S. M. F. D'Ossoli. . . 538.9-10
— Prose writers of Germany. 2d ed. Philadel-
phia, 1852. 8° 545.1
HEDGES and evergreens. Warder, J. A. 166.15
HEGEL, G. W. F. Philosophy of history. Transl.
by J. Sibree. London, 1857. p.8° 855.8
HEGNER, U. Gesammelte Schriften. Berlin,
1828-30. 5v. 8° 1014.4

Contents. — Vol. I. Auch ich war in Paris. II. Die
Molkenkur. III. Saly's Revolutionstage. IV. Briefe
aus dem bernerischen Oberlande; Tagebuch einer
Reise nach München; Berg-Land-und Seereise. V.
Aus dem Leben eines Geringen, Leben Johann
Rudolf Schellenbergs, Anton Graff's, Johann Kaspar
Kuster's, Johann Heinrich Troll's; Beitrag zur Be-
zeichnung des Künstlers, wie er seyn sollte; Gedichte;
Gedanken, Meynungen, Urtheile.

HEIDELBERG : a romance. James, G. P. R. . . . 463.1&8
HEIDENMAUER, The. Cooper, J. Fenimore . . 760.25-29
HEIMSKRINGLA, The : or, chronicle of the kings
of Norway. Snorro Sturleson 924.3
HEINE, H. Gedichte. Hamburg, 1851-4. 3v. 16°. 1016.5

Contents. — Vol. I. Buch der Lieder, 12te Aufl.
II. Neue Gedichte, 3te Aufl. III. Romanzero.

— Reisebilder. 4te und 5te Aufl. Hamburg,
1848-56. 4v. 16° 1037.8
HEIR of Redclyffe : a novel. Yonge, C. M. . . . 786.1-6
HEIR of Wast-Wayland : a tale. Howitt, M. . . . 459.8-9
HEIRESS, The : a novel. Pickering, E. 805.3
HEIRESS of Bruges, The. Grattan, T. C. 798.8
HELDENBUCH, Neues. Sporschil, J. 1016.2
HELEN : a tale. Edgeworth, M. . . . . v.X. of 467.1-3
HELFENSTEIN, E. Hugo : a legend of Rockland
lake. Ed. by E. O. Smith. 2d ed. N. York,
1851. 12° 449.4
HELIODORUS, Longus and Achilles Tatius. Tr.
by R. Smith. London, 1855. p.8° 844.10
HELOISE : a tale. Robinson, T. A. L. v. J. . . . 449.14-15
HELPS, A. Companions of my solitude. Repr.
from Eng. ed. Boston, 1852. 16° 909.4
— Friends in council : a series of readings, and
discourse thereon. Boston, 1849. 12° . . . 878.4
— Fruits of leisure, or essays in the intervals of
business. 2d Am. from 5th Eng. ed. New
York, 1852. 12° 888.22
— Spanish conquest in America, and its relation
to slavery. London, 1855-57. 3v. 8° . . . 254.2
HEMANS, F. D. Complete works, ed. by her sister.
From last English ed. New York, 1851.
2v. 16° 347.2-3

Contents. — Vol. I. England and Spain; Wallace's
invocation to Bruce; Abencerrage; Widow of Crescentius; Tales and historic scenes; Restoration of the
works of art to Italy; Modern Greece; Translations
from Camoens and others; Italian literature; The
sceptic; Tale of the secret tribunal; The last Constantine; Sebastian of Portugal; The siege of Valencia,
dram. poem; The forest sanctuary; Lays of many
lands; Miscellaneous pieces; Dartmoor; Welsh melodies; Hymns for childhood; De Chatillon, trag.; Miscellaneous pieces. II. The vespers of Palermo, trag.;
Songs of the Cid; Records of woman; Miscellaneous
poems ; Songs of the affections ; National lyrics;
Lyrics; Songs of Spain; Songs for summer hours;
Songs of captivity; The league of the Alps; Scenes
and hymns of life; Female characters of scripture;
Sonnets, devotional and memorial; Records of the
spring of 1834; Records of the autumn of 1834; De-
spondency and aspiration; Thoughts during sickness;
Critical remarks on the genius of Mrs. Hemans;
Juvenile poems.

— The forest sanctuary and other poems. Boston, 1827. 8° . . . . v.II. of 324.2
— League of the Alps, siege of Valencia, vespers of Palermo and other poems. Boston,
1826. 8° 324.2

HEMANS, F. D. Poems. Boston, 1827. 2v. 18° . 347.5

Contents. — Vol. I. The siege of Valencia, a dram.
poem; The vespers of Palermo, a trag.; The league
of the Alps, poem. II. The forest sanctuary ; Lays
of many lands ; Miscellaneous poems.

— Poems. A new collection. Boston, 1828.
2v. 18° 347.4

Contents. — Vol. I. Review of the forest sanctuary;
Restoration of the works of art to Italy; The Aben-
cerrage; The widow of Crescentius; Alaric in Italy;
Night scene in Genoa; Troubadour and Richard;
Translations from Camoens, etc. II. The sceptic;
Modern Greece; Dartmoor; Meeting of Wallace and
Bruce; The last Constantine; Greek songs; Songs of
the Cid; Belshazzar's Feast; Song of the battle of
Morgarten; The meeting of the bards; Hymns on the
works of nature.

— Records of woman, and other poems. Bos-
ton, 1828. 8° . . . . v.II. of 324.2
— Chorley, H. F. Memorials of 596.8
— Hughes, Mrs. Memoir of the life and writ-
ings of 596.9
HENDERSON, E. Residence in Iceland, 1814-15.
2d ed. Edinburgh, 1819. 8° 668.1
HENDERSON, W. Homœopathy fairly represented.
Reply to Simpson. 1st American ed. Phila-
delphia, 1854. 8° 157.2
HENDERSON, W. A. Modern domestic cookery.
Boston, 1844. 12° 189.2
HENFREY, A. Outlines of structural and physio-
logical botany. London, 1847. 12° 169.17
— Rudiments of botany. London, 1849. 18° . 169.32
HENLEY, Robert, *Lord.* Memoirs of the earl of
Northington. London, 1831. 12° 588.15
HENNINGSEN, C. F. Campaign with Zumalacar-
regui. London, 1836. 2v. 12° 917.3
HENRI, or the web and woof of life. Cambridge,
W. G. 489.7
HENRI II. of France. Anecdotes of the court of.
Benger, E. O. 594.2-8
HENRI III. et sa cour : drame historique. Du-
mas, A. 1078.6
HENRI IV. of France. Abbott, J. S. C. 559.13-17
— Bethune, M. de, *Duke of Sully.* Life and
reign of 609.3
— Costello, L. S. A legendary tour to the
country of 654.2
HENRI V., Jeunesse de, comédie. Duval, A. . . 1078.5
HENRIADE, La. Poëme. Voltaire, F. M. A. de . 1076.18
HENRIETTE d' Angleterre, duchesse d' Orléans.
Histoire de Mme. M. A. P. de la V. Lafa-
fayette 1078.17
HENRY, C. S. Epitome of the history of philos-
ophy. New York, n.d. 2v. 18° 820.45
HENRY, M. Memoir of Philip Henry. Abr. from
the ed. of J. B. Williams. N. York, n.d. 12° 1107.12
— Memoir of. Williams, J. B. 119.18
HENRY, Patrick, Life of, by A. H. Everett.
Sparks's American biography . . . . v.XI. of 529.1
— Life and character of. Wirt, W. 513.18
HENRY, Rev. Philip, Memoir of. Henry, Rev. M. 1107.12
HENRY of Huntingdon. Chronicle, comprising
the history of England from invasion of
Julius Cæsar to Henry II. [etc.] London,
1853. p.8° 856.3
HENRY IV. (the play.) Printed from contempo-
rary MS. Ed. by J. O. Halliwell. 342.27
HENRY V. Henry of Monmouth, or memoirs of
the life and character of. Tyler, J. E. . . . 552.4
HENRY VI. (the play.) First sketches of the
second and third parts. Shakespeare, W. . 342.14
HENRY VIII. Herbert, W. Memoirs of 558.1-3
— Turner, S. Reign of 955.3
— Tytler, P. F. Life of 558.4
HENRY De Pomeroy : A legend. Bray, A. E. . . 448.10
HENRY Esmond, Esq., History of. Thackeray,
W. M. 501.6-10
HENRY Masterton. James, G. P. R. 464.4
HENRY of Ofterdingen : a romance. Hardenberg,
F. F. v. 708.13

HENRY Smeaton: a Jacobite story. James, G.
P. R. 463.13
HENRY Woodville. A tale. Opie, A. 469.34-35
HENSLOW, J. S. Principles of descriptive and
physiological botany. London, 1836. 16°. 408.6
HENSLOWE, P. Diary, 1591-1609, edited by J. P.
Collier. London, 1845. 8° 342.28
HENSMAN, R. Civil engineering. Lectures on
the exhibition 199.16
HENSON, J. Story of his own life. With an in-
troduction by Mrs. H. B. Stowe. Boston,
1858. 12° 526.12
HENTZ, C. L. Mrs. Eoline: or Magnolia vale.
Philadelphia, [1852.] 12° 445.13
— Ernest Linwood: a novel. Boston, 1856. 12°. 445.1-10
— Linda: or, the young pilot of the Belle Cre-
ole. Philadelphia, [1850.] 12° 445.11
— Lost daughter, and other stories. Philadel-
phia, [1857.] 12° 445.15
— Love after marriage: and other stories. Phila-
delphia, [1857.] 12° 446.1
— Planter's Northern bride. Philadelphia, 1854.
2v. 12° 446.3-5
— - Same. Philadelphia, [1854.] 12°. . . . 446.2
— Rena: or, the snow-bird. A tale. Philadel-
phia, [1851.] 12° 445.12
— Robert Graham. A sequel to "Linda." Phila-
delphia, [1855.] 12° 445.14
— Tadeuskuud: an histor. tale. Boston, 1825. 12° 489.11-12
HEPTAMERON. Novellen. Dingelstedt, F. . . 1034.22
HÉQUET, G. Mme. de Maintenon. Paris, 1853. 12° 1078.52
HERBERT, E., of Cherbury. Life — written by him-
self. London, 1826. 8° 563.5
HERBERT, G. Life [by Walton,] and writings;
with the "Synagogue." Boston, 1851. 12° 345.18
— Life of. Walton, I. 589.5
HERBERT, H. J. G., Earl of Carnarvon. Portugal
and Gallicia, with a review of the state of
the Basque provinces. 3d ed. Lon., 1848. 12°. 889.8
HERBERT, H. W. American game in its season.
New York, 1853. 12° 174.8
— The brothers. A tale of the Fronde. New
York, 1835. 2v. 12° 498.6
— Captains of the old world. N. Y., 1851. 12°. 948.8
— Captains of the Roman republic. New York,
1854. 12° 948.7
— Frank Forester's field sports of N. America.
6th ed. New York, n.d. 8° 174.4-6
— Frank Forester's fish and fishing in United
States and British provinces. 3d ed., with
supplement. New York, 1851. 8° 174.2-3
— Frank Forester's horse and horsemanship of
America. New York, 1857. 2v. 4° 171.1
— Memoirs of Henry VIII.; with the fortunes
of his wives. New York, 1855. 12° . . . 555.1-3
— Oliver Cromwell. New York, 1856. 12° . . . 558.5
— Persons and pictures from the histories of
France and England. New York, 1851. 12° 548.6
— Roman traitor. Phila., 1853. 2v. in 1. 12° . 436.15
— Sporting scenes and characters. Philadelphia,
n.d. 2v. 12° 174.7

Contents. — Vol. I. My shooting box; The deer-
stalkers. II. The Warwick woodlands; Tom Draw's
visit to Pine brook; The Quorndon hounds.

— The dog, by Dinks, Mayhew, and Hutchinson.
Ed. by Frank Forester. N. York, 1857. 12° 177.4
HERBERT Lacy: a novel. Lister, T. H. 777.1
HERBERT Milton: or, Almacks revisited 769.5
HERCULANEUM, Last days of. A poem. Athers-
tone, E. 349.9-10
HERDER, J. G. von. Spirit of Hebrew poetry,
transl. by J. Marsh. Burlington, 1833. 2v. 12° 1087.17
HERDER, Briefe von 1034.10
HERE and hereafter: or, the two altars. Athern, A. 478.5
HERIOT, G. Travels through the Canadas. Phila-
delphia, 1813. 12° 629.23
HERMENEUTICS. Legal and political. Lieber, F. 134.12
HERMSPRONG: by Robert Bage. Barbauld, A. L.
British novelists. . . . . v.XLVIII. of 779.1

HERNIA, abdominal, Anatomy and treatment of.
Cooper, Sir A. 151.1
HERODOTUS. Transl. by W. Beloe. New York,
n.d. 3v. 18° 830.20
— New and literal version of H., Edited by H.
Cary. London, 1852. p.8° 814.1
— Life of Homer, ascribed to H. Translated . 824.5
— Notes on. Turner, D. W. 855.3
— An analysis and summary of. Wheeler, J. T. 855.2
— Life and travels of. Wheeler, J. T. 547.12
HEROES and hero-worship. Carlyle, T. 885.13
HEROES, The: or, Greek fairy tales. Kingsley, C. 484.12
HEROES, Biography of American. Wilson, T. . . 527.8
HEROIC tales of ancient Greece. Niebuhr, B. G. . 728.9
HEROINES of the missionary enterprise. Eddy,
D. C. 539.13
HERON, R. Journey through the Western counties
of Scotland, 1792. Perth, 1793. 2v. 8° . . . 646.1
— Notes and illustrations to Junius. 873.10
HERSCHEL, Sir J. F. W. Discourse on the study of
natural philosophy. London, 1831. 16°. . 398.4
— - Same. New ed. New York, 1851. 12°. . 149.5
— Essays from the Edinburgh and Quarterly re-
views. London, 1857. 8° 144.18
— Outlines of astronomy. 4th ed. London,
1851. 8° 146.5
— - Same. London, 1849. 8° 146.6
— Astronomy. New ed. London, 1834. 16°. . 398.10
— Treatise on astronomy. New ed. London,
1851. 12° 149.16
— - Same. New ed., with preface and quest.
by S. C. Walker. Philadelphia, 1836. 12°. 149.15
See Great Britain, Admiralty Manual of
scientific enquiry 149.3-4
HERSHBERGER, H. R. The horseman, to which
is annexed, a sabre exercise. New York,
1844. 12° 197.18
HERTHA: A novel. Bremer, F. 455.14-18
HERVÉ, F. A residence in Greece and Turkey.
[London], 1837. 2v. 8° 683.8
HERVEY, G. W. Rhetoric of conversation. New
York, 1853. 12° 405.9
HERVEY, J. Memoirs of the reign of George II.
Ed. by J. W. Croker. Philadelphia, 1848.
2v. 12° 553.7
HERVEY, T. K. Book of Christmas. New York,
1845. 12° 989.2
HESIOD, Callimachus and Theognis. Works,
translated into English prose by J. Banks.
London, 1856. p.8° 854.2
HESS, J. G. Life of Ulrich Zwingle. Translated
by L. Aikin. London, 1812. 12° 545.27
HESSISCHE Land und Volk. Müller, E. 1029.5
HETHERINGTON, W. M. History of the West-
minster assembly of divines. New York,
1853. 12° 1106.15
HEWES, G. R. T. Traits of the tea party, being a
memoir of Hewes. New York, 1835. 18° . 219.4
HEWINS, J. M. Hints concerning church music.
Boston, 1856. 12° 209.1
HEYWOOD, J. Pardoner and Frere. Childe, F. J. 356.1
HEYWOOD, T. Apology for actors. London,
1841. 8° 342.2
— Fair maid of the exchange. Ed. by B. Field
London, 1845. 8° 342.29
— 1st and 2d parts of K. Edward IV., with an
introduction by B. Field. London, 1842. 8° 342.12
— and Rowley, W. Fortune by land and sea.
Ed. by B. Field. London, 1845. 8° 342.29
HIAWATHA, The song of. Longfellow, H. W. . 343.1-5
HIBBERD, S. Rustic adornments for homes of
taste. 2d ed. London, 1857. 12° 207.11
HICKEY, W. Constitution of the United States,
etc., 6th ed. Philadelphia, 1853. 12° . . . 299.2-3
HICKOK, L. P. Rational cosmology. New York,
1858. 8° 163.26
HIDDEN path, The: a novel. Hawes, V. 805.26
HIDE and seek: a novel. Collins, W. W. 754.1-5
HIEMPSAL'S history of the African settlements.
See Phenix, The 808.8

HIEROGLYPHS, Egyptian. Study of. Birch, S.. 957.8
HIGBEE, E. Y. Address at the funeral of Dr.
Wainwright. Wainwright, J. M. 1083.13
HIGGINS, W. M. Philosophy of sound and history of music. London, 1838. 16° 149.18
— The earth, its physical condition and its phenomena. New York, n.d. 18° 810.73
HIGGINSON, E. Spirit of the Bible. London, 1853-55. 2v. 12° 1106.4
HIGGINSON, F. The ocean, its depths and phenomena. London, 1857. 8° 146.14
HIGGINSON, T. W. Woman's rights tracts . . . 878.8
HIGH latitudes, Letters from. Blackwood, F. T.. 708.1
HIGH ways and by ways. Grattan, T. C. 798.3
HIGHLAND treason, The : a drama. Holland, E. G. 338.10
HIGHLAND widow, The. Scott, Sir W. 480.18-21
HIGHLANDERS. Stewart, Col. D. Sketches of the 987.2
— Stewart, W. G. Amusements, and popular superstitions of the 989.11
HIGHLANDS, Wild sports and natural history of the. St. John, C. 899.10
HIGHLANDS and Highland clans. History of the. Browne, J. 985.3
HIGHTON, E. Electric telegraph. Lond., 1852. 16° 819.9
HILDEBRAND, pope Gregory VII. Greisley, Sir R. 543.7
HILDRETH, R. Banks, banking and paper currencies. Boston, 1840. 12° 136.23
— History of the United States [1497-1789.] N. York, 1849. 3v. 8° 303.2
— - Same. Revised ed. N. York, 1854. 3v. 8° 303.3
— History of the United States [1789-1821.] N. York, 1851-52. 3v. 8° 303.2
— - Same. Revised ed. N. York, 1855. 3v. 8° 303.3
— Japan, as it was and is. Boston, 1855. 12°. . 938.2-3
— - Same. Boston, 1855. 12° 708.3
— Theory of politics. New York, 1853. 12° . . 134.10
— White slave ; or memoirs of a fugitive. Boston, 1852. 12° 796.18
— - Same. London, 1853. 16° 795.19
HILDRETH, S. P. Pioneer history of the Ohio valley and N. W. territory. Cinn., 1848. 8° 245.3
HILL, Mrs. E. The widow's offering. New London, Conn., 1852. 12° 539.14
HILL, G. C. Capt. John Smith : a biography. Boston, 1858. 12° 528.13
— General I. Putnam : a biography. Boston, 1858. 12° 528.10
HILL, G. J. Story of the war in La Vendée, and the little Chouannerie. New York, n.d. p.8° 1008.13
HILL, J. Life and writings of Hugh Blair. Philadelphia, 1808. 8° 575.10
HILL, R. A naturalist's sojourn in Jamaica. Gosse, P. H. 178.7
HILL, Rev. R., Memoir of. Jones, Wm. 578.4
HILL, S. S. Travels in Siberia. London, 1854. 2v. 12° 707.8
— Travels on the shores of the Baltic. London, 1854. 12° 687.20
HILL and valley : a tale. Martineau, H.. . v.II. of 749.2-3
HILLARD, G. S. Six months in Italy. Boston, 1853. 2v. 12° 679.7-9
— Life of Capt. John Smith . . . . v. I. of 518.5
HILLHOUSE, J. A. Dramas, discourses, [etc.] Boston, 1839. 2v. 16° 356.20

Contents. — Vol. I. Demetria ; Hadad ; Percy's masque. II. The judgment, a vision ; Sachem's wood, a poem ; Discourses ; (1.) On the choice of an era in epic and tragic writing. (2.) On the relations of literature to a republican government. (3.) On the life and services of Lafayette ; The hermit of Warkworth, a ballad by Thomas Percy.

HILLIARD, H. W. Speeches and addresses. New York, 1855. 8° 873.3
HILLS of the Shatemuc : a novel. Warner, S. . . 794.1-6
HIMALAYAN journals : or, notes of a naturalist. Hooker, J. D. 695.9
HINCHLIFF, T. W. Summer months among the Alps. London, 1857. 12° 667.14
HIND, J. R. Illustrated London astronomy. London, 1853. 8° 147.12

HIND, J. R. The solar system. N. Y., 1852. 12°. 146.26
HINDOOS, The, including a description of India. London, n.d. 2v. 12° 839.16
HINDOOS, India and the. Ward, F. De W. 709.6
HINDOSTAN. Foster, J. Communication of Christianity to the people of 878.19
See also : India.
HINES, Rev. G. Oregon : its history, condition and prospects. Buffalo, 1851. 12° 637.4
HINGHAM, Mass., History of. Lincoln, S. jr. . . 227.19
HINMAN, R. R. Part sustained by Connecticut in the revolution. Hartford, 1842. 8° 213.7
HINTS and sketches. New York, 1839. 12° 888.21
HIPSLEY, W. Equational arithmetic, applied to interest, annuities, etc. London, 1852. 16°. 829.20
HIRELING, The, and the slave. Grayson, W. J. 349.3
HIRTIUS, Aulus. Supplementary books of Cæsar's commentaries, attributed to 824.3
HISTOIRE d'Albert et Isabelle, par Ch. D. Bruxelles, n.d. 12° 1075.14
HISTORIC doubts on the life of Richard III. Walpole, H. 989.10
HISTORICAL account of the circumnavigation of the globe. New York, n.d. 18° 810.76
HISTORICAL collections of Virginia. Howe, H. . 235.2
HISTORICAL magazine. Vol. I., [12 Nos., Jan. to Dec., 1857.] Boston, 1857. 8° 273.1
HISTORICAL parallels from original historians. Malkin, J. H. 839.12
HISTORICAL scenes, Paris. See Paris 849.19
HISTORICAL Society of Mass. See Mass. Hist. Soc.
HISTORICAL Society of Pennsylvania. Braddock's expedition, by Sargent, W. 244.1
HISTORICAL studies. Greene, G. W. 947.9
HISTORICAL and critical essays. De Quincey, T. . 895.16
HISTORICAL and descrip. acc. of Ireland, Greenl'd, and the Faroe islands. N. York, 1851. 18°. 820.35
HISTORIETTEN. Kossak, E. 1037.14
HISTORY. Abbott, J. General course of. 948.1
— Ancient. Rollins, C. 952.1
— Arnold, T. Lectures on modern 947.11
— Cantù, C. Storia di cento anni, 1750-1850 . . 1046.10
— - Tre discorsi sulla storia universale. . . . 1046.12
— Chateaubriand, F. A. de. Mélanges historiques 1069.13
— Davidson, D. Connexion of sac. and profane. 1089.34
— Follen, C. T. C. Essay on . . . . v.V. of 877.1
— Goodrich, S. G. Universal 951.2
— Juste, T. Précis de l'histoire moderne . . . 1075.16
— Hegel, G. W. F. Philosophy of 855.8
— Keightley, T. Outlines of 368.1
— Lord, J. Modern H. fr. Luther to Napoleon. 947.4
— Lucas, S. History as a condition of social progress 139.9
— McBurney, I. Cyclopædia of universal . . . 947.5
— Miller, G. History philosophically illustrated, A.D. 476 to A.D. 1789 . . . . 859.6
— Millot, C. F. X. Elements of 945.3
— Moke, H. G. Précis de l'histoire universelle. 1065.40
— Müller, J. von. Universal 949.4
— Munsell, J. Every-day book of history . . . 947.1
— Nicolas, Sir N. H. Chronology of 368.2
— Schlegel, K. W. F. von. Lectures on modern. 848.1
— - The philosophy of 818.3
— Seymour, F. G. Romance of ancient 959.3
— Smyth, W. Lectures on modern . . . . . 943.3 & 7
— Taylor, W. C. Manual of ancient and mod.. 952.2
— Thierry, A. Dix ans d'études historiques . . 1076.13
— Trimmer, Mrs. S. Lessons in ancient 129.32
— Tytler, A. F. Elements of general 956.13
— Weber, G. Outlines of universal 952.3
— White, J. The eighteen Christian centuries. 1105.1

NOTE. — For the history, civil, ecclesiastical, military, literary, etc., of various countries, see the names of those countries ; and for the history of arts, sciences, literature, and the like, see the terms appropriate to each.

HISTORY of Berkshire, Mass. Pittsfield, [Mass.,] 1829. 12° 227.9
HISTORY of Dublin, N. H., and proceedings at centennial celebration, 1852. Boston, 1855. 8° 225.1

HISTORY of Napoleon and France. Lond., 1852. 18° 1009.15
HISTORY of New Ipswich, N. H. Boston, 1852. 8° 234.6
HISTORY of Rome. London, [1834-35.] 2v. 16°. 378.2
HISTORY of St. Domingo. New York, 1824. 8°. . 264.3
HISTORY of silk, cotton, linen, wool, etc. New
 York, 1845. 8° 195.4
HISTORY of the mutiny at Spithead and the Nore.
 London, 1842. 16° 389.5
HISTORY of the Protestant church in Hungary.
 Translated by J. Craig. Introduction by J.
 H. Merle d' Aubigné. Boston, 1854. 12°. . 1095.9
HISTORY of wonderful inventions. Lond., 1849. 12° 197.20
— - Same. New York, n.d. 12° 197.21
HITCHCOCK, E. Geology, mineralogy, botany and
 zoology of Massachusetts, with atlas. Am-
 herst, 1833. 8° 163.10
— Geology of the globe. Boston, 1853. 8° . . 163.11
— Lectures on diet, regimen and employment.
 2d edition. Amherst, 1831. 8° 158.4
— Religion of geology and its connected sci-
 ences. Boston, 1854. 12° 167.21-22
— Religious truth, illustrated from science.
 Boston, 1857. 12° 1088.5
HITCHCOCK, E. A. Remarks upon alchemy and
 the alchemists. Boston, 1857. 12° 197.4
HIVE, The, and honey bee. Richardson . . v.III. of 169.15
HIVE, The, of "the bee hunter." Sketches.
 Thorpe, T. B. 794.14
HOADLY, C. J. Records of the colony of N. Haven. 234.9
HOBART, J. H. Christian's manual, containing
 dialogues and prayers. 6th ed. New York,
 1844. 12° 1099.16-17
— Companion for the altar. 22d ed. N.Y., 1850. 12° 118.10
HOBART, N. Life of Swedenborg. 3d ed. by B.
 Worcester. New York, 1850. 16° 545.17
HOBBES, T. Analysis of Aristotle's rhetoric.
 See Aristoteles 814.8
HOBBIE, H., Memoir of. Armstrong, R. G. . . . 119.11
HOCHELAGA depicta : history and present state of
 Montreal. Bosworth, N. 265.4
HOCHELAGA : or, England in the new world. War-
 burton, E. 627.19-20
HOCKER, N. Das Moselthal von Nancy bis Kob-
 lenz. Leipzig, 1855. 16° 1029.3
— Der Rhein von Mainz bis Köln. Leipzig,
 1857. 16° 1029.21
HOEFER, E. Bewegtes Leben. Geschichten. Stutt-
 gart, 1856. 16° 1037.9
  Contents. — Erzahlungen eines alten Fidlers; Der
  Onkel Stephan ; Aus einer Familie ; Die hellen
  Fenster; Der wilde Heide.
HOFFMAN, C. F. The vigil of faith, and other
 poems. New York, 1842. 12° 358.4
— Life of Jacob Leisler. Sparks's American
 biography . . . . v.XIII. of 529.1
HOFFMANN, D. Chronicles of Cartaphilus, the
 wandering Jew. London, 1853. 2v. 8°. . 901.5
HOFFMANN, E. T. A. (W.) Gesammelte Schriften.
 Berlin, 1844-45. 12v. 16° 1027.5
  Contents. — Vols. I.—IV. Die Serapions Bruder,
  gesammelte Erzahlungen u. Mahrchen. V. Nacht-
  stucke. VI. Die Elixiere des Teufels. VII. Fanta-
  siestucke in Callot's Manier; Vorrede von Jean Paul;
  Jacques Callot; Ritter Gluck; Kreisleriana, No. 1-6;
  Don Juan; Nachricht von den neuesten Schicksalen
  des Hundes Berganza; Der goldne
  Topf; Die Abentheuer der Sylvester-Nacht; Kreisle-
  riana. VIII. Lebensansichten des Katers Murr. IX.
  Klein Zaches genannt Zinnober; Prinzessin Brambilla. X. Seltsame Leiden eines Theater-Direktors;
  Meister Floh. XI.—XII. Erzahlungen aus Hoffmann's letzten Lebensjahren : Die Doppeltganger;
  Die Rauber; Die Irrungen; Die Geheimnisse; Der Ele-
  mentargeist; (12.) Datura fastuosa; Meister Johannes
  Wacht; Die Marquise de la Pivardiere; Die Vision
  auf dem Schlachtfelde bei Dresden; Haimatochare;
  Der Feind; Neueste Schicksale eines abentheuer-
  lichen Mannes ; Des Vetters Eckfenster; Die Ge-
  nesung.
— Contes fantastiques, trad. d l'allemande. Bruxelles, 1830. 4v. 16° 1070.11
  Contents. — Vol. I. Sur Hoffmann et les compositions fantastiques, par Walter Scott; Le Marjorat;

HOFFMANN, E. T. A. (W.), continued.
  Le Sanctus; Salvator Rosa; La vie d'artiste. II. Le
  violon de Cremone; Marino Falieri; Le bonheur au
  jeu; Le choix d'une fiancee; Le spectre fiancé. III.
  Le pot d'or; Les aventures de la nuit de Saint-Syl-
  vestre; Maitre Martin le tonnelier et ses apprentis.
  IV. La princesse Brambilla ; L'homme au sable;
  Gluck; Don Juan.
— Fairy tales. Boston, 1857. 16° 737.14
— Rolandsitten. Goldsmith of Paris. Transl.
 Omnibus of modern romance 801.3
— Strange stories. Fr. the German. Bos., 1855. 12° 737.13
— The golden pot. Translated, with notice of
 the author by T. Carlyle . . . . v.II. of 418.1
HOFFMANN von Fallersleben, A. H. Gedichte.
 Octav Ausg. 3te Aufl. Hannover, n.d. . . 1027.4
HOFLAND, B. Domestic tales. N. Y., 1852. 16° 719.13
— Energy : a tale. Boston, 1848. 18° 878.22
— Moral tales for the young. N. Y., 1852. 18°. 719.14-15
— The unloved one. New York, 1844. 8° . . . 802.15
HOGARTH, G. Musical history, biography, and
 criticism. London, 1838. 2v. 12° 209.9
HOGG, Jabez. The microscope ; its history, con-
 struction, and application. London, 1854. 8° 144.2
HOGG, James. The Ettrick shepherd. Poetical
 works, with an autobiogr. Glasgow, 1855.
 5v. 12° 355.8
  Contents. — Vol. I. Queen's wake. . . . . II.
  Pilgrims of the sun; . . . . Mountain bard. II.
  Queen Hynde. IV. Poetic mirror; Mador of the
  Moor; Russiadde. . . . . V. Life; Songs.
— Noctes ambrosianæ. See Wilson, J. 865.1
— The three perils of man. A romance. Lon-
 don, 1822. 3v. 12° 769.6
HOGG, T. J. Life of Percy Bysshe Shelley. Lon-
 don, 1858. 2v. 8° 585.14
HOLBERG, L., Baron von. Journey to the world
 under ground. By Nich. Klimius. Lon-
 don, 1742. 12° 799.11
HOLBROOK, J. Ten years among the mail-bags.
 Boston, 1856. 12° 884.6-9
HOLBROOK, S. F. Threescore years ; an autobiog-
 raphy. Boston, 1857. 16° 525.6-7
HOLBROOK, S. P. Sketches by a traveller. Bos-
 ton, 1830. 12° 878.15
HOLCROFT, T. Memoirs, by himself. London,
 1816. 3v. 12° 507.14
— - Same. London, 1852. 16°. 409.8
— - Same. London, 1852. 16° 597.15
HOLLAND. Abbott, J. Rollo in 659.17-21
— Bell, R. Wayside pictures through 675.5
— Davies, C. M. History of 914.1
— Family tour through South. 389.2
— Meeter, E. Institutions, etc. of 917.4
— Motley, J. L. Rise of the Dutch republic . . 923.1-4
— Murray, J. Handbook for 649.19
HOLLAND, E. G. Essays ; and a drama in five
 acts. Boston, 1852. 12° 338.10
HOLLAND, J. and Everett, J. Life and writings
 of J. Montgomery. London, 1854. 4v. 8°. 584.17
HOLLAND, John. Memoirs of Rev. John Sum-
 merfield. Introd. by J. Montgomery. New
 York, n.d. 12° 1107.10
HOLLAND, John, Esq. Present state of the manu-
 factures in metals. Lond., [1831-34.] 3v. 16° 408.10
HOLLAND, J. G. The bay path : tale of New Eng-
 land colonial life. New York, 1857. 12° . . 415.1-2
— History of Western Massachusetts. Spring-
 field, 1855. 2v. 12° 227.14
HOLLAND, Lord. See Fox, H. R. and H. E.
HOLLAND, S. S., Lady. Memoirs of Sydney Smith.
 London, 1855. 2v. 8° 583.18
— - Same. New York, 1855. 2v. 12° 583.19
HOLLAND, W. M. Life and opinions of Martin
 Van Buren. Hartford, 1835. 12° 517.20
HOLLEY, H. Genius and character of. Caldwell, C. 534.1
HOLLINGS, J. F. Life of Cicero. London, 1839. 16° 389.7
— Life of Gustavus Adolphus, king of Sweden.
 London, 1838. 16° 389.6
HOLLWAY, J. G. Month in Norway. London,
 1853. 16° 669.7

HOLMES, A. Annals of America, from 1492 to 1826. 2d ed. Cambridge, 1829. 2v. 8° 304.9
— Life of Ezra Stiles. Boston, 1798. 8° . . . 534.12
HOLMES, E. Life of Mozart, including his correspondence. New York, 1845. 12° . . . 545.21
HOLMES, M. J., Mrs. Tempest and sunshine. New York, 1854. 12° 416.4
HOLMES, O. W. Homœopathy and its kindred delusions. Boston, 1842. 12° 158.1
— Poems. London, 1846. 16° 344.15–16
— - Same. New and enlarged ed. Boston, 1853. 16° 344.13–14
HOLMES, W. R. Sketches on the shores of the Caspian. London, 1845. 8° 674.3
HOLSTEIN, H. L. V. D. Memoirs of Bolivar and his principal generals. London, 1830. 2v. 12° 539.1
— Memoirs of La Fayette. New York, 1824. 12° 617.4
HOLT, E. Life of George III. London, 1820. 2v. 8° 553.8
HOLTEI, K. von. Die Vagabunden. Roman. Breslau, 1852. 4v. 16° 1035.8
— Vierzig Jahre. Berlin and Breslau. 1843–50. 8v. 16° 1035.7
HOLTON, I. F. New Granada: twenty months in the Andes. New York, 1857. 8° 633.2
HOLY land, The. Bulfinch, S. G. H. L. and its inhabitants 1089.24
— Clarke, E. D. Travels in 689.6
— Dorr, B. Notes of travel in 686.12
— Hahn-Hahn, I. Travels in 687.10
— Irby, C. L. and Mangles, J. Travels in . . . 889.25
— Kitto, J. Physical geography of 840.25
— Lamartine, A. de. Journey in 687.15
— Lindsay, A. W. C., Lord. Letters on . . . 693.16
— Martineau, H. Eastern life 686.1–4
— Pfeiffer, I. Visit to 879.5
— Prime, W. C. Tent life in 686.7–11
— Russell, M. The holy land 810.33
— Spencer, J. A. Travels in 686.6
    See also: Palestine.
HOLY living and dying. Taylor, J. 848.7
HOLY Scriptures. See Bible.
HOLY week. England, J. Ceremonies of the, in the Vatican 1098.18
— Wiseman, N. Offices and ceremonies of the. 1098.3
HOMANS, J. S. Sketches of Boston and vicinity. Boston, 1851. 16° 229.7
HOME, H., Lord Kames. Art of thinking, [with] a life of the author. New York, 1818. 12°. 129.11
— Elements of criticism. Ed. by A. Mills. New ed. New York, 1853. 12° 403.3
HOME. How to make home happy. Jones, W. 877.10
HOME. A book for the family. Tweedie, W. K. 898.15
HOME: a tale. Sedgwick, C. M. 729.14–17
HOME as found: a novel. Cooper, J. F. . . . 760.33–37
HOME of the mutineers. Philadelphia, 1854. 18° 1109.8
HOME for all. Fowler, O. S. 207.10
HOME, or family cares and family joys. Bremer, F. 455.10
HOME, or life in Sweden: a novel. Bremer, F. . . 817.4
HOME, or the iron rule: a story. Ellis, S. S. . . 804.10
HOME education. Taylor, I. 137.6
HOME influence: a tale. Aguilar, G. 764.2–4
HOME scenes and home sounds. Stephens, H. M. 489.18
HOME studies. Upton, R. A. 188.28
HOMŒOPATHIA, Elementary treatise upon. Jahr, G. H. G. 158.20
HOMŒOPATHY. Henderson, W. H. fairly represented 157.2
— Holmes, O. W. H. and its kindred delusions. 158.1
— Simpson, J. Y. Its tenets and tendencies . . 157.1
HOMERIC ballads, translated by W. Maginn . . . 346.4
HOMERUS. Iliad and Odyssey. Translated by W. Cowper. . . . . .v.XI–XIV. of 337.1
— - Same. Translated by A. Pope. N. Y., n.d. 3v. 18° 830.21
— Iliad. Ed. by Felton. Boston, 1833. 8° . . . 315.4
— - Same. Literally transl. by T. A. Buckley. New York, 1856. 12° 315.5
— - Same. London, 1853. p.8° 824.4
— - Same. Translated by W. Cowper. Ed. by R. Southey, with notes by M. A. Dwight. New York, 1850. 8° . . . . .315.3&6
— - Same . . . . .v.VII. of 817.11

HOMERUS. Iliad. Transl. by A. Pope. London, 1853. 2v. 12° 879.1
— - Same, with "Gay's welcome fr. Greece." Revised by W. C. Armstrong. 5th edition. Hartford, 1853. 8° 315.2
— - Same. Notes by J. S. Watson, with Flaxman's designs. London, 1857. p.8° 835.13
— Odyssey, etc. Translated by T. A. Buckley. London, 1851. p.8° 824.5
— - Translated by W. Cowper. Edited by R. Southey . . . . .v.VIII. of 817.11
— - Translated by A. Pope. London, 1853. 12° 879.2
— - Same. [and Batrachomyomachy.] Philadelphia, 1828. 2v. 18° 369.20
— - Same. Ed. by J. S. Watson, with Flaxman's designs. London, 1858. p.8° 835.15
— - Same, with "Conclusion of the notes" by Broome. Revised by W. C. Armstrong. Hartford, 1853. 8° 315.2
— Fables. Translated into verse. Dryden, J. . 315.17
HOMES abroad: a tale. Martineau, H. . . .v.X. of 749.2–3
HOMES of British poets. Howitt, W. 896.1–2
HOMES for the people. Wheeler, G. 207.8
HOMES, rural, or sketches of houses, etc. Wheeler, G. 207.9
HOMEWARD bound: a tale. Cooper, J. F. 760.30–32
HONDURAS. Baily, J. Description of 266.4
— Squier, E. G. H. and the inter-oceanic railway. 263.1
— Wells, W. V. Explorations and adventures in. 621.2
    See also: America.
HONE, W. Every-day book and table book. London, 1837–39. 3v. 8° 892.12
— Year book of recreation. London, 1839. 8°. 892.13
HONEY-BEE. Bevan, E. Its natural history, etc. 165.8
— Frarière, A. de. Les abeilles et l' apiculture. 1078.11
— Huber, F. Natural history of the 165.22
— Langstroth, L. L. The hive, and honey bee. 165.23
— The honey bee. From the Quarterly review. London, 1852. 16° 165.29
HONOUR triumphant. Forde, J. 342.18
HOOD, C. Warming buildings by hot water; ventilation, etc. 3d ed. London, 1855. 8° . . 207.3
HOOD, E. P. John Milton, the patriot and poet. London, 1852. 18° 586.24
— Self-education. 2d edition. London, 1852. 18° 129.20
— Uses of biography. London, 1852. 18° . . . 878.24
— William Wordsworth: a biography. London, 1856. 12° 584.20
HOOD, G. History of music in New England. Boston, 1846. 16° 209.7
HOOD, T. Poetical works, with account of the author. Boston, 1854–57. 4v. 16° 318.1–5
    Contents. — Vol. I. Plea of the midsummer fairies; Hero and Leander; Lycus the Centaur; Two peacocks of Bedfont; Two swans; Dream of Eugene Aram; Elm tree; Haunted house; Song of the shirt; . . . . Sonnets. II. Miss Kilmansegg and her precious leg; Tale of a trumpet; Irish schoolmaster; The forge; Last man; The season; . . . . III. Lost heir; . . . . IV. Love and lunacy; . . . . Odes and addresses.
    NOTE. — In the set numbered 5, the contents of the first two volumes differ somewhat from the above.
— Prose and verse. N.Y., 1845. 2 parts in 1. 12° 498.4
— Tylney Hall. A novel. Phila., 1834. 2v. 12° 498.3
— Whimsicalities. N. Y., 1852. 12° 896.17
HOOK, J. Pen Owen. A romance. London, 1822. 3v. 12° 809.8
— Percy Mallory. Edinburgh, 1824. 3v. 12° . . 809.7
HOOK, T. E. Cousin Geoffry: a novel. Philadelphia, 1840. 2v. in 1. 12° 809.10
— Maxwell: a tale. London, 1830. 3v. 12° . . 807.5
— Ned Musgrave. New ed. London, 1854. 16° 809.9
— Sayings and doings. 1st ser. London, 1824. 3v. 12° 809.1
— - Same. Philadelphia, 1824. 2v. 12° . . . 809.4
— - Same. 2d series. London, 1825. 3v. 12° . 809.2
— - Same. 2d series. Phila., 1825. 2v. 12° . . 809.5
— - Same. 3d ser. New ed. London, 1828. 3v. 12° 809.3
— - Same. 3d series. Phila., 1828. 2v. 12° . . 809.6
— T. Hook: a sketch. 4th ed. Lond., 1853. 16° 586.25
HOOKER, E. W. Memoirs of Mrs. S. L. H. Smith. 3d edition. New York, n.d. 12° 1107.13

HOOKER, J. D. Himalayan journals : or, notes of a naturalist. London, 1854. 2v. 8° 695.9
HOOKER, R. Works — with life by Walton — arranged by J. Keble. 3d American edition. New York, 1851. 2v. 8° 1103.4

Contents. — Vol. I. Ed.'s preface; Life, by Walton, with appendices; Laws of eccles. polity, b. 1–5. II. Same, [concluded]; Sermons; Travers' supplication; Hooker's answer.

— Life, by I. Walton 589.5
HOOKER, W. Child's book of nature. Part I. Plants. II. Animals. III. Air, water, heat, etc. New York, 1857. 16° 177.32
HOOKER, W. J. Journal of a tour in Iceland in 1809. 2d edition. London, 1813. 2v. 8°. . 668.2
HOOPER, J. J. Simon Sugg's adventures [and] widow Rugby's husband, [etc.] Philadelphia, n.d. 12° 726.15
HOOPER, W. H. Ten months among the tents of the Tuski. London, 1853. 8° 694.12
HOOREBEKE, E. van. Précis d'instruction criminelle. Bruxelles, n.d. 12° 1065.21
HOPE, I. Britanny and the Bible. Lond., 1852. 12° 409.9
— Britanny and the chase. London, 1853. 12°. 409.9
HOPE, Sir J. Despatch after the battle of Corunna. 830.42
HOPE on ! hope ever ! Howitt, M. 459.10–12
HOPES. A tale. Bremer, F. 817.1–2
HÖPFNER, J. L. F. Briefe von 1031.10
HOPKINS, E. Exposition of the ten commandments. New York, n.d. 12° 1107.19
HOPKINS, E. J. The organ : its construction, preceded by a history by E. F. Rimbault. London, 1855. 8° 204.3
HOPKINS, J. H. The American citizen — his rights and duties. New York, 1857. 12° 134.17
HOPKINS, M. Miscellaneous essays and discourses. Boston, 1847. 8° 1106.2
HOPKINS, S. Youth of the old dominion. Boston, 1856. 12° 478.8
HOPKINS, W. Elements of trigonometry. Lib. Us. Kn. 365.12
HOPPER, I. T. A true life. Child, L. M 525.10–15
HORATIUS Flaccus, Q. Works. Translated by C. Smart, [with text.] Phila., 1808. 2v. 18°. 369.4
— — Same. New edition. London, 1853. p.8° 814.11
— Horace. Translated by P. Francis, with an appendix. New York, n.d. 2v. 18° 830.16
— Satires, epistles, and art of poetry ; done into English by S. Dunster. 3d ed., corr. London, 1719. 8° 315.7
HORN, J. E. Brüssel nach seiner Vergangenheit und Gegenwart. Leipzig, 1855. 16° 1029.7
HORN, Philip, Count, Trial of. Schiller, J. C. F. v. 818.10
HORN-BOOK, Sailor's. Law of storms. Piddington, H. 145.18
HORNE, G. Works, life, etc., by W. Jones. New York, 1853. 2v. 8° 1083.7

Contents. — Life ; Caution to the readers of Mr. Law; Essays on various subjects; Use of the Hebrew language; Com. on the Psalms. II. Discourses; State of the case between Newton and Mr. Hutchinson; Apology for certain gentlemen in the Univ. of Oxford; Life and death of St. John the Baptist; Letters on infidelity; Charge to the clergy of Norwich.

HORNE, R. H. New spirit of the age. New York, 1844. 12° 878.23
HORNE, T. H. Compendious introduction to the study of the Bible. 9th ed. Lond., 1852. 12° 1088.28
HORNER, F. Memoirs and correspondence, edited by L. Horner. Boston, 1853. 2v. 8° . . . 582.6
HOROLOGY. Carpenter, W. B. 146.25
HORSE. Martin, W. C. L. History of the 840.44
— Richardson, H. D. The horse . . . . v.1 of 169.15
— Stephen, Sir G. Adventures in search of a. . 164.8
— Stewart, J. Stable economy 165.18
— Youatt, W. Structure and diseases of the . . 165.16
HORSE and horsemanship of America. Herbert, H. W. 171.1
HORSEMAN. Hershberger, H. R. 197.18
HORSEMANSHIP, Method of. Baucher, F. 164.7

HORSES and hounds : on their management. London, 1855. 12° 177.12
HORSES. Linsley, D. C. Morgan horses, etc. . . . 165.17
— Stewart, J. Management of 165.18
— Youatt, W. Treatise on draught 172.17
HORSE'S foot. Miles, W. 165.18
HORSE Shoe Robinson : a novel. Kennedy, J. P. 726.4–6
HORTENSE. Genlis, Mme. de 449.20
HORTICULTURE. Lindley, J. Theory of 164.16
— Lemaire, C. Traité d' H. pratique 1065.32
See also: Garden, Gardening, Flowers, etc.
HORTICULTURIST, The suburban. Loudon, J. C. 164.4
HORTON, R. G. Life and public service of James Buchanan. New York, 1856. 12° 517.10
HOSIERY, Haberdashery and. Perkins, E. E. . . 199.38
HOSKING, W. Guide to the regulation of buildings in towns. London, 1848. 12° 207.13
— Treatises on architecture and building 201.4
HOSPITALS and sisterhoods. 2d ed. Lond., 1855. 16° 139.7
HOTTENTOT, The. Passages of missionary life. Merriman, Archd. 578.7
HOUNDS. Practical treatise on 177.12
HOUSE of the seven gables. Hawthorne, N. . . . 457.3–5
HOUSEHOLD angel in disguise : a novel. Baker, H. N. W. 476.3
HOUSEHOLD education. Martineau, H. 137.19
HOUSEHOLD of Sir Thomas More. New York, 1852. 12° 469.6–7
HOUSEHOLD science, Handb'k of. Youmans, E. L. 188.5
HOUSEHOLD words. Dickens, C. 871.1
HOUSEKEEPER. Ellet, Mrs. E. F. Practical . . 187.1
See also: Domestic economy.
HOUSES for the humbler classes. Wilds, W. . . . 207.4
HOUSEWIFE. *See* Domestic economy.
HOUSTON, S. Life. New York, 1855. 12° 517.15
HOUZEAU, J. C. Physique du globe et météorologie. Bruxelles, n.d. 12° 1065.22
— Règles de climatologie. Bruxelles, n.d. 12°. 1065.23
HOW I became a Unitarian. Boston, 1852. 12°. . 117.6
HOW to be a lady : a book for girls. Newcomb, H. 469.21
HOW to be a man : a book for boys. Newcomb, H. 469.20
HOW to do business : a pocket manual. N. York, 1857. 12° 136.25
HOW to observe. Geology. De la Beche, H. T. . 163.19
HOW to write : a pocket manual of composition and letter writing. New York, 1857. 12°. 406.12
HOWADJI. Curtis, G. W. H. in Syria 686.19–21
— Nile notes of a 698.6–7
HOWARD, F. Colour as a means of art. London, 1849. 12° 208.7
— Imitative art : a manual of details for the sketcher, etc. London, n.d. 12° 208.19
HOWARD, G. W. F., *earl of Carlisle*. Diary in Turkish and Greek waters. Boston, 1855. 12° 683.12–13
— Lectures in aid of popular education. New ed. London, 1853. 12° 409.3
HOWARD, H., *earl of Surrey*. Poems. London, 1831. 16° 329.11
HOWARD, J. Brown, J. B. Memoirs of the public and private life of 575.12
— Dixon, W. H. J. Howard and the prison world of Europe 575.14
— Field, J. Life of 575.13
— Life of. Soc. Us. Kn. 589.14
HOWARD, L. Seven lectures on meteorology. 2d ed., rev. London, 1843. 16° 145.28
HOWE, H. Historical collections of Virginia. Charleston, S. C., 1852. 8° 235.2
HOWE, Mrs. J. W. Passion flowers. Boston, 1854. 18° 345.17
— The world's own : [a play.] Boston, 1857. 16° 345.16
— Words for the hour. Boston, 1857. 12° . . . 345.15
HOWE, R., *Earl*. Life of. Barrow, Sir J. 564.7
HOWE, S. G. Historical sketch of the Greek revolution. 2d ed. New York, 1828. 12° . . . 918.4
HOWELL, J. W., Letters-memorial of. Pitcairn, D. 599.13
HOWELL, M. J. Handbook of dressmaking. London, 1845. 12° 199.1

HOWELL, M. J. Handbook of millinery, [with] an essay on corset-making. Lond., 1847. 8° 199.2

HOWISON, J. Sketches of Up. Canada, and recollections of the U. States. Edin., 1821. 8°. 637.1

HOWISON, R. R. History of Virginia. Philadelphia, 1846-48. 2v. 8°. 236.2

HOWITT, A. M. An art-student in Munich. Boston, 1854. 16° 207.16-17

HOWITT, M. Poetical works of Howitt, Milman and Keats. Philadelphia, 1840. 8° 332.6

Contents. — Howitt : The seven temptations; Hymns and fireside verses; Birds and flowers; Tales. Milman : Fazio, a tragedy; Samor, a heroic poem; Anne Boleyn, dramatic poem; Martyr of Antioch, a dramatic poem ; Belshazzar, dramatic poem; Fall of Jerusalem. Keats : Endymion ; Lamia ; Isabella ; Eve of St. Agnes; Hyperion.

— Artist wife, and other tales. N. Y., n.d. 12°. 459.3-7
— Ballads and other poems. New ed. N. York, 1848. 12° 545.12
— Castle of fools. [Also, The village on the heath.] London, 1852. 16° 469.11
— Heir of Wast-Wayland, a tale. N. Y., 1851. 12°. 459.8-9
— Hope on ! hope ever ! N. Y., 1851. 18°. 459.10
— Same. Boston, 1845. 18° 459.11-12
— Memoir of Elihu Burritt 898.3
— My own story. New York, 1853. 18° 459.18-19
— My uncle, the clockmaker. N. York, 1845. 18°. 459.14
— Pictorial calendar of the seasons, embodying Aikin's calendar. London, 1854. p.8° 825.10
— Sowing and reaping. New York, 1851. 18°. 459.15-16
— Which is the wiser : a tale. N. York, 1852. 18°. 459.17
— Wood Leighton : a novel. Lond., 1836. 3v. 12°. 459.1
— Same. London, 1847. 16° 459.2
— Work and wages. New York, 1850. 18° 459.13

HOWITT, W. Boy's adventures in the wilds of Australia. Boston, 1855. 16° 719.4-6
— Country year-book. New York, 1850. 12° 478.7
— Homes and haunts of the most eminent British poets. New York, 1847. 2v. 12° 896.1-2
— Land, labor, and gold : or, two years in Victoria. Boston, 1855. 2v. 12° 705.19
— Same. London, 1855. 2v. 12° 705.17
— Life and adventures of Jack of the mill. New York, 1844. 8° 802.16
— Rural life of England. London, 1838. 2v. 12° 896.4
— Same. Fr. the 2d Lon. ed. Phila., 1841. 8° 986.5
— Student-life of Germany. Philad., 1842. 8°. 663.6
— Tallangetta, a story of Australian life. London, 1857. 2v. 12°. 705.9
— Visits to remarkable places. 1st ser. 3d Am. ed. Philadelphia, 1851. 2v. 12°. 896.3
— and M. Literature and romance of Northern Europe. London, 1852. 2v. 12° 404.5
— Stories of English and foreign life. London, 1853. p.8° 825.5

Contents. — Margaret von Ehrenberg, the artist-wife; The Meldrum family; Sir Peter and his pigeon; The Wood-nook-wells, or neighbours' quarrels ; Leaves from the diary of a poor schoolmaster; The Hunnybuns at the sea-side; Some love-passages in the lives of every-day people; The hunt; The two squires; The poacher's progress.

HOWLAND, E. A. American housekeeper. Worcester, [1845.] 12° 188.26
HOWLAND, J., Life of. Stone, E. M. 525.8
HOWLEY, E. Concise history of the English constitution. London, 1857. 12° 987.7
HOYLAND, J. Customs, habits, and present state of the gypsies. York, 1816. 8° 955.6
HOYT, E. Antiquarian researches, comprising a history of the Indian wars. Greenfield, Mass., 1824. 8° 245.8
HUARD, A. Epitome of chemistry. Transl. by J. B. Fessenden. Boston, 1857. 12° 155.23
HUBBACK, M. The three marriages. Philadelphia, 1855. 12° 428.9
HUBBARD, F. M. Life of Wm. R. Davie. v.XXV. of 529.1
HUBBARD, J. N. Life and times of Major Moses Van Campen. Bath, N. Y., 1842. 12° 528.4
HUBBARD, W. General history of New England. Cambridge, 1815. 2v. 8° . v.V. and VI. of 278.2

HUBBELL, M. S. Memorial : or, life and writings of an only daughter, [M. E. Hubbell.] Boston, 1857. 12° 538-11
— Shady side : or, life in a country parsonage. Boston, 1853. 12° 417.14-18
HUBER, F. Natural history of bees. New ed. London, 1841. 12° 165.22
HUBER, T. Erzählungen. Leipzig, 1830-3. 6v. 16°. 1035.3
HUC, M. l'Abbé. Christianity in China, Tartary, and Thibet. London, 1857. 2v. 8°. 113.4
— Journey through the Chinese empire. 2d ed. London, 1855. 2v. 8° 706.1
— Same. New York, 1855. 2v. 12°. 706.2-3
— Travels in Tartary, Thibet and China, 1844-45-46. 2d ed. London, n.d. 2v. 12°. 706.4
— Same. London, 1852. p.8° 409.10
— Same. Translated by W. Hazlitt. London, n.d. 2v. p.8°. 879.6-7
HUDIBRAS : a poem. Butler, S. 314.13
HUDSON, C. Doubts concerning the battle of Bunker's hill. Boston, 1857. 16° 217.14
HUDSON, D. History of Jemima Wilkinson. Geneva, N. Y., 1821. 12° 539.12
HUDSON, Hend. Life of. H. R. Cleveland. v.X. of 529.1
HUDSON, H. N. Lectures on Shakspeare. 2d ed. New York, 1848. 2v. 12° 357.6-8
HUDSON'S bay territory. Notes of a twenty-five years' service in the. M'Lean, J. 704.19
HUET, P. D. Memoirs, by himself. Translated by J. Aikin. London, 1810. 2v. 8°. 613.9
HUFELAND, C. W. Art of prolonging life. Ed. by E. Wilson. Boston, 1854. 12° 157.27
— Same. London, 1853. 16° 158.14
HUFF, G. Electro-physiology. 2d ed. New York, 1853. 12° 157.8
HUGHES, Mrs. Memoir of the life and writings of Mrs. Hemans. Philadelphia, 1839. 12° 596.9
HUGHES, S. Treatise on gas-works. London, 1853. 16° 829.15
— Survey of metropolitan roads. Law, H. 819.33
HUGHES, W. The Australian colonies. London, 1852. 12° 409.11
HUGHES, W. C. American miller and mill-wright's assistant. Philadelphia, 1851. 12°. 199.14
HUGO, V. Bug-Jargal. Dernier jour d' un condamné ; Claude Gueux ; Littérature et philosophie mêlées. Paris, 1855. 12° 1066.19
— Han d' Islande ; Mélanges littéraires. Paris, 1853. 12° 1066.18
— Hans of Iceland, [and Claude Gueux.] London, n.d. 12° 498.14
— Notre Dame de Paris. Paris, 1855. 12° 1075.40
— Poésies. Paris, 1853-54. 2v. 12° 1066.20

Contents. — Vol. I. Les Orientales: Les Voix intérieures ; Les rayons et les ombres. II. Odes et ballades; Les feuilles d'automne ; Les chants du crépuscule.

— Théâtre. Paris, 1853-54. 3v. 12° 1066.21

Contents. — Vol. I. Lucrèce Borgia: Marion Delorme; Marie Tudor; La Esmeralda; Ruy Blas. II. Hernani; Le Roi s'amuse; Les Burgraves. III. Angelo; Procès D'Angelo et D'Hernani; Cromwell.

HUGO : a legend of Rockland lake. Helfenstein, E. 449.4
HUGUENOT family, Memoirs of a. Fontaine, J. 617.11
— The priest and the. See Bungener, L. 1066.2-3
HULL, Gen. Wm. Defence before general court marshal at Albany, 1814, with an address to the citizens of the U. S. Boston, 1814. 12° 217.15
— Revolutionary services and civil life. [Ed.] by M. Campbell. New York, 1848. 8° 513.2
HULSE, G. A. Sunbeams and shadows, buds and blossoms. New York, 1851. 12° 478.12
HULSEAN lectures. Trench, R. C. 1106.12
HUMAN body and its connection with man. Wilkinson, J. J. G. 157.6
HUMAN life, or practical ethics. De Wette, W. M. L. de 127.6
HUMAN nature in its fourfold state. Boston, T. 1109.9
— Burnap, G. W. Rectitude of. 1088.3
— Dewey, O. Discourses on 1086.11
— Sunderland, L. Book of. 125.11

HUMAN races, The unity of the. Smyth, T. . . .   176.5
HUMAN species, The natural hist. of the. Smith,
    Lt. Col. C. H. 176.4
    See also: Ethnography, Man, etc.
HUMAN understanding, An essay concerning.
    Locke, J. 122.5
HUMBOLDT, Baron F. H. A. von. Aspects of na-
    ture. Translated by Mrs. Sabine. Phila-
    delphia, 1850. 12° 167.12
— - Same. Translated by E. C. Otté and H. G.
    Bohn. London, 1850. p.8° 816.6-7
— Climate, inhabitants, etc., of Mexico, with
    notes by J. Taylor. London, 1824. 8° . . .   633.4
— Cosmos. Translated by E. C. Otté and B. H.
    Paul. London, 1849-52. 4v. p.8° 816.3
— - Same. New York, 1851-52. 12° . . 146.15-16
— Institutions and monuments of the ancient
    inhabitants of America. Translated by H.
    M. Williams. London, 1814. 2v. 8° . . .   256.2
— Introduction to meteorological essays of F.
    D. Arago 145.17
— Travels to the equinoctial regions of America.
    London, 1852-53. 3v. p.8° 816.13
— Macgillivray, W. Travels and researches of.   810.54
— Klencke, P. F. H. Life of 545.7
HUMBOLDT, Bar. K. W. v. Letters to a female
    friend, transl. from the 2d German ed. by
    Cath. M. A. Couper. London, 1849. 2v. 12°   544.20
— Life, by Schlesier 545.7
HUME, D. History of England, to the abdication
    of James II. Boston, 1851. 6v. 12° 963.1
— - Same, with continuation, by T. Smollett
    and J. R. Miller. Philadelphia, 1832. 4v. 8°   963.1
— - Same, by Hume, Smollett, Miller and
    Wright. London, 1836. 3v. 8° 962.3
— - Same, by Hume, Smollett and Farr. Lon-
    don, n.d. 3v. 8° 961.1
— Life and correspondence. Burton, J. H. . . .   582.12
HUMMING birds, A general history of. Martin,
    W. C. L. 179.2
HUMOR, The cyclopædia of wit and. Burton, W. E.   901.7
HUMOR, wit and wisdom, Quotations of 469.51
HUMOROUS poetry of the English language. Par-
    ton, J. 324.15
HUMPHREYS, D. Life and exploits of Israel Put-
    nam. Hartford, 1851. 12° 528.7
— Same. With a sketch of Bunker hill battle,
    by S. Swett. Boston, 1818. 16° 528.9
HUMPHREYS, H. N. Coin collector's manual. Lon-
    don, 1853. 2v. p.8° 826.8
HUMPHRY Clinker, The expedition of, by To-
    bias Smollett. Barbauld's British novel-
    ists . . . . v.XXX.-XXXI. of 779.1
HUNDRED years ago, 1755 to 1756. Historical
    sketch. Hutton, J. 988.1
HUNGARY. Bowring, J. Sketch of the language
    and literature of 316.2
— Brace, C. L. H. in 1851 . . . .   667.5-6
— Görgei, A. My life and acts in 547.14
— History of the Protestant church in 1095.9
— Klapka, G. Memoirs of the war of indepen-
    dence in 928.10
— Paget, J. Remarks on condition, etc. of . . .   667.16
— Pardoe, J. H. and her institutions, 1839-40 .   928.1
— Pulszky, T. Tales and traditions of 767.2-3
— Scenes of the civil war, 1848-9 . . . .   928.2
— Stiles, W. H. Revolution in, 1848-9 . . . . .   924.2
— and its revolutions, with memoir of Kossuth.
    London, 1854. p.8° 827.5
HUNT, F. Library of commerce. v.I. New York,
    1845. 12° 136.30
    Contents.— Vol. I. Commercial intercourse with
    China, repr. from Knight, with additions by F. Hunt.
    II. History of the British corn laws by J. C. Platt.
    III. Commercial delusions, embracing the Mississippi
    scheme, and the South Sea bubble, by C. Mackay.
— Worth and wealth. Maxims for merchants.
    New York, 1856. 12° 136.20
HUNT, G. H. Outram and Havelock's Persian cam-
    paign. [Also, a] summary of Persian hist.
    by G. Townsend. London, 1858. 12° 938.9

HUNT, H. K. Glances and glimpses. Boston,
    1856. 12° 886.3
HUNT, J. Hours of reflection. n.p. 1845. 12° . .   349.22
HUNT, J. H. Leigh. Autobiography. New York,
    1850. 2v. 12° 584.13
— Book for a corner: selections in prose and
    verse. 1st series. New York, 1852. 12° . .   806.15
— - Same. 2d series. N. Y., 1852. 12° 806.16
— Essays and miscellanies. Phila., 1851. 12° .   807.6
— Imagination and fancy: or, selections from the
    English poets and an essay. New ed. New
    York, 1848. 16° 348.7-8
— Men, women and books. N. Y., 1847. 2v. 12°   908.1
— Poetical works. London, 1832. 8° 332.13
— Stories from the Italian poets. New York,
    1846. 12° 335.14
HUNT, R. Elementary physics. London, 1851. 12°   149.13
— - Same. New ed. London, 1855. p.8° . . .   826.13
— Light in its chemical relations. 2d ed. Lon-
    don, 1854. 8° 145.13
— Manual of photography. 4th ed. London,
    1854. p.8° 197.14
— Poetry of science, or studies of nature. 2d
    ed. London, 1849. 8° 145.15
— - Same. 3d ed. London, 1854. p.8° 826.11
HUNTER, H. Sacred biography. N. Y., 1844. 8°.   541.4
HUNTER, J. D. Manners and customs of several
    Indian tribes, with author's life. Philadel-
    phia, 1823. 8° 625.9
— Memoirs of a captivity among the Indians.
    London, 1823. 8° 244.9
HUNTER, Wm. S. jr. Guide from Niagara falls to
    Quebec. Boston, 1857. 12° 629.13
HUNTER naturalist. Romance of sporting. Web-
    ber, C. W. 171.3-5
— Wild scenes and song birds. Webber, C. W.   171.4
HUNTER's feast: a novel. Reid, M. 716.1-10
HUNTER's life in South Africa. Cumming, R.
    G. 697.10-13
HUNTINGTON, F. D. Sermons for the people.
    Boston, 1856. 12° 1086.8-9
HUNTINGTON, J. V. Lady Alice, or the new Una.
    New York, 1849. 8° 802.3
HUNTINGTON, Lady Selina, and her friends.
    Knight, H. C. 1107.7
HUNTINGTON, Mrs. S., Memoirs of. Wisner, B. B.   538.22
HUNTLEY, H. Seven years' service on the slave
    coast of W'n Africa. London, 1850. 2v. 12°.   698.15
HUNTLEY, Lydia. See Sigourney, Mrs. L. H.
HURLBUT, W. H. Gan-Eden: or, pictures of
    Cuba. Boston, 1854. 12° 627.23
HURRY-GRAPHS. Willis, N. P. 904.1-2
HUSBANDRY, American. Buel, J. 169.29
— Lectures on Roman. Daubeny, C. 165.11
    See also: Agriculture.
HUTCHINSON, Anne, Life of, by Ellis, G. E.
    Sparks's Am. biog. . . . . v.XVI. of 529.1
HUTCHINSON, L. Life of Col. Hutchinson. 7th ed.
    London, 1848. p.8° 818.13
HUTCHINSON, T. J. Impressions of Western Af-
    rica. London, 1858. 12° 667.3
HUTCHINSON, Col. W. N. Dog-breaking 177.4
HUTTEN, U. von, der Ritter, der Gelehrte, u. s. w.
    Bürck, A. 1025.5
HUTTON, J. A hundred years ago, 1755 to 1756.
    Historical sketch. London, 1857. 12° . . .   988.1
HUYDENS, G. Histoire du Marquisat d'Anvers.
    Bruxelles, n.d. 12° 1075.18
HYDE, E., Earl of Clarendon. History of the re-
    bellion and civil wars in England. Oxford,
    1819. 3v. in 6. 8° 977.1
— History of the rebellion and civil wars in Ire-
    land. London, 1720. 8° 975.5
— Enquiry into the character of. Ellis, G. A. .   566.14
— Corresp. with Sir. R. Browne . . . . v.IV. of 977.4
HYDER Ali Khan, History of. Maistre de la
    Tour, M. 547.17
HYDRAULIC machines. Ewbank, T. Account of.   195.3
HYDRAULICS. Ferguson, J. Lectures on 146.8
— Millington, Prof. Hydraulics. Library of
    Useful Knowledge. . . . . v.I. of 365.14

HYDROSTATICS. Brougham, H., *Lord.* Hydrostatics. Lib. Us. Kn. . . . . v.I. of 365.14
— Familiar introduction to 149.39
— Ferguson, J. Lectures on 146.8
— Jamieson, A. H. descriptive and const'ctive. 144.13
— Lardner, D. Treatise on 398.9
HYGIÈNE. Sovet, M. le Dr. H. privée et publique. 1065.53
  See also : Health.
HYMNS. Bowring, J. H. and devotional pieces. 349.18
— Spitta, C. J. P. Christliche Lieder 1034.18
HYPATIA : or new foes with an old face. Kingsley, C. 484.11
HYPERION, a romance. Longfellow, H. W. . . . 438.5–7

ICELAND. Blackwood, F. T. Scenes in I. in 1856. 708.1
— Henderson, E. Journal in, 1814–15 . . . . . 668.1
— Historical and descriptive account of 820.35
— Hooker, W. J. Tour in, 1809 . . . . 668.2
— Howitt, W. and M. Literature of 404.5
— Miles, P. Rambles in 668.12
— Pfeiffer, I. Journey to 668.20
— — Same; with essay on Icelandic poetry, etc. 668.19
ICHTHYOLOGY. *See* Jardine's Naturalists' Library, v.XXXV.–XL. 179.1
— Swainson, W. Natural history of fishes . . . 408.1
— Yarrell, W. History of British fishes 172.11
  See also : Fish, Fish-breeding, etc.
IDA MAY : a story. Pike, M. H. 416.9–11
IDLEWILD : or, a home on the Hudson. Willis, N.P. 904.16
IDOMEN, or the vale of Yumuri. Brooks, M. S. . 469.27
IGNORANCE, Evils of popular. Foster, J. 878.19
ILLINOIS. Birkbeck, M. Letters from. 629.21
— Ford, T. History of, 1818–47 . . . . 237.6
— Gerhard, F. I. as it is 237.7
ILLUSTRATED book of English songs from the 16th to 19th century. 3d ed. Lond., n.d. 12° 869.7
ILLUSTRATED book of Scotch songs from the 16th to 19th century. London, n.d. 12°. . . 869.8
ILLUSTRATED London instructor. Lond., 1850. 8° 405.3
ILLUSTRATED London reading book. London, 1852. 8° 405.2
ILLUSTRATIONS of lying. Opie, A. . . . v.III. of 801.4–6
ILLUSTRATIONS of the history and practices of the Thugs. London, 1851. 8° 937.3
ILLUSTRIOUS personages of Gt. Britain, Portraits of. Lodge, E. 815.1
ILSLEY, C. P. Forest and shore, or legends of the pine tree state. Boston, 1856. 12° 428.1
IMAGINATION, Pleasures of. [A poem.] Akenside, M. 358.25
IMAGINATION and fancy. Hunt, J. H. L. 348.7–8
IMITATIVE art. Manual for the sketcher. Howard, F. 208.19
IMMACULATE conception of the Virgin. Bryant, J. D. 1098.17
IMMERMANN, K. L. Die Epigonen [Roman.] 2te Aufl. Berlin, 1854. 3v. 16° 1037.5
IMMORTALITY. Plato. The I. of the soul, Dialog. on 898.22
— Sears, E. H. Athanasia, or foregleams of. . . 118.18
— Mussey, A. B. Man a soul 1099.18
  See also : Theology.
IMPERIAL guard of Napoleon. Headley, J. T. . . 1008.5
IMPHEE and Sorgho. Olcott, H. L. 166.12
IMPOSTURE, deception, etc. Sketches of 399.5
INCHBALD, Mrs. E. British theatre. Collection of plays with biographical and critical remarks. London, 1808. 25v. 18° 354.1
  Contents. — Vols. I.–V. W. Shakspeare: (1.) Comedy of errors; Romeo and Juliet; Hamlet; King John; King Richard III.; (2.) King Henry IV., part 1–2; Merchant of Venice; King Henry V.; Much ado about nothing; (3.) As you like it; Merry wives of Windsor; King Henry VIII.; Measure for measure; Winter's tale; (4.) King Lear; Cymbeline; Macbeth; Julius Cæsar; Antony and Cleopatra; (5.) Coriolanus; Othello; Tempest; Twelfth night. — Ben Jonson: Every man in his humour. VI. Beaumont and Fletcher: Rule a wife and have a wife; The chances.— P. Massinger: New way to pay old debts. — N. Lee: Rival queens. — J. Dryden: All for love. VII. T. Southern : Isabella, or the fatal marriage; Oroonoko. — J. Racine: Distressed mother, transl. by A. Philips.

INCHBALD, Mrs. E., *continued.*
— Voltaire: Zara, transl. by A. Hill. — H. Brooke: Gustavus Vasa. VIII. G. Farquhar: The constant couple ; The inconstant; Recruiting officer; Beaux stratagem. — J. Addison : Cato. IX. J. Vanbrugh: The provoked wife; The provoked husband. — C. Cibber: Love makes a man; She wou'd and she wou'd not ; The careless husband. X. N. Rowe: Tamerlane; The fair penitent; Jane Shore; Lady Jane Grey. — J. Hughes: Siege of Damascus. XI. S. Centlivre: The busy body ; The wonder; Bold stroke for a wife. — G. Lillo: George Barnwell; Fatal curiosity. XII. T. Otway: The orphan; Venice preserved.—R. Steele: The conscious lovers.—E. Young: The revenge.—J. Gay: The beggars' opera. XIII. W. Congreve: Love for love; The mourning bride. — Voltaire: Mahomet, the impostor, transl. by J. Miller. — J. Thomson: Tancred, and Sigismunda.— B. Hoadly : The suspicious husband. XIV. C. Macklin: The man of the world.—E. Moore: The foundling; The gamester. — W. Whitehead: The Roman father.—W. Shirley: Edward the black prince. XV. J. Brown: Barbarossa.—A. Murphy: The way to keep him; All in the wrong; The Grecian daughter; Know your own mind. XVI. W. Wycherly: (altered by D. Garrick) The country girl.—G. Colman, *the elder:* The jealous wife. — Colman and Garrick : The clandestine marriage. — H. Hartson : The countess of Salisbury. — J. Home : Douglas. XVII. O. Goldsmith: The good natured man; She stoops to conquer.—I. Bickerstaffe: Love in a village; The maid of the mill; Lionel and Clarissa. XVIII. R. Cumberland: The brothers; The West Indian ; The Jew; First love ; Wheel of fortune. XIX. J. F. de La Harpe : The earl of Warwick, transl. by T. Franklin. — R. B. Sheridan : The rivals; The duenna. — H. Cowley : The belle's stratagem; A bold stroke for a husband. XX. F. Reynolds: The dramatist. — R. Jephson: The count of Narbonne.—G. Colman, *the younger :* Inkle and Yarico; The battle of Hexham ; The surrender of Calais. XXI. *(By the same) :* The mountaineers; The iron chest; The heir at law; John Bull; The poor gentleman. XXII. J. O'Keefe: The castle of Andalusia; Fontainbleau; Wild Oats. — J. Burgoyne : The heiress. — H. Jones : The earl of Essex. XXIII. E. Inchbald : Such things are; Every one has his fault; Wives as they were, and maids as they are; Lovers' vows, altered from Kotzebue; To marry, or not to marry. XXIV. T. Holcroft: The road to ruin; The deserted daughter. — A. F. F. v. Kotzebue: The stranger. — J. Baillie : De Monfort.— L. S. Mercier: The point of honor, transl. from " Le Deserteur" by C. Kemble. XXV. T. Morton : The way to get married; A cure for the heart-ache; Speed the plough; The school of reform. — J. Tobin : The honey moon.

— — Same. 4v. Containing a portion of the above . . . .· 357.15
  Contents. — Vol. I. Speed the plough; Cure for the heart-ache; School of reform; Wild oats. II. Deserted daughter; Road to ruin; Such things are; To marry or not to marry. III. First love; Jew; Wheel of fortune ; The way to keep him ; The Grecian daughter. IV. The mountaineers; John Bull; Poor gentleman; The dramatist.

— Collection of farces. London, 1809. 7v. 18°   354.2
  Contents. — Vol. I. Mme. de Genlis: The child of nature, transl. fr. " Zélie." — Mrs. Inchbald : The wedding day. — Damaniant : The midnight hour, transl. fr. the " Guerre ouverte." — J. Kenney: Raising the wind; Matrimony, altered from the French; Elia Rosenberg. — W. B. Ibbetson: The blind boy.— Mrs. H. Cowley: Who's the dupe.—C. Macklin: Love a-la-mode. II. T. Dibdin : The birth-day, altered from Kotzebue ; The Jew and the doctor. — J. Whiteley: The Irishman in London, altered by W. Macready. — J. O'Keefe: The prisoner at large. The poor soldier; The farmer; The Highland reel.— R. Jephson: Two strings to your bow. — C. Dibdin: The deserter. III. W. Pearce: Hartford bridge; Netley abbey. — T. Knight: The turnpike gate. — P. Hoare : Lock and key.—J. Reed: The register office. —A. Murphy: The apprentice.—R. B. Sheridan: The critic. — I. Bickerstaffe: The sultan. — Mrs. F. M. Brooke: Rosina. IV. I. Jackman: All the world's a stage. — D. Garrick: The lying valet. — A. Murphy: The citizen ; Three weeks after marriage. — Shakspeare: Catherine and Petruchio, altered by D. Garrick. — I. Bickerstaffe: The padlock. — D. Garrick: Miss in her teens.—C. Dibdin: The Quaker.—D. Garrick: The guardian. V. D. Garrick: High life below stairs: Bon ton.—H. Fielding: The mock doctor. — C. Coffey: The devil to pay. — D. Garrick: The Irish

INCHBALD, Mrs. E., *continued.*

widow. — S. Foote: The minor; The mayor of Garratt; The lyar. — T. Doggett: Flora, or hob in the well, altered by John Hippisley from the " Country wake." VI. G. Colman, *the elder:* The deuce is in him.—J. Hawkesworth: Edgar and Emmeline.— J. Burgoyne: Richard Cœur de Lion; The maid of the oaks.—K. O'Hara: Tom Thumb.—J. Cobb: The doctor and the apothecary; The first floor.—S. Birch: The adopted child. — J. P. Kemble: The farm house, taken fr. Johnson's Country lasses. VII. G. P. Kemble: Lodoiska; G. Colman, jr.; Ways and means.—J. Tobin: The school for authors.—K. O'Hara: Midas.— C. Dibdin: The waterman.— S. Foote: The author. —A. Murphy: The old maid.— R. Dodsley: The miller of Mansfield. — G. Colman, *the elder:* Comus, altered from Milton.

— A simple story . . . . v.XXVIII. of 778.1
— Nature and art . . . . v.XXVII. of 778.1
INDEPENDENCE, Declaration of. Constitutional text book 290.1
— Constitutions 282.8
    See also: United States.
INDIA, Acland, C. Manners and customs of . . . 889.2
— Allen, D. O. Ancient and modern. 934.1-2
— Campbell, D. Overland journey to 709.18
— Cary, A. F. C. Journal kept in 696.1
— Chapman, J. Cotton and commerce of. . . . 135.10
— Corner, Miss. J. I., pictorial, descriptive and historical 835.2
— Elphinstone, M. History of. 934.3
— Heber, R. Upper provinces of, 1824-25 . . . 708.20
— I., its government, religion, manners and customs 839.16
— Keppel, G. Journey from I. to England . . . 695.5
— Ludlow, J. M. Races and history of British. 939.2
— Mackenzie, C. Six years in 707.11
— Martineau, H. British rule in 989.5
— Mead, H. Sepoy revolt 939.3
— Murray, H. Account of British 810.51
—   - History of British 989.1
— Orlich, L. von. Travels in 695.3
— Pococke, E. I. in Greece, or truth in mythol. 956.10
— Roberts, E. Scenes in 838.10
— Robertson, W. Knowledge the ancients had of . . . . v.III. of 943.4
— Royle, J. F. Arts and manufactures of . . . 199.16
— Taylor, B. I. in 1853 . . . . 708.17-19
— Thornton, E. British empire in 985.1
— Thugs, History and practices of 937.3
— Ward, F. De W. I. and the Hindoos 709.6
INDIAN archipelago, Native races of. Earl, G. W. 176.2
INDIAN biography. Thatcher, B. B. 249.6
INDIAN captivities. Drake, S. G. 245.9-10
INDIAN character and manners. Johnston, C. . . 639.9
INDIAN in his wigwam. Schoolcraft, H. R. . . . 245.6
INDIAN nullification in Mass. Apes, W. 249.3
INDIAN rebellion, causes and results. Duff, A. . 939.4
INDIAN relations of the U. S. and Great Britain, 1783-95. Stone, W. L. 513.12
INDIAN sketches during an expedition to the Pawnees. Irving, J. T. jr. 628.3
INDIAN traits. Thatcher, B. B. 249.4
INDIAN tribes West of the Mississippi. Hunter, J. D. 625.9
— Thirty years with. Schoolcraft, H. R. . . . 244.4
INDIAN wars bordering on the Conn. Hoyt, E. . 245.8
INDIAN wars of the West. Flint, T. 249.2
INDIANA, Early trials and sketches. Smith, O. H. 235.8
INDIANS. Bouton, N. Hist. of the anc. Penacooks 224.3
-- Case of the Seneca Indians of N. Y. 244.8
— Catlin, G. Manners, etc., of the N. American. 245.1
— Copway, G. History of the Ojibway nation. 249.1
— Drake, S. G. History of the I. of N. America. 244.5
— Gardiner, A. F. Visit to the I. of Chili . . . 635.18
— Halkett, J. Notes respecting the I. of N. A.. 245.5
— Hunter, J. D. Captivity among the I. of N. A. 241.9
— M'Kenney, T. L. Travels among the Amer. 625.3
— Moore, J. B. Memoir of the Penacook . . . 224.18
— Murray, C. A. Residence among the Pawnees. 639.3
— Parkman, F. jr. War of against the colonies. 244.2-3
-- Pinckard, G. Observations on the I. of S. A. 635.7

INDIAN. Schoolcraft, H. R. Notes on Iroquois . 224.6
— - Indian tales and legends 489.9
— Tanner, J. Captivity and advent. among the. 245.4
— Trumbull, H. History of engagem'ts with the. 245.7
  See also: Black Hawk, Jemison, M., Tecumseh, Thayendanegea, etc.
INDIES. See West Indies.
INDUCTIVE philosophy, Spirit of. Powell, B. . . . 147.23
INDUS, Voyage on the. Burnes, A. 694.11
INDUSTRIAL drawing. Mahan, D. H. 203.6
INDUSTRIAL education, Necessity of. Playfair, L. 199.16
INDUSTRIAL information, Boy's book of. Noyce, E. 196.15
INDUSTRIAL resources of the S. and W. states. De Bow, J. D. B. 296.2
INDUSTRY of all nations, Cyclopædia of. Knight, C. 196.2
INDUSTRY of the Rhine. Banfield, T. C. 840.1
INEBRIATING liquors, Manufacture and use of. Morewood, S. 196.9
INFANCY. Combe, A. The physiological and moral management of 158.17
— West, C. Diseases of. 151.20
INFANTRY tactics. See United States. 199.39
INFIDELITY. Comprising Jenyns, Leslie, Lyttelton, and Watson, etc. New York, n.d. 16° 119.9

  Contents. — Jenyns' internal evidence ; Leslie's short method; Lyttelton's conversion of Paul; Watson's reply to Gibbon and Paine; A notice of Hume on miracles; Starkie's examination of same. An extract from West on the resurrection.

— Crichton, A. Converts from 830.28
— Morison, J. Counsels to young men on modern 1109.16
— Nelson, D. Cause and cure of 1107.16
— Pearson, T. Aspects, causes, etc., of 1083.11
  See also: Evidences of Christianity, and Theology.
INFUSORIA. Living and fossil. Pritchard, A. . . . 175.3
INGERSOLL, C. J. Second war between the United States and Great Britain. Phila., 1845. 4v. 8° 215.9
INGLIS, H. D. Journey through Ireland during 1834. 3d ed. London, 1835. 2v. 646.5
— Journey through Norway, Sweden and Denmark. Edinburgh, 1829. 18° 830.47
— - Same. 4th ed. London, 1837. 12° 668.7
— Rambles in the footsteps of Don Quixote. London, 1837. 12° 673.5
— Spain. 2d ed. London, 1837. 2v. 12° . . . 675.14
— Switzerland, the South of France and the Pyrenees. London, 1837. 12° 663.14
— - Same. Edinburgh, 1831. 2v. 18° 830.65
— The Tyrol: with a glance at Bavaria. London, 1833. 2v. p.8° 663.15
INGOLDSBY legends. Barham, R. H. 345.6
INGRAHAM, J. H. The Cruiser of the Mist. New York, 1845. 8° 801.1
INGULPH'S chronicle of the abbey of Croyland, with the continuations, by Peter of Blois. Translated by H. T. Riley. Lond., 1854. p.8° 856.8
INHERITANCE, The: a novel. Ferrier, S. 777.12
INHERITANCE, The, and other sketches. Töpffer, R. 469.12
INITIALS, The : a story of modern life. Tautphœus, Baroness 474.11-12
IN memoriam. [A poem.] Tennyson, A. 334.21
INQUIRE within. [A receipt book.] New York, 1857. 12° 188.32
INQUIRY into the tendency of the separation of convicts to produce disease and derangement. Philadelphia, 1849. 8° 135.13
INSANITY. Barlow, J. Man's power over himself to prevent, etc. . . . . v.I. of 850.25
— Cooke, W. Mind and the emotions in relation to disease 137.4
— Millingen, J. G. Management of the insane. 139.26
— Rush, B. Observations on diseases of the mind 122.11
— Upham, T. C. Imperfect and disordered mental action 820.7
  See also: Intellectual science.
INSCRIPTIONS on grave stones in Northampton, etc. Bridgman, T. 228.3

INSECT architecture. Rennie, J. 839.13
INSECT life, Episodes of 175.8
INSECT miscellanies. London, n.d. 12° 839.14
— - Same. Boston, 1832. 12° 849.14
INSECT transformations. London, n.d. 12° . . . 839.15
— - Same. Boston, 1831. 12° 849.15
INSECTS. Harris, T. W. I. of New England injurious to vegetation 165.1
— Newman, E. Familiar introduction to the history of. 175.7
— Rennie, J. and Westwood, J. O. Natural history of 810.9
— Swainson, W. History and natural arrangement of 408.3
See also : Entomology, Natural Hist. etc.
INSPIRATION of the Scriptures. See Bible and Theology.
INSTINCT. Brougham, H., Lord. Dialogues on . 840.8
— Kemp, T. L. Indications of 409.2
— Paine, M. Discourse on 125.10
— Swainson, W. I. of animals 408.4
INSTITUTION of civil engineers. Manufacture of rotating chambered-breech fire arms. By S. Colt. London, 1854. 8° 195.23
INSTITUTIONS of the Greeks and Romans, Treatise on. Fosbroke, T. D. 378.3
INSTRUCTIVE tales. Trimmer, S. 759.1
INSTRUCTOR's manual. Hall, S. R. 129.24
See also : Education.
INSTRUMENTS. Brewster, D. Treatise on new philosophical 144.12
— Heather, J. F. Treatise on mathematical . . 819.23
— Kentish, T. Treatise on a box of 199.9
INSUBORDINATION : an Am. story, Arthur, T. S. 449.11
INSURANCE. See Martou, E. Inst. de prévoyance. 1065.38
INTELLECTUAL powers. Abercrombie, J. Inquiries concerning 124.20-21
INTELLECTUAL science. Aristotle's metaphysics. 854.4
— Bailey, S. Formation of opinions 137.33
— Barlow, J. Connec'n of physiology and. v.I. of 850.25
— Bockshammer, G. F. Freedom of the will . . 1099.9
— Brodie, B. C. Mind and matter 125.6
— - Psychological inquiries 129.18
— Brougham, H. Dialogues on instinct 840.7
— Comte, A. Positive philosophy 124.10
— Durfee, J. Panidea : or, omnipresent reason, as the Logos 122.8
— Edwards, J. Freedom of the will 124.6
— Feuchtersleben, E. v. Dietetics of the soul . 129.15
— Greek philosophy . . . . v.II. of 850.25
— - Greek philosophy, from Socrates to the coming of Christ . . . . v.II of 850.25
— Hare Brothers. Guesses at truth 139.11
— Haven, J. Mental philosophy 124.8
— Home, H., Lord Kames. Art of thinking . . 129.11
— Kant, I. Critique of pure reason 855.5
— Lewes, G. H. Comte's philosophy of the sciences 826.9
— Locke, J. Philosophical works 827.4
— - Human understanding 820.65
— Mackay, C. Extraordinary delusions 870.8
— Paine, M. The soul and instinct 125.10
— Philosophical theories and experience . . v.I.of 850.25
— Schlegel, F. von. Æsthetic works 838.8
— Scott, Sir W. Demonology 840.13
— Symonds, J. A. Sleep and dreams 125.23
— Taylor, I. The world of mind 125.7
— Tennemann, W. A. History of philosophy . 855.1
— Upham, T. C. Disordered mental action . . . 820.7
— - Mental philosophy 125.4
— Wayland, F. Elements of intellectual philos. 124.14
See also : Education, Ethics, Insanity, Metaphysics, Philosophy, etc.
INTER-OCEANIC railway, The Honduras. Squier, E. G. 263.7
INTEREST, Essays on. McCulloch, J. R. 135.4
See also : Mathematics.
INTRODUCTION to practical organic chemistry. Philadelphia, 1846. 16° . . . . v.I. of 850.25
INTRODUCTION to vegetable physiology. Philadelphia, 1846. 16° . . . . v.III. of 850.25

INVASION, The : a novel. Griffin, G. 807.1
INVENTIONS. Beckmann, J. History of 818.8-9
— History of wonderful 197.20
— Novelties, I., etc., in arts and manufactures . 199.26
— Somerset, E., Marq. of Worcester. Century of. 199.27
INVENTOR's guide. Phillips, W. 196.18
INVENTOR's manual of legal principles. Curtis, G. T. 196.17
INVERTEBRATA. Gould, A. A. Report on the I. of Massachusetts 175.2
— Owen, R. Comparative anatomy and physiology of 172.15
— Siebold, C. T. von. Anatomy of 175.1
ION : a tragedy. Talfourd, T. N. 356.13
IONIAN islands, History of the republic of. Jervis-White-Jervis, H. 918.10
IOWA handbook for 1856. Parker, N. H. 237.16
IRBY, C. L. and Mangles, J. Travels in Egypt and Nubia, Syria and the Holy Land. London, 1844. p.8°. 889.25
IRELAND : a tale. Martineau, H. . . . . . v.IX. of 749.2-3
IRELAND. Barrington, Sir J. Legislative union between Great Britain and 986.6
— Barrow, J. A tour round 646.17
— Bigelow, A. Rambles in some parts of . . . 648.16
— Cockayne, T. O. History of 989.13
— Gordon, J. History of 975.3
— Greg, R. P. Mineralogy of 163.8
— Haskins, G. F. Travels in 658.14
— Hayes, E. The ballads of 316.5
— Hyde, E. Rebellion and civil wars of 975.5
— - Historical view of the affairs of 977.1
— Inglis, H. D. Journey throughout, in 1834 . 646.5
— Kohl, J. G. Scotland, England and 647.5
— Marmion, A. Maritime ports of 975.4
— Mills, A. Literature and literary men of . . . 402.2
— Moore, T. History of 368.5
— Nicholson, A. Famine in 646.18
— - Tour through 647.22
— O'Connor, A. The state of 647.6
— Sampson, W. History of 575.8
— Taylor, W. C. Civil wars of 830.68
— - History of 810.52
— Thackeray, W. M. Sketches in 501.11
— Weld, C. R. Vacations in 646.4
See also : Great Britain.
IRELAND's welcome to the stranger. Nicholson, A. 647.22
IRENE : or, the autobiography of an artist's daughter. Fairfield, G. G. 804.6
IRETON, H., Biography of 399.7
IRISH bar. Curran, W. H. Sketches of 598.4
— Sheil, R. L. Sketches of 598.5
IRISH balls, Essay on. Edgeworth, M. . . v.I. of 467.1-3
IRISH character, Sketches of. Hall, A. M. 804.1-2
IRISH eloquence. Phillips, Curran and Grattan . . 862.3-8
IRISH history, Outlines of 989.4
IRISH life, Lights and shadows of. Hall, A. M. . 776.12
IRISH nation, Rise and fall of. Barrington, Sir J. 986.6
IRISH peasantry, Stories of. Hall, A. M. 776.10
IRISH settlers in North America. McGee, T. D. . 309.2
IRISH sketch-book, 1842. Thackeray, W. M. . . . 508.1
IRISH tales. Illustrated by Cruikshank. 815.2
IRISHMEN, Lives and times of the United. Madden, R. R. 598.1-3
IRON. Fairbairn, W. Application of, to building. 194.1
— Manufacture of. Lib. Us. Kn. 199.34
— Mushet, D. Papers on I. and steel 194.7
— Overman, F. Manufacture of 195.6
IRON cousin, The. Clarke, M. C. 434.6-7
IRON manufacture of Great Britain. Truran, W. . 191.5
IRON mask, The. Dumas, A. 735.1
— Ellis, G. J. W. A. History of 615.9
IRON metallurgy, Element. treat. on. Rogers, S. B. 195.8
IRON roads, History, construction of. Williams, F. S. 195.13
IRON ships, The compass in. Scoresby, W. . . . 196.7
IROQUOIS, the, Notes on. Schoolcraft, H. R. . . 244.6
IRRAWADDI, Up and down the 709.10
IRVING, D. Lives of Scottish writers. Edinburgh, 1850. 2v. in 1. 12° 586.13

IRVING, J. T. jr. Indian sketches. Philadelphia, 1835. 2v. 12°. 628.3
IRVING, T. Conquest of Florida. N.Y., 1851. 12° 237.11
IRVING, W. Works. New edition. New York, 1849-53. 15v. 12°. *Containing:*
  1. Knickerbocker's history of New York . . 387.2-4
  2. Sketch-book 387.5-10
  3-5. Columbus and his companions 397.1-3
  6. Bracebridge hall 397.4-8
  7. Tales of a traveller 397.9-13
  8. Astoria 407.1-3
  9. Crayon miscellany 407.4-5
  10. Bonneville's adventures 407.6-8
  11. Oliver Goldsmith 407.9-12
  12, 13. Mahomet and his successors 407.13-16
  14. Conquest of Granada 408.12-14
  15. The Alhambra 408.15-19
— Works. Loudon, 1854. 10v. p.8°. 367.2-3
   Contents. — Vol. I. Salmagundi ; Knickerbocker's N. Y. II. Sketch book ; Life of O. Goldsmith. III. Bracebridge Hall ; Abbotsford and Newstead Abbey. IV. Alhambra ; Tales of a traveller. V. Conquest of Granada and Spain. VI. Columbus. VII. Columbus and his companions. VIII. Astoria ; Tour on the prairies. IX. Mahomet. X. Capt. Bonneville and T. Irving's conquest of Florida.

— Complete works, with memoir. Paris, 1834. 1v. in 2. imp.8° 901.1
   Contents. — Part I. Memoir ; Salmagundi ; History of New York ; Sketch book ; Bracebridge Hall ; Tales of a traveller. II. Life and voyages of Christopher Columbus ; Voyages and discoveries of the companions of Columbus ; Chronicle of the conquest of Granada ; The Alhambra.

— Abbotsford and Newstead abbey. Philadelphia, 1835. 16° 438.18
— Alhambra. Philadelphia, 1832. 2v. in 1. 12° 438.20
— Astoria, or an enterprise beyond the Rocky mountains. Philadelphia, 1836. 2v. 8° . . 625.5
— Bracebridge hall. Phila., 1830. 2v. in 1. 12° 438.19
— - Same. London, 1845. p.8° 889.26
— History of New York. By Diedrich Knickerbocker. New ed. Phila., 1838. 2v. 12° 438.17
— - Same. London, 1836. 16° 389.8
— Life and voyages of Christopher Columbus. Abridged. Boston, 1839. 12° 544.18
— - Same. 2d ed. London, 1841. 16° . . . 389.9
— Life of Washington. London, 1856-7. 4v. 12° 516.6-10
— - Same. New York, 1855-57. 4v. 8°. . . 511.1-4
— Oliver Goldsmith : a biography. London, 1849. p.8° 583.14
— - Same, with selections from his writings. New York, n.d. 2v. 18° 820.28
— Rocky mountains, or incidents in the far West. Philadelphia, 1837. 2v. 12° 639.14
— Sketch book of Geoffrey Crayon. New ed. London, 1858. 2v. 16° 389.10
— Tales of a traveller. New edition. London, 1848. p.8° 889.27
— Tour on the prairies. Philadelphia, 1835. 12° 639.15
— Voyages and discoveries of the companions of Columbus. London, 1831. 16° 389.11
— Wolfert's roost, etc. New York, 1855. 12° . 438.13-16
— and Paulding, J. K. Salmagundi. 1st ser. New ed. New York, 1835. 2v. 12° . . . 438.22
— - Same. 2d series. N. Y., 1835. 2v. 12° . 438.21
— - Same. New York, 1808. 2v. 18° . . . 759.13
— Biographical sketch of T. Campbell. Stone, W. L. 237.14
— Biography and remains of M. M. Davidson . 538.12
ISAAC Comnenus : a play. Taylor, II. 355.7
ISAACO. Death of M. Park. *See* Park, M. . . 820.11
ISABEL, the young wife. Jeaffreson, J. C. . . . 478.6
ISABELLA Orsini. Racconto. Guerrazzi, F. D. . 1057.5
ISAIAH, Book of. *See* Bible.
ISHAM, W. Mud cabin, or the character and tendency of British institutions. New York, 1853. 12° 135.21
ISLAND world, The : or Madagascar, Java, Iceland, etc. Nordhoff, C. 939.5

ISNARDO o sia il milite romano. Racconto italico. Colleoni, G. 1049.3
ISOTTA. Novella. Cantù, C. 1046.13
ISRAEL, Tae, of the Alps. Muston, A. 879.13
   See also: Waldenses.
ISRAELITISH nation, History of the. Wise, I. M. 1085.7
   See also: Jews.
ISTHMUS, Practicability of commerce through the Mexican. Robinson, W. D. 254.8
ISTRIA, Dora d', Comtesse. *Pseud. See* Ghika, Helen.
ITALIAN journey : or, the sisters abroad. Channing, B. II. 678.17
ITALIAN painters, Mems. of the early. Jameson, A. 840.23
ITALIAN poets, Stories from the. Hunt, J. H. L. 335.14
ITALIAN republics, History of the. Sismondi, J. C. L. S. de 378.4
ITALIAN sights and papal principles. Jarves, J. J. 678.9
ITALY. Balbo, C. Storia d' 1046.9
— Beckford, W. Travels in 675.18
— - I., with sketches of Spain and Portugal . 679.6
— Bell, J. Observations on 679.3
— Beyle, II. Chroniques Italiennes 1067.16
— - Histoire de la peinture en 1067.24
— Botta, C. Storia d', sino al 1789 . . . . . 1048.2
— - Storia d', dal 1789 al 1814 . . . . 1048.1
— Bruen, M. Essays on scenes in 679.5
— Colquhoun, J. C. Life in I. in the olden time. 915.5
— Cooper, J. F. Gleanings in Europe 679.4
— Dickens, C. Pictures from 481.12-16
— Eustace, J. C. Classical tour through . . . 675.1
— Göthe, J. W. v. Letters from . . . . v.II. of 838.3-4
— Guicciardini, F. Istoria d' 1048.3
— Haskins, G. F. Travels in 658.14
— Headley, J. T. Letters from 676.18
— Hillard, G. S. Six months in 679.7-9
— Kugler, F. Schools of painting in 208.12
— Laing, S. Social and political state of . . . 409.14
— Lanzi, A. L. History of painting in 828.4
— - Storia pittorica della 1058.13
— Lemaistre, J. G. Travels in, after the peace of Amiens 654.3
— Lyman, T. jr. Political state of 915.3
— MacFarlane, C. Popular customs, sports, etc., of the South of 840.36
— - Romance of history 419.6
— Mariotti, L. Views of its history and lit. . . 917.1
— Matthews, H. Tour in 679.14
— Miraglia, B. Condizione della letteratura I. . 1059.7
— Moore, J. Society and manners in 675.4
— Murray, J. and Blewitt, O. Handbooks of Northern, Southern, and Middle I. 649.4
— Pfeiffer, I. Visit to 879.5
— Piozzi, II. L. Observations and reflections in. 676.1
— Ranalli, F. Istorie Ital., 1846-53 . . . . . 1057.8
— Raumer, F. v. I. and the Italians 678.4
— Rochau, A.L. v. Wanderings thro. the cities of 678.1
— Rose, W. S. Letters from the North of . . . 675.3
— Sforzosi, L. History of 810.74
— Shelley, Mrs. Lives of eminent literary and scientific men of 398.1
— Simond, L. A tour in Sicily and 675.2
— Sinclair, J. D. An autumn in 830.53
— Spaulding, W. I. and the Italian islands . . 820.51
— Turnbull, R. Genius of 676.6
— Valery, A. C. P. Curiosités et anecdotes . . 1065.2
   See also: Names of various parts of Italy.
IVANHOE. Scott, Sir W. 460.39-40
IVIMEY, J. John Milton ; his life and times. New York, 1833. 12° 586.23
IVORS : a novel. Sewell, E. M. 424.9-12
IVRY : a song of the Huguenots. Macaulay, T. B. 324.13
IZARD, R. Correspondence and memoir, from 1774 to 1804. New York, 1844. 12° 216.11

JACK Jugler : a play. Child, F. J. 356.1
JACK of the mill, Life of. Howitt, W. 802.16
JACK Tier : or the Florida reef. Cooper, J. F. 760.38-40
JACKSON, A. Baldwin, J. G. Sketch of . . . 518.7
— Eaton, J. II. Life of 517.3

JACKSON, A. Frost, J. Pictorial life of 517.1
— Waldo, S. P. Memoirs of 517.2
JACKSON and New Orleans. Walker, A. 215.15
JACKSON, F. History of the early settlement of
    Newton. Boston, 1854. 12° 227.5
JACKSON, J. Letters to a young physician. Bos-
    ton, 1855. 12° 157.23-24
JACKSON, J., jr. Memoir, with letters and medi-
    cal cases. Ed. by J.J., sen. Boston, 1835. 8°. 523.13
JACKSON, J. G. Empire of Morocco, and the dis-
    trict of Suse, [with] an account of Timbuc-
    too. Philadelphia, 1810. 12° 699.11
JACKSON, W. A man of sorrows : or, the life of
    W. J. 3d ed., enlarged. Boston, 1842. 12° . 534.15
JACOB Faithful : a novel. Marryat, Capt. F. . . 745.13
JACOB, S. History of the Ottoman empire. By
    S. J., Col. Procter, J. E. Riddle, and J. M'-
    Conechy. 2d ed., rev. London, 1854. 12°. 956.11
JACOBITE ballads. Thornbury, G. W. 316.3
JACOBITES of 1715 and 1745. Memoirs of the.
    Thomson, A. T. 562.2
JACOBS, T. J. Scenes in the Pacific ocean. New
    York, 1844. 12° 708.11
JACQUERIE, (La,) ou les insurrections des pay-
    sans. Paris, 1853. 12° 1078.25
— Scènes féodales. Drame. Mérimée, P. . . . 1069.6
JAHN, J. Biblical archæology. Translated by T.
    C. Upham. 5th ed. New York, 1853. 8°. . 1103.5
— Hebrew commonwealth, with history of the
    Jews, to Adrian. From Basnage. Transl.
    by C. E. Stowe. London, n.d. 8° 1085.8
JAHR, G. H. G. Treatise on homœopathia. Trans.
    by E. Bayard. New York, 1845. 12°. . . . 158.20
JAMAICA. Bleby, H. Facts and incidents in . . 127.20
— Gosse, P. H. A naturalist's sojourn in . . . 178.7
— - The birds of 178.16
— Phillippo, J. M. Its past and present state . . 264.2
JAMES I. Aikin, L. Memoirs of the court of . . 552.8
— Birch, T. Court and times of 552.10
— Chambers, R. Life of 830.59
— D'Israeli, I. Character of . . . . . v.III. of 897.5-6
— Goodman, G. Court of 552.7
— Harris, W. Historical and critical account of
    the life and writings of 552.9
— Secret history of the court of 552.6
JAMES II. Ainsworth, W. H. Hist'cal romance. 802.7
— Carrel, J. B. N. A. Fox's history of the
    reign of 837.10
— Lord Lonsdale's reign of 837.10
JAMES, duke of Monmouth, Life of. Roberts, G. . 566.5
JAMES, G. P. R. Ancient regime : a tale. London,
    1841. 3v. p.8° 464.7
— Arabella Stuart. A romance. Lond., 1844.3v. 12° 463.21
— - Same. New York, 1844. 12° . . . . 463.2&18-20
— Arrah Neil. A romance. New York, 1844. 8° 463.3-4
— Attila. A romance. New York, 1837. 2v. 12°. 464.6
— Beauchamp : or, the error. New York, 1847. 8° 463.1
— - Same. London, 1848. 3v. 12° 463.26
— Castle of Ehrenstein. [A novel.] New York,
    1847. 8° 463.2
— - Same. London, 1847. 3v. 12° 463.24
— Charles Tyrrell. A novel. New York, 1845.
    2v. in 1. 16° 463.30
— Commissioner. New York, 1851. 8°. 463.11
— The convict. A tale. London, 1847. 3v. 12° 463.28
— Corse de Leon. A romance. New York, 1845.
    2v. in 1. 16° 463.29
— Dark scenes of history. Lond., 1849. 3v. 12° 463.27
— Desultory man. London, 1836. 3v. 12° . . 464.1
— The false heir : a novel. New York, 1843. 8° 463.2 & 16
— - Same. London, 1843. 3v. 12° 463.17
— Forest days : a romance. New York, 1843. 8° 463.1
— The gipsy. A tale. New York, 1836. 2v.
    [in 1.] 12° 464.2-3
— Heidelberg. A romance. New York, 1846. 8° 463.1 & 8
— Henry Masterton. London, 1832. 3v. 12° . . 464.4
— - Same. New York, 1832. 2v. 12° 464.8
— Henry Smeaton : a Jacobite story. New York,
    n.d. 8° 463.13
— History of Charlemagne. N. Y., n.d. 18°. . 810.60

JAMES, G. P. R. History of chivalry. New York,
    n.d. 18° 810.20
— History of Edward the Black Prince. Lond.,
    1836. 2v. 8° 552.3
— King's highway. A novel. London, 1840.
    3v. 12° 463.25
— Life and times of Louis XIV. New ed. Lon-
    don, 1851. 2v. p.8° 858.3
— Life of Richard Cœur de Lion. London, 1841-
    1849. 4v. 8° 552.2
— - Same. New ed. London, 1854. 2v. p.8°. 827.7
— Margaret Graham. New York, 1847. 8° . . 463.7
— Mary of Burgundy : or, the revolt of Ghent.
    New York, 1853. 2v. 12° 464.11
— - Same. Philadelphia, 1848. 8° 463.6
— Morley Ernstein : or, the tenants of the heart.
    2d ed. London, 1843. 3v. 12° 464.5
— Philip Augustus. New York, 1831. 2v. 12° . 464.10
— The robber. A tale. New York, 1846. 2v. 12° 464.9
— Rose d'Albret. A romance. N. Y., 1844. 8° 463.9
— Russell : a tale of the reign of Charles II.
    London, 1847. 3v. 12° 463.15
— - Same. New York, 1847. 8° 463.14
— Story without a name. New York, 1852. 8°. 463.12
— Sir Theodore Broughton : or, laurel water.
    New York, 1848. 8° 463.5
— Ticonderoga. A romance. N. Y., 1854. 8°. 463.10
— Lives of foreign statesmen. . . v.II.-V. of 388.7
JAMES, H. Christianity the logic of creation.
    New York, 1857. 12° 1088.7
— Lectures and miscellanies. N. Y., 1852. 12°. 885.7
— Nature of evil. New York, 1855. 12° 1088.26
JAMES, J. A. Anxious inquirer after salvation.
    New York, n.d. 16° 119.23
— - Same. New York, 1853. 18° 1109.25
— Christian professor addressed. N. Y., 1838. 12° 118.8
— Christian progress. New York, n.d. 16° . . 119.22
— Pastoral addresses, chiefly on Christian duty.
    New York, 1852. 12° 1088.30
— Young man from home. New York, n.d. 16° 119.28
JAMES Leganger, Passages from the life of. Car-
    len, E. 766.1
JAMES, Marian. The elder sister. N. Y., 1855. 12°.498.15-16
JAMES, Maria. Wales and other poems, with an
    introd. by A. Potter. New York, 1839. 12° 358.1
JAMES, W. Naval history of Great Britain. 1793-
    1827. New ed., with additions, by Capt.
    Chamier. London, 1837. 6v. 8° 986.2
JAMES, Epistle of. See Bible.
JAMESON, Mrs. A. Commonplace book of thoughts.
    London, 1854. p.8° 876.13
— - Same. New York, 1855. 12° 877.9
— Diary of an ennuyée. From the last London
    ed. Boston, 1857. 18° 469.50
— - Same. Boston, 1833. 12° 658.8
— Loves of the poets. From last London ed.
    Boston, 1857. 18° 359.11
— Memoirs and essays, art, literature, etc. Lon-
    don, 1846. 12° 876.14
— Memoirs of celebrated female sovereigns.
    New York, n.d. 2v. 18° 810.44
— Memoirs of the early Italian painters, and of
    the progress of painting in Italy. London,
    1845. 2v. 18° 840.23
— Public galleries of art in and near London.
    London, 1842. 12° 208.9
— Sisters of Charity and the communion of labor.
    Boston, 1857. 12° 127.23-24
— Sketches in Canada. New ed. London, 1852.
    12° 629.24
— - Same. New ed. London, 1852. p.8° . . 409.12
— Winter studies and summer rambles in Cana-
    da. London, 1838. 3v. 12° 629.10
JAMESON, R. Discovery and adventure in the
    polar seas. 810.15
— History of British India 810.51
— Narrative of discov. and adventure in Africa . 810.18
JAMESTOWN, English plantation at. Banvard, J. 228.15
JAMESTOWN, Voyage of the, on her errand of
    mercy. Forbes, R. B. 296.5

JAMIESON, A. Mechanics of fluids, comprising hydrostatics. 2d edition. London, 1848. 8° 144.13
JANE Bouverie. Sinclair, C. 456.9-11
JANE Eyre. Brontë, C. 435.2-8
JANE Talbot: a tale. Brown, C. B. 757.4
JANNEY, S. M. Life of Penn; with selections from his correspondence and autobiography. 2d edition. Philadelphia, 1852. 8° 523.14
JAPAN. Golownin, W. M. J. and the Japanese . 708.14
— Hildreth, R. J. as it was and is 708.3
— Hawks, F. L. J. expedition, 1852-54. . . . 701.2
— Spalding, J. W. J. and around the world . . 708.4
— Taylor, B. J. in 1853 . . . . .708.17-19
— Tomes, R. U. States expedition to, abridged. 708.5
JAPANESE, Manners and customs of the 708.2
JAPHET in search of a father. Marryat, Capt. F. . 745.10
JARDINE, D. Criminal trials. Narrative of the gunpowder plot. London, [1836?] 2v. 12°. 839.4
— Same. v.I. Boston, 1832. 16°. 849.11
— Narrative of the gunpowder plot. London, 1857. 12° 977.6
JARDINE, Sir W. Naturalist's library. Edinburgh, [1840]-1852. 40v. 16° n.d. 179.1

Contents.—Vol. I.—XIV. Ornithology. (1—4.) Birds of Great Britain and Ireland. (5.) Sunbirds; (6—7.) Humming-birds; (8.) Gamebirds, by the editor; (9.) Pigeons; (10.) Parrots, by P. J. Selby. (11—12.) Birds of Western Africa; (13.) Flycatchers, by W. Swainson. (14.) Gallinaceous birds, by the editor. XV.—XXVII. Mammalia. (15.) Introduction to mammalia, by C. H. Smith. (16.) Lions, tigers, etc. by the editor. (17.) British quadrupeds, by W. Macgillivray. (18—19.) Dogs; (20.) Horses, by C. H. Smith. (21.) Deer, antelopes, camels, etc.; (22.) Goats, sheep, oxen, etc.; (23.) Thick skinned quadrupeds, by the editor. (24.) Marsupialia; or, pouched animals, by G. R. Waterhouse, Esq. (25.) Amphibious carnivora; (26.) Whales, etc., by Robt. Hamilton, M. D. (27.) Monkeys, by the editor. XXVIII.—XXXIV. Entomology. (28.) Introduction to entomology, by J. Duncan. (29.) British butterflies; (30.) Moths, sphinxes, etc., by J. Duncan. (31.) Foreign butterflies; (32.) Exotic moths, etc., by J. Duncan. (33.) Beetles, by J. Duncan. (34.) Bees. XXXV.—XL. Ichthyology. (35.) Treating of the nature, structure, and economical uses of fishes, by J. S. Bushnan. (36,37.) British fishes, by R. Hamilton. (38.) Fishes of the perch family, by the editor. (39,40.) Fishes of British Guiana, by R. H. Schomburgk, Esq.
Note.—Each vol. contains a biographical notice of some celebrated naturalist. See Naturalists.

JARVES, J. J. Art hints. Architecture, sculpture, and painting. New York, 1855. 12° 208.16
— History of the Hawaiian islands. 3d edition. Honolulu, 1847. 8° 931.6
— Italian sights and papal principles. New York, 1856. 12° 678.9
— Parisian sights and French principles. New York, 1852. 12° 654.17
— — Same. 2d series. New York, 1855. 12° . 1008.9
— Why and what am I? confessions of an inquirer. Part I. Boston, 1857. 12°. 766.10
JAUFRY the knight, and the fair Brunissende. From the French version of Mary Lafon, by A. Elwes. New York, 1857. 8° 735.2
JAY, J. The federalist. See Madison, J. 285.4
— Life and times of. Flanders, H. 523.3
— Life of, with selections from his correspondence. Jay, W. 512.13
— Life of. Renwick, H. B. 820.33
JAY, Rev. W. Autobiography: ed. by G. Redford and J. A. James. N. Y., 1855. 2v. 12° 575.15
— Christian contemplated. New York, n.d. 16° 119.14
JAY, W. Causes and consequences of the Mexican war. Boston, 1849. 12° 259.5
— Life of John Jay, with selections from his correspondence. New York, 1833. 2v. 8°. 512.13
— Miscellaneous writings on slavery. Boston, 1853. 12° 118.3
JEAFFRESON, J. C. Isabel, the young wife and the old love. New York, 1857. 12° 478.6
JEAMES's diary. Thackeray, W. M. 509.15-17
JEAN Paul. See Richter, J. P. F. 1036.1
JEANNE d'Arc. See Joan of Arc.

JEANS, H. W. Navigation and nautical astronomy. London, 1853. 16° 829.30
JEBB, J. and Knox, A. Thirty years' correspondence. Ed. by C. Forster. Phila., 1835. 2v. 8° 575.5
JEFFERSON, T. Writings. Ed. by H. A. Washington. Washington, 1853-54. 9v. 8° . . 286.1
Contents.—Vol. I. Autobiography and correspondence. II.—VII. Correspondence. VII.—VIII. Official papers. VIII. Biographical sketches. IX. Manual of parliamentary practice; The anas, and miscellaneous papers.
— Memoir, correspondence and miscellanies. Ed. by T. J. Randolph. Charlottesville, 1829. 4v. 8° 523.17
— Notes on Virginia. 9th Am. ed. Bost., 1802. 16° 239.15
— Baldwin, J. G. Sketch of. 518.7
— Carpenter, S. C. Memoirs of 523.16
— Dwight, T. Character of 517.16
— Randall, H. S. Life of. 512.2
— Rayner, B. L. Life of. 517.24
— and Cabell, J. C. Early history of the university of Va. Richmond, 1856. 8°. . . 294.2
JEFFREY, F., Lord. Contributions to the Edinburgh review. Phila., 1850. 4v. in 1. 8° . 863.6
— Jonathan Swift. [Repr. from Edinburgh review.] London, 1853. 12° 409.3
— Samuel Richardson. [Repr. from Edinburgh review.] London, 1853. 12° 409.3
— Life, with selections from his correspondence. Cockburn, H., Lord 568.3
JEFFREYS, G., Judge, Memoirs. Woolrych, H. W. 568.4
JELLALABAD, Seizure and defence of. Gleig, G. R. 899.11
JEMISON, M. (Deh-He-Wä-Mis.) Life. Seaver, J. E. 539.3
JENKS, J. W. Rural poetry of the English language. Boston, 1856. 8° 314.3
JENNER, E. Life, with correspondence. Baron, J. 573.1
JENNINGS, R. Social delusions concerning wealth and want. London, 1856. 16° 139.13
JENNY. Roman. Lewald, F. 1024.11
JENYNS, L. Observations in meteorology. London, 1858. 8° 145.24
JENYNS, S. Internal evidence of the Christian religion 119.9
JERRMANN, E. Pictures from St. Petersburg. Translated by F. Hardman. N. Y., 1852. 12° 687.23
— Same. London, 1853. 12° 409.13
JERROLD, D. Writings. Collected ed. London, 1851-54. 8v. 12° 905.1
Contents. — Vol. I. St. Giles and St. James. II. Men of character. III. Mrs. Caudle's curtain lectures; Story of a feather; Sick giant and Doctor dwarf. IV. Cakes and ale. V. Punch's letters to his son; Punch's complete letter writer; Sketches of the English. VI. A man made of money; Chronicles of Clovernook. VII. Comedies. VIII. Comedies and dramas.
— Dreamer and worker. New York, 1847. 8°. 802.36
— History of St. Giles and St. James. New York, 1845. 8° 802.35
— Specimens of wit. Ed. by B. Jerrold. Boston, 1858. 16° 884.18
JERUSALEM. Barclay, J. T. City of the great king 684.3
— Johnson, S. B. Three years in. 689.14
— Milman, H. H. Fall of: a poem. 369.2
— Maundrell, H. Journey from Aleppo to. . . . 684.9
— Tasso, T. Gerusalemme liberata 1047.5
— — J. delivered: a poem. 317.1
JERVIS, J. Earl of St. Vincent. Memoirs of. Tucker, J. S. 564.5
JERVIS-WHITE-JERVIS, H. Manual of field operations. London, 1852. 8° 197.9
— History of Corfù, and the republic of the Ionian islands. London, 1852. 12° 918.10
JERVIS-WHITE-JERVIS, M., Lady. Boyhood of great painters. London, 1853. 16° 548.14
JESSE, E. Gleanings in natural history. Philadelphia, 1833. 18° 178.38
JESSE, J. H. Court of England during the reign of the Stuarts. London, 1840. 4v. 8°. . . 976.1
— Court of Eng. from 1688 to the death of Geo. II. London, 1843. 3v. 8° 976.2

JESSE, J. H. George Selwyn and his contemporaries. London, 1843-44. 4v. 8° 563.2
— Memoirs of the pretenders and their adherents. London, 1845. 2v. 8° 553.5
— - Same. Philadelphia, 1846. 2v. 12° . . . 979.8
JESSE, W. Life of G. Brummell. Philadelphia, 1844. 8° 892.10
— - Same. Philadelphia, 1844. 2v. in 1. 8°. 566.1
— Russia and the war. London, 1854. 8° . . . 927.7
JESUIT, Der. Spindler, K. 1026.5
JESUIT missions in North America. Kip, Wm. I. . 1088.12
JESUITISM in its rudiments. Taylor, I. 1098.8
JESUITS. Nicolini, G. B. History of 835.3
— Saint Priest, A. de. Fall of 889.3
— Steinmetz, A. History of 1095.7
JESUS, Historical minutes of the Society of. Butler, C. 617.14
See Christ.
JEUNESSE. Souvenirs de. Nodier, Ch. 1076.2
JEW, The: a novel. Spindler, K. 802.4
JEWESS, The. See Livonian tales 889.31
JEWETT, I. A. Passages in foreign travel. Boston, 1838. 2v. 12° 657.4
JEWISH literature. Steinschneider, M. 402.9
JEWITT, J. R. Captivity among the savages of Nootka Sound. Ithaca, N. Y., 1849. 16°. . 629.31
JEWS. Adams, H. History of the, A.D., 70-1800. 949.6
— Jahn, J. History of the, to A.D., 17 . . . . 1085.8
— Milman, H. H. History of the 810.1
— Prideaux, H. O. and N. Testament connected in the history of the 1093.12
— Wise, I. M. Hist. of the Israelitish nation . 1085.7
JEWSBURY, G. E. History of an adopted child. New York, 1853. 16° 469.2
— Zoe: the history of two lives, n.p., n.d. 8°. 802.23
JEWSBURY, M. J. Letters to the young. From 3d London ed. Boston, 1835. 12° 137.29
— Three histories: an enthusiast; a nonchalant; a realist. [Fiction.] Boston, 1831. 12° . . 469.1
JILT, The: a novel. Curtis, Miss 802.31
JOAN of Arc. Michelet, J. 1078.34
— Southey, R. Poem. 311.4
— Stanhope, P. H. Life of 609.6
See also: Maid of Orleans.
JOB, Book of. See Bible.
JOBSIADE. Komisches Heldengedicht. Kortum, C. A. 1037.13
JOBSON, F. J. America and Am. Methodism, with preface by J. Hannah. London, 1857. 8° . 625.22
JOCASTA: a tragedy, from the Phœnissæ of Euripides. Transl. by Gascoigne, G. and Kinwelmarsh, F. See Child, F. J. 356.1
JOCELYN, R., Lord. Six months with the Chinese expedition. 2d ed. London, 1841. 12°. 709.16
JOHN, Gospel and epistles of. See Bible.
JOHN Bull and Brother Jonathan, The diverting history of. Paulding, J. K. 797.10
JOHN Halifax, gentleman. Muloch, D. M..v.II. of 762.1-2
JOHN Railton: or, read and think. Robson, W. 449.19
JOHN True. Harper's story books. Abbott, J. v.VI.of 739.1
JOHNS, C. A. A week at the Lizard. [London, 1848.] 16° 659.29
— Flowers of the field. 2d ed. London, n.d. 12° 169.24
JOHNSON, A. B. Encycl. of instruction: or apologues and breviats on man and manners. New York, 1857. 12° 127.8
— Guide to the right understanding of our Am. Union. New York, 1857. 12° 297.16
— Treatise on banking, etc. 136.17
JOHNSON, C. W. Farmer's encyclopædia. Ed. by G. Emerson. Philadelphia, 1848. 8° . . . 164.1
JOHNSON, F. H. Sketches in the South of France and the Pyrenees. London, 1857. 12° . . . 654.7
JOHNSON, James, M. D. Change of air, or the pursuit of health. London, 1831. 8° 153.4
JOHNSON, James, Tribute to the memory of. Livermore, G. 524.13
JOHNSON, James, Esq. and J. H. Patentee's manual, or law of let. pat. 2d ed. Lon., 1858. 8°. 133.10
JOHNSON, R. M. Authentic biography of. [By W. Emmons.] Boston, 1834. 12° 527.9

JOHNSON, S. Works: with essay on his life and genius by A. Murphy. 3d complete Am. ed. New York, 1851. 2v. 8° 901.6
Contents. — Vol. I. The rambler; The adventurer; The idler; Rasselas; Theodore; The fountains; Letters; Irene, a tragedy; Miscellaneous poems. II. Lives of the poets; Lives of eminent persons; Political tracts; Philological tracts, etc.; Miscellaneous tracts, etc.; Dedications; Opinions on questions of law; Reviews and criticisms; Journey to the Western islands of Scotland; Prayers and meditations.
— Life and writings. Ed. by W. P. Page. New York, 1844-47. 2v. 18° 820.23
Containing: Life and miscellaneous essays.
— Considerations on the corn laws 125.22
— Idler . . . . v.XXXIII. of 850.24
— Lives of the English poets and other eminent persons. London, 1831. 16° 586.20
— Lives of English poets. With notes by P. Cunningham. London, 1854. 3v. 8° . . . 582.11
— - Same. New ed. New York, 1841. 3v. 12°. 586.22
— Rambler . . . . v.XIX.-XXII. of 850.24
— Rasselas, prince of Abyssinia: a tale. London, 1810. 12° . . . . v.XXVI. of 778.1
— - Same. Hartford, 1850. 12° 759.10
— Tour to the Hebrides, with some poetical pieces. Boswell, J. 869.1
— Boswell, J. Life of 869.2-6
— Piozzi, H. L. Anecdotes of 588.12
— Religious life and death. New York, 1850. 12° 584.12
JOHNSON, S. B. Hadji in Syria: or, three years in Jerusalem. Philadelphia, 1858. 16° 689.14
JOHNSON, T. T. and Thurston, S. R. California and Oregon. 4th ed. Philad., 1851. 12° . . 239.8
JOHNSTON, C., Capture, detention, and ransom of. New York, 1827. 12° 639.9
JOHNSTON, C., M. R. G. S. Travels in Southern Abyssinia. London, 1844. 2v. 8° 697.1
JOHNSTON, G. History of British zoöphytes. 2d ed. London, 1847. 2v. 8° 178.1
— Introduction to conchology. Lond., 1850. 8°. 175.6
JOHNSTON, J. F. W. Applications of chemistry and geology to agriculture. New edition. New York, n.d. 12° 164.14
— Chemistry of common life. N.Y., 1855. 2v. 12° 156.15
— Notes on N. America. Boston, 1851. 2v. 12° 624.16-17
— Relations which science bears to agriculture. New York, 1850. 12° 164.15
JOHNSTON, W. England as it is in the middle of the 19th century. London, 1851. 2v. 12° . 979.4
JOHNSTONE, C. The reverie: or, a flight to the paradise of fools. 3d ed. Dublin, 1776. 2v. 12° 429.7
JOHNSTONE, Chev. de. Rebellion in 1745 and 1746. Translated. 3d ed. London, 1822. 8° . . . 976.7
JOHNSTONE, J. Life and writings of S. Parr. London, 1829. 2v. 8° 571.1
JOHNSTONE, W. Letters descriptive of Prince Edward's Island. Dumfries, 1822. 12° . . 629.19
— Travels in Prince Edward's Island. Edin., 1824. 12° 629.19
JOINERY, Treatise on. Encycl. Britannica 201.4
See also: Carpentry, and Architecture.
JOINVILLE, J. de. Crusade of St. Louis 846.6
JOMINI, H. de. Art of war. Translated by O. F. Winship and E. E. McLean. N.Y., 1854. 12° 197.10
— Campaign of Waterloo. Transl. N.Y., 1853. 12° 987.10
JONCE Smiley, the Yankee boy who had no friends. Weld, H. H. 802.6
JONES, D. Value of annuities and reversionary payments. London, 1843. 2v. 8° 365.8
JONES, D. S., Memorial of. Jones, W. A. 526.11
JONES, E. C. Harp of Sylva. Poems. Philadelphia, 1841. 12° 338.22
JONES, G. History of ancient America. The Tyrian æra. 3d ed. London, 1843. 8° . . . 254.1
JONES, H. Poems. London, 1749. 12° 338.6
JONES, H. B. Animal chemistry in its application to stomach and renal diseases. London, 1850. 8° 155.16
JONES, J. Attempts in verse, and essay on our uneducated poets, by R. Southey. London, 1831. 8° 584.5

JONES, J. P. Life and corresp. N. York, 1830. 8° 513.6
— Mackenzie, A. S. Life of 528.6
— Sherburne, J. H. Life of 528.5
JONES, J. S. The carpenter of Rouen. A dramatic tale. Boston, 1849. 12° 498.8-9
JONES, S. Practical phrenology. Boston, 1836. 12° 124.15
JONES, T. R. The aquarian naturalist. London, 1858. 12° 175.10
— Outline of the organisation of the animal kingdom. 2d edition. London, 1855. 8° . 172.10
— Natural history of animals. London, 1845-52. 2v. 12° 177.10
JONES, Sir W., Life of. Shore, J. 583.11
JONES, W. Memoir of Rev. Rowland Hill. 5th edition. London, 1853. 16° 578.4
JONES, W., F. S. A. Health for the million. London, 1858. 16° 157.33
— How to make home happy. Lond., 1857. 12° 877.10
JONES, W., Esq. Contin. of hist. of modern Europe. See Russell, W. 943.5
JONES, W. A. Memorial of D. S. Jones. New York, 1849. 12° 526.11
— Characters and criticisms. N.Y., 1857. 2v. 12° 888.11
JONSON, B. Works; with memoir of life and writings by [B. W. Procter.] Lond., 1838. 8° 322.2

Contents. — Life; Ancient commendatory verses on B. J.; Every man in his humour; Every man out of his humour; Cynthia's revels; Poetaster, or, his arraignment; Sejanus, his fall; Volpone, or the fox; Epicoene, or the silent woman; The alchemist; Catiline, his conspiracy; Bartholomew fair; The devil is an ass; The staple of news; The new inn; The magnetic lady; A tale of a tub; The sad shepherd; Fall of Mortimer; The case is altered; Entertainments; Masques; Epigrams; The forest; Underwoods; Leges convivales; Translations from the Latin poets; Timber, or discoveries made upon men and matter; The English grammar; Jonsonus Virbius, or the memory of Ben Jonson; Glossary; Index.

— Conversations with Drummond, of Hawthornden. Ed. by D. Laing. Lond., 1842. 8° 342.7
— Verses to the memory of. Ford, J. . . . v.11. of 353.9
JORDAN, Expedition to the river. Lynch, W. F. 684.5-6
JORTIN, J., Memoirs of. Disney, J. 575.7
JOSEPH, The history of: a poem. Rowe, E. . . . 369.25
JOSEPHINE. Abbott, J. S. C. History of 560.17-22
— Headley, P. C. Life of 606.7
— Le Normand, M. A., M'lle. Historical and secret memoirs of 606.1-6
— Memes, J. S. Memoirs of 810.34-38
— and Napoleon I. Confidential correspondence. 605.6
JOSEPHIUS, Fl. Works, translated, with notes, by W. Whiston. Philadelphia, 1851. 2v. 8°. 946.2

Contents.— Vol. I. Jewish antiquities. II. J. antiq.; Life; Jewish war; Against Apion; Dissertations.

-- Works. From the London edition of 1827. Philadelphia, 1831. 2v. 8° 946.3
Contents as above.

— Jewish war. Transl. by R. Traill. Boston, 1858. 8° 946.1
JOURNAL of a few months in Portugal, etc. London, 1847. 2v. 12° 673.4
JOURNAUX. Hist. des journaux en France, de 1789 à 1799. Monseignat, C. de 1078.44
JOURNEY to the world underground, by N. Klimius. See Holberg, L. v. 799.11
JOWETT, B. Notes on Romans, Galatians, and Thessalonians. See Bible 1093.14
JOYCE, J. Introduction to the arts and sciences. New ed. London, 1852. p.8° 859.4
— Scientific dialogues. Ed. by Pinnock and Griffith. London, 1852. p.8° 826.18
— - Same. Enlarged ed. London, 1855. p.8° 826.17
JUDAISM and Christianity, Relation between. Palfrey, J. G. 1083.16
JUDD, S. Margaret; a tale. Rev. ed. Boston, 1851. 2v. 12° 488.17
— Philo, an evangeliad. Boston, 1850. 12° . 358.7
— Richard Edney and the governor's family: a tale. Boston, 1850. 12° 488.6
— Life and character of. Hall, A. 534.21
JUDE, Der. Spindler, C. 1026.4

JUDEA, Scenes in. Ware, W. 808.12
JUDICIAL hist. of Massachusetts. Washburn, E. 297.2
JUDSON, Adoniram. Conant, H. C. Character and labors of 536.4
— Wayland, F. Life and labors of 536.1-3
JUDSON, Mrs. Ann H. Knowles, J. D. Memoir of. 539.20
— Willson, A. W. Life of 538.4-5
JUDSON, Mrs. E. C. Great secret, or how to be happy. 4th ed. New York, 1849. 18° . . . 789.7
— Kathayan slave, etc. Boston, 1853. 12° . . . 1108.11
— Memoir of Sarah B. Judson. New rev. ed., with notes. New York, 1851. 18° 539.19
— Life of. Willson, A. W. 538.4-5
JUDSON, Mrs. S. B. Memoir of. Judson, E. C. . 539.19
— Life of. Willson, A. W. 538.4-5
JUICES in the animal body, Motion of the. Liebig, J. 155.14
JUKES, J. B. Excursions in and about Newfoundland. London, 1842. 2v. 12° 629.9
JULIA Howard: a romance. Bell, Mrs. M. . . . 802.13
JULIAN; a tragedy. Mitford, M. R. 804.4
JULIAN and his generation: an historical picture. Neander, J. A. W. 516.11
JULIUS, and other tales, from the German. Translated by W. H. Furness 756.10
JULLIAN, P. L. P. de. Memoir of Joseph Fouché. Ed. by A. de Beauchamp. Tr. Bost., 1825. 8° 613.4
JUNIUS, Letters of, with notes by R. Heron. Philadelphia, 1804. 2v. 8° 873-10
JUNIUS: including letters under other signatures, correspondence with Wilkes, and private letters to Woodfall. Edited by J. Wade. London, 1850. 2v. p.8° 848.5
JUNIUS discovered. Griffin, F. 877.12-13
JUNIUS unmasked, or Lord G. Sackville proved to be J. With app. Boston, 1828. 12° . . . 877.11
JUNG-STILLING, J. H. Heinrich Stilling. Translated by S. Jackson. London, 1835. 2v. 12° 546.19
— Theobald, or the fanatic. Translated by S. Schaeffer. Philadelphia, 1846. 12° 769.12
JUNOT, L. P., duchesse d' Abrantès. Histoire des salons de Paris. Bruxelles, 1837-38. 6v. 12° 1068.15
— Memoirs of Napoleon, his court and family. New York, 1854. 2v. 8° 603.3
— Scènes de la vie espagnole. Bruxelles, 1836. 2v. 16° 1068.2
JUPITER Ammon, Adventures in the oasis of. St. John, B. 899.9
JURISPRUDENCE, Medical. Taylor, A. S. . . . 151.5
See also: Law.
JUSTE, T. Charlemagne. 2de édition. Bruxelles, 1848. 12° 1075.9
— Histoire grecque. Bruxelles, n.d. 12° . . . 1065.24
— Précis de l' histoire moderne. Bruxelles, n.d. 2v. 12° 1075.16
— Précis de l' histoire du moyen age. Bruxelles, n.d. 5v. 12° 1075.15
— Précis de l' histoire romaine. Brux., n.d. 12° 1065.25
JUSTINUS. [Works; also those of] Cornelius Nepos and Eutropius. Translated by J. S. Watson. London, 1853. p.8° 834.16
JUVENALIS, D. J. Translated by C. Badham. New York, n.d. 18° 830.22
— Satires [with those] of Persius, Sulpicia, and Lucilius. Transl. London, 1852. p.8° . . 824.13
JUVENILE budget reopened. Aikin, J. 499.12-13
JUVENILE delinquents; their condition and treatment. Carpenter, M. 135.16
JUVENILE poems, Selections of. Park, R. . . . 349.11

KAEMTZ, L. F. Meteorology, with notes by Ch. Martins, and appendix by L. Lalanne. Tr. by C. O. Walker. London, 1845. 12° . . 147.21
KAFFIR, The. Passages of missionary life. Merriman, Archd. 578.7
KAFFIRS of South Africa, Sporting scenes amongst the. Drayson, A. W. 692.3
KAFIRS of Natal and the Zulu country. Shooter, J. 693.2
KAH-GE-GA-GAH-BOWH. See Copway, G.
KAMES, Lord. See Home, H.
KAMTCHATKA. Cochrane, J. D. Pedestrian jour. to 830.46

KAMTCHATKA. Dobell, P. Travels in 666.2
KANE, E. K. U. S. Grinnell expedition in search
of Sir John Franklin. New York, 1854. 8° 702.2-6
— Arctic explorations, 1853–55. 2d Grinnell ex-
pedition in search of Franklin. Philadel-
phia, 1856. 2v. 8° 703.1-9
— Biography of. Elder, W. 524.9
KANSAS. Gihon, J. L. Gov. Geary's administra-
tion in 239.2
— Gladstone, T. H. Englishman in 239.5
— Hale, E. E. History of 629.2
— Robinson, H. A. Six months in, etc. 239.3
KANSAS region, The. Greene, M. 239.6
KANT, I. Critique of pure reason. Translated by
J. M. D. Meiklejohn. London, 1855. p.8° . 855.5
KAPPER, S. Die böhmischen Bäder. Leipzig,
1857. 16° 1029.11
KARR, J. B. A. Contes et nouvelles. Paris,
1856. 16° 1078.16
    Contents.— Les Willis; Un diamant; Berthe et Ro-
    dolphe; Bouret et Gaussin; Midi a quatorze heures;
    Jobisme; Un homme et une femme; Une visite à
    l'arsenal; Pour ne pas être treize; Voyage dans Paris;
    Histoire d'un voisin.
— Geneviève. Nouv. éd. Paris, 1853. 12° . . . 1067.14
— Une poignée de vérités. Mélanges philoso-
phiques. Paris, 1853. 12° 1067.15
KARS. Lake, A. Defence of 987.1
— - K. and our captivity in Russia 988.11
KASIMIRSKI, M. Trad. nouv. du Koran. See Mo-
hammed 1066.22
KATE Coventry: an autobiography. Melville, G.
J. W. 802.40-41
KATE Walsingham: a novel. Pickering, E. . . . 805.17
KATER, H. and Lardner, D. Treatise on mechan-
ics. New ed. London, 1849. 16° 398.8
— - Same. From London ed. Cambridge,
1831. 16° 149.26
— - Same. Philadelphia, 1838. 16° 149.19-20
KATHARINE Ashton: a novel. Sewell, E. M. . . 424.8
KATHARINE Walton, or the rebel of Dorchester.
Simms, W. G. 790.25-29
KATHAYAN slave, The. Judson, E. 1108.11
KATMANDU, the capital of Nepaul. Journey to.
Oliphant, L. 709.12
KAVANAGH: a tale. Longfellow, H. W. 438.8-12
KAVANAGH, J. Adèle: a tale. New York, 1858. 12° 454.1-3
— Daisy Burns: a tale. 9th ed. N. Y., 1854. 12° 454.4
— Grace Lee: a tale. New York, 1855. 12° . . 454.12
— Nathalie: a tale. New York, 1854. 12° . . 454.5-6
— Rachel Gray: a tale. New York, 1856. 12° 454.7-11
— Saint-Gildas: or the three paths. Boston,
1856. 12° 454.13
KAY, S. Travels and researches in Caffraria. Lon-
don, 1833. 12° 698.22
KAYE, J. W. Life and correspondence of Sir
John Malcolm. London, 1856. 2v. 8° . . . 565.1
KEATING, W. H. Expedition to St. Peter's river,
etc., under S. H. Long. London, 1825. 2v. 8° 624.11
— - Same. Philadelphia, 1824. 2v. 8° 625.10
KEATS, J. Poetical works. Parts I.–II. N. Y.,
1846. 12° 334.24-25
    Contents.— Endymion, a poetic romance; Lamia;
    Isabella, or, the pot of Basil; The eve of St. Agnes;
    Hyperion; Miscellaneous poems.
— - Same. See Howitt, M. 332.6
— - Same. With a life. Boston, 1854. 16°. . 347.6
KEBLE, J. The Christian year, Thoughts in verse.
36th edition. Oxford, 1849. 8° 1083.20
KEDGE anchor, The: or sailors' assistant. Brady,
W. 194.6
KEEPERS of the great seal of England, Lives of.
Campbell, J. 568.1
KEEPING house and house keeping: a tale. Hale,
S. J. 729.10
KEHAMA, The curse of. Southey, R. 359.1
KEIGHTLEY, T. Fairy mythology. New edition,
revised and enlarged. London, 1850. p.8°. 846.10
— History of England. From 2d London ed.
New York, 1840-42. 5v. 18° 820.26

KEIGHTLEY, T. History of Greece. London,
1835. 12° 959.7
— History of Rome; edited by J. T. Smith.
Boston, 1839. 12° 959.4-5
— History of the Roman empire. Edited by J.
T. Smith. Boston, 1841. 12° 957.6
— History of the war of independence in Greece.
Edinburgh, 1830. 2v. 18° 830.61
— Mythology of ancient Greece and Italy. 11th
American edition. New York, 1852. 18°. . 1087.25
— Outlines of history. New edition. London,
[1850.] 16° 369.1
KELLAND, Prof. Transatlantic sketches. Edin-
burgh, 1858. 16° 629.32
KELLY, J. F. Dan Marble: a biographical sketch.
New York, n.d. [1851?] 12° 519.6
KELLY, M. Reminiscences. London, 1826. 2v. 8° 597.1
KELLY, W. K. History of Russia. London, 1855.
2v. p.8° 827.6
— Continuation of the history of the house of
Austria; with a translation of Hartig's gen-
esis of the Austrian revolution of 1848.
Coxe, W. 828.3
KELT, T. Mechanic's text book. Added, valuable
hints by J. Frost. Boston, 1850. 12°. . . 198.4
KEMBLE, F. A. Journal. [1832.] Philadelphia,
1835. 2v. 12° 639.2
— Year of consolation. N.Y., 1847. 2v. in 1. 12° 676.7-10
KEMBLE, J. M. Social and political state of Eu-
rope. [1686-1716.] London, 1857. 8° . . . 563.1
KEMBLE, J. P., Life of. Boaden, J. 597.5
KEMP, E. How to lay out a garden. 2d edition.
London, 1858. sm.8° 175.11
KEMP, T. L. Indications of instinct. London,
1854. 12° 409.2
— Natural history of creation. Lond., 1852. p.8° 409.31
— Phasis of matter; outline of modern chemis-
try. London, 1855. 2v. 12° 156.22
KEMPIS, T. à. Imitation of Christ. Transl. 3d
American edition. New York, 1850. 12° . . 1007.28
KENDALL, G. W. Texan Santa Fé expedition. 6th
edition. New York, 1850. 2v. 12° 638.7
KENILWORTH: a novel. Scott, Sir W 460.60-61
— a melo-drama founded on the novel. Scott,
Sir W. 355.11
KENNEDY, E. Obstetric auscultation; with legal
notes by J. Smith, and illustrations by I. E.
Taylor. New York, 1843. 12° 153.8
KENNEDY, G. Dunallan: or, know what you
judge. Philadelphia, n.d. 12° 808.15
— Father Clement: a R. Catholic story. From
6th Edinburgh ed. Newark, N. J., 1851. 18° 808.16
KENNEDY, J. Conversations on religion with
Lord Byron and others. London, 1830. 8° 585.6
KENNEDY, J. P. Horse shoe Robinson. Revised
edition. New York, 1852. 12° 726.4-6
— Life of William Wirt. New edition. Phila-
delphia, 1852. 2v. 12° 517.11
— Rob of the bowl: a legend of St. Inigoe's.
Revised edition. New York, 1854. 12°. . . 726.3
— Swallow barn: or a sojourn in the old domin-
ion. Revised edition. New York, 1851. 12° 726.2
KENRICK, J. Phœnicia. London, 1855. 8° . . . 956.4
KENRICK, W. New American orchardist. 2d ed.,
enlarged. Boston, 1835. 12° 169.7
KENT, J. Commentaries on American law. 7th
ed. New York, 1851. 4v. 8° 133.2
KENTISH, T. Treatise on a box of instruments.
Philadelphia, 1852. 12° 199.9
KENTON, S., Biographical sketch of. McDonald, J. 518.8
KENTUCKY. Collins, L. Historical sketches of . 235.5
— M'Nemar, R. The K. revival. 1089.20
KENYON, J. A day at Tivoli: with other verses.
London, 1849. 8° 346.2
— Poems. London, 1838. 8° 345.1
KEOKUK, Sketches of. Drake, B. 539.7
KEPLER, J., Life of. Brewster, Sir D. 820.34
KEPPEL, A. Life of. Keppel, T. 564.4
KEPPEL, G. Journey from India to England in
1824. Philadelphia 1827. 8° 695.5

KEPPEL, H. Expedition to Borneo for the suppression of piracy. New York, 1846. 12° . 707.14
KEPPEL, T. Life of Augustus, visc. Keppel. London, 1842. 2v. 8° 564.4
KER, H. Travels through the western interior of the United States, 1808–16. Elizabethtown, 1816. 8° 626.2
KETTELL, S. Specimens of American poetry, with critical and biographical notices. Boston, 1829. 3v. 12° 339.4
KEW conservatories, Wanderings through, etc. See Soc. for promoting Christian Knowl.. . 178.22
KHANIKOFF. Bokhara: its Amir and its people. Transl. by C. A. De Bode. London, 1845. 8° 694.4
KIDD, J. Adaptation of external nature to the physical condition of man. London, 1852. p.8° 826.3
KIDD, S. China. London, 1841. 8° 696.8
KIDD, Capt. W. Historical sketch of. Campbell, W. W. 589.2
KIDDER, D. P. Mormonism and the Mormons. New York, 1852. 16° 1009.27
— and Fletcher, J. C. Brazil and the Brazilians. Philadelphia, 1857. 8° 263.2-5
KINDT, J. De la vapeur et de ses applications. Bruxelles, n.d. 12° 1065.27
— De l'industrie du coton, de la laine, et de la soie. Bruxelles, n.d. 12° 1065.28
— Industrie linière. Bruxelles, n.d. 12° 1065.26
KING Arthur: a poem. Lytton, E. B. 346.11
KING, J. A. Twenty-four years in the Argentine republic. London, 1846. 8° 263.8
KING, R. Journey to the Arctic ocean, under Capt. Back, 1833-5. London, 1836. 2v. 12° . . 704.18
KING, W. Political and literary anecdotes of his own times. 2d ed. London, 1819. 12° . 588.15
— Political and literary anecdotes of his own times. Boston, 1819. 12° 888.19
KING, W. R. Obituary addresses on the death of. See United States 523.10
KINGLAKE, A. W. Eöthen, or traces of travel brought home from the East. New York, 1845. 12° 544.11
— - Same. New ed. London, 1854. 12° . . . 409.6
— - Same. New ed. New York, 1850. 12°. . 687.13
KING's highway, The: a novel. James, G. P. R.. 463.25
KING's own, The: a novel. Marryat, F. 745.14
KING's theatre, Seven years of. Ebers, J. 353.12
KINGSLEY, C. Adventures of Sir Amyas Leigh. Boston, 1855. 12° 484.9-10
— Alton Locke: an autobiography. New York, 1851. 12° 484.13-14
— Andromeda, and other poems. Bost., 1858. 12° 324.18
— Glaucus: or the wonders of the shore. Boston, 1855. 16° 178.27
— Heroes: or, Greek fairy tales. Bost., 1856. 16° 484.12
— Hypatia. [Novel.] 2d ed. Boston, 1854. 2v. 16° 484.11
— Sir W. Raleigh, with other papers. Boston, 1859. 12° 804.6-10
— Two years ago. Boston, 1857. 12° 484.1-8
— Yeast: a problem. New York, 1855. 12° . .484.15-16
KINGSLEY, J. L. Life of Ezra Stiles. Sparks's American biography . . . . .v.XVI. of 529.1
KINGSTON, W. H. G. Fred Markham in Russia. New York, 1858. 16° 709.14
KINKEL, J. G. Otto der Schütz. Rheinische Geschichte. 19te Aufl. Stuttgart, 1856. 18° . 1039.4
KINNEAR, J. G. Cairo, Petra and Damascus in 1839. London, 1841. 12° 689.13
KINNEY expedition. History of the. Wells, W. V. 266.8
KINWELMARSH, F. Jocasta. See Child, F. J.. . 356.1
KIP, W. I. Catacombs of Rome. N. Y., 1851. 12° 1088.13
— Christmas holidays in Rome. N. Y., 1846. 12° 678.18
— Early conflicts of Christianity. New York, 1850. 12° 1088.14
— Early Jesuit missions in North America. New York, 1846. 12° 1088.12
KIPPING, R. Treatise on masting, mast-making and rigging. London, 1854. 16° 819.38

KIPPIS, A. Life of J. Butler. 1108.10
— Voyages round the world performed by Capt. Cook, with his life. New York, n.d. 16° . 820.66
KIRBY, R. S. Wonderful and eccentric museum: or, magazine of remarkable characters. London, 1820. 5v. 8° 894.1
KIRBY, W. Power, etc. of God, manifested in the creation of animals. New ed. London, 1853. 2v. p.8° 826.2
KIRK, E. N. Sermons delivered in England and America. New York, 1840. 12° 1099.2
KIRKALDY, Sir W. Memoirs and adventures of. Edinburg, 1849. 12° 566.9
KIRKLAND, C. M. Holidays abroad: or, Europe from the West. New York, 1849. 2v. 12°. 648.14-15
— Memoirs of Washington. N. York, 1857. 12°. 515.4
KIRKLAND, S., Life of. Lothrop, S. K. . v.XXV. of 529.1
KIRKMAN, T. P. First lessons in geometry, algebra, and trigonometry. London, 1852. 16°. 829.35
KITCHEN, Christianity in the. Mann, Mrs. H.. 188.24
KITCHINER, W. Art of prolonging life. Philadelphia, 1823. 16° 158.21
— The cook's oracle. 3d ed. London, 1821. 12°. 189.5
— - Same. From last London edition, with appendix. Boston, 1822. 12° 189.6
— Economy of the eyes. London, 1824. 16° . . 158.12
KITTO, J. Lost senses. I. Deafness ; II. Blindness. London, 1845-53. 2v. 18° 840.24
— Physical geography of the Holy Land. London, 1848. 18° 840.25
— Scripture lands. London, 1850. p.8° 815.7
— Uncle Olliver's travels in Persia. Lon., n.d. 18° 689.18
— and Taylor, J. Popular cyclopædia of Biblical literature. Boston, 1851. 8° 1083.8
KLAPKA, Gen. G. Memoirs of the war in Hungary. Trans. by O. Wenckstern. London, 1850. 2v. 12° 928.10
KLEIST, H. von. Gesammelte Schriften. Berlin, 1826. 3v. 16° 1026.2

Contents. — I. Die Familie Schroffenstein; Penthesilea: Amphitryon. II. Der zerbrochene Krug; Das Kätchen von Heilbronn; Prinz Friedrich von Homburg; Die Hermannsschlacht. III. Erzählungen; Robert Guiskard; Gedichte.

KLENCKE, P. F. H. and Schlesier, G. Lives of the brothers Humboldt. N. York, 1853. 12°. 545.7
KLIMIUS, N. Pseud. See Holberg, L.
KLIPSTEIN, L. F. Selections from the Anglo-Saxon literature. New York, 1849. 2v. 8°. 404.4
KLOSTERHEIM: a tale. De Quincey, T. . . v.II. of 905.3
KNAPEN, D. M. Mechanic's assistant: a treatise on mensuration. New York, 1850. 12°. . . 198.5
KNAPP, A. I. Roots and ramifications of divers words. London, 1857. 16° 406.17
KNAPP, F. Chemical technology: or chemistry applied to the arts. London, 1848-51. 3v. 8°. 144.3-4
KNAPP, G. C. Christian theology. Trans. by L. Woods, jr. 7th Am. ed. Philad., 1858. 8°. 1083.4
KNAPP, J. F. Country rambles in England, with notes, etc., by S. F. Cooper. Buffalo, 1853. 12°. 177.35
KNAPP, S. L. Bachelors, and other tales. New York, 1836. 12° 498.12
— Biographical sketches of eminent lawyers, statesmen, etc. Boston, 1821. 8° 524.10-11
— Lectures on Am. literature. N. Y., 1829. 8°. 402.3
— Life of Daniel Webster. Boston, 1831. 12°. 526.26
KNELB, P. H. Narratives of an old traveller. Philadelphia, 1856. 8° 668.5
— Perilous incidents in the lives of sailors and travellers. Philadelphia, 1856. 8° 668.5
KNICKERBOCKER's history of New York. See Irving, W.
KNIGHT, C. Capital and labour, including the results of machinery. London, 1853. 18°. 840.26
— Cyclopædia of London. London, 1851. 8°. 974.2
— Cyclopædia of the industry of all nations. New York, 1851. 8° 196.2
— The elephant viewed in relation to man. London, 1844. 18° 840.21

KNIGHT, C. Half hours of English history. Complete ed. London, 1853. 8° 975.2
— Half hours with the best authors. N. York, 1849. 4v. 12° 865.3
— - Same. 3d ed. London, 1854. 4v. 12° . . 865.2
— Knowledge is power: productive forces of society. London, 1855. p.8° 138.7
— London. London, 1851. 6v. 8° 961.2
— Volume of varieties. London, 1844. 18° . . 840.27
— William Caxton: a biography. Lon., 1844. 18°. 840.28
KNIGHT, C. Weekly and monthly volumes. Lond. 14 vols. 18° Containing :
Banfield, T. C. Industry of the Rhine. . . . 840.1
Blaze de Bury, Mme. Molière and the Fr. classical drama 840.3
— Racine and the Fr. classical drama . . . 840.4
Book of table talk. 2v. 840.2
Brougham, H. Dialogues on instinct . . . 840.7–8
Historical sketches of statesmen in the time of Geo. III. I.–III. series. 6v. 840.5
— Discourses. 1. Science ; II. Political science 840.6
Butler, S. Hudibras and other works. Ed. by A. Ramsay 840.9
Cabinet portrait gallery of British worthies. 12v. 840.10–11
Chaucer, G. Canterbury tales. Ed. by J. Saunders. 2v. 840.12
Craik, G. L. Bacon, his writings and his philosophy. 3v. 840.13
— History of British commerce. 3v. . . . 840.14
History of literature and learning in England. 6v. 840.15
Pursuit of knowledge under difficulties. 3v. 840.16
— - Same. Illustrated by female examples 840.17
Davis, J. D. The Chinese: a description of China and its inhabitants. 4v. 840.18
Dennis, G. The Cid: a chronicle 840.19
Dodd, G. Textile manufactures of Great Britain. 6v. 840.20
Grenville, G. N. T. L'd Nugent. Lands classical and sacred. 2v. 840.48
Gresham, Sir T. Life of 840.22
Jameson, A. Early Italian painters. 2v. . . 840.23
Kitto, J. Lost senses. I. ser. Deafness ; II. ser. Blindness. 2v. 840.24
— Physical geography of the Holy Land . 840.25
Knight, C. Capital and labour 840.26
— Elephant, The, viewed in relation to man. 840.21
— Volume of varieties. 840.27
— William Caxton: a biography 840.28
Lamb, C. and M. Tales fr. Shakspere. 2v. . 840.29
Lane, E. W. Arabian tales and anecdotes . . 840.30
— Modern Egyptians. 3v. 840.31
Lankester, E. Vegetable substances used for food. 2v. 840.32
Lewes, G. H. Biographical history of philosophy. I.–II. ser. 4v. 840.34
— Spanish drama. Lope de Vega and Calderon 840.35
— Camp of refuge. 2v. 840.40
— The Dutch in the Medway 840.37
— Legend of Reading abbey 840.33
MacFarlane, C. Popular customs, sports, etc., of the South of Italy. 840.36
— Romance of travel. The East. 2v. . . . 840.38–39
Malkin, J. H. Historical parallels. 3v. . . 840.41
Martin, W. C. L. History of the dog . . . 840.43
— History of the horse 840.44
Martineau, H. The billow and rock 840.42
Memoirs of a working man. 840.45
Mind amongst the spindles 840.46
Nicolay, C. G. The Oregon territory 840.47
Paley, W. Natural theology. Notes by Brougham and Bell. 4v. 840.49
Paris, its historical buildings, and its revolutions 840.50
Planché, J. R. History of British costume . 840.51
Plutarchus. Civil wars of Rome. Translated by G. Long. 5v. 850.1

KNIGHT, C. Weekly and monthly volumes, continued.
Pompeii, its destruction and re-discovery . . 850.2
Poole, S. The Englishwoman in Egypt. 3v. 850.3
Pratt, A. Flowers and their associations . . 850.4
— Field, garden, and woodland 850.5
Rennie, J. Bird architecture 850.7
— Bird miscellanies 850.8
— Insect architecture. 2v. 850.6
Saunders, J. Pictures of Eng. life. Chaucer. 850.9
Secret societies of the middle ages. 850.13
Settlers and convicts ; or the Australian backwoods 850.10
Sketch of the history of monkeys 850.11
Sketches in natural history. Mammalia. 6v. 850.12
Sketches of popular tumults 850.14
Smith, S. Philosophy of health. 2v. 850.15
Spenser and his poetry. Ed. by G. L. Craik. 3v. 850.16
Tasso, T. Godfrey of Bulloigne, or the recovery of Jerusalem. 2v. 850.19
Traill, C. P. Backwoods of Canada 850.17
Thorne, J. Rambles by rivers. 4v. [v.I. missing.]. 850.18
Vieusseux, A. Napoleon Bonaparte. 2v. . . 850.20
Wittich, W. Curiosities of physical geography. 2v. 850.21
— Western coast of Norway 850.22
Wornum, R. N. The epochs of painting . . 850.23
KNIGHT, E. C. Dinarbas, continuation of Rasselas. London, 1790. 16° 799.5
KNIGHT, F. Thorn cottage, or the poet's home. A memorial. Boston, 1855. 12° 536.5
KNIGHT, H. C. Lady Huntington and her friends. New York, n.d. 12° 1107.7
— Life of J. Montgomery. Boston, 1857. 12°. 584.16
KNIGHTHOOD and its times. Mills, C. . . . 945.2
KNIGHTS and their days. Doran, J. 948.6
KNIGHTS of Malta, Achievements of. Sutherland, A. 830.63
KNIGHTS of St. John of Jerusalem, History of. Taaffe, J. 915.1
KNIGHTS of the round table. Prince Arthur . . 850.29
KNIGHTS templars 849.5
KNORRING, Baroness. Peasant and his landlord. Translated by M. Howitt. New York, 1848. 12° 418.8–9
KNOUT, The, and the Russians. Lagny, G. de . . 927.6
KNOWLEDGE. Bailey, S. Progress of. . . . 878.14
— Dick, T. Improvement of society by the diffusion of 810.58–59
— Park, R. Systematic survey of 194.10
KNOWLEDGE is power. Productive forces of society. Knight, C. 138.7
KNOWLES, J. Life of H. Fuseli. 543.5
KNOWLES, J. D. Memoir of Ann H. Judson. 4th edition. Boston, 1851. 18°. 539.20
— Memoir of Roger Williams. Boston, 1834. 12° 536.6
KNOWLES, R. B. Use of sunshine. N.Y., 1852. 12° 458.6
KNOX, A. Correspondence with J. Jebb. . . . 575.5
KNOX, A. E. Game birds and wild fowl. London, 1850. 12° 177.11
— Ornithological rambles in Sussex. 2d ed. London, 1850. 12° 177.16
KNOX, J. P. Historical account of St. Thomas, W. I. New York, 1852. 12° 264.7
KOBELL, F. v. Sketches from the mineral kingdom. 826.5
KOCH, C. W. History of the revolutions in Europe. Edinburgh, 1828. 3v. 18°. 830.45
KOENIG, H. J. Die Clubisten in Mainz. [Roman.] Leipzig, 1847. 3v. 16° 1015.1
— König Jerôme's Carneval. Geschichtlicher Roman. Leipzig, 1855. 3v. 16° 1015.2
— William Shakspeare. Ein Roman. 2te Aufl. Leipzig, 1850. 2v. in 1. 16°. 1015.3
KOHL, J. G. Austria: Vienna, Prague, Hungary, etc. London, 1843. 8° 667.2
— Ireland, Scotland and England. Lond., 1844. 8° 647.5
— Russia: St. Petersburgh, Moscow, Kharkoff, etc. London, 1844. 8° 674.5
KOHLRAUSCH, F. History of Germany. Transl. by J. D. Haas. New York, 1852. 8° 925.2–3

KOLFF, D. H. jr.   Voyages through the Moluccan archipelago, 1825-26. Translated by G. W. Earl. London, 1840. 8° 705.7

KÖLN, Von Minden nach.   Schücking, C. B. L. .   1029.18

KÖNIG Jérôme's Carneval. Roman. Koenig, H. J.   1015.2

KÖNIGIN, Die, der Nacht.   Roman.   Schücking, C. B. L. 1017.3

KÖNIGSWINTER, W. M. v.   *See* Müller v. Königswinter.

KONINGSMARKE : or, old times in the new world. Paulding, J. K. 797.7

KOORDISTAN.   Layard, A. H.   Visit to the Christians of 685.11

— Rich, C. J.   Narrative of a residence in . . .   694.7

— Southgate, H.   Tour through 687.3

KORAN.   *See* Mohammed.

KÖRNER, T.   Sämmtliche Werke.   4te ges. Ausg. Berlin, 1853.   4v.   16°. 1038.6

   Contents. — Vol. I. Charakteristik u. Biographie des Dichters; Leyer und Schwert; Nachtrag aus des Dichters Nachlasse; Vermischte Gedichte; Nachtrag, Ungedrucktes; Jugendscherze. II.–III. Dramat. Werke; Toni; Zriny; Hedwig. (3.) Rosamunde; Joseph Heyderich, oder, deutsche Treue, eine wahre Anekdote; Die Braut; Der graue Domino; Der Nachtwächter; Der Vetter aus Bremen; Die Gouvernante. IV. Das Fischermädchen; Lyr. Drama; Der vierjährige Posten, Singspiel; Die Bergknappen, Oper; Alfred der Grosse, Oper; Der Kampf mit dem Drachen, Singspiel; Erzählungen; Mündliche Erzählungen, schriftlich bearbeitet von Caroline Pichler; Briefe; Gedichte deutscher Dichter auf Theodor und Emma Korner; Gedichte englischer Dichter; Englische Uebersetzungen Korner'scher Gedichte.

— Songs and ballads.   Transl. by C. T. Brooks.   316.6

KORTUM, C. A.   Die Jobsiade.   Ein grotesk-komisches Heldengedicht.   7te Aufl. Leipzig, 1854.   16° 1037.13

KOSSAK, E.   Historietten.   Berlin, 1856.   16°. . .   1037.14

KOSSUTH, L.   Select speeches.   Abridged by F. W. Newman.   New York, 1854.   12° 866.4

— Memoir of 827.5

KOTZEBUE, A. F. F. von.   Theater. Leipzig, 1840-41.   40v.   16° 1039.1

   Contents. — Vol. I. Der Eremit auf Formentera; Menschenhass und Reue; Die Indianer in England. II. Die Sonnenjungfrau; Das Kind der Liebe; Der weibliche Jakobiner Klubb. III. Der Spiegelritter; Bruder Moritz, der Sonderling; Die edle Lüge; Der Papagei. IV. Sultan Wampum, oder die Wünsche; Graf Benjowsky, oder die Verschwörung auf Kamtschatka; Die Spanier in Peru, oder Rollas Tod. V. Armuth und Edelsinn; Der Mann von vierzig Jahren; Die Negersklaven; Die Verleumder. VI. Die Witwe und das Reitpferd; Der Wildfang; Der Graf von Burgund; Falsche Scham. VII. La Peyrouse; Die Versöhnung; Die Verwandtschaften; Die Unglücklichen. VIII. Der Opfer-Tod; Das Dorf im Gebirge; Die silberne Hochzeit. IX. Die Corsen; Der alte Leibkutscher Peter des Dritten; Ueble Laune; Johanna von Montfaucon. X. Schreibepult, oder, die Gefahren der Jugend; Der Gefangene; Der hyperboralische Esel, oder die heutige Bildung; Das neue Jahrhundert; Der Taubstumme, oder, der Abbé de l'Épée. XI. Lohn der Wahrheit ; Das Epigramm; Die kluge Frau im Walde, oder, Der stumme Ritter. XII. Die Zurückkunft des Vaters ; Octavia ; Die beiden Klingsberg. XIII. Gustav Wasa; Bayard. XIV. Der Besuch, oder, Die Sucht zu glänzen; Des Teufels Lustschloss : Die barmherzigen Brüder; Cleopatra; Unser Fritz; Die schlaue Wit-we, oder, Die Temperamente; Der Hahnenschlag: Ariadne auf Naxos. XV. Die deutschen Kleinstädter; Die französischen Kleinstädter ; Der Wirrwarr, oder, Die Muthwillige; Die Hussiten vor Naumburg im Jahre 1432. XVI. Hugo Grotius; Der Schauspieler wider Willen; Das Urtheil des Paris; Die Tochter Pharaonis; Rübezahl; Incognito; Die Uhr und die Mandeltorte; Sultan Bimbambum, oder, Der Triumph der Wahrheit. XVII. Don Ranudo di Colibrados ; Pagenstreiche; Der todte Neffe; Die hübsche kleine Putzmacherin; Der Gimpel auf der Messe; Hygea; Die Sparbüchse, oder, Der arme Kandidat. XVIII. Mädchenfreundschaft, oder; Der tarkische Gesandte; Der Trunkenbold; Eduard in Schottland, oder, Die Nacht eines Flüchtlings; Der Vater von ungefähr; Der Abschied; Heinrich Reuss von Plauen, oder, Die Belagerung von Marienburg; Die Stricknadeln. XIX. Die Schule der Frauen; Fanchon, das Leiermädchen; Die gefährliche Nachbarschaft; Das Kost-

KOTZEBUE, A. F. F. von, *continued.*

   lichste : Eulenspiegel. XX. Die Brandschatzung; Das verlorne Kind; Die Organe des Gehirns; Blinde Liebe; Carolus Magnus ; Der Sammtrock. XXI. Das liebe Dörrchen; Der Kaiser und der Rosenstock; Kaiser Claudius; Das Lustspiel am Fenster; Das Strandrecht; Das Posthaus in Treuenbrietzen; Der Leineweber; Der Stumme; Die Erbschaft; Der Graf von Gleichen; Der Deserteur. XXII. Der Russe in Deutschland; Die Unvermählte; Das Gespenst; Die englischen Waren. XXIII. Die Seeschlacht und die Meerkatze; Das Landhaus an der Heerstrasse; Der kleine Deklamator; Der Hagestolz und die Korbe; Die Abendstunde; Ubaldo; Das Intermezzo, oder, der Landjunker zum ersten Male in der Residenz. XXIV. Der blinde Gärtner, oder die blühende Aloe; Herr Gottlieb Merks, der Egoist und Kritikus; Pandorens Büchse ; Die Zerstreuten ; Der häusliche Zwist ; Des Esels Schatten, oder, der Prozess in Krähwinkel; Die kleine Zigeunerin ; Der verbannte Amor, oder, die argwöhni'schen Eheleute; Die Feuerprobe; Blind geladen. XXV. Der arme Minnesinger; Die Komödiantin aus Liebe; Das zugemauerte Fenster; Die Glücklichen; Sorgen ohne Noth und Noth ohne Sorgen; Das arabische Pulver; Feodore. XXVII. Die alten Liebschaften; Das Thal von Almeria; Der Lügenfeind; Die Quäker; Das unsichtbare Mädchen; Pachter Feldkümmel von Tippelskirchen; Die neue Frauenschule. XXVIII. Die Belagerung von Saragossa, oder, Pachter Feldkümmels Hochzeitstag; Max Helfenstein; Die Rosen des Herrn von Malesherbes; Die beiden kleinen Auvergnaten; Die Masken; Der arme Poet; Das gethcilte Herz; Die respektable Gesellschaft. XXIX. Der Brief aus Cadix; Die deutsche Hausfrau; Belas Flucht; Ungarns erster Wohlthäter; Die Ruinen von Athen; Der Fluch eines Römers; Die Nachtmütze des Propheten Elias; Die seltene Krankheit. XXX. Zwei Nichten für Eine; Braut und Bräutigam in einer Person; Die Prinzessin von Cacambo; Pervonte, oder, die Wünsche; Die Alpenhütte; Hans Max Giesbrecht von der Humpenburg, oder, die neue Ritterzeit; Der Kasicht. XXXI. Adelheid von Wulfingen; Der Kosak und der Freiwillige; Babbel, oder, Aus zwei Uebeln das Kleinste; Der schelmische Freier ; Die Rückkehr der Freiwilligen, oder, das patriotische Gelübde; Wer weiss wozu das gut ist; Der Shawl. XXXII. Die Kreuzfahrer; Der Schutzgeist; Die Grossmama. XXXIII. Die Beichte; Der Westindier, von Cumberland ; Der Verschwiegene wider Willen, oder, die Fahrt von Berlin nach Potsdam; Die Seelenwanderung, oder, der Schauspieler wider Willen auf eine andere Manier; Der Edukationsrath; Drei Väter auf Einmal ; Die Uniform des Feldmarschalls Wellington. XXXIV. Der Rehbock, oder, die schuldlosen Schuldbewussten ; Rudolph von Habsburg und König Ottokar von Böhmen; Des Hasses und der Liebe Rache. XXXV. Der Freimaurer; Der Ruf ; Der Citherschläger und das Gaugericht ; Die Bestohlenen ; Der gerade Weg der beste; Die Brillen-Insel; Der Kiffhäuser-Berg. XXXVI. Alfred; Der hölzerne Sabel, oder, die Heerschau; Die Waste; Die Einladungskarte; Marie; Der Vielwisser. XXXVII. Der Spiegel, oder, Lass das bleiben; La Peyrouse; Der Rothmantel; Der Kapitän Belronde; Die Verkleidungen; Der fürstliche Wildfang, oder, Fehler und Lehre. XXXVIII. Der Selbstmorder; Die Rosenmädchen; Gisela; Das Taschenbuch; Die entlarvte Fromme, oder, Ein Probchen vom Zeitgeiste. XXXIX. Der deutsche Mann und die vornehmen Leute; Hermann und Thusnelde; Menschenhass und Reue; Die eifersüchtige Frau. XL. Biographische Nachrichten über A. von Kotzebue; Pfalzgraf Heinrich; Verlegenheit und List; Die Frau vom Hause; Der Flussgott Niemen und Noch Jemand; Noch Jemands Reise-Abenteuer ; Das Liebhaber-Theater vor dem Parlament; Die schöne Unbekannte; Alphabetisches Verzeichniss aller A. von Kotzebue'schen Theaterstücke und Inhalt zu dieser Ausgabe in 40 Bänden.

— Life and literary career ; with the journal of his exile. London, 1827.   2v.   18° . . .   549.2

— Lover's vows.   Translated by Mrs. Inchbald. London, 1798.   8° 353.7

— Most remarkable year in the life of.   Transl. by Rev. B. Beresford. London, 1806. 3v. 16°   548.24

KOTZEBUE, O. v.   Voyage of discovery into the S. Sea and Beering's Straits.   [Translated by H. E. Lloyd.] London, 1821.   3v.   8°. .   702.12

KRUMMACHER, F. A.   Parables, with illustrations. Translated from the 7th German edition. London, 1854.   16° 736.13

KRUMMACHER, F. W. Elijah the Tishbite. From
the German. New York, n.d. 16° 119.6
— Select discourses 1096.9
KRÜSI, H. Principles of perspective. New York,
1857. 8° 201.6
KUGLER, F. Schools of painting in Italy. Ed.
by Sir C. L. Eastlake. London, 1842. 12° . 208.14
— - Same. 2d ed., with much additional mat-
ter. London, 1851. 2v. 12° 208.21
KÜHNE, F. G. Die Freimaurer. Roman. Frank-
furt, a. M., 1855. 3v. in 1. 8° 1013.4
— Quarantäne im Irrenhause. Leipzig, 1835. 8° 1016.4
— Wien in alter u. neuer Zeit. Leipzig, 1855. 16° 1029.4
KURDISTAN. See Koordistan.
KÜRNBERGER, F. Der Amerika-Müde. Roman.
Frankfurt, a. M., 1855. 8° 1013.9
KURNIK, M. Breslau und die schlesischen Eisen-
bahnen. Leipzig, 1856. 16° 1029.9
KURTEN, P. Art of manufacturing soaps, with
receipts for making candles. Philadelphia,
1854. 12° 198.11–12
KURZ, H. Der Sonnenwirth. Frankfurt, a. M.,
1855. 8° 1013.6
KUZZILBASH, The : a tale of Khorasan. Fraser,
J. B. 807.6

LA BOËTIE, E. de. Servitude volontaire, avec préf.
de Lamennais. Bruxelles, 1836. 18° . . . 1069.16
LABOR. Jameson, A. Communion of 127.23–24
— Lieber, F. Essays on 820.47
See also: Political econ'y and social science.
LABORDE, L. E. S. J. comte de. Journey through
Arabia Petræa to Mt. Sinai. 2d ed. Lon-
don, 1838. 8° 685.8
LA BROUSSE, M. de. The mulberry tree, abridged,
with notes, etc., by W. H. Vernon. Boston,
1828. 8° 136.2
LACON, or many things in few words. Colton,
C. C. 885.8
LACROIX-MARLES, J. Life of Mary Stuart. Boston,
1856. 12° 594.11
LADD, J. B. Literary remains, with life by W. B.
Chittenden. New York, 1832. 12° 898.7
LADIES of Great Britain, Letters of royal and
illustrious. Green, M. A. E. 596.5
LADIES' medical oracle. Mott, Mrs. 158.3
LADY of the lake : a poem. Scott, Sir W. . . . 359.15
LADY Alice : a novel. Huntington, J. V. . . . 802.3
LADY Lee's widowhood. Hamley, E. B. . . 802.37–38
LADY Willoughby, or diary of a wife and mother
in the 17th century. Fr. 2d London ed. N.
York, 1851. 12° 777.7
LADY's guide to perfect gentility. Thornwell, E. 127.11
LA FAYETTE, General M. P. J. R. Y. G. de M. de.
Complete history of, embracing an account
of his tour. Hartford, 1851. 12° 617.2
— Cloquet, J. Private life of 617.1
— Headley, P. C. Life of 617.3
— Holstein, H. L. V. D. Memoirs of 617.4
— Levasseur, A. L. in America 639.5
— Sarrans, B. L. et la revolution de 1830 . . . 617.5
LA FAYETTE, M. M. P. de la V. de. Histoire d'
Henriette d' Angleterre. Paris, 1853. 12°. 1078.17
LA FAYETTE, M'lle de, on le siècle de Louis XIII.
Genlis, C'tesse de 1066.15
LA FONTAINE, A. Village pastor and his children.
Translated. From London ed. of 1803. New
York, 1810. 2v. 12° 799.13
LA FONTAINE, J. de. Fables [précédées d'une vie
de La F. et d'Ésope.] Paris, 1846-17. 2v. 18° 1069.7
— Fables et œuvres diverses. Notice, etc. par
Walckenaer. Paris, 1854. 12° 1066.11
— Fables translated from the French by E.
Wright. 2d ed. Boston, 1841. 12° 332.1
LA FORCE, C. R. de C. de. Cabinet des Fées,
etc. . . . . .v.VI. of 1077.1
LAFORET, N. J. Études sur la civilisation euro-
péenne. Bruxelles, n.d. 12° 1065.29
LAGARDE, M. Histoire du duché de Limbourg.
Bruxelles, 1848. 12° 1075.8

LAGARDE, M. Histoire du duché de Luxembourg.
Bruxelles, n.d. 2v. 12° 1075.20
LA GIRONIÈRE, P. P. de. Twenty years in the
Philippines. Abridged. London, 1853. 12° 409.21
— - Same. New York, 1854. 12° 705.13–14
LAGNY, G. de. The knout and the Russians. Tr.
by J. Bridgeman. New York, 1854. 12° . . 927.6
LAHARPE, J. F. de. Lycée, ou cours de littéra-
ture. Nouv. éd. Paris, 1817. 16v. 18° . . 1079.15
LA HODDE, L. de. Secret societies and republican
party of France, 1830-48. Transl. Phila-
delphia, 1856. 8° 1004.4
LAING, A. G. Travels in Western Africa. Lon-
don, 1825. 8° 692.4
LAING, J. Voyage to Spitzbergen, 1806-7. Lon-
don, 1815. 8° . . . . v.II. of 668.2
— - Same. New ed. Edinburgh, 1825. 12° . 704.20
LAING, S. Notes on France, Prussia, Switzer-
land, Italy and other parts of Europe. 1st
series. London, 1854. 12° 409.14
— Residence in Norway, 1834-36. New edition.
London, 1854. 12° 409.15
LAISHLEY, R. Popular history of British birds'
eggs. London, 1858. 16° 177.27
LAKE, A. Defence of Kars, from authentic docu-
ments. London, 1857. 8° 987.1
— Kars and our captivity in Russia. London,
1856. 12° 988.11
LAKE of the woods, Long's expedition to the.
Keating, W. H. 624.11
LAKE Superior, Physical character of. Agassiz, L. 624.1
LAKES, Sketches of a tour to the, etc. McKenney,
T. L. 625.4
LAMARTINE, A. P. de. Œuvres diverses. Brux-
elles, 1836. 2v. 16° 1068.13

Contents. — Vol. I. Poésies. II. Poésies; Politique
rationnelle; Considérations préliminaires sur la question a proposer par l' Academie de Macon: Des devoirs
civils du curé; Discours de réception à l'Academie-
Destinées de la poesie.

— Celebrated characters. New York, 1854-56.
3v. 12° 547.4
— Christophe Colomb. Paris, 1853. 12° . . . 1078.19
— Chute d' un ange. Bruxelles, 1838. 2v. 18° 1068.12
— French revolution of 1848. Translated. 1st
American ed. Boston, 1849. 2v. in 1. 12°. 1008.1
— - Same. London, 1852. p.8° 848.3–4
— Geneviève, histoire d' une servante. Paris,
1853. 12° 1066.23
— Girondists, translated by H. T. Ryde. Lon-
don, 1849-50. 3v. p.8° 828.6
— History of Turkey, translated. New York,
1855. 12° 918.9
— Les confidences—confidential disclosures. Tr.
by E. Plunkett. New ed. New York, 1857. 12° 885.9
— Past, present and future of the republic. New
York, 1850. 12° 134.11
— Restoration of monarchy in France. Transl.
by Capt. Rafter. London, 1854. p.8° . . . 837.9
— - Same. New York, 1851-53. 4v. 12° . . . 1007.1
— Travels in the East, with memoir of the
author. Edinburgh, 1850. 2v. 12° 687.15
LAMB, C. Works. [Ed. by T. N. Talfourd.] Lon-
don, 1850. 4v. p.8° 874.6

Contents. — Vol. I. Life and letters. II. Final memorials. III. Essays of Elia. IV. Rosamund Gray: Essay; Letters under assumed signatures; Curious fragments: Mr. H—, farce; Poems; Sonnets; John Wood-
vil, tragedy; The witch, dramatic sketch of the 17th
century; Miscellaneous.

— Works, with life, by Talfourd. New York,
1838. 2v. 8° 874.2–3

Contents. — Vol. I. Letters; Poems; The wife's trial;
(drama.) II. Elia; Rosamund Gray, [a tale.]; Christ's
hospital; Essays; Mr. H., a farce.

— Adventures of Ulysses. London, 1839. 16°. 759.9
— Essays of Elia. New York, 1852. 8° 884.2–4
— - Same. New York, 1855. 8° 802.10
— - Same. New York, 1851. 8° 884.4

LAMB, C. Sketches and letters. Edited by T. N. Talfourd. New York, 1848. 12° 874.5
— Same. 2d ed. New York, 1849. 12° . . . 874.4
— Specimens of English dramatic poets about the time of Shakspere. New York, 1845. 2v. in 1. 12° 356.2
— - Same. New ed. New York, 1848. 2v. in 1. 12° 356.6
— - Same. New ed. London, 1854. p.8°. . . 356.9
— and M. Tales from Shakspere. London, 1844-46. 2v. 24° 840.29
LAMB, Gen. J. Life and times. Leake, I. Q. . . 513.5
LAMB, R. Journal during the American war to 1783. Dublin, 1809. 8° 213.13
LAMBERT, A. T. Mother's advice to her son and daughter. 1st Am. ed. Boston, 1844. 8° . 139.21
LAMBERT, J. Travels through Lower Canada and the U. S. A. 1806-8. London, 1810. 3v. 8°. 625.20
LAMBERT Lilly. Pseud. See Goodrich, S. G.
LA MENNAIS, H. F. R. de. Paroles d'un croyant. Bruxelles, 1838. 12° 1068.14
— People's own book. Translated by N. Greene. Boston, 1839. 24° 129.34
— Servitude volontaire, Préface, etc., par. See Boëtie, E. de 1069.16
LAMOTHE-LANGON, Bar. E. L. de. Evenings with Cambacérès. London, 1837. 2v. 8° . . . 1004.3
LAMOTTE, A. H. de. Un choix de fables de. See Florian, J. P. C. de 1066.14
LA MOTTE-FOUQUÉ, K. de, Baroness. The modern Lothario. Novel. Omnibus of modern romance 801.3
LA MOTTE-FOUQUÉ, Fr. H. K., Baron de. Ausgewählte Werke. Ausg. letzter H'd. Halle, 1841. 12v. 16° 1026.7
    Contents. — Vols. I.—III. Der Held des Nordens, Heldenspiel. 1. Sigurd der Schlangentodter. 2. Sigurd's Rache. 3. Aslanga. IV.—VI. Der Zauberring, Ritterroman. VII. Sintram und seine Gefährten; Nordische Erzahlung, nach Albrecht Durer. VIII. Undine, Erzahlung IX. Die beiden Hauptleute; Das Galgenmannlein; Der unbekannte Kranke; Novellen. X. Der Geheimrath; Der Siegeskranz, Legende; Das Schwerdt des Fursten; Eugenie; Rose. XI. Adler und Lowe; Norlandssage; Rosaura und ihre Verwandten, Erzahlung; Eginhard und Emma, Schauspiel. XII. Die Nacht im Walde, Sage; Gedichte.
— Aslauga's knight. Transl. with biographical notice. See Carlyle, T. . . . . . . v.I. of 418.1
— Undine: or, the water-spirit and Sintram and his companions. Transl. N. Y., 1845. 12° 416.13
— Same. Philadelphia, 1854. 12° 416.14
LAMPING, C. and France, A. de. The French in Algiers. Translated by Lady Duff Gordon. London, 1845. 12° 889.18
LAMPLIGHTER, The: a novel. Cummins, M. . 447.11-15
LAMPREDI, G. M. Lettere di—sulla Virginia e sulla Oreste di Alfieri 1046.3
LANCASTER, D. The history of Gilmanton, [N. H.] Gilmanton, 1845. 8° 224.24
LANCASTER, History of the Northern half of. Wilder, D. 227.12
LANCELOTT, F. The queens of England and their times, [1066-1849.] N. Y., 1848. 2v. 12° . 593.2
LANCES of Lynwood, The: a novel. Yonge, C. M. 786.11
LAND we live in; a sketch-book of the British empire. London, n.d. 4v. 4° 641.1
LANDED property, Transfer, management, etc. of. Ryde, E. 194.12
LANDER, R. Journal in Africa. Clapperton, H. 693.8
LANDER, R. and J. Journal of an expedition to the Niger. New York, n.d. 3v. 18° . . . 840.45
— - Same. 2d ed. London, 1838. 2v. 16° . . 380.12
LANDON, L. E. Ethel Churchill: or, the two brides, 2d ed. Phila., 1838. 2v. in 1. 12° 498.18
LANDOR, W. S. Dry sticks fagoted. Edinburgh, 1858. 8° 332.10
LANDS, Classical and sacred. Grenville, G. N. T. 840.48
LANDSBOROUGH, D. History of British sea-weeds. 2d ed. London, 1851. sq.12° 178.31
— History of British zoophytes. London, 1852. sq.16° 178.30

LANDSCAPE gardening. Downing, A. J. Theory and practice of 203.8-10
— Field, M. Essay on 203.16
— and architecture. Repton, H. 203.19
    See also: Agriculture, Architecture, etc.
LANE, E. W. Arabian tales and anecdotes. London, 1845. 18° 840.30
— Manners and customs of the modern Egyptians. London, n.d. 2v. 12° 839.8
— - Same. London, 1836. 2v. 12° 959.2
— - Same. London, 1846. 3v. 24° 840.31
LANETON parsonage: a tale. Sewell, E. M. . . . 425.6
LANGDON, Mary. Pseud. See Pike, M. H.
LANGHORNE, J. Letters between Theodosius and Constantia. New ed. London, 1770. 2v. 12°. 429.12
LANGON, Baron. See Lamothe-Langon.
LANGSTROTH, L. L. On the hive and the honey bee. Northampton, 1853. 12° 165.23
LANGUAGE, Balch, Wm. S. Lectures on 406.25
— Richardson, C. On the study of 406.14
— Schlegel, K. W. F. von. Philosophy of . . 828.8-9
LANGUAGES, On the origin of. Smith, A. 817.10
— Rousseau. Origine des langues . . . . v.XI. of 1069.1
    See also: Dictionary, Grammar, Rhetoric.
LANKESTER, E. Vegetable substances used for the food of man. London, n.d. 12° 840.8
— - Same. Boston, 1832. 12° 859.3
— - Same. New York, 1840. 18° 820.63
— - Same. London, 1846. 2v. 18° 840.32
LANMAN, C. Adventures in the wilds of N. Am. ed by C. R. Weld. London, 1854. 12°. . . 409.16
— Adventures, etc. With appendix by C. Hardy. Philadelphia, 1856. 2v. 8° 623.3
— Letters from the Alleghany mountains. New York, 1849. 12° 628.11
LANMAN, J. H. Hist. of Michigan. N. Y., n.d. 18°. 820.41
LANZI, L. History of painting in Italy. Trans. by G. W. D. Evans. London, 1831. 2v. 12°. 208.13
— - Same. Transl. by T. Roscoe. New ed., rev. London, 1847. 3v. p.8° 828.4
— Storia pittorica della Italia. 6a edizione. Milano, 1823. 6v. 16° 1058.13
LAOCOON, an essay on painting and poetry. Lessing, G. E. 209.14
LAPHAM, I. A. Geographical and topographical description of Wisconsin. Milwaukie, Wis., 1844. 16° 239.16
LA PLATA. Record of a cruise. Stewart, C. S.. 635.14
LA PORTE, Jos. de. La bibliothèque des fées et des génies. Cabinet des Fées. v.XXXIV. of 1077.1
L'ARDÈCHE. See Laurent de l'Ardèche.
LARDNER, D. Cabinet cyclopædia. London. 132v. 16°. Containing:

        History.
Keightley, T. Outlines of history 368.1
Nicolas, Sir N. H. Chronology of history . . 368.2
Mackintosh, Sir J. History of England, 10v. 368.3
Scott, Sir W. History of Scotland. 2v. . . 368.4
Moore, T. History of Ireland. 4v. 368.5
Crowe, E. E. History of France. 3v. 368.6
Wilson, J. History of Switzerland, by . . . 368.7
Dunham, S. A. History of Spain and Portugal. 5v. 368.8
— History of the Germanic empire. 3v. 368.9
Fergus, H. Hist. of the United States. 2v. 368.10
Thirlwall, C. History of Greece. 8v. . . . 368.11
History of Rome. 2v. 378.2
Fosbroke, T. D. Arts, manufactures, etc., of the Greeks and Romans. 2v. 378.3
Sismondi, J. C. L. S. de. History of the Italian republics 378.4
Dunham, S. A. Europe during the middle ages. 4v. 378.6
Bell, R. History of Russia. 3v. 378.7
Grattan, T. C. History of the Netherlands . 378.8
Dunham, S. A. History of Poland 378.9
— History of Denmark, Sweden, and Norway. 3v. 378.10
Cooley, W. D. Maritime and inland discovery. 3v. 378.11

LARDNER, D. Cabinet cyclopædia, *continued*.
Stebbing, H. The Christian church, to A.D.
1492. 2 v. 388.1
Sismondi, J. C. L. S. de. Fall of the Roman
empire. 2v. 378.5
Stebbing, H. History of the reformation. 2v. 388.2
Biography.
Gleig, G. R. Brit. military commanders. 3v. 388.3
Southey, R. British admirals. 5v. 388.5
Roscoe, H. Lives of eminent Brit. lawyers . 388.4
Mackintosh, J., Forster, J. and Courtenay,
T. P. British statesmen. 7v. 388.6
Crowe, E. E. and James, G. P. R. Foreign
statesmen. 5v. 388.7
Shelley, M. W. [G.,] and others. Literary
and scientific men of Italy, Spain, and Por-
tugal. 3v. 398.1
— Lit. and scientific men of France. 2v. 388.8
Bell, R. English poets. 2v. 398.2
Dunham, S. A., Bell, R. and others. Lit. and
scient. men of Great Britain and Ireland. 3v. 398.3
Natural Philosophy, etc.
Herschel, J. F. W. Preliminary discourse . 398.4
Powell, B. History of natural philosophy . 398.5
Lardner, D. Arithmetic 398.6
— Geometry 398.7
Kater, H. and Lardner, D. Mechanics . . . 398.8
Lardner, D. Hydrostatics and pneumatics . 398.9
Herschel, Sir J. F. W. Treatise on astronomy. 398.10
Brewster, D. Treatise on optics 398.11
Lardner, D. Treatise on heat 398.12
Donovan, M. Treatise on chemistry 398.13
Lardner, D. and Walker, C. V. Electricity,
magnetism, and meteorology. 2v. 398.14
De Morgan, A. Essay on probabilities . . . 398.15
Natural History.
Swainson, W. Preliminary discourse on the
study of natural history 398.16
— Geography and classification of animals. 398.17
— Nat. hist. and classific. of quadrupeds . . 398.18
— Animals in menageries 398.19
— Natural history and classification of
birds. 2v. 398.20
— Fishes, amphibians, and reptiles. 2v. . . 408.1
— Shells and shell fish 408.2
— and Shuckard, W. E. Insects 408.3
— Habits and instincts of animals 408.4
— Taxidermy, with the biography of zoölo-
gists, etc. 408.5
Henslow, J. S. Principles of descriptive and
physiological botany 408.6
Phillips, J. Treatise on geology. 2v. . . . 408.7
Useful Arts.
Donovan, M. Domestic economy. 2v. . . . 408.8
Porter, G. R. Manufacture of silk 408.9
Holland, J. Manufactures in metals. 3v. . 408.10
Porter, G. R. Manufacture of porcelain and
glass 408.11
— Handbooks of natural philosophy and astron.
I.-III. course. Phila., 1855-7. 3v. 12°. . 147.18-19
Contents. — First course: Mechanics, hydrostatics,
hydraulics, pneumatics, sound, optics. Second course:
Heat, magnetism, common electricity, voltaic electric-
ity. Third course: Meteorology, astronomy.
— Lectures on science and art. [Various eds.]
New York, 1851. 2v. 8° 144.14-17
— and Walker, C. V. Manual of electricity,
magnetism and meteorology. London, 1841-
[44.] 2v. 16° 398.14
— Museum of science and art. v.I.-XII. London, 1854-56. 7v. 12° 147.20
Contents. — Part I. The planets; Are they inhabited
worlds ? Weather prognostics; Popular fallacies; Latitudes and longitudes; Lunar influences; Meteoric
stones and shooting stars; Railway accidents; Light.
II. Air; Locomotion by river and railway in the United
States; Cometary influences; Water; The potter's art;
Fire. III.—IV. Locomotion and transport, their influence and progress; The moon; The earth; Terres-
trial heat; The sun; The electric telegraph; Earthquakes and volcanoes; The barometer; The safety

LARDNER, D. Museum of sci. and art, *continued*.
lamp; Whitworth's micrometric apparatus; Steam.
V.—VI. The steam engine; The eye; The atmosphere; Time; Pumps; Spectacles; The kaleidoscope;
Clocks and watches; Microscopic drawing and engraving; The locomotive; The thermometer; The new
planets; Le Verrier and Adam's planet; Magnitude
and minuteness. VII.—VIII. The almanac; Colour;
Optical images; The looking-glass; The tides; How
to observe the heavens; The stellar universe; Man;
Magnifying glasses; Instinct and intelligence; The
solar microscope ; Camera lucida; Magic lantern ;
Camera obscura. IX. — X. The microscope; The
white ants, their manners and habits; The surface
of the earth; Science and poetry; The bee, its character and manners; Steam navigation; Thunder and
lightning, and the Aurora Borealis; Electro-motive
power. XI.—XII. The printing press; The crust
of the earth ; The stereoscope; Comets; The pre-
Adamite earth; Eclipses; Sound.
— Popular essays on scientific subjects. Lon-
don, 1852. 12° 147.21
Contents. — Steam; Artificial light; Photography;
Electro-metallurgy; Electric telegraph; Pottery; Glass
manufacture; Railways; Steam marine; Essays on
the earth; Essays on industrial subjects, by Baron C.
Dupin, M. Chevalier, S. Lemoinne, and H. Berlioz.
— Popular geology. London, 1855. 12° . . 163.22
— Railway economy. New York, 1850. 12° . . 195.24
— Steam engine, rudimentary treatise. 3d ed.
London, 1853. 16° 819.24
— Steam engine familiarly explained. Additions
by J. Renwick. 5th American from 5th
London ed. Philadelphia, 1840. 8° . . . 195.16
— - Same. 8th ed., revised and improved.
London, 1851. 12° 198.16
— Treatise on arithmetic. London, 1834. 16°. 398.6
— Treatise on geometry. London, 1840. 16° . . 398.7
— Treatise on heat. London, 1833. 16° 398.12
— Treatise on hydrostatics and pneumatics. Lon-
don, 1831. 16° 398.9
— Mechanics. Kater, H. 149.19-20
— Newton's optics, and pneumatics. Lib. of
Useful Knowledge . . . . . . v.I. of 365.14
LA RIVE, A. de. Treatise on electricity. Transl.
by C. V. Walker. London, 1853-58. 3v. 8° 145.7
LA ROCHEJAQUELEIN, M. L. V. de D. Memoirs.
Tr. from the French. Edinburgh, 1827. 18° 830.27
LARRABEE, W. C. Wesley and his coadjutors.
Cincinnati, 1851. 2v. 16° 578.9
LA SALLE, R. C. de. Life of, by J. Sparks . v.XI. of 529.1
LAS CASES, M. J. E. D., *Count* de. Private life
and conversations of Napoleon at St.
Helena. London, 1824. 4v. 8° 603.2
— — Same. Boston, 1823. 4v. 8° 603.1
— Souvenirs de Napoléon I. Paris, 1854. 12°. . 1078.45
LAST days of Pompeii: a novel. Lytton, Sir E. B. 465.24
LAST of the barons: a novel. Lytton, Sir E. B. 465.18
LAST of the Mohicans. Cooper, J. F. 770.13-16
LASTEYRIE, *Count* C. P. de. History of auricular
confession. Translated by C. Cocks. Lon-
don, 1848. 2v. 12° 1008.10
LATHAM, R. G. The English language. 3d ed.
London, 1850. 8° 402.7
— Handbook of the English language. Lon-
don, 1851. 12° 403.12
— - Same. New York, 1852. 12° 406.2
— Logic in its application to language. London,
1856. 12° 403.6
— Man and his migrations. New York, 1852. 12° 176.6
— Native races of the Russian empire. London,
1854. 12° 176.1
LATINORUM, Corpus poetarum. Walker, W. S. . 353.1
LATOUR, A. L. Hist. memoir of the war in W.
Florida and La. in 1814-15. Transl. Phila-
delphia, 1816. 8° 246.1
— Atlas to the same. Pl.II.-IX. Philadelphia,
1816. Folded 8°. 246.2
LATROBE, C. J. Rambler in Mexico, 1834. New
York, 1836. 12° 629.14
LATTER-DAY pamphlets. Carlyle, T. 885.15
LATTER-DAY saints, or history of the Mormons.
Gunnison, J. W. 1087.8
See also: Mormons.

LAUBE, H. Gräfin Chateaubriant. Roman. 2te
   Aufl. Leipzig, 1846. 3v. in 1. 16° 1029.24
LAURENT, P. E. Manual of ancient geography.
   New ed. Oxford, 1840. 8° 954.5
LAURENT de l' Ardèche, P. M. Hist. of Napoleon.
   From the French. 2v. in 1. N. Y., n.d. 8° 604.10
LAURIE, T. Dr. Grant and the mountain Nestor-
   ians. Boston, 1853. 12° 686.5
LAURRINGTONS, The : a novel. Trollope, F. . . . 787.7
LAVELEYE, E. de. Histoire des rois francs.
   Bruxelles, n.d. 2v. 12° 1075.13
LA VENDÉE, Story of the war in. Hill, G. J. . . 1008.13
LAVENGRO, the scholar, the gipsy, the priest.
   Borrow, G. 478.2-3
LAW. Anthon, J. The law student 133.4
 — Bemis, G. Report of the case of J. W. Web-
   ster 133.3
 — Blackstone, W. Commentaries on the laws
   of England 133.6
 — - The student's Blackstone ; edited by R.
   M. Kerr 133.12
 — Burke, P. Trials connected with the aristoc-
   racy 133.8-9
 — - Trials connected with the upper classes . 133.9
 — Burton, J. H. Criminal trials in Scotland . . 987.4
 — Chandler, P. W. American criminal trials. . 297.17
 — Closset, A. de. Éléments de droit civil . . . 1065.12
 — Criminal law, Principles of . . . . . v.III. of 850.25
 — Criminal trials, supplying illustrations of his-
   tory 839.4
 — Cushing, L. S. Law and practice of legisla-
   tive assemblies 133.1
 — Feuerbach, A. R. v. Remarkable criminal
   trials 133.7
 — Freedley, E. T. Legal adviser 133.11
 — Goudebien, fils, J. Éléments de droit com-
   mercial 1065.16
 — Gibbons, D. Law of contracts 819.36
 — Hoorebeke, E. van. Précis d' instruction
   criminelle 1065.21
 — Jardine, D. Criminal trials 849.11
 — Johnson, J. and J. H. Patentee's manual . . 133.10
 — Kent, J. Commentaries on American 133.2
 — Lieber, F. Legal and political hermeneutics. 134.12
 — Roelker, B. Manual for notaries public . . . 133.5
 — Schnermans, H. Précis de droit criminel . . 1065.48
 — Simons, C. Éléments de droit civil 1065.50-51
 — Taylor, A. S. Medical jurisprudence 151.5
 — Wines, E. C. Laws of the Hebrews 1083.2
   See also : Constitution, Property, State. . .
LAW, H. Art of constructing and repairing roads.
   London, 1850. 16° 819.33
 — Mathematical tables. London, 1853. 16° . . 829.26
 — Manuel pratique de construction. [Trad. de
   l' anglais.] Bruxelles, 1850. 12° 1075.32
 — Rudiments of civil engineering. New edition.
   London, 1852. 4v. in 2. 16° 819.11
 — Treatise on logarithms. London, 1853. 16° . 829.26
LAW, J. Son système et son époque. Cochut, P. A. 1078.30
LAWRENCE, A. Diary and correspondence. Ed.
   by his son, W. R. Lawrence. Bost., 1855. 8° 524.1-2
 — Life of. Thayer, W. M. 526.20
LAWRENCE, E. Lives of British historians. New
   York, 1855. 2v. 12° 586.11-12
LAWRENCE, F. Life of H. Fielding. London,
   1855. 12° 584.3
LAWRENCE, Capt. J. Biography, with interesting
   papers. New Brunswick, 1813. 18° 529.5
 — Memoir of. Niles, J. M. 527.7
LAWRENCE, J. jr. A selection from [his] writ-
   ings. New York, 1833. 12° 907.3
   Contents. — Life of Algernon Sidney ; Dialogues
   of the dead ; A dream ; Poetry of Burns ; Mission to
   Panama ; English comedy ; Poetical pieces.
LAWRENCE, M. W. Light on the dark river : or,
   mem. of H. A. L. Hamlin. 3d ed. Boston,
   1854. 12° 538.6-8
LAWRENCE, Sir T., Life and correspondence of.
   Williams, D. E. 556.3
LAWRENCE, W., Memoir of. Lothrop, S. K. . . 524.3

LAWRIE Todd : a novel. Galt, J. 788.6
LAWSON, J. Ontwa : the son of the forest ; with
   notes by L. Cass. New York, 1822. 8° . . 349.1
LAWSON, J. P. Remarkable conspiracies during
   the 15th, 16th and 17th centuries. Edinb.,
   1829. 2v. 18° 830.51
LAWYER, The : or, success in life. Tuthill, L. C. . 525.20
LAWYERS. Knapp, S. L. Biographical sketches
   of eminent 524.10-11
 — Roscoe, H. Lives of eminent British 388.4
LAY of the last minstrel. Scott, Sir W. 359.14
LAY preacher, The. Dennie, J. 1089.32
LAYARD, A. H. Discoveries among the ruins of
   Nineveh and Babylon. New York, 1853. 8°. 685.12-13
 — Nineveh and its remains. N.Y., 1850. 2v. 8° 685.11
 — - Same. New York, 1851. 2v. 12° 685.7
 — - Same. New York, 1854. 12° 685.14-16
 — Popular account of discoveries at Nineveh.
   New ed. London, 1852. 12° 685.19
 — - Same. New York, 1854. 12° 685.18
 — The discoveries of, applied to the elucidation
   of holy writ. Bonomi, J. 835.14
LAYS of ancient Rome. Macaulay, T. B. 324.13
LEADING pursuits and leading men. Freedley,
   E. T. 296.3
LEAF and flower pictures, and how to make them.
   New York, 1857. 12° 168.1
LEAGUE of the Alps : a poem. Hemans, F. . . . 324.2
LEAKE, I. Q. Memoir of the life and times of
   Gen. J. Lamb. Albany, 1850. 8° 513.5
LEAKE, W. M. Travels in the Morea. London,
   1830. 3v. 8° 683.1
LEARNING, Dignity and advancement. Bacon, F. 826.7
LEATHER-DRESSING, Art of. Fontenelle, J. De . 194.11
LEATHER-STOCKING tales. See Cooper, J. F.

   Contents. — Deerslayer ; Last of the Mohicans ;
   Pathfinder ; Pioneers ; Prairie.

LEATHER work, Complete guide to 199.7
LEAVES from a family journal. Souvestre, E. . . 767.9
LEBANON, Three weeks in 689.16
LE BAS, C. W. Life of Archb'p Cranmer. Lon-
   don, 1833. 2v. 12° 578.2
 — Life of Wiclif. London, 1832. 12° 578.1
LEBENSFRAGE, Eine. Roman. Lewald, F. . . . 1024.10
LECLERC, J. M. J. Traité de drainage. Brux-
   elles, n.d. 12° 1065-30
LECLERCQ, T. Œuvres. Proverbes dramatiques.
   1e-4e sér. Nouv. éd., par SteBeuve et
   Mérimée. Paris, n.d. 4v. 12° 1066.24
LECOUNT, P. Practical treatise on railways. Ed-
   inburgh, 1851. 12° 195.25
LECTURES on the results of the exhibition. Lon-
   don, 1852. 12° 199.16

   Contents. — Dr. Whewell: Inaugural ; De la Beche:
   Mining ; R. Owen: Animal products ; Jacob Bell:
   Chemical processes ; Dr. L.Playfair: Industrial edu-
   cation ; Prof. Lindley: Substances used as food ; Prof.
   Solly : Vegetable substances : Prof. Willis: Machines ;
   J. Glaisher, Esq. : Philosophical instruments ; R.
   Hensman, Esq. : Civil engineering ; Prof. Royle:
   Manufactures of India ; Capt. Washington : Life
   Boats.

LEDDERHOSE, K. F. Life of P. Melanchthon. Tr.
   by G. F. Krotel. Philadelphia, 1855. 12° . 545.9
LEDYARD, J. Life of. Sparks, J. 523.15
LEE, C. Memoirs, political and military essays :
   also letters. New York, 1792. 12° 528.11
 — Life of. By Sparks, J. . . . . . . v. XVIII. of 529.1
LEE, C. A. Elements of geology. N. Y., n.d. 18°. 820.71
LEE, E. B. Life of J. P. F. Richter, with his auto-
   biography. New York, 1850. 12° 545.13
 — Memoirs of Rev. J. Buckminster, and Rev. J.
   S. Buckminster. Boston, 1849. 12° 535.9
 — - Same. 2d ed. Boston, 1851. 12° 535.8
 — Naomi : or, Boston two hundred years ago.
   Boston, 1848. 16° 437.7
 — - Same. 2d ed. Boston, 1848. 12° 437.6
 — - Parthenia : or, the last days of paganism.
   Boston, 1858. 12° 437.3-5

LEE, Harriet. Canterbury tales. New York, 1857.
2v. 12° 437.2
LEE, Henry. Memoirs of the war in the Southern
department of the United States. New ed.
Washington, 1827. 8° 216.2
LEE, Mrs. H. F. Life and times of Martin Luther.
Philadelphia, 1852. 16° 545.25
— Life of Thomas Cranmer. Philad., 1852. 16°. 578.5
— Memoir of P. Toussaint. Boston, 1854. 16°. 539.10–11
— Sketches of sculpture and sculptors. Boston,
1854. 2v. 12° 208.23
— Sketches of the old painters. Philadelphia,
1852. 16° 209.13
— Sketches and stories from life: for the young.
Boston, 1850. 16° 469.8
LEE, M. E. Social evenings: or, historical tales.
Boston, 1840. 18° 469.25–26
LEE, Dr. R. Last days of Alexander and the first
days of Nicholas. 2d ed. London, 1854. 8°. 547.16
LEE, Mrs. R. Taxidermy. 6th ed. Lond., 1843. 12° 177.25
LEE, Prof. R. H. Memoir of the life of R. H.
Lee. Philadelphia, 1825. 2v. 8°. 515.6
LEE, S. Canterbury tales. N. York, 1857. 12° . . 437.1
LEEDS, W. H. Rudimentary architecture. 3d ed.
London, 1854. 16° 819.12
LEFRANÇOIS, E. Notions de mécanique générale.
Bruxelles, n.d. 12° 1065.31
LEGACY for young ladies. Barbauld, A. L. . . . 137.31
LEGAL adviser. Freedley, E. T. 133.11
LEGAL tales. Three courses and a dessert 815.2
LEGAL and political hermeneutics. Lieber, F. . . . 134.12
LEGARÉ, H. S. Writings. Prefaced by a memoir.
Charleston, 1845–46. 2v. 8° 872.3
LEGEND of Montrose. Scott, Sir W. 460.34–38
LEGENDS of the library at Lilies. Grenville, G.
N. T. and A. L., Lord and Lady Nugent . . 777.11
LEGENDS and lyrics. Procter, A. A. 339.8
LEGGE, T. Latin play of Richardus tertius . . . 342.20
LEGISLATIVE assemblies in the U. S. A., Practice
of. Cushing, L. S. 133.1
LEGOUVÉ, E. Histoire morale des femmes. 3e
éd. Paris, 1848. 12° 1078.9
LEIGHTON, R. Whole works. Life by J. N. Pear-
son. New York, 1852. 8° 1083.6
Contents. — Life and Doddridge's preface; Commentary on the I. Ep. of Peter; Meditations; Fragment on Psalm vii.; Expository lectures; Lectures on
the Gospel by Matthew; Sermons; Exposition of the
creed; Expos. of the Lord's prayer; Expos. of the ten
commandments; Short catechism; Theological lectures; Exhortation to students; Valedictory oration;
Moderate episcopacy; Fragment on Ezra ix.; Charges;
Rules for a holy life; Appendix, containing biogr.
notices and letters.

LEILA, or the island: [a tale.] Tytler, A. F. . . . 719.1
LEILA: a novel. Lytton, E. B. 466.7–9
LEIPSIC campaign. Gleig, G. R. 409.7
LEIPZIG, Die Schlachten bei. Berneck, K. G. v. 1029.2
LEISLER, J., Life of, by C. F. Hoffman. Sparks,
J. American biography . . . . . . v.XIII. of 529.1
LEISURE labors. Cobb, J. B. 877.6
LEMAIRE, C. Horticulture pratique. Bruxelles,
n.d. 12° 1065.32
LEMAISTRE, J. G. Travels in France, Switzerland,
Italy and Germany. London, 1806. 3v. 8° 654.3
LE MARCHAND, Mme. F. D. de V. Boca. Cabinet
des Fées . . . . v.XVIII. of 1077.1
LEMOINNE, J. Essays on industrial subjects.
Lardner, D. 147.21
LEMURS, Natural history of 839.17
LENAERTS, J. De l'organisation provinciale en
Belgique. Bruxelles, n.d. 12° 1065.33
L'ENCLOS, Story of Ninon de. Damours, L. . . . 892.10
LENDY, A. F. Elements of fortification. London,
1857. 12° 197.8
LENNOX, Mrs. C. R. The female Quixote; or,
the adventures of Arabella. London, 1820.
2v. 12° . . . . v.XXIV. & XXV. of 778.1
LE NORMAND, M. A. Secret memoirs of the
Empress Josephine. Translated by J. M.
Howard. New ed. Phila., 1854. 2v. 12° 606.1–6

LENTNER, J. F. Novellenbuch. Magdeburg, 1848.
3v. 16° 1036.3
Contents.—Vol. I. Luststudien; Unser lieben Frauen
neue Kirche; Der Wildschatz. II. Stentorello; Die
Pantoffeln; Diebsgeläste; Zwei Stunden; III. Trau-
benkuren; Der Flüchtling Veranderungen.

LEO X., Life and pontificate of. Roscoe, W. . . . 818.2
LEOMINSTER, Mass., History of. Wilder, D. . . . 227.12
LEONARD, P. Western coast of Africa. Phila-
delphia, 1833. 12° 699.10
LEONOR de Guzman: a tragedy. Boker, G. H. v.I. of 335.2
LEONORA: a tale. Edgeworth, M. . . . v.VII. of 467.1–3
LE PRINCE de Beaumont, Mme. M. "Contes des
Fées." Cabinet des Fées . . . . v.XXXV. of 1077.1
LEPSIUS, K. R. Discoveries in Egypt, Ethiopia
and Sinai, 1842–45. London, 1853. p.8°. . 856.6
— – Same. 2d ed. London, 1853. 8° 693.11
— Tour from Thebes to Sinai, 1845. Translated
by C. H. Cottrell. London, 1846. 16° . . . 699.16
LEREBOURS, N. P. Treatise on photography.
Translated by J. Egerton. Lond., 1843. 8° 197.13
LE SAGE, A. R. Histoire de Gil Blas. Paris, 1816.
4v. 18° 1068.19
— Adventures of Gil Blas. Translated by Smol-
lett. London, 1797. 3v. 18° 779.3
— – Same. London, n.d. 8° 801.7
LESLEY, J. P. Coal and its topography. Phila-
delphia, 1856. 16° 197.6
LESLIE, C. Short method with the deists; and
truth of Christianity demonstrated 119.9
LESLIE, C. R. Handbook for young painters.
London, 1855. 12° 208.17
LESLIE, E. The behaviour book. A manual for
ladies. 4th ed. Philadelphia, 1851. 12° . 127.12–17
— New receipts for cooking. Phila., n.d. 12° . 188.7
LESLIE, J. Discovery and adventure in the polar
seas. Murray, H. 810.15
LESLIE, Madeline. Pseud. See Baker, H. N. W.
LESSING, G. E. Gesammelte werke. Leipzig,
1841. 10v. 16° 1019.1
Contents. — Vol. I. Sinngedichte; Anhang; Lieder;
Anhang; Oden; Fabeln und Erzählungen; Frag-
mente; Die Juden; Der Freigeist; Doctor Faust;
Werther der Beasere. II. Miss Sarah Sampson;
Philotas; Minna von Barnhelm; Emilia Galotti. III.
Nathan der Weise. IV. Briefe aus dem zweiten
Theile der Schriften, 1753; Ein Vade Mecum für den
Herrn Sam. Gotth. Lange, 1754; Rettungen des
Horaz; Abhandlungen über die Fabel; Vorrede zum
ersten–vierten Theile der Schriften; Vorrede zu den
vermischten Schriften des Herrn Christlob Mylius;
Vorbericht zu den preussischen Kriegsliedern in den
Feldzügen 1756 und 1757 von einem Grenadier 1758;
Vorrede zu Friedrichs von Logau Sinngedichten;
Vorreden zu Diderot's Theater. V. Aus den Briefen
die neueste Literatur betreffend; Sophocles; Wie die
Alten den Tod gebildet; Antiquarische Briefe. VI.
Laokoon oder über die Gränzen der Malerei und
Poesie; Ueber das Epigramm und einige Epigram-
matisten. VII.—III. Hamburgische Dramaturgie;
Ueber Meusels Apollodor; Vom Alter der Oelmalerei,
aus dem Theophilus Presbyter. IX. Zur Geschichte
und Literatur; Aus den Schätzen der herzogl. Bibli-
othek zu Wolfenbüttel; Theologische Streitschriften;
Ernst und Falk; Gespräche für Freimaurer; Noch
nähere Berichtigung des Mährchens von tausend
Ducaten, oder Judas Ischarioth dem Zweiten; Die
Erziehung des Menschengeschlechts. X. Briefe von
Lessing; Einige Worte über G. E. Lessing und seine
Schriften.

— Education of the human race. London, 1858.
18°. pp.79 . . . . 138.8
— Laocoon, or painting and poetry. Translated
by E. C. Beasley. Introduction by T. Bur-
bidge. London, 1853. 16° 209.14
LESTER, C. E. Artists of America; a series of
biographical sketches. N. Y., 1846. 8°. . . 524.14
— Condition and fate of England. New York,
1842. 2v. 12° 988.9
— Glory and shame of England. New York,
1842. 2v. 12° 646.12
My consulship. N. Y., 1853. 2v. 12° 678.6
— and Foster, A. Life and voyages of Americus
Vespucius. New York. 1846. 8° 544.1

LETTERE sulla pittura, etc. Bottari, G. 1049.1
LETTER to a young piano-forte player. 2d edition.
  London, 1830. 12° 199.28
LETTERS from abroad. Sedgwick, C. M. 648.8
LETTERS from Madras during the years 1836-39.
  London, 1846. 12° 889.28
LETTERS from the shores of the Baltic. London,
  1844. 12° 889.29
LETTERS from the South by a Northern man.
  Paulding, J. K. 888.18
LETTERS of " an Englishman " on Louis Napoleon
  and the coup d'état. London, 1852. 12° . . 1009.6-7
LETTERS-OF-MARQUE of the war of 1812. Cogges-
  hall, G. 215.8
LETTERS to my unknown friends. Lond., 1853. 16° 127.32
LETTER-WRITING, A pocket manual of 496.12
LETTICE Arnold : a tale. Marsh, A. 795.8
LETTSOM, W. G. Mineralogy of Great Britain.
  Greg, R. P. 163.8
LEUTRE, Ch. de. Histoire de la révolution belge
  en 1830. Bruxelles, n.d. 3v. in 1. 12° . . . 1065.34
LEVANT, Cruise to the. Colton, W. 678.16
LEVANT, Monasteries in the. Curzon, R. 689.8-9
LEVASSEUR, A. Lafayette in America in 1824-25.
  Translated by J. D. Godman. Philadelphia,
  1829. 2v. 12° 639.5
LEVELLING, Treatise on. Castle, H. J. 196.6
LEVÊQUE, Mme. L. C. " Le Prince des Aigues-
  Marines" et "Le Prince Invisible."v.XXIV.of 1077.1
LEVER, C. Charles O'Malley, the Irish dragoon.
  Philadelphia, n.d. 8° 501.14-15
— The Daltons : or, three roads in life. New
  York, 1852. 8° 501.19
— Dodd family abroad. New York, 1854. 8° . . 501.18
— Martins of Cro'Martin. New York, 1856. 8°.501.16-17
LE VERT, Mme. O. W. Souvenirs of travel. New
  York, 1857. 2v. 12° 648.13
LEVIEN, E. Hist. of Greece. See Hamilton, W. D. 829.38
LEVIS, J., Sixty years of the life of. New York,
  1831. 2v. 12° 597.13
LEVITICUS, Book of. See Bible.
LEWALD, F. Eine Lebensfrage. Roman. Leip-
  zig, 1845. 2v. 16° 1024.10
— Jenny. Roman. Leipzig, 1843. 2v. 16° . . 1024.11
LEWES, G. H. Biographical history of philosophy.
  London, 1852-53. 4v. 18° 840.34
— - Same. New York, 1857. 2v. 8° 547.1
— - Same. London, 1857. 8° 122.4
— Comte's philosophy of the sciences. London,
  1853. p.8° 826.9
— Life of Robespierre, with correspondence.
  London, 1849. 12° 615.1
— Life and works of Goethe. Bost., 1856. 2v. 12° 545.5-6
— Sea-side studies. Edinburgh, 1858. 8° . . . 178.2
— Spanish drama. Lope de Vega and Calderon.
  London, 1846. 18° 840.35
LEWIS, A. Poems. Boston, 1831. 12° 348.20
LEWIS, E. J. American sportsman. Phila., 1855. 8° 172.2
LEWIS, G. C. Credibility of the early Roman his-
  tory. London, 1855. 2v. 8° 953.4
LEWIS, M. G. Journal of a residence in the W. I.
  London, 1845. 12° 889.30
— Life and correspondence. Lond., 1839. 2v. 8° 582.10
LEWIS, T. The six days of creation. 2d edition.
  Schenectady, 1855. 12° 146.17
— Introduction to mythology. See Dwight,
  M. A. 1083.10
LEWIS and Clarke's expedition. History of.
  Allen, P. 820.52
LEXINGTON, History of the battle of. Frothing-
  ham, R. jr. 214:2-8
LEXINGTON papers. Sutton, R. 975.11
LEYDEN, J. Discoveries in Africa. See Murray, H. 692.10
L'HÉRITIER, M'lle M. J. " La tour ténébreuse
  et les Jours lumineux." Cabinet des
  Fées. . . . . . . v.XII. of 1077.1
LIAGRE, J. Élements de géométrie et de topog-
  raphie. Bruxelles, n.d. 12° 1065.35
— Traité élémentaire de topographie. Bruxelles,
  n.d. 12° 1065.36

LIBERIA, or Mr. Peyton's experiments. Hale, S.J. 488.3
LIBERTY. Bunsen, C. C. J. Dangers to religious. 134.9
— Eliot, S. History of 134.7
— - Passages from the history of 135.22
LIBRARIES. See Bibliothèque industrielle . . . 1075.30-39
— Bibliothèque nationale 1075.7-29
— Bohn, H. G. Antiquarian library. . . . . 846 & 856
— - Classical library. . . . . . 814 & 824
— - Ecclesiastical library 845.1-10
— - Illustrated library . . . . . . 815 & 825
— - Philological and philosophical library . 855.1-6
— - Scientific library. . . . . . 816 & 826
— - Standard library. . . . . . 817 & 827
— Constable, A. Miscellany. 830.25-71
— Encyclopédie populaire. 1065.4
— Harper. Classical library 830.8-24
— - Family library 810.1
— Jardine, W. Naturalists' library 179.1
— Knight's weekly and monthly volume. . . . 840 & 850
— Lardner, D. Cabinet cyclopædia 368.1
— Murray, J. Family library 379.1
— - Home and colonial library 889.1-34
— National illustrated library . . . . . . 869 & 879
— Putnam, G. P. Story library. 738.1
— Small books on great subjects 850.25
— Library of useful knowledge. 365.1-17
— Library of entertaining knowledge . . . . . 839 & 849
— Sparks, J. L. of American biography 529.1
— Traveller's library 409.1
— Weale's series . . . . . . 819 & 829
LIBRARY of biography. Remarkable women. 1st
  ser. Boston, 1858. 12° 547.5
LIBYAN desert, Adventures in the. St. John, B. . 698.21
LIDDELL, H. G. History of Rome to the estab-
  lishment of the empire. London, 1857. 12° 957.4
LIEBER, F. Civil liberty and self-government.
  Philadelphia, 1853. 2v. 12° 134.13
— Essays on property and labor. New York,
  1843. 18° 820.47
— Great events described by distinguished his-
  torians. Boston, [1840.] 12° 947.12
— Legal and political hermeneutics. Enlarged
  ed. Boston, 1839. 12° 134.12
— Reminiscences of an intercourse with Niebuhr
  in Rome. Philadelphia, 1835. 12° 588.7
— Stranger in America. London, 1835. 2v. 12° 628.19
LIEBIG, J. Complete works on chemistry. Phil-
  adelphia, n.d. 8° 156.1

  Contents. — Agricultural chemistry; Animal chemistry; Motion of the juices; Potato disease.

— Agricultural chemistry. London, 1855. 12° 155.24
— Animal chemistry. Ed. by W. Gregory. 3d
  ed., enlarged. Part I. London, 1846. 8° . 155.4
— Chemistry in its application to agriculture
  and physiology. Ed. by L. Playfair and
  W. Gregory. 4th ed., revised and enlarged.
  London, 1847. 8° 164.6
— Chemistry and physics in relation to physiol-
  ogy and pathology. 2d ed. Lond., 1847. 8° 155.21
— Chemistry of food. Ed. by W. Gregory.
  London, 1847. 8° 155.7
— Familiar letters on chemistry. 3d ed. Lon-
  don, 1851. 16° 156.32
— Handbook of organic analysis. Ed. by A.
  W. Hofmann. London, 1853. 12° 156.23
— Motion of the juices in the animal body. Ed.
  by W. Gregory. London, 1848. 8° 155.14
— Organic chemistry, in its application to agri-
  culture and physiology. Ed. by L. Play-
  fair. 1st. Am. ed., with introd. and notes,
  by J. W. Webster. Cambridge, 1841. 8° 155.25
LIFE and adventures of Major R. S. Potter. By
  Pheleg van Trusedale. N. York, 1858. 12°. 427.1
LIFE. Giles, H. Christian thought on 1088.27
— Gosse, P. H. L. in its lower, intermediate,
  and higher forms 178.15
— Hufeland, C. W. Art of prolonging 157.27
— Kitchiner, W. Art of prolonging 158.21
— Schlegel, K. W. F. von. Philosophy of . . . 825.8-9

LIFE-ANNUITIES. J. De Witt's treatise on. . . . 545.16
   See also : Assurance, etc. . . . . . .
LIFE-BOATS, Lectures on, by Capt. Washington . 199.16
LIFE and love in Norway. Mügge, T. 415.3
LIFE and manners. De Quincey, T. 895.10
LIFE here and there. Willis, N. P. 904.3-5
LIFE in earnest. Hamilton, J. 1109.26-28
LIFE in the clearings. Moodie, S. S. 636.12-18
LIFE in the itinerancy. New York, 1856. 12°. . 417.10
LIFE in the new world. Sealsfield, C. 735.5-6
LIFE in the wilds. Martineau, H. . . . . . v.I. of 749.2-3
LIFE lore : lessons from the childhood of Nolan
   Fairfield. London, 1847. 12°. 449.5
LIFE of a sailor. Chamier, F. 737.1
LIFE studies : or, how to live. Baillie, J 548.12
LIFE thoughts. Beecher, H. W. 1086.16
LIFE's discipline : a tale. Robinson, T. A. L. v. J. 449.12
LIGHT. Its chemical relations. Hunt, R. . . . 145.13
 — Double refraction and polarization of . . v.I.of 365.14
 — Nature, sources, effects, etc., of 149.32
   See also : Optics.
LIGHT dragoon, The. Gleig, G. R. 726.1
LIGHT in dark places. Neander, A. 858.7
LIGHT of truth, and pleasure of light. Milledge-
   ville, 1827. 12° 1099.19
LIGHTHOUSES, Treatise on. Stevenson, A. . . . 819.34-35
LIGHTING buildings, Remarks on. Reid, D. B. . . 207.2
LIGHTS and shadows of Irish life. Hall, A. M. . 776.12
LILLO, G. Dramatic works, with memoir, by T.
   Davies. 2d ed. London, 1810. 2v. 12° . . 356.18

   Contents. — Vol. I. Life; Silvia, an opera; George
Barnwell; The life of Scanderbeg ; The Christian
hero. II. Fatal curiosity; Marina; Elmerick; Bri-
tannia and Batavia, a masque; Arden of Feversham.

LILY, The, and the bee. Warren, S. 767.18
LIMA, Journey to. Markham, C. R. 633.20
LIMA, Residence in. Smith, A. 633.21
LIMAN, Campaign of the. Jones, J. P. 513.6
LIMBOURG. Histoire du duché de. Lagarde, M. 1075.8
LIMES, cements, mortars, etc. Burnell, G. R. . . 199.19
LINCOLN, A. H. *See* Phelps, A. H.
LINCOLN, B. Life of, by F. Bowen. Sparks's Am.
   biography . . . . v.XXIII. of 529.1
LINCOLN, S. jr. History of Hingham, Mass.
   Hingham, 1827. 12° 227.19
LINCOLN, Mass., A history of the town of. Shat-
   tuck, L. 224.20
LINDA, the young pilot. Hentz, C. L. 445.11
LINDEN, Liele. *Pseud.* Chestnut Wood: a tale. 416.3
LINDLEY, J. Botany, in four parts. Lon., 1838. 8°. 365.15
 — Introduction to the natural system of botany.
   London, 1830. 8°. 164.3
 — Ladies' botany. London, 1837. 2v. 8° . . . 164.2
 — School botany. London, 1839. 16°. 169.25
 — Theory of horticulture. 2d Am. ed., with
   notes by A. J. Downing. N. Y., 1852. 12°. 164.16
 — Substances used as food. 199.16
LINDSAY, A. W. C., *Lord.* Letters on Egypt,
   Edom, and the Holy Land. London, 1838.
   2v. 12°. 693.16
LINE of life. Forde, J. 342.18
LINEN, History of. History of silk, etc. 195.4
 — Industrie linière. Kindt, L. 1065.26
LINGARD, J. Hist. of England, A.C. 55 to A.D.
   1689. New ed. London, 1837. 13v. 16°. 969.3
 — - Same. 5th ed. Paris, 1840. 8v. 8° . . . 964.2
 — - Sadler's abridg. Paris, 1836. 12° . . . 968.4
LINN, E. A. Life and services of L. F. Linn.
   New York, 1857. 8° 523.1
LINSLEY, D. C. Morgan horses : a premium es-
   say. New York, 1857. 12°. 165.17
LINTOT, Mme. C. C. de. "Contes." Cabinet des
   Fées. . . . . v.XXXII. of 1077.1
LION killer, adventures of the. Gerard, J. . . . 697.14-18
LIONEL Lincoln : a novel. Cooper, J. F. 760.41-44
LIPPINCOTT, S. J. C. *(Grace Greenwood.)* Haps
   and mishaps of a tour in Europe. Boston,
   1854. 16°. 658.5-7
 — Poems. Boston, 1851. 16°. 369.1
 — Stories and legends for children. Boston,
   1857. 16°. 729.9

LIST, F. Political economy. Translated by G. A.
   Matile. Notes by H. Richelot. Essay and
   notes by S. Colwell. Philadelphia, 1856. 8°. 135.8
LISTER, T. H. Herbert Lacy : [a novel.] London,
   1828. 3v. 12° 777.1
LISTON, R. Elements of surgery. Notes and add.
   by S. D. Gross. 4th Am. ed. Phila., 1846. 8° 151.17
LITERARY addresses, delivered at various popular
   institutions. 1st-3d ser. Lond., 1855. 3v. 16° 866.10
LITERARY and scientific men of America. Lives of.
   Wynne, J. 518.3-4
 — of Great Britain. Lives of. Dunham, S. A. 398.3
LITERARY character, illustrated. D'Israeli, I. . . 402.5
LITERARY essays and characters. Hallam, H. . . 868.19
LITERARY history of the New Testament. Lon-
   don, 1845. 8° 1085.5
LITERARY life, Recollections of. Mitford, M. R. 896.12
LITERARY men of Italy, Spain, and Portugal.
   Lives of. Shelley, M. W. 398.1
LITERARY reminiscences. De Quincey, T. . . 895.11-13
LITERATURE. Brande, W. T. Dictionary of . . 135.1
 — Carcano, G. Della letteratura rusticale . . . 1056.10
 — D'Israeli, I. Amenities of 404.8
 — - Curiosities of 897.7-8
 — Gilfillan, G. L. and literary men 548.3
 — Gilman, S. Contributions to 887.5
 — Goodrich, S. G. Ancient and modern 406.9
 — Grant, J. Walks in the world of 898.19
 — Grimké, T. S. Character and objects of . . . 878.9
 — Hamilton, Sir W. Discussions on 872.1
 — Jameson, A. Essays illustrative of 876.14
 — La Harpe, J. F. Cours de L. anc. et mod. . . 1079.15
 — Moir, D. M. Poetical L. of past half century. 406.10
 — Montgomery, J. Lectures on general . . . 810.64-65
 — Ossoli, S. M. F. d'. L. and art 403.18
 — Ripley. G. Handbook of 406.22
 — Soane, G. New curiosities of 402.11
 — Staël Holstein, Mme. de. Influence of L.
   upon society 868.14
 — Tannehill, W. Hist. of L. to the xv. century. 402.8
 — Tuckerman, H. T. Characteristics of 548.5
 — Whipple, E. P. Lectures on subjects con-
   nected with 875.13
 — White, C. Essays in 403.17

   NOTE. — For the literature of particular countries
and languages, see under their several names.

LITTLE Dorrit. Dickens, C. 472.4-9
LITTLE duke, The. Yonge, C. M. 786.12
LITTLE Louvre, The. Harper's story books. Ab-
   bott, J. . . . . v.III. of 739.1
LIVE and learn. Over 1000 mistakes corrected.
   New York, n.d. 12° 406.16
LIVE and let live. Sedgwick, C. M. 729.12-13
LIVERMORE, A. A. Discourses. Bost., 1854. 12° 1086.18
 — War with Mexico reviewed. Bost., 1850. 12° 259.4
LIVERMORE, G. Tribute to the memory of J.
   Johnson. Boston, 1855. 8° 524.13
LIVES and voyages of Drake, Cavendish, and
   Dampier. New York, n.d. 18° 810.41
LIVES of Balboa, Cortes, and Pizarro. Boston,
   1840. 18°. 539.21-22
LIVES of British physicians. London, 1830. 16°. 389.13
LIVES of Columbus and Americus Vespucius.
   Boston, 1840. 18° 547.21
LIVES of eminent individuals celebrated in Amer-
   ican history. [From Sparks's American bi-
   ography.] Boston, [1839.] 3v. 12° 538.5

   Contents. — Vol. I. Life of J. Stark, by E. Everett;
D. Brainerd, by O. W. B. Peabody : R. Fulton, by J.
Renwick; Capt. J. Smith, by G. S. Hillard. II. Ethan
Allen, by J. Sparks; Sebastian Cabot, by C. Hay-
ward, jr.; Henry Hudson, by H. R. Cleveland; Jos.
Warren, by A. H. Everett; Israel Putnam, by. W. B.
O. Peabody ; David Rittenhouse, by J. Renwick.
III. William Pinkney, by H. Wheaton; Sir Henry
Vane, by C. W. Upham; Anthony Wayne, by J.
Armstrong; William Ellery, by E. T. Channing;
Rich. Montgomery, by J. Armstrong.

   See also : Biography.

LIVING. Mayo, H. Philosophy of 158.9
 — Ticknor, C. Philosophy of 810.72
LIVING orators in America. Magoon, E. L. . . . 518.16

LIVINGSTONE, D. Cambridge lectures. Introduction and life of Dr. L., by W. Monk. Cambridge, 1858. 16° 804.4
— Missionary travels and researches in South Africa. New York, 1858. 8° 691.1–11
LIVIUS, T. History of Rome. Translated by G. Baker. Boston, 1823. 6v. in 3. 8° . . . 946.4
— - Same. New York, n.d. 5v. 18° 830.19
— - Same. Translated by Spillan, Edmonds and M'Devitte. London, 1850–53. 4v. p.8° 814.4
LIVONIAN tales. The disponent. The wolves. The Jewess. London, 1846. 12° 889.31
LIZARD, A week at the. Johns, C. A. 659.29
LIZZIE Leigh. A story. Dickens, C. 491.1–6
LLOYD, E. Mathematical geography. Library of Useful Knowledge . . . . v.III. of 365.14
LLOYD, H. J. Physical geography. Library of Useful Knowledge . . . . v.III. of 365.14
LLOYD, W. F. Sketch of life of R. Raikes and of the history of Sunday Schools. New York, 1852. 16° 578.13
LOAMY soils, Treatise on. Donaldson, J. . . . 829.3
LOBEIRA, V. de. Amadis of Gaul. London, 1803. 4v. 12° 779.2
LOCAL loiterings in the vicinity of Boston. Boston, 1845. 12° 228.9
LOCKE Amsden: or, the schoolmaster. Thompson, D. P. 726.10
LOCKE, J. Philosophical works. [Ed.] by J. A. St. John. London, 1824. 2v. p.8° 827.4

Contents. — Vol. I. Essay concerning the human understanding. II. Same; Appendix; Elements of nat. philosophy; Reading and study for a gentleman.

— Conduct of the understanding 820.65
— Essay concerning human understanding. New ed. New York, 1824. 2v. in 1. 8° 122.5
— - Same. And treatise on the conduct of the understanding. Philadelphia, 1853. 8° . . 122.6
LOCKHART, J. G. Adam Blair. Edinb., 1822. 16° 769.7
— Adam Blair and Matthew Wald. Edinburgh, 1843. 12° 769.9
— Ancient Spanish ballads. 4th ed. London, 1853. 16° 316.14
— - Same. Transl. with notes. New ed., with essay on the Cid. New York, 1842. 8° . . 316.1
— History of Matthew Wald. Edinb., 1824. 16° 769.8
— History of Napoleon Buonaparte. 3d ed. London, 1835. 2v. 16° 389.14
— - Same. New York, 1843. 2v. 18° 810.2–3
— Life of Robert Burns. Edinburgh, 1828. 18° 830.39
— Life of Sir W. Scott. Phila., 1839. 7v. 12° 585.2
— Reginald Dalton. New York, 1823. 2v. 12°. 798.12
— Valerius: a Roman story. New York, 1835. 2v. 12° 489.4
— Noctes ambrosianæ. See Wilson, J. 865.1
LOCKS. Denison, E. B. L. and clocks 197.7
— Manuel du serrurier 1075.38
— Tomlinson, C. Construction of 829.17
LOCOMOTION, Elementary treatise on. Sewell, J. 829.10
LOCOMOTIVE engines. Pambour, F. M. G. de . . 195.15
— Manner of constructing. Norris, S. 198.17
See also: Steam engine.
LOCKWOOD, H. H. See United States, Navy Dep.
LODGE, E. Portraits of illustrious personages of Great Britain. London, 1849–50. 8v. p.8°. 815.1
LOFTUS, W. K. Travels in Chaldæa and Susiana. London, 1857. 8° 694.1
LOFTY and the lowly. McIntosh, M. J. 437.14
LOG cabin and hard cider melodies. Boston, 1840. 18° 229.6
LOG college. Biographical sketches of the founder and principal alumni of. Alexander, A. . . 1089.8
LOG of a privateersman, a hundred years ago. Marryat, F. 745.1
LOGAN, J. Poems and tragedy of Runnamede, with life of author. New ed. Edinburgh, 1805. 12° 349.24
LOGARITHMS and mathemat. tables. Bowditch, N. 135.3
— - Same. Law, H. 829.26
LOGIC. Aristoteles. Organon: or, logical treat. 834.12

LOGIC. Coppée, H. Elements of 124.18
— Devey, J. L.: or, the science of inference . . 855.4
— Gerhart, E. V. Outline treatise on 403.8
— Hamilton, W. G. Parliamentary 125.22
— Latham, R. G. L. in its applic. to language. 403.6
— Law, H. Essay on 829.40
— Mahan, A. Science of 403.7
— Mill, J. S. System of 122.13
— Watts, I. L.: or, the right use of reason . . 139.4
— Whately, R. Elements of 129.16
See also: Evidence.
LOKMAN. Contes et fables indiennes de Bidpaï et de . . . . v.XVII. of 1077.1
LOMÉNIE, L. de. Beaumarchais and his times. Transl. by H. S. Edwards. N.Y., 1857. 12° 615.4
LONDINIANA: or, reminiscences of the British metropolis. Brayley, E. W. 989.7
LONDON Times, Essays from the 899.13–14
— - Same. 2d series 899.15
LONDON. Abbott, J. Rollo in 659.5–7
— Austin, W. Letters from, 1802–3 . . . . . . 647.2
— Cunningham, P. L. in 1853 . . . . 649.21
— Grant, J. Sketches of 646.13
— - Great metropolis 868.8
— Head, F. B. L. and the North Western railway 889.23
— Illustrated L. instructor 405.3
— Jameson, A. Handbook to galleries of art in. 208.9
— Knight, C. 961.2
— - Cyclopædia of 974.2
— M'Culloch, J. R. L. in 1850–51 . . . . . . 409.21
— Mayhew, H. L. labor and L. poor 974.1
— Miller, T. Picturesque sketches of 646.14
— Redding, C. The stranger in 987.11
— Ritchie, J. E. The London pulpit 128.7
— Smith, C. M. Curiosities of L. life 884.17
— Surr, T. S. A winter in 429.8
— Sutton, R. Court of L. at the end of 17th century 975.11
— Thomson, R. Chronicles of L. bridge. . . 379.7
— Vanderkiste, R. W. Mission among dens of. 127.25
LONG, G. Cyclopædia of political knowledge. London, 1853. 4v. p.8° 859.5
— Egyptian antiquities in the British museum. London, 1846. 2v. 12° 839.7
— France and its revolutions, 1789–1848. London, 1850. 4° 1001.1
— Geography of America and the West Indies. London, 1841. 8° 365.3
— and Porter, G. R. Geography of Gt. Britain. Pt. I. England and Wales. London, n.d. 8° 365.10
LONG, S. H. Expedition to St. Peter's river, Lake Winnepeck, etc., 1823. See Keating, W. H. 625.10
LONGCHAMPS, M. and Rengger, J. R. Francia's reign in Paraguay 266.3
LONGEVITY. Bell, J. Treatise on regimen and . 157.21
— Fitch, S. S. Laws of 158.7
— Smith, T. S. Promotion of 850.15
LONGFELLOW, H. W. Poems. New ed. Boston, 1854. 2v. 16° 333.1–9

Contents. — Vol. I. Voices of the night; Earlier poems; Translations; Ballads; Children of the Lord's supper; Miscellaneous; Poems on slavery; Spanish student. II. Belfry of Bruges; Songs; Sonnets; Translations; Evangeline; The seaside and the fireside.

— Courtship of Miles Standish and other poems. Boston, 1858. 16° 375.2–6
— Evangeline: a tale of Acadie. 10th ed. Boston, 1856. 16° 333–10
— Golden legend. Boston, 1855. 16° 333.11–13
— Hyperion: a romance. N. Y., 1839. 2v. in 1. 12° 438.5
— - Same. 4th ed. Boston, 1847. 16° 438.7
— - Same. 14th ed. Boston, 1854. 16° 438.6
— Kavanagh: a tale. Boston, 1849. 16° 438.8–11
— - Same. 7th ed. Boston, 1855. 16° 438.12
— Outre-mer: a pilgrimage. 5th ed. Boston, 1852. 16° 658.18–20
— Poets and poetry of Europe. With introduction and biograph. notices. N.Y., 1855. 8° 322.1

LONGFELLOW, H. W. Proverbes dramatiques.
Portland, 1830. 12° 1078.10
— Song of Hiawatha. Boston, 1855. 16°. . 343.1–5
— Voices of the night. Cambridge, 1839. 16° . 343.6
— Waif, The: a collection of poems. Cambridge, 1845. 16° 333.14
LONG ISLAND. Giraud, J. P. jr. Birds of. . . . 172.7
— Thompson, B. F. History of 234.11
LONGUEVILLE, A. G. de Bourbon, duchesse de. Youth of. Cousin, V. 617.12
LONGUS, Romances of. 844.10
LONG vacation ramble in Norway and Sweden, by X and Y. Cambridge, 1857. 12°. 668.8
LONSDALE, Lord Visc. See Lowther, J.
LOO-CHOO island, Voyage of discov'y to. Hall, B. 696.5
LOOK to the end, or the Bennets abroad. Ellis, S. S. 804.13
LOOM and the lugger. Martineau, H. . v.XVII. of 749.2 3
LOOMIS, E. Progress of astronomy, especially in the U. S. New York, 1851. 12° 146.13
— - Same. 3d ed. New York, 1856. 12° . . 146.22
LOOMIS, J. R. Elements of geology. Boston, 1852. 12° 163.20
LOPE de Vega and Calderon. Lewes, G. H. . . . 840.35
LORAIN, P. Origine et fondation des États Unis 1497–1620. Revu par Guizot. Paris, 1853. 12° 1078.13
LORD, D. N. Figurative language. New York, 1854. 12° 406.5
LORD, E. The epoch of creation, with introduction by R. W. Dickinson. N. Y., 1851. 12° 1106.16
LORD, J. Modern history from Luther to Napoleon. Philadelphia, n.d. 8° 947.4
LORD, W. W. André: a tragedy. New York, 1856. 12° 338.3
LORD and Lady Harcourt: a novel. Sinclair, C. . 456.1
LORD of the isles: a poem. Scott, Sir W. 359.17
LORDS, Random recollections of the house of. Grant, J. 868.9
LORENZO Benoni: a novel. Ruffini, G. 756.3–4
LORENZO de' Medici, Life of. Roscoe, W. 818.6
LORGNETTE, The, or studies of the town. Mitchell, D. G. 476.11
LORING, J. S. The hundred Boston orators, 1770–1852. Boston, 1852. 8° 282.5–6
LOS GRINGOS, or an inside view of Mexico and California, Wise, H. A. 627.24
LOSSING, B. J. Biographical sketches of the signers of the declaration of independence. New York, n.d. 12° 518.10
— Field-book of the revolution. New York, 1851–52. 2v. 8° 211.1–8
— History of the fine arts. New York, n.d. 18° 820.9
— Our countrymen, or memoirs of eminent Americans. Philadelphia, 1855. 12°. . . . 518.11
— Pictorial history of the United States. For schools and families. New York, 1857. 12° 309.8
— A history of the United States. For families and libraries. New York, 1857. 8° 304.1
— 1776, or the war of independence. New ed. New York, 1852. 8° 213.8–9
LOST daughter, The, and other tales. Hentz, C. L. 445.15
LOTHROP, Amy. Pseudon. See Warner, A. B.
LOTHROP, S. K. History of the church in Brattle street, Boston. Boston, 1851. 12° . . . 297.22
— Memoir of William Lawrence. Bost., 1855. 8° 524.3
— Life of Samuel Kirkland . . . . . . v.XXV. of 529.1
LOTUS eating: a summer book. Curtis, G. W. . 625.28
LOUDON, J. C. The suburban horticulturist. London, 1842. 8° 164.4
LOUDON, J. W. Gardening for ladies. Ed. by A. J. Downing. 2d American ed. New York, 1857. 12° 164.9–13
LOUIS II. de Bourbon, prince of Condé, Life of. Stanhope, P. H. 889.10
LOUIS XI., History of. Commines, P. de 857.4
LOUIS XIV. Astié, J. F. L. and the writers of his age 1008.10
— James, G. P. R. Life and times of 858.3
— Pardoe, J. L. and the court of France . . . 616.5–9

LOUIS XIV. Saint Simon, L. de R. L. and the regency 615.2
— - L. et sa cour 1078.18
— Voltaire, F. M. A. de. Siècle de 1076.19
LOUIS XV. Saint Simon, L. de R. Le régent et la cour de France, sous la minorité de . . 1078.51
— Voltaire, F. M. A. de. Abstract of the age of. 1005.7
LOUIS XVI. Edgeworth, C. S. Last hours of . . 615.8
LOUIS XVII. Beauchesne, A. de. The life, suffering, and death of 615.5–6
— Hanson, J. H. Identity of L. XVII. and Rev. E. Williams 615.7
LOUIS XVIII. Crowe, E. E. History of the reign of 1005.3
LOUIS Philippe. Boutmy, M. Personal history of. 616.10
— La Hodde, L. de. L. and the revol. of Feb. 1004.4
— Poore, B. P. Rise and fall of 1009.1
LOUISA von Plettenhaus: the journal of a poor young lady. Fr. the Ger. N. Y., 1857. 16°. 755.2–5
LOUISIANA. Bunner, E. History of 820.69
— Gayarré, C. Colonial history of 235.12
— - History of. Spanish domination 235.13
— Latour, A. L. War in W. Florida and 246.1
— Scalsfield, C. Les émigrés français dans la . 1078.24
— Stoddard, A. Sketches of 236.6
L'OUVERTURE, T., Life of. Beard, J. R. 539.2
LOUVRE, The: or, biography of a museum. St. John, B. 654.12
LOVAT, S., Lord, Life of. Burton, J. H. 566.6
LOVE after marriage, and other stories. Hentz, C. L. 446.1
LOVE and duty: a tale. Opie, A. 469.44
LOVE and intrigue. Schiller, F. von 818.12
LOVE match: a novel. Maberly, K. C. 769.2
LOVE, mystery, and superstition. Opie, A. v.III. of 801.4–6
LOVE's dream: a petite opera. London, 1821. 8°. 355.11
LOVE story: a fragment from "The doctor." Southey, R. 409.1
LOVER's pilgrimage, The. Silver, Mrs. 428.6
LOVER's vows: a play. Kotzebue, A. F. F. von. 353.7
LOVES of the poets. Jameson, A. 359.11
LOW, D. Domesticated animals of the British islands. London, 1853. 8° 165.7
LOWE, Sir H. Letters and journals of. See Forsyth, W. History of the captivity of Napoleon 605.5
LOWELL, A. C. Introduction to geometry. Boston, 1843. 12° 148.1
— Seed-grain for thought and discussion. Boston, 1856. 2v. 12° 124.22
— Theory of teaching. Boston, 1841. 12°. . 137.25
LOWELL, C. Sermons chiefly occasional. Boston, 1855. 12° 1086.2
— Sermons chiefly practical. Boston, 1855. 12°. 1086.3
LOWELL, J. jr. Life and character of. Everett, E. 1083.17
LOWELL, J. R. Biglow papers. 3d ed. Boston, 1853. 16° 896.13–14
— Conversations on some of the old poets. 2d ed. Cambridge, 1846. 16°. 344.17–18
— Fable for critics. New York, 1848. 12° . . 346.18
— Poems. 2d ed. Cambridge, 1844. 12°. . . . 346.17
— Vision of Sir Launfal. 4th ed. Bost., 1851. 16°. 346.17
LOWELL as it was and is. Miles, H. A. 227.20
LÖWIG, C. Organic and physiolog. chemistry. Transl. by D. Breed. Philad., 1853. 8° . . 156.4
LOWTHER, Jr Vis. Lonsdale. Reign of James II. 837.10
LOYALISTS. Curwen, S. Biographical notices of many American 213.4
— Sabine, L. Biography of the American . . . 213.1
LOYOLA and Jesuitism. Taylor, I. 1098.8
LUBERT, Mlle. de. Lionnette et Coquerico, Le prince glacé et la princesse étincelante, La princesse Camion . . . . . . v.XXXIII. of 1077.1
LUCANUS, M. A. Pharsalia. Translated by H. T. Riley. London, 1853. p.8° 834.5
LUCAS, S. History as a condition of social progress. London, 1853. 16° 139.9
LUCIAN, Comedies of. Transl. by W. Maginn . . 346.4
LUCILIUS, C. S. Satires, transl. by L. Evans . . 824.13
LUCK of Barry Lyndon. Thackeray, W. M. . . . 508.5–8

LUCRETIA: or the children of night. Lytton,
　　E. B. 465.31-34
LUCRETIUS Carus, T. Nature of things. Poem.
　　Translated into prose by J. S. Watson.
　　[Also the poetical version of J. M. Good.]
　　London, 1851. p.8° 824.9
LUCY Howard's journal. Sigourney, L. H. . . . 906.6
LUDLOW, F. The hasheesh eater. New York,
　　1857. 12° 884.10
LUDLOW, J. M. British India, its races and his-
　　tory. Cambridge, 1858. 2v. 16° 939.2
LUDUS Coventriæ. Halliwell, J. O. 342.3
LUDWIG, O. Zwischen Himmel und Erde, Erzäh-
　　lung. Frankfurt a M., 1856. 16° 1035.4
LUISA Strozzi. Storia del secolo XVI. Ro-
　　sini, G. 1057.10
LUKE, St. Gospel of. See Bible.
LUMISDEN, A. Memoirs of. Dennistoun, J. . . 556.6
LUND, T. Short and easy course of algebra. 2d
　　ed. Cambridge, 1851. 12° 149.27
LUNDIE, J. C. Memoir of Mary Lundie Duncan.
　　New York, n.d. 16° 119.7
LUNGS, Six lectures on uses of the. Fitch, S. S. 158.7
LUNT, G. Age of gold, and other poems. Boston,
　　1843. 12° 349.14
— Culture, a poem: Boston, 1843. 12° 338.13
— Three eras of New England. Boston, 1857. 12° 888.7
LUSSAN, M. de. Les veillees de Thessalie. Cabi-
　　net des fées . . . . . . v.XXVI.-XXVII. of 1077.1
LUTFULLAH, [a Mohammedan] Autobiography.
　　Ed. by E. B. Eastwick. London, 1857. 8° · 547.9
LUTHER, M. Autobiography. Transl. by J. P.
　　Lawson. Edinburgh, 1836. 12° 1099.24
— Mémoires, par lui-même: traduit par M.
　　Michelet. Bruxelles, 1840. 2v. 18° . . . 1079.3
— Memoirs, collected by M. Michelet, and trans.
　　by W. Hazlitt. London, 1846. 12° 515.23
— Table talk. Transl. by W. Hazlitt. London,
　　1848. 12° 877.15
— - Same. New ed., with life, by A. Chalmers.
　　London, 1857. p.8° 837.8
— Lee, H. F. Life and times of 545.25
— Sears, B. Life of 545.24
LUXEMBOURG, Histoire du duché de. Lagarde, M. 1075.20
LYCÉE, ou cours de littérature. Laharpe, J. F. . 1079.15
LYCIA. Fellows, Sir C. Travels and researches in. 687.6
— Spratt, T. A. B. Travels in 683.7
LYELL, C. Elements of geology. 1st American
　　ed. Philadelphia, 1839. 12° 163.16
— Manual of elementary geology. From 4th ed.
　　New York, 1853. 8° 163.1
— - Same. Reprinted from 5th ed. New York,
　　1855. 8° 163.2-3
— Principles of geology. New ed. New York,
　　1854. 8° 163.5-6
— - Same. 9th ed. Boston, 1853. 8° 163.7
— Second visit to the United States. New York,
　　1850. 2v. 12° 628.2
— Travels in North America in 1841-42, with
　　geolog. observations on the United States,
　　Canada and Nova Scotia. New York, 1852.
　　2v. in 1. 12° 628.1
LYLIE'S Endymion compared with Oberon's vis-
　　ion. Halpin, N. J. 342.15
LYMAN, S. P. Life and memoirs of D. Webster.
　　New York, 1853. 2v. 16° 525.23
LYMAN, T. A few weeks in Paris [in 1814.] 1st.
　　American ed. Boston, 1814. 12° 1009.16
LYMAN, T. jr. Diplomacy of the United States.
　　1778-1814. Boston, 1826. 8° 297.4
— Political state of Italy. Boston, 1820. 8° . . 9.5.3
LYNAM, R. History of the Roman emperors. Ed-
　　ited by J. T. White. London, 1850. 2v. 8° 956.1
LYNCH, A. C. Rhode Island book. Providence,
　　1841. 12° 888.9
LYNCH, W. F. Narrative of the United States ex-
　　pedition to the Jordan and Dead sea. 6th
　　ed. Philadelphia, 1849. 8° 684.5-6
LYND, J. First book of etymology. Revised ed.
　　Philadelphia, 1848. 12° 493.3

LYON, G. F. Attempt to reach Repulse Bay in 1824.
　　London, 1825. 8° 625.11-12
— Residence and tour in Mexico, 1826. London,
　　1828. 2v. 12° 628.4
LYTERIA: a dramatic poem. Quincy, J. P. . . . 345.13
LYTTELTON, Lord G. Conversion of St. Paul . . 119.9
LYTTON, Sir E. G. E. L. Bulwer. Novels. New
　　York, 1843-46. 3v. 8° 465.1
　　Contents. — Vol. I. Pelham; Disowned; Devereux;
　　Paul Clifford. II. Ernest Maltravers; Alice; Last of
　　the Barons; Lucretia. III. Eugene Aram; Last days
　　of Pompeii; Rienzi; Pilgrims of the Rhine.
— Alice: a novel. New York, 1838. 2v. 12° . . 465.17
— - Same. London, 1854. 12° 465.16
— Athens, its rise and fall. New York, 1852.
　　2v. 12° 957.7
— Caxtons, a family picture. N. Y., n.d. 8° . 465.28
— - Same. New ed. London, 1854. p.8° . . . 465.30
— - Same. London, 1855. 16° 465.29
— Devereux: a tale. N. Y., 1836. 2v. in 1. 12° 465.8
— - Same. London, 1852. p.8 . . . . 465.9
— - Same. London, 1855. 16° 465.10
— Disowned: a novel. New York, 1836. 2v. in 1.
　　12° 465.5
— - Same. London, 1852. p.8° 465.6
— - London, 1855. 16° 465.7
— England and the English. New York, 1833.
　　2v. 12° 898.13
— Ernest Maltravers: a novel. New York, 1837.
　　2v. 12° 465.15
— - Same. London, 1854. 12° 465.13
— - Same. With Alice. London, 1851. 2v.
　　p.8° 465.14
— Eugene Aram: a tale. N. Y., 1832. 2v. 12° . 465.22
— - Same. New York, 1836. 2v. in 1. 12° . . 465.19
— - Same. London, 1853. p.8° 465.20
— - Same. London, 1854. 12° 465.21
— Godolphin: a novel. Philadelphia, 1833. 2v.
　　12° 466.12
— - Same. London, 1854. 16° 466.13
— - Same. London, 1854. p.8° 466.14
— Harold, the last of the Saxon kings: a novel.
　　London, 1853. p.8° 466.5
— - Same. London, 1855. 16° 466.4
— King Arthur: a poem. Phila., 1851. 2v. 12° 346.11
— Lady of Lyons: a drama. N. Y., n.d. 16° . 356.14-15
— Last days of Pompeii: a novel. New York,
　　1834. 2v. in 1 . . . . 465.23
— - Same. London, 1854. p.8° 465.24
— - Same. London, 1854. 16° 465.25
— Last of the barons: a novel. London, 1853.
　　p.8° 465.18
— Leila: a tale. New York, 1838. 12° 466.8
— - Same. And Calderon, the courtier. Lon-
　　don. 1853. p.8 . . . . 466.7
— - Same. London, 1855. 16° 466.9
— Lucretia: a novel. New York, 1846. 8° . . 465.31-32
— - Same. London, 1853. p.8° 465.33
— - Same. London, 1855. 16° 465.34
— My novel. London, 1854. 2v. p.8° 466.16
— - Same. London, 1855. 2v. 16° 466.17
— - Same. New York, 1852. 8° 466.15
— New Timon: a romance. 3d American, from
　　4th Lond. ed. Phila., 1849. 12° 346.10
— Night and morning: a novel. New York,
　　1850. 8° 465.1
— - Same. London, 1854. p.8° 465.2
— - Same. London, 1854. 16° 465.3
— Paul Clifford. London, 1848. p.8° 465.12
— - Same. London, 1854. 16° 465.11
— Pelham. London, 1835. 2v. in 1. 12° . . . 465.2
— - Same. London, 1853. p.8° 465.3
— - Same, with notice of the author. Lond.,
　　1854. 16° 465.4
— Pilgrims of the Rhine: a novel. London,
　　1854. 16° 465.27
— - Same. London, 1854. p.8° 465.26
— Rienzi: a novel. London, 1854. 16° 466.6
— Zanoni: a novel. London, 1853. p.8° . . . 466.11
— - Same. London, 1853. 12° 466.10

LYTTON, Lady R. L. Bulwer. Bianca Cappello: a historical romance. N. Y., 1843. 12°. . . . 466.18

MABEL Vaughan: a tale. Cummins, M. S. . . . 447.1–10
MABERLY, K. C. Emily: a novel. London, 1840. 3v. 12° 769.1
— Love-match: a novel. Lond., 1841. 3v. 12°. 769.2
— Melanthe: a tale. London, 1843. 3v. 12°. . 769.3
MACARIO Spaccalancia. Cantù, I. 1046.11
McARTHUR, D., Biographical sketch of. McDonald, J. 518.8
MACAULAY, T. B. Biographical and historical sketches. New York, 1857. 12° 884.10
— Biographies of illustrious men. Bost., 1857. 12° 547.7
— Comic dramatists of the restoration. London, 1853. p.8°. 409.18
— Critical and miscellaneous essays. New ed. Philadelphia, 1851. 12° 863.1–4
— - Same. New ed. Phila., 1853. 5v. 12°. 867.4
— Gladstone on church and state. [From the Edinburgh review.] London, 1851. p.8° . 409.20
— History of England from the accession of James II. Boston, 1849–56. 4v. 12°. . . . 966.2
— - Same. New York, 1854–56. 4v. 12° . . . 966.3–4
— Horace Walpole, [an essay.] Lond., 1852. 8° 409.17
— Lays of ancient Rome ; with Ivry and the Armada. Boston, 1856. 12° 324.13
— Life and writings of Addison. Lond., 1852. p.8° 409.17
— Lord Bacon, [an essay.] London, 1852. p.8° 409.17
— Lord Byron, [an essay.] London, 1853. p.8° 409.18
— Lord Clive, [an essay.] London, 1853. p.8°. 409.19
— Ranke's history of the popes. [From the Edinburgh review.] London, 1851. p.8° . 409.20
— Speeches on parliamentary reform. London, 1854. p.8°. 409.18
— Warren Hastings, [an essay.] London, 1852. p.8° 409.19
— William Pitt, earl of Chatham ; [an essay.] London, 1851. p.8° 409.20
M'BURNEY, J. and Niel, S. Cyclopædia of universal history. London, 1855. p.8° 947.5
M'CALL, H. History of Georgia. [1584–1783.] Savannah, 1811–16. 2v. 8° 234.15
M'CARTNEY, W. Origin and progress of the United States. Philadelphia, 1847. 12° . . 309.3
McCLURE, A. W. Translators revived; mem. of the authors of the English version of the Holy Bible. New York, 1853. 12° 548.10
McCLURE, R. Le M., Discovery of the North-west passage by. Osborn, S. 704.4
M'CONECHY, J. and others. Ottoman empire. See Jacob, S. 956.11
M'CORMICK, R. C. jr. Visit to the camp before Sevastopol. New York, 1855. 12° 687.19
M'COSH, J. Divine government. 5th edition. Edinburgh, 1856. 8° 113.8
McCULLOCH, J. R. Bills of exchange 136.17
— Dictionary of commerce and commercial navigation. Ed. by H. Vethake. Philadelphia, 1851. 2v. 8° 135.9
— Essays on interest, exchange, coins, paper-money and banks. Philadelphia, 1851. 8°. 135.4
— London in 1850–51. London, 1851. p.8° . . 409.21
— Principles of political economy. 4th edition. Edinburgh, 1849. 8° 136.1
— Principles, practice, and history of commerce. Library of Useful Knowledge 365.15
— Russia and Turkey. London, 1854. 12° . . 409.28
— Universal gazetteer. N. Y., 1848–51. 2v. 8° 951.3
McDONALD, J. Biographical sketches of Massie, McArthur, Wells and Kenton. Dayton, O., 1852. 12° 518.8
McDOUGALL, G. F. Voyage of H. M. S. "Resolute," in search of Sir J. Franklin, 1852–54. London, 1857. 8° 703.10
McELLIGOTT, J. N. American debater. New York, 1855. 12° 134.20
McFARLAN, D. Revivals of the 18th century. With three sermons by Whitefield. Edinburgh, [n.d.] 12° 118.9

MACFARLANE, C. Camp of refuge. Historical novelette. London, n.d. [2v. in 1.] 18°. . 469.49
— - Same. London, 1844. 2v. 18° 840.40
— Dutch in the Medway. London, 1845. 18° . . 840.37
— Legend of Reading abbey. London, 1845. 18° 840.33
— Lives and exploits of banditti and robbers. London, 1837. 16° 379.16
— Popular customs, sports, etc., of the South of Italy. London, 1846. 18° 840.36
— Romance of history. Italy. 2d ed. London, 1832. 3v. 16° 419.6
— Romance of travel. The East. Lond., 1846–47. 2v. 18° 840.38–39
— Turkey and its destiny ; journeys in 1847–8. Philadelphia, 1850. 2v. 12° 687.2
— - Same. London, 1850. 2v. 8° 685.6
— and Craik, G. L. Pictorial hist. of England . 962.2
MACFARLANE, R. Hist. of propellers and steam-navigation ; with biographies. New York, 1851. 12° 198.19
M'FINGAL: a modern epic poem. Trumbull, J. . 314.9
McGEE, T. D. Irish settlers in North America. Boston, 1851. 12° 309.2
— Protestant reformation in Ireland, 1540 to 1850. Boston, 1853. 12° 1089.10
MACGILLIVRAY, W. British quadrupeds. Jardine's nat. lib. . . . . v.XVII. of 179.1
— Molluscous animals of Scotland. 2d edition. London, 1844. 12° 178.23
— A. von Humboldt in America and Asiatic Russia. New York, n.d. 18° 810.54
McHARG, C. K. Life of Talleyrand ; with speeches, etc. New York, 1857. 12° 617.10
MACHIAVELLI, N. History of Florence, and The Prince. New translation. Lond., 1851. p.8° 828.7
MACHINERY. Babbage, C. Economy of 198.30
— Fenwick, T. Simplification of. 195.21
— Glynn, J. Constructing of cranes 819.26
— Knight, C. Results of 139.24
— Tate, T. Construction of 199.18
— Weisbach, J. Mechanics of 195.2
MACHINES and tools, Lecture on. Willis, R. . . . 199.16
M'ILVAINE, C. P. Evidences of Christianity. 9th ed. New York, n.d. 12° 1107.1
MACILWAIN, G. Memoirs of J. Abernethy, with a view of his lectures, etc. N. Y., 1853. 12° 588.8
MACINTOSH, A. F. Military tour in European Turkey, Crimea, etc. Lond., 1854. 2v. 12°. 687.8
M'INTOSH, C. Book of the garden. Edinburgh, 1853–55. 2v. 8° 165.6
McINTOSH, M. J. Charms and countercharms. 5th ed. New York, 1849. 12° 437.18
— The lofty and the lowly. New York, 1853. 2v. 12° 437.14
— Two lives, or to seem and to be. 2d ed. New York, 1847. 12° 437.16–17
— - Same. New York, 1853. 12° 437.15
— Violet, or the cross and the crown. Boston, 1856. 12° 437.11–13
— Woman in America. New York, 1850. 12°. . 888.23
MACKARNESS, M. [Formerly Miss Planché.] Sibert's wold: a tale. Boston, 1856. 12°. . .476.9–10
— Sunbeam stories. Boston, 1856. 12° 476.7–8

   Contents. — Trap to catch a sunbeam: "Only." a tale; A merry Christmas; Dream chintz; Old Jolliffe; Sequel to old Jolliffe; Cloud with the silver lining; Star in the desert.

MACKAY, A. The Western world, or travels in the U. S. in 1846–47. From 2d London ed. Philadelphia, 1849. 2v. 12°. 628.5
MACKAY, C. Memoirs of extraordinary popular delusions, and the madness of crowds. 2d ed. London, 1852. 2v. 12° 879.8–9
MACKAY, Mrs. The family at Heatherdale. New York, 1855. 18° 490.7
M'KENNEY, T. L. Memoirs, with travels among the Indians. 2d ed. N. Y., 1846. 2v. in 1. 8° 625.3
— Tour to the lakes, Chippeway Indians, etc. Baltimore, 1827. 8° 625.4

MACKENZIE, A. Voyages from Montreal to the Frozen and Pacific oceans, 1789 and 1793, with an account of the fur trade. 1st. Am. ed. New York, 1802. 8°. 625.19

MACKENZIE, A. S. American in England. New York, 1835. 2v. 12°. 658.15

— Life of S. Decatur. Sparks's Am. biog.v.XXI. of 529.1

— Life of Paul Jones. New York, 1848. 2v. 16°   528.6

— Life of O. H. Perry. New York, n.d. 2v. 18°   820.31

— Year in Spain. 3d edition. New York, 1836. 3v. 12°. 679.2

MACKENZIE, C. Five thousand receipts in all the arts. 4th Am. ed. Philadelphia, 1829. 8°.   187.3

— — Same. New Am. ed. Phila., 1858. 8°. .   187.4–9

MACKENZIE, Mrs. C. Life in the missiou, the camp and the Zenáná, or six years in India. New York, 1853. 2v. 12°. 707.11

MACKENZIE, D. L. Dictionary of English synonyms. London, 1854. 16°. 406.20

MACKENZIE, H. Miscellaneous works. 3d ed. New York, 1853. 12°. 798.14

Contents.— Memoir, by Sir W. Scott; Man of feeling; Papers from the Lounger; Man of the world; Julia de Roubigné; Papers from the Mirror.

— Man of feeling. New ed. London, 1800. 16°   798.15

— — Same. With Julia de Roubigné .v.XXIX. of 779.1

— The Mirror. 8th ed. London, 1790. 3v. 16°   878.21

MACKENZIE, J. Memoirs of J. Calvin. 2d ed. London, 1818. 12°. 1108.9

MACKIE, J. M. Life of Tai-Ping-Wang, chief of the Chinese insurrection. N. Y., 1857. 12°   547.8

— Life of S. Gorton. Sparks's Am. biog.v.XV. of 529.1

MACKINNON, Capt. Atlantic and transatlantic sketches, afloat and ashore. London, 1852. 2v. 12°. 628.9

MACKINTOSH, Sir J. Lives of eminent British statesmen. London, 1831–39. 7v. 16°. . .   388.6

— Miscellaneous works. Phila., 1850. 8°. . . .863.8 & 17

— Life. Ed. by R. J. Mackiutosh. From 2d London ed. Boston, 1853. 2v. 8°. 582.9

— Memorials of. McLeod, N. 588.3

— Wallace, W. and Bell, R. History of England. London, 1830–1840. 10v. 16°. . . .   368.3

MACKNIGHT, T. B. D'Israeli. A literary and political biography. London, 1854. 8°. . .   582.14

— Life and times of Edmund Burke. London, 1858. 2v. 8°. 572.4

MACLAREN, J. Sketch of the history of the currency. London, 1858. 8°. 136.10

M'LEAN, J. Twenty-five years in the Hudson's Bay territory. London, 1849. 2v. 12°. . .   704.19

M'LEHOSE, A. C. (*Clarinda.*) Correspondence with Burns, and memoir 586.14

M'LEOD, D. Life of Mary, Queen of Scots. New York, 1857. 12°. 594.10

M'LEOD, J. Voyage to the Yellow sea. Philadelphia, 1818. 8°. 696.11

McLEOD, N. Earnest student. Memoirs of J. Mackiutosh. 5th ed. Edinb., 1855. p.8°. .   588.3

— Home school. 3d ed. Edinburgh, 1856. 16°   129.19

M'MAHON, B. American gardener's calendar, with memoir by J. J. Smith. 11th ed. Philadelphia, 1857. 8°. 165.3

M'NALLY, W. Evils and abuses in the naval and merchant service. Boston, 1839. 12°. . .   135.20

MACNEILL, H. Poetical works. New ed. Philadelphia, 1815. 12° 348.12

Contents.— The pastoral; The harp; The links o' Forth; Scotland's scaith; Waes o' war; Songs, etc.

M'NEMAR, R. Kentucky revival. Cinc., 1808. 16° 1089.20

MACNISH, R. Philosophy of sleep. 1st Am. ed. New York, 1834. 12°. 157.28

MACOMB, A. Memoir of. Richards, G. H. . . .   528.20

M'QUEEN, J. Orator's touchstone. New York, 1854. 12°. 405.8

MACQUEEN, J. The war. Who's to blame? or, the Eastern question investigated. London, 1854. 8°. 986.7

M'VICKAR, J. Memoir of E. D. Griffin 534.10

MACY, O. History of Nantucket. Bost., 1835. 12°   227.8

MADAGASCAR, History of. Ellis, W. 934.5

MADDEN, R. R. Infirmities of genius. Philadelphia, 1833. 12°. 887.7

— Life and times of Robert Emmet. Also mem. of T. A. Emmet. New York, 1857. 12°. . .   598.15

— Literary life and corresp. of the Countess of Blessington. New York, 1855. 2v. 12°   595.8–9

— Travels in Turkey, Egypt, Nubia and Palestine, in 1824–27. 2d ed. Lond., 1833. 2v. 12°   687.9

— Twelve months' residence in the West Indies, [1833–34.] London, 1835. 2v. 12°. 635.21

— United Irishmen, their lives and times. 1st– 3d ser. London, 1842–46. 7v. 12°. 598.1–3

MADEIRA. Dix, J. A. A winter in 675.8

— March, C. W. Sketches and adventures in .   675.12

— White, R. Climate and scenery of 264.6

MADELINE: a tale. Opic, A. . . . . .v.I.of 801.4–6

MADISON, J. Papers: being his correspondence, and reports of debates during the congress of the confederation, and in the federal convention: published under the superintendence of H. D. Gilpin. Wash., 1840. 3v. 8°   285.3

— Hamilton, A. and Jay, J. The Federalist . .   285.4

MADONNA d'Imbevera. Racconto. Cantù, C. . .   1040.13

MADRAS. Heber, R. Journey to 889.24

— Maitland, J. C. Letters from, 1836–39 . . .   889.28

MADRE, Una. Racconto. Thouar, P. 1058.3

MADRID, Attaché in. Calderon de la Barca, F. E. I. 675.10–11

MAESTRAZZI, E. Giovanua d'Angio. Race. stor. Milano, 1852. 12°. 1056.13

MAFFITT, J. N. Pulpit sketches, sermons, and devotional fragments. Boston, 1828. 12°. . .   1099.1

MAGDALEN church'd, The. Regnault Warin, J. J.   429.1

MAGDALEN Hepburn : a story. Oliphant, M. . .   753.11

MAGIC. Apuleius Madaurensis, L. Discourse on.   834.15

— Brewster, D. Letters on natural 379.10

— Ennemoser, J. History of . . . . . . .v.II. of 826.12

See also: Occult sciences, Supernaturalism, etc.

MAGICIAN'S own book. New York, 1857. 12° . .   197.23

MAGINN, W. Fraserian papers. Life of the author, by R. S. Mackenzie. N. Y., 1857. 12°   884.12

— Homeric ballads and comedies of Lucian. Annot. by R. S. Mackenzie. N. Y., 1856. 12°   346.4

— Odoherty papers. Annot. by R. S. Mackenzie, New York, 1855. 2v. 12°. 867.7

— Noctes Ambrosianæ. See Wilson, J. 865.1

MAGOUN, E. L. Living orators in America. New York, 1850. 12°. 518.16

— Orators of the American revolution. 4th ed. New York, 1850. 12°. 528.1

— Westward empire. New York, 1856. 12°. .   948.2

MAGNETISM. Bersot, E. Sur le M. animal . . .   1078.41

— Davis, D. jr. Manual of 149.2

— Harris, Sir W. S. Rudimentary 819.8

— Lardner, D. Manual of 398.14

— Roget, P. M. Lib. Us. Kn. 365.14

— Scoresby, W. Compass in iron ships 195.7

See also: Animal magnetism, Electricity.

MAGUIRE, J. F. Rome, its ruler and institutions. London, 1857. 8°. 919.1

MAGYAR, City of the. Pardoe, J. 928.1

MAGYARS, Poetry of the. Bowring, J. 316.2

MAHAN, A. Modern mysteries. Boston, 1855. 12°   125.2

— Science of logic. New York, 1857. 8°. . . .   403.7

MAHAN, D. H. Industrial drawing. N. Y., 1852. 8°   203.6

MAHOMET. See Mohammed.

MAHON, Lord. See Stanhope, P. H.

MÄHRCHEN. Andersen, H. C. 1035.11

— Brentano, C. 1013.8

MAID, The, of Orleans: a romantic chronicle. New York, 1850. 8°. 802.10

MAID of Orleans : an hist. drama. Schiller, J. C. F. v. 818.11

MAIDEN and married life of Mary Powell. New York, 1852. 16°. 469.3–5

MAILLARD, N. D. History of Texas. Lond., 1842. 8°   236.5

MAILLY, E. Principes de la science du calcul. Arith. et alg. Bruxelles, n.d. 12°. . . .   1065.37

MAIN, R. Rudiment. astronomy. Lond., 1852. 16°   829.27

MAINE. Springer, J. S. Forest life in 628.18

— Williamson, W. D. History of, 1602 to 1820   234.1

MAINTENON, Mme. de. Roman historique. Genlis, Ctsse. de 1066.16
— - Same. 4e éd. 2v. 1068.4
— Héquet, G. Histoire de 1078.52
MAISTRE de la Tour. Hist. of Hyder Ali Khan. Dublin, 1774. 2v. in 1. 12° 547.17
MAISTRE, Comte X. de. Œuvres complètes. Nouv. éd. Paris, 1854. 12° 1067.9
    Contents. — Voyage autour de ma chambre; Expédition nocturne; Le lépreux de la cité d'Aoste; Les prisonniers du Caucase; La jeune Sibérienne.
MAITLAND, F. L. Surrender of Bonaparte. Boston, 1826. 12° 1009.8
MAITLAND, J. F. Letters from Madras during 1836–39. Loudon, 1846. 12° 889.28
MAÎTRE d'armes, Memoir of a. Dumas, A. . . . 409.5
MAIZE in milk: a Christmas story. Simms, W. G. 790.53-55
MAJOR Jones's scenes in Georgia. Thompson, W. T. 726.14
MA-KA-TAI-ME-SHE-KIA-KIAK: or, Black Hawk. Life, dictated by himself. Boston, 1834. 12° 539.6
MALACOLOGY: a treatise on. Swainson, Wm. . . 408.2
    See also: Conchology, and Mollusca.
MALAYAN waters, Journal in. Osborn, S. 708.13
MALCOLM, Sir J. Sketches of Persia. London, 1845. 12° 889.33
— Life and correspondence of. Kaye, J. W. . . 565.1
MALCOLM, J., Esq. Campaign in the Pyrenees and South of France 830.42
MALCOM, H. Travels in South Eastern Asia. 5th ed. Boston, 1840. 2v. 12° 709.3-4
— - Same. 8th ed. Cincinnati, 1849. 12° . . 709.5
MALDEN bi-centennial book. 227.18
MALEPEYRE, F. Arts of tanning, currying, etc. See Fontenelle, J. de 194.11
MALIBRAN, Mme., Memoirs of. Merlin, Countess de 615.10
MALKIN, B. H. Astronomy. Lib. Us. Kn. v.III. of 365.14
MALKIN, F. History of Greece. London, 1829. 8° 365.6-7
MALKIN, J. H. Historical parallels. Bost., 1831. 12° 849.12
— - Same. London, 1846. 2v. 12° 839.12
— - Same. London, 1846. 3v. 18° 840.41
MALLET, P. H. Northern antiquities. Translated by T. Percy, and edited by I. A. Blackwell. New ed. London, 1847. p.8° 846.2
MALLET-DU-PAN, J. Memoir and correspondence, collected by A. Sayous. Lond., 1852. 2v. 8° 613.6
MALLEVILLE. A Franconia story. Abbott, J. v.I. of 738.4
MALTA. Bigelow, A. Travels in 676.2
— Brydone, J. Tour through 679.11
— Taaffe, J. History of the knights of 915.1
— Wilson, S. S. Sixteen years in 683.2
— Zauli Sajani, I. Ultimi giorni dei cavalieri di. 1059.1
MALVINA: See Cottin, M. J. R. 1069.12
MAMMALIA. History of the 850.12
— Introductions to . . . . v.XV.–XXVII. of 179.1
— Menageries. 839.17
— Waterhouse, G. R. Natural history of . . . 172.6
— White, A. Popular history of 177.33
MAMMON: or, covetousness. Harris, J. 1109.13
MAN. Atkinson, H. G. Laws of the nature and development of 137.18
— Combe, G. Constitution of 124.9
— Kidd, J. Adaptation of nature to condition of. 826.3
— Latham, R. G. M. and his migrations. . . . 176.6
— Moore, G. M. and his motives 125.20
— Mudie, R. M. in his physical structure and adaptations 176.7
— Omalius d' Halloy, J. J. d'. Des races humaines 1065.43
— Prichard, J. C. Natural history of 173.3
— Wilkinson, J. J. G. Human body in connection with 157.6
    See also: Ethnography, Human race, Races, etc.
MAN as he is. [By R. Bage.] Lond., 1792. 4v. 12° . 799.3
— - Same. 2d ed. London, 1796. 4v. 16° . . 799.2
MAN of feeling: a novel. Mackenzie, H. 798.15
MAN of sorrows. Jackson, W. 534.15
MANCHESTER strike: a tale. Martineau, H. v.VII.of 749.2-3

MANDEVILLE, Sir J. Narrative of. Wright, T. . . 846.7
MANFREDO Palavicino. Stor. ital. Rovani, G. . . 1057.6
MANGANESE, New methods of determining the value of. Fresenius, C. R. 156.21
MANGIN, V. Camille: a novel 801.2
MANGLES, J. and Irby, C. L. Travels in Egypt, Nubia, Syria, and the Holy Land 889.25
MANHATTANER in New Orleans. Hall, A. O. . . 629.15
MANILLA, Rambles in. Ball, B. L. 708.6-7
MANLY exercises. Walker, D. 197.24
MANN, H. Lectures on education. Bost., 1850. 12° 137.8
— Slavery: letters and speeches. Bost., 1853. 12° 866.6
— Thoughts for a young man. Boston, 1850. 16° 139.20
MANN, H., Mrs. Christianity in the kitchen. Boston, 1857. 8° 188.24
MANN, J. American bird-keeper's manual. Boston, 1848. 16° 177.24
MANN, W. Poems, sacred, philanthropic and rural. Plymouth, 1846. 16° 349.4
MANNERS and minor morals.
— Abbott, J. S. C. Child at home 1109.14
— - Mother at home 119.12
— Alcott, W. A. Moral philosophy of courtship and marriage 127.5
— - Young woman's guide 139.16
— American gentleman's guide to politeness . . 127.33
— Barbauld, A. L. Legacy for young ladies . . 137.31
— Chandler, M. G. Elements of character . . . 118.11
— Chesterfield's letters to his son 873.9
— Child, L. M. The mother's book 137.28
— Droz, J. Art of being happy 139.5
— Eliot, W. G. Lectures to young men 127.26
— - Lectures to young women 127.27
— Etiquette for gentlemen 129.35
— Hale, Sir M. Advice to his grandchildren . . 139.6
— James, J. A. Young man from home 119.28
— Jewsbury, M. J. Letters to the young . . . 137.29
— Lambert, A. T. Mother's advice 139.21
— Leslie, E. The behaviour book; for ladies . 127.12-17
— Letters to my unknown friends 127.32
— McLeod, N. The home school 129.19
— Mann, H. Thoughts for a young man . . . 139.20
— Mother's friend 139.18
— Muzzey, A. B. The young maiden 127.29
— Sedgwick, C. M. Means and ends 129.22
— Sigourney, L. H. Letters to young ladies . . 127.18
— - Letters to mothers 139.2
— Sprague, W. B. Letters to a daughter 1109.12
— Thornwell, E. Lady's guide to gentility . . 127.11
— Tuthill, L. C. Young lady's home 137.24
— Waterbury, J. B. Considerations for young men 1109.17
— Whitman, J. Young ladies' aid 129.21
MANNERS and customs of the Japanese, in the 19th century. London, 1841. 12° 708.2
— - Same. New York, 1848. 18° 820.36
MANNERS of the day: a novel. Gore, C. G. . . . 776.9
MANSFIELD, C. B. Paraguay, Brazil, and the Plate, in 1852-3. Life by C. Kingsley. Cambridge, 1856. 12° 635.10
MANSFIELD, E. D. American education. New York, 1851. 8° 137.3
— Life of Gen. W. Scott. New York, 1846. 12°. 517.14
— The Mexican war: its origin and victories. New York, 1848. 12° 259.1
— - Same. 10th edition. New York, 1852. 12° 259.2
MANSFIELD park: a novel. Austen, J. 758.5
MANTELL, G. A. Geological excursions round the Isle of Wight. 3d ed. London, 1854. p.8°. 826.10
— Petrifactions and their teachings. London, 1851. p.8° 816.11
— Wonders of geology. 6th edition. London, 1848. 2v. p.8° 836.4
— - Same. 7th edition; revised by T. R. Jones. London, 1857. p.8° 836.5
MANUAL of scientific enquiry 149.3-4
MANUAL of the arts for young people. Boston, 1857. 12° 197.19
MANUAL of the practical naturalist. Bost., 1831. 12° 849.17
MANUEL du serrurier. Bruxelles, 1853. 12° . . . 1075.38

MANUFACTURES. Aikin, A. Illustrations of arts and 199.17
— Alcan, M. Manuel du tisserand 1075.33
— Baird, R. H. American cotton spinner. . . . 199.5
— Banfield, T. C. M. of the Rhine. . . . . v.II.of 840.1
— Birch, S. History of ancient pottery. . . . 196.1
— Dodd, G. M. of Great Britain 840.20
— History of silk, cotton, linen, wool and other fibrous substances 195.4
— Holland, J. M. in metal 408.10
— Iron manufactures. Library of Useful Knowl. 199.34
— Kindt, J. De l'industrie du coton, de la laine, et de la soie 1065.28
— – Industrie linière 1065.26
— Mason, G. C. Application of art to 197.1
— Materials of. Vegetable substances 849.9
— Novelties, inventions, etc. 199.26–30
— Overman, F. M. of iron 195.6
— - M. of steel 199.12
— Pellatt, A. Curiosities of glass-making . . . 196.11
— Prideaux, T. S. Economy of fuel in 829.9
— Scott, R. Practical cotton spinner. 195.5
— Truran, W. Iron M. of Great Britain . . . 191.5
— Ure, A. Dictionary of 146.2
MANZONI, A. Tragedie e poesie scelte. Brusselle, 1837. 2v. 12° 1058.8

> Contents. — Vol. 1. L'unite de temps et de lieu dans la tragédie; Notizie storiche sul conte di Carmagnola; Il conte di Carmagnola' tragedia; Il nome di Maria, poema; Il cinque Maggio, poema. II. Notizie storiche sull' Adelchi; Adelchi, tragedia; Discorso sopra alcuni punti della storia longobardica in Italia; Inni.

— I promessi sposi. Storia della colonna infame. 6a ed. Milano, 1856. 2v. 12° 1058.6
— I promessi sposi. The betrothed. New translation. New York, 1845. 2v. 12° 488.2
MANZONI, G. Favole e regole per bene scrivere. Con cinque novelle del P. A. Cesari. Biog. del P. A. Bresciani. Parma, 1842. 16° . . 1058.7
MARBLE, D. A biographical sketch. Kelly, J. F. 519.6
MARBLE worker's manual. From the French. Transl. by M. L. Booth. N. Y., 1856. 12°. 199.10
MARBLES in the British museum 209.15
MARCET, J. Conversations on chemistry. 15th ed. London, 1846. 2v. 16° 155.26
— Conversations on natural philosophy. 10th edition. London, 1843. 12° 149.1
— Lessons on animals, vegetables and minerals. London, 1844. 18° 178.36
— Popular introductions to natural philosophy. Library of Useful Knowledge . . . . v.11. of 365.14
— Scenes in nature; or, conversations on land and water. Boston, 1840. 16° 169.23
MARCET, W. Composition of food, and how it is adulterated. London, 1856. 8° 155.15
MARCH, C. W. Reminiscences of Congress. 3d edition. New York, 1851. 12° 526.22
— Sketches and adventures in Madeira, Portugal and Spain. New York, 1856. 12° 675.12
MÄRCHEN. See Mährchen.
MARCO Paul's voyages and travels. Springfield armory. Abbott, J. 738.5–7
MARCO Polo. See Polo, M.
MARCO Visconti. Storia del trecento. Grossi, T. 1056.14
MARETZEK, M. Crotchets and quavers. New York, 1855. 12° 428.10
MARGARET: a tale of the real and the ideal. Judd, S. 488.7
MARGARET Graham. James, G. P. R. 463.7
MARGARET Lyndsay, Trials of. Wilson, J. . . . 759.7
MARGARET Maitland, Some passages in the life of. Oliphant, M. 753.12
MARGARET: or, prejudice at home. New York, 1854. 12° 449.17
MARGARET Percival, a novel. Sewell, E. M. . . 425.17
MARGARET Percival in America. Hale, E. E. and L. P. 425.16
MARGARET Smith's journal, 1678–9. Whittier, J. G. 777.8
MARGGRAFF, H. Ernst Schulze geschildert. Leipzig, 1855. 16° . . . . v.V. of 1037.10
— Fritz Beutel. Eine Münchhauseniade. Frankfurt a M. 1856. 8° 1013.10

MARGHERITA Pusterla. Racconto. Cantù, C. . . 1046.13
MARGINALIA, Essays and. Coleridge, H. 875.14
MARGUERITE d'Angoulême, queen of Navarre, Life of. Freer, M. W. 544.12
MARIA Stuart, ein Trauerspiel. Schiller, J. C. F. v. 1038-5
MARIAN, or a young maid's fortunes: a novel. Hall, A. M. 776.13
MARIE Antoinette. Abbott, J. S. C. Hist. of . 569.13–16
— Campan, J. L. H. G. Court of 645.3
— Weber, J. Memoirs of 613.1
MARIE de Bernière: a tale. Simms, W. G. . . . 790.53–55
MARIE de Medicis, queen of France, Life of. Pardoe, J. 543.1
MARIE Stuart. See Mary, Queen of Scots.
MARILLAC, M. de. Assassinat du Maréchal D'Ancre. Paris, 1853. 12° 1078.33
MARINE engines. Rudimentary treatise on. Murray, R. 829.12
MARINER, W. Account of the natives of the Tonga islands. Compiled by J. Martin. 3d ed. Edinburgh, 1827. 2v. 18° 830.33
MARINO Faliero: Drame hist. Delavigne, C. . . 1078.3
MARION, F., Life of. Simms, W. G. . . . 528.14–15
MARIOTTI, L. Italy, its history and literature. London, 1841. 2v. 12° 917.1
— Memoir of Fra Dolcino and his times. London, 1853. 8° 544.16
MARITIME adventure. History of. Goodrich, F. B. 701.10
MARITIME discovery. Cabot, S. Review of the history of 564.10
— Cooley, W. D. History of 378.11
MARITIME ports of Ireland, Hist. of. Marmion, A. 975.4
MARK, St., Gospel of. See Bible.
MARKHAM, C. R. Cuzco and Lima. Lon., 1856. 8° 633.20
MARKHAM, Mrs. Pseud. See Penrose, E.
MARLBOROUGH, Duchess of. Memoirs. See Thomson, A. T. 594.1
MARLBOROUGH, Duke of. See Churchill, J.
MARLES, J. Lacroix. See Lacroix-Marles, J.
MARLOWE, C. Works, with notes and life by A. Dyce. London, 1850. 3v. 8° 356.5

> Contents. — Vol. 1. Acct. of M. and his writings; Tamburlaine, parts 1, 2, tragedy; The Jew of Malta, tragedy. II. Faustus; Same, with a later text; Ballad of Faustus; Edward the second, trag.; Massacre at Paris, trag.; Dido, tragedy. III. Hero and Leander; Ovid's elegies; Epigrams; First book of Lucan; Minor poems.

MARMION, A. History of the maritime ports of Ireland. London, 1855. 8° 975.4
MARMONT, A. F. L. V. de. Present state of the Turkish empire. Transl. by F. Smith. 2d ed. London, 1854. 12° 918.8
MARMONTEL, J. F. Memoirs, written by himself. Transl. Edinburgh, 1808. 4v. 12° 609.8
MARONCELLI, P. Appendix to memoirs of Andryane, A. . . . . v.II. of 544.10
MAROON, The: a legend of the Caribbees. Simms, W. G. 790.53–55
MAROONS, Crimes by our government against the. Giddings, J. R. 237.19
MARQUESAS islands, Four months in. Melville, H. 899.2
MARQUETTE, J., Life of. Sparks's Am. biog. v.X. of 529.1
MARRIAGE, Moral philosophy of. Alcott, W. A. 127.5
MARRIAGE of wit and wisdom: an ancient interlude. Halliwell, J. O. 342.30
MARRIED life. Follen, E. L. Sketches of . . . 429.5
— Parkes, Mrs. W. Relations and duties of . . 189.1
MARRIED or single: a novel. Sedgwick, C. M. . 436.1–5
MARRYAT, F. Children of the New Forest. New York, 1848. 12° 745.6
— Frank Mildmay, or the naval officer. New York, 1857. 12° 745.11
— Jacob Faithful: or the adventures of a waterman. New York, 1857. 12° 745.13
— Japhet in search of a father. N. Y., 1857. 12° 745.10
— King's own. New York, 1857. 12° 745.14
— Log of a privateersman one hundred years ago. New York, 1847. 8° 745.1
— Masterman Ready. New ed. Lon., 1857. p.8° 835.9

MARRYAT, F. Mr. Midshipman Easy. N. York, 1857. 12° 745.5
— - Same. Rev. ed. Boston, 1836. 2v. 12° . 745.4
— Newton Forster : or, the merchant service. New York, 1857. 12° 745.9
— Pacha of many tales. New York, 1857. 12° . 745.2
— Percival Keene. New York, 1857. 12° . . . 745.15
— Peter Simple. New York, 1857. 12° 745.7
— Phantom ship. New York, 1857. 12° 745.12
— Poacher. New York, 1857. 12° 745.3
— Second series of a diary in America. Philadelphia, 1840. 12° 628.7
— Snarleyyow, or the dog fiend. New York, 1857. 12° 745.8
MARRYING too late. A tale. Wood, G. 498.5
MARSDEN, J. B. History of the later Puritans, 1642-1662. 2d ed. London, 1854. 8° 1085.17
MARSH, A. Angela a novel. Lond., 1848. 3v. 12° 795.9
— Country vicarage. [Also : Tale of an oak tree : poem.] London, 1852. 16° 469.9
— Emilia Wyndham. New York, n.d. 8° . . . 795.6
— - Same. London, 1848. 16° 795.7
— Lettice Arnold. A tale. London, 1850. 2v. 12° 795.8
— Mordaunt hall. A novel. N. Y., n.d. 8° . . 795.10
— - Same. London, 1849. 3v. 12° 795.11
— Professional visits of le docteur noir. [Also : Sealed orders and Limoelan.] London, 1852. 16° 469.10
— Protestant reformation in France. Philadelphia, 1851. 2v. 12° 1008.2
— Time the avenger. London, 1851. 3v. 12° . . 795.5
— - Same. New York, 1851. 8° 795.4
— Triumphs of time. N. Y., 1844. 8° 795.1
— Wilmingtons. A novel. London, 1850. 3v. 12° 795.3
— - Same. New York, 1850. 8° 795.2
MARSH, G. P. The camel. His organization, habits and uses. Boston, 1856. 16° 177.17
MARSH, J. Remains, [ed. by J. Torrey,] with a memoir. Boston, 1843. 8° 534.4
MARSHALL, C. Diary kept during the American revolution. v.1. Phila., 1839-49. 12° . . . 217.13
MARSHALL, J. Life of George Washington. 2d ed. Phila., 1840. 2v. 8° 515.2
— Writings upon the federal constitution. Boston, 1839. 8° 134.4
MARSHALL, T. W. Episcopal polity of the church. Edited by J. M. Wainwright. New York, 1844. 12° 118.6
MARSHFIELD, Mass., Memorials of. Thomas, M. A. 227.10
MARSHPEE Indians, Nullification of laws relative to. Apes, W. 249.3
MARTEL, C. Principles of colouring in painting. London, 1855. 16° 208.8
MARTIN, F. X. History of North Carolina. New Orleans, 1829. 2v. 8° 236.7
MARTIN, T., Macaulay, T. B. and others. Biographies of illustrious men 547.7
MARTIN, W. C. L. General history of humming-birds. London, 1852. 16° 179.2
— History of the dog. London, 1845. 18° . . . 840.43
— History of the horse. London, 1845. 18° . . 840.44
MARTIN Chuzzlewit. Dickens, C. 471.7-10
MARTIN Toutrond : or, a Frenchman in London. Morier, J. 469.17
MARTINEAU, H. Billow and rock : a tale. London, 1846. 18° 840.42
— British rule in India. London, 1857. 16° . . 989.5
— Deerbrook : a novel. London, 1839. 3v. 12° . 749.1
— Eastern life, present and past. Phila., 1848. 8° 686.1
— - Same. London, 1850. 8° 686.2-4
— Essential faith of the universal church. Boston, 1833. 18° 1099.28
— Five years of youth. 1st American ed. Boston, 1832. 18° 749.5
— Household education. Phila., 1849. 18° . . . 137.19
— Illustrations of political economy. Boston, 1832-35. 19v. 12° 749.2-3

MARTINEAU, H., continued.
Contents. — Vol. I. Life in the wilds. II. The hill and the valley. III. Brooke and Brooke Farm. IV. Demerara. V. Ella of Garveloch. VI. Weal and woe in Garveloch. VII. A Manchester strike. VIII. Cousin Marshall. IX. Ireland. X. Homes abroad. XI. For each and for all. XII. French wines and politics. XIII. The charmed sea. XIV. Berkeley the banker, part 1. XV. Berkeley the banker, part 2. XVI. Messrs. Vanderput and Snoek. XVII. The loom and the lugger, part 1. XVIII. The loom and the lugger, part 2. XIX. Sowers not reapers.
— Letters on man's nature, to H. G. Atkinson . 137.18
— Life in the sick-room. Introduction to American ed. by E. L. Follen. Boston, 1844. 12° 878.2
— - Same. 2d American ed. Boston, 1845. 16° 1100.7
— Miscellanies. Boston, 1836. 2v. 12° 868.2
— Poor laws and paupers illustrated. The parish : a tale. Boston, 1833. 18° 749.4
— Retrospect of western travel. London, 1838. 3v. 12° 626.10
— Society in America. New York, 1837. 2v. 12° 628.17
— The faith as unfolded by many prophets. Boston, 1833. 18° 1099.20
MARTINEAU, J. Miscellanies. Boston, 1852. 12° 1086.17
Contents. — The life, character and works of Dr. Priestley ; The life and correspondence of T. Arnold, D. D. ; Church and state ; Theodore Parker's discourse of religion ; Phases of faith ; The church of England ; The battle of the churches.
— Studies of Christianity. Ed. by W. R. Alger. Boston, 1858. 12° 1086.14
MARTINS of Cro' Martin : a novel. Lever, C. . . 501.16-17
MARTIUS, K. F. P. von. See Spix and Martius.
MARTOU, E. Études sur les institutions de prévoyance. Bruxelles, n.d. 12° 1065.38
MARTYN, H. Journal and letters. Edited by S. Wilberforce. 1st American ed. New York, 1851. 12° 576.4
— Memoir of. Sargent, J. 576.3
MARTYRIA : legend of the reign of Edward VI. Mountford, W. 488.8-9
MARTYRS. Butler, A. Lives of the 541.5
— Chateaubriand, Vte. de. Les martyrs 1066.7
— Fox, J. Book of 1101.2
— Tayler, C. B. Memorials of the English . . 1094.10
MARTYRS' triumph, and other poems. Mellen, G. 338.14
MARVEL, Ik. Pseud. See Mitchell, D. G.
MARY Barton : a tale of Manchester life. Gaskell, E. C. 794.15
MARY Bell : a Franconia story. Abbott, J. . v.IV. of 738.4
MARY Erskine : a Franconia story. Abbott, J. v.III. of 738.4
MARY, Queen of England. Turner, S. Reign of. 965.4
— Tytler, P. F. England under the reign of . . 974.4
MARY, Queen of Scots. Abbott, J. History of . 599.7-12
— Bell, H. G. Life of 810.21-28
— Benger, E. O. Memoirs of 594.2-8
— Lacroix-Marles, J. Life of 594.11
— McLeod, D. Life of 594.10
— Mignet, F. A. A. Histoire de 1066.25
— - History of 554.4
MARY Stuart : historical drama. Schiller, F. v. . 818.11
MARY of Burgundy : or, the revolt of Ghent. James, G. P. R. 463.6
MARYLAND, History of, 1633-60. Bozman, J. L. . 235.3
MARYS, The, or the beauty of female holiness. Philip, R. 1089.21
MASCARON, J. Oraison funèbre de Turenne . . . 1066.5
MASIUS, H. Studies from nature. Translated by C. Boner. London, 1855. 8° 178.3
MASON, G. C. Application of art to manufactures. New York, 1858. 12° 197.1
MASON, J. Treatise on self-knowledge. New York, n.d. 12° 1100.11
MASON, J., Maj. Life of. Ellis, G. E. Sparks's American biography . . . . v.XIII. of 529.1
MASON, L. Musical letters from abroad. Festivals of 1852. New York, 1854. 12° 209.6
MASONIC institution, Letters on. Adams, J. Q. . 134.6
MASONRY. Dobson, E. Stone cutting and . . . 819.17 18
— Nicholson, P. Treatise on stone cutting and 202.3
— Treatise on. Encyclopædia Britannica 201.4

MASS and rubrics of the Roman Catholic church.
Cotter, J. R. 1008.23
MASSACHUSETTS. Barber, J. W. Historical col-
lections relating to 223.8
— Barry, J. S. History of 223.3
— Baylies, F. Mems. of New Plymouth, 1620–41. 223.11
— Bradford, A. History of 223.9–10
— Bradford, W. Hist. of Plym. plantation. v.III. of 278.4
— Carpenter, W. H. History of 228.11–12
— Hayward, J. Gazetteer of 229.2
— Hitchcock, E. Geology, mineralogy, botany
and zoology of 163.10
— Holland, J. G. History of Western 227.14
— Morton, N. New England's memorial. . . . 223.14
— Oliver, P. Puritan commonwealth of 223.4
— Thornton, J. W. Landing at Cape Anne. . . 223.2
— Washburn, E. Judicial history of 207.2
— Young, A. Chronicles of the first planters of. 223.12
— - Chronicles of the Pilgrim fathers 223.13

For the history of the divisions of this State, see
names of counties, towns, etc., as follows: Acton;
Attleboro'; Berkshire; Beverly; Boston; Boxford;
Bradford; Bridgewater; Cambridge; Concord; Dan-
vers; Dedham; Dorchester; Duxbury; Eastham;
Framingham; Georgetown; Groton; Hingham; Leo-
minster; Lincoln; Lowell; Malden; Marshfield;
Medford; Nantucket; Natick; Newburyport; Orleans;
Pepperell; Plymouth; Rowley; Salem; Scituate;
Shrewsbury; Watertown; Wellfleet; Weston.

— [Report] Manual of the mulberry tree. By
J. H. Cobb. New ed. Boston, 1833. 12°. 169.10
— Report on the invertebrata of Massachusetts.
By A. A. Gould. Cambridge, 1841. 8°. . . 175.2
MASSACHUSETTS Charitable Mechanic Associa-
tion. Annals, compiled by J. T. Bucking-
ham. Boston, 1853. 8° 294.5
MASSACHUSETTS Historical Society's collections.
First ser., from 1792–1809. Boston. 10v. 8° 278.1
— - Same. Second ser., from 1814–23. 10v. 8° 278.2
— - Same. Third ser., from 1825–49. 10v. 8° 278.3
— - Same. Fourth ser., from 1852–58. 4v. 8° 278.4
MASSACRE in Boston in 1770, Reminiscences of
the. Hewes, G. R. T. 219.4
MASSEY, G. Poetical works. Boston, 1857. 18°. 359.9
— Poems and ballads. From the 3d London ed.
New York, 1854. 12° 334.1
MASSIE, N. Biogr. sketches of. McDonald, J. . 518.8
MASSINGER, P. Plays, with notes by W. Gifford,
London, 1805. 4v. 8° 353.8

Contents. — Vol. I. Introd.; Essay, etc., by Dr. Ferriar; Virgin-martyr; Unnatural combat; Duke of Milan. II. Bondman; Renegado; Parliament of love;
Roman actor; Great Duke of Florence. III. Maid
of honour; The picture; Emperor of the East; Fatal
dowry; New way to pay old debts. IV. City madam;
The guardian; A very woman; Bashful lover; The
old law.

— - Same. 3d ed. London, 1840. 8° 353.4

Contents. — Same as above.

— Plays, adapted for family reading. New
York, 1831. 3v. 18° 357.14

Contents. — Vol. I. Life; Virgin-martyr; Great
Duke of Florence; Bondman; Maid of honour. II.
Duke of Milan; The city madam; Unnatural com-
bat; The picture; Selections from the Roman actor.
III. New way to pay old debts; Fatal dowry; Em-
peror of the East; A very woman; Bashful lover.

MASTERMAN Ready: a sea tale. Marryat, F. . . 835.9
MASTER'S house: a tale of Southern life. By
Logan. New York, 1854. 12° 796.13
MASTICS, Treatise on. Burnell, G. R. 819.32
MASTING, mast-making, etc. Kipping, R. . . . 819.38
MASTODON giganteus of N. American. Warren, J. C. 170.1
MATERIA medica. See Medicine.
MATHEMATICAL dictionary. Davies, C. 147.1
MATHEMATICAL geography. Lloyd, E. . v.III. of 365.14
MATHEMATICAL instruments. Heather, J. F.
Treatise on 199.21
— Keutish, T. Treatise on a box of 199.9
MATHEMATICAL tables. See Tables.
MATHEMATICIAN, The. Davies, T. S. 147.9

MATHEMATICS. Brougham, H. and Routh, E. J.
Analytical view of Newton's principia . . . 147.6
— De Morgan, A. Connection of number and
magnitude 147.16
— Gregory, O. M. for practical men 147.2
— Hamilton, W. R. Lectures on quaternions . 147.7
— Hann, J. Treatise on conic sections 829.22
— Peirce, B. Curves, functions and forces . . . 148.2
— The study and difficulties of. Library of Use-
ful Knowledge 365.12
— See also: Algebra, Arithmetic, Assurance,
Astronomy, Geometry, Mechanics, Optics,
etc.
MATHER, C. Sufferings of Margaret Rule 229.5
— Life of Peabody, W. B. O. . . . . . v.VI. of 529.1
MATINS and vespers. Bowring, J. 349.18
MATTHEW, St., Gospel of. See Bible.
MATTHEW of Westminster, Flowers of history,
especially such as relate to Britain, to A.D.
1307. London, 1853. 2v. p.8° 856.5
MATTHEW Paris. English hist. from 1235 to 1273.
Translated by J. A. Giles. London, 1852–54.
3v. p.8° 856.1
— Flowers of history ascribed to. Roger of
Wendover 846.9
MATTHEW Wald, History of. Lockhart, J. G. . 769.9
MATTHEWS, H. Diary of an invalid in Italy,
France, etc., 1817–19. London, 1835. 16°. . 679.14
MATTHIÆ, A. G. History of Greek and Roman
literature. Translated from 3d ed. Oxford,
1841. 12°. 406.11
MATTHIAS, B. Rules of order in deliberative
bodies. 5th ed. Philadelphia, 1851. 18°. 139.22
MATTISON, H. Spirit-rapping unveiled. New
York, 1853. 12° 125.19
MAUD and other poems. Tennyson, A. 334.17–18
MAUNDER, S. History of the world. Ed. by J.
Inman. New York, 1853. 2v. 8° 951.5
MAUNDEVILLE, Sir J. See Mandeville, Sir J.
MAUNDRELL, H. Journey from Aleppo to Jeru-
salem, A.D. 1697; also, a journey from Cairo
to Mt. Sinai. Translated by Bp. Clayton.
London, 1810. 8° 684.9
— Narrative of travels in Palestine 846.7
MAUREL, J. The Duke of Wellington, his char-
acter, actions and writings. 3d ed. Lon-
don, 1853. 12° 558.8
MAURITIUS, Narrative of a visit to. Backhouse, J. 692.13
MAURY, J. S. Principles of eloquence. N. Y.,
n.d. 18° 830.4
MAURY, L. F. A. Les fées du moyen-age. Paris,
1843. 12° 1078.2
MAURY, M. F. Physical geography of the sea.
New York, 1855. 8° 145.1
— - Same. New ed. New York, 1857. 8°. . 145.2–6
MAURY, S. M. Statesmen of America in 1846.
London, 1847. 12° 525.1
MAVERICK, A. and Briggs, C. F. History of the
Atlantic cable 196.16
MAVERICK, S. Trial of British soldiers for the
murder of S. M. and others, 5th March,
1770 in Boston 219.1
MAW, H. L. Passage from the Pacific to the At-
lantic, descending the Amazon. London,
1829. 8° 633.13
MAXIMILIAN II. of Austria, Times of. Ranke, L. 409.27
MAXWELL, A. M. A run through the United
States in 1840. London, 1841. 2v. 12°. . . 626.9
MAXWELL, W. H. Border tales and legends of the
Cheviots and the Lammermuir. London,
1852. 16° 807.12
— The field-book. London, 1833. 8° 174.1
— Victories of Wellington and the British ar-
mies. New ed. London, 1852. p.8° 825.3
— and Dickens, C. Pic-nic papers 452.4
MAXWELL: a novel. Hook, T. E. 807.5
MAY, E. J. Bertram Noel: a story for youth.
London, n.d. 12°. 805.27
MAY Flower, and miscel. writings. Stowe, H. B. 806.3
MAY Martin, and other tales. Thompson, D. P. . 726.11

MAYER, B. Mexico as it was, and as it is. 3d ed. Philadelphia, 1847. 8° 254.5
MAYGRIER, J. P. Midwifery illustrated. Transl. by A. S. Doane. 6th ed. N. Y., 1850. 8° . 151.3
MAYHEW, E. Dogs, and their management . . . 177.4
MAYHEW, H. London labour, and the London poor. London, 1851. 2v. 8° 974.1
— Peasant-boy philosopher — (founded on the early life of Ferguson.) New York, 1855. 12° 589.4
— Wonders of science ; or, young Humphry Davy. New York, 1856. 16° 149.21
MAYHEW, I. Means and ends of universal education. New York, 1857. 12° 137.5
MAYHEW, J. Life and writings of. Bradford, A. 534.2
MAYO, H. Philosophy of living. 3d ed. London, 1851. 16° 158.9
— Popular superstitions ; with an account of mesmerism. From 3d London ed. Philadelphia, 1852. 12° 1099.3
MAZARIN, Vie du Cardinal. Corne, H. 1078.22
MEAD, H. The sepoy revolt ; its causes and consequences. London, 1857. 8° 937.1
— - Same. London, 1858. 16° 939.3
MEADE, W. Old churches, ministers, and families of Virginia. Philadelphia, 1857. 2v. 8° . . 236.1
MEANS and ends. Sedgwick, C. M. 129.22
MEARES, J. Voyages made in 1788-89, from China to the N. W. coast of America. London, 1791. 2v. 8° 623.13
MECCA, Pilgrimage to. Burton, R. F. 689.10
MECHANIC, The. Mach. II. M.'s tables . . 198.6
— Kelt, T. M.'s text-book 198.4
— Nicholson, J. Operative 196.8
— Templeton, W. M.'s workshop companion . . 199.36
MECHANICAL philosophy. Carpenter, W. B. . . 146.25
— Coues, S. E. Outlines of a system of. 147.17
MECHANICS, Familiar introd. to the principles of. 149.37
— Fenwick, T. Four essays on practical 195.21
— Ferguson, J. Lectures on select subjects in . 146.8
— Glynn, J. Cranes and machinery for raising heavy bodies 199.20
— Jamieson, A. M. of fluids for practical men . 144.13
— Kater, H. Treatise on 140.19-20
— Lardner, D. Library of Useful Knowl. . v.I. of 365.14
— Lefrançois, E. Notions de M. générale . . . 1065.31
— Moseley, H. Illustrations of. 839.1
— Renwick, J. The elements of 196.5
— Tomlinson, C. Principles of, and their application 819.6
— Weisbach, J. M. of machinery 144.8
— Whewell, W. M. of engineering 195.20
MECHANICS' assistant : a practical treatise on mensuration 198.5
MECHANISM. Baker, T. Elements of 829.29
— Tate, T. Elements of 199.18
MECHI, J. J. Irrigation with liquid manure . . . 836.1
MECKLENBURG county, N. C. Declaration of independence by the citizens of. 235.6
MEDFORD, Mass., History of. Brooks, C. 224.5
MEDICAL biography of the U. S. Thacher, J. . . 523.11
MEDICAL biography, American. Williams, S. W. 523.12
MEDICAL botany. Griffith, R. E. 152.11
MEDICAL chemistry, Handbook of. Bowman, J. E. 157.11
MEDICAL jurisprudence. Taylor, A. S. 151.5
MEDICI, Lorenzo de, Life of. Roscoe, W. 543.11
MEDICINE. Acton, W. Diseases of the urinary and generative organs 151.21
— Ashwell, S. Diseases peculiar to women . . 151.16
— Bartlett, E. Fevers of the United States . . . 152.12
— Beasley, H. Pocket formulary 153.6
— Bell, J. On regimen and longevity 157.21
— Bowditch, H. I. Young stethoscopist 153.10
— Churchill, F. Diseases of women 151.11
— Condie, D. F. Diseases of children 152.6
— Cooper, Sir A. Abdominal hernia 151.1
— Cornell, W. M. Ship and shore physician and surgeon 157.56
— Dunglison, R. Medical lexicon 151.14
— - New remedies, with formulæ 151.15
— - Practice of 152.1
— - Therapeutics and materia medica 152.4

MEDICINE. Fallot, L. Aperçu de la M., dans ses rapports avec les maladies internes . . 1065.14
— Fitch, S S. Uses of the lungs, and longevity. 158.7
— Gregory, G. Lectures on eruptive fevers . . 152.13
— Griffith, R. E. Universal formulary 152.9
— Hall, M. Respiration in drowning 157.5
— Hall, W. W. Consumption 157.12
— Handbook of domestic 826.14
— Hitchcock, E. Diet, regimen, and employment 158.4
— Hufeland, C. W. Art of prolonging life . . 157.27
— Jackson, J. Letters to a young physician . 157.23-24
— Kennedy, E. Obstetric auscultation 153.8
— Kitchiner, W. Art of prolonging life 158.21
— Macnish, R. Philosophy of sleep 157.28
— Maygrier, J. P. Midwifery illustrated . . . 151-3
— Meigs, C. D. Woman, her diseases, etc. . . 151.10
— - Obstetrics 152.2
— Neill, J. Compendium of 153.5
— Mohr, F. Practical pharmacy 152.10
— Morfit, C. Pharmaceutical manipulations . . 155.2
— Mott, L. Ladies' medical oracle 158-3
— Neill, J. Compendium of medical science . . 153.5
— Paine, M. Materia medica and therapeutics. 153.9
— Parker, E. H. Mother's hand-book 157.15
— Payen, A. Substances alimentaires 1078.37
— Pereira, J. Materia medica and therapeutics. 152.7
— - Treatise on food and diet 157.3
— Ramsbotham, F. H. Process of parturition. 151.2
— Raspail, F. V. Domestic 829.37
— Ricord, P. Syphilis 151.22
— - Venereal diseases 153.2
— Smith, T. S. Promotion of human longevity. 850.15
— Sunderland, L. Theory of nutrition 157.31
— Sweetser, W. Treatise on digestion 157.29
— Tanner, T. H. Manual of the practice of . . 155.27
— Tilt, E. J. Women at the critical periods . 158.18
— Tweedie, A. Fever and its modifications . . 153.11
— Vidal, A. Venereal diseases 152.5
— Walker, A. Pathology 158.2
— Warren, J. C. Etherization 157.22
— Watson, T. Principles and practice of physic. 151.6-9
— Wesley, J. Primitive physic 157.36
— West, C. Diseases of infancy and childhood. 151.20
— Whitehead, J. Causes and treatment of abortion and sterility 153.3
— Wilson, E. Diseases of the skin 153.1
— - On healthy skin, with treatment of cutaneous diseases 157.14
— Wood, G. B. Treatise on the practice of . . 152.3
— - and Bache, F. Dispensatory of the United States 151.12
    See also : Anatomy, Disease, Health, Surgery ; also the names of various diseases.
MEDITERRANEAN. Napier, E. Excursions along the shores of the 675.15
— Schroeder, F. Shores of the 676.5
— Willis, N. P. Summer cruise in the 676.11-15
MEDWAY, Dutch in the. Mac Farlane, C. 840.37
MEDWIN, T. Conversations of Lord Byron. New York, 1824. 12° 898.20
MEETER, E. Holland, its institutions, etc. London, 1857. 12° 917.4
MEIGS, C. D. Obstetrics ; the science and art. 2d ed. Philadelphia, 1852. 8° 152.2
— Woman, her diseases and remedies. 3d ed. Philadelphia, 1854. 8° 151.10
MEINHOLD, J. W. Mary Schweidler ; the amber witch. Transl. by Lady D. Gordon. New York, 1845. 12° 416.13
— - Same. London, 1844. 12° 889.34
— Sidonia, the sorceress. New York, n.d. 8° . 802.1
MELANCHOLY, Anatomy of. Burton, R. 872.7-9
MELANCHTHON, P., Life of. Ledderhose, K. F. . 545.9
MELANTHE : or, the days of the Medici. A tale. Maberly, K. C. 769.3
MELAS, T. Erwin von Steinbach ; ein Roman. Hamburg, 1834. 3v. 16° 1035.2
MELBOURNE, and the Chincha isl'ds. Peck, G. W. 705.21
MELISH, J. Travels in the United States of Am., 1806-11, and through G. Britain and U. Canada. Philadelphia, 1812. 2v. 8° 623.7

MELLEN, G. Martyr's triumph, and other poems. Boston, 1833. 12° 338.14
— Sad tales and glad tales. Boston, 1828. 12° . 489.13
MELLICHAMPE : a legend of the Santee. Simms, W. G. 790.17-21
MELVILL, H. Bible thoughts. N. York, n.d. 16° 119.17
MELVILLE, G. J. W. Kate Coventry : an autobiography. Boston, 1856. 8° 802.40-41
MELVILLE, H. Confidence man ; his masquerade. New York, 1857. 12° 736.10
— Moby Dick : or, the whale. N. Y., 1851. 12°. 735.9
— Omoo. Adventures in the South seas. London, 1847. 12° 899.1
— - Same. 5th ed. New York, 1847. 12° . . 736.1
— - Same. 6th ed. New York, 1852. 12° . . 736.5
— Piazza tales. New York, 1856. 12° 736.11
— Pierre : or, the ambiguities. N. Y., 1852. 12° 736.8
— Redburn : his first voyage. New York, 1849. 12° 736.6
— Typee : a peep into Polynesian life. New York, 1846. 12° 736.4
— - Same. London, 1846. 12° 899.2
— - Same. Revised ed. New York, 1847. 12° 736.2-3
— - Same. With sequel. N. Y., 1847. 12°. . 736.1
— White jacket : or, the world in a man-of-war. New York, 1850. 12° 736.7
MEMES, J. S. History of sculpture, painting and architecture. Edinburgh, 1829. 18° 830.48
— Memoirs of the Empress Josephine. Edinburgh, 1831. 18° 830.67
— - Same. New York, 1855. 18° 810.34-38
MEMOIRS of a working-man. London, 1845. 18°. 840.45
MEMORABILIA of Socrates. Xenophon 844.4
MEMORIALS of the late war. [1806-15.] Edinburgh, 1828. 2v. 18° 830.42
MEMORIES of youth and manhood. Willard, S. . 525.16
MEMORY and hope. Boston, 1851. 8° 346.1
MEN and manners. Hazlitt, W. Essays on . . . 886.11
— Shenstone, W. Essays on 850.27
MEN and things, Short essays on. Baker, J. L. . 136.16
MEN and women : poems. Browning, R. 335.4-5
MEN of capital : a novel. Gore, C. G. 776.8
MEN of character. Jerrold, D. . . . . v.II. of 906.1
MEN of the time. New York, 1852. 12° 548.1-2
MEN, women and books. Selection of sketches, essays, etc. Hunt, J. H. L. 908.1
MENAGERIES of the Zoological society. Bennett, E. T. 172.19-20
MENAGERIES. Natural history of monkeys, opossums and lemurs. London, 1850. 12° . . . 839.17
— Quadrupeds, described and drawn from living subjects. Boston, 1830-32. 2v. 12° . . . 849.16-17
— - Same. London, 1848. 3v. 12° 839.18
MENDELSSOHN-BARTHOLDY, T. Life and works of. Benedict, J. 545.4
MEN'S wives. Thackeray, W. M. 508.18-20
MENSURATION. Baker, T. Treatise on 829.22
— Haswell, C. H. M. and practical geometry . 147.25
MENZEL, W. History of Germany. Transl. by Mrs. Horrocks, from 4th German ed. London, 1848-9. 3v. p.8° 848.2
MERCANTILE correspondence. Anderson, W. . . 136.21
MERCANTILE guide for the United States. Freedley, E. T. 296.3
MERCEDES of Castile. Cooper, J. F. 760.45-49
MERCER, J. Lyric poems. 2d ed., with additions. London, 1804. 16° 358.18
MERCHANT, The : or, success in life. Tuthill, L. C. 525.19
MERCHANT's manual. Foster, B. F. 136.22
MERCIER, L. S. Tableau de Paris. Vie de Mercier, etc., par Desnoiresterres. Paris, 1853. 12° 1076.1
MERCK, J. H. Briefe von 1034.10
MEREDITH, L. A. My home in Tasmania. London, 1852. 2v. 12° 705.16
— - Same. New York, 1853. 12° 707.10
— Residence in N. S. Wales, 1839-44. London, 1844. 12° 899.3
MÈRES rivales, Les : ou la Calomnie. Genlis, Mme. de 1008.7

MÉRIMÉE, P. Chronique du temps de Charles IX. Bruxelles, 1855. 18° 1069.4
— Colomba. From the French. Bost., 1856. 12° 787.12
— History of Peter the cruel, king of Castile and Leon. London, 1849. 2v. 12° 546.18
— La Jaquerie. Famille de Carvajal. [Drames.] Bruxelles, 1828. 18° 1069.6
— Théâtre de Clara Gazul. Bruxelles, 1828. t.I. 18° 1069.6

Contents. — Les Espagnols en Danemarck ; Une femme est un diable ; L'amour africain ; Inès Mendo, ou le préjugé vaincu ; Inès Mendo, ou le triomphe du préjugé ; Le ciel et l' enfer.

— Voyage dans le midi de la France. Bruxelles, 1835. 12° 1069.3
— Voyage dans l' ouest de la France. Bruxelles, 1837. 18° 1069.2
MERIVALE, C. History of Rome under the emperors. Part III. The Augustan age. London, 1843. 8° 365.9
MERLE d' Aubigné, J. H. History of the reformation. Transl. by H. White. New York, n.d. 5v. 12° 1107.13
— - Same. Hartford, 1852. 4v. in 2. 12° . . . 1095.10
— - Same. Philadelphia, 1843. 8° 1085.13
MERLIN, Countess de. Memoir of Mme. Malibran. London, 1840. 2v. 12° 615.10
MÉROVINGIENS, Récits des temps. Thierry, A. . 1076.14
MERRIE England in the olden time. Daniel, G. . 978.1
MERRIMACK river, A week on. Thoreau, H. D. . 623.17
MERRIMAN, Archdeacon. The Kafir, the Hottentot, etc. Passages of missionary life. London, 1854. 16° 578.7
MERRY Christmas : a story. Mackarness, M. . . 476.7-8
MERRY Mount : a romance of Massachusetts colony. Motley, J. L. 476.4-5
MERRY tales of the three wise men of Gotham. Paulding, J. K. 797.11
MERRY wives of Windsor, First sketch of the . . 342.8
MERZ, H. Christliche Frauenbilder. 2te Ausg. Stuttgart, 1855. 2v. 12°. 1014.3
MESMERISM. Bersot, E. M. et le magnétisme animal 1078.41
— Mayo, H. Account of 1099.3
— Townshend, C. H. Facts in 125.17
See Animal magnetism.
MESOPOTAMIA. Buckingham, J. S. Travels in. 694.16
— Fraser, J. B. from the earliest ages . . . 820.54
— Southgate, H. Visit to the Syrian church in. 118.15
MESSAGES of the presidents of the U. S. from 1789-1849. Williams, E. 296.4
METALLIC wealth of the U.S. Whitney, J. D. . . 163.1
METALLURGY. Connaissance des métaux 1075.54
— Holland, J. Present state of manufactures in metal 408.10
— Mitchell, J. Manual of practical assaying. . 144.10
— Napier, J. Ancient workers in metal 199.4
— Overman, F. Treatise on 195.7
— Phillips, J. A. Chemistry of the metals. . . 196.14
— - Manual of 196.14
— - Mining and records of 196.12
— Piggot, A. S. Chemistry and M. of copper. 198.10
— Rogers, S. B. Elementary treatise on iron . 195.8
— Smee, A. Elements of electro-M. 196.13
METAMORPHOSES. Ovidius Naso, P. 824.7
METAMORPHOSES, or the golden ass. Apuleius. Madaurensis, L. 834.15
METAPHYSICAL science applied to the evidences of religion. Bowen, F. 125.8
METAPHYSICS. See Intellec. science, and Philos.
METASTASIO, P. Opere. Prato, 1820. 14v. in 7. 16° 1049.2

Contents. — Vol. I. Vita ; Didone abbandonata ; Siroe ; Catone in Utica. II. Ezio ; Alessandro nell' Indie ; Artaserse ; Adriano in Siria. III. Demetrio ; Issipile ; Olimpiade ; Demofoonte. IV. La clemenza di Tito ; Achille in Sciro ; Ciro riconosciuto ; Temistocle. V. Zenobia ; Antigono ; Ipermnestra ; Semiramide. VI. Attilio Regolo ; Il re pastore ; L'eroe cinese ; Nitteti. VII. Il trionfo di Clelia ; Romolo ed Ersilia ; Il Ruggiero ; Giustino. VIII. Drammi sacri : Per la festività del Santo natale ; La passione ; Sant' Elena al Calvario ; La morte d'Abel ; Giuseppe ricon-

METASTASIO, P., *continued.*
   osciuto; Betulia liberata; Gioas re di Giuda; Isacco.
   IX. Poesie profani: La contesa de' Numi; Il tempio
   dell' eternità; L'asilo d'amore; Le grazie vendicate;
   Il sogno di Scipione; Il palladio conservato; Il Parnaso accusato e difeso; La pace tra la virtù e la bellezza ; Astrea placata ; Il natal di Giove; L'amor
   prigioniero; Il vero omaggio; La danza; L'isola disa-
   bitata. X. Le Cinesi; Il ciclope; Il sogno; Alcide al
   bivio; Egeria; Il Parnaso confuso; Il trionfo d'amore;
   Partenope; La rispettosa tenerezza; Tributo di ris-
   petto e d'amore ; La gara ; La ritrosia disarmata ;
   L'ape; L'Atenaide. XI. La corona; La pace fra le
   tre Dee; La Galatea; L'Endimione; Gli orti espe-
   ridi; L'Angelica serenata; Cantate. XII. Epitalamj;
   Sonetti; Canzonette, ec. XIII. Estratto dell' arte
   poetica d'Aristotele. XIV. Dell' arte poetica di Q.
   Orazio Flacco. Traduzioni; Lettere ; Seutenze e
   massime.
— Vie de. Beyle, H 1007.18
METCALFE, F. The Oxonian in Thelemarken, or
   notes of travel in Norway. London, 1858.
   2v. 12°. 666.3
METEOROLOGY. Arago, F. D. J. Meteorological
   essays. 145.17
— Bassnett, T. Mechanical theory of storms . 145.25
— Brocklesby, J. Elements of 145.27
— Butler, T. B. Philosophy of the weather . . 145.26
— Daniell, J. F. Elements of 145.16
— Drew, J. Practical. 149.17
— Greenwood, G. Rain and rivers 145.14
— Houzeau, J. C. Physique du globe, et 1005.22
— Howard, L. Lectures on 145.28
— Jenyns, L. Observations in 145.24
— Kaemtz, L. F. Complete course of 147.21
— Lardner, D. Manual of 398.14
— Muller, J. Principles of . . . . 144.11&19
— Piddington, H. Sailor's horn-book for the
   law of storms 145.18
— Prout, W. M. with reference to natural the-
   ology 826.16
— Redfield, W. C. Storms of the Atlantic coast. 145.22
METHODISM. Jobson, F. J. America and Amer-
   ican. 625.22
— Taylor, I. Wesley and 1108.4
METHODIST Episcopal church. Doctrines and dis-
   cipline. New York, 1848. 12° 129.8
METHODIST Episcopal pulpit. Clark, D. W. . . 1096.16
METHODIST ministers, Lives of. Gorrie, P. D. . . 535.14
METRICAL romances, Specimens of early English.
   Ellis, G. 846.5
METROPOLITAN pulpit. Grant, J. 1099.11
MEULDER, L. de. Le calcul mental et le calcul
   chiffré. Bruxelles, n.d. 12° 1065.30
MEXICAN revolution, Memoirs of. Robinson,
   W. D. . . . . 254.4&8
MEXICAN travel. Taylor, J. Bayard 627.17
MEXICO. Bullock, W. Six months in 633.9
— Calderon de la Barca, F. E. Life in 633.7
— Carleton, J. H. Hist. of the battle of Buena
   Vista. 259.8
— Carpenter, W. W. Travels and adventures in. 638.8
— Clavigero, F. S. History of 254.7
— Diaz, B. Discovery and conquest of. 254.6
— Domenech, E. Missionary adventures in . . 633.3
— Edwards, F. S. Campaign with Col. Doniphan. 623.20
— Ferry, G. Vagabond life in 638.3
— Gregg, J. Nine years' residence in Northern. 239.12
— Hall, B. Journal written on the coasts of. . 639.7
— Humboldt, A. von. Ancient inhabitants of
   America 256.2
— - Climate, inhabitants, productions, and
   mines of 633.4
— - Equinoctial regions of America 816.13
— Jay, W. M'n war. Causes and consequences. 259.5
— Ker, H. Particular description of 626.2
— Latrobe, C. J. Rambler in 629.14
— Livermore, A. A. War with, reviewed . . . 259.4
— Lyon, G. F. Tour and residence in 628.4
— Mansfield, E. D. Origin, etc., of Mex'n war. 259.1-2
— Mayer, B. M. as it was and as it is 254.5
— Other side, The. War between M. and the
   U. S. 259.3
— Poinsett, J. R. Notes on M. in 1822 . . . . 256.3

MEXICO. Prescott, W. H. Conquest of 252.1-2
— Ripley, R. S. The war with 252.4
— Ruxton, G. F. Adventures in 638.5-6
— Semmes, R. Service afloat and ashore. . . . 623.15
— Stevens, I. I. Campaigns of Rio Grande, etc. 623.9
— Tempsky, G. F. v. Journey in, 1853-55 . . . 633.8
— Thompson, W. Recollections of 633.5
— Thorpe, T. B. Our army on the Rio Grande . 259.6-7
— Tudor, H. Narrative of a tour in 638.1
— Ward, H. G. M. in 1827 . . . . 633.6
— Wilson, R. A. M. and its religion, 1851-54. . 256.4
— Wise, H. A. Inside view of 627.24
MEYER, E. Studien zu Goethe's Faust. Altona,
   1847. 8° 1034.4
MEYERN, W. F. v. Dya-Na-Sore, oder ; Die Wand-
   erer. 3te Aufl. Wien, 1840-41. 5v.16° . . 1037.15
MIALL, J. G. Footsteps of our forefathers. Bos-
   ton, 1852. 12° 1086.22
MICHAEL Angelo Buonarroti. *See* Buonarroti.
MICHAEL Armstrong, the factory boy. Trollope, F. 787.6
MICHAUD, J. F. History of the crusades. Transl.
   by W. Robson. New York, 1853. 3v. 12°. 1095.12
MICHELET, J. History of France. Transl. by G.
   H. Smith. New York, 1845-51. 2v. 8° . . 1003.2-3
— Hist. of the Roman republic. Transl. by
   W. Hazlitt. London, 1847. 12°. 919.5
— - Same. New York, 1847. 12°. 919.4
— Jeanne d'Arc. Paris, 1856. 12°. 1078.34
— Modern history. New York, n.d. 18° . . . 820.64
— The people. Transl. by G. H. Smith. New
   York, 1846. 12°. 124.17
— Women of the French revolution. Phila.,
   1855. 12°. 1008.6-7
MICHIGAN, History of. Lanman, J. H. 820.41
MICROSCOPE, The. Carpenter, W. B. The M. and
   its revelations 178.21
— Catlow, A. Drops of water 178.29
— Hannover, A. Construction and use of . . . 145.19
— Hogg, J. History, construction, etc. of . . . 144.2
— Pereira, J. Lectures on 156.29
— Quekett, J. Treatise on the use of . . . . 144.1 & 6
— Schacht, H. Application of, to vegetable an-
   atomy 145.23
MIDDLE ages, The. Berington, J. Literary hist. of. 404.9
— Dunham, S. A. History of Europe during . 378.6
— Greene, G. W. History and geography of . 947.10
— Hallam, H. State of Europe during 945.1
— Juste, T. Histoire du 1075.15
— Secret societies of 850.13
MIDDLEBURY, Conn. History of. Cothren, W. . 225.2
MIDNIGHT sun ; a pilgrimage. Bremer, F. . . . 455.4-5
MIDSHIPMAN Easy: a novel. Marryat, F. . . . 745.5
MIDSUMMER eve ; a fairy tale. Hall, A. M. . . 804.3
MIDSUMMER medley for 1830. Smith, H. . . . 797.6
MIDSUMMER night's dream, Illustrations of. Hal-
   liwell, J. O. 342.26
MIDWIFERY. *See* Medicine.
MIER, Texian expedition against the city of, 1842.
   Green, T. J. 623.10
MIGNET, F. A. A. Antonio Perez et Philippe II.
   3e éd. Paris, 1854. 12°. 1066.26
— Charles V. son abdication, son séjour et sa
   mort à Yuste. 2de éd. Paris, 1854. 8° . 1065.1
— Histoire de Marie Stuart. Paris, 1854. 2v.12° 1066.25
— History of Mary, Queen of Scots. London,
   1851. 2v. 8° 554.4
— History of the French revolution, 1789-1814.
   From Lond. ed. New York, 1827. 8° . . . 1005.6
— Hist. of the French revol. London, 1846. 12° 1008.15
— - Same. London, 1856. p.8°. 837.3
MILBURN, M. M. Sheep and shepherding. Lon-
   don, n.d. 16° . . . . v.I. of 169.15
— The cow. New ed. London, n.d. 16°. v.I.of 169.15
MILBURN, W. H. Rifle, axe, and saddle-bags, and
   other lectures. New York, 1857. 12°. . . 808.14
MILE stones in our life journey. Osgood, S. . . . 1088.22
MILES, H. A. Altar at home, prayers. 7th ed.
   Boston, 1857. 12°. 118.16
— Lowell as it was, and as it is. Lowell, 1845. 18° 227.20
MILES, P. Nordurfari: or, rambles in Iceland.
   New York, 1854. 12° 668.12

MILES, W. The horse's foot, and how to keep it sound. New York, 1851. 12°. 165.18
MILES Wallingford ; a novel. Cooper, J. F. . . . 760.6-8
MILITARY and naval resources of European Nations. Wraxall, L. 947.3
MILITARY art and science. Colt, S. Manufacture of rotating chambered-breeched fire arms . 195.23
— Brialmont, A. Précis d' art militaire 1065.9
— Grafton, H. D. Treatise on the camp and march. 197.11
— Jervis-White-Jervis, H. Manual of field operations. 197.9
— Jomini, H. de. Art of war. 197.10
— Lendy, A. F. Elements of fortification . . . 197.8
— Root, N. W. T. Military and gymn. exercises. 137.9
— Scott, Gen. W. U. States infantry tactics . . 199.39
— U. States Navy. Exercises in small arms and field artillery 194.8
MILL, J. S. System of logic, ratiocinative and inductive. 3d ed. London, 1851. 2v. 8°. . 122.13
MILL, Mrs. Woman's rights tracts. 878.8
MILLEDULCIA. New York, 1847. 8°. 886.7
MILLER, G. History philosophically illustrated. 3d ed. London, 1848-49. 4v. p.8°. 859.6
MILLER, H. Cruise of the Betsey. Bost., 1858. 12° 167.6
— First impressions of England and its people. Boston, 1853. 12°. 646.7-9
— Foot-prints of the Creator. Memoir by L. Agassiz. Fr. 3d Lond. ed. Bost., 1851. 12° 167.15-17
— Geology of the Bass rock ; its civil and eccl. history by Dr. M'Crie. N. Y., 1851. 16° . . 167.27
— My schools and schoolmasters. Bost., 1854. 12° 586.5-7
— Old red sandstone. From 4th London edition. Boston, 1851. 12° 167.24-26
— Scenes and legends of the North of Scotland. From 2d London ed. Boston, 1851. 12° . . 646.3
— Testimony of the rocks ; with memorials of the author. Boston, 1857. 12° 167.2-5
— - Same. Edinburgh, 1857. 12°. 167.1
— Life and times of. Brown, T. N. 586.8
— Reply to M.'s testimony of the rocks. 169.19
MILLER, J. R. History of England. See Hume, D. 963.1
MILLER, S. Life of J. Edwards Sparks's American biography . . . . v.VIII. of 529.1
— Discourse in Murray street church, N. Y. . . 1083.5
MILLER, S. F. Bench and bar of Georgia. Memoirs and sketches. Phila., 1858. 2v. 8°. 294.3
MILLER, T. History of the Anglo-Saxons 3d edition. London, 1852. 12° 988.8
— - Same. 3d ed. London. 1856. p.8° 835.6
— Pictures of country life and summer rambles. London, 1847. 12° 906.4
— Picturesque sketches of London, past and present. London, n.d. 12°. 646.14
— - Same. London, n.d. 12°. 879.10
MILLER, W. A. Elements of chemistry. Part III. Organic. London, 1857. 8° 156.5
MILLINERY, Hand-book of. Howell, M. J. 199.2
MILLINGEN, J. G. History of duelling. London, 1841. 2v. 8° 985.4
— Treatment and management of the insane. London, 1840. 18° 139.26
MILLINGTON, J. Hydraulics. Lib. Us. Kn. v.f. of 365.14
MILLOT, C. F. X. Elements of general history. Translated. Salem, 1796. 5v. 8° 945.3
MILLS. Fenwick, T. An essay upon. 195.21
— Glynn, J. Water employed to drive 829.14
MILLS, A. Literature and literary men of Great Britain and Ireland. N. Y., 1851. 2v. 8°. 402.2
MILLS, C. History of chivalry. Phila., 1844. 8°. 945.2
MILL-WRIGHT and miller's guide. Evans, O. . . 195.9
MILL-WRIGHT's and miller's assistant. Hughes, W. C. 199.14
MILMAN, E. A. The wayside cross ; or, a tale of the Carlist war. London, 1847. 12° 899.4
MILMAN, H. H. Poetical works. Lond., 1839. 3v. 16° 327.9
    Contents. — Vol. I. Fall of Jerusalem; Martyr of Antioch; Belshazzar. II. Samor, lord of the bright city, and minor poems. III. Anne Boleyn, a dramatic poem; Fazio, a tragedy; Nala and Damayanti; Death of Yajnadatta; Extracts from the Mahabharata; The deluge.

MILMAN, H. H. Poetical works. 332.6
    Contents. — Fazio; Samor; Anne Boleyn; Martyr of Antioch; Belshazzar; Fall of Jerusalem; Miscellaneous poems.
— Fall of Jerusalem. London, 1853. 16° 369.2
— History of Christianity; notes by J. Murdock. New York, 1844. 8°. 1085.3
— History of the Jews. N. Y., 1843. 3v. 18° . . 810.1
— - Same. 2d edition. London, 1830. 3v. 16° 389.15
MILNE, W. C. Life in China. London, 1857. 12° 697.9
MILNE-EDWARDS, H. See Edwards, H. M.
MILNER, T. Life of I. Watts, D.D. London, 1834. 8°. 574.9
MILNES, R. M. Poems of many years. New ed. Boston, 1846. 16°. 334.2
MILNOR, J., Life of. Stone, J. S. 1107.17
MILTON, J. Poetical works ; prefixed, the life of the author. London, 1808. 18°. 359.4
    Contents. — Paradise lost; Paradise regained; Samson agonistes; Lycidas; L'Allegro; Il Penseroso; Arcades; Comus; Sonnets; Odes; Miscellanies; Translations; Psalms.
— - Same ; with notes and life by H. Stebbing, and Channing's essay. London, 1847. 16°. 359.3
    Contents. — Same as above, added: Elegiarum liber; Epigrammatum liber; Sylvarum liber.
— - Same. New ed. With notes and life by J. Mitford. Boston, 1850. 2v. 8° 312.3-5
    Contents. — Vol. I. Life; Paradise lost, b. 1-10. II. Same, concluded; Paradise regained; Samson agonistes; Lycidas; Il Penseroso; L'Allegro; Arcades ; Miscellaneous poems ; Sonnets ; Psalms ; Poemata ; Elegiarum liber ; Epigrammatum liber; Sylvarum liber.
— Poetical works. London, 1851. 3v. 12° . . . 329.6
    Contents. — Vol. I. Paradise lost, b. 1-4. II. Same, b. 5-12; Paradise regained. III. Samson agonistes; Miscellaneous poems; Sonnets; Psalms; Elegiarum liber; Epigrammatum liber; Sylvarum liber.
— - Same. Edited by Sir E. Brydges. New York, 1852. 8° 312.6
— Paradise lost ; with notes by Sir E. Brydges. Philadelphia, 1851. 8° 312.7
— - Same. Edited by J. R. Boyd. New York, 1853. 12° 312.8
— - Same. Life of author by H. Stebbing. Philadelphia, 1853. 18° 359.2
— Prose works ; with notes, etc., by J. A. St. John. London, 1848-52. 5v. p.8° 838.7
    Contents. — Vol. I. Defence of the people of England; Second defence; Eikonoklastes. II. Tenure of kings and magistrates; Areopagitica; Tracts on the commonwealth; Observations on Ormond's peace; Letters of state; Brief notes on Dr. Griffith's sermon; Reformation in England ; Prelatical Episcopacy ; Reason of church government urged against prelacy; True religion, heresy, schism ; Toleration ; Civil power in ecclesiastical causes. III. Likeliest means to remove hirelings out of the church; Animadversions upon the remonstrant's defence against Smectymnuus; Apology for Smectymnuus; Doctrine and discipline of divorce; Judgment of Martin Bucer concerning divorce ; Tetrachordon; Colasterion; Tractate on education; Declaration for the election of John III. king of Poland; Familiar letters. IV. Treatise on Christian doctrine, compiled from the Holy Scriptures alone, transl. by C. R. Sumner. V. Second book of the same; History of Britain; History of Moscovia; Accedence commenced grammar.
— Hayley, W. Life of 583.8
— Ivimey, J. Life and times of 586.23
— Symmons, C. Life of 583.6
— Todd, H. J. Life and writings of 583.7
— Coleridge, S. T. Lectures on. 332.7
— Hood, E. P. The patriot and the poet 586.24
— Ring, M, M. und seine zeit. Hist. Roman. . 1013.14
MIMIC life. Ritchie, A. C. 475.1-12
MINA, Gen X., Expedition of. Robinson, W. D. . 254.4-8
MIND. See Intellectual science, Insanity, Education, etc.
MIND amongst the spindles ; from the Lowell offering. London, 1845. 18° 840.46
MINER, C. History of Wyoming. Phila., 1845. 8° 234.12
MINERALOGY. Ansted, D. T. Element. course of. 163.24
— Chapman, E. J. Practical 163.12

MINERALOGY. Dana, J. D. System of 163.9
— Marcet, J. H. Lessons on minerals 178.36
— Nichol, J. Manual of 163.25
— Omalius d'Halloy, J. J. d'. Traité sur 1065.41
— Overman, F. Practical 197.16
— Phillips, W. Outlines of 163.18
— - Elementary introduction to 163.21
— Sowerby, H. Popular 169.28
— Varley, D. Rudimentary treatise on 819.5
      See also: Geology, Natural history, etc.
MINER's daughter: a story. Dickens, C. 491.1-6
MINER's guide and metallurgist's directory. Orton,
      J. W. 199.35
MINES. Cornwall: its M. and miners 658.17
— Murchison, J. H. British M. as a means of
      investment 136.32
— Ure, A. Dictionary of 146.2
MINIFIE, W. Text-book of geometrical drawing
      3d ed. Baltimore, 1851. 8°. 203.1-5
— - Same. 5th ed. With appendix on the
      theory of colors. Baltimore, 1857. 8° . . . 203.3-5
MINING and metallurgy, Records of. Phillips,
      J. A. 196.12
MINISTER, E. and son. Complete guide to practi-
      cal cutting. 2d ed. London, n.d. 8° 194.2
MINISTERING children: a tale. N. Y., 1854. 12°. 416.7
MINNAY Sotor river, Canoe voyage up. Feathers-
      tonhaugh, G. W. 623.14
MINNESOTA. Andrews, C. C. Tour through . . . 237.10
— Bond, J. W. M. and its resources 237.8
— Neill, E. D. History of 235.14
— Oliphant, L. M. and the far West 236.10
— Parker, N. H. Handbook for 1856-7 . . . . . 237.18
— Seymour, E. S. Sketches of 638.9
MINOR drama. [In 7v.] See Wemyss, F. C. . . . 364.2
MINSTRELS' gift, containing songs and ballads.
      Turner, J. W. 338.19
MINSTRELSY, ancient and modern. Motherwell. 348.5
      See also: Ballads.
MINTURN, R. B. jr. From New York to Delhi.
      New York, 1858. 12° 706.9
MIRABEAU, H. G. Riquetti, Comte de. Recollec-
      tions of. Dumont, P. E. L. 613.3
— Souvenirs sur. Dumont, P. E. L. 1079.1
MIRACLES. Cumming, J. Lectures on 116.4
— Trench, R. C. Notes on 1093.8
      See also: Evidences of Christianity, Theol-
      ogy, etc.
MIRAGLIA, B. Cinque novelli calabresi. Firenze,
      1856. 16° 1059.7
MIRANDA's [Don F. de] attempt to effect a revolu-
      tion in S. America. Biggs, J. 266.7
MIRICK, B. L. History of Haverhill, Mass. Haver-
      hill, 1832. 12° 227.17
MIRROR of olden time in America. Pritts, J. . . . 245.2
MIRZA, The: a novel. Morier, J. 808.2
MISERRIMUS. New York, 1833. 18° 429.11
MISCELLANIES of literature. D'Israeli, I. 897.5-6
MISSIONARY enterprise, Heroines of. Eddy, D. C. . 539.13
MISSIONS. Allen, D. O. Christianity in India . . 934.1-2
— Coke, T. M. established in the W. Indies . . 264.5
— Crowe, F. Gospel in Central America 1087.4
— Dibble, S. Sandwich Islands mission 1108.7
— - Thoughts on 119.20
— Ellis, W. Christian M. in Madagascar 934.5
— Foster, J. Communication of Christianity to
      the people of Hindostan 878.19
— Gammell, W. History of American Baptist. 1106.10
— Huc, L'abbé. Christianity in China, Tartary
      and Thibet 113.4
— Kip, W. I. Early Jesuit missions in N. Am. 1088.12
— Russell, M. Christianity in the S. Sea islands. 938.13
— Shea, J. G. Catholic missions among the
      Indians of United States 1098.7
— Williams, J. Missionary enterprises in the
      South Sea islands 1087.15
MISSISSIPPI, The. Beltrami, J. C. Description of
      the course of 625.18
— Flint, T. Ten years in the valley of 236.4
— Hart, A. M. History of the M. valley 237.12

MISSISSIPPI, The. Monette, J. W. Discovery and
      settlement of the valley of 234.14
MISSOURI penitentiary, Imprisonment in. Thomp-
      son, G. 138.2
MISTAKES, One thousand, corrected 406.16
MISTERI di Firenze. Panzani, A. 1057.7
MITCHELL, D. G. Battle summer in Paris, 1848.
      New York, 1852. 12° 884.11
— Fresh gleanings of continental Europe. New
      York, 1851. 12° 669.2-3
— Lorgnette, The: or, studies of the town. 10th
      ed. New York, 1853. 2v. 12° 476.11
— Reveries of a bachelor. By Ik Marvel. 14th
      ed. New York, 1853. 12° 476.13
— - Same. 17th ed. New York, 1854. 12° . . 476.12
MITCHELL, J. Falsifications of food. London,
      1848. 12° 156.28
— Manual of practical assaying. 2d ed. Lond.,
      1854. 8° 144.10
MITCHELL, N. Early settlement of Bridgewater,
      Mass. Boston, 1840. 8° 224.6
MITCHELL, O. M. Orbs of heaven. 4th ed. Lon-
      don, 1853. 12° 879.11
— Planetary and stellar worlds. New York,
      1851. 12° 145.27
MITFORD, M. R. Works, prose and verse. Phila-
      delphia, 1850. 8° 804.4

      Contents. — Our village; Belford Regis; Country
      stories; Finden's tableaux; Foscari; Julian; Rienzi;
      Charles the First.

— Atherton and other tales. Boston, 1854. 12° 794.13
— Country stories. London, 1850. 16° 779.4
— Recollections of a literary life. New York,
      1852. 12° 896.12
MITFORD, W. History of Greece. Prefaced by
      memoir by Lord Redesdale. Revised by
      W. King. London, 1838. 8v. 8° 944.1
MOBY-DICK; or, the whale. Melville, H. 736.9
MODEL republic: its glory or its fall 207.13
MODERN accomplishments: a novel. Sinclair, C. 456.8
MODERN British essayists. Phila., 1848-51. 8v. 8° 863.1-18

      Contents. — Vol. I. T. B. Macaulay. II. A. Alison.
      III. S. Smith. IV. J. Wilson. V. T. Carlyle. VI.
      F. Jeffrey. VII. Talfourd and Stephen. VIII. Sir
      J. Mackintosh.

MODERN chivalry: a romance. Brackenridge,
      H. H. 498.19
MODERN flirtations: a novel. Sinclair, C. 456.12-15
MODERN Lothario: a rom. La Motte Fouqué, K. de 801.3
MODERN pilgrims: a novel. Wood, G. 428.4
MODERN society: a novel. Sinclair, C. 456.2
MODERN standard drama. See Sargent, E.
MODONA-OLIVETTI, N. Il vachero, stor. geno-
      vese, del secolo XVII. Firenze, 1856. 12° 1059.10
MOHAMMED. Koran. Transl., with notes and pre-
      lim. discourse, by G. Sale. New ed., with
      mem. of the translator, etc. Phila., 1853. 8° 113.5
— Le Koran. Trad. par Kasimirski. Nouv. éd.
      Paris, 1852. 12° 1066.22
— Bush, G. Life of 810.12
— Green, S. Life of 389.4
— Irving, W. M. and his successors . . v.IX. of 367.2-3
— Ockley, S. M. and his successors 828.5
MOHAMMED Ali Pasha. Account of the proceed-
      ings of, 1801-43. Yates, W. H. 955.8
MOHR, Der, oder das Haus Holstein-Gottorp in
      Schweden. Crusenstolpe, M. J. v. 1025.8
MOHR, F. and Redwood, T. Practical pharmacy.
      Ed. by W. Procter, jr. Philadelphia, 1849. 8° 152.10
MOIR, D. M. Poetical literature of the last half
      century. 2d ed. Edinburgh, 1852. 16° . . 406.10
— Poetical works. Ed. by T. Aird, with mem.
      Edinburgh, 1852. 2v. 16° 327.7
MOKE, H. G. Histoire de la littérature française.
      Bruxelles, n.d. 4v. 12° 1075.27
— Moeurs, usages, fêtes, etc., des Belges. Brux-
      elles, n.d. 2v. 12° 1075.11
— Précis de l'histoire universelle. Bruxelles,
      n.d. 3v. 12° 1066.40

MOLIÈRE, J. B. P. Œuvres complètes, avec des
   notes. Paris, 1854. 4v. 8° 1067.1
   Contents. — Vol. I. L'étourdi, ou les contre-temps;
   Le dépit amoureux; Les précieuses ridicules; Sganarelle; Don Garcie de Navarre; L'école des maris; Les
   fâcheux; L'école des femmes. II. La critique de
   l'école des femmes; L'impromptu de Versailles; Le
   mariage forcé; La princesse d'Élide; Don Juan;
   L'amour médecin ; Le misanthrope ; Le médecin
   malgré lui; Mélicerte; Pastorale comique; Le Sicilien.
   III. L'imposteur, ou le Tartuffe ; Amphitryon ;
   L'avare; George Dandin, ou le mari confondu; Mons.
   de Pourceaugnac; Les amants magnifiques. IV. Le
   bourgeois gentilhomme; Psyché; Les fourberies de
   Scapin; La comtesse d'Escarbagnas ; Les femmes
   savantes; Le malade imaginaire; Poésies diverses.
— Œuvres, avec des notes. Paris, 1853. 2v. 12°   1076.3
   Contents. — Vol. I. Vie; L'étourdi; Le dépit amo-
   reux ; Les précieuses ridicules; Sganarelle; L'école
   des maris; Les fâcheux; L'école des femmes; La
   critique de l'école des femmes; L'impromptu de Versailles; Le mariage forcé; Don Juan; L'amour mede-
   cin; Le misanthrope; Le médecin malgré lui. II. Le
   Tartuffe; Amphitryon; L'avare; George Dandin; M.
   de Pourceaugnac; Le bourgeois gentilhomme; Les
   fourberies de Scapin; La comtesse d'Escarbagnas;
   Les femmes savantes; Le malade imaginaire.
MOLTKE, *Baron v.* The Russians in Bulgaria
   and Rumelia in 1828-29. From the Ger-
   man. London, 1854. 8° 924.3
MOLUCCAN archipelago, Voyages through, 1825-26.
   Kolff, D. H. 705.7
MOLLUSCA, Manual of. Woodward, S. P. . . .   175.12
MOLLUSCOUS animals of Scotland, History of.
   Macgillivray, W. 178.23
   See also : Conchology and Malacology.
MONACA di Casa. Racconto moderno. Gugliel-
   mucci, V. 1056.1
MONACA di Monza. Storia del secolo XVII.
   Rosini, G. 1057.11
MONALDI: a tale. Allston, W. 755.1
MONARCHS retired from business. Doran, J. . .   918.5
MONASTERIES in the Levant, Visit to. Curzon, R.   689.8-9
MONASTERY, The. Scott, Sir W. 460.49
MONCRIF, F. A. P. de. Contes . . . . . v.XXV. of 1077.1
— Les aventures de Zéloïde et d'Amanzarif-
   dine . . . . v.XXXII. of 1077.1
MONETTE, J. W. Discov. and settlement of the
   valley of the Mississippi. N. Y., 1846. 2v. 8°   231.14
MONGE, G. Theory of shadows and perspective.   829.8
MONIKINS, The : a novel. Cooper, J. F. 770.34-37
MONK, G., An hist'l study, 1608-70. Guizot, F. P. G.   568.11
MONK, M. Awful disclosures of the Hotel Dieu
   Nunnery, Montreal. New York, 1836. 12°   1098.24
MONKEYS. Jardine Sir W. Nat. hist. of. v.XXVII. of 179.1
— Knight, C. History, etc., of 850.11
— Natural history of 839.17
MONMOUTH, J., *Duke of,* Life, progresses, and re-
   bellion of. Roberts, G. 566.5
MONOD, A., Krummacher, F. W., Tholuck, A. F.
   G. and Müller, J. Select discourses. Tr.
   by H. C. Fish and D. W. Poor. N. Y., 1858. 12°   1096.9
MONROE, J. Tour of observation in 1817 through
   the N. E. and N. W. departments of the
   Union. Philadelphia, 1818. 12° 629.3
MONSEIGNAT, C. de. Histoire des journaux en
   France, de 1789 à 1799. Paris, 1853. 12° . .   1078.44
— Le Cid campéador, chronique. Paris, 1853. 12°   1078.36
MONTAGU, E. Letters. Ed. by M. Montagu. Bos-
   ton, 1825. 3v. 12° 596.7
MONTAGU, M. W. Works. [Ed. by J. Dallaway.]
   London, 1803. 5v. 12° 899.21
   Contents. — Vol. I. Memoirs, by J. Dallaway; Let-
   ters written before the year 1717; The enchiridion of
   Epictetus. II. Letters during Mr. Wortley's embassy.
   III. Same: Letters to the Countess of Mar; Letters to
   Mr. Wortley, 1739 to 1761. IV. Letters, 1746 to 1756.
   V. Letters during her last residence abroad; Poems;
   Essays.
— Letters and works. Ed. by Lord Wharncliffe.
   2d ed. London, 1837. 3v. 8° 595.3
   Contents. — Vol. I. Memoir, by Mr. Dallaway; In-
   troductory anecdotes; The court of George I.; State of
   party at the accession of George I.; Letters. II. Let-
   ters. III. Letters ; The enchiridion of Epictetus;
   Essays; Poems.

MONTAIGNE, M. de. Works. Ed. by W. Hazlitt.
   3d ed. Philadelphia, 1851. 8° 873.7
— Essays. 9th ed. London, 1811. 3v. 8° . . .   873.8
— A biography. St. John, B. 583.20
MONTALEMBERT, *C'te* C. de. Life of St. Elizabeth
   of Hungary. Transl. New York, 1854. 12°   517.15
— Political future of England. Fr. the French.
   London, 1856. 12° 988.3
MONTENEGRO, Dalmatia and. Wilkinson, J. J. G.   925.5
MONTEREY, Storming and surrender of. Thorpe,
   T. B. 259.7
MONTEZ, Lola. Lectures, including her auto-
   biography. New York, 1858. 12° 894.5
MONTGOMERY, H. Life of Zachary Taylor. 20th
   ed. Auburn, 1851. 12° 517.6
MONTGOMERY, J. Poetical works, with memoir,
   by R. W. Griswold. Boston, 1853. 2v. in 1. 8°   311.5
   Contents. — Vol. I. Prison amusements; Wanderer
   of Switzerland; West Indies; World before the flood;
   Greenland; Pelican island; Chronicle of angels; Songs
   on the abolition of negro slavery, 1834; Sonnets, imi-
   tations, and translations. II. Thoughts on wheels;
   Climbing boy's soliloquies; Songs of Zion, being imi-
   tations of the Psalms; Narratives; Tributary poems;
   Miscellaneous poems.
— Lectures on poetry and general literature.
   London, 1833. 12° 405.14
— Same. New York, n.d. 18° 810.64-65
— Lives of literary and scientific men of Italy,
   Spain, and Portugal 398.1
— Poet's portfolio ; or, minor poems. London,
   1835. 16° 348.13
— Baillie, J. Biography of 518.12
— Holland, J. Life and writings of 584.17
— Knight, H. C. Life of 584.16
MONTGOMERY, *Don J.* Bernardo del Carpio.
   Transl. by J. G. Marvin. Boston, 1843. 8°   802.5
MONTGOMERY, R. Life of. Armstrong, J. v.III. of 518.5
MONTGOMERY'S Tippecanoe almanac for 1841, con-
   taining the life of Harrison. Phil., n.d. 8°   517.4
MONTHOLON-SÉMONVILLE, C. T. de. Captivity of
   Napoleon at St. Helena. London, 1846. 4v. 8°   1006.1
MONTHS, Book of the. Soane, G. 402.11
MONTIGNY. Stratagems of chess, illustrated on
   [120] plates. 3d ed. London, 1817. 12° . .   197.30
MONTREAL. Bosworth, N. Early history and
   present state of 265.4
— Mackenzie, A. Voyages from, to the frozen
   ocean 625.19
MONTROSE, Legend of. Scott, Sir W. 460.34-38
MONTROSE, *Marq. of.* Memoirs of. Grant, J. . . .   565.8
MONTROSE and the covenanters, their characters
   and conduct. Napier, M. 975.9
MONZA, La monaca di. Rosini, G. 1057.11
MOODIE, S. S. Flora Lyndsay. New York, n.d. 12°   794.9
— Life in the clearings, versus the bush. New
   York, n.d. 12° 636.12-18
— Roughing it in the bush; or, life in Canada.
   New York, 1852. 2v. 12° 636.3-11
MOOR, Traces of the Roman and 675.6-7
MOORE, C. C. George Castriot, king of Albania.
   New York, 1850. 12° 547.10
MOORE, F. American eloquence, with sketches
   and notes. New York, 1857. 2v. 8° 861.1
— Songs and ballads of the Am. revolution.
   With notes. New York, 1856. 12° 314.2
MOORE, G. Man and his motives. N. Y., n.d. 12°   125.20
MOORE, H. Memoir of Ethan Allen. Plattsburgh,
   N. Y., 1834. 12° 528.19
MOORE, John, *M.D.* Society and manners in
   France, Switzerland, and Germany. 5th ed.
   London, 1783. 2v. 8° 657.3
— Same. Paris, 1803. 2v. 16° 679.15
— View of society and manners in Italy. Bos-
   ton, 1792. 8° 675.4
MOORE, Sir J. Life of. Moore, J. C. 564.9
MOORE, J. B. Annals of Concord, N. H., 1726 to
   1823. Concord, 1824. 12° 224.18
MOORE, J. C. Life of Sir John Moore. London,
   1833. 2v. 8° 564.9

MOORE, T. Poetical works complete. N. Y., 1852. 8° 311.2
  Contents. — Odes of Anacreon, transl. with notes ;
  Odes; Epigrams from the Anthologia; Juvenile poems; Poems relating to America; Corruption and
  intolerance; The skeptic; Twopenny post bag; Intercepted letters; Satirical and humorous poems; Irish
  melodies; National airs; Sacred songs; Evenings in
  Greece; Legendary ballads; Set of glees; Ballads,
  songs, miscellaneous poems, etc. ; Songs from the
  Greek anthology; Unpublished songs; Lalla Rookh;
  Political and satirical poems; The Fudge family in
  Paris; Fables for the Holy Alliance; Rhymes on the
  road; Miscellaneous poems; The loves of the angels;
  Satirical and humorous poems; The Fudges in England; Songs from M. P., or the bluestocking; Miscel-
  laneous poems; The epicurean, a tale; Alciphron, a
  fragment.
— Epicurean ; a tale. New ed. N. Y., 1841. 12° 759.6
— Fudge family in Paris. 5th ed. London,
  1818. 16° 358.17
— History of Ireland. New ed. London, 1840–
  1846. 4v. 16° 308.5
— Life of Lord Byron, with his letters and jour-
  nals. London, [1851.] 6v. 16° 585.13
— - Same. Phila., 1846. 2v. 8° 585.7
— - Same. Phila., 1853. 2v. in 1. 8° 585.3
— Life of Sheridan. New York, 1853. 2v. 12° . 508.6–9
— Life and death of Lord E. Fitzgerald. New
  York, 1831. 2v. 12° 508.14
— - Same. Paris, 1831. 12° 508.13
— Melodies, songs, [etc.] New York, 1822. 12° 369.16
— Notes from letters to J. Power, with introduc-
  tory letter from T. C. Croker. New York,
  [1854.] 8° 896.7
— Travels of an Irish gentleman in search of a
  religion. Baltimore, 1847. 12° 1089.3
— Memoirs, journal and correspondence. Ed. by
  Lord J. Russell. London and Boston, 1853–
  1856. 8v. p.8° 588.16
— - Same. New York, 1857. 2v. 8° 582.3
— Dickens, C. and others. Pic-nic papers . . . 462.4
MOORS of Spain. Florian, J. P. C. de. 820.70
  See also : Moor.
MORA, A. H. de. Narrative of imprisonment and
  escape from Spain. Translated by W. H.
  Rule. London, 1856. 16° 1008.22
MORAL philosophy. Abercrombie, J. Philosophy
  of the moral feelings 810.57
— Combe, G. Duties of man 139.19
— Dymond, J. Principles of morality 125.9
— Paley. W. M. and political philosophy . . . 1009.35
— Salzmann, C. G. Morality for children . . . 429.9
— Smith, A. Theory of M. sentiments 817.10
— Smith, S. Elementary sketches of 125.16
— Southey, R. Moral essays 139.23
— Wayland, F. Elements of 125.14
— Whewell, W. Elements of morality 127.31
— Winslow, H. Elements of 127.3
  See also : Ethics.
MORAL tales for the young. Hofland, B. 719.14–15
MORAL tales. Guizot, Mme. E. C. P. de M. . . . 737.16
MORALS, minor. *See* Manners and Minor morals.
MORDAUNT Hall, or a September night. Marsh, A. 795.11
MORE, C. Life of Sir T. More, with a biographi-
  cal preface by J Hunter. London, 1828. 8° 562.5
MORE, H. Works. New York, 1847. 7v. 12° . . 907.2
  Contents. — Vol. I. Repository tales. II. Cœlebs in
  search of a wife; Essays ; Moriana. III. Christian
  morals; Moral sketches; Reflections on prayer. IV.
  Practical piety; Life and writings of St. Paul. V.
  Manners of the great; Religion of the fashionable
  world; Tragedies; Poems. VI. Strictures on female
  education; Sacred dramas. VII. Hints for forming
  the character of a princess; Spirit of prayer; Bible
  rhymes.
— - Same. 1st complete American ed. New
  York, 1855. 2v. 8° 1094.5
  Contents. — Vol. I. Poems; Sacred dramas; Stories for
  persons of the middle rank; Allegories; Tales; Fema'e
  education; Practical piety; Tragedies. II. Hints for
  forming the character of a young princess; Christian
  morals; Character and practical writings of St. Paul;
  Cœlebs in search of a wife; Foreign sketches; Domestic sketches; Reflections on prayer; Spirit of prayer.

MORE, H. Christian morals. 1st Amer. ed. New
  York, 1813. 18° 129.26
— Cœlebs in search of a wife. From 2d London
  ed. New York, 1809. 2v. 12° 769.14
— Memoirs of. Roberts, W. 595.11
MORE, Sir T. Utopia. Translated by G. Burnet.
  London, 1849. 12° 759.5
— Same. With the new Atlantis, by Lord
  Bacon, and an analysis of Plato's republic,
  by J. A. St. John. London, 1838. 16° . . . 888.14
— Household of 469.6–7
— More, C. Life of 562.5
— Roper, W. Life of 589.9
MORE worlds than one, the creed of the philoso-
  pher, and hope of the Christian. Brewster,
  Sir D. 146.28
MOREA, The. Gell, W. Journey in 683.3
— Leake, W. M. Travels in 683.1
MOREDUN, a tale of the 1210. New York, 1855. 8° 802.33
MORELL, C. *Pseudon. See* Ridley, J.
MORELL, J. D. Speculative philosophy of Eu-
  rope in the 19th century. N. Y., 1853. 8° . 122.3
MOREWOOD, S. History of the manufacture and
  use of inebriating liquors. Dublin, 1838. 8° 196.9
MORFIT, C. Chemistry applied to the manufac-
  ture of soap and candles. New ed. Phila-
  delphia, 1856. 8° 194.5
— and Cl. Chemical and pharmaceutical manip-
  ulations. 2d ed. Philadelphia, 1857. 8° . . 155.2
MORGAN, Gen. D. Life of. Graham, J. 528.3
MORGAN, *Lady* S. O. France. Four app. on law,
  finance, medicine and political opinion in
  France, by Sir T. C. Morgan. Philadelphia,
  1817. 8° 1003.4
— Life and times of Salvator Rosa. London,
  1824. 2v. 8° 542.1
MORGAN horses. Linsley, D. C. 165.17
MORGANTE maggiore : poema. Pulci, L. 1056.2
MORIER, J. Adventures of Haji Baba of Ispahan.
  Paris, 1824. 3v. 12° 808.7
— - Same. London, 1851. 12° 808.4
— - Same. Philadelphia, 1855. 12° 808.6
— Adventures of Haji Baba in England. Lon-
  don, 1850. 12° 808.5
— Ayesha, the maid of Kars. Lond., 1834. 3v. 12° 418.3
— Journey through Persia, Armenia and Asia
  Minor. 1808–9. Philadelphia, 1816. 8° . . 694.15
— Martin Tontrond, or adventures of a French-
  man in London. London, 1852. 16° 469.17
— The Mirza. London, 1841. 3v. 12° 808.2
— Zohrab, the hostage : a novel. New York,
  1833. 2v. 12° 808.3
MORIN, F. Saint François d' Assise et les Fran-
  ciscains. Paris, 1853. 12° 1078.46
MORISON, J. Counsels to young men, on infidelity
  and the evidences of Christianity. New
  York, n.d. 16° 1109.16
MORISON, J. H. Life of Jeremiah Smith. Boston,
  1845. 12° 523.19
MORLEY, H. Gossip. London, 1857. 8° 885.17
— Life of Bernard Palissy, the potter. Boston,
  1853. 2v. 16° 546.17
— Life of G. Cardano. London, 1854. 2v. 12° . 546.16
— Life of Henry Cornelius Agrippa von Net-
  tesheim. London, 1856. 2v. 8° 546.15
MORLEY Ernstein : or, the tenants of the heart.
  James, G. P. R. 464.5
MORMONS, The ; with mem. of Jos. Smith. Lon-
  don, 1852. 12° 879.42
— Ferris, B. G. History, doctrines, etc. of . . . 1035.14
— - The M. at home 637.6
— Gunnison, J. W. History of 1087.8
— Kidder, D. P. M. and Mormonism 1099.27
MORNING call : a table book of literature. Ellis,
  S. S. 804.5
MORNING communings with God. Sturm, C. C. . 837.11
MORNING watches. Bremer, F. 1094.3
MOROCCO. Jackson, J. G. Account of the em-
  pire of 699.11
— Urquhart, D. Travels in 675.9

MORRELL, Capt. Four voyages to the South Sea, 1822-31. New York, 1853. 8° 702.7
MORRELL, Capt. B. Adventures in the Pacific ocean. Jacobs, T. J. 708.11
MORRIS, G., The life of. Sparks, J. 515.12
MORRIS, L. Papers of, 1738 to 1746. New Jersey Historical Society 283.2
MORSE, J. Annals of the American revolution. Hartford, 1824. 8° 213.15
— and Parish, E. A compendious history of New England. Charlestown, 1804. 12° . . 228.8
MORT d'Arthur. History of Prince Arthur. . . . 850.29
MORTARS, concretes, etc. Burnell, G. R. 199.19
MORTON, P. Geometry, plane, solid and spherical. London, 1830. 8° 365.4
MORTON, N. New England's memorial. 6th ed. Also, Governor Bradford's history, [etc.] Boston, 1855. 8° 223.14
MOSCHUS, Idylls. Translated into prose by J. Banks, and into verse by J. M. Chapman. . 834.6
MOSELEY, H. Lectures on astronomy. 3d edition. London, 1850. 12° 147.13
— Mechanics. Revised by J. Renwick. New York, 1844. 18° 830.1
— Mechanical principles of engineering and architecture. 2d ed. London, 1855. 8° . . . 203.20
MOSELTHAL, von Nancy bis Koblenz. Hocker, N. 1029.3
MOSHEIM, J. L. v. Institutes of ecclesiastical history. Translated by J. Murdock. 5th ed. New York, 1852. 3v. roy.8° 1085.2
MOSLEM. El-Mukattem. Lands of the. 684.8
— Strauss, G. L. M. and Frank. 918.14
MOSQUITO shore, Adventures on the. Bard, S. A. 623.21
MOSS-SIDE: a novel. Hawes, J. 805.18-22
MOSSES from an old manse. Hawthorne, N. . . . 457.1-2
MOTHER at home. Abbott, J. S. C. 119.12
MOTHERLESS children. Baker, Mrs. H. N. 735.15
MOTHER'S advice to her son and daughter. Lambert, A. T. 139.21
MOTHER'S book, The. Child, L. M. 137.28
MOTHER'S friend, The. New York, 1835. 18°. . . 139.18
MOTHER'S hand-book. Parker, E. H. 157.15
MOTHER'S recompense: a tale. Aguilar, G. . . . 764.6-8
MOTHERS, Letters to. Sigourney, L. H. 139.2
MOTHERS of England. Ellis, S. S. 908.3
MOTHERWELL, W. Minstrelsy ancient and modern, with historical introduction and notes. Boston, 1846. 2v. 16° 348.5
— Posthumous poems. Boston, 1851. 12° 348.6
MOTHS, The book of. Brown, T. 830.69-70
   See also: Entomology.
MOTLEY, J. L. Merry mount: romance of the Massachusetts colony. Boston, 1849. 12° . 476.4-5
— Rise of the Dutch republic. N.Y., 1856. 3v. 8° 923.1-4
MOTT, L. Ladies' medical oracle. Bost., 1834. 12° 158.3
MOULDING and founding, A treatise on. Overman, F. 199.6
MOUNTAIN, A. S. H. Memoirs and letters. Ed by Mrs. Mountain. London, 1857. 12° . . . 565.6
MOUNTAINS, Letters from the. Grant, A. 909.3
MOUNTFORD, W. Euthanasy: or happy talk towards the end of life. Boston, 1852. 12°. 1088.19-20
— Martyria: a legend of the reign of Edward VI. 2d edition. Boston, 1850. 12° 488.8-9
— — Same. 1st American ed. Boston, 1846. 16° 488.10
— Thorpe, a quiet English town, and human life therein. Boston, 1852. 12° 488.11
MOWATT, A. C. See Ritchie, A. C. M.
MOZART, J. C. W. A. Beyle, H. Vie de 1067.18
— Holmes, E. The life of 545.21
— Schlictegroll. Life of. See Carpani, G. 545.20
MRS. ARMYTAGE: or, female domination. Gore, Mrs. C. F. 489.8
MUCK manual for farmers. Dana, S. L. 169.31
MUD cabin, The. Isham, W. 135.21
MUDIE, R. The earth. Philadelphia, 1836. 12° . 169.18
— Feathered tribes of the British islands. 4th ed. London, 1854. 2v. p.8° 825.12
— Guide to the observ. of nature. N.Y., n.d. 18° 810.56
— Man in his physical structure and adaptation. Boston, 1838. 12° 176.7
MUDIE, R. Popular guide to the observation of nature. London, 1832. 18° 830.71
MÜFFLING, F. K. F. v. Missions to Constantinople and St. Petersburg. Transl. by D. Jardine. London, 1855. 16° 689.15
— Passages from my life. Ed. by P. Yorke. London, 1853. 8° 542.4
MÜGGE, T. Gesammelte novellen. Leipzig, 1842-43. 6v. 16° 1035.12
   Contents. — Vol. I. Angelica; Die Emigranten. II. Rosalie; Zwei Bräute; Lebensmagie; Paul Jones. III. Neffe und Nichte. IV. Liebe in alter Zeit; Swinemünde und Ragen; Der gefährliche Gast. V. Jakobine; Herz und Welt; Das Medaillon; Der Weg zum Glück; Ein Abenteuer in Holland. VI. Das Gold der Pinheiro's; Simon.
— Erich Randal. Hist. Roman. Frankfurt a. M., 1856. 8° 1013.13
— Life and love in Norway: a tale. Transl. by E. J. Morris. 6th ed. Phila., 1858. 12° . . 415.3
MÜHLBACH, L. Pseud. See Mundt, K.
MÜHLENBERG, H. A. Life of Peter Mublenberg. Philadelphia, 1849. 12° 528.2
MULBERRY tree. La Brousse. M. de. Cultivation of the 136.2
— Massachusetts. Growth of the 169.10
MULDER, G. J. Chemistry of vegetable and animal physiology. Transl. by Dr. P. F. H. Fromberg. Introd. and notes by J. F. W. Johnston. Edinburgh, 1849. 8° 155.8
— Chemistry of wine. Edit. by H. B. Jones. London, 1857. 16° 156.26
MÜLLER, E. Das hessische Land und Volk. Leipzig, 1857. 16° 1029.5
MÜLLER, F. v. Goethe and his contemporaries. Austin, S. 897.9
MÜLLER, J. Principles of physics and meteorology. London, 1847. 8° 144.11
— — Same. 1st Am. ed. Philad., 1848. 8° . . 144.19
MÜLLER, Jul. Select discourses by. See Monod, A. 1096.9
MÜLLER, Joh. v. Universal history. Trans. Boston, 1837. 4v. 12° 949.4
MÜLLER, K. O. and others. Attica and Athens. Transl. by J. I. Lockhart. London, 1842. 8° 955.7
— Literature of anc. Greece. Lond, 1840. v.1. 8° 365.11
MÜLLER, O. Charlotte Ackermann. Roman. Frankfurt a. M., 1854. 8° 1013.12
MÜLLER, W. Gedichte. Miniatur-Ausgabe. Leipzig, 1850. 2v. 24° 1039.5
MÜLLER von Königswinter, W. Münchener Skizzenbuch. Leipzig, 1856. 16° 1029.17
MULOCH, D. M. Novels. N.Y., 1852-56. 2v. 12° 762.1-2
   Contents. — Vol. I. Olive; The Ogilvies; Avillion, and other tales. II. Agatha's husband; The head of the family; John Halifax.
— Avillion, and other tales. New York, 1854. 8° 762.3
— John Halifax, gentleman. N. York, 1856. 8° 762.4-8
— Nothing new. Tales. New York, 1857. 8° 762.9-11
— A woman's thoughts about women. London, 1858. 12° 874.7
— — Same. New York, 1858. 12° 874.8-11
MÜNCHENER Skizzenbuch. Müller von Königswinter, W. 1029.17
MUNDT, K. Aphra Behn. Roman. Berlin, 1849. 3v. 16° 1016.7
— Der Zögling der Gesellschaft. Berlin, 1850. 2v. 16° 1016.6
— Friedrich der Grosse und sein Hof. 2te Aufl. Berlin, 1855. 3v. 18° 1039.6
— Carmela oder die Wiedertaufe. Roman. Hannover, 1844. 16° 1034.17
MUNDY, G. C. Our antipodes. Residence in the Australasian colonies. 3d ed. London, 1855. 705.1
MUNICH, An art-student in. Howitt, A. M. . . 207.16-17
MUNRO, Sir T., Life of. Gleig, G. R. 899.5
MUNSELL, J. Every-day book of history and chronology. New York, 1858. 8° 947.1
MURAT, A. America and the Americans. Transl. by H. J. Bradfield. New York, 1849. 12° . 207.20
MURAT, H. J. de C. "Les nouveaux contes des Fées" . . . . v.1. of 1077.1

MURDOCK, J. The New Testament. Transl. from the Syriac Peshito version. *See* Bible . . . 1093.7
MURDOCK, J. E. and Russell, W. Vocal culture in elocution. Boston, 1845. 12° 137.16
MURCHISON, J. H. British mines as a means of investment. 2d ed. London, 1855. 16° . . 136.32
MURPHY, A. Life and genius of Dr. Johnson . . 901.6
MURPHY, E. Agricultural instructor. 3d ed. Dublin. 16° . . . . v.II. of 169.15
MURPHY, R. Treatise on the theory of algebraical equations. London. 1839. 8° 365.15
MURRAY, A. M. Letters from the United States, Cuba, and Canada. New York, 1856. 12° . 639.18
MURRAY, C. A. Travels in North America during 1834–36. New York, 1839. 2v. 12° 639.3
MURRAY, H. British America. N. Y., 1848. 2v. 18° 820.8
— Discoveries in Africa. 2d ed. Edinburgh, 1818. 2v. 8° 692.10–11
— Discov. in North America. Lond., 1829. 2v. 8° 625.14
— and others. Brit. India. N. Y., 1844. 3v. 18° 810.51
— - Same. London, 1853. 16° 989.1
— and others. Encyclopædia of geography. Philadelphia, 1846. 3v. 8° 952.4
— and others. Discovery and adventure in Africa. New York, 1844. 18° 810.18
— and others Discov. and adven. in the Polar seas and regions. New York, n.d. 18° . . 810.15
MURRAY, H. A. Lands of the slave and free: or, Cuba, U. S. and Canada. Lond., 1857. 16° . 627.4
MURRAY, J. Family library. London, 1829–51. 75v. 16°
Contents:
Aytoun, W. E. Life and times of Richard I. 379.1
Barrow, *Sir* J History of the mutiny and seizure of H. M. S. Bounty 389.1
— Life of Peter the Great 389.16
Blunt, J. J. Reformation in England 379.2
Brewster, *Sir* David. Letters on natural magic 379.10
— - Same. 6th ed.. . . . . 379.3
— Life of Sir Isaac Newton 379.4
Bucke, C. Life of J. Churchill, duke of Marlborough 379.5
— Ruins of ancient cities. 2v. 379.6
Chronicles of London bridge. 379.7
Coleridge, H. N. Six months in the West Indies in 1825. . . . . 379.8
Cunningham, A. Lives of British painters, sculptors and architects. 6v. 379.9
Court and camp of Buonaparte. 379.11
Davenport, R. A. The Bastile and its captives. 379.12
— Lives of individuals who raised themselves from poverty 379.13
— Narratives of peril and suffering. 2v.. . 379.14
— Life of Ali Pasha 379.15
De Foe, D. Journal of the plague 379.17
Edmonds, C. R. Life and times of General Washington. 2v. 379.18
Eustace, J. C. A classical tour through Italy. 3v. 379.19
Gleig, G. R. British empire in India. 4v. . . 389.3
Green, S. Life of Mahomet 389.4
Hollings, J. F. Life of Gustavus Adolphus. 389.6
— Life of Cicero 389.7
Irving, W. Knickerbocker's history of N. Y 389.8
— Life and voyages of Columbus 389.9
— The sketch-book of Geoffrey Crayon . . 389.10
— Voyages and discoveries of the companions of Columbus 389.11
Lander, R. and J. Expedition to explore the course of the Niger 389.12
Lives of British physicians. 389.13
Lockhart, J. G. History of Napoleon Buonaparte. 389.14
MacFarlane, C. Lives and exploits of banditti and robbers 379.16
Milman, H. H. History of the Jews. 3v... 389.15
Mutiny at Spithead and the Nore. 389.5
Palgrave, Fr. History of the Anglo-Saxons. 389.17
Rennie, J. and Westwood, J. O. Natural history of insects. 2v. 389.18

MURRAY, J. Family library, *continued.*
Roscoe, T. Life and writings of M. de Cervantes. 399.1
Scott, W. Letters on demonology and witchcraft 399.2
Ségur, P. P., *Comte de.* Expedition to Russia. 2v. 399.3
Sketches of imposture, deception and credulity 399.5
Smedley, E. Sketches from Venetian hist. 2v. 399.4
Southey, R. Life of Nelson 399.6
Trials of Charles I. and some of the regicides. 399.7
Tour through South Holland, and across the Netherlands, to Ostend 389.2
Tytler, A. F. Universal history to the beginning of the 18th century. 6v. 399.8
Tytler, P. F. Lives of Scottish worthies. 3v. 399.9–10
Wesley, J. Compendium of natural philosophy. 3v. 399.11
Williams, J. Life of Alexander the Great. . 399.12
MURRAY, J. Handbooks, viz. Art of travel. *See* Galton, F 649.17
— - Belgium and the Rhine. Lond., 1852. 12° 649.7
— - Central Italy. *See* Blewitt, O. 649.6
— - The continent. 10th ed. Lond., 1854. 12° 649.19
— - Devon and Cornwall. 3d ed. London, 1856. 12° 649.2
— - Egypt. *See* Wilkinson, J. G. 649.13
— - France. 5th ed. London, 1854. 12° . . . 649.1
— - Greece *See* Bowen, G. F. 649.8–9
— - Northern Europe. Part I.–II. New ed. London, 1849. 2v. 12° 649.11
— - Northern Italy Part I.–II. 5th ed. London, 1854. 2v. 12° 649.4
— - Portugal. London, 1855. 12° 649.16
— - Rome. *See* Blewitt, O. 649.10
— - Southern Germany. 7th ed. London, 1855. 12° 649.5
— - Southern Italy. *See* Blewitt, O. 649.3
— - Spain. *See* Ford, R. 649.12
— - Switzerland and the Alps. 6th ed. London, 1854. 12° 649.18
— - Turkey. 3d ed. London, 1854. 12° . . .649.14–15
MURRAY, J. Home and colonial library. London, 1843–49. 49v. p.8°
Contents:
Acland, C. Manners and customs of India. . 889.2
Barrow, J. Life and voyages of Sir F. Drake. 889.13
Borrow, G. Bible in Spain. 889.4
— Gypsies of Spain. 889.5
Buxton, T. F. Memoirs and correspondence by his son 889.6
Campbell, T. Lives of the British poets. . . 889.7
Darwin, C. Voyage of a naturalist around the world 889.12
Drinkwater, J. Siege of Gibraltar. 889.14
Edwards, W. H. Voyage up the river Amazon 889.15
Ford, R. Gatherings from Spain 889.17
French in Algiers. Transl. by Lady Gordon. 889.18
Gleig, G. R. Campaigns at Washington and N. Orleans, 1814–15. . . . . 889.19
— Life of Robert, first Lord Clive 889.9
— Sale's brigade in Afghanistan 889.11
— Life of Sir Thomas Munro 889.5
Hay, J. H. D. Western Barbary, its wild tribes and savage animals 889.20
Haygarth, H. W. Bush life in Australia. . . 889.21
Head, F. B. Journeys across the pampas . . 889.22
— Stokers and pokers 889.23
Heber, R. Travels through India. 2v. . . . 889.24
Herbert, H. J. G. Journey in Portugal and Galicia 889.8
Irby, *Capt.* C. L. and Mangles, J. Travels in the Holy Land, Egypt, etc. 889.25
Irving, W. Bracebridge hall 889.26
— Tales of a traveller 889.27
Letters from Madras, by a lady 889.28
Letters from the shores of the Baltic. 889.29
Lewis, M. G. Residence in the West Indies . 889.30
Livonian tales 889.31
Malcolm, *Sir* J. Sketches of Persia 889.33

MURRAY, J. Home and colonial library, *continued.*
  Meinhold, J. W. Amber witch, translated by
    Lady D. Gordon 889.34
  Melville, H. Omoo: or, the South Sea islanders.   899.1
  — Typee: or, the Marquesas islands. . . .   899.2
  Meredith, L. A. Sketches of N. S. Wales,
    1839-44 . . . . 899.3
  Milman, *Capt.* E. A. The wayside cross: or, a
    tale of the Carlist war 899.4
  Musgrave, P.: or, missionary life in Canada.
    Edited by J. Abbott 889.1
  Residence at Sierra Leone, by a lady 899.6
  Ripa, *Father.* Residence at the court of Peking.   899.7
  Ruxton, G. F. Adventures in Mexico 899.8
  Saint-Priest, A. de. History of the fall of the
    Jesuits 889.3
  Schimmer, K. A. Sieges of Vienna, by the
    Turks 889.16
  Southey, R. Lives of Cromwell and Bunyan. 889.11
  St. John, B. Adventures in the Lybian desert.   899.9
  St. John, C. Wild sports and natural history
    of the Highlands 899.10
  Stanhope, P. H. Historical essays 889.32
  — Life of Louis, prince of Condé 889.10
  Steffens, H. Adventures on the road to Paris,
    1813-14 . . . . 899.12
— Modern cookery book, based on the work of
  Mrs. Rundell. New and revised ed. Lon-
  don, 1853. 12° 189.8
MURRAY, L. Power of religion on the mind. From
  the 18th ed. New York, 1854. 12° . . . 1084.16
— Memoirs, by himself. Continued by E. Frank.
  York, Eng., 1826. 8° 574.12
MURRAY, P. J. Life of John Banim. London,
  1857. 16° 586.21
MURRAY, R. Marine engines and steam vessels.
  2d ed. London, 1852. 16° 829.12
MURRAY, T. B. Pitcairn;—the island, the people
  and the pastor. 2d ed. London, 1853. 16°.   939.6
MURRAY street church lectures 1083.5
MUSAEUS, J. A. Carlyle's German romance. v.I. of 418.1
MUSEUM, the. Abbott, J. . . . . v.VI. of 739.1
MUSEUM, Kirby's wonderful and eccentric 894.1
MUSEUM of science and art. Lardner, D. . . . 147.20
— The Louvre, or biography of a. St. John, B.   654.12
MUSGRAVE, G. M. A ramble through Normandy.
  London, 1855. 12° 654.11
MUSGRAVE, P. Memoirs of a Ch. of Eng. mission
  in the N. A. colonies. London, 1846. 12°.   889.1
MUSHET, D. Papers on iron and steel. London,
  1840. 8° 194.7
MUSIC. Bird, J. Gleanings from the history of . 209.3
— Burgh, A. Anecdotes of 209.8
— Butler, C. A letter on 617.14
— Calcott, J. W. Grammar of 209.12
— Catel, C. S. On harmony 204.1
— Cherubini, L. Counterpoint and fugue 204.2
— Chorley, H. F. Recollec. and criticisms on
  modern German 209.5
— Dubourg, G. The violin 209.2
— Fétis, E. Les musiciens belges 1075.29
— Fétis, F. J. M. explained to the world . . . 209.10
— — La M. mise a la portée de tout le monde . 1078.58
— — Traité élémentaire de musique 1065.15
— Gardiner, W. M. and friends 204.7
— — M. of nature 204.6
— Harris, J. Treatise concerning 209.4
— Hewins, J. M. Hints concerning church . . 209.1
— Higgins, W. M. History of 149.18
— Hood, G. History of music in N. England . 209.7
— Hopkins, E. J. The organ 204.3
— Letter to a young piano-forte player 199.28
— Music and the art of dress. From the Quart.
  Rev. London, 1852. 16° 209.11
— Seidel, J. J. The organ 204.8
— Singer's companion 207.20
— Spencer, C. C. Church modes 204.5
— — The piano-forte 889.6
— — Treatise on 829.5
— Stafford, W. C. A history of 809.57
— Webb, G. J. Cultivation of pure tone . . . 137.16
— Weber, G. Theory of composition 204.4

MUSICAL hist., biog., and criticism. Hogarth, G.   209.9
MUSICAL letters from abroad. Mason, L. 209.6
MUSICAL terms, Dictionary of. Warner, J. F. . 204.4
MUSPRATT, *Dr.* S. Use of the blowpipe. *See* Platt-
  ner, Prof. 155.18
MUSSET, A. de. Comédies et proverbes. Paris,
  1853. 2v. 12° 1066.27
    Contents. — Vol. I. André del Sarto; Lorenzaccio;
    Les caprices de Marianne; Fantasio; On ne badine
    pas avec l'amour; La nuit vénitienne; Barberine. II.
    Le chandelier; Il ne faut jurer de rien; Un caprice;
    Il faut qu'une porte soit ouverte ou fermée; Louison;
    On ne saurait penser à tout; Carmosine; Bettine.
MUSTAPHA, Ali, Life of. Stanhope, L. 918.2
MUSTON, A. The Israel of the Alps. Transl. by
  W. Hazlitt. London, 1852. p.8° 879.13
MUTINEERS, Home of the 1109.8
MUTINY at Spithead and the Nore 389.5
MUTINY of the Bounty. Barrow, Sir J. 810.42
MUZZEY, A. B. Man a soul, or evidences of Chris-
  tianity. Boston, 1842. 16° 1099.18
— The young maiden. Boston, 1840. 12°. . . 127.29
MY brother's keeper: a novel. Warner, A. B. . . 794.7
MY consulship. Lester, C. E. 678.6
MY courtship and its consequences. Wikoff, H. . 794.18
MY novel. Lytton, E. B. 466.15-17
MY own story. Howitt, M. 459.18-19
MY uncle, the clockmaker. Howitt, M. 459.14
MYRTLE, H. Cats and dogs. London, 1857. 16°. 177.28
MYRTILLA; a fairy extravaganza. Rice, G. E. . . 356.22
MYSTERIES, modern, explained and exposed.
  Mahan, A. 125.2
MYSTERIOUS stranger; a novel. Opie, A. 469.48
MYSTIC, the. A poem. Bailey, P. J. 344.9
MYTHOLOGICAL fables. Vanden Heuvel, Mrs. . . 345.8
MYTHOLOGY. Bulfinch, T. Age of fable . . . 1087.23-24
— Dwight, M. A. Grecian and Roman 1083.10
— Grey, Sir G. Polynesian 1087.20
— Keightley, T. Fairy 846.10
— The M. of ancient Greece and Italy 1087.25
— Pococke, E. Truth in 956.10
— Prichard, J. C. Egyptian 1083.9
— Thorpe, B. Northern 1087.19
    See also: Fairy and Supernaturalism.

NAMUR, Histoire du comté de. Borgnet, J. . . . 1075.12
NAN Darrell, or the gipsy mother: a novel. Pick-
  ering, E. 805.5
NAOMI, or Boston two hundred years ago. Lee,
  E. B. 437.6-7
NANTUCKET, History of. Macy, O. 227.8
NAPIER, C. J. William the conqueror. Ed. by
  Sir W. Napier. London, 1858. 12°. . . . 415.4
— Life and opinions of, by W. F. P. Napier . . 565.5
NAPIER, *Lt. Col.* E. Shores of the Mediterranean.
  London, 1842. 2v. 12°. 675.15
— Reminiscences of Syria. London, 1843.
  2v. 12° 693.15
NAPIER, E. E. Excursions in Southern Africa.
  London, 1849. 2v. 12°. 692.15
NAPIER, J. Chemistry applied to dyeing. Phila-
  delphia, 1853. 12° 197.3
— Ancient workers and artificers in metal. Lon-
  don, 1856. 12° 199.4
NAPIER, M. Montrose and the Covenanters. Lon-
  don, 1838. 2v. 8° 975.9
NAPIER, W. F. P. English battles and sieges in
  the peninsula. London, 1855. 8° 1007.8
— History of the war in the peninsula and South
  of France. 1807-14. London, 1828-40. 6v. 8° 1004.2
— — Same. From 4th ed. Phila., 1842. 4v. 8° 1004.1
— Life of Sir C. Napier. London, 1857. 4v. 8°. 565.5
— Sir C. Napier's administration of Scinde.
  London, 1854. 8° 937.2
NAPLES. Beyle, H. 1067.27
— Porzio, C. La congiura de' baroni di Napoli
  contra il re Ferdinando I. 1059.9
— Reumont, A. von. N. under Spanish do-
  minion 827.2
NAPOLEON I. Confidential correspondence of the
  emperor and Josephine. With notes by J.
  S. C. Abbott. New York, 1856. 12° . . . 665.6

NAPOLEON I. Confidential correspondence with his brother Joseph. Translated. N. Y., 1856. 2v. 12° 605.7
— Memoirs dictated by himself at St. Helena. Vols. 1—4. Historical miscellanies. Vols. 1—3. 2d ed. London, 1823–24. In all 7v. 8° . . . 602.5
— - Same. V. 1—4. London, 1823–24. 4v. 8° . . . 603.4
— Memoirs, 1815. Translated by B. E. O'Meara. Philadelphia, 1820. 12° 605.10
— Abbott, J. S. C. History of 601.1–8
— - Napoleon at St. Helena 602.2–1
— Antommarchi, F. Napoleon's exile 602.7
— Bausset, L. F. J. de. Memoirs of the court of . 603.5
— Bourrienne, L. A. F. de. Memoirs of 830.60
— Chateaubriand, R. F. A. de. Portrait of Bonaparte 609.7
— Court and camp of Bonaparte 810.39–40
— Cockburn, Sir G. Buonaparte's voyage to St. Helena 1009.10
— Fleury de Chaboulon, P. de A. É. Private life, return and reign of, in 1815 . . . . 604.9
— Forsyth, W. Captivity of N. at St. Helena . 605.5
— Fortescue, H. Two conversations with the emperor . . . . v.III. of 603.1
— Goldsmith, L. Secret hist. of the cabinet of . 1009.14
— Gregorovius, F. Sketch of the early life of . 1007.5
— Hazlitt, W. Life of Napoleon Buonaparte . 605.4
— Headley, J. T. N. and his marshals 605.1–2
— History of N. and France 1009.15
— Junot, Mme. L. P. Memoirs of N., his court and family 603.3
— Las Cases, M. J. E. D. de. Souvenirs de l' empereur . . . . v.III. of 1078.45
— - Private life of N. at St. Helena 603.1–2
— Laurent de l'Ardèche. History of 604.10
— Lockhart, J. G. The history of 810.2–3
— Maitland, F. L. Surrender of Buonaparte, and residence on board the Bellerophon . . 1009.8
— Montholon-Sémonville, C. T. de. Captivity at St. Helena 1006.1
— O'Meara, B. E. N. in exile, or a voice from St. Helena 605.8–9
— Pelet de la Lozère, J. N. in council 1008.14
— Saint Hilaire, E. M. de. N. et la grande armée. 1068.16
— Savary, A. J. M. R. Memoirs of 602.6
— Scott, Sir W. Life of 601.1–8
— Thiers, L. A. The consulate and the empire. 1002.6
— Vieussieux, A. Sayings and deeds of 830.20
— Warden, Wm. Conduct and conversations of N. on board the Northumberland and at St. Helena 1009.9
— Whately, R. Historic doubts relative to . . 838.15
NAPOLEON III. Political and historical works, with memoirs to 1852. London, 1852. 2v. 8° 134.5

Contents. — Vol. I. Political life; Political reveries; Ideas of a new constitution; Switzerland, political and military; Ideas of Napoleonism; Historical fragments; The revolutions of 1688 and 1830. II. Analysis of the sugar question; Extinction of pauperism; A few words relative to Jos. Bonaparte; Opinions; Governments and their supporters; Reply to M. de Lamartine; The past and future of artillery; L'Idée Napoléonienne, 1840; Revision of the constitution, 1851; Miscellaneous papers, etc.; Papers relating to the coup d'état.

— Review of his life, character, and policy. London, 1857. 8° 601.11
— Roth, E. Life of 604.12
— St. John, J. A. Biography of 604.13
— The empire, and the coup d'état 1009.6–7
NARES, E. Universal history, continued. See Tytler, A. F. 820.1
NARRATIVE of the loss of the Amazon. London, 1852. 16° 989.9
NASH, J. A. The progressive farmer, a scientific treatise. New York, 1853. 12° 168.4
NASH, T. Pierce Penniless's supplication to the devil, with an introduction by J. P. Collier. London, 1842. 8° 342.11
NASSAU, Bubbles from the Brunnens of. Head, Sir F. B. 667.18
NATCHEZ, Les. Chateaubriand, F. A. de. . . . 1059.14

NATHALIA Borissovna, Life and times of. Heard, J. A. 516.14
NATHALIE: a tale. Kavanagh, J. 454.5–6
NATICK, History of. Bacon, O. N. 224.8
— - Same. Biglow, W. 224.12
NATIONAL constituent assembly, History of, from May, 1848. Corkran, J. F. 1008.3
NATIONAL illustrated library. London, 1852–54. 32v. 12°.
Contents:
Boswell, J. Tour to the Hebrides with S. Johnson 869.1
— Life of S. Johnson 869.2–6
Bunyan, J. Pilgrim's progress 869.9
Dumas, A. Pictures of travel in the South of France 869.10
Gautier, T. Wanderings in Spain 869.12
Homer. Iliad, translated by A. Pope. 2v. . . 879.1
— Odyssey, translated by A. Pope 879.2
Huc. Travels in Tartary, Thibet and China, translated by W. Hazlitt. 2v. 879.6–7
Illustrated book of English songs, from 16th to 19th century 869.7
Illustrated book of Scottish songs from 16th to 19th century 869.8
Mackay, C. Extraordinary delusions and the madness of crowds. 2v. 879.8–9
Miller, T. Picturesque sketches of London . 879.10
Mitchell, O. M. The orbs of heaven 879.11
Mormons, with memoirs of the life and death of J. Smith 879.12
Muston, A. Israel of the Alps, translated from the French by W. Hazlitt 879.13
Neale, F. A. Residence in the capital of Siam. 879.14
Pfeiffer, I. Iceland and the Scandinavian North 879.3
— A woman's journey round the world . . 879.4
— Visit to the Holy Land, Egypt and Italy. 879.5
Pope, A. Memoir, with correspondence . . . 869.13
Rabbe, A. and Duncan, A. Hist. of Russia. 2v. 869.11
Russell, W. Boyhood and early life of extraordinary men 879.15
Walton, I. and Cotton, C. The complete angler 879.19
Wilkes, C. Narrative of the U. S. exploring expedition. 2v. 879.16–18
NATURAL history of quadrupeds. N. Y., n.d. 18° 820.10
NATURAL history. The elephant. N. Y., n.d. 18° 820.59
— Brown, T. Butterflies, sphinxes and moths . 830.69
— Catlow, A. Drops of water—their inhabitants. 178.29
— Cooper, S. F. Rural hours 168.2–3
— Darwin, C. Voyage of the Beagle 707.12–13
— Goodrich, S. G. Anecdotes of the animal kingdom 169.14
— Gosse, P. H. Life in its several forms . . . 178.15
— Gould, A. A. Naturalist's library 172.1
— Humboldt, A. v. Equinoctial regions of Am. 816.13
— Jardine, W. Naturalist's library. 40v. . . . 179.1
— Jesse, E. Gleanings in 178.38
— Jones, T. R. Natural history of animals . . 177.10
— Kemp, T. L. Natural history of creation . . 409.31
— Lee, R. Taxidermy: or, the art of preparing objects of 177.25
— Marcet, Mrs. J. H. Scenes in nature 169.23
— Myrtle, H. Lessons in 177.28
— Oken, L. Physio-philosophy 166.2
— Phenomena of nature. See Bell, H. G. . . . 830.32
— Plinius Secundus, C. Natural history . . . 844.7
— Samuelson, J. The earth-worm and the common house-fly 175.13
— Sketches in 850.12
— Swainson, W. Study of 398.16
— - Taxidermy 408.5
— Vestiges of the N. H. of creation 149.36
— Waterton, C. Essays on 177.20
— Wood, J. G. Illustrated 177.9

NOTE. — For the natural history of districts, etc., see the name of each; and, for the several branches of natural history, see Conchology, Crustacea, Entomology, Mammalia, Ornithology, Zoology, Zoophytes, etc., and also, Animals, Aquarium, Birds, Cattle, Dog, Fishes, Horse, Insects, Ocean, etc.

NATURALIST. Broderip, W. J. Leaves from the
  note book of a 178.5
— Knapp, J. F. Journal of a 177.35
— Manual of the practical. 849.17
— Quatrefages, A. de. Rambles of a 654.10
— Thompson, E. P. The note-book of a 178.6
NATURALISTS, Lives of distinguished. *See* Jar-
  dine, Sir W. Naturalist's library 179.1
  Namely :

	Vol.		Vol.
Aldrovandi, U.	17.	Le Vaillant, F.	12.
Aristotle	14.	Linnæus, Sir C.	6.
Azara, F. d'	19.	Merian, M. S.	30.
Banks, Sir J.	38.	Pallas, P. S.	18.
Barclay, J.	24.	Pennant, T.	7.
Bewick, T.	10.	Peron, F.	25.
Bruce, J.	11.	Pliny	9.
Buffon, G. C. le C.	27.	Raffles, Sir T. S.	8.
Burckhardt, J. L.	40.	Ray, J.	33.
Camper, P.	21.	Rondelet, W.	36.
Cuvier, G.	16.	Salviani, H.	35.
Dru Drury	15.	Schomburgk, R. H.	39.
Geer, C. de	28.	Sibbald, Sir R.	1.
Gesner, C.	20.	Sloane, Sir H.	23.
Haller, A. von	13.	Smellie, W.	2.
Huber, F.	34.	Swammerdam, J.	28.
Humboldt, A. von	37.	Walker, J.	3.
Hunter, J.	22.	Werner, A. G.	29.
Lacepède, Comte de	26.	Wilson, A.	4.
Lamarck, J. B. P. de	31.	Willughby, F.	5.
Latreille, P. A.	32.		

NATURAL philosophy. Bird, G. Elements of . . 149.24
— Euler, L. Letters on 810.55
— Herschel, Sir J. F. W. Preliminary discourse
  on the study of 149.5
— Hunt, R. Elementary physics: an introd. to. 826.13
— Lardner, D. Handbooks of 147.18–19
— Marcet, J. H. Conversations on 149.1
— Powell, B. History of 398.5
— Renwick, J. First principles of 149.25
— Society for the diff. of us. knowl. Introduc. to 365.14
— Tate, T. Elementary course of 149.37
— Tomlinson, C. Rudimentary treatise on . . 819.2
— Wesley, J. A compendium of 399.11
  See also : Physics, and the various branches
  of natural philosophy, as Electricity, Heat,
  Light, Optics, Pneumatics, Sound, etc.
NATURAL theology. *See* Theology.
NATURE. Addresses and lect's. Emerson, R. W. 876.6–7
NATURE: on freedom of mind, and other poems.
  Boston, 1839. 12° 338.21
NATURE of things: a poem. Lucretius Carus . . 824.9
NATURE. Bacon, F. Interpretation of 826.7
— Bell, H. G. Remarkable phenomena of. . . 830.32
— Bigelow, J. N. in disease 157.25–26
— Bucke, C. Beauties, harmon's and sublim's of. 820.46
— Gardiner, W. The music of 204.6
— Good, J. M. Book of 172.8
— Hooker, W. Child's book of 177.32
— Humboldt, A. von. Aspects of 167.12
— Marcet, J. H. Scenes in 169.23
— Masius, H. Studies from 178.3
— Mudie, R. Guide to the observation of . . . 810.56
— Oersted, H. C. The soul in N. 816.15
— Saint Pierre, J. H. B. de. Studies of 173.4
— Schele de Vere. Stray leaves fr. the book of. 178.8–9
— Schoedler, F. The book of 145.20
— Trimmer, S. Introd. to the knowledge of . . 129.30
— Tucker, A. The light of N. pursued 1094.4
NAUNTON, Sir R. Fragmenta regalia. Cary, R.. 563.8
NAVAJO country, Military reconnaissance from
  Santa Fé to the. Simpson, J. H. 623.5
NAVAL architect. Bland, J. Form of ships and boats 829.16
— Creuze, A. F. B. Theory and practice of . . 191.4
— Griffiths, J. W. Treatise on 191.1
— Kipping, R. Masting and rigging 819.38
— Peake, J. Rudiments of 199.22
— Washington, *Capt.* Lecture on the progr. of. 199.16
NAVAL art and science. Blunt, J. Shipmaster's
  assistant 135.2
— Bowditch, N. Practical navigator 135.3
— Boyd, J. M^PN. Manual for naval cadets . . . 199.3
— Exercises in small arms and field artillery,
  for U. S. naval service 194.8

NAVAL art and science. Greenwood, J. Rudi-
  mentary treatise on navigation 819.39
— Jeans, H. W. Navigation and nautic. astron. 829.30
— M'Nally, W. Evils and abuses in the naval
  and merchant service exposed 135.20
— Piddington, H. Sailor's horn-book. 145.18
— Wrottesley, J., *Lord.* Navigation . . v.III. of 365.14
NAVAL and milit. resources of European nations.
  Wraxall, L. 947.3
NAVAL monument, 1812–15. Bowen, A. 215.11
NAVAL worthies of Queen Elizabeth's reign. Me-
  moirs of the. Barrow, J. 564.8
NAVARINO. Account of the battle of. James, W. 986.2
NEAL, D. History of the Puritans, 1517–1688,
  with life and notes by J. O. Choules. New
  York, 1844. 2v. 8° 1085.16
NEALE, A. Spanish campaign of 1808. Memo-
  rials of the late war . . . . v.I. of 830.42
NEALE, F. A. Narrative of a residence at the cap-
  ital of Siam. London, 1852. 12° 879.14
NEALE, W. J. Gentleman Jack. Philadelphia,
  1837. 2v in 1. 12° 737.6
NEANDER, J. A. W. History of the Christian
  religion and church. Transl. by J. Torrey.
  New ed. Rev. by A. J. W. Morrison. Lon-
  don, 1850–52. 8v. p.8° 858.1
— - Same. Tr. by J. Torrey. v.I.–IV., [var.
  eds.,] Boston, 1852, with v.V. published from
  the posthumous papers, by K. F. Th.
  Schneider. Boston, 1854. 5v. 8° 1103.1
— Life of Jesus Christ. Transl. from the 4th
  Ger. ed. by J. M'Clintock and C. E. Blu-
  menthal. London, 1851. p.8° 848.8
— Julian and his generation, an historical pic-
  ture. New York, 1850. 12° 546.11
— Memorials of Christian life, including Light
  in dark places. Transl. by J. E. Ryland.
  London, 1852. p.8° 858.7
— Planting and training of the church. Also
  Antignostikus. Transl. by J. E. Ryland.
  London, 1851. 2v. 12° 848.9
NEBRASKA, History of Kanzas and. Hale, E. E. 629.2
NECKER de Saussure, A.-A. Étude de la vie des
  femmes. Bruxelles, 1840. 12° 1068.8
— Progressive education, translated by Mrs.
  Willard and Mrs. Phelps. Boston, 1835. 12° 137.7
NECROMANCERS, Lives of the. Godwin, W. . . . 125.1
NED Myers: or, life before the mast. Cooper,
  J. F. 770.38–40
NED Musgrave. Hook, T. 809.9
NEELE, H. Romance of the history of England.
  London, 1828. 3v. 12° 419.2
— - Same. London, 1833. 3v. 16° 419.3
— - Same. 2d ed. London, 1828. 3v. 12° . . 419.1
NEFF, F. Letters and biography. From the
  French of Bost. London, 1843. 16° 544.15
NEFF, J. K. Army and navy of America. Phila-
  delphia, 1845. 8° 215.10
NEIGHBOR Jackwood. Trowbridge, J. T. 796.1–10
NEIGHBORS, The: a story. Bremer, F. 455.11–13
NEILL, E. D. Hist. of Minnesota. Phila., 1858. 8° 235.14
NEILL, J. and Smith, F. G. Compendium of med-
  ical science. 2d ed. Philadelphia, 1852 . . 153.5
  Contents. — Handbooks of anatomy; of physiology;
  of surgery; of obstetrics; of materia medica and thera-
  peutics; of chemistry; of the practice of medicine.
NELL, W. C. Colored patriots of the American
  revolution, with an introducion by H. B.
  Stowe. Boston, 1855. 12° 216.8
NELSON, D. Cause and cure of infidelity. New
  York, 1841. 12° 1107.16
NELSON, H., Life of. Southey, R. 810.4–7
NEMESIS of power. St. John, J. A. 139.14
NENNIUS. History of the Britons. *See* Giles, J. A. 846.4
NEPAUL, Journey to Katmandu, the capital of.
  Oliphant, L. 709.17
NERO, History of. Abbott, J. 549.19
NESTORIAN Christians. Perkins, J. 695.1
NESTORIANS. Laurie, T. Dr. Grant and the
  mountain N. 686.5

NESTORIANS. Shiel, *Lady*. Notes on the N. . . 695.12
NETHERLANDS, Family tour across the 389.2
— Grattan, T. C. History of the 378.8
— Wolf, J. W. Niederländische Sagen. 1013.17
  See also : Holland.
NEUROLOGICAL system of anthropology. Buchanan, J. R. 124.5
NEUTRALITY of 1793, Letters on the. Hamilton, A. 285.4
NEUVAINE, La, de la chandeleur. Nodier, C. . . . 1076.2
NEVER too late to mend, romance. Reade, C. . . 414.1–10
NEVILLE, L. Edith Allen; or, sketches of a life in Virginia. Richmond, 1855. 12° 777.6
NEVINS, W. Practical thoughts. N. Y. n.d. 16° 1109.19
— Thoughts on popery. New York. n.d. 16°. 119.27
NEW age of gold, The. Romaine, R. D. 526.2
NEWBURYPORT, Mass. Cushing, C. History and present state of 228.7
— Smith, E. V. History of 224.15
NEW Caledonia, 1774—1854. Brainne, C. 1078.50
NEW Church, Theology of the. Swedenborg, E. 1084.2
NEWCOMB, H. How to be a lady. 14th ed. Boston, 1854. 18° 469.21
— How to be a man. 14th ed. Boston, 1854. 18° 469.20
— Young lady's guide. Revised ed., with an address on female education. N. Y., 1853. 12° 1088.21
NEWCOMES, The. Thackeray, W. M. 501.1–5
NEWELL, H. Life and writings. Phila., n.d. 18° 539.23
NEW England and her institutions. By one of her sons. Boston, 1835. 12° 228.10
NEW England. Barber, J. W. History and antiquities of 237.5
— Bartlett, W. H. Founders of 223.1
— Drake, S. G. History of the discovery and settlement of 222.1
— Dwight, T. Travels in. 624.5
— Elliott, C. W. The N. E. history, 986–1776. . 223.6
— Felt, J. B. Customs of. 224.21
— - Ecclesiastical history of 1085.1
— Hubbard, W. General history of. . v.V.–VI. of 278.2
— Morton, N. Memorial of. 223.14
— Morse, J. History of 228.8
— White, H. Early history of 228.4
— Winthrop, J. History of, from 1630 to 1649 . 223.7
  See also : Plymouth and the several states, and other divisions included within N. E.
NEW England life, stories of. Russell, M. 417.9
NEW England tale, A. Sedgwick, C. M. 436.9–10
NEW family receipt-book from the records of the patent office, London. Boston, 1847. 12° . 188.4
NEW forest, The : a novel. Smith, H. 797.4
NEWFOUNDLAND in 1842. Bonnycastle, R. H. . . 629.8
— Jukes, J. B. Excursions in and about 629.9
NEW Granada. Twenty months in the Andes. Holton, I. F. 633.2
NEW Hampshire. Barstow, G. History of . . . 234.3
— Felton, A. C. Festival of the sons of, 1853. . 234.5
— Hayward, J. Gazetteer of 229.1
— Stone, J. W. Festival of the sons of, 1849 . . 234.4
  See also : the names of the following towns, etc., viz. Concord, Dublin, Gilmanton, New Ipswich, Newton, Portsmouth, White Mt's.
NEW Haven, Conn. Records of, 1638 to 1649 . . . 234.9
NEW Ipswich, N. H., History of, etc. *See* History. 234.6
NEW Jersey. Selections from the correspondence of the executive of N. J., 1776 to 1786. Newark, N. J., 1848. 8° 213.10
— Barber, J. W. History and antiquities of. . 237.5
— Gordon, T. F. Gazetteer of the state of . . . 235.7
— - The history of 235.7
NEW Jersey Historical Society. Papers of Gov. L. Morris, from 1738 to 1746. N. Y., 1852. 8° 283.2
NEW Jerusalem on earth. Porter, W. H. 1084.8
NEW Jerusalem doctrines. Swedenborg, E. von. 1084.12
NEW London, Conn., History of, 1612–1852. Caulkins, F. M. 225.3
NEWMAN, E. Introd. to the hist. of insects; new ed. of the grammar of entomology. London, 1841. 8° 175.7
NEWMAN, F. W. Regal Rome. Introd. to Rom. hist. New York, 1852. 12° 919.6

NEWMAN, J. H. Discourses to mixed congregations. Boston, 1853. 12° 1096.25
NEWMAN, S. P. Political economy. Andover, 1835. 12° 136.27
NEW Mexico. Bartlett, J. R. Explorations, etc. connected with boundary commission . . . 624.2
— Davis, W. W. H. New M. and her people. . 623.18
— Edwards, F. S. Campaign in, with Col. Doniphan. 623.20
— Sage, R. B. Scenes in 639.16
NEW Netherland. O'Callaghan, E. B. 234.8
NEW Orleans. Gleig, G. R. Brit. army at, in 1815. 899.19
— Hall, A. O. The Manhattaner in 629.15
— Walker, A. Battle of 215.15
NEW pastoral, The. Read, T. B. 325.8
NEW Plymouth. *See* Plymouth.
NEWS out of purgatory. Tarlton, R. 342.19
NEWSBOY, The. Smith, E. O. 806.2
NEWSPAPER literature, Specimens of. Buckingham, J. T. 868.3
NEW sketches of everyday life : a diary. Bremer, F. 455.2–3
NEW South Wales. Notes and sketches of. Meredith, L. A. 899.3
  See also : Australia, Victoria, etc.
NEW spirit of the age. Horne, R. H. 878.23
NEW Testament. *See* Bible.
NEWTON, I. Brewster, D. The life of 379.4
— Brougham, H. Analytical view of Newton's Principia. 147.6
— Lardner, D. N.'s optics . . . . . . v.II. of 365.14
NEWTON, J. Life, by himself, continued by R. Cecil. New York, n.d. 16° 119.24
NEWTON Forster : or, the merchant service. Marryat, Capt. F. 745.9
NEWTON, Mass., Early settlement of. Jackson, F. 227.5
NEWTOWN, Queen's county, New York, Annals of. Riker, J. jr. 224.4
NEW York aristocracy. New York, 1851. 12°. . . 868.21
NEW York city. Darby, W. Tour from the city of New York to Detroit 625.8
— Francis, J. W. Old N. Y.: or reminiscences of the past 60 years 237.3
— Minturn, R. B. jr. From N. Y. to Delhi . . . 706.9
— Valentine, D. T. History of the city of . . . 236.11
— Wallys, P. What a boy saw in his visit to. . 629.17
NEW York, State of. Barber, J. W. History and antiquities of 237.5
— Brodhead, J. R. History of, from 1609 to 1664. 234.10
— Dwight, T. Travels in 624.5
— Hammond, J. D. Hist. of political parties in. 234.13
— Irving, W. Knickerbocker's history of . . . 389.8
— O'Callaghan, E. B. Hist. of, under the Dutch. 234.8
  See also : the names of the several counties, towns, etc.: as Orange co., Long Island, etc.
NEW York Historical Society. Memoir on N. E. boundary by A. Gallatin, and speech by D. Webster, 1843. New York, 1843. 8° 297.7
NEW York speaker, The. Edgarton, W. P. 405.5
NEW world. Tappan, H. P. A step from the new world to the old 659.25
— Warburton, E. Hochelaga : or, England in . 627.19–20
  See also : Old world.
NEW Zealand. Dieffenbach, E. Travels in 705.3
— Grey, Sir G. Ancient history of the N.Z. race. 1087.20
— Rise and progress, etc., of. *See* Rise. 705.15
— Russell, M. History of 938.13
NEW Zealanders, The : containing a narrative of the first discovery. London, n.d. 12° . . . 849.1
— - Same. Boston, 1830. 12° 849.18
NGAMI, Lake. Andersson, C. J. 692.2
NIAGARA falls. Guide from, to Quebec. Hunter, W. S. jr. 629.13
NICARAGUA. Baily, J. Description of. 266.4
— Robinson, W. D. Practicability of opening a commerce at the lake of 255.1
— Squier, E. G. N.; its people, scenery, monuments, etc. 621.3
— Wells, W. V. Walker's expedition to. 266.8
NICCOLINI, G. B. Arnaldo da Brescia. Tragedia. 3a ed. Firenze, 1852. 12° 1056.8

NICCOLINI, G. B. Filippo Strozzi. Tragedia. Vita di Filippo e documenti. Firenze, 1847. 12°. 1056.9
NICCOLÒ de' Lapi, ovvero i Palleschi e i Piagnoni. Azeglio, M. d' 1056.21
NICHOL, J. P. Architecture of the heavens. New York, 1840. 12° 149.7
— - Same. 9th ed. London, 1851. 8° 144.5
— Cyclopædia of the physical sciences. London, 1857. 8° 145.8
— Phenomena and order of the solar system. From last Edinburgh ed. N. Y., 1842. 12°. 147.22
— Thoughts on the system of the world. Edinburgh, 1846. 8° 146.11
— - Same. 1st Am. ed. Boston, 1848. 12° . . 145.12
NICHOLAS I., Czar of Russia. Christmas, H. Brief memoir of his life and reign 546.20
— Gilson, A. Private life, etc. 918.16
— Lee, R. First days of 547.16
— Smucker, S. M. Reign of 546.10
NICHOLAS, Sir E. Correspondence with Charles I. Evelyn, J. 977.4
NICHOLAS Nickleby. Dickens, C. 461.24–29
NICHOLS, C. I. J. Woman's rights tracts. 878.8
NICHOLSON, A. Famine in Ireland in 1847, 1848, and 1849. New York, 1851. 12° 646.18
— Ireland's welcome to the stranger. New York, 1847. 12° 647.22
NICHOLSON, J. Operative mechanic; with supplements by Dupin, Taylor and Warr. 4th ed. London, 1853. 8° 196.8
NICHOLSON, P. Principles of architecture; also, rules for shadows. 6th ed., revised and corrected by J. Gwilt. London, 1848. 8° . . . 202.5
— Student's instructor in the five orders of architecture. New ed. London, 1845. 8° . . . 203.22
— Treatise on masonry and stone cutting. New edition. London, 1839. 8° 202.3
NICOL, J. Manual of mineralogy. Edinburgh, 1849. 12° 163.25
NICOLAS, Sir N. H. Chronology of history. London, 1833. 16° 368.2
— History of the navy of Great Britain. London, 1847. 2v. 8° 986.1
— Life and times of Sir C. Hatton. London, 1847. 8° 573.3
— Life of W. Davison. London, 1823. 8° . . . 562.4
— Junius' letters, Analysis, etc., of 848.5
NICOLAY, C. G. Physical geography. London, 1858. 12° 167.7
— Oregon territory. London, 1846. 18° 840.47
NICOLINI, G. B. History of the Jesuits. London, 1854. p.8° 835.3
NIEBUHR, B. G. Heroic tales of ancient Greece. From the German. Ed. by Felix Summerly. [H. Cole.] London, 1844. 16° 728.9
— History of Rome. Translated. New edition. London, 1851. 3v. 8° 954.6
— Lectures on ancient ethnography and geography. Translated from the German ed. of Dr. Isler, by L. Schmitz. Lond., 1853. 2v. 8° 955.3
— Lectures on Roman history. Translated by Chepmell and Demmler. London, 1852. 3v. 16° 959.8
— Life and letters. [Ed. and translated by S. Winkworth.] New York, 1852. 12° . . . 583.2
— - Same. 2d ed. London, 1852. 3v. 8° . . 583.1
— Intercourse with N. in Rome. Lieber, F. . . 588.7
NIEDERLÄNDISCHE Sagen. Wolf, J. W. 1013.17
NIEL, S. Cyclop. of history. See McBurney, I. . 947.5
NIGER. Allen, W. Expedition to the river . . . 693.9
— Lander, R. and J. Expedition to the river . 389.12
NIGHT and morning. Romance. Lytton, E. B. . 466.1–3
NIGHTS at sea, or naval life during the war. London, 1852. 16° 469.19
NIGHTS in a blockhouse. Watson, H. C. . . 733.3–4
NIGHT-SIDE of nature, or ghosts and ghost-seers. Crowe, C. 124.23
NILE. Furniss, W. Charms of the. 608.19
— Werne, F. Expedition to discover the source of the white Nile. 693.14

NILE boat, The. Bartlett, W. H. 684.1
NILE notes of a Howadji. Curtis, G. W. 608.1–5
NILES, J. M. Life of O. H. Perry, with memoir of Lawrence. 2d ed. Hartford, 1821. 12°. 527.7
NINA : a tale. Bremer, F. 817.3
NINETEENTH century, Introduction to the history of the. Gervinus, G. G. 949.12–13
NINEVEH. Bonomi, J. N. and its palaces 685.10
— Buckingham, J. S. Ruins of N. Babylon, etc. 694.16
— Fergusson, J. Palaces of N. restored 694.9
— Layard, A. H. Discov. among the ruins of.685.12–13
— - N. and its remains 685.11
— Rich, C. J. Site of ancient N. 694.7
— Vaux, W. S. W. N. and Persepolis 956.14
NISBET J. Annals of San Francisco. Soulé, F. . . 235.10
NIXON, F. R. Cruise of the Beacon in Bass's straits. London, 1857. 16° 707.9
NOAD, H. M. Chemical manipulation and analysis. New ed. London, 1852. 8° 155.9
— Manual of electricity. 4th ed. Part I. Electricity and galvanism. London, 1855. 8°. 145.12
NOBLE, G. W. Edmond Dantes. Phila., 1849. 8° 735.4
NOBLE, L. L. The course of empire. Voyage of life, etc., of T. Cole, with selections from his letters. New York, 1853. 12° 525.9
NOBLE, S. Plenary inspiration of the Scriptures asserted. Cincinnati, 1839. 12° 1086.26
NOBLE deeds of American women. Clement, J. . 538.2–3
NOCTES ambrosianæ. Wilson, J. 865.1
NODIER, C. E. Contes. Nouvelle éd. Paris, 1844. 12° 1067.5
    Contents. — Trilby ; La feé aux miettes ; Contes divers en prose; Contes en vers.
— Nouvelles. Paris, 1843. 12° 1067.6
    Contents. — Souvenirs de jeunesse; Mademoiselle de Marsan; Inès de las Sierras; [La neuvaine de la Chandeleur.]
— Romans. Paris, 1843. 12° 1067.7
    Contents. — Jean Sbogar; Le peintre de Salzbourg; La meditation du cloître; Adele; Therese Aubert.
— Souvenirs de jeunesse, suivis de M'lle de Marsan, et de La neuvaine de la Chandeleur. 6e éd. Paris, 1855. 12° 1076.2
— Souvenirs de la révolution et de l'empire. Nouv éd. Paris, 1850. 2v. 12° 1067.8
NOEL, B. W. Christian baptism. N. Y., 1850. 12° 1099.25
— Union of church and state. N. Y., 1849. 12°. 128.3
NOEL Bertram : a story for youth. May, E. J. . . 805.27
NOLTE, V. Fifty years in both hemispheres. N. York, 1854. 12° 884.5
NONCHALANT, The history of a. Jewsbury, M. J. 469.1
NON-METALLIC elements, Lectures on the. Faraday, M. 156.33
NOON-TIDE leisure. Drake, N. 746.12
NOOTKA Sound, A captivity of three years among the savages of. Jewitt, J. R. 629.31
NORDHOFF, C. Stories of the island world. New York, 1857. 16° 939.5
— Whaling and fishing. Cincinnati, 1856. 16°. 728.7
NORMAN, B. M. Rambles in Yucatan. 4th ed. N. York, 1844. 8° 621.4
NORMAN Maurice. An Am. drama. Simms, W. G. 348.1–2
NORMANS. Conquête de l'Angleterre par les Normands. Thierry, A. 1075.11
NORMANBY, Marquis of. See Phipps, C. M.
NORMANDY. Excursions in 654.14
— Musgrave, G. M. A ramble through 654.11
— St. John, J. A. Journal of a residence in . . 850.64
— Ordericus Vitalis. Ecclesiastical history of . 856.7
NORMANDY, A. Commercial handbook of chemical analysis. London, 1850. 12° 156.20
— Introduction to H. Rose's chemical analysis. London, 1849. 8° 155.13
NORRIS, M. Life and times of Mme. de Staël. London, 1853. 12° 615.11
NORRIS, S. Handbook for locomotive engineers and machinists. Philadelphia, 1852. 12°. 198.17
NORSE-FOLK, The : or, a visit to the homes of Norway and Sweden. Brace, C. L. 668.9–11
NORTH, Christopher, Recreations of. Wilson, J. 863.10

NORTH. A journey due N. Sala, G. A 666.1
NORTH, The, and the South. Chase, H 297.18
NORTH America. *See* America.
NORTHAMPTON, Brief annals of. *See* Bridgman, T. 228.3
NORTHAMPTON grave yards, Inscriptions in.
    Bridgman, T 228.3
NORTHANGER abbey: a novel. Austen, J . .v.V. of 758.3
NORTH-BRITAIN, Sketches of rambles in some
    parts of. Bigelow, A 648.16
NORTHBROOKE, J. Treatise against dicing, danc-
    ing, plays and interludes, with other idle
    pastimes. London, [1577, reprint.] 1843. 8° 342.13
NORTH Carolina. Declaration of independence by
    the citizens of Mecklenburg county. Raleigh,
    n.d. 8° 235.6
— Martin, F. X. History of 236.7
— Swain, D. L. British invasion of 235.6
— Wheeler, J. H. Hist. sketches of, 1584-1851. 235.6
NORTHCOTE, J. Fables, reëdited by Miss Corner,
    embellished by A. Crowquill. London,
    1854. 8° 735.3
— Life of Titian. London, 1830. 2v. 8° 543.3
— Memoirs of Sir J. Reynolds. Philadelphia,
    1817. 8° 556.1
NORTHEND, C. Teacher and parent. 2d ed., Bos-
    ton, 1853. 12° 137.17
NORTH-EAST passage, Voyage for the purpose of
    exploring a. Kotzebue, O. v. 702.12
NORTH-EASTERN boundary, Memoir on the 297.7
NORTH-EASTERN voyages of discovery, History
    of. Burney, J 702.15
NORTHERN antiquities. Mallet, P. H 846.2
NORTHERN mythology. Thorpe, B 1087.19
NORTHERN travel. Taylor, J. B 668.13-17
NORTHERN worthies, Lives of. Coleridge, H . . . 589.10
NORTHMEN. Smith, J. T. Discovery of America
    by the 309.6
— Wheaton, H. History of the 925.1
NORTHMORE, T. Washington: or, liberty restored.
    A poem. Baltimore, 1809. 12° 358.15
NORTH Star, Cruise of the yacht. Choules, J. O. 647.9-12
NORTH-WEST coast. Franchere, G. Voyage to
    the, 1811-14 . . . . 626.7
— Swan, J. G. Three years' residence in Wash-
    ington territory 626.5-6
NORTH-WEST passage, The. Brown, J 701.11
— Meares, J. Observations on the probable ex-
    istence of a 623.13
— Osborn, S. Discovery of a, in 1850-51 . . . . 704.4
— Parry, W. E. Three voyages for the discovery
    of a 820.22
— Ross, J. Voyage of discovery for a 703.11
    See also : Arctic, Polar, etc.
NORTHWESTERN territory, Notes on the early set-
    tlement of the. Burnet, J 236.3
— Journal of a tour into the. Harris, T. M . . 693.13
NORTH-WEST territories, History of the. Green-
    how, R 235.9
    See also : California, Oregon, etc.
NORTON, A. Evidences of the genuineness of the
    gospels. Cambridge, 1844-46. 3v. 8° . . 1093.13
— Internal evidences. Boston, 1855. 8° 1093.11
— Reasons for not believing the doctrines of
    Trinitarians. 2d ed., with additions and life.
    Boston, 1856. 12° 1086.15
— Tracts concerning Christianity. Cambridge,
    1852. 8° 1095.3

    Contents. — Defence of liberal Christianity; Extent
    and relations of theology; Thoughts on true and false
    religion; Views of Calvinism; The latest form of infi-
    delity; Modern German school of infidelity; Objec-
    tion to faith in Christianity as resting on historical
    facts and critical learning.

— A translation of the Gospels, with notes. *See*
    Bible 1093.5
NORTON, C. E. S. Altamont: or, the charity sis-
    ter. New York, 1852. 8° 802.2
— Stuart of Dunleath. New York, 1851. 8° . . 802.17
NORTON, J. Memoir of John Cotton. New York,
    1842. 18° 539.24

NORWAY. Dunham, S. A. History of 378 10
— Forbes, J. D. N. and its glaciers 663.1
— Forester, T. N. in 1848 and 1849 . . . . . . 668.3
— Hollway, J. G. A month in 669.7
— Howitt, W. and M. Literature of 404.5
— Inglis, H. D. A journey through 668.7
— Laing, S. A residence in, 1834-36 . . . . . 409.15
— Long vacation ramble, by X and Y 668.8
— Metcalfe, F. Notes of travel in the S. W. of. 666.3
— Murray, J. Handbook 649.11
— Pfeiffer, I. Travels in N 668.20
— Price, E. Norway and its scenery 825.7
— Snorro Sturleson. Chron. of the kings of . . 924.4
— Unprotected females in 668.18
— Wittich, W. A visit to the western coast of. 850.22
NORWAY, [Maine.] History of. Noyes, D 227.1
NOSES, Notes on. *See* Notes 176.8
NOTA, A., Comedies of. Goldoni, C 345.3
NOTABILITIES in France and Eng. Chasles, V. E. P. 868.7
NOTARIES public, Manual for. Roelker, B. . . . 133.5
NOTES and queries, Selections from. Milledulcia. 883.7
NOTES from books, in four essays. Taylor, H. . . 403.4
NOTES on noses. London, 1852. 16° 176.8
NOTHING new. Tales. Muloch, D. M 762.9-11
NOTHING to do: a tilt at our best society. Bos-
    ton, 1857. 12° 344.24
NOTHING to do: an accompaniment to "Nothing
    to wear." By a lady. N. Y., 1857. 12° . . 344.25
NOTHING to eat. [Poem.] Illustr. N. Y., 1857. 12° 344.23
NOTHING to say. Thomson, M. M 344.26
NOTHING to wear. Butler, W. A 344.22
NOTICES to correspondents, consisting of ten
    thousand answ. to quest. London, n.d. 16° 885.11
NOTRE Dame de Paris. Hugo, V 1075.40
NOTT, J. C. and Gliddon, G. R. Indigenous races
    of the earth. Monographs by Maury, Pulsz-
    ky, and Meigs. Philadelphia, 1857. 8° . . 171.2
— Types of mankind: or, ethnolog. researches.
    Philadelphia, 1854. 8° 173.1-2
NOTT, Sam'l, jr. Sermons from the fowls of the
    air and the lilies of the field. 2d ed. Bos-
    ton, 1835. 12° 1099.8
NOUVELLE-CALÉDONIE. Voyages, missions,
    mœurs, colonisation. Brainne, C 1078.50
NOVA Scotia. Dawson, J. W. Acadian geology. 163.23
— Haliburton, T. C. Historical and statistical
    account of 265.2
— Lyell, C. Geological observations on 628.1
— Williams, C. R. Exiles of 217.12
NOVELTIES, inventions, and curiosities, in arts and
    manufactures. 3d ed. London, 1853. 16° 199.26&30
NOVUM organum. Bacon, F 825.7
NOW-A-DAYS. New York, 1854. 12° 794.19
Now and then: a novel. Warren, S. 767.15-17
Now or never: a story. Adams, W. T 729.4-6
NOYCE, E. The boy's book of industrial inform-
    ation. London, 1858. 12° 196.15
NOYES, D. The history of Norway, [Maine.]
    Norway, 1852. 8° 227.1
NOYES, G. R. Collection of theological essays
    from various authors. Boston, 1856. 12° . 1096.7
— New translation of the Hebrew prophets.
    See Bible 118.7
NOYES, J. O. Roumania, the border land of the
    Christian and the Turk. N. York, 1857. 12° 686.14
NUBIA, Belzoni, G. Operations and discov. in. 693.12
— Hahn-Hahn, I. Travels in 687.10
— Irby, C. L. Travels in 889.25
— Madden, R. R. Travels in 687.9
— Prime, W. C. Boat-life in 698.8-12
— Russell, M. N. and Abyssinia 810.61
— Saint John, J. A. N. and Egypt 693.5
NUGENT, *Lord. See* Grenville, G. N. T.
NUMA Pompilius. *See* Florian, J. P. C 1079.5
NUMBER and magnitude, The connexion of. De
    Morgan, A 147.16
NUNNERIES *See* Convents.
NUTRITION, Theory of. Sunderland, L 157.31
NUTTALL, T. Introduction to botany. Boston,
    1827. 12° 169.1

NUTTALL, T. Introduction to botany. 2d ed., with additions. Cambridge, 1830. 12° 169.2
— Travels into Arkansas territory, 1819. Philadelphia, 1821. 8° 624.8

OAKFIELD: or, fellowship in the East. Arnold, W. D. 418.6-7
OAK-OPENINGS: or, the bee hunter. Cooper, J.F. 770.41-44
OAK tree, Tale of an. Poem. Marsh, A. 469.9
OASIS, The. Child, L. M. 139.17
OASIS of Jupiter Ammon. St. John, B. 608.21
OBERKIRCH, Baroness H. L. d'. Memoirs by herself. London, 1852. 3v. 8° 546.12
OBERLIN, J. F. Memoirs. Transl. by C. F. Barnard. 2d Am. ed. Boston, 1845. 16° . . . 545.22
OBERON: a poem. Wieland, C. M. 315.15
OBERON'S vision compared with Lylie's Endymion. Halpin, N. J. 342.15
O'BRIEN, P. Journal of a residence in the Danubian principalities, 1853. London, 1854. 12° 663.12
O'BRIEN, W. S. Principles of government, with notes. Am. ed. Boston, 1856. 12° 135.17
OBSOLETE and provincial English, Dictionary of. Wright, T. 855.7
OBSTETRICS. See Medicine.
O'CALLAGHAN, E. B. Hist. of New Netherland: or, N. Y. under the Dutch. N. Y., 1846. 8° . 234.8
OCCULT sciences. Salverte, E. 125.24
— Smedley, E. 125.5
OCEAN, The. Gosse, P. H. 178.10-11
— Higginson, F. The O., its depths and phenom. 146.14
— Kingsley, C. Glaucus, or the wonders of the shore 178.27
See also: Aquarium.
OCKLEY, S. History of the Saracens. 5th ed. London, 1848. p.8° 828.5
O'CONNELL, J. Recollections during a parliamentary career, 1833 to 1848. Lond., 1849. 2v. 12° 988.4
O'CONNOR, A. State of Ireland. London, 1843. 8° 647.6
O'CONNOR, T. War between the U. States and G. Britain, 1812-15. 3d ed. N. Y., 1816. 12° 217.7
— - Same. 2d ed. New York, 1815. 12°. . . 217.6
OCTAGON mode of building. Fowler, O. S. 207.10
ODOHERTY papers. Maginn, W. 867.7
ŒDIPUS: a musical drama, transl. Sophocles . . 355.11
OEHLENSCHLÄGER. See Öhlenschläger.
OERSTED. See Örsted.
OFEN, Wiedereroberung von. Roman. Pichler, C. 1025.9
OGG, Mr. Heat. Lib. Us. Kn. . . . . .v.I. of 365.14
OGILVIES, The: a novel. Muloch, D. M. v.I. of 762.1-2
OGLETHORPE, J. Harris, T. M. Memorials of . 513.10
— Sparks, J. Life of, by W. B. O. Peabody. v.XII. of 529.1
OHIO river, Course of the. Beltrami, J. C. 625.18
OHIO valley. Hildreth, S. P. First examination. 245.3
OHIO, State of. Harris, T. M. Geographical and historical account of. 639.13
— Taylor, J. W. History of, 1650-1787 . . . . . 237.4
ÖHLENSCHLÄGER, A. G. Aladdin: a dramatic poem, transl. by T. Martin. Lond., 1857. 12° 334.23
— Correggio, tragedy,[and] Sappho, by Grillparzer, with autobiography of Öhlenschläger. Boston, 1846. 12° 489.16
— Étude biographique. Deumier, J. Le F. . . . 1078.23
OJIBBEWAY Indians in Europe 645.4
OJIBWAY nation, Traditional history of. Copway, G. 249.1
O'KEEFFE, J. Recollections. London, 1826. 2v. 8° 597.2
OKEN, L. Elements of physio-philosophy. London, 1847. 8° 166.2
OLCOTT, H. A. The torchlight: or, through the wood. New York, 1856. 12° 428.11
OLCOTT, H. S. Sorgho and imphee: the sugar canes. New York, 1857. 12° 166.12
OLD bachelor, The. Wirt, W. 850.30
OLD brewery, The, and the new mission house at the five points. New York, 1854. 12° . . . 808.13
OLD curiosity shop, The. Dickens, C. 461.17-23
OLD elm, The, and the fountain on Boston common. Burnham, E. J. 349.12
OLD engagement, The: a spinster's story. Day, J. 478.14

OLDFIELD, A. Faithful memoirs of. Egerton, W. 597.6
OLD Jolliffe: a story. Mackarness, M. 476.7-8
OLD Mortality. Scott, Sir W. 460.22-26
OLD Nick: a satirical story. Dubois, E. 709.12
OLD portraits and modern sketches. Whittier, J. G. 887.6
OLD red sandstone. Miller, H. 167.24-26
OLD sports of England. London, 1835. 16° . . . 589.14
OLD Testament canon, Critical history and defence of. Stuart, M. 1097.24
OLD and New Testament, The, connected in the history of the Jews. Prideaux, H. 1093.12
OLD world, The, and the new. Dewey, O. 669.1
OLD world, The, and the new: a novel. Trolloppe, F. 807.4
OLIN, S. Life and letters. N. Y., 1853. 2v. 12° . 534.19
OLIPHANT, L. Journey to Katmandu. London, 1852. 16° 709.17
— - Same. New York, 1852. 12° 709.12
— Minnesota and the far West. Edinburgh, 1855. 8° 236.10
— Russian shores of the Black sea in 1852. New York, 1854. 12° 689.3-5
— - Same. Edinburgh, 1853. 8° 674.2
OLIPHANT, M. Adam Graeme of Mossgray. New York, n.d. 12° 753.13
— Days of my life: an autobiography. New York, 1857. 12° 753.6-10
— Magdalen Hepburn. A story of the Scottish reformation. New York, n.d. 12° . . . 753.11
— Margaret Maitland. N. Y., 1851. 12°. . . . 753.12
— The Athelings: [a romance.] New York, 1857. 8° 753.5
— Zaidee: a romance. Boston, 1856. 8° . . . 753.1-4
OLIVE: a novel. Muloch, D. M. . . . . . .v.I.of 762.1-2
OLIVER, P. Puritan commonwealth, of Massachusetts. Boston, 1856. 8°. 223.4
OLIVER Cromwell: a novel. Herbert, H. W. . . . 558.5
OLIVER Newman: a N. E. tale in verse. Southey, R. 349.20
OLIVER Optic. Pseud. See Adams, W. T.
OLIVER Twist, Adventures of. Dickens, C. 461.6-10
OLLAPODIANA papers. Clark, W. G. 873.5
OLMSTED, D. Compendium of astronomy. New York, 1839. 12° 149.8-9
— Introduction to astronomy. Stereotype ed. New York, 1850. 8° 146.4
— Letters on astronomy. Boston, 1840. 12° . 149.11-12
OLMSTED, F. L. Journey in the seaboard slave states. New York, 1856. 12°. 627.5
— Journey through Texas. N. Y., 1857. 12° . .627.6-11
— Walks and talks of an American farmer in England. Part I.-II. N. Y., 1852-57. 12° . .646.10-11
OLNEY, S. Life of. Williams, C. R. 528.12
OLYMPIODORUS. Life of Plato. See Plato.v.VI. of 814.3
OMALIUS d'Halloy, J. J. d'. Des races humaines. Bruxelles, n.d. 12° 1065.43
— Géologie. Bruxelles, n.d. 12° 1065.42
— Minéralogie. Bruxelles, n.d. 12° 1065.41
O'MEARA, B. E. Napoleon in exile. New York, 1853. 2v. 12° 605.8-9
OMNIBUS of modern romance. N. Y., 1844. 2v. 8° 801.2-3
Contents.—Vol. I. The princess of Wolfenbuttel, by H. Zschokke; The post-captain; Camille, tr. from the Fr. of V. Mangin; The fatal whisper, by J. Galt; The sisters; The curate, by F. Bremer. II. Frank Heartwell, or fifty years ago, by B Tiller; First and second love, by H. C. Crawford; The goldsmith of Paris, tr. from the German of E. T. A. Hoffmann; Rolandsitten, or the deed of entail, tr. from the German of E. T. A. Hoffmann; The wife hunter, tr. from the German of Caroline Pichler; The modern Lothario, by the Baroness la Motte Fouqué.

OMOO. Adventures in the South seas. Melville, H. 736.1
OMPHALOS. An attempt to untie the geological knot. Gosse, P. H. 163.17
ONDERDONK, H. jr. Revolutionary incidents of Queen's county, N. Y. New York, 1846. 12° 217.17
ONE fault: a novel. Trollope, F. 787.8
ONE year: a tale of wedlock. Carlen, E. F. . . . 766.4-5
ONLY: a tale for young and old. Mackarness, M. 476.7-8

ONLY a fiddler: a novel. Andersen, H. C. 766.8
ONTWA, the son of the forest: a poem. Lawson, J. 349.1
ONYX ring, The: a fiction. Sterling, J. 756.11
OPERATIVE mechanic. Nicholson, J. 196.8
OPIE, A. Complete works. Phila., 1853. 3v. 8° 801.4–6

Contents. — Vol. I. Madeline; Adeline Mowbray;
The black velvet pelisse; The death-bed; The fashionable wife, and untashionable husband; The robber; The mother and son; Love and duty; The soldier's return; The brother and sister; The revenge;
The uncle and nephew; Murder will out; The
orphan; The father and daughter; Happy faces, or
benevolence and selfishness. II. Lady Anne and
Lady Jane; Austin and his wife; The mysterious
stranger; Appearance is against her; Valentine's eve;
Mrs. Arlington, or all is not gold that glitters; Propo-
sals of marriage; White lies; Henry Woodville; The
quaker and the young man of the world; A tale of
trials, told to my children; The ruffian boy; The welcome home, or the ball. III. Temper: A woman's
love; A wife's duty; The two sons; The opposite
neighbor; Love, mystery, and superstition; After the
ball, or the two Sir Williams; False or true, or the
journey to London; The confessions of an odd-tem-
pered man; Illustrations of lying, in all its branches.

— All is not gold that glitters. Lond., 1846. 18° 469.28–29
— Appearance is against her: a tale. London,
        1847. 18° 469.38–39
— A wife's duty: a tale. London, 1847. 18° . 469.36–37
— Brother and sister [and Henry Woodville.]
        London, 1847. 18° 469.34–35
— Father and daughter. London, 1845. 18° . . 469.42
— Father and son, and other tales. London,
        1845. 18° 469.43
— Happy faces [and The revenge.] London,
        1847. 18° 469.32–33
— Love and duty: a tale [and Confessions of an
        odd-tempered man.] London, 1847. 18° . . 469.44
— Mysterious stranger and The orphan [also
        Black velvet pelisse.] London, 1846. 18°. 469.48
— Opposite neighbor, and Woman's love. Lon-
        don, 1847. 18° 469.46–47
— Ruffian boy: a tale, [and "After the ball."]
        London, 1846. 18° 469.45
— Stage coach, and other tales. Lond., 1845. 18° 469.30–31
— White lies. Tales. London, 1847. 18° . . 469.40–41
— Memorials of the life of. Brightwell, C. L. . 595.4
OPIE, J. Lectures on painting. Barry, J. 816.2
OPINIONS, Formation and public. of. Bailey, S. 125.18
OPIUM-EATER, Confessions of an English. De
        Quincey, T. 895.2–6
OPIUM trade. Evils of the. Sirr, H. C. 696.2
OPOSSUMS, The natural history of. Menageries . 839.17
OPPOSITE neighbor: a tale. Opie, A. 469.46–47
OPTICAL instruments. Description of by A.
        Pritchard 365.14
OPTICS. Brewster, Sir D. A treatise on 149.35
— - Optics. Lib. Us. Kn. 365.14
— Ferguson, J. Lectures on selected subjects in. 146.8
— Galbraith, I. Manual of 149.33
— Lardner, D. Newton's optics 365.14
— Pereira, J. Lectures on polarized light . . 156.29
— Woodward, C. Introduction to the study of
        polarized light 145.21
        See also: Microscope, Light, Eyes, etc.
OPTIMIST, The: a series of essays. Tuckerman,
        H. T. 898.9
ORANGE county, N. Y., History of. Eager, S. W. 236.12
ORATORS, Dialogue on. Tacitus, C. C. . . v. II. of 834.1
ORATORS in America. Magoon, E. L. 518.16
ORATORS of Boston, The hundred. Loring, J. S. 282.5–6
ORATORS of France. Cormenin, L. M. de la H. . 617.9
ORATORS of the American revolution. Magoon,
        E. L. 528.1
ORATOR'S touchstone, The. McQueen, H. 405.8
ORATORY. Cicero, M. T. O. and orators 844.9
— Quintilianus, M. F. Institutes of 854.1
— Tacitus, C. Dialogue concerning. 872.11
        See also: Eloquence, Elocution, Rhetoric.
ORBS, The, of heaven. Mitchell, O. M. 879.11
ORCHARDIST, The new American. Kenrick, W. . 169.7
        See also: Agriculture.

ORDERICUS Vitalis. Ecclesiastical history of Eng.
        and Normandy. Tr. Lond., 1853–54. 2v. p.8° 856.7
OREGON. Greenhow, R. History of. 235.9
— Hines, G. Oregon, its history, condition and
        prospects. 637.4
— Johnson, T. T. California and 239.8
— Nicolay, C. G. An account of 840.47
— Palmer, J. O., its inhabitants, climate, soil, etc. 627.21
— Parkman, F. jr. Sketches of the O. trail . . 626.12–14
— Sage, R. B. Scenes in 639.16
        See also: North-west territory.
ORGAN, The. Hopkins, E. J. Its history, etc... 204.3
— Seidel, J. J. The O. and its construction . . 204.8
        See also: Music.
ORGANIC analysis, Handbook of. Liebig, J. . . . 156.23
        See also: Chemistry.
ORGANON, The: or, logical treatises. Aristoteles. 834.12
ORIENT, Poems of the. Taylor, J. B. 345.21
        See also: East.
ORIENTAL acquaintance; or, letters from Syria.
        DeForest, J. W. 687.17
ORLANDO Furioso. Ariosto, L. 345.2
ORLEANS, Mass., History of. Pratt, E. 224.22
ORLEANS, House of. Taylor, W. C. 1005.4
ORLÉANS, Histoire du siège d'. Quicherat, J. . . 1078.42
ORLICH, L. v. Travels in India. Translated by
        H. E. Lloyd. London, 1845. 2v. 8°. . . . 695.3
ORMOND: or, the secret witness. Brown, C. B. . 757.2
ORNITHOLOGY. Gosse, P. H. Popular British . 178.17
— Jardine, Sir W. . . . . v. I.–XIV. of 179.1
— Knox, A. E. Game birds and wild fowl . . . 177.11
— - Ornithological rambles in Sussex 177.16
— Laishley, R. Popular history of British birds'
        eggs 177.27
— Martin, W. C. L. General history of hum-
        ming-birds 179.2
— Mudie, R. Feathered tribes of the British
        Islands 825.12
— Wilson, A. American 172.4
        See also: Birds.
OROSIUS, Anglo-Saxon version of, by Alfred.
        Pauli, R. 856.4
ORPHAN, The. Opie, A. 469.48
ORPHAN niece, The. Novel. Pickering, E. 805.4
ORSINI, F. Austrian dungeons in Italy. Transl.
        London, 1856. 16° 919.7
ÖRSTED, H. C. Soul in nature, with supplement-
        ary contributions and life. Lond., 1852. p.8° 816.15
ORSUA, The expedition of. Southey, R. 266.9
ORTHOPHONY: or, vocal culture in elocution.
        Murdoch, J. E. 137.10
ORTON, J. R. Camp fires of the red men. New
        York, 1855. 12° 736.12
ORTON, J. W. Miner's guide and metallurgist's
        directory. New York, 1849. 12° 199.35
OSBORN, S. Discovery of the N. W. passage, by
        Capt. R. Le M. M'Clure. London, 1856. 8° 704.4
— Quedah: or, stray leaves from a journal in
        Malayan waters. London, 1857. 12° . . . 708.13
— Stray leaves from an Arctic journal, 1850–51.
        New York, 1852. 12° 709.7–8
OSBORNE, F. Memoirs of the reigns of Queen
        Elizabeth and James I. 552.6
OSBURN, W. Monumental history of Egypt. Lon-
        don, 1854. 2v. 8° 955.1
OSCANYAN, C. The sultan and his people. New
        York, 1857. 12° 686.13
OSCEOLA, the Seminole. Reid, M. 716.11–14
OSGOOD, F. S. Wreath of wild flowers from New
        England. London, 1838. 12° 348.10
OSGOOD, S. God with men. Boston, 1853. 12° . 117.8
— The hearth stone. New York, 1854. 12° . 886.4–6
— Mile-stones in our life-journey. New York,
        1855. 12° 1088.22
OSLER, E. Life of Admiral Vis. Exmouth. Lon-
        don, 1835. 12° 568.10
OSSIAN. Poems; transl. by Macpherson, with dis-
        sertation on the era and poems of O. by
        Blair, etc. New York, 1841. 12° 315.10–11
— - Same. New ed. London, 1790. 2v. 8°. 315.8

OSSOLI, S. M. F. d'. At home and abroad: or, America and Europe. Edited by A. B. Fuller. 2d ed. Boston, 1856. 12° 654.5–6
— Literature and art; with introduction by H. Greeley. New York, 1852. 12° 403.18
— Memoirs. [Prepared by Rev. J. F. Clarke, Rev. F. H. Hedge, W. H. Channing, and R. W. Emerson.] Boston, 1852. 2v. 12° ... 538.9–10
— Woman in the 19th century. Edited by A. B. Fuller, with introduction by H. Greeley. Boston, 1857. 12° 885.10
OSTEOLOGY; Analytical view of the researches on fossil. Brougham, H. 840.8
See also: Anatomy, compar., and Geology.
OTHEMAN, E. Memoirs and writings of H. M. Pickard. Boston, 1845. 12° 538.1
OTHER side, The; or notes for the hist. of the war between Mexico and the United States. Transl. by A. C. Ramsay. N. Y., 1850. 12° 259.3
OTIS, Mrs. H. G. The Barclays of Boston. Boston, 1854. 12° 417.2–7
OTIS, J. Life of. By F. Bowen ...... v.XII. of 529.1
— Life of. Tudor, W. 513.3
OTRANTO, The castle of. Walpole, H. 758.1
OTTER, W. Life and remains of E. D. Clarke. New York, 1827. 8° 583.10
OTTO der Schütz, Rhein. Geschichte. Kinkel, J. G. 1039.4
OTTOMAN empire. Jacob, S. History of. ... 956.11
— Ranke, L. In the 16th and 17th centuries . . 913.1
— Upham, E. History of the 830.49
See also: Turkey.
OTWAY, T. Works. With a life, enlarged from that of Dr. Johnson. London, 1812. 2v. 8° 353.10
Contents. — Vol. I. Alcibiades; Don Carlos; Prince of Spain; Titus and Berenice, with the cheats of Scapin; Friendship in fashion; Soldier's fortune. II. The atheist, or the second part of the Soldier's fortune; The orphan; History and fall of Caius Marius; Venice preserved; Poems and letters.
OUDE, tour through. Sleeman, W. H. 707.5
See also: India.
OUR college, from an undergraduate's scribbling book. London, 1857. 12° 885.3
OUR first families. A novel. Phila., 1855. 12° .. 428.8
OUR parish; or annals of pastor and people. Boston, 1854. 12° 417.11–12
OUR village. Mitford, M. R. 864.4
OUTLINES of Irish history. London, 1829. 12° .. 989.4
OUTRE-MER. Longfellow, H. W. 658.18–20
OVERMAN, F. Manufacture of iron [and a chapter on steel.] Philadelphia, 1850. 8° 195.6
— Manufacture of steel. Philadelphia, 1851. 12° 199.12
— Moulder's and founder's pocket guide. Philadelphia, 1851. 12° 199.6
— Practical mineralogy, assaying and mining. Philadelphia, 1851. 12° 197.16
— Treatise on metallurgy. New York, 1852. 8° 195.7
OVIDIUS Naso, P. Ovid, transl. by Dryden, Pope, Congreve, Addison, and others. N. York, 1852. 2v. 18° 830.17
— Fasti, Tristia, etc. Transl. by H. T. Riley. London, 1851. p.8° 824.6
— Heroïdes, etc. Transl. by H. T. Riley. London, 1852. p.8° 824.8
— Metamorphoseon, libri XV. cum ver. Angl. By J. Clarke. 8th ed. Glocester, 1790. 8° 357.2
— Metamorphoses, in Eng. prose; with the Latin text and notes. 3d ed. London, 1759. 8° 357.1
— Metamorphoses. Tr. into Eng. prose by H. T. Riley. London, 1851. p.8° 824.7
— Fables. Dryden, J. 315.17
OWEN, J. Forgiveness of sin. New York, n.d. 12° 1109.3
OWEN, R. Anatomy and physiology of invertebrate animals. London, 1843. 8° 172.15
— Anatomy and physiology of vertebrate animals. Pt. I. Fishes. London, 1846. 8° .. 172.16
— History of British fossil mammals and birds. London, 1846. 8° 172.21
— Principal forms of the skeleton and of the teeth. Philadelphia, 1854. 12° 177.5
— Lecture on animal products. 199.16

OWEN, W. F. W. Voyages to the shores of Africa, Arabia, and Madagascar. Lond., 1833. 2v. 8° 702.8
OXFORD prize poems. 8th ed. Oxford, 1834. 12° 349.15
OXFORD, Conn. History of. Cothren, W. 225.2
OXONIAN, The, in Thelemarken. Metcalfe, F. ... 666.3

PAALZOW, A. v. Godwie castle. [Roman.] Breslau. 1855. 3v. 16° 1017.5
— Jakob van der Nees [Roman.] Breslau, 1855. 3v. 16° 1017.8
— Ste. Roche. [Roman.] Breslau, 1855. 3v. 16° 1017.6
— Thomas Thyrnau. [Roman.] Breslau, 1855. 3v. 16° 1017.7
PACHA of many tales. Marryat, F. 745.2
PACIFIC. Bates, D. B. Four years on the P. coast. 708.12
— Beechey, F. W. Voyage to the 702.13
— Cheever, H. T. The island-world of the ... 705.11
— Erskine, J. E. Cruise among the islands of the Western 696.7
— Hines, G. Life on the plains of the 637.4
— Jacobs, T. J. Scenes, incidents, and adventures in the 708.11
See also: South seas.
PAGE, H. Memoir of. Hallock, W. A. 1109.15
PAGE, J. W. Uncle Robin in his cabin, and Tom without one. 2d ed. Richmond, 1853. 12° 796.12
PAGET, J. Hungary and Transylvania. Fr. new London ed. Philadelphia, 1850. 12° . . . 667.16
PAGGI, i fratelli, di Genova. Discorso. Bottari, G. 1059.13
PAINE, M. Materia medica and therapeutics. New York, 1848. 12° 153.9
— The soul and instinct: a discourse. Enl. ed. New York, 1849. 12° 125.10
PAINE, R. T. jr. Works in verse and prose. Boston, 1812. 8° 524.17
Contents. — Life; College exercises; Miscellaneous poems; Odes and songs; Orations; Theatrical criticisms; Sketch of Spain.
PAINE, T. Political writings. Middletown, N. J., 1837. 2v. 8° 287.3
Contents. — Vol. I. Life of Paine; Common sense; Epistle to the Quakers; The crisis; Public good; Letter to the Abbé Raynal; Letter to Washington; Letter from Washington to Paine; On government, etc.; Address from Bordentown; Invasion of England; To the inhabitants of La.; To the citizens of Pa. on the proposal for calling a convention; Polit. and mil. affairs of Europe; English navy; Gov. Lewis's speech; Of gun boats, etc.; Resolutions of Mr. Hale; Letters to Lewis on prosecution of Farmer; "Will there be war"? Royal pedigree. II. Prospects on the Rubicon; Rights of man; Letter to the authors of the Republican; Letter to the Abbé Sieyes; Address to the addressers; Letters to Lord Onslow; First principles of government; Speech in French nat. convention; Letters to Mr. Sec. Dundas; English system of finance; To the people of France; Reasons for preserving the life of Louis Capet; Agrarian justice; Letter to the sheriff of Sussex; Letters to Macdonald; Propriety of bringing Louis XVI. to trial, and on the respite of sentence; Louisiana and emissaries; Challenge to the federalists; Liberty of the press; Cullen, alias Carpenter; Affairs of England; Cheetham; Letter to Dr. Mitchell; To the citizens of N. Y.; To the federal faction; Memorial to Congress; To the speaker of the Ho. of Reps.
— Life of. Cheetham, J. 513.14
PAINTER, gilder, and varnisher's companion. 2d ed. Philadelphia, 1851. 12° 199.11
PAINTERS. Jervis-White-Jervis, Lady M. Boyhood of great. 548.14
— Lee, H. F. Historical sketches of the old . . 209.13
— Leslie, C. R. A hand-book for young. . . . 208.17
— Ruskin, J. Modern 206.4–7
— Vasari, G. Lives of the most eminent 848.6
PAINTING. Allston, W. Lectures on art 208.10
— Barry, J., Fuseli, H. and Opie, J. Lectures on. 816.2
— Bottari, G. Lettere sulla pittura 1049.1
— Dodge, P. P., its rise and progress 208.15
— Eastlake, C. L. A history of oil P. 205.1
— Field, G. Grammar of colouring 819.19
— Harris, J. Treatise concerning 209.4
— Jameson, A. The progress of, in Italy ... 840.23

PAINTING. Jarves, J. J. Art hints 208.16
— Lessing, G. E. Limits of 209.14
— Martel, C. Colouring in 208.8
— Memes, J. S. History of 830.48
— Phillips, T. History and principles of . . . 205.2
— Reynolds, Sir J. Discourses on 858.4
— Ruskin, J. Lecture on 203.2
— - Pre-Raphaelitism 206.3
— Wornum, R. N. The epochs of 850.23
PAINTING on glass. Fromberg, E. O. Essay on
the art of 819.28
— Gessert, M. A. Rudimentary treatise on . . 819.27
See also: Æsthetics, Beauty, Colors, Fine
Arts, Taste, etc.; and for the different
schools of painting, see their several
names.
PAJON, H. Contes. Cabinet des Fées. v.XXXIV. of 1077.1
PALESTINE. Chateaubriand, R. F. A. de. Travels
in P. in 1806-7 . . . . 685.7
— Madden, R. R. Travels in 687.9
— Pierpont, J. Airs of P.: a poem 369.17
— Robinson, E. Biblical researches in 1103.7
— Russell, M. P. from the earliest period . . 810.33
— Three weeks in 689.16
— Stanley, A. P. P. and Sinai 684.7
— Stewart, R. W. Journey to 685.3
— Upham, T. C. Letters from 657.5
— Van de Velde, C. W. M. Journey through . 694.13
— Wright, T. Early travels in 846.7
See also: Holy Land, East, etc.
PALEY, W. Works. new ed. Phila.. n.d. 8° . . 113.6
Contents. — Life; Moral and political philosophy;
Evidences of Christianity; Natural theology; Tracts;
Horæ Paulinæ; Clergyman's companion; Sermons.
— Evidences of Christianity, with life of the au-
thor. New York, 1824. 32° 1099.34
— Horæ Paulinæ [and] Clergyman's companion.
New York, 1824. 32° 1099.37
— Moral and polit. philosophy. N. Y., 1824. 32° 1099.35
— Natural theology with notes, etc., by Lord
Brougham and Sir Ch. Bell. Lond., 1845-51.
4v. 18° 840.49
— - Same. With notes, etc., by Brougham,
Bell, and Potter. New York, 1847. 2v. 18° 820.4
— - Nat. theol. and tracts. N. Y., 1824. 32° . 1099.36
— Sermons. N. Y., 1824. 32° 1099.38
PALFREY, J. G. Lowell lectures on the evi-
dences of Christianity, with life of J. Low-
ell, jr., by E. Everett. Boston, 1843. 2v. 8° 1083.17
— Relation between Judaism and Christianity.
Boston, 1854. 8° 1083.16
PALFREY, W., Life of. By J. G. Palfrey. v. XVII. of 529.1
PALGRAVE, F. History of the Anglo-Saxons.
London, 1837. 16° 389.17
PALISSY, B., Life of. Morley, H. 546-17
PALMER, J. Travels over the Rocky mts. to the
mouth of the Columbia river. Cin., 1852. 12° 627.21
PALO Alto, Battle of. Thorpe, T. B. 259.6
PALOMBE, ou la femme honorable. Camus, J. P. 1078.12
PAMBOUR, F. M. G. de. Treatise on locomotive
engines. 2d ed. London, 1840. 8° 195.15
PAMPAS, Journeys across the. Head, F. B. . . . 889.22
PAMELA: a novel. Richardson, S. . . . . v.I.-IV. of 768.1
PANAMA. Griswold, C. D. Isthmus of. 629.16
— Tomes, R. P. in 1855 . . . . 629.26
PANIDÉA: or, an omnipresent reason. Durfee, J. 122.8
PANORAMA and other poems. Whittier, J. G. . . 345.9
PANORAMIC view from Bunker hill monument.
Boston, 1848. sm.4° 235.15
PANTOLOGY: a survey of human knowledge.
Park, R. 194.10
PANTOMIME, The, of life. Dickens, C. 402.1
PANZANI, A. Misteri di Firenze. Firenze, 1854.
2v. 16° 1057.7
PAPAL conspiracy exposed. Beecher, E. 1098.9
PAPAL states, Handbook of the. Blewitt, O. . . . 649.6
PAPER currencies. Hildreth, R. 136.23
PAPER money, Essays on. McCulloch, J. R. . . . 135.4
See Bank, Political economy, etc.
PAPERS for the people. Chambers, W. 386.1-2
PARA: or, the banks of the Amazon. Warren, J. E. 636.30-31

PARABLES. Cumming, J. Lectures on our Lord's. 116.5
— Krummacher, F. A. 736.13
— Trench, R. C. P. of our Lord 1093.9
— Notes and illustrations of the parables of the
New Testament. 1089.15
See also: Bible.
PARADISE lost. Milton, J. 359.2
— Hayley, W. Conjectures on the origin of . . 583.8
— Todd, H. J. Inquiry into the origin of . . . 583.7
PARAGREENS in Paris. Reßßßini, G. 755.12
PARAGUAY. Dobrizhoffer, M. Account of the Abi-
pones of 266.2
— Mausfield, C. B. 635.10
— Rengger, J. R. Dr. Francia's reign in 266.3
— Robertson, J. P. and W. P. Letters on . . . 635.11
PARDEE, R. G. Manual for the cultivation of the
strawberry, etc. 3d rev. ed. New York,
1856. 12° 165.26
PARDOE, J. City of the Magyar. Hungary in
1839-40. London, 1840. 3v. 12° 928.1
— City of the Sultan. 4th ed. Lond., 1854. 16° 689.17
— Court and reign of Francis I., king of France.
Philadelphia, 1849. 2v. 12° 616.2
— Life of Marie de Medicis. 2d ed. London,
1852. 3v. 8° 543.1
— Louis XIV. and the court of France in the
17th century. New York, 1848-55. 2v. 12°. 616.3-9
— Reginald Lyle: a novel. New York, 1854. 12° 416.8
— The rival beauties: a novel. N. Y., 1855. 8°. 802.42
— The river and the desert. Phila., 1858. 2v. 12° 608.21
PARDONER and frère: a play, by J. Heywood. . . 356.1
PAREA, A. Novelle di. See Soave, F. 1058.2
PARINI, G. Versi e prose. Firenze, 1856. 12°. . 1056.12
Contents. — Su la vita e le opere di G. Parini; Il
giorno, poema; Poesie liriche; Poesie piscevoli; Poe-
sie pastorali, campestri e pescatorie; Versi sciolti;
Poesie drammatiche; Saggi di traduzione libere;
Frammenti; Prose; Della nobiltà, dialogo; De'
principii delle belle lettere.
PARIS and its historical scenes. London, n.d
2v. 12° 849.2
— - Same. Boston, 1831. 2v. 12° 849.19
— - Same. New ed. London, 1849. 18° . . . 840.50
PARIS. Abbott, J. Rollo in 659.8
— Gay and Girardin, Mmes. Parisian letters. . 609.5
— Head, F. B. Paris in 1851 . . . . 654.18
— Jarves, J. J. Parisian sights and French
principles. 654.17
— Junot, L. P. Histoire des salons de 1068.15
— Lyman, T. P. during the residence of the al-
lied sovereigns 1009.16
— Mercier, L. S. Tableau de 1076.1
— Phipps, C. H. P. in 1848 . . . . 1002.4
— Sanderson, J. The American in 654.15
— Steffens, H. Adventures on the road to . . . 899.12
— Thackeray, W. M. P. sketch book 509.5-7
— Tricolored sketches in, 1851-2-3 . . . . . . 1008.8
— Trollope, F. P. and the Parisians in 1835 . . 657.1-2
PARISH, E. History of New England. Morse, J. 228.8
PARISH, The: a tale. Martineau, H. 749.4
PARK, H. G. A voice from the parsonage, with an
introductory chapter by E. A. Park. 2d ed.
Boston, 1855. 12° 417.8
PARK, L. J. Memoir of Eliz. Carter. Boston,
1841. 16° 599.10
PARK, M. Life and travels of, with later discover-
ies. New York, n.d. 18° 820.11
PARK, R. Juvenile and miscellaneous poems.
Philadelphia, 1836. 12° 349.11
— Pantology: or, a systematic survey of human
knowledge. Philadelphia, 1841. 8° 194.10
PARKER, E. G. Golden age of American oratory.
Boston, 1857. 12° 866.3
PARKER, E. H. The mother's hand-book. New
York, 1857. 12° 157.15
PARKER, N. H. Iowa handbook for 1856. Boston,
1856. 12° 237.16
— Minnesota handbook for 1856-57. Boston,
1857. 12° 237.18
PARKER, S. Tour beyond the Rocky mountains,
1835-37. Ithaca, N. Y., 1838. 12° 628.8

PARKER, T. Discourse of matters pertaining to
religion. 3d ed. Boston, 1847. 12°. . . . 1086.20
— Public function of woman 878.8
— Sermons of theism, atheism, and the popular
theology. Boston, 1853. 12°. 1086.19
— Opinions of, reviewed. Walker, J. B. 1094.13
PARKES, W. Domestic duties. 3d American ed.
New York, 1829. 12°. 188.30
PARKINSON, R. Tour in America in 1798-1800.
London, 1805. 2v. 8° 624.13
PARKMAN, F. An offering of sympathy to the
afflicted. 2d ed. Boston, 1833. 18° . . 1089.25
PARKMAN, F. jr. California and Oregon trail. N.
York, 1849. 12° 626.12-13
— Conspiracy of Pontiac. Boston, 1851. 8° . . 244.2-3
— Prairie and Rocky mountain life. 3d ed. New
York, 1852. 12° 626.14
— Vassall Morton: a novel. Boston, 1856. 12°.795.15-17
PARKYNS, M. Life in Abyssinia. New York, 1856.
2v. in 1. 12° 697.5-6
PARLEY, Peter. See Goodrich, S. G.
PARLIAMENTARY practice. Cushing, L. S. Manual. 139.25
— - Lex P. Americana 133.1
— Matthias, B. Rules of order in 139.22
PARLIAMENTARY reform, Speeches on. Macaulay,
T. B. 409.18
PARLOR dramas. Fowle, W. B. 356.9
PARME, La chartreuse de. Beyle, H. 1067.28
PARNELL, T. Poetical works, [with life of Zoilus.]
London, 1852. 16° 329.7
    Contents. — Life, by J. Mitford; Hesiod, or the rise
    of woman; Songs; A fairy tale; Vigil of Venus; Ho-
    mer's Batrachomuomachia; The hermit; The life of
    Zoilus.
PARR, S. Memoirs of. Johnstone, J. 574.1
PARRY, E. Memoirs of Sir W. E. Parry. Lon-
don, 1857. 12° 565.4
PARRY, W. The last days of Lord Byron. Lon-
don, 1825. 8° 585.5
PARRY, W. E. Three voyages for the discovery
of a Northwest passage. N.Y., [1845.] 2v. 18° 820.22
— Memoirs of, by E. Parry 565.4
PARSONS, T. Essays. 3d ed. Boston, 1855. 16°. 875.9
— - Same. 2d series. Boston, 1856. 12°. . . 875.10
PARSONS, T. W. Poems. Boston, 1854. 16° . . 346.3
PARSONS, U. Life of Sir W. Pepperrell. Boston,
1855. 8° 513.19-20
PARTHENIA, or the last days of paganism. Lee,
E. B. 437.3-5
PARTISAN: a romance of the revolution. Simms,
W. G. 790.13-16
PARTON, J. Humorous poetry of the English
language. Chaucer to Saxe, with notes.
New York, 1856. 12° 324.15
— Life and times of A. Burr. N. Y., 1858. 12° .515.9-11
PARTON, S. P. Fern leaves from Fanny's port-
folio. Fiction. Auburn, 1853. 12° . . . 755.8
— Fern leaves. Second series. Auburn, 1854. 12° 755.5
— Fresh leaves, by Fanny Fern. N.Y., 1857. 18° 755.11
— Playday book, by Fanny Fern. New York,
1857. 16° 755.10
— Rose Clark: a novel. By Fanny Fern. New
York, 1856. 12° 755.7
— Ruth Hall. By Fanny Fern. N. Y., 1855. 12° 755.9
PARTURITION. See Medicine.
PARTY. See Political science.
PASCAL, B. Miscellaneous writings, with intro-
duction and notes by G. Pearce. London,
1849. 8° 874.1
    Contents. — Letters; Treatise on the geometrical
    spirit; Authority in matters of philosophy; On the
    passion of love; On the art of persuasion, or elo-
    quence; Thoughts on eloquence and style; Miscella-
    neous thoughts; Conversations; Thoughts on the
    Jesuits and the Jansenists; Thoughts on the pope and
    the church; Conversation on his work on religion.
— Provincial letters. Translated by T. M'Crie.
2d ed. Edinburgh, 1848. 12°. 127.28
PASCAL, J. Or a glimpse of convent life. Con-
sin, V. 545.8
PASSAGES from the diary of a late physician. Warren, S. 767.19

PASSION flowers. Howe, J. W. 345.17
PASSMORE, J. C. Introductory essay on the life
and writings of Bishop Butler. 139.1
PAST and present. Carlyle, T. 878.16
PAST, present and future. Carey, H. C. 136.4
PAST meridian. Sigourney, L. H. 808.18
PASTORAL theology. Vinet, A. R. 1088.17
PATHOLOGY. See Medicine.
PATAGONIA, The captive in. Bourne, B. F. . . . 635.16-17
PATENT office, Guide to the. Curtis, G. T. . . . 196.17
PATENT rights, Rules, forms, etc., for securing.
Phillips, W. 196.18
PATENTEE's manual. Johnson, J. 133.10
PATHFINDER, The: [a novel.] Cooper, J. F. . . .770.20-25
PATHOLOGY. See Medicine.
PATIENT Grissil: a comedy. Dekker, T. 342.6
PATMORE, C. K. Angel in the house. The be-
trothal. Boston, 1856. 16° 334.6-11
— Same. The espousals. Boston, 1856. 16° 334.12-16
PATON, A. A. Highlands and islands of the
Adriatic. London, 1849. 2v. 8°. 667.4
— Servia in 1843-44. London, 1845. 12° . . 666.4
PATRICK, S. Discourse concerning prayer. Ed.
by F. E. Paget. New York, 1841. 12°. . . 1097.27
PATTISON, S. R. Chapters on fossil botany. Lon-
don, 1849. 12°. 169.6
— The earth and the word, or geology for Bible
students. Philadelphia, 1858. 12° 167.28
PAUL, B. H. Manual of technical analysis. See
Bolley, P. A. 836.3
PAUL and Virginia, with memoir of the author.
Saint-Pierre, H. J. B. de. 729.1
PAUL Clifford, a novel. Lytton, E. B. 465.11-12
PAUL Creyton. Pseud. See Trowbridge, J. T.
PAUL Fane, [a tale.] Willis, N. P. 794.12
PAUL Ferroll. A tale from 4th Eng. ed. N. York,
1856. 12° 795.12-14
PAULDING, H. Cruise of the Dolphin, among the
islands of the Pacific ocean. N. Y., 1831. 24° 709.19
PAULDING, J. K. Book of St. Nicholas; from the
Dutch of Dom. Nicholas Ægidius Ouden-
arde. New York, 1836. 12° 797.13
— Dutchman's fireside; a tale. 5th ed. New
York, 1837. 2v. 12° 797.9
— History of John Bull and Brother Jonathan.
New ed. New York, 1835. 12° 797.10
— Koningsmarke, or old times in the new world.
New ed. New York, 1836. 2v. 12° 797.7
— Letters from the South. N. York, 1817. 2v. 12° 639.10
— - Same. New York, 1835. 2v. 12° 888.18
— Life of Washington. N. Y., n.d. 2v. 18°. . 810.71
— Merry tales of the three wise men of Gotham.
New York, 1839. 12° 797.11
— Tales of the good woman. New ed. New
York, 1836. 2v. 12° 797.12
PAULDING, J. K. and others. Salmagundi. See
Irving, W. 759.13
PAULI, R. Life of Alfred the Great. Transl. [Also,]
Alfred's version of Orosius, with a transl.
London, 1853. p.8° 856.4
PAWNEE tribe of Indians, Summer residence with
the. Murray, C. A. 639.3
PAXTON, P. Stray Yankee in Texas. New York,
1853. 16°. 626.16-18
PAYEN, A. Des substances alimentaires. 3e éd.
Paris, 1856. 12°. 1078.37
PAYSON, E. Memoir of. Cummings, A. 119.26
— Memoir and select thoughts of. Cummings, A. 534.6
PEABODY, A. P. Conversation, its faults and
graces. Boston, 1856. 16°. 406.13
— Lectures on Christian doctrine. 2d ed. Bos-
ton, 1844. 12°. 1106.9
— - Same. New ed. Boston, 1857. 12° . . . 117.13
PEABODY, Eph. Christian days and thoughts.
Boston, 1858. 12°. 117.12
— Sermons, with a memoir. Boston, 1857. 12° 1086.5
PEABODY, E. P. Æsthetic papers. Boston, 1849. 8° 873.6
PEABODY, O. W. B. Life of I. Putnam. Sparks,
J. American biography . . . . v.II. of 518.5
— Life of J. Sullivan . . . . v.XIII. of 529.1
PEABODY, W. B. O. Literary remains. Ed. by E.
Peabody. Boston, 1850. 12° 876.12

PEABODY, W. B. O. Sermons, with a mem. by his brother. Boston, 1849. 12° 1088.4
— Life of D. Brainerd. . . . . v.VIII. of 529.1
— Life of C. Mather. . . . . v.VI. of 529.1
— Life of J. Oglethorpe. . . . . v.XII. of 529.1
— Life of A. Wilson . . . . v.II. of 529.1
PEAKE, J. Rudiments of naval architecture. London, 1849-1851. 2v. in 1. 12° 199.22
PEARCE, G. Introduction and notes to a new transl. of the misc. writings of B. Pascal. . 874.1
PEARCE, S. Memoir of. 1109.18
PEARL fishing. Choice stories. Dickens, C. . . . 472.3
PEARSON, H. Memoir of C. Buchanan. N. York, n.d. 16° 1109.22
— - Same. Boston, 1818. 12° 578.8
PEARSON, J. An exposition of the creed with app. revised by W. S. Dobson. N. York, 1851. 8° 1103.2
PEARSON, J. N. Life of R. Leighton 1083.6
PEARSON, T. Infidelity ; its aspects, causes, and agencies. New York, 1854. 8° 1083.11
PEASANT and landlord. Knorring, Baroness. . . 418.8-9
PEASANT boy philosopher, The. Mayhew, H. . . 589.4
PEASANTS' war in France. See Jacquerie, La. . . 1078.25
PECK, G. Appeal to scripture, the rule of faith and practice. New York, 1852. 12° 129.9
— Wyoming, its history and romantic adventures. New York, 1858. 12° 237.2
PECK, G. W. Melbourne, and the Chincha isl'ds, with sketches of Lima. N. Y., 1854. 12°. . 705.21
PECK, J. M. Life of Daniel Boone . . . v.XXIII. of 529.1
PECK, W. G. Mathematical dictionary. See Davies, C. 147.1
PEDRO the Cruel, king of Castile and Leon, Life of. Mérimée, P. 546.18
PEEL, Sir R. Memoirs. London, 1853-57. 2v. 12° 566.4
    Contents. — Vol. I. The Roman Catholic question, 1828-29. II. The new government, 1834-35; Repeal of the corn laws, 1845-46.
PEERAGE, Romance of the. Craik, G. L. 566.8
PEERS and parvenus : a tale. Gore, C. G. . . . 776.5
PEG Woffington, a novel. Reade, C. 415.5
PEIRCE, B. Elementary treatise on algebra. 6th ed. Boston, 1850. 12° 148.4
— Elementary treatise on curves, functions, and forces. Boston, 1846-52. 2v. 12° 148.2
— Elementary treatise on plane and solid geometry. Boston, 1851. 12°. 148.3
— Plane and spherical trigonometry. New ed. Boston, 1852. 8° 147.3
PEIRCE, C. H. Drugs, etc., as to their adulterations. Cambridge, 1853. 12° 155.13
PEKING, Thirteen years' residence at the court of. Ripa 899.7
PELAYO : or the cavern of Covadonga. New York, 1836. 12°. 338.5
PELET de la Lozère, J. Napoleon in council. Tr. by B. Hall. Edinburgh, 1837. 12° 1008.14
PELHAM : a novel. Lytton, Sir E. B. 465.2-4
PELLARIN, C. Life of Fourier. 2d ed. N. York, 1848. 12° 545.11
PELLATT, A. Curiosities of glass making. London, 1849. 8° 196.11
PELLEW, E. Visc. Exmouth. Life of. Osler, E. 568.10
PELLICO, S. Prose. Firenze. 1856. 12° 1057.2
PENACOOK Indians. See Indians.
PENCILLINGS by the way. Willis, N. P. 657.9
PENDENNIS, The history of, Thackeray, W. M. . 401.11-15
PENINSULA. See Spain.
PENN, G. Mems. of Sir W. Penn. Lond., 1833. 2v. 8° 564.1
PENN, W. Clarkson, T. Private and public life of. 526.19
— Dixon, W. H. An historical biography . . . 526.17
— Ellis, G. E. Life of. Sparks, J. . . v.XXII. of 529.1
— Janney, S. M. Life, with correspond., etc. . 523.14
— Weems, M. L. Life 526.18
PENNINGTON, M. Life of Elizabeth Carter. 1st. Am ed. Boston, 1809. 8° 595.5
PENNSYLVANIA. Barber, J. W. History of . . . 237.5
— Day, S. Historical collections of the state of. 235.1
— Peck, G. Wyoming, its history, etc. 237.2
— Pleasant peregrination through 639.19
— Pritts, J. History of the early settlement of. 245.2

PEN Owen : a romance. Hook, J. 809.8
PENROSE, E. History of England. New ed., with questions by E. Robbins. N. Y., 1852. 12° 968.3
— History of France. Prepared for schools by J. Abbott. New York, 1848. 12°. . . . 1007.4
— History of Germany. New ed. Lond, 1853. 12° 928.4
PEOPLE, The. Michelet, J. 124.17
PEOPLE I have met. Willis, N. P. 904.7-10
PEOPLE'S own book. Lamennais, H. F. R. de . 129.34
PEPPERELL, history of. Butler, C. 224.14
PEPPERRELL, Sir W., Life of. Parsons, U. . . 513.19-20
PEPYS, S. Diary and correspondence, with life and notes by Lord Braybrooke. 3d ed. London, 1848-49. 5v. 8° 977.5
PERCIVAL Keene : a novel. Marryat, F. 745.15
PERCY, S. and R. Percy anecdotes, original and selected. London, n.d. 20v. 18° 909.7
— - Same. With American A. N.Y., 1850. 8° 892.3
— - Same. New York, 1858. 8° 892.4-8
PERCY, T. Reliques of ancient English poetry, with a glossary. London, 1839. 8° 332.3
PERCY Mallory. Hook, J. 809.7
PERCY Ranthorpe. Gore, C. G. 776.4
PEREIRA, J. Lectures on polarized light, [and] on the microscope. Edited by B. Powell. 2d ed. London, 1854. 16° 156.29
— Materia medica and therapeutics. 3d Am. ed., by J. Carson. Philadelphia, 1852-54. 2v. 8° 152.7
— Treatise on food and diet. Ed. by C. A. Lee. New York, n.d. 8° 157.3
PEREZ, Antonio, et Philippe II. Mignet, F. A. A. 1066.26
PERFUMERY, Art of. Piesse, G. W. S. 198.13
PERIL and suffering, Narr. of. Davenport, R. A. 379.14
PERILOUS adventures. Davenport, R. A. 820.56
PERILS and captivity of the Picard family. Edinburgh, 1827. 18° 830.31
PERKINS, E. E. Haberdashery and hosiery. 8th ed. London, 1853. 18° 199.38
PERKINS, E. T. Na Motu ; or, reef-rovings in the South seas. New York, 1854. 8° 705.6
PERKINS, J. Residence in Persia among the Nestorians. Andover, 1843. 8° 695.1
PERKINS, J. H. Memoir and writings. Ed. by W. H. Channing, 1851. 2v. 12° 525.4
PERKINS, T. H. Memoir of. Cary, T. G. . . . 524.4
PERRAULT, C. Contes des fées. Paris, An. IX., [1801.] 12° 1068.1
    Contents. — Le chaperon rouge ; Les fées ; La barbe bleue : La belle au bois dormant ; Le chat botté, Cendrillon ; Riquet à la houpe ; Le petit poucet ; L'adroite princesse ; Griselidis ; l'eau d'anc ; Les souhaits ridicules.
— Précis de la vie et des ouvrages de C. P. avec l'analyse de ses contes . . . . . . v.I. of 1077.1
PERRY, A. Harold and Rosaline, with other poems. Boston, 1846. 12° 369.5
PERRY, O. H. Elliott, J. D. Review of controversy between Com. Perry and Elliott. . . 527.10
— Mackenzie, A. S. The life of. 820.31
— Niles, J. M. The life of 527.7
PERRY, W. C. The Franks. London, 1857. 8°. . 925.6
PERSEPOLIS. Fergusson, J. Palaces of, restored. 694.9
— Francklin, W. Remains of the palace of. . . 694.10
— Rich, C. J. Narrative of a journey to 694.8
— Vaux, W. S. W. Nineveh and. 956.14
PERSIA. Binning, R. B. M. Journal of two years' travel in 685.1
— Ferrier, J. P. Caravan journeys in 694.3
— Francklin, W. Tour from Bengal to. . . . 694.10
— Fraser, J. B. Hist. and descriptive account of. 810.68
— Hunt, G. H. Campaign of Outram and Havelock. 938.9
— Kitto, J. Uncle Olliver's travels in 689.18
— Malcolm, J. Sketches of. 889.33
— Morier, J. A journey through. 694.15
— Perkins, J. Eight years in. 695.1
— Sheil, Lady. Life and manners in 695.12
— Shoberl, F. Description of. 938.11
— Southgate, H. Narrative of a tour through . 687.3
— Townsend, G. Summary of Persian history. Hunt, G. H. 938.9

PERSIUS Flaccus, A. Persius; translated by Sir W. Drummond. New York, n.d. 18°. . . . 830.22
— Satires; transl. into prose by L. Evans, and into verse by W. Gifford. Juvenalis, D. J. 824.13
PERSPECTIVE. Krüsi, H. Principles of. 201.6
— Pyne, G. Treatise on 819.14
— Taylor, B. Principles of linear 205.5
   See also: Drawing.
PERSUASION; a novel. Austen, J. . . . . . . v. V. of 758.3
PERTHES, F. C., Life and times of, by C. T. Perthes. Edinburgh, 1858. 12°. 545.14
— Biography of, by J. Baillie 548.12
PERTHES, F. M. Life of John Chrysostom; transl. from the German by A. Hovey and D. B. Ford. Boston, 1854. 12°. 547.20
PERU. Hall, B. Journal on the coast of. 639.7
— - Same . . . . v.II. and III. of 830.25
— Prescott, W. H. History of the conquest of. 252.3
— Smith, A. A residence in Lima 633.21
— Sutcliffe, T. Sixteen years in 633.17
— Temple, E. Travels in 633.12
— Trueba y Cosio, Don T. de. History of the conquest of. 830.62
— Tschudi, J. J. v. Travels in, 1838–42. . . . . 635.12
PERVERSION: or, the causes, etc., of infidelity. A tale for the times. Conybeare, W. J. . . . 777.10
PESCHEL, C. F. Elements of physics; translated by E. West. London, 1845–46. 3v. 16°. . 149.29
PESTILENCE. See Plague.
PESTS of the farm. Richardson, H. D. . . . v.II. of 169.15
PETER, 1st and 2d epistles of. See Bible.
PETER of Blois. Continuation of "Ingulph's Chronicle." Ingulph. 856.8
PETER the Cruel, History of. Mérimée, P. . . . 546.18
PETER the Great. Banks, J. Life of 546.21
— Barrow, Sir J. Life of 810.66
— Bradford, S. H. History of 546.22
PETER Parley. Pseud. See Goodrich, S. G.
PETER Pindar. Pseud. See Wolcot, J.
PETER Schlemihl in America: [a novel.] Wood, G. 808.1
PETER Simple. Marryat, F. 745.7
PETER, W. Poets and poetry of Greece and Rome, by various translators. Phila., 1847. 8°. . 315.1
PETERS, A. R., A memoir of. Clark, J. A. . . . 119.15
PETERS, Rev. H., A history of. Peters, S. 575.9
PETERS, S. History of the Rev. Hugh Peters. New York, 1807. 8°. 575.9
PETIS de La Croix, F. Les mille et un jour. Contes persans traduits en français. . v.XIV.–XV. of 1077.1
PETRA in 1839. Kinnear, J. G. 689.13
PETRARCA, F. Opere filosofiche. Milano, 1833. 16° 1059.11
   Contents. — Del modo di governare ottimamente uno stato; Libro degli uffici e delle virtù di un capitano; Della vera sapienza, dialogo; Il segreto del Petrarca o vero le sue confessioni.
— Rime. 4a ed. Firenze, 1851. 12°. 1056.3
— Campbell, T. Life and times of. 543.6
— Sade, J. F. P. A. de. Memoirs. [Dobson's ed.] 548.25
PETRIFACTIONS and their teachings. Mantell, G. A. 816.11
   See also: Geology.
PETTIGREW, T. J. Chronicles of the tombs. London, 1857. p.8°. 856.13
PEVERIL of the peak. Scott, Sir W. 470.13–15
PEYTON, Sir E. Catastrophe of the house of Stuart. See "Secret history," etc. 552.6
PFEIFFER, I. A lady's voyage round the world. Translated by Mrs. Sinnett. New edition. London, 1852. 12°. 409.23
— - Same. Translated from the German. 3d edition. London, 1852. 12°. 879.4
— A lady's second journey round the world. New York, 1856. 12°. 708.10
— Journey to Iceland and travels in Sweden and Norway. Translated by C. F. Cooper. New York, 1852. 12°. 668.20
— - Same. Translated from the German. London, 1852. 12°. 879.3
— - Same. 2d ed. London, 1853. 12°. 668.19
— Visit to the Holy Land, Egypt, and Italy. 2d ed. London, 1853. 12°. 879.5

PHÆDON: or, a dialogue on the immortality of the soul. Plato 808.22
PHÆDRUS, with the appendix of Gudius. Translated by C. Smart. N. Y., 1852. 18°. v.II. of 830.16
— Translated into prose by H. T. Riley, and into verse by C. Smart. See Terentius Afer, P.. 834.11
PHŒNICIA. Kenrick, J. [Description and history of] 956.4
PHANTASMAGORIA of fun. Edited by A. Crowquill. London, 1843. 2v. 12°. 449.1
PHANTOM ship: a novel. Marryat, F. 745.12
PHANTOM world. See Supernaturalism.
PHARMACY. See Medicine.
PHARSALIA, The. Transl. into English prose by H. T. Riley. Lucanus, M. A. 834.5
PHELPS, A. H. Botany for beginners. New York, 1847. 18°. 169.16
— Familiar lectures on botany. 3d ed. Hartford, 1852. 12°. 169.3
PHENIX, The: a collection of old and rare fragments. New York, 1835. 12°. 898.8
PHIGALEIAN marbles in the British Museum. Ellis, Sir H. 839.9
PHILEMON, Epistle to. See Bible.
PHILIP II. of Spain. Mignet, F. A. A. Philippe II. et Antonio Perez 1066.26
— Prescott, W. H. Reign of 922.1–7
— Watson, R. Reign of 542.2
PHILIP III. of Spain. Reign of. Watson, R. . . . 542.2
PHILIP Augustus of France, Capefigue, B. H. R. Histoire de P. A. 1066.6
- James, G. P. R. P. A.: or, the brothers in arms. [A novel.]. 464.10
PHILIP. History of King Philip. Abbott, J. S. C. 579.7
PHILIP, J. Researches in South Africa. London, 1828. 2v. 8°. 692.8
PHILIP, R. The Marys: or, female holiness. New York, 1836. 18°. 1089.21
PHILIP Van Artevelde: a dramatic romance. Taylor, H. 346.16
PHILIPPART, J. Memoirs and campaigns of Charles John [Bernadotte] prince royal of Sweden. Baltimore, 1815. 8°. 542.3
PHILIPPIANS, Epistle to the. See Bible.
PHILIPPINES, Twenty years in the. La Gironière, P. P. de 705.13–14
PHILLIPPO, J. M. Jamaica, its past and present state. Philadelphia, 1843. 12°. 264.2
— The United States and Cuba. London, 1857. p.8° 625.21
PHILLIPS, C. Curran and his contemporaries. New York, 1851. 12°. 598.11
— Speeches. New York, 1817. 8° 866.1
— Curran, J. P. and Grattan, H. Irish eloquence, [with] appeal of R. Emmet. Phil., 1854. 8°. 862.3–8
PHILLIPS, J. Treatise on geology. London, 1837–39. 2v. 16°. 408.7
PHILLIPS, J. A. Manual of metallurgy. 2d ed. London, 1854. 12°. 196.14
— and Darlington, J. Records of mining and metallurgy. London, 1857. 12°. 196.12
PHILLIPS, S., Memoir of. Taylor, J. L. 523.2
PHILLIPS, T. History and principles of painting. London, 1833. 8°. 205.2
PHILLIPS, Wendell. Speech on woman's rights. See Woman's 878.8
PHILLIPS, Willard. The inventor's guide. Boston, 1837. 12°. 196.18
PHILLIPS, Wm. Elementary introduction to mineralogy. New ed. by Brooke and Miller. London, 1852. 12°. 163.18
— Outlines of mineralogy and geology. 4th ed. London, 1826. 8°. 163.21
PHILO: an evangeliad. Judd, S. 358.7
PHILO Judæus. Works, transl. by C. D. Yonge. London, 1854–55. 4v. p.8° 845.7–8
PHILOSOPHERS. Diogenes Laërtius. Lives and opinions of eminent 834.10
— Fénelon, F. de S. de La M. Lives of the ancient 820.42
   See also: Philosophy.

PHILOSOPHICAL instruments. Brewster, D. Treatise on 144.12
— Glaisher, J. Lecture on 199.16
PHILOSOPHICAL theories and experiences. From 2d London ed. Philadelphia, 1846. 16°.v. I. of 850.25
PHILOSOPHICAL writers, Essays on. De Quincey, T. 895.20
PHILOSOPHY. Butler, W. A. History of ancient. 124.7
— Cousin, V. History of modern 124.4
— - Introduction to the history of 122.2
— Fleming, W. Vocabulary of 125.30
— Gerhart, E. V. Introduction to the study of. 403.8
— Hamilton, Sir W. Philosophy 122.12
— - Discussions on 872.1
— Henry, C. S. History of 820.45
— Lewes, G. H. Biographical history of. . . . 840.34
— Tenneman, W. A. History of 855.1
See also: Intellectual science, and Natural philosophy.
PHILOSOPHY of the plays of Shakspere unfolded. Bacon, D. 353.3
PHILOSOPHY of rhetoric. Campbell, G. 405.6
PHILOSOPHY of skepticism and ultraism. Walker, J. B. 1094.13
PHILOSOPHY of the plan of salvation. Walker, J.B 1086.21
PHILOSOPHY of the seasons. Duncan, H. 1089.7
PHILOSTORGIUS, Ecclesiastical history of. Sozomenus Hermias. 845.9–10
PHILOTHEA: a romance. Child, L. M. 488.15
PHIPPS, C. H., Marq. of Normanby. A year of revolution: a journal kept in Paris in 1848. London, 1857. 2v. 8° 1002.4
— The contrast: a novel. London, 1832. 3v. 12° 489.17
PHIPS, Sir W. Life of, by F. Bowen . . . . v.VII. of 529.1
PHŒNIX, John. Pseud. See Derby, G. H.
PHŒNIXIANA; or sketches and burlesques. Derby, G. H. 806.1
PHOTOGRAPHY. Delamotte, P. H. The practice of. 197.15
— Halleur, G. C. H. Art of. 829.11
— Hunt, R. Manual of 197.14
— Lerebours, N. P. Treatise on 197.13
— Price, L. Photographic manipulation 197.12
PHRENOLOGY. Bridges, F. P. made practical . . 124.26
— Combe, G. System of 124.2
— Jones, S. Practical 124.15
— Spurzheim, J. G. P. or mental phenomena . 124.1
See also: Intellectual science.
PHYSIC. See Medicine.
PHYSICAL geography. Ansted, D. T. Elementary course of 163.24
— Fitch, G. W. Outlines of 167.8
— Guyot, A. Earth and man 167.18
— Houzeau, J. C. Physique du globe 1065.22
— Maury, M. F. Phys. geog. of the sea 145.16
— Mudie, R. The earth 169.18
— Nicolay, C. G. Principles of 167.7
— Somerville, M. Physical geography 167.9–10
— Wittich, A. Curiosities of 850.21
See also: Geology, Meteorology, etc.
PHYSICAL sciences. Nichol, J. P. Cyclopædia of 145.8
— Somerville, M. Connexion of the 149.22
See also: Physics.
PHYSICAL theory of another life. Taylor, I. . . . 1108.2
PHYSICIAN, Letters to a young. Jackson, J. . . . 157.23–24
PHYSICIANS, Lives of British 389.13
— Eminent living, of Paris. Sketches, etc. . . . 609.1
See also: Medical biography.
PHYSICS. Airy, G. B. Gravitation. 146.24
— Arnott, N. Elements of 145.10
— Buff, H. P. of the earth. 149.31
— Hunt, R. Elementary P. 149.13
— Müller, J. Principles of 144.11
— Peschel, C. F. Elements of 149.29
— Plateau, J. et Quetelet, A. Physique 1065.44
— Tomlinson, C. Principes de physique générale 1075.31
— Whewell, W. General physics considered with reference to natural theology 826.4
See also: Astronomy, Hydraulics, Hydrostatics, Light, Magnetism, Mechanics, Meteorology, Natural philosophy, Optics, Pneumatics, Sound, Telegraph, etc.

PHYSIOGNOMY, A poem. Bartlett, J. 878.12
PHYSIOGNOMY, Comparative. Redfield, J. W. . . 122.7
PHYSIOLOGY, Animal. Barlow, J. Connection between P. and intellectual philosophy. v. I. of 850.25
— Carpenter, W. B. Manual of 149.23
— Combe, A. P. applied to health 810.69
— Cutter, C. Anatomy and 158.6
— Edwards, H. M. Animal mechanism and . . 177.23
— Fowler, O. S. Animal and mental 157.13
— Gluge, le docteur. Physiologie 1065.17
— Griscom, J. H. Animal mechanism and . . . 810.78
— Liebig, J. Chemistry in its applications to . 164.6
— Motion of the juices in the animal body . . . 155.14
— Smith, S. Animal physiology 365.12
See also: Medicine.
PHYSIOLOGY, Vegetable. Goadby, H. Text-book of. 173.5
— Gray, Asa 166.5
— Mulder, G. J. The chemistry of 155.8
— Phytology, or. Lib. Us. Kn. 365.12
PIANO forte. Letter to a P. F. player. Instructions for practising 199.28
— Spencer, C. C. Art of playing upon 829 6
PIAZZA tales. Melville, H. 736.11
PICARD family. Sufferings of, after the wreck of the Medusa. See Perils and captivity 830.31
PICCIOLA, or, the prisoner of Fenestrella. Saintine, X. B. 478.11
PICCOLOMINI, The, a drama, transl. from Schiller. Coleridge, S. T. . . . . v.III. of 327.10
PICHLER, K. Die Wiedereroberung von Ofen. Wien, 1829. 2v. 16° 1025.9
— Denkwürdigkeiten aus meinem Leben. Wien, 1844. 4v. in 2. 16° 1035.9
— The wife hunter; a novel 801.3
PICKARD, H. M. Memoir of, and writings. Otheman, E 538.1
PICKERING, C Races of man. Prefixed, a synopsis of the nat. hist. of man, by J. C. Hall. New ed. London, 1850. p.8° 815.3–6
PICKERING, E. The expectant, a novel. Philadelphia, 1842. 2v. 12° 805.16
— - Same. Philadelphia, n.d. 8° 805.10
— The fright. Philadelphia, 1847. 8° 805.1
— - Same. New York, n.d. 8° 805.2
— The grandfather, a novel. New York, 1844. 8° 805.6 7
— The grumbler, a novel. New York, 1844. 8°. 805.9
— The heiress, a novel. New York, 1845. 8° . . 805.3
— Kate Walsingham. London, 1850. 3v. 12° . 805.17
— Nan Darrell, or the gipsy mother. Philadelphia, n.d. 8° 805.5
— The orphan niece. Philadelphia, n.d. 8° . . 805.4
— The poor cousin: a novel. Phila., n.d. 8° . 805.14–15
— The prince and the pedlar. Phila., n.d. 8° . 805.13
— The quiet husband. Phila., n.d. 8° 805.11–12
— The squire. Philadelphia, n.d. 8° 805.8
PICKERING, W. Aldine edition of the British poets. London. 53v. 16°. Contents:
Akenside, M. With memoir by A. Dyce . . . 310.1
Beattie, J. With memoir, by A. Dyce. . . . 319.2
Burns, R. With memoir, by Sir N. H Nicolas. 3v. 319.3
Butler, S. With memoir, by J. Mitford. 2v. 319.4
Chaucer, G. With life by Sir N. H. Nicolas. 6v. 319.5
Churchill, C. Mem. and notes, by Tooke. 3v. 319.6
Collins, W. With notes and memoir, by A. Dyce, and essay by Sir E. Brydges 329.1
Cowper, W. With a memoir, by Sir N. H. Nicolas. 3v 310.7
Dryden, J. Poetical works, ed., with life, by J. Mitford. 5v 310.8
Falconer, W. With memoir, by J. Mitford. 329.2–3
Goldsmith, O. Memoir and notes, by J. Mitford 329.4
Gray, T. Works with life, by J. Mitford. 5v. 339.2
Howard, H., Earl of Surrey. With memoir, by Sir N. H. Nicolas. 329.11
Milton, J. Poetical works. Memoir, by J. Mitford. 3v 329.6
Parnell, T. With memoir, by J. Mitford . . 329.7
Pope, A. With memoir, by A. Dyce. 3v . . . 339.3
Prior, M. With memoir, by J. Mitford 2v. 329.8

PICKERING, W., *continued.*
Shakespeare, W. Poems. Memoir, by A.
    Dyce 329.9
Spenser, E. With memoir, by J. Mitford. 5v. 329.10
Swift, J. With memoir, by J. Mitford. 3v.. 329.12
Thomson, J. With memoir, by Sir N. H.
    Nicolas. 2v. 329.13
White. H. K. With memoir, by Sir N. H.
    Nicolas 329.5
Wyatt, T. With mem., by Sir N. H. Nicolas. 339.1
Young, E. With memoir, by J. Mitford. 2v. 329.14
PICKWICK papers. Dickens, C. 461.11-16
PIC-NIC papers. Dickens, C. 462.4
PICTORIAL calendar of the seasons. Howitt, M.. 825.10
PICTORIAL history of the Russian war, 1854-55.
    Edinburgh, 1856. 8° 924.1
PICTORIAL narratives. New York, n.d. 12° . . 1109.2
PICTURE galleries of England. Hazlitt, W. . . . 207.19
PICTURES from Italy. Dickens, C. 892.10
PICTURES from the battle fields. By the " Roving
    Englishman." 2d ed. London, 1855. p.8° 988.5-6
PICTURES of early life. Embury, E. C. 878.27
PICTURES of the world. Ward, R. P. 787.3
PIDDINGTON, H. Sailor's horn-book for the law
    of storms. 2d ed. London, 1855. 8° . . . 145.18
PIERCE, F., Life of. Hawthorne, N. 517.27-28
PIERCE Penniless' supplication to the devil.
    Nash, T. 342.11
PIERCE, W. L. The year: a poem. New York,
    1813. 18° 369.8
PIERPONT, J. Airs of Palestine: a poem. 3d ed.,
    revised. Boston, 1817. 18° 369.17
PIERRE, or the ambiguities: a tale. Melville, H. 736.8
PIESSE, G. W. S. Art of perfumery. London,
    1855. 12° 198.13
PIGGOT, A. S. Chemistry and metallurgy of cop-
    per. Philadelphia, 1858. 12° 198.10
PIGNOTTI, L. Storia della Toscana. Capolago,
    1843. 5v. 16° 1058.1
PIGS, Domestic; their origin and varieties, man-
    agement, etc. Richardson, H. D.. . . v.I. of 169.15
PIKE, J. G. Guide for disciples, abridged. New
    York, n.d. 18° 119.3
— Religion and eternal life. New York, n.d. 16° 119.5
PIKE, M. H. Agnes: a novel. Boston, 1858. 12° 427.2-4
— Ida May: a story. Boston, 1854-55. 12° . . 416.9-11
PIKE, Z. M. Life of, by H. Whiting. . . . v.XV. of 529.1
PILGRIM celebration at Plymouth, Mass. Aug.
    1, 1853. See Account, etc. 224.17
PILGRIM'S progress. Bunyan, J. 869.9
PILGRIMS of the Rhine. Lytton, E. B.. . . . . 465.27
PILGRIMS of Walsingham. Strickland, A. . . . 787.9-11
PILGRIMS. Banvard, J. Plymouth and the . . . 228.14
— Bartlett, W. H. Pilgrim fathers 223.1
— Bridgman, T. Pilgrims of Boston and their
    descendants 223.5
— Young, A. Pilgrim fathers of Plymouth. . 223.13
    See also : New England.
PILLANS, J. Elementary teaching chiefly in refer-
    ence to the parochial schools of Scotland.
    2d ed. Edinburgh, 1829. 12° 1099.23
PILLET, R. M. Views of England. Boston,
    1818. 12° 988.10
PILOT, The : a tale of the sea. Cooper, J. F. . . 780.1-5
PINCKARD, G. Notes on the West Indies, and
    the Indians of South America. 2d ed. Lon-
    don, 1816. 2v. 8° 635.7
PINDARUS. Pindar, translated by C. A. Wheel-
    wright. New York, 1852. 18° 830.23
— Odes translated into prose by D. W. Turner,
    [also,] a metrical version by A. Moore.
    London, 1852. p.8° 824.11
PINKNEY, W. Life by his nephew, Rev. W. Pink-
    ney. New York, 1853. 8° 512.10
— - Life, by H. Wheaton . . . . v.III. of 518.5
PIONEER history. Hildreth, S. P. 245.3
PIONEERS, The : a descriptive tale. Cooper, J.F. 770.26-30
PIOZZI, H. L. Anecdotes of Samuel Johnson. 2d
    ed. London, 1786. sm.8° 588.12
— Journey through France, Italy, and Germany.
    London, 1789. 2v. 8° 676.1

PIRATE, The. Scott, Sir W. 470.1-5
PITCAIRN, D. Perfect peace: letters-memorial of
    John W. Howell. From 9th London ed.
    New York, 1845. 18° 599.13
PITCAIRN'S island. Barrow, Sir J. P.'s island and
    its inhabitants 810.42
— Home of the mutineers. See Home 1109.8
— Murray, T. B. Pitcairn's island, the people
    and the pastor 939.6
— Smith, A. Life of the captain of the island
    of Pitcairn 519.5
PITRAT, J. C. Paul and Julia: or, the church of
    Rome. Boston, 1855. 12° 1098.19
PITT, W., *earl of Chatham.* Essay on. Macau-
    lay, T. B. 409.20
PITT, W., *Rt. Hon.* Life. Tomline, G. 563.3
PITTS street chapel lectures. Delivered in Boston,
    1858, by clergymen of six different denomi-
    nations. Boston, 1858. 12° 1086.1

    Contents. — I. Lecture, by Rev. W. R. Clark,
    "Why am I a Methodist?" II. By Rev. T. B.
    Thayer, "Why are you a Universalist?" III. By
    Rev. J. N. Sykes, "Why am I a Baptist?" IV. By
    Rev. N. Adams, "Why am I a Trinitarian Congre-
    gationalist?" V. By Rev. G. M. Randall, "Why
    am I a Churchman ?" VI. By Rev. O. Dewey,
    "Why am I a Unitarian ?" VII. By Rev. T. S.
    King, " Spiritual Christianity."

PIZARRO, F., Life of 539.21-22
PLACE, A, in thy memory. De Kroyft, S. H. . . 878.3
PLAGUE in London, in 1665. De Foe, D. . . . 379.17
PLAGUE in Florence, in 1348. Descrizione della
    pestilenza. Boccaccio, G. 1059.3
PLANCHE, G. Essai sur Adolphe. Constant, B . 1066.8
PLANCHÉ, J. R. Fairy tales, selected from Per-
    rault and others. London, 1858. 12° . . . 737.9
— History of British costume. Lond., 1849. 12° 839.3
— - Same. London, 1847. 18° 840.51
PLANCHÉ, M. See Mackarness, Mrs. M.
PLANETARY and stellar worlds. Mitchel, O. M. 146.21
PLANT, The : a biography. Schleiden, M. J. . . 164.5
PLANTAGENETS and the Tudors. Forster, J. . . 894.3
PLANTER'S Northern bride. Hentz, C. L. . . . 446.2-5
PLANT hunters among the Himalayas. Reid, M. 728.1-5
PLANTS, Classes and orders of. Lindley, J. . . . 169.25
    See also : Botany.
PLASTERING, Rudim. treatise on. Burnell, G. R. 819.32
PLATE, The river. Mansfield, C. B. 635.10
    See also : La Plata.
PLATEAU, J. et Quetelet, A. Physique. 1re partie,
    etc. Bruxelles, n.d. 12° 1065.44
PLATER, E. Life of the Countess Emily Plater.
    New York, 1842. 12° 599.4
PLATO. Works, translated by Henry Cary, Henry
    Davis, and George Burges. London,
    1849-54. 6v. p.8° 814.3

    Contents. — Vol. I. The apology of Socrates; Crito;
    Phædo; Gorgias; Protagoras; Phædrus; Theætetus;
    Euthyphron and Lysis, by Henry Cary. . . . .
    II. The republic; Timæus and Critias, by Henry Da-
    vis. . . . . III. Meno; Euthydemus; The Soph-
    ist; The statesman; Cratylus; Parmenides and the
    banquet, by George Burges. . . . IV. Philebus;
    Charmides; Laches; Menexenus; Hippias Major;
    Hippias Minor; Ion; First Alcibiades ; Second Alci-
    biades; Theages; The rivals; Hipparchus; Minos;
    Clitopho; The Epistles, by George Burges. . . . .
    V. The laws, by George Burges. . . . . VI. The
    doubtful works; Epinomis; Axiochus; Eryxias; On
    virtue; On justice; Sisyphus; Demodocus; Defini-
    tions; Timæus Locrus, with lives of Plato, by Dio-
    genes Laertius, Hesychius and Olympiodorus; Intro-
    ductions to his doctrines, by Alcinous, and to the
    dialogues by Albinus; The doctrines of Plato, by
    Apuleius; The notes of Thomas Gray, and a general
    index to the entire work.

— Divine dialogues, [and] Apology of Socrates.
    Transl., with dissertations and notes, by
    Dacier. 3d ed., rev. and cor. Lond, 1845. 12° 1089.1
— Phædon: or, a dialogue on the immortality
    of the soul. 1st Am. ed. N. Y., 1833. 16° 898.22
— Republic. Analysed by J. A. St. John.
    More, Sir T. 888.14

PLATTNER, and Muspratt, S. Use of the blow-
pipe. 3d ed., enl. London, 1854. 8° 155.18
PLAUTUS, M. A. Comedies. Transl. by Henry T.
Riley. London, 1852. 2v. p.8° 824.12
PLAY and study. By Mrs. M. Leslie, [Mrs.
Baker.] Boston, 1858. 16° 735.16
PLAY-DAY book. Parton, S. P. 755.10
PLAYES, A treatise against vaine. Northbrooke, J. 342.13
PLAYFAIR, L. Lecture on industrial education .   199.16
PLEASANT peregrination through parts of Penn-
sylvania. Philadelphia, 1836. 18° 639.19
PLEASURES of imagination: a poem. Akenside, M.   358.25
PLEIAD, the. Abridgments from seven writers
on the evidences of Christianity. Wrang-
ham, F.   830.41
PLINIUS Secundus, C. Letters, [transl.,] with re-
marks, by W. Melmoth. Bost., 1809. 2v. 12°   898.17
— Natural history. Transl., etc., by J. Bostock
and H. T. Riley. London, 1855–57. 6v. p.8°   844.7
PLUTARCHUS. Lives. Transl. by J. and W. Lang-
horne. New York, 1851. 4v. 12° 517.11
— - Same. Cincinnati, 1856. 8° 541.6–7
— Select lives. Transl., with notes, by G. Long.
London, 1844–48. 5v. 18° 850.1
PLYMOUTH, Mass. Account of the pilgrim celebra-
tion at, 1853 . . . .   224.17
— Banvard, J. P. and the pilgrims 228.14
— Baylies, F. Historical memoir of P. colony.   223.11
— Bradford, W. Hist. of P. plantation. v.III. of 278.4
— Morton, N. Gov. Bradford's history of P.
colony 223.14
— Thacher, J. History of the town of P., from
its first settlement 227.11
— Young, A. Chronicles of P. colony 223.13
PNEUMANEE: or, the fairy of the 19th century.
Cunningham, J. W. 777.4
PNEUMATICS, Lectures on select subjects in. Fer-
guson, J. 146.8
— Lardner, D. Treatise on. 398.9
— - Pneumatics. Libr. of Useful Knowl. v.I. of 365.14
— Science made easy. Familiar introduction to
the principles of 149.39
— Tomlinson, C. Rudimentary treatise on. . . .   819.10
See also: Natural philosophy.
POACHER, The. A novel. Marryat, F. 745.3
POCKET miscellany. Chambers, W. 367.1
POCOCKE, E. India in Greece: or, truth in my-
thology. London, 1852. 12° 956.10
POE, E. A. Works with mem. by R. W. Griswold,
etc. New York, 1855–56. 4v. 12° 887.1–2

    Contents. — Vol. I. Tales. II. Poems and tales.
    III. The literati. IV. Arthur Gordon Pym, etc.

POEMS of established reputation. Baltimore, 1803.
12° 358.24

    Contents. — Vol. I. The art of preserving health, by
    J. Armstrong. II. The minstrel, or the progress of
    genius, by J. Beattie. III. The pleasures of imagina-
    tion, by M. Akenside. IV. The task, by W. Cowper.

POETARUM Latinorum corpus. Walker, W. S. . . .   353.1
POETICAL literature of the past half century.
Moir, D. M. 406.10
POETICAL litera. of the West. Gallagher, W. D. .   338.1
POETRY of life, The. Ellis, S. S. 804.7
POETRY of science. Hunt, R. 145.15
POETRY. Aristoteles. Treatise on the poetic . .   814.8
— Harris, J. Treatise concerning 209.4
— Lessing, G. E. Limits of 209.14
— Montgomery, J. Lectures on 405.14
POETRY. Collections:
Adams, H. G. Poetical quotations. 344.21
Aikin, J. British poets 312.1
Alger, W. R. Poetry of the East. 315.12–13
Aytoun, W. E. Ballads of Scotland. 375.1
Bowring, J. Ancient poetry of Spain 316.9
— Poetry of the Magyars 316.2
— Russian poets 315.14
British satirist 369.13
Brooks, C. T. German lyrics 316.8
— Songs and ballads 316.6
Bryant, W. C. Selec. from American poets. .   820.24

POETRY, continued.
Campbell, T. Spec. of the British poets . . .   343.14
Dictionary of quotations from British poets .   358.5
Doran, J. Bentley ballads 316.13
Dryden, J. Fables; translated from Homer,
Ovid, etc. 315.17
Dulcken, H. W. German songs 316.7
Ellis, G. Specimens of early English poets .   316.11
Evans, T. Old ballads 316.4
Finlay, J. Scottish historical and romantic
ballads 316.10
Gallagher, W. D. Poetical literature of the
West 338.1
Griswold, R. W. Female poets of America .   314.7
— Poets and poetry of America 314.4–6
— Poets and poetry of England, 19th cent. .   311.7
— Sacred poets of England and America. .   314.8
Hale, S. J. Dictionary of poetic quotations .   312.2
Halleck, F. G. Selections from the British
poets. 820.25
Hayes, E. Ballads of Ireland. 316.5
Hazlitt, W. Select poets of Great Britain . .   312.9
Howitt, M. Poetical works of Howitt, Mil-
man and Keats. 392.6
Illustrated book of English songs. 16th to
19th century 869.7
Illustrated book of Scottish songs. 16th to
19th century. 869.8
Jenks, J. W. Rural poetry of the English
language 314.3
Kettell, S. American poetry. 339.4
Lockhart, J. G. Ancient Spanish ballads . .   316.1
Maginn, W. Homeric ballads and comedies
of Lucian 346.4
Moore, F. Songs and ballads of the American
revolution 314.2
Oxford prize poems 349.15
Parton, J. Humorous poetry 324.15
Percy, T. Reliques of anc. English poetry. .   332.3
Peter, W. Poets and poetry of Greece and
Rome 315.1
Poems of established reputation 358.24
Procter, B. W. English songs. 345.11
Rogers, C. Modern Scottish minstrel 316.12
Selections from female poets. 369.15
Smith, C. W. Book of recitations 356.25
Specimens of British poets 369.12
Southey, R. British poets, 1400–1658 . . . .   312.11
Thornbury, G. W. Songs of the cavaliers and
roundheads 316.3
Walker, W. S. Corpus poetarum latinorum .   353.1
Wreath, The. A collection of poems 369.9

    NOTE.—For different forms of poetry, as the drama,
    and for the poetry of various countries, see their sev-
    eral names.

POETS. De Quincey, T. Essays on the 895.15
— Griswold, R. W. P. and poetry of England.   311.7
— Suetonius Tranquillus, C. Lives of the an-
cient 844.8

    For other collections of the lives of poets, see Biog-
    raphy.

POGGIO Bracciolini. The life of. Shepherd, W. .   543.8
POINSETT, J. R. Notes on Mexico in 1822. Phila-
delphia, 1824. 8° 256.3
POKERS, Stokers and. Head, F. B. 889.23
POLAND. Dunham, S. A. A history of 378.9
— Fletcher, J. History of 810.30
— Saxton, L. C. The fall of, with its history .   927.8
— Stephens, J. L. Incidents of travel in. . .   689.1–2
POLAR sea. Franklin, J. Journey to the shores
of the. 704.5
— Wrangel, F. v. Narrative of an expedition to.   820.49
POLAR seas. Bellot, J. R. Journal of a voyage
in the 617.13
— Murray, H. Discovery and adventure in the.   810.15
See also: Arctic, Antarctic, N. W. Passage,
etc.
POLARIZATION. See Optics.
POLICEMAN, Recollections of a. Waters, T. . . .   905.5
POLISH tales. Gore, C. G. 776.6
POLITENESS. See Manners and Minor morals.

POLITICAL economy. Anderson, W. Practical
    mercantile correspondence 136.21
— Bowen, F. Principles of 135.7
— Brouckere, C. de. Principes d' économie poli-
    tique 1065.10
— Carey, H. C. Essay on wages 136.7
— - Past, present and future 136.4
— Cairnes, J. E. Character and logical method of.   136.11
— Chalmers, T. P. E. in connection with the
    moral state and prospects of society 136.29
— Chapman, J. Cotton and commerce of India.   135.10
— Everett, A. H. New ideas on population . .   136.6
— Foster, B. F. Merchants' manual 136.22
— Franklin, B. Essays on . . . . .v.II. of 286.2
— Hamilton, A. Reports on public credit, manu-
    factures, commerce, finance, etc. . . . v.III. of 285.1
— Hunt, F. Library of commerce 136.30
— - Worth and wealth. Maxims for merchants.   136.20
— Jennings, R. Social delusions concerning
    wealth and want 139.13
— Knight, C. Results of machinery 139.24
— Lieber, F. On property and labour 820.47
— List, F. National system of 135.8
— Maclaren, J. History of the currency. . . .   136.10
— M'Culloch, J. R. Principles of 136.1
— - Essays on interest, coins, paper money,
    etc. 135.4
— Martineau, H. Illustrations of 749.2-3
— Murchison, J. H. British mines as a means
    of investment 136.32
— Newman, S. P. Elements of 136.27
— Potter, A. Objects, uses, and principles of .   830.3
— Ricardo, D. Political economy 136.3
— Senior, N. W. Political economy 136.28
— Smith, A. Wealth of nations 136.33
— Smith, E. P. Manual of 136.19
— Southey, T. Colonial sheep and wools . . .   136.9
— Sterling, P. J. Gold discoveries and their
    probable consequences 136.12
— Taylor, R. C. Statistics of coal 135.6
— Wayland, F. Elements of 136.14
— Whitney, J. D. Metallic wealth of the U. S..   163.1
    See also: Agriculture, Banking, Business,
    Capital, Commerce, Currency, Manufac-
    tures, Taxation, Useful arts, etc.
POLITICAL science. Adams, J. Independence of
    the judiciary . . . . .v.III. of 283.1
— - Defence of the constitutions of the United
    States . . . . .v.IV.-VI. of 283.1
— Aristoteles. The politics 834.9
— Brougham, H. Discourse of 840.6
— Remarks on party 840.5
— Camp, G. S. Democracy 820.40
— Coleridge, S. T. Statesman's manual . . .v.I. of 886.2
— - Constitution of church and state . . .v.VI. of 886.2
— Guizot, F. P. G. History of civilization . . .   837.5
— - Origin of representative government . . .   817.7
— Macaulay, T. B. Parliamentary reform . . .   409.18
— Long, G. Cyclopædia of political knowledge.   859.5
— Madison, J. The federalist 285.4
— Paley, W. Political philosophy 1009.35
— Rousseau, J. J. Du contrat social . . .v.II. of 1069.1
— Southey, R. Political essays 139.23
— Theory of human progression 134.18
— Washington, G. Political legacies. 297.6
— Williams, E. Statesman's manual 296.4
    See also: Constitutions, Government. Re-
    public, etc.
POLITICS. Brougham, H. Opinions on 888.2
— Brownson, O. A. Essays and reviews on . .   1086.31
— General register. P. and literature in Eur.
    and Am. in 1827 . . . .   830.38
— Hildreth, R. Theory of 134.10
POLLOK, R. Course of time, with memoir of the
    author. Ed. by W. C. Armstrong. Hartf.
    1851. 12° 345.5
POLLY Peablossom's wedding, and other tales.
    Thompson, W. T.. . . . .   726.14
POLO, M. Travels. Ed. by H. Murray. N. York,
    1845. 18° 820.67

POLYNESIA. Acc't of the islands in the South Sea.
    Russell, M.. . . . .   820.55
POLYNESIAN researches. Ellis, W. 707.4
POLYNESIAN mythology. Grey, Sir G. 1087.20
POMPEII: its past and present state, chiefly from
    W. Clarke. London, n.d. 2v. 12° 849.3
— - Same. Boston, 1833. 12° 849.20
— - Same. New ed. London, 1853. 18° . .   850.2
— Last days of. Lytton, E. B. 465.24
— Last night of. A poem. Fairfield, S. L. . . .   358.2
PONSARD, F. Théâtre complet. Paris, 1851. 12°   1067.4
    Contents. — Lucrèce, tragédie; Agnes de Méranie,
    trag. ; Charlotte Corday, trag. ; Horace et Lydie,
    comédie.
PONTIAC, Conspiracy of. Parkman, F. jr. 244.2-3
PONTIC epistles. Transl. by H. T. Riley. Ovid-
    ius Naso, P. 824.6
POOLE, S. The Englishwoman in Egypt. Lon-
    don, 1842-46. 3v. 18° 859.3
POOR. See Social science.
POOR cousin, The, a novel. Pickering, E.. . . . .805.14-15
POOR laws and paupers. Martineau, H. 749.4
POOR rich man and rich poor man. Sedgwick, C.
    M. 729.11
POORE, B. P. Rise and fall of Louis Philippe.
    Boston, 1848. 12° 1009.1
POPE, A. Complete poetical works. Hartf. 1851.
    2v. 12° 335.1
    Contents. — Vol. I. Memoir; Author's preface; Pas-
    torals ; Translations and imitations ; Imitations of
    English poets; Windsor forest; Odes for music; Eloisa
    to Abelard; Elegy to the memory of a lady; Prologues
    and epilogues; Battle of the frogs and mice; 1740, a
    poem; Miscellanies; Fugitive pieces; Epigrams; Epi-
    taphs; Johnson's criticisms on epitaphs; Commenda-
    tory poems. II. Essay on man; Moral essays; Satires
    of Dr. Donne; Epistles and satires of Horace; Essay
    on criticism; Rape of the lock; The Dunciad; Mis-
    cellaneous epistles; Imitations of English poets; Eloisa
    to Abelard; Prologues and Epilogues; Key to the
    lock.
— Poetical works. London, 1851. 3v. 16° . . .   339.3
    Contents. — Vol. I. Memoir of Pope ; Pastorals ;
    Messiah; Windsor forest; The rape of the lock; Eloisa
    to Abelard; Sappho to Phaon; The fable of Dryope;
    Vertumnus and Pomona ; The first book of Statius
    Thebais. II. An essay on criticism; An essay on
    man; Universal prayer; Moral essays; Ode for music
    on St. Cecilia's day ; Epistle to Robert, earl of Oxford
    and Mortimer; Epistles; Prologues; Epigrams; Imi-
    tations of English poets. III. Satires, epistles, and
    odes of Horace, imitated; Satires of Dr. John Donne,
    versified; Epitaphs; The Dunciad.
— Poetical works. Ed. by R. Carruthers. Lon-
    don, 1858. v.1. p.8° 835.16
    Contents. — Vol. I. Translations and imitations ;
    Imitations of English poets; Pastorals; Windsor for-
    est; Messiah, a sacred eclogue; The temple of fame ;
    Ode on St. Cecilia's day. . . . An essay on crit-
    icism; The rape of the lock; Eloisa to Abelard; Epis-
    tles; Epitaphs; An essay on man; The universal
    prayer; Moral essays.
— Memoir, with extracts from his correspond-
    ence. London, 1853. 12° 869.13
— Carruthers, R. The life of 835.12
— Johnson, S. Life of 586.20
POPERY. See Roman Catholic church.
POPES. Daunou, P. C. F. Temporal power of
    the 919.2
— Macaulay, T. B. Review of Ranke's popes
    of R. 409.20
— Ranke, L. History of the 838.1
— Wiseman, N. Recollections of the last four.   1098.1
    See Roman Catholic church.
POPKIN, J. S. Memorial. Ed. by C. C. Felton.
    Cambridge, 1852. 16° 534.20
POPULAR antiquities of Great Britain. Brand, J.   846.8
POPULAR English specimens of the Greek dra-
    matic poets. Æschylus 359.6
POPULAR tales. Guizot, Mme. C. P. 737.15
POPULAR tumults, Sketches of 134.16
POPULATION, New ideas on. Everett, A. H. . . .   136.6
PORCELAIN. Bohn, H. G. Guide to the knowl-
    edge of 835.11

PORCELAIN. Porter, G. R. Manufacture of . . . 408.11
PORPHYRIUS. Introduction to the Organon. Aristoteles 834.12
PORSON, R. Anecdotes and reminiscences of. Barker, E. H 584.8
PORSONIANA. Rogers, S. Table talk 877.16
PORTE Crayon. See Strother, David H.
PORTER, A. M. Don Sebastian, or the house of Braganza: a historical romance. Exeter, 1835. 2v. 32° 789.12
PORTER, C. B. Silver cup of sparkling drops. Boston, 1857. 12° 888.20
PORTER, D. Journal of a cruise to the Pacific ocean, in the Essex, 1812-14. 2d ed. New York, 1822. 2v. 8° 702.11
PORTER, E. Analysis of the principles of rhetorical delivery. 2d ed. Andover, 1828. 12° . 405.16
PORTER, G. R. Manufacture of porcelain and glass. London, 1832. 16° 408.11
— Treatise on the silk manuf. London, 1831. 16° 408.9
— and Long, G. Geography of Great Britain . 365.10
PORTER, J. Scottish chiefs; a romance. Brattleborough, 1818. 3v. 18° 789.5
— — Same. New York, 1856. 12° 789.4
— Sir E. Seaward's narrative of his shipwreck. Abridged ed. London, 1832. 12° 409.24
— — Same. 2d ed. London, 1832. 3v. 16° . . 429.2
— Thaddeus of Warsaw: a novel. Hartford, 1851. 2v. in 1. 18° 789.6
PORTER, Sir J. Turkey, its history and progress, cont. by Sir. G. Larpent. Lond., 1854. 2v. 8° 685.9
PORTER, W. H. The heavenly union, or new Jerusalem on earth. [Also common and scripture proverbs explained.] Bost., 1850. 16° 1084.8
— — Same. Boston, 1850. 12° 1084.13
PORTER, W. T. Hunting and shooting in North America. Hawker, P. 172.3
PORTFOLIO, A poet's. Montgomery, J. 348.13
PORTLAND sketch book, The. Stephens, A. S. . 888.10
PORTLAND, Summary history of. Willis, W. . . 234.2
PORTLOCK, J. E. Treatise on geology. 3d ed. London, 1853. 16° 819.4
PORTO Rico, Notices of. Turnbull, D. 635.3
PORTRAITS, Galleries of. Gilfillan, G. 548.3-4
PORTRAITS of illustrious personages of Great Britain. Lodge, E. 815.1
PORTSMOUTH, N. H., Annals of. Adams, N. . . . 224.26
PORTUGAL. Beckford, W. Sketches of 679.6
— - Tour in 675.18
— Busk, M. M. History of 365.1
— Costigan, A. W. Sketches of society and manners in 679.10
— Dunham, S. A. The history of 368.8
— Forrester, J. J. Prize essay on 673 3
— Froissart, J. The ancient chronicles of . . . 1003.1
— Herbert, H. J. G. Account of 889.8
— Historic sketches of. Lib. Us. Kn. 979.11
— Journal of a few months' residence in 673.4
— March, C. W. Sketches and adventures in . 675.12
— Matthews, H. Tour in 679.14
— Murray, J. Handbook, etc., of 649.16
— Shelley, W. Literary and scientific men of . 398.1
— Sketches of 675.12
PORZIO, C. Congiura de' baroni di Napoli contra il re Ferdinando I. Firenze, 1855. 16° . . . 1059.9
POSEY, T. Memoir of. Hall, J. . . . . . v.XIX. of 529.1
POSITIVE philosophy. Comte, A. 124.10
POST captain, The. Omnibus of modern romance. 801.2
POSTE, B. Britannic researches: or, rectifications of anc. Brit. hist. London, 1853. 8° 985.2
POTIPHAR papers, The. Curtis, G. W. 476.14-15
POTOMAC, Voyage of the, round the world. Reynolds, J. N. 701.8
POTTER, A. Handbook for readers and students. 4th ed. New York, n.d. 18° 820.60
— Political economy, its objects and principles. New York, n.d. 18° 830.3
— Preliminary observations and notes to Paley's natural theology. Paley, W. 820.4
— Principles of science applied to the arts. Boston, 1840. 12° 197.5

POTTER, A. and Emerson, G. B. The school and schoolmaster. Boston, 1843. 12°. 137.14-15
POTTER, Major R. S. Pseud. Life and adventures of 427.1
POTTERY. Bohn, H. G. A guide to the knowledge of 835.11
— Birch, S. History of ancient. 196.1
See Porcelain.
POULTRY. Bement, C. N. Poulterer's companion. 168.8
— Bennett, J. C. Poultry book. 168.7
— - A treatise on domestic fowls 168.7
— Brown, D. J. American poultry yard 168.6
— - Origin, history, etc. of different breeds of. 168.6
— Richardson, H. D. Domestic fowl and ornamental . . . . v.III. of 169.15
— Ysabeau, A. Des oiseaux de basse cour . . . 1075.3
POVERTY, Blessings of. Bartlett, J. 878.12
See also: Social science.
POWELL, B. Essays on the spirit of the inductive philosophy, unity of worlds, and the philosophy of creation. London, 1855. 12°. . . . 147.23
— History of natural philosophy. Lond., 1834. 16° 398.5
POWELL, C. F. Life of Zachary Taylor, with sketches of Maj. Ringgold and others. N. York, 1846. 8° 517.5
POWELL, Mary. Maiden and married life of . . 469.3-5
POWELL, T. Living authors of America. 1st series. New York, 1850. 12° 518.15
— Living authors of England. New York, 1849. 12° 586.9-10
PRACTICAL piety. More, H. . . . . v.IV. of 907.2
PRACTICAL thoughts. Nevins, Wm. 1109.19
PRAED, W. M. Poetical works, [including the Troubadour.] New York, 1854. 12°. . . . 346.5
PRAIRIE, The. A tale. Cooper, J. F. 770.31-33
PRAIRIES. Gregg, J. Commerce of the 628.16
— Irving, W. A tour on the 639.15
PRANK; or the philosophy of tricks and mischief. Abbott, J. . . . . v.III. of 739.1
PRATT, A. Dawnings of genius. New York, 1850. 18° 548.26
— Flowers and their associations. Lond., 1846. 18° 850.4
— The field, garden, and woodland. 2d ed. London, 1841. 16° 169.33
— - Same. 3d ed. London, 1847. 18° 850.5
PRATT, E. History of Eastham, Wellfleet, and Orleans, Mass. Yarmouth, 1844. 8° . . . 224.22
PRAY, L. G. History of Sunday schools and of religious education. Boston, 1847. 12° . . 1108.8
PRAYER. See Theology.
PREACHER, The. [Whitefield.] Ryle, J. C. . . 1088.32-33
— and the king. Bourdaloue and Louis XIV. Bungener, L. 1096.4-6
PREBLE, E. Life of. Sabine, L. . . . . . v.XXII. of 529.1
PRECAUTION; a novel. Cooper, J. F. 780.6-10
PRELUDE, The, or growth of a poet's mind. Wordsworth, W. 344.1-2
PRENTICE, G. D. Biography of Henry Clay. Hartford, 1831. 12° 517.26
PRENTISS, S. S. Memoir, ed. by his brother. N. York, 1855. 2v. 12° 525.3
PRE-RAPHAELITISM. Ruskin, J. 206.3
PRESCHAC, de. Les contes moins contes que les autres. Cabinet des Fées. . . . . . . v.V. of 1077.1
PRESCOTT, W. H. Biographical and critical miscellanies. New York, 1845. 8° 872.2
— - Same. London, 1856. 12° 865.4-9
— History of the conquest of Mexico. New York, 1853. 3v. 8° 252.1-2
— - Same. London, 1857. 2v. 12° 258.1-6
— History of the conquest of Peru. New York, n.d. 2v. 8° 252.3
— - Same. London, 1858. 2v. 12° 258.7-12
— History of the reign of Ferdinand and Isabella. Boston, 1838. 3v. 8° 912.1-2
— - Same. 2d ed. Boston, 1838. 3v. 8° . . 912.3
— - Same. London, 1854. 2v. 12° 929.2-7
— History of the reign of Philip II. Boston, 1855. 2v. 8° 922.1-7
— - Same. London, 1857. 2v. 12° 929.8-13

PRESCOTT, W. H. Life of Charles V. after his abdication. *See* Robertson, W. . . . . v.III. of 912.4-5
— Life of C. B. Brown . . . . .v.I. of 529.1
PRESENT age, The, and inner life. Davis, A. J. 122.10
PRESIDENT's daughters, The. Bremer, F. 455.6-9
PRESIDENTS ot the U. States, Memoirs, addresses and messages of. Williams, E. 296.4
PRESS, The, and the public service. London, 1857. 12° 868.6
PRETENDERS, the, Memoirs of. Jesse, J. H. . . . 553.5
PRETENDERS and their adherents. Memoirs of. Jesse, J. H. 979.8
PREVENTION better than cure. Ellis, S. S. 804.11
PRICE, E. Norway and its scenery. Edited by T. Forester. London, 1853. p.8° 825.7
PRICE, L. Manual of photographic manipulation. London, 1858. 12° 197.12
PRICHARD, J. C. Egyptian mythology. Prelim. essay, by A. W. v. Schlegel, translated. London, 1838. 8° 1083.9
— Natural history of man. 4th ed. By E. Norris. London, 1855. 2v. 8° 173.3
PRIDE and lowliness. Thynn, F. 342.4
PRIDE and prejudice: a novel. Austen, J. . v.II. of 758.3
PRIDEAUX, H. Old and New Testament connected in the history of the Jews. Life prefixed. 2d American ed. Baltimore, 1833. 2v. 8° 1093.12
PRIDEAUX, T. S. Economy of fuel. London, 1853. 16° 829.9
PRIEST, The. [Bishop Latimer.] Ryle, J. C. . 1088.32-33
PRIEST, J. American antiquities, and discoveries in the West. 3d ed. Albany, 1833. 8°. . . 256.1
PRIESTLEY, J. Views of Christian truth, piety, and morality. With a memoir by H. Ware, jr. Cambridge, 1834. 12° 1099.10
PRIME, S. I. Travels in Europe and the East. New York, 1855. 2v. 12° 647.8
PRIME, W. C. Boat life in Egypt and Nubia. New York, 1857. 12° 698.8-12
— Tent life in the Holy Land. New York, 1858. 12° 686.7-11
PRINCE, T. Portions of the chronology of New England. *See* Morton, N. 223.14
PRINCE Edward Island, Travels in. Johnstone, W. 629.19
PRINCE, The. Machiavelli, N. 828.7
PRINCE, The, and the pedlar. Pickering, E. . . . 805.13
PRINCESS of Wolfenbuttel: a novel. Zschokke, H. Omnibus of modern romance 801.2
PRINCESSE Aurélie, La. Comédie. Delavigne, C. . 1078.7
PRINCESSES of England from the Norman conquest. Green, M. A. E. 594.13
PRINCESSES of England connected with the succession of G. B. Strickland, A. 593.4-5
PRINTING, Dictionary of the art of. Savage, W. . 196.4
PRIOR, J. Memoir of Edmund Burke. New ed. Boston, 1854. 2v. 16° 588.17
PRIOR, M. Poetical works. London, 1835. 2v. 16° 329.8
   Contents. — Vol. I. Life, by J. Mitford; Miscellaneous poems and imitations. II. Miscellaneous poems; Alma, or the progress of the mind; Solomon, or the vanity of the world; Miscellaneous poems; The turtle and sparrow; Down-hall, a ballad; Songs; Miscellaneous.
PRISON discipline. Adshead, J. Prisons and prisoners 135.12
— Chesterton, G. L. Revelations of prison life. 135.14
— Inquiry into the separation of convicts. . . . 135.13
— Thompson, G. P. life and reflections 138.2
PRISON of Weltevreden. Gibson, W. M. 707.6-7
PRISON-WORLD of Europe, John Howard and the. Dixon, W. H. 575.14
PRISONER of state in the fortress of Spielberg. Andryane, A. 544.10
PRISONER's memoirs: or, Dartmoor prison. Andrews, C. 219.2
PRITCHARD, A. History of infusoria, living and fossil. London, 1841. 8° 175.3
— Description of optical instruments. . . v.II. of 365.14
PRITTS, J. Mirror of olden time. Border life. Abingdon, Va., 1849. 8° 245.2

PRIVATE anecdotes of foreign courts. London, 1827. 2v. 8° 1005.5
PRIVATEERS. History of the American P. of the war of 1812. Coggeshall, G. 215.8
PROBABILITIES, Essay on. De Morgan, A. . . . 398.15
— Quetelet, A. Théorie des probabilités 1065.45
— Treatise on probability. Lib. Us. Kn. 365.12
   See also: Reversionary payments.
PROBABILITY an aid to faith. Tupper, M. F. v.II. of 887.3
PROBUS: or, Rome in the third century. Ware, W. 808.11
PROCTER, A. A. Legends and lyrics. New York, 1858. 12° 339.8
PROCTER, B. W. Dramatic scenes, with other poems. Boston, 1857. 12° 334.22
— English songs, and other small poems. Boston, 1844. 16° 358.12
— — Same. New and enlarged ed. Boston, 1851. 12° 345.11
— Essays and tales in prose. Boston, 1853. 2v. 16° 875.4
PROCTER, G. History of the Ottoman empire. *See* Jacob, S. 956.11
— — Historical essays. Stoddart, J. 988.7
PROFESSIONAL visits: a tale. Marsh, A. 469.10
PROFESSOR: a tale. Brontë, C. 435.13-17
PROFESSOR's lady, The. Auerbach, B. 802.18
PROGRESS and prejudice: a novel. Gore, C. G. . 776.11
PROGRESSION, Theory of human 134.18
PRÖHLE, H. Harzbilder. [Sitten u. Gebräuche a.d. Harzgebirge.] Liepzig, 1855. 16°. . 1029.14
PROJECTION, Treatise on orthographic. Binns, W. 206.8
   See also: Drawing.
PROMESSI sposi, I. Manzoni, A. 1058.6
— — Same; translated 488.2
PROPELLERS. *See* Engineering, Steam engine, etc.
PROPERTY. Lieber, F. Essays on P. and labour. 820.47
— Simons, C. Des modes d' acquérir et de transmettre la propriété 1065.50
— Sugden, E. Handbook on P. law. 134.24
   See also: Law.
PROPHETIC studies. Lectures on Daniel. Cumming, J. 116.10
   See Bible.
PROPRIA quae maribus, a jeu d' esprit. Reade, C. 415.8
PROSE writers of America. Griswold, R. W. . . . 872.12
PROTESTANT, The: a tale of the reign of Queen Mary. Bray, A. E. 448.10
PROTESTANTISM. Balmes, J. P. and Catholicity compared 1083.3
— Beecher, E. P. defended 1098.9
   See also: Ecclesiastical history, Reformation, Roman Catholic church, etc.
PROUT, W. Chemistry, etc., with reference to natural theology. 4th ed., by J. W. Griffiths. London, 1855. p.8° 826.16
PROVERBIAL philosophy. Tupper, M. F. . v.IV. of 887.3
PROVERBS, Book of P. *See* Bible.
PROVERBS. Bohn, H. G. Polyglot of foreign. . 856.14
— Leclercq, T. Proverbes dramatiques. 1066.24
— Longfellow, H. W. Manuel de P. dramatiques. 1078.10
— Ray, J. Handbook of. 856.12
— Trench, R. C. Lectures on the lessons in . . 1106.14
PROVINCIAL English, Dictionary of. Wright, T. 855.7
PROVINCIAL letters. Pascal, B. 127.28
PROVOST, The: a fiction. Galt, J. 788.14
PROWESS, Narratives of personal. Pritts, J. . . 245.2
PRUE and I. Curtis, G. W. 794.10
PRUSSIA. Atkinson, E. W. Memoirs of the Queens of. 546.1
— Gillies, J. Reign of Frederic II. 546.4
— Laing, S. Social and political state of. . . . 409.14
— Murray, J. Handbook for the continent . . 649.19
— Ranke, L. History of P. in the 17th and 18th centuries 925.7
— Vehse, K. E. Memoirs of the court of . . . 546.7
PSALMS, Book of. *See* Bible.
PSALTER und Harfe, Christl. Lieder. Spitta, C. J. P. 1034.18

PSYCHOLOGY. Brodie, B. C. Psyc. inquiries . . 129.18
— Follen, C. T. C. Fragment of a work on. v.III.of 877.1
— Sunderland, L. Book of. 157.30
   See also: Intellectual science, Philosophy, etc.
PUBLIC characters. Brougham, H. Sketches of. 888.3
— Robertson, I. L. Sketches of 518.9
PUBLIC men of the revolution. Sullivan, W... 213.3
PUBLIC rights, duties and interests, Speeches upon questions relating to. Brougham, H.... 862.1
PUBLIC service, The press and the 868.6
PUBLIC speaking, Art of extempore. Rippingham, J. 405.13
PUBLIUS Syrus, Choice sayings of. *See* Phenix, The 898.8
PULASKI, *Count* K., Life of. Sparks, J... v.XIV. of 529.1
PULCI, L. Il Morgante maggiore. Poema. Firenze, 1855. 2v. 12°. 1056.2
PULPIT. Fowler, H. Sketches of the American . 534.9
— Grant, J. The metropolitan 1099.11
— Ritchie, J. E. The London 128.7
— Sprague, W. B. Annals of the American . . 113.1
— Spring, G. The power of the 116.2
PULSZKY, F. and T. White, red, black: sketches of American society in the United States. New York, 1853. 2v. 12° 627.3
PULSZKY, T. Memoirs of a Hungarian lady; introduction by F. Pulszky. Phila., 1850. 12° 546.9
— Tales and trad. of Hungary. N. Y., 1852. 12° 767.2-3
PUNCHARD, G. History of Congregationalism, A.D. 250 to 1616. Salem, 1841. 12° 1099.13
PUNCH's letters and complete letter writer. Jerrold, D. . . . . v.V. of 906.1
PUNCH's prize novelists. Thackeray, W. M... 508.2-4
PUNCTUATION, Treatise on English. Wilson, J.. 405.17
PUNISHMENT, Ground and reason of, by T. Lewis. *See* Cheever, G. B., on capital P. 135.23
   See also: Prison discipline.
PUNJAB frontier, A year on the, in 1848-49. Edwards, H. B. 695.6
PUPIL, The, of Raphael. New York, 1843. 12° . 489.21
PURITAN, The. [R. Baxter.] Ryle, J. C... 1088.32-33
PURITANS. Marsden, J. B. History of the later, 1642-62 . . . . 1085.17
— Neal, D. History of the 1085.16
— Tales of the 769.11
   See also: Ecclesiastical history. N. Eng., etc.
PURLEY, Diversions of. Tooke, J. H. 402.10
PURSUIT of knowledge under difficulties. Craik, G. L. 125.12-13
PUSCHIN, A. Racconti poetici, tradotti da L. Delàtre. Firenze, 1855. 16° 1059.12
   Contents. — Cenni intorno alla vita di A. Puschin; Il prigioniero del Caucaso; Il conte Nulin; Li Zingari; La fontana di Bakcisarai; Eugenio Anieghin; Pultava.
PUTLITZ, G. zu. Was sich der Wald erzählt. 19te Aufl. Berlin, 1856. 16° 1039.2
— What the woods talk about. Translated by H. W. Carstens. 878.5
PUTNAM, I. Cutter, W. Life of. 528.8
— Hill, G. C. Biography of 528.10
— Humphreys, D. Essay on the life of. 528.7-9
— Peabody, O. W. B. Life of. . . . . . . v.II. of 518.5
PUTNAM, E. Receipt book. New and enlarged edition. Boston, 1856. 16° 188.21
PUTNAM, G. P. Monthly magazine, January, 1853, to June, 1855. New York. 5v. 8°. 880.1
— Story library. New York, 1856-58. 4v. 12° . 738.1
   Contents. — Vol. I. The modern story-teller, or the best stories of the best authors. II. The baked head, and other tales. III. Stories for Christmas and winter evenings. IV. *Wanting.* V. Sea stories.
PYCROFT, J. Course of English reading. Ed. by J. A. Spencer. New York, 1854. 12° . . . 405.19-20
— - Same. 2d edition. London, 1850. 12° . . 405.18
PYNE, G. Perspective for beginners. 4th edition. London, 1852. 16° 819.14
PYRENEES. Costello, L. S. Béarn and the. . . . 654.2
— Ellis, S. S. Summer and winter in the. . . . 654.16
— Inglis, H. D. The P. in 1830 . . . . 663.14

PYRENEES. Johnson, F. H. Sketches of the . . 654.7
PYROMETER, The: by T. S. Traill . . . . v.II. of 365.14
PYRRHUS, History of. Abbott, J. 549.20-24

QUADROON, The. Reid, M. 717.1-2
QUADRUPEDS. Bell, T. A history of British . . 172.18
— Bennett, E. T. 172.19
— Menageries, The. Q. described 849.16-17
— Natural history of, etc. 820.10
— Swainson, W. Nat. hist. and classification of. 308.18
   See also: Mammalia.
QUAKERS. Barclay, R. Princip. and doctrines of. 1095.4
— Sewel, W. History of the 1085.10
   See also: Friends.
QUALITATIVE chemical analysis. Fresenius, C. R. 155.10
— System of instruction in. Fresenius, C. R.. 155.11
QUARANTÄNE im Irrenhause. Kühne, F. G. . . 1016.4
QUARLES, F. Emblems, divine and moral. [Poetry.] New York, 1854. 16° 1108.12
— - Same. New York, 1816. 32° 369.24
QUARRELS of authors. D'Israeli, I. . . . . v.II. of 897.5-6
QUARRYING of stone, Treatise on. Burgoyne, Sir J. 819.25
QUARTERLY review, Papers from the. New York, 1852. 12° 899.16
QUATERNIONS, Lectures on. Hamilton, W. R... 147.7
QUATRE Bras and Waterloo. Eaton, C. A. 1008.16
QUATREFAGES, A. de. Rambles of a naturalist, in France, Spain and Sicily. Translated by E. C. Otté. London, 1857. 2v. 12° 654.10
QUATREMÈRE de Quincy, A. C. Life of Raphael. *See* Duppa, R. 835.7
QUEBEC, Tour from Hartford to. Silliman, B. . 628.26
QUEECHY; a novel. Warner, S. 793.5-10
QUEENHOO-HALL; a romance. Strutt, J. 499.6
QUEENS before the conquest. Hall, M. 594.12
QUEENS of England. Doran, J. Lives of the, of house of Hanover 593.3
— Lancelott, F. 593.2
— Strickland, A. Lives of the 592.1-4
QUEENS county, N. Y., Revolutionary incidents of. Onderdonk, H. 217.17
QUEEN'S rangers. Simcoe, J. G. Journal of the, during the revolution. 212.2
QUEKETT, J. Treatise on the use of the microscope. 2d ed. London, 1852. 8°. 144.6
— - Same. 3d. ed., with add. Lond., 1855. 8° 144.1
QUENTIN Durward. Scott, Sir W. 470.19-25
QUESNEL, P. The gospels, with moral reflections on each verse. Bible 1093.3
QUETELET, A. Astronomie. Bruxelles, n.d. 12° 1065.46
— Physique. Plateau, J. 1065.44
— Théorie des probabilités. Bruxelles, n.d. 12° 1065.45
QUICHERAT, J. Siège d' Orléans. Paris, 1854. 12° 1078.42
QUICKBORN. Groth, K. 1024.2
QUIET husband, The: a novel. Pickering, E. . . 805.11-12
QUINCY, E. Wensley, a story. Boston, 1854. 16° 765.11-14
QUINCY, J. History of Harvard University. 2v. Cambridge, 1840. 8° 294.1
— Life of J. Q. Adams. Boston, 1858. 8° . . . 512.1
QUINCY, J. P. Charicles, a dramatic poem. Boston, 1856. 12° 346.7
— Lyteria, a dramatic poem. Boston, 1854. 16° 345.13
— - Same. 2d ed. Boston, 1855. 16° 345.14
QUINTILIANUS, M. F. Institutes of oratory. Translated by J. S. Watson. Lond., 1856. 2v. p.8° 854.1
QUITS, a novel. Tautphœus, Baroness 474.1-10
QUOTATIONS. Adams, H. G. Cyclop. of poetical. 344.21
— Bartlett, J. A collection of familiar 344.20
— Dictionary of. 358.5
— Hale, S. J. Dictionary of poetical 312.2
— Riley, H. T. Dictionary of Latin and Greek. 854.3
— Shakespeare, W. Shakespearian. 357.4
QUOTATIONS of humor, wit, and wisdom. Boston, 1849. 18° 469.51

RABBE, A. and Duncan, J. Hist. of Russia. London, 1854. 2v. 12° 869.11
RACES of man. Gobineau, A. de. Diversity of . 176.3
— Nott, J. C. Indigenous races of the earth . . 171.2
— Omalius d'Halloy, J. J. de. Des races humaines 1065.43

RACES of man. Pickering, C. 815.3–6
    NOTE. — For the native races of each continent and country, see their several names. See also Man, Human race, Ethnography, etc.
RACHEL Gray, a tale, founded on fact. Kavanagh, J.454.7–11
RACHEL Kell, a tale. New York, 1853. 12°. . . 449.6
RACHEL, *M'lle. See* Félix, R.
RACINE, J. Théâtre complet, précédé d'une notice par M. Auger. Paris, 1854. 12° 1076.4
    Contents. — Notice sur la vie et les ouvrages de R.; La Thébaïde; Alexandre le Grand; Andromaque; Les Plaideurs; Britannicus; Bérénice; Bajazet; Mithridate; Iphigénie; Phèdre; Esther; Athalie.
— Beyle, H. Études sur le romantisme, R. and Shakespeare 1067.23
— R. and the French drama. Blaze de Bury, *Mme.* 840.4
RADCLIFFE, A. Gaston de Blondeville, roman. With memoir of the author. Lond., 1839. 12° 777.5
— Mysteries of Udolpho, romance. London, 1810. 3v. 12° . . . . . . v.XLV.–XLVII. of 779.1
— Romance of the forest. London, 1810. 2v. 12° . . . . v.XLIII.–XLIV. of 779.1
RADCLIFFE, J. N. Fiends, ghosts, and sprites. London, 1854. 12° 124.24
RAFFLES, T. Memoirs of the Rev. Thomas Spencer. 3d Am. ed. Boston, 1814. 8°. 575.1
RAFINESQUE-SCHMALZ, C. S. Travels and researches in N. America and S. Europe. Philadelphia, 1836. 12°. 629.11
RAGUSA, History of. Wilkinson, J. G. 925.5
RAHEL. *See* Varnhagen von Ense, K. A.
RAIKES, H. Memoir of Sir J. Brenton, reëdited by his son. 2d ed. London, 1855. 12°. . . 565.7
RAIKES, R. Life of. Lloyd, W. F. 578.13
RAIKES, T. Portion of journal, comprising life in London and Paris in 1831–47. 2d ed. London, 1856–57. 4v. 8° 566.7
RAILROADS. Handbook for locomotive engineers. 198.17
— Haskoll, W. D. Assistant engineers' railway guide 195.18
— Lardner, D. Railway economy. 195.24
— Lecount P. Treatise on railways 195.25
— Pambour, F. M. G. de. Treatise on locomotive engines 195.15
— Stephenson, R. M. Railway details 829.1
— Williams, F. S. Our iron roads—their hist. . 195.13
— With, E. Means of preventing R. R. accidents. 198.14
— Vose, G. L. Handbook of R. R. construction. 195.11
    NOTE. — For the railroads of individual countries, see the names of those countries. See also, Engineering, Locomotion, Steam engine, etc.
RAIN and rivers; or Hutton and Playfair against Lyell and all comers. Greenwood, G. . . . 145.14
RALE, S. Life of, by C. Francis. Sparks, J. v.XVII. of 529.1
RALEIGH, Sir W. Discovery of the empire of Guiana. London, 1848. 8° 266.1
— Kingsley, C. R. and his times 894.6–10
— Tytler, P. F. Life of. 568.8
RAMBLER, The. Johnson, etc. . . . v.XIX.–XXII. of 850.24
RAMBLES in the footsteps of Don Quixote. Inglis, H. D. 673.5
RAMBLES by rivers. Thorne, J. 850.18
RAMSAY, A. Works, with life of the author, by G. Chalmers, and essay by Lord Woodhouselee. London, 1852. 3v. 12° 326.4
    Contents. — Vol. I. Life; Essay on the genius and writings of Ramsay, by A. F. Tytler, (L'd W.); Serious poems; Elegiac; comic. II. Pastoral poems; Lyric; Satiric. III. Epigrammatical and epistolary poems; Fables and tales; Appendix.
RAMSAY, D. History of the American revolution. Philadelphia, 1789. 2v. 8° 214.12
— Life of George Washington, with notes, and biog. sketch of the author. Ithaca, N. Y., 1840. 515.5
— Same. Ithaca, 1840. 8° 515.3
RAMSEY, J. G. M. The annals of Tennessee. Philadelphia, 1853. 8° 235.4
RAMSBOTHAM, F. H. The process of parturition. 6th Am. ed. Philadelphia, 1851. 8° 151.2
RANALLI, F. Le istorie italiane dal 1846 al 1853. Firenze, 1855. 4v. 8° 1057.8

RAN away to sea. Reid, M. 727.1–10
RANDALL, H. S. Life of Jefferson. N.Y.,1858. 3v. 8° 512.2
RANDOLPH, J. Baldwin, J. G. Sketch of 518.7
— Garland, H. A. Life of 525.2
— Sawyer, L. Biography of 523.18
RANDOM recollections of the House of Lords. Grant, J. 868.9
— of the House of Commons. Grant, J. 868.10
RANGERS, The, and regulators of the Tanaha. Arrington, A. W. 488.4
RANK, J. Aus dem Böhmerwalde. Leipzig, 1851. 3v. 12° 1036.9
— Poetisches-Reise-Album. Leipzig, 1855. 16° 1029.6
— Schillerhäuser. Leipzig, 1856. 16° 1029.12
— Vier Brüder aus dem Volke. Roman. Leipzig, 1844. 16° 1035.10
RANKE, L. Civil wars and monarchy in France, 16th and 17th centuries. Transl. by M. A. Garvey. New York, 1853. 12° 1007.6
— Ferdinand I. and Maximilian II. of Austria. Germany after the reformation. London, 1853. p.8° 409.27
— History of the popes, 16th and 17th centuries. 2d ed., transl. by S. Austin. London, 1841. 3v. 8° 1085.19
— - Same. Transl. by E. Foster. London, 1847–50. 3v. p.8° 838.1
— History of Servia. Tr. by Mrs. Kerr, [and] Slave provinces of Turkey, by C. Robert. London, 1853. p.8° 827.1
— House of Brandenburg, and history of Prussia, 17th and 18th centuries. Tr. by A. and D. Gordon. London, 1849. 3v. 8°. 925.7
— Ottoman and Spanish empires in 16th and 17th centuries. Philadelphia, 1845. 8°. . . 913.1
— Reformation in Germany. Transl. by S. Austin. Philadelphia, 1844. 8° 1085.12
— - Same. 2d ed. London, 1845. 3v. 8° . 1085.20
— Review of Ranke's history of the popes. Macaulay, T. B. 409.20
RANTOUL, R. jr. Memoirs, speeches, and writings. Ed. by L. Hamilton. Boston, 1854. 8° 512.12
RAPE of the bucket: a poem. Tassoni, A. 345.4
RAPHAEL. Quatremère de Quincy. Life of . . . 835.7
— Harford, J. S. Memoir of 543.2
RASPAIL, F. V. Domestic medicine. Ed. by G. L. Strauss. London, 1853. 16° 829.37
RASSELAS, prince of Abyssinia, History of. Johnson, S. 759.10
RAUMER, F. L. G. v. America and the American people. Transl. by W. W. Turner. New York, 1846. 8° 297.1
— Contributions to modern history. Frederick II. and his times. London, 1837. 12° . . . 546.8
— England in 1835. Translated by S. Austin. London, 1836. 3v. 12° 979.2
— England in 1841. Transl. by H. E. Lloyd. London, 1842. 2v. 12° 979.3
— History of the 16th and 17th centuries. Trans. London, 1835. 2v. 12° 927.9
— Italy and the Italians. London, 1840. 2v. 12° 678.4
RAY, J. Handbook of proverbs. Index and additions by H. G. Bohn. London, 1857. p.8°. 856.12
RAYMOND, G. Life and enterprises of R. W. Elliston, comedian. London, 1857. 16° . . . 597.16
RAYNER, B. L. Life of Thomas Jefferson, with selec. from his private corresp. 1834. 12°. 517.24
READ, H. F. Dramatic poems. Boston, 1848. 8° 332.4
    Contents. — Medea; Erminia, a tale of Florence; The new world.
READ, T. B. Sylvia and other poems. Philadelphia, 1857. 12° 349.13
— The new pastoral. Philadelphia, 1855. 16°. 325.8
READE, C. Christie Johnstone: a novel. Boston, 1855. 12° 415.7
— Clouds and sunshine, [and] Art: a dramatic tale. Boston, 1855. 12° 415.6
— "It is never too late to mend:" a romance. Boston, 1856. 2v. 12° 414.1–10
— Peg Woffington: a novel. Boston, 1855. 12° 415.5

READE, C. Propria quae maribus, and The box
   tunnel. Boston, 1857. 12° 415.8
— White lies : a novel. Boston, 1858. 12° . . 415.9–13
READERS and students. Handbook for. Potter, A. 820.60
READIEST reckoner, The. Simpson, S. 136.34
READING abbey, Legend of. Mac Farlane, C. . . 840.33
READING book, The illustrated London 405.2
READING, Course of English. Pycroft, J . . 405.18–20
REALIST, The history of a. Jewsbury, M. J . . . 469.1
REASON why, The. Reasons for things imper-
   fectly understood. London, n.d. 12° . . . 198.3
REASON, Critique of pure. Kant, I. 855.5
REASON and Faith. Rogers, H. 117.1
REBECCA and Rowena. Thackeray, W. M. . . 508.15–17
REBELLION and civil wars in England. Hyde, E. 977.1
REBELLIONS in Scotland in 1745 and 1746. Me-
   moirs of the. Johnstone, Chevalier de . . 976.7
— - Hist. of the. Chambers, R. 830.34
— - from 1638 till 1660. Chambers, R. 830.44
— - in 1689 and 1715. Chambers, R. 830.50
RECEIPTS. Handbook of. Branston, T. F. . . . 198.1
   See also : Domestic economy.
RECKONER, Readiest ever invented. Simpson, S. 136.34
RECOLLECTIONS of a life-time. Goodrich, S. G. . 526.4
RECOLLECTIONS of a parliamentary career. O'Con-
   nell, J. 988.4
RECOLLECTIONS of a Southern matron. Gilman, C. 437.8–10
RECORDED will : or, truth and not fiction. Bos-
   ton, 1855. 12° 428.13
RECORDS of the Bubbleton parish. Boston, 1854.
   12° 417.13
RECORDS of woman. Hemans, F. D. B. . . v.II. of 324.2
RECREATIONS of Christopher North. Wilson, J. 863.10
RECREATIVE arts. Apperley, C. J. The chase,
   the turf and the road. 177.14
— Baucher, F. Method of horsemanship. . . . 164.7
— Forrest. G. Every boy's book. 197.25
— Games for all seasons. 197.29
— Hawker, P. Instructions to young sports-
   men. 172.3
— Herbert, H. W. American game in its season. 174.8
— - Sporting scenes and characters. 174.7
— Lewis, E. J. The American sportsman . . . 172.2
— Magician's own book 197.23
— Montigny. Stratagems of chess 197.30
— Root, N. W. T. School amusements. 137.9
— Salzmann, C. G. Gymnastics for youth . . . 137.2
— Sawyer, F. W. Plea for amusements 129.14
— Strutt, J. Sports and pastimes 195.10
— Turf characters. 177.13
— Walker, D. Manly exercises. 197.24*
— Walker, G. The chess player 197.28
— Webber, C. W. The romance of sporting . . 171.3–5
   See also : Angling, Chess, Field, Game,
   Games, Hunting, Sporting, etc.
REDBURN : his first voyage. Melville, H. 736.6
REDDING, C. History and description of modern
   wines. 3d ed. London, 1851. p.8° 815.10
— The stranger in London, with a sketch of the
   great exhibition. London, 1851. 16° 987.11
REDESDALE, Lord. See Mitford, J. F.
RED fawn of the flower land. Reid, M. 716.11–14
REDFIELD, J. W. Comparative physiognomy ;
   men and animals. N. Y., 1852. 8° 122.7
REDFIELD, W. C. Prevailing storms of the Atlan-
   tic coast. New York. 8° 145.22
REDGAUNTLET : a novel. Scott, Sir W. 480.5–7
RED River settlement, its rise, etc. Ross, A. . . 623.16
RED rover, The : a tale. Cooper, J. F. 780.11–15
REDSKINS, The : or, Indian and Injin. Cooper,
   J. F. 780.18–21
REDWOOD : a tale. Sedgwick, C. M. 436.6–8
REDWOOD, T. Practical pharmacy. Mohr, F. . 152.10
REED, H. Lectures on English literature. Phila-
   delphia, 1855. 16° 406.8
— Lectures on the British poets. Philadelphia,
   1857. 2v. 12° 346.9
— Lectures on English history and tragic poetry,
   as illustrated by Shakspeare. Philadel-
   phia, 1855. 12° 968.2
— Life of Joseph Reed. Sparks, J. . . v.XVIII. of 529.1

REED, W. B. Life and correspondence of Joseph
   Reed. Philadelphia, 1847. 2v. 8° 513.1
REEDS of the Tiber : a story. Genlis, Mme. de . 759.15
REEVE [or Reeves] C. The old English
   baron. A Gothic story. London, 1810.
   12° . . . . v.XXII. of 778.1
REFLECTION, Aids to. Coleridge, S. T. . . v.I. of 886.2
— Hours of. Hunt, J. 349.22
REFORM in parliament. Macaulay, T. B. Speeches
   on 409.18
— Wright, T. History of . . . . v.III. of 962.3
REFORMERS before the reformation. Bonnechose,
   É. de 1085.9
REFORMATION. Blunt, I. J. Sketch of the R. in
   England 379.2
— Davies, C. M. Rise and progress of the R. in
   Holland 914.1
— Ghika, H. Switzerland, the pioneer of the . 914.2
— Marsh, A. Protestant R. in France 1008.2
— Stebbing, H. History of the R. 388.2
   See also : Ecclesiasti'l hist., Protestantism.
REFORMS, Hints towards. Greeley, H. 877.3
REFRACTION. See Light.
REGENERATION. Sears, E. H. 1106.11
   See also : Theology.
REGICIDES, Trials of some of the. Trials of
   Charles I., etc. 399.7
REGINALD Dalton. Lockhart, J. G. 798.12
REGINALD Lyle. Pardoe, J. 416.8
REGINALD Reverie. See Mellen, G.
REGIMEN and longevity. Bell, J. 157.21
REGNAULT, H. V. Elements of chemistry. Tr.
   by Betton. Ed. by Booth and Faber. 3d ed.
   Philadelphia, 1856. 2v. 8° 155.1
REGNAULT-WARIN, J.B.J.I.P. Magdalen church-
   yard. Translated by S. Mackay. Boston,
   1809. 2v. 12° 429.1
REICHENBACH, K. Magnetism, electricity, [etc.]
   in their relations to the vital force. Parts
   I.–II. Transl. with notes, by W. Gregory.
   London, 1850. 8° 145.9
REID, D. B. Rudiments of chemistry. 4th ed.
   London, 1851. 18° 156.35
— Ventilation in American dwellings. Introd.
   by E. Harris. New York, 1858. 8° 207.1
— Ventilation, warming, lighting, and sound.
   London, 1844. 8° 207.2
REID, H. The steam engine. 3d ed. London,
   1851. 12° 198.29
REID, M. The boy hunters. Boston, 1853. 12° . 718.1
— The bush-boys ; or, adventures in South
   Africa. Boston, 1856. 16° 718.8–12
— English family Robinson ; the desert home.
   Boston, 1854. 16° 718.13–14
— Forest exiles : a novel. Boston, 1857. 12° . . 718.15
— Hunter's feast. New York, n.d. 12° 716.1–10
— Osceola the Seminole. New York, n.d. 12° 716.11–14
— Plant hunters, with illustr. Boston, 1858. 12° 728.1–5
— Quadroon : a novel. New York, [1856.] 12°. 717.1–2
— Ran away to sea. Boston, 1858. 12° 727.1–10
— Rifle rangers. A novel. New York, n.d. 8° 715.1–3
— Scalp hunters. A novel. New York, 1856. 12° 717.8–11
— War trail : a romance of the prairie. New
   York, 1857. 12° 715.4–13
— White chief : a legend of North Mexico. New
   York, n.d. 12° 717.3–7
— Young Yägers. Boston, 1857. 16° 718.3–7
— Young voyageurs. Boston, 1854. 12° 718.2
REIFFENBERG, F. A. F. T., Baron de, and Vander-
   vin, J. E. Histoire du comté de Hainaut.
   Bruxelles, n.d. 3v. 12° 1075.19
REINHOLD, C. Gesammelte novellen und Erzähl-
   ungen. Bremen, 1847–48. 3v. 16° 1024.13
   Contents. — Vol. I. Die Kinder der Fremde. II.
   Real und ideal. III. Die Karfreitags-Christen.
REISEBILDER. Heine, H. 1037.8
REJECTED addresses. Smith, H. and J. 325.3
RELIQUES of ancient English poetry. Percy, T. . 332.3
RELIGIO-MEDICI. Browne, Sir T. . . . . . v.II. of 846.11
RELIGION. See Theology, Ecclesiastical history,
   Evidences of Christianity, Mythology, etc.

RELLSTAB, L. Gesammelte Schriften. Leipzig, 1843–1854. 20v. 12° 1014.2

Contents. — Vols. I.–IV. 1812. Ein historischer Roman, 4e Aufl. V. Sagen und romantische Erzählungen; Waldhulde oder der Wolfsbrunnen; Elsbeth, eine Sage vom Ilsenstein; Jaromir, eine romantische Erzählung; Berghold, eine romantische Erzählung; Das Hochzeitfest, nach einer italienischen Sage; Harzbilder und Harzsagen. VI. Kunst-novellen; Theodor; Julius; Edmund, musikalische Skizzen; Donna Anna, ein Bruchstück aus dem Leben der Künstler und Vornehmen; Drei Blätter aus dem Tagebuche eines Reisenden, eine poetisch-musikalische Skizze; Der Goldschmied von Augsburg, eine Erzählung. VII. Novellen: Die Steinkohlengruben; Die Räuber im Schwarzwalde. VIII. Novellen: Die Badereise; Der Wildschütz. IX. Auswahl aus der Reisebildergallerie des Verfassers; Erste Abtheilung : Empfindsame Reisen im Jahre 1832; Zweite Abtheilung; Reise-Idyllen, Skizzen, Portraits und Jeremiaden aus dem Jahre 1835 ; Vermischte Aufsätze; Die Cholera im Fürstenthume Scheeran; Ludwig Devrient; Wilhelmine Schroder-Devrient. X. Vermischte Schriften: Neue empfindsame Reisen; Kritiken und vermischte Aufsätze. XI. Dramatische Werke: Karl der Kühne, Herzog von Burgund, Trauerspiel; Bianca, Trauerspiel; Franz von Sickingen, Histor. Tragödie. XII. Gedichte. XIII.–XIV. Algier und Paris im Jahre 1830; Neue Auflage. XV. James Skey, eine Erzählung; Die Gemsjäger, ein Bruckstück aus meinem Reise Tagebuche ; Die Gewerke, eine Erzählung; Die Brüder, eine Erzählung im Volkston; Reise durch's Riesengebirge, in zerstreuten Blättern. XVI. Die Artilleristen, eine Novelle; Osraim der Suchaer, frei nach orientalischen Mittheilungen; Die Kameraden, eine Erzählung im Volkston. XVII. Die Venetianer, eine Novelle; Die Strandbewohner, eine Novelle; Der Pflegesohn, frei nach dem Französischen. XVIII. Elvira, eine Erzählung; Müller und Müller, eine aus den Acten gezogene Geschichte; Aus Heinrich's Denkwürdigkeiten, Wahrheit, nicht Dichtung; Drei Tage an den Ufern des Orinoko, skizzirte Erzählung, frei nach dem Englischen. XIX. Dramatische werke; Eugen Aram, Trauerspiel; Die Venetianer, Drama; Die drei Tanzmeister, Posse. XX. Musikalische Beurtheilungen.

REMARKABLE characters. Kirby, R. S. Wonderful and eccentric museum 894.1
REMEDIES, with formulæ for their administration. Dunglison, R. 151.15
REMINISCENCES of the last sixty-five years. Thomas, E. S. 216.6
REMINISCENCES of thought and feeling. Boston, 1853. 16° 138.5
RENA, or the snow-bird : a novel. Hentz, C. L. . 445.12
RENGGER, J. R. and Longchamps. Reign of Dr. Francia in Paraguay. London, 1827. 8° . . 266.3
RENNIE, J. Architecture of birds. Lond. n.d. 12° 839.2
— - Same. Boston, 1831. 12° 849.10
— - Same. New ed. London, 1844. 18° . . . 850.7
— Bird miscellanies. London, 1847. 18° . . . 850.8
— Domestic habits of birds. London, 1848. 12° 839.11
— Faculties of birds. London, 1848. 12° . . . 839.10
— Insect architecture. Boston, 1830. 12° . . . 849.13
— - Same. New edition. London, 1845. 2v. 18° 850.6
— - Same. 4th ed. London, n.d. 12° 839.13
— Natural history of birds. N. York, 1850. 18° 820.5
— and Westwood, J. O. Natural history of insects. New York, 1843. 2v. 18° 810.9
— - Same. 2d ed. London, 1829–38. 2v. 16° 389.18
RENNELL, Maj. J. Topography of ancient Babylon. Rich, C. J. 694.8
RENWICK, H. B. and J. Lives of John Jay and Alexander Hamilton. N.Y., n.d. 18° . . . 820.33
RENWICK, J. Elements of mechanics. Phila., 1832. 8° 196.5
— First principles of natural philosophy. New York, 1846. 12° 149.25
— Life of Dewitt Clinton. New York, n.d. 18° 820.30
— Life of Robert Fulton . . . . v.I. of 518.5
— Life of D. Rittenhouse . . . . v.II. of 518.5
— Life of B. Thompson, *Count Rumford*. v.XV. of 529.1
REPRESENTATIVE government, Origin of. Guizot, F. P. G. 817.7
REPRESENTATIVE men. Seven lectures. Emerson, R. W. 876.5

REPTILES, The natural history of. Swainson, W. 408.1
   See also : Natural history.
REPTON, H. Landscape gardening and architecture. New ed., by J. C. Loudon. London, 1840. 8° 203.19
REPUBLIC, The, of the United States ; its duties to itself and its relations to other countries. New York, 1848. 12° 297.19
REPUBLIC. Cicero, M. T. Treatise on the 834.14
— Cunynghame, A. A glimpse at the great Western republic 629.28
— Plato. The republic . . . . v.II. of 814.3
— Lamartine, A. de. The past, the present, and the future of the 134.11
— Tocqueville, A. de. R. of United States of America 134.3
REPUBLICAN party of France, History of. La Hodde, L. 1004.4
REPUBLICANISM. Austin, B. Constitutional republicanism in opposition to fallacious federalism 297.11
   See also : Government, Political science, etc.
REPULSE Bay, Attempt to reach. Lyon, G. F. . 625.11–12
RESCUED nun, The : a novel. St. Leger, Baron . 802.24
RESIDENCE at Sierra Leone ; by a lady. London, 1849. 12° 899.6
RESIDENCES, Designs of cheap, country and village. Ritch, J. W. 201.1–2
RESOLUTE, Voyage of discovery ship. M'Dougall, G. F. 703.10
RESTORATION of belief. Cambridge, 1855. 12° . . 1086.28
RESTORATION of monarchy in France, History of the. Lamartine, A. de. 837.9
RETRIBUTION, a tale of passion. Southworth, E. D. E. N. 456.16
RETZ, *Card.* de, Memoirs of. *See* Gondi, J. F. P. de. 613.10
REUBEN Apsley : a novel, Smith, H. 797.3
REUBEN Medlicott. Novel. Savage, M. W. . . . 438.4
REUMONT, A. v. Carafas of Maddaloni : or, Naples under Spanish dominion. Lond., 1854. p.8° 827.2
REVELATION, Book of the. *See* Bible.
REVELS at court, in the reigns of Elizabeth and James I. Cunningham, P. 342.5
REVENGE, The : a tale. Opie, A. 469.32–33
REVERE, J. W. A tour of duty in California. Ed. by J. N. Balestier. N. Y., 1849. 12° . . 637.5
REVERIE, The : or, a flight to the paradise of fools. Johnstone, C. 429.7
REVERIES of a bachelor. Mitchell, D. G. 476.12
REVERSIONARY payments. Jones, D. 365.8
   See also : Probabilities.
REVETT, N. Antiquities of Athens and other monuments of Greece. Stuart, J. 835.17
— Corrections and remarks on " Travels in Greece." Chandler, R. 683.5
REVIVALS of the 18th century. Macfarlan, J. . . 118.9
REVOLUTION, Causes and forms of. St. John, J. A. 139.14
REVOLUTION, History of the, in Europe. Koch, C. W. 830.45
   See also : American, English, French ; and for revolutions in other countries, see their several names.
REYNOLDS, F. Life and times; by himself. London, 1826. 2v. 8° 597.4
REYNOLDS, Sir J. Literary works. Edited by H. W. Beechey. London, 1852. 2v. p.8° . . . 858.4

Contents. — Vol. I. Memoir ; Discourse 1–8. II. Discourse 9–15; The Idler, nos. 76, 79, 82; Journey to Flanders and Holland; Art of painting, by C. A. Du Fresnoy; Annotations on Du Fresnoy's poems ; Du Fresnoy's sentiments on the principal painters of the two last ages; Parallel between poetry and painting; Epistle to Mr. Jervas ; Chronological list of painters; Alphabetical list of painters.

— Memoirs of, with an analysis of his discourses. Northcote, J. 556.1
REYNOLDS, J. N. Voyage of the Potomac during the circumnavigation of the globe, 1831–34. New York, 1835. 8° 701.8
— Pacific and Indian oceans : or, the South Sea exploring expedition. New York, 1841. 8° 704.6
RHEDER und Matrose. Willkomm, E. 1013.2

RHETORIC. Aristoteles. Treatise on 814.8
— Baron, A. Manuel abrégé de 1065.3
— Campbell, G. Philosophy of. 405.6
— Cicero, M. T. Rhetorical invention . v. IV. of 824.10
— Hervey, G. W. R. of conversation. 405.9
— Porter, E. Analysis of rhetorical delivery . 405.16
— Theremin, F. Outlines of a systematic . . . 405.7
— Whately, R. Elements of 406.21
    See also : Elocution, and Oratory.
RHETORICIANS, Lives of the. Suetonius Tran-
    quillus, C. 814.8
RHIND, W. History of British India. Murray, H. 810.51
RHINE. Abbott, J. Rollo on the 659.22-24
— Banfield, T. C. Industry of the 840.1
— Buddeus, A. Eisenbahnfahrt und Wander-
    ungen im süddeutschen Rheinland 1029.16
— Cooper, J. F. Excursion up the 654.9
— Family tour up the 389.2
— Headley, J. T. Alps and the. 676.18
— Hocker, N. Der Rhein von Mainz bis Köln. 1029.21
— Legaré, H. S. Journal of the 872.3
— Murray, J. Handbook for Belgium and the. 649.7
— - The R. from Holland to Switzerland. . . 649.19
— Thackeray, W. M. Legend of the 508.15-17
RHODE Island bar, Memoirs of the. Updike, W. . 518.1-2
RHODE Island book. Lynch, A. C. 888.9
RHODES, Knights of. Taaffe, J. 915.1
RHONE, Recollections of the. Pardoe, J. 668.21
RHYMES of travel, ballads and poems. Taylor,
    J. B. 345.19
RIBAULT, J., Life of. Sparks, J. . . . . . v.XVII. of 529.1
RICANNERIES, Les. Recueil d' anecdotes, etc.
    Paris, 1817. 18°. 1069.10
RICARDO, D. Principles of political economy and
    taxation. 2d ed. London, 1819. 8°. . . . 136.3
RICCI, A. M. Gli sposi fedeli. Stor. italo-goth.,
    romantica. 2a ediz. Milano, 1837. 16° . . 1058.11
RICCI, S. de. Female convents. Secrets of nun-
    neries disclosed. Compiled by De Potter.
    Edited by T. Roscoe. N. Y., 1834. 12°. . 1098.13-15
RICE, G. E. Blondel : a historic fancy. Boston,
    1854. 12° 356.22
— Myrtilla : a fairy extravaganza. Boston,
    1854. 12° 356.22
— Old play in a new garb. (Hamlet.) 2d ed.
    Boston, 1853. 12° 356.22
RICE, J. H. and B. H. Memoir of J. B. Taylor.
    2d ed. New York. 16° 1100.21
— Discourse delivered in Murray st. church . . 1083.5
RICH, C. J. Journey to the site of Babylon in
    1811, and to Persepolis. London, 1839. 8°. 694.8
— Residence in Koordistan and Nineveh, with
    voyage to Bagdad. London, 1836. 2v. 8°. 694.7
RICH, E. The occult sciences. Smedley, E. . . . 125.5
RICHARD I. Abbott, J. History of 559.8-12
— Aytoun, W. E. Life and times of 379.1
— Crusade of R. Cœur de Lion 846.6
— James, G. P. R. Life of R. Cœur-de-Lion . . 552.2
RICHARD II. Abbott, J. History of 579.8-12
RICHARD III. Abbott, J. History of 579.13-17
— Brooke, C. The ghost of : a poem 342.21
— Field, W. The true tragedy of 342.20
— Halsted, C. A. R. III. as duke of Gloucester
    and king of England 552.5
— Walpole, H. Historic doubts on the life of. 989.10
RICHARD Edney and the governor's family. Judd,
    S. 488.6
RICHARD Hurdis : a tale of Alabama. Simms,
    W. G. 790.47-51
RICHARD of Cirencester, on the ancient state of
    Britain. Giles, J. A. 846.4
RICHARD of Devizes. Narrative of the crusade
    of Richard, Cœur de Lion 846.6
RICHARDS, G. H. Memoir of A. Macomb. New
    York, 1833. 12° 528.20
RICHARDS, T. A. Appleton's illustrated hand-
    book of American travel. N. Y., 1857. 8°. 639.17
RICHARDS, W. C. Electron : a telegraphic epic.
    New York, 1858. 12° 339.7
RICHARDSON, C. On the study of language. An
    exposition of Tooke. London, 1854. 16°. . 406.14

RICHARDSON, G. F. Introduction to geology.
    New ed. London, 1851. p.8°. 816.10
RICHARDSON, H. D. Rural handbooks. London,
    n.d. 4v. 16° 169.15

    Contents. — Vol. I. The horse, by Richardson ; The cow, by Milburn ; The sheep, by Milburn ; The pig, by Richardson. II. Agricultural instructor, by Murphy ; Pests of the farm, by Richardson ; Land drainage, by Donald. III. The dog ; Domestic fowl ; The hive and the honey bee. IV. The flower garden, by Glenny ; Flax, by Ward ; Soils and manures, by Donaldson.

— Dogs ; their origin and varieties. New York,
    1847. 12° 177.15
RICHARDSON, *Sir* J. Arctic searching expedition.
    N. Y., 1852. 12° 704.8-9
RICHARDSON, Jas. Travels in the great desert of
    Sahara in 1845-46. London, 1848. 2v. 8°. 693.1
— Écarté : or, the salons of Paris. New York,
    1829. 2v. 12° 807.7
RICHARDSON, S. Works, with sketch of his life
    and writings, by E. Mangin. London, 1811.
    19v. 12° 768.1

    Contents.—Vol. I. Life and writings of Richardson ; Eulogy, from the French of Diderot. I.—IV. Pamela. V.—XII. Clarissa Harlowe. XIII.—XIX. Sir Charles Grandison.

— Correspondence : biographical account by A.
    L. Barbauld. London, 1804. 6v. 12° . . . 599.2
— Review of the correspondence of. Jeffrey, F. 409.3
RICHARDSON, T. Chemical technology. Ronalds,
    E.. . . . . 155.20
RICHE, B. Farewell to the militarie profession.
    Eight novels publ. in 1581. Lond., 1846. 8°. 342.32
RICHELIEU, A. du P. Vie du cardinal de. Corne, II. 1078.38
RICHES, The race for. Arnot, W. 127.7
RICHMOND, L. Annals of the poor. New ed.
    New York, 1852. 12° 119.2

    Contents. — The dairyman's daughter ; The negro servant ; The young cottager ; The cottage conversation ; A visit to the infirmary.

— Life. New York, 1848. 16° 599.11
RICHTER, J. P. F. Sämmtliche werke. Berlin,
    1840-42. 33v. 16° 1036.1

    Contents.—Vols. I.—II. Vorwort des Herausgebers ; Ankündigung der Herausgabe meiner sämmtlichen Werke ; Die unsichtbare Loge. III. Leben des Quintus Fixlein aus fünfzehn Zettelkasten gezogen, und einigen Jus de tablette. IV. Aus des Teufels Papieren. V.—VIII. Hesperus oder 45 Hundsposttage. IX. Grönländische Prozesse oder satirische Skizzen. X. Jean Paul's biographische Eclustigungen unter der Gehirnschale einer Riesin, eine Geistergeschichte ; Satirischer appendix ; Der Jubelsenior, ein Appendix ; Appendix des appendix oder meine Christnacht. XI.—XII. Blumen-Frucht-und Dornenstücke ; oder Ehestand, Tod und Hochzeit des Armenadvokaten F. St. Siebenkäs. XIII. Das Kampaner Thal, oder über die Unsterblichkeit der Seele nebst einer Erklärung der Holtzschnitte unter den zehn Geboten des Katechismus ; Jean Paul's Briefe und bevorstehender Lebenslauf ; Konjektural-Biographie. XIV. Palingenesien. XV.—XVI. Titan. XVII. Komischer Anhang zum Titan ; Clavis Fichtiana ; Das heimliche Klaglied der jetzigen Männer, eine Stadtgeschichte ; Die wunderbare Gesellschaft in der Neujahrsnacht. XVIII.—XIX. Vorschule der Aesthetik nebst einigen Vorlesungen in Leipzig über die Parteien der Zeit. XX.—XXI. Flegeljahre. XXII. Levana oder Erziehlehre. XXIII. Levana-oder Erziehlehre ; Ergänzblatt zur Levana ; Freiheits-Büchlein. XXIV. Dr. Katzenbergers Dadreise ; nebst einer Auswahl verbesserter Werkchen. XXV. Friedenspredigt an Deutschland ; Dämmerungen für Deutschland ; Mars und Phöbus Thronwechsel ; Politische Fastenpredigten. XXVI. Leben Fibels des Verfassers der Bienrodischen Fibel ; Des Feldpredigers Schmelzle Reise nach Flätz ; Nebst der Beichte des Teufels bei einem Staatsmanne. XXVII. Museum ; Ueber die deutschen Doppelwörter. XXVIII. Der Komet, oder Nikolaus Marggraf. XXIX. Der Komet, Fortsetzung ; Briefe an F. H. Jakobi. XXX.—XXXI. Herbst-Blumine, oder gesammelte Werkchen aus Zeitschriften. XXXII. Gesammelte Aufsätze und Dichtungen. XXXIII. Selina, oder ueber die Unsterblichkeit der Seele ; Vorläufige Gedanken ; Inhaltsverzeichniss von Jean Paul's sämmtlichen Werken.

RICHTER, J. P. F. Flower, fruit, and thorn pieces.
    Transl. by E. H. Noel. 1st-2d series. Bos-
    ton, 1845. 2v. 12° 887.8
— Walt and Vult, or the twins. Transl. by Mrs.
    E. B. Lee. Boston, 1846. 2v. 16° 808.8
— Carlyle, T. Memoir; Schmelzle's journey
    and Quintus Fixlein. German rom. . v.III. of 418.1
— Lee, E. B. Life of R. 545.13
RICORD, P. Letters on syphilis, with an introduc-
    tion by A. Latour. Transl. by W. P. Latti-
    more. Philadelphia, 1852. 8° 151.22
— Venereal diseases. Transl. by A. S. Doane.
    7th ed. Philadelphia, 1853. 8° 153.2
RIDDLE, J. E. History of the Ottoman empire.
    Jacob, S. 956.11
RIDGE, B. Health and disease. London, 1858. 12°   157.35
RIDLEY, J. Tales of the genii. New ed. London,
    1857. p.8° 835.10
— Les contes des génies . . . . v.XXIX.-XXX. of 1077.1
RIENZI, the last of the Roman tribunes. Novel.
    Lytton, E. B. 466.6
RIENZI, trag. Mitford, M. R. 804.4
RIFLE, axe and saddle-bags. Milburn, W. H. . . .   898.14
RIFLE rangers. Reid, M. 715.1-3
RIGAULT, H. Étude littéraire sur Camus et le ro-
    man chrétien au XVIIe. siècle. See Camus,
    J. P.   1078.12
RIGGING of ships. Treatise on. Kipping, R. . .   819.38
RIKER, J. jr. Annals of Newtown, N. Y. New
    York, 1852. 8° 224.4
RILEY, H. T. Dictionary of Latin quotations, with
    a select. of Gr. quot. London, 1856. p.8° .   854.3
RIMBAULT, E. F. History of the organ. Hop-
    kins, E. J. 204.3
RING, M. John Milton und seine Zeit. Hist. Ro-
    man. Frankfurt, a. M. 1857. 8° 1013.14
RIO Grande, Campaigns of the. Stevens, I. I. . .   623.9
— Our army on the. Thorpe, T. B. 259.6
RIO de Janeiro, travels. Gerstäcker, F. 636.1
RIPA, Father. Memoirs during thirteen years' resi-
    dence at the court of Peking. Lond., 1844. 12°   899.7
— - Same. Transl. by F. Prandi. New York,
    1846. 12° 544.11
RIPLEY, G. and Taylor, J. B. Handbook of litera-
    ture and the fine arts. New York, 1852. 8°   406.22
RIPLEY, R. S. War with Mexico. New York,
    1849. 2v. 8° 252.4
RIPPINGHAM, J. The art of extempore public
    speaking. London, 1813. 12° 405.13
RIQUETTI. See Mirabeau.
RISE and progress of religion. Doddridge, P. . .   119.10
RISE and progress of Australia, Tasmania, and
    New Zealand. London, 1857. 12° 705.15
RITCH, J. W. American architect. Cheap coun-
    try and village residences. N. Y., n.d. 4°. 201.1-2
RITCHIE, A. C. M. Autobiography of an actress.
    Boston, 1854. 16° 538.17-21
— Mimic life; or before and behind the curtain.
    Boston, 1856. 12° 475.1-12
— Plays, [Armand and Fashion,] new and rev.
    ed. Boston, 1855. 16° 356.16
— Twin roses; a narrative. Boston, 1857. 12° .   475.13
RITCHIE, J. E. The London pulpit. 2d ed. Lon-
    don, 1858. 16° 128.7
RITCHIE, J. S. Wisconsin and Lake Superior. 3d
    ed. Philadelphia, 1858. 12° 237.9
RITCHIE, L. Romance of history. France. New
    York, 1831. 2v. 12° 419.4
— - Same. 4th ed. London, 1832. 3v. 16°.   419.5
— Schinderhannes, the robber of the Rhine.
    London, 1833. 16° 758.9
— - Same. London, 1848. 16° 758.8
— Pic-nic papers. Dickens, C. 462.4
RITTENHOUSE, D. Life of, by J. Renwick. See
    Lives of eminent individuals . . . . v.II. of 518.5
— Life of. Barton, W. 524.12
RITTER, vom Geiste. Roman. Gutzkow, K. F. .   1015.4
RIVAL beauties, The; a novel. Pardoe, J. . . .   802.42
RIVALS, The. Tracy's ambition; a novel. Grif-
    fin, G. 807.2

RIVERS. Rain and; or Hutton and Playfair
    against Lyell. Greenwood, G. 145.14
ROADS. Gillespie, W. M. Manual of R. and road-
    making 195.19
— Law, H. Art of constructing and repairing .   819.33
ROB of the bowl; a legend of St. Inigoe's. Ken-
    nedy, J. P. 726.3
ROBBER, The; a tale. James, G. P. R. 464.9
ROBBERS, The; a tragedy. Schiller, J. C. F. v. .   478.1
ROBERT, C. Slave provinces of Turkey. Ranke, L.   827.1
ROBERT Graham. Sequel to Linda. Hentz, C. L.   445.14
ROBERT Merry's museum. Goodrich, S. G. . .   907.1
ROBERTS, E. Scenes and characteristics of Hin-
    dostan. Philadelphia, 1836. 12° 938.10
ROBERTS, G. Life, progresses, and rebellion of
    James, duke of Monmouth. London, 1844.
    2v. 12° 566.5
ROBERTS, O. W. Narrative of voyages and excur-
    sions in Central America. Edinb., 1827. 18°   830.35
ROBERTS, R. House servant's directory. Bos-
    ton, 1827. 12° 189.4
ROBERTS, W. Looker on. See British Essay-
    ists . . . . v. XLI. of 850.24
ROBERTS, W., Esq. Memoirs and correspondence
    of Hannah More. New York, 1851. 2v. 12°   595.11
ROBERTSON, D. Reports of the trials of Aaron
    Burr. Philadelphia, 1808. 2v. 8° 296.6
ROBERTSON, F. W. Sermons preached at Trinity
    chapel, Brighton. 1st series from 3d Lon-
    don ed. Boston, 1857. 12° 1086.6
— - Same. 2d series from 4th London ed.
    Boston, 1858. 12° 128.1
— - Same. 3d series from 2d London ed.
    Boston, 1858. 12° 128.2
ROBERTSON, I. L. Sketches of public characters,
    living and dead. New York, 1830. 12° . . .   518.9
ROBERTSON, J. B. Life of K. W. F. von Schlegel.   818.3
ROBERTSON, J. P. and W. P. Letters on Para-
    guay. London, 1838. 3v. 12° 635.11
ROBERTSON, W. Works. N. Y., 1848-50. 3v. 8°   943.4

    Contents. — Vol. I. America. II. Charles V. III.
    Scotland and India.

— History of America abridged, with mem. of R.
    by D. Stewart. New York, 1848. 18° . . .   830.5
— History of the reign of Charles V. Abridged
    ed. New York, n.d. 18° 830.6
— - Same, [continued by] W. H. Prescott.
    Boston, 1857. 3v. 8° 912.4-5
— Life and writings of. Stewart, D. 582.1
ROBESPIERRE, F. M. J. I. de, Life of. Lewes, G. H.   615.1
ROBIN Hood, An historical sketch of. Campbell,
    W. W. 589.2
ROBINSON Crusoe. De Foe, D. 735.9
ROBINSON, E. and Smith, E. Biblical researches
    in Palestine, Mount Sinai and Arabia Pe-
    træa. Boston, 1841. 3v. 8° 684.4
— - Same. 2d ed. London, 1856. 3v. 8° . .   1103.7
ROBINSON, H., Biography of. Wilson, D. 428.5
ROBINSON, H. A. Six months in Kansas. Bos-
    ton, 1856. 12° 239.3
ROBINSON, J. Works; with mem. and annot. by
    R. Ashton. Boston, 1851 3v. 12° . . .   1087.10

    Contents. — Vol. I. Memoir of Dr. Robinson; New
    essays, or observations divine and moral; A defence
    of the doctrine propounded by the synod at Dort,
    against John Murton and his associates. II. A justi-
    fication of separation from the church of England,
    against Mr. Richard Bernard and his invective. III.
    A just and necessary apology of certain Christians;
    Religious communion, private and public; The peo-
    ple's plea for the exercise of prophecy; A treatise of
    the lawfulness of bearing of the minister in the church
    of England; An appeal on truth's behalf; An answer
    to a censorious epistle; A catechism, being an appen-
    dix to the foundation of the Christian religion, gath-
    ered into six principles, by Rev. Wm. Perkins.

ROBINSON, M. Vacenza: a novel. 3d ed. Lon-
    don, 1792. 2v. 12° 429.10
— Walsingham: a domestic story. London,
    1797. 4v. 12° 429.3

ROBINSON, T. A. L. v. J. Heloise; or the unre-
vealed secret: a tale. New York, 1850. 12°.449.14-15
— Languages and literature of the Slavic na-
tions. Preface by E. Robinson. N. York,
1850. 12° 404.7
— Life's discipline: a tale of Hungary. New
York, 1851. 12° 449.12
— The exiles. New York, 1853. 12° 449.13
ROBINSON, W. D. Mexican revolution and Mina's
expedition. Philadelphia, 1820. 8° . . . 255.1
— Memoirs of the Mexican revolution and Mi-
na's expedition. London, 1821. 2v. 8°. . 254.4-8
ROBISON, John. Treatise on carpentry. See
Encyclopædia Britannica 201.4
ROB ROY. Scott, Sir W. 460.17-21
ROBSON, W. John Railton; or; read and think.
London, 1854. 12° 449.19
ROCCA, M. de. War of the French in Spain.v. II.of 830.42
ROCHAU, A. L. v. Wanderings through the cities
of Italy. London, 1853. 2v. 12° 678.1
ROCHE, R. M. Children of the abbey. Hartford,
1822. 2v. 18° 789.8
ROCHELLE, Le siège de La. Genlis, Mme. de . . 1069.15
ROCKS, Voices from the See Voices 169.19
ROCKY mountains, Exploring expedition to the.
Frémont, J. C. 628.13-15
— Irving, W. Scenes, incidents, etc., among
the 639.14
— Palmer, J. Journal of travels over the . . . 627.21
— Parker, S. Journal of a tour beyond the. . . 628.8
— Parkman, F. jr. R. M. life 626.14
— Ruxton. G. F. Adventures in the 638.5-6
— Sage, R. B. Scenes in the 639.4
ROD and the staff, The. Stone, T. T. 118.17
RODOLPHUS: a Franconia story. Abbott, J. v.VI.of738.4
ROE, A. S. The star and the cloud; or, a daugh-
ter's love. New York, 1857. 12° 726.13
— Time and tide; or, strive and win. N. York,
1852. 12° 726.12
— True to the last; or, alone on a wide, wide
sea. New York, 1858. 12° 735.14
ROELKER, B. Constitutions of France. Boston,
1848. 12° 134.14
— Manual for notaries public. N. Y., 1853. 8° . 133.5
ROGER de Hoveden. Annals, comprising the his-
tory of England from A.D. 732 to A.D. 1201.
London, 1853. 2v. p.8° 856.2
ROGER of Wendover. Flowers of history. Tr.
by J. A. Giles. London, 1849. 2v. p.8° . . 846.9
ROGERS, C. Modern Scottish minstrel, with
memoirs of the poets, [etc.] Edinburgh,
1855-57. 6v. 12° 316.12
ROGERS, H. Defence of the Eclipse of faith, etc.
Boston, 1854. 12° 117.10
— Eclipse of faith, or visit to a sceptic. 5th ed.
Boston, 1854. 12° 117.11
— Greyson letters. Boston, 1857. 12° 885.6
— Reason and faith, and other miscellanies.
Boston, 1853. 12° 117.1
— New biographies. See Macaulay, T. B. . . . 547.7
ROGERS, S. Table talk; to which is added Por-
soniana. New York, 1856. 12° 877.16
ROGERS, S. B. Elementary treatise on iron metal-
lurgy. London, 1857. 8° 195.8
ROGERS, T. J. New American biographical dic-
tionary. 2d ed. Easton, Pa., 1823. 12° . . 518.14
ROGET, P. M. Electricity, electro-magnetism,
galvanism, magnetism . . . . v.II. of 365.14
— Thesaurus of English words. Ed. by B.
Sears. Boston, 1854. 12° 403.13
ROI, Le, des canaries; conte. Saintine, X. B. . . 1078.39
ROKEBY: a poem. Scott, Sir W. 359.16
ROLAND, M. J. P. Lettres autographes à Bancal
des Issarts. Introd. par Ste. Beuve. Brux-
elles, 1836. 16° 1079.2
— History of. Abbott, J. S. C. 569.23-27
ROLAND von Berlin. Roman. Häring, W. . . . 1024.6
ROLANDSITTEN. Fiction. Hoffmann, E. T. A. [W.] 801.3
ROLLIN, C. Ancient history, with a life by J.
Bell. Cincinnati, 1852. 2v. 8° 952.1

ROLLO in Geneva. Abbott, J. 659.12-16
— in Holland. Abbott, J. 659.17-21
— in London. Abbott, J. 659.5-7
— in Paris. Abbott, J. 659.8
— in Switzerland. Abbott, J. 659.9-11
— on the Atlantic. Abbott, J. 659.1-4
— on the Rhine. Abbott, J. 659.22-24
ROMAINE, R. D. New age of gold, or life and adventures. Boston, 1856. 12° 526.2
ROMAN antiquities. Adam, A. 954.7
— Ampère, J. J. Rome 1066.1
— Becker, W. A. Gallus, or R. scenes in the
times of Augustus 957.2
— Burton, E. Antiquities and curiosities of
Rome 919.3
— Daubeny, C. Lectures on R. husbandry . . . 165.11
— Fosbroke, T. D. Treatise on the arts, institu-
tions, etc., of the Romans 378.3
ROMAN Catholic church. Decrees of the council
of Trent. Translated by J. Waterworth.
New York, 1848. 8° 1085.18
— Cotter, J. R. Mass and rubrics of. Transl. 1098.23
— Dannou, P. C. F. History of the court of
Rome. 919.2
— Dowling, J. History of Romanism 1085.15
— Nevins, W. Thoughts on popery 119.27
— Peel, Sir R. Roman Catholic question . v.I. of 566.4
— Pitrat, J. C. Mysteries, hypocrisy and cruelty
of the. 1098.19
— Seymour, M. H. Evenings with the Roman-
ists 1098.16
— Spirit of popery. See Spirit 119.1
— Steele, R. Romish ecclesiastical history of
late years. [1714.] 949.11
See also: Popes.
ROMAN exile, The. Gajani, G. 678.2-3
ROMAN literature. Matthiæ, A. G. A manual of. 406.11
— Peter, W. Specimens of the poets and poetry
of Rome 315.1
ROMAN mythology. Dwight, M. A. 1083.10
ROMAN nights. Verri, A. 809.11
ROMAN traitor, The: a novel. Herbert, H. W. . 436.15
ROMANCE of history. Egypt. Seymour, F. G. . 959.3
— England. Neele, H. 419.1-3
— France. Ritchie, L. 419.4-5
— Italy. Macfarlane, C. 419.6
— Spain. Trueba y Cosio. Don T. de 419.7
ROMANCE of the fashionable world. Batchelder,
E. 339.6
ROMANCE of the peerage. Craik, G. L. 566.8
ROMANS, Epistles to the. See Bible.
ROMANTIC composition. Beyle, H. Études sur
le romantisme 1067.23
— Ellis, G. Rise and progress of, in France and
England 846.5
ROMANY Rye, The: a sequel to Lavengro. Bor-
row, G. 802.22
ROMANZETTI, Tre, di varii autori. [scelti da L.
Carrer.] Venezia, 1841. 12° 1058.12
Contents. — Gli amori d'Abrocome e d'Anzia, di
Senofonte Efesio tradotti da Antonmaria Salvini; I
compassionevoli avvenimenti d'Erasto; Le strane ed
innocenti corrispondenze del conte Sigismondo
d'Arco colla principessa Claudia Felice d'Innspruck.
ROMBERT: a tale of Carolina. New York, 1835.
2v. 12° 478.16
ROME. Arnold, T. History of Rome 953.2-3
— Later Roman commonwealth 956.3
— Beckett, G. A. à. Comic history of Rome. . 956.9
— Beyle, H. Rome 1067.27
— - Promenades dans 1067.20
— Blewitt, O. Handbook for Rome 649.10
— Bonner, J. Child's history of Rome 959.11
— Daunou, P. C. F. History of the court of. . 919.2
— Eaton, E. C. Rome in the 19th century . . . 678.5
— Eliot, S. The ancient Romans. History of
liberty 134.7
— Elton, C. A. History of the R. empire . . . 548.11
— Ferguson, A. History of the Rom. republic. 830.7
— Gibbon, E. Decline and fall. 953.6

ROME. Goldsmith, O. History of 952.5
— Graham, M. Three months in mountains East of 676.3
— History of 378.2
— Juste, T. Précis de l' histoire romaine . . . 1065.25
— Keightley, T. The history of 959.4–5
— Lewis, G. C. Inquiry into the credibility of the early Roman history 953.4
— Liddell, H. G. History of Rome to the establishment of the empire 957.4
— Livius, T. History of 814.4
— Lynam, R. Roman emperors 956.1
— Maguire, J. F. R., its ruler and its institu. 919.1
— Merivale, C. R. under the emperors . . . 365.9
— Michelet, J. History of the Roman republic. 919.4–5
— Newman, F. W. Regal Rome 919.6
— Niebuhr, B. G. History of Rome 954.6
— - Lectures on Roman history 959.8
— Schmitz, L. History of Rome to the death of Commodus 957.3
— Sismondi, J. C. L. S. de. Fall of. 378.5
— Trimmer, S. A general outline of R. history. 129.28
ROMER, I. F. Pilgrimage to Egypt, Nubia, and Palestine. 2d ed. London, 1847. 2v. 8°. 693.13
ROMILLY, S. Memoirs by himself, with a selection from his correspondence. 3d ed. London, 1841. 2v. 16° 589.11
ROMULUS, History of. Abbott, J. 549.27–28
RONALDS, E. and Richardson, T. Chemical technology. 2d ed. London, 1855. 2v. 8°. . 155.20
ROOT, N. W. T. School amusements, or how to make the school interesting. New York, 1857. 12° 137.9
ROOTS and ramifications of the English language. Knapp, A. J. 406.17
ROPER, W. Life of Sir T. More. New ed., by S. W. Singer. Chiswick, 1822. 12°. . . 589.9
ROQUETTE, O. Waldmeisters Brautfahrt. Märchen. 16te. Auflage. Stuttgart, 1855. 24° 1039.3
ROSA, Salvator, The life and times of. Morgan, S. O. 542.1
ROSAS, J. M. de. Administration of. King, J. A. 263.8
ROSCOE, H. Life of W. Roscoe. Boston, 1833. 2v. 12° 513.10
— Lives of eminent British lawyers. London, 1830. 16° 388.4
ROSCOE, T. Life and writings of Miguel de Cervantes Saavedra. London, 1839. 16°. . . . 399.1
— Memoir of W. Roscoe 543.11
— German novelists : tales selected from ancient and modern authors, transl. with critical and biographical notices. London, 1826. 12° 418.2
ROSCOE, W. Life and pontificate of Leo X. 5th ed. London, 1846. 2v. p.8° 818.2
Life of Lorenzo De' Medici. New ed., with memoir. London, 1842. 16°. 543.11
Same. 10th ed. London, 1851. p.8° . . . 818.6
Life of. Roscoe, H. 543.10
ROSE, H. Chemical analysis, qualitative and quantitative. Transl., with notes and additions by A. Normandy. Lond., 1849. 2v. 8° 155.12
ROSE, W. S. Letters from the North of Italy. London, 1819. 2v. 8° 675.3
ROSE and the ring: a fireside pantomime. Thackeray, W. M. 508.21–23
ROSE Clark: a novel. Parton, S. P. F. 755.7
ROSE D' Albret, or troublous times : a romance. James, G. P. R. 463.9
ROSE of Tistelön : a tale. Carlén, E. 766.3
ROSENKRANZ, J. K. F. Göthe und seine Werke. 2te Aufl. Königsberg, 1856. . . . . . . 1034.5
ROSINI, G. Il conte Ugolino della Gherardesca. Romanzo storico. 2a edizione. Milano, 1843. 3v. 16° 1057.12
— La monaca di Monza. [Storia del secolo XVII.] 25a ed. Milano, 1853. 16° 1057.11
— Luisa Strozzi. Storia del secolo XVI. Firenze, 1850. 12° 1057.10
ROSS, A. Red river settlement, with account of the native races. London, 1856. 8° 623.16

ROSS, J. Voyage for exploring Baffin's bay and a N. W. passage. 2d ed. Lond., 1819. 2v. 8° 703.11
ROSS, J. C. Voyage of discovery and research in the antarctic regions, 1839–43. London, 1847. 2v. 8° 702.14
ROSSIGNOL, Un, pris au trébuchet. Récit. Saintine, X. B. 1078.39
ROSSINI, J., Vie de. Beyle, H. 1067.26
ROTH, E. Life of Napoleon III. Boston, 1856. 12° 604.12
ROTHELAN, romance of the English hist. Galt, J. 788.7
ROTHMAN, R. W. History of astronomy . v.III. of 365.14
ROUGE, Le, et le noir, chronique du XIX. siècle. Beyle, H. 1067.17
ROUGHING it in the bush. Moodie, S. 636.3–11
ROUMANIA, the border land of Christian and Turk. Noyes, J. O. 686.14
ROUMELIA, The Russians in, 1828–29. Moltke, Baron von 924.3
ROUMELI, Travels through, during an eventful period. Urquhart, D. 689.11
ROUNDHEADS, Songs of the. Thornbury, G. W.. 316.3
ROUND table, The: a collec. of essays. Hazlitt, W. 886.10
ROUSSEAU, J. J. Œuvres. Paris, 1819. 20v. 12° 1069.1
    Contents.—Vol. I. Discours et lettres. II. Paix perpétuelle ; Polysynodie de St. Pierre ; Du contrat social; Gouvernement de Pologne; Lettres à Butta-Foco. III.—V. Julie, ou la nouvelle Héloïse. VI.—VII. Émile, ou de l'éducation. VIII. Same; Émile et Sophie. IX. Lettres de la Montagne. X. Lettre à M. D'Alembert ; De l'imitation théatrale; Narcisse, comédie; Les prisonniers de guerre, comédie ; Pygmalion, scène lyrique ; L'engagement téméraire, comédie; Les muses galantes, ballet; Le devin du village, intermède; Lettre; La découverte du nouveau monde, tragédie; Fragmens d'Iphis, tragédie; Fragmens de Lucrèce, tragédie. XI. Sur la musique ; Sur l'origine des langues ; Lettres. XII.—XIII. Dictionnaire de musique. XIV. Mélanges ; Poésies; Fragmens pour un dictionnaire de botanique. Lettres. XV.—XVI. Les confessions. XVII. Lettres; Les rêveries du promeneur solitaire. Rousseau juge de Jean Jacques. XVIII.—XX. Correspondance, 1732–1771.
— La reine fantasque . . . . v.XXVI. of 1077.1
ROUSSELL, N. Catholic and Protestant nations compared, with introd. by B. Noel. Boston, 1855. 8° 1103.6
ROUTH, E. J. Analytical view of Newton's principia. Brougham, H. 147.6
ROUTLEDGE, G. American handbook, and guide through the United States. Lond., 1854. 16° 620.29
ROUVROY, Louis de. Memoirs. See Saint Simon, Duke of 615.2
ROVANI, G. Manfredo Palavicino, stor. ital. Milano, 1845. 4v. 12° 1057.6
ROVIGO, Duke of. Memoirs. See Savary, A. J. M. R. 602.6
ROWCROFT, C. Australian Crusoes : or, adventures in the wilds of Australia. From 6th London ed. Philadelphia, 1853. 16° . . 737.7
ROWE, Mrs. E. Poetical works, incl. history of Joseph, and life. London, n.d. 32° . . . 369.25
ROWE, N. Works. New ed., prefixed, a life. London, 1792. 2v. 12° 356.21
    Contents.— Vol. I. Ambitious step-mother; Tamerlane; The fair penitent; The biter. II. Ulysses ; The royal convert; Jane Shore; Jane Gray; Poems on several occasions.
ROWLANDSON, Mrs. M. Narrative of captivity with the Indians, by herself. 6th ed. Lancaster, 1828. 16° 249.5
ROWLEY controversy, History of the. Chatterton, T. 346.6
ROWLEY, Mass., History of. Gage, T. 227.6
ROWLEY, W. Fortune by land and by sea, by T. Heywood, and W. Rowley 342.29
ROWSON, S. Charlotte Temple : a tale. Hartford, 1829. 18° 789.10
ROXBURY, Conn., History of. Cothren, W. . . . 225.2
ROYLE, J. F. Arts and manufactures of India . . 199.16
RUDIMENTARY chronology. London, 1854. 16° . . 829.39
RUDIMENTARY treatises on various subjects in science. Weale, J. 83v. . . . . 819&829
RUFFIAN boy, The: a tale. Opie, A. 409.45

RUFFINI, G. Doctor Antonio. A tale. Edinburgh, 1855. 16° 756.5
— - Same. New York, 1856. 16° 755.6-9
— Lorenzo Benoni. Edinburgh, 1853. 12° . . . 756.4
— - Same. New York, 1853. 12° 756.3
— The Paragreens on a visit to the Paris universal exhibition. New York, 1857. 16° . . 756.12
RUGBY, School days at 434.8-11
— School. Sermons preached in the chapel of. Arnold, T. 137.32
RUHE ist die erste Bürgerpflicht. Roman. Häring, W. 1024.5
RUINS. Les ruines, ou méditations sur les révolutions des empires. Volney, C. F. 1075.41
RUINS of ancient cities. Bucke, C. 379.6
RUINS of sac. and historic lands. Lond., 1853. 16° 949.10
RULE of faith and practice. Peck, G. 129.9
RULE, Margaret, Sufferings of. Calef, R. 229.5
RULES of order. See Parliamentary practice.
RUMELIA. See Roumelia.
RUMFORD, Count. See Thompson, B.
RUNDELL, Mrs. Domestic cookery. London, 1853. 12° 189.9-10
RUNNAMEDE: a tragedy. Logan, J. 349.24
RUPERT and the cavaliers. Warburton, E. . . . 553.6
RURAL and domestic economy. Miles, W. The horse's foot, and how to keep it sound . . . 165.18
— Richardson, H. D. Rural handbooks . . . 169.15
— Stewart, J. Stable economy 165.18
— Warder, J. Hedges and evergreens 166.15
— Ysabeau, A. Traité de l'élève du bétail . . 1075.2
   See also: Agriculture, Gardening, Drainage, Honeybee, Horse, Poultry, Veterinary surgery, etc.
RURAL essays. Downing, A. J. 165.5
RURAL hours. Cooper, S. F. 168.2-3
RURAL letters and thought at leisure. Willis, N. P. 904.15-17
RURAL literature. Carcano, G. Della letteratura rusticale 1056.10
RURAL poetry of the Eng. language. Jenks, J. W. 314.3
RURALITY. Original tales. Talbot, M. E. . . . 449.16
RUSCONI, C. Enrico Valieri. Firenze, 1847. 12° 1056.29
RUSH, B. Diseases of the mind. Phila., 1827. 8° 122.11
RUSH, J. Philosophy of the human voice. 3d ed., enl. Philadelphia, 1845. 8° 405.1
RUSH, R. Washington in domestic life. Philadelphia, 1857. 8° 511.8
RUSKIN, J. Elements of drawing. N.Y., 1857. 12° 205.11
— - Same. London, 1857. 12° 205.12-16
— Lectures on architecture and painting, 1853. New York, 1854. 12° 205.2
— Modern painters. Part I.-V. New York, 1856-58. 4v. 8° 205.4-7
— Notes on the construction of sheepfolds. New York, 1851. 12° 205.3
— Political economy of art. London, 1857. 12° 208.25
— Pre-Raphaelitism. New York, 1851. 12° . 205.3
— Seven lamps of architecture. N.Y., 1849. 12° 208.24
— Turner gallery at Marlborough House, 1856-1857. 3d edition. London, 1857. 8° . . . 205.1
RUSSELL, J. Tour in Germany and S. province of Austria, in 1820-22. From 2d Edinburgh ed. Boston, 1825. 8° 643.5
— Same. New ed. Edinburgh, 1828. 2v. 18° 830.43
RUSSELL, J. jr. History of the war of 1812-15. Hartford, 1815. 8° 215.12
RUSSELL, John. History of the United States. Philadelphia, 1838. 12° 309.5
RUSSELL, M. Ancient and modern Egypt. New York, n.d. 18° 810.29
— - Same. 10th ed., [enlarged.] London. 1853. 12° 957.9
— History and present condition of the Barbary States. New York, 1845. 18° 810.70
— Life of Oliver Cromwell. Edinburgh, 1829. 2v. 18° 830.54
— - Same. New York, 1852. 2v. 18° 810.62-63
— Nubia and Abyssinia; their civil history, etc. New York, n.d. 18° 810.61
— Palestine: or, the Holy Land. N.Y., n.d. 18° 810.33

RUSSELL, M. Polynesia: account of the islands of the South Sea. New York, 1848. 18° . . . 820.55
— - Same. London, 1853. 16° 938.13
RUSSELL, Martha. Stories of New England life. Boston, 1857. 12° 417.9
RUSSELL, R. North America; its agriculture and climate. Edinburgh, 1857. 8° 623.4
RUSSELL, Lady R., Letters of. Phila., 1854. 12° 596.2
— - Same. London, 1853. 2v. 8° 596.3
RUSSELL, W., LL.D. History of modern Europe epitomized. London, 1857. 8° 947.6
— - Same; continued by W. Jones. New York, 1845. 3v. 8° 943.5
RUSSELL, W. Esq. Extraordinary men; their boyhood and early life. London, 1853. 12°. 879.15
RUSSELL, W. Introductory remarks on declamation. See Edgarton, W. P. 405.5
— and Murdoch. J. E. Orthophony, or vocal culture in elocution. 137.16
RUSSELL, W. H. British expedition to the Crimea. Revised edition. London, 1858. 8° 984.1
RUSSELL, Historical memoirs of the house of. Wiffen, J. H. 975.7
RUSSELL: a tale of the reign of Charles II. James, G. P. R. 463.14-15
RUSSIA. Bell, R. A history of. 378.7
— Clarke, E. D. Travels in. 2v. 689.6
— Cobden, R. R. and the Eastern question . . 928.5
— Cochrane, J. D. Pedestrian journey through. 674.6
— Custine, Marquis de. R. in 1839 . . . . . . 409.4
— Englishwoman in. 687.24
— Forster, M. Briefe aus Südrussland 1029.13
— Fowler, G. Lives of the sovereigns of . . . 544.22
— Gurowski, Count A. de. R. as it is 927.1-2
— Hamley, E. B. War in Southern 928.7-8
— Haxthausen, Bar. v. The Russian empire. . 674.1
— Jesse, W. R. and the war 927.7
— Kelly, W. K. History of, to the present time. 827.6
— Kingston, W. H. G. Fred Markham in . . . 709.14
— Kohl, J. G. St. Petersburg, Moscow, etc. . 674.5
— Latham, R. G. Native races of. 176.1
— McCulloch, J. R. Description of. 409.28
— Macgillivray, W. Humboldt's journeys in Asiatic 810.54
— Murray, J. Handbook for Northern Europe. 649.11
— Oliphant, L. Russian shores of the Black Sea. 674.2
— Rabbe, A. History of 869.11
— Sala, G. A. Notes of a residence in 666.1
— Schnitzler, J. H. Secret history of, under Alexander I. and Nicholas 925.4
— Ségur, P. P. de. Expedition to, 1812. . . . 399.3
— - Same. 820.43-44
— Seymour, H. D. R. on the Black Sea and Sea of Azof. 685.5
— Slade, A. Travels in, 1838-39. . . . . . . 663.9
— Spencer, E. Turkey, Russia, etc. 687.21-22
— Spottiswoode, W. Tarantasse journey thro' Eastern. 674.7
— Stephens, J. L. Incidents of travel in 689.1-2
— Wilbraham, R. Travels in the Trans-Caucasian provinces of 674.4
RUSSIAN and English conversation, Manual of. Cornet, J. 406.19
RUSSIAN discoveries between Asia and America. Coxe, W. 702.17
RUSSIAN empire, The. Its resources, government and policy. Cincinnati, 1855. 12° 927.3-4
RUSSIAN poets, Specimens of. Bowring, J. . . . 315.14
RUSSIAN princesses, Captivity of two, in Caucasus. Verderevsky, M. 687.1
RUSSIAN war, Pictorial history of. See Pictorial history 924.1
RUSSIANS. Brooks, S. Russians of the South . . 409.2
— Lagny, G. de. The knout and the 927.6
— Moltke, Baron v. The R. in Bulgaria and Rumelia, in 1828-29 . . . . 924.3
RUSSO-TURKISH campaigns of 1828-29. Chesney, F. R. 918.5-7
RUSTIC adornments for homes of taste. Hibberd, S. 207.11
RUTH: a novel. Gaskell, E. C. 435.1
RUTH Hall: domestic tale. Parton, S. P. 755.9

RUTLEDGE, J., Life and times of. Flanders, H. . 523.3
RUXTON, G. F. Adventures in Mexico and the
    Rocky Mountains. New York, 1848. 12° . 638.5-6
— - Same. London, 1847. 12° 899.8
— Life in the far West. New York, 1849. 12°. 628.22-23
RYDE, E. Text-book for architects, engineers, sur-
    veyors, etc. Added, chapters on agriculture
    and landed property, by Prof. Donaldson.
    London, 1854. 8° 194.12
RYLE, J. C. The priest, puritan and preacher. New
    York, 1856. 18° 1088.32-33
RYLE, T. American liberty and government ques-
    tioned. London, 1855. 12° 134.15

SABBATH evening readings of the New Testament.
    See Cumming, J. 116.8,15,16
SABBATH morning readings on the Old Testament.
    Cumming, J. 116.18
SABINE, L. American loyalists. Boston, 1847. 8° 213.1
— Duels and duelling, with historical essay. Bos-
    ton, 1855. 12° 947.14
— Life of E. Preble. Sparks, J. . . . . . v.XXII. of 529.1
SACCHETTI, Fr. Novelle scelte. Parma, 1852. 16° 1058.10
SACKVILLE, Lord George, proved to be Junius . . 877.11
SACONTALÁ : or, the fatal ring, an Indian drama.
    Translated from the Sanscrit and Pracrit.
    See Cálidás 351.8
SACRA privata. Wilson, T. 1109.30
SACRED biography : or, the history of the patri-
    archs. Hunter, H. 511.4
SACRED philosophy. God revealed in the process
    of creation. Walker, J. B. 1089.7
SACRED poets of England and America. Griswold,
    R. W. 314.8
SAD tales and glad tales. Mellen, G. 489.13
SADE, J. F. T. A. de. Life of Petrarch, collected
    from the "Mémoires," by Mrs. Dobson.
    1st American ed. Boston, 1809. 2v. 24° . 548.25
SAEWULF, Narrative of. Wright, T. 846.7
SAFFELL, W. T. R. Records of the revolutionary
    war. New York, 1858. 12° 216.12
SAFFORD, W. H. Life of H. Blennerhassett. Cin-
    cinnati, 1853. 12° 517.12-13
SAGE, R. B. Scenes in the Rocky mountains, Ore-
    gon and California, [etc.] Phila., 1846. 12° 639.16
— - Same. 2d ed. Phila., 1854. 12° 639.4
SAGEN, Niederländische. Wolf, J. W. 1013.17
SAGEN und romantische Erzählungen. Rellstab,
    L. . . . . v.V. of 1014.2
SAHARA, Travels in the desert of, 1845-6. Rich-
    ardson, J. 693.1
SAILOR'S assistant. Brady, W. 194.6
SAILOR'S sea-book. Greenwood, J. 819.39
SAILOR'S horn book for the law of storms. Pid-
    dington, H. 145.18
SAILORS, Perilous incidents in the lives of. Kneib,
    P. H. 668.5
SAINCLAIR : or, the victim to the arts and sciences.
    Genlis, Mme. de 449.20
ST. AUGUSTINE, Fa. Banvard, J. The Spanish
    settlement at 228.15
— Fairbanks, G. R. History and antiquities of. 234.16
ST. DOMINGO, History of the island of 264.3
SAINT DOMINIQUE et les dominicains. Caro, E. 1078.35
SAINT ÉVREMOND, C. M. de St. D. de. Œuvres
    choisies, par M. Hippeau. Paris, 1852. 12° 1067.13

    Contents. — Notice sur St. Évremond: Œuvres his-
    toriques; Critique littéraire: Philosophie morale; Poé-
    sies diverses; Choix de lettres.

SAINT FÉLIX, J. de. Aventures de Cagliostro.
    Paris, 1854. 12° 1078.29
SAINT GENOIS, J. de. Les voyageurs belges. Brux-
    elles, n.d. 2v. 12° 1075.10
SAINT GILDAS : a tale. Kavanagh, J. 454.13
ST. GILES and St. James. Jerrold, D. . . . v.I. of 906.1
SAINT HILAIRE, E. M. de. Histoire de la garde
    impériale. La Haye, 1846-47. 4v. 16° . . 1068.17
— Histoire populaire de Napoléon et de la grande
    armée. Bruxelles, 1845. 3v. 12° 1068.16
ST. HYACINTHE. Histoire du Prince Titi.
    v.XXVII-XXVIII. of 1077.1

SAINT JOHN, B. Adventures in the Libyan desert,
    and the oasis of Jupiter Ammon. London,
    1849. 12° 899.9
— - Same. New York, 1849. 12° 698.21
— Montaigne, the essayist. A biography. Lon-
    don, 1858. 2v. 12° 583.20
— The Louvre : or, biography of a museum.
    London, 1855. 12° 654.12
ST. JOHN, C. Wild sports and natural history of
    the Highlands. Lond., 1846. p.8° 899.10
ST. JOHN, H. Lord Bolingbroke. Works. Phila-
    delphia, 1841. 4v. 8° 891.3

    Contents. — Vol. I. Life: Letter to Sir W. Wind-
    ham written in 1717; Reflections upon exile: The occa-
    sional writer, Nos. 1—3. ; First vision of Camillick;
    Answer to the London Journal; Answer to defence of
    the inquiry into the reasons of the conduct of Gt.
    Britain; remarks on the history of England: On lux-
    ury; Good and bad ministers; Policy of the Athenians;
    Power of the prince, and freedom of the people. II.
    A dissertation upon parties; Letters on the study and
    use of history. III. Letter occasioned by one of
    Abp. Tillotson's sermons; Letters or essays, addressed
    to Alexander Pope. IV. Essays continued; Frag-
    ments or minutes of essays; Index.

ST. JOHN, Mrs. H. Audubon: his adventures and
    discoveries. New York, 1856. 16° 529.2
ST. JOHN, J. A. Analysis of Plato's republic.
    More, T. 888.14
— Egypt and Nubia. London, 1845. 8° 693.5
— Journal of a residence in Normandy. Edin-
    burgh, 1831. 18° 830.64
— Lives of celebrated travellers. New York,
    1844-47. 3v. 18° 810.47
— Louis Napoleon ; a biogr. London, 1857. 12° 604.13
— Nemesis of power. Revolution. London,
    1854. 18° 139.14
— Preliminary essay and notes to Locke's works. 827.4
ST. JOHN of Jerusalem, Holy, military, sovereign
    order of. Taaffe, J. 915.1
ST. LEGER, B. The rescued nun. N.Y., 1843. 12° 802.24
ST. LEON, Tale of the 16th century. Godwin, W. 419.8
SAINT NICHOLAS, The book of. Paulding, J. K. . 797.13
ST. PAUL, Life and epistles of. Conybeare, W. J. 113.9
ST. PETERSBURG. Jerrmann, E. Pictures from . 409.13
— Müffling, Bar. F. K. F. v. Missions to 689.15
ST. PETER'S river, Expedition to the source of.
    Keating, W. H. 625.10
SAINT PIERRE, J. H. B. de. Paul and Virginia.
    With mem. of the author. Phila., 1854. 12° 729.1
— Studies of nature. Transl. by H. Hunter, with
    notes by B. S. Barton. Phila., 1808. 3v. 8° 173.4

    Vol. III. contains: Paul and Virginia ; Arcadia;
    Wishes of a recluse; Coffee house of Surat; Indian
    cottage.

SAINT PRIEST, A. de. Fall of the Jesuits in the
    eighteenth century. Transl. Lond., 1845. 12° 889.3
ST. RONAN'S well. Scott, Sir W. 480.1-4
SAINT-SIMON, L. de R. duc de. Le regent et la cour
    de France, 1715-23. Paris, 1853. 12° . . . 1078.51
— Louis XIV. et sa cour. Paris, 1853. 12° . . . 1078.18
— Memoirs on the reign of Louis XIV., and the
    regency. Abr. from the French. London,
    1857. 4v. 12° 615.2
ST. THOMAS, W. I., Hist. account of. Knox, J. P. 264.7
ST. VALENTINE'S day. Chronicles of the Canon-
    gate. 2d ser. Scott, Sir W. 480.22-26
ST. VINCENT, Earl of. See Jervis, J.
ST. VINCENT of Paul, Life of. Butler, C. 617.14
SAINTE-BEUVE, C. A. Volupté. 3me éd. Paris,
    1845. 12° 1076.20
— Lettres de Mme. Roland. Introduction par
    Ste.-Beuve 1079.2
— Notice sur Leclercq, T. 1063.24
STE MARIE, Cte. Algeria in 1845. Lond., 1846. 12° 698.23
SAINTINE, X. B. Picciola, the prisoner of Fenes-
    trella. 3d ed. Philadelphia, 1843. 12° . . 478.11
— - Same. 17th ed. Bruxelles, 1853. 18° . . 1068.11
— The real Robinson Crusoe. Transl. by A. T.
    Wilbur. Boston, 1851. 16° 737.8
— Un rossignol, etc. Récits dans la tourelle.
    Paris, 1856. 12° 1078.39

SAINTINE, X. B. Woman's whims. Transl. by F. Robinson. New York, 1850. 12° . . . . . 878.6 & 13
SAINTS' everlasting rest. Baxter, R. 1087.3
SAINTS, Lives of the fathers, martyrs, etc. Butler, A. 541.5
SALA, G. A. A journey due North, Russia in 1856. London, 1858. 12° 666.1
SALAD for the social. Saunders, F. 898.5
SALAD for the solitary. Saunders, F. 898.4
SALE, G. Discourse preliminary to the Koran. See Mohammed 113.5
SALE, Lady. Disasters in Afghanistan, 1841-2. London, 1843. 12° 987.6
SALE, Sir R. H. Sale's brigade in Afghanistan. Gleig, G. R. 899.11
SALEM, Mass., Annals of. Felt, J. B. 227.13
SALEM witchcraft. Calef, R. 229.5
SALLET, F. v. Gedichte. 3te Aufl. Hamburg, 1852. 16° 1034.15
SALLUSTIUS, C. C. Sallust. Transl. by W. Rose. New York, n.d. 18° 830.10
— Sallust, Florus, and Velleius Paterculus. Transl. by J. S. Watson. Lond., 1852. p.8° 834.4
SALMAGUNDI. Irving, W. . . . . . . v.I. of 367.2-3
SALOONS, Celebrated. Gay, Mme. S. 609.5
SALT, H. Life and correspondence of. Halls, J. J. 563.7
SALT lake, A visit to. Chandless, W. 626.3
SALT water bubbles, or life on the wave. Sleeper, J. S. 737.5
SALVADOR, Description of. Baily, J. 266.4
SALVATION, Philos. of the plan of. Walker, J. B. 1086.21
SALVERTE, E. The occult sciences. Transl. by A. T. Thomson. New York, 1847. 2v. 16° . . 125.24
SALZMANN, C. G. Elements of morality, for the use of children. Transl. 1st Balt. ed. Baltimore, 1811. 12° 420.9
— Gymnastics for youth; freely translated. Philadelphia, 1803. 8° 137.2
SAM Slick's wise saws, etc. Haliburton, T. C. . . 489.2
SAMPSON, W. Memoirs, including a sketch of the history of Ireland. 2d ed. Leesburg, Va., 1817. 8° 575.8
— Additions to the history of Ireland. See Taylor, W. C. 810.52
SAMUELSON, J. The earthworm and the common housefly. London, 1858. 12° 175.13
SANBORN, C. W., and Chase, H. The North and the South 207.18
SANCHONIATHO. History of the creation. See Phenix, The 898.8
SAND, George. Pseud. See Dudevant, Mme. M. A.
SANDERSON, J. Sketches of Paris. Phila., 1838. 12° 898.12
— - Same. 3d ed. Philadelphia, 1847. 2v. 12° 654.15
SANDERSON, R. Life of. Walton, I. 589.5
SANDFORD and Merton, The history of. Day, T. . 729.22
SANDS, R. C. Writings in prose and verse. New York, 1834. 2v. 8° 873.4
SANDSTONE, The old red. Miller, H. 167.24-26
SANDWICH islands. Bingham, H. Residence of twenty-one years in the 934.4
— Cheever, H. T. Life in the 705.20
— Dibble, S. History of the S. I. mission . . . 1108.7
— Stewart, C. S. A residence in 705.10
See also: Hawaiian Islands.
SANDWICH island notes, by a Häolé. New York, 1854. 12° 705.12
SANFORD, E. History of the U. S. before the revolution, with acc't of the aborigines. Philadelphia, 1819. 8° 305.1
SAN Francisco, The annals of. Soulé, F. 235.10
SAN Marino, Memorie storiche della repubblica di. Delfico, M. 1046.16
SANNILLAC, a poem. Whiting, H. 338.4
SAN Salvador, Notes on. Squier, E. G. 263.1
SANTA Fé. Gregg, J. The journal of a S. F. trader. 628.16
— Kendall, G. W. Narrative of the expedition to. 638.7
— Simpson, J. H. Military reconnaissance from, to the Navajo country 623.5
SANTAREM, E. F. de B. y S. Vic.de. Researches respecting Americus Vespucius and his voyages. Transl. by E. V. Childe. Boston, 1850. 12° 259.10-11

SAPPHO, a tragedy; by Grillparzer. See Öhlenschläger, A. G. 489.16
SARACEN. Taylor, J. B. Lands of the 686.15-18
— Oekley, S. History of the 828.5
SARGENT, E. Arctic adventure by sea and land. Boston, 1857. 12° 704.10-16
— Fleetwood, or the stain of birth. A novel. New York, 1845. 12° 480.10
— Modern standard drama. N. York, 1846. 15v. 12° . . . . 363.1 & 364.1

Contents.— Vol. I. Ion, by T. N. Talfourd; Fazio, H. H. Milman; The Lady of Lyons, by E. L. Bulwer; Richelieu, by E. L. Bulwer; The wife, by J. S. Knowles; The honeymoon, by J. Tobin; The school for scandal, by R. B. Sheridan; Money, by E. L. Bulwer, with a memoir and portrait of Mrs. A. C. Mowatt. II. The stranger, by A. F. Kotzebue; Grandfather Whitehead, by M. Lemon; Richard III., by W. Shakspeare; Love's sacrifice, by G. W. Lovell; The gamester, by E. Moore; Cure for the heartache, by T. Morton; The hunchback, by J. S. Knowles; Don Cæsar De Bazan, by Dumanoir and Dennery, with a memoir of Mr. Charles Kean. III. The poor gentleman, by G. Colman, jr.; Hamlet, by W. Shakspeare; Charles II., by J. H. Payne; Venice preserved, by T. Otway; Pizarro, by R. B. Sheridan; The love-chase, by J. S. Knowles; Othello, by W. Shakspeare; Lend me five shillings, by J. M. Morton, with a portrait and memoir of Mr. William E. Burton. IV. Virginius, by J. S. Knowles; The king of the commons, by J. White; London assurance, by D. I. Bourcicault; The rent-day, by D. Jerrold; Two gentlemen of Verona, by W. Shakspeare; The jealous wife, by G. Colman, sen.; The rivals, by R. B. Sheridan; Perfection, by T. H. Bayly, with a Memoir of Mr. James H. Hackett. V. A new way to pay old debts, by P. Massinger; Look before you leap, by G. W. Lovell; King John, by W. Shakspeare; The nervous man, by W. B. Bernard; Damon and Pythias, by J. Banim; The clandestine marriage, by G. Colman, sen.; William Tell, by J. S. Knowles; The day after the wedding, by Mrs. C. Kemble; with a portrait and memoir of George Colman, the elder. VI. Speed the plough, by T. Morton; Romeo and Juliet, by W. Shakspeare; Feudal times, by J. White; Charles the twelfth, by J. R. Planché; The bridal, by J. S. Knowles; The follies of a night, by J. R. Planché; The iron chest, by G. Colman, jr.; Faint heart never won fair lady, by J. R. Planche, with a portrait and memoir of Sir E. Bulwer Lytton. VII. Road to ruin, by T. Holcroft; Macbeth, by W. Shakspeare; Temper, by R. Bell; Evadne, by R. L. Sheil; Bertram, by C. Maturin; The duenna, by R. B. Sheridan; Much ado about nothing, by W. Shakspeare; The critic, by R. B. Sheridan; with a portrait and memoir of Richard Brinsley Sheridan. VIII. The apostate, by R. L. Sheil; Twelfth night, by W. Shakspeare; Brutus, by J. H. Payne; Simpson and Co., by J. Poole; Merchant of Venice, by W. Shakspeare; Old heads and young hearts, by D. Bourcicault; The mountaineers, by G. Colman, jr.; Three weeks after marriage, by A. Murphy; And memoir of Mr. George H. Barrett. IX. Love, by J. S. Knowles; As you like it, by W. Shakspeare; Elder brother, by Beaumont and Fletcher; Werner, by Byron; Glapppus, by G. Griffin; Town and country, by T. Morton; King Lear, by W. Shakspeare; Blue devils, by G. Colman, jr.; And a portrait and memoir of Mrs. Shaw. X. Henry the eighth, by W. Shakspeare; Married and single, by J. Poole; Henry the fourth, part I., by W. Shakspeare; Paul Pry, by J. Poole; Guy Mannering, by D. Terry; Sweethearts and wives, by J. Kenney; The serious family, by M. Barnett; She stoops to conquer, by O. Goldsmith, with a portrait and memoir of Miss Charlotte Cushman. XI. Julius Cæsar, by W. Shakspeare; Vicar of Wakefield, by J. S. Coyne; Leap year, by J. B. Buckstone; The catspaw, by D. Jerrold; The passing cloud, by B. Bernard; The drunkard, by W. H. Smith; Rob Roy, by I. Pocock; George Barnwell, by G. Lillo, with a memoir of Mrs. John Sefton. XII. Ingomar, by M. Lovell; The two friends, by R. Lacy; Corsican brothers, by E. Grangé & X. de Montepin; Heir-at-law, by G. Colman, jr.; Sketches in India, by T. Morton; Jane Shore, by N. Rowe; Mind your own business, by M. Lemon; Writing on the wall, by T. and J. M. Morton, with a memoir of Tros. S. Hamblin. XIII. Soldier's daughter, by A. Cherry; Marco Spada, by J. P. Simpson; Sardanapalus, by Lord Byron; The robbers, by F. Schiller; Douglas, by Dr. Home; Nature's nobleman, by H. O. Pardey; Civilization, by J. H. Wilkins; Katharine & Petruchio, by W. Shakspeare, with a portrait and memoir of Edwin Forrest. XIV. Game of love, by J. Brougham;

SARGENT, E., *continued.*
  Midsummer-night's dream, by W. Shakespeare: Ernestine, by W. Robertson: Ragpicker of Paris, by E. Stirling; Flying Dutchman, by E. Fitzball; Hypocrite, by S. Smith; Therese, by J. H. Payne; La Tour de Nesle, by V. Hugo; with a portrait and memoir of John Brougham. XV. Ireland as it is, by J. A. Amherst; Sea of ice, anonymous; Seven clerks, by T. E. Wilks; Game of life, by J. Brougham; Forty thieves, anonymous; Bryan Boroihme, by J. S. Knowles; Romance and reality, by J. Brougham; Ugolino, by J. B. Booth, with a portrait and memoir of Barney Williams.

SARGENT, *Rev.* J. Memoir of Henry Martyn, with essay and app. by [B. B. Edwards.] 3d ed. Boston, 1836. 12° 576.3
SARGENT, J., *M. D.* Notes on Cuba. Boston, 1844. 12° 629.4-5
SARGENT, L. M. Dealings with the dead. Boston, 1856. 2v. 12° 228.1
— Reminiscences of Samuel Dexter. Boston, 1857. 16° 519.3
SARGENT, N. Life of Dr. L. F. Linn 523.1
SARGENT, W. The history of an expedition [Braddock's] against fort Du Quesne in 1755. Philadelphia, 1855. 8° 244.1
SARRANS, B. Memoirs of Lafayette, and of the revolution of 1830. Boston, 1833. 2v. 12° .   617.5
SARTOR resartus. Carlyle, T. 878.16
SATANSTOE. Cooper, J. F. 780.22-25
SATIRIST, British. *See* British satirist 369.13
SAUNDERS, F. Salad for the solitary. New York, 1853. 12° 898.4
— Salad for the social. New York, 1856. 12° . .   898.5
SAUNDERS, J. Cabinet pictures of English life. Chaucer. London, 1845. 18° 850.9
SAVAGE, M. W. Bachelor of the Albany. London, 1848. 12° 438.1
— Same. New York, 1848. 12° 438.2-3
— Reuben Medlicott; or the coming man. New York, 1852. 12° 438.4
SAVAGE, W. Dictionary of the art of printing. London, 1841. 8° 196.4
SAVARY, A. J. M. R. Memoirs of Napoleon. 2d ed. London, 1835. 4v. 8° 602.6
SAVONAROLA, G., Memoirs of. Harford, J. S. . .   543.2
SAVOY, Travels through the Alps of. Forbes, J. D.   663.2
SAWYER, F. W. Plea for amusements. New York, 1847. 16° 129.14
SAWYER, L. Biography of John Randolph. New York, 1844. 8° 523.18
SAXE-WEIMAR-EISENACH, B., *Duke of.* Travels through N. America during the years 1825 and 1826. Philadelphia, 1828. 2v. in 1. 8° .   623.11
SAXTON, C. M. Architectural publications. Ritch, J. W. 201.1-2
SAXTON, L. C. Fall of Poland, with the history of the country from its origin. New York, 1851. 2v. 8° 927.8
SAYINGS and doings. Hook, T. Series I.-III. .   809.1-3
SCALP hunters; or, adventures among the trappers. Reid, M. 717.8-11
SCANDAL. Bickford, J. T. 416.12
SCANDERBEG. George Castriot, surnamed S., Life of. Moore, C. C. 547.10
SCANDINAVIA, Ancient and modern. Crichton, A.   820.39
SCANDINAVIAN popular tales and traditions. Thorpe, B. 846.12
SCANDINAVIAN North, Iceland and the. Pfeiffer, I.   668.19
SCARLET letter: romance. Hawthorne, N. 437.6-9
SCENERY, science, and art. Ansted, D. T. . . .   208.2
SCENERY-SHOWING and other writings. Burton, W.   449.7-8
SCENES and thoughts in Europe. Calvert, G. H. .   647.14
SCENES in my native land. Sigourney, L. H. . .   868.17
SCENES in the practice of a N. Y. surgeon. Dixon, E. H. 428.2
SCENES of the civil war in Hungary, 1848-9. Philadelphia, 1850. 12° 928.2
SCHACHT, H. The microscope and its application to vegetable anatomy and physiology. 2d ed. London, 1853. 12° 145.23

SCHAEFER, J. W. Goethe's Leben. Bremen, 1851. 2v. 12° 1034.9
SCHAFF, P. Life and labors of St. Augustine. Translated. New York, 1854. 12° 544.17
— Political, social, and religious character of the United States. New York, 1855. 12° 1088.10
SCHAMYL, the sultan, warrior, etc. Wagner, F. .   409.28
SCHAYES, A. G. B. Hist. de l'architecture en Belgique. 2e éd. Bruxelles, 1853. 2v. 12° . .   1005.47
SCHEFER, L. Ausgewählte Werke. Berlin, 1845. 12v. 16° 1018.2

  Contents. — Vol. I. Künstlerehe; Die weisse Henne; Die Deportirten. II. Der Waldbrand; Unglückliche Liebe; Der Zwerg. III. Die Osternacht; Die lebendige Madonna; Palmerio; Der Kuss des Engels. IV. Der Gekreuzigte, oder Nichts Altes unter der Sonne; Die Davecke, oder die Leiden einer Kenigin; Lenore di San-Sepolero. V. Violante Beccaria; Der Sclavenhändler; Die Perserin. VI. Der Bauchredner; Die Erbtände; Der Seelenmarkt. VII. Die Osternacht; Das Verbrechen zu irren. VIII. Die Pflegetochter; Die Prinzeninseln; Ein Weihnachtsfest in Rom. IX. Göttliche Comödie in Rom; Der heimliche König der Armenier. X. Gedichte; Für Liebende; Legenden; Balladen; Fabeln; Vermischte Gedichte; Für Künstler; Epigramme; Hymnen; Dithyramben. XI.-XII. Laienbrevier; Erstes-Zweites Halbjahr.

— The artist's married life. Tr. by Mrs. J. R. Stodart. London, 1853. 12° 416.16
SCHEFFEL, J. V. Ekkehard, Gesch. aus dem 10ten Jahrhundert. Frankfurt a M., 1855. 8° . .   1013.11
SCHELE de Vere. Stray leaves from the book of nature. New York, 1855. 12° 178.8-9
SCHERZER, C. Travels in the free states of Central America. London, 1857. 2v. 12° . . .   638.2
SCHILLER, J. C. F. von. Sämmtliche Werke. Stuttgart, 1847. 12v. 16° 1019.2

  Contents. — Vol. I. Nachrichten von Schillers Leben; Charlotte von Schiller; Gedichte der ersten und zweiten Periode; Metrische Uebersetzungen; Gedichte der dritten Periode. II. Die Räuber, Schauspiel; Die Verschwörung des Fiesco zu Genua, ein republicanisches Trauerspiel; Kabale und Liebe, ein bürgerliches Trauerspiel; Der Menschenfeind, Fragment. III. Metrische Uebersetzungen; Iphigenie in Aulis, uebersetzt aus dem Euripides; Scenen aus den Phönicierinnen des Euripides; Don Carlos, Infant von Spanien, ein dramatisches Gedicht. IV. Wallenstein, ein dramatisches Gedicht, erster Theil; Wallensteins Lager; Die Piccolomini; Zweiter Theil; Wallensteins Tod. V. Maria Stuart; Die Jungfrau von Orleans; Die Braut von Messina, oder die feindlichen Brüder. VI. Wilhelm Tell; Die Huldigung der Künste; Macbeth, ein Trauerspiel von Shakspeare; Turandot, Prinzessin von China, ein tragikomisches Mährchen nach Gozzi. VII. Phädra, Trauerspiel von Racine; Der Parasit oder die Kunst sein Glück zu machen, ein Lustspiel nach dem Französischen; Der Neffe als Onkel, Lustspiel in drei Aufzügen, aus dem Französischen des Picard; Nachlass; (1.) Demetrius; (2.) Warbeck; (3.) Die Maltheser; (4.) Die Kinder des Hauses. VIII. Geschichte des Abfalls der vereinigten Niederlande von der spanischen Regierung. IX. Geschichte des dreissigjährigen Kriegs. X. Prosaische Schriften; Erste Periode; Ueber den Zusammenhang der thierischen Natur des Menschen mit seiner geistigen; Ueber das gegenwärtige deutsche Theater; Der Spaziergang unter den Linden; Eine grossmüthige Handlung aus der neuesten Geschichte; Die Schaubühne als eine moralische Anstalt betrachtet; Zweite Periode; Der Verbrecher aus verlorener Ehre, eine wahre Geschichte; Spiel des Schicksals, ein Bruchstück aus einer wahren Geschichte; Der Geisterseher, aus den Papieren des Grafen von O—; Philosophische Briefe; Briefe über Don Carlos; Was heisst und zu welchem Ende studirt man Universalgeschichte? eine akademische Antrittsrede; Etwas über die erste Menschengesellschaft nach dem Leitfaden der mosaischen Urkunde; Die Sendung Moses; Die Gesetzgebung des Lykurgus und Solon. XI. Ueber Völkerwanderung, Kreuzzüge und Mittelalter; Uebersicht des Zustands von Europa zur Zeit des ersten Kreuzzugs, ein Fragment; Universalhistorische Uebersicht der merkwürdigsten Staatsbegebenheiten zu den Zeiten Friedrichs I.; Geschichte der Unruhen in Frankreich welche der Regierung Heinrichs IV. vorangingen, bis zum Tode Karls IX.; Herzog von Alba bei einem Frühstück auf dem Schlosse zu Rudolstadt, im Jahre 1547; Denkwürdigkeiten aus

SCHILLER, J. C. F. von, *continued.*

dem Leben des Marschalls Vieilleville; Vorrede zu
der Geschichte des Malteserordens nach Vertot von
M. N. bearbeitet; Vorrede zu dem ersten Theile der
merkwürdigen Rechtsfälle nach Pitaval; Ueber
Anmuth und Würde; Ueber das Pathetische; Ueber
den Grund des Vergnügens an tragischen Gegen-
ständen; Ueber die tragische Kunst; Zerstreute
Betrachtungen über verschieden aesthetische Gegen-
stände. XII. Ueber die ästhetische Erziehung des
Menschen, in einer Reihe von Briefen; Ueber die
nothwendigen Gränzen beim Gebrauch schöner For-
men; Ueber naive und sentimentalische Dichtung;
Ueber den moralischen Nutzen aesthetischer Sitten;
Ueber das Erhabene; Gedanken über den Gebrauch
des Gemeinen und Niedrigen in der Kunst; An den
Herausgeber der Propyläen; Ueber Bürgers Gedichte;
Ueber den Gartenkalender auf das Jahr 1795; Ueber
Egmont, Trauerspiel von Goethe; Ueber Matthissons
Gedichte.

— Works. Early dramas and romances. Transl.
chiefly by H. G. Bohn. London, 1853. p.8°   818.12

  Contents.—The robbers; Fiesco; Love and intrigue;
Demetrius; The ghost seer; The sport of destiny.

— Historical dramas. London, 1850. p.8° . . .   818.11

  Contents. — Don Carlos; Mary Stuart; The Maid of
Orleans; The bride of Messina.

— Historical works, translated by G. Moir. Edinburgh, 1828. 2v. 18° 830.36

  Contents. — Vol. I. Life; Thirty years' war. II.
Thirty years' war; Trial of Counts Egmont and Horn;
The siege of Antwerp.

— Continuation of the revolt of the Netherlands,
[etc.] London, 1847. p.8° 818.10
— Correspondence with Körner, with biogra-
phy, etc., by L. Simpson. London, 1849.
3v. 12° 876.16
— Ghost-seer, from the German. v.I. London,
1849. 16° 798.9
— Maria Stuart. Trauerspiel. 5te Auflage. Tü-
bingen, 1815. 16° 1038.5
— Minor poems. Translated by J. H. Merivale.
London, 1844. 16° 355.6
— Piccolomini, and the death of Wallenstein.
Coleridge, S. T. . . . . v.III. of 327.10–11
— Robbers: a tragedy. 3d ed. Lond., 1797. 8°   478.1
— Schiller's und Goethe's Xenien Manuscript.
Berlin, 1856. 8° 1013.15
— Supplemente zu Schiller's Werken. Stutt-
gart, 1840-41. 4v. 16° 1019.3
— The characters of. Ellet, E. F. 908.7
— Life, and examination of the works of. Car-
lyle, T. 545.12
— Life and lectures on the dramas of. Follen,
C. T. C. . . . . v.IV. of 877.1
SCHILLERHÄUSER. Rank, J 1029.12
SCHILLER's Leben. Schwab, G. 1035.1
SCHIMMELPENNINCK, M. A. Life, ed. by Chr. C.
Hankin. London, 1858. 2v. 12° 595.12
SCHIMMER, K. A. Sieges of Vienna by the Turks.
London, 1847. p.8° 889.16
SCHINDERHANNES, the robber of the Rhine.
Ritchie, L. 758.8
SCHINDLER, A. Life of Beethoven, ed. by J.
Moscheles, including his correspondence,
[transl., etc.] London, 1841. 2v. 12° . . .   545.3
SCHLATTER, M. Life, travels and labors among
the Germans in Pennsylvania, etc. Har-
baugh, H. 534.18
SCHLEGEL, A. W. v. Lectures on dramatic art
and literature, translated by J. Black, rev.
by A. J. W. Morrison. London, 1846. p.8°   818.7
— Preliminary essay to Egyptian mythology.
Prichard, J. C. 1083.9
SCHLEGEL, K. W. F. v. Æsthetic works, transl.
by E. J. Millington. Lond., 1849. p.8° . .   838.8
— Lectures on modern history, translated by L.
Purcell and R. H. Whitelock. London,
1849. p.8° 848.1
— Philosophy of history, translated, with memoir, by J. W. Robertson. 6th ed. Lon-
don, 1848. p.8° 818.3

SCHLEGEL, K. W. F. v. Philosophy of life and
philosophy of language, translated by A.
J. W. Morrison. London, 1847. p.8° 828.8-9
SCHLEGELS, Anecdotes of the. Schiller, J. C. F. v.   876.16
SCHLEIDEN, M. J. Poetry of the vegetable world,
ed. by A. Wood. 1st American ed. Cin-
cinnati, 1853. 8° 166.9-10
— The plant: a biography, translated by A.
Henfrey. London, 1848. 8° 164.5
SCHLESIER, G. Life of W. v. Humboldt. Klencke,
P. F. H. 545.7
SCHLESISCHE Gebirge, Das. Gottschall, R. . . .   1029.19
SCHLICHTEGROLL, Life of Mozart. Carpani, G .   545.20
SCHLOENBACH, A. Zwölf Frauenbilder aus der
Goethe-Schiller Epoche. Hanover, 1856. 16°   1024.1
SCHLOSS [ein] am Meer. Roman. Schücking,
C. B. L. 1017.2
SCHLOSS Hainfeld, or a winter in lower Styria.
Hall, B. 667.21
SCHMITZ, L. History of Greece. N. Y., 1851. 12°   958.3
— History of Rome to A.D. 192. Andover,
1847. 12° 957.3
SCHNITZLER, J. H. Secret history of the court
and government of Russia. Lond., 1854. 2v.8°   925.4
SCHOEDLER, F. Book of nature; physics, astron-
omy, chemistry, etc. 3d ed., transl. from
6th Ger. ed. by H. Medlock. Lond., 1855. 8°   178.4
— — Same. 1st American, from 2d English ed.
Philadelphia, 1853. 8° 145.20
SCHOELCHER, V. Life of Handel. Lond., 1857. 8°   545.2
SCHOMBURGK, R. H. History of Barbados. Lon-
don, 1848. 8° 264.1
— Natural history of the fishes of British Gui-
ana . . . . v.XXXIX.-XL. of 179.1
SCHOOL and the schoolmaster. Potter, A. 137.14-15
SCHOOL amusements. Root, N. W. T. 137.9
SCHOOLCRAFT, H. R. Algic researches. Indian
tales and legends. 1st series. New York,
1839. 2v. 12° 489.9
— Life and character of Lewis Cass. Albany,
1848. 8° 523.8
— Notes on the Iroquois: or contributions to
American hist., antiq., etc. Albany, 1847. 8°   244.6
— Indian in his wigwam. New York, 1848. 8°   245.6
— Thirty years with the Indian tribes, 1812-42.
Philadelphia, 1851. 8° 244.4
SCHOOL days at Rugby. Boston, 1857. 12° . . . 434.8-11
SCHOOL days of eminent men. Timbs, J. 589.3
SCHOOLS. Miller, H. My S. and schoolmasters. 586.5-7
  See Education.
SCHOPENHAUER, J. My youthful life. London,
1847. 2v. 12° 548.21
SCHOUW, J. F. The earth, plants and man; and
sketches from the mineral kingdom; by F.
von Kobell. London, 1852. p.8° 826.5
SCHROEDER, F. Shores of the Mediterranean.
New York, 1846. 2v. 12° 676.5
SCHUBERT, F. Locale for photographic opera-
tions. Halleur, G. C. H. 829.11
SCHÜCKING, C. B. L. Der Bauernfürst. Roman.
Leipzig, 1851. 2v. 16° 1017.1
— Die Königin der Nacht. Roman. Leipzig,
1852. 16° 1017.3
— Ein Schloss am Meer. Roman. Leipzig,
1843. 2v. 16° 1017.2
— Ein Staatsgeheimniss. Roman. Leipzig, 1854.
3v. 16° 1034.19
— Eine Eisenbahnfahrt durch Westfalen. Leip-
zig, 1855. 16° 1029.20
— Von Minden nach Köln. Leipzig, 1855. 16°   1029.18
SCHÜRMANS, H. Précis de droit criminel. Brux-
elles, n.d. 12° 1005.48
SCHULZE, E. K. F. Sämmtliche poetische Werke.
Leipzig, 1855. 5v. 16° 1037.10

  Contents.—Vols. I.—II. Cäcilie, ein romantisches
Gedicht. III. Poetisches Tagebuch; Reise durch das
Weserthal; Sonette; Psyche; Ein griechisches Märchen in sieben Buchern. IV. Elegien; Epistelu;
Vermischte Gedichte; Die bezauberte Rose; Ein
romantisches Gedicht. V. Ernst Schulze nach
seinen Tagebüchern und Briefen, u. s. w. geschildert
von Hermann Marggraff.

SCHWAB, G. Schiller's Leben. 2r. Druck. Stuttgart, 1844. 8° 1035.1
SCHWANN, T. Anatomie du corps humain. Bruxelles, n.d. 12° 1065.49
SCHWARZWÄLDER Dorfgeschichten. Erzählungen. Auerbach, B. .... 1037.1 & 3
SCHWEIDLER, Mary, the amber witch. Meinhold, J. W., ... 889.34
SCIENCE. Bigelow, J. Application of science to the useful arts 198.7-8
— Brande, W. T. Dictionary of 135.1
— Brougham, H. Objects, advantages and pleasures of .... v.1. of 365.14
— Grimké, T S. Reflections on the character and objects of 878.9
— Hitchcock, E. Religious truth illustrated from 1088.5
— Hunt, R. Poetry of science: or, studies of the physical phenomena of nature 145.15
— Lardner, D. Lectures on 144.14-17
— - Museum of 147.20
— Mayhew, H. Wonders of 149.21
— Potter, A. S. applied to the domestic and mechanic arts.......... 197.5
— Timbs, J. Things not generally known 149.28
— - Year-book of facts in science and art ... 159.2
SCIENCE and revealed religion, Connexion between. Wiseman, N. 1098.20
SCIENCE made easy. Chemistry, mechanics, hydrostatics and pneumatics. Philadelphia, 1837. 16° 149.39
SCIENCES, History of the inductive. Whewell, W. 122.9
SCIENTIFIC dialogues. Joyce, J. 826.17
SCIENTIFIC discovery, Annual of, 1850-58. Wells, D. A. 159.1
SCIENTIFIC enquiry, Manual of. Great Britain .. 149.3-4
SCINDE, Sir C. Napier's administration of. Napier, Sir W. 937.2
SCIOGRAPHY, or examples of shadows. Gwilt. J. 205.4
See also: Architecture and Drawing.
SCIPIO's dream: translated by C. R. Edmonds. Cicero, M. T. 824.2
SCITUATE, Mass., History of. Deane, S. 224.23
SCOFFERN, J. Philosophy of common life. London, 1857. 12° 157.9
SCORESBY, W. Account of the arctic regions. Edinburgh, 1820. 2v. 8° 702.10
— The compass in iron ships. London, 1854. 8° 195.7
SCOTLAND. Abbott, J. A summer in 647.18-21
— Aytoun, W. E. Ballads of 375.1
— Bagehot, W. Estimates of some Scotchmen. 563.9
— Burton, J. H. Criminal trials in....... 987.4
— Carus, C. G. King of Saxony's journ. through. 647.3
— Caswall, H. S. and the Scottish church. ... 1089.12
— Chambers, R. Domestic annals of...... 974.3
— - Rebellions of Montrose and others, 1638-1660. .... 830.44
— - Rebellions in S. under Dundee and Mar, 1689-1715. .... 830.50
— - History of the rebellion in 1745-46 .... 830.34
— Cockburn, H. Memorials of his time ... 568.5
— Froissart, J. The ancient chronicles of. .. 1001.2
— Heron, R. Journey through the W. counties of, 1792 .... 646.1
— Irving, D. Lives of Scottish writers 586.13
— Johnstone. Rebellions, 1745-46 ...... 976.7
— Kohl, J. G. Travels in........... 647.5
— Macgillivray, W. Molluscous animals of. . 178.23
— Miller, H. Scenes and legends of 646.3
— Napier, M. Montrose and the covenanters.. 975.9
— Scott, Sir W. History of 368.4
— Sinclair, C. S. and the Scotch 647.17
— Stanhope, P H. Insurrection of 1745 .... 989.6
— Stewart, D. Character, manners and state of the highlanders 987.2
— Stewart, W. G. Popular superstitions and amusements of the highlanders 989.11
— Strickland, A. Lives of the queens of.... 593.4-5
— Tytler, P. F. History of, 1249-1643 ..... 987.7
— Wilson, J. Voyage round the coasts of ... 646.6
See also: Highlands, Scottish.

SCOTT, C. H. The Danes and the Swedes, a visit to Denmark, etc. London, 1856. 12°. 668.4
SCOTT, G. G. Remarks on secular and domestic architecture. London, 1857. 8° 203.17
SCOTT, J., Earl of Eldon, Life of. Twiss, H. ... 552.6
SCOTT, R. Practical cotton-spinner, enlarged by O. Byrne. Philadelphia, 1851. 8° 195.5
SCOTT, T. The Holy Bible, with notes. See Bible. 1001.1
SCOTT, Sir W. Works, with a biography. Philadelphia, 1852-53. 10v. 8° 902.1
    Contents.—Vol. I. Minstrelsy of the Scottish border; Sir Tristrem; Lay of the last minstrel; Ballads translated, or imitated from the German; Marmion; Lady of the lake; Miscellaneous poems; Rokeby; Vision of Don Roderick; Lord of the Isles; Occasional poems; Bridal of Triermain; Harold the dauntless; Field of Waterloo; Songs and miscellanies. II. Waverley; Guy Mannering; Antiquary; Rob Roy; Black dwarf; Old Mortality. III. Heart of Mid Lothian; Bride of Lammermoor; Legend of Montrose; Ivanhoe; Monastery; Abbot. IV. Kenilworth; Pirate; Fortunes of Nigel; Peveril of the Peak; Quentin Durward. V. St. Ronan's well; Redgauntlet; Betrothed; Talisman; Woodstock. VI. Highland widow; Two drovers; My aunt Margaret's mirror; Tapestried chamber; The laird's Jock; Fair maid of Perth; Anne of Geierstein; Count Robert of Paris; Castle dangerous; Surgeon's daughter. VII. Tales of a grandfather; History of Scotland. VIII. Life of John Dryden; Life of J. Swift; Biographical notices of the novelists; Dramatic works; Paul's letters to his kinsfolk; Eyrbiggia-Saga; Essay on chivalry, romance and the drama; Religious discourses; Demonology and witchcraft. IX. Life of Napoleon. X. Life of S. by J. G. Lockhart.
— Poetical works. New York, 1818-19. 6v. 18° 359.13
    Contents. — Vol. I. The lay of the last minstrel. II. The vision of Don Roderick; Ballads and lyrical pieces; Thomas the rhymer. III. Marmion. IV. The lady of the lake; The field of Waterloo. V. Rokeby. VI. The lord of the isles.
— Poetical works, with a sketch of his life, by J. W. Lake. Philadelphia, 1846. 8° 336.1
    Contents. — Life; Lay of the last minstrel; Dance of death, etc.; Marmion; The lady of the lake; Rokeby; Lord of the isles; Thomas the rhymer; Harold the dauntless; The bridal of Triermain; Vision of Don Roderick; The field of Waterloo; Halidon hill; Ballads and lyrical pieces; Miscellanies.
— Poetical works. New ed. N. Y., 1850. 2v. 12° 336.13
    Contents.—Vol. I. Lay of the last minstrel; Marmion; Lady of the lake; The bridal of Triermain; Poetry from the border minstrelsy. II. Rokeby; Lord of the isles; Vision of Don Roderick; Harold the dauntless; The field of Waterloo; Songs and miscellanies; Ballads translated from the German; Songs; Miscellaneous poems; Poetry from the border minstrelsy.
— Poetical works, with life of the author. New York, 1852. 16° 336.14
    Contents. — Lay of the last minstrel; Marmion; Lady of the lake; Don Roderick; Rokeby; Ballads; Lyrics, and songs.
— Poetical works. New York, 1853. 6v. 12°. 336.2
    Contents. — Vol. I. Lay of the last minstrel; Ballads translated from the German; Songs; The poacher; Miscellaneous poems; Poetry published in border minstrelsy. II. Marmion; Occasional pieces. III. Lady of the lake; The vision of Don Roderick. IV. Rokeby; The bridal of Triermain. V. The lord of the isles; The field of Waterloo; Songs and miscellanies. VI. Harold the dauntless; Dramatic pieces, viz. Halidon hill; Macduff's cross; Doom of Devorgoil; Auchindrane, or the Ayrshire tragedy.
— Halidon hill: a dramatic sketch from Scottish history. Philadelphia, 1822. 16°. . 358.21
— Lady of the lake. Baltimore, 1812. 18°. . 359.15
— - Same. New ed. New York, 1857. 12°. . 336.3-7
— Lay of the last minstrel, ballads and lyrical pieces, with a life. London, 1835. 18°. ... 359.14
— Lord of the isles. Boston, 1815. 18°. 359.17
— Marmion. New ed. New York, 1857. 12°. 336.8-12
— Rokeby: a poem. Baltimore. 1813. 18°. ... 359.16
— Waverley novels. Library ed. From last rev. ed. Boston, 1852-53. 27v. 12°
    Contents:
    1. Waverley, or 'tis sixty years since ... 460.2-5
    2. Guy Mannering.............. 460.7-10
    3. Antiquary................. 460.11-16

SCOTT, Sir W. Waverley novels, *continued.*

4. Rob Roy 460.19-21
5. Black dwarf, Old mortality 460.22-25
6. Heart of Mid-Lothian 460.28-33
7. Bride of Lammermoor, Legend of Montrose 460.35-38
8. Ivanhoe 460.39-46
9. Monastery 460.51-54
10. Abbot 460.55-59
11. Kenilworth 460.60-63
12. Pirate 470.2-5
13. Fortunes of Nigel 470.7-12
14. Peveril of the Peak 470.15-18
15. Quentin Durward 470.21-25
16. St. Ronan's well 480.1-4
17. Redgauntlet 480.5-7
18. The betrothed, The talisman 480.8-13
19. Woodstock 480.14-17
20. Highland widow, Two drovers 480.18-21
21. St. Valentine's day 480.22-26
22. Anne of Geierstein 480.27-30
23. Count Robert of Paris 480.31-34
24-26. Castle dangerous, Tales of a grandfather. 1st series. Scottish history . 480.36-39
 Tales, etc. 2d series. Scottish history 480.42-45
27. Tales of a gandfather. 3d series. Same. 480.48-51
 4th series. Stories of France 490.3-6
— The antiquary. Edinb., 1816-18. 3v. 12° . . 460.12
— - Same. Boston, 1821. 8° 460.13
— Fortunes of Nigel. Boston, 1822. 8° 470.6
— Guy Mannering. Philadelphia, 1820. 12° . . 460.11
— Ivanhoe. Boston, 1820. 8° 460.47
— - Same. New York, 1823. 2v. in 1. 12° . 460.48
— Kenilworth. Boston, 1821. 8° 460.65
— - Same, 4th Am. ed. Phila., 1824. 2v. 12° 460.64
— Monastery. Edinburgh, 1820. 3v. 12° . . . 460.50
— - Same. Boston, 1820. 8° 460.49
— Peveril of the peak: a romance. New York, 1823. 2v. 12° 470.13
— - Same. Boston, 1823. 8° 470.14
— Pirate. Boston, 1822. 8° 470.1
— Quentin Durward. Edin., 1823. 3v. 12° . . 470.20
— - Same. Philadelphia, 1823. 2v. 12° . . 470.19
— Rob Roy. Edinburgh, 1818. 3v. 12° . . 460.17
— - Same. Boston, 1821. 8° 460.18
— Tales of my landlord. Black Dwarf; Old Mortality. Boston, 1821. 8° 460.26
— - Same. 2d ser. Heart of Mid-Lothian. Boston, 1821. 8° 460.27
— - Same. 3d ser. Bride of Lammermoor. Legend of Montrose. Boston, 1821. 8° . . 460.34
— Waverley; or, 'tis sixty years since. Edinburgh, 1814. 3v. 12° 460.6
— - Same. Boston, 1820. 8° 460.1
— Waverley anecdotes, illustrative of the novels and romances of Scott. Bost., 1833. 2v. 16° 470.26
— History of Scotland. London, 1830. 2v. 16° 368.4
— Letters on demonology and witchcraft. London, 1830. 16° 399.2
— - Same. New York, 1848. 18° 810.13
— Life of Napoleon, with view of the French revolution. Exeter, 1828. 2v. 8° 604.8
— - Same. Exeter, 1827. 2v. 8° 604.7
— - Same. Philadelphia, 1858. 3v. in 1. 8°. 604.5-6
— - Same. Philadelphia, 1858. 2v. in 1. 8°. 604.1-4
— Lives of the novelists. Phila., 1825. 2v. 12° 586.19
— Tales of a grandfather. 1st ser. Stories from Scottish history. Phila., 1853. 2v. in 1. 16° 480.35
— - Same. 2d ser. Phila., 1853. 2v. in 1. 16°.480.40-41
— - Same. 3d ser. Phila., 1853. 2v. in 1. 16°.480.46-47
— - Same. 4th ser. Stories from the history of France. Phila., 1853. 2v. in 1. 16° . . 490.1-2
— Ancient British drama. Lond., 1810. 3v. roy.8° 331.2

Contents.—Vol. I. The four P's, Heywood; Ferrex and Porrex, Sackville; Returne from Pernassus, anon.; Damon and Pithias, Edwards; Gammer Gurton's needle, anon.; Alexander and Campaspe, Lyly; Edward II., Marlow; The heir, May; The bird in a cage, Shirley; The Jew of Malta, Marlow; The wits, Davenant; Sir John Oldcastle, [part 1,] anon.; Life and death of Thomas Lord Cromwell, anon.;

SCOTT, Sir W., *continued.*

London prodigal, anon.; The puritan, anon.; Yorkshire tragedy, anon.; George a Greene, anon.; Jeronimo, anon.; The Spanish tragedy, anon.; The honest whore, Dekkar. II. Malcontent, Marston; All fools, Chapman; Eastward hoe, Jonson and others; The revenger's tragedy, Tourneur; The dumb knight, Machin; Miseries of inforced marriage, Wilkins; Lingua, Brewer; Merry devil of Edmonton, anon.; A mad world my masters, Middleton; Ram alley, Barry; Roaring girl, Middleton; City match, Mayne; Muse's looking-glass, Randolph; A woman killed with kindness, Heywood; A match at midnight, Rowley; The gamester, Shirley; Microcosmus, Nabbes; Greene's Tu Quoque, Cook; Albumazar, Tomkis. III. The white devil, Webster; The hog hath lost his pearl, Tailor; Four prentices of London, Heywood; The antiquary, Marmion; The ordinary, Cartwright; Jovial crew, Brome; Old couple, May; Andromana, Shirley; Mayor of Quinborough, Middleton; Grim, the collier of Croydon, anon.; City nightcap, Davenport; Parson's wedding, Killegrew; Adventures of five hours, Tuke; Elvira, Digby; Widow, Jonson and others; Dutchess of Malfy, Webster; The rebellion, Rawlins; Witch, Middleton.

— Modern British drama. Lond., 1811. 5v. roy.8° 331.1

Contents.—Vol. I. *Tragedies:* Two noble kinsmen, Shakespeare and Fletcher; A king and no king, Beaumont and Fletcher; The maid's tragedy, Beaumont and Fletcher; Thierry and Theodoret, Beaumont and Fletcher; Philaster, Beaumont and Fletcher; Bonduca, Beaumont and Fletcher; The false one, Beaumont and Fletcher; The bondman, Massinger; The fatal dowry, Massinger and Field; The broken heart, Ford; The rival queens, Lee; Theodosius, Lee; All for love, Dryden; Don Sebastian, Dryden; The orphan, Otway; Venice preserved, Otway; Isabella, Southern; Oroonoko, Southern; The mourning bride, Congreve; Tamerlane, Rowe; The fair penitent, Rowe; Jane Shore, Rowe; Lady Jane Gray, Rowe; Cato, Addison; Distrest mother, Philips; Siege of Damascus, Hughes. II. *Tragedies:* The revenge, Young; The brothers, Young; Mariamne, Fenton; Geo. Barnwell, Lillo; Fatal curiosity, Lillo; Arden of Feversham, Lillo; Zara, Hill; King Charles I., Havard; Gustavus Vasa, Brooke; Mahomet, Miller; Tancred and Sigismunda, Thomson; Irene, Johnson; Roman father, Whitehead; Elfrida, Mason; Caractacus, Mason; Gamester, Moore; Boadicea, Glover; Earl of Essex, Jones; Barbarossa, Brown; Douglas, Home; Cleone, Dodsley; Orphan of China, Murphy; Zenobia, Murphy; Grecian daughter, Murphy; Earl of Warwick, Franklin; Matilda, Franklin; Countess of Salisbury, Hartson; Mysterious mother, Walpole; Comus, Milton; Fair apostate, Macdonald. III. *Comedies:* Every man in his humour, Jonson; Volpone, Jonson; The alchemist, Jonson; Rule a wife and have a wife, Fletcher; The chances, Fletcher; New way to pay old debts, Massinger; The committee, Howard; The rehearsal, Buckingham; Key to the rehearsal; Country girl, Wycherly; Plain dealer, Wycherly; Old bachelor, Congreve; Double dealer, Congreve; Love for love, Congreve; Way of the world, Congreve; Provoked wife, Vanbrugh; Confederacy, Vanbrugh; Mistake, Vanbrugh; Provoked husband, Vanbrugh and Cibber; Spanish friar, Dryden; Love makes a man, Cibber; She would and she would not, Cibber; Careless husband, Cibber. IV. *Comedies:* Hypocrite, Cibber; Constant couple, Sir Harry Wildair, The inconstant, The recruiting officer, Beaux stratagem, Farquhar; The funeral, The tender husband, Conscious lovers, Steele; Busy body, Wonder, Bold stroke for a wife, Centlivre; Drummer, Addison; Miser, Fielding; Suspicious husband, Hoadly; Way to keep him, Murphy; Falstaff's wedding, Kenrick; Jealous wife, Colman; Clandestine marriage, Colman and Garrick; Good natured man, She stoops to conquer, Goldsmith; The brothers, The West Indian, Cumberland; The riva's, Sheridan. V. *English opera and farce:* Comus, Milton; Cheats of Scapin, Otway; Beggars' opera, Gay; Contrivances, Cranonhotor thologus, Carey; Tom Thumb, Fielding; Mock doctor, Fielding; Intriguing chambermaid, Fielding; Devil to pay, Coffey; King and miller of Mansfield, Sir John Cockle at court, Dodsley; Lying valet, Miss in her teens, Lethe, Male coquette, Guardian, Neck or nothing, Peep behind the curtain, Irish widow, Bon ton, High life below stairs, Garrick; Taste, Englishman in Paris, Knights, Englishman returned from Paris, The author, The minor, The liar, The orators, Mayor of Garratt, The patron, The commissary, The devil upon two sticks, The lame lover, The maid of Bath, Foote; The appren-

SCOTT, Sir W., *continued*.

tice, The upholsterer, The old maid, The citizen, Three weeks after marriage, Murphy ; Love-a-la-mode, Mack∂in; Love in a village, Maid of the mill, The padlock, Bickerstaff ; Dr. Last in his chariot, Bickerstaff and Foote; The sultan, Bickerstaff; The deuce is in him, Colman; Midas, O'Hara; Maid of the oaks, Burgoyne; Two misers, O'Hara ; The critic, Sheridan; Rosina, Mrs. Brooke.

— Allan, G. Life of, and notices of his writings. 585.1
— Lockhart, J. G. Memoirs of the life of . . . 585.2
SCOTT, W. Infantry tactics. U. S. war departm't. 199.39
— Life of. Mansfield, E. D. 517.14
SCOTTISH ballads, historical and romantic. Finlay, J. 316.10
SCOTTISH chiefs: romance. Porter, J. 789.4
SCOTTISH minstrel, Modern. Rogers, C. 316.12
SCOTTISH songs, Illustrated book of 869.8
SCOTTISH worthies, Lives of. Tytler, P. F. . . .399.9-10
SCOTT, The: a novel. Simms, W. G. 790.22-24
SCREW-PROPELLER, Treatise on the. Bourne, J. 191.3
SCRIBE, A. E. Œuvres choisies. Paris, 1845. 5v. 12° 1076.6

Contents. — Vol. I. La nuit d'un garde national; Le nouveau Pourceaugnac ; Le solliciteur; Les deux précepteurs; Une visite à Bedlam; La somnambule; L'ours et le Pacha; Le secrétaire et le cuisinier; Frontin, mari-garçon; L'intérieur d'une étude; Michel et Christine; Mémoires d'un Colonel de Hussards; La loge du portier; L'intérieur d'un bureau; Le menteur véridique; La maîtresse au logis. II. Le coiffeur et le perruquier; La mansarde des artistes; La haine d'une femme; La quarantaine; Le plus beau jour de la vie; Le charlatanisme; Les premières amours; Le confident; La demoiselle à marier; Simple histoire; L'ambassadeur; Le mariage de raison. III. L'héritière; Le diplomate; La marraine; La manie des places; Avant, pendant, et après; Un mariage d'inclination; Louise ou la réparation; La seconde année; Une faute; La famille de Riquebourg. IV. Le budget d'un jeune ménage; Toujours; Les malheurs d'un amant heureux; La chanoinesse; Etre aimé ou mourir; La pensionnaire mariée; Clermont ou une femme d'artiste; Le parrain; Rodolphe; Valérie. V. Le mariage d'argent; Bertrand et Raton; L'ambitieux; La Camaraderie; La calomnie; Le verre d'eau.

SCRIPTURES. *See* Bible.
SCULPTURE. Bottari, G. Lettere sulla scultura . 1049.1
— Cunningham, A. Lives of British sculptors. 379.9
— Ellis, Sir H. (Townley gallery of,) in British Museum 849.6
— Jarves, J. J. Art hints. 208.16
— Lee, H. F. Familiar sketches of S. and sculptors. 208.23
— Memes, J. S. History of. 830.48
— Vasari, G. Lives of the most eminent sculptors. 848.6
SEA, Physical geography of the. Maury, M. F. . 145.1-6
SEA-BOARD slave states, journey, etc. Olmsted, F.L. 627.5
SEALED orders, a tale. Marsh, A. 469.10
SEA-LIONS, The, or the lost sealers. Cooper, J. F.780.26-29
SEALSFIELD, C. Gesammelte Werke. Stuttgart, 1845-47. 15v. in 14. 16° 1027.6

Contents. — Vols. I.–III. Der Legitime und die Republikaner. IV.–VI. Der Virey und die Aristokraten, oder Mexico im Jahr 1812. VII.–VIII. Morton oder die grosse Tour. IX.–XIII. Lebensbilder aus der westlichen Hemisphäre. [Including] IX. George Howard's Esq. Brautfahrt. X. Ralph Doughby's Esq. Brautfahrt. XI.–XII. Pflanzerleben. XIII. Nathan, der Squatter-Regulator. XIV.–XV. Das Cajütenbuch oder nationale Charakteristiken.

— Cabin book; or national characteristics. Tr. by S. Powell. London, 1852. 12° 735.7
— Les émigrés français dans la Louisiane, [1800-1804.] Paris, 1853. 12° 1078.24
— Life in the new world. New York, n.d. 8°. 735.5-6
SEALY, T. H. Broad grins from China. London, 1852. 16° 469.16
SEARLE, J Life, character, and genius of Ebenezer Elliott, the corn law rhymer. London, 1850. 18° 599.12
SEARS, B. Life of Luther. Philadelphia, n.d. 18° 545.24
— Edwards, B. B. and Felton, C. C. Classical studies. Boston, 1849. 12° 403.16

SEARS, E. H. Athanasia ; or foregleams of immortality. Boston, 1858. 12° 118.18
— Regeneration. Boston, 1853. 12° 1096.21
— - Same. 5th ed. Boston, 1856. 12° 1106.11
SEARS, R. History of the Bible, with notes and engravings. 3d ed. New York, 1844. 2v. in 1. 8° 1085.4
— Pictorial history of the American revolution. New York, 1846. 8° 305.2
SEA-SIDE book. Harvey, W. H. 178.26
SEA-SIDE studies. Lewes, G. H. 178.2
SEASONS. Duncan, H. Sacred philosophy of the. 1089.7
— Griffiths, T. Chemistry of the four. 156.6
— Howitt, M. Pictorial calendar of the 825.10
SEAVER, J. E. Life of M. Jemison. Deh-he-wämis. 4th ed., with notes. N. Y., 1856. 12° 539.3
SEAWARD, Sir E. Narrative of his shipwreck. Porter, J. 400.24
SEA-WEEDS. Gifford, I. British. 169.21
— Landsborough, D. Popular history of British. 178.31
SECCHIA rapita, La, poema. Tassoni, A. 345.4
SECRET history of the court of James I., by F. Osborne. Edinburgh, 1811. 2v. 8° 552.6
SECRET proceedings and debates of the convention for forming the constitution of the U. S. Richmond, 1839. 12° 209.6
SECRET societies of France, Hist. of, from 1830 to 1848. La Hodde, de 1004.4
SECRET societies of the middle ages. Lond., n.d. 12° 849.5
— - New ed. London, 1848. 18° 850.13
SEDGWICK, Prof. A. Brougham, H. Objects of science. 820.72
— Livingston, D. Prefatory letter by A. S. . . 894.4
SEDGWICK, C. M. A New England tale and miscellanies. New York, 1852. . . . . . . .436.9-10
— Clarence ; or a tale of our own times. Rev. ed. New York, 1849. 12° 436.11-14
— Home. New ed. Boston, 1854. 18° 729.14-17
— Letters from abroad. New York, 1841. 2v. 12° 648.8
— Live and let live. New York, 1837. 18° . . .729.12-13
— Married or single? a novel. N. Y., 1857. 2v. 12° 436.1-5
— Means and ends, or self-training. Boston, n.d. 18° 129.22
— - Same. 2d ed. New York, n.d. 18° 729.18
— Memoir of Joseph Curtis. New York, 1858. 16° 537.4
— Redwood, a tale. Rev. ed. New York, 1850. 12° 436.6-8
— The poor rich man, and the rich poor man. New York, n.d. 729.11
— Tales and sketches. 2d ser. N. York, 1844. 18° 729.19
— Memoir of L. M. Davidson. Sparks, J. v.VII. of 529.1
SEED-GRAIN for thought and discussion. Lowell, A. C. 124.22
SEELY, J. B. The wonders of Elora. 2d ed. London, 1825. 8° 695.7
SÉGUR, Mme. de. *Née Rostopchine.* Nouveaux contes des fées. Paris, 1857. 12° 1078.43
SÉGUR, A. J. P. de. Women—their condition and influence. London, 1803. 3v. 16° 139.15
SÉGUR, L. P. de. Memoirs and recollections—written by himself. London, 1825-26. 2v. 8° 613.2
SÉGUR, P. P. de. Expedition to Russia. New York, n.d. 2v. 18° 820.43-44
— - Same. 8th ed. London, 1840. 2v. 16° . 399.3
SEIDEL, J. J. The organ and its construction. 2d ed. London, 1855. 8° 204.8
SELBORNE, Natural history of. White, G. 178.19
SELBY, P. J. Nat. hist. of parrots [and] pigeons. Jardine, W. . . . . .v.IX.-X. of 179.1
SELDEN, J. Table-talk—with biog., pref., and notes, by S. W. Singer. London, 1847. 16° 877.17
SELECT temperance tracts. New York, n.d. 12° 1109.4
SELECTIONS from female poets. Boston, 1857. 18° 369.15
SELECTION of English synonyms. [Rev'd by R. Whately.] 1st Am. ed., from 2d London. Boston, 1852. 12° 403.11
SELF, or, the world as it goes. A novel. Gore, Mrs. C. F. 776.7
SELF-CULTIVATION recommended. Taylor, I. . . 129.23
SELF-CULTURE, Thoughts on. Grey, M. G., and Shirreff, E. 124.12-13

SELF-DEVOTION; or, the history of Katharine
　Randolph. Campbell, H. 	768.2
SELF-EDUCATION; twelve chapters for young
　thinkers. Hood, E. P. 	129.20
SELF-FORMATION; or, the history of an individual
　mind. London, 1837. 2v. 12° 	137.22
SELF-GOVERNMENT. Lieber, F. 	134.13
SELF-KNOWLEDGE, A treatise on. Mason, J. . . 	1209.11
SELF-TAUGHT men, Biog. of. Edwards, B. B. . . 518.18-19
SELF-TRAINING. Sedgwick, C. M. 	129.22
FÉLIS, N. J. Le Prince Désiré. Cabinet des
　Fées . . . . v.XXXV.of 1077.1
SELKIRK, A., Life of. De Foe, D. 	735.8
SELWYN, G. A., and his contemporaries. Jesse,
　J. H. 	563.2
SEMMES, R. Service afloat and ashore during the
　Mexican war. Cincinnati, 1851. 8° 	623.15
SENECA, Morals, etc. By Sir R. L' Estrange.
　Boston, 1794. 12°. 	129.10
SENECA Indians, Case of the 	244.8
SENIOR, N. W. Political economy, from the En-
　cyc. Metrop. 2d ed. London, 1850. 12° . . . 	136.28
SENNAAR, Expedition to. English, G. B. . . . 	693.4
SENSE and sensibility: a novel. Austen, J. . v.I. of 758.3
SENSES. Kitto, J. The lost senses. 	840.24
— Wilson, G. Five gateways of knowledge . . 	138.6
SENTIMENTAL journey through France and Italy.
　Sterne, L. 	908.10
SEPOY revolt, its causes and its consequences.
　Mead, H. 	937.1
SERMONS, Cyclopædia of. Burns, J. 	1083.15
SERMONS of eminent divines of the church of
　England. London, 1856. 16° 	866.11
　　See also: Ballou, H.; Buckminster, J. S.;
　　Bushnell, H.; Cecil, R.; Discours. in Mur-
　　ray street church; Greenwood, F.W. P.;
　　Huntington, F. D.; Kirk, E. N.; Liver-
　　more, A. A.; Lowell, C.; Maffitt, J. N.;
　　Monod, A., and others; Newman, J. H.;
　　Nott, S. jr.; Paley, W.; Peabody, E.;
　　Peabody, W. B. O.; Robertson, F. W.;
　　South, R.; Spurgeon, C. H.; Trench, R. C.;
　　Trimmer, S.; Wainwright, J. M.; Way-
　　land, F.; Whitefield, G.
SERRURIER, Manuel du 	1075.38
SERVANTS' directory. Roberts, R. 	189.4
SERVIA in 1843 and 1844. Paton, A. A. 	666.4
SERVIA and the Servian revolution. Ranke, L. . 	827.1
SERVICE afloat and ashore during the Mexican
　war. Semmes, R. 	623.15
SERVITUDE volontaire. La Böetie, E. de 	1069.16
SETTLERS and convicts, or recollections of the
　Australian backwoods. London, 1847. 18° 	850.10
SEVASTOPOL, Visit to the camp before. McCor-
　mick, R. C. jr. 	687.19
SEVEN poor travellers: a tale. Dickens, C. . . . 491.1-6
SEVEN years of the king's theatre. Ebers, J. . . 	353.12
SEVENTEEN hundred and seventy-six. Lossing,
　B. J. 	213.8
SÉVIGNÉ, M. de R. de. Lettres, avec les notes de
　tous les commentateurs. Paris, 1853. 6v. 12° 1076.5
— Mémoires touchant la vie et les écrits de.
　Walckenaer, Baron. 	1067.31
SEWARD, A. Memoirs of Dr. Darwin, with anec-
　dotes and criticisms. Philadelphia, 1804. 8° 	573.5
— Poetical works, with correspondence. Ed. by
　W. Scott. Edinburgh, 1810. 3v. 8° 	340.8
　　Contents. — Vol. I. Biographical preface; Literary
　　correspondence. II. Miscellaneous poems; Monody
　　on Major André; Miscellaneous poems. III. Louisa, a
　　poetical novel; Sonnets; Translations.
SEWARD, W. H. Life and public services of J. Q.
　Adams. Auburn, 1849. 12° 	517.25
— Life of, etc. Baker, G. E. 	526-3
SEWEL, W. History of the Quakers. New York,
　1844. 2v. 8° 	1085.10
SEWELL, E. M. Amy Herbert. Ed. by W. Sewell.
　New York, 1844. 8° 	425.1-2
— Earl's daughter. Ed. by Rev. W. Sewell.
　New York, 1851. 16° 	426.1-4

SEWELL, E. M. Experience of life. New York,
　1853. 12° 	424.1-2
— Gertrude. Ed. by Rev. W. Sewell. 5th Am.
　ed. New York, 1852. 12° 425.11-15
— Ivors. New York, 1857. 2v. 12° 	424.9-12
— Journal kept during a summer tour, for the
　children. 3 parts in 1 vol. New York,
　1852. 12° 	659.28
　　Contents. — Pt. 1. From Ostend to the lake of Con-
　　stance. 2. From the lake of Constance to the Sim-
　　plon. 3. From the Simplon through part of the Tyrol
　　to Genoa.
— Katherine Ashton. New York, 1854. 2v. 12° 	424.8
— Laneton parsonage: Tale. Pt.I.-III. Ed.
　by Rev. W. Sewell. Pt.I. 4th Am. ed. New
　York, 1849. 3v. 12° 	425.6
— - Same. 5th Am. ed. New York, 1850-51.
　3v. 12° 	425.3-5
— Margaret Percival. Ed. by Rev. W. Sewell.
　New York, 1850. 2v. 12° 	425.17
— Ursula: a tale of country life. New York,
　1858. 2v. 12° 	424.3-7
— Walter Lorimer and other tales. [viz: Em-
　blems of life; Lost inheritance.] New
　York, 1849. 12° 	425.7-10
SEWELL, J. Steam and locomotion. London,
　1852-53. 2v. in 1. 16° 	829.10
SEWELL, W. Hawkstone: a tale. 7th Am. ed.
　New York, 1849. 2v. 12° 	428.3
SEYD, E. California and its resources. London,
　1858. 8° 	236.9
SEYMOUR, E. S. Sketches of Minnesota. New
　York, 1850. 12° 	638.9
SEYMOUR, F. G. Romance of ancient history.
　Egypt. London, 1834. 2v. 12° 	959.3
SEYMOUR, H. D. Russia on the Black sea and
　sea of Azof. London, 1855. 8° 	685.5
SEYMOUR, M. H. Evenings with the Romanists.
　Philadelphia, 1855. 12° 	1008.16
SFORZOSI, L. History of Italy, translated by N.
　Greene. New York, 1847. 18° 	810.74
SHABBY genteel story. Thackeray, W. M. . . . 509.1-3
SHADOW and perspective. Heather, J. F. . . . 	829.8
　　See also: Drawing.
SHADOWS, with rules for their projection. Gwilt,
　J. 	205.4
SHADY side, or life in a country parsonage. Hub-
　bell, M. S. 417.14-18
SHAKERISM, Progress of. M'Nemar, R. 	1089.20
SHAKERS. Brown, T. Account of the. 	1089.13
— Dyer, J. Narrative elucidating character,
　etc., of Mary Dyer 	1089.14
SHAKESPEARE, W. Works, in eight volumes.
　Edinburgh, 1795. 8v. 12° 	337.2
　　Contents. — Vol. I. Tempest; Midsummer night's
　　dream; Two gentlemen of Verona; Merry wives of
　　Windsor; Measure for measure. II. Missing. III.
　　All 's well that ends well; Twelfth night; Comedy of
　　errors; Winter night's tale; King John. IV. King
　　Richard 2d; King Henry 4th; King Henry 6th; King
　　Henry 6th, part 1. V. King Henry 6th, parts 2, 3;
　　King Richard 3d; King Henry 8th. VI. King Lear;
　　Timon of Athens; Titus Andronicus; Coriolanus.
　　VII. Julius Cæsar; Antony and Cleopatra; Cymbe-
　　line; Troilus and Cressida. VIII. Romeo and Juliet;
　　Hamlet; Othello; Glossary and index.
— Works, with notes and life, by Rev. H. N.
　Hudson. Boston, 1851, '52, '54, '55 and '56.
　11v. 16° 	325.1
　　Contents. — Vol. I. Tempest; Two gentlemen of
　　Verona; Merry wives of Windsor; Twelfth night.
　　II. Measure for measure; Much ado about nothing;
　　Midsummer night's dream; Love's labour's lost. III.
　　Merchant of Venice; As you like it; All 's well that
　　ends well; Taming of the shrew. IV. Winter's tale;
　　Comedy of errors; Macbeth; King John. V. King
　　Richard 2; First and second parts of King Henry 4;
　　King Henry 5. VI. 1st to 3d parts of King Henry
　　6. VII. Richard 3; Henry 8; Troilus and Cres-
　　sida. VIII. Timon of Athens; Coriolanus; Julius
　　Cæsar; Antony and Cleopatra. IX. Cymbeline;
　　Titus Andronicus; Pericles; King Lear. X. Romeo
　　and Juliet; Hamlet; Othello. XI. Life; History of
　　the Drama; General criticism; Poems and Sonnets.

SHAKESPEARE, W. Works, ed. by J. P. Collier. New York, 1853. 8v. 12° 326.2

   Contents. — Vol. I. History of the English drama and stage; Life of Shakespeare; Tempest; Two gentlemen of Verona; Merry wives of Windsor. II. Measure for measure; Comedy of errors; Much ado about nothing; Love's labour's lost; Midsummer night's dream; Merchant of Venice. III. As you like it; Taming of the shrew; All's well that ends well; Twelfth night; Winter's tale. IV. King John; King Richard 2; King Henry 4, parts 1, 2; King Henry 5. V. King Henry 6, parts 1, 2, 3; King Richard 3; King Henry 8. VI. Troilus and Cressida; Coriolanus; Titus Andronicus; Romeo and Juliet; Timon of Athens. VII. Julius Cæsar; Macbeth; Hamlet; King Lear; Othello. VIII. Antony and Cleopatra; Cymbeline; Pericles; Venus and Adonis; Rape of Lucrece; Sonnets; Lover's complaint; Passionate pilgrim.

— Comedies, histories, tragedies and poems, with a biography and studies, by C. Knight. Pict. ed. London, 1853. 8v. 8° 322.4

   Contents. — Comedies: Vol. I. Two gentlemen of Verona; Comedy of errors; Love's labour's lost; All's well that ends well; Taming of the shrew; Midsummer night's dream; Merchant of Venice. II. Much ado about nothing; Merry wives of Windsor; As you like it; Twelfth night; Measure for measure; Winter's tale; Tempest. Histories: III. King John; King Richard 2; King Henry 4, parts 1 and 2; King Henry 5. IV. King Henry 6, parts 1, 2, 3; King Richard 3; King Henry 8; Tragedies: V. Romeo and Juliet; Hamlet; Othello; Timon of Athens; King Lear; Macbeth. VI. Troilus and Cressida; Cymbeline; Coriolanus; Julius Cæsar; Antony and Cleopatra; Titus Andronicus; Pericles; VII. Venus and Adonis; Rape of Lucrece; Sonnets; Lover's complaint; Passionate pilgrim; Biography. VIII. Studies of Shakespere; Shakespere's critics; Indexes.

— Dramatic works, with corrections of Johnson, Steevens, [etc.] Rev. by I. Reed. New York, 1821. 10v. 12° 326.1

   Contents. — Vol. I. Author's life; Dr. Johnson's preface; Learning of Shakespeare; Tempest; Two gentlemen of Verona; Merry wives of Windsor. II. Measure for measure; Comedy of errors; Merchant of Venice; As you like it. III. Midsummer night's dream; Much ado about nothing; Love's labour's lost; Taming of the shrew. IV. All's well that ends well; Twelfth night; Winter's tale; Macbeth. V. King John; Richard 2; Henry 4, parts 1 and 2. VI. King Henry 5; King Henry 6, parts 1, 2, and 3. VII. Richard 3; Henry 8; Coriolanus. VIII. Julius Cæsar; Antony and Cleopatra; Timon of Athens; Titus Andronicus. IX. Troilus and Cressida; Cymbeline; King Lear; Romeo and Juliet. X. Hamlet; Othello; Pericles.

— Dramatic works, with a life, by C. Symmons, and a glossary. Chiswick, 1828. 8v. in 4. 32° 359.18

   Contents. — Vol. I. Tempest; Two gentlemen of Verona; Merry wives of Windsor; Twelfth night; Measure for measure. II. Much ado about nothing; Midsummer night's dream; Love's labour's lost; Merchant of Venice; As you like it. III. All's well that ends well; Taming of the shrew; Winter's tale; Comedy of errors; Macbeth. IV. King John; King Richard 2; King Henry 4; King Henry 5. V. King Henry 6; King Richard 3. VI. King Henry 8; Troilus and Cressida; Timon of Athens; Coriolanus. VII. Julius Cæsar; Antony and Cleopatra; Cymbeline; Titus Andronicus; Pericles. VIII. King Lear; Romeo and Juliet; Hamlet; Othello.

— Dramatic works, with notes, sketch of life, [etc.,] by C. H. Wheeler. London, 1834. 8° 322.3
— Dramatic works, with life and notes. Boston, 1851. 7v. 8° 313.1-2

   Contents. — Vol. I. Life of Shakespeare, his will, etc.; Preface of the players; Tempest; Two gentlemen of Verona; Merry wives of Windsor; Twelfth night; Measure for measure; Much ado about nothing. II. Love's labour's lost; Merchant of Venice; Midsummer night's dream; As you like it; All's well that ends well; Taming of the shrew. III. Winter's tale; Comedy of errors; Macbeth; King John; Richard 2; Henry 4, part 1. IV. Henry 4, part 2; Henry 5; Henry 6, parts 1–3. V. Richard 3; Henry 8; Troilus and Cressida; Timon; Coriolanus. VI. Julius Cæsar; Antony and Cleopatra; Cymbeline; Titus Andronicus; Pericles. VII. King Lear; Romeo and Juliet; Hamlet; Othello.

SHAKESPEARE, W. Poetical works, with notes. Boston, 1851. 8° . . . . v. VIII. of 313.1

   Contents. — Venus and Adonis; The rape of Lucrece; Sonnets; Illustration of the sonnets; A lover's complaint; Passionate pilgrim; Verses among the additional poems to Chester's love's martyrs; Illustrations of a lover's complaint, passionate pilgrim, etc.; Supplementary notice to the poems; Supplementary notice to the Roman plays.

— Poems. London, 1842. 16° 329.9
— Beauties, with notes. Ed. by W. Dodd. London, 1752. 2v. 12° 357.12
— Dictionary of Shakespearian quotations. Philadelphia, 1853. 12° 357.4
— First sketch of merry wives of Windsor. Ed. by J. O. Halliwell. London, 1842. 8° . . . 342.8
— King Henry IV., printed from a contemporary MS. Ed. by J. O. Halliwell. London, 1845. 8° 342.27
— First sketches of 2d and 3d parts of King Henry VI. Ed. by J. O. Halliwell. London, 1843. 8° 342.14
— Bacon, D. Philosophy of the plays of,—unfolded 353.3
— Beyle, H. Études sur le romantisme 1067.23
— Clarke, M. C. Girlhood of Shakespeare's heroines 325.15
— Coleridge, S. T. Lectures on 332.7
— Collier, J. P. Emendations from folio 1632 . 357.9
— Craik, G. L. The English of 356.7
— Davies, T. Observations on the plays of . . 353.11
— Guizot, F. P. G. S. and his times 357.5
— Halliwell, J. O. S. and the early English drama 342.30
— Hazlitt, W. Characters of 356.23
— Hudson, H. N. Lectures on 357.6-8
— Koenig, H. William Shakspeare. Roman . . 1015.3
— Lamb, C. and M. Tales from S. for young persons 840.29
— Reed, H. Lectures on English history and tragic poetry, as illustrated by 968.2
— Walker, W. S. Versification of 326.3
— White, R. G. Scholar of. Studies of text, etc. 353.2
— Skottowe, A. Life of 583.17
— Tweddell, G. His times and contemporaries. 357.18
— Ward, J. Notices of 977.2

SHAKESPEARE society. London, 1841–1846. 32v. 8° 342.1-32

   Contents:

  1. Mem. of E. Alleyn. By J. P. Collier. 1841. 342.1
  2. Gosson's school of abuse. 1841. . . . . . 342.2
  3. Heywood's apology for actors. 1841 . . . 342.2
  4. Coventry mysteries. Ed. by Halliwell. 1841. . . . . 342.3
  5. Thynn's pride and lowliness. 1841. . . . 342.4
  6. Patient Grissil, a comedy by Dekkar, etc. 1841 . . . . 342.6
  7. Revels at court in Elizabeth and James's reigns. 1842. . . . . 342.5
  8. Jonson's conversations with Drummond. Laing. 1842. . . . . 342.7
  9. First sketch of merry wives of Windsor. Halliwell. 1842 . . . . 342.8
 10. Fools and jesters; Armin's nest of ninnies. Collier. 1842 . . . . 342.9
 11. Old play of Timon. A. Dyce. 1842 . . . 342.10
 12. Nash's Pierce Penniless. Collier. 1842. 342.11
 13. Heywood's Edward IV. Field. 1842 . . 342.12
 14. Northbrooke against dicing, etc. Collier. 1843 . . . . 342.13
 15. First sketches of Henry VI. Halliwell. 1843 . . . . 342.14
 16. Oberon's vision compared with Lylie's Endymion. Halpin. 1843 . . . . 342.15
 17. Chester Whitsuntide plays, part I. Wright. 1843 . . . . 342.16
 18. Alleyn papers. Collier. 1843 . . . . . . 342.17
 19. Two tracts by Forde the dramatist. Collier. 1843 . . . . 342.18
 20. Tarlton's jests, News out of purgatory, and Life. Halliwell. 1844 . . . . 342.19

SHAKESPEARE society, *continued.*

21. True tragedy of Richard III., and Legge's Richardus Tertius. 1844 . . . .   342.20
22. Ghost of Richard III., a poem by Brooke.(?) 1844 . . . .   342.21
23. Sir Thomas More, a play. Ed. by A. Dyce. 1844 . . . .   342.22
24. Shakespeare society's papers. Vols. I., II. 1844–1845 . . . .   342.23
25. Taming of a shrew, and the wife lapped in morel's skin. T. Amyot. 1844 . . .   342.24
26. Fairy mythology of midsummer night's dream. Halliwell. 1845 . . . .   342.26
27. Reprint of a contemporary MS. of Henry IV. Halliwell. 1845 . . . .   342.27
28. Diary of Philip Henslowe. Collier. 1845.   342.28
29. Fair maid of the exchange. Heywood; and, Fortune by land and sea, by Heywood and Wm. Rowley. 1846 . . . .   342.29
30. Marriage of wit and wisdom. Halliwell. 1846 . . . .   342.30
31. Memoirs of actors in Shakespeare's plays. Collier. 1846 . . . .   342.31
32. Riche, his farewell to the militarie profession. 1846 . . . .   342.32

SHALER, W. Sketches of Algiers. Boston, 1826. 8°   915.4
SHARP, James, *A'b'p of St. Andrews.* Life and times of. Stephen, T. 574.10
SHARP, John, *A'p'b of York.* Life, etc. of. Sharp, T.   574.11
SHARP, R. Letters and essays in prose and verse. 2d ed. London, 1834. 16° 878.18
SHARP, T. Life of John Sharp. Ed. by T. Newcome. London, 1825. 2v. 8° 574.11
SHARPE, S. Hist. of Egypt till A.D. 640. 3d ed. London, 1852. 2v. 8° 954.3
— Notes on Eng. version of N. Testament. London, 1856. 16° 1089.18
SHATTUCK, L. Hist. of Concord, Mass., and adjacent towns. Boston, 1835. 8° 224.20
SHAW, W. S. Memorials of. Felt, J. B. 537.1
SHEA, J. G. Catholic missions among the Indian tribes of the U. S., 1529–1854. N. Y., 1855. 12°   1098.7
SHEEP and wools, Rise, progress, and present state of colonial. Southey, T. 136.9
SHEEP and shepherding. Milburn, M. M. . .   169.15
SHEEPFOLD in the waters. Biernatzki, J. C. . .   884.1
SHEEPFOLDS, Notes on the constr. of. Ruskin, J.   206.3
SHEFFIELD, *Lord.* Holroyd, J. B. *See* Gibbon, E.
SHEIL, *Lady.* Glimpses of life and manners in Persia, etc. London, 1856. 12° 695.12
SHEIL, R. L. Sketches of the Irish bar, with memoir and notes, by R. S. Mackenzie. New York, 1854. 2v. 12° 598.5
SHELLEY, M. W. Frankenstein, or the modern Prometheus. Rev. and cor. Lond., 1849. 16°   798.9
— Literary and scientific men of France. London, 1838–39. 2v. 16° 388.8
— and others. Literary and scientific men of Italy, Spain, and Portugal. Lond., 1835–37. 3v. 16° 398.1
SHELLEY, P. B. Poetical works, ed. by Mrs. Shelley. Philadelphia, 1851. 8° 311.9–12

    Contents. — Queen Mab; Alastor, or the spirit of solitude; The revolt of Islam; Prometheus unbound; The Cenci; Hellas; Œdipus Tyrannus, or Swellfoot the tyrant; Early poems; Poems written 1816–22; Translations.

— Essays, letters from abroad, translations, and fragments. New ed. Lond., 1852, 2v. 16°   875.15
— Life of. Hogg, T. J. 585.14
— Last days of. Trelawny, E. J. 585.9–11
SHELLS, Treatise of recent and fossil. Woodward, S. P. 175.12
SHELLS of the British Islands, Manual of the land and fresh water. Turton, W. 175.9
SHELLS, Nat. classification of. Swainson, W. . .   408.2
   See also: Conchology, Mollusca, etc.
SHELTON, F. W. Chrystalline: a romance. New York, 1854. 12° 769.10
— Rector of St. Bardolph's. N. Y., 1853. 12°.   428.7

SHENSTONE, W. Poetical works, with life [by R. Dodsley.] London, 1804. 32° 369.26
— Essays on men and manners, a life by S. Johnson, and character by Dodsley. London, n.d. 24° 850.27
SHEPHERD, W. Life of Poggio Bracciolini. Liverpool, 1837. 8° 543.8
SHEPPARD, F. Constitutional text-book. Philadelphia, 1857. 12° 299.4
SHEPPARD, J. Notices of J. Foster. 858.8
SHEPPARD Lee: a novel. Bird, R. M. 498.11
SHERBURNE, J. H. Life of Paul Jones. London, 1825. 12° 528.5
SHERER, M. Military memoirs of the Duke of Wellington. London, 1830. 2v. 16° 558.10
— Tales of the wars of our own times. London, 1829. 2v. 12° 799.6
SHERIDAN, F. Memoirs of Miss Sidney Bidulph. 5th ed. London, 1796. 5v. 12° 768.3
SHERIDAN, R. B. Dramatic works, with a memoir. London, 1848. p.8° 828.10

    Contents. — Life; The rivals; St. Patrick's day; The duenna; The school for scandal; The critic; Trip to Scarborough; Pizarro; Verses to the mem. of Garrick.

— Speeches. London, 1842. 3v. 8° 861.6
— Memoirs of the life of. Moore, T. 598.6–9
SHERLEY, A. R. and T. The three brothers: or, adventures in Persia, Russia, Turkey, Spain, etc. London, 1825. 12° 687.16
SHERMAN, J. Memoir of William Allen. London, 1851. 12° 568.6
SHERWOOD, M. M. Life, with extracts from Mr. Sherwood's journal. London, 1857. 8° . .   595.13
SHETLAND and the Shetlanders. Sinclair, C. . .   646.19
SHEW, J. Water-cure manual. 9th thousand. New York, 1849. 12° 157.19–20
SHIP and shore. Colton, W. 678.10–16
SHIPMASTER's assistant, The. Blunt, J. 135.2
SHIPP, J. The K'Haunie Kinch-Walla: or, the Eastern story teller. London, 1852. 12°. .   719.16
SHIPS and boats, Hints on principles to regulate forms of. Bland, W. 829.16
SHIPWRECK, The; and other poems. Falconer, W.   359.5
SHIPWRECKS of the royal navy, Narratives of. Gilly, W. O. S. 988.12
SHIRLEY. Brontë, C. 435.11
SHIRLEY, Mass., History of. Butler, C. 224.14
SHIRREFF, E. Thoughts on self culture. Grey, M. G. 124.12–13
SHIRREFF, P. A tour through N. America. Edinburgh, 1835. 8° 624.10
SHOBERL, F. Persia; a description of the country, government, etc. Philadelphia, 1828. 12°.   938.11
SHOOTER, J. Kaffirs of Natal and the Zulu country. London, 1857. 8° 693.2
SHORE, J., *Lord Teignmouth.* Memoirs of the life, writings and correspondence of Sir William Jones. Philadelphia, 1805. 8° 583.11
SHREWSBURY, Mass., History of. Ward, A. H. .   224.19
SHUCKARD, W. E. History and natural arrangement of insects. Swainson, W. 408.3
SIAM. Bowring, J. Kingdom and people of, in 1855. . . . .   696.3
— China, pictorial, descriptive and historical, Some account of 825.8
— Neale, F. A. Siam and the Siamese 879.14
SIBERIA. Atkinson, T. W. Oriental and Western.   701.1
— Dobell, P. Travels in 666.2
— Erman, A. Travels in 709.1
— Hill, S. S. Travels in 707.8
— Kotzebue, A. von. Journal of exile to 549.29
SIBERIAN Tartary, Pedestrian journey through. Cochrane, J. D. 674.6
SIBERT's Wold. A tale. Mackarness, M. 176.9–10
SIBILLA Odaleta, Episodio delle guerre d' Italia alla fine del secolo XV. Varese 1059.2
SIBLEY, J. L. History of the town of Union, Maine. Boston, 1851. 12° 227.2
SIBORNE, W. History of the war in France and Belgium, in 1815. 2d ed. London, 1844. 2v 8°. Atlas in folio. 1005.2

SICILIAN vespers, War of the. Amari, M. 915.6
SICILY. Bigelow, A. Travels in 676.2
— Brydone, P. Tour through 679.11
— Murray, J. The Sicilies 649.3
— Simond, L. Tour in 675.2
— Tuckerman, H. T. Sicily: a pilgrimage . . . 678.19
— Spallanzani, L. Travels in the two Sicilies . 676.4
SICK giant and the doctor dwarf. Jerrold, D. v.III.of 905.1
SICK room, Life in the. Martineau, H. 878.2
SICKNESS and health of the people of Bleaburn.
    2d ed. Boston, 1853. 16°. 449.10
SIDEREAL heavens, illustrative of the character of
    the Deity, etc. Dick, T. 820.6
SIDNEY Bidulph, Miss, Memoirs of. Sheridan, F. 768.3
SIDNEY, H. Diary of the times of Charles II. Ed.,
    with notes, by R. W. Blencowe. London,
    1843. 2v. 8°. 553.4
SIDNEY, S. Three colonies of Australia. 2d ed.
    London, 1853. 8°. 705.2
SIDONIA, the sorceress. Meinhold, W. 802.1
SIEBENKÄS, F. S. Married life, death, etc., of J.
    P. F. Richter. 887.8
SIEBOLD, C. T. E. v. and Stannius, H. Compara-
    tive anatomy of the invertebrata. Transl.
    and edited by W. I. Burnett. v.I. Boston,
    1854. 8°. 175.1
SIEBOLD, P. F. v. See Manners of the Japanese . 708.2
SIEGE of Valencia. Poem. Hemans, F. D. . . . 324.2
SIERRA Leone, Residence at 899.6
SIGHT and hearing; how preserved and how lost.
    Clark, J. H. 157.10
SIGNERS of the declaration of independence. Los-
    sing, B. J. 518.10
SIGNS of the times. Bunsen, C. C. J. 134.9
— Cumming, J. 116.3
SIGOURNEY, L. H. Examples from the 18th and
    19th centuries. 1st series. N. Y., 1857. 12° 548.17
— Letters to mothers. 6th ed. N. Y., 1845. 12° 139.2
— Letters to young ladies. 16th edition. New
    York, 1848. 12°. 127.18
— Lucy Howard's journal. N. Y., 1858. 12° . . 905.6
— Moral pieces in prose and verse. Hartford,
    1815. 12°. 349.7
— Past meridian. New York, 1854. 12° 848.18
— Scenes in my native land. Boston, 1845. 16° 868.17
— Select poems. 10th ed., revised. Philadelphia,
    1852. 12°. 348.11
— Western home, and other poems. Phila-
    delphia, 1854. 12°. 338.17
SIGURD. Travels in Palestine. See Wright, T. . 846.7
SILENT revolution, The: or, the future effects of
    steam and electricity. Garvey, M. A. . . . 199.23
SILK. Cobb, J. H. Directions for the culture of. 199.29
— History of. See History 195.4
— Kindt, J. De l'industrie de la soie. 1065.28
— Porter, G. R. Origin, progress, etc., of the S.
    manufacture 408.9
SILLIMAN, B. Tour between Hartford and Quebec,
    1819. 2d ed., corrected. New Haven, 1824. 12° 628.26
— Visit to Europe in 1851. N. Y., 1854. 2v. 12° 648.6-7
SILVER cup of sparkling drops. Porter, C. B. . . 888.20
SILVER, Mrs. The lover's pilgrimage and a trial
    of affection. Boston, 1846. 12° 428.6
SIMCOE, J. G. Military journal. History of the
    queen's rangers during the revolution, with
    memoir of the author. N. Y., 1844. 8° . . 212.2
SIMMS, W. G. Beauchampe, sequel to Charlemont.
    New ed. New York, 1856. 12°. . . .790.35-39
— Border beagles: a tale. N. Y., 1855. 12° . . 800.3-7
— Charlemont: a tale. New York, 1856. 12°. 800.23-26
— Confession: or, the blind heart, a domestic
    story. New ed. New York, 1856. 12° . .790.44-46
— Eutaw, sequel to the forayers. New ed. New
    York, 1856. 12°. 800.18-22
— The forayers. New York, 1855. 12° 800.12-17
— Guy rivers. New ed. N. Y., 1855. 12° . .800.8-11
— History of S. Carolina. Charleston, 1842. 12° 237.17
— Katharine Walton. New ed. N. Y., 1854. 12° 790.25-29
— Life of the Chevalier Bayard. N. Y., 1847. 12° 547.13
— Life of Francis Marion. N. Y., 1844. 12° . .528.14-15

SIMMS, W. G. Marie de Berniere; The Maroon;
    Maize in milk. Philadelphia, 1853. 12°. .790.53-55
— Mellichampe: a legend of the Santee. New
    ed. New York, 1854. 12° 790.17-21
— Norman Maurice, an American drama, and
    other poems. 4th ed., revised and cor-
    rected. Philadelphia, 1853. 12°. 348.1-2
— The partisan: a romance. New ed. New
    York, 1854. 12° 790.13-16
— Poems. New York, 1853. 2v. 12° 348.3
    Contents. — Vol. I. Norman Maurice; Atalantis;
    Tales and traditions of the South; City of the silent.
    II. Southern passages and pictures; Historical and
    dramatic sketches; Scripture legends; Francesca da
    Rimini.
— Richard Hurdis: a tale. New ed. New York,
    1855. 12° 790.47-51
— The scout. New ed. New York, 1856. 12° 790.22-24
— Southward ho! a novel. N. Y., 1854. 12° . 790.40-43
— The sword and the distaff: a story of the
    South. Philadelphia, 1853. 12° 790.52
— Vasconselos: a romance. N. Y., 1857. 12° . 800.28
— Vision of Cortes, Cain, and other poems.
    Charleston, 1829. 16° 369.14
— The wigwam and the cabin. Tales of the
    South. 1st series. Philadelphia, 1853. 12° 800.27
— Woodcraft: a story of the South. New ed.
    New York, 1854. 12° 790.30-34
— The Yemassee: a romance. New ed. New
    York, 1854. 12° 790.8-12
SIMON Suggs' adventures and travels. Philadel-
    phia, n.d. 12° 726.15
SIMOND, L. Tour and residence in Great Britain,
    1810-11, and appendix on France. 2d ed. Ed-
    inburgh, 1817. 2v. 8°. 645.3
— Tour in Italy and Sicily. London, 1828. 8°. 675.2
— Switzerland. Journal of a tour and residence
    in that country, 1817-19. Lond., 1822. 2v. 8° 663.3-4
SIMONDE de Sismondi, J. C. L. See Sismondi, J.
    C. L. S. de.
SIMONDS, T. C. History of South Boston. Bos-
    ton, 1857. 12°. 227.4
SIMONS, C. Eléments de droit civil. La propriété.
    Bruxelles, n.d. 12°. 1065.50
— De la propriété, et de ses modifications. Brux-
    elles, n.d. 12° 1065.51
SIMPLICISSIMUS, Die Abenteuer des. Roman.
    Grimmelshausen, C. v. 1025.4
SIMPLON, From the lake of Constance to the.
    Sewell, E. M. 659.28
SIMPSON, J. H. Military reconnaissance, from Santa
    Fé to the Navajo country. Philadelphia,
    1852. 8° 623.5
SIMPSON, J. Y. Homœopathy — its tenets and ten-
    dencies. 1st American ed. Phila., 1854. 8° 157.1
SIMPSON, S. and Wise, E. Readiest reckoner ever
    invented. 6th ed. London, 1847. 16° . . . 136.34
SIMPSON, T. Discoveries on the N. coast of Amer-
    ica, 1836-39. London, 1843. 8° 625.2
SINAI. Dumas, A. Travelling sketches in . . . 709.20
— Laborde, L. E. S. J., *Comte de*. Journey to . 685.8
— Lepsius, K. R. Tour from Thebes to the pen-
    insula of 699.16
— Discoveries in 693.11
— Maundrell, H. Journey from Grand Cairo to. 684.9
— Robinson, E. Biblical researches in 684.4
— Stanley, A. P. S. and Palestine in connec-
    tion with their history 684.7
— Stewart, R. W. Journey to S. and Palestine. 685.3
SINCLAIR, C. Beatrice. New York, n.d. 12° . . . 456.3-7
— Jane Bouverie. New York, 1851. 12° . . .456.9-11
— Lord and Lady Harcourt. Phila., 1851. 12° 455.1
— Modern accomplishments. New York, 1849. 12° 455.8
— Modern flirtations. New York, n.d. 12° . .456.12-15
— Modern society. New York, 1854. 12° . . . 456.2
— Scotland and the Scotch. N. Y., 1840. 12° 647.17
— Shetland and the Shetlanders. N. Y., 1840. 12° 646.19
SINCLAIR, J. D. An autumn in Italy. Edin-
    burgh, 1829. 18°. 830.53
SINGER'S companion, The. New York, 1854. 12° 207.20

SINTRAM and his companions. La Motte Fouqué,
   F. H. K. de 416.13-14
SIR Michael Scott: a romance. Cunningham, A. 777.3
SIR Roger de Coverley. Addison, J. 409.1
SIR Theodore Broughton. James, G. P. R. . . . 463.5
SIR Thomas More: a play. Ed. by A. Dyce. Lon-
   don, 1844. 8° 342.22
SIRR, H. C. China and the Chinese. The opium
   trade, [etc.] London, 1849. 2v. 8° 696.2
SISMONDI, J. C. L. S. de. Fall of the Roman em-
   pire. London, 1834. 2v. 16° 378.5
— History of the crusades against the Albigen-
   ses. Transl. Philadelphia, 1843. 12° . . . 949.5
— History of the Italian republics. London,
   1832. 16° 378.4
— Literature of the South of Europe. Trans. by
   T. Roscoe. 3d ed. London, 1850. 2v. p.8° 818.4
SISTERHOODS. See Hospitals and sisterhoods . 139.7
SISTERS, The, or warnings and words. See Omni-
   bus of modern romance 801.2
SISTERS abroad, The: or, an Italian journey.
   Channing, B. H. 678.17
SISTERS of charity. Jameson, A. 127.23-24
SIX days of creation. Lewis, T. 146.17
SIX months in Italy. Hillard, G. S. 679.7-9
SIX years in a man-of-war. Holbrook, S.F. . . 525.6-7
SIXTEENTH and seventeenth centuries, History of
   the. Raumer, F. von 927.9
SKELETON, Principal forms of the. Owen, R. . . 177.5
SKEPTICISM, Philosophy of. Walker, J. B. . . . 1094.13
SKETCH, A, of the history of monkeys. London,
   1848. 18° 850.11
SKETCH book, The. Irving, W. . . . . . v.III. of 367.2-3
SKETCHER, The. Eagles, J. 208.1
SKETCHES by a traveller. Holbrook, S. P. . . . 878.15
SKETCHES by Boz. Dickens, C. 461.1-5
SKETCHES from life. Blanchard, L. 877.18
SKETCHES in natural history. Mammalia. Lon-
   don, 1849. 6v. in 5. 18° 850.12
SKETCHES of eminent living surgeons and physi-
   cians of Paris. Translated by E. Bartlett.
   Boston, 1831. 12° 669.1
SKETCHES of history, life, and manners in the
   United States. New Haven, 1826. 12° . . . 629.20
SKETCHES of imposture, deception, and credulity.
   2d ed. London, 1840. 16° 399.5
SKETCHES of married life. Follen, E. L. 429.5
SKETCHES of popular tumults. London, 1837. 12° 134.16
— - Same, London, 1847. 18° 850.14
SKETCHES and stories from life. Lee, H. F. . . 469.8
SKIN, diseases of the. See Medicine.
SKINNER, T. H. Discourse delivered in Murray
   street church. See Discourses, etc. 1083.5
SKOTTOWE, A. Life of Shakspeare, and essays on
   the ancient theatres. London, 1824. 2v. 8° 583.17
SLADE, A. Travels in Germany and Russia.
   London, 1840. 8° 663.9
SLATER, S., Memoir of. White, G. S. 524.5
SLAVERY. Adams, N. South-side view of . . . 127.21
— American Anti-S. Soc. S. in the U. States . 127.1
— Bacon, L. Essays on 127.10
— Bleby, H. Death struggles of 127.20
— Canot, T. Twenty years of an African slaver. 609.2
— Carey, H. C. Why the slave trade exists, and
   how it may be extinguished 1096.23
— Chambers, W. Slavery and colour in America. 297.8
— Follen, C. T. C. Address on . . . . . v.V. of 877.1
— Fuller, R. S. as a scriptural institution . . 1109.23
— Helps, A. Relation of the Spanish conquests
   in America to 254.2
— Huntley, H. Service on the slave coast of
   Africa 698.15
— Jay, W. Miscellaneous writings on 118.3
— Mann, H. Letters and speeches on 866.6
— Olmsted, F. L. Journey through the sea-
   board slave states 627.5
— Stephen, G. Anti-slavery recollections . . 1080.17
— Stirling, J. Letters from the slave states . . 627.1
— Thornton, T. C. Inquiry into the history of. 127.9
   See West Indies

SLAVIC nations, Language and literature of the.
   Robinson, T. A. L. v. J. 404.7
SLAVONIC nations, Remarks on. Wilkinson,
   J. G. 925.5
SLEEMAN, W. H. A journey through Oude, in
   1849-50, with correspondence relative to the
   annexation. London, 1858. 2v. 8°. 707.5
SLEEP, The philosophy of. Macnish, R. 157.28
SLEEP and dreams. Symonds, J. A. 125.23
SLEEPER, J. S. Salt water bubbles: or, life on
   the wave. Boston, 1854. 12° 737.5
SMALL arms, Exercises in. See United States.
SMALL books on great subjects, No. I.-XII. Philadelphia, 1846-47. 3v. 16° 850.25
    Contents.—Vol. I. No.1. Philosophical theories and
   philosophical experience ; 2. Connection between
   physiology and intellectual science, by J. Barlow; 3.
   Man's power over himself to prevent or control insanity, by J. Barlow; 4. Introduction to practical organic
   chemistry. II. No. 5. Brief view of Greek philosophy
   to the age of Pericles; 6. Brief view of Greek philosophy from the age of Socrates to the coming of Christ;
   7. Christian doctrine and practice in the second century; 8. An exposition of vulgar and common errors
   adapted to the year of grace MDCCCXLV. III. No. 9.
   Introduction to vegetable physiology with references
   to the works of De Candolle, Lindley, etc.; 10. Principles of criminal law; 11. Christian sects in the 19th
   century; 12. The general principles of grammar.
SMEDLEY, E. History of France, 843-1529. London, 1836. 8° 365.5
— Sketches from Venetian history. London,
   1831-38. 2v. 16° 399.4
— - Same. New York, 1846. 2v. 18° 810.49
— Taylor, W. C., Thompson, H. and Rich, E.
   Occult sciences. London, 1855. 12° 125.5
SMEE, A. Electro-metallurgy. 3d ed. London,
   1851. 12° 196.13
SMILES, S. Life of George Stephenson. From
   the 4th London ed. Boston, 1858. 12° . . 588.4-6
SMILES and frowns. A novel. Wentz, S. A. . . 777.9
SMITH, Adam. Nature and causes of the wealth of
   nations. Aberdeen, 1848. 12° 136.33
— Theory of moral sentiments. New ed. Lon-
   don, 1853. p.8° 817.10
SMITH, Albert. Comic tales and sketches. Lon-
   don, 1852. 16° 728.11
SMITH, Alexander. City poems. Boston, 1857. 12° 324.11
— Poems. Boston, 1853. 16° 324.12
SMITH, Capt. Alexander. Life of A. Smith, cap-
   tain of the island of Pitcairn, by himself.
   Boston, 1819. 12° 519.5
SMITH, Archibald. Peru as it is: a residence in
   Lima, and other parts of the republic. Lon-
   don, 1839. 2v. 12° 633.21
SMITH, C. The old manor house. London, 1820.
   2v. 12° . . . . v.XXXVI.-XXXVII. of 779.1
SMITH, C. H. Natural history of the human spe-
   cies. Ed. by S. Kneeland, jr. Boston, 1851.
   12° 176.4
— Introd. to mammalia and natural history of
   dogs and horses. Jardine, W. v.XV.,
                        XVIII.-XX. of 179.1
SMITH, C. M. Curiosities of London life. London, 1853. 12° 884.17
SMITH, C. W. Book of recitations, a collection
   from the best poets and dramatists. Lon-
   don, 1857. 16° 356.25
SMITH, Eli. Travels in Palestine. Robinson, E. . 684.4
SMITH, Elias. Life, conversion, etc. Portsmouth,
   1816. 12° 539.8
SMITH, Elizabeth. Fragments in prose and verse,
   with life, by H. M. Bowdler. Bost., 1810. 12° 599.7
SMITH, E. H. Black Hawk, and scenes in the West,
   a national poem. New York, 1849. 12° . . 338.11
SMITH, E. O. Newsboy. New York, 1854. 12°. . 806.2
SMITH, E. P. Manual of political economy. New
   York, 1853. 12° 136.19
SMITH, E. R. The Araucanians, or, notes of a tour
   in Chili. New York, 1855. 12° 635.9
SMITH, E. V. History of Newburyport, Mass.
   Newburyport, 1854. 8° 224.15

SMITH, F. G. Analytical compendium of medical science. *See* Neill, J. 153.5
SMITH, G. Visit to each of the consular cities of China, 1844-46. New York, 1847. 12° . . 696.14-15
SMITH, H. Adam Brown, the merchant. New York, 1843. 8° 802.21
— Arthur Arundel, a tale. New York, 1844. 8° 802.20
— Brambletye house, or, cavaliers and round-heads. London, 1826. 3v. 12° 797.1
— - Same. Boston, 1826. 3v. 12° 797.2
— Festivals, games, and amusements. New York, 1847. 48° 810.31
— Gaieties and gravities. New York, 1852. 12° 899.17-18
— Midsummer medley for 1830. London, 1830. 2v. 12° 797.6
— The new forest, a novel. London, 1829. 3v. 12° 797.4
— Pic-nic papers. *See* Dickens, C. 482.4
— Reuben Apsley. London, 1827. 3v. 12° . . . 797.3
— The Tor hill. London, 1826. 3v. 12° . . . 797.5
— and J. Poetical works, with biogr. sketch. Ed. by E. Sargent. New York, 1857. 8° . . 324.14

Contents. — Poems, by Horace Smith; Miscellaneous; Humorous poems, by James Smith; London lyrics; Miscellaneous; Rejected addresses [by Horace and James Smith]; Notes to "Rejected addresses."

— Rejected addresses. From 22d London ed. Boston, 1851. 12°. 325.3
SMITH, H. I. Education. New York, 1845. 18°. 829.53
SMITH, J. Memoirs, letters, and comic miscellanies, in prose and verse. Ed. by H. Smith. London, 1840. 2v. 12° 584.1
SMITH, Hon. J. Life of. Morison, J. H. 523.19
SMITH, Capt. J. Hill, G. C. Biography of 528.13
— Hillard, G. S. Life of . . . . v.I. of 518.5
SMITH, Joseph. Life of. *See* Mormons. 879.12
SMITH, Joseph A. Productive farming. N. York, 1843. 12° 169.9
SMITH, J. C. Correspondence and miscellanies, with an eulogy, by W. W. Andrews. New York, 1847. 12° 898.6
SMITH, J. E. Memoir and correspondence. Ed. by Lady Smith. London, 1832. 2v. 8° . . 573.7
SMITH, J. H. Causes which led to the death of Major André. London, 1808. 8° 565.3
SMITH, J. P. Relation between the Holy Scriptures and parts of geological science; with the literary life of the author. 5th ed. London, 1852. p.8° 816.11
SMITH, J. T. The discovery of America by the Northmen, in the 10th century. 2d ed. London, 1842. 12° 309.6
SMITH, J. V. C. Pilgrimage to Egypt. Boston, 1852. 12° 698.18
— Turkey and the Turks. Boston, 1854. 12° . 918.12-13
SMITH, L. L. Questions to accompany Taylor's manual of ancient history. N. York, 1851. 8° 955.2
SMITH, O. H. Early Indiana trials and sketches. Cincinnati, 1858. 8° 235.8
SMITH, Sydney. Works. Phila., 1844. 3v. 12°. 867.3
— Works. Philadelphia, 1851. 8° 863.11, 14-15
— Works. Boston, 1856. 8° 863.12-13
— Selections from the writings of S. Smith. London, 1854. 12° 409.25
— Sketches of moral philosophy. New York, 1850. 12° 125.16
— Wit and wisdom, with memoir and notes, by E. A. Duyckinck. New York, 1856. 12° . . 896.5-6
— Memoir, with selection from letters of. Holland, S. S. 583.18-19
SMITH, S. C. Chile con carne; or the camp and the field. New York, 1857. 12° 623.19
SMITH, S. L. H., Memoir of. Hooker, E. W. . . . 1107.18
SMITH, Rev. T., *of Portland*, Journal of. *See* Willis, W. 234.2
SMITH, T. S. Animal physiology. Lib. Us. Knl. 365.12
— Illustrations of the divine government, with an app. by T. Whittemore. Boston, 1831. 12° 1089.2
— Philosophy of health. 5th ed. London, 1851. 2v. 18° 850.15

SMITH, W. History of Greece, to the Roman conquest. Boston, 1854. 12° 958.4
— - Same. New York, 1854. 12° 958.1-2
— - Same. With notes and continuation, by C. C. Felton. Boston, 1855. 8° 952.7
SMITH, W. H. Canada, past, present, and future. Toronto, n.d. 2v. 8° 265.1
SMITH, Wm. Hawkes. Letters on social science. Birmingham, 1839. 16° 139.1-2
SMITH, Sir W. Sidney. Life and correspondence. Barrow, J. 564.3
SMOKE, Prevention of. Williams, C. W. 195.14
SMOLLETT, T. History of England. *See* Hume, D. . . . . 962.3&963.1
— Humphry Clinker . . . . . v.XXX.-XXXI. of 779.1
— Anderson, R. Life of, etc. 584.9
SMUCKER, S. M. Arctic explorations and discoveries during the 19th century. New York, 1857. 12° 704.17
— Court and reign of Catherine II. New York, 1855. 12° 546.10
— Life and times of Alexander Hamilton. Boston, 1857. 12° 517.9
— Memoir of J. C. Frémont. 517.19
SMUGGLERS of the Swedish coast. A romance. Carlen, E. 766.2
SMYTH, T. History of the Westminster assembly. New York, 1844. 12° 1096.19
— Unity of the human races. From the American edition. Edinburgh, 1851. 12° 176.5
SMYTH, W. Lectures on the French revolution. New edition. London, 1855. 2v. p.8° . . . 837.2
— Lectures on modern history. New ed. London, 1851. 2v. p.8° 827.8-9
— - Same. Cambridge, [Eng.,] 1840. 2v. 8°. 943.7
— - Same. 3d American ed.; with additions by J. Sparks. Boston, 1851. 8° 943.3
SNARLEYYOW: or, the dog-fiend. Marryat, F. . . 745.8
SNELLAERT, A. Histoire de la littérature flamande. Bruxelles, n.d. 12° 1075.28
SNODGRASS, W. D. Discourse delivered in Murray street church 1083.5
SNORRO Sturleson. The Heimskringla; chronicle of the kings of Norway. Translated, etc., by by S. Laing. London, 1844. 2v. 8° . . . 924.4
SNOW, H. Spirit-intercourse; incidents of personal experience. Boston, 1853. 12° . . 125.26-27
SNOW, W. P. Two years' cruise off Tierra del Fuego, the Falkland Islands, Patagonia, and in the Plate. London, 1857. 2v. 12° . . . 708.9
SNOWFLAKES and sunbeams: or, the young fur traders. Ballantyne, R. M. 728.12-16
SOANE, G. New curiosities of literature and book of the months. 2d ed. London, 1849. 2v. 12° 402.11
SOAPS, Manufacture of, including recent discoveries. Kurten, P. 198.11-12
SOAP and candles, Chemistry, applied to the manufacture of. Morfit, C. 194.5
SOAVE, F. Novelle morali. Nuov. ed. Livorno, 1851. 12° 1058.2
SOCIAL science. Ballou, A. Practical Christian socialism. 134.2
— Brouckere, C. de. La charité et l'assistance publique 1065.11
— Brownson, O. A. Essays and reviews on . . 1086.31
— Carpenter, M. Juvenile delinquents. 135.16
— Dick, T. Improvement of society. 810.58
— Fitzhugh, G. Sociology for the South 135.19
— Fourier, F. C. M. Œuvres complètes 1064.2
— Haley, W. D. Words for the workers 137.27
— Jameson, A. Communion of labor 127.23-24
— Jennings, R. Delusions concerning wealth and want 139.13
— Karr, J. B. A. Une poignée de vérités. . . . 1067.15
— La Boëtie, E. D. Servitude volontaire 1069.16
— Lucas, S. History as a condition of social progress 139.9
— Martineau, H. Poor-laws and paupers: a tale. 749.4
— Michelet, J. The people 124.17
— Segur, A. J. P. de. Women; their condition and influence 139.15

SOCIAL science. Smith, W. H. Letters on 139.12
— Theory of human progression 134.18
— Thouissen, J. J. Le socialisme dans le passé. 1005.57
— - Le socialisme et ses promesses 1005.56
— Woman's rights tracts 878.8
  See also: Prison discipline, Slavery, Tem-
    perance, Woman, etc.
SOCIAL distinction: or, hearts and homes. Ellis,
  S. S. 804.8
SOCIAL evenings: or, historical tales. Lee, M. E. 469.25-26
SOCIETY. Withington, W. Growth of thought
  as affecting the progress of 124.16
SOCIETY for the diffusion of useful knowledge.
  Library of entertaining knowledge. Lond.,
  various dates. 43v. 12°.
  Contents:
  Clarke, W. Pompeii: chiefly from the jour-
    nals of W. C. 849.3
  Craik, G. L. Pursuit of knowledge under dif-
    ficulties. 2v. 849.4
  Davis, J. F. A general description of China
    and its inhabitants. 2v. 839.5
  Ellis, H. Elgin marbles. 2v. 839.9
  — Townley gallery. 2v. 849.6
  Jardine, D. Criminal trials. 2v. 839.4
  Lane, E. W. Modern Egyptians. 2v. 839.8
  Lankester, E. Vegetable substances used for
    the food of man 849.8
  Long, G. Egyptian antiquities. 2v. 839.7
  Malden, H. Eminent men. 4v. 839.6
  Malkin, J. H. Historical parallels. 2v. . . . 839.12
  Manners of the Hindoos. 2v. 839.16
  New Zealanders 849.1
  Paris and its historical scenes. 2v. 849.2
  Planché, J. R. British costume. 839.3
  Rennie, J. Bird architecture. 839.2
  — Faculties of birds 839.10
  — Habits of birds 839.11
  — Insect architecture 839.13
  — Menageries, nat. hist. of monkeys, etc. . 839.17
  — Menageries. Quadrupeds. 3v. 839.18
  — and Westwood, J. O. Insect miscellanies. 839.14
  — - Insect transformations 839.15
  Secret societies of the middle ages 849.5
  Trail, C. P. Backwoods of Canada 839.1
  Vegetable substances used in the arts 849.7
  Vegetable substances; materials of manu-
    factures 849.9
SOCIETY for the diffusion of useful knowledge.
  Library of entertaining knowledge. Boston,
  various dates. 15v. 12°.
  Contents:
  Clarke, W. Pompeii; chiefly from the jour-
    nals of W. C. 849.20
  Craik, G. L. Pursuit of knowledge under dif-
    ficulties 849.21
  Jardine, D. Criminal trials 849.11
  Lankester, E. Vegetable substances used for
    the food of man 859.3
  Malkin, J. H. Historical parallels. 849.12
  New Zealanders 849.18
  Paris and its historical scenes 849.19
  Rennie, J. Architecture of birds 849.10
  — Insect architecture. 849.13
  — Insect miscellanies 849.14
  — Insect transformations 849.15
  — Menageries 849.16
  — Menageries, v. II. and Prac. naturalist . 849.17
  Vegetable substances used in the arts 859.1-2
SOCIETY for the diffusion of useful knowledge.
  Library of useful knowledge. 22v. and 1v.
  atlas. London. 8° 365.1-17
  Contents:
  Brougham, H. Account of Lord Bacon's
    novum organon scientiarum 365.11
  Busk, M. M. History of Spain and Portugal,
    B.C. 1000 to A.D. 1814 . . . . 365.1
  De Morgan, A. The differential and integral
    calculus 365.2
  History of the American revolution 365.11

SOCIETY for the diff. of use. knowl., *continued.*
  Jones, D. On the value of annuities and re-
    versionary payments 365.8
  Lindley, J. Botany 365.15
  Long, G. Geography of America and the
    West Indies 365.3
  — and Porter, G. R. Geography of Great
    Britain 365.10
  Malkin, F. History of Greece 365.6-7
  M'Culloch, J. R. Treatise on the principles,
    practice and history of commerce 365.15
  Mathematical and miscellaneous tracts 365.12
    Contents. — Elements of trigonometry by W. Hop-
    kins; Elements of spherical trigonometry, by A. De
    Morgan; On the study and difficulties of mathemat-
    ics; Animal mechanics, by Sir C. Bell; Vegetable
    physiology ; Animal physiology, by T. S. Smith;
    Objects, advantages, and pleasures of science, by
    Brougham; On the manufacture of iron; On proba-
    bility; Art of brewing, by Booth.
  Merivale, C. History of Rome under the em-
    perors 365.9
  Morton, P. Geometry, plane, solid and spher-
    ical 365.4
  Müller, K. O. History of the literature of
    ancient Greece. v. I. 365.11
  Murphy, R. Treatise on the theory of alge-
    braical equations 365.15
  Natural philosophy. 3v. 8° 365.14
    Contents. — Vol. I. Objects, advantages, and pleas-
    ures of science, by H. Lord Brougham; Mechanics,
    [three treatises, by D. Lardner]; Hydrostatics, [by
    Lord Brougham]; Hydraulics, [by J. Millington];
    Pneumatics, [by D. Lardner]; Heat, [by Mr. Ogg];
    Optics, [by Sir D. Brewster]; Double refraction and
    polarization of light, [by the same] with an explana-
    tion of scientific terms, and an index prefixed [by D.
    Booth]. II. Popular introductions to natural philos-
    ophy, [by Mrs. J. Marcet]; Newton's optics, [by D.
    Lardner]; Description of optical instruments, [by A.
    Pritchard]; The thermometer and pyrometer, [by T.
    Stewart Traill:] Electricity, Galvanism, Magnetism,
    Electro-magnetism, [by P. M. Roget] with an expla-
    nation of scientific terms, and an index [by D. Booth.]
    III. Astronomy, [by Sir B. H. Malkin]; History of
    astronomy, [by R. W. Rothman]; Mathematical geog-
    raphy, [by E. Lloyd]; Physical geography, [by H. J.
    Lloyd], and Navigation, [by J. Lord Wrottesley.] with
    an explanation of scientific terms, and an index, [by
    D. Booth.]
  Smedley, E. History of France, A.D. 843-
    1529 . . . . 365.5
  Vaughan, R. History of England, 1603-1688. 365.16
  Vieusseux, A. History of Switzerland . . . 365.9
  Waddington, G. History of the church,
    from the earliest ages to the reformat'u. 2v. 365.13
  Waud, S. W. Algebraical geometry, arith-
    metic and algebra, with examples of their
    progress 365.17
  Youatt, W. The horse, with a treatise on
    draught 172.17
  — Cattle, their breeds, etc. 172.13
— Historic sketches. Spain and Portugal. Lon-
  don, 1835. 2v. in 1. 16° 979.11
— Historical pictures. England. London, 1835-
  1836. 3v. in 2. 16° 979.10
— History of the American revolution. 1st Am.
  ed. Boston, 1832. 18° 219.3
— Lives of Bertrand Du Guesclin and John
  Howard. London, 1840. 16° 589.14
— Manufacture of iron. Philadelphia, 1837. 18° 199.34
— Results of machinery. Philadelphia, 1831. 18° 139.24
SOCIETY for the promotion of Christian knowl-
  edge. Conservatories at Kew. London,
  n.d. 16° 178.22
— Light, its nature, sources, effects and applica-
  tions. London, n.d. 16° 149.32
— Three weeks in Palestine and Lebanon. Bos-
  ton, 1836. 16° 689.16
SOCIETY for the reform of colonial government.
  Charters of the old English colonies in
  America, with introduction and notes, by
  Samuel Lucas. London, 1850. 8° 305.3

SOCRATES. The god of Socrates. Apuleius . . . 834.15
— Plato. Apology of. Translated 1089.1
SOCRATES Scholasticus. Ecclesiastical history.
    Translated. London, 1853. p.8° 845.3-4
SOILS and manures. Donaldson, J. . . . . v.IV. of 169.15
SOIRÉES, Les, de Neuilly. Esquisses dram. et
    hist. Cave et Dittmer 1079.13
SOLAR system. Hind, J. R. 146.26
— Mitchell, O. M. Orbs of heaven 879.11
— Nichol, J. P. Phenomena and order of . . . 147.22
SOLARI, C. H. B. Letters. London, 1845. 16° . 541.21
SOLDIER's fortune, from the French, by Mrs. A.
    Marsh. London, 1852. 16° 469.15
SOLITARY, The: a tale. Bremer, F. 817.1-2
SOLITUDE. Consolations of. See Consolations . 338.15
— Story, J. The power of. A poem 358.14
SOLL und Haben. Roman. Freytag, G. 1035.5
SOLOMON, S. Guide to health, or advice to both
    sexes. 52d ed. New York, n.d. 12° 158.8
SOLLY, E. Lecture on vegetable substances used
    in the arts and manufactures 199.16
SOME account of the English stage fr. 1660 to 1830.
    Bath, 1832. 10v. 8° 351.1
SOMERSET, E., Marq. of Worcester. Century of
    inventions, with memoir by C. F. Parting-
    ton. London, 1825. 12° 199.27
SOMERVILE, W. The chase. See Falconer, W.. 359.5
SOMERVILLE, M. Connexion of the physical
    sciences. 8th ed. London, 1849. 12° . . . 149.22
— Mechanism of the heavens. London, 1831. 8° 146.7
— Prelim. dissertation on the mechanism of the
    heavens. Philadelphia, 1832. 18° 149.38
— Physical geography. New Am. [from 3d Eng.]
    ed., with notes, [etc.] by W. S. W. Rusch-
    enberger. Philadelphia, 1855. 12° 167.9-10
— - Same. 2d Am. ed., with additions. Phil-
    adelphia, 1850. 12° 167.11
SONGS of labor. Whittier, J. G. 325.7
SONGS of summer. Stoddard, R. H. 344.6-7
SONNENWIRTH, Der. Volks-Rom. Kurz, H.v.IV. of 1013.6
SONNINI, C. N. S. de M. Travels in Greece and
    Turkey. London, 1801. 2v. 8° 683.9
SONORA. Bartlett, J. R. Explorations, etc., con-
    nected with the boundary commission. . . 624.2
— Wells, W. V. History of the S. expedition . 266.8
SOPHIA Dorothea, Consort of George I., Me-
    moirs of. 2d ed. London, 1846. 2v. 8° . . 554.5
SOPHOCLES, [Tragedies.] Translated by T. Franck-
    lin. New York, n.d. 18° 830.14
— Tragedies, translated by T. A. Buckley. New
    ed. London, 1849. p.8° 814.5
— Œdipus, a musical drama, adapted by J. S.
    Faucit. London, 1821. 8° 355.11
SORGHO and imphee. Olcott, H. S. 166.12
SORROW, The discipline of. Eliot, W. G. 1089.22
SOTO, H. de, The conquest of Mexico by. Ir-
    ving, T. 237.11
SOUL. Feuchtersleben, E. v. Dietetics of the . 129.15
— Gallaudet, T. H. Child's book on the 1109.29
SOUL and instinct, Discourse on the. Paine, M. . 125.10
SOUL in nature. Örsted, H. C. 816.15
SOULÉ, F., Gihon, J. H. and Nisbet, J. Annals of
    San Francisco. New York, 1855. 8° 235.10
SOUND. Brewer, E. C. S. and its phenomena . . 199.32
— Higgins, W. M. Philosophy of 149.18
— Reid, D. B. Communication of 207.2
SOUTH, J. F. Household surgery. 1st Am. from
    2d London ed. Philadelphia, 1850. 12° . . 157.7
SOUTH, R. Sermons. New ed. Phila, 1852-53. 4v. 8° 1094.2
SOUTH, Letters from the. Paulding, J. K. 639.10
SOUTH AFRICA. Cumming, R. G. Hunter's life
    in 697.10-12
— Drayson, A. W. Sporting scenes in 692.3
    See also: Africa.
SOUTH Boston, History of. Simonds, T. C. . . . 227.4
SOUTHBURY, Conn. History of. Cothren, W. . . 225.2
SOUTH Carolina, History of. Simms, W. G. . . 237.17
SOUTH seas, Adventures of British seamen in
    the 830.26
— Melville, H. Narrative of adventures in the 899.1

SOUTH seas. Morrell, B. Four voyages to the . 702.7
— Perkins, E. T. Reef-rovings in the 705.6
— Stewart, C. S. Visit to the 705.22
— Williams, J. Missionary enterprises in the
    South Sea islands 1087.15
SOUTH side view of slavery. Adams, N. 127.21
SOUTHENNAN: [a tale.] Galt, J. 788.3
SOUTHERN states, Early history of the. Goodrich,
    S. G. 239.14
SOUTHERN and Western states, Industrial resour-
    ces of the. De Bow, J. D. B. 296.2
SOUTHEY, C. Chapters on churchyards. New
    York, 1842. 12° 878.10
SOUTHEY, R. Poetical works, complete. New ed.
    London, 1850. 8° 311.13
    Contents. — Prefaces; Joan of Arc; The vision of the
    Maid of Orleans; The triumph of woman; Wat Tyler;
    Poems concerning the slave trade; Botany Bay
    eclogues; Sonnets; Monodramas; Amatory poems of
    Abel Shufflebottom ; Lyric poems; Songs of the
    American Indians; Occasional pieces; The retro-
    spect; Hymn to the penates; English eclogues; Non-
    descripts; The devil's walk; Inscriptions; Carmen
    triumphale for 1814; Odes; The warning voice; On
    the portrait of Bishop Heber; Epistle to Allan Cun-
    ningham; Op eene Verzameling van mijne Afbeel-
    dingen; Thalaba the destroyer; Ballads and
    metrical tales; A tale of Paraguay; All for love; The
    pilgrim to Compostella; The curse of Kehama; Rod-
    erick, the last of the Goths; The poet's pilgrimage to
    Waterloo; Carmen nuptiale; Funeral song for the
    princess Charlotte of Wales; A vision of judgment;
    Oliver Newman, a New England tale; Miscellaneous
    poetical remains.
— Complete poetical works. New ed., including
    "Oliver Newman," etc. New York, 1850. 8° 311.3-4
    Contents. — Joan of Arc; The vision of the Maid of
    Orleans; Juvenile and minor poems ; Thalaba the
    destroyer; Madoc; Ballads and metrical tales; Curse
    of Kehama ; Roderick, the last of the Goths; The
    poet's pilgrimage to Waterloo; Carmen nuptiale; A
    funeral song; A vision of judgment; Oliver Newman,
    a New England tale.
— A love story, edited by J. W. Warter. Lon-
    don, 1853. 12° 409.1
— Common place book, [1st] 2d series. New
    York, 1849-50. 2v. 8° 872.6
— Curse of Kehama. New York, 1811. 2v. in 1. 12° 359.1
— Doctor, etc. Edited by J. W. Warter. New
    ed. London, 1853. 8° 892.11
— Essays, moral and polit. Lond., 1832. 2v. 16° 139.23
— Expedition of Orsua and the crimes of Aguirre.
    Philadelphia, 1821. 12° 266.9
— Letters from England, by Espriella. London,
    1807. 3v. 16° 679.13
— Life and correspondence, ed. by C. C. Southey.
    New York, 1851. 8° 582.7-8
— Life of Nelson. New York. 18° 810.4-7
— - Same. London, 1814. 2d ed. 2v. 16° . . . 558.9
— - Same. New ed. London, 1840. 16° . . . 399.6
— Life of Oliver Cromwell. New York, 1852. 16° 589.13
— Oliver Newman, with other poetical remains.
    London, 1845. 12° 349.20
— Select biographies. Cromwell and Bunyan.
    London, 1844. 12° 889.11
— Select works of the British poets, from Chau-
    cer to Johnson, with biographical sketches.
    London, 1831. 8° 342.11
— Life of W. Cowper. See Cowper, W. v.I.-III. of 817.11
— Essay on the lives and works of uneducated
    poets. See Jones, J. 584.5
— and Bell, R. Lives of the British admirals.
    London, 1833-40. 5v. 16° 388.5
— Browne, C. T. Life of 584.6-7
— Cottle, J. Reminiscences of 586.17
SOUTHEY, T. Colonial sheep and wools, from 1846.
    London, 1851. 8° 136.9
— - Same. London, 1852. 8° 136.9
— Chronological history of the West Indies.
    London, 1827. 3v. 8° 264.4
SOUTHGATE, H. Tour through Armenia, Kurdis-
    tan, Persia, and Mesopotamia. London,
    1840. 2v. 12° 687.3

SOUTHGATE, H. Visit to the Syrian church of
  Mesopotamia. New York, 1844 . . . . . . 118.15
— War in the East. 2d ed. New York, 1855. 18° 989.12
SOUTHWARD ho! Simms, W. G. 790.40–43
SOUTHWORTH, E. D. E. N. Retribution: a tale of
  passion. Philadelphia, 1855. 12° 455.16
— The three beauties. Philadelphia, 1858. 12° . 455.17
SOUVENIRS of travel. Le Vert, O. W. 648.13
SOUVESTRE, É. Attic philosopher in Paris. New
  York, 1854. 16° 767.11
— - Same. London, 1853. 12° 767.10
— Brittany and La Vendée. New York, 1857. 12° 767.4–8
— Confessions of a working man. Translated
  from 3d ed. London, 1853. 12° 767.10
— Leaves from a family journal. New York,
  1855. 12° 767.9
SOUZA, A. F. de. Charles et Marie. Nouv Éd.
  Bruxelles, 1827. 18° 1079.10
— Émilie et Alphonse. Bruxelles, 1828. 2v. in 1.
  18° 1079.8
— Eugénie et Mathilde. Bruxelles, 1827. 3v.
  in 1. 18° 1079.9
— La Comtesse de Fargy. Paris, 1828. 4v. in 1.
  18° 1079.7
SOVEREIGNS of modern Europe. Ellis, G. J.
  W. A. 548.28
SOVET, le Dr. Éducation physique de l' enfance.
  Bruxelles. 2v. in 1. 12° 1065.52
— Hygiène privée et publique. Bruxelles. 12° 1065.53
SOWERBY, G. B. Popular history of the aquarium.
  London, 1857. 12° 178.18
SOWERBY, G. B. junr. Conchological manual. 4th
  ed. London, 1852. 8° 175.5
SOWERBY, H. Popular mineralogy. London, 1850.
  16° 169.28
SOWERS not reapers. Martineau, H. . . . . .v.XIX.of 749.2
SOWING and reaping. Howitt, M. 459.15–16
SOYER, A. Culinary campaign. Historical remi-
  niscences of the late war. London, 1857. 16° 884.15
— Shilling cookery for the people. London, 1854. 189.11
SOZOMENUS. Ecclesiastical history. Also, the
  eccl. hist. of Philostorgius translated by E.
  Walford. London, 1855. p.8° 845.9–10
SPAIN. Beckford, W. Sketches of 679.6
— - Tour in 675.18
— Borrow, G. The Bible in 673.1
— Bowring, J. Ancient poetry and romances of. 316.9
— Busk, M. M. History of 365.1
— Calderon de la Barca, F. E. I. Attaché in
  Madrid 675.10–11
— Carleton, G. Anecdotes of the war in . . . 565.2
— Clark, W. G. Gazpacho, or summer months in. 675.13
— Condé, J. A. Dominion of the Arabs in . . . 827.3
— Cushing, C. Reminiscences of. 679.1
— Cushing, C. W. Letters descriptive of public
  monuments, etc., in 888.13
— Dix, J. A. A summer in 675.8
— Dunham, S. A. History of. 368.8
— Dunlop, J. S. during the reigns of Philip IV.
  and Charles II 913.3
— Florian, J. P. C. de. Moors of 820.70
— Ford, R. Gatherings from 889.17
— — - Hand-book for 649.12
— Froissart, J. Ancient chronicles of 1001.2
— Gautier, T. Wanderings in 869.12
— George, A. Annals of the queens of 544.4
— Hamilton, T. Annals of the Peninsular cam-
  paigns, 1808–14 . . . . 1009.4
— Inglis, H. D. Rambles in the footsteps of
  Don Quixote 673.5
— - Spain 675.14
— Irving, W. Conquest of . . . . . .v.V. of 367.2–3
— Mackenzie, A. S. A year in 679.2
— March, C. W. Sketches and adventures in . . 675.12
— Napier, W. F. P. War in the Peninsula, 1807
  to 1814 . . . . 1004.1
— Neale, A. Spanish campaign of 1808 . . .v.I.of 830.42
— Prescott, W. H. History of Ferdinand and
  Isabella 912.3
— - History of Philip II 922.1–7

SPAIN. Rocca, M. de. War of the French in.v.II.of 830.42
— Shelley, M. W. Literary and scientific men of. 398.1
— Society of Us. Knowl. Historic sketches . . 979.11
— Stirling, W. Artists of 543.4
— Traces of the Roman and Moor in 675.6–7
— Trueba y Cosio, T. de. Romance of history . 419.7
— Urquhart, D. Travels in 675.9
— Vane-Stewart, C. W. The Peninsular war . 1009.5
— Wallis, S. T. S., her institutions, etc. . . .675.16–17
— Walton, W. Revolutions of, 1808–36 . . . . 913.4
  See also: Spanish.
SPALDING, J. W. Japan and around the world.
  Three visits. New York, 1855. 12° 708.4
SPALDING, W. History of English literature. 2d
  ed. Edinburgh, 1853. 12° 404.16
— Italy and the Italian islands. New York, 1848.
  3v. 18° 820.51
SPALLANZANI, L. Travels in the two Sicilies and
  Apennines. London, 1798. 4v. 8° 676.4
SPANGENBERG, A. G. Life of Nicholas Lewis,
  Count Zinzendorf. Transl. by S. Jackson.
  London, 1838. 8° 545.26
SPANISH ballads. Lockhart, J. G. 316.1
SPANISH conquest in America. Helps, A. 254.2
SPANISH drama. Lope de Vega and Calderon.
  Lewes, G. H. 840.35
SPANISH empire in the 16th and 17th centuries.
  Ranke, L. 913.1
SPANISH literature. Bouterwek, F. History of. 404.10
— Ticknor, G. History of 402.1
SPANISH school of painting, History of. Head, E. 208.21
SPARKS, J. Correspondence of the American re-
  volution; letters to Washington. Boston,
  1853. 4v. 8° 213.3
— Diplomatic correspondence of the American
  revolution. Boston, 1829–30. 12v. 8° . . . 216.7
— Library of American biography. New York,
  1846–51. 25v. 16° . . . . 529.

  Contents. — Vol. I. John Stark, by E. Everett ;
  C. B. Brown, by W. H. Prescott; R. Montgomery, by
  J. Armstrong; E. Allen, by J. Sparks. II. A. Wilson,
  by W. B. O. Peabody; Capt. J. Smith, by G. S. Hil-
  lard. III. Life and treason of B. Arnold, by J. Sparks.
  IV. A. Wayne, by J. Armstrong; H. Vane, by C. W.
  Upham. V. J. Eliot, the apostle to the Indians, by
  C. Francis. VI. W. Pinkney, by H. Wheaton; W.
  Ellery, by E. T. Channing; C. Mather, by W. B. O.
  Peabody. VII. Sir W. Phips, by F. Bowen; I. Putnam,
  by O. W. B. Peabody; Memoir of L. M. Davidson, by C. M.
  Sedgwick; D. Rittenhouse, by J. Renwick. VIII. J.
  Edwards, by S. Miller; D. Brainerd, by W. B. O. Pea-
  body. IX. Baron Steuben, by F. Bowen; S. Cabot,
  by C. Hayward, jr.; W. Eaton, by C. C. Felton. X.
  R. Fulton, by J. Renwick; J. Warren, by A. H. Ev-
  erett ; H. Hudson, by H. R. Cleveland ; Fatner
  Marquette, by J. Sparks. XI. R. C. de La Salle, by
  J. Sparks; P. Henry, by A. H. Everett. XII. J. Otis,
  by F. Bowen; J. Oglethorpe, by W. B. O. Peabody.
  XIII. J. Sullivan, by O. W. B. Peabody; J. Leisler,
  by C. F. Hoffman; N. Bacon, by W. Ware; J. Mason,
  by G. E. Ellis. XIV. R. Williams, by W. Gammell;
  T. Dwight, by W. B. Sprague; Count Pulaski, by J.
  Sparks. XV. B. Thompson, count of Rumford, by
  J. Renwick; Z. M. Pike, by H. Whiting; S. Gorton,
  by J. M. Mackie. XVI. E. Stiles, by J. L. Kingsley;
  J. Fitch, by C. Whittlesey; A. Hutchinson, by G. E.
  Ellis. XVII. J. Ribault, by J. Sparks; S. Rale, by C.
  Francis; W. Palfrey, by J. G. Palfrey. XVIII. C.
  Lee, by J. Sparks; J. Reed, by H. Reed. XIX. L.
  Calvert, by G. W. Burnap; S. Ward, by W. Gam-
  mell; T. Posey, by J. Hall. XX. N. Greene, by G.
  W. Greene. XXI. S. Decatur, by A. S. Mackenzie.
  XXII. E. Preble, by L. Sabine; W. Penn, by G. E.
  Ellis. XXIII. D. Boone, by J. M. Peck; B. Lincoln,
  by F. Bowen. XXIV. J. Ledyard, by J. Sparks.
  XXV. W. R. Davie, by F. M. Hubbard; S. Kirkland,
  by S. K. Lothrop.
  For a selection of lives from the above, see Lives of
  eminent individuals, etc.

— Life of George Washington. Boston, 1853. 8° 511.5-7
— Life of Gouverneur Morris, his correspondence and miscellaneous papers. Boston,
  1832. 3v. 8° 515.12
— Life of John Ledyard. Cambridge, 1828. 8°. 523.15
SPAULDING, J. H. Historical relics of the White
  mountains. Boston, 1855. 12° 239.11

SPECIES, Unity or plurality of. *See* Ethnology, Races of men, etc.

SPECIMENS of the British poets. Reigns of Henry VIII.-Geo. III. London, 1809. 2v. 18° . 369.12

SPECTATOR, The. Addison, J. 873.12

SPECULATIVE philos. of Europe. Morell, J. D. . 122.3

SPEECHES of eminent British statesmen. London, 1855-57. 2v. 16° 866.12

SPENCER, C. C. Art of playing the piano forte. London, 1853. 16° 829.6

— Concise explanation of the church modes. 2d ed. London, 1846. sm.4° 204.5

— Treatise on music. 4th ed. London, 1851. 2v. in 1. 16° 829.5

SPENCER, E. Fall of the Crimea. Lond., 1854. 12°. 928.6

— Germany and the Germans. 2d ed. London, 1836. 2v. 8° 663.7

— Turkey, Russia, the Black sea, and Circassia. Illustrated by engravings and a map. London, 1854. 12° 687.21-22

SPENCER, H. Essays: scientific, political, and speculative. London, 1858. 8° 863.18

SPENCER, J. A. The East. Sketches of travel in Egypt and the Holy Land. Lond., 1850. 12° 686.6

SPENCER, Rev. T., Memoirs of the life of. Raffles, T. 575.1

SPENCER, W. V. Boston theatre : a collection of scarce acting tragedies, comedies, [etc.] Boston, 1855-57. 15v. 12° 355.9

Contents. — Vol. I. Moll Pitcher, by J. S. Jones; The forest rose, by S. Woodworth; Swiss swains, by B. Webster; The bachelor's bedroom, by C. Mathews; Sophia's supper, by H. R. Addison; A Roland for an Oliver, by T. Morton; Black-eyed Susan, by D. Jerrold; John Bull, by G. Colman, jr. II. Satan in Paris, by Charville and E. Damarin; More blunders than one, by T. G. Rodwell; Rosina Meadows, by C. H. Saunders; The dumb belle, by J. R. Planché; My aunt, by S. J. Arnold; Spring and autumn, by J. Kenney; Six degrees of crime, by F. S. Hill; Limerick boy, by J. Pilgrim. III. Presumptive evidence, by J. B. Buckstone ; Man and wife, by S. J. Arnold; The sergeant's wife, anon.; Masks and faces, by T. Taylor and C. Reade; Merry wives of Windsor, by W. Shakspeare; Nature and philosophy, anon.; Agnes De Vere, by J. B. Buckstone; Shandy Maguire, by J. Pilgrim. IV. Wild Oats, by J. O'Keeffe; Michael Erle, by T. E. Wilks; Teddy the tiler, by G. H. Rodwel ; Spectre bridegroom, by W. T. Moncrieff; Idiot witness, by J. T. Haines; Willow copse, by D. P. Bourcicault ; Matteo Falcone, by W. H. Oxberry; People's lawyer, by J. S. Jones. V. Jenny Lind, by A. B. Reach ; Comedy of errors, by W. Shakspeare; Lucretia Borgia, by V. Hugo and J. M. Weston; Surgeon of Paris, by J. S. Jones; Patrician's daughter, by J. W. Marston; The two Buzzards, by J. M. Morton; Shoemaker of Toulouse, by F. S. Hill; Momentous question, by E. Fitzball. VI. Love and loyalty, by W. J. Robson; The robber's wife, by I. Pocock; The happy man, by S. Lover; The dumb girl of Genoa, by J. Farrell; The wreck ashore, by J. B. Buckstone; Clari, the maid of Milan, by J. H. Payne; The miller and his men, by I. Pocock; Wallace, by W. Barrymore, embellished with a portrait and accompanied by a memoir of Mr. J. B. Howe. VII. Madelaine, anon.; Betsey Baker, by J. M. Morton; The fireman, by S. D. Johnson; No. 1, round the corner, by W. Brough; Teddy Roe, by E. Stirling; Grist to the mill, by J. R. Planché; Object of interest, by J. H. Stocqueler; Two loves and a life, by T. Taylor and C. Reade. VIII. Anne Blake, by J. W. Marston; My fellow clerk, by J. Oxenford; Bengal tiger, by C. Dance; The steward, by S. Beazley; Capt. Kyd, by J. S. Jones; Nick of the woods, by L. H. Medina; The marble heart, by C. Selby; Laughing hyena, by Benj. Webster. IX. Second love, by J. P. Simpson ; The victor vanquished, by C. Dance; Our wife, by J. M. Morton; The dream at sea, by J. B. Buckstone; My husband's mirror, by W. W. Clapp, jr.; Yankee land, by C. A. Logan; Norah Creina, by E. Stirling; Good for nothing, by J. B. Buckstone. X. The first night, anon.; The rake's progress, by W. L. Rede; The pet of the petticoats, by J. B. Buckstone; The Eton boy, by E. Morton ; The wandering minstrel, by H. Mayhew ; Wanted, 1000 spirited young milliners, for the gold diggings, by J. S. Coyne ; Poor Pillicoddy, by J. M. Morton; The breach of promise, by J. B. Buckstone. XI. The mummy, by W. B. Bernard; The review, by G. Colman, jr.; The lady of the lake, adapt. by T.

SPENCER, W. V. Boston theatre, *continued.*

Dibdin; Still waters run deep, by T. Taylor; The man of many friends, by J. S. Coyne; Love in livery, by J. P. Wooler; Antony and Cleopatra, by C. Selby, The scholar, by J. B. Buckstone. XII. Helping hands, by T. Taylor; Aladdin, anon.; Trying it on, by W. Brough; The stage-struck Yankee, by O. E. Durivage; My young wife and my old umbrella, by B. Webster: The last man, by G. D. Pitt; The belle's stratagem, by H. Cowley; Crinoline, by R. B. Brough. XIII. Old and young, by J. Salmon; A family failing, by J. Oxenford; The young scamp, by E. Stirling: The adopted child, by S. Birch; The turned head, G. A. à Beckett; A match in the dark, by C. Dance; Advice to husbands, by C. S. Lancaster ; Raffaelle the reprobate, by T. E. Wilks. XIV. Ruth Oakley, by T. Williams and A. Harris; The British slave, by J. B. Howe; The Siamese twins, by G. A. à Beckett; A life's ransom, by J. W. Marston; Sent to the tower, by J. M. Morton; Giralda, by B. Webster; Time tries all, by J. Courtney; Ella Rosenberg, by J. Kenney. XV. Somebody else, by J. R. Planché; The warlock of the glen, by C. E. Walker; Zelina, by C. A. Somerset; The ladies' battle, anon.; The art of acting, anon.; The brigand, by J. R. Planché: The lady of the lions, by O. E. Durivage; Neighbor Jackwood, by J. T. Trowbridge.

SPENSER, E. Poetical works, with observations on the Faerie Queene, by G. S. Hillard. 1st Am ed. Boston, 1839. 5v. 8° 323.1

Contents. — Vol. I. Essay on the life and writings of Spenser; Introductory observations on the Faerie Queene; The Faerie Queene, b. 1, 2, canto vi. II. Same, b. 2, canto vii. — book 4, canto i. III. Same, book 4, canto ii. — book 5, canto xii. IV. Same, book 6; The shepheard's calender; Muiopotmos. V. The ruines of time; The teares of the Muses; Virgil's gnat; Prosopopois, or Mother Hubberd's tale; The ruines of Rome; Three visions; Daphnaida; Colin Clout; Astrophel; Dolefull lay of Clorinda; Mourning muse of Thestylis; Pastorall æglogue upon the death of Sir Philip Sidney; An elegie; An epitaph; Prothalamion; Amoretti, or sonnets;Poems; Epithalamion; Fowre hymnes.

— Poetical works. London, 1839. 5v. 16° . . 329.10

Contents. — Vol. I. Life by J. Mitford; The Faerie Queene, books 1, 2, canto vii. II. Same, book 2 canto viii.—b. 4, canto ii. III. Same, book 4, canto iii.—6, canto i. IV. Same, book 6, canto ii.—vii.; Colin Clout; Virgil's gnat; Shepheard's calender. V.Fowre hymnes; Three visions; Mother Hubberd's tale; Prothalamion; Epithalamion; Poems; Amoretti, or sonnets; Daphnaida; Astrophel; Doleful lay of Clorinda; Mourning muse of Thestylis; A pastoral æglogue ; An elegie; An epitaph; Teares of the Muses; The ruines of Rome; The ruines of time; Muiopotmos; Brittain's Ida.

— S. and his poetry, ed. by G. L. Craik. London, 1845. 3v. 18° 850.16

— Essay on the life and writings of. Hart, J. S. 324.1

SPHINXES, Book of. Brown, T. 830.69-70

SPIELBERG, Memoirs of a prisoner in the fortress of. Andryane, A. 544.10

SPINDLER, K. Der Bastard. Stuttgart, 1839. 4v. 16° 1026.6

— Der Jesuit. Stuttgart, 1847. 3v. in 1. 16° . 1026.5

— Der Jude. Stuttgart, 1839. 4v. 16° 1026.4

— The Jew : fiction. New York, 1844. 8° . . . 802.4

SPINDLES, Mind amongst the. *See* Mind. . . . 840.46

SPINOZA, B. Ein Denkerleben Auerbach, B. . . . 1037.2

SPIRIT of life : poem. Clark, W. G. 338.10

SPIRIT of popery, The. New York, n.d. 16° . . 119.1

SPIRIT of the age, The: or, contemporary portraits. Hazlitt, W. . . . . v.V. of 867.2

SPIRIT of the East, The. Urquhart, D. 694.6

SPIRIT history of man, Vestiges of the. Dunlap, S. F. 122.16

SPIRITUAL writings. Swedenborg, E. 1084.1

SPIRITUALISM. Brownson, O. A. The spirit rapper 125.3

— Davis, A. J. Present age and inner life . . . 122.10

— Dods, J. B. Spirit manifestations examined and explained 1096.24

— Edmonds, J. W. Spiritualism 122.14-15

— Gordon, W. R. Three-fold test of modern. 1096.18

— Hammond, C. Light from the spirit world . 124.25

— Hayden, W. B. The phenomena of modern. 125.25

— Mahan, A. Modern mysteries explained and exposed 125.2

SPIRITUALISM. Mattison, H. Spirit rapping un-
veiled 125.19
— Snow, H. Spirit intercourse 125.26-27
— Werner, H. Guardian spirits 1084.14
SPITHEAD and the Nore, Mutiny at. *See* History
of, etc. 380.5
SPITTA, C. J. P. Psalter und Harfe. Leipzig, 1856.
16° 1034.18
SPITZBERGEN. Blackwood, F. T. S. in 1856 . . . 708.1
— Laing, J. Account of 704.20
SPIX, J. B. v. and Martius, C. F. P. v. Travels in
Brazil, 1817-20. [Transl. by H. E. Lloyd.]
London, 1824. 2v. 8° 633.18
SPORSCHIL, J. Neues Heldenbuch für die
deutsche Jugend. 4te Aufl. Braunschweig,
1818. 3v. in 1. 8° 1016.2
SPORTING. Drayson, A. W. Scenes amongst the
Kaffirs 602.3
— Hammond, S. H. Adventures with the rifle
and the rod 174.9
Maxwell, W. H. Sports and pastimes of the
British islands 174.1
See also : Recreative arts.
SPOSI fedeli. Storia italo-gotica-romantica. Ricci,
A. M. 1058.11
SPOTORNO, G. B. Memoir of Columbus. *See*
Columbus, C. 544.3
SPOTTISWOODE, W. Tarantasse journey through
Eastern Russia in 1856. London, 1857. 12° 674.7
SPRAGUE, C. Poetical and prose writings. New
and rev. ed. Boston, 1850. 12° 325.9-10

Contents. — Curiosity; Shakespeare ode; Centennial
ode; Miscellaneous poems: Prose: — American independence; On intemperance.

SPRAGUE, J. T. Origin, progress, and conclusion
of the Florida war. New York, 1848. 8° . 244.7
SPRAGUE, W. B. Annals of the American pulpit.
New York, 1857-58. 4v. 8° 113.1
— Discourse delivered in Murray street church. 1083.5
— Letters to a daughter. 11th Am. ed. New
York. 16° 1109.12
— Life of T. Dwight. Sparks, J. . . . . v.XIV. of 529.1
— Visits to European celebrities. Boston,
1855. 12° 648.9
SPRATT, T. A. B. and Forbes, E. Travels in Lycia,
etc. London, 1847. 2v. 8° 683.7
SPRING, A. Botanique. Bruxelles, n.d. 12° . . 1065.54
SPRING, G. Bible not of man. New York. 12° . . 1107.14
— Discourse delivered in Murray street church. 1083.5
— First things — revealed to mankind. 3d ed.
New York, 1852. 2v. 12° 116.1
— The power of the pulpit. 2d ed. New York,
1854. 12° 116.2
SPRINGER, J. S. Forest life on the rivers of
Maine and New Brunswick. New York,
1851. 12° 628.18
SPRINGFIELD armory. Abbott, J. 738.5-7
SPRINGFIELD, History of. Bliss, G. 227.15
SPURGEON, C. H. Sermons. 1st series, with in-
troduction and biography by E. L. Magoon.
New York, 1858. 12° 1096.10
— Sermons. 2d-4th series. N. Y., 1857-58. 3v. 12° 1096.10
SPURZHEIM, J. G. Phrenology, physiological,
philosophical. 5th Am. ed. New York,
1846. 2v. in 1. 8° 124.1
— Funeral oration on. Follen, C. T. C. . . v.V. of 877.1
SPY, The: a tale. Cooper, J. F. 780.30-34
SQUIER, E. G. Nicaragua, its people, scenery,
monuments, etc. New York, 1852. 2v. 8° . 621.3
— Notes on Central America. N. Y., 1855. 8° . 263.1
— States of Central America, their geography,
etc. New York, 1858. 8° 263.7
SQUIRE, The: a novel. Pickering, E. 805.8
STAATSGEHEIMNISS. Roman. Schücking, C. B. L. 1034.19
STABLE economy. *See* Rural and domes. economy.
STAAL, M. J. C. D. Mme. de. Deux années à la
Bastille, 1718-20. Paris, 1853. 12° . . . 1078.26
STAËL-HOLSTEIN, A. L. G. N. de. Considerations
on the French revolution. Translated from
original MS. New York, 1818. 2v. 8° . . 1004.6

STAËL-HOLSTEIN, A. L. G. N. de. Corinne, ou l'
Italie. Nouv. éd. Genève, 1831. 2v.
18° 1079.4
— - Same. Paris, 1846. 2v. in 1. 16° 1079.12
— - Same. Nouv. éd. Notice par Mme.
Necker de Saussure. Paris, 1853. 12° . . 1076.9
— Corinna, or Italy. London, 1822. 4v. 12° . . 757.10
— - Same. Translated by Isabel Hill. Phil-
adelphia, 1851. 12° 757.6
— - Same. With memoir. London, 1854. 12° 757.7-9
— De l' Allemagne. Bruxelles, 1832. 3v. 18°. 1069.9
— - Same. Avec préface par Marmier. Nouv.
éd. Paris, 1852. 12° 1076.10
— - Same. Paris, 1853. 16° 1076.7
— Germany. New York, 1814. 3v. in 2. 12° . . 667.20
— Delphine. Philadelphia, 1836. 3v. 12° . . . 488.1
— Influence of literature upon society. From
2d London ed. Boston, 1813. 2v. in 1. 12° 868.14
— Mémoires [dix années d' exil.] Autres ouv-
rages posthumes — notice par Mme. Necker
de Saussure. Nouv. éd. Paris, 1845. 12° . 1076.8
— Life of. Norris, M. 615.11
STAFFORD, W. C. History of music. Edinburgh,
1830. 18° 830.57
STAGE. Collier, J. P. Early English 342.17
— Some account of the English 351.1
— Wood, W. B. Personal recollections of the. 356.12
See also : Theatre.
STAGE coach, The, and other tales. Opie, A. . . 469.30-31
STANDISH, Miles, Courtship of. Longfellow, H. W. 375.2-6
STANFORD, J. F. Rambles in Thuringian Sax-
ony. London, 1842. 8° 663.10
STANHOPE, L. Greece in 1823-24, and life of Mus-
tapha Ali. London, 1824. 8° 918.2
STANHOPE, P. D. *Lord Chesterfield.* Works, in-
cluding life. 1st Am. ed. N. Y., 1853. 8° . 873.9
Contents. — Life ; Speech on the stage-licensing
bill; Two speeches on the "gin act" ; Letters to his
son; Miscellaneous pieces; Index.
STANHOPE, P. H., *Earl, formerly Lord Mahon.*
Historical essays. London, 1849. 12° . . . 889.32
— History of England, 1713-83. New York,
1849. 2v. 8° 963.2
— Joan of Arc. [An essay.] London, 1853. 16° 609.6
— Life of Belisarius. Philadelphia, 1846. 12° . 545.13
— Life of Louis, prince of Condé. London,
1845. 12° 880.10
— - Same. New York, 1845. 12° 617.19
— "The forty-five;" [with] Letters of prince
Charles Stuart. London, 1851. 12° 989.6
STANLEY, A. P. Life and correspondence of T.
Arnold. 2d Am. from last London ed. New
York, 1846. 8° 574.2-3
— Sinai and Palestine, with maps and plans.
New York, 1857. 8° 684.7
— 1st Corinthians: Notes, etc. *See* Bible. . . . 1093.15
STANLEY Buxton: a novel. Galt, J. 788.1
STANLEY, E. Familiar history of birds. 6th ed.
London, 1854. 16° 177.26
STANLEY, G. Painters of the Dutch and Flemish
schools. London, 1855. p.8° 826.15
STANNIUS, H. Comparative anatomy. Siebold,
C. T. E. v. 175.1
STANSBURY, P. Pedestrian tour in North Amer-
ica, in 1821. New York, 1822. 12° 629.22
STAR and the cloud, The. Roe, A. S. 726.13
STAR in the desert: [a tale.] Mackarness, M. . . 476.7-8
STAR papers. Beecher, H. W. 885.4-5
STARK, J., Life of, by E. Everett. Sparks, J. v.I. of 518.5
STARLING, E. Noble deeds of woman. Boston,
1850. 12° 547.6
STARS. Dick, T. Celestial scenery 810.77
— - Sidereal heavens 820.6
— Mitchell, O. M. Stellar worlds 870.11
— Nichol, J. P. On the system of the world. . 146.11
— Wilson, G. Stars and their inhabitants . . . 409.31
STATE. *See* Government, Political science, etc.
STATE trials, modern. Townsend, W. C. 975.6
STATESMEN. Brougham, H. S. of the time of
George III. 568.7
— Crowe, E. E. Lives of eminent foreign . . . 358.7

STATESMEN. Forster, J. S. of the commonwealth of England 562.3
— Knapp, S. L. Biogr. sketches of eminent. . 524.10–11
— Mackintosh, Sir J. Lives of eminent British. 388.6
— Maury, S. M. S. of America in 1845 . . . . . 525.1
STATICS and dynamics, Principles and practice of. Baker, T. 829.28
    See also : Hydrostatics, Hydraulics, Natural philosophy, Physics, etc.
STAUNTON, H. Chess-player's companion. London, 1849. p.8° 816.4
— Chess-player's handbook. 2d ed. London, 1848. p.8° 816.1
— Chess tournament. London, 1852. p.8° . . . 826.1
STEAM boat, The: a novel. Galt, J. 788.13
STEAM engine. Adcock, H. Rules and data for the. 198.30
— Armstrong, R. Construction and management of steam boilers. 819.41
— Bourne, J. Catechism of the. 198.24
— ·· Treatise on the. 191.2
— Burn, R. S. Its history and mechanism . . . 195.22
— Ewbank, T. Progressive development of the. 195.3
— Galloway, E. History and progress of the . 195.17
— Garvey, M. A. Future effects of steam. . . . 199.23
— Kindt, J. De la vapeur et de ses applications. 1065.27
— Lardner, D. Steam engine explained and illustrated 195.16
— ·· Rudimentary treatise on the 819.24
— Macfarlane, R. History of propellers and steam navigation 198.18–19
— Murray, R. Rudimentary treatise on steam vessels 829.12
— Reid, H. A popular account of the 198.29
— Sewell, J. Elementary treatise on S. and locomotion 829.10
— Templeton, W. Practical examinator on the. 198.21
— Woodcroft, B. Origin and progress of steam navigation 195.12
    See also : Engineering.
STEBBING, H. Chivalry and the crusades. Edinburgh, 1830. 2v. 18° 830.56
— History of the Christian church. London, 1833. 2v. 16° 388.1
— History of the reformation. London, 1836. 2v. 16° 388.2
STEEL. Mushet, D. Practical and experimental papers on. 194.7
— Overman, F. Essay on the manufacture of . 195.6
    See also : Iron.
STEELE, A. Chief of the pilgrims: or, life and times of Elder Brewster ; illustrated. Philadelphia, 1857. 8° 223.15
STEELE, *Sir* R. Papers in the Spectator. Addison, J. 830.2
— Biography of. Forster, J. 894.3
— Papers in the Tatler. Brit. essayists. v.I.–V. of 850.24
— Papers in the Guardian. British essayists . . . . v.XVI.–XVIII. of 850.24
— Romish ecclesiastical history of the late years. London, 1714. 16° 949.11
STEFFENS, H. Adventures on the road to Paris, 1813–14. Translated. London, 1848. 12° . . 899.12
— Novellen. Gesammt Ausgabe. Breslau, 1837–1838. 16v. 16° 1029.22
    Contents. — Vol. I. Gebirgs-Sagen: Als Anhang: Die Trauung, eine Sage des Nordens; Hiezu die letzten Worte des Pfarrers von Mittelfahrt auf Seeland, von F. W. J. v. Schelling. II.–VI. Die Familien Walseth und Leith, Novellen. VII.–XII. Die vier Norweger, Novellen. XIII.–XVI. Malkolm, Eine norwegische Novelle.
STEINMETZ, A. History of the Jesuits. Philadelphia, 1848. 2v. 8° 1095.7
STEINSCHNEIDER, M. Jewish literature ; a hist. essay. From the German. Lond., 1857. 8° 402.9
STENDHAL. *Pseud. See* Beyle, H.
STENOGRAPHY, Academical. Williams, T. 403.2
STEPHEN, King of England, The acts of. Henry of Huntingdon 856.3
STEPHEN, G. Adventures of a gentleman in search of a horse. Philadelphia, 1857. 12° 164.8
— Antislavery recollections. London, 1854. 12° 1089.17

STEPHEN, J. Critical and miscellaneous essays. Philadelphia, 1843 12° 867.5
— - Same. Philadelphia, 1850. 8° 863.9
— Lectures on the history of France. New York, 1852. 8° 1002.1
— - Same. 3d edition, with additions. London, 1857. 2v. 8° 1002.2
STEPHEN, T. Life of Archbishop Sharp of St. Andrews. London, n.d. 8° 574.10
STEPHENS, A. Memoirs of John Horne Tooke. London, 1813. 2v. in 1. 8° 583.3
STEPHENS, A. S. Fashion and famine: [a tale.] New York, 1854. 12° 416.5
— Portland sketch book. Portland, 1836. 12° . 888.10
STEPHENS, H. Book of the farm ; notes by J. S. Skinner. New York, 1851. 2v. 8° 165.4
STEPHENS, H. M. Home scenes and home sounds. Boston, 1854. 12° 489.18
STEPHENS, J. L. Incidents of travel in Central America and Yucatan. 12th ed. New York, 1856. 2v. 8° 621.5–9
— - Same. Revised ; with additions by F. Catherwood. London, 1854. 8° 621.10
— Incidents of travel in Egypt, Arabia, etc. 4th edition. New York, 1838. 2v. 12°. 699.1–2
— Incidents of travel in Greece, Turkey, Russia and Poland. 7th ed. N. Y., 1849. 2v. 12° 689.1–2
— Incid. of travel in Yucatan. N.Y., 1858. 2v. 8° 621.10–14
STEPHENSON, G., Life of. Smiles, S. 588.4–6
STEPHENSON, R. M. Railways. An introductory sketch. Part I. London, 1850. 16° 829.1
STEPS towards heaven. Arthur, T. S. 1105.17
STEREOSCOPE, The : its history, etc. Brewster, D. 207.18
STERILITY, Causes and treatment of. Whitehead, J. 153.3
STERLING, J. Essays and tales. Edited, with memoir, by J. C. Hare. Lond., 1848. 2v. 12° 886.1
— Onyx ring. With biographical preface by C. Hale. Boston, 1856. 12° 756.11
— Life of. Carlyle, T. 584.15
STERNBERG, A. v. Diane. Roman. Berlin, 1842. 3v. 16° 1037.11
STERNE, L. Works : with life of the author, by himself. New York, 1813–14. 6v. 12° . . . 908.10
    Contents.— Vol. I.–II. Life and opinions of Tristram Shandy. III. Sentimental journey through France and Italy : History of a watchcoat. IV.–V. Sermons. VI. Letters ; The Koran ; or life, etc. of tria juncta in uno.
STETHOSCOPIST. *See* Medicine.
STEUBEN, F. W. A., *Baron*, Life of, by F. Bowen. Sparks, J. . . . . v.IX. of 529.1
STEVENS, I. I. Campaigns of the Rio Grande and Mexico. New York, 1851. 8° 623.9
STEVENSON, A. Treatise on lighthouses. London, 1850. 3v. in 1. 16° 819.34–35
STEWART, C. S. Brazil and La Plata. New York, 1856. 12° 635.14
— Residence in the Sandwich islands. Introduction and notes, by Rev. W. Ellis. 5th edition. Boston, 1839. 12° 705.10
— Visit to the South seas. N. Y., 1833. 2v. 12° 705.22
STEWART, Col. D. Sketches of the character, etc. of the Highlanders of Scotland. 2d ed. Edinburgh, 1822. 2v. 8° 987.2
STEWART, Dugald. Life and writings of W. Robertson. London, 1801. 4° 582.1
— Memoir of A. Smith 817.10
STEWART, J. Stable economy. From 3d Eng. ed. With notes, etc., by A. B. Allen. N. York, 1851. 12° 165.18
STEWART, R. W. The tent and the khan ; a journey to Sinai and Palestine. Edinb., 1857. 8° 685.3
STEWART, W. G. Superstitions of the Highlanders. New ed. London, n.d. 16° 989.11
STICKNEY, Sarah. *See* Ellis, S. S.
STIFTER, A. Studien. Pesth, 1855. 3v. 8° . . . 1025.1
    Contents.— Vol. I. Der Condor; Feldblumen; Das Haidedorf; Der Hochwald; Die Narrenburg. II. Die Mappe meines Urgrossvaters; Abdias; Das alte Siegel; Brigitta. III. Der Hagestolz; Der Waldsteig; Zwei Schwestern; Der beschriebene Tännling.
STILES, E. Holmes, A. The life of 524.12
— Kingsley, J. L. Life of. *See* Sparks, J. v.XVI. of 529.1

STILES, W. H. Austria in 1848–49. New York, 1852. 2v. 8° 924.2
STILLING. See Jung-Stilling, H. J.
STIRLING, Earl of. See Alexander, W.
STIRLING, J. Letters from the slave states. London, 1857. 12° 627.1
STIRLING, P. J. The gold discoveries and their probable consequences. Edinburgh, 1853. 8° 136.12
STIRLING, W. Annals of the artists of Spain. London, 1848. 3v. 8° 543.4
— Cloister life of Charles V. From 2d London ed. Boston, 1853. 12° 617.6–8
— Velasquez and his works. London, 1855. 16° 899.20
STÖCKHARDT, J. A. Chemical field lectures for agriculturists, transl. and ed., with notes, by J. E. Teschemacher. Cambridge, 1853. 12° 156.14
— — Same. Ed. by A. Henfrey. London, 1855. p.8° 836.1
— Principles of chemistry. Transl. by C. H. Peirce. 4th Am. ed. Cambridge, 1851. 12° 156.9–10
— — Same. Transl. by C. H. Peirce. New ed. London, 1852. p.8° 816.8–9
STOCQUELER, J. H. Life of the duke of Wellington. London, 1852–53. 2v. 8° 564.11
STODDARD, A. Sketches of Louisiana. Philadelphia, 1812. 8° 236.6
STODDARD, R. H. Poems. Boston, 1852. 12° . . 344.8
— Songs of summer. Boston, 1857. 12° 344.6–7
STODDART, Sir J., and others. Historical essays and dissertations. London, n.d. 12° . . . 988.7

> Contents. — Vol. I. Uses of history as a study, by Sir J. Stoddart. II. Europe at the fall of the Roman empire in the West, by Col. G. Procter. III. Rise, growth, etc., of the feudal system, by Col. Procter. IV. Rise, progress and results of the crusades, by Col. Procter. V. Remarks on the French revolution, by Lord Brougham. VI. English nation, what and whence we are, by Prof. E. Creasy.

STOKERS and pokers. Head, F. B. 889.23
STOKES, J. The cabinet-maker and upholsterer's companion. Philadelphia, 1850. 12° 190.24
STOLEN child, The. Galt, J. 788.11
STOMACH and renal diseases. Jones, H. B. . . . 155.16
See also: Medicine.
STONE, Mrs. The cotton lord. New York, 1845. 8° 802.11
STONE, E. M. History of Beverly, Mass., 1630–1842. Boston, 1843. 12° 227.3
— Life and recollections of J. Howland. Providence, 1857. 12° 525.8
STONE, J. S. Memoir of James Milnor. New York, n.d. 12° 1107.17
STONE, J. W. Festival of the sons of New Hampshire. Boston, 1850. 8° 234.4
STONE, T. T. The rod and the staff. 2d ed. Boston, 1856. 16° 118.17
STONE, W. L. Border wars of the American revolution. New York, n.d. 2v. 18° . . . 820.62
— Life of Joseph Brant, incl. the border wars of the Am. revol. Cooperstown, 1845–46. 2v. 8° 513.12
— Poetry and history of Wyoming, containing Campbell's Gertrude, and a biogr. of the author by W. Irving. New York, 1841. 12° . 237.14
STONE cutting. Burgoyne, J. 819.25
— Dobson, E. Rudimentary treatise on masonry and 819.17–18
— Nicholson, P. Treatise on 202.3
STORCH, L. Ansgewählte Romane und Novellen. Leipzig, 1855–56. 12v. 16° 1016.9

> Contents. — Vol. 1. Vorwärts-Hans. II. Der Glockengiesser. III.—V. Kunz von Kauffungen. VI. Waldmeister. VII.—IX. Die Heideschenke. X. Der Stockfischfang. XI.—XII. Der Freibeuter.

— Ein deutscher Leinweber. Leipzig, 1846–50. 9v. 16° 1016.8
STORIES from "Blackwood." New York, 1852. 12° 469.22
STORIES of an old maid. Girardin, É. de 478.15
STORIES of Eng. and for. life. Howitt, W. and M. 825.5
STORIES of the study. Galt, J. 788.5
STORIES, Yule-tide. Thorpe, B. 846.12
STORMS. See Meteorology.
STORY, J. Familiar exposition of the constitution of the U. S. New York, 1852. 12° 135.38

STORY, J. Miscellaneous writings. Ed. by W. W. Story. Boston, 1852. 8° 872.5
— The power of solitude, poem. Salem, 1804. 12° 358.14
— Life and letters. Story, W. W. 512.3
STORY, R. Memoir of Isabella Campbell. 3d ed. Greenock, 1830. 18° 590.14
STORY, W. W. Life and letters of J. Story. Boston, 1851. 2v. 8° 512.3
— Poems. Boston, 1856. 12° 335.3
STORY of a feather. Jerrold, D. . . . . . v.III. of 903.1
STORY without a name. James, G. P. R. 463.12
STOUGHTON, J. Philip Doddridge—his life, with introd. by J. G. Miall. Boston, 1853. 12° 576.6
STOWE, H. E. B. Autographs for freedom. London, 1853. 16° 899.23
— Dred, a tale. Boston, 1855. 2v. 12° 806.4–12
— The Mayflower, and miscellaneous writings. Boston, 1855. 12° 806.3
— Sunny memories of foreign lands. Boston, 1854. 2v. 12° 658.1–4
— The Christian slave, a drama, founded on Uncle Tom's Cabin. Boston, 1855. 12° . . . 357.11
— Uncle Tom's Cabin. Boston, 1852. 2v. 12°. 796.10–17
— — Same. London, 1852. 12° 796.15
STRABO. Geography. Tr. by H. C. Hamilton and W. Falconer. Lond., 1854–57. 3v. p.8° 844.3
STRAIN, I. G. Journal in Chili and the Argentine provinces, in 1849. New York, 1853. 12° . 635.13
STRAIT gate, The. Abbott, J. . . . . v.I. of 739.1
STRANGE, Sir R., Memoirs of. Dennistoun, J. . . 556.6
STRANGE stories. Hoffmann, E. T. A. [W.] . . . 757.13
STRATEGY. See Military art and science.
STRAUSS, G. L. Moslem and Frank. Lon., 1854. 12° 918.14
STRAUSS and the Gospels. Bremer, F. 1094.3
STRAWBERRY, Cultivation of the. Pardee, R. G. 165.25
STRICKLAND, A. Lives of the queens of England. Philadelphia, 1853. 12v. in 6. 12° 592.1–4

> Contents. — Vol. I. Matilda of Flanders, A.D. 1067; Matilda of Scotland, 1100; Adelicia, 1120; Matilda of Boulogne, 1136; Eleanora of Aquitaine, 1154; Berengaria, 1191; Isabella of Angoulême, 1200; Eleanor of Provence, 1236; Eleanora of Castile, 1273; Marguerite, 1299; Isabella of France, 1308; Philippa, 1327; Anne of Bohemia, 1399; Isabella of Valois, 1397; Joanna, 1402; Katherine of Valois, 1402; Margaret, 1444; Elizabeth Woodville, 1464; Anne of Warwick, 1475. II. Elizabeth of York, 1486; Katharine of Arragon, 1509; Anne Boleyn, 1533; Jane, 1536; Anne of Cleves, 1539; Katharine Howard, 1540; Katharine Parr, 1543; Mary, 1553. III. Elizabeth Tudor, 1558; Anne of Denmark, 1603. IV. Henrietta Maria, 1638; Catharine of Braganza, 1661; Mary of Modena, 1685. V. Same; Mary second, 1688; Anne, 1702. VI. Same, continued.

— Lives of the queens of Scotland, and English princesses connected with the succession of Great Britain. New York, 1851–57. 6v. 12° 593.4–5

> Contents. — Vol. I. Margaret Tudor; Magdalene of France; Mary of Lorraine. II. Same; Lady Margaret Douglas. III.—VI. Mary Stuart.

— Pilgrims of Walsingham. N. Y., 1854. 12° 787.9–11
STRIFE and peace. Bremer, F. 455.2–3
STROTHER, D. H. Virginia illustrated: by Porte Crayon. New York, 1857. 8° 623.1–2
STROZZI, F. Vita e documenti. Niccolini, G. B. 1055.9
STRUTT, J. Queenhoo-Hall, a romance; and Ancient times, a drama. Edinb., 1808. 4v. 16. 499.6
— Sports and pastimes of the people of England. New ed. by W. Hone. London, 1850. 8° . 195.10
STUART, A. M. See Willson, A. M.
STUART, J. Three years in North America. From 2d London ed. New York, 1833. 2v. 12° . 639.6
STUART, James, and Revett, N. Antiquities of Athens. 3d ed. London, 1858. p.8° 835.17
STUART, I. W. Life of Capt. Nathan Hale. Hartford, 1856. 12° 528.21
STUART, M. Commentary on the book of Daniel. 1093.4
— Commentary on the book of Proverbs 1097.23
— Commentary on Ecclesiastes 1097.25
— Commentary on the epistle to the Romans. 1097.1
— Critical history and defence of the Old Testament canon. New York, 1849. 12° 1097.24
— Miscellanies. Andover, 1846. 12° 118.5

STUART of Dunleath: a novel. Norton. C. E. S. . 802.17
STUDENT-LIFE of Germany. Howitt, W. 663.6
STUDIES of nature. Saint Pierre, J. H. B. de . . . 173.4
STUDIO, The: or, illustrations of drawing. Abbott, J. . . . . v.IV. of 739.1
STURGE, J. and Harvey, T. The West Indies in 1837. London, 1838. 8° 635.8
STURM, C. C. Morning communings with God. Translated by W. Johnstone. 7th ed. London, 1858. p.8° 837.11
STUYVESANT: a Franconia story. Abbott, J. . . . . v.VIII. of 738.4
STYLES, J. Early blossoms; or, biographical notices, with specimens. London, 1819. 12° 878.11
   Contents. — John Bowdler, jr.; Michael Bruce; Daniel Parken; William Isaac Roberts.
STYRIA, A winter in lower. Hall, B. 667.21
SUBALTERN, The. Gleig, G. R. 979.5
SUBLIME and beautiful, Origin of our ideas of the. Burke, E. 125.28–29
SUCCESS in life. The merchant. Tuthill, L. C. . 525.19
SUDBURY, Mass., A notice of. Barry, W. 224.7
SUETONIUS Tranquillus, C. Lives of the twelve Cæsars. Transl. of A. Thomson, revised by T. Forester. London, 1855. p.8° 844.8
SUGDEN, E. Lord St. Leonards. Handy book on property law. From 5th London ed. New York, 1858. 12° 134.24
SULLIVAN, J., Life of, by O. W. B. Peabody v.XIII. of 529.1
SULLIVAN, W. Familiar letters on public characters, 1783 to 1815. Boston, 1834. 8° 207.9
— Historical causes and effects, from the fall of the Roman empire to 1517. Boston, 1838. 12° 949.3
— Public men of the revolution, in a series of letters, with biography of the author, by J. T. S. Sullivan. Philadelphia, 1847. 8° . . . 213.3
SULLY, Duke of. See Béthune, M. de.
SULPICIA. Satire. Transl. by L. Evans. Juvenalis, D. J. 824.13
SULTAN. Oscanyan, C. The S. and his people. . 686.13
— Pardoe, J. The city of the 689.17
SUMMER rambles, Pictures of. Miller, T. 906.4
SUMMER time in the country. Willmott, R. A. . 899.19
SUMMERFIELD, C. Pseud. See Arrington, A. W.
SUMMERFIELD, J. Holland, J. Life and ministry of. 1107.10
— Willett, W. M. Life of 574.7
SUMMERLY, F. Pseud. for H. Cole. See Niebuhr, B. G.
SUMNER, C. Orations and speeches. Bost., 1850. 12° 866.7
— Recent speeches and addr. Boston, 1856. 12° 866.8
SUMNER, W. H. History of East Boston, with biogr. sketches of its early proprietors. Boston, 1858. 8° 233.1
SUNBEAMS and shadows: a novel. Hulse, G. A. 478.12
SUNDAY schools. Pray, L. G. History of 1108.8
— Lloyd, W. F. Sketch of the history of. . . . 578.13
SUNDERLAND, L. Book of health. 2d ed. New York, 1852 . . . . 157.30
— Book of human nature. New York, 1853. 12° 125.11
— Book of psychology. New York, 1853. 12°. 157.30
— Theory of nutrition. Boston, 1855. 12° . . . 157.31
SUNNY memories of foreign lands. Stowe, H. B. 658.1–1
SUNRISE within the tropics. An account of the Yoruba mission. Tucker, Miss. 699.14
SUNSHINE on daily paths. Dickens, C. 462.22–26
SUPERIOR, Lake, its physical character, etc. Agassiz, L. 624.1
— its commerce and navigation. Ritchie, J. S. 237.9
SUPERNATURALISM. Brierre de Boismont, A. Hallucinations 122.1
— Calmet, A. The phantom world 1106.6
— Crowe, C. Night side of nature 124.23
— Ferriar, J. Theory of apparitions 118.13
— Radcliffe, J. N. Fiends, ghosts, and sprites . 124.24
SUPERSTITIONS. Brand, J. Origin of vulgar customs, ceremonies and 910.8
— Mayo, H. Popular S. and the truths therein. 1009.3
— Stewart, W. G. S. of the Highlanders of Scotland 989.11

SURGEONS. Eminent living S. of Paris, See Sketches, etc. 609.1
SURGERY. Burggraeve, le Dr. Chirurgie 1065.8
— Chelius, J. M. System of 152.8
— Cooper, S. Dictionary of 151.19
— Druitt, R. Principles and practice of modern. 151.18
— Fergusson, W. System of practical 152.14
— Liston, R. Elements of 151.17
— South, J. F. Household S.: or, hints on emergencies 157.7
— Wilson, W. J. E. The dissector 153.7
   See also: Anatomy, and Medicine.
SURR, T. S. A winter in London: a novel. 8th ed. London, 1806. 3v. 12° 429.8
SURVEYING, Treatise on land. Castle, H. J. . . 196.6
   See also: Geometry, and Trigonometry.
SUSIANA. Travels and researches in. Loftus, W. K. 694.1
SUSPIRIA de profundis. De Quincey, T. 895.2–6
SUSSEX, Ornithological rambles in. Knox, A. E. 177.16
SUTCLIFF, R. Travels in some parts of North America, in 1804–6. Phila., 1812. 12° . . . 628.29
SUTCLIFFE, T. Sixteen years in Chili and Peru. London, 1841. 8° 633.17
SUTHERLAND, A. Achievements of the Knights of Malta. Edinburgh, 1830. 2v. 18° 830.63
SUTTON, R. Lord Lexington. Lexington papers: or, the courts of London and Vienna, [1700.] London, 1851. 8° 975.11
SWAIN, C. Poems. Boston, 1857. 18° 359.10
SWAIN, D. L. British invasion of North Carolina in 1776. [No imprint.] 8° 235.6
SWAINSON, W. Animals in menageries. London, 1838. 16° 398.19
— Birds of Western Africa . . . . . v.XI.–XII. of 179.1
— Discourse on the study of natural history. London, 1834. 16° 398.16
— Geography and classification of animals. London, 1835. 16° 398.17
— Habits and instincts of animals. London, n.d. 16° 408.4
— Natural history and classification of birds. London, 1836–37. 2v. 16° 398.20
— Natural history and classification of quadrupeds. London, 1835. 16° 398.18
— Natural history of fishes, amphibians and reptiles. London, 1838–39. 2v. 16°. . . . 408.1
— Taxidermy, with the biography of zoologists, [etc.] London, 1840. 16° 408.5
— Treatise on malacology. London, 1840. 16°. 408.2
— and Shuckard, W. E. History and natural arrangement of insects. London, 1840. 16° 408.3
SWALLOW barn; or, a sojourn in the old dominion. Kennedy, J. P. 726.2
SWAN, J. G. Northwest coast; or, three years in Washington territory. N. York, 1857. 12° 626.5–6
SWEDEN. Dunham, S. A. History of 378.10
— Fryxell, A. History of 928.3
— Howitt, W. and M. Literature of 404.5
— Inglis, H. D. Journey through part of . . . 668.7
— Long vacation ramble through 668.8
— Murray, J. Handbook for Northern Europe. 649.11
— Pfeiffer, I. Travels in 668.20
— Philippart, J. Memoirs and campaigns of Charles John, prince royal of. 512.3
— Scott, C. H. Swedes; a visit to Denmark, etc. 668.4
SWEDENBORG, E. v. Angelic wisdom concerning the divine providence. 3d Am. ed. Boston, 1851. 12° 1084.9
— Angelic wisdom concerning divine love and the divine wisdom. Boston, 1847. 12° . . . 1084.10
— Apocalypse revealed: from the Lond. rev. ed. St. Clairsville, O., 1848. 8° 1084.3
— Compendium of the theological writings of, with introd. and life. Boston, 1853. 8° . . 1084.1
— Concerning heaven and hell. Bost., 1851. 12° 1084.11
— Delights of wisdom concerning conjugial love, [etc.] Boston, 1852. 8° 1084.4–5
— Divine love and divine wisdom. [From Lond. ed., 1840.] Boston, 1841. 12° 1084.7

SWEDENBORG, E. v. Doctrines of the new Jerusalem. Transl. fr. the Latin. Boston, 1839. 12° 1084.12
— Heavenly arcana which are in the sacred Scripture. [Commentary on] Genesis, Exodus. *See* Bible 1084.6
— True Christian religion. New York, 1851. 8° 1083.12
— - Same, new transl. Boston, 1849. 8° . . . 1084.2
— Clissold, A. Pract'l nature of the doctrines of. 1084.15
— Hobart, N. Life of 545.17
— Wilkinson, J. J. G. S. a biography 545.18
SWEETSER, W. Treatise on digestion. Boston, 1837. 12° 157.29
SWETT, S. Sketch of Bunker hill battle. Humphreys, D. 528.9
SWIFT, J. Gulliver's travels, illust. N. Y., 1854. 18° 738.5
— Poetical works. London, 1833–34. 3v. 16° . 329.12
— [Select] works; with a life of the author by J. Mitford, and notes by W. C. Taylor. New York, 1853. 12° 738.2

Contents. — Gulliver's travels; Tale of a tub; Battle of the books, etc.; Life of the author, by Rev. John Mitford, and notes, by W. C. Taylor.

— Review of the works of. Jeffrey, Fr. 409.3
SWINDELL, J. G. Treatise on well-digging, boring, [etc.] 3d ed. London, 1854. 16° . . . 819.22
SWITZERLAND. Abbott, J. Rollo in 659.9–11
— Agassiz, L. A journey to 663.8
— Bruen, M. Essays on scenes in 679.5
— Christoffel, R. Reformation in 1085.14
— Cooper, J. F. Sketches of 654.9
— Coxe, W. Travels in 663.11
— Ferguson, R. Swiss men and mountains . . 409.26
— Forbes, J. A month in Switzerland in 1848 . 669.6
— Ghika, H. S. the pioneer of the reformation. 914.2
— Inglis, H. D. So. of France, and 663.14
— Laing, S. Social and political state of 409.14
— Lemaistre, J. G. Travels in S. after the peace of Amiens 654.3
— Matthews, H. Tour in 679.14
— Moore, J. Society and manners in 657.3
— Murray, J. Handbook 649.18
— Simond, L. Tour in 663.3–4
— Vieusseux, A. History of 365.9
— Williams, H. M. A tour in 669.8
— Wilson, J. History of 368.7
— Zschokke, J. H. D. History of 917.2
SWORD and distaff: a story of the South. Simms, W. G. 790.52
SYLVIA; or, the last shepherd. Read, T. B. . . . 349.13
SYMES, M. Embassy to the kingdom of Ava, 1795. 2d ed. London, 1800. 3v. 8° 696.6
— - Same, with Bell's, H. G., Narrative of the operations in the Birmese empire. Edinburgh, 1827. 2v. 18° 830.29
SYMMONS, C. Life of John Milton. 3d ed. London, 1822. 8° 583.6
SYMONDS, J. A. Sleep and dreams. 2d ed. London, 1851. 8° 125.23
SYMONDS, W. Memoirs; ed. by J. A. Sharp. London, 1858. 8° 564.2
SYNAGOGUE, The, in imitation of Herbert. Herbert, G. 345.18
SYNONYMES. Crabb, G. English 403.1
— Graham, G. F. English 403.9–10
— Mackenzie, D. L. English 405.20
— Selection of English 403.11
— Taylor, W. English S. discriminated 403.15
See Words.
SYRIA. Curtis, G. W. The Howadji in 686.19–21
— Hahn-Hahn, I. Travels in, by a German countess 687.10
— Irby, C. L. Travels in 889.25
— Napier, E. Reminiscences of 693.15
— Van de Velde, C. W. M. Journey through . 694.13
SYRIAC Peshito version of the New Testament. A literal translation from the, by J. Murdock. *See* Bible 1093.7

TAAFFE, J. History of the order of St. John of Jerusalem. London, 1852. 4v. in 2. 8° . . 915.1

TABLE talk: or, selections from the Ana. Edinburgh, 1827. 18° . . . . '. . . 830.30
— Table talk, Book of. *See* Book 840.2
— Hazlitt, W. Opinions on books, men, etc..v.I.of 867.2
— Luther, M. Table talk 837.8
— Rogers, S. Table talk 877.16
TABLE traits, with something on them. Doran, J. 188.20
TABLES, Mathematical, etc. Bowditch, N. Practical navigator 135.3
— Byrne, O. Practical model calculator 194.4
— Haswell, C. H. Mechanics' 198.6
— Law, H. Mathematical 829.26
— Ryde, E. Text-book for architects, [etc.] . . 194.12
— Simpson, S. and Wise, E. Readiest reckoner ever invented 136.34
— Winslow, E. S. Computist's manual 136.26
TACITUS, C. C. Works; with an essay, notes, etc., by A. Murphy. New ed. N.Y., 1851. 8° 872.11
— Works; the Oxford translation revised. London, 1854. 2v. p.8° 834.17
TACTICS. *See* Military art and science.
TADEUSKUND, the last king of the Lenape. Hentz, C. L. 489.11–12
TAGGART, C. Poems. Providence, 1834. 12° . 338.12
TAI-PING-WANG, chief of the Chinese insurrection, Life of. Mackie, J. M. 547.8
TALBA, The: or, the moor of Portugal. Bray, A.E. 448.14
TALBOT, M. E. Rurality; desultory tales. Providence, 1830. 12° 449.16
TALBOT, S., Life of. Tuckerman, H. T. 529.3–4
TALE of a tub. Swift, J. 738.2
TALES and takings. Watson, J. V. 897.10
TALES from the German. Furness, W. H. 756.10
TALES from the German; translated by N. Greene. Velde, F. C. van der 799.7
TALES from the German of Heinrich Zschokke. 767.12
TALES from Shakespeare. Lamb, C. and M. . . . 840.29
TALES of an American landlord: or, life South of the Potomac. New York, 1824. 2v. in 1. 12° 418.5
TALES for girls and boys. Hawthorne, N. . . . 457.10
TALES for mothers. Bouilly, J. N. 498.13
TALES for the marines. Wise, H. A. 737.3–4
TALES of a grandfather. 1st–3d series. Scottish history. *See* Scott, Sir W.
— 4th series. Stories of France. *See* Scott, Sir W.
TALES of a traveller. Irving, W. . . . . . . v.IV. of 367.2–3
TALES of Flemish life. Conscience, H. 488.16
TALES of my landlord. *See* Scott, Sir W.

Contents. — Black dwarf; Bride of Lammermoor; Heart of Mid-Lothian.

TALES of the crusaders. Scott, Sir W. 480.8–13

Contents. — Betrothed; Talisman.

TALES of the good woman. Paulding, J. K. . . . 797.12
TALES of the genii. Ridley, J. 835.10
TALES of the Puritans. New Haven, 1831. 12° . 769.11
TALES of the wars of our own times. Sherer, M. 799.6
TALFOURD, T. N. Critical and miscellaneous writings. 2d Am. ed. Philadelphia, 1850. 8° . 863.9
— - Same. 3d American ed. Boston, 1854. 8° 863.16
— Ion: a tragedy, in five acts. 2d edition. New York, 1837. 12° 356.13
— Supplement to "Vacation rambles." London, 1854. 16° 669.5
— Vacation rambles, and thoughts. 2d edition. London, 1845. 12° 667.13
TALISMAN, The. Scott, Sir W. 480.8–13
TALLANGETTA: the squatter's home. Howitt, W. 705.9
TALLEYRAND-PERIGORD, C. M. Life. London, 1834–36. 4v. 8° 614.1
— Life of. McHarg, C. K. 617.10
TALLMADGE, N. P. Appendix to "Spiritualism." Edmonds, J. W. 122.14–15
TALVI. *Pseud.* *See* Robinson, T. A. L. v. J.
TANGLEWOOD tales for girls and boys. Hawthorne, N. 457.10
TAMING of a shrew. Amyot, T. 342.24
TANNEHILL, W. Sketches of the history of literature. Nashville, 1827. 8° 402.8

TANNER, J. Narrative of captivity and adventures among the Indians in N. A. N.Y., 1830. 8° ... 245.4

TANNER, T. H. Practice of medicine. 1st Amer. from 3d London ed. Philadelphia, 1858. 12° ... 155.27

TANNING, Art of. Fontenelle, J. de ... 194.11

TANSUR, J. P. Poem on the true use of the drama. Boston, 1838. 12° ... 358.27

TAPPAN, H. P. Step from the new world to the old, and back again. N.Y., 1852. 2v. 12°. ... 659.25

TAPPAN, W. B. Poems. Philadelphia, 1834. 18° 369.10

TARANTASSE journey through Eastern Russia. Spottiswoode, W. ... 674.7

TARBELL, J. A. Sources of health: or, mental and physical hygiene. Boston, 1855. 16° ... 158.10

TARLIER, J. Description géograph. de la Belgique, [et atlas général de géographie moderne.] Bruxelles, n.d. 12° ... 1065.55

TARLTON, R. Jests, and news out of purgatory; with notes, and some account of his life, by J. O. Halliwell. London, 1844. 8° ... 342.19

TARTARY. Clarke, E. D. Travels in ... v.I.-II. of 689.6
— Cochrane, J. D. Pedestrian tour through Siberian ... 830.46
— Huc, Abbé. Christianity in ... 113.4
— - Travels in, 1844-46 ... 706.4
— Tu-Li-Shin. Chinese embassy to the Khan of the Tourgouth Tartars, 1712-15 ... 694.5

TASMANIA, My home in. Meredith, L. A. ... 705.16

TASSO, T. Aminta, poesie, e i discorsi sull' arte poetica. Firenze, 1824. 32° ... 1047.9
— La Gerusalemme liberata—col riscontro della conquistata. Padova, 1828. 3v. in 2. 18° ... 1047.8
— - Same—preceduta da un discorso di Ugo Foscolo. 4a ed. Firenze, 1853. 12° ... 1047.5
— Prose filosofiche. Firenze, 1847. 2v. 12° ... 1047.4

Contents.—Vol. I. Discorso intorno a Torquato Tasso; Il Porzio ovvero delle virtù; Il padre di famiglia; Il Costantino ovvero della clemenza; Il Manso ovvero dell' amicizia; Il Beltramo ovvero della cortesia; Il Rangone ovvero della pace; Forno primo ovvero della nobiltà; Forno secondo ovvero della nobiltà; Il Gonzaga ovvero del piacere onesto; Il G nzaga secondo ovvero del giuoco; Il Minturno ovvero della bellezza. II. Della dignità; I Bagni ovvero della pietà; La Molza ovvero dell' amore; Il cavaliere amante e la gentil donna amata; Il forestiero napoletano ovvero della gelosia; Il Romeo ovvero del giuoco; Il Malpiglio ovvero della corte; Il Malpiglio secondo ovvero del fuggir la moltitudine; Il nifo ovvero del piacere; Il messaggiero; Il Cataneo ovvero delle conclusioni; Conclusioni amorose; Discorso sopra due questioni amorose; Il secretario; Dell' ufficio del siniscalco; Del maritarsi; Dell' amor vicendevole fra il padre e il figliuolo; Del giuramento falso; Della virtù eroica e della carità; Della virtù femminile e donnesea; Della gelosia; Dell' arte del dialogo; Discorso di Torquato Tasso sopra varj accidenti della sua vita.

— Lettere ed altre prose. Parma, 1847. 2v. 16° 1047.7

Contents.—Vol. I. Lettere scelte. II. Lettere scelte; Il secretario; Riposta di Roma a Plutarco; Intorno alla sedizione nata nel regno di Francia l'anno 1585; Sopra varj accidenti della vita di T. Tasso. Dialoghi.

— Lettere. Firenze, 1853-55. 5v. 12° ... 1047.6
— Jerusalem delivered. Translated by John Hoole. New ed. London, 1807. 2v. 12°. 317.16
— - Same. 1st Am. from 8th London ed. Newburyport, 1810. 2v. 8° ... 317.1
— - Same. 7th ed. London, 1844-53. 2v. 18° 830.19
— - Same. From the Italian, by E. Fairfax. 1st Am. from 7th London ed. Introductory essay by L. Hunt, and lives of Tasso and Fairfax, by C. Knight. New York, 1851. 2v. in 1. 12° ... 317.2
— - Same. Translated by J. H. Wiffen. 3d Am. from last English ed. N. Y., 1851. 16° 317.4
— - Same. With a life. 5th edition. London, 1854. p.8° ... 835.1
— Jerusalem delivered. Translated by A. C. Robertson. Edinburgh, 1853. 12° ... 317.3
— Love, madness and imprisonment of. Wilde, R. H. ... 544.14
— Torquato, T. Schauspiel. Göthe, J. W. v. 1038.2
— Göthe's Tasso erläutert. Düntzer, J. H. J. 1034.7

TASSONI, A. Rape of the bucket. Transl. with notes by J. Atkinson. London, 1827. 2v. 12° 345.4

TASTE. Alison, A. Essays on the nature and principles of ... 129.12
— Burke, E. Origin of our ideas of the sublime and beautiful ... 125.29
— Cousin, V. The true, the beautiful and the good ... 124.3
— - Philosophy of the beautiful ... 125.21
— Taylor, Jane. Pleasures of ... 129.13

TASTU, Mme. A. Notice littéraire sur Madame de Genlis ... 1066.17

TATE, T. Elements of mechanism. 3d ed. London, 1855. 12° ... 199.18
— Elementary course of natural and experimental philosophy. London, 1855. 2v. 18° 149.37

TATLER, The, and the Guardian. London, n.d. 8° 873.11
— See British essayists ... v. I.-V. of 850.24

TAUTPHOEUS, Baroness. The initials: a story. 3d Am. ed. Philadelphia, 1852. 12° ... 474.11
— - Same. Philadelphia, n.d. 12° ... 474.12
— Quits: a novel. Phila., 1857. 2v. [in 1.] 12° 474.1-10

TAXATION, Principles of. Ricardo, D. ... 136.3

TAXIDERMY. Lee, R. ... 177.25
— Swainson, W. ... 408.5

TAYLER, C. B. Facts in a clergyman's life. New York, 1849. 12° ... 449.2
— Memorials of the English martyrs. New York, 1853. 12° ... 1094.10

TAYLER, J. J. Christian aspects of faith and duty. 2d ed. London, 1855. 12° ... 1096.17

TAYLOR, A. S. Medical jurisprudence. 3d Am. ed., by E. Hartshorne. Phila., 1853. 8° ... 151.5

TAYLOR, Brook. Linear perspective. New ed., by J. Jopling. London, 1835. 8° ... 205.5

TAYLOR, F. W. The flag-ship, or a voyage round the world. New York, 1840. 2v. 12°. ... 708.8

TAYLOR, H. Edwin the fair, and other poems. 3d ed. London, 1852. 16° ... 355.7
— Notes from books. London, 1849. 12°. ... 403.4
— Notes from life, in seven essays. From 3d London ed. Boston, 1853. 16° ... 898.21
— Philip van Artevelde: a dramatic romance. Cambridge, 1835. 2v. in 1. ... 346.16

TAYLOR, I. Fanaticism. New ed., rev. London, 1843. 16° ... 1108.5
— Home education. 1st Am. from 2d London ed. New York, 1838. 12° ... 137.6
— Introductory essay to Edwards on the will. Edwards, J. ... 124.6
— Loyola, and Jesuitism in its rudiments. New York, 1851. 12° ... 1098.8
— Memoirs of Jane Taylor. Boston, 1845. 16°. 599.10
— Natural history of enthusiasm. Boston, 1830. 12° ... 1108.3
— Physical theory of another life. New York, 1836. 12° ... 1108.1
— Self-cultivation recommended. 3d Am. ed. Ithaca, 1842. 12° ... 129.23
— The world of mind. London, 1857. 12° ... 125.7
— Wesley and Methodism. New York, 1852. 12° 1108.4

TAYLOR, Rev. Jas. Cyclopædia of biblical literature. Kitto, J. ... 1083.8

TAYLOR, Jas. Bayard. Cyclopædia of modern travel. Cincinnati, 1856. 8° ... 621.1
— Eldorado, comprising Mexican travel. 2d ed. New York, 1850. 2v. 12° ... 627.17
— - Same. New York, 1857. 12° ... 627.12-16
— Handbook of literature, etc. Ripley, G. 406.22
— Journey to Central Africa. N. Y., 1857. 12° 699.4-9
— Lands of the Saracen. New York, 1857. 12° 686.15-18
— Northern travel. Sweden, Denmark, and Lapland. New York, 1858. 12° ... 668.13-17
— Poems of the Orient. Boston, 1855. 16° ... 345.21
— Rhymes of travel, ballads and poems. 2d ed. New York, 1849. 12° ... 345.19
— Romances, lyrics and songs. Bost., 1852. 12° 345.20
— Views a-foot: or, Europe seen with knapsack and staff. Preface by N. P. Willis. 15th ed. New York, 1853. 12° ... 657.12-14
— - Same. 20th ed. New York, 1856. 12° ... 657.15-19

TAYLOR, Jas. Bayard. A visit to India, China, and
    Japan in 1853. New York, 1855. 12°....708.17–19
TAYLOR, Jas. Brainerd, Memoir of. Rice, J. H.
    and B. H.................1109.21
TAYLOR, J. W. History of Ohio, 1650–1787. Cin-
    cinnati, 1854. 12°.............237.4
TAYLOR, Jane. Writings. New York, n.d. 3v. 12° 868.12

Contents. — Vol. I. Memoirs and correspondence;
Poetical remains and essays in rhyme. II. Contributions of Q. Q. III. Correspondence between a mother
and her daughter at school; Original poems for infant
minds; and Display, a tale.

— Contributions of Q. Q. N. Y., 1826. 2v. 12°. 1089.6
— Pleasures of taste, and other stories, with life
    by S. J. Hale. Boston, 1839. 18°...... 129.13
— Memoirs of, by I. Taylor........... 599.10
TAYLOR, Jeremy. Practical works, with bio-
    graphical memoir. Lond., 1850. 2v. roy.8° 1101.3

Contents. — Vol. I. Biographical memoir of Taylor;
Liberty of prophesying; Sermons, Part I. Twenty-
seven sermons for the summer half-year; Part 2.
Twenty-five sermons for the winter half-year; Part 3.
Miscellaneous sermons. II. Rule and exercise of holy
living; Rule and exercise of holy dying; The golden
grove, or manual of daily prayers and litanies; Psalter
of David; Collection of offices, or forms of prayer in
cases ordinary and extraordinary; The worthy com-
municant; Christian consolations; Discourse of the
nature, offices, and measures of friendship, with rules
of conducting it; Letters to persons changed in their
religion; Contemplations of the state of man in this
life, and in that which is to come.

— Holy living and dying. London, 1851. p.8°. 848.7
— Predecessors, contemporaries and successors
    of. Willmott, R. A............. 578.6
TAYLOR, Col. John. Arator: agricultural essays.
    2d ed. Georgetown, D. C., 1814. 12°.. 169.12
TAYLOR, John L. Memoir of Samuel Phillips.
    Boston, 1856. 8°............. 523.2
TAYLOR, R. C. Statistics of coal, brought down
    to 1854, by S. S. Haldeman. 2d ed. Phila-
    delphia, 1855. 8°............. 135.6
TAYLOR, T. Editor and compiler of the life of
    Haydon. Haydon, B. R......... 556.7–9
TAYLOR, W. English synonyms discriminated.
    London, 1856. 16°............ 406.15
TAYLOR, W. C. History of Ireland. Edinburgh,
    1831. 2v. 18°.............. 830.68
— - Same. New York, 1847. 2v. 18°...... 810.52
— Manual of ancient history. Revised by C. S.
    Henry. 5th ed. N. Y., 1851. 8°...... 955.2
— - Same. And modern history, with a chap-
    ter on the United States. 7th ed. New
    York, 1852. 8°............. 952.2
— Memoirs of the house of Orleans. London,
    1849. 3v. 8°.............. 1005.4
— The occult sciences. Smedley, E....... 125.5
— Questions to accompany T.'s manual of an-
    cient history. Smith, L. L......... 955.2
TAYLOR, Z. Frost, J. Life of........ 517.8
— Fry, J. R. Life of........... 517.7
— Montgomery, H. Life of......... 517.6
— Powell, C. F. Life of.......... 517.5
TEA. Ball, S. Cultivation and manuf. of, in China. 136.5
— Fortune, R. Tea countries of China and the
    Himalaya.............. 706.7
TEA party, Traits of the Boston. Hewes, G. R. T.. 219.4
TEACHING. *See* Education.
TECHNOLOGY. *See* Useful arts.
TECUMSEH. Brock, *Sir I.* Notices of...... 556.10
— Drake, B. Life of........... 539.5
TEETH. Owen, R. Forms of the....... 177.5
— Harris, C. A. Dental surgery........ 151.13
TEGG, T. Chronology, from the earliest period.
    3d ed. London, 1824. 12°........ 949.7
— Dictionary of chronology. New ed. New
    York, 1854. 16°............ 947.2
— Young man's book of knowledge. 1st Am.
    from the 20th London ed. N. Y., 1834. 12° 138.1
TEGNÉR, E., *Bishop.* Children of the Lord's
    supper. Longfellow, H. W.....v.I. of 333.1–9

TEHRAN, A winter's journey from Constantinople
    to. Fraser, J. B............. 694.17
TEIGNMOUTH, *Lord. See* Shore, Sir J.
TELEGRAPH. Bois, V. Télégraphie électrique. 1078.32
— Briggs, C. F. The story of the...... 196.16
— Davis, D. Book of the........ 149.10
— Highton, E. Electric......... 819.9
— Turnbull, L. Historical account of the rise,
    progress, and condition of........ 194.9
    See also: Electricity, Magnetism, *etc.*
TELEMACHUS, The adventures of. Fénélon, F.
    de S. de La M.............759.11–12
— Les aventures de. Fénélon, F.de S. de La M. 1008.3
TEMPER. [A novel.] Opie, A.....v.III. of 801.4–6
TEMPER and temperament. [A novel.] Ellis, S. S. 804.12
TEMPERANCE. Carpenter, W. B. The physiol-
    ogy of............... 139.8
— - Use and abuse of alcoholic liquors.... 157.17
— Forbes, J. Physiological effects of alcoholic
    drinks............... 127.19
— Select T. tracts. *See* Select......... 1109.4
TEMPERANCE reformation. Armstrong, L. His-
    tory of.............. 127.22
— Forbes, J. Origin and progress of the... 127.19
TEMPEST and sunshine : a novel. Holmes, M. J. 416.4
TEMPLE, E. Travels in Peru. Lond., 1830. 2v. 8° 633.12
TEMPLE, Launcelot. *Pseud. See* Armstrong, J.
TEMPLES and tombs of Nubia, Egypt, and Pales-
    tine in 1845–46. Romer, I. F....... 693.13
TEMPLETON, W. Operative mechanic's workshop
    companion. 3d ed. London, 1853. 18°.. 199.36
— Practical examiner on steam and the steam
    engine. Philadelphia, 1853. 12°...... 198.21
TEMPSKY, G. F. von. Mitla, a journey in Mexico,
    Guatemala and Salvador, 1853–55. Ed. by J.
    S. Bell. London, 1858. 8°........ 633.8
TEN commandments, Exposition of the. Hop-
    kins, E.............. 1107.19
TEN thousand a year. A novel. Warren, S...767.14–15
TEN thousand Greeks, Travels in the track of the.
    Ainsworth, W. F............ 687.12
TEN years, 1830–1840, The hist. of. Blanc, J. J. L. 1002.5
TENNANT, W. Anster fair, with other poems.
    Boston, 1815. 18°........... 309.11
TENNEMANN, W. A. History of philosophy.
    Transl. by Arthur Johnson. London, 1852.
    p.8°............... 855.1
TENNESSEE, Annals of. Ramsey, J. G. M..... 235.4
TENNYSON, A. In memoriam. Boston, 1851. 16° 334.21
— Maud and other poems. Boston, 1855. 16°. 334.17–18
— Poems, [including The princess.] New ed.
    Boston, 1854. 2v. 12°.........334.19.20
TENT, The, and the altar. Cumming, J...... 116.17
TENT life in the Holy Land. Prime, W. C.... 686.7
TERENTIUS Afer. P. Comedies and fables of
    Phaedrus. Transl. by H. T. Riley. Lon-
    don, 1853. p.8°............ 834.11
TERRIBLE tractoration. Fessenden, T. G..... 349.19
TERSTEEGEN, G., Biography of. Baillie, J.... 548.12
TERTULLIAN, Antignostikus, or the spirit of.
    Neander, J. A. W........... 848.9
TESTAMENT, New. *See* Bible.
TESTIMONY of the rocks. Miller, H.......167.1–5
TESTS, Chemical. *See* Chemical tests, Chemistry.
TESTUDINATA, N. American. Agassiz, L.....v.I. of 170.2
TEXAS. Bartlett, J. R. Explorations, etc., con-
    nected with the boundary commission.... 624.2
— Braman, D. E. E. Information about.... 239.10
— Domenech, E. Missionary adventures in.. 633.3
— Foote, H. S. Texas and the Texans.... 639.1
— Kendall, G. W. Texan Santa Fé expedition. 638.7
— Olmsted, F. L. Journey through......627.6–11
— Maillard, N. D. History of........ 236.5
— Paxton, P. A stray Yankee in......626.16–18
— Sage, R. B. Scenes in.......... 639.16
— Yoakum, H. History of T. from 1685 to 1846. 235.11
TEXIAN expedition against Mier. Green, T. J.. 623 10
TEXT book for architects, engineers, surveyors,
    solicitors, auctioneers, land-agents, and
    stewards. Ryde, E........... 194.12

THACHER, J. American medical biography. Boston, 1828. 2v. in 1. 8°. 523.11
— History of the town of Plymouth, from 1620. 2d ed., enl. Boston, 1835. 12°. 227.11
— Journal during the American revolutionary war, with appendix. 2d ed., rev. and cor. Boston, 1827. 8°. 214.9
THACHER, S. C. Memoir of J. S. Buckminster. v.I. of 117.5
THACKERAY, W. M. Ballads, Boston, 1856. 16°. 325.6
— Book of snobs. New York, 1852. 16°. . . . 509.4
— Confessions of Fitz-Boodle, and some passages in the life of Major Gahagan. New York, 1852. 16° 509.8-11
— English humorists of the eighteenth century. New York, 1853. 12° 586.1-4
— Great Hoggarty diamond. N. York, n.d. 8° 501.12-13
— Hist. of Henry Esmond, Esq. N.Y., 1852. 8°. 501.6-10
— Hist. of Pendennis. New York, 1854. 2v. 8° 491.11-15
— Irish sketch book,1842. New ed. Lon.,1857. 12° 508.1
— Jeames's diary, A legend of the Rhine ; and Rebecca and Rowena. N. Y., 1853. 16° .508.15-17
— Journey from Cornhill to Grand Cairo. New York, 1846. 12° 658.10-11
— Luck of Barry Lyndon. N.York, 1853. 2v. 16° 508.5-8
— Men's wives. New York, 1852. 16° 508.18-20
— Mr. Brown's letters, with The proser, and other papers. New York, 1853. 16°. . .508.12-14
— Newcomes. New York, 1855. 2v. in 1. 8°. . 501.1-5
— Paris sketch book. New York, 1852. 2v. 16° 509.5-7
— Punch's prize novelists; Fat contributor, and Travels in London. New York, 1853. 16°. 508.2-4
— Shabby genteel story and other tales. New York, 1853. 12° 509.1-3
— Sketches in Ireland. Philadelphia, n.d. 8° . 501.11
— The rose and the ring: a fireside pantomime. New York, 1855. sq.16° 508.21-23
— Vanity fair. New York, n.d. 8°. 491.7-10
— Yellowplush papers. N. York, 1852-53. 16°. .508.9-11
THADDEUS of Warsaw: a novel. Porter, J. . . . 789.6
THAMES, The. Rambles by rivers. Thorne, J.
v.IV. of 850.18
THATCHER, B. B. Indian biography. N.Y., 1832. 18° 249.6
— — Same. New York, 1848. 2v. 18°. 810.50
— — Indian traits. New York, 1810. 2v. 18°. . 249.4
THAYENDANEGEA, [Brant,] Life of. Stone, W. L. 513.12
THAYER, W. M. The poor boy and merchant prince. Life of A. Lawrence. Boston, 1857. 12° 526.20
THEATRE. Constant, B. de. Réflexions sur le T. allemand. 1066.8
— Dunlap, W. History of the American. . . . 353.5-6
— Ebers, J. Seven years of the king's 353.12
See also : Drama, Plays, Stage.
THEISM. See Theology.
THELEMARKEN, The Oxonian in. Metcalfe, F. . 666.3
THEOBALD, or the fanatic. Jung-Stilling, J. H.. 769.12
THEOCRITUS. Idylls [with those] of Bion and Moschus, and the war-songs of Tyrtæus. Translated by J. Banks and J. M. Chapman. London, 1853. p.8° 834.6
THEODORE, or the gamester's progress. A poetic tale. London, 1802. 8° 369.6
THEODORE, or the skeptic's conversion. De Wette, W. M. L.. . . . . 1088.18
THEODORETUS and Evagrius. History of the church, A.D. 322-427 and 431-594. London, 1854. p.8° 845.5-6
THEODOSIUS and Constantia, Letters between. Langhorne, J. 429.12
THEODRIC: a poem. Campbell, T.. . . . . . . 346.13
THEOGNIS, The works of. Translated into prose by J. Banks, and into verse by J. H. Frere. See Hesiodus 851.2
THEOLOGY and religion. Abbott, J. Young Christian 1087.7
— - The corner stone. 1087.16
— - Way to do good 1087.6
— Adams, H. View of religions. 1099.5
— Adams, J. Q. Letters on the Bible and its teachings 120.36

THEOLOGY, continued.
— Adams, N. Christ a friend 1106.1
— - The communion Sabbath. 1106.3
— - The friends of Christ. 1083.19
— Adams, W. Sacred allegories 1094.9
— - The three gardens. 1086.27
— Alleine, R. Heaven opened 1107.5
— Arnold, T. Serm. preached in Rugby school. 137.32
— - Works 1083.14
— Arthur, T. S. Steps towards heaven 1106.17
— Ballou, H. Nine sermons on important subjects 1089.4
— - Sermons on doctrinal subjects 1089.19
— Ballou, H. 2d. Ancient history of Universalism 1099.12
— Barclay, R. Apology for the true Christian divinity. 1095.4
— Barrett, B. F. The golden reed 1088.15
— Baxter, R. Call to the unconverted 1087.3
— - Practical writings 1094.8
— - Saints' everlasting rest. 1087.3
— Bayne, P. Christian life, social and individ'l.1086.12-13
— Beecher, C. E. The Bible and the people . . 1086.4
— Beecher, E. Conflict of ages. 1105.20-21
— Beecher, H. W. Life thoughts 1086.16
— Bell, C. The hand as evincing design 139.3
— Bible. See Bible.
— Binney, T. Is it possible to make the best of both worlds ? 118.22
— Boston, T. Crook in the lot. 1089.29
— - Human nature 1109.9
— Bowen, F. Metaphysical and ethical science applied to the evidences of religion 125.8
— Bremer, F. Morning watches 1094.3
— Brownson, O. A. Charles Elwood, or the infidel converted 1109.6
— - Essays and reviews on T. 1086.31
— Bryant, J. D. Immaculate conception of the Virgin Mary 1098.17
— Buchanan, J. Modern atheism 1096.8
— Buckminster, J. S. Works 117.5
— Bunsen, C. C. J. Signs of the times. 113.3
— Bunyan, J. Pilgrim's progress 1094.7
— - Works 1101.4
— Burnap, G. W. Miscellaneous writings . . . 1107.11
— - Rectitude of human nature. 1088.3
— Burnet, G. Exposition of the XXXIX articles 1103.3
— Burns, J. Cyclopædia of sermons 1083.15
— Bushnell, H. Sermons for the new life . . . 1088.9
— Butler, J. Analogy of religion 1108.10
— Cecil, R. Works. 1087.5
— Chalmers, T. Adaptation of nature to man. . 826.6
— - Posthumous works. 1108.6
— Channing, W. E. Works 117.3
— Chase, I. Baptismal tracts for the times . . . 1089.11
— Chateaubriand, R. F. A. de. Selections from " Genius of Christianity ". 1088.16
— Cheap repository tracts 1108.13
— Cheever, G. B. Lectures on Pilgrim's progress 1094.6
— Child, L. M. Progress of religious ideas . . 1095.6
— Christmas, H. Echoes of the universe . . . 1106.5
— Clark, D. W. Methodist Episcopal pulpit. . 1095.16
— Clarke, J. F. Christian doctrine of prayer . 1109.24
— Clissold, A. Practical nature of the doctrines of Swedenborg 1084.15
— Constitutions of the apostles. 1083.1
— Conybeare, W. J. Life and epistles of St. Paul 113.9
— Cooke, P. Divine law of beneficence 119.13
— Cotter, J. R. Mass and rubrics of the Roman Catholic church 1098.23
— Crabbe, G. Outline of a system of natural . 1083.18
— Crofton, D. Genesis and geology 118.20
— Cumming, J. Church before the flood . . . 116.11
— - Signs of the times 116.3
— - Tent and the altar 116.17
— - The end 116.19
— - Voices of the day. 116.12

THEOLOGY, *continued.*

— Cumming, J. Voices of the dead 116.13
— - Voices of the night 116.14
— Dana, M. S. B. Letters on the doctrine of
the Trinity. 1106.8
— De Quincey, T. Theological essays 905.2
— Derby, E. H. The Catholic. Letters, etc.. . 1098.12
— Dewey, O. Controversial theology 1086.10
— - Discourses on human nature 1086.11
— - On the nature of religion 117.9
— - Reviews upon quest. in controversial T.. 1086.10
— De Wette, W. M. L. Theodore: or, the skep-
tic's conversion. 1088.18
— Doddridge, P. Rise and progress of religion. 119.10
— Dow, L. Writings 1083.21
— Duncan, H. Sacred philosophy of the seasons. 1089.7
— Dunlap, S. F. Spirit history of man 122.16
— Edwards, B. B. Writings with memoir . . . 1096.12
— Edwards, J. Works 1094.1
— Eliot, W. G. Discipline of sorrow 1089.22
— - Unity of God 1086.23
— Ellis, G. E. Half century of the Unitarian
controversy. 113.7
— England, J. Ceremonies of holy week and
Easter Sunday 1098.18-21
— - Nature and ceremonies of the mass . . . 1098.21
— - Works 1095.2
— Erskine, T. Freeness of the gospel 1088.25
— Evelyn, J. History of religion 1095.8
— Farley, S. Discourses on theology and specul.
topics 117.7
— Fénelon, F. de S. de la M. Pious reflections. 1089.33
— Flavel, J. Christ knocking at the door of the
sinner's heart. 1107.4
— - The fountain of life 1107.3
— - Method of grace 1107.6
— Fountain of living waters 129.25
— Furness, W. H. Jesus and his biographers . 1101.5
— Gallaudet, T. H. Child's book on the
soul. 1109.29
— Giles, H. Christian thought on life 1088.27
— Godwin, B. Philosophy of atheism 1088.34
— Goodrich, C. A. Religious ceremonies and
customs 1099.4
— Grant, J. Metropolitan pulpit 1099.11
— Gurney, J. J. Habitual love to God as a pre-
paration for heaven. 1089.27
— Hall, R. Works 1089.16
— Hamilton, J. Life in earnest 1109.26-28
— Hare, J. C. Mission of the comforter 1106.7
— Harris, J. Great commission 1088.1
— - Great teacher. 1088.2
— - Mammon 1109.13
— Herder, J. G. von. Spirit of Hebrew poetry. 1087.17
— Hitchcock, E. Religious truth illus. from
science 1088.5
— Hobart, J. H. Christian's manual 1099.16-17
— - Companion for the altar 118.10
— Hooker, R. Works 1103.4
— Hopkins, E. Exposition of the ten command-
ments 1107.19
— Hopkins, M. Misc. essays and discourses . . 1106.2
— Horne, G. Works 1083.7
— How I became a Unitarian 117.6
— Infidelity; comprising Jenyns, Leslie, Lyt-
telton, etc. 119.9
— Jahn, J. Hebrew commonwealth and hist.
of the Jews. 1085.8
— James, H. Nature of evil 1087.18
— James, J. A. Anxious enquirer directed . . 1109.25
— - Christian professor addressed 118.8
— - Christian progress 119.22
— - Pastoral addresses 1088.30
— Jay, W. Christian contemplated 119.14
— Keble, J. Christian year. 1083.20
— Kempis, T. à. Imitation of Christ. 1097.28
— Kidd, J. Adaptation of nature to man. . . . 826.1
— Kitto, J. Cyclopædia of biblical literature. . 1083.8
— Knapp, G. C. Lectures on Christian. 1083.4
— Krummacher, F. W. Elijah the Tishbite . . 119.6

THEOLOGY, *continued.*

— Lasteyrie, Cte. C. P. de. History of auricular
confession 1098.10
— Leighton, R. Works. 1083.6
— Lewis, T. The six days of creation 146.17
— Lord, E. The epoch of creation 1106.16
— M'Cosh, J. Of the divine government . . . 113.8
— Maffitt, J. N. Pulpit sketches, sermons, and
devotional fragments. 1099.1
— Martineau, H. Essential faith of the univer-
sal church 1099.28
— - The faith as unfolded by many prophets . 1099.29
— Martineau, J. Miscellanies 1086.17
— - Studies of Christianity 1086.14
— Mason, J. Treatise on self-knowledge . . . 1109.11
— Melvill, H. Bible thoughts 119.17
— Miles, H. A. Altar at home: prayers 118.16
— More, H. Works 1094.5
— Morison, J. Counsels to young men. 1109.16
— Mountford, W. Euthanasy 1086.19-20
— Murray, L. Power of religion on the mind . 1084.16
— Muzzey, A. B. Man a soul. 1099.18
— Nelson, D. Cause and cure of infidelity . . 1107.16
— Nevins, W. Practical thoughts 1109.19
— - Thoughts on popery 119.27
— Noble, S. Plenary inspiration of the Scrip-
tures asserted 1086.26
— Noel, B. W. Christian baptism 1099.25
— Norton, A. Reasons for not believing the
doctrines of the Trinitarians 1086.15
— — Tracts concerning Christianity 1095.3
— Noyes, G. R. Coll. of theological essays . . 1096.7
— Osgood, S. God with men. 117.8
— Owen, J. Forgiveness of sin 1109.3
— Paley, W. Horæ Paulinæ 1099.37
— - Natural theology and tracts 1099.36
— - Sermons 1099.38
— Parker, T. Matters pertaining to religion. . 1086.20
— - Theism, atheism, and the popular the-
ology 1086.19
— Patrick, S. Discourse concerning prayer . . 1097.27
— Pattison, S. R. The earth and the word. . . 167.28
— Peabody, A. P. On Christian doctrine. . . . 117.13
— Peabody, E. Christian days and thoughts. . 117.12
— Pearson, J. Exposition of the creed 1103.2
— Pearson, T. Infidelity, its causes, etc. . . . 1083.11
— Peck, G. Appeal to Scripture, the rule of
faith and practice 129.9
— Philip, R. The Marys, or female holiness. . 1089.21
— Pictorial narratives 1109.2
— Pike, J. G. Guide for young disciples . . . 119.3
— - Religion and eternal life 119.5
— Pitrat, J. C. Paul and Julia. 1098.19
— Pitts street chapel lectures. 1086.1
— Porter, W. H. The heavenly union 1084.8-13
— Priestley, J. Christian truth, piety and mo-
rality. 1099.10
— Prout, W. Chemistry, meteorology and the
function of digestion considered with refer-
ence to natural theology 826.16
— Restoration of belief 1086.28
— Richmond, L. Annals of the poor. 119.2
— Robinson, E. Biblical researches in Palestine. 1103.7
— Robinson, J. Works 1087.10
— Rogers, H. Defence of the eclipse of faith . 117.10
— - The eclipse of faith. 117.11
— - Reason and faith and other miscellanies. 117.1
— Sears, E. H. Athanasia 1096.21
— - Regeneration. 1099.1
— Sears, R. History of the Bible 1085.4
— Seymour, M. H. Evenings with Romanists. 1098.16
— Sharpe, S. Notes on English version of New
Testament 1089.18
— Smith, T. S. Illustrations of the divine gov-
ernment 1089.2
— Spirit of popery 119.1
— Spring, G. Bible not of man. 1107.14
— - First things revealed to mankind 116.1
— - Power of the pulpit 116.2
— Stone, T. T. The rod and the staff. 118.17

THEOLOGY, *continued.*
— Stuart, M. Crit. hist. and defence of the
   Old Testament canon 1097.24
— - Miscellanies 118.5
— Swedenborg, E. v. Angelic wisdom concern-
   ing divine providence 1084.9–10
— - Apocalypse revealed 1084.3
— - Compendium of the theolog. writings of. 1084.1
— - Concerning heaven and hell 1084.11
— - Delights of wisdom concerning conjugial
   love 1084.5
— - Divine love and divine wisdom 1084.7
— - Doctrines of the new Jerusalem 1084.12
— - The true Christian religion 1084.2
— Tayler, J. J. Christian aspects of faith and
   duty 1095.17
— Taylor, I. Physical theory of another life . 1108.1–2
— Taylor, Jeremy. Holy living and dying . . . 848.7
— - Practical works 1101.3
— Trench, R. C. Hulsean lectures 1106.12
— - Notes on the parables 1093.9
— Trimmer, S. Help to the unlearned in the
   study of the Scriptures 129.6
— - Prayers and meditations 129.29
— Tucker, A. Light of nature pursued 1094.4
— Tulloch, J. Theism 1087.9
— Turner, S. Sacred history of the world . . . 810.43
— Venn, H. Complete duty of man 1107.15
— Vinet, A. R. Pastoral 1088.7
— Walker, J. B. God revealed in the creation
   and by Christ 1086.7
— - Philosophy of the plan of salvation . . . 1086.21
— - Philosophy of skepticism and ultraism . 1094.13
— Ware, H. Works 117.4
— Ware, H. jr. Formation of the Christian
   character 1089.31
— Werner, H. Guardian spirits 1084.14
— Whately, R. Scripture revelations concern-
   ing a future state 1086.24
— Wheatly, C. Illustrations of the book of
   common prayer 838.6
— Whitman, B. Letters to a Universalist . . . 1089.5
— Willison, J. The afflicted man's companion. 1109.5
— Wilson, J. Unitarian principles confirmed
   by Trinitarian testimonies 1094.14
— Wilson, T. Sacra privata 1109.30
— Wines, E. C. Laws of the Hebrews 1083.2
— Wiseman, N. Ceremonies of holy week . . . 1098.3
— - Connexion between science and revealed
   religion 1098.20
— - Essays on various subjects 1098.2
— - Real presence of Christ in the eucharist . 1098.4
— Woodbridge, J. Practical religion 1088.23
— Zollikofer, G. J. Exercises of piety 1088.11
   See also: Bible, Ecclesiastical history, Evi-
   dences, Mythology, Sermons, etc.
THEOLOGY of inventions. Blakely, J. . . . 1087.14
THEORY of human progression. Boston, 1851. 12° 134.18
THERAPEUTICS. *See* Medicine.
THÉRÈSE: or, the orphan of Geneva. A melo-
   drama; translated from the French. 10th
   edition. London, n.d. 8° 355.11
THEREMIN, F. Eloquence a virtue: or, a system-
   atic rhetoric. Translated by W. G. T. Shedd.
   Andover, 1854 12° 405.7
THERMOMETER and pyrometer, Treatise on, by T.
   S. Traill . . . . v.II. of 365.14
THERSITES: a play. Child, F. J. 356.1
THESSALONIANS, Epistles to the. *See* Bible
THIBET, Christianity in. Huc, M. l'abbé . . . 113.4
— Travels in, 1844–46. Huc, M. l'abbé 706.4
THIERRY, J. N. A. Conquête de l'Angleterre par
   les Normands. 8e et 9e éd. Paris, 1851. 4v. 12° 1076.11
— Conquest of England by the Normans. Trans-
   lated by W. Hazlitt from 7th Paris edition.
   London, 1847. 2v. 978.6
— - Same. London, 1856. 2v. p.8° 837.6
— Dix ans d'études historiques. 6e éd. Paris,
   1851. 12° 1076.13
— Essai sur l'histoire du tiers état. 2e éd. Paris,
   1853. 2v. 12° 1076.15

THIERRY, J. N. A. Formation and progress of the
   tiers état. Tr. by F. B. Wells. Lond., 1855.
   2v. 12° 1008.17
— Lettres sur l'histoire de France. 9e éd. Paris,
   1851. 12° 1076.12
— Récit des temps mérovingiens. 4e éd. Paris,
   1851. 2v. 12° 1076.14
THIERS, L. A. Histoire de la révolution française.
   11e et 16e éd. Paris, 1846–53. 8v. 12° . . 1076.16
— History of the French revolution. Transl. by
   F. Shoberl. 3d American edition. Phila-
   delphia, 1852. 4v. [in 2.] 8° 1002.7
— History of the consulate and the empire of
   Napoleon. London, 1856. 8° 1002.6
THINGS not generally known. Timbs, J 149.28
— - Same. Wells, D. A. 806.10
THINKING, Introduction to the art of. Home, H. 129.11
THIRLWALL, C. History of Greece. London,
   1835–40. 8v. 16° 368.11
— - Same. New York, 1848–51. 2v. 8° . . . 952.6
THIRTY-NINE articles of the church of England,
   Exposition of the. Burnet, G. 1103.3
THIRTY years' view of the American government.
   Benton, T. H. 282.1–4
THIRTY years' war. Chapman, B. History of the. 546.5
— Schiller, J. C. F. v. History of the 830.36
THIS, that and the other. Chandler, E. L. . . . 448.1–8
THOLUCK, F. A. G., Discourses by. Monod, A. . 1093.9
THOMAS, C. Farmingdale: [a novel] N.Y., 1854. 12° 794.11
THOMAS, E. S. Reminiscences of the last 65 years.
   Also, sketches of his own life and times.
   Hartford, 1840. 2v. 8° 216.6
THOMAS, J. Travels in Egypt and Palestine.
   Philadelphia, 1853. 12° 699.3
THOMAS, J. J. Farm implements and the princi-
   ples of their construction. N. Y., 1854. 12° 165.12
THOMAS, M. A. Memorials of Marshfield, Mass.
   Boston, 1854. 12° 227.10
THOMPSON, B., *Count Rumford,* Life of, by J.
   Renwick . . . . v.XV. of 529.1
THOMPSON, B. F. History of Long Island. New
   York, 1839. 8° 234.11
THOMPSON, D. P. Gaut Gurley: or, the trappers
   of Umbagog. A tale. Boston, 1857. 12° . 726.9
— Green mountain boys. A tale. Revised ed.
   Boston, 1854. 12° 726.8
— Locke Amsden: or, the schoolmaster. Bos-
   ton, 1856. 12° 726.10
— May Martin, and other tales of the Green
   mountains. New ed. Boston, 1856. 12° . . 726.11
THOMPSON, E. P. The note book of a naturalist.
   London, 1845. 12° 178.6
THOMPSON, G. Prison life and reflections. Hart-
   ford, 1849. 12° 138.2
THOMPSON, H. The occult sciences. Smedley, E. 125.5
THOMPSON, J. P. Photographic views of Egypt.
   Boston, 1854. 12° 698.24
THOMPSON, P. History and antiquities of Boston,
   [England.] Boston, 1856. roy.8° 962.1
THOMPSON, W. Recollections of Mexico. New
   York, 1846. 8° 633.5
THOMPSON, W. T. Maj. Jones' scenes in Georgia.
   Philadelphia, 1848. 12° 726.14
— Polly Peablossom's wedding, and other tales.
   Edited by T. A. Burke. Phila., 1851. 12° . 726.14
THOMPSON, Z. History of Vermont. Burlington,
   1853. 8° 234.7
THOMSON, Mrs. A. T. Memoirs of the court and
   times of King George II. and Queen Caro-
   line. London, 1850. 2v. 8° 554.6
— Memoirs of the Duchess of Marlborough.
   London, 1839. 2v. 8° 594.1
— Memoirs of the Jacobites of 1715 and 1745.
   London, 1845–46. 3v. 8° 562.2
THOMSON, J. Poetical works. Lond., 1847. 2v. 16° 329.13
   Contents. — Vol. I. Memoir by Sir Harris Nicolas;
   Miscellaneous poems; Songs; Prologues, etc.; Bri-
   tannia; Liberty. II. The seasons; Castle of indolence.
— The seasons. London, 1825. 16° 358.13
— - Same. With life by P. Murdoch. New
   York, 1820. 18° 349.26

THOMSON, M. M. Nothing to say. [Poem.] New York, 1857. 12° 344.26
THOMSON, R. Chronicles of London bridge. 2d edition. London, 1839. 16° 379.7
— Illustrations of the history of Great Britain. Edinburgh. 1828. 2v. 18° 830.37
THOMSON, R. D. Cyclopædia of chemistry. London, 1854. 8° 156.7
— School chemistry. London, 1848. 16° 156.31
THOMSON, S. Wanderings among the wild flowers. 3d ed. London, 1855. 12° 169.22
THOMSON, W. History of Philip III. of Spain. Watson, R. . . . . v.II. of 542.2
THONISSEN, J. J. Le socialisme dans le passé. Bruxelles, n.d. 3v. in 1. 12° 1065.57
— Le socialisme et ses promesses. Bruxelles, n.d. 2v. in 1. 12° 1065.56
THORBURN, G. Life and writings, prepared by himself. New York, 1852. 12° 588.11
THOREAU, H. D. Walden: or, life in the woods. Boston, 1854. 16° 428.14–15
— A week on the Concord and Merrimack rivers. Boston, 1849. 12° 623.17
THORNBURY, G. W. Songs of the cavaliers and roundheads, Jacobite ballads, etc. London, 1857. 12° 316.3
THORNE, Dr.: a novel. Trollope, A. 485.1–5
THORNE, J. Rambles by rivers. London, 1844–49. 4v. 18° 850.18
THORNTON, B. The connoisseur. v.XXX.–XXXII.of 850.24
THORNTON, E. British empire in India. London, 1841. 6v. 8° 985.1
THORNTON, J. W. Landing at Cape Anne. Boston, 1854. 8° 223.2
THORNTON, T. C. An inquiry into the history of slavery. Washington, 1841. 12° 127.9
THORNWELL, E. Lady's guide to perfect gentility. New York, 1856. 12° 127.11
THORPE, B. Northern mythology, comprising traditions and superstitions. Lond., 1851–52. 3v. 12° 1087.19
— Yule-tide stories. London, 1853. p.8°. 846.12
THORPE, T. B. Hive of the bee hunter. N. York, 1854. 12° 794.14
— Our army at Monterey. Phila., 1847. 16° . . 259.7
— Our army on the Rio Grande. Phila., 1846. 12° 259.6
THORPE, a quiet English town, and human life therein. Mountford, W. 488.11
THOUAR, P. Letture graduali, ed una scelta di esemplari di buono stile. Firenze, 1855. 3v. 16° 1056.18
— Nuovi racconti. 3a ed. Firenze, 1855. 16°. . 1056.17
— Racconti per fanciulli. 3a ed. Firenze, 1853. 16° 1056.6
— Racconti pei giovanetti. Firenze, 1852. 16° 1055.16
— Racconti popolari. Firenze, 1855. 16° 1059.6
— Una madre, racconto. Firenze, 1847. 16° . . 1058.3
THOUGHT, Growth of, as affecting the progress of society. Withington, W. 124.16
THOUGHT and feeling, Reminiscences of. See Reminiscences, etc. 138.5
THOUGHTS and things, at home and abroad. Burritt, E. 898.3
THOUGHTS, feelings and fancies. Bovee, C. N. . . 877.2
THOUGHTS on missions. Dibble, S. 119.20
THOUSAND and one days; a companion to the Arabian nights. Introduction by Miss Pardoe. Baltimore, 1858. 12° 737.12
THRASHING machines, Essay upon. Fenwick, T. 195.21
THREE beauties, The: a novel. Southworth, E. D. E. N. 456.17
THREE brothers, The. Sherley, Sir A. 687.16
THREE courses and a dessert; illustrated by G. Cruikshank. 5th ed. London, 1852. p.8°. 815.2
THREE eras of New England. Lunt, G. 888.7
THREE gold dollars, The. Abbott, J. . . . v.VII. of 739.1
THREE histories, The, enthusiast, nonchalant, realist. Jewsbury, M. J. 469.1
THREE marriages, The; or, life at a watering place. Hubback, M. 428.9

THREE perils of man: romance. Hogg, J. 769.6
THREE wise men of Gotham. Paulding, J. K. . . 797.11
THREE years in North America. Stuart, J. . . . 639.6
THUCYDIDES. History of the Peloponnesian war. Translated by Rev. H. Dale. London, 1851. 2v. in 1. p.8° 814.2
— Same. Transl. by W. Smith. New ed., cor. and rev. New York, 1852. 2v. 18°. . 830.18
— Analysis and summary of. Wheeler, J. T. . . 855.6
THUGS, Illustrations of the history and practices of the 937.3
THURINGIA. Bechstein, L. Der Sagenschatz und die Sagenkreise des Thüringerlandes. . . . 1025.3
— Bock, A. Die Thüringische Eisenbahn . . . 1029.8
— Stanford, J. F. Rambles and researches in Th Saxony 663.10
THURSTON, L. G., Memoir of. New York, n.d. 16° 119.16
THURSTON, S. R. Overland route to Oregon, etc. Johnson, T. T. 239.8
THYNN, F. Debate between pride and lowliness. Reprinted, with introduction by J. P. Collier. London, 1841. 8° 342.4
TIA fingida; or, the pretended aunt. Cervantes Saavedra, M. de 857.3
TIBULLUS, A. Works, transl. into prose by W. K. Kelly, with a metrical version. Catullus, C. Val. 844.2
TICKNOR, C. Philosophy of living. N.Y., 1846. 18° 810.72
TICKNOR, G. History of Spanish literature. New York, 1849. 3v. 8° 402.1
— Memoir of N. A. Haven 524.15
TICONDEROGA: a romance. James, G. P. R. . . . 463.10
TIECK, L. Schriften. Berlin, 1828–46. 20v. 16° 1018.1

Contents. — Vol. I. Vorbericht; Kaiser Octavianus, ein Lustspiel mit Prolog. II. Leben und Tod der heiligen Genoveva, ein Trauerspiel; Der Abschied, ein Trauerspiel; Leben und Tod des kleinen Rothkäppchens, eine Tragodie. III. Fortunat, ein Mährchen mit Prolog. IV.–V. Phantasus: (IV.) Der blonde Eckbert; Der getreue Eckart; Der Runenberg; Liebeszauber; Liebesgeschichte der schonen Magelone und des Grafen Peter von Provence; Die Elfen; Der Pokal. (V.) Der Blaubart, ein Mährchen; Der gestiefelte Kater, ein Kindermährchen; Die verkehrte Welt, ein historisches Schauspiel; Leben und Thaten des kleinen Thomas, genannt Daumchen, ein Mährchen. VI.–VII. William Lovell, mit Vorbericht. VIII. Abdallah, eine Erzahlung; Die Bruder, eine Erzahlung; Almansor, ein Idyll; Das grüne Band, eine Erzahlung. IX. Arabesken; Denkwürdige Geschichtschronik der Schildbürger; Die sieben Weiber des Blaubart; Leben des berühmten Kaisers Abraham Tonelli, eine Autobiographie; Das jüngste Gericht, eine Vision. X. Prinz Zerbino oder die Reise nach dem guten Geschmack, gewissermassen, eine Fortsetzung des gestiefelten Katers. XI. Vorbericht; Karl von Berneck, Trauerspiel; Das Ungeheuer und der verzauberte Wald, ein musikalisches Mährchen; Alla Moddin, ein Schauspiel. XII. Herr von Fuchs, ein Lustspiel nach dem Volpone des Ben Jonson. Epicoene, oder das stille Frauenzimmer, ein Lustspiel von Ben Jonsen; Die Theegesellschaft, ein Lustspiel. XIII. Mährchen: Die Heymonskinder; Melusine; Dramatische Gedichte: Ein Prolog; Der Autor, ein Fastnachtsspiel; Fragmente: Magelone; Prolog; Aus dem alten Heldengedicht vom Konig Rother; Der erste Akt des Donauweibes. XIV. Erzahlungen und Novellen: Schicksal; Die männliche Mutter; Die Rechtsgelehrten; Die Versohnung; Der Fremde; Die Freunde; Peter Lebrecht, 1 Theil; Der Geheimnissvolle, Novelle. XV. Erzahlungen: Peter Lebrecht, [II. Theil.]; Die beiden merkwürdigsten Tage aus Siegmund's Leben, Ulrich, der Empfindsame; Fermer, der Geniale; Der Naturfreund; Die gelehrte Gesellschaft; Der Psycholog; Der Roman in Briefen; Ein Tagebuch. XVI. Franz Sternbald's Wanderungen, eine altdeutsche Geschichte. XVII. Novellen: Die Gemalde; Die Verlobung; Die Reisenden; Musikalische Leiden und Freuden. XVIII. Novellen: Das Fest zu Kenelworth; Dichterleben, in zwei Theilen. XIX. Novellen; Glück giebt Verstand; Der funfzehnte November; Tod des Dichters. XX. Novellen: Der Jahrmarkt; Der Hexen-Sabbath.

— Popular tales. Carlyle, T. . . . . v.II. of 418.1
Contents. — The fair-haired Eckbert; The trusty Eckhart; The Runenberg; The goblet; The elves.
TIERRA del Fuego, Cruise off. Snow, W. P. . . . 798.9

TIERS état, Formation and prog. of the. Thierry, J. N. A. 1008.17
TIFFANY, O. Brandon, or a hundred years ago. New York, 1858. 16° 415.14
TIFFANY, O. jr. The Canton Chinese, or sojourn in the celestial empire. Boston, 1849. 12° 697.8
TIGRI, G. Canti popolari toscani. Firenze, 1856. 12° 1056.4
TILES, Treatise on the manufacture of. Dobson, E. 819.16
TILLER, B. *Pseud.* Frank Heartwell, or fifty years ago. Omnibus of modern romance . 801.3
TILT, E. J. Health of women at the critical periods. New York, 1851. 18° 158.18
TIMBER. *See* Connaissance des bois 1075.37
— Turnbull, W. Treatise on strength and stiffness of 196.10
See also: Architecture, Bridge, Carpentry, Joinery, etc.
TIMBOO and Fanny. Abbott, J. . . . . v.II. of 739.1
TIMBOO and Joliba. Abbott, J. . . . . v.II. of 739.1
TIMBS, J. Curiosities of history. London, 1857. 16° 949.9
— Popular errors explained and illustrated. New ed. London, 1857. 16° 197.22
— School days of eminent men. Lond., 1858. 16° 589.3
— Things not generally known. 2d ed. London, 1856. 12° 149.28
— Year-book of facts in science and art. [In 1851, extra vol. on the great exhibition.] London, 1839-58. 21v. 16° 159.2
TIMBUCTOO. Adams, R. American sailor in the city of 692.7
— Caillié, R. Travels to 693.10
TIME and tide, or strive and win. Roe, A. S. . . . 726.12
TIME, the avenger: a novel. Marsh, A. 795.4
TIMELY retreat, The, or a year in Bengal before the mutinies. Wallace-Dunlop, M. and R. 695.10
TIMON: a play. Ed. by A. Dyce. London, 1842. 8° 342.10
TIMOTHY, 1st and 2d epistles. *See* Bible.
TISSOT, P. F. Notice sur Béranger. Béranger, P. J. de 1068.9
TITIAN Vecelli, The life of. Northcote, J. 543.3
TITMARSH, Michael Angelo. *See* Thackeray, W. M.
TITUS, Epistle to. *See* Bible.
TIVOLI, A day at, with other verses. Kenyon, J. 346.2
TOCQUEVILLE, A. de. Republic of U. S. A., and its political institutions. Translated by H. Reeves, with preface and notes by J. C. Spencer. New York, 1851. 2v. in 1. 8° . . 134.3
— The old regime and the revolution. Transl. New York, 1856. 12° 1008.11
TODD, H. J. Illustr. of the lives and writings of Gower and Chaucer. London, 1810. 8° . . 312.10
— Life and writings of John Milton. London, 1826. 8° 583.7
— Life of Archbishop Cranmer. London, 1831. 2v. 8° 574.8
TODD, S. H. Occasional poems. Boston, 1851. 16° 338.12
TOLLA: a tale of modern Rome. About, E. . . . 478.13
TOMES, R. Americans in Japan: the expedition under Com. Perry. New York, 1857. 12° . 708.5
— Panama in 1855. New York, 1855. 16° . . . 629.26
TOMLINE, G. Memoirs of the Right Hon. W. Pitt. Philadelphia, 1821. 2v. 8° 563.3
TOMLINSON, C. Pneumatics. London, 1852. 16° 819.10
— Principes de physique générale. Trad. de l' Anglais. Bruxelles, 1850. 12° 1075.31
— Rudimentary mechanics. 3d ed. London, 1854. 16° 819.6
— Study of natural philosophy. Lond., 1851. 16° 819.3
— Same. 3d ed. London, 1853. 16° 819.2
— Treatise on the construction of locks. London, 1853. 16° 829.17
— Treatise on warming and ventilation. London, 1850. 16° 819.40
TONGA islands, Natives and language of. Mariner, W. 830.33
TONNA, Charlotte Elizabeth. Falsehood and truth. Liverpool, 1841. 16° 469.23
— Personal recollections. New York, n.d. 16°. 1100.20

TOOKE, J. H. Diversions of Purley. New ed., by R. Taylor. London, 1840. 8° 402.10
— Exposition of the Diversions of Purley. Richardson, C. 406.14
— Memoirs of. Stephens, A. 583.3
TOOKE, W. Life of Catharine II. of Russia. 3d ed. London, 1799. 3v. 8° 546.2
TÖPFFER, R. Gesammelte Schriften. [Genfer Novellen und Das Pfarrhaus.] Leipzig, 1847-52. 7v. 12° 1036.4
— Inheritance and other sketches. London, 1852. 16° 469.12
TOPOGRAPHIE, Traité élémentaire de. Liagre, J. 1055.36
TORCHLIGHT, The, or through the wood: a novel. Olcott, H. A. 428.11
TOR hill, The: a novel. Smith, H. 797.5
TORREY, J. Memoir of J. Marsh. *See* Marsh, J. 534.4
TOUSSAINT, P. [*Not* L'Ouverture.] Memoir of. Lee, H. F. 539.10-11
TOWNLEY gallery of classic sculpture. Ellis, Sir H. 849.6
TOWNS, Drainage of. Dempsey, G. D. 819.21
TOWNSEND, C. H. Facts in mesmerism. New York, 1843. 12° 125.17
TOWNSEND, G. Summary of Persian history. Hunt, G. H. 938.9
TOWNSEND, W. C. Modern state trials. London, 1850. 2v. 8° 975.6
TOWNSHEND, T. Poems. London, 1796. 12° . . 348.18
TOXICOLOGY, Manual of practical. Christison, R. 158.5
TRACES of the Roman and Moor, through Lombardy and Spain. New York, 1853. 12° . . 675.6-7
TRACTS, Cheap repository. *See* Cheap 1108.13
TRADES. *See* Useful arts.
TRAIL, C. P. The backwoods of Canada. London, n.d. 12° 839.1
— - Same. New ed. London, 1846. 18° . . . 850.17
— Stories of the Canadian forest. New York, 1857. 16° 728.17
TRAILL, T. S. Thermometer and pyrometer. Lib. Us. Kn. . . . . v.II. of 365.14
TRAIN, G. F. American merchant in Europe, Asia and Australia. Introduction by F. Hunt. New York, 1857. 12° 705.18
— Young America in Wall street. New York, 1857. 12° 877.7
TRAITS of travel. Grattan, T. C. 798.1
TRAJAN, Life of. Arnold, T. Later Roman commonwealth. 956.3
TRÄLINNAN: a story. Bremer, F. 817.1-2
TRANSATLANTIC sketches. Kelland, Prof. 629.32
TRANSLATORS, The, of the English version of the Bible, revived. McClure, A. W. 548.10
TRANSYLVANIA. Bowring, J. Language and literature of 316.2
— Paget, J. T. Remarks on the condition of . 667.16
TRAP to catch a sunbeam: a story. Mackarness, M. 476.7-8
TRAVEL. Abbott, J. The Rollo books 659.1-24
— Galton, F. Art of 199.25
— Häring, W. Reise-Pitaval. 1029.10
— Heine, H. Reise-bilder 1037.8
— MacFarlane, C. The romance of 840.38-39
— Taylor, J. B. Cyclopædia of modern 621.1
NOTE. — For travels in various countries, see under their several names. *See also:* Murray, J., Handbooks.
TRAVELLER. Beyle, H. Mémoires d' un touriste. 1067.21
— Kneib, P. H. Narratives of an old 668.5
— Williams, W. Northern and Eastern traveller's guide 639.12
See also: Adventures; Arctic; Antarctic; Discoveries; North West passage; Polar voyages, South seas, etc.
TRAVELLERS, Hand books for. *See* Murray, J.
TRAVELLER'S library. London. 31v. 12°.
Addison, J. Sir Roger de Coverley, from the Spectator 409.1
Brooks, S. Russians of the South; [and] Kemp, L. Indications of instinct; in 1v. . 409.2
De Custine's Russia 409.4
Dumas, A. Memoirs of a maitre d'armes . . 409.5

TRAVELLER'S library, *continued.*

Ferguson, R. Swiss men, etc.; [and] Barrow's Tour on the continent 409.26
Gleig, G. R. Leipsic campaign 409.7
Holcroft, T. Memoirs 409.8
Hope, I. Britanny and the Bible; [and] Britanny and the chase 409.9
Howard, G. F. W., *Earl of Carlisle.* Lectures and addresses; [and] Lord Jeffrey's essays on Swift and Richardson; in 1v. 409.3
Huc, M. Travels through Tartary, Thibet, and China 409.10
Hughes, W. The Australian colonies 409.11
Jameson, A. Sketches in Canada 409.12
Jerrmann, E. Pictures from St. Petersburg. 409.13
Kinglake, W. Eöthen: or, traces of travel brought home from the East 409.6
Laing, S. Notes of a traveller. 409.14
— Residence in Norway during 1834-'35-'36. 409.15
Lannan, C. Adventures in the wilds of N.A. 409.16
Macaulay, T. B. Addison, Walpole and Lord Bacon 409.17
— Byron, Comic dramatists, [and] speeches on parliamentary reform, in 1v. 409.18
— Essays, on Warren Hastings and Lord Clive 409.19
— Essays on Chatham, Ranke's Popes, and Gladstone's Church and state 409.20
McCulloch, J. R. London in 1850 and 1851; [and] La Gironière, P. de. Twenty years in the Philippines 409.21
Our coal and our coal-pits 409.22
Pfeiffer, I. Voyage round the world 409.23
Porter, J. Seaward's narrative abridged . . . 409.24
Smith, S. Selections. v.I 409.25
Turkey, and Ranke's Ferdinand I. and Maximilian II. 409.27
Wagner, F. Schamyl, [and] McCulloch, J. R. Russia and Turkey 409.28
Wellington, Memoir of the Duke of; [and] Cockayne's life of Turenne 409.30
Werne, F. African wanderings. Transl. . . . 409.29
Wilson, G. Electricity and the electric telegraph; [and] Kemp's Nat. hist. of creation. 409.31
TRAVELLERS, Lives of celebrated. St. John, J. A. 810.47
TRAVELLING bachelor: or, notions of the Americans. Cooper, J. F. 780.40-44
TRAVELS of an Irish gentleman in search of a religion. Moore, T. 1089.3
TREBIZOND, Empire of, 1204-1461. Finlay, G. . . 956.5
TREDGOLD, T. Treatises on masonry and joinery. Encyclopædia Britannica 201.4
TRELAWNY, E. J. Recollections of the last days of Shelley and Byron. Boston, 1858. 16°. 585.9-11
TRELAWNEY of Trelawne. A legend of Cornwall. Bray, A. E. 448.9
TREMAINE: a novel. Ward, R. P. 787.2
TREMENHEERE, H. S. Constitution of the United States compared with our own. London, 1854. 12° 299.5
— Notes on public subjects made during a tour in the U. S. and Canada. London, 1852. 12° 297.12
TRENCH, R. C. Calderon; his life and genius, with specimens. New York, 1856. 12° 898.11
— English, past and present. New York, 1855. 12° 403.19
— Hulsean lectures for 1845 and 1846. From 2d London ed. Philadelphia, 1854. 12°. . . . 1106.12

Contents. — Vol. I. Fitness of Holy Scripture for unfolding the spiritual life of men. II. Christ the desire of all nations, or, the unconscious prophecies of heathendom.

— Lessons in proverbs. New York, 1853. 12°. 1105.14
— Notes on the miracles. 2d American edition. New York, 1852. 8° 1093.8
— Notes on the parables. 2d American ed. New York. 1852. 8° 1093.9
— On the authorised version of the New Testament. New York, 1858. 12° 128.6
— Poems. New York, 1856. 12° 324.17

TRENCH, R. C. Sermons preached before the University of Cambridge. New York, 1857. 12° 1106.13
— Study of words. From 2d London edition. New York, 1853. 12° 406.6-7
TRENCK, *Bar.* F. v. der. Life, by himself; transl. by T. Holcroft. 2d ed. London, 1789-92. 4v. 12° 547.18
— - Same. London, n.d. 18° 547.19
TRESCOT, W. H. Diplomacy of the revolution. New York, 1852. 12° 217.16
— Diplomatic history of the administrations of Washington and Adams. Boston, 1857. 12° 297.5
TREVES, Pilgrimage to. Anthon, C. E. 667.12
TREVOR, A. Life and times of William III. London, 1835-36. 2v. 8° 553.1
TRIAL of the British soldiers for the murder of Crispus Attucks and [others.] Bost., 1824. 12° 219.1
TRIALS of Charles I. and of some of the regicides. 2d ed. London, 1838. 16° 309.7
TRIALS. *See* Law.
TRICOLORED sketches in Paris, 1851-53. New York, 1855. 12° 1008.8
TRIFOLIUM, A. Carstens, H. W. 878.5
TRIGONOMETRY. De Morgan, A. Elements of spherical. Library of Useful Knowledge . 365.12
— - T. and double algebra 147.14
— - T. and trigonometrical analysis 147.16
— Hann, J. Plane and spherical 829.23-24
— Hopkins, W. Elements of. Libr. of Us. Kn. 365.12
— Kirkman, T. P. Mnemonical lessons in . . . 829.35
— Peirce, B. Plane and spherical 147.3
TRIMMER, S. Abridgment of New Testament. *See* Bible 120.2
— Fabulous histories. Treatment of animals. 11th edition. London, 1821. 12° 129.4
— Geographical companion to Mrs. T.'s histories. New ed. London, 1816. sm.12° . . . 129.27
— Help to the unlearned in the study of the Scriptures. 4th ed. London, 1818. 2v. 12° 129.6
— History of England, in easy lessons. London, 1820. 2v. 12° 969.5
— Instructive tales. 2d ed. London, 1812. 12° 759.1
— Introduction to the knowledge of nature, and reading the Scriptures. 16th ed. London, 1819. 12° 129.30
— Miscellaneous pieces from the Family Magazine. London, 1818. 12° 888.16
— Outline of ancient history. London, 1820. 12° 129.32
— Outline of Roman history. London, 1821. 12° 129.28
— Prayers and meditations. London, 1819. 12° 129.29
— Questions to Mrs. T.'s histories. London, 1817. 12° 129.31
— Questions to Mrs. T.'s History of England. London, 1817. 12° 129.33
— The economy of charity. Lond., 1801. 2v. 12° 129.7
— Sacred history; selected from the Scriptures. *See* Bible 129.1
— Sermons for family reading. Abridged. 2d edition. London, 1812. 12° 129.5
TRINIDAD, its geography, natural resources, etc. De Verteuil, L. A. A. 635.2
TRINITARIANS. Reasons for not believing the doctrines of. Norton, A. 1086.15
TRINITY, Reply to arguments in support of the doctrine of the. Dana, M. S. B. 1106.8
TRISTIA. Translated by H. T. Riley. Ovidius Naso, P. 824.6
TRISTRAM Shandy, Life and opinions of. Sterne, L. 908.10
TRIUMPHS of time: a novel. Marsh, A. 795.1
TROLLOPE, A. Doctor Thorne: a novel. New York, 1858. 12° 485.1-5
TROLLOPE, F. Laurringtons, The: or, superior people; [a novel.] London, 1844. 3v. 12° 787.7
— Life and adventures of Michael Armstrong, the factory boy: [a novel.] London, 1840. 2v. 8° 787.6
— One fault: a novel. London, 1840. 3v. 12°. 787.8
— The old world and the new: a novel. London, 1849. 3v. 12° 807.4
— Paris and the Parisians in 1835. N.Y., 1836. 8° 657.1-2

TROLLOPE, F. Young love: a novel. London, 1841. 3v. 12°. 807.3
TROPICS, Health trip to the. Willis, N. P. . . . 636.19-28
TROTTER, J. B. Latter years of C. J. Fox. 3d ed. London, 1811. 8°. 555.2
TROWBRIDGE, J. T. Neighbor Jackwood. Boston, 1857. 12°. 795.1-10
TROYES, J. de. Secret history of Louis XI. Commines, P. de 857.4
TRUE, beautiful and good, Lect. on the. Cousin, V. 124.3
TRUE Christian religion. Swedenborg, E. v. . . . 1083.12
TRUE glory of woman. Harbaugh, H. 896.8
TRUE to the last; or, alone on a wide, wide sea. Roe, A. S. 735.14
TRUEBA y Cosio, T. de. Conquest of Peru. Edinburgh, 1830. 18°. 830.62
— Life of Hernan Cortes. Edinburgh, 1829. 18° 830.55
— Romance of history, Spain. 2d ed. London, 1830. 3v. 16°. 449.7
TRUMBULL, H. History of the discovery of America: landing of the Pilgrims, etc. Boston, 1832. 8°. 215.7
TRUMBULL, J. Autobiography, reminiscences and letters, 1756-1841. London, 1841. 8°. . . . 213.6
— Poetical works, containing McFingal, Progress of dulness, etc. Hartford, 1820. 2v. 8° 314.9
TRURAN, W. Iron manufacture of Great Britain. London, 1855. 4°. 191.5
TRUTH. See Intellectual science.
TRYON county, N. Y., Annals of, during the revolution. Campbell, W. W. 217.11
TSCHUDI, J. J. v. Travels in Peru, 1838-42. Transl. by T. Ross. New ed. New York, 1852. 12° 635.12
TU-LI-SHIN. Chinese embassy to the Khan of the Tourgouth Tartars, 1712-15. Transl. by G. T. Staunton. London, 1821. 8°. 694.5
TUBULAR and other iron girder bridges. Dempsey, G. D. 819.30
TUCKER, A. Light of nature pursued. From 2d Lond. ed., with life by H. P. St. J. Mildmay. Cambridge, 1831. 4v. 8°. 1094.4
TUCKER, Miss. Abbeokuta; or, sunrise within the tropics. New York, 1853. 12°. 699.14
TUCKER, G. History of the United States, to end of 26th Cong. in 1841. Phila., 1856-57. 4v. 8° 304.4
TUCKER, J. S. Memoirs of the Earl of St. Vincent. London, 1844. 2v. 8°. 564.5
TUCKER, L. American husbandry. Buel, J. . . . 169.29
TUCKERMAN, H. T. Artist-life; or, sketches of American painters. New York, 1847. 12°. 526.8
— Biographical essays. Boston, 1857. 8°. . . 547.2
— Characteristics of literature. [1st and] 2d ser. Philadelphia, 1849-51. 2v. 12°. 548.5
— Essay on the poetry of Mrs. Browning. See Browning, E. B. 335.11
— Life of Com. Silas Talbot. N. York, 1850. 18° 529.3-4
— Memorial of Horatio Greenough. New York, 1853. 12°. 526.9
— Month in England. 2d ed. N. York, 1854. 12°.646.15-16
— Optimist; a series of essays. N. York, 1852. 12°. 808.9
— Poems. Boston, 1851. 12°. 325.12
— Sicily, a pilgrimage. New York, 1852. 12°. . 678.19
TUDOR, H. Narrative of a tour in North America, 1831-32. London, 1834. 2v. 8°. 638.1
TUDOR, W. Letters on the Eastern states. New York, 1820. 16°. 228.5-6
— Life of James Otis. Boston, 1823. 8°. . . . 513.3
— Miscellanies. Boston, 1821. 12°. 888.15
— Gebel Teir. Boston, 1829. 12°. 799.8-9
TUGGS's at Ramsgate, The. Dickens, C. 462.1
TULLOCH, J. Theism, the witness of reason and nature to a creator. New York, 1855. 12°. 1087.9
TUMULTS, Sketches of popular. See Sketches, etc. 134.16
TUPPER, M. F. Complete works. Authorized ed. Philadelphia, 1851. 4v. 12°. 887.3

Contents. — Vol. I. The crock of gold; The twins, and Heart. II. An author's mind; Essays; Probabilities. III. Ballads for the times, and other poems. IV. Proverbial philosophy; A modern pyramid; and the poems of King Alf. d

TUPPER, M. F. Heart: a social novel. New York, 1845. 12°. 794.8
— The twins: a domestic novel. N. Y., 1845. 12° 794.8
TURENNE, H. de La T. d'A. Vte. de, Life of. Cockayne, T. O. 409.30
TURF characters; the officials and the subalterns: by Martingale. London, 1852. 16°. . . . 177.13
TURKEY and Christendom. Repr. from the Edin. review. London, 1853. 12°. 409.27
TURKEY. Bessé, A. de. History, statistics, and religious condition of the Turkish empire . 689.12
— Clarke, E. D. Travels in . . . . . . v.1.-11. of 689.6
— Dorr, B. Notes of travel in 686.12
— Frontier lands of the Christian and the Turk. 685.2
— Hahn-Hahn, I. Travels in 687.10
— Hervé, F. A residence in 683.8
— Howard, G. W. F. Diary in Turkish and Greek waters 683.12-13
— Lamartine, A. De. History of 918.9
— McCulloch, J. R. Description of 409.28
— McFarlane, C. T. and its destiny 685.6
— Mackintosh, A. F. A military tour in European 687.8
— Madden, R. R. Travels in 687.9
— Marmont, A. F. L. V. de. Present state of the Turkish empire 918.8
— Murray, J. Handbook for 649.14-15
— Noyes, J. O. Roumania, the border land of the Christian and the Turk 686.14
— Oscanyan, C. The sultan and his people . . . 683.13
— Pardoe, J. City of the sultan 689.17
— Porter, Sir J. T., its history and progress . 685.9
— Ranke, L. Slave provinces of, by C. Robert . 827.1
— Sonnini, C. S. Travels in 683.9
— Spencer, E. T., Russia, etc. 687.21-22
— Smith, J. V. C. T. and the Turks 918.12-13
— Stephens, J. L. Incidents of travel in 689.1-2
See also: East, Ottoman empire, and Constantinople.
TURKISH evening entertainments. Ahmed Ibn Hemdem 737.10-11
TURKS. Gilson, A. T. in Europe—their rise and decadence, by F. Bouvet 918.16
— Schimmer, K. A. Sieges of Vienna by the . 889.16
— White, C. Domestic manners of the 687.11
TURNBULL, D. Cuba, with notices of Porto Rico and the slave trade. London, 1840. 8°. . . . 635.3
TURNBULL, L. Electro-magnetic telegraph. 2d ed. Rev. and impr. Philadelphia, 1853. 8° 194.9
TURNBULL, P. E. Austria. London, 1840. 2v. 8° 667.1
TURNBULL, R. Christ in history. Bost., 1854. 12° 1106.18
— Genius of Italy. 3d ed. N. York, 1852. 12°. 676.6
TURNBULL, W. On the strength and stiffness of timber. London, 1833. 8°. 196.10
TURNER, D. W. Notes on Herodotus. 2d ed. London, 1853. p.8°. 855.3
TURNER, E. Elements of chemistry. 2d ed. London, 1828. 8°. 155.5
— Same, with notes by F. Bache. 5th Am. fr. 5th London ed. Philadelphia, 1835. 8° 156.11
— Same. 8th ed., by Baron Liebig and W. Gregory. London, 1847. 2v. 8°. 155.6
TURNER, J. W. Minstrel's gift. Also, Melodies for the flute, and an opera. Bost., 1854. 12° 338.19
TURNER, S. History of the Anglo Saxons to the Norman conquest. 6th ed. London, 1836. 3v. 8°. 965.1
— History of England during the middle ages. 3d ed. London, 1830. 5v. 8°. 935.2
— History of the reign of Henry VIII. 3d ed. London, 1828. 2v. 8°. 965.3
— History of the reigns of Edw. VI., Mary and Elizabeth. 3d ed. London, 1835. 2v. 8°. 965.4
— Sacred hist. of the world. N. Y., n.d. 3v. 18° 810.43
— Same. 8th ed. London, 1848. 3v. 8°. . . 1095.11
TURNER gallery at Marlborough House, 1856-57. Ruskin, J. 206.1
TURNER's companion. Philadelphia, 1851. 12°. . 199.15
TURTON, W. Land and fresh water shells of the British islands. New ed. by J. E. Gray. London, 1840. 12°. 175.9

TUSCANY. Blewitt, O. T. and the Papal states.   649.6
— Pignotti, L. Storia della Toscana 1058.1
TUSCULAN disputations, transl. by Yonge. Cicero,
    M. T. 834.7
TUSKI, Ten months among the tents of the.
    Hooper, W. H. 694.12
TUTHILL, L. C. Success in life: the lawyer.
    New York, 1850. 12° 525.20
— - The merchant. New York, 1850. 12° . .   525.19
— Young lady's home. New Haven, 1839. 12°   137.24
TUTOR's ward, The: a novel. N. York, 1852. 8°   802.14
TUTTLE, J. F. Life of W. Tuttle. 2d ed., abr.
    New York, n.d. 16° 539.25
TWEDDELL, G. Shakspere, his times and contem-
    poraries. London, 1852. 12° 357.10
TWEEDIE, A. Treatise on continued fever. Lon-
    don, 1832. 12° 153.11
TWEEDIE, W. K. Home: a book for the family.
    London, 1857. 16° 898.15
TWELVE stars of our republic. Williams, E. . .   513.13
TWICE-TOLD tales. Hawthorne, N. 457.14
TWILIGHT hours of an artist. Brackett, E. A. . .   348.19
TWIN roses, a narrative. Ritchie, A. C. 475.13
TWINS, The: a tale. Bremer, F. 817.1-2
TWINS, The: a dramatic novel. Tupper, M. F. .   794.8
TWISS, H., Life of [J. Scott,] Lord Chancellor
    Eldon, with corresp. Phila., 1844. 2v. 8°   562.6
Two admirals, The: a novel. Cooper, J. F. . . . 780.35-39
Two baronesses, The: romance. Andersen, H. C.   766.9
Two drovers; a tale. Scott, Sir W. 480.18-21
Two guardians: or home in this world. Yonge,
    C. M. 786.10
Two lives: or, to seem and to be. McIntosh,
    M. J. 437.15-17
Two millions: a poem. Butler, W. A. 344.27
Two sons, The: a tale. Opie, A. . . . . . v.III. of 801.4-6
Two years ago. Kingsley, C. 484.1-8
Two years before the mast. Dana, R. H. jr. . . 820.12-21
TYLER, J. E. Memoirs of Henry V. London,
    1838. 2v. 8° 552.4
TYLER, M. W. A book without a title. Boston,
    1855. 12° 478.10
TYLNEY Hall: a novel. Hood, T. 498.3
TYPEE, a peep at Polynesian life. Melville, H. . 736.1-3
TYPES of mankind. Nott, J. C. 173.1-2
TYROL, The. Inglis, H. D. 663.15
— Murray, J. Handbook of Southern Germany.   649.5
— Sewell, E. M. Summer tour through 659.28
TYRTÆUS. War songs, transl. into prose by J.
    Banks, and into verse by R. Polwhele. See
    Theocritus 834.6
TYTLER, A. F., Lord Woodhouselee. General his-
    tory, ancient and modern, continued by E.
    Nares. Concord, N. H., 1825. 12° 956.13
— Questions for T.'s history. Concord, N. H.,
    1825. 12° 956.13
— Universal history, from the creation to the
    18th century. 3d ed. London, 1839. 6v. 16°   399.8
— and Nares, E. Same, [v. VI.] to the death of
    Geo. III. New York, n.d. 6v. 16° 820.1
TYLER, Ann F. Leila: or the island. N.Y., 1853. 12°   719.1
— Leila in England. New York, 1853. 12° . . .   719.2
— Leila at home. N. Y., 1853. 12° 719.3
TYTLER, P. F. England under Edward VI. and
    Mary. London, 1839. 2v. 8° 974.4
— History of Scotland, 1249-1603. Edinburgh,
    1841-43. 9v. 12° 978.7
— Life of Henry VIII., with biog. sketches of
    his contemporaries. London, 1850. 16° . .   558.4
— Life of T. Craig. Edinburgh, 1823. 16° . . .   589.12
— Life of Sir W. Raleigh. London, 1851. 12°. .   568.8
— Life of the admirable Crichton. 2d ed. Ed-
    inburgh, 1823. 12° 589.8
— Lives of Scottish worthies. London, 1831-38.
    3v. 16° 399.9-10
— Progress of discovery on the Northern coasts
    of America. New York, 1846. 18° 810.53
— - Same, with additions. London, 1853. 12°   627.18

UDE, L. E. The French cook. Philad., 1828. 12°   189.7

UGOLINO della Gherardesca, Il conte. Romanzo
    storico. Rosini, G. 1057.12
UHLAND, J. L. Alte hoch und niederdeutsche
    Volkslieder. Stuttgart, 1844-45. 2v. 8°. .   1016.1
— Gedichte. Wohlfeile Ausg. 4te Aufl. Stutt-
    gart, 1856. 12° 1027.2
— Songs and ballads. Brooks, C. T. 316.6
ULI, der Knecht, ein Volksbuch. Bitzius, A. . . 1034.13
ULYSSES, The adventures of. Lamb, C. 759.9
UNCLE Frank's pleasant pages. Woodworth, F. C.   498.10
UNCLE Horace: a novel. Hall, A. M. 776.15
UNCLE Olliver's travels in Persia. Kitto, J. . . .   689.18
UNCLE Robin in his cabin in Va. Page, J. W. . .   796.12
UNCLE Sam's palace: a novel. Wellmont, E. . .   488.5
UNCLE Tom's cabin. Stowe, H. B. 790.15-17
UNDINE: or the water-spirit. La Motte Fouqué,
    F. H. K. de 416.13-14
UNGER, F. Botanical letters to a friend. Transl.
    by D. B. Paul. London, 1853. 12° 166.14
UNGEWITTER, F. H. Europe, past and present.
    New York, 1850. 12° 947.13
UNION, Me., A hist. of the town of. Sibley, J. L.   227.2
UNITARIANISM. Eliot, W. G. Discourses on the
    unity of God 1086.23
— Ellis, G. E. Half-century of the U. contro-
    versy 113.7
— How I became a Unitarian. 117.6
— Wilson, J. U. principles confirmed by Trini-
    tarian testimonies. 1094.14
    See also: Theology.
UNITED Irishmen. Madden, R. R. 508.1-3
UNITED States. Exercises in small-arms and field
    artillery. [Prepared by H. H. Lockwood.]
    Philadelphia, 1852. 8° 194.8
— Infantry tactics. By Maj. Gen. Scott. New
    ed. New York, 1857. 3v. 18° 199.39
— Narrative of the exploring expedition, 1838
    to 1842. By C. Wilkes. Phila., 1845-51. 5v. 8° 701.6-7
— - Same. London, 1852. 2v. 12° 879.16-18
— Obituary addresses on the death of Daniel
    Webster. Washington, 1853. 8° 512.7
— Obituary addresses on the death of W. R.
    King. Washington, 1854. 8° 523.10
— Abdy, E. S. Residence and tour in the, in
    1833-34 . . . .   629.7
— Agassiz, L. Contributions to the natural his-
    tory of 170.2
— Arfwedson, C. D. U. S. in 1832-34 . . . . .   624.12
— Baird, R. H. Cotton spinner of America . .   199.5
— Bancroft, G. History of 301.1-3
— Bartlett, J. R. Mexican boundary commis'n.   624.2
— Bonner, J. Child's history of the 309.12
— Bowen, A. Naval register of the, for 1815 . .   215.11
— Brissot de Warville, J. P. New travels in the.   625.16
— Chevalier, M. Society, manners and politics
    in the 624.3
— Cobbett, W. A year's residence in. 629.25
— Combe, G. Notes on the, during 1838-40. . .   637.2
— Cooper, J. F. History of the navy of 215.1-7
— Cunynghame, A. Glimpse at the great West-
    ern republic. 629.28
— Curwen, S. Journal and letters, 1775-84 . . .   213.4
— Davis, E. The half-century, 1800-50, Changes
    in the 297.10
— De Roos, F. F. Travels in the 624.14
— Dixon, J. Tour through a part of the 637.8
— Duhring, H. Remarks on the U. S. with re-
    gard to the state of Europe. 297.14
— Duncan, J. M. Travels through part of the,
    1818-19 . . . .   628.24
— Eliot, S. Manual of the history of, 1492-1850.   309.1
— Fergus, H. History of the Western world .   368.10
— Finch, I. Travels in 624.7
— Frost, J. Pictorial history of the 304.5-6
— Godman, J. D. American natural history . .   172.12
— Goodrich, C. A. A history of the 309.9
— Grahame, J. Colonial history of the. 304.3
— Hale, S. History of 820.27
— Hall, J. First settlement of the Western sec-
    tions of.   237.1

UNITED States. Hall, S. R. School history of. . 309.10
— Hamilton, J. C. History of, in the writings of A. Hamilton 304.2
— Hamilton, S. History of the national flag of. 216.7
— Hildreth, R. History of the 303.2–3
— Izard, R. Correspondence, 1774–1804 . . . . . 216.11
— Ker, H. Travels through the Western interior of 626.2
— Lambert, J. Travels through the, in 1806–8 . 625.20
— Lanman, C. Adventures in the wilds of the . 623.3
— Lee, H. Memoirs of the war in the Southern department of the, 1777–1782 . . . . . . 216.2
— Lorain, P. Origine et fondation des États-Unis d'Amérique. 1078.13
— Lossing, B. J. History of the 304.1
—   - Pictorial field-book of the revolution. . 211.1–8
— Lyell, Sir C. Travels in the 628.1
—   - Second visit to the 628.2
— Lyman, T. jr. Diplomacy of the 297.4
— Mackay, A. Travels in the U. S. in 1847–47 . 628.5
— M'Cartney, W. Origin and progress of the . 309.3
— Maxwell, A. M. A run through the, 1840 . . 626.9
— Melish, J. Travels in the 623.7
— Monroe, J. Tour through the N. E. and N. W. of, 1817 . . . . 629.3
— Murray, A. M. Letters from the 639.18
— Murray, H. Discoveries and travels in the . 625.14
— Murray, H. A. Travels in the 627.4
— Phillippo, J. M. U. S. and Cuba. 625.21
— Pulszky, F. A. American society in the. . . 627.3
— Republic of. Duties to itself and relations to other countries 297.19
— Routledge, G. Tourists' guide through the . 629.29
— Russell, J. History of the. 309.5
— Sabine, L. American loyalists. 213.1
— Sanford, E. History, before the revolution. . 305.1
— Schaff, P. Political, social and religious character of the. 1088.10
— Secret proceedings and debates, in Convention for forming the Constitution 299.6
— Shirreff, P. Comprehensive view of the. . . 624.10
— Sketches of history, life and manners in the. 629.20
— Sullivan, W. Public characters and public events, 1783–1815 . . . . 297.9
— Thomas, E. S. Reminiscences of sixty-five years from 1776. . . . . 216.6
— Tocqueville, A. de. The republic of the . . 134.3
— Tremenheere, H. S. Constitution of the, compared with that of Great Britain . . . 299.5
— Tucker, G. History of, to 1841 . . . . 304.4
— Urquhart, D. Boundary differences between U. S. and Great Britain. 297.7
— Van Santvoord, G. Chief justices of the . . 523.4
— Watson, E. Men and times of the revolution. 513.9
— Weld, C. R. Vacation tour in the 629.1
— Whitney, J. D. Metallic wealth of the . . . 163.1
— Williams, E. Messages of the presidents of the, from 1789 to 1849. . . . . 296.4
— Wortley, E. S. Travels in the 628.20–21
    See also: America, American revolution, Constitution of the U. S., War of 1812–15, and the names of the several states, and other divisions of the country, as New England, The West, etc.
UNITED States practical receipt book. Philadelphia, 1844. 12° 188.1
UNITY of worlds. See Astronomy, and Worlds.
UNIVERSAL history. See History.
UNIVERSALISM. Ballou, H. Ancient history of. 1099.12
— Whitman, B. Friendly letters to a Universalist on divine rewards and punishments. 1089.5
    See also: Theology.
UNIVERSE, The, no desert, the earth no monopoly. Boston, 1855. 2v. in 1. 12° 119.6
UNIVERSE. See Cosmography, Stars, Worlds.
UNIVERSITY. Bristed, C. A. Five years in an English University. 884.14
— Hamilton, Sir W. Discussions on U. reform. 872.1
UNIVERSITY of Virginia, The. Jefferson, T. Early history of. 294.2

UNLOVED one, The: a domestic story. Hofland, B. 802.15
UNPROTECTED females in Norway, or the pleasantest way of travelling there. London, 1857. 12° 668.18
UP-COUNTRY letters: edited by Prof. B. New York, 1852. 12° 489.3
UPDIKE, W. Memoirs of the Rhode Island bar. Boston, 1842. 12° 518.1–2
UPHAM, C. W. Life of J. C. Fremont. Boston, 1856. 12° 517.17–18
— Life of Sir Henry Vane . . . . v.III. of 518.5
UPHAM, E. History of the Ottoman empire till 1828. Edinburgh, 1829. 2v. 18° 830.49
UPHAM, T. C. Imperfect and disordered mental action. New York, 1848. 18° 820.7
— Letters written from Europe, Egypt, and Palestine. Brunswick, 1855. 12° 657.5
— Life of Mme. Guyon, with some account of Fénélon. New York, 1851. 2v. 12° 617.15–16
— Mental philosophy; intellect and sensibilities. New York, 1848. 2v. 12° 125.4
UPHOLSTERY. Stokes, J. The upholsterer's companion 199.24
UPTON, R. A. Home studies. Boston, 1856. 12°. 188.28
URE, A. Dictionary of arts, manufactures and mines, [with] supplement. 11th ed. New York, 1851. 8° 146.2
URINARY organs. See Medicine.
URN-BURIAL. Browne, Sir T. . . . . v.III.of 846.11
URQUHART, D. Boundary differences between Great Britain and the U. S. Glasgow, 1840. 8° 297.7
— Pillars of Hercules, or Spain and Morocco in 1848. New York, 1850. 2v. 12° 675.9
— Spirit of the East, travels through Roumeli. Philadelphia, 1839. 2v. 12° 689.11
—   - Same. 2d ed. London, 1839. 2v. 8° . 694.6
URSULA: a tale of country life. Sewell, E. M. . 424.3–7
USCOCS, History of the. Wilkinson, J. G. . . 925.5
USE and abuse of alcoholic liquors. Carpenter, W. B. 157.17
USE of sunshine: a novel. Knowles, R. B. . . 458.6
USEFUL arts. Alcan, M. Manuel du tisserand . 1075.33
— Bigelow, J. U. A. in connexion with the applications of science 198.8
— Book of trades. Circle of the U. A. 199.37
— Burnell, G. R. Well-sinking and boring. . . 819.22
— Complete guide to ornamental leather work . 199.7
— Denison, E. B. Clock and watch making . . 829.4
—   - Clocks and locks 197.7
— Dyer and color maker's companion. 190.13
— Dodd, G. British manufactures. 840.20
— Fontenelle, J. de, and Malepeyre, F. R. Arts of tanning, currying and leather dressing . 194.11
— Fosbroke J. D. Arts, manufactures, etc. of the Greeks and Romans 378.3
— Guillery, H. Technologie 1065.19
— Hazen, E. Popular technology, or professions and trades 820.50
— Howell, M. J. Hand-book of millinery . . . 199.2
—   - Hand-book of dress making 199.1
— Hughes, S. Manufacture of coal gas 829.15
— Knapp, F. Chemistry applied to the arts, etc. 144.3–4
— Manual of the arts, for the young 197.19
— Manuel du serrurier 1075.38
— Marble worker's manual 199.10
— Minister, E. and son. Guide to practical cutting. 194.2
— Overman, F. The moulder's and founder's guide 199.6
— Painter, gilder, and varnisher's companion . 190.11
— Perkins, E. E. Haberdashery and hosiery . 199.38
— Porter, G. R. Manufacture of porcelain and glass 408.11
—   - Manufacture of silk 408.9
— Ronalds, E. Chemistry applied to the arts and manufactures. 155.20
— Stokes, J. Cabinet maker and upholsterer's companion 199.24
— Templeton, W. Operative mechanic's workshop companion 199.36

USEFUL arts. Tomlinson, C. Construction of
locks. 829.17
— Wiggins, J. Embanking lands from the sea. 829.13
See also: Agriculture, Chemistry, Domestic Economy, Food, Glass, Manufactures,
Mill-wright, Photography, and the names
of numerous trades.
USES and abuses of air. Griscom, J. H. 207.14
UTAH. Carvalho, S. N. Incidents of travel in U. 626.11
See Mormons.
UTOPIA, or the happy republic. More, Sir T. . . 759.5

VACATION rambles and thoughts. Talfourd, T. N. 667.13
VACHERO, Il. Storia Genovese del XVIIa secolo.
Modona-Olivetti, N. 1059.10
VAGABOND life in Mexico. Ferry, G. 638.3
VAGABUNDEN, Die. Roman. Holtei, K. v. . . . 1035.8
VALDENSES. *See* Waldenses.
VALE of cedars ; or, the martyr, a novel. Aguilar, G. 764.16–22
VALENTINE, D. T. History of the city of New
York. New York, 1853. 8° 236.11
VALENTINE'S eve. Opie, A. . . . . v.II. of 801.4–6
VALERIUS. A Roman story. Lockhart, J. G. . . 489.4
VALERY, A. L. P. Curiosités et anecdotes italiennes. Paris, 1842. 8° 1065.2
VALLEY, The, of the Shenandoah. New York,
1824. 2v. 12° 799.1
VALPARAISO. Gerstäcker, F. Travels 636.1
VALVASSORI Bresciani, Racconto. Ercoliani, L. 1058.9
VANBRUGH, Sir J. Plays. London, 1776. 2v. 12° 356.19

Contents. — Vol. I. Account of the life and writings
of the author; The relapse ; The provoked wife ;
Æsop; The false friend. II. The confederacy; The
mistake; The country-house; A journey to London;
The provoked husband.

VAN BUREN, M. Life and political opinions of.
Holland, W. M. 517.20
VAN CAMPEN, M. Life and times of. Hubbard,
J. N. 528.4
VANCENZA ; or the dangers of credulity. Robinson, M. 429.10
VANDEN HEUVEL, *Mrs.* Mythological fables.
Transl. by Dryden, Pope, [etc.] New
York, 1837. 12° 345.8
VANDERKISTE, R. W. Mission among the dens of
London. London, 1854. 16° 127.25
VANDERVIN, J. E. Histoire du comté de Hainaut. *See* Reiffenberg, F. A. F. T. . . v.III.of 1075.19
VAN DE VELDE, C. W. M. Narrative of a journey
through Syria and Palestine, 1851-52. London, 1854. 2v. 8° 694.13
VANE, Sir H., Life of, by C. W. Upham . . v.III. of 518.5
VANE-STEWART, C. W. *Marq. of Londonderry.*
Narrative of the war in Germany and France
in 1813 and 1814. Philadelphia, 1831. 12° . . 1009.3
— Story of the Peninsular war. New ed., with
additions. New York, 1848. 12° 1009.5
VANITY fair. A novel without a hero. Thackeray, W. M. 491.7–10
VAN SANTVOORD, G. Lives and services of the
chief justices of the U. S. N. York, 1854. 8° 523.4
VAN SCHAACK, H. C. Life of Peter Van Schaack,
embracing selections from his correspondence. New York, 1842. 8° 513.4
VAN TRUSEDALE, Pheleg. *Pseud.* Life and adventures of Major Potter. 427.1
VARESE, — Sibilla Odaleta. [Romanzo istor.]
Firenze, 1831-32. 3v. in 1. 18° 1059.2
VARNHAGEN von Ense, K. A. Biographische
Denkmale. 2te Aufl. Berlin, 1846. 5v. 12° 1026.3

Contents. — Vol. I. Graf Wilhelm zur Lippe; Graf
Matthias von der Schulenburg; König Theodor von
Corsica. II. Freiherr Georg von Derfflinger; Fürst
Leopold von Anhalt-Dessau. III. Fürst Blücher von
Wahlstadt. IV. Paul Flemming; Freiherr Friedrich
von Canitz ; Johann von Besser. V. Graf Ludwig
von Zinzendorf.

— Rahel. Ein Buch des Andenkens für ihre
Freunde. Berlin, 1834. 3v. 8° 1014.1
VARIETIES, A volume of. Knight, C. 810.27

VARLEY, D. Treatise on mineralogy. Parts I.-II.
London, 1849. 16° 819.5
VARNISHER'S companion. *See* Painter 199.11
VASARI, G. Lives of eminent painters, sculptors,
and architects. London, 1850-52. 5v. p.8° 848.6
VASCONSELOS, a romance of the new world.
Simms, W. G. 800.28
VASSALL Morton. [A novel.] Parkman, F. . . . 795.15–17
VATHEK ; an Arabian tale. Beckford, W. 799.14
VAUGHAN, R. Life and opinions of John de Wycliffe. London, 1828. 2v. 8° 575.3
— History of England, 1603-88. London, 1840.
8° 365.16
— History of England under the house of Stuart. London, 1840. 2v. 8° 965.5
VAUX, C. Villas and cottages for the U. S. New
York, 1857. 8° 203.15
VAUX, W. S. W. Nineveh and Persepolis. 3d ed.
London, 1851. 8° 955.14
VEGETABLE physiology, An introduction to. *See*
Introduction . . . . v.III. of 850.25
VEGETABLE substances. Materials of manufactures. London, n.d. 12° 849.9
— Description and history of. *See* Description. 849.7
— used for the food of man. Lankester, E. . . 840.32
VEGETABLE world, Poetry of the. Schleiden, M.
J. . . . . v.II. 166.9–10
VEGETABLES, Lessons on. Marcet, J. 178.36
See also: Botany.
VEHSE, K. E. Memoirs of the court, aristocracy,
and diplomacy of Austria. London, 1856.
2v. 8° 927.10
— Memoirs of the court of Prussia. Transl. by
F. C. F. Demmler. London, 1854. 8° . . . 546.7
VELAZQUEZ, D. R. de Silva y. Velazquez and his
works. Stirling, W. 899.20
VELDE, C. F. Van der. Christina and her court, a
tale. New York, 1845. 8° 801.1
— Tales from the German. Transl. by N. Greene,
Boston, 1837. 2v. 12° 799.7

Contents. — Vol. I. Arwed Gyllenstierna. II. The
Lichtensteins; The sorceress; The anabaptist.

VELLEIUS Paterculus, C. Transl. by J. S. Watson. Sallustius Crispus, C. 834.4
VELVET cushion, The, [a tale.] Cunningham, J.
W. 429.13
VENEREAL diseases. *See* Medicine.
VENICE. Flagg, E. V. from 1797 to 1849. . . . . 678.7–8
— Hazlitt, W. C. Origin and rise of the republic of 915.2
— Smedley, E. Sketches from Venetian history. 399.4
VENN, H. Complete duty of man. New ed. New
York, n.d. 12° 1107.15
VENTILATION. Bernan, W. History and art of. 207.15
— Eckstein, G. F. Remarks on 207.12
— Griscom, J. H. Uses and abuses of air . . . 207.14
— Hood, C. Treatise on 207.3
— Reid, D. B. V. in American dwellings . . . 207.1–2
— Tomlinson, C. V. of houses, mines, ships, etc. 819.40
— Wyman, M. Treatise on 207.5
VERDEREVSKY, — . Captivity of two Russian
princesses in the Caucasus. Transl. by H.
S. Edwards. London, 1857. 12° 687.1
VÉRICOUR, L. R. de. Modern French literature,
revised, with notes by W. S. Chase. Boston, 1848. 12° 404.12
— The life and times of Dante. London, 1858. 12° 544.9
VÉRITÉS, Une poignée de. Mélanges philosophiques. Karr, J. B. A. 1067.15
VERMONT. Carpenter, W. H. History of 228.13
— Hayward, J. Gazetteer of 229.3
— Thompson, Z. History of, natural, civil, and
statistical 234.7
VERNON: or, conversations about old times in
England. Abbott, J. . . . . v.IX of 739.1
VERPLANCK, G. C. On the objects, etc. of science.
Brougham, H. 820.72
VERRI, A. Roman nights : or, the tomb of the
Scipios. New York, 1825. 2v. 12° 809.12
— - Same. With notes by H. W. Hilliard.
Philadelphia, 1850. 12° 809.11

VERSIFICATION. Boscaven, H. Manuel de . . . 1065.6
— Everett, Erastus. System of English 406.4
VERTEBRATE animals. See Anatomy, Comparative.
VESPERS of Palermo. A poem. Hemans, F. D. . 324.2
VESPRO siciliano. Amari, M. La guerra del . . . 1046.7
VESPUCIUS, A. Lester, C. E. Life and voyages of. 544.1
— Life of. See Lives, etc. 547.21
— Santarem, E. F. de B. y S. Researches re-
specting 259.10–11
VESTAL, The ; or, a tale of Pompeii. Gray, T. . . 429.6
VESTIGES of the natural history of creation. [At-
tributed to R. Chambers.] 10th ed., with ad-
ditions. London, 1853. 8° 1087.1
— - Same. With a sequel. N. Y., n.d. 16° . 149.36
— - Explanations: a sequel. 2d ed. London,
1816. 12° 1087.2
VETERINARY surgery. Clater, F. Every man his
own farrier 197.17
— Miles, W. The horse's foot, etc. 165.18
— Youatt, W. Structure and diseases of the
horse 165.16
See also: Rural and domestic economy.
VEVA: or, the war of the peasants: a tale. Con-
science, H. 488.18
VICAR of Wakefield: a tale. Goldsmith, O. . . . 759.2–4
VICARS, H. S. J., Memorials of. N. Y., 1856. 18° 578.3
VICARS, J. England's worthies. London, 1845. 12° 588.13
VICTORIA: or, the world overcome. Chesebro',
C. 775.11
VICTORIA. Howitt, W. Two years in 705.17–19
— Wathen, G. H. V. in 1854 . . . . 707.15
— Westgarth, W. V. and the Australian gold
mines 705.8
VIDAL, A. Treatise on venereal diseases, trans-
lated and edited by G. C. Blackman. New
York, 1854. 8° 152.5
VIDOCQ, E. F. Memoirs, by himself. Philadel-
phia, 1834. 8°. 613.5
VIELÉ, E. L. "Following the drum." New York,
1858. 12°. 626.4
VIENNA. Adair, Sir R. Mission to the court of. 667.3
— Kühne, F. G. Wien in alter u. neuer Zeit . . 1029.4
— Schimmer, K. A. Sieges of V. by the Turks. 889.16
— Sutton, H. M. V. at the end of the 17th
century 975.11
VIER Brüder aus dem Volke. Roman. Rank, J. 1035.10
VIEUSSEUX, A. History of Switzerland. Lon-
don, 1840. 8° 365.9
— Napoleon Bonaparte, — his sayings and his
deeds. London, 1846. 2v. 18° 850.20
VIEWS a-foot. Taylor, J. B. 657.15–19
VIGIL, The, of faith: a poem. Hoffman, C. F. . . 358.4
VIGIL of Venus. Catullus, C. V. 844.2
VIGNY, A. V. de. Cinq Mars. 11e éd. La vérité
dans l'art ; discours de réception à l'Acad-
émie. Paris, 1855. 12° 1067.12
VILLAGE. Howitt, M. The V. on the heath: a
tale 409.11
— La Fontaine, A. V. pastor and his children :
a novel 799.13
VILLAS and cottages, Designs for. Vaux, C. . . . 203.15
VILLEMAIN, A. F. Essai sur l' oraison funèbre.
See Bossuet, J. B. 1066.5
VILLENEUVE, G. S. B. de. La belle et la bête.
v.XXVI. of 1077.1
VILLETTE: a novel. Brontë, C. 435.9–10
VINCI, L. da, Life and works of. Brown, J. W. . . 543.9
VINET, A. R. Pastoral theology ; translated and
ed. by T. H. Skinner. N. Y., 1853. 12° . . 1088.17
— Jaqueline Pascal: a glimpse at Port Royal.
Cousin, V. 545.8
VIOLIN, Some account of the. Dubourg, G. . . . 209.2
VIOLET : or, the cross and the crown. McIntosh,
M. J. 437.11–13
VIRGILIUS Maro, P. Works. Translated by David-
son. New ed. London, 1850. p.8°. 814.10
— The eclogues, georgics, and the Æneid. New
York, 1852. 2v. 18°. 830.13
VIRGINIA. Howe, H. Historical collections of. 235.2
— Howison, R. R. History of 236.2

VIRGINIA. Jefferson, T. Notes on the state of . 239.15
— Meade, W. Old churches, ministers, and fami-
lies of 236.1
— Pritts, J. Early history of. 245.2
VIRGINIA, Historical and philosophical society of.
Discoveries in the West until 1519, and
voyages to N. A., 1520–73. Richmond, 1848. 8° 625.1
VIRGINIA, Early history of the University of.
Jefferson, T. 294.2
VIRGINIA: or, light on a dark saying. Abbott, J.v.II.of739.1
VISION of Columbus: a poem. Barlow, J. 314.1
VISION of Sir Launfal: a poem. Lowell, J. R. . . 346.17
VISITS to remarkable places. Howitt, W. 896.3
VITAL force, Electricity, heat, light, etc., in their
relations to the. Reichenbach, K. v. 145.9
See also: Animal magnetism, Mesmerism, etc.
VITTORIA Colonna. Deumier, J. Le F. 1078.47
VOCABULARY of philosophy. Fleming, W. . . . 125.30
VOICE. Rush, J. Philosophy of the human . . . 405.1
See also : Elocution.
VOICE, A, from the parsonage. Park, H. G. . . . 417.8
VOICE, A, to America: or, the model republic, its
glory or its fall. New York, 1855. 12°. . . 297.13
VOICES from the rocks : a reply to Hugh Miller's
testimony of the rocks. London, 1857. 12°. 109.19
VOICES of the day. Cumming, J. 116.12
VOICES of the dead. Cumming, J. 116.13
VOICES of the night. Cumming, J. 116.14
VOICES of the night. Longfellow, H. W. 343.6
VOLCANOS. Daubeny, C. Active and extinct . . 163.14
— Wittich, W. V. and earthquakes. . . . .v.II. of 850.21
See also : Geology.
VOLKSLIEDER, Alte hoch und niederdeutsche.
Uhland, J. L. 1016.1
VOLNEY, C. F. C. de. Les ruines; et la loi naturelle.
10e éd. Paris, 1822. 8° 1075.41
VOLTAIRE, F. M. A. de. La Henriade, poème [sui-
vie d' opuscules.] Paris, 1853. 12°. 1076.18
Contents—(Opuscules.) Essai sur les guerres civiles;
Essai sur les poetes; Poeme de Fontenoy; Discours
sur l'homme; Poëmes sur la loi naturelle et sur le
desastre de Lisbonne; Temple du gout, et temple de
l'amitié.
— Siècle de Louis XIV. Paris, 1854. 12° 1076.19
— Age of Louis XIV. Translated, with notes,
by R. Griffith. London, 1779–81. 3v. 8° . . 1005.7
— Théatre. Paris, 1853. 12° 1076.17
Contents. — Œdipe ; Brutus; Zaire ; La mort de
César; Alzire ; Le Fanatisme; Mérope; Sémiramis;
Rome sauvée; L'Orphelin de la Chine; Tancrede.
— Memoirs by himself, with life by Condorcet.
See Condorcet, M. J. A. N. de 609.4
VOLUPTÉ, conte. Sainte Beuve, C. A. 1076.20
VOSE, G. L. Handbook of railroad construction.
Boston, 1857. 8° 195.11
VOYAGES. Saint Génois, J. de. Les voyageurs
belges, au XIII.–XIX. siècle 1075.10
VOYAGES round the world. Belcher, Sir E. Nar-
rative of, 1836–42 . . . . 702.9
— Campbell, A. Voyage from 1806 to 1812 . . . 709.9
— Cook, J. Voyages, 1768–79 . . . . 820.66
— Darwin, C. Voyage of the Beagle 889.12
— Defoe, D. New voyage 709.2
— Delano, A. Three voyages 704.1–2
— Pfeiffer, I. A woman's 879.4
— - A lady's second 708.10
— Reynolds, J. N. Voyage of the Potomac . . 701.8
— Taylor, F. W. The flag-ship 708.8
— Wilkes, C. Exploring expedition 701.6–7
See South seas, Pacific, etc.
VULGAR errors. Browne, Sir T. . . . . . . .v.I. of 846.11
— An exposition of. See Exposition. . . .v.II. of 850.25
VULLIET, M. The geography of nature, transl.
by a lady. Boston, 1856. 12° 167.13

WADDINGTON, G. History of the church to the
reformation. London, 1831–33. 2v. 8° . . 365.13
WADE, J. England's greatness, its rise and progress in government, [etc.] Lond., 1856. 12° 987.9
WAGES, Essay on the rate of. Carey, H. C. . . . 136.7

WAGNER, F., and Bodenstedt, F. Schamyl, the sultan, warrior, and prophet of the Caucasus. London, 1854. 12° 409.28

WAGSTAFF, W. R. History of the Society of Friends. Part I., [in Europe.] N.Y., 1845. 8° 1085.11

WAIF, The : a collection of poems. Longfellow, H. W 333.14

WAINWRIGHT, J. M. Memorial volume. Thirty-four sermons ; Address by E. Y. Higbee ; Memoir by G. W. Doane. N. Y., 1856. 8° 1083.13

WAKEFIELD, E. G. England and America : social and political state of both. N. Y., 1834. 8°. 645.1

WALCKENAER, C. A., Baron de. Mémoires touchant la vie et les écrits de Mme. la Marquise de Sévigné. Paris, 1845–52. 5v. 12° 1037.31

— Sur la vie de La Fontaine. See La Fontaine . 1066.11

WALDAU, Max. Pseud. See Hauenschild, R. G. S. v.

WALDEN : or, life in the woods. Thoreau, H. D. 428.14–15

WALDENSES, Authentic details of the 1096.1

— Baird, R. Present state of the 1096.13

— Muston, A. Israel of the Alps 879.13

See also : Albigenses.

WALDMEISTERS Brautfahrt, Märchen. Roquette, O. 1039.3

WALDO, S. P. Life and character of S. Decatur, with notices of the Am. navy. Hartf.,1821. 12° 527.6

— Memoir of Andrew Jackson. Hartf., 1818. 12° 517.2

WALES and other poems. James, M. 358.1

WALKER, Alexander, of Eng. Beauty in woman. Ed. by an Am. physician. N. Y., 1843. 12° 138.4

— Pathology, founded on the natural system of anatomy and physiology. N. York, 1842. 12° 158.2

WALKER, Alexander. Jackson and New Orleans. N. Y., 1856. 12° 215.15

WALKER, C. V. Electrotype manipulations. From 13th London ed. Phila., 1844. [Vol. I.] 12° 199.33

— Manual of electricity, magnetism, and meteorology. Lardner, D. . . . . . v.II. of 398.14

WALKER, D. British manly exercises. Philadelphia, 1837. 16° 198.31

— Same, revised by "Craven," [Capt. Carleton.] 10th ed. London, 1857. p.8° . . . 835.5

— Same. From 9th Lond. ed. Phila.,1856. 12° 197.24

WALKER, G. Art of chess play. 4th ed. London, 1846. 12° 197.26

— The chess player, with additions by W. S. Kenny. Boston, 1841. 12° 197.28

WALKER, John. Elements of elocution. 3d ed. London, 1806. 8° 405.4

WALKER, Jonathan. Trial and imprisonment, with a sketch of his life. Boston, 1845. 12° 526.13

WALKER, J. B. God revealed in the creation, and by Christ. Boston, 1855. 12° 1086.7

— Philosophy of the plan of salvation. Introductory essay by C. E. Stowe. New ed. Boston, 1855. 12° 1086.21

— Philosophy of skepticism and ultraism. [In ans. to Theo. Parker.] N. Y., 1857. 12° . . 1094.13

WALKER, W. S. Corpus poetarum latinorum. Londini, 1835. 8° 353.1

Index auctorum : Catullus ; Lucretius ; Virgilius ; Tibullus ; Propertius ; Ovidius ; Horatius ; Phædrus ; Lucanus ; Persius ; Juvenalis ; Martialis ; Sulpicia ; Statius ; Silius Italicus ; Valerius Flaccus ; Calpurnius Siculus ; Ausonius ; Claudianus ; Supplementum in Virgilium.

WALKER, W. Expedition to Nicaragua, with a memoir of Gen. W. Wells, W. V. 266.8

WALKS and talks of an American farmer in England. Olmsted, F. L. 646.10–11

WALKS and wanderings in the world of literature. Grant, J. 898.19

WALLACE : a Franconia story. Abbott, J. 738.4

WALLACE, Sir W., of Elderslie, Life of. Carrick, J. D. 830.58

WALLACE, H. B. Art and scenery in Europe, [with other papers.] Phila., 1857. 12° . . . 208.3

WALLACE-DUNLOP, M. and R. The timely retreat ; or, a year in Bengal before the mutinies. London, 1858. 2v. 12° 695.10

WALLACE, Prof. History of British India. Murray, H. 810.51

WALLACE, W. and Bell, R. Continuation of the history of England. Mackintosh, Sir J. . . 368.3

WALLENSTEIN, The death of : a drama, transl. from Schiller by Coleridge, S. T. . . v.III. of 327.10

— Schiller, F. C. J. v. W.'s camp : a historical drama 818.10

— Willkomm, E. W. historicher Roman. . . . 1037.12

WALLER, E. Poetical works, with life. Bell's 2d ed. Edinburgh, 1784. 2v. in 1. 18° 369.23

Contents.—Vol. I. Miscellanies. II. Epistles ; Songs ; Epigrams ; Epitaphs ; Fragments ; Divine poems, etc.

WALLIS, S. T. Spain, her institutions, politics, and public men. Boston, 1853. 12° 675.16–17

WALLYS, P. About New York. N. York, 1857. 12° 629.17

WALPOLE, H. Castle of Otranto, with memoir of the author. London, 1840. 12° 758.1

— Historic doubts on the life of Richard III. Dublin, 1768. 12°. 989.10

— Letters. Ed. by Peter Cunningham. London, 1845. 8v. 8° 572.3

— Macaulay, T. B. Review of letters of H. W. to Sir H. Mann 409.17

— Warburton, E. Memoirs of 572.2

WALSH, J. H. Domestic medicine and surgery. London, 1858. 16° 157.32

WALSH, R. Notices of Brazil in 1828–29. 2v in 1. Boston, 1831. 12°. 266.6

WALSINGHAM, or the pupil of nature : a domestic story. Robinson, M. 429.3

WALT and Vult : or, the twins. Richter, J. P. F. 808.8

WALTHAM, Mass. History and family memorials of. Bond, H. 224.1

WALTHAM : a novel. London, 1853. 16° 798.11

WALTON, I. Account of the life and death of R. Hooker. Hooker, R. . . . . v.I. of 1103.4

— Lives of Donne, Wotton, Hooker, Herbert, and Sanderson, with account of the author by T. Zouch. New edition, with notice. New York, 1846. 12° 589.5

— and Cotton, C. The complete angler, with notes and lives. London, 1842. 12° 177.2

— Same, with preface, notes, and appendix by the Am. ed., [G. W. Bethune.] Parts I. and II. New York, 1852. 12° 177.3

— Same. New ed. by "Ephemera." London, 1853. 12° 879.19

— Same. Ed. by E. Jesse. Papers on fishing tackle, etc., by H. G. Bohn. London, 1856. p.8° 835.8

WALTON, W. Revolutions of Spain, from 1808 to 1836. London, 1837. 2v. 8° 913.4

WANDERER. D'Arblay, F. B. The W.: or, female difficulties. A novel 499.1

— Meyern, W. F. v. Die Wanderer, oder : Dya-Na-Sore 1037.15

WANDERING Jew, The. Chronicles from Cartaphilus. Hoffman, D. 901.5

WAR of 1812–15. Armstrong, J. Notices of . . . 217.4

— Bowen, A. Naval monument 215.11

— Brackenridge, H. M. The war between the United States and Great Britain 217.5

— Dwight, T. Policy of the U. S. which led to. 305.4

— Coggeshall, G. Hist. of Am. privateers, etc. 215.8

— Gilleland, J. C. History of 219.6

— Headley, J. T. Second war with England . . 217.2–3

— Hull, Gen. W. Defence before a court martial. 217.15

— Ingersoll, C. J. Sketches of 215.9

— O'Connor, T. Impartial history of. 217.6

— Russell, J. jr. History of 215.12

— Williams, J. S. Invasion and capture of Washington 217.1

WAR, The [Crimean] : or, voices from the ranks. London, 1855. 16° 989.3

— or, the Eastern question investigated. Macqueen, J. 986.7

See Crimea, Russia, Turkey, etc.

WAR, Memorials of the late, 1806–15. See Memorials, etc. 830.42

WAR; its accordance with the principles of Christianity. Dymond, J. 127.2
WAR. *See* Military art and science; Moral philosophy, etc.
WARAGA: or, charms of the Nile. Furniss, W. . 698.19
WARBURTON, E. Conquest of Canada. New York, 1850. 2v. 12° 265.3
— Crescent and the cross. New ed. New York, 1850. 2v. in 1. 12° 689.7
— Hochelaga: or, England in the new world. New York, 1846. 12° 627.19-20
— Memoirs of H. Walpole and his contemporaries. London, 1851. 2v. 8° 572.2
— Memoirs of Prince Rupert, and the cavaliers. London, 1849. 3v. 8° 553.6
WARD, A. H. History of Shrewsbury, Mass. Boston, 1847. 8° 224.19
WARD, F. de W. India and the Hindoos. New York, 1851. 12° 709.6
WARD, H. The Cape and the Kaffirs. 3d edition. London, 1851. 12° 699.15
WARD, H. G. Mexico in 1827. Lond., 1828. 2v. 8° 634.6
WARD, Rev. John. Diary, 1648 to 1679. London, 1839. 8° 977.2
WARD, James. Flax: its cultivation and preparation . . . . v.IV. of 169.15
WARD, R. P. Chatsworth: or, the romance of a week. New York, 1844. 8° 787.1
— De Vere: or, the man of independence. London, 1827. 4v. 12° 787.4
— - Same. New York, 1831. 2v. 12° 787.5
— Pictures of the world. London, 1839. 3v. 12° 787.3
— Tremaine. [Novel.] London, 1833. 3v. 12° 787.2
WARD, S. Life of, by W. Gammell . . . . v.XIX. of 529.1
WARDEN, W. Letters written on board the Northumberland and at St. Helena, [respecting] Napoleon Buonaparte. Phila., 1817. 12°. . 1009.9
WARDER, J. A. Hedges and evergreens. New York, 1858. 12° 166.15
WARE, H. Inquiry into the evidences of religion. Cambridge, 1842. 2v. 12° 118.12
WARE, H. jr. Works. Boston, 1846-47. 4v. 12° 117.4

Contents. — Vols. I.–II. Miscellaneous writings. I. Recollections of J. Anderson; How to spend holy time; Poetry of mathematics; Village funeral; Sabbath with my friend; How to spend a day; Robert Fowle; Poetry. II. Life and character of Rev. J. E. Abbott; Memoir of N. Parker, D. D.; Biographical notice of Rev. T. Prentiss, a sermon; State of the times; To the Unitarian community; Address before York Co. Unitarian Association; Duties of the pulpit and pastoral office; Duties of young men; Faith once delivered to the saints; Questions relating to the Christian name, etc., answered; Essays on personal religion; Letters on the genuineness of 1 John v. 7; Letter to Nehemiah Adams; Hints on extemporaneous preaching. III.–IV. Sermons. [IV.] Formation of the Christian character; Progress of the Christian life.

— Formation of the Christian character. Cambridge, 1831. 18° 1089.31
WARE, J. Life of Henry Ware, jr. Boston, 1846. 2v. 12° 535.7
— - Same. New edition. Boston, 1849. 12° . 535.6
WARE, M. L., Memoir of. Hall, E. B. 535.3-5
WARE, W. Aurelian: or, Rome in the 3d century. New York, 1849. 2v. 12° 808.10
— Julian: or, scenes in Judea. 2d edition. New York, 1856. 2v. in 1. 12° 808.12
— Life of N. Bacon . . . . v.XIII. of 529.1
— Probus: or, Rome in the 3d century. New York, 1838. 2v. 12° 808.11
— Sketches of European capitals. Bost., 1851. 12° 648.4-5
— Works and genius of W. Allston. Boston, 1852. 12° 208.11
— Zenobia: or, the fall of Palmyra. 8th edition. New York, 1850. 2v. 12° 808.9
WARLEIGH. [A novel.] Bray, A. E. 448.12
WARMING. Bernan, W. History and art of . . . 207.15
— Hood, C. W. by hot water. 207.3
— Reid, D. B. Remarks on 207.2
Tomlinson, C. Rudimentary treatise on . . . 819.40
See also Heat.

WARNER, A. B. Dollars and cents: by Amy Lothrop. New York, 1852. 2v. 12° . . . 793.11-13
— My brother's keeper. New York, 1855. 12°. 794.7
WARNER, H. W. Liberties of America. New York, 1853. 12°. 207.15
— Preface, notes, and appendix to autobiography of C. Caldwell. *See* Caldwell, C. . . . 524.6
WARNER, J. F. Dictionary of musical terms. Boston, 1841. 8° 204.4
WARNER, Col. Seth, Memoir of. Chipman, D. . . 528.22
WARNER, Susan. Hills of the Shatemuc. New York, 1856. 12°. 794.1-6
— Queechy. New York, 1852. 2v. 12° 793.7-10
— - Same. New York, 1856. 2v. in 1. 12°. . 793.5-6
— Wide, wide world. 16th ed. N.Y., 1852. 2v. 12° 793.1
— - Same. New ed. New York, 1856. 12°. . 793.2-4
WARREN, J. C. Etherization. Boston, 1848. 12° 157.22
— Mastodon giganteus of North America. Boston, 1852. 4° 170.1
— Preservation of health. Boston, 1854. 16°. . 158.19
WARREN, John E. Para: or, the banks of the Amazon. New York, 1851. 12° 636.30-31
WARREN, Gen. J., Life of, by A. H. Everett. Sparks, J. . . . . v.II. of 518.5
WARREN, M. History of the American revolution. Boston, 1805. 3v. 8° 214.10
WARREN, S. Moral and professional duties of attorneys. New York, 1849. 12° 134.25
— Now and then: a novel. New York, 1848. 12° 767.16-17
— Passages from the diary of a late physician. From 5th London ed. N. Y., 1853. 3v. 18° 767.19
— Ten thousand a year. Philadelphia, 1840-41. 6v. in 2. 12°. 767.14-15
— The lily and the bee; an apologue of the Crystal palace. New York, 1851. 16°. . . . 767.18
WARRENIANA; with notes. Boston, 1851. 12°. . 325.2
WARREN, Maine, Annals of the town of. Eaton, C. 227.7
WAR-TRAIL, The: a romance. Reid, M. 715.4-13
WARVILLE. *See* Brissot de Warville, J. P.
WÄRWOLF, Der: Roman. Häring, W. 1024.9
WASHBURN, E. Judicial history of Massachusetts, 1630-1775. Boston, 1840. 8° 297.2
WASHINGTON, G. Epistles, domestic, confidential and official. New York, 1796. 8° . . . 216.5
— Writings, with life and illustrations by J. Sparks. Boston, 1835-40. 12v. 8° 287.2

Contents. — Vol. I. Life by Sparks. II. Writings: Part 1, Letters before the American revolution. March, 1754, to May, 1775. III. Part 2, Correspondence and papers relating to the American revolution. June, 1775, to July, 1776. IV. Correspondence. July, 1776, to July, 1777. V. Correspondence. July, 1777, to July, 1778. VI. Correspondence. July, 1778, to March, 1780. VII. Correspondence. March, 1780, to April, 1781. VIII. Correspondence. April, 1781, to Dec., 1783. IX. Part 3, Private correspondence. Dec., 1783, to April, 1789. X. Part 4, Correspondence, official and private. May, 1789, to Nov., 1794. XI. Correspondence. Nov., 1794, to Dec. 1799. XII. Part 5, Speeches and messages to congress; Proclamations; Addresses; Indexes. *Each vol. has also an appendix.*

— Farewell address. *See* Constitutional text book 299.1
— Political legacies. Boston, 1800. 8° 207.6
— Reprint of letters to Jos. Reed. Philadelphia, 1852. 8°. 216.4
— Essay on the character and influence of. Guizot, F. P. G. 518.17
— Letters of eminent men to. Sparks, J. . . . 213.2
— Bancroft, A. Life of 519.2
— Edmonds, C. R. Life and times of 379.18
— Headley, J. T. Life of 515.1
— Hickey, W. Prominent political acts of . . . 299.2-3
— Irving, W. Life of 511.1-4
— Kirkland, C. M. Memoirs of 515.4
— Marshall, J. Life of 515.2
— Paulding, J. K. Life of 810.71
— Ramsay, D. Life of 515.3
— Rush, R. W. in domestic life 511.8
— Sparks, J. Life of 511.5-7
— Witt, Cornelis de. Histoire de, et de la fondation de la république des États Unis . . 1067.30

WASHINGTON, G. and John Adams. Memoirs of the administrations of. Gibbs, G. 285.5
— - Diplomatic history of the administrations of. Trescot, W. H. 297.5
WASHINGTON and his generals. Headley, J. T. . 516.1-5
WASHINGTON, Memoirs of the mother and the wife of. Conkling, M. C. 538.14-16
WASHINGTON, or liberty restored : a poem. Northmore, T. 358.15
WASHINGTON, Capt. Lecture on life-boats and the progress of naval architecture 199.16
WASHINGTON city, British army at, in 1814. Gleig, G. R. 889.19
— History of the invasion and capture of. Williams, J. S. 217.1
WASHINGTON, Conn., History of. Cothren, W. . 225.2
WASHINGTON territory, Three years' residence in. Swan, J. G. 626.5-6
WAS sich der Wald erzählt. Märchen. Putlitz, G. zu 1039.2
WATAUGA association, from 1769 to 1777. Ramsey, J. G. M. 235.4
WATCH-MAKING, Rudimentary treatise on. Denison, E. B. 829.4
See also : Clocks, and Horology.
WATER, Drops of. Catlow, A. 178.29
WATER-CURE manual. Shew, J. 157.19-20
WATER-DRINKER, Memoirs of a. Dunlap, W. . 539.26
WATER power applied to flour mills, etc. Glynn, J. 829.14
WATER wheels, Essay upon. Fenwick, T. 195.21
WATER-WITCH: a tale. Cooper, J. F. 780.45-48
WATERBURY, J. B. Considerations for young men. New York, n.d. 18° 1109.17
WATERHOUSE, G. R. Natural history of the mammalia. London, 1846-48. 2v. 8° . . 172.6
— Marsupialia, or pouched animals. Jardine, Sir W. . . . . v.XXIV. of 179.1
WATERLOO. Eaton, C. A. Quatre Bras and . . 1008.16
— Jomini, H., Baron de. Campaign of 987.10
— Siborne, W. Details of the battle of 1005.2
WATERS, T. Recollections of a policeman. New York, 1852. 12° 906.5
WATERTON, C. Essays on natural history, with autobiography. 1st, 2d and 3d series. London, 1851-57. 3v. 12° 177.20
— Wanderings in South America, etc. 2d ed. London, 1828. 8° 633.16
WATERTOWN, Mass. Bond, H. Early history and family memorials of 224.1
— Francis, C. Historical sketch of 224.2
WATHEN, G. H. The golden colony, or Victoria in 1854. London, 1855. 12° 707.15
WATKINS, J. Life, poetry and letters of E. Elliott, the corn law rhymer. London, 1850. 12° . 586.18
WATSON, E. Men and times of the revolution. Ed. by W. C. Watson. New York, 1856. 8° 513.9
WATSON, H. C. Nights in a block-house. Philadelphia, 1853. 8° 733.3-4
WATSON, J. V. Tales and takings, sketches and incidents. New York, 1857. 12° 897.10
WATSON, Richard, Bishop. Reply to Gibbon, or an apology for Christianity. With an appeal to infidels. See Infidelity. 119.9
— Anecdotes of life of, by himself. Phila., 1818. 8° 575.2
WATSON, Robert. Reigns of Philip II. and III. of Spain, [continued] by W. Thomson. 1st Am. ed. New York, 1818. 2v. 8° 542.2
WATSON, T. Principles and practice of physic. Rev. with add., by D. F. Condie. 3d Am. from last Lond. ed. Philadelphia, 1853. 8° 151.6-9
WATT, J., Historical éloge of. Arago, D. F. . . 573.6
WATTS, I. Logic. 3d Am. ed. Exeter, 1806. 12° 139.4
— Life, times, and correspondence of. Milner, T. 574.9
WAUD, S. W. Algebraical geometry. Lond. 1835. 8° 365.17
WAVERLEY, or 't is sixty years since. Scott, Sir W. 460.2-5
WAVERLEY anecdotes, illustrative of the novels and romances of Scott. Scott, Sir W. . . . 470.26
WAVERLEY, Remarks on the series of novels called. Adolphus, J. 868.16
WAY to do good. Abbott, J. 1087.6

WAYLAND, F. Correspondence on slavery. Fuller, R. 1109.23
— Discourse delivered in Murray street church. See Discourses, etc. 1083.5
— Elements of intellectual philosophy. Boston, 1854. 12° 124.14
— Elements of political economy. Boston, 1851. 12° 136.14
— Moral science. Stereo. ed. Boston, 1843. 12° 127.4
— - Same. Boston, 1851. 12° 125.14
— Memoir of the life and labors of Rev. A. Judson. Boston, 1853. 2v. 12° 536.1-3
— Principles and practices of Baptist churches. New York, 1857. 12° 1088.8
— University sermons. 3d ed. Boston, 1850. 12° 1096.22
WAYLAND, J. Recollections of real life in England. Introduction by F. Wayland. New York, 1848. 18° 899.22
WAYNE, A., Life of, by J. Armstrong. Sparks, J. . . . . v.III. of 518.5
WAYSIDE cross, The, or the raid of Gomez: a tale. Milman, E. A. 809.4
WEAL and woe in Garveloch, a tale. Martineau, H. . . . . v.VI. of 749.2-3
WEALE, J. Series of rudimentary works for the use of beginners. London, var.d. 86v. 16°
Contents:
Allen, C. B. On cottage building. Lond., 1854. 819.29
Andrews, G. H. Agricultural engineering. 1852-53. 3v. 829.2
Armstrong, R. On steam boilers. 1850 . . 819.41
Baker, T. Elements of mechanism. 1852 . . 829.29
— On mensuration. 1850 . . . . 829.25
— Statics and dynamics. 1851 . . . . . . 829.28
Bland, W. On the form of ships. 1852 . . . 829.16
Burgoyne, Sir J. Blasting and quarrying stone. 1852 . . . . 819.25
Burnell, G. R. On limes, cements, etc. 1850. 819.32
Cox, H. Integral calculus. 1852 . . . . . . 829.32
Dempsey, G. D. Drainage of districts and lands. 1854 . . . . 819.20
— Drainage of towns and buildings. 1849 . 819.21
— Tubular and other iron girder bridges. 1850 . . . . 819.30
Denison, E. B. Clock and watch making. 1850. 829.4
Dobson, E. Art of building. 1854 . . . . . . 819.15
— Foundations and concrete works. 1850 . 819.31
— Manufacture of bricks and tiles. 1850. . 819.16
— Masonry and stone-cutting. 1849 . . . 819.17-18
Donaldson, Prof. Clay lands and loamy soils. 1852 . . . . 829.3
Euclides. Elements. Notes and essay on logic, by H. Law 829.40
Field, G. Rudiments of the painter's art. 1850. 819.19
Fownes, G. Rudimentary chemistry. 1854 . 819.1
Fromberg, E. O. Painting on glass. 1851 . . 819.28
Garbett, E. L. Principles of design in architecture. 1850 . . . . 819.13
Gessert, M. A. Painting on glass. 1851 . . . 819.27
Gibbons, D. Law of contracts for services. 1849-50 . . . . 819.36
Glynn, J. Cranes and machinery for raising heavy bodies. 1854 . . . . 199.20
— Power of water to drive mills, etc. 1853 . 829.14
Greenwood, J. Sailor's sea-book. 1850 . . 819.39
Haddon, J. Differen. calculus. Examp. 1851. 829.34
— Elements of algebra. 1850 . . . . 829.21
Halleur, G. C. H. Art of photography. 1854. 829.11
Hann, J. Analytical geometry. 1850 . . . . 829.22
— Integral calculus. Examples. 1850 . . . 829.33
— Plane trigonometry. 1854 . . . . 829.23
— Spherical trigonometry. 1849 . . . . . . 829.24
Hamilton, W. D. Outlines of the history of England. 1852-53 . . . . 829.36
— Outlines of the history of Greece. 2v. 1853-54 . . . . 829.38
Harris, W. S. Rudimentary electricity. 1853. 819.7
— Rudimentary magnetism. 2v. 1850-52 . 819.8
Heather, J. F. Descriptive geometry. 1851. 829.8
— Mathematical instruments. 1853 . . . . 819.23

WEALE, J., *continued.*

Highton, E. Electric telegraph. 1852.... 819.9
Hipsley, W. Equational arithmetic. 1852.. 829.20
Hughes, S. On gas works. 1853 .... 829.15
Jeans, H. W. Navigation and nautical as-
tronomy. 1853 . . . . 829.30
Kipping, R. Treatise on masting, etc. 1854. 819.38
Kirkman, T. P. First lessons in geometry,
algebra, and trigonometry. 1852 . . . . . 829.35
Lardner, D. Steam engine. 1853 . . . . . 819.24
Law, H. Art of constructing roads. 1850. 819.33
— On logarithms. 1853 . . . . 829.26
— Rudiments of civil engineering. 2v. 1852. 819.11
Leeds, W. H. Rudimentary architecture. 1854. 819.12
Main, R. Rudimentary astronomy. 1852 . . 829.27
Murray, R. Marine engines, etc. 1852 . . 829.12
Peake, J. Naval architecture. 2v. 1849–51. 819.37
Portlock, J. E. Treatise on geology. 1853 819.4
Prideaux, T. S. Economy of fuel. 1853 . . 829.9
Pyne, G. Perspective for beginners. 1852. 819.14
Raspail, F. V. Domestic medicine. 1853 . . 829.37
Rudimentary chronology. 1854 . . . . . . 829.39
Sewell, J. Steam and locomotion. 1852–53. 829.10
Spencer, C. C. Art of playing the piano. 1853. 829.6
— Treatise on music. 1854 . . . . 829.5
Stephenson, R. M. Railway details. 1850. 829.1
Stevenson, A. Treatise on lighthouses. 1850.819.34–35
Swindell, J. G. Well-digging, boring, etc. 1854. 819.22
Tomlinson, C. On construction of locks. 1853. 829.17
— On warming and ventilation. 1850 . . . 819.40
— Pneumatics. 1852 . . . . 819.10
— Rudimentary mechanics. 1854 . . . . . 819.6
— Study of natural philosophy. 1851–53. 819.2–3
Varley, D. Treatise on mineralogy. 1849 . . 819.5
Weale, J. Dictionary of terms in architect-
ural engineering. 1849–50 . . . . 819.26
Wiggins, J. Embanking lands from the sea.
1852 . . . . 829.13
Woodward, S. P. Manual of the mollusca.
2v. 1851–54 . . . . 829.7
Woolhouse, W. S. B. Differential calculus.
1854 . . . . 829.31
Young, J. R. Key to treatise on arithmetic.
1853 . . . . 829.19
→ Treatise on arithmetic. 1854 . . . . . 829.18
— Dictionary of terms in architecture, engineer-
ing, etc. London, 1849–50. 16° 819.26
WEALTH and want, Social delusions concerning.
Jennings, R. 139.13
WEALTH of nations. Smith, A. 136.33
WEATHER, Philosophy of the. Butler, T. B. . . . 145.26
See also: Meteorology.
WEAVING. Manuel du tisserand. Alcan, M. . . 1075.33
WEBB, G. J. Cultivation of pure tone. Murdoch,
J. E. 137.16
WEBBER, C. W. The hunter-naturalist. Wild
scenes and song-birds. N. York, 1854. 8°. 171.4
— Hunter-naturalist. Romance of sporting.
Philadelphia, n.d. 8° 171.3–5
WEBER, George. Universal history. Transl. by
M. Behr, revised by F. Bowen. 3d ed. Bos-
ton, 1854. 8° 952.3
WEBER, Gottfried. Theory of musical composi-
tion. Transl. by J. F. Warner. Boston,
1841–46. 2v. in 1. 8° 204.4
WEBER, J. Memoirs of Maria Antoinette. Transl.
by R. C. Dallas. London, 1805–12. 3v. 8°. 613.1
WEBSTER, A. L. The improved housewife. 20th
ed. Boston, 1856. 12° 188.8
WEBSTER, D. Works. 6th ed. Boston, 1853. 6v. 8° 284.1–2

Contents. — Vol. I. Biographical memoir, by E.
Everett. I.–II. Speeches on various public occasions. III. Speeches in convention to amend the
constitution of Massachusetts. III.–V. Speeches in
congress. V.–VI. Legal arguments. VI. Diplomatic and official papers.

— Speech on the North Eastern boundary. *See*
New York Historical Society 297.7
— Private correspondence. Ed. by F. Webster.
Boston, 1857. 2v. 8° 512.4–5

WEBSTER, D. Life, containing numerous anec-
dotes. Philadelphia, 1853. 16° 526.25
— Banvard, J. Illustrations of the life and char-
acter of 526.24
— Boston-Memorial of. Ed. by G. S. Hillard . 512.6
— Constitutional text-book. Selections from
the writings of 299.1
— Knapp, S. L. Life of 526.26
— Lyman, S. P. Life and memorials of 526.23
— March, C. W. Biography of 526.22
— U. States. Obituary addresses on the occa-
sion of the death of 512.7
WEBSTER, J. W. Trial for the murder of G. Park-
man. Bemis, G. 133.3
WEBSTER, N. Papers on political, literary, and
moral subjects. New York, 1843. 8° . . . 873.2
WEBSTER, N. jr. History of animals. New Ha-
ven, 1812. 16° 177.31
WEEMS, M. L. Life of Benjamin Franklin. 6th
ed. Philadelphia, 1822. 12° 517.23
— Life of William Penn. Philadelphia, 1829. 16° 526.18
WEISBACH, J. Mechanics of engineering. Lon-
don, 1847–48. 2v. 8° 144.8
— — Same. 1st Am. ed. By W. R. Johnson.
Philadelphia, 1848–49. 2v. 8° 105.2
WEISS, C. History of the French protestant refu-
gees. Transl. by H. W. Herbert. N. York,
1854. 2v. 12° 1095.13
WELD, C. R. Tour in the United States and Can-
ada. London, 1855. 12° 620.1
— Vacations in Ireland. London, 1857. 12° . . 646.4
WELD, H. H. Franklin's autobiography, with a
narrative of his public life. *See* Franklin, B. 523.6
— Jonce Smiley. By Ezekiel Jones, Esq. New
York, 1845. 8° 802.6
WELD, I. jr. Travels through the states, and U.
and L. Canada, 1795–97. 3d ed. London,
1800. 2v. 8° 625.15
WELDON, *Sir* A. Court and character of King
James. *See* Secret history 552.6
WELL digging. Rudimentary treatise on. Swin-
dell, J. G. 819.22
WELL spent hour, The. Follen, E. L. 738.8
WELLESLEY, A. *Duke of Wellington.* Life, mil-
itary and civil. London, 1852. p.8° . . . 825.4
— Memoir. London, 1852. 12° 409.30
— Brialmont, A. Life of 565.9
— Egerton, F. Life and character of 558.11
— Maurel, J. Life of 558.8
— Maxwell, W. H. Victories of W., and the
British armies 825.3
— Sherer, M. Military memoirs of 558.10
— Stocqueler, J. H. Life of 564.11
WELLFLEET, Mass. Comprehensive history of.
Pratt, E. 224.22
WELLINGTON, Duke of. *See* Wellesley, A.
WELLMONT, E. Uncle Sam's palace. Boston,
1853. 12° 488.5
WELLS, A. M. Poems and juvenile sketches.
Boston, 1830. 12° 338.24
WELLS, D. A. Annual of scientific discovery,
1850–58, [1850–51 assisted by G. Bliss, jr.]
Boston, 1850–58. 9v. 12° 159.1
— Things not generally known. New York,
1857. 12° 896.10
WELLS, Capt. W., Biographical sketch of. Mc-
Donald, J. 518.8
WELLS, W. V. Explorations and adventures in
Honduras, with sketches of travel in Central
America. New York, 1857. 8° 621.2
— Walker's expedition to Nicaragua. N. York,
1856. 12° 266.8
WELLSTED, J. R. Travels to the city of the ca-
liphs, including a voyage to Arabia. Lon-
don, 1840. 2v. 8° 693.3
WEMYSS, F. C. Minor drama. New York, n.d.
7v. 12° 363.2

Contents. — Vol. I. The Irish attorney, by W. B.
Bernard; Boots at the Swan, by C. Selby; How to pay
the rent, by T. Power; The loan of a lover, by J. R.

WEMYSS, F. C., *continued*.

Planché: The dead shot, by J. B. Buckstone; His last legs, by W. B. Bernard; The invisible prince, by J. R. Planché; The golden farmer, by B. Webster, with memoir of Mr. John Sefton. II. The pride of the market, by J. R. Planché; Used up, by C. Mathews; The Irish tutor, by R. Butler, the earl of Gleugall; The barrack-room, by T. H. Bayley; Luke the labourer, by J. B. Buckstone; Beauty and the beast, by J. R. Planché; St. Patrick's eve, by T. Power; Captain of the watch, by J. R. Planché, with memoir of Miss Catherine Wemyss. III. The secret, by Moncrieff; White horse of the Peppers, by S. Lover; The Jacobite, by J. R. Planché; The bottle, by T. P. Taylor; Box and Cox, by J. M. Morton; Bamboozling, by T. E. Wilks; The widow's victim, by C. Selby; Robert Macaire, by C. Selby, with memoir of Mr. F. S. Chanfrau. IV. Secret service, by J. R. Planché; The omnibus, anon.; The Irish lion, by J. B. Buckstone; Maid of Croissey, by Mrs. C. Gore; The old guard, anon.; Raising the wind, by J. Kenney; Slasher and Crasher, by J. M. Morton; Naval engagements, by C. Dance, with memoir of Rose Telbin. V. Cockneys in California, by J. S. Coyne; Bombastes Furioso, by T. B. Rhodes; The Irish ambassador, by J. Kenney; The weathercock, by T. J. Allingham; Who speaks first? by C. Dance; Macbeth travestie, by W. K. Northall; Delicate ground, by C. Dance; All that glitters is not gold, by T. and J. M. Morton, with memoir of W. A. Goodall. VI. Grimshaw, Bagshaw, and Bradshaw, by J. M. Morton; Bloomer costume, by E. Stirling; Born to good luck, by T. Power; 'T would puzzle a conjuror, by J. Poole; Rough diamond, by J. B. Buckstone; Two Bonnycastles, by J. M. Morton; Kiss in the dark, by J. B. Buckstone; Kill or cure, by C. Dance, with memoir of F. M. Kent. VII. Box and Cox married and settled, by J. S. Coyne; St. Cupid, by D. Jerrold; Go-to-bed-Tom, by T. Morton; The lawyers, by S. Lawrence; Jack Sheppard, by J. B. Buckstone; The Toodles, anon.; The mobcap, by H. Paul; Ladies beware, anon., with memoir of Sol. Smith.

WENSLEY: a story without a moral. Quincy, E. 765.11–14
WENTZ, S. A. Smiles and frowns. N. Y., 1857. 12° 777.9
WEPT of Wish-ton-wish, The. Cooper, J. F. . 780.50–53
WERNE, F. African wanderings, transl. London, 1852. p.8° 409.29
— Expedition to the White Nile. From the German. London, 1849. 2v. 12° 693.14
WERNER, H. Guardian spirits. Transl., with parallels, from E. Swedenborg, by A. E. Ford. New York, 1847. 12° 1084.14
WERTHER: Briefe Goethe's meistens aus seiner Jugendzeit. *See* Göthe, J. W. v. 1034.11
WESLEY, J. Compendium of natural philosophy. New ed. London, 1836. 3v. 16° 399.11
— Primitive physic. Revised and enlarged by W. M. Cornell. Boston, 1858. 12° 157.36
— Larrabee, W. C. W. and his coadjutors . . 578.9
— Taylor, I. W. and Methodism 1108.4
WESLEY family, Memoirs of the. Clarke, A. . . 535.12
WEST, C. Diseases of infancy and childhood. 2d American ed. Philadelphia, 1854. 8° 151.20
WEST, G. Extract from West on the resurrection. 119.9
WEST, The. Brackenridge, H. M. Recollections of persons and places in 239.7
— Carvalho, S. N. Incidents of travel 626.11
— De Bow, J. D. B. Industrial resources of the Southern and Western States 296.2
— Flagg, E. A tour beyond the mountains . . 629.18
— Gregg, J. Scenes in the Western prairies . . 239.12
— Hall, J. Commerce and navigation of 239.9
— - History, life, and manners of 239.13
— - Letters from 257.1
— Ruxton, G. F. Life in the far West 628.22–23
— Sigourney, L. H. The Western home . . . 338.17
See also: America, and United States.
WESTCOTT, T. Life of John Fitch. Phila., 1857. 12° 525.5
WEST country of England, Tales of the. *See* Three courses and a dessert 815.2
WESTERN empire, History of the, from Charlemagne to Charles V. Comyn, R. 1004.7
WESTERN travel, Retrospect of. Martineau, H. . 626.10
WESTERN world. Fergus, H. History of the . . 368.10
— Mackay, Alex. Travels in the United States in 1846–47 . . . . 628.5

WESTGARTH, W. Victoria and the Australian gold mines in 1857, etc. London, 1857. 8° . 705.8
WEST Indies. Baird, R. W. I. in 1849 . . . . . 628.6
— Coke, T. History of the 264.5
— Coleridge, H. N. Six months in the W. I. in 1825 . . . . 379.8
— Davy, J. W. I. before and after slave emancipation 635.4
— Day, C. W. Five years' residence in the . . 635.20
— Gurney, J. J. A winter in the 635.5
— Halliday, Sir A. Natural and physical history of the 635.19
— Lewis, M. G. Journal of a residence among the negroes of the 889.30
— Long, G. Geography of the 305.3
— Madden, R. R. Twelve months' residence in. 635.21
— Pinckard, G. Notes on the 635.7
— Southey, T. Chronological history of the . 264.4
— Sturge, J. W. I. in 1837 . . . . 635.8
See also: the names of the several islands.
WESTMINSTER assembly of divines. *See* Ecclesiastical history.
WESTON, Mass. Historical and family memorials. Bond, H. 224.1
WESTPHALIA. Schücking, L. Eine Eisenbahnfahrt durch Westfalen 1029.20
— Secret tribunals of. *See* Secret societies. . . 849.5
WESTWARD empire. Magoon, E. L. 948.2
WESTWOOD, J. O. Entomologist's text book. London, 1838. 12° 178.35
— Natural history of insects. Rennie, J. 810.9
WHALE fishery. Cheever, H. T. The whale and his captors 728.8
— Laing, J. Some account of the 704.20
— Macy, O. Rise and progress of the 227.8
— Nordhoff, C. Whaling and fishing. 728.7
WHAT the woods talk about, by Gustav zu Putlitz. Carstens, H. W. 878.5
WHATELY, R. Elements of logic. Only correct Am. from 8th London ed. N. Y., 1852. 18°. 129.16
— Elements of rhetoric. New York, n.d. 18°. 406.21
— Historic doubts relative to Napoleon Buonaparte, and historic certainties respecting the early history of America. N. Y., 1853. 12°. 868.15
— Scripture revelations concerning a future state. Philadelphia, 1855. 12°. 1086.24
— Introduction to remains of Copleston. Copleston, E. 555.5
WHEATLY, C. Illustration of the book of common prayer. London, 1850. p.8° 838.6
WHEATON, H. History of the Northmen, or Danes and Normans. Philadelphia, 1831. 8° . . . 925.1
— Scandinavia, ancient and modern. Crichton, A. 820.39
— Life of W. Pinkney. Sparks, J. . . . . v.III. of 518.5
WHEATON, R. Memoir; with selections from his writings. Boston, 1854. 16° 525.17–18
WHEELER, G. Homes for the people. New York, 1855. 12° 207.8
— Rural homes. New York, 1851. 12° 207.9
WHEELER, J. H. Historical sketches of North Carolina, 1584 to 1851. Phila., 1851. 2v. 8° 235.6
WHEELER, J. T. Analysis and summary of Herodotus. 2d London ed., 1854. p.8° 855.2
— Analysis and summary of Thucydides. London, 1855. p.8° 855.6
— Life and travels of Herodotus; an imaginary biography. New York, 1856. 2v. 8° 547.12
WHEWELL, W. Astronomy and general physics considered with reference to natural theology. London, 1852. p.8° 826.4
— Elements of morality, including polity. New ed., rev. and cor. London, 1848. 2v. 12°. 127.31
— History of the inductive sciences. With add. 3d ed. New York, 1858. 2v. 8° 122.9
— Inaugural lecture delivered before the society of arts, manufactures and commerce. . . . 199.16
— Mechanics of engineering. Camb. 1841. 8°. 195.20
— Plurality of worlds, with an introduction by E. Hitchcock. Boston, 1854. 12° 146.18–21
— Syllabus to Bp. Butler's discourses. Butler, J. 139.1

WHICH is the wiser, or, people abroad. Howitt, M.   459.17
WHICHER, M. F., (formerly Miss Berry.) Widow Bedott papers. With introduction by A. B. Neal. New York, 1855. 12° 428.16
WHIMSICAL woman, The. A novel. Carlen, E. F.   766.6
WHIMSICALITIES. Hood, T. 896.17
WHIPPLE, E. P. Essays and reviews. New York, 1848-49. 2v. 12° 875.11
— - Same. 2d ed. Boston, 1851. 2v. 16°. . .   875.12
— Lectures on subjects connected with literature and life. 3d ed. Boston, 1850. 12° 875.13
WHITE, A. Popular history of British crustacea. London, 1857. sq.12° 178.28
— Popular history of mammalia. London, 1850. 12° 177.33
WHITE, Rev. C., D.D. Essays in literature and ethics. Boston, 1853. 12° 403.17
WHITE, C. Three years in Constantinople. 2d ed. London, 1846. 3v. 12° 687.11
WHITE, G. Natural history of Selborne, with additions by Sir W. Jardine. Edinburgh, 1829. 18° 830.52
— - Same. Philadelphia, 1832. 18° 178.37
— - Same. [Without additions.] N. York, 1847. 18° 820.48
— - Same. New ed., with notes by E. Blyth and R. Mudie. London, 1850. 12° . . .   178.19
— - Same. With notes by J. G. Wood. London, 1853. 12° 178.20
— - Same, ed. by E. Jesse. London, 1851. p.8°   815.8
WHITE, G. S. Memoir of S. Slater, with a history of the cotton manufacture. 2d ed. Philadelphia, 1836. 8° 524.5
WHITE, H. Early history of New England. 8th ed. Concord, 1843. 12° 228.4
WHITE, H. K. Complete works, with life by Southey. Boston, 1829. 8° 324.4-5
    Containing: — Miscellaneous poems; Gondoline; Time; Childhood; The Christiad; Prose remains, and Melancholy hours.
— Poetical works, [with life by Sir N. H. Nicolas.] London, 1840. 16° 329.5
— Life and remains. London, 1825. 12°. . . .   335.12
— - Same. London, 1827. 12° 358.11
— Memoir by Southey, and poetical remains, with introduction by Rev. J. Todd. Boston, 1853. 12° 324.6
WHITE, Rev. J. Landmarks of the history of Greece. London, 1857. 16° 957.12
— The eighteen Christian centuries. Edinburgh, 1858. 12° 1105.1
WHITE, John. Voyage to the China sea. Boston, 1823. 8° 623.12
WHITE, J. Blanco. Life by himself. Ed. by J. H. Thom. London, 1845. 3v. 12° 575.16
WHITE, R. Madeira, its climate and scenery. Ed. by J. Y. Johnson. 2d ed. Edinb., 1857. 12°   264.6
WHITE, R. G. Shakespeare's scholar. New York, 1854. 8° 353.2
WHITE, W., Life of. Wilson, B. 534.3
WHITE acre vs. Black acre. Reported by J. G. [Fiction.] Richmond, 1856. 12° 796.11
WHITEBOY, The: a story of Ireland in 1822. Hall, A. M. 805.11
WHITE chief, The: a legend of North Mexico. Reid, M. 717.3-7
WHITE hoods, The; Bray, A. E. 448.17
WHITE jacket: or, the world in a man-of-war; a novel. Melville, H. 736.7
WHITE lies: a tale. Opie, A. 469.40-41
WHITE lies: a novel. Reade, C. 415.9-13
WHITE mountains. Spaulding, J. H. Historical relics of the 239.11
— Willey, B. G. Incidents in W. M. history.   239.1
WHITE, red, and black. Sketches of American society. Pulszky, F. and T. 627.3
WHITE rose, The: a domestic tale. Bray, A. E. . .   448.10
WHITE slave: or memoirs of a fugitive: a tale. Hildreth, R. 796.18
WHITEFIELD, G. Eighteen sermons. Boston, 1820. 12° 1099.22
— Macfarlan, D. Three sermons by W. . . .   118.9

WHITEHEAD, J. Causes and treatment of abortion and sterility. Philadelphia, 1848. 8°.   153.3
WHITING, H. Life of Z. M. Pike. Sparks, J. v.XV. of 529.1
WHITMAN, B. Letters to a Universalist on divine rewards and punishments. Camb., 1833. 12°   1089.5
WHITMAN, J. Young ladies' aid. Portl., 1838. 16°   129.21
WHITMAN, Z. G. History of the Ancient and Honorable Artillery company, 1637-1842. Boston, 1842. 8° 294.6
WHITING, H. Sannillac, a poem, with notes by L. Cass and H. R. Schoolcraft. Boston, 1831. 8°   338.4
WHITNEY, J. D. Metallic wealth of the United States. Philadelphia, 1854. 8° 163.1
WHITTIER, J. G. Leaves from Margaret Smith's journal, 1678-79. Boston, 1849. 16° 777.8
— Old portraits and modern sketches. Boston, 1850. 16° 887.6
— The panorama and other poems. Boston, 1856. 16° 345.9
— Poems, illustrated. Boston, 1850. 8° 332.8-9
— Songs of labor, and other poems. Boston, 1851. 16° 325.7
WHITTLESEY, C. Life of J. Fitch. Sparks, J. v.XVI. of 529.1
WHY and what am I. Jarves, J. J. 766.10
WICLIF, J. Le Bas, C. W. Life of 578.1
— Vaughan, R. Life and opinions of 575.2
WIDDIFIELD, H. New cook book. Philadelphia, 1856. 12° 188.9-10
WIDE, wide world, The: a tale. Warner, S. . . . 793.1-4
WIDOW Bedott papers. Whicher, M. F. 428.16
WIDOW Rugby's husband. Hooper, J. J. 726.15
WIDOW of Luzi; a tale. Genlis, Mme. de . . .   759.15
WIDOW's marriage: a comedy. Boker, G. H. v.II. of 335.2
WIDOW's offering: an authent. narrative. Hill, E.   539.14
WIELAND, C. M. Sämmtliche Werke. Leipzig, 1839-40. 36v. 16° 1028.1

Contents.—Vol. I.—II. Die Abenteuer des Don Sylvio von Rosalva. III. Poetische Werke; Musarion; Die Grazien, ein Gedicht; Der verkagte Amor, ein Gedicht; Nadine, eine Erzählung; Erdenglück; Celia an Damon, nach dem Englischen; Bruchstücke von Psyche, einem unvollendet gebliebenen allegorischen Gedichte; Das Leben ein Traum: Aspasia, oder die platonische Liebe: Anmerkungen. IV.—VI. Geschichte des Agathon. VII.—VIII. Der goldne Spiegel, oder die Könige von Scheschian; eine wahre Geschichte aus dem Scheschianischen übersetzt. IX. Geschichte des weisen Danischmend. X.—XII. Poetische Werke. XIII.—XIV. Geschichte der Abderiten. XV. Der neue Amadis [Gedicht.] XVI.—XVII. Peregrinus Proteus [in Gesprächen im Elysium.] XVIII. Agathodamon. XIX. Diogenes von Sinope; Das Hexameron von Rosenhain. XX. Oberon, ein romantisches Heldengedicht; Nachrichten von Wielands Leben. XXI. Menander und Glycerion; Krates u. Hipparchia; Koxkox und Kikequetzel. XXII.—XXIV. Aristipp. XXV. Die Natur der Dinge, oder die vollkommenste Welt, ein Lehrgedicht; Moralische Briefe in Versen; der Anti-Ovid: Der Frühling; Erzählungen in Versen. XXVI. Briefe von verstorbenen an hinterlassene Freunde, [in Versen.] Die Prüfung Abrahams, Gesänge; Hymne auf Gott; Psalmen; Erinnerungen an eine Freundin; Cyrus ein unvollendtes Heldengedicht. XXVII. Araspes und Panthea; Bonifaz Schleichers Jugendgeschichte; Der Stein der Weisen, Die Salamandrin und die Bildsäule; Göttergespräche. XXVIII. Dramatische Werke. XXIX.—XXXVI. Vermischte Schriften.

— Oberon, a poem, from the German, by W. Sotheby, with biog. notices, and a review. 1st Am. from 3d Lond. edition. Newport, R. I., 1810. 2v. in 1. 12° 315.15
— Les aventures merveilleuses de Don Silvio de Rosalva. Tr. par Mme. d'Ussieux. v.XXXVI. of 1077.1
— Sketches and anecd. of. Schiller, J. C. F. v.   876.16
WIELAND: or, the transformation. Brown, C. B.   757.1
WIEN in alter und neuer Zeit. Kühne, F. G. . .   1029.4
WIFE hunter, The. Transl. from German of C. Pichler 801.3
WIFE's duty: a tale. Opie, A. 469.36-37
WIFFEN, J. H. Memoirs of the house of Russell. London, 1833. 2v. 8° 975.7

WIGGINS, J. Embanking lands from the sea. London, 1852. 16° 829.13

WIGHT, Isle of, Geological excursions round the. Mantell, G. A. 826.10

WIGWAM and the cabin. Tales of the South. Simms, W. G. 800.27

WIKOFF, H. Adventures of a roving diplomatist. New York, 1857. 8° 887.4

— My courtship and its consequences. New York, 1855. 12° 794.18

WILBERFORCE, R. I. and S. Life of W. Wilberforce. London, 1838. 5v. 12° 576.5

WILBERFORCE, S. History of the Protestant Episcopal church in America. 2d ed. London, 1846. 12° 1099.26

WILBERFORCE, W., Life of. Wilberforce, R. I. and S. 576.5

WILBRAHAM, R. Travels in Trans-Caucasian Russia. London, 1839. 8° 674.4

WILBUR, H. Pseud. See Lowell, J. R.

WILD flowers, Wanderings among. Thomson, S. 169.22

WILDE, R. H. Love, madness and imprisonment of Torquato Tasso. New York, 1842. 2v. 12° 544.14

WILDE, W. R. Austria, its institutions, etc. Dublin, 1843. 12° 667.17

WILDER, D. History of Leominster, Mass., from 1701 to 1852. Fitchburg, 1853. 12° 227.12

WILDFELL hall, The tenant of. Brontë, A. . . 435.18-19

WILD sports of the West. Gerstäcker, F. 628.25

WILDS of the U. S. and British American provinces, Adventures in. Lanman, C. 623.3

WILDS, W. Art of building cottages of earthen walls. On bricks, lime, etc. Lond., 1835. 8° 207.4

WILHELM Meister's apprenticeship and travels. Göthe, J. W. 756.1-2

WILHELM Tell: a historical drama. Schiller, J. C. F. v. 818.10

WILKES, C. Narrative of the U. S. exploring expedition, 1838-42. Phila., 1845-51. 5v. 8° 701.6-7

— - Same. London, 1852. 2v. 8° 879.16-18

— Voyage round the world: embracing the principal events of the U. S. exploring expedition. New York, 1851. 12° 701.9

WILKES, J. Correspondence and memoirs of his life, by J. Almon. London, 1805. 5v. 12° 589.1

WILKIE, Sir D., Life of. Cunningham, A. . . . 556.2

WILKINS, P., Life and adventures of, or History of the flying islanders. Boston, 1828. 2v. 18° 799.16

WILKINSON, E. Letters during the invasion and possession of Charleston, S. C., by the British. New York, 1839. 12° 216.10

WILKINSON, J. G. Dalmatia and Montenegro, and remarks on the Slavonic nations. London, 1848. 2v. 8° 925.5

— Hand book for Egypt. New ed. London, 1847. 12° 649.13

— Popular account of the ancient Egyptians. Abridged. New York, 1854. 2v. 12° . . . 959.1

— The Egyptians in the time of the Pharaohs. [And] Introduction to the study of Egyptian hieroglyphs, by S. Birch. London, 1857. 12° 957.8

WILKINSON, J. J. G. Emanuel Swedenborg: a biography. Boston, 1849. 16° 545.18

— The human body and its connection with man. Philadelphia, 1851. 12° 157.6

WILKINSON, J. W. Hands not hearts: a novel. New York, 1850. 8° 802.9

WILKINSON, J. History of. Hudson, D. 539.12

WILL, The. See Intellectual science.

WILL, H. Outlines of chemical analysis. Translated from 3d German ed. by D. Breed and L. H. Steiner. Boston, 1855. 8° 156.2

— Alkalimetry. Fresenius, C. R. 155.21

WILLARD, E. Last leaves of American history. New York, 1849. 12° 309.11

WILLARD, S. Memories of youth and manhood. Cambridge, 1855. 2v. 16° 525.16

WILLETT, W. Life of Summerfield. Philadelphia, 1857. 8° 574.7

WILLEY, B. G. Incidents in White mountain history; [With] A guide to the White mountains. Boston, 1856. 12° 235.1

WILLIAM of Malmesbury. Chronicle of the kings of England, to the reign of king Stephen. Ed. by J. A. Giles. London, 1847. p.8° . . 846.3

WILLIAM the conqueror. Abbott, J. History of. 559.6-7

— Napier, C. A historical romance 415.4

WILLIAM III., Life and times of. Trevor, A. . . 553.1

WILLIAMS, C. R. Biography of Gen. Barton and of Capt. Olney. Providence, 1839. 12° . . 528.12

— Neutral French, or exiles of Nova Scotia. 2d ed. Providence, n.d. 12° 217.12

WILLIAMS, C. W. Combustion of coal, and prevention of smoke. London, 1854. 8° . . . 195.14

WILLIAMS, D. E. Life and correspondence of Sir Thomas Lawrence. London, 1831. 2v. 8° 556.3

WILLIAMS, E. Statesman's manual, messages, [etc.,] of presidents of U. S., 1789-1849, [etc.] New York, 1849. 3v. 8° 296.4

— The twelve stars of our republic. New York, 1850. 8° 513.13

WILLIAMS, Rev. E. and Louis XVII., Identity of. Hanson, J. H. 615.7

WILLIAMS, F. S. Our iron roads, their history, [etc.] London, 1852. 8° 195.13

WILLIAMS, H. M. Poems. London, 1786. 2v. 12° 349.21

Contents.—Vol. I. Odes; Sonnets; Misc. poems. II. Peru, in six cantos; Poems.

— Tour in Switzerland, and present state of Paris. Dublin, 1798. 2v. 16° 669.8

WILLIAMS, Rev. J. Life and actions of Alexander the Great. 2d ed. London, 1829. 16° . . . 399.12

— - Same. New York, 1843. 18° 810.8

WILLIAMS, Rev. J., first minister of Deerfield. Memoir of. See Williams, Stephen W. . . 539.16-17

WILLIAMS, Rev. J., missionary. Missionary enterprises in the South Sea islands. London, 1838. 12° 1087.15

WILLIAMS, J. B. Memoir of Matthew Henry. New York, n.d. 18° 119.18

— Memoirs of Sir M. Hale. London, 1835. 12° 568.9

WILLIAMS, J. S. Invasion and capture of Washington. New York, 1857. 12° 217.1

WILLIAMS, R., Life of, by W. Gammell. Sparks, J. . . . . v.XIV. of 529.1

— Memoir of. Knowles, J. D. 536.6

WILLIAMS, R. F. Shakspeare and his friends. New York, 1847. 8° 801.8

WILLIAMS, S. Wells. The middle kingdom. A survey, etc., of the Chinese empire. 3d ed. New York, 1851. 2v. 8° 696.12

WILLIAMS, Stephen W., M. D. American medical biography. Greenfield, Mass., 1845. 8° . . 523.12

— Biographical memoir of Rev. J. Williams, first minister of Deerfield. Greenfield, 1837. 12° 539.16-17

WILLIAMS, Theophilus. Academical stenography. London, 1826. 8° 403.2

WILLIAMS, Thomas. Cottage Bible, with explanatory notes. See Bible. 1091.2

WILLIAMS, W. Appleton's new and complete U. S. guide-book for travellers. 2v. in 1. New York, 1850. 16° 639.11

— Appleton's Northern and Eastern traveller's guide. New ed. New York, 1853. 18° . . 639.12

— Appleton's Southern and Western traveller's guide. New York, 1850. 16° 639.11

WILLIAMS, W. R. Introduction to Jaqueline Pascal. Cousin, V. 545.8

WILLIAMS, Sir W. F. Kars and our captivity, etc. Lake, A. 988.11

WILLIAMSON, W. D. History of the state of Maine, fr. 1602-1820. Hallowell, 1853. 2v. 8° 234.1

WILLIBALD. Narrative of early travels in Palestine. See Wright, T. 846.7

WILLIE and the mortgage. Abbott, J. . . . . v.I. of 739.1

WILLIS, N. P. Dashes at life with a free pencil. New York, [1845.] 8°. 891.1

Contents. — 1. High life in Europe, and American life. II. Inklings of adventure. III. Loiterings of travel. IV. Ephemera.

— - Same. Pt. IV. Ephemera. N. Y., 1851. 8°   891.2
— Famous persons and places. New York, 1854. 12° 657.7–8
— Fun-jottings. New York, 1853. 12° 904.11–13
— Health trip to the tropics. N. Y., 1853. 12° 636.19–28
— Hurry-graphs. 2d ed. New York, 1851. 12° 904.1–2
— Life here and there. New York, 1850. 12° . . 904.3–5
— Out-doors at Idlewild. New York, 1855. 12°   904.16
— Paul Fane, or parts of a life else untold. A novel. New York, 1857. 12° 794.12
— Pencillings by the way. Phila., 1836. 2v. 12°   657.9
— - Same. New York, 1852. 12° 657.10–11
— People I have met. New York, 1850. 12° . .904.7–10
— Poem delivered before Soc. of United Bro's, Brown Univ., 1831. With other poems. N. York, 1831. 8° 324.3
— Poems, sacred, passionate, and humorous. Complete ed., rev. New York, 1850. 8° . .343.7–13
— Rural letters. New York, 1849. 12° 904.15
— - Same. New York, 1851. 12° 904.17
— Summer cruise in the Mediterranean. New York, 1853. 12° 676.11–15
— - Same. Auburn, 1853. 12° 676.16–17
WILLIS, R. Lecture on machinery and tools. . . 199.16
WILLIS, W. Journals of the Rev. T. Smith and the Rev. S. Deane. Portland, 1849. 8° . . 234.2
WILLISON, J. The afflicted man's companion. N. York, n.d. 12° 1109.5
WILLKOMM, E. Die Familie Ammer [Deutsche Sitten-roman.] Frankfurt a M., 2v. in 1. 8° 1013.5
— Rheder und Matrose. Roman. Frankfurt a M., 1857. 8° 1013.2
— Von Berlin nach Hamburg. Leipzig, 1855. 16° 1029.15
— Wallenstein. Historischer Roman. Leipzig, 1844. 4v. 16° 1037.12
WILLMOTT, R. A. Jeremy Taylor, his predecessors, contemporaries, and successors. 2d ed. London, 1848. 16° 578.6
— Journal of summer time in the country. N. York, 1852. 12° 899.19
WILLOUGHBY, *Lady.* Passages from the diary of a wife and mother in the seventeenth century. New York, 1851. 12° 777.7
WILLSON, A. M. Lives of Mrs. A. H. Judson, and Mrs. S. B. Judson, with a sketch of Mrs. E. C. Judson. Auburn, 1854. 12° 538.4–5
WILMINGTONS, The. A novel. Marsh, A. 795.2
WILSON, A. American ornithology. With notes by Jardine, [and] a synopsis of Am. birds, by T. M. Brewer. New York, 1854. 8° . . 172.4–5
— and Bonaparte, C. J. L. L. American ornithology. Ed. by R. Jameson. Edinburgh, 1831. 4v. 18° 177.34
— Life of. By W. B. O. Peabody. Sparks, J. v. II. of 529.1
WILSON, B. Life of William White. Philadelphia, 1839. 8° 534.3
WILSON, D. Henrietta Robinson. New York, 1855. 12° 428.5
WILSON, D., *F.S.A., Scott.* Oliver Cromwell and the protectorate. London, 1854. 16°. . . 558.6–7
WILSON, D., *B'p.* Expository lectures on the epistle to the Colossians. New York, 1846. 12° 1097.26
— Introductory essay to Quesnel's gospels. *See* Bible 1093.3
WILSON, G., *M.D.* Electricity and the electric telegraph. With the chemistry of the stars. London, 1852. 12° 400.31
— Five gateways of knowledge. Philadelphia, 1857. 12° 138.6
WILSON, James, *M.P.* Capital, currency, and banking. London, 1847. 8° 136.8
WILSON, James, *F.R.S.E.* Voyage round the coasts of Scotland. Edinburgh, 1842. 2v. 12° 646.6
— History of British India. Murray, H. 810.51

WILSON, James, *F.R.S.E.* Narrative of adventure and discovery in Africa. Murray, H. . . . 810.18
— Sketches of the natural history of the North American regions, with Tytler's progress of discovery, etc. Tytler, P. F. 810.53
WILSON, John, *Boston.* Treatise on English punctuation. 3d ed. Boston, 1855. 16° 405.17
— Unitarian principles confirmed by Trinitarian testimonies. Boston, 1855. 12° . . . 1094.14
WILSON, John, *Prof.* Noctes Ambrosianæ, by J. Wilson, W. Maginn, J. G. Lockhart, J. Hogg, etc. Ed. by R. S. Mackenzie. New York, 1854. 5v. 12° 865.1
— Recreations of Christopher North. Philadelphia, 1850. 8° 863.10
— The foresters. New edition. Edinburgh, 1840. 12° 759.8
— Trials of Margaret Lyndsay. A tale. Boston, 1845. 12° 759.7
WILSON, John. History of Switzerland. London, 1832. 16° 368.7
WILSON, J. L. Western Africa; its history and prospects. New York, 1856. 12° 938.1
WILSON, R. Poems. Boston, 1856. 16° 349.17
WILSON, R. A. Mexico and its religion. New York, 1855. 12° 256.4
WILSON, S. F. History of the American revolution. Baltimore, 1834. 12° 216.9
WILSON, S. S. The Greek mission, or sixteen years in Malta and Greece. London, 1839. 8° . . 683.2
WILSON, T. Biography of American heroes. 2d ed., rev. New York, 1821. 2v. 12° 527.8
WILSON, T., *B'p.* Sacra privata. Private meditations and prayers. New ed. New York, 1851. 32° 1109.30
WILSON, W. Memoir of the life and times of D. Defoe. London, 1830. 3v. 8° 582.13
WILSON, W. J. Erasmus. Anatomist's vade mecum. 6th ed. London, 1851. 12° 157.34
— Diseases of the skin. 4th Am. ed. Philadelphia, 1857. 8° 153.1
— Dissector. Ed. by P. B. Goddard. New ed. Philadelphia, 1851. 12°. 153.7
— Healthy skin, with treatment of cutaneous diseases. New York, 1846. 12° 157.14
— System of human anatomy. 2d Am. ed. Philadelphia, 1844. 8° 151.4
WINCKELMANN, J. History of ancient art among the Greeks. Transl. by G. H. Lodge. London, 1850. 8° 205.7
WINE. Donovan, M. Wine making . . . . . v.I. of 408.8
— Mulder, G. J. Chemistry of 156.26
— Redding, C. History and description of modern wines 815.10
WINES, E. C. Laws of the ancient Hebrews. New York, 1853. 8°. 1083.2
— Hints on popular education. Phila., 1838. 12° 137.10
WING-AND-WING, The: or, le feu follet. Cooper, J. F. 780.54–58
WINNIPEEK, Lake, Long's expedition to the source of. Keating, W. H. 624.11
WINSLOW, C. F. Cosmography: or, philosophical views of the universe. Boston, 1853. 16° . 118.14
WINSLOW, E. S. Computist's manual of facts. 5th ed. Boston, 1855. 12° 130.26
WINSLOW, *Rev.* H. Elements of moral philosophy. New York, 1856. 12° 127.3
— Woman as she should be. 5th ed. Boston, 1843. 12° 1088.29
WINSLOW, H. L., Memoir of. Winslow, M. . . . 1109.10
WINSLOW, M. Memoir of H. L. Winslow. New York, n.d. 16° 1109.10
WINSLOW, Mrs. M., Biography of. Baillie, J. . . 548.12
WINSOR, J. History of Duxbury, Mass. Boston, 1849. 8° 224.9
WINTER in London. Surr, T. S. 429.8
WINTERSLOW: Essays and characters written there. Hazlitt, W. 878.26
WINTHROP, J. History of New England, 1630 to 1649. Boston, 1853. 2v. 8° 223.7

WINTHROP, R. C. Addresses and speeches. Boston, 1852. 8° 861.4
WIRT, W. Letters of the British spy. 4th ed Baltimore, 1811. 18° 909.6
— - Same. 10th ed. New York, 1832. 12° . . 909.5
— Life and character of Patrick Henry. Philadelphia, 1817. 8° 513.18
— - Same. 3d ed. Philadelphia, 1818. 8°. . 513.16
— - Same. Rev. ed. Ithaca, N. Y., 1850. 12°. 513.15
— - Same. 15th ed. Hartford, 1852. 8° . . . 513.17
— The old bachelor. Baltimore, [1818.] 2v. 18° 850.30
— Life of. Kennedy, J. P. 517.11
WISCONSIN. Lapham, I. A. Geographical and topographical description of 239.16
— Ritchie, J. S. W. and its resources. [Also] The constitution of the state 237.9
WISDOM of the ancients. Bacon, F. 868.20
WISE, E. The readiest reckoner. Simpson, S. . 136.34
WISE, H. A. Los Gringos : or, Mexico, California, and Peru. New York, 1849. 12°. . . . 627.24
— Tales for the marines. By Harry Gringo. New York, 1855. 12° 737.3-4
WISE, I. M. History of the Israelitish nation. v.I. Albany, 1854. 8° 1085.7
WISEMAN, N. Ceremonies of holy week in the papal chapels. London, 1839. 8° 1098.3
— Connexion between science and revealed religion. 4th ed. Baltimore, 1852. 2v. 16° 1098.20
— Essays on various subjects. Lond., 1853. 3v. 8° 1098.2
    Contents. — Vol. I. Controversy concerning 1 John v. 7; Catholic versions of Scripture; Parables and miracles of the New Test. ; Letters to J. Poynder, on popery in alliance with heathenism; Authority of the holy see in S. America; On ecclesiastical organization; Fate of sacrilege; On prayer and prayer books; On national holidays; On the minor rites and offices of the church; Ancient and modern catholicity; Actions of the N. Testament. II. Hampden controversy ; Tracts for the times; Froude's remains; High church theory of dogmatical authority; Catholic and Anglican churches ; Anglican system ; Protestantism of the Anglican church; Unreality of the Anglican belief ; Position of the high church theory at the close of 1847 ; Fourth of October. III. Papers on history, antiquities and art; Spain; Pope Boniface VIII. ; St. Elizabeth of Hungary ; Council held at Constantinople A.D. 1109; On the writings of St. Ephrem; Account of a recently discovered Christian inscription ; Remarks on Lady Morgan's statement regarding St. Peter's chair ; The Roman forum ; Christian art; Spanish and English national art; Superficial travelling; Italian guides and tourists; Religion in Italy ; Italian gesticulation; Early Italian academies; Sense v. science.
— Fabiola : or, the church of the catacombs. London, 1855. 16° 809.13
— Lectures on the principal doctrines and practices of the Catholic church. 3d Am. from last Lond. ed. Baltimore, 1851. 2v. in 1. 12° 1098.5
— Real presence of the body and blood of Christ in the eucharist. Fr. Lond. ed. Balt.,1852. 12° 1098.4
— Recollections of the last four Popes. London, 1858. 8° 1098.1
WISNER, B. B. Memoirs of Mrs. S. Huntington. 4th ed. Boston, 1833. 12° 538.22
WIT and wisdom of the Rev. S. Smith 896.5-6
WIT, Specimens of Douglas Jerrold's 884.18
WIT, The cyclopædia of. Burton, W. E. . . . 901.7
    See also : Humor.
WITH, E. Railroad accidents. Introduction by A. Perdonnet. Transl. by G. F. Barstow. Boston, 1856. 12° 198.14
WITHINGTON, W. Growth of thought as affecting the progress of society. Boston, 1851. 12° 124.16
WITCHCRAFT. Calef, R. Wonders of the invisible world 229.5
— Scott, Sir W. Letters on 399.2
WITT, C. de. Histoire de Washington. Étude hist. sur W. par Guizot. Paris, 1855. 12° 1067.30
WITT, J. de, Life and times of. Barnwell, R. G.. 545.16
WITTICH, W. Curiosities of physical geography. London, 1853. 2v. 18° 850.21
— Visit to the Western coast of Norway. London, 1848. 18° 850.22

WIVES. Child, L. M. Biographies of good wives. 548.8-9
— Ellis, S. S. The wives of England. . . pt.II. of 804.7
WOEHLER, F. Analytical chemist's assistant. Translated, with additions, by O. M. Lieber. Philadelphia, 1852. 12° 156.16
WOLCOT, J. Works of Peter Pindar. London, 1797. 3v. 12° 348.16
    Contents. — Vol. I. Odes to Royal academicians; The Lousiad, i.—iv.; Bozzy and Piozzi; Ode upon ode; Instructions to a laureat; Brother Peter to brother Tom; Peter's prophecy; Epistle to Sir Joseph Banks on the election of a president to the Royal society; Peter's pension, a solemn epistle to a sublime personage. II. Sir Joseph Banks and the emperor of Morocco, a tale; Epistle to a failing minister; Subjects for painters; Expostulatory odes to a great duke and a little lord; A benevolent epistle to master John Nichols, printer; A Rowland for an Oliver; Advice to the future laureat; Epistle to James Bruce, Esq.; The rights of kings; Odes to Mr. Paine, (Thomas); The remonstrance, also The magpie and robin, etc.; More money, or instruction to Mr. Pitt; Odes of importance, or, the wolves, the bear, etc.; The tears of S . Margaret, likewise Mrs. Robinson's handkerchief; A pair of lyric epistles to Lord Macartney; Odes to Kien Long. III. Epistle to the pope, on his keeping a disorderly house; Pathetic odes to the duke of Richmond; The Lousiad, canto v.; Hair powder, a plaintive epistle to Mr. Pitt; Frogmore fête, an ode for music; Royal tour and Weymouth amusements; Pindariana, or Peter's portfolio; Convention bill, an ode.

WOLDEMAR, Der falsche : Roman. Häring, W. . 1024.8
WOLF, J. W. Fairy tales ; edited by K. R. H. Mackenzie. London, 1855. 16° 719.10
— Neiderländische Sagen. Leipzig, 1843. 8°. . 1013.17
WOLF-BOY of China ; or, incidents in the life of Lyu-Payo. Dalton, W. 728.6
WOLFERT's roost. Irving, W. 438.13-16
WOLFF, J. Mission to Bokhara. N. Y., 1845. 8°. 695.2
WOLSEY, T., Cardinal. Cavendish, G. Life of.. 566.10
— Galt, J. Life of 566.11
WOLVES, The. Livonian tales 889.31
WOLZOGEN, K. v. Cordelia. Leipzig, 1840. 2v. 16° 1035.6
WOMAN. Beecher, C. E. Remedy for wrongs of. 868.13
— Graves, A. J. W. in America 820.61
— Harbaugh, H. The true glory of 896.8
— Legouvé, É. Histoire morale des femmes . . 1078.9
— McIntosh, M. J. W. in America 888.23
— Merz, H. Christliche Frauenbilder 1014.3
— Muloch, D. M. A woman's thoughts about women 874.7
— Necker de Saussure, Mme. A. A. Étude de la vie des femmes 1068.8
— Ossoli, S. M. F. d'. W. in the 19th century . 885.10
— Saintine, X. B. Woman's whims . . . . 878.6 & 13
— Ségur, A. J. P. de. The condition and influence of W. in society 139.15
— Starling, E. Noble deeds of 547.6
— Winslow, H. Woman as she should be . . . 1088.29
WOMAN's record. Hale, S. J. 541.1
WOMAN's rights tracts. Boston, 1854. 12° 878.8
WOMAN's love : a novel. Opie, A. 469.46-47
WOMAN's trials, Tales of. Hall, A. M. 776.14
WOMEN. Aguilar, G. The W. of Israel. . . . 766.11-15
— Ellet, E. F. W. of the American revolution . 538.13
— Ellis, S. S. W. of England. 804.7
— Library of biography. Remarkable W. of different nations and ages. 547.5
— Michelet, J. W. of the French revolution. . 1008.6-7
    NOTE. — For works on the health and diseases of women, see Medicine.
WONDER book for girls and boys. Hawthorne, N. 737.17
WONDERFUL inventions. See History of. 197.21
WONDERFUL and eccentric museum. Kirby, R. S. 804.1
WONDERFUL tales from Denmark. Andersen, H. C. 719.8
WONDERS of geology. Goodrich, S. G. 169.13
WOOD, G. Marrying too late. New York, 1857. 12° 498.5
— Modern pilgrims. Boston, 1855. 2v. 12° 428.4
— Peter Schlemihl in America. Phila., 1848. 12° 808.1
WOOD, G. B. Treatise on the practice of medicine. 3d ed. Philadelphia, 1852. 2v. 8°. . . . 152.3
— and Bache, F. Dispensatory of the United States. 9th ed. Philadelphia, 1851. 8° . . 151.12

WOOD, J. History of the administration of J. Adams, 1797–1801. Phila., 1846. 12° 309.7
WOOD, J. G. Illustrated natural history. New York, 1854. 16° 177.9
— Sketches and anecdotes of animal life. London, 1854. 16° 178.24
WOOD, M. A. E., Miss. See Green, M. A. E., Mrs.
WOOD, W. B. Personal recollections of the stage. Philadelphia, 1855. 12° 356.12
WOOD-LEIGHTON. A novel. Howitt, M. 459.1
WOODBRIDGE, J. Practical religion recommended in a series of letters. N. Y., 1857. 12° . . . 1088.23
— Discourse delivered in Murray street church. See Discourses 1083.5
WOODBURY, Conn., History of ancient. Cothren, W. 225.2
WOODCRAFT: or, hawks about the dovecote. Simms, W. G. 790.30–34
WOODCROFT, B. Origin and progress of steam navigation. London, 1848. sm.4° 195.12
WOODEN booksellers, and miseries of authorship. Fessenden. T. G. 349.19
WOODLAND, field and garden. Pratt, A. . . . 850.5
WOODLAND gleanings. An account of British forest trees. London, 1853. 16° 109.20
WOODS, D. B. Sixteen months at the gold diggings. New York, 1851. 12° 637.3
WOODS, L. sen. Discourse delivered in Murray street church. See Discourses, etc. 1083.5
WOODSTOCK. Scott, Sir W. 480.14–17
WOODWARD, C. Introduction to the study of polarized light. 2d ed. London, 1851. 8° 145.21
WOODWARD, S. P. Manual of the mollusca: or, recent and fossil shells. 3 parts. London, 1851–56. 12° 175.12
— Same. Pt. I.–II. London, 1851–54. 2v. 16° 829.7
WOODWORTH, F. C. Uncle Frank's pleasant pages for the fireside. New York, 1857. 12° . . . 498.10
WOODWORTH, S. Additions to festivals, games, etc. Smith, H. 810.31
WOOL, History of. See History of silk. 195.4
— Kindt, J. De l' industrie de la laine . . . 1065.28
— Southey, T. Colonial, home and foreign wools 136.9
WOOLHOUSE, W. S. B. Differential calculus. Elements. 2d ed. London, 1854. 16° 829.31
WOOLRYCHE, H. W. Memoirs of the life of Judge Jeffreys. London, 1827. 8° 568.4
WORCESTER, N. Bible news. 5th ed. Boston, 1854. 12° 118.1
WORCESTER, Marquis of. See Somerset, E.
WORDS. Roget, P. M. Thesaurus of English . . 403.13
— Trench, R. C. The study of 406.6–7
See Language.
WORDS for the hour. Howe, J. W. 345.15
WORDSWORTH, C. Athens and Attica. London, 1836. 8° 683.6
— Memoirs of W. Wordsworth. Edited by H. Reed. Boston, 1851. 2v. 16° 584.21
WORDSWORTH, W. Complete poetical works. Edited by H. Reed. Philadelphia, 1851. 8° . 311.1

Contents. — Poems written in youth; Poems referring to the period of childhood; Poems founded on the affections; Poems on the naming of places; Poems of the fancy; Poems of the imagination; Miscellaneous sonnets; Memorials of a tour in Scotland; Poems dedicated to national independence and liberty; Sonnets dedicated to liberty and order; Sonnets upon the punishment of death; Memorials of a tour on the continent; The river Duddon; Yarrow revisited; Poems, composed or suggested during a tour in the summer of 1833; Memorials of a tour in Italy, 1837; The white doe of Rylstone; Ecclesiastical sonnets; Poems of sentiment and reflection; Evening voluntaries; Miscellaneous poems; Selections from Chaucer, modernized; Inscriptions; Poems referring to the period of old age; Epitaphs and elegiac pieces; The prelude; The excursion; Appendix, prefaces, etc., etc.

— Poetical works. New ed. London, 1849–50. 6v. 18° 359.12

Contents. — Vol. I. Poems written in youth; Poems referring to the period of childhood; Poems founded

WORDSWORTH, W., continued.

on the affections. II. Poems on the naming of places; Poems of the fancy; Poems of the imagination; Miscellaneous sonnets. III. Memorials of a tour in Scotland; Poems dedicated to national independence and liberty; Memorials of a tour on the continent; Memorials of a tour in Italy; The river Duddon; Yarrow revisited, and other poems. IV. The white doe of Rylstone; Ecclesiastical sonnets; Evening voluntaries; Poems, composed in the summer of 1833; Poems of sentiment and reflection; Sonnets dedicated to liberty and order; Sonnets upon the punishment of death. V. Miscellaneous poems; Inscriptions; Selections from Chaucer, modernized; Poems referring to the period of old age; Epitaphs and elegiac pieces; Appendix, prefaces, etc., etc. VI. The excursion.

— The excursion: a poem. N. Y., 1850. 12° . . 344.3–4
— The prelude: an autobiographical poem. New York, 1850. 12° 344.1–2
— Yarrow revisited, and other poems. Boston, 1835. 16° 344.5
— Hood, E. P. A biography of 584.20
— Wordsworth, C. Memoirs of 584.21
WORK: or, plenty to do and how to do it. Brewster, M. M. 1099.20–21
WORK and wages: or, life in service. Howitt, M. 459.13
WORKERS, Words for the. Haley, W. D. 137.27
WORKING man, Memoirs of a 840.45
WORKING man's way in the world. The autobiography of a printer. N. Y., 1854. 12° . . . 767.1
WORLD, The. Blake, J. L. Characteristics of all nations 947.8
— Fisher, R. S. Book of the 951.4
— Goodrich, S. G. Pictorial geography of the. 951.1
— Maunder, S. A history of 951.5

NOTE. — See also: Astronomy, Solar system, etc. For voyages round the world, see Voyages.

WORLD, The. Moore, E. See British Essayists. v.XXVI.–XXIX. of 850.24
WORLD'S own, The. Howe, J. W. 345.16
WORLDS. Brewster, D. More worlds than one . 146.28
— Dick, T. Plurality of. 810.77
— Powell, B. Unity of 147.23
— Whewell, W. The plurality of. 146.18–21
WORMLEY, M. E. Amabel, a family history. New York, 1853. 12° 416.2
— Our cousin Veronica. New York, 1855. 12°. 416.1
WORNUM, R. N. The epochs of painting characterized. London, 1847. 24° 850.23
WORTH and wealth. Hunt, F. 136.20
WORTHEN, W. E. Appleton's cyclopædia of drawing. New York, 1857. 8° 201.5
WORTHIES, Cabinet portrait gallery of British . 840.10–11
WORTHIES of England, History of the. Fuller, T. . 574.5
WORTHINGTON, E. History of Dedham, Mass. 1827. 8° 224.16
WORTLEY, E. S. Travels in the U. S., etc., during 1849–50. New York, 1851. 12° . . . 628.20–21
WOTTON, Sir H., The life of. Walton, I. 589.5
WRANGELL, F. v. Expedition to the Polar sea in 1820–1823. New York, 1845. 18° 820.49
WRANGHAM, F. The Pleiad, from seven writers on the evidences of Christianity. Edin., 1828. 18° 830.41
WRAXALL, L. Naval and military resources of the principal European nations. London, 1856. 8° 947.3
WREATH, The: a collection of poems. Hartford, 1824. 24° 369.9
WREATH of wild flowers from New England. Osgood, F. S. 348.10
WREN, Sir C., Life and times of. Elmes, J. . . . 203.18
WRIGHT, F. See Darusmont, F. W.
WRIGHT, S., Life and times of. Hammond, J. D. 523.9
WRIGHT, T. The Chester plays. Lond., 1843. 8° 342.16
— Dictionary of obsolete and provincial English. London, 1857. 2v. p.8° 855.7
— Early travels in Palestine. London, 1848. p.8° 846.7
— Essays on England in the middle ages. London, 1846. 2v. 12° 988.13

WRIGHT, T. History of the reigns of George IV. and William IV. *See* Hume, D.... v.III. of 962.3
— Literature, superstitions and history of England in the middle ages. Lond., 1846. 2v. 12° 987.3
— Queen Elizabeth and her times: a series of original letters. Lond., 1838. 2v. 8° . . . 554.2
WROTTESLEY, J., L'd., Navigation by . . . v.III. of 365.14
WUNNISSOO : or, the vale of Hoosatunnuk. Allen, W. 338.8
WUTHERING heights : a novel. Brontë, E. . . . 455.12
WYANDOTTÉ : or, the hutted knoll ; a tale. Cooper, J. F. 790.1–6
WYATT, *Sir* T. Poetical works. Lond., 1831. 16° 339.1
WYCLIFFE, J. de. *See* Wiclif, J.
WYMAN, M. Practical treatise on ventilation. Boston, 1846. 12° 207.5
WYNNE, J. Lives of eminent literary and scientific men of America. New York, 1850. 12° . 518.3–4
WYOMING. Miner, C. A history of 234.12
— Peck, G. History, etc. 237.2
— Stone, W. L. Poetry and history of 237.14

XENIEN manuscript, Schiller's and Göthe's. *See* Schiller, J. C. F. v. 1013.15
XENOPHON. Works. Tr. by A. Cooper, Spelman, Smith, Fielding, and others. N.Y., 1852. 8° 872.10
— Minor works, transl. by J. S. Watson. London, 1857. p.8° 844.6
— Anabasis. Transl. by E. Spelman. [Also the Cyropædia.] New York. 2v. 18° . . 830.8
— Anabasis; and memorabilia of Socrates. Transl. by J. S. Watson. London, 1854. p.8° 844.4
— Cyropædia and the Hellenics, transl. by Watson and Dale. London, 1855. p.8° 844.5
XENOPHON Ephesius. Gli amori d' Abrocome e d' Anzia. *See* Romanzetti. 1058.12
XERXES the Great, History of. Abbott, J. . . . 549.25–26

YALE, C. Life of the Rev. Jeremiah Hallock. New York, n.d. 12° 1107.2
YANKEE stories. Haliburton, T. C. 489.1
YANKEE travels through Cuba. By Demoticus Philalethes. New York, 1856. 16° 626.15
YARRANTON, A., Account of. Dove, P. E. . . . 588.1
YARRELL, W. History of British fishes. 2d ed. London, 1841. 2v. 8° 172.11
YARROW revisited, and other poems. Wordsworth, W. 344.5
YATES, R. Notes of proceedings of the convention for forming the constitution of the United States, 1787. *See* Secret proceedings. 299.6
YATES, W. H. Modern Egypt. Lond., 1843. 2v. 8° 955.8
YEAR, The : a poem. Pierce, W. L. 369.8
YEAR book of daily recreation, etc. Hone, W. . . 892.13
YEAR book of science and art. Timbs, J. 159.2
YEAR of consolation. Kemble, F. A. 676.7–10
YEAR of revolution in Paris, in 1848. Phipps, C. H. 1002.4
YEAR nine, The : a tale of the Tyrol. London, 1858. 12° 434.1
YEAST, a problem. Kingsley, C. 484.15–16
YELLOWPLUSH papers, The. Thackeray, W. M. . 508.9–11
YELLOW Sea, Narrative of a voyage to the. McLeod, J. 696.11
YEMASSEE, The, a romance of Carolina. Simms, W. G. 790.8–12
YEZIDIS, or devil-worshippers, Account of a visit to the. Layard, A. H. 685.14–16
YOAKUM, H. History of Texas, 1685 to 1846. New York, 1856. 2v. 8° 235.11
YONGE, C. D. Hist. of England. Lond., 1857. p.8° 966.1
YONGE, C. M. Beechcroft, a tale. N. Y., 1856. 12° 786.8–9
— Castle builders. New York, 1855. 12° . . . 786.7
— Daisy chain : or, aspirations. New York, 1856. 2v. 12° 775.1–10
— Dynevor terrace : or, the clue of life. New York, 1857. 2v. 8° 785.1–10
— Heartsease : or, the brother's wife. New York, 1855. 2v. 12° 784.1–6
— Heir of Redclyffe. New York, 1855. 2v. 12° 786.1–6
— Lances of Lynwood. New York, 1856. 16° . 786.11

YONGE, C. M. Little duke : or, Richard the fearless. [With illustr.] London, 1855. sq.16° 786.12
— Two guardians : or, home in this world. New York, 1855. 12° 786.10
YOUATT, W. Cattle ; breeds, management, and diseases. London, n.d. 8° 172.13
— History of the horse. Martin, W. C. L. . . . 840.44
— The dog. Ed. by E. J. Lewis. Philadelphia, 1852. 8° 172.22–23
— The horse, with a treatise on draught. London, 1831. 8° 172.17
— On the structure and diseases of the horse. Brought down by W. C. Spooner. Breeds in the United States by H. S. Randall. Auburn, 1855. 12° 165.16
YOUMANS, E. L. Handbook of household science. New York, 1857. 12° 188.5–6
YOUNG, A. Chronicles of the pilgrim fathers, 1602 to 1625. Boston, 1841. 8° 223.13

Contents. — Gov. Bradford's history of Plymouth colony; Bradford's and Winslow's journal; Cushman's discourse on the state of the colony; Winslow's relation; Winslow's brief narration; Gov. Bradford's dialogue; Gov. Bradford's memoir of Elder Brewster; Letters.

— Chronicles of the first planters of the colony of Massachusetts Bay. Boston, 1846. 8°. 223.12

Contents. — White's brief relation; Hubbard's narrative; The company's records; Gov. Cradock's letter to Captain Endicott; Instructions to Endicott; Form of government; Allotment of the lands; Agreement with the ministers; Higginson's journal of his voyage; Higginson's New England's plantation; Considerations for planting New England; Agreement at Cambridge; Company's letters to Higginson and Endicott; Humble request; Dudley's letter to the Countess of Lincoln; R. Clap's memoirs; Early records of Charlestown ; Wood's description of Massachusetts; John Cotton's life and letters; R. Mather's journal; Thacher's narrative of his shipwreck; Shepard's memoir of his own life.

YOUNG, E. Works. New ed., rev. and cor. London, 1813. 3v. 8° 314.12

Contents. — Vol. I. Life; The complaint, or, night thoughts. II. Last day; The force of religion; Love of fame; Epistles to Mr. Pope; Paraphrase on part of the book of Job; Ocean, an ode; Sea piece; Busiris, king of Egypt, tragedy. III. The revenge, tragedy; The brothers, tragedy; The centaur not fabulous, in six letters on the life in vogue.

— Poetical works. London, 1852. 2v. p.8° . . . 329.14

Contents. — Vol. I. Life, by J. Mitford; The complaint, or night-thoughts. II. The last day; The force of religion; Love of fame; Ocean, an ode; Paraphrase on part of the book of Job; Miscellaneous; Reflections on the public situation of the kingdom; Resignation; On the death of Queen Anne; The instalment; Epistles.

YOUNG, J. The Christ of history. New York, 1856. 12° 1087.13
YOUNG, J. R. Treatise on arithmetic. 2d ed. London, 1854. 16° 829.18
— Key to rudimentary treatise on arithmetic. London, 1853. 16° 829.19
YOUNG, T. Notes to treatise on carpentry by Prof. Robison 201.4
YOUNG, W. T. Life and services of Gen. Lewis Cass. 2d ed. Detroit, 1852. 8° 526.7
YOUNG, The. *Note.* For books of advice to young people, see Manners and Minor morals.
YOUNG America in Wall street. Train, G. F. . . . 877.7
YOUNG Christian. Abbott, J. 1087.7
YOUNG emigrants, The. Boston, 1830. 12° . . . 449.9
YOUNG housekeeper's friend. Cornelius, M. H. . 188.25
YOUNG love : a novel. Trollope, F. 807.3
YOUNG maiden, The. Muzzey, A. B. 127.29
YOUNG man's book of knowledge. Tegg, T. . . . 138.1
YOUNG prima donna. The romance of the opera. Grey, Hon. Mrs. 802.26–27
YOUNG rifleman's comrade. Philadelphia, 1827. 12° 737.2
YOUNG voyageurs, or the boy hunters of the North. Reid, M. 718.2

YOUNG Yägers, The. Reid, M. 718.3–7
YOUTH of the old dominion. Hopkins, S. 478.8
YOUTH's companion and counsellor. Chambers, W. 138.9
YSABEAU, A. Culture des plantes fourragères.
    Bruxelles, n.d. 12° 1075.6
— De l' élève etc. des oiseaux de la basse cour et
    des lapins. Bruxelles, n.d. 12° 1075.3
— Traité de l' élève et de l' engraissement du
    bétail. Bruxelles, n.d. 2v. in 1. 12° . . . 1075.2
— Traité des arbres fruitiers. Bruxelles, n.d. 1075.5
— Traité des engrais et amendements. Bruxelles,
    n.d. 12° 1075.4
— Traité des opérations agricoles. Bruxelles,
    n.d. 12° 1075.1
YUCATAN. Fancourt, C. St. J. History of 635.6
— Norman, B. M. Rambles in 621.4
— Stephens, J. L. Incidents of travel in 621.5–10
YVAN and Callery. Insurrection in China. See
    Callery 938.6

ZAIDEE : a romance. Oliphant, M. 753.1–4
ZANOLINI, A. Il diavolo del Sant' Ufficio. Storia
    bolognese. Capolago, 1847. 3v. 12° . . . 1057.9
ZANONI : a novel. Lytton, E. B. 465.10–11
ZAULI Sajani, I. Ultimi giorni dei cavalieri di
    Malta, 1841. 2v. in 1. 16° 1059.1
ZELUCO : a novel, by J. Moore. v.XXXIV.–XXXV. of 779.1
ZENEIDA, or ideal perfection : a tale. Genlis,
    Mme. de 759.15
ZENOBIA, or the fall of Palmyra: a historical ro-
    mance. Ware, W. 808.9
ZINCALI, The. See Gypsies.
ZINZENDORF, N. L., Life of. Spangenberg, A. G. 545.26
ZOE, the history of two lives. Jewsbury, G. E. . 802.23
ZÖGLING der Gesellschaft. Rom. Mundt, K. . . 1016.6
ZOHRAB, the hostage: [a novel.] Morier, J. . . . 808.3
ZOLLIKOFER, G. J. Exercises of piety. Transl.
    by J. Manning, abridged, corrected, etc.,
    by T. M. Harris. Boston, 1855. 12° . . . 1088.11
ZONCADA, A. Tre racconti. [Il pittore di Arlem.
    L' amor filiale. Un duello.] Milano, 1850.
    12° 1056.15

ZOOLOGY. Agassiz, L. The principles of 177.6–7
— Bennett, E. T. Gardens and menageries of
    the zoological society 172.19–20
— Broderip, W. J. Zoological recreations . . . 177.8
— Carpenter, W. B. Zoology 836.6
— Hannon, J. Traité élémentaire de zoologie . 1065.20
    See also : Natural history, and the branches
    of zoology there enumerated.
ZOOLOGISTS, Biography of. Swainson, W. . . .   408.5
ZOOPHYTES. Johnston, G. A history of the
    British 178.1
— Landsborough, D. Popular history of British. 178.30
ZOROASTER, The oracles of. See Phenix, The . . 808.8
ZOUAVE before Sebastopol, Recollections of a.
    Maynard, F. 1008.18
ZSCHOKKE, J. H. D. Fool of the nineteenth cen-
    tury, and other tales. New York, 1845. 12° 767.12

    Contents. — Florian, the fugitive of the Jura; Mar-
    ble and Conrad; Oliver Flyeln, a fool of the 19th cen-
    tury; Hortensia: asleep and awake.

— History of Switzerland, continued to 1848 by
    E. Zschokke, translated by F. G. Shaw.
    New York, 1855. 12° 917.2
— The princess of Wolfenbuttel 801.2
— Tales from the German, by P. Godwin. New
    York, 1845. 2v. in 1. . . . .   767.12

    Contents. —Vol. I. Fool of the 19th century; Har-
    monius; Jack Steam; Floretta; New Year's eve. II.
    Illumination, or, the sleepwalker; The broken cup;
    Jonathan Frock; The involuntary journey; Leaves
    from the journal of a poor vicar in Wiltshire.

ZULU country, The Kafirs of the. Shooter, J. . .   693.2
ZUMA, or the tree of health: A tale. Genlis,
    Mme. de 759.15
ZUMALA-CARREGUI, T., Striking events of a cam-
    paign with, in Navarre, and the Basque
    provinces. Henningsen, C. F. 917.3
ZWINGLI, U. Hess, J. G. Life of 545.27
— Christoffel, R. Life of. 1085.14
ZWISCHEN Himmel und Erde. Erzählung.
    Ludwig, O. 1035.4

BOOKS OF REFERENCE

IN THE READING ROOM.

ADLER, G. J. Dictionary of the German and English languages. 4th ed. N. Y., 1854. 8° ... L.9

ALEXANDER, J. H. Dictionary of weights and measures, anc. and mod. Balt., 1850. 8°.. L.10

ALLEN, W. American biographical dictionary. 3d ed. Boston, 1857. 8° K.1

AMERICAN almanac, The, for the year 1858. Boston, 1857. 12° C.8

AMERICAN literature, Cyclopædia of. Duyckinck, E. A. and G. L. L.11

AMERICANISMS, Dictionary of. Bartlett, J. R... M.6

ANDREWS, E. A. Copious and critical Latin-English lexicon, founded on the Latin-German lexicon of W. Freund. New York, 1854. 8° K.8

ANGLO-SAXON and Eng. dictionary. Bosworth, J. M.5

ANTIQUITIES, Dictionary of Greek and Roman. Smith, W. K.12

APPLETON, D. and Co. Dictionary of machines, mechanics, engine-work, and engineering. New York, 1851-52. 2v. 8° K.4

ARCHITECTURE. Nicholson, P. Encyclopædia of. U.1

— Stuart, R. A dictionary of K.11

ARNAULT, A. V. and others. Biographie nouvelle des contemporains. Paris. 1820-25. 20v. 8° E.1

ASTRONOMY. Johnston, A. K. Atlas of ....

— Society for Diffusion of Useful Knowledge. Six maps of the stars ....

ATLAS. Black, A. and C. General atlas .....

— Colton, G. W. A. of the world ....

— Findlay, A. G. Classical atlas M.2

— - Modern atlas M.1

— Soc. for Diff. Usef. Knowl. Maps, with index.

BALDWIN, T. and Thomas, J. Gazetteer of the United States. Philadelphia, 1854. 8° .. C.11

BARETTI, J. Spanish and English dictionary. Neuman, H. E.2

BARTLETT, J. R. Dictionary of Americanisms. New York, 1848. 8° M.6

BELL, J. System of geography, popular and scientific, illustrated by maps and engravings. London, 1851-53. 6v. 8° M.9

BIBLE. Holy Bible. New York, 1854. 8° L.6

— Brown, Rev. J. Dictionary of the L.7

— Cruden, A. Concordance to the L.8

BIOGRAPHICAL dictionary. Allen, W. American. K.1

— Arnault, A. V., etc. Biographie nouvelle des contemporains E.1

— Blake, J. L. Universal V.3

— Godwin, P. Handbook of biography..... C.4

— Gorton, J. A general M.10

— Hale, S. J. Woman's record K.6

— O'Byrne, W. R. Naval L.2

— Rose, H. J. General D.1

— Smith, W. Greek and Roman K.13

BIOGRAPHICAL sketches. See Men of the time . C.10

BLACK, A. and C. General atlas of the world, by S. Hall, W. Hughes, etc. New ed. Edinburgh, 1854. fol. ....

BLAKE, J. L. A biographical dictionary, including 2000 articles of American biography. 13th ed. Philadelphia, 1856. 8° V.3

BOAG, J. Imperial lexicon of the English language, [illustrated.] Edinb., n.d. 2v. 8° V.6

BOSWORTH, J. Anglo-Saxon and English dictionary. London, 1849. 8° M.5

BOUVIER, J. Law dictionary, adapted to the laws of the United States and of the several states. 6th ed. Philadelphia, 1856. 2v. 8° L.3

BRITISH Islands, Gazetteer of the. Sharp, J. A.. M.7

BROWN, G. Grammar of English grammars. With an introduction, historical and critical. New York, 1851. 8° L.12

BROWN, J. A dictionary of the Bible, with a life of the author. From 12th Edinburgh ed. New York, 1848. 8° L.7

BRYAN, M. Dictionary of painters and engravers. New ed., rev. and enlarged by G. Stanley. London, 1853. 8° K.3

CHRONOLOGY. Haydn, J. The dictionary of dates . M.8

— Putnam, G. P. The world's progress, a dictionary of dates................ C.13

CLARKE, M. C. Concordance to Shakspere. [London,] n.d. 8° K.2

CLASSICAL atlas, to illustrate ancient geography. Findlay, A. G. M.2

CLASSICAL dictionary, A new, of Greek and Roman mythology, etc. Smith, W. K.13

COLTON, G. W. and Fisher, R. S. Atlas of the world. Accomp. by descriptions, geographical, statistical and historical, by R. S. Fisher. New York, 1856. 2v. 14°.....

Contents.— Vol. I. America. II. Europe, Asia, Africa, etc.

COMMERCE, and commercial navigation, Cyclopædia of. Homans, J. S. U.2

CONCORDANCE to the Holy Scriptures. Cruden, A. L.8

CONCORDANCE to Shakspere. Clarke, M. C... K.2

CONTEMPORAINS, Biographie nouvelle des. Arnault, A. V. and others E.1

CRAIG, J. New universal dictionary of the English language. London, 1849. 2v. 8° .. V.9

CRESY, E. Encyclopædia of civil engineering. London, 1847. 8° C.12

CRUDEN, A. Complete concordance to the Holy Scriptures, with introduction by Rev. D. King. Boston, 1854. 8° L.8

CYCLOPÆDIA. Duyckinck, E. A. and G. L. C. of American literature. L.11

— Godwin, P. C. of biography........ C.4

— Homans, J. S. C. of commerce and commercial navigation U.2

— National, etc. C. of useful knowledge F.2

— New American N.2

— Penny cyclopædia T.2

— Tomlinson, C. C. of useful arts, etc. U.3

See also: Encyclopædia.

DATES. See Chronology.

DICTIONARY of scientific terms. Hoblyn, R. D. . C.6

DICTIONARY of select and popular quotations, from the Latin, French, Greek, Spanish, and Italian langg. 6th Am. ed. Phila., 1852. 12° C.7

DICTIONARY. *See* Anglo-Saxon, English, French, German, Greek, Italian, Latin, Spanish; *see also:* Antiquities, Architecture, Bible, Chronology, Commerce, Engravers, Law, Machines, Mythology, Painters, Quotations, Scientific terms, Weights and measures; *and compare* Cyclopædia and Encyclopædia.

DOD, C. R. Peerage of Great Britain and Ireland for 1855. London, [1855.] 12° C.9

DUYCKINCK, E. A. and G. L. Cyclopædia of American literature. New York, 1855. 2v. 8° . L.11

ENCYCLOPÆDIA Americana. New ed. Edited by F. Lieber, assisted by E. Wigglesworth and T. G. Bradford. Supplementary volume, ed. by H. Vethake. Boston, 1853. 14v. 8° . N.1

ENCYCLOPÆDIA Britannica, with preliminary dissertations on the history of the sciences. [Ed. by M. Napier.] 7th ed. Edinburgh, 1842. 21v. 4° S.1 T.1

ENCYCLOPÆDIA. Cresy, E. E. of civil engineering. C.12
— Moore, J. W. Complete E. of music U.4
— Nicholson, P. E. of architecture U.1
See also: Cyclopædia.

ENGINEERING, Appleton's dictionary of K.4
— Cresy, E. Encyclopædia of civil C.12
— Tomlinson, C. Cyclopædia of U.3

ENGLISH language. Boag, J. Imperial lexicon of the V.6
— Craig, J. A new dictionary of the V.9
— Ogilvie, J. Imperial dictionary of the. . . . V.2
— Richardson, C. New dictionary of the . . . V.1
— Walker, J. Rhyming dictionary of the . . . F.1
— Webster, N. Dictionary of the V.4
— Worcester, J. E. Critical dictionary of the . V.8
— - Pronouncing dictionary of the M.4
See also: Grammar, Americanisms.

ENGRAVERS, Biog. and crit. dict. of. Bryan, M. . K.3

FELLER, F. X. de. Dictionnaire historique. Nouv. éd. T.1–8, supplém., 9–12. Paris, 1818–20. 12v. 12° D.2

FINDLAY, A. G. Classical atlas, to illustrate ancient geography. London, 1853. 8° M.2
— Modern atlas. 5th ed. London, 1853. 8° . . M.1

FISHER, R. S. Statistical gazetteer of the United States. New York, 1853. 8° K.10

FLEMING, *Prof.* and Tibbins, J. French and English and English and French dictionary. Tables of verbs by C. Picot. [Ed.] by J. Dobson. 6th ed., rev. and corrected. Philadelphia, 1852. 8° V.7

FOWLER, W. C. English grammar, with a history of the origin and development of the language. New York, 1851. 8° L.13

FRENCH and English dictionary. Fleming, *Prof.* and Tibbins, J V.7
— Pronouncing. Spiers, A. and Surenne, G. J. . V.5
— Phraseological. Tarver. J. C. L.1

GAZETTEER of the British Islands. Sharp J. A. . M.7
— of Scotland. *See* Topographical K.7
— of the United States. Baldwin, T. C.11
— - Fisher, R. S. Statistical K.10
— of the world. Ed. by a member of the R. G. S. Edinburgh, n.d. 7v. 18° U.5
— Lippincott's pronouncing G. *See* Thomas, J. U.6

GEOGRAPHY, popular and scientific. Bell, J. . . M.9
See also: Gazetteer.

GERMAN dictionary. *See* New English-German . C.1

GERMAN and English dictionary. Adler, G. J. . L.9

GODWIN, P. Handbook of universal biography. New York, 1852. 12° C.4

GORTON, J. General biographical dictionary. New ed., to which is added a supplementary vol. London, 1851. 4v. 8° M.10

GRAMMAR, English. Fowler, W. C. L.13
GRAMMAR of English grammars. Brown, G. . . L.12

GREEK-ENGLISH lexicon. Liddell, H. G., and Scott, R. K.9

GREEK and Roman antiquities, Dictionary of. Smith, W. K.12
GREEK and Roman biography, Dictionary of. Smith, W. K.13
GREEK lexicon, Illustrated companion to the. *See* Rich, A. C.5

HALE, S. J. Woman's record: or, sketches of distinguished women. Illustrated. 2d ed., with additions. New York, 1855. 8° K.6
HAYDN, J. Dictionary of dates. 5th ed. London, 1851. 8° M.8
HOBLYN, R. D. Dictionary of scientific terms. New York, 1850. 12° C.6
HOMANS, J. S. and J. S. Homans, jr. Cyclopædia of commerce and commercial navigation. New York, 1858. 8° U.2

ITALIAN and English dictionary. Millhouse, J. . C.2

JOHNSTON, A. K. Atlas of astronomy, 18 plates. Ed. by J. R. Hind. Edinb., 1855. 4° . . .

LATIN-ENGLISH lexicon. Andrews, E. A. K.8
LATIN lexicon, Illustr. companion to the. Rich, A. C.5
— Phraseological. Yonge, C. D. C.3
LAW dictionary. Bouvier, J. L.3
LEXICON. *See* Dictionary.

LIDDELL, H. G. and Scott, R. Greek-English lexicon, based on Passow, with additions by H. Drisler. New York, 1854. 8° K.9

LIPPINCOTT's pronouncing gazetteer of the world. *See* Thomas, J. U.6

LITERATURE, Cyclop. of American. Duyckinck, E. A. and G. L. L.11

MACHINES, Dictionary of, Appleton's K.4
MANUFACTURES, Cyclopædia of. Tomlinson, C. . U.3
MASSACHUSETTS. Revised statutes, 1835, with constitutions of the United States and of Mass., under the supervision of T. Metcalf and H. Mann. Boston, 1836. 8° L.4
— Supplement to revised statutes: general laws, 1836–53. Ed. by T. Metcalf, L. S. Cushing, and H. Gray, jr. v.I. Boston, 1854. 8° . . . L.5
MEASURES, Dictionary of. Alexander, J. H. . . L.10
MECHANICS, Appleton's dictionary of K.4
MEN of the time. Biographical sketches of eminent living characters: also Women of the time. London, 1856. 12° C.9
MILLHOUSE, J. New English and Italian dictionary. 2d ed. [Vol. 1, Eng.-Ital., vol. 2, Ital.-Eng.] Milan, 1857. 2v. 8° C.2
MINING, Cyclopædia of. Tomlinson, C. U.3
MOORE, J. W. Encyc. of music. Boston, 1854. 8° U.4
MUSIC, Encyclopædia of. Moore, J. W. U.4
MYTHOLOGY, Dictionary of Greek and Roman. *See* Smith, W. K.13

NATIONAL cyclopædia of useful knowledge. London, 1853. 12v. in 6. 8° F.2
NAVAL biographical dictionary. O'Byrne, W. R. L.2
NAVIGATION, Dictionary of commercial. Homans, J. S. U.2
NEUMAN, H. and Baretti, D. Dictionary of the Spanish and English languages. Boston, 1850. 2v. 8° E.2
— Seoane's Neuman and Baretti, by M. Velazquez de la Cadena. Pronouncing dictionary of the Spanish and English languages. New York. 1853. 8° K.5
NEW American cyclopædia. Ed. by G. Ripley and C. A. Dana. New York, 1858. 8° . . . N.2
NEW English-German and German-English dictionary. Philadelphia, 1849. 2v. in 1. 8° . C.1
NICHOLSON, P. Encyclopædia of architecture. Ed. by E. Lomax and T. Gunyon. New ed. London, n.d. 2v. 4° U.1

O'BYRNE, W. R. Naval biographical dictionary of her Majesty's navy. London, 1849. 8° . L.2

OGILVIE, J. Imperial dictionary, English, technological and scientific. Illustrated. Glasgow, 1853. 2v. 8° V.2

PAINTERS, Biograph. and crit. dict. of. Bryan, M.   K.3
PEERAGE, etc., of Great Britain, 1855. Dod, C. R.   C.9
PENNY cyclopædia. *See* Society for the diffusion of useful knowledge T.2
PUTNAM, G. P. The world's progress, a dictionary of dates. New York, 1851. 12° C.13

QUOTATIONS, Dictionary of, Latin, Greek, French, etc. *See* Dictionary, etc. C.7

RHYMING dictionary. Walker, J. F.1
RICH, A. Illustrated companion to the Latin dictionary and Greek lexicon: a glossary of all the words representing visible objects. London, 1849. 8° C.5
RICHARDSON, C. New dictionary of the English language [with a preliminary essay.] London, 1839. 2v. 4° V.1
ROMAN antiquities, Dictionary of Greek and. Smith, W. K.12
ROMAN biography, A dictionary of. Smith, W. .   K.13
ROSE, H. J. General biographical dictionary. London, 1853. 12v. 8° D.1

SCIENTIFIC terms, Dictionary of. Hoblyn, R. D.   C.6
SCOTLAND, Gazetteer of. *See* Topographical . .   K.7
SHAKSPERE, Concordance to. Clarke, M. C. . . .   K.2
SHARP, J. A. New gazetteer of the British islands. London, 1852. 2v. 8° M.7
SMITH, W. Dictionary of Greek and Roman antiquities. 2d ed. London, 1854. 8° K.12
— Dictionary of Greek and Roman biography and mythology. London, 1849. 3v. 8° . .   K.13
— New classical dictionary. Revised by C. Anthon. New York, 1851. 8° M.3
SOCIETY for the diffusion of useful knowledge. Penny cyclopædia [and] supplement, ed. by. G. Long. London, 1833-51. 29v. roy.8° . .   T.2
— Maps, [and index, by J. Mickleburgh.] London, 1846. 2v. in 1. Atl. fol. . . . . . .
   Contents.— Vol. I. Europe and Asia. II. Africa and America.
— Six maps of the stars. London, 1830. Atl. fol.
   Note. — Bound with Maps, above.

SPANISH. Neuman, H. and Baretti, D. Spanish and English dictionary E.2
— Seoane's Neuman and Baretti K.5
SPIERS, A. and Surenne, G. J. French and English pronouncing dictionary, rev. and enl. by G. P. Quackenbos. New York, 1853. 8°   V.2
STARS, Six maps of. Society for the diff. of us. kn.
STATISTICS. *See* Gazetteer.
STUART, R. Dictionary of architecture. Philadelphia, 1851. 3v. in 2. 8° K.11

TARVER, J. C. Royal phraseological English-French, and French-English dictionary. London, 1845-50. 2v. 8° L.1
THOMAS, J. and Baldwin, T. Lippincott's pronouncing gazetteer of the world. Philadelphia, 1855. 8° U.6
TOMLINSON, C. Cyclopædia of useful arts, manufactures, mining and engineering. With an introd. essay on the exhibition of 1851. Illustrated. London, 1851. 2v. 8° . .   U.3
TOPOGRAPHICAL, statistical and historical gazetteer of Scotland. Glasgow, 1843. 2v. 8° .   K.7

USEFUL arts, Cyclopædia of. Tomlinson, C. . . .   U.3

WALKER, J. Rhyming dictionary of the English language. 3d ed. Lond., 1819. 2v. in 1. 8°   F.1
WEBSTER, N. American dictionary of the English language. Ed. by C. A. Goodrich. Springfield, 1853. 4° V.4
WEIGHTS and measures, Dictionary of. Alexander, J. H. L.10
WOMAN'S record. Hale, S. J. K.6
WOMEN of the time, Biographical sketches of celebrated. *See* Men of the time. C.10
WORCESTER, J. E. Universal and critical dictionary of the English language. Boston, 1853. 8° V.8
— Pronouncing, explanatory and synonymous dictionary of the English language. Boston, 1855. 8° M.4

YONGE, C. D. Phraseological English-Latin dictionary. New ed. Part I.-II. Lond., 1856. 12°   C.3

PERIODICALS.

THE following works, either Periodicals, or partaking of the character of Periodicals, are received regularly at the Library. The latest portions of them which may have come to hand, will be found. arranged upon the tables, in the *large* Reading Room, in alphabetical order, beginning at the north-west corner with the letter A, and ending with the leite. Z at the north-east corner.

The letters affixed to the titles signify respectively, *m.* monthly, ½*m.* twice a month, 2*m.* once in two months, *d.* daily, *w.* weekly, *a.* annually, ½*y.* semi-annually, *q.* quarterly, *un.* uncertain, etc.

ALBION. New York . . . . fol. *w.*
ALLGEMEINE Zeitung. Augsburg . . . . 4° *d.*
AMERICAN Agriculturist. New York . . . . . . 4° *m.*
AMERICAN Farmers' Magazine. New York . . . 8° *m.*
AMERICAN Journal of Dental science. Phila. . 8° *q.*
AMERICAN Journal of Insanity. Utica. . . . . 8° *q.*
AMERICAN Journal of the Medical sciences, (Hays'.) Philadelphia. . . . . 8° *q.*
AMERICAN Journal of Science and arts. (Silliman's.) New Haven. . . . . 8° 2*m.*
AMERICAN Phrenological Journal. New York. . 4° *m.*
AMERICAN Publishers' Circular. New York . . . 4° *w.*
AMERICAN Quarterly Church Review and ecclesiastical register. New Haven. . . . . . . 8° *q.*
AMERICAN Rail-road Journal. New York . . . . 4° *w.*
ANNALS and Magazine of Natural History. London . . . . 8° *m.*

ANNALES de Chimie et de physique. Paris. . . . 8° *m.*
ANNALES d' Hygiène publique et de Médecine Légale. Paris . . . . 8° *q.*
ANNALES Médico-Psychologiques. Paris . . . . 8° *q.*
ANNALES des Sciences Naturelles. Paris. . . . . 8° *m.*
ARCHIV für Naturgeschichte. Berlin . . . . . . 8° *un.*
ARCHIV für das Studium der neueren Sprachen und Literaturen. Braunschweig. . . . . . 8° *un.*
ARTIZAN, The. London . . . . 4° *m.*
ART Journal. London . . . . 4° *m.*
ATHENÆUM. London . . . . 4° *w.*
ATLANTIC Monthly. Boston . . . . 8° *m.*

BANKERS' Magazine. New York . . . . 8° *m.*
BANKERS' Magazine. London . . . . 8° *m.*
BENTLEY'S Miscellany. London . . . . 8° *m.*
BIBLICAL Repertory. Philadelphia . . . . 8° *q.*

BIBLIOTHECA Sacra and Biblical Repository. Andover. . . . . 8° q.
BIBLIOTHÈQUE Universelle. Revue Suisse et étrangère. Genève. . . . . 8° m.
BLACKWOOD's Edinburgh Magazine. Edinburgh. 8° m.
BLÄTTER für literarische Unterhaltung. Leipzig. 4° w.
BOSTON Medical and Surgical Journal. Boston. 8° w.
BRAITHWAITE's Retrospect of practical Medicine and Surgery. New York. . . . . 8° ½y.
BRITISH and Foreign Medico-Chirurgical Review. London. . . . . 8° q.
BRITISH Quarterly Review. London. . . . . . . 8° q.
BROWNSON's Quarterly Review. New York. . . 8° q.
BUILDER, The. London. . . . . fol. w.
BULLETIN de l' Académie Impériale de Médecine. Paris. . . . . 8° ½m.
BULLETIN de la Société Géologique de France. Paris. . . . . 8° un.
BULLETIN général de Thérapeutique médicale et chirurgicale. Paris. . . . . 8° ½m.
CENDRILLON; Journal de tous les Travaux de Dames. Paris. . . . . 8° m.
CHAMBERS's Journal. London and Edinburgh. . 8° m.
CHESS Monthly. New York. . . . . 8° m.
CHRISTIAN Examiner. Boston. . . . . 8° 2m.
CHRISTIAN Observer. London. . . . . 8° m.
CHRISTIAN Review. Baltimore. . . . . 8° q.
CHURCH Review. See Amer. Quar. Ch. Review.
CIVIL Engineer and Architect's Journal. London. 4° m.
COLBURN's New Monthly Magazine. London. . 8° m.
COLBURN's United Service Magazine, and Naval and Military Journal. London. . . . . . . 8° m.
COMPTES Rendus des séances de l' Académie des Sciences. Paris. . . . . 4° w.
COSMOPOLITAN Art Journal. New York. . . . . 4° q.
COURRIER des États-Unis. New York. . . . . . fol. w.
DE BOW's Review, Industrial Resources, etc. N.O. fol. m.
DUBLIN Quarterly Journal of Medical Science. Dublin. . . . . 8° q.
DUBLIN Review. London. . . . . 8° q.
DUBLIN University Magazine. Dublin. . . . . . 8° m.
DWIGHT's Journal of Music. Boston. . . . . . . 4° w.
ECLECTIC Magazine of foreign literature. N. Y. 8° m.
ECLECTIC Review. London. . . . . 8° m.
ECONOMIST. London. . . . . fol. w.
EDINBURGH Medical Journal. Edinburgh. . . . 8° m.
EDINBURGH New Philosophical Journal. Edinb. 8° q.
EDINBURGH Review. London. . . . . 8° q.
EMERSON's Magazine and Putnam's Monthly. New York. . . . . 8° m.
EVENING Mail. London. . . . . fol. tri-w.
EXAMINER, The. London. . . . . fol. w.
FRASER's Magazine. London. . . . . 8° m.
GAZETTE des Hôpitaux. Paris. . . . . fol. tri-w.
GENTLEMAN's Magazine and historical review. London. . . . . 8° m.
GODEY's Lady's Book. Philadelphia. . . . . . . 8° m.
GRAHAM's Illustrated Magazine. Philadelphia. . 8° m.
HARPER's New Monthly Magazine. New York. 8° m.
HARPER's Weekly. New York. . . . . fol. w.
HEIDELBERGER Jahrbücher der Literatur. Heidelberg. . . . . 8° m.
HISTORICAL Magazine; and Notes and Queries concerning the antiquities, history and biography of America. New York. . . . . . . 4° m.
HOME Journal. New York. . . . . fol. w.
HORTICULTURIST, and Journal of rural art and taste. New York. . . . . 8° m.
HOUSEHOLD Words. London. . . . . 8° w.
HUNT's Merchants' Magazine, and Commercial Review. New York. . . . . 8° m.
ILLUSTRATED London News. London. . . . . . fol. w.
ILLUSTRATED News of the World. London. . . fol. w.
ILLUSTRATED Times. London. . . . . fol. w.
ILLUSTRATION, Journal Universel. Paris. . . . fol. w.
IRISH Quarterly Review. Dublin. . . . . 8° q.
JOURNAL de Médecine, et de Chirurgie pratique. Paris. . . . . 8° m.

JOURNAL des Débats. Paris. . . . . fol. d.
JOURNAL des Savants. Paris. . . . . 4° m.
JOURNAL of the Franklin Institute. Philadelphia. 8° m.
KNICKERBOCKER. New York. . . . . 8° m.
KRITISCHE-UEBERSCHAU der deutschen Gesetzgebung und Rechtswissenschaft. München. 8° un.
LABOURER's Friend: the Magazine of the Society for improving the condition of the labouring classes. London. . . . . 8° m.
LANCET. London. . . . . 4° w.
LITERARY Gazette. London. . . . . 4° w.
LITTELL's Living Age. Boston. . . . . 8° w.
LONDON, Edinburgh and Dublin Philosophical Magazine. London. . . . . 8° m.
MATHEMATICAL Monthly. Cambridge. . . . . . 4° m.
MASSACHUSETTS Teacher. Boston. . . . . 8° m.
MECHANICS' Magazine. London. . . . . 8° m.
MEDICAL Times and Gazette. London. . . . . . 4° w.
METHODIST Quarterly Review. New York. . . 8° q.
MINING and Statistical Magazine. New York. . 8° m.
MISSIONARY Herald. Boston. . . . . 8° m.
MONITEUR Universel. Paris. . . . . fol. d.
MONTHLY Religious Magazine, and Independent Journal. Boston. . . . . 8° m.
MÜLLERS Archiv für Anatomie, Physiologie und wissenschaftliche Medicin. Berlin. . . . 8° un.
MUSICAL World. New York. . . . . 4° w.
NATIONAL Review. London. . . . . 8° q.
NAUTICAL Magazine. London. . . . . 8° m.
NEW-ENGLANDER. New Haven. . . . . 8° q.
NEW England Historical and Genealogical Register. Boston. . . . . 8° q.
NEW Jerusalem Magazine. Boston. . . . . 8° m.
NEWTON's London Journal of Arts and Sciences. London. . . . . 8° m.
NEW Orleans Medical and Surgical Journal. New Orleans. . . . . 8° 2m.
NEW York Journal of Medicine. New York. . . 8° 2m.
NEW York Musical Review. New York. . . . . . 4° ½m.
NORTH American Medico-Chirurgical Review. Philadelphia. . . . . 8° 2m.
NORTH American Review. Boston. . . . . 8° q.
NORTH British Review. Edinburgh. . . . . . . 8° q.
NOTES and Queries. London. . . . . 4° w.
NUMISMATIC Chronicle, and Journal of the Numismatic Society. London. . . . . 8° q.
PUBLISHERS' Circular. London. . . . . 8° ½m.
PUNCH. London. . . . . 4° w.
QUARTERLY Journal of the Chemical Society. London. . . . . 8° q.
QUARTERLY Journal of the London Geological Society. London. . . . . 8° q.
QUARTERLY Journal of Microscopical Science. London. . . . . 8° q.
QUARTERLY Review. London. . . . . 8° q.
RANKING's Abstract of the Medical Sciences. London. Reprinted, Philadelphia. . . . . 8° ½y.
REVUE des deux Mondes. Paris. . . . . 8° ½m.
REVUE Médicale française et étrangère. Paris. . 8° ½m.
SATURDAY Review. London. . . . . fol. w.
SCIENTIFIC American. New York. . . . . fol. w.
SÉANCES et Travaux de l'Académie des Sciences, Morales et Politiques. Compte Rendu. Paris. 8° 2m.
SHARPE's London Magazine. London. . . . . . 8° m.
SOUTHERN Literary Messenger. Richmond. . . 8° m.
SPECTATOR. London. . . . . 8° w.
TAIT's Edinburgh Magazine. Edinburgh. . . . . 8° m.
TITAN. London. . . . . 8° m.
UNIVERSALIST Quarterly. Boston. . . . . 8° q.
VETERINARIAN. London. . . . . 8° m.
WESTMINSTER Review. London. . . . . 8° q.
ZEITSCHRIFT für Musik. Leipzig. . . . . 4° w.

SUPPLEMENT TO THE INDEX.

CONTAINING A LIST OF THE BOOKS PLACED IN THE LOWER HALL, FROM DEC. 20, 1858,
TO MARCH 26, 1859.

Shelf. No.

ABBOTT, J. Rollo in Rome. Boston, 1858. 16°. 669.9–13

ABBOTT, J. S. C. The empire of Austria. New York, 1859. 12° 927.11–13

ABEEL, D. Residence in China [etc.], 1830–1833. With an essay by B. W. Noel. London, 1835. Sm. 12° 709.23

ADAMS, W. B. English pleasure carriages. London, 1837. 8° 194.17

ADAMS, W. T. Poor and proud; or, the fortunes of Katy Redburn. Boston, 1859. 16° . . 748.4

ADDISON, J. Works, with notes by R. Hurd. Additions collected and edited by H. G. Bohn. New ed. London, 1856. 6v. 16° . . 847.7

Contents. — Vol. I. Poems on several occasions; Ovid's metamorphoses; Essay on Virgil's Georgics; Rosamond, an opera; Cato, a tragedy; Poemata; Dialogues upon the usefulness of ancient medals, especially in relation to the Latin and Greek poets; Three sets of medals, illustrated by the ancient poets in the foregoing dialogues; Remarks on several parts of Italy, in the years 1701, 1702, 1703. II. The tatler; The spectator. III. The spectator. IV. The spectator; The guardian; The lover; The present state of the war, and the necessity of an augmentation considered; The late trial and conviction of Count Tariff; The whig-examiner; The freeholder. V. The freeholder; On the Christian religion; The drummer, or the haunted house, comedy; A discourse on ancient and modern learning; Appendix, containing pieces by Addison, not hitherto published in any collected edition of his works; The tatler; The plebeian [by Steele]; Letters. VI. Letters; Second appendix, containing miscellanies and gleanings; Translations of Addison's Latin poems; Addison's Latin prose; Official documents; Addisoniana; General index.

AFTERNOON (The) of unmarried life. London, 1858. 12° 904.19

— - Same. New York, 1859. 12° 903.6

AHN, F. A new method of learning the German language. First course. 1st Am. fr. 8th Lond. ed. New York, 1859. 12° 1034.24

AIMWELL stories. Jessie; or, trying to be somebody. By Walter Aimwell. Boston, 1859. 16° 748.3

AINSWORTH, W. F. Travels in Asia Minor, Mesopotamia, Chaldea, and Armenia. London, 1842. 2v. 12° 688.5

ALDERSON, E. H. Selections from charges and other papers. London, 1858. 12° 558.14

ALDRICH, T. B. Ballad of Babie Bell, and other poems. New York, 1859. 12° 375.10

ALEXANDER, J. E. Expedition into the interior of Africa. London, 1858. 2v. 12° 688.4

ALMÆ Matres. London, n. d. 16° 386.3

AMBROSOLI, A. Componimenti dramatici ad uso della infanzia. Milano, 1852–3. 3v. in 1. 24° 1059.22

AMORY, T. C. Life of James Sullivan. Boston, 1859. 2v. 8° 522.1

ANDREWS, J. Journey from Buenos Ayres to Potosi, Arica, Santiago de Chili, and Coquimbo, 1825–6. London, 1827. 2v. 16°. . . 637.11

ANDROS, R. S. S. United States customs guide. Boston, 1859. 12° 309.13

ARABIAN days' entertainments. Transl. by H. P. Curtis. Boston, 1858. 12° 736.14

Shelf. No.

ARAGO, F. Biographies of distinguished scientific men. Translated by W. H. Smyth, Rev. B. Powell, and Robt. Grant. Boston, 1859. 2v. 16° 549.31–32

ARCHER, T. C. Economic botany. London, 1853. 16° 168.13

— First steps in economic botany. London, 1854. 16° 168.20

ARIOSTO, L. Orlando Furioso. Translated by W. S. Rose. New ed. London, 1858. Vol. 1. p. 8° 847.9

ARNOLD, S. G. History of Rhode Island. Vol. 1, 1636–1700. New York, 1859. 8° 233.2

ARPA Cristiana; inni della chiesa cattolica: versione di P. B. Silorata. Torino, 1848. 12° . 1045.2

ATHERN, A. Step by step; or, Delia Arlington. Boston, 1857. 12° 479.2

BACON, T. S. Both sides of the controversy between the Roman and Reformed churches. New York, 1859. 12° 1105.13

BAINBRIDGE, R. Guide to the conservatory. London, 1842. 12° 168.19

BAKER, Mrs. H. N. Howard and his teacher; The sister's influence [etc.] Boston, 1859. 16°. 748.1

— Trying to be useful. Boston, 1859. 16° . . . 748.2

BALBO, C. Delle speranze d'Italia 5a ed. Firenze, 1855. sm.8° 1045.3

BALLOU's pictorial drawing-room companion. Boston, 1851–55. 9v. 4° 860.1

BARHAM, T. F. Philadelphia; or, the claims of humanity. London, 1858. 12° 138.13

BATCHELDER, S. Poetry of the bells. Cambridge, 1858. 12° 375.14

BELL, J. British theatre. Comedies — operas — tragedies. London, 1791–93. 18v. 18°. . . 450.1

Contents. — Comedies: Vol. I. The country girl, altered from Wycherly by David Garrick; Rule a wife and have a wife, Beaumont and Fletcher; The alchymist, altered from Ben Jonson; Love for love, by William Congreve; Love makes a man, or the fop's fortune, by Colley Cibber. II. The busy body, by Mrs. S. Centlivre; The chances, as altered from Beaumont and Fletcher by His Grace the Duke of Buckingham; The tender husband, or the accomplished fools, by Sir Richard Steele; The beaux' stratagem, by Geo. Farquhar; The Spanish fryar, or the double discovery, by Mr. John Dryden. III. The gamesters, as altered by Garrick from James Shirley and C. Johnson; The conscious lovers, by Sir Richard Steele; Every man in his humour, by Ben Jonson, as altered by David Garrick; The careless husband, by Colley Cibber; The provoked husband, or a journey to London, by Sir John Vanbrugh and C. Cibber. IV. Amphitryon, or the two Socias, altered from Dryden by Dr. John Hawkesworth; The foundling, by Mr. Edward Moore; The good-natured man, by Dr. Oliver Goldsmith; The brothers, by Richard Cumberland; The minor, by Samuel Foote. V. The miser, by Henry Fielding; The way to keep him, by Arthur Murphy; She stoops to conquer, or the mistakes of a night, by Dr. Goldsmith; The country lasses, or the custom of the manor, by Mr. Charles Johnson; The fair quaker of Deal, or the humours of the navy, by Mr. Charles Shadwell. VI. The West Indian, by Richard Cumberland; The hypocrite, altered from C. Cibber, by Isaac Bickerstaff; The city wives' confederacy, by Sir J. Vanbrugh; The committee, by the Hon. Sir R. Howard; The wonder, a

BELL, J. British theatre, *continued*.

woman keeps a secret! by Mrs. S. Centlivre. VII. A bold stroke for a wife, by Mrs. Centlivre; The suspicious husband, by Dr. B. Hoadly; The recruiting officer, by G. Farquhar; All in the wrong, by A. Murphy; The constant couple, or a trip to the jubilee, by G. Farquhar. VIII. The school for lovers, by W. Whitehead; The fashionable lover, by R. Cumberland; The school for wives, by H. Kelly; The clandestine marriage, by G. Colman and D. Garrick; The drummer, or the haunted house, by J. Addison. IX. The double gallant, or the sick lady's cure, by C. Cibber; She wou'd and she wou'd not, or the kind impostor, by C. Cibber; The refusal, or the ladies' philosophy, by C. Cibber; The jealous wife, by G. Colman; The natural son, by R. Cumberland. *Operas:* X. Comus, a mask, by J. Milton; The maid of the mill, by I. Bickerstaff; The school for fathers, or Lionel and Clarissa, by I. Bickerstaff; Love in a village, by I. Bickerstaff; The beggars' opera, by J. Gay. *Tragedies:* XI. Venice preserved, or a plot discovered, by T. Otway; The fair penitent, by Nicholas Rowe; Zara, from the Zaïre of Voltaire, by A. Hill; Douglas, by J. Home; The mourning bride, by Mr. W. Congreve. XII. The orphan, or the unhappy marriage, by T. Otway; Cato, by J. Addison; The distrest mother, translated by A. Philips, from the Andromaque of Racine; The Earl of Essex, by H. Jones; Jane Shore, by N. Rowe. XIII. Cleone, by Mr. R. Dodsley; Zimena, or the heroic daughter, by C. Cibber; All for love, or the world well lost, by Mr. Dryden; Tamerlane, by N. Rowe; Isabella, or the fatal marriage, altered from T. Southern. XIV. Tancred and Sigismunda, by Mr. J. Thomson; George Barnwell, by G. Lillo; The Grecian daughter, by A. Murphy; The gamester, by Mr. E. Moore; The Earl of Warwick, translated from La Harpe, by Dr. W. Francklin. XV. Philaster, altered from Beaumont and Fletcher; The Carmelite, by R. Cumberland; Alzira, translated from Voltaire, by A. Hill; Œdipus, by Dryden and Lee; Medea, by Mr. R. Glover. XVI. The Albion queens, or the death of Mary Queen of Scots, by J. Banks; Edward the black prince, or the battle of Poictiers, by W. Shirley; Boadicea, by Mr. Glover; Lady Jane Gray, by N. Rowe; Oroonoko, by T. Southern. XVII. Theodosius, or the force of love, by N. Lee; The revenge, by E. Young; The Roman father, altered from Mr. W. Whitehead; The siege of Damascus, by J. Hughes; The rival queens, or the death of Alexander the Great, by Nathaniel Lee. XVIII. The battle of Hastings, by R. Cumberland; The choleric man, by R. Cumberland; The discovery, by Mrs. F. Sheridan; King Charles I., by Mr. W. Havard; The Countess of Salisbury, by Hall Hartson.

BELVILLE, J. H. Manual of the barometer. 2d edition. London, 1849. sm.8° 148.13

BENTWRIGHT, J. The American horse-tamer. New York, 1858. 12° 168.9

BERRIMAN, M. W. Militiaman's manual. New York, 1858. 12° 187.13

BETTI, S. L'illustre Italia. Dialoghi. 5a ed. Torino, 1853 . . . . . . 1059.17

BIANCHETTI, G. Dello scrittore italiano : [e] degli uomini di lettere. Ed. riveduta. Firenze, 1855. 12° 1045.7

BIANCIARDI, S. Letture offerte ai fanciulli e ai giovinetti italiani. Livorno, 1853. 16° 1059.19

BIOT, J. B. Elementary astronomy; ed. by Rev. H. Goodwin. Cambridge, 1850. 8° 148.10

BISHOP, G. Every woman her own lawyer. New York, [1858.] 12° 134.26

BLONDE and brunette. [A story.] New York, 1858. 12° 485.13

BOAS, E. Schiller's Jugendjahre. Hrsg. v. W. v. Maltzahn. Hannover, 1856. 2v. 16° . . . 1023.6

BOHN, H. G. Hand-book of games. London, 1850. 16° 836.13-17

BOSANQUET, S. R. "Vestiges of the natural history of creation" examined and exposed. 2d edition. London, 1845. 12° 167.31

BOYES, J. F. Life and books. London, 1859. 12° 385.10

BREMER, F. Father and daughter. Translated by M. Howitt. Philadelphia, n.d. 12° . . . 496.6-10

BREWSTER, Sir D. The kaleidoscope: its history, theory, and construction. 2d ed. London, 1858. 16° 148.12

— On magnetism : [from] the Encyclopædia Britannica. Edinburgh, 1838. 12° 148.11

BROGLIE, A. de. Etudes morales et littéraires. Paris, 1853. 12° 1064.16

BROUGH, J. C. Fairy tales of science. London, 1859. 12° 148.9

BROWN, J., *M.D.* Locke and Sydenham, with other papers. Edinburgh, 1858. 12° . . . 894.13

BROWN, J. [of Barnwell]. Sixty years' gleanings from life's harvest. Camb. [Eng.], 1858. 12° 556.11

BROWNSON, O. A. The convert : or, leaves from my experience. New York, 1857. 12° . . . 1105.9

BRYANT, J. D. Redemption. A poem. Philadelphia, 1859. 12° 385.11

BRYANT, W. C. Letters of a traveller. 2d series. New York, 1859. 8° 666.9

BUCKLAND, F. T. Curiosities of natural history. From 4th London ed. New York, 1859. 12° 177.38

BULFINCH, T. The age of chivalry. Boston, 1859. 12° 948.9

BULLAR, J. and H. A winter in the Azores; and a summer at the baths of the Furnas. London, 1841. 2v. 8° 634.1

BUSHNELL, H. Nature and the supernatural as constituting the one system of God. 3d ed. New York, 1858. 8° 122.18

BUTLER, C. Historical memoirs of the English, Irish, and Scottish Catholics. 3d ed. London, 1822. 4v. 8° 541.9

BRYDGES, S. E. Recollections of foreign travel. London, 1825. 2v. 16° 688.3

CAMBRIDGE, Eng., University of. Prize poems. Cambridge, 1859. 12° 375.20

CANTÙ, C. Letture giovanili. 10a-14a ediz. Milano, 1846-51. 4v. in 2. 16° 1059.18

— La Lombardia nel secolo XVII. Milano, 1854. 16° 1045.5

— Storia della città e della diocesi di Como. Firenze, 1856. 2v. 8° 1045.8

CARLYLE, T. History of Frederick the Great. New York, 1858. 2v. 12° 542.6-8

— Life of Robert Burns. New York, 1859. 18° 589.15

CARPENTER, M. Juvenile delinquents. London, 1853. 12° 138.17

CARY, A. Pictures of country life. N.Y., 1859. 12° 507.14

CASKET of entertaining and useful reading. New York, 1843. 12° 148.17

CATLOW, A. Garden botany. Lond., 1855. sq.16° 168.14

— Greenhouse botany. London, 1857. 16° . . . 168.16

CATLOW, M. E. British entomology. 2d edition. London, 1852. 16° 178.39

CAVALCA, D. Specchio di Croce, ridotto alla sua vera lezione, per cura di B. Sorio. Venezia, 1840. 16° 1059.21

CELNART, Mme. Manuel de la bonne compagnie. Nouvelle édition. Paris, 1852. 12° 1079.18

CHAMBERS, R. Domestic annals of Scotland, from the reformation to the revolution. Edinburgh, 1858. 2v. 8° 984.5

— History of Scotland. New edition. London, 1849. 2v. in 1. 16° 999.7

— Traditions of Edinburgh. Edinb., 1856. 16° 999.8

CHAPONE, Mrs. H. Posthumous works, and correspondence, with life and character. London, 1807. 2v. 16° 138.20

CHARLESWORTH, M. L. The ministry of life. A tale. New York, 1858. 12° 479.3

CHATEAUBRIAND, R. F. A. de. Atala, René, les Abencerages, suivis du voyage en Amérique. Paris, 1854. 12° 1064.6

— Itinéraire de Paris à Jerusalem. Paris, 1854. 2v. 12° 1064.11

CHEVALIER, M. Probable fall in the value of gold. Transl. by R. Cobden. Manchester, 1859. 8° 138.24

COALE, W. E. Hints on health. Boston, 1857. 12° 158.24

COBBETT, W. Cottage economy. 17th ed. London, 1850. 12° 189.19

— Legacy to labourers, in six letters. 3d ed. London, 1835. 32° 139.29

— Legacy to parsons, in six letters. 6th edition. London, 1835. 32° 139.28

COBBETT, W. Protestant reformation in England and Ireland. London, 1853–57. 2v. 12°. . 1105.11

COLMAN, G. Broad grins: tales in verse. 8th ed. London, 1839. 16° 385.8

COLWELL, S. The way and means of payment. Philadelphia, 1859. 8° 132.5

CORNWALLIS, C. Correspondence. Edited with notes by Charles Ross. Lond., 1859. 3v. 8° 561.1

COUSIN, V. Jacqueline Pascal. Bruxelles, 1845. 18° 1064.20

CROKER, T. C. Popular songs of Ireland. London, 1839. 12° 385.6

CROLY, G. Poetical Works. London, 1830. 2v. in 1. 12° 375.17

— Salathiel: a story. Cincinnati, 1858. 2v. in 1. 12° 507.1

CROWE, E. E. History of France. Vol. I. London, 1858. 8° 1003.6

CUMMINS, G. D. Life of Mrs. Virginia Hale Hoffman. Philadelphia, 1859. 12° 539.27

DALLAWAY, H. Manual of heraldry. London, 1828. 12° 948.15

DANDOLO, (C. T.) Il Settentrione dell' Europa e dell' America sin 1789. Milano, 1853. 2v. sm.8° 1045.12

DANSKIN, (W. A.) How and why I became a spiritualist. Boston, 1858. 12° 1105.7

DARU, P. Ant. Noel Bruno de. Histoire de la république de Venise. 3e éd. Paris, 1826. 18° 1064.23

DANTE Alighieri. Transl. by I. C. Wright. 4th edition. London, 1857. p.8° 847.11

DARLINGTON, Wm. American weeds and useful plants. Revised by George Thurber. New York, 1859. 12° 166.19

DAVIS, J. F. The Chinese. New ed. London, 1845–51. 3v. in 2. 12° 939.7

— Vizier Ali Khan: or, the massacre of Benares. London, 1844. 16° 939.8

DAVIS, S. M. Life and times of Sir Philip Sidney. Boston, 1859. 12° 558.12–13

DAVY, Sir H. Fragmentary remains; with a sketch of his life, by John Davy. London, 1858. 8° 554.7

DEBORAH's diary. Sequel to "Mary Powell." London, n.d. 12° 507.2

DEXTER, H. M. Street thoughts. Bost., 1859. 12° 804.14

DITSON, G. L. Crescent and French crusaders. New York, 1859. 12° 919.17

DORAN, J. New pictures and old panels. London, 1859. 12° 904.18

DOTEN, E. Hesper, the home-spirit. Boston, 1859. 12° 507.3

DOUBLEDAY, T. Financial, monetary and statistical history of England. Lond., 1847. 8°. 984.3

DOUGLAS, Sir Howard. Naval warfare with steam. London, 1858. 8° 194.13

DOWNING, A. J. Theory and practice of landscape gardening. 6th ed., with suppl. by H. W. Sargent. New York, 1859. 8° . . . 202.10

DRAYSON, A. W. The earth we inhabit. London, 1859. 12° 167.32

DRYDEN, J. Poetical works. London, 1857. 16° 385.7

DUNLOP, J. Drinking usages of the United Kingdom. 7th ed. London, 1844. 16° 999.6

— Universal tendency to association analyzed and illustrated. London, 1840. 16° . . . 138.19

EDGAR, J. G. Wars of the roses. Lond., 1859. 12° 999.3

EDUCATORE (L') ed il narratore istorico italiano. Firenze, 1856. 2v. sm.8° 1045.11

ELLIOTSON, J. Human physiology. With much of Blumenbach's Institutiones physiologicæ. 5th ed. London, 1840. 8° 153.13

ELLIOTT, G. D. Journal of my life during the French revolution. London, 1859. 8° . . . 1006.2

ELLIS, Rev. W. Three visits to Madagascar, during 1853, 1854, 1856. London, 1858. 8° . . . 682.2

EMINENT men and popular books. Lond., 1859. 16° 549.33

EVANS, F. W. Shakers. With biographies of Ann Lee [and others]. N. Y., 1859. 12° . . 1105.15

EYNARD, C. Lucques et les Burlamacchi. Souvenirs de la réforme en Italie. Paris, 1848. 12° 1064.17

FANE, H. E. Five years in India. London, 1842. 2v. 12° 688.7

FARADAY, M. Chemistry and physics. London, 1859. 8° 143.3

FARRAR, F. W. Eric: or, little by little. New York, 1859. 12° 496.11–14

FÉLICE, G. de. History of the Protestants of France. Transl. from the 2d ed. by P. E. Barnes. London, 1853. 16° 1007.10

FELTON, J. H. The decimal system. New York, 1858. 12° 134.27

FERGUSON, F. Bible election: or, letters on the Calvinistic controversy. Glasgow, 1854. 12° 128.21

FERGUSON, R. English surnames. London, 1858. 12° 999.10

FERRIER, J. P. History of the Afghans. Transl. by Capt. W. Jesse. London, 1858. 8° . . . 934.8

FICQUELMONT, Comte de. Lord Palmerston, l' Angleterre, et le continent. Bruxelles, 1852–53. 2v. 12° 1064.9

FIRENZUOLA, A. Opere, ridotte a miglior lezione, e corredate di note da B. Bianchi. Firenze, 1848. 2v. 12° 1045.9

FLETCHER, M. The Methodist. Introduction by W. P. Strickland, D.D. N.Y., 1859. 2v. 12° 507.15

FLINT, C. L. Milch cows and dairy farming. Boston, 1858. 12° 172.24

FORBES, J. D. Danger of superficial knowledge. London, 1849. 16° 138.22

FORSTER, J. G. A. Sämmtliche Schriften. Hrsg. v. dessen Tochter. Mit einer charakteristik Forster's von G. G. Gervinus. Leipzig, 1843. 9v. 12° 1023.3

Contents.—Vols. I.–II. Vorrede; Einleitung; Johann Reinhold Forster's und Georg Forster's Reise um die Welt in den Jahren 1772 bis 1775. III. Ansichten vom Niederrhein von Brabant, Flandern, Holland, England und Frankreich im April, Mai, und Junius 1790. IV.–VI. Kleine Schriften. VII.–VIII. Johann Georg Forster; Von G. G. Gervinus; Briefwechsel. IX. Briefwechsel; Sakontala, oder der entscheidende King; Ein indisches Schauspiel von Kalidas.

FOSTER, J. Fosteriana. Ed. by H. G. Bohn. London, 1858. p.8° 857.7

FOSTER brothers (The). New York, 1859. 12° . 506.1

FROUDE, J. A. History of England from the fall of Wolsey to the death of Elizabeth. 2d ed. London, 1858. 4v. 8° 984.2

GALLENGA [A.] (Marriotti). Castellamonte, autobiographical sketch of Italian life. 2d ed. London, 1856. 2v. in 1. 12° 507.5

— Present state and prospects of Italy. Lond., 1848. 12° 937.6

GALT, J. Life and studies of B. West. 2d ed. London, 1817–20. 2v. in 1. 8° 527.12

GARDNER, G. Travels in Brazil, 1836–41. 2d ed. London, 1849. 8° 634.2

GAVAZZI, A. The last four popes: an answer to Dr. Wiseman. London, 1858. 12° 1098.25

GEIKIE, A. Story of a boulder. Edinburgh, 1858. 12° 167.29

GENLIS, Mme. de. Alphonse ou le fils naturel. 3e éd. Paris, 1824. 2v. 16° 1064.12

GÉRARD, G. Le cabinet des fées. New York, 1859. 12° 1064.3

GESTA Romanorum. [Moral stories.] Transl. from the Latin by Rev. C. Swan. London, 1824. 2v. 12° 128.16

GIBBONS, J. S. Banks of New York, and the panic of 1857. New York, 1858. 12° 135.24

GIOBERTI, V. Riforma cattolica della chiesa; frammento pubblicato per cura di G. Massari. Torino, [1856.] 12° 1059.15

GOSSE, P. H. Canadian naturalist. London, 1840. 12° 177.39

GÖTHE, J. W. v. Briefe und Aufsätze aus den Jahren 1766–86. Hrsg. durch. A. Schöll. Weimar, 1846. 16° 1023.5
— Novels and tales. Transl. chiefly by R. D. Boylan. London, 1854. p.8° 847.1
— Poems and ballads. Transl. by W. E. Aytoun and T. Martin. Edinburgh, 1859. 12° . . 375.22
GRANTHAM, J. Iron as a material for ship-building. London, 1842. 8° 194.14
GREEN, H. Selections from prescriptions of American practitioners. N.Y., 1858. 12° . . 153.12
GREGORY, W. Inorganic chemistry. 4th Am. ed. Added, Physics of chemistry. By J. M. Sanders. New York, 1857. 8° 143.1
— Organic chemistry. 4th Am. ed., by J. M. Sanders. New York, 1857. 8° 143.2
GROSS, A. Manuel du petit four ou patisserie légère. Nouv. éd. Paris, Roret, 1851. sm.12° 1079.17
GUERRAZZI, F. D. Isabella Orsini: a hist. novel. New York, 1859. 12° 485.12
— La Battaglia di Benevento, storia del secolo XIII. Livorno, 1849. 2v. sm.8° 1045.10
GUIZOT, F. P. G. Origines du gouvernement représentatif en Europe. Bruxelles, 1851. 2v. 12° 1064.5
GULLICK, T. J., and Timbs, J. Painting popularly explained. London, 1859. 16° 209.16
GÜTZLAFF, K. F. A. China opened. Revised by Rev. A. Reed. London, 1838. 2v. 12° . . . 688.6
— Journal of three voyages along the coast of China, Siam, etc., 1831, 1832, and 1833. Introd. essay by Rev. W. Ellis. 3d ed. London, n.d. sm.8° 688.8

HAGGARD, E. Myra; or, the rose of the East. London, 1857. 12° 375.19
HALF-HOURS with the microscope. Illustrated by T. West. London, n.d. 18° 178.44
HALL, B. Patchwork. 2d ed. London, 1841. 3v. 16° 689.21
HALL, Mrs. S. C. Midsummer eve. New York, 1848. 12° 507.17
HALLAM, H. Constitutional history of England. Henry VII.,—George II. 8th ed. London, 1855. 3v. 16° 396.2
— Europe during the middle ages. 11th ed. London, 1855. 3v. 16° 396.1
— Literature of Europe, in the 15th, 16th, and 17th centuries. 5th ed. London, 1855. 4v. 16° 396.3
HALLECK, F. G. Poetical works. New York, 1858. 12° 375.11
HARDING, J. D. Drawing models. 2d ed. Lond., 1854. 16° 209.17
HARRISON, J. B. Contamination of water by the poison of lead. London, 1852. 16° 158.25
HAWKINS, W. G. Life of J. H. W. Hawkins. Boston, 1859. 12° 527.11–13
HEDLEY, O. D. Who invented the locomotive engine? London, 1858. 8° 194.19
HERVÉ, A. Manuel des alliages métalliques. Paris. Roret, 1859. 12° 1079.19
HINTS for the table. London, 1859. 16° 189.15
HISTORICAL magazine. Vol. II. New York, 1858. 4° 273.1
HISTORY of shipwrecks and disasters at sea. London, 1833–35. 4v. 18° 699.17
HISTORY of the Jews. 1st Am. ed. Pref. notes and index by W. C. Brownlee. New York, 1812. 12° 1105.14
HITCHCOCK, E. A. Swedenborg, a hermetic philosopher. New York, 1858. 12° 1084.17
HOFFMEISTER, K. Schiller's Leben. Ergänzt u. hrsg. von H. Viehoff. 2e Ausgabe. Stuttgart, 1851. 3v. 16° 1023.11
HOLLAND, J. Poems. Boston, 1858. 12° 375.21
HOLLAND, J. G. Bitter-sweet: a poem. New York, 1859. 12° 375.16
HOLMES, O. W. Autocrat of the breakfast table. Boston, 1858. 12° 903.1–5

HOMERUS. Batrachomyomachia; hymns [etc.]; Hesiod's works and days; Musæus; Hero and Leander; Juvenal's fifth satire. Transl. by G. Chapman, with notes by R. Hooper. London, 1858. sq.16° 385.5
— The Iliad, transl. by G. Chapman, with introduction and notes by R. Hooper. London, 1857. 2v. sq.16° 385.3
— The Odyssey, transl. by G. Chapman, with notes by R. Hooper. London, 1857. 2v. 16° 385.4
HOPKINSON, J. Jr. Working of the steam engine explained by the indicator. 2d ed. London, 1857. 8° 194.18
HORNBY, Mrs. E. In and around Stamboul. Phila. n.d. 12° 666.6
HORNE, R. H. The poor artist; or, seven eye-sights and one object. London, 1850. 16° . . 209.18
HOVEY, A. Life and times of Rev. Isaac Backus. Boston, 1858. 12° 535.15
HUME, D. The student's Hume. A history of England, abridged, and continued to 1858. London, 1859. 12° 909.1
HUNGERFORD, J. The old plantation. New York, 1859. 12° 507.9
HUNT, F. K. The fourth estate: a history of newspapers. and of the liberty of the press. London, 1850. 2v. sm.8° 909.5
HUNT, J. H. Leigh. Table-talk: imaginary conversations of Pope and Swift. London, 1851. 16° 905.4
HYMNS of the ages. Introduction by Rev. F. D. Huntington. Boston, 1859. 12° 375.8

INSURANCE guide and hand-book. Lond. [1857]. 8° 132.3

JERDAN, W. Autobiography. London, 1852–53. 4v. 8° 587.1
JERROLD, B. Life and remains of Douglas Jerrold. London, 1859. 12° 588.18–19
JOHNS, M. Boy's book of modern travel and adventure. London, 1859. 16° 748.7
JOHNSON, A. C. Peasant life in Germany. New York, 1858. 12° 666.7
JONES, J. Tables of annuities and assurances. London, 1843. 8° 132.2
JONES, J. M. Naturalist in Bermuda. London, 1859. 8° 177.37

KAY, J. Social condition and education of the people of England and Europe. London, 1850. 2v. 12° 128.16
KEMBLE, F. A. Poems. Boston, 1859. 12° . . . 375.9
KEMP, E. How to lay out a garden. From 2d Lond. ed. New York, 1858. 12° 175.14
KENNY, C. Manual of chess. New York, 1859. 16° 209.19
KIMBALL, J. W. Heaven. Boston, 1857. 12° . . 1105.10
KIPPING, R. On sails and sailmaking. London, 1858. 16° 196.22
KNAPP, S. L. Life of Lord Timothy Dexter. Boston, 1858. 12° 519.7
KNIGHT, C. Once upon a time. London, 1854. 2v. 16° 507.7

LAISHLEY, R. History of British birds' eggs. London, 1858. 16° 178.42
LANMAN, C. Dictionary of the United States congress. Philadelphia, 1859. 8° 522.4
LATHAM, R. G. Natural history of the varieties of man. London, 1850. 8° 174.10
LAWS and practice of whist. N,Y., 1859. sq.18° . 189.20
LEDRU-ROLLIN, A. A. Décadence de l'Angleterre. Bruxelles, 1850. 2v. 12° 1064.8
LEE, H. Sylvan Holt's daughter. N.Y., 1859. 12° 485.14
LEMOINNE, J. Wellington from a French point of view. London, 1852. 16° 578.14
LEWALD, J. K. A. Das Jugendleben Friedrichs des gr. Stuttgart, 1847. 2v. in 1. sm.8° . . 1023.4
LINDSAY, A. W. C., Lord. History of Christian art. London, 1847. 3v. 8° 202.9
LINDSAY, W. L. British lichens. Lond., 1856. 16° 168.18

LOOMIS, E. Elements of natural philosophy. New York, 1858. 12° 148.6
LOVIOT, F. A lady's captivity among Chinese pirates. Transl. by A. B. Edwards. London, n.d. 18° 709.21
LOWELL, R. T. S. The new priest in Conception Bay. Boston, 1858. 2v. 12° . . . 496.1-5
LYTTON, Sir E. G. E. L. Bulwer. What will he do with It? A novel. New York, 1859. 8° . 501.20-24

McINTOSH, M. J. Meta Gray; or, what makes home happy. New York, 1859. 12° 427.5
MACKENZIE, R. S. Tressilian and his friends. Philadelphia, 1859. 12° 506.3
MADDEN, R. R. Cuba: its resources, progress, and prospects. London, 1853. 12° 266.10
MADINIER, P. et Lacoste, G. de. Guide du cultivateur du sorgho à sucre. Paris, 1856. 12° 1064.18
MAISTRE, J. M. de. Lettres et opuscules inédits. Notice biogr. par son fils. 2de éd. Paris, 1853. 2v. 12° 1064.4
MAN and his dwelling-place. London, 1859. 12° . . 128.19
— — Same. New York, 1859. 12° 128.20
MANGNALL, R. Historical and miscellaneous questions. Imp. ed. London, n.d. 18° . . 939.9
MANTELL, G. A. Invisible world revealed by the microscope; or, thoughts on animalcules. New ed. London, 1850. 16° 178.43
MARCET, J. Conversations on land and water. 5th ed. London, 1852. 16° 148.16
— Rich and poor. London, 1851. sm.18° 138.21
MARENCO, C. Tragedie inedite; liriche e La Pia de'Tolomei. Firenze, 1856. 12° 1045.6
MARRIOTTI, L. See Gallenga.
MARSH, C. C. Science of double-entry bookkeeping. New York, 1858. 8° 132.1
MARSH, H. Comparative view of the churches of England and Rome. 3d ed., with app. London, 1841. 16° 128.15
MARTIN, L. Aimé. Éducation des mères de famille ou de la civilisation du genre humain par les femmes. 3e éd. Bruxelles, 1842. 12° 1064.13
MASON, T. M. Creation by the immediate agency of God. London, 1845. 8° 167.30
MASSEY, W. England during the reign of George III., 1745-80. London, 1855-58. 2v. 8° . 983.1
MASSON, D. The life of John Milton. Vol. I., 1608-1639. Boston, 1859. 8° 561.2
MAUNDER, S. Biographical treasury. 10th ed. London, 1856. 12° 549.35
MAXWELL, W. H. Irish rebellion in 1798; and Emmett's insurrection in 1803. 4th ed. London, 1854. 8° 984.4
MAYO, A. D. Symbols of the capital. New York, 1859. 12° 138.23
MECHI, J. J. How to farm profitably. London, 1859. 16° 168.10
MENZIES, H. Early ancient history, or the anti-Greek period. London, 1858. 12° 948.10
MERCHANT'S and banker's register for 1859. New York, 1859. 8° 132.4
MÉRIMÉE, P. Episode de l'histoire de Russie—les faux Démétrius. Paris, 1854. 12° 1064.7
MIGNET, F. A. A. Notices et portraits historiques et littéraires. 3e éd. Paris, 1854. 2v. 12°. 1064.15
MILL, J. S. On liberty. London, 1859. 12° 138.26
MILLINGTON, E. J. Heraldry in history, poetry, and romance. London, 1858. 12° 948.11
MILTON, J. Paradise lost. Boston, 1847. 18° . . . 450.4
MITFORD, M. R. Our village: sketches of rural character and scenery. New ed. 1st and 2d series. London, 1856-57. 2v. 16° 507.6
MOFFAT, R. Missionary labours in S. Africa. London, 1842. 8° 682.3
MÖLLHAUSEN, B. Journey from the Mississippi to the Pacific. Introd. by Alex. Von Humboldt. Transl. by Mrs. P. Sinnett. Lond., 1858. 2v. 8° 623.22
MOORE, A. Notes from Plymouth pulpit. From discourses of H. W. Beecher. New York, 1859. 12° . . . . , 1105.3

MORGAN, J. F. England under the Norman occupation. London, 1858. 12° 999.2
MORGAN, Lady S. O. Passages from my autobiography. New York, 1859. 12° 508.18
MORRIS, J. G. Quaint sayings and doings concerning Luther. Philadelphia, 1859. 12° 1105.4
MULOCH, D. M. A hero; Bread upon the waters Alice Learmont. New ed. N.Y., 1859. 12°. 507.16
MURRAY, J. Handbook for travellers in Syria and Palestine. Part I., II. Lond, 1858. 2v. 12° 683.2

NASH, S. Morality and the state. Columbus, 1859. 12° 128.17
NEWCOMB, H. Cyclopædia of missions. New York, 1854. 8° 1092.4
NEW Jerusalem church. Manual for Sabbath schools. New York, 1859. 12° 128.22
NEW Jerusalem. Centenary of the New Jerusalem. Twelve addresses. N. Y., 1859. 8° 1082.2
NEWMAN, F. W. Phases of faith. 5th ed. Lond., 1858. 12° 128.12
— The soul: its sorrows and its aspirations. 6th ed. London, 1858. 12° 128.11
NICHOLLS, H. G. The forest of Dean: an historical and descriptive account. Lond., 1858. 12° 989.15
NOYCE, E. Outlines of creation. Lond., 1858. 12° 148.7

OGILVIE, G. The master-builder's plan, indicated in the forms of animals. Lond., 1858. 12°. 177.36
OLIPHANT, M. The laird of Norlaw: a Scottish story. New York. 1859. 12° 507.10-12
OLIVE and the pine. Boston, 1859. 12° 375.15
OPPORTUNITIES for industry; or, a thousand chances to make money. Phila., 1859. 12°. 138.25
ORDERICUS Vitalis. Ecclesiastical history of England and Normandy. Transl., with notes, by T. Forester. Vols. III., IV. London, 1854. 2v. p.8° 856.7
OUR little ones in heaven. Boston, 1858. 18°. . . 339.9

PAGE, T. J. La Plata, Argentine confederation and Paraguay. New York, 1859. 8° 622.3
PAGET, J. Inquiry into the charges brought by Lord Macaulay against William Penn. London, 1858. 12° 999.4
PALADINI, L. A. Manuale per le giovinette italiane. 2a edizione. Firenze, 1856. 16°. 1059.20
PALFREY, J. G. History of New England. Vol. I. Boston, 1858. 8° 232.1-5
PALGRAVE, Sir F. The merchant and the friar. London, 1844. 16° 507.8
PARDOE, J. Episodes of French history during the consulate and the first empire. New York, 1859. 12° 1007.9
PASLEY, Sir C. W. On limes, cements, mortars. [etc.] 2d ed. London, 1847. 8° 191.16
PETERS, De Witt C. Life and adventures of Kit Carson. New York, 1858. 8° 522.2
PICTORIAL handbook of London. Lond., 1854. p.8° 847.10
PORZIO, C. Opere, pubblicate per cura di C. Monzani. 2a ed. Firenze, 1855. 12° 1045.4
PIESSE, G. W. S. Chymical, natural, and physical magic. London, 1858. 16° 189.16
PIGOTT, G. Manual of Scandinavian mythology. London, 1859. 16° 128.9
PILGRIMAGE to the land of Burns. Deptford, 1822. 16° 645.6
PINKERTON, J. N. Sleep and its phenomena. London, 1859. 16° 158.26
POPULAR geography of plants. By M. C. Edited by C. Daubeny. London, 1855. 16°. 168.17
POLO, Marco. Travels. Ed. by T. Wright. London, 1854. p.8° 857.6
POWELL, B. Unity of worlds and of nature. 2d ed. London, 1856. 16° 128.13
PRATT, A. Common things of the sea coast. London, 1856. 16° 177.40
PRESCOTT, W. H. History of the reign of Philip the Second of Spain. Vol. III. Boston, 1859. 8° 921.1-10

PROGRESSIVE speaker and common school reader
  Boston, 1858. k°. 385.2
PULLAN, Mrs. Lady's manual of fancy work.
  New York, 1859. 12°. 187.12
PUNCHARD, G. View of congregationalism.
  Introd. essay by R. S. Storrs. 3d ed. Bos-
  ton, 1856. 12°. 1105.12

QUINCY, J. The life of John Quincy Adams. Boston, 1858. 8°. 522.3

RAINEY, G. Formation of shells, bone [etc.]
  London, 1858. p.8°. 175.15
READ, G. Baker's assistant. 2d ed. Lond., 1854. 16° 189.18
— Cookery, confectionery, and pickling. Lon-
  don, 1850. 16°. 189.17
READINGS for young men, merchants, and men of
  business. Repr. from London ed. Boston,
  1859. 12°. 138.11
REDPATH, J. The roving editor. New York,
  1859. 12°. 299.8
REID, T. Works. Preface, notes, and supple-
  mentary dissertations, by Sir William
  Hamilton. Prefixed, Stewart's life of Reid.
  Edinburgh, 1846. 8°. 864.2
REYBAUD, M. Roch Louis. Jérôme Paturot à la
  recherche de la meilleure des républiques.
  Bruxelles, 1849. 4v. 18°. 1064.22
RICE, H. Mount Vernon, and other poems. Bos-
  ton, 1858. 12°. 375.12
RICE, N. P. Trials of a public benefactor. New
  York, 1859. 12°. 158.27
RICHARDSON, W. H. Jr. Boot and shoe manufac-
  turer's assistant and guide. Boston, 1858. 8° 196.20
RICHTER, J. P. Sketches of and from Jean Paul
  Richter. London, 1859. 12°. 545.23
RICORD, F. W. History of Rome, for the use of
  schools. New York, 1859. 12°. . . 948.12-14
ROBERTS, M. History of the Mollusca. London,
  1851. 16°. 178.40
ROBERTS, M. Voices from the woodlands, de-
  scriptive of forest trees [etc]. London,
  1850. 16°. 108.12
ROBERTSON, F. W. Lectures and addresses. Bos-
  ton, 1859. 12°. 894.12
ROBERTSON, J. P. and W. P. Letters on South
  America. London, 1843. 3v. 16°. 637.10
ROBERTSON, W. P. A visit to Mexico, with ad-
  ventures on the way. London, 1853. 2v. 16° 638.10
ROBINSON, E. Memoir of Rev. Wm. Robinson.
  New York, 1859. 8°. 536.7
ROE, A. S. True to the last. New York, 1858. 12° 735.14
ROLLE, H. Mémoires de Jérôme Paturot. Brux.,
  1843. 2v. 18°. 1064.21
ROSSE, J. W. Index of dates. Vol. I. London,
  1858. . . . . 857.8
RUSKIN, J. The true and the beautiful. Selected
  from the works of J. R. Notice of the
  author by L. C. Tuthill. New York, 1859.
  12°. 206.17
RUSSELL, Lord John. Life and times of Charles
  James Fox. Vol. I. London, 1859. 12°. . 577.1
RYDER, G. M. Gillian ; and other poems. Philadelphia, 1858. 12°. 375.7

SAINTE-AULAIRE, Le Marquis de. Les derniers
  Valois, les Guise et Henri IV. Paris,
  1854. 12°. 1064.10
SAINTE-BEUVE, C. A. Nouveaux portraits et cri-
  tiques littéraires. Bruxelles, 1836. 3v. 16° 1064.19
— Tableau de la poésie française, au XVIe
  siècle. Paris, 1843. 12°. 1064.14
SALA, G. A. A journey due North Notes in
  Russia. Boston, 1858. 12°. 666.5
SCHEDEL, H. E. The emancipation of faith. Ed.
  by G. Schedel. New York, 1858. 2v. 8°. . 1082.1
SCHILLER, C. v. Briefe von Schiller's Gattin.
  Hrsg. v. H. Düntzer. Leipzig, 1856. 16°. . 1023.8
SCHILLER, J. C. F. v. Briefwechsel mit Körner.
  Berlin, 1847. 4v. 12°. 1023.7

SCHILLER, J. C. F. v. Briefwechsel zwischen
  Schiller u. W. v. Humboldt. Mit Vorerin-
  nerung ueber S. von W. v. Humboldt.
  Stuttgart, 1830. 16°. 1023.9
— Nachträge zu Schiller's sämmtlichen Werken.
  Hrsg. v. E. Boas. Neue Ausgabe. Stuttgart,
  1840-53. 3v. 16°. 1032.1
— Schiller's Briefe. Hrsg. v. Dr. H. Döring.
  Altenburg, 1846. 2v. 16°. 1033.1
— Schiller's Gedichte erläutert von H. Viehoff.
  Neue Aufl. Stuttgart, 1856. 3v. 16°. . . . 1023.10
SCHMIDT, J. Geschichte der deutschen Literatur
  im 19ten Jahrhundert. 2te Aufl. Leipzig,
  1855. 3v. 8°. 1023.2
SCHOPENHAUER, J. Sämmtliche Schriften. Ber-
  lin, 1830-31. 24v. 18°. 1033.2
SCORESBY, W. Adventurous life of W. Scoresby.
  London, 1851. 8°. 578.15
— American factories and their female opera-
  tives. London, 1845. 12°. 196.21
— Zoistic magnetism. London, 1849. 8°. . . 194.15
SCOURING of the white horse. Boston, 1859. 16°.434.12-17
SCOTT, Sir W. Recollections. London, 1837. 16° 587.2
SEWELL, W. Christian morals. New ed. Lon-
  don, 1849. 16°. 128.14
SEYMOUR, C. C B. Self-made men. New York,
  1858. 12°. 543.13
SHAW, C. Description of Boston. Boston, 1817.
  12°. 228.16
SHAW, J. A gallop to the antipodes. London,
  1858. 12°. 687.25
SHEIL, Rev. Dr. The Bible against protestantism
  and for catholicity. 5th ed. Boston, 1859. 12° 1105.16
SHERIDAN, R. B. Speeches, with a sketch of his
  life. London, 1842. 3v. 8°. 864.1
— Dramatic works, with a memoir. London,
  1857. p.8°. 847.2-6
SHIRREFF, E. Intellectual education. London,
  1858. 12°. 138.12
SIDNEY Grey: a tale of school life. New York,
  1859. 16°. 748.5
SIGOURNEY, Mrs. L. H. The daily counsellor.
  Hartford, 1859. 12°. 375.18
SILLIMAN, B., Jr. First principles of physics ; or,
  natural philosophy. Philadelphia, 1859.
  12°. 148.5
SILLOWAY, T. W. Text-book of modern carpen-
  try. Boston, 1858. 12°. 196.19
SIMMONDS, P. L. Curiosities of food. London,
  1859. 12°. 189.14
SIMON, J. Sanitary condition of London. Lon-
  don, 1854. 8°. 138.15
SMEATON and lighthouses. [Biogr.] London,
  1844. sm.12°. 196.23
SMITH A. A month at Constantinople. 3d ed.
  London, 1851. 16°. 689.20
— Evening parties. London, n.d. 32°. . . . 450.5
SMITH, C. H. J. Parks and pleasure grounds.
  London, 1852. 12°. 207.21
SMITH, S. My thirty years out of the senate, by
  Maj. Jack Downing. New York, 1859. 12°. 309.14
SMITH, W. Thorndale ; or, the conflict of opinions.
  Boston, 1859. 12°. 894.11
SOMERVILLE, M. Connection of the physical sci-
  ences. 9th ed. London, 1858. 12°. 148.8
SOUTHEY, C. B. Tales of the factories. Edinb.,
  1833. 16°. 385.9
SPURGEON, C. H. Spurgeon's gems. New York,
  1858. 12°. 1105.6
STANLEY, A. P. Life and correspondence of
  Thomas Arnold. 5th ed. London, 1845.
  2v. 8°. 576.8
STANLEY, C. H. Chess player's instructor. New
  York, 1859. 18°. 189.21
STARK, R. M. Popular history of British mosses.
  London, 1854. 16°. 108.15
STAUNTON, H. The chess-player's handbook. 2d
  ed. London, 1848. 16°. 836.8-12
STEINMETZ, A. Japan and her people. London,
  1859. 12°. 709.22

STILES, J. D. Twelve messages from the spirit John Quincy Adams. Boston, 1859. 8° .. 122.19

STRICKLAND, A. Lives of the Queens of Scotland. Vol. VII. New York, 1859. 12° ... 503.4–5

STRICKLAND, Major. Twenty-seven years in Canada West. Ed. by Agnes Strickland. London, 1853. 2v. in 1. 12° 635.23

SUTTON, T. Dictionary of photography. London, 1858. 8° 187.11

TAYLOR, I. Logic in theology, and other essays. London, 1859. 12° 128.23

— Restoration of belief. Cambridge, 1855. 12°. 128.10

TERENTIUS Afer, P. Comedies. Transl. by H. T. Riley. Blank verse translation by Geo. Colman. New York, 1859. 12° 385.1

THACKERAY, W. M. Christmas books; Mrs. Perkins' ball; Our street; Dr. Birch. New ed. London, 1857. 16° 509.15

THAYER, W. M. The poor girl and true woman. From the life of Mary Lyon and others. Boston, 1859. 16° 138.10

THOMPSON, J. P. Memoir of Rev. David Tappan Stoddard. New York, 1858. 12° 535.16–17

THOMPSON, W. Outline of the laws of thought. From 4th Lond. ed. Cambridge, 1859. 12°. 128.18

THOMSON, W. M. The land and the book. New York, 1859. 2v. 8° 688.1

TIMBS, J. Curiosities of London. London, 1855. 16° 999.9

— Year-book of facts. Lond., 1859. 16°. Vol. XXII. of 159.2

TOMMASÉO, N. Fede e bellezza. 4a ed. Milano, 1852. 12° 1045.1

— Nuove speranze d'Italia. Firenze, 1848. 12°. 1059.16

TRAIN, G. F. Spread-eaglelsm. N.Y., 1859. 12°. 299.9

TYLER, S. The progress of philosophy. Philadelphia, 1858. 12° 122.17

UHDEN, H. F. New England theocracy. Boston, 1859. 12° 1105.8

UNITED STATES. Exploration of the Valley of the Amazon. Part I., Herndon. Part II., Gibbon. With maps. Washington, 1854. 4v. 8° 622.1–2

UNPROTECTED females in Sicily, Calabria, and on the top of Mount Ætna. London, 1859. 12° 677.1

VANDENHOFF, G. Common sense. A satire in verse. Boston, 1858. 12° 375.13

VANE-STEWART, C. W. Tour in the north of Europe in 1836–37. London, 1838. 2v. in 1. 8° 666.8

VERDIZOTTI, G. M. Favole morali antiche volgarizzate. Milano, 1822. 16° 1059.23

VERGNAUD, P. Manuel des Jeunes Gens, ou sciences, arts, et récréations qui leur conviennent. Paris, Roret, 1831. 2v. sm.12° . 1079.16

WALMSLEY, H. M. Algeria during the Kabyle war. London, 1858. 12° 689.19

WALPOLE, H. Letters. Ed. by P. Cunningham. Vol. IX. London, 1859. 8° 572.3

WARREN, S. Development of the present age. New ed. Edinburgh, 1854. sm.8° 138.18

— Duties of attornies and solicitors. 2d ed Edinburgh, 1851. 16° 139.27

— Miscellanies critical, imaginative, and juridical. Contributed to Blackwood. Edinb., 1855. 2v. 16° 507.4

WARREN, T. R. Dust and foam; or, three oceans and two continents. New York, 1859. 12°. 706.10

WATKINS, J. Life of R. B. Sheridan. 3d ed. London, 1818. 2v. 8° 572.5

WATSON, A. American home garden. New York, 1859. 12° 166.20

WAYLAND, F. Sermons to the churches. New York, 1858. 12° 1105.5

WELLS, D. A. Annual of scientific discovery for 1859. Boston, 1859. 12° ... Vol. X. of 159.1

WHATELY, R. Errors of Romanism. Essays. 3d series. 5th ed. London, 1856. 8° ... 128.8

WHITE, A. Popular history of birds. London, 1855. 16° 178.41

WHITE, W. A month in Yorkshire. London, 1858. 8° 645.5

WHITTEMORE, T. Autobiography. Bost., 1859. 12° 535.18

WHITWORTH, J. Miscellaneous papers on mechanical subjects. London, 1858. 8° 194.20

WILKS, W. and M. The three archbishops: Lanfranc—Anselm—A'Becket. London [1858]. 12° 542.7

WILLIAMS, C. Narratives of travellers in Africa. London, 1859. 12° 707.16

WILLIAMS, S. F. Elements of mechanics and hydrostatics. Cambridge, 1854. 16° 148.14

WILMER, L. A. Life, travels, and adventures of Ferdinand de Soto. Philadelphia, 1858. 8° 541.8

WILSON, J. Mechanics' and builders' price-book. New York, 1859. 12° 187.14

WILSON, R. A. History of the conquest of Mexico. Philadelphia, 1859. 12° 255.2

WINTER, C. T. Six months in British Burmah. London, 1858. 12° 706.11

WOOD, W. M. Fankwei; or the San Jacinto in the seas of India, China, and Japan. New York, 1859. 12° 706.12

NOTE.—Additional copies of many books in the original Index have been procured for the Library; but it has not been thought necessary to repeat their titles in this Supplement.

PUBLIC LIBRARY OF THE CITY OF BOSTON.

SECOND SUPPLEMENT TO THE INDEX.

CONTAINING A LIST OF THE BOOKS PLACED IN THE LOWER HALL, FROM MARCH 26, 1859,
TO OCTOBER 20, 1859.

ABBOTT, J. Harper's Story Books. New York.
n.d. 16°.
The Alcove 440.45–46
The Alps 440.39–40
American history 440.29–30
Ancient history 440.25–26
Aunt Margaret 440.1–2
Bruno 440.55–56
Carl and Jocko 440.67–68
Congo 440.47–48
Dialogues 440.30–31
Elfred 440.17–18
Emma 440.37–38
The engineer 440.37–38
English history 440.27–28
Franklin 440.21–22
Gibraltar Gallery 440.43–44
The great elm 440.49–50
Harper's Establishment 440.19–20
Jasper 440.65–66
John Trne 440.31–32
Judge Justin 440.61–62
Lapstone 440.57–58
The little Louvre 440.13–14
Little Paul 440.71–72
Minigo 440.63–64
The museum 440.35–36
Orkney 440.59–60
Prank 440.15–16
The strait gate 440.5–6
The studio 440.23–24
Three gold dollars 440.41–42
Timboo and Fanny 440.11–12
Timboo and Joliba 440.9–10
Vernon 440.53–54
Viola 440.69–70
Virginia 440.7–8
Willie 440.3–4
— History of Alexander the Great. New York,
1857. 16° 550.1–2
— — King Alfred, of England. New York,
1850. 16° 550.19–20
— — Charles I., of England. N.Y., 1854. 16° 550.31–32
— — Charles II., of England. N.Y., 1854. 16° 550.33–34
— — Cyrus the Great. New York, 1857. 16° . 550.5–6
— — Darius the Great. New York, 1851. 16° 550.11–12
— — Queen Elizabeth. New York, 1858. 16° 550.35–36
— — Hannibal. New York, 1857. 16° 550.9–10
— — Julius Cæsar. New York, 1859. 16° . . 550.13–14
— — Mary Queen of Scots. N. Y., 1859. 16° 550.37–38
— — Nero. New York, 1854. 16° 550.15–16
— — Pyrrhus. New York, 1854. 16° 550.17–18
— — Richard I., of England. N.Y., 1857. 16° 550.23–24
— — Richard II., of England. N.Y., 1858. 16° 550.25–26
— — Richard III., of England. N.Y., 1858. 16° 550.27–28
— — Romulus. New York, 1854. 16° 550.3–4
— — William the Conqueror. N.Y., 1859. 16° 550.21–22
— — Xerxes the Great. N. Y., 1854. 16° . . 550.7–8
— — Rollo in Naples. Boston, 1858. 16° . . 677.10–11
— — — Scotland. Boston, 1857. 16° . . . 677.18–19
ABBOTT, J. S. C. Empire of Russia. New York,
1860. 12° 927.14
— French Revolution of 1789. N. Y., 1859. 8° . 1001.3–7
— History of Henry IV., of France. New York.
1856. 16° 550.29–30

ABBOTT, J. S. C. Hernando Cortez. N. Y., 1855.
16° 550.45–46
— — Madame Roland. N. York, 1858. 16° . 550.39–40
— — Maria Antoinette. N. York, 1857. 16° . 550.41–42
— — King Philip. New York, 1857. 16° . . 550.43–44
— — Napoleon Bonaparte. N. Y., 1855. 2v. 8° 611.1–2
ABOUT, E. The Roman question. Transl. by H.
C. Coape. New York, 1859. 12° 1098.26
— La question romaine. Bruxelles, 1859. 8° . 1074.34
ACCOUNT of Laura Bridgman. 2d edition. Lon-
don, 1845. 32° 539.32
ACCOUNTS of shipwrecks and of other disasters
at sea. Brunswick, Me., 1823. 12° 699.18
ACTING proverbs ; or, drawing-room theatricals.
London, 1858. 12° 385.17
ADAMS, H. G. Cage and singing birds. New ed.
London, 1859. 18° 176.13
ADOLPHUS, J. L. Letters from Spain in 1856 and
1857. London, 1858. 12° 666.19
AGASSIZ, Mrs. First lessons in natural history.
Boston, 1859. 12° 176.15
AGNEL, H. R. The book of chess. N. Y., 1859. 12° 187.18
AINSWORTH, W. Researches in Assyria, Babylo-
nia, and Chaldea. London, 1838. 8° 946.5
ALCOTT, W. A. Forty years in the wilderness of
pills and powders. Boston, 1859. 12° . . 536.10
— The house I live in. Ed. by T. C. Girtin. 9th
ed. London, 1857. 32° 139.42
ALL about it: or, the history of common things.
New York, 1859. 12° 187.17
ALLEN, Mrs. S. S., and others. The mother's as-
sistant. Boston, 1853. 8° 126.10
ALLEN, R. L. The American farm book. N. Y.,
1858. 12° 166.21
ALMOST a heroine. Boston, 1859. 12° 497.13
ALTHAUS, J. Treatise on medical electricity.
London, 1859. 8° 163.15
ANDERSON, R. Observations upon the Pelopon-
nesus and Greek islands made in 1829. Bos-
ton, 1830. 12° 689.22
ANDREWS, A. History of British journalism.
London, 1859. 2v. 8° 395.1
ARABIAN nights' entertainments. Transl. by Rev.
E. Forster. London, 1856. 8° 711.1
— — Same. Transl. by E. W. Lane. N. Y.,
1856. 2v. 12° 744.1–3
ARNOLD, Dr. J. M. Ishmael ; or, a natural history
of Islamism. London, 1859. 8° 1104.4
ARNOLD, T. Life of Hannibal. N.Y., 1860. 18° . 550.61
ARROWSMITH, A. Compendium of ancient and
modern geography. London, 1839. 8° . . . 942.3
ARTHUR, W. The successful merchant. 20th ed.
London, 1858. p.8° 587.6
ATHERSTONE, E. The fall of Nineveh. A poem.
London, 1847. 2v. 8° 374.1
AUTRICHE et son gouvernement. Paris, 1859. 8° 1074.25
AYERST, W. The Jews of the nineteenth century.
London, 1848. 12° 115.15
AZEGLIO, M. d'. Ettore Fieramosca ; or the chal-
lenge of Barletta. Boston, 1859. 12° . . . 917.7

BADEAU, A. The vagabond. New York, 1859. 12° 903.8
BAILLIE, J. The missionary of Kilmany ; being
a memoir of Alexander Paterson. 14th ed.
Edinburgh, 1859. 24° 1008.32

BAKER, H. N. and A. R. Theology in romance. Boston, 1859. 2v. 18° 468.13
BALFOUR, C. L. Morning dewdrops. 4th ed. London, 1859. 12° 168.25
BALL, J. Peaks, passes, and glaciers. London, 1859. 8° 666.12
BALLANTYNE, R. M. The coral island. London, 1858. 16° 748.8
— Ungava: a tale of Esquimaux land. London, 1858. 12° 748.15
BARANTE, Baron de. Le parlement et La Fronde. La vie de Mathieu Molé. Paris, 1859. 8°. 1074.1
BARCLAY, S. Personal recollections of the American revolution. New York, 1859. 12° . . 217.10
BARTOLI, D., and Maffei, J. P. Life of St. Francis Xavier. Pref. by Dr. Faber. 1st Am., from Lond. ed. Baltimore, 1859. 12° 612.11
BASHAM, W. R. On dropsy. London, 1858. 8°. 153.18
BAUTAIN, M. Art of extempore speaking. New York, 1859. 12° 396.5
BEDE, C. Adventures of Mr. Verdant Green. London, 1858. 12° 506.9
BEECHER, H. W. Fruits, flowers, and farming. New York, 1859. 12° 163.30
— New star papers. New York, 1859. 12° . . . 115.3
BELCHER, J. Historical sketches of hymns. Philadelphia, 1859. 12° 557.9
BELL, J. Treatise on baths. 2d ed. Philadelphia, 1859. 12° 153.28
BENNETT, J. C. History of the saints; an exposé of mormonism. Boston, 1842. 12° 115.14
BERQUIN, A. de. The children's friend. New York, 1857. 2v. in 1. 12° 727.11-12
BEST method of doing common things. 4th ed. London, n.d. 18° 189.37
BIBLE: Notes on the Acts of the Apostles. By M. W. Jacobus. New York, 1859. 12° . . . 115.5
BICKERSTETH, J. L. Memoir. Lond., n.d. 32°. 189.34
BIRCHALL, J. England under the Normans and Plantagenets. London, 1858. 8° 993.2
BISHOP, J. English laws respecting landlords, tenants, and lodgers. London, n.d. 32° . . 128.34
BITZIUS, A. Gesammelte Schriften. Bde 8—12. Berlin, 1856. 16° 2025.1

Contents. — Vols. VIII—X. — Erzählungen und Bilder aus dem Volksleben der Schweiz. XI. Jakobs, des Handwerksgesellen, Wanderungen durch die Schweiz. XII. Dursli, der Branntweinsaufer, oder: der heilige Weihnachtsabend.

BLAKEY, R. Angling; or, how to angle and where to go. New ed. Lond., 1858. 12°. . 168.22
— Old faces in new masks. London, 1859. 12°. 905.10
BLANCHET, P. Maistre Pierre Pathelin. Nouv. Ed. Notes par P. L. Jacob. Paris, 1859. 12° 1074.30
BOAS, E. Schiller und Goethe im Xenienkampf. Stuttgart, 1851. 2 Thle. 1851. 8° 1032.3
BORDEAUX wine and liquor dealers' guide. New York, 1858. 12° 189.22
BOSTON. Dedication of the Public Library. Boston, 1858. 8° 202.1
BOULLÉE, A. Essai sur la vie, le caractère et les ouvrages de J. E. M. Portalis. Paris, 1859. 8° 1074.2
BOUTWELL, G. S. Educational topics and institutions. Boston, 1859. 12° 138.30
BOWMAN, A. Common things of every day life. London, 1857. 12° 189.31.36
— The Kangaroo hunters. London, 1859. 12° . 747.13
BRABAZON, E. J. Historical tales of the Muslims in Spain. London, 1853. 18° 457.6
BREAKFAST, dinner, and tea. New York, 1859. 12° 905.12
BREWSTER, C. W. Rambles about Portsmouth. Portsmouth, 1859. 8° 233.5
BRIGHTWELL, C. L. Heroes of the laboratory and the workshop. London, 1859. 12° . . . 530.54
BRITISH birds. The water birds. Lond., n.d. 18° 176.12
BRITISH land birds. London, n.d. 18° 176.11
BRITISH Museum, (The). Edinburgh, 1859. 12°. 207.24
BRITISH workman, (The). London, 1856. Fol. . 990.1
BROCK, Mrs. C. Children at home. London, 1859. 12° 487.2

BROCK, Mrs. C. Working and waiting. London, 1859. 12° 487.5
BROOKES, J. Manners and customs of the English nation. London, n.d. 12° 999.16
BROUGHTON, Lord. Italy: remarks made in several visits, 1816—1854. London, 1859. 2v. 8° 666.10
BROWN, J. Sixty years' gleanings from life's harvest. New York, 1859. 12° 556.12
BROWN, T. The taxidermists' manual. 14th ed. London, 1858. 16° 178.46
BROWN, W. S. Chemistry for beginners. 2d ed. Boston, 1855. 12° 158.29
BROWNING, M. Forty-four years of the life of a hunter. Philadelphia, 1859. 12° 748.20
BUCHANAN, R. Notes of a clerical furlough, spent chiefly in the Holy Land. Lond., 1859. 12° 688.11
BUCKLEY, T. A. The dawnings of genius. 4th ed. London, 1857. 12° 550.59
BUNSEN, C. C. J. Life of Martin Luther. With essays by Carlyle and Hamilton. N. Y. [1859]. 18° 550.50
BURGON, J. W. Memoir of Patrick Fraser Tytler. 2d ed. London, 1859. 12° 587.8
BURKE, Sir B. Vicissitudes of families. London, 1859. 12° 998.3
BURROUGHS, W. Adventures of a trooper in the Australian constabulary. Lond., 1859. 12° 709.26
BUSCH, Dr. M. Guide for travellers in Egypt. Tr. by W. C. Wrankmore. London, 1858. 12°. 698.26
BUSK, H. The navies of the world. Lond., 1859. 12° 947.15
BUTLER, C. Guide to useful knowledge. 12th ed. London, n.d. 32° 128.37
BUTTS, I. R. The business-man's law cabinet. Boston, 1859. 8° 132.9

CAIRD, J. Prairie farming in America. New York, 1859. 12° 167.30
CALKINS, N. A., and Adams, W. T. The universal speaker. Boston, 1859. 12° 396.11
CAMPBELL, J. L. Manual of scientific and practical agriculture. Philadelphia, 1859. 12°. 168.23
CAMPBELL, Lord. Shakespeare's legal acquirements considered. London, 1859. 8° 585.12
CARPENTER, H. S. Here and beyond. New York, 1859. 12° 128.25
CARPENTER, W. B. Animal physiology. New ed. London, 1859. p.8° 853.1
— Vegetable physiology and systematic botany. Ed. by E. Lankester. London, 1858. p.8°. 853.2
CASWALL, H. The city of the mormons. Lond., 1843. 18° 630.24
CATHERINE II. Memoirs, written by herself. Preface by A. Herzen. Tr. from the French. London, 1859. 12° 513.15
— — Same. New York, 1859. 12° 513.10
CHADWICK, W. Life and times of Daniel Defoe. London, 1859. 8° 577.2
CHALLEN, J. Igdrasil; or, the tree of existence. Philadelphia, 1859. 12° 585.16
CHAPMAN, R. A treatise on ropemaking. London, 1858. 24° 209.26
CHATFIELD, P. The tin trumpet. New York, 1859. 12° 905.10
CHERRY and Violet. By the author of "Mary Powell." 2d ed. London, n.d. 12° 507.18
CHESS handbook, (The). Philadelphia, 1859. 12° 187.16
CHEVALIER, M. La baisse probable de l'or. Paris, 1859. 8° 1074.3
CHOICE notes from "Notes and queries." Folk lore. London, 1859. 12° 894.16
CHOICE notes from "Notes and queries." History. London, 1858. 12° 929.18
CLARENCE, S. "Not a minute to spare." London, n.d. 24° 139.35
CLARK, G. F. History of Norton, Bristol County, 1669-1859. Boston, 1859. 12° 227.21
CLARKE, J. E. Heart-music for working people. London, 1857. 24° 375.25
COLE, S. W. The American veterinarian. New York, 1859. 16° 169.34

COMFORT, J. W. Practice of medicine on Thomsonian principles. 6th ed. Philadelphia, 1859. 8° 153.14
CONSCIENCE, H. La guerre des paysans. Paris, 1855. 18° 1074.33
CONSTRUCTION of dwelling-houses. 2d ed. London, 1851. 12° 209.21
COOKE, P. St. G. Scenes and adventures in the army. Philadelphia, 1859. 12° 637.14
COOKERY; or how to live well. 10th ed. London, n.d. 32° 189.32
COOKMAID'S complete guide. New edition. London, n.d. 12° 189.29
COOLIDGE, A. J. & Mansfield, J. B. History and description of New England. Vol. I. Boston, 1859. 8° 233.4
COOPER, J. F. The pathfinder. New ed. New York, 1857. 12° 800.29-30
— The pilot. New ed. New York, 1856. 12°. 800.33
— The prairie. New ed. New York, 1858. 12° . 800.31-32
— The red rover. New ed. N. York, 1858. 12° . 800.34-35
COOPER, T. Parliamentary short-hand. London, 1858. 24° 128.35
COPELAND, R. M. Country life. Boston, 1859. 8° 164.19
COPLEY, E. The complete cottage cookery. London, 1859. 32° 189.33
— Lads of the factory. London, n.d. 32° . . . 139.39
COPPÉE, H. Elements of rhetoric. Philadelphia, 1859. 12° 396.4
COUSIN Minnie's tales for young christians. n. p. n.d. 24° 450.23
COUSIN, V. Secret history of the French court. Tr. by M. L. Booth. N. Y., 1859. 12° . . 1009.17
COXE, A. C. Impressions of England, or sketches of English scenery and society. 2d ed. New York, 1856. 12° 645.13
COZZENS, F. S. Acadia. New York, 1859. 12°. . 637.18
CRAWFORD, M. S. Life in Tuscany. New York, 1859. 12° 666.18
CRAWLEY, R. Chess; its theory and practice. London, n.d. 32° 209.24
CRICKET field, (The). Boston, 1859. 12° 198.33
CURWIN, M. E. Sketches of the campaign in Northern Mexico in 1846–47. New York, 1853. 12° 259.12
CUVILLIER-FLEURY. Dernières études historiques et littéraires. T. I.–II. Paris, 1859. 12° . . 1074.18

DADD, G. H. On the diseases of cattle. Boston, 1859. 12° 167.27
DALTON, W. The English boy in Japan. London, 1858. 16° 748.12
DANA, D. D. The fireman. Boston, 1858. 12° . . 309.4
DANA, R. H., Jr. To Cuba and back. Boston, 1859. 12° 637.15-17
DASENT, G. W. Popular tales from the Norse. 2d ed. Edinburgh, 1859. 12° 748.22
— Same. New York, 1859. 12° 748.18
DAVYS, G. The saving bank. New ed. Saffron Walden, n.d. 18° 450.21
DEAN, W. The China mission. N. Y., 1859. 12° 115.9
DE FOREST, J. W. Seacliff. Boston, 1859. 12°. . 506.15
DELAMER, E. S. Flax and hemp. Their culture and manipulation. London, 1859. 18° . . 167.35
— The kitchen garden. New ed. Lond., 1859. 18° 168.26
— Pigeons and rabbits. New ed. 1858. 12° . . 168.21
DELTOUR, F. Les ennemis de Racine au XVIIe siècle. Paris, 1859. 8° 1074.4
DEMOGEOT, J. Tableau de la littérature française au XVIIe siècle. Paris, 1859. 8°. . . . 1074.5
DE QUINCEY, T. The avenger; a narrative, and other papers. Boston, 1859. 12° 905.5-8
— Logic of political economy. Boston, 1859. 12° 905.12
DESBARROLLES, M. Two French artists in Spain. Tr. by C. Mac Farlane. London, 1851. 12° 666.17
DICKENS, C. Christmas stories. Philadelphia, n.d. 2v. 12° 500.1-2
— David Copperfield. Philadelphia, n.d. 2v. 12° 500.3-4
— A house to let. Philadelphia, n.d. 8° . . . 472.9-10
— Martin Chuzzlewit. Phila., n.d. 2v. 12° . . 500.5-6

DICKENS, C. Nicholas Nickleby. Philadelphia., n.d. 2v. 12° 500.7-8
— Oliver Twist. Philadelphia, n.d. 8° 472.11
— Pickwick papers. Phila., n.d. 2v. 12° . . . 500.9-10
DICKSON, J. Unity of physical sciences. London, 1859. 12° 148.30
DISRAELI, B. Coningsby. New ed. London, 1859. 12° 752.1
— Contarini Fleming. New ed. Lond. 1858. 12° 752.2
— Henrietta Temple. New ed. Lond., 1858. 12° 752.3
— Sybil; or the two nations. New ed. London, 1858. 12° 752.4
— Tancred. New ed. London, 1858. 12° . . . 752.5
— Venetia. New edition. London, 1858. 12° . 752.6
D'ISRAELI, I. Curiosities of literature. 10th ed. London, 1858. 8° 392.4
DIXON, F. B. Law of shipping, and merchant's and shipmaster's guide. N. York, 1859. 8° 132.8
DODD, G. The curiosities of industry. London, 1853. 8° 167.33
DOMESTICATED and wild animals. Lond., 1856. 12° 178.47
DONNE, A. Mothers and infants, nurses and nursing. Tr. from the French. Bost., 1859. 12° 155.29
DÜRING, H. Schiller und Goethe. Leipzig, 1852. 16° 2016.5
DOWLING, J. G. Introduction to the critical study of ecclesiastical history. London, 1838. 8° 1082.3
DRESSER, C. Unity in variety. London, 1859. 8° 164.18
DRURY, A. H. The inn by the seaside. An allegory. London, 1852. 16° 1098.34
DU DEFFAND, Mme. Correspondance inédite. T. I.–II. Paris, 1859. 8° 1074.20
DUDEVANT, Mme. La guerre. Paris, 1859. 8°. . 1074.22
DU HAMEL, M. le Cte. L'Italie l'Autriche et la guerre. Paris, 1859. 8° 1074.9
DUN, F. Veterinary medicines. 2d ed. Edinburgh, 1859. 8° 166.31
DUNDONALD, T., Earl of. Narrative of services in the liberation of Chili, Peru, and Brazil, from Spanish and Portuguese domination. London, 1859. 8° 263.9
DURIVAGE, F. A. Life scenes, sketched in light and shadow from the world around us. Boston, 1853. 12° 487.8
DUTIES of human life. Translated from a Sanscrit MS. Ed. by J. Perkins. W. Killingly, Conn., 1858. 12° 126.11
DWIGHT, B. W. Modern philology. New York, 1859. 8° 392.5

EDDY, D. C. The Percy family. A visit to Ireland. Boston, 1859. 16° 645.7
EICHENDORFF, J. F. v. Ahnung und Gegenwart. Roman. Nürnberg, 1815. 16° 2025.3
ELLIOTT, E. Poems. London, 1833-5. 3v. 12° . . 385.21
ELLIS, R. The chemistry of creation. London, n. d. 18° 148.22
ELWYN, A. L. Glossary of supposed Americanisms. Philadelphia, 1859. 12° 396.7
ERITIS sicut Deus. Anonymer Roman. Hamburg, 1854. 3v. 12° 2025.2
ERNEST Carroll. Boston, 1858. 12° 497.9-10
ESQUIROS, A. La Néerlande et la vie Hollandaise. Paris, 1859. 2v. 16° 1074.19
ESSAY on intuitive morals. Part 1. 1st Am. ed. Boston, 1859. 12° 139.33
ETYMOLOGY made easy. London, 1856. 32° . . 128.36
EVANS, A. J. Beulah. New York, 1859. 12° . . 497.11
EVANS, M. Adam Bede. N. Y., 1859. 12° . . . 506.4-6
EVERTS, W. W. Manhood; its duties and responsibilities. N. Y., 1859. 12° 138.31
EXPERIMENTS with Sorghum sugar cane. Cincinnati, n.d. 18° 168.32

FABER, G. S. Napoleon III. the man of prophecy. 1st Am. ed. N. Y., 1859. 24° 1009.18
FACTS for everybody. London, n.d. 12° 126.4
FAIRBANKS, C. B. Aguecheek. Bos., 1859. 12° . . 666.13
FAIRFIELD, J. Life of Sumner Lincoln Fairfield. N. Y., 1846. 12° 339.28

FAR off; or, Asia and Australia described. London, 1856. 2v. 12° 939.10

FEUCHTWANGER, L. Popular treatise on gems. N. Y., 1859. 12° 163.27

FIELD, H. M. Summer pictures from Copenhagen to Venice. N. Y., 1859. 16° 666.11-16

FIRST lessons in the history of the United States. Boston, 1856. 12° 309.18

FISHER, G. Young man's companion. New ed. Corr. by Rev. G. N. Wright. London, 1856. 12° 128.27

FISKE, D. W. Book of the first American chess congress. N. Y., 1859. 12° 207.23

FISON, Mrs. W. Hints for the earnest student. 2d. ed. London, 1854. 12° 128.33

FLEMING, W. Vocabulary of philosophy. 2d. ed. London, 1858. 12° 125.31

FLINT, C. L. Grasses and forage plants. 4th ed. Boston, 1859. 8° 167.29

FOLLEN, E. L. Home dramas. Bos., 1859. 12° . 395.10

FONBLANQUE, A. How we are governed. London, 1859. 18° 136.35

FOOTSTEPS of St. Paul. London, 1859. p.8° . . 115.11

FORBES, E. Natural history of the European seas. Ed. by R. Godwin-Austen. Lond., 1859. 12° 176.16

FOSTER, J. Fosteriana. Ed. by H. G. Bohn. London, 1858. p.8° 857.7-8

FOWNES, G. Manual of elementary chemistry. Ed. by R. Bridges. Phila. 1859. 12° . . . 148.31

FOXE, J. Foxe's book of martyrs. Abridged by Theo. A. Buckley. London, 1858. 12° . . . 1098.33

FRAMJEE, D. The Parsees. Lond., 1858. 12° . . 939.11

FRANCATELLI, C. E. The modern cook. From 9th Lond. ed. Philadelphia, n.d. 8° . . . 187.19

FREEDLEY, E. T. Leading pursuits and leading n n. Philadelphia, 1856. 8° 132.11

FREEMAN, N. C. The twilight dream. Phila., 1853. 12° 385.14

FREER, M. W. Henry III. King of France and Poland; his court and times. Lond., 1858. 3v. p.8° 1007.11

FRENCH, H. F. Farm drainage. New York, 1859. 12° 164.17

FROEBEL, J. Seven years' travel in Central America. London, 1859. 8° 622.4

FULLER, H. Sparks from a locomotive. N. Y., 1859. 12° 905.11

GARIBALDI, G. Life, written by himself. Tr. by T. Dwight. New York, 1859. 12° . . . 542.12

GARWOOD, J. The million-peopled city. London, 1853. 12° 126.9

GASKELL, A. Mary Barton. N. Y., 1856. 8° . . 801.10

— My Lady Ludlow. New York, 1858. 8° . . 802.46-47

GEFFROY, A. Lettres inédites de la Princesse des Ursins. Paris, 1859. 8° 1074.7

GELDART, Mrs. T. Stories of England. 5th ed. London, n. d. 18° 999.19

GELDART, T. Truth is everything. New York, 1859. 18° 748.16

GERUZEZ, E. Histoire de la littérature française pendant 1789—1800. Paris, 1859. 12° . . . 1074.29

GIBBON, E. Life of Mahomet. Notes by D. Milman and Dr. W. Smith. New York, n.d. 18° 550.47

GILBART, J. W. The logic of banking. London, 1859. 12° 133.14

GIUSTINIAN, S. Four years at the Court of Henry VIII. Tr. by R. Brown. London, 1854, 2v. 8° 908.1

GOSSE, P. H. Letters from Alabama — relating to natural history. London, 1859. 12° . . . 176.14

GRANDEFFE, A. de. Pie IX. et l'Italie. Nouv. Éd. Paris, 1859. 8° 1074.24

GRENVILLE, R. P. T. Memoirs of the Court of George IV. 1820—1830. London, 1859. 2v. 8° 983.3

GRETTON, A. L. V. Vicissitudes of Italy. Lond., 1859 12° 917.5

GUIZOT, F. Memoirs to illustrate the history of my own time. Tr. by J. W. Cole. London. Vol. II. 1859. 8° 1003.5

GUTHRIE, G. J. Surgery of war in Portugal, Spain, France, &c. 6th ed. London, 1855. 8° 155.32

GUY Livingstone; or "thorough." New York, 1857. 12° 497.6

HALCOMBE, J. J. The speaker at home. And: Stone, W. H. Physiology of speech. Lond., 1859. 12° 395.9

HALE, S. J. Sketches of American character. 4th ed. Boston, 1833. 18° 150.25

HALLECK, H. W. Elements of military art and science. 2d. ed. New York, 1859. 12° . . 198.32

HAMILTON, J. C. History of the United States, as traced in the writings of A. Hamilton. New York, Vol. III.-IV. 1859. 8° 304.2

HAMILTON, Sir W. Lectures on metaphysics and logic. Edited by Rev. H. L. Mansel, and J. Veitch. Boston, 1859. 8° 873.14

HAMPDEN, A. Hartley Norman. New York, 1859. 12° 496.16

HANGER, C. H. Proverbial and moral thoughts. Boston, 1859. 16° 375.23

HARPER's New Monthly Magazine. New York, 1850-1858. 17v. 8° 880.3

HARRISON, W. The light of the forge. London, 1853. 18° 1098.31

HASTINGS, Marquis of. Private journal. Edited by Marchioness of Bute. London, 1858. 2v. 12° 707.17

HAVEN, J. Moral philosophy. Boston, 1859. 12°. 126.8

HEADLAND, F. W. The action of medicines in the system. Philadelphia, 1859. 8° . . . 153.16

HEADLEY, J. T. Life of General H. Havelock. New York, 1859. 12° 577.3

HEQUEMBOURG, C. L. Plan of the creation. Boston, 1859. 12° 1105.19

HERBERT, H. W. Guy Carleton. New York, 1859. 12° 736.15

— Hints to horse-keepers. New York, 1859. 12° 166.26

HERODOTUS. History. Tr. by G. Rawlinson. New York. Vol. I. 8° 941.1

HILL, R. Post Office reform. 4th ed. London, 1838. 8° 133.15

HINTS for early education. 16th ed. London, 1853. 18° 128.32

HISTORY and adventure. London, 1858. 2v. 12°. 376.3

HISTORY of the Indian revolt and of the expeditions to Persia, China, and Japan. London, 1859. 8° 931.1

HODGES, R. M. Practical dissections. Cambridge, 1858. 12° 157.37

HOLBEIN, H. Dance of death. With a dissertation by F. Douce. Introd. by T. F. Dibdin. London, 1858. p.8° 843.5

HOLLEY, O. L. Life of Franklin. Bost., 1848. 12° 519.8

HOLMES, A. Parties and their principles. New York, 1859. 12° 299.11

HOME book of household economy. New ed. London, 1857. 12° 189.25

HOOK, T. E. Life and remains, by Rev. R. H. D. Barham. 4th ed. London, 1850. 2v. 12° . 587.9

HOOKER, Sir W. J. Kew gardens. 17th ed. London, 1858. 12° 167.34

HOPKINS, S. The puritans, during the reigns of Edward VI. and Queen Elizabeth. Boston, 1859. Vol. I. 8° 982.3

HOUSEHOLD truths for working men. New ed. London, n.d. 16° 189.38

HOWITT, M. History of the United States. London, 1859. 2v. 12° 305.5

HUMBOLDT, F. H. A. v. The island of Cuba. Translated by J. S. Thrasher. New York, 1856. 8° 637.21

— Life, travels and books. Introduction by B. Taylor. New York, 1859. 12° 542.13

HUMBOLDT, W. v. Sphere and duties of government. Transl. by J. Coulthard. London, 1854. 8° 126.2
HUME, D. The student's Hume. A history of England to 1688, abridged and continued to 1858. New York, 1859. 12° 998.5
HUNT, J. Philosophy of the voice and speech. London, 1859. 8° 155.31
HUNT, V. D. The horse and his master. London, 1859. 12° 166.29

ILLNESS prevented or speedily cured. London, n.d. 32° 139.43
INDUSTRIAL and social position of women. London, 1857. 8° 126.1
INGRAHAM, J. H. The pillar of fire; or, Israel in bondage. New York, 1859. 12° 1105.21
— The Prince of the house of David. N. York, 1859. 12° 1105.17
— The South-West. New York, 1835. 2v. in 1. 8° 639.23
INTERNATIONAL monthly magazine of literature, science and art. N. York. [1850-1852.] 5v. 8° 870.2
IRELAND, J. B. Wall street to Cashmere. New York, 1859. 8° 682.5
IRVING, W. Life of George Washington. London, 1859. Vol. V. 12° 516.6-10
— — Same. New York, 1859. 8° 511.1-4

JAEGER, B. Life of North American insects. N. York, 1859. 12° 175.16
JAMES, G. P. R. The cavalier. Philadelphia, 1859. 12° 464.12
— Memoirs of great commanders. New ed. London, 1858. 8° 557.6
JENKINS, J. S. The new clerk's assistant. New York, 1856. 8° 132.10
JENYNS, L. Observations in meteorology. London, 1858. 8° 148.20
JESSE, E. Anecdotes of dogs. Lond., 1858. p.8° 843.1
JOHNES, M. Boy's book of modern travel and adventure. New York, 1859. 12° 727.14
JONES, R. Lectures and tracts on political economy. Ed. by Rev. Wm. Whewell. London, 1859. 8° 132.6
JUSSIEU, A. H. L. De. The elements of botany. Tr. with additions by J. H. Wilson. London, n.d. p.8° 853.4

KAPP, F. Life of Frederick William von Steuben. Introduction by G. Bancroft. New York, 1859. 12° 514.1
KATE Felton, or a peep at realities. Bost., 1859. 12° 506.17
KAVANAGH, J. A summer and winter in the Two Sicilies. Leipzig, 1858. 2v. in 1. 12° . . . 666.15
KELLY, W. K. Proverbs of all nations. London, 1859. 12° 396.9
KIDDER, K. P. Guide to apiarian science. Burlington, Vt., 1858. 12° 167.31
KING, E. F. Ten thousand wonderful things. London, n.d. 12° 196.25
KINGSLEY, C. The good news of God. N. York, 1859. 12° 115.4
KINGSLEY, H. Recollections of Geoffrey Hamlyn. Boston, 1859. 12° 503.10-11
KINGSTON, W. H. G. Old Jack, a man-of-war's man. London, 1859. 12° 748.13
KINKEL, Mme. Counterparts. Boston, 1859. 8°. 502.1-7
— — Same. London, 1854. 3v. 8° 505.8
— Almost a heroine. Boston, 1859. 12° 497.13
KIP, L. Army life on the Pacific. N. Y., 1859. 12° 249.7
KIRBY, M. & E. Plants of land and water. London, n.d. 32° 169.36
— Truth is always best. London, 1858. 15° . . 748.10
KLIPPART, J. H. The wheat plant. Cin., 1860. 12° 168.33
KNIGHT, C. Popular history of England. London, 1856-58. 4v. 8° 982.1
KNIGHTON, W. The private life of an Eastern king. New ed. London, 1857. 12° 550.56
KOCH, C. W. The Crimea from Kertch to Perekop. London, 1855. 12° 689.23

KRUDNER, Baron de. La Sainte alliance et les nationalités. Paris, 1859. 8° 1074.21
KURTZ, J. H. History of the old covenant. Tr. by J. Martin and Rev. A. Edersheim. Philadelphia, 1859. 2v. 8° 1104.2

LA FORGE, A. de. L'Autriche devant l'opinion. Paris, 1859. 8° 1074.11
— La guerre c'est la paix. Paris, 1859. 8° . . . 1074.13
LAIGHTON, A. Poems. Boston, 1859. 12° 385.13
LAMARTINE, A. de. Life of Christopher Columbus. New York, n.d. 18° 549.37
— Life of Oliver Cromwell. New York, n.d. 18° 550.49
LANG, J. Wanderings in India. Lond., 1859. 8° . 709.24
LANGSTROTH, L. L. Treatise on the hive and honey-bee. 3d ed. N. York, 1859. 12° . . . 166.23
LEARNING to act. London, n.d. 32° 139.38
— to converse. London, n.d. 32° 128.38
— to feel. London, n.d. 18° 159.34
— to think. London, n.d. 12° 139.37
LESSONS from nature. New ed. Lond., 1857. 32° 139.44
LETTERS to the working classes. Glasgow, 1856. 12° 128.28
LEVER, C. Davenport Dunn. Phila., n.d. 8°. 802.45.48
LEWIN, T. Invasion of Britain by Julius Cæsar. London, 1859. 8° 982.2
LIEBER, F. On civil liberty and self-government. Enlarged ed. Phila., 1859. 8° 133.13
LIEBIG, J. v. Letters on modern agriculture. Ed. by J. Blyth. London, 1859. 12° 166.25
— — Same. New York, 1859. 12° 167.28
LINDSAY, A. W. C., Lord. Letters on Egypt, Edom, and the Holy Land. 5th ed. Lond., 1858. p.8° 843.7
LIVING for self and living for others. London, n.d. 32° 450.21
LOCKE, J. Life and letters. [Ed. by] Lord King. New ed. London, 1858. p.8° 857.11
LOVER, S. Lyrics of Ireland. London, 1858. 12° 374.2
— Rory O'More. New ed. London, 1859. 12°. 497.7
LYTTON, R. B. Poems by Owen Meredith. Boston, 1859. 18° 450.17

MACAULAY, T. B. Life of Frederick the Great. New York, 1859. 18° 557.1
— Life of William Pitt. Preceded by the life of Earl of Chatham. New York, [1859.] 18°. 557.2
MAC FARLANE, C. A life of Marlborough. 2d ed. London, 1854. 12° 550.55
MACGREGOR, J. Law of reformatories. Lond., 1856. 8° 126.3
— Our brothers and cousins: A tour in Canada and the States. London, 1859. . . . . . . 639.20
MACKARNESS, M. The golden rule. London, 1859. 12° 748.17
MACKAY, C. Life and liberty in America. New York, 1859. 12° 637.20
MACKEY, A. G. Masonic jurisprudence. New York, 1859. 12° 135.25
MAJENDIE, V. D. Up among the Pandies. Lond., 1859. 12° 709.25
MALCOLM, G. F. India and the Indian mutiny. Philadelphia, 1858. 12° 999.14
MANN, R. J. A guide to astronomical science. London, n.d. 18° 148.23
— The knowledge of life, vegetable and animal. 2d ed. London, n.d. 18° 169.38
MANSEL, H. L. Limits of religious thought. 1st Amer. fr. 3d Lond. ed. Boston, 1859. 12°. 115.1
MANTELL, G. A. The medals of creation; or, first lessons in geology. 2d ed. London, 1854. 2v. p.8° 853.3
— The wonders of geology. 7th ed. Rev. by T. R. Jones. London, Vol. II., 1858. p.8°. . 836.5
MARCET, Mrs. J. Rich and poor. London, 1851. 32° 139.40
MARGUERITTES, J. de. Italy and the war of 1859. Introd. by R. S. Mackenzie. Philadelphia, 1859. 12° 917.6
MASSON, D. British novelists and their style. Boston, 1859. 12° 395.7

MASSON, D. Essays on English poets. Cambridge, 1856. 8° 576.9
— Life of Milton. With an estimate of his character, by Lord Macaulay. N. Y., 1859. 18°. 550.52
MEMOIR of Robert Haldane, and Jas. Alexander Haldane. New York, [1858.] 12° 1105.22
MEMORIALS of early genius. London, 1858. 12°. 550.57
MEN who have risen. A book for boys. London, n.d. 16° 557.3
MICHIELS, A. Secret history of the Austrian government. London, 1859. 12° 928.11
MILBURN, W. H. Ten years of preacher-life. New York, 1859. 12° 535.19
MILLER, H. Popular geology. Introductory résumé by Mrs. Miller. Boston, 1859. 12° 166.24
MILLER, J., and Lizars, J. Alcohol and tobacco. Philadelphia, 1859. 12°. 126.6
MILLER, T. The British wolf-hunter. London, 1859. 18° 748.11
MILMAN, H. H. Life of Thomas à Becket. New York, 1860. 18°. 550.62
MILTON, J. Poems, with notes by T. Keightley. London, 1859. 2v. 8° 321.1
MITCHELL, J. W. Five essays. Ed. by S. W. Mitchell. Phila., 1859. 12°. 155.30
MITCHELL, O. M. The planetary and stellar worlds. London, 1859. 12° 148.21
MONOD, A. Woman; her mission and life. Tr. from the French. New York, 1858. 12° . . 139.32
MONROE, J. Science and art of chess. N. York, 1859. 12° 187.15
MOORE, N. F. Ancient mineralogy. 2d ed. New York, 1859. 16°. 176.9
MOORMAN, J. J. The Virginia springs, and springs of the South and West. Phila., 1859. 12° 638.11
MORE, M. Mendip annals. Ed. by A. Roberts. 3d ed. London, 1859. 12° 1098.28
MORPHY, P. Exploits and triumphs. N. York, 1859. 12° 196.26
MORRISON, T. Manual of school management. Glasgow, 1859. 8° 128.26
MOTLEY, J. L. Histoire de la Republique des Provinces-Unies. Trad. par M. Guizot. Paris, 1859. 2v. 8°. 1074.8
MUDIE, R. Autumn; or, the causes and effects of the decay of nature. London, [1837.] 18°. 148.27
— Spring; or, the causes and effects of the renovations of nature. London, [1837.] 18°. . 148.25
— Summer; or, the causes and effects of the nuptials of nature. London, [1837.] 18° . . . 148.26
— Winter; or, the causes and effects of the repose of nature. London, [1837.] 18° 148.28
MUIRHEAD, J. P. Life of James Watt. N. York, 1859. 12° 587.4
MULOCH, D. M. A life for a life. N.Y., 1859. 12°. 495.6
MUNN, B. Practical land drainer. New York, 1855. 12° 166.22
MURRAY, H. The African continent. Recent exploring expedition, by J. M. Wilson. London, 1853. 12° 697.19
MURRAY, J. Handbook for Kent and Sussex. London, 1858. p.8° 645.11
— Handbook for Surrey, Hampshire, and the Isle of Wight. London, 1858. p.8° . . . 645.12
"MY station and its duties." New ed. London, n.d. 32° 139.45

NAPOLEON dynasty, (The). N. York, 1860. 8° . . 611.3
NAPOLEON III. Napoleonic ideas. Tr. by J. A. Dorr. New York, 1859. 12° 136.37
— L'Empereur Napoléon III. et l'Italie. 5me ed. Paris, 1859. 8° 1074.6
NEANDER, A. History of the Christian religion and church. Transl. by J. Torrey. New ed. London, 1858. Vol. IX. p.8° 858.1
— Lectures on the history of the Christian dogmas. London, 1858. 2v. p.8° 818.10
NEW dictionary of quotations from the Greek, Latin, and modern languages. Fr. last Lond. ed. Paris, 1859. 8° 806.12

NIGHT of toil, (The). 4th ed. Lond., 1854. 12° . **115.18**
NIGHTINGALE, F. Notes on Hospitals. London, 1859. 8° 153.17
NISARD, D. Études d'histoire et de littérature. Paris, 1859. 12° 1074.17
NORTHEND, C. The teacher's assistant. Boston, 1859. 12° 126.7
NORTON, Mrs. C. E. S. The dream, and other poems. New York, 1845. 12° 385.15
NOVELTIES, inventions, and curiosities in arts and manufactures. 5th ed. Lond., 1858. 18°. 209.22

OBSERVING eye (The). 4th ed. Lond., n.d. 18°. 169.35
OGDEN, J. Science of Education. Cin., 1859. 12° 138.34
OLD man's rambles (The). New ed. London, 1852. 12° 1098.29
OLIPHANT, M. Agnes Hopetoun's schools and holidays. Boston, 1859. 12° 748.9
ORLÉANS, Madame [Hélène] la Duchesse d'. 6me ed. Paris, 1859. 8° 1074.12
— Same. Translated from the French by Mrs. Austin. London, 1859. 8°. 616.11
ORMSBY, R. McK. History of the whig party. Boston, 1859. 12° 299.10
OSSOLI, S. M. F. d'. Summer on the lakes, in 1843. Boston, 1844. 12° 639.22
OUR farm of four acres. London, 1859. 12° . . 166.27
OUR living painters. London, 1859. 12° . . . 537.6
OUTLINES of social economy. 2d ed. London, 1859. 18° 128.31
OWEN, J. B. Business without Christianity. n.p. n.d. 18° 138.35

PAGET, J. Inquiry into the charges brought by Lord Macaulay against Wm. Penn. Edinburgh, 1858. 8° 999.17
PAINE, C. Tent and harem. New York, 1859. 12° 688.10
PALEY, W. Moral philosophy; with annotations by Richard Whately. London, 1859. 8° . . 1105.20
PALISSY, Madame. The provocations of. 3d ed. London, 1855. 12° 487.1
PALMER, J. W. The new and the old; or, California and India. New York, 1859. 12° . . 637.19
PARDOE, J. Rival beauties. New York, 1855. 8° 802.49
PARKER, T. Experience as a minister. Boston, 1859. 8°. 115.6-8
PARSONS, T. Memoir of Theophilus Parsons. Boston, 1859. 12° 536.8-9
PASHA papers (The). Epistles of Mohammed Pasha. New York, 1859. 12° 903.11
PAUTET, J. Le pape, l'Autriche et l'Italie. Paris, 1859. 8° 1074.23
PEARL (The), of days; or, the advantages of the Sabbath. Philadelphia, 1859. 8° 139.30
PEEL, Sir R. Life. New ed. London, 1859. 12° 550.58
PEEP (A) into architecture. By Eliza Chalk. 2d ed. London, 1847. 4° 209.20
PEEP of day; or, a series of religious instruction. London, 1859. 32° 139.41
PERCIVAL, J. G. Poetical works. Boston, 1859. 2v. 18° 450.18
PETER the Great. Life of. N.Y. [1859.] 2v. 18°. 550.51
PHELPS, Mrs. L. Hours with my pupils. New York, 1859. 12° 138.28
PHILLIPPS, G. J. System of mining coal and metalliferous veins fully explained. Philadelphia, 1858. 12° 196.24
PHILLIPS, B. Scrofula; its nature, causes, prevalence, and principles of treatment. London, 1846. 8° 152.19
PHILLIPS, W. Conquest of Kansas, by Missouri and her allies. Boston, 1856. 12° 239.17
PHILP, R. K. The history of progress in Great Britain. London, 1859. 8° 984.6
PICTURES of heroes, and lessons from their lives. London, n.d. 12° 550.64
PITT, J. How to brew good beer. London, 1859. 12° 189.24
PLUTARCH's lives. Corr. and rev. by A. H. Clough. Boston, 1859. 5v. 8° 511.10
POCKET schoolmaster (The). Boston, 1859. 24°. 406.26

POE, E. A. Poetical works. N. Y., 1859. 18° . 450.19
POLITIQUE Napoléonienne en Italie. Paris, 1859. 8° 1074.26
POLLARD, E. A. Black diamonds. N.Y., 1859. 12° 126.5
POLSON, A. Law and lawyers. London, 1858. 12° 136.36
POPE, A. Poetical works. Ed. by R. Carruthers. New ed. London, vol. II., 1858. p. 8° . . . 835.16
PORTER, W. T. Spirit of the times. Vols. 9—21. New York 1839—1851. 13v. Fol. 890.2
PRAED, W. M. Poetical works. New ed. New York, 1860. 2v. 12° 376.2
PROGRESSIVE lessons in social science. London, 1850. 18° 138.36
PRIME, S. The Bible in the Levant ; or, the life and letters of Rev. C. M. Righter. New York, 1859. 12° 688.9
PRUTZ, R. E. Das Engelchen. Roman. Leipzig. 1851. 3v. 16° 2025.4

QUACKENBOS, G. P. A natural philosophy. New York, 1859. 12° 148.29
QUESTION de Cuba. Paris, 1859. 8° 1074.28
QUINTON, J. A. Heaven's antidote to the curse of labor. Pref. notice by Rev. S. H. Tyng. Philadelphia, 1859. 18° 139.31

RAMROD broken (The) ; or, the Bible in favor of the moderate use of liquors. Bost., 1859. 12° 128.24
RAMSAY, E. B. Reminiscences of Scottish life and character. 3d ed. Edinburgh, 1859. 12°. 395.8
RAMSAY, W. Elementary manual of Roman antiquities. London, 1859. 12° 948.17
RAND, E. S. Life memories. Boston, 1859. 12°. 375.24
READE, C. "Love me little, love me long." New York, 1859. 12° 415.15-19
RECREATIONS of a southern barrister. Introd. by Rev. J. G. Jones. Philadelphia, 1859. 8°. 905.13
RECTORY of Moreland. Boston, 1859 12° . . . 497.12
RÉPONSE d'un Italien aux deux brochures l'Empereur Napoléon III., et l'Italie. Paris, 1859. 8° 1074.27
REYBAUD, Mme. C. Faustine. 2me ed. Paris, 1858. 12° 1074.31
— La dernière bohémienne. Paris, 1856. 12°. 1074.32
RHODES, G. Tents and tent-life. [Added] The practice of encamping an army. New ed. London, 1859. 8° 196.27
RICHMOND, A. The first twenty years of my life. Philadelphia, 1859. 12° 537.5
RICHTER, Jean Paul, Sketches of and from. London, 1859. 12° 395.3
RIVES, W. C. Life and times of James Madison. Boston, 1859. Vol. I. 8° 522.6
ROBBINS, C. Memoir of Maria Elizabeth Clapp. Boston, 1858. 18° 539.31
ROGERS, S. Recollections. London, 1859. 18°. 395.5
ROMIEU, Mme. La femme au XIXe siècle. Paris, 1859. 12° 1074.15
RONDELET, A. Du spiritualisme en économie politique. Paris, 1859. 8° 1074.14
ROPES, H. A. Cranston house. Boston, 1859. 12° 496.15
ROSS, A. Adventures of the first settlers on the Oregon river. London, 1849. 12° 637.22
ROSSE, J. W. An index of dates. London. Vol. I. A—I. 1858. p.8° 857.10
ROUGH, D. Narrative of a journey through the north of New Zealand. London, n.d. 32°. 709.28
ROWTON, F. The female poets of Great Britain. Philadelphia, 1849. p.8° 321.2
RÜCKERT, F. Gedichte. Frankfurt a. M., 1851. 2v. in 1. 24° 2016.6
— Nal und Damajante. 3te Aufl. Frankfurt a. M., 1845. 24° 2016.7
RUSCHENBERGER, W. S. W. Three years in the Pacific. Philadelphia, 1834. 8° 633.22
RUSKIN, J. The two paths : being lectures on art. New York, 1859. 12° 207.22
RUSSELL, C. W. Life of Card. Mezzofanti. London, 1858. 8° 542.14
RUSSELL, Lord J. The life and times of Charles James Fox. London, Vol. II., 1859. 12° . 577.1

RUSSELL, M. Palestine ; or the Holy Land. London, 1857. 12° 947.16
RUSSELL, W. Extraordinary women. London, 1857. 8° 536.19

SAINTINE, X. Chrisna, the queen of the Danube. Tr. by A. T. Wood. New York, 1859. 8°. 802.44
SALA, G. A. Gaslight and daylight. Lond., 1859. 12° 903.9
SARGANT, W. L. Social innovators and their schemes. London, 1858. 12° 138.27
SARGEANT, A. M. The housemaid's complete guide and adviser. New ed. London, n.d. 24°. 189.28
— The maid-of-all-work's guide. New ed. London, n.d. 18° 189.30
SAUNDERS, F. Mosaics. New York, 1859. 12°. 905.9
SAVAGE, J. '98 and '48. The modern revolutionary history and literature of Ireland. New York, 1856. 12° 993.4
SCHAFF, P. History of the Christian church, A. D., 1–311. New York, 1859. 8° 1092.5
SCHIMMELPENNINCK, M. A. The principles of beauty in nature, art and human character. Ed. by C. C. Hankin. London, 1859. 8° . . 138.32
SCHOOL home (The) of Thornvale. Lond., 1859. 12° 128.29
SCHOOLCRAFT, H. R. The myth of Hiawatha, and other legends of the Indians. Phila., 1856. 12° 485.15
SCHWAB, G. Gedichte. 4te Aufl. Stuttgart, 1851. 24° 2016.8
SCOTT, A. J. Christian statesmen : a lecture. n. p., 1855. 18° 138.35
SEDDON, T. Memoirs and letters. Lond., 1858. 12° 557.4
SENIOR, N. W. A journal kept in Turkey and Greece. London, 1859. 8° 688.13
SHELLEY, Lady. Shelley Memorials. [Added] an essay on Christianity, by P. B. Shelley. Boston, 1859. 12° 587.5
SHILLABER, B. P. Knitting-work : wrought by Ruth Partington. Boston, 1859. 12° . . . 487.7
SHIRREFF, E. Why should we learn! London, 1859. 16° 138.29
SIMMS, W. G. Cassique of Kiawah. New York, 1859. 12° 800.36-40
SIMPSON, A. Life and travels of Thomas Simpson. London, 1845. 8° 704.21
SIMPSON, J. Y. Obstetric memoirs and contributions. Ed. by W. O. Priestley and H. R. Storer. Philadelphia, 1855, 1856. 2v. 8° . 153.20
SIMPSON, L. F. The handbook of dining. Lond. 1859. 12° 189.23
SLOAN, S. City and suburban architecture. Philadelphia, 1859. 4° 200.1
— Constructive architecture. Phila. 1859. 4°. 201.8
SMITH, E. E. Three eras of woman's life. Boston, 1859. 12° 497.1-5
SOCIETY for promoting Christian knowledge. The industrial handbook. London, 1853. 18°. . 189.35
SOUTHEY, R. Life of Wesley. Ed. by Rev. C. C. Southey. Notes by Rev. D. Curry. New York, 1847. 2v. 12° 578.16
SOUTHWORTH, E. D. E. N. Lady of the isle. Philadelphia, n.d. 12° 506.7
STAPLETON, A. G. George Canning and his times. London, 1859. 8° 567.1
STEEL, R. Doing good. London, 1858. p.8° . . 115.12
STEINMETZ, A. Japan and her people. London, 1859. 12° 938.14
STEPHENS, H. and Norton, J. P. The farmer's guide to agriculture. N. York, 1858. 2v.8° 161.1
STERLING, J. Strafford : a tragedy. Lond., 1843. 16° 375.26
STERNBERG, A. F. v. U. Berühmte deutsche Frauen des 18ten Jahrhunderts. Leipzig, 1848. 2v. in 1. sm. 8° 1032.2
STONE, J. S. Memoir of the life of A. V. Griswold. Philadelphia, 1844. 8° 536.12
STORY (The) of Italy. London, 1859. 12° . . . 917.8
STORY of the massacre of St. Bartholomew's day. London, 1849. 18° 450.20
STOWE, H. B. The minister's wooing. New York, 1859. 12° 495.1-5

STRICKLAND, A. Lives of the queens of Scotland. Elizabeth Stuart. Vol. VIII. N. Y., 1859. 12°   593.4
STRICKLAND, J. M. Rome, regal and republican. London, 1854. 12°   948.16
STUART, I. W. Life of Jonathan Trumbull, Sen. Gov. of Connecticut. Boston, 1859. 8°...   522.5
SUCCESS in business; or, Bible principles illustrated. London, n.d. 32°   139.36
SUCCESSFUL men of modern times. Lond., n. d. 32°   550.63
SWEAT, M. J. M. Highways of travel. Boston, 1859. 12°...   666.20
SWINTON, W. Rambles among words. N. York, 1859. 12°...   396.6

TALES of other lands. London, n.d. 32°....   450.22
TANNER, T. H. Treatise on the diseases of infancy and childhood. Phila., 1859. 12°   155.28
TAYLOR, B. Travels in Greece and Russia. New York, 1859. 12°   688.12
TAYLOR, Mrs. H. N. Jack, the chimney sweeper. Boston, 1859. 12°   748.21
TAYLOR, I. Transmission of ancient books to ancient times. New ed. London, 1859. 8°   395.4
TAYLOR, N. W. Moral government of God. New York, 1859. 2v. 8°...   1101.1
— Revealed theology. New York, 1859. 8°...   1104.3
TAYLOR, T. A. Memoir of the Rev. Oliver A. Taylor. Boston, 1853. 12°   539.29
TEACHER'S indicator (The) and parent's manual. Cincinnati, 1859. 12°   138.33
TEGETMEIER, W. B. Manual of domestic economy. 4th ed. London, 1858. 32°   189.27
TENNYSON, A. Idyls of the king. Boston, 1859. 16°   385.20
TEXIER, E. Tableau de Paris. 1852. 2v. 4°...   830.1
THIERRY, J. N. A. Formation and progress of the Tiers État in France. Tr. by Rev. F. B. Wells. London, 1859. 2v. in 1. p.8°...   857.12
THIERS, A. The Mississippi bubble: a memoir of John Law. Tr. by F. S. Fiske. N.Y. 1859. 12°.   587.7
THOMPSON, J. H. Memoir of David Hale. New York, 1850. 12°...   536.13
TIMBS, J. Things not generally known. 2d ser. London, 1859. 12°...   148.18
TODD, J. The angel of the iceberg. Northampton, 1859. 12°...   718.14
TONNA, C. E. Glimpses of the past. London, 1858. 12°   487.3
— Judah's lion. London, 1859. 12°...   487.4
TRENCH, R. C. Glossary of English words. New York, 1859. 12°...   396.8
TROLLOPE, A. The Bertrams. N. York, 1859. 12° 505.12-14
TROLLOPE, T. A. A decade of Italian women. London, 1859. 2v. 12°...   513.14
— Tuscany in 1849 and 1859. London, 1859. 12°   917.9
TUCKERMAN, H. T. Mental portraits. London, 1853. 8°...   557.10
TULLOCH, J. Leaders of the reformation. Luther, Calvin, Latimer, Knox. Edinburgh, 1859. 12°   115.10

USEFUL arts employed in the production of clothing. 2d ed. London, 1851. 18°...   209.25
— employed in the production of food. 3d ed. London, 1857. 12°...   189.26

VALE, G. Life of Thomas Paine, with his letters to Washington. New York, 1859. 8°...   514.2
VAPEREAU, G. L'année littéraire et dramatique. 1re année, 1858. Paris, 1859. 8°...   1071.16
VENEDY, J. England. Leipzig, 1845. 3v. 16°.   2016.1
-- Ireland. Leipzig, 1844. 2v. 16°...   2016.2
"VICTORY won (The)." A memorial. 15th ed. London, 1859. 18°...   1098.30
VIEHOFF, H. Goethe's Gedichte erläutert, u. s. w. Düsseldorf, 1846-1853. 3v. 16°...   2016.4
— Goethe's Leben. 2te Ausg. Stuttgart, 1854. 4v. 16°...   2016.3

VOYAGES round the world. London, 1857. 12°.   707.18
VRAIE question (La.) France — Italie — Autriche. Paris, 1859. 8°...   1074.10

WALPOLE, H. Journal of the reign of George the Third, 1771-1783. Ed. with notes by Dr. Doran. London, 1859. 2v. 8°...   983.2
WALTER Thornley; or, a peep at the past. New York, 1859. 12°...   505.16
WARD, Mrs. Hardy and Hunter. Lond., 1858. 12° 748.19
— Telescope teachings. London, 1859. 12°...   148.19
WATT, James, and the steam engine. London, n.d. 32°...   209.23
WEBB, Rev. T. W. Celestial objects for common telescopes. London, 1859. 12°...   148.24
WELD, C. R. The Pyrenees west and east. London, 1859. 8°...   665.11
WHARTON, F. A treatise on theism. Philadelphia, 1859. 12°...   1105.18
WHAT we did in Australia. Ed. by G. B. Earp. London, 1853. 18°...   709.27
WHATELY, R. Explanations of the bible and prayer-book. London, 1858. 18°...   1098.27
WHITE, J. History of France. N. York, 1859. 8° 1001.8
WHITE, W. Northumberland, and the Border. London, 1859. 8°...   645.9
WHITECAR, W. B. Jr. Four years aboard the whaleship. Philadelphia, 1860. 12°...   745.16
WHITNEY, A. Poems. New York, 1859. 12°..   385.18
WHITTIER, J. G. Literary recreations and miscellanies. Boston, 1854. 8°...   905.14
WHO is to have it? A novel. London, 1859. 12°   407.8
WIFFEN, J. H. Life of Torquato Tasso. New York, 1859. 18°...   550.45
WILCOX, C. M. Rifles and rifle practice. N. York, 1859. 12°...   196.28
WILLIAMS, R. F. The secret passion. New York, n.d. 8°...   801.9
— Shakespeare and his friends. N.York, n.d. 8°.   801.9
— The youth of Shakespeare. N. York, n.d. 8°.   801.9
WILLIAMS, T. and Calvert, J. Fiji and the Fijians. Ed. by G. S. Rowe. N. Y., 1859. 8°.   934.9
WILLIS, N. P. The convalescent. N. Y. 1859. 12°.   903.7
WILLMOTT, R. A. Pleasures and advantages of literature. New ed. London, 1857. 18°.   395.6
WILSON, G. The five gateways of knowledge. 2d ed. Cambridge, 1857. 18°...   128.30
WISEMAN, N. Sermons, lectures, and speeches. Dublin, 1859. 12°...   615.10
— Same. Boston, 1859. 12°...   615.8
WOOD, G. B. Treatise on therapeutics and pharmacology. Phila. 2v. 8°. 1855, 1856...   155.21
WOOD, J. G. Common objects of the country. London, 1858. 12°...   178.45
— Common objects of the sea-shore. London, 1859. 18°...   168.24
— My feathered friends. London, 1858. 18°...   176.16
WORBOISE, E. J. Life of Thomas Arnold. Lond., 1859. 12°...   578.17
WORNUM, R. N. A sketch of the history of painting. New ed. London, 1859. p.8°...   200.18
WORTHEN, W. E. Appleton's cyclopædia of drawing. New York, 1857. 8°...   201.7
WRAXALL, L. The armies of the great powers. London, 1859. 12°...   948.18
WYNTER, A. Pictures of town and country life. London, 1855. 12°...   395.2

YONGE, C. D. Parallel lives of ancient and modern heroes. London, 1858. 12°...   545.29
YONGE, C. M. Ben Sylvester's word. New York, 1859. 18°... 786.13-22
— Kenneth: or, the rear guard of the grand army. New York, 1855. 12°...   786.23
YOUNG botanists (The). London, n.d. 32°...   169.37
YOUNG men of the Bible. Boston, 1859. 12°...   115.2

THIRD SUPPLEMENT TO THE INDEX.

CONTAINING A LIST OF THE BOOKS PLACED IN THE LOWER HALL, FROM OCTOBER 20, 1859,
TO DECEMBER, 13, 1860.

Shelf. No.

ABBOTT, J. American history. New York, 1860.
Vols. 1-2. 16° 308.1
— The Florence stories. Grimkie. New York,
1860. 16 . . . . 717.3
— History of Genghis Khan. N. Y. 1860. 16°. 550.76
— History of Nero. New York, 1853. 16°. . . 550.67
— History of Peter the Great. N. Y. 1860. 16°.550.71-75
ABBOTT, J. S. C. South and north. N. Y.1859.12° 637.26
ABOUT, E. La question romaine. Bruxelles,
1859. 8° 1074.34
— The king of the mountains. Transl. by Mary
L. Booth. Boston, 1861. 12° 495.9
ADAMS, W. H. D. Neptune's heroes, or, the sea-
kings of England. London, 1861. 12°. . . 578.19
ADAMS, W. T. Little by little; or, the cruise of
the Flyaway. Boston, 1861. 12° 747.6
ADLER, G. J. Handbook of German literature.
New York, 1857. 12° 2013.5
ÆSCHYLUS. Ex novissima recensione Friderici
A. Paley. New York, 1860. 18° 395.15
AGASSIZ, L. J. R. Lake Superior: its physical
character, vegetation, and animals. Bos-
ton, 1850. 8° 1622.1
ALCOTT, Mrs. H. H. Isora's child. N. Y. 1855. 12°. 485.16
ALCOTT, W. A. The laws of health. Boston,
1859. 12° 1173.2
ALLSTON, W. Monaldi: a tale. Bost. 1841. 12°. 1785.5
ALTHAUS, J. Treatise on medical electricity.
Philadelphia, 1860. 12° 158.34
AMERICAN Christian record. New York, 1860. 12°. 114.12
ANDERSEN, H. C. The sand-hills of Jutland.
Boston, 1860. 12° 485.19
ANNALS of England. Oxford, 1858. 3v. 18°. . 998.9
ANSTED, D. T. Geological gossip. London, 1860.
16° 168.38, 158.40
ANTISELL, T. Manufacture of photogenic or hy-
dro-carbon oils. New York, 1859. 8° . . . 194.21
APELLES and his contemporaries. Bost. 1860. 16°. 487.11
ARGYLL, duke of. See Campbell, G. D.
ARNOLD, S. G. History of Rhode Island. Vol. II.
New York, 1860. 8° 233.3
ART recreations. Boston, 1860. 12° 207.25
ARTHUR, W. Italy in transition. N. Y. 1860. 12°. 928.13
ATKINSON, T. W. Travels in the regions of the
upper and lower Amoor. London, 1860. 8°. 681.2

BABSON, J. J. History of Gloucester, including
the town of Rockport. Gloucester, 1860. 8°. 225.5
BACHI, P. Teatro scelto italiano. Cambrigia,
1829. 12° 1055.2
Contents. – L'Aminta di Tasso; L'Artaserse di Me-
tastasio; La Griselda di Goldoni; La Merope di Maf-
fei; Il Saul di Alfieri.
BAIRD, S. J. The Elohim revealed in the creation
and redemption of man. Phila. 1860. 8°. 1092.7
BAKEWELL, F. C. Great facts. N. Y. 1860. 12°. 187.22
— Natural evidence of a future life. London,
1835. 8° 122.21
BALL, J. Peaks, passes, and glaciers. 5th edition.
London, 1860. 12° 1666.1
BANCROFT, G. History of the United States.
Vol. 8. [The American revolution. Vol. 2.]
Boston, 1860. 8° 212.3-5, 291.1-7
BARBER, J. Treatise on gesture. Camb. 1831. 12°. 395.21
BARON-WILSON, M. Memoirs of Harriot, duchess
of St. Albans. Philadelphia, 1860. 2v. 12°. 598.20

Shelf. No.

BARTHÉLEMY, J. J. Voyage du jeune Anachar-
sis en Grèce. Paris, 1834. 2v. 12° . . . 2065.2
BARTHOLOMEW, W. N. Linear perspective ex-
plained. Boston, 1859. 8° 204.9
BARTLETT, D. W. Life and services of Hon. Abra-
ham Lincoln. Added, a sketch of Hannibal
Hamlin. New York, 1860. 12° 527.21
BARTOLOMMEO, F. da S. Concordio. Ammaestra-
menti degli antichi. Milano, 1808. 8° . . . 1055.4
BARWELL, Mrs. Infant treatment. Revised and
enlarged. New York, 1844. 12° 187.29
BATEMAN, J. Life of Daniel Wilson. Boston,
1860. 8° 571.1
BATES, S. P. Lectures on mental and moral cul-
ture. New York, 1860. 12° 126.15
BAYLDON, R. Treatise on road legislation. Lon-
don, 1857. 8° 134.29
BEARD, J. R. Self-culture. Manchester, n.d. 12°. 148.40
BEECHER, C. E. An appeal to the people, as au-
thorized interpreters of the Bible. New
York, 1860. 12° 114.2
BEECHER, E. The concord of ages. New York,
1860. 12° 115.21
BELGIOJOSO, C. T., princesse de. Ermina. Récits
turco-asiatiques. Paris, 1856. 16° 2049.4
BELL, J. Life, speeches, and public services of
John Bell. With a sketch of the life of Ed-
ward Everett. New York, 1860. 12° . . . 528.25
BELL, J. D. A man. Philadelphia, 1860. 12°. . 893.11
BELLOWS, H. W. Re-statements of Christian doc-
trine. New York, 1860. 12° 114.8
BENEDICT, D. Fifty years among the baptists.
New York, 1860. 12° 114.9
BENEDICT, E. C. A run through Europe. New
York, 1860. 12° 665.5
BESANT, W. H. Hydrostatics and hydrodynamics.
Cambridge, 1859. 8° 194.22
BIBLICAL reason why. New York, 1859. 12° . . 1104.6
BICKERSTETH, E. H. The rock of ages. Intro-
duction by F. D. Huntington. Boston, 1860.
12° 1104.15
BIGELOW, J. History of the cemetery of Mount
Auburn. Boston, 1860. 12° 229.10
BIRCHALL, J. England under the Normans and
Plantagenets. London, n.d. 12° 998.14
BISSETT, A. The strength of nations. London,
1859. 16° 133.17
BLACKWELL, E. The laws of life. Lond. 1859. 16°. 126.36
BOKER, G. H. Calaynos: a tragedy. Philadelphia,
1848. 12° 374.21
BOLLAERT, W. Antiquarian researches in New
Granada, Equador, Peru, and Chili. Lon-
don, 1860. 8° 266.11
BOMBET, L. A. C. Life of Haydn, and life of Mo-
zart. Providence, 1820. 12° 1545.4
BONNECHOSE, F. P. E. B. de. Géographie de la
France. Paris, 1847. 8° 1074.38
BOOTH, M. L. Clock and watch maker's manual.
New York, 1860. 12° 186.1
— History of New York. New York, 1859. 8°. 232.7
BOURNE, J. Catechism of the steam engine. New
edition. London, 1859. 16° 187.25
BOWRING, Sir J. A visit to the Philippine Is-
lands. London, 1859. 8° 682.6
BOYD, J. R. Memoir of Philip Doddridge. New
York, 1860. 12° 578.18

Shelf. No.

Boys and their rulers. London, 1853. 12° 126.29
Bray, A. E. Trials of the heart. New edition. London, 1845. 16° 448.18
Bree, C. R. Species not transmutable. London, n.d. 12° 174.12
Brinley, F. Life of William T. Porter. New York, 1860. 12° 528.23
Brontë, C. Jane Eyre. New York, 1848. 8° . . 1780.4
Brontë, E. Agnes Grey. Philadelphia, n.d. 8°. 803.6
Brooks, S. Aspen court : a story of our own time. New York, 1856. 12° 487.18
Brougham, H., lord. Tracts mathematical and physical. London, 1860. 12° 148.37
Browning, E. B. Aurora Leigh. N. Y. 1857. 12°. 335.6-8
— Napoleon III in Italy. New York, 1860. 12°. 374.18
Buckland, F. T. Curiosities of natural history. 2d series. London, 1860. 12° . . . vol. II of 177.38
Bucknill, J. C. Unsoundness of mind in relation to criminal acts. 2d ed. London, 1857. 16°. 126.35
Buffon, G. L. L. de. Morceaux choisis. Paris, 1842. 18° 2069.1
Bulfinch, T. Age of chivalry. Boston, 1859. 12°. 1935.1
— The boy inventor : a memoir of Matthew Edwards. Boston, 1860. 16° 537.7-26
Burke, Sir B. Vicissitudes of families. 2d ser. London, 1860. 12° . . . . vol. II of 998.3
Burn, R. S. Handbook of the mechanical arts. 2d edition. Edinburgh, 1860. 12° 205.12
— Illustrated architectural engineering and mechanical drawing-book. 2d ed. rev. London, 1856. 8° 205.10
— Year book of agricultural facts. Edinburgh, 1860. 12° 168.35
Burnett, P. H. The path which led a protestant lawyer to the catholic church. New York, 1860. 8° 1092.6
Burrowes, J. F. The thorough-bass primer. 20th ed. Boston, n.d. 12° 209.34
Burrows, M. Pass and class. Oxford, 1860. 12°. 395.23
Burton, R. F. Lake regions of central Africa. London, 1860. 2v. 8° 681.1
— - Same. New York, 1860. 8° 681.3
Bury, C. The insnared. Philadelphia, 1847. 8°. 803.4
Busk, H. The rifle, and how to use it. 5th ed. London, 1859. 12° 209.37
Butler, S. Hudibras. Ed. by H. G. Bohn. London, 1859. 2v. p.8° 847.13
Buxton, C. Slavery and freedom in the British West Indies. London, 1860. 12° 269.1

Caird, J. Sermons. Edinburgh, 1858. p.8° . . 114.17
Calderon de la Barca, F. E. Life in Mexico. Boston, 1843. 2v. 12° 1634.4
Callcott, M., lady. Little Arthur's history of England. New edition. London, 1859. 18°. 908.8
Campbell, C. History of Virginia. Philadelphia, 1860. 8° 232.6
Campbell, G. D., duke of Argyll. Presbytery examined. 2d ed. London, 1849. 16°. . . 1104.9
Carlen, E. F. One year : a tale of wedlock. N. York, 1853. 12° 1785.10
Carlton, R. The new purchase : or seven and a half years in the far west. New York, 1843. 2v. 12° 634.4
Carlyle, T. Critical and miscellaneous essays. Boston, 1860. 4v. 8° 803.3
— Life of John Sterling. Boston, 1851. 12° . . 1595.1
Carpenter, M. Reformatory schools. London, 1851. 8° 126.28
Carter, T. Curiosities of war, and military studies. London, 1860. 16° 908.10
Castle, T. Manual of surgery. 4th ed. Boston, 1859. 18° 158.32
Channing, W. Etherization in childbirth. Boston, 1848. 8° 162.4
Chanter, C. Over the cliffs. Boston, 1861. 12°. 495.12
Chapin, E. H. The crown of thorns. Boston, 1860. 12° 1104.10
Charlesworth, M. L. Ministering children : a story. New York, n.d. 18° 1785.14

Shelf. No.

Chase, G. W. Digest of masonic law. New York, 1859. 12° 126.22
Chateaubriand, R. F. A. de. The martyrs. Ed. by O. W. Wight. New York, 1859. 12° . . 115.20
Cheeseman, L. Ishmael and the church. Philadelphia, 1860. 12° 1104.19
Cheever, G. B. Studies in poetry. Boston, 1830. 12° 376.4
Chevreul, M. E. The principles of colours. Transl. by C. Martel. 3d ed. London, 1859. p.8° 853.9
Churchill, J. F. Pulmonary phthisis. N. Y. n.d. 8° 153.23
Claiborne, J. F. H. Life and times of General Samuel Dale. New York, 1860. 12° 527.14
Cler, General. Reminiscences of an officer of Zouaves. Transl. from the French. New York, 1860. 12° 1005.5
Cobbett, W. Life of Andrew Jackson. New York, 1837. 18° 519.9
Cobbold, R. H. Pictures of the Chinese. London, 1860. 12° 938.15
Cochrane, T., earl of Dundonald. Autobiography of a seaman. Vol. I-II. Second edition. London, 1860. 8° 577.5
Coggeshall, G. Historical sketch of commerce and navigation. New York, 1860. 8° . . . 912.5
Collins, P. McD. A voyage down the Amoor. New York, 1860. 12° 677.22
Collins, T. W. Humanics. New York, 1860. 8° 882.2
Collins, W. After dark. New York, n.d. 8° . 752.7
— The woman in white. New York, 1860. 8°. 752.8-12
Combe, G. Constitution of man. 5th Am. ed. Boston, 1835. 12° 1173.1
Contributions in rhyme. By a septuagenarian. Edinburgh, 1860. 12° 374.20
Coquerel fils, A. Jean Calas et sa famille. Paris, 1858. 12° 2065.4
Cornell, W. M. How to enjoy life. Philadelphia, 1860. 12° 158.39
Corner cupboard, The : or, facts for everybody. New York, [1859.] 12° 187.20
Cottle, J. Reminiscences of Coleridge and Southey. New York, 1847. 16° 1595.2
Coultas, H. What may be learned from a tree. New York, 1860. 8° 164.22
Crosby, N. Annual obituary notices for 1858. Boston, 1859. 8° 522.10
Crowe, E. E. The history of France. Vol. II. London, 1860. 8° 1003.6
Cumming, J. The great tribulation. 2d ser. New York, 1860. 12° 111.15
Cummins, M. S. El Fureidis. Boston, 1860. 12°. 441.1-10
Cust, Sir E. Annals of the wars of the eighteenth century. London, 1858-60. 5v. 16°. 919.13
Custis, G. W. P. Recollections and private memoirs of Washington. N. Y. 1860. 8° . . 522.12-13
Czerny, C. Letters to young ladies on the art of playing the piano-forte. Boston, n.d. 8°. 209.27
— Treatise on thorough-bass. Transl. by J. A. Hamilton. Boston, n.d. 12° 209.33

Dall, C. H. "Woman's right to labor." Three lectures. Boston, 1860. 12° 395.20
Dallas, A. R. C. Felix Alvarez. New York, 1818. 2v. 12° 479.4
Darwin, C. The origin of species. London, 1859. 12° 176.17
— - Same. New York, 1860. 12° 176.18
Davies, T. A. Answer to Hugh Miller and theoretic geologists. New York, 1860. 12° . . 167.39
Dawson, J. W. Archaia ; or cosmogony and natural history of the Hebrew scriptures. Montreal, 1860. 12° 167.38
Day, H. N. The art of elocution. Revised edition. Cincinnati, 1860. 12° 395.12
Dead shot, The, or sportsman's complete guide. By Marksman. London, 1860. 12° 175.19
Degerando. See Gérando, J. M. de.

	Shelf. No.
DEMAUS, R. Class-book of English prose. Edinburgh, 1860. 12°	394.6
— The prose and prose writers of Britain. Edinburgh, 1860. 12°	587.12
DEUTSCHES Lesebuch für Anfänger. Cambridge, 1826. 12°	2013.2
DIARY of a Samaritan. New York, 1860. 12°	237.22
DICKENS, C. All the year round. Vol. I. London, 1859. 8°	851.1
— Fortune Wildred. New York, n.d. 8°	472.13
— Household words. Vols. 14, 15. New York, 1851–5. 2v. 8°	881.1
— — Vols. 16–19. New York, 1856–59. 4v.	871.1
— Round of stories by the Christmas fire. New York, 1853. 8°	472.14
— Short stories. Philadelphia, n.d. 12°	500.11
— A tale of two cities. Phila. n.d. 8°	472.12
DIXON, J. Guide to the practical study of diseases of the eye. Philadelphia, 1860. 12°	158.33
DOBELL, S. Poems. Boston, 1859. 18°	450.26
DODGE, P. Sculpture: and the plastic art. Boston, 1850. 12°	207.30
DOMENECH, E. Seven years' residence in the deserts of North America. London, 1860. 2v. 8°	622.7
DONALDSON, S. J. jr. Lyrics and other poems. Philadelphia, 1860. 16°	374.12
DOUGLAS, S. A. Life. New York, 1860. 12°	527.18
DRAPER, B. H. The juvenile naturalist. New York, 1842. 16°	168.37
DRESSER, C. Popular manual of botany. Edinburgh, 1860. 12°	168.41
DREW, J. Practical meteorology. 2d ed. Edited by F. Drew. London, 1860. 12°	148.44
DU COURET, L. Life in the desert. New York, 1860. 12°	696.16
DUFRESNE, A. Stories of Henry and Henrietta. Translated by H. B. A. Boston, 1860. 12°	747.1
DUMAS, A. Le comte de Monte-Cristo. Paris, 1846. 6v. 16°	2065.5
— The count of Monte-Cristo. Lond. 1858. 16°	479.9
DUN, F. Veterinary medicines. 2d edition. Edinburgh, 1859. 8°	164.21
DUNDONALD, T. earl of. See Cochrane, T.
DUNSTER, H. P. The discoveries of Columbus and of the English in America. London, n.d. 12°	269.2
DUREAU de La Malle, A. J. C. A. Économie politique des Romains. Paris, 1840. 2v. 8°	2034.4
DWIGHT, B. W. The higher Christian education. New York, 1859. 12°	126.16
— Modern philology. New York, 1859. 12°	392.6
EAMES, J. A. The budget closed. Bost. 1860. 12°	665.8
EARDLEY-WILMOT, J. E. Reminiscences of Thomas Assheton Smith. 2d edition. London, 1860. 8°	567.2
EBONY idol, The. New York, 1860. 12°	784.8
EDGAR, J. G. The crusades and the crusaders. London, 1860. 12°	947.17
EDKINS, J. The religious condition of the Chinese. London, 1859. 16°	125.34
EDWARD the Sixth's Latin grammar. 13th edition. London, 1859. 12°	395.17
EDWARD the Sixth's first Latin book. 3d edition. London, 1859. 12°	395.18
EDWARDS, A. B. Summary of English history. London, 1856. 16°	999.20
EDWARDS, Mrs. C. M. The rainbow side. New York, 1858. 12°	487.13
EICHENDORFF, J. F. v. Zur Geschichte des Dramas. Leipzig, 1854. 12°	2016.13
ELLACOMBE, H. T. Remarks on belfries and ringers. London, 1859. 8°	205.11
ELLEN Parry, or trials of the heart. New York, 1850. 12°	487.21
ELLET, E. F. Women artists in all ages and countries. New York, 1859. 12°	544.23
ELLIOTT, W. Carolina sports by land and water. New York, 1859. 12°	637.23
ELLIS, S. S. Chapters on wives. New York, 1860. 12°	905.18
— Pictures of private life. New York, 1846. 8°	803.10
— A voice from the vintage. Boston, 1843. 8°	122.22
ENCYCLOPÆDIA metropolitana. Greek and Roman philosophy and science. London, 1853. 8°	395.14
ERNEST Carroll. A novel. Boston, 1858. 12°	1783.2
ERÖRTERUNG der Fragen über Verfassung und Reformen in Oesterreich. Leipzig, 1859. pp.32. 8°	1032.8
EVANS, D. M. Commercial crisis, 1857–58, and the stock exchange panic of 1859. London, 1859. 8°	132.12
EVANS, M. J. Adam Bede. New York, 1859. 12°.	505.1-5
— The mill on the Floss. N. Y. 1860. 12° .	505.11-15
EVENINGS at Haddon hall. Illustrations by G. Cattermole. London, n.d. p.8°	853.14
EVERETT, E. The life of George Washington. New York, 1860. 12°	514.3, 1524, 2-24
— The Mount Vernon papers. N. Y. 1860. 12°	893.7
— Orations and speeches. Vol. III. Boston, 1859. 8°	861.7
FAIRHOLT, F. W. Gog and Magog. The giants in Guildhall. London, 1859. 18°	909.21
— Tobacco: its history and associations. London, 1859. p.8°	946.6
FAMILY cyclopædia, The, or domestic library. n.p. 1854. 12°	187.27
FARADAY, M. Lectures on the various forces of matter. Edited by Wm. Crookes. London, 1860. 12°	148.39
— — Same. New York, 1860. 12°	148.43
FERNALD, W. M. God in his providence. Boston, 1859. 12°	115.17
FERRERO, E. The art of dancing. New York, [1859.] 12°	209.38
FEUILLET, O. Romance of a poor young man. New York, 1859. 8°	803.12
FICHTE, I. H. Contributions to mental philosophy. Transl. by J. D. Morell. London, 1860. 12°	126.23
FILIPPI, D. A. Italienische Sprachlehre. 7e Aufl. Wien, 1843. 8°	2013.3
FIRST impressions. n.p. n.d. 16°	450.32
FIRST steps to thorough bass. Boston, n.d. 12°	209.30
FLANDERS, H. Exposition of the constitution of the United States. Philadelphia, 1860. 12°	299.12
FONBLANQUE, A. Rights and wrongs. London, 1860. 12°	187.23
FORBES, D. The history of chess. Lond. 1860. 8°	205.13
FORBES, J. D. Theory of glaciers. Edinb. 1859. 8°.	143.9
— Tour of Mont Blanc and Monte Rosa. Edinburgh, 1855. 12°	669.14
FORBES, Sir W. Memoirs of a banking-house. London, 1860. 8°	132.14
FORDE, W. Class-book, or new piano primer. Boston, n.d. 12°	209.35
FORESTER, T. Paris and its environs. London, 1859. p.8°	853.11
FORSTER, J. Arrest of the five members by Charles the first. London, 1860. p.8°	908.13
FOSTER, B. F. Commercial book-keeping. Boston, 1836. 8°	133.16
FRAMJEE, D. The Parsees. London, 1858. 12°	937.8
FRANCIS, J. Annals of life assurance. London, 1853. 12°	133.19
FRASER, J. B. Tales of the caravanserai. Philadelphia, 1853. 12°	479.6
FREEMAN, G. E. and Salvin, F. H. Falconry, its claims, history and practice. London, 1859. 8°	176.20
FRENCH, S. Minor drama. New York, n.d. 14v. 12° [Two sets]	384.1-2

Contents. — Vol. I. Temptation, or, the Irish emigrant, by John Brougham; Paddy Carey, or, the boy of Clogheen, by Tyrone Power; The two Gregories, or, luck in a name; King Charming, or, the blue bird of paradise, by J. R. Planché; Po-ca-hon-tas, or, the gentle savage, by John Brougham; The clockmaker's hat; The married rake, by Charles Selby; Love and

FRENCH, S. continued.

murder, by John Brougham. II. A morning call, by Charles Dance ; Popping the question, by John B. Buckstone ; Deaf as a post, by T. Poole ; The new footman, by Chas. Selby ; A pleasant neighbor, by Mrs. Eliza Planché ; Paddy the piper, by James Pilgrim ; Brian O'Linn ; Irish assurance and Yankee modesty ; The Musard ball, or love at the academy, by John Brougham. III. Ireland and America, or scenes in both ; A pretty piece of business, by Thos. Morton ; The Irish broom-maker, or, a cure for dumbness, by C. A. F. Wood ; To Paris and back for five pounds, by John M. Morton ; That blessed baby, by J. George Moore ; Our gal, by S. D. Johnson ; The Swiss cottage, or, why don't she marry ? by Thos. H. Bayly ; The young widow, or a lesson for lovers, by Thos. G. Rodwell. IV. The Irish post, by J. Planché ; My neighbor's wife, by Alfred Bunn ; The Irish tiger, by John M. Morton ; P. P. or, the man and the tiger, by Tom Parry ; To oblige Benson, altered from the French, by Tom Taylor ; State secrets, or the tailor of Tamworth ; The Irish Yankee, or, the birth-day of freedom, by John Brougham. V. A good fellow, by Chas. M. Walcott ; Cherry and Fairstar ; Galo Breezely, or, the tale of a tar, by J. B. Johnstone ; Our Jeminay, or, Connecticut courtship, by H. J. Conway ; The miller's maid ; by John F. Saville ; An awkward arrival, by J. Stirling Coyne ; A conjugal lesson, by H. Danvers ; Crossing the line, or, crowded houses, by G. Almar. VI. My wife's mirror, by Ed. G. P. Wilkins ; Life in New York, or, Tom and Jerry on a visit, by John Brougham ; The middy ashore, by Wm. B. Barnard ; The crown prince, or the buckle of brilliants, by Thos. E. Wilks ; The two queens, by John B. Buckstone ; A thumping legacy, by John M. Morton ; The unfinished gentleman, by Chas. Selby ; The house dog, by Thos. Higgie. VII. The demon lover, or, my cousin german, by John Brougham ; Matrimony, altered from the French by Jas. Kenney ; In and out of place, by S. D. Johnson ; I dine with my mother, adapted by Charles McLachlan ; Hiawatha, or ardent spirits and laughing water, by Chas. M. Walcott ; Andy Blake, or the Irish diamond, by Dion Boureicault ; Love in '76, an incident of the revolution, by Olive Bunce ; Romance after marriage, or, the maiden wife, by Frank B. Goodrich and Frank L. Warden. VIII. One coat for two suits, by Chas. M. Walcott ; A decided case, by John Brougham ; The daughter, by Thos. Haynes Bayly ; No ! a coroner's inquisition, by A. O. Hall ; Love in humble life, by J. H. Payne ; Family jars ; Personation, or fairly taken in, by Mrs. C. Kemble. IX. The children in the wood, by Thos. Morton ; Winning a husband, by Macfarren ; Day after the fair, by G. A. Somerset ; Make your wills ! by E. Mayhew and G. Smith ; The rendezvous, by R. Ayton ; My wife's husband, by F. Challis ; Monsieur Tonson, by Moncrieff ; The illustrious stranger, by F. Kenney. X. Mischief-making, by J. B. Buckstone ; A live woman in the mines, or, Pike county ahead ; The corsair, or, the little fairy at the bottom of the sea, by Wm. Brough ; Shylock, or, the merchant of Venice preserved, by F. Talfourd ; The spoiled child, by Prince Hoare ; The evil eye, by J. B. Phillips ; Nothing to nurse, by Chas. M. Walcott ; Wanted — a widow, with immediate possession, by Dion Boureicault and Chas. Seymour. XI. The lottery ticket, or, the lawyer's clerk, by J. B. Buckstone ; Fortune's frolic, or the ploughman turned lord, by Allingham ; Is he jealous ? by Beaseley ; The married bachelor, by P. P. O'Callaghan ; A husband at sight, by J. B. Buckstone ; The Irishman in London, by Macready ; Animal magnetism, or mesmerism, by Mrs. Inchbald ; High-ways and by-ways, by B. Webster. XII. Columbus el filibustero ! ! by J. Brougham ; Harlequin Blue-Beard, the great bashaw, or the good fairy triumphant over the demon of discord ; Ladies at home, or, gentlemen, we can do without you, by J. G. Millengen, M.D. ; A phenomenon in a smock frock, by Wm. Brough ; Comedy and tragedy, from the French of M. R. Fournier, translated by Wm. Robson ; Opposite neighbors, by J. H. Paul ; The Dutchman's ghost, or, all right, by S. Barry ; The persecuted Dutchman, or, the original John Schmidt, by S. Barry. XIII. Promotion, or, a morning at Versailles, by J. R. Planché ; A fascinating individual, or, too agreeable by half, by H. Danvers ; Neptune's defeat, or, the seizure of the seas, by John Brougham ; Mrs. Caudle's curtain lecture, by E. Stirling ; Shakespeare's dream, by J. Brougham ; The lady of the bed-chamber, by J. Brougham ; The Irish widow, by D. Garrick ; Take care of little Charley, by J. Brougham. XIV. The Musard ball, or love at the academy, by John Brougham ; The great tragic revival, by John Brougham ; High, low, Jack, and the game, or the

FRENCH, S. continued.

card party, by J. R. Planché and Chas. Dance ; A gentleman from Ireland, by Fitzjames O'Brien ; Tom and Jerry, or life in London, by Moncrieff ; The village lawyer ; The captain's not a-miss, by T. E. Wilks ; Amateurs and actors, by R. B. Peake.

— **Standard drama.** New York, n.d. 13v. 12°. 383.1-2

Contents.—Vol. II. Jane Eyre, by John Brougham ; Pauline, translated from the French ; Aline, or the rose of Killarney, by E. Stirling ; David Copperfield, adapted by J. Brougham ; The rose of Ettrick vale, or, the bridal of the Borders, by T. J. Lynch ; Wenlock of Wenlock, or, the spirit of the black mantle, by T. E. Wilks ; Married life, by J. B. Buckstone ; Camille, or the fate of a coquette, by Alex. Dumas, jr. III. The bold dragoons, by Morris Barnett ; Ernest Maltravers, by Miss L. Medina ; Eustache Baudin, by J. Courtney ; Henriette the forsaken, by J. B. Buckstone ; Tom Cringle, or, Mat of the iron hand, by E. Fitzball ; The three guardsmen, or, the queen, the cardinal, and the adventurer, by Chas. Rice ; The Æthiop, or the child of the desert, by Wm. Dimond ; Night and morning, adapted by John Brougham. IV. The French spy ; or, the siege of Constantina, a military drama, by J. T. Haines ; The wept of Wish-ton-wish, from J. F. Cooper's novel ; The evil genius, by B. Bernard ; Ben Bolt, by J. B. Johnstone ; The sailor of France, or, the republicans of Brest, by J. B. Johnstone ; The red mask, or, the wolf of Lithuania, by J. Brougham ; Grimaldi, or, the life of an actress, by Dion Boureicault ; The wedding-day, by Mrs. Inchbald. V. The minerali, or, the dying gift, by H. G. Plunkett ; Retribution, by Tom Taylor ; Jonathan Bradford, or, the murder at the roadside inn, by E. Fitzball ; Ben the boatswain, or sailors' sweethearts, by T. E. Wilks ; Peter Wilkins, or, the flying islanders ; Esmeralda, or, the deformed of Notre Dame, by E. Fitzball ; The last days of Pompeii, taken from Bulwer's novel, by L. Medina ; Dred, or the dismal swamp, by John Brougham. VI. All's fair in love, by J. Brougham ; Hofer, the Tell of the Tyrol, by E. Fitzball ; Self, by Mrs. S. F. Bateman ; Cinderella, or the fairy and little glass slipper ; The phantom, by Dion Boureicault ; Franklin, by J. Brougham ; The gun-maker of Moscow, by John Brougham ; The love of a prince, or, the court of Prussia, by Chas. Gayler. VII. The son of the night, by C. Gayler ; Rory O'More, by S. Lover ; The golden eagle, or, the privateer of '76, by J. B. Howe ; Rienzi, a tragedy, by Miss Mitford ; The broken sword, by Wm. Dimond ; Rip Van Winkle, by Chas. Burke ; Isabelle, or woman's life, by J. B. Buckstone ; The heart of Mid-Lothian, from Sir Walter Scott's novel, by Thos. Dibdin. VIII. Angelo, or the actress of Padua, translated from the French by G. à Becket ; The floating beacon, or Norwegian wreckers, by Edward Ball ; The bride of Lammermoor, by J. W. Calcraft ; The cataract of the Ganges, or the Rajah's daughter, by W. T. Moncrieff ; The Robber of the Rhine, by G. Almar ; The school of reform, or, how to rule a husband, by T. Morton ; The wandering boys, or, the Castle of Olival ; Mazeppa, or the wild horse of Tartary, dramatized by H. M. Milner. IX. Young New York, by E. G. P. Wilkins ; Victims, by Tom Taylor ; Romance after marriage, or, the maiden wife, by F. B. Goodrich and F. L. Warden ; The brigand, by J. R. Planché ; The poor of New York ; Ambrose Gwinnett, or, the sea-side story, by D. Jerrold ; Raymond and Agnes, the travellers benighted, or the bleeding nun of Lindenberg, by M. G. Lewis ; The gambler's fate, or thirty years of a gamester's life, by H. M. Milner. X. Father and son, or, the rock of Charbonniere, by E. Fitzball ; Massaniello, or, the dumb girl of Portici, by G. Milner ; Sixteen string Jack, by L. Rede ; The youthful queen, by Shannon ; The skeleton witness, or the murder at the mound, by W. L. Rede ; The innkeeper of Abbeville, or the ostler and the robber, by E. Fitzball ; The miller and his men, by I. Pocecke ; Aladdin, or, the wonderful lamp. XI. Adrienne, the actress, or, the reigning favorite, by John Oxenford ; Undine, or, the spirit of the waters, by G. Soane ; Jessie Brown, or the relief of Lucknow, by D. Boureicault ; Asmodeus, or the little devil's share, adapted from the French of Scribe, by Thos. Archer ; The Mormons, or life at Salt Lake city, by Thos. D. English ; Blanche of Brandywine ; Viola, by E. Maturin ; Deseret deserted, or, the last days of Brigham Young. XII. Americans in Paris, or, a game of dominoes ; Victorine, or, "I'll sleep on it," by J. B. Buckstone ; The wizard of the wave, or, the ship of the avenger, by J. T. Haines ; The castle specter, by M. G. Lewis ; Horseshoe Robinson ; or the battle of King's mountain, by C. W. Tayleure ; Arman, or the peer and the peasant, by A. C. Mowatt ; Fashion, or, life

Shelf. No.

FRENCH, S. Standard drama, *continued.*
In New York, by A. C. Mowatt ; A glance at New York. XIII. The inconstant, or wine works wonders, by G. Farquhar ; Uncle Tom's Cabin, or, life among the lowly, dramatized by G. L. Aiken ; The guide to the stage, by L. T. Rede ; The veteran, or, France and Algeria, by J. L. Wallack ; The miller of New Jersey, or, the prison-hulk, by J. Brougham ; The dark hour before morn, by John Brougham and F. B. Goodrich ; Midsummer night's dream, by Shakespeare ; Art and artifice, or, woman's love, by J. Brougham. XIV. The Jewess ; or, the council of Constance, by W. T. Moncrieff ; To parents and guardians ; Dombey and son, dramatized by John Brougham ; The little treasure, by A. Harris ; The king's rival, or, the court and the stage, by Tom Taylor, and Chas. Reade ; The carpenter of Rouen, or, the massacre of St. Bartholomew, by J. S. Jones ; The pilot, from Cooper's novel, by E. Fitzball ; The tempest, by Wm. Shakespeare.

FROM hay-time to hopping. By the author of Our farm of four acres. London, 1860. 12° . . 487.22

FROTHINGHAM, N. L. Metrical pieces. Boston, 1855. 12° 1395.6

FULLER, F. Five years' residence in New Zealand. London, 1859. 8° 707.20

GAJANI, G. The Roman exile. Bost. 1856. 12°. 1785.11
GANGOOLY, J. C. Life and religion of the Hindoos. Boston, 1860. 12° 938.16
GARDEN, The, that paid the rent. London, 1860. 12° 168.34
GARIBALDI, G. Garibaldi: an autobiography. Edited by A. Dumas. Transl. by Wm. Robson. London, 1860. 12° 557.17
GARLAND of Flora. Boston, 1829. 8° 166.32
GARRATT, A. C. Electro-physiology and electro-therapeutics. Boston, 1860. 8° 162.2
GASKELL, A. Right at last. New York, 1860. 12°. 506.21
GELDART, *Mrs.* T. A popular history of England. New York, 1860. 12° 998.17
GEMS from British poets. Sacred. London, 1838. 24° 450.30
GEORGE, A. Annals of the queens of Spain. New York. 2v. 1850. 12° 1545.3
GÉRANDO, J. M. de. Self-education. Transl. by E. P. Peabody. 3d ed. Boston, 1860. 12° . . 126.13
GESSNER, S. Sämmtliche Werke. Wien, 1792-3. 2v. 12° 2016.10
GIBSON, W. The revival in Ireland, 1859. Introduction by Rev. B. Stow. Bost. 1860. 12°. 1104.12
GIRARDIN, D. de. Lettres parisiennes. Paris, 1856. 2v. 16° 2065.13
GISEKE, R. The rose of the parsonage. Philadelphia, 1854. 12° 486.7
GIULAY, — Kriegsführung in der Lombardei. Hersfeld, 1859. pp.39. 8° 1032.5
GODWIN, P. The history of France. Vol. I. New York, 1860. 8° 1001.9
GOETHE, J. W. v. Faust: a dramatic poem. Transl. by A. Hayward. 1st Am. fr. 3d. London ed. Lowell, 1840. 16° 1395.2
— Goethe's correspondence with a child. Boston, 1860. 12° 905.15
— Sorrows of Werter. New ed. Lond. 1793. 18°. 487.12
GOODRICH, S. G. Moral tales. Bost. 1840. 2v. 18°. 450.27
GORE, C. G. The dean's daughter. Auburn, n.d. 12° 487.10
— Mammon, or the hardships of an heiress. New York, n.d. 12° 497.15
GOSSE, P. H. Evenings at the microscope. New York, 1860. 12° 148.32
GRAHAME, F. R. The archer and the steppe. London, n.d. 12° 927.15
GRATTAN, T. C. Civilized America. London, 1859. 2v. 8° 622.6
GRATTON, C. J. The gallery. A sketch of parliamentary reporting and reporters. London, 1860. 16° 997.2
GRAY, G. H. The mystic circle and hand-book of masonry. 5th edition. Cincin. 1859. 12° . 126.12
GREELEY, H. An overland journey from New York to San Francisco. N. Y. 1860. 12° . . 637.24

Shelf. No.

GROSS, J. B. The heathen religion in its development. Boston, 1856. 12° 115.22
GROTE, *Mrs.* G. Memoir of the life of Ary Scheffer. London, 1860. 8° 542.16
GRUND, F. J. Thoughts on the present position of Europe. Philadelphia, 1860. 12° 947.19
GUERICKE, H. E. F. Manual of church history. Translated by W. G. T. Shedd. Andover, 1857. 8° 1082.4
GUIDE to the stars. New ed. London, 1860. 8°. 143.10
GUIZOT, F. P. G. Memoirs to illustrate the history of my own time. Translated by J. W. Cole. Vol. III. London, 1860. 8° 1003.5
GUIZOT, M. G., *son.* Alfred le grand, ou l'Angleterre sous les Anglo-Saxons. Paris, 1856. 16° 2065.12
GUROWSKI, A. G. Slavery in history. New York, 1860. 12° 946.9
GUTHRIE, T. Christ and the inheritance of the saints. Edinburgh, 1859. 12° 114.16
GUYARD, A. Les fils de la fée noire. Paris, 1853. 12° 2065.1

HABITS of good society. From the last Lond. ed. New York, 1860. 12° 126.26
HALL, W. W. Bronchitis, and kindred disease. 9th ed. New York, 1859. 12° 158.37
— Consumption. 2d edition. N. Y. 1860. 12°. 158.35
— Health and disease. 3d edition. New York, 1860. 12° 158.36
— Journal of health. New York, 1854-59. 6v. 8°. 154.1
HAMILTON, J. C. History of the United States. Vols. V., VI. New York, 1860. 8° 304.2
HANNA, W. Wycliffe and the Huguenots. Edinburgh, 1860. 12° 998.15-16
HARBAUGH, H. Poems. Philadelphia, 1860. 12°. 374.4
HARDWICK, C. The history of friendly societies. London, 1859. 12° 187.24
HARE, J. C., and A. W. Guesses at truth. From 5th London ed. Boston, 1861. 12° 1173.4
HARPER's magazine. Vol. 18. N. Y. 1859. 8°. . 880.3
HARRISON, W. H. Waldemar, a tale of the thirty years' war. Philadelphia, 1834. 12° . . . 479.8
HARRY Coverdale's courtship. N. York, n.d. 12°. 487.14
HARRY Lee, or hope for the poor. New York, 1859. 12° 487.9
HARTWIG, G. The sea and its living wonders. London, 1860. 8° 143.8
HASE, C. Life of Jesus. Tr. by J. F. Clarke. Boston, 1860. 16° 114.13
HAWES, V. Nemesis. New York, 1860. 12° . . 784.7
HAWTHORNE, N. The marble faun. Boston, 1860. 2v. 12° 505.6-10
HAYES, I. I. Arctic boat journey in the autumn of 1854. Boston, 1860. 12° 706.18
HAYNE, P. H. Avolio, a legend. Bost. 1860. 12°. 374.5
HAZLITT, W. Characters of Shakespeare's plays. New York, 1845. 12° 374.7
HEAD, J. H. Home pastimes, or tableaux vivants. Boston, 1860. 12° 385.22
HELPER, H. R. The impending crisis of the South. New York, 1860. 12° 297.24,25
HELPS, A. Friends in council. New series. From the English edition. Boston, 1860. 2v. 12°. 126.19
HENRY, C. S. On social welfare and human progress. New York, 1861. 12° 883.1
HENSMAN, A. P. Handbook of the constitution. London, 1860. 12° 998.18
HERBERT, G. The temple, and other poems. 2d ed. Vol. II. London, 1858. 16° 1395.1
HERODOTUS, History. New version by Geo. Rawlinson, assisted by Sir H. Rawlinson and Sir J. G. Wilkinson. Vols. II.-IV. New York, 1859, 60. 3v. 8° 941.1
HILL, G. C. Daniel Boone, the pioneer of Kentucky. New York, 1860. 12° 527.17
HILL, S. S. Travels in Peru and Mexico. London, 1860. 2v. 12° 634.3
HILL, T. Jesus the interpreter of nature. Boston, 1860. 16° 114.10

Shelf. No.

HISTORICAL magazine, The. Vol. III. New York, 1859. 4° 273.1

HISTORY and progress of education. By Philobiblius. New York, 1860. 12° 126.25

HITTELL, T. H. The adventures of James Capen Adams. Boston, 1860. 12° 527.23

HOCKIN, J. B. Hints on photography. London, 1860. 12° 185.3

HODSON, W. S. R. Twelve years of a soldier's life in India. Ed. by G. H. Hodson. From 3d English edition. Bost. 1859. 12° . 557.11, 13, 14

HOFLAND, T. C. The British angler's manual. Ed. by E. Jesse. London, 1848. p.8° . . . 176.21

HOGARTH, G. Memoirs of the opera in Italy, France, Germany and England. London, 1851. 2v. 12° 905.19

HOGG, J. Familiar anecdotes of Sir Walter Scott. New York, 1834. 12° 589.19

— The queen's wake. A poem. New York, 1848. 16° 450.34

HOLBROOK, A. The normal, or methods of teaching. New York, 1859. 12° 126.14

HOLLAND, J. G. Gold-foil hammered from popular proverbs. New York, 1859. 12° . . . 903.13

— Miss Gilbert's career. New York, 1860. 12°. 495.8

HOLLINGSHEAD, J. Odd journeys in and out of London. London, 1860. 12° 645.18

— Under Bow bells. London, 1860. 16° 497.17

HOLMES, O. W. The professor at the breakfast table; with the story of Iris. Boston, 1859. 12° 903.14–17

HOME is home. New York, 1851. 12° 774.12

HOOD, T. Memorials. Edited by his daughter. Preface and notes by his son. Boston, 1860. 2v. 12° 587.20

— Tylney hall. London, 1857. 16° 1795.3

— Whims and waifs. London, 1860. 12° . . . 374.15

HOOKER, W. Natural history. N. Y. 1860. 12°. 176.22

HOPKINS, S. The Puritans. Vol. II. Boston, 1860. 8° 982.3

HORATIUS Flaccus, Q. Opera omnia. Ex recensione A. J. Macleane. New York, 1860. 18° 395.16

— The odes of Horace. Transl. by T. Martin. Boston, 1861. 24° 450.31

— Works with English notes, by J. L. Lincoln. New York, [1851.] 12° 394.4

HOUDIN, R. Memoirs, written by himself. Ed. by Dr. R. S. Mackenzie. Phil. 1859. 12°. 615.13

HOW to talk: a pocket manual of conversation. New York, 1857. 12° 395.13

HOWARD, J. H. Athletic and gymnastic exercises. London, 1860. 12° 205.14

HOWE, J. W. A trip to Cuba. Boston, 1860. 12°. 637.25

HOWITT, M. Popular history of the United States. New York, 1860. 2v. 12° 305.6

HUBBACK, Miss. Kate Penrose. N. York, n.d. 8° 803.7

HUMBOLDT, F. H. A. v. Ansichten der Natur. Stuttgart, 1849. 2 Bde. 12° 2025.5

— Letters to Varnhagen von Ense from 1827 to 1858. Transl. by F. Kapp. N. York, 1860. 12°. 893.4

HUNGARY and its revolutions to the 19th century; with a memoir of Louis Kossuth. London, 1854. 16° 1825.2

HUNT, L. The old court suburb, or memorials of Kensington. 3d edition. London, n.d. 12°. 903.20

HUNTINGTON, F. D. Christian believing and living. Boston, 1860. 12° 114.7

— Sermons for the people. Boston, 1856. 12° . 1115.1

IDELER, C. L. and Nolte, H. Handbuch der französischen Sprache und Literatur. Berlin, 1848–9. 2v. 8° 2064.1

INGRAHAM, J. H. The sunny south. Philadelphia, 1860. 12° 207.27

JACKSON, J. Letters to a young physician. Boston, 1855. 12° 1155.1

JAMES, G. P. R. Leonora D'Orco. New York, 1857. 8° 464.13

— Lord Montagu's page. Phila. 1858. 12° . . . 464.14

Shelf. No.

JAMES, M. The elder sister. N. York, 1855. 12° 1783.1

JEAFFRESON, J. C. A book about doctors. London, 1860. 2v. 12° 883.5

JEANS, T. The Tommiebeg shootings; or, a moor in Scotland. London, 1860. 12° 486.11

JENYNS, L. Observations in meteorology. London, 1858. 8° 148.33

JERROLD, B. The French under arms. London, 1860. 12° 1009.19

JERVIS, J. B. Railway property. New York, 1861. 12° 185.4

JOHNES, M. Prince Charlie the young chevalier. New York, 1859. 12° 557.12

JOUSSE, J. A catechism of music. From 19th London ed. Boston, n.d. 18° 209.36

JUDSON, E. C. Life and letters. By A. C. Kendrick. New York, 1860. 12° 539.33

KARADSCHITSCH, W. S. Volksmärchen der Serben. Berlin, 1854. 4° 2016.12

KAVANAGH, J. Adèle: a tale. New York, 1858. 12° 1785.8

— Madeline. New York, 1852. 12° 774.11

— Rachel Gray. New York, 1856. 12° 1785.13

— Women of Christianity. London, 1852. 12°. 595.14

KEDDIE, W. Cyclopædia of literary and scientific anecdote. From London edition. Columbus, 1859. 12° 394.1

KEIGHTLEY, T. Account of the life, opinions, and writings of John Milton. London, 1859. 8° 587.11

KENNEDY, J. P. Quodlibet: by Solomon Secondthoughts. Second ed. Phila. 1860. 12° 297.26

KETTELL, T. P. Southern wealth and northern profits. New York, 1860. 8° 292.4

KING, T. S. The white hills. Bost. 1860. sm.4°. 225.4

KING, W. H. Lessons on steam, the steam engine, propellers, etc. Revised by J. W. King. New York, 1860. 8° 202.11

KINGSLEY, C. Sermons for the times. N. York, 1856. 12° 1104.14

KINGSTON, W. H. G. Peter the whaler. N. York, 1855. 16° 747.5

KLOPSTOCK, M. and F. Memoirs. Trans. from the German. Phila. 1810. 12° 1545.6

KNIGHT, C. Popular history of England. Vols. V., VI. London, 1859, 60. 8° 982.1

KNORR, J. Methodical guide for teachers of music on the piano-forte. Tr. by G. A. Schmitt. Boston, n.d. 12° 209.32

KOHL, J. G. Kitchi-Gami. Wanderings round Lake Superior. London, 1860. 8° 622.5

KÜLLIKER, A. Manual of human microscopic anatomy. London, 1860. 8° 154.2

KOSSUTH and the Hungarian war. Philadelphia, 1851. 12° 928.12

KOTZEBUE, A. F. F. v. Dramatic works. Transl. by C. Smith. New York, 1800–1801. 3v. 8°. 374.19

KRAPF, J. L. Travels, and missionary labors in Eastern Africa. Appendix by E. G. Ravenstein. London, 1860. 8° 692.16

— Same. Boston, 1859. 12° 1694.1

KURTZ, J. H. Manual of sacred history. Tr. by C. F. Schaeffer. 7th ed. Phila. 1860. 12°. 1104.17

— Text-book of church history. Vol. I. Phila. 1860. 8° 1104.16

LADY'S tour round Monte Rosa. London, 1859. p.8° 666.23

LAFEVER, M. Beauties of modern architecture. New edition. New York, 1855. 8° 204.11

LAMARTINE, A. M. L. Prat de. Life of Mary Stuart. New York, 1860. 18° 550.69

LAMSON, A. The church of the first three centuries. Boston, 1860. 8° 1092.10

LANDOR, R. E. The fountain of Arethusa. London, 1848. 2v. 12° 893.9

LANE, B. I. Responses on the use of tobacco. New York, 1846. 12° 187.28

Shelf. No.

LATHBURY, T. The Spanish armada, A. D. 1588.
London, 1840. 18° 998.7

LAUD, W. Autobiography. Oxford, 1839. 16° . 589.17

LAW of the territories. Philadelphia, 1859. 12° . 299.13

LAWRENCE, A. Diary and correspondence. Edited by his son. Boston, 1860. 12° 1525.1-10

LAYCOCK, T. Mind and brain. Edinburgh, 1860.
2v. 12° 905.17

LEE, H. Against wind and tide. New York, 1860.
12° 497.19

— Hawksview. New York, 1860. 12° 486.5-6

LEE, T. J. Tables and formulæ useful in surveying, geodesy, and practical astronomy. 2d ed. with additions. Washington, 1853. 8°. 143.6

LESAGE, A. R. Adventures of Gil Blas. Transl. by T. Smollett. New ed. Lond. 1859. p.8°. 853.12

LESLIE, E. Leonilla Lynmore; or, a lesson for young wives. Phila. 1848. 8° 803.1

LESLIE, C. R. Autobiographical recollections. Ed. by T. Taylor. Boston, 1860. 12° . . . 587.18

LEVASSEUR, A. La Fayette en Amérique en 1824 et 1825. Paris, 1829. 2v. 8° 2064.5

LEVER, C. Davenport Dunn. Phila. n.d. 8° . . 802.48

— Gerald Fitzgerald, "the chevalier." New York, 1859. 8° 762.15

— Kate O'Donoghue. Philadelphia, n.d. 8° . . 502.12

LEWALD, F. Lake-house. Tr. from the German by Nath'l. Greene. Boston, 1861. 12° . . . 495.11

LEWES, G. H. Physiology of common life. New York, 1860. 2v. 12° 158.30

— Studies in animal life. New York, 1860. 12°. 176.24

LEWIS, Lady T. The semi-detached house. Boston, 1860. 12° 495.7

LIARDET, F. Professional recollections of seamanship. Portsea, 1849. 8° 143.7

LIDDELL, H. G. Life of Julius Cæsar. N. York, 1860. 18° 550.70

LIFE'S lesson : a tale. New York, 1854. 12° . . 487.19

LILLYWHITE, F. The English cricketer's trip to Canada and the United States. London, 1860. 12° 639.26

LINCOLN, A. Life, speeches, and services. New York, 1860. 12° 528.24

— and Douglas, S. A. Political debates. Columbus, 1860. 8° 292.5

LISTER, T. H. Granby ; a tale of modern society. London, n.d. 18° 479.10

LIVES of eminent persons. Library of useful knowledge. London, 1833. 8° 365.18

LOST principle, The, or sectional equilibrium. By "Barbarossa." Richmond, Va. 1860. 8° . 292.9

LOUIE's last term at St. Mary's. N. Y. 1860. 12°. 486.10

LOWELL, R. T. S. Fresh hearts that failed three thousand years ago. Boston, 1860. 12° . . 374.16

LÖWENTHAL, J. Morphy's games New York, 1860. 12° 186.4

LUCK of Ladysmede. Boston, 1860. 8° 803.11

LUNT, G. Radicalism in religion, philosophy, and social life. Boston, 1858. 12° 2095.2

LYELL, Sir C. Second visit to the United States. New York, 1849. 2v. 12° 1634.6

LYTTON, E. G. E. L. Bulwer. Eva, and the pilgrims of the Rhine. Leipzig, 1842. 16° . . 468.14

LYTTON, R. B. Lucille. Boston, 1860. 24° . . 450.29

MACAULAY, T. B. Biographies, contributed to the Encyclopædia Britannica. Edinb. 1860. 12°. 587.14

— Critical and miscellaneous essays and poems. New edition. New York, 1860. 12° . . . 905.20

— Lays of ancient Rome ; with Ivry, and the Armada. Boston, 1856. 16° 1395.4

M'CLINTOCK, F. L. Fate of Sir John Franklin and his companions. London, 1859-60. 12°. 706.13-18

M'COSH, J. The intuitions of the mind. London, 1860. 8° 123.2

MACDUFF, J. R. Memoirs of Bethany. New York, 1859. 12° 126.24

— Memoirs of Gennesaret. New York, 1859. 12°. 114.4

MACGREGOR, J. Three days in the East. London, 1853. 24° 709.29

MACKAY, C. Jacobite songs and ballads of Scotland from 1688 to 1746. London, 1861. 12°. 376.7

MACKIE, S. J. First traces of life on the earth. London, 1860. 12° 167.41

MADEMOISELLE Mori : a tale of modern Rome. Boston, 1860. 12° 505.16

MAGUIRE, J. F. Rome : its ruler and its institutions. New York, 1858. 12° 1935.2

MAIDEN sisters, The. A tale. Leipzig, 1859. sm. 4° 479.11

MALEY, A. J. Historical recollections of the reign of William IV. London, 1860. 2v. 12° . . 998.11

MAMIANI, della Rovere, T. Rights of nations. Tr. by R. Acton. London, 1860. 8° . . . 132.13

MANSEL, H. L. Metaphysics, or the philosophy of consciousness. Edinburgh, 1860. 8° . . 893.6

MARCET, W. On chronic alcoholic intoxication. London, 1860. 12° 126.39

MARCH, C. W. Reminiscences of congress. New York, 1850. 12° 1525.1

MARCY, R. B. The prairie traveller. New York, 1859. 16° 639.25

MARMONT, A. F. L. Visse de, duke of Ragusa. Voyage en Hongrie, Transylvanie, etc. Paris, 1837-8. 5v. 8° 2064.2

MARRYATT, F. The little savage. New ed. London, 1858. 16° 747.4

— Poor Jack. Philadelphia, n.d. 8° 745.17

MARSH, A. Evelyn Marston. N. York, 1856. 8°. 803.13

MARSH, G. P. Lectures on the English language. New York, 1860. 8° 394.2, 392.7

MARSH, Mrs. G. P. Wolfe of the knoll. New York, 1860. 12° 374.13

MARSHMAN, J. C. Memoirs of Sir Henry Havelock. London. 1860. 8° 577.4

MASON, G. C. Reunion of the sons and daughters of Newport. Newport, 1859. 12° 227.22

MASSEY, W. History of England during the reign of George the Third. Vol. III. London, 1860. 8° 983.1

MATHEWS, Mrs. C. Life and correspondence of Charles Mathews. New ed. Lond. 1860. 12°. 587.17

MAXWELL, J. S. The czar, his court and people. New York, 1849. 12° 677.23

MAXWELL, W. H. Captain O'Sullivan. N. York, 1855. 8° 803.2

MAYHEW, E. The illustrated horse-doctor. London, 1860. 8° 173.6

MAYHEW, —. The fear of the world. New York, 1860. 8° 803.3

MEADE, W. Manual for students preparing for examination at Apothecary's hall. London, 1839. 12° 158.31

MEDHURST, W. H. China, its state and prospects. Boston, 1838. 12° 938.4-5

— - Same. London, 1857. 8° 934.11

MENZEL, W. German literature. Transl. by Felton. Boston, 1840. 3v. 12° 893.10

METRICAL translations from Goethe, Schiller, Uhland, Heine, and others. London, 1852. 8° 322.7

MICHELET, J. L'oiseau. Paris. 2de ed. 1856. 16°. 2065.6

— L'amour. Paris, 1859. 12° 1074.36

MILBURN, W. H. Pioneers, preachers, and people of the Mississippi valley. N. York, 1860. 12°. 1104.7

MILL, J. Analysis of the mind. London, 1829. 2v. 8° 122.20

MISSING link, The. By L. N. R. London, 1860. 16° 126.32

MITCHEL, O. M. Popular astronomy. New York, 1860. 12° 148.38

MOGES, Marquis de. Baron Gros's embassy to China and Japan in 1857-58. Lond. 1860. 12°. 697.21

MONTALEMBERT, C. F. de. Pie IX, et la France en 1849 et en 1859. Londres, 1859. 8° 1074.37

MONTI, V. Tragedie. Torino, 1830. 16° 2049.2

MOORE, G. H. The treason of major-general Charles Lee. New York, 1860. 8° 292.2

MORE, M. Mendip annals. Ed. by A. Roberts. London, 1859. 12° 126.33

Shelf. No.

MORIN, A. Ideas of mechanics. Tr. by J. Bennett. New York, 1860. 8° 194.24

MORPHY, P. Games of chess. Notes by J. Löwenthal. London, 1860. p.8° 853.5-8

MORRELL, A. J. Narrative of a voyage to the south Atlantic ocean in 1829-31. New York, 1833. 12° 099.19

MORRIS, F. O. Anecdotes in natural history. London, 1860. 16° 176.19

MORRIS, G. P., and Willis, N. P. Prose and poetry of Europe and America. 7th ed. N. York, 1848. 8° 321.3

MOTLEY, J. L. Histoire de la république des Provinces-Unies. Tom. III., IV. Paris, 1859-60. 8° 1074.8

MULOCH, D. M. A life for a life. N. Y. 1859. 12° 495.6

— Same. New York, 1859. 8° 762.12-14

— Poems. Boston, 1860. 16° 374.8

MURRAY, A. M. Letters from the United States, Cuba, and Canada. New York, 1856. 12° . 1634.2

MURRAY, E. An artist's life in Morocco, Spain, and the Canary Islands. Lond. 1859. 2v. 8°. 664.1

MURRAY, J. Handbook for India. London, 1859. 2v. p.8° 645.14

— Handbook of travel-talk. London, 1855. 16°. 395.11

MY life, and what shall I do with it? By an old maid. London, 1860. 12° 883.4

NEWMAN, E. Grammar of entomology. London, 1835. 18° 189.41

NICHOLS, I. Hours with the evangelists. Vol. 1. Boston, 1859. 8° 112.1

NIGHTINGALE, F. Notes on nursing. New York, 1860. 12° 186.5-25, 27-56

NORTHEND, C. The national orator. New York, 1859. 12° 395.10

NORTON, C. E. Notes of travel and study in Italy. Boston, 1860. 12° 666.22

NOUVELLES danoises, traduites par Xavier Marmier. Paris, 1855. 16° 2065.9

NUNNELEY, T. The organs of vision: their anatomy and physiology. London, 1858. 8° . . 153.24

O'CONNELL, J. Experience during a parliamentary career from 1833 to 1848. London, 1849. 2v. 8° 893.8

OERSTED, H. C. The soul in nature. London, 1852. 12° 1825.1

OLIPHANT, L. The earl of Elgin's mission to China and Japan in 1857-59. New York, 1860. 8° 701.12-13

— Patriots and filibusters, or incidents of political and exploratory travel. Edinb. 1860. 12°. 656.1

OLIPHANT, M. Harry Muir. New York, 1853. 16°. 487.20

OLIVER, E. B. Text book of music. Bost. n.d. 12°. 209.28

OLMSTEAD, F. L. A journey in the back country. New York, 1860. 12° 638.12

— A journey in the seaboard slave states. London, 1856. 12° 1634.5

ORLEANS, H. L. E. duchess of. A memoir. Transl. by Mrs. Austen. 2d ed. London, 1860. 8°. 614.2

— Memoir of the duchess of Orleans, by the marquesse de H. Transl. from the French. New York, 1860 12° 618.1

OSBORN, H. S. Palestine, past and present. Philadelphia, 1859. 8° 942.4

OSBORN, S. The career and fate of Sir John Franklin. London, 1860. 18° 707.19

OSSOLI, M. F. d'. Life without and life within. Ed. by A. B. Fuller. Boston, [1859.] 12° . 903.18

OUTLAW, The. New York, 1855. 2v. 12° . . . 497.16

OWEN, A. A lost love. New ed. revised. London, 1858. 12° 497.18

OWEN, R. D. Footfalls on the boundary of another world. Phila. 1860. 12° 114.5

PAGE, D. Handbook of geological terms and geology. Edinburgh, 1859. 12° 167.40

PAGET, J. Lectures on surgical pathology. 2d Am. ed. Phila. 1860. 8° 153.22

PALEY, W. The evidences of Christianity. Annotations by Whately. New York, 1860. 8°. 1092.9

PALFREY, J. G. History of New England. Vol. II. Boston, 1860. 8° 232.1-5

PALLISER, J. The solitary hunter. New edition. London, 1860. 12° 189.43

PARDOE, J. The jealous wife. N. York, 1855. 8° 803.8

PARKER, E. G. Reminiscences of Rufus Choate. New York, 1860. 12° 515.13

PARKER, T. Two christmas celebrations. Boston, 1859. sm.4° 114.6

PARRISH, E. Introduction to practical pharmacy. 2d ed. Phila. 1859. 8° 153.25

PARSONS, J. Minor theatre, The. Vol. IV. London, 1794. 18° 450.28

    Contents. — The commissary, by Saml. Foote; The lame lover, by Saml. Foote; Taste, by S. Foote; Edgar and Emmeline, by Dr. Hawkesworth; The author, by S. Foote.

PARTON, J. Life of Andrew Jackson. N. York, 1860. 3v. 8° 522.7-8

— Life and times of Aaron Burr. 13th ed. New York, 1860. 8° 1524.1

PASCAL, B. Thoughts, letters, and opuscules. Tr. by O. W. Wight. New York, 1859. 12° 115.19

PATTERSON, J. B. National character of the Athenians. New ed. Edinburgh, 1860. 12° . . 946.8

PATTERSON, R. H. The new revolution, or the Napoleonic policy in Europe. Edinburgh, 1860. 8° 1002.8

PATTON, J. H. The history of the United States of America. New York, 1860. 8° 292.3

PEABODY, A. P. Lectures on christian doctrine. New ed. Boston, 1848. 12° 115.18

— Memorial of John W. Foster. Portsmouth, 1852. 12° 536.14

PEABODY, E. Sermons, with a memoir. Boston, 1857. 12° 2095.1

PEEL, Sir L. Life of Sir Robert Peel. London, 1860. 8° 587.19

PELLICO, S. Tre nuove tragedie. Torino, 1852. 18°. 2049.5

PEMBERTON, J. D. Vancouver's island and British Columbia. London, 1860. 8° 264.8

PEPPER, J. H. The boy's play-book of science. London, 1860. 16° 186.2

PEPYS, Lady C. Journey from Kiev to Eaux-Bonnes on a plank. 1859. London, 1860. 2v. 12° 607.22

PERRENS, F. T. Jérome Savonarole. 2de éd. Paris, 1853. 16° 2065.7

PETRARCA, F. Sonnets, triumphs, and other poems. Transl. by various hands. Life by T. Campbell. London, 1859. p.8° 847.12

PFEFFEL, G. C. Poetische Versuche. Wien, 1791-2. 3v. 12° 2019.3

PHILLIPS, J. A., and Darlington, J. Mining and metallurgy. London, 1857. 12° 187.30

PICHOT, A. Life and labours of Sir Charles Bell. London, 1860. 12° 587.13

PICKERING, E. The grumbler. Phila. n.d. 8°. 1784.16

PIDDINGTON, H. The sailor's horn-book. London, 1860. 8° 143.5

PINNEY, J. A key to the attainment of the full term of life. London, 1860. 8° 162.1

PIRIE, M. Flowers, grasses, and shrubs. London, n.d. 12° 168.40

PLAIN words about sickness. By a doctor's wife. London, 1860. 12° 168.39

PLATO. Apology and Crito; with notes by W. S. Tyler. New York, 1860. 12° 385.23

— Platonic dialogues for English readers. By W. Whewell. Vol. 1. Cambridge, [Eng.] 1859. 12° 126.18

PLUTARCHUS. Greek history. Revised and arranged by A. H. Clough. Lond. 1860. 12°. 946.10

POLITICAL text-book for 1860. N. York, 1860. 8°. 292.6

POPE, H E. The corsair and his conqueror. London, 1860. 12° 688.51

POWELL, B. Christianity without Judaism. London, 1857. p.8° 114.19

Shelf No.

POWELL, B. *continued.*
— The order of nature. Lond. 1859. 8° 114.18
— The unity of worlds and of nature. 2d ed. London, 1856. p.8° 114.20
PRACTICAL Swiss guide. 4th ed. Lond. 1859. 12°. 645.15
PRACTICAL treatise on dyeing and calico-printing. Supplement by R. Macfarlane. New York, 1860. 8° 194.23
PRATT, A. Common things of the sea-coast. London, n.d. 18° 189.42
PRATT, J. H. Treatise on the figure of the earth. Cambridge, 1860. 12° 148.41
PRESCOTT, G. B. History of the electric telegraph. Boston, 1860. 12° 185.1
PREUSSEN, der Bund und der Frieden. Hannover, 1859. pp.20. 8° 1032.6
PRIME, S. I. Letters from Switzerland. New York, 1860. 12° 665.1
PROUT, *Father.* The reliques of father Prout. Collected by Rev. F. Mahony. New ed. rev. London, 1860. p.8° 853.16
PUNSHON, W. M. Sermons. Introd. by Rev. W. H. Milburn. New York, 1860. 12° 1104.13

QUINCY, J. Essays on the soiling of cattle, and an address. Boston, 1859. 8° 164.20
QUITMAN, J. A. Life and correspondence. By J. F. H. Claiborne. New York, 1860. 2v. 12°. 528.26

RANKIN, W. J. M. A manual of the steam engine and other prime movers. London, 1859. 12°. 307.26
RATHBONE, *Mrs.* R. Colloquies of Edward Osborne. By the author of "Mary Powell." London, 1860. 16° 468.17
— Old Chelsea bun house. By the author of "Mary Powell." London, 1860. 16° 507.19
RAUMER, F. L. G. v. Briefe aus Frankfurt und Paris, 1848, 49. Leipzig, 1849. 2v. 12° . . 2025.6
RAWLINSON, G. Historical evidence of the truth of the scripture records. Notes tr. by Rev. A. N. Arnold. Boston, 1860. 12° 114.14
READE, C. The eighth commandment. Boston, 1860. 12° 893.13
REAL, The, and the beau-ideal. Lond. 1860. 12°. 479.12
RECENT inquiries in theology. From 2d London ed. Boston, 1860. 12° 112.2
RECREATIONS in shooting. By Craven. New ed. London, 1859. p.8° 853.13
RECREATIONS of a country parson. Bost. 1861. 12°. 883.2-3
REDDING, C. Every man his own butler. 3d ed. enlarged. London, 1853. 16° 207.29
REDPATH, J. Life of Captain John Brown. Boston, 1860. 12° 527.15-16
REID, M. Odd people. New York, 1860. 16° . . 176.27
RICE, G. E. Nugamenta, a book of verses. Boston, 1860. 12° 374.17
RICHARDS, T. A. Appleton's companion handbook of travel. New York, 1860. 12° . . . 638.14
RICHARDSON, J. Practical treatise on mechanical dentistry. Phila. 1860. 8° 162.5
RICHTER, J. P. F. Der Komet, oder Nikolaus Marggraf. Berlin, 1820. 2v. 16° 2019.2
— Extracts, selected and translated by Georgiana, lady Chatterton. London, 1859. 12°. 905.21
— Politische Fastenpredigten während Deutschlands Marterwoche. Stuttgart, 1817. 16°. 2019.1
RITCHIE, J. E. About London. London, 1860. 12°. 998.19
ROBERTSON, F. W. Sermons on St. Paul's epistles to the Corinthians. Boston, 1860. 16°. 126.27
ROCHETTE, D. R. Tableau des catacombes de Rome. 2de éd. Paris, 1853. 16° 2065.11
ROGERS, J. W. Sewerage system of London. etc. London, [1857.] pp.48 and xxviii. 8°. 205.9
RONGE, J. and B. Guide to the English Kinder Garten. 2d ed. London, 1858. 4° 123.1
ROSSE, J. W. An index of dates. Vol.II. K-Z. London, 1859. p.8° 857.9
ROWELL, G. A. The cause of rain. Oxford, 1859. 8°. 143.4
RUSH, R. Occasional productions, political, diplomatic, and miscellaneous. Phila.1860. 8°. 882.4

RUSKIN, J. The elements of perspective. New York, 1860. 12° 205.8
RUSSELL, W. H. My diary in India in 1858-59. London, 1860. 2v. 12° 939.12
ST. JOHN, C. H. Poems. Boston, 1860. 16° . . 374.9
ST. JOHN, W. C. Catechism of the history of Newfoundland. Boston, 1855. 18° 259.13
SALA, G. A. Lady Chesterfield's letters to her daughter. London, 1860. 12° 905.16
— Looking at life. London, 1860. 12° 893.5
— Twice round the clock. London, n.d. 8° . . 893.2
SALMON fishing in Canada. By a resident. Edited by J. E. Alexander. London, 1860. 8° . . 175.18
SAMSON, G. W. Spiritualism tested. Boston, 1860. 16° 148.36
SAMUELSON, J., and Hicks, J. B. The honey-bee, its natural history, habits, and anatomy. London, 1860. 12° 176.28
SARGANT, W. L. Robert Owen, and his social philosophy. London, 1860. 8° 587.16
SAVAGE, J. Our living representative men. Phila. 1860. 12° 527.19
SAWYER, F. W. Hits and Hints. Boston, 1860. 16°. 297.23
SAXE, J. G. The money-king. Boston, 1860. 12°. 374.3
SCARTH, J. Twelve years in China. Edinburgh, 1860. 12° 937.7
SCHALLER, C. A. Handbuch der klassischen Literatur der Deutschen von Lessing bis auf gegenwärtige Zeit. Halle, 1812-16. 2v. 8°. 2013.4
SCHILLER, J. C. F. v. Maria Stuarda. Tragedia trad. del cav. A. Maffei. Firenze, 1852. 18°. 2049.3
— Wallenstein, ein dramatisches Gedicht. Tübingen, 1816. 16° 2016.9
SCHIMMELPENNINCK M. A. Memoirs of Port Royal. 5th ed. London, 1858. 3v. 12° . . 1006.3
— Sacred musings. Preface by Rev. J. Baylee. London, 1860. p.8° 1104.8
SCHLEGEL, F. History of literature, ancient and modern. London, 1859. p.8° 857.13
SCHLÖZER, C. v. A. L. v. Schlözers öffentliches und Privatleben aus Originalurkunden. Leipzig, 1828. 2v. 8° 2013.1
SCHMIDT, H. I. Course of ancient geography. New York, 1860. 12° 946.7
SCHMIDT-WEISSENFELS. Oesterreich und Napoleon III. im Streit um Italien. Prag. 1859. 8° 1032.7
SCHOLEFIELD, J. Hints for improvements in the authorized version of the New Testament. 4th ed. Cambridge, 1857. 16° 126.30
SCHULLER, J. C. Romänische Volkslieder. Hermannstadt, 1859. sq.16° 2025.7
SCRIVER, C. Gotthold's emblems : or, invisible things understood by things that are made. Boston, 1860. 12° 126.17
SEARS, B. Life of Luther. Phila. n.d. 18° . . 1545.1
SECKER, W. The nonsuch professor. Introd. by C. P. Krauth. New York, 1860. 12° 114.1
SECRET out, The, or, one thousand tricks with cards. New York, 1859. 12° 187.21
SEWARD, W. H. Life and speeches. Boston, 1860. 12° 527.22
— Works. Ed. by G. E. Baker. New York, 1853. 3v. 8° 294.7
SEWELL, E. M. History of the early church. New York, 1860. 18° 947.20
SHAKESPEAR, *Capt.* H. Wild sports of India. London, 1860. 12° 707.21
— Same. Boston, 1860. 12° 176.26
SHAKESPEARE, W. Beauties of Shakespeare. Ed. by Rev. W. Dodd. New ed. London, 1851. 12° 364.4
— Henry the Eighth. Ed. by Rev. J. Hunter. London, 1860. 12° 364.3
— New exegesis of Shakespeare. Edinburgh, 1859. 12° 394.5
— Religious and moral sentences from Shakespeare. From Eng. ed. Introd. by F. W. Huntington. Boston, 1859. 12° 374.6

Shelf. No.

SHEDD, W. G. T. Lectures upon the philosophy of history. Andover, 1857. 12°. 947.18

SHELLEY, M. W. Shelley memorials. Boston, 1859. 12°. 1595.5

SHERER, M. Military memoirs of Wellington. Philadelphia, 1833. 2v. 12°. 1579.1

SHOT-GUN and sporting rifle. London, 1859. 12°. 174.11

SIDDONS, J. H. Norton's hand-book to Europe. New York, 1860. 12°. 609.15

SIDNEY, Sir P. Miscellaneous works. Life by W. Gray. Boston, 1860. 8°. 893.1

SIMEON, C. Stray notes on fishing and natural history. Cambridge, [Eng.] 1860. p.8°. . 175.17

SIMMS, W. G. History of South Carolina. New York, 1860. 12°. 237.21

SIMPSON, J. Y. Obstetric memoirs and contributions. Ed. by W. O. Priestley and H. R. Storer. Philadelphia, 1855-53. 2v. 8°. . 153.20

SLEEPER, J. S. Jack in the forecastle. Boston, 1860. 12°. 745.18

SMALL beginnings, or the way to get on. London, n.d. 12°. 747.2

SMILES, S. Brief biographies. Boston, 1861. 12°. 589.18
— Self-help; with illustrations of character and conduct. London, 1859. 16°. 126.20
— - Same. Boston, 1860. 16°. 126.21

SMITH, A. The Pottleton legacy. Philadelphia, 1849. 8°. 803.9
— Wild oats and dead leaves. Lond. 1860. 12°. 495.10

SMUCKER, S. M. History of the four Georges. New York, 1860. 12°. 554.8

SMITH, Mrs. Olympia Morata, her times, life, and writings. 4th edition. London, 1840. 16°. 599.15

SOAVE, F. Novelle morali. Parigi, 1833. 2v. 18°. 2049.1

SOCIETY for diffusion of useful knowledge. Barlow's tables of squares, cubes, etc. London, 1860. 12°. 148.42

SOUVESTRE, É. Chroniques de la mer. Nouv. éd. Paris, 1856. 12°. 2065.3
— Scènes de la vie intime. Nouv. éd. Paris, 1856. 12°. 2065.10

SPENCER, H. Education, intellectual, moral and physical. New York, 1861. 12°. 123.3

SPENCER, W. V. Boston theatre. Vols. XVI.-XXIV. Boston, n.d. 12°. 355.9

Contents.—Vol. XVI. The wonder, by Mrs. S. Centlivre ; The rights of man, by O. S. Leland ; Robert Emmett, by Jas. Pilgrim ; My husband's ghost, by J. M. Morton ; Fighting by proxy, by J. Kenney ; Two can play at that game, by E. Pierron and A. Lafferrière ; Unprotected female, by J. S. Coyne ; Green bushes, by J. B. Buckstone. XVII. Flowers of the forest, by J. B. Buckstone ; Forty and fifty, by T. H. Bayly ; Who stole the pocket-book, by J. M. Morton ; A bachelor of arts, by P. Hardwicke ; My son Diana, by A. Harris ; The midnight banquet ; Unwarrantable intrusion, by J. M. Morton ; Mr. and Mrs. White, by R. J. Raymond. XVIII. A quiet family, by W. Suter ; Husband of an hour, by E. Falconer ; Love's labour lost, by W. Shakespeare ; The naiad queen, by J. S. Dalrymple ; Caprice, by O. S. Leland ; Cool as a cucumber, by W. B. Jerrold ; Sudden thoughts, by T. E. Wilks ; Jumbo Jum. XIX. The cradle of liberty, by Capt. S. E. Glover ; A blighted being, by T. Taylor ; Little Toddlekins, by C. Matthews ; The lost ship, by T. Townsend ; A lover by proxy, by D. Bourcicault ; Maid with the milking pail, by J. B. Buckstone ; Country squire, by C. Dance ; Perplexing predicament, by C. Selby. XX. Fraud and its victims, by J. S. Coyne ; Dr. Dilworth, by J. Oxenford ; Out to nurse, by T. Williams ; Putnam, the iron son of 76, by N. H. Bannister ; The king and deserter, by J. M. Maddox ; A lucky hit, by H. Paul ; The dowager, by C. Matthews ; La Fiammina, by W. W. Clapp. XXI. A hard struggle, by W. Marston ; Gwinneth Vaughan, by M. Lemon ; The love knot, by J. S. Coyne ; Metamora, a burlesque, by J. Brougham ; Dreams of delusion, by J. P. Simpson ; The shaker lovers, by S. D. Johnson ; Ticklish times, by J. M. Morton ; Twenty minutes with a tiger. XXII. Miralda, or the justice of Tacon, by M. M. Ballou ; Heads or tails ? by J. P. Simpson ; A soldier's courtship, by J. Poole ; Lavater, or not a bad judge, by J. R. Planché ; The noble heart, by G. H. Lewes ; Coriolanus, by W. Shakespeare ; The winter's tale, by W. Shakespeare ; Servant's legacy, by J. Pilgrim.

Shelf. No.

SPENCER, W. V. continued.
XXIII. Eveleen Wilson, by J. Pilgrim ; Nick Whiffles, by Dr. J. H. Robinson ; The queen's heart ; Dying for love, by J. M. Morton ; The pirate's legacy, by C. H. Saunders ; An alarming sacrifice, by J. B. Buckstone ; The valet de sham, by C. Selby ; Nicholas Nickleby, by E. Stirling. XXIV. The last of the pigtails, by C. Selby ; King René's daughter, from the Danish of Henrik Herz ; The grotto nymph, by A. W. Thaxter ; The charcoal burner, by G. Almar ; Adelgitha, by M. G. Lewis ; A devilish good joke, by T. Higgie ; A twice told tale, by J. P. Wooler ; Pas de fascination, by J. S. Coyne.

SPRAGUE, P. Speeches and addresses. Boston, 1858. 8°. 882.3

SQUIER, E. G. Nicaragua ; its people, scenery, and monuments. Rev. ed. N. Y. 1860. 8°. 622.8

STANLEY, A. P. Life and correspondence of Thomas Arnold. 3d Am. fr. last Lond. ed. Boston, 1860. 2v. 12°. 587.10

STARK, C. Memoir and correspondence of Gen. John Stark. Concord, 1860. 8°. 522.11

STARS and the angels. Philadelphia, 1860. 12°. 148.35

STEDMAN, E. C. Poems, lyrical and idyllic. New York, 1860. 12°. 385.24
— The Prince's ball. New York, 1860. 12°. 376.5

STEVENS, A. History of methodism. New York, 1858. 2v. 12°. 114.3

STEWART, W. G. Lectures on the mountains. London, 1860. 2v. 12°. 907.1

STIGANT, W. A vision of Barbarossa. London, 1860. 12°. 374.14

STOPFORD, E. A. The religious revival in Belfast. 6th ed. Dublin, 1859. 8°. 113.10

STORIES from Italian writers with literal interlinear translation. 1st Am. ed. Phila. 1832. 16°. 1055.3

STOWE, H. B. Dred, a tale of the great Dismal swamp. London, 1856. 12°. 1785.15
— The minister's wooing. N. Y. 1859. 12°. . 495.1-5
— Uncle Tom's cabin. Boston, 1852. 2v. 12°. 1785.12

STREET, A. B. Woods and waters ; or the Saranacs and Racket. New York, 1860. 12°. . 638.13

STRICKLAND, A. The royal sisters. Boston, 1845. 18°. 487.16

SYMES, J. Principles of surgery. Lond. 1856. 8°. 153.26

TAYLOR, J. B. At home and abroad. New York, 1860. 12°. 688.14
— Poems of home and travel. Bost. 1855. 12°. 1395.3

TAYLOR, I. Ultimate civilization. Lond. 1860. 12°. 395.19

TEMPLETON, T. The adventures of my cousin Smooth. New York, 1855. 12°. 487.15

TENNENT, Sir J. E. Ceylon : an account of the island, physical, historical, and topographical. 4th ed. rev. London, 1860. 2v. 8°. 934.10

TENNEY, S. Geology, for teachers, etc. Philadelphia, 1860. 12°. 167.37

THACKERAY, W. M. The English humorists of the eighteenth century. N. Y. 1853. 12°. 1595.4
— The four Georges. New York, 1860. 12°. . 555.2
— Lovel the widower. New York, 1860. 8°. . 502.13
— The Virginians. New York, 1859. 8°. . . 502.8-11

THAT's it, or plain teaching. By the author of The reason why. London, 1860. 8°. . . . 186.26

THAYER, W. M. The bobbin boy. Bost. 1860. 16°. 527.20

THOMAS, C. W. Adventures on the west coast of Africa. New York, 1860. 12°. 697.20

THOREAU, H. D. Walden, or life in the woods. Boston, 1854. 16°. 1634.3

THORNBURY, W. Life in Spain. N. Y. 1860. 12°. 666.21

THREE nights in a lifetime. New York, 1845. 8°. 803.5

THÜMMEL, M. A. v. Poetische Schriften. Wien, 1792. sm. 16°. 2019.4

TIMBS, J. Anecdote biography. Lond. 1860. p.8°. 587.15
— Curiosities of science. 2d ser. Lond. 1860. 12°. 207.28
— School-days of eminent men. From London ed. Columbus, 1860. 12°. 557.15
— Stories of inventors and discoverers in science and the useful arts. Lond. 1860. 12°. 186.3
— - Same. New York, 1860. 12°. 187.26

TIMROD, H. Poems. Boston, 1860. 16°. 374.10

Shelf. No.

TOCQUEVILLE, A. C. H. de. The old regime and the revolution. Transl. by J. Bonner. New York, 1856. 12° 1006.4
— L'ancien régime de la revolution. Paris, 1856. 8° 2063.1
TODD, S. E. The young farmer's manual. New York, 1860. 12° 168.36
TOMLINSON, C. The dew-drop and the mist. London, n.d. 12° 168.42
TRELAWNY, E. J. Recollections of the last days of Shelley and Byron. Boston, 1858. 16° . 1595.3
TRENCH, R. C. Notes on the parables of our Lord. Condensed. New York, 1861. 12° . 1104.18
— The story of Justin Martyr. 4th ed. London, 1857. 18° 126.31
TROLLOPE, A. Barchester towers. New edition. London, 1860. 12° 485.17
— Castle Richmond. New York, 1860. 12° . . 486.8
— Doctor Thorne: a novel. N. York, 1858. 12°. 1785.4
— The Kelleys and the O'Kelleys. New York, 1860. 12° 486.1–4
— The three clerks. New York, 1860. 12° . .500.18–20
— The warden. New ed. London, 1860. 12°. 485.18
— The West Indies and the Spanish main. London, 1859. 12° 263.10
— — Same. New York, 1860. 12° 263.11
TROLLOPE, T. A. Life of Vittoria Colonna. New York, 1859. 18° 550.68
TUNER's guide, The. Boston, n.d. pp.72. 12° . 209.29
TUTHILL, L. C. The boarding-school girl. 9th ed. Boston, 1856. 16° 450.33
TYLER, W. S. Memoir of Rev. Henry Lobdell. Boston, 1859. 12° 536.15
TYNDALL, J. The glaciers of the Alps. London, 1860. 12° 665.4
— — Same. Boston, 1861. 8° 665.7
TYTLER, P. F., and Taylor, J. The history of Scotland. Adapted to tuition by Alex. Reid. 8th edition. Edinburgh, 1859. 12° . 998.6

ULLMANN, C. The sinlessness of Jesus. Transl. from 6th German ed. Edinb. 1858. p.8°. . 1104.5
UNITED States. Report of the select committee on the Harper's ferry invasion. Washington, 1860. 8° 292.10
UNITED States magazine. N. York, 1857. 2v. 8°. 870.3

VAIL, E. A. De la littérature et des hommes de lettres des États Unis d'Amérique. Paris, 1841. 8° 2063.2
VAUGHAN, R. Revolutions in English history. Vol. 1. New York, 1860. 8° 982.4
VIDOCQ, E. F. Memoirs, written by himself. Philadelphia, n.d. sm. 8° 1615.1
VINET, A. History of French literature in the eighteenth century. Transl. by Rev. J. Bryce. Edinburgh, 1854. 8° 394.3
VOGT, C. Studien zur gegenwärtigen Lage Europas. Genf u. Bern, 1859. 8° 1032.10

WALLACE-DUNLOP, M., and R. How we spent the autumn, or wanderings in Brittany. London, 1860. 12° 665.3
WALTHAM: a novel. Philadelphia, 1833. 12° . . 479.7
WALTON, I. Lives. Account of the author by Thomas Zouch. New edition. Boston, 1860. 8° 1595.6
WARD, M. Les harems du nouveau monde, vie des femmes chez les Mormons. Trad. par B. H. Révoil. Paris, 1856. 16° 2063.8
WARDEN, R. B. A familiar view of man and law. Columbus, 1860. 8° 882.1
WARE, W. Palmyra. Edinburgh, 1839. 8° . . . 1780.1
WARNER, S., and A. B. Say and Seal. Philadelphia, 1860. 2v. 12° 774.1–10
WARREN, J. Written music remodelled and invested with the simplicity of an exact science. Boston, 1860. 4° 204.10

WARREN, J. C. Life. Compiled by Edward Warren, M.D. Boston, 1860. 2v. 8° 522.9
WARREN, S. The merchant's clerk, and other tales. New York, 1856. 12° 479.5
WAS hat Preussen gesagt, gethan? Politik gegenüber œsterreich und Frankreich. Leipzig, 1859. 8° 1032.9
WASHINGTON, E. K. Echoes from Europe. Philadelphia, 1860. 8° 665.6
WATER cure in America. New York, 1848. 12° . 158.38
WAYLAND, F. Intellectual philosophy. Boston, 1854. 12° 1173.3
WELD, C. R. Two months in the Highlands, Orcadia, and Skye. London, 1860. 8° . . 645.16
WELLS, D. A. Annual of scientific discovery for 1860. Boston, 1860. 12° . . . . . . v.11 of 159.1
WESTCOTT, B. F. Introduction to the study of the Gospels. Cambridge, 1860. 12° 1104.11
WETHERILL, C. M. The manufacture of vinegar. Philadelphia, 1860. 12° 185.2
WHARTON, G., and P. The queens of society. London, n.d. 2v. 8° 542.15
— — Same. New York, 1860. 12° 542.17
— The wits and beaux of society. London, n.d. 2v. 8° 555.1
WHEAT and tares. New York, 1860. 12° 486.9
WHITE, J. The eighteen christian centuries. From Edinburgh ed. Phila. 1859. 12° . . . 115.16
WHITE, W. All round the wrekin. London, 1860. 12° 645.17
WHITMAN, S. H. Edgar A. Poe and his critics. New York, 1860. 12° 374.11
WHITTIER, J. G. Home ballads. Bost. 1860. 12°. 376.6
WIFE's domain, The. By Philothalos. London, 1860. 12° 158.41
WILLETT, W. M. Life and times of Herod the Great. Philadelphia, 1860. 12° 557.16
WILLIAMS, F. S. Wonders of the heavens. London, 1852. 12° 207.27
WILLIAMS, J. B. Memoirs of Rev. Matthew Henry. 3d ed. London, 1829. 12° 589.16
WILLMOTT, R. A. Pleasures, objects, and advantages of literature. New ed. Lond. 1857. 12°. 395.22
WILLS, A. Wanderings among the high Alps. London, 1856. p.8° 665.2
WILLS, W. H. Old leaves, gathered from household words. New York, 1860. 12° 903.19
WILSON, G. The five senses. Phila. 1840. 12° . 904.21
WINSLOW, F. On obscure diseases of the brain. London, 1860. 8° 162.3
WISEMAN, N., card. Recollections of the last four popes, and of Rome in their times. Boston, 1858. 12° 1545.2
WOMEN of worth. New York, 1860. 12° 550.66
WOOD, G. B. Treatise on therapeutics and pharmacology. Philadelphia, 1856. 2v. 8° . . 153.21
WOOD, Mrs. H. Danesbury house. New York, 1860. 12° 487.17
WOOD, J. G. Illustrated natural history. London, n.d. 8° 171.6
WOODBURY, I. B. Elements of musical composition and thorough bass. Boston, n.d. 12°. 209.31
WOOLSEY, T. D. Introduction to the study of international law. Boston, 1860. 12° . . . 299.14
WRAXALL, L. Life in the sea. Lond. 1860. 8° . 176.25
WROTTESLEY, J., lord. Thoughts on government and legislation. London, 1860. p.8° . . . 133.18
WYLIE, Mrs. M. The gospel in Burmah. New York, 1860. 12° 114.11
WYNTER, A. Curiosities of civilization. London, 1860. 12° 893.12
YANKEE notions. Boston, 1858. 12° 438.15
YONGE, C. M. Beechcroft. New York, 1855. 12°. 1785.7
— The castle-builders. New York, 1855. 12° . 1785.6
— Friarswood post-office. N. Y. 1860. 18° . .497.20–22
YOUATT, W. The pig. Rewritten by S. Sidney. London, 1860. 12° 176.23
YOUNG lady's book, The. London, n.d. p.8° . 853.15

Shelf. No.

YOUNG men of the bible. A series of lectures by distinguished clergymen. Boston, 1859. 12° 544.21

ZINGERLE, I., and J. Kinder-und Hausmärchen aus Süddeutschland. Regensburg, 1854. 12° 2016.11

Shelf. No.

ZINGERLE, I. and J. continued.
— Kinder-und Hausmärchen. Innsbruck, 1852. sm.4° 2016.14
ZSCHOKKE, J. H. D. Histoire de la nation suisse. Arau, 1832. 16° 2065.14
— The sleep-walker. A tale from the German. Boston, 1842. 18° 468.16

FOURTH SUPPLEMENT TO THE INDEX.

CONTAINING A LIST OF THE BOOKS PLACED IN THE LOWER HALL, FROM DECEMBER 13, 1860,
TO NOVEMBER 1, 1861.

Shelf. No.

ABBOTT, J. Stories of Rainbow and Lucky. Up the river. New York, 1861. 16° 747.11

ABBOTT, J. S. C. Italy, from the earliest period to the present day. New York, [1860]. 8° . 917.10

ABEL, C. D. Elementary principles of machinery. London, 1860. 16° 1169.37

ABERDEEN (Geo.) Earl of. See Gordon, Geo.

ABOUT, E. F. V. Rome of to-day. N. Y. 1861. 12°. 665.10

ADAMS, F. C. An outcast; or virtue and faith. New York, 1861. 12° 486.18

ADAMS, N. Agnes and the little key. 5th ed. Boston, 1859. 12° 477.1

— Evenings with the doctrines. Bost. 1861. 12°. 113.14

— The sable cloud, a southern tale. Boston, 1861. 16° 486.20

ADAMS, W. T. Try again, a story. Boston, 1861. 16° 747.12

ADDISON, J. Sir Roger De Coverley. By the Spectator. Notes by W. H. Wills. London, 1852. p.8° 1655.22

ADVENTURES with animals. Zoological notes and anecdotes. London, n.d. 12° 176.35

AGASSIZ, L. J. R. Contributions to the natural history of the United States of America. Vol. III. Boston, 1860. 4° 170.2

AGUILAR, G. Home influence. Leipzig, 1859. 24°. 410.1

— The mother's recompense. Leipzig, 1859. 24°. 410.2

AIMWELL stories. See Simonds, W.

AINSWORTH, W. H. The flitch of bacon. Leipzig, 1854. 24° 410.3

— Jack Sheppard. Leipzig, 1846. 24° 720.1

— The Lancashire witches, Leipzig, 1849. 24°. 410.4

— Mervyn Clitheroe. Leipzig, 1858. 24° . . . 410.5

— Ovingdean grange. Leipzig, 1860. 24° . . . 720.2

— Saint James's, or the court of Queen Anne. Leipzig, 1844. 24° 410.6

— The spendthrift. Leipzig, 1856. 24° 410.7

— The star-chamber. Leipzig, 1854. 24° 410.8

— Windsor Castle. Leipzig, 1844. 24° 410.9

AIRD, T. The old bachelor in the old Scottish village. 2d ed. Edinburgh, 1857. 12° . . 477.9

AKENSIDE, M. Poetical works. Life by Rev. A. Dyce. Boston, 1854. 18° 1316.1

ALEXANDER, J. W. Forty years' familiar letters. Ed. by J. Hall. New York, 1860. 2v. 8° . 577.10

ALLAN, J. McG. The intellectual severance of men and women. London, 1860. 16° . . . 1159.16

ALLEN, J. Life of [Thomas Cochrane], the Earl of Dundonald. London, 1861. 16° 579.18

ALLEN, J. H. Hebrew men and times. Boston, 1861. 12° 113.18

ALLEN, S. M. Fibrilia: a practical and economical substitute for cotton. Bost. 1861. 12°. 166.33

ANDERSON, W. Practical mercantile correspondence. 11th ed. London, 1860. 12° 1159.7

ARAGO, F. D. J. History of my youth. Transl. by Rev. B. Powell. London, 1855. p.8° . . . 1655.17

AREY, H. W. Girard college and its founder. Philadelphia, 1854. 12° 537.29

ARNOLD, M. On translating Homer. London, 1861. p.8° 1325.8

— Popular education of France. London, 1861. 8° 122.25

ATKINSON, J. C. Sketches in natural history. London, 1861. 12° 176.29

Shelf. No.

ATKINSON, T. W. Travels in the regions of the upper and lower Amoor. N. Y. 1860. 8° . 682.8

AUGUSTINUS, A. St. Confessions. Edited by W. G. T. Shedd. Andover, 1860. 12° 1115.19

AULDJO, J. Ascent to the summit of Mont Blanc, in Aug. 1827. 3d ed. London, 1856. p.8° . 1655.1

BABRIUS. Fables. Transl. from the text of Sir G. C. Lewis, by Rev. J. Davies. London, 1860. 16° 396.13

BACHI, P. Grammar of the Italian language. New ed. Boston, 1838. 12° 2048.1

— Raccolta di favole morali. Boston, 1835. 12°. 2049.6

— Scelta di prose italiane. Cambridge, 1828. 8°. 2048.2

BAINE, A. C. Divine faith and natural reason. Baltimore, 1861. 12° 1115.3

BAINES, E. Visit to the Vaudois of Piedmont. London, 1858. p.8° 1655.7

BALLANTYNE, R. M. Hudson's Bay; or, life in the wilds of N. America. Bost., 1859. 16°. 747.25

BALZAC, H. de. The alchemist. Transl. by O. W. Wight and F. B. Goodrich. New York, 1861. 12° 485.21

BARNARD, G. Landscape painting in water-colours. London, 1861. 8° 202.13

BARNARD, J. G. Sea-coast defence. New York, 1861. 8° 205.18

BARROW, J. Tour on the continent by rail and road, in Germany, Austria, etc. London, 1859. p.8° 1655.2

BAUSMAN, B. Sinai and Zion; or, a pilgrimage through the wilderness to the land of promise. Philadelphia, 1861. 12° 688.16

BEATON, P. Creoles and coolies; or five years in Mauritius. London, 1859. 12° 997.6

BEATTIE, J. Poetical works. Memoir by Rev. A. Dyce. Boston, 1854. 18° 1316.2

BÉDARRIDE, J. Les Juifs en France, en Italie, et en Espagne. 2ème éd. Paris, 1861. 8° . . 2063.7

BECK, T. R. and J. Medical jurisprudence. 11th ed. Revised by C. R. Gilman. Philadelphia, 1860. 2v. 8° 162.7

BEDE, C. Glencreggan; or, a Highland home in Cantire. London, 1861. 2v. 8° 656.5

BELISLE, D. W. History of Independence hall. Philadelphia, 1859. 12° 216.14

BELL, A. N. A knowledge of living things. New York, 1860. 12° 176.33

BENTON, J. G. Course of instruction in ordnance and gunnery. New York, 1861. 8° 204.14

BERRIMAN, M. W. The militiaman's manual. 2d ed. New York, 1861. 12° 1208.1

BESELER, W. Das deutsche Interesse in der italienischen Frage. Leipzig, 1859. 60 pp. 8°. 2025.10

BIBLE. Notes on the Gospels. Matthew. By J. H. Morison. 2d ed. Boston, 1861. 12° . . 1115.17

BICKERSTETH, E. H. The Rock of ages. Introd. by F. D. Huntington. Boston, 1860. 12° . 1115.9

BIGELOW, J. Expositions of rational medicine. Prefixed, The paradise of doctors, a fable. Boston, 1858. 69 pp. 12° 157.38

BLACKSTONE, W. Commentaries on the laws of England. With notes, Field's analysis, and a life of the author, by Geo. Sharswood. Philadelphia, 1860. 4v. in 2. 8° . . 132.18

Shelf. No.

BLAIKIE, A. View of the sects in the United States. 2d ed. Boston, 1855. 12° 1115.4
— Position of the schools of Presbyterians in the United States. Bost. 1860. 59 pp. 16°. 1115.11
BOARDMAN, A. A defence of phrenology. New York [1847]. 12° 1158.10
BODENSTEDT, F. *See* Wagner, F.
BOHN, H. G. Index verborum to Bohn's Dictionary of Latin quotations. London, 1860. 12°. 1158.2
— Pictorial hand-book of modern geography. London, 1861. p.8° 854.11
BOOK (The) and its story. By L. N. R. New York, 1861. 12° 1115.8
BOTTA, A. C. L. Hand-book of universal literature. New York, 1860. 12° 386.5
BOUVIER, H. M. Familiar astronomy. Philadelphia, 1857. 8° 143.15
BOUVIER, J. Institutes of American law. Philadelphia. New ed. 1858. 4v. 8° 131.1
BOWDITCH, W. R. On coal-gas. London, 1860. 68 pp. 8° 205.21
BOWMAN, A. Bear-hunters of the Rocky Mountains. London, 1861. 16° 747.14
BOYD, A. K. P. Recreations of a country parson. 2d ser. Boston, 1861. 12° 883.2-3
BRADSHAW. Guide through Paris and its environs. London, n.d. 84 pp. 24° 1659.1
— Hand-book for Belgium and the Rhine. London, n.d. 24° 1659.3
— Hand-book to France. London, n.d. 24° . 1659.2
— Hand-book to Switzerland and the Tyrol. London, n.d. 24° 1659.4
BRÉHAUT, T. C. Cordon training of fruit trees. London, 1860. 12° 168.43
BREMER, F. Life in the old world. Transl. by M. Howitt. Philadelphia, [1861.] 2v. 12°. 665.9
— Two years in Switzerland and Italy. Transl. by M. Howitt. London, 1861. 2v. 12° . . 665.14
BRESSLAU, M. H. Compendious Hebrew grammar. London, 1855. 84 pp. 16° 1169.5
— Hebrew and English dictionary, London, 1855-6. 2v. 16° 1169.5
BRIZEUX, J. A. P. Œuvres complètes. Paris, 1861. 2v. 12° 2065.28
Contents. — Vol. I. Marie ; Les Bretons ; La harpe d'Armorique ; Sagesse de Bretagne. II. La fleur d'or ; Histoires poétiques ; Cycle ; Poétique nouvelle.
BROCK, W. Biographical sketch of Sir Henry Havelock. Leipzig, 1858. 24° 720.3
BRONTË, C. Jane Eyre. Leipzig, 1850. 24° . . 410.10
— The professor. Leipzig, 1857. 24° 410.11
— Shirley. Leipzig, 1849. 24° 410.12
— Villette. Leipzig, 1853. 24° 410.13
BRONTË, E. and A. Wuthering Heights and Agnes Grey. Leipzig, 1851. 24° 410.14
BROOKS, S. The Russians of the South. London, 1855. p.8° 1655.6
— The silver cord. New York, 1861. 8° 502.16
BROOKS, S. H. On the erection of dwelling-houses. London, 1860. 16° 1169.42
BROTHERS, S. Wool and woollen manufactures of Great Britain. London, 1859. 8° 193.1
BROUGHAM, H. *lord.* England and France under the House of Lancaster. New ed. London, 1861. 8° 903.1
BROWN, J. Horæ subsecivæ. [Reviews and essays.] 2d ser. Edinburgh, 1861. 12°. v.2 of 894.13
BUCKE, C. The book of human character. London, 1837. 2v. 16° 1899.1
BUCKINGHAM, *Duke of. See* Grenville, R. P. T. N. B. C.
BUCKLE, H. T. History of civilization in England. Vol. II. London, 1861. 8° 942.1
BUNSEN, C. C. J. Egypt's place in universal history. Transl. from the German by C. H. Cottrell. V. III-IV. Lond. 1859-60. 2v. 8°. 954.4
BUNYAN, J. The pilgrim's progress. Leipzig, 1855. 24° 410.15
BURNELL, G. R. Rudiments of hydraulic engineering. Part I.-II. London, 1858. 10° . . 1159.1

BURNS, R. Poetical works. Leipzig, 1845. 24°. 410.16
BUSH wanderings of a naturalist. London, 1861. 16° 176.31
BUSHNELL, H. Christian nurture. New York, 1861. 12° 113.19
BUSINESS life: the experience of a London tradesman. 2d ed. London, 1861. 16° 1138.3
BUTLER, S. Poetical works. Boston, 1857. 2v. 18° 1316.3
Contents. — Vol. I. Memoir by Rev. J. Mitford ; Hudibras. II. Miscellaneous poems.
BUTT, I. The history of Italy, from the abdication of Napoleon I. London, 1860. 2v. 8°. 914.3
BYRON, G. G. N. *lord.* Works. Leipzig, 1842. 5v. 24° 720.1
Contents. — Vol. I. Don Juan. II. Childe Harold's pilgrimage ; The Giaour ; The Corsair ; Lara ; The siege of Corinth ; Parisina ; The prisoner of Chillon ; Mazeppa ; Beppo. III. The bride of Abydos ; The island ; Hours of idleness ; English bards and Scotch reviewers ; The age of bronze ; Hints from Horace ; The curse of Minerva ; The waltz ; The lament of Tasso ; Ode on Venice ; The prophecy of Dante ; Ode to Napoleon Buonaparte ; Monody on the death of Sheridan ; The dream ; The vision of judgment ; The Morgante Maggiore of Pulci ; Francesca of Rimini ; The blues. IV. Hebrew melodies ; Domestic pieces ; Manfred ; Cain ; The deformed transformed ; Heaven and earth. V. Marino Faliero, doge of Venice ; The two Foscari ; Sardanapalus ; Werner, or the inheritance ; Appendix ; A fragment ; Parliamentary speeches.
CALEF, R. and Mather, C. Salem witchcraft. Notes by S. P. Fowler. Salem, 1861. 12°. 228.17
CALKINS, N. A. Primary object lessons. New York, 1861. 16° 1133.4
CAMPAN, J. L. H. Genet. Lettres de deux amies. Paris, 1825. 16° 2065.34
CAMPBELL, J. F. Popular tales of the West Highlands. Edinburgh, 1860. 2v. 12° . . 479.13
CAMPBELL, T. Poetical works. Notes by Rev. W. A. Hill. Boston, 1860. 18° 1316.4
CAMPE, J. H. Die Entdeckung von Amerika. 12te Aufl. Braunschweig, 1830. 3v. 18° . . 2019.10
CAMPIN, F. Hand-turning. London, 1861. 16°. 185.21
CARLIER, A. Le mariage aux États-Unis. Paris, 1860. 12° 2065.18
CARLYLE, A. Autobiography. Boston, 1861. 8°. 578.20
CARLYLE, T. The French revolution. Leipzig, 1851. 3v. 24° 410.17
— History of Frederick the Great. Leipzig, 1858. 5v. in 3. 24° 410.18
CARNEGIE, G. M. *countess of Northesk.* The sheltering vine. Selections [for devotion]. Introd. by R. C. Trench. Lond. 1861. 12°. 1115.12
CASWALL, H. The American church and the American union. London, 1861. 12° . . . 1116.3
CATLIN, G. The breath of life; or, mal-respiration. New York, 1861. 76 pp. 8° 154.4
CAZALET, W. W. The human voice. New York, 1860. 46 pp. 12° 1157.1
CHALLAMEL, J. B. M. A. Histoire anecdotique de la Fronde, 1643 à 1653. Paris, 1860. 12°. 2065.24
CHAMBERS, R. Cyclopædia of English literature. Philadelphia, 1859, 60. 2v. 8° 392.8
CHANNING, W. E. Poems. Bost. 1843, 47. 2v. 12°. 1325.1
CHAPIN, E. H. Living words. Introductory letter by Rev. T. S. King. Boston, 1860. 12°. 113.13
CHARLESWORTH, M. L. England's yeomen. London, 1861. 16° 486.13
— Same. New York, 1861. 12° 495.14
CHATTERTON, *Lady* G. Memorials, personal and historical of admiral lord Gambier. London, 1861. 2v. 8° 577.6
CHATTERTON, T. Poetical works. Notices of his life. Boston, 1857. 2v. 18° 1316.5
CHILD, F. J. English and Scottish ballads. Boston, 1857-1859. 8v. 18° 1316.6
Contents. — Vol. I. Romances of chivalry, and legends of the popular heroes of England ; Ballads of fairies, elves, magic, and ghosts. II.-IV. Love ballads. V. Robin Hood ballads. VI. Border and historical ballads. VII. Historical ballads. VIII. Miscellaneous ballads ; General index.

Shelf. No.

CHURCHILL, C. Poetical works. Notes and life by W. Tooke. Boston, 1854. 3v. 18° . . 1316.7

Contents. — Vol. I. Life ; Rosciad; Apology to the Critical reviewers ; Night ; Prophecy of famine; Epistle to Hogarth. II. The duellist; Gotham; The author; The conference. II. III. The ghost.

CLARK, R. W. The African slave-trade. Boston, [1860.] 16° 2109.5

CLARKE, H. Hand book of comparative philology. London, 1859. 16° 1169.17

— Dictionary of the English language. London, 1855. 16° 1169.4

— Grammar of the English tongue. 2d ed. London, 1859. 18° 1169.12

CLEVELAND, C. D. Compendium of classical literature. Philadelphia, 1861. 12° . . . 386.4

COCHIN, J. D. M. Manuel des salles d'asile. 5ème éd. Paris, 1857. 8° 2063.15

COCKAYNE, T. O. Life of marshal Turenne. London, 1859. p 8° 1655.14

COLERIDGE, S. T. Poems. Edited by D. and S. Coleridge. Leipzig, 1860. 24° 410.19

— Poetical and dramatic works, with a memoir. Boston, 1854. 3v. 18° 1316.8

Contents. — Vol. I. Memoir of the author ; Poems written in youth ; The ancient mariner ; Christabel; Sibylline leaves. II. Sibylline leaves; Poems written in later life ; Remorse, a tragedy ; Zapolya, a Christmas tale. III. The Piccolomini, or, the first part of Wallenstein; The death of Wallenstein.

COLLINS, W. Wilkie. After dark [tales]. Leipzig, 1856. 24° 410.20

— The crossed path. Philadelphia, n.d. 12° . 752.16

— Hide and seek. Leipzig, 1856. 2v. 24° . . 720.5

— A plot in private life, and other tales. Leipzig, 1859. 24° 410.21

— The woman in white. Leipz. 1860. 2v. in 1. 24°. 410.22

COLLINS, William. Poetical works. Bost. 1859. 18° 1316.9

COMER, G. N. Book-keeping rationalized. Boston, 1861. 12° 1133.5–6

— Manual of practical navigation. Boston, 1860. 8° 143.14

CONNOLLY, T. W. J. The romance of the ranks. London, 1859. 2v. 12° 468.20

COOK, E. Poems. New ed. London, 1861. 16° . 396.14

COOKE, G. W. Conquest and colonisation in North Africa. Edinburgh, 1860. 12° . . . 917.12

COOKE, M. C. The seven sisters of sleep ; history of seven prevailing narcotics. London, n.d. 12° 158.44

CORÉ, F. Guide commercial des constructeurs-mécaniciens. Paris, 1860. 8° 2063.14

CORNWALL: its mines and miners. London, 1857. p.8° 1655.23

CORNWALLIS, K. The prince of Wales in America. New York, 1860. 12° 638.15

COTSELL, G. Treatise on ships' anchors. London, 1856. 16° 1169.32

COWPER, W. Poetical works. Boston, 1859. 3v. 18° 1316.10

Contents, as on p. 43 of the catalogue printed 1859. Shelf. No. 358.22.

CRAIK, G. L. Outlines of the history of the English language. 3d ed. London, 1859. 12° . 1158.3

— Spenser, and his poetry. London, 1845. 18° . 1819.2

CRICKET field (The). Boston, 1859. 12° . . . 1205.1

CROKER, T. C. A walk from London to Fulham. London, 1860. 12° 645.19

CROSWELL, W. Poems, sacred and secular. Ed. by A. C. Coxe. Boston, 1861. 16° . . . 450.36

CROWE, C. Susan Hopley. London, 1855. 12° . 486.15

CURMER, L. Tombeau de Napoléon Ier. Paris, 1853. 12° 2065.25

CURRY, J. P. Volunteers' camp and field book. New York, 1861. 18° 1199.10

CURTIS, G. W. Trumps : a novel. New York, 1861. 12° 784.13

CUST, *Hon. Lady.* The invalid's own book. 2d ed. London, 1856. 16° 185.14

CUSTINE, A. *marq.* de. Russia. Lond. 1856. p.8°. 1655.5

Shelf. No.

DALTON, W. Lost in Ceylon. London, 1861. 12°. 747.7

— The white elephant. New York, 1860. 16° . 747.13

D'ARBLAY, *Mme.* F. B. Evelina. Leipz. 1850. 24°. 410.23

DAVEY, M. B. Icnusa ; or reminiscences of a two years' residence in the island of Sardinia. Bath, n.d. 12° 665.11

DAVIS, N. Carthage and her remains. N. York, 1861. 8° 942.6

DAWSON, H. B. Battles of the United States by sea and land. Illustrated by A. Chappel. New York, [1858.] 2v. 4° 221.1

DEAN, A. Commercial law for business men. New York, 1861. 8° 132.15

DE CRESSY. By the author of "Still waters." Leipzig, 1857. 24° 720.6

DEMPSEY, G. D. Locomotive engine in all its phases. 2d ed. London, 1857. 16° . . . 1169.31

DE FOE, D. Robinson Crusoe. Leipz. 1845. 24°. 410.24

DE QUINCEY, T. Letters on self-education. London, n.d. 12° 386.8

DICEY, E. Rome in 1860. Cambridge, 1861. 12°. 917.14

DICKENS, C. All the year round. Vols. 2-4. London, 1860-61. 2v. 8° 851.1

— American notes. Leipzig, 1842. 24° 410.25

— Battle of life ; and The haunted man. Leipzig, 1856. 24° 720.7

— Bleak house. Leipzig, 1852. 2v. 24° 410.26

— A christmas carol in prose. The chimes. The cricket on the hearth. Leipzig, 1846. 24°. 410.27

— David Copperfield. Leipzig, 1849. 2v. 24°. 410.28

— Dombey and son. Leipzig, 1847, 48. 2v. 24°. 410.29

— Great expectations. Philadelphia [1861]. 12°. 482.2

— Hard times. Leipzig, 1854. 24° 410.30

— Hunted down ; [and] The uncommercial traveller. Leipzig, 1860. 24° 410.31

— Little Dorrit. Leipzig, 1856, 57. 2v. 24° . . 410.32

— Martin Chuzzlewit. Leipzig, 1844. 2v. 24°. 410.33

— Master Humphrey's clock. Leipzig, 1846. 2v. 24° 410.34

— A message from the sea ; and The uncommercial traveller. Philadelphia, n.d. 8°. 482.1

— Nicholas Nickleby. Leipzig, 1843. 2v. 24°. 410.35

— - Same. New York, 1861. 4v. 12° 483.3

— Oliver Twist. Leipzig, 1843. 24° 410.36

— - Same. N. York, 1861. Vols. 1-2. 12° . . 483.2

— Pickwick papers. N. York, 1861. 4v. 12° . . 483.1

— - Same. Leipzig, 1842. 2v. 24° 720.8

— Pictures from Italy. Leipzig, 1846. 24° . . 720.9

— Sketches. Leipzig, 1843. 24° 720.10

— A tale of two cities. Leipzig, 1859. 24° . . 720.11

DICTIONARY of contemporary biography. London, 1861. 8° 555.4

DICTIONARY of daily wants. London, 1861. 8° . 185.10

DISRAELI, B. Alroy. New ed. London, 1859. 12°. 752.15

— - Same. Leipzig, 1846. 24° 410.37

— Coningsby. Leipzig, 1844. 24° 410.38

— Contarini Fleming. Leipzig, 1846. 24° . . 720.12

— Henrietta Temple. Leipzig, 1859. 24° . . . 410.39

— Ixion in heaven. The infernal marriage. Popanilla. Count Alarcos. New ed. London, 1859. 12° 752.14

— Sybil. Leipzig, 1845. 24° 720.13

— Tancred. Leipzig, 1847. 24° 720.14

— Venetia. Leipzig, 1858. 24° 410.40

— Vivian Grey. Leipzig, 1859. 24° 410.41

— The young duke. New ed. Lond. 1859. 12°. 752.13

DIXON, W. H. Personal history of Lord Bacon. Boston, 1861. 12° 587.21

DODDS, J. Fifty years' struggle of the Scottish covenanters, 1638-88. 2d ed. Edinb. 1860. 16°. 2109.2

DONNE, J. Poetical works, with a memoir [by Walton]. Boston, 1855. 18° 1316.11

DOROTHY. By the author of "Still waters." Leipzig, 1857. 24° 410.42

DRAYSON, *Capt.* Military surveying and sketching. London, 1861. 16° 205.2

DRURY, A. H. Misrepresentation ; a novel. 2v. Lond. 1859. 12° 485.20

DRYDEN, J. Poetical works. Bost. 1859. 5v. 18°. 1316.12

Contents, as on p. 50 of the catalogue printed, 1859. Shelf No. 319.8.

Shelf. No.

DU CHAILLU, P. B. Explorations and adventures in equatorial Africa. London, 1861. 8°. . 683.14

DUMAS, A. The Garibaldians in Sicily. Translated by E. Routledge. London, 1861. 16°. 917.15

— Memoirs of a maitre d'armes ; or 18 months at St. Petersburg. Transl. by the marq. of Ormonde. London, 1857. p.8° 1655.22

DURRIEU, X. The present state of Morocco. London, 1854. p.8° 1655.10

DUSSIEUX, L. E. Les grand faits de l'histoire de France racontés par les contemporains. T. II. Le moyen âge. Paris, 1860. 8° . . . 2063.23

DWIGHT, B. W. Modern philology. 2d ed. New York, 1860. 8° 392.6

EAMES, J. A. Another budget ; or things which I saw in the East. Boston, 1855. 12° . . . 688.17

EDEN, E. Easton and its inhabitants. London, 1860. 16° 500.17

EDERSHEIM, A. History of the Jewish nation. 2d ed. Edinburgh, 1857. 12° 945.4

EDWARDS, S. The Russians at home. London, 1861. 8° 928.15

ELLIS, J. The avoidable causes of disease, insanity, and deformity. New York, 1860. 12°. 154.5

ELWES, A. Dictionary of the Italian, English, and French languages. Lond. 1855. 3v. 16°. 1169.11

— Dictionary of the Spanish and English languages. London, 1854. 16° 1169.1

— French-English dictionary. London, 1854-55. 2v. 16° 1169.7

— Grammar of the Italian language. 2d ed. London, 1854. 16° 1169.19

— Grammar of the Spanish language. London, 1852. 16° 1169.15

EMERSON, R. W. The conduct of life. Boston, 1860. 12° 883.9

EMMONS, N. Works. Ed. by J. Ide. [Life by E. A. Park.] Boston, 1842. 4v. 8° 1082.5

ENFANS studieux (Les) qui se sont distingués. 8me éd. Paris, 1824. 32° 2069.2

ÉTAT de l'Europe à la fin de 1860. Paris, 1861. 8°. 2063.22

EVANS, D. M. Facts, failures, and frauds. London 1859. 12° 133.22

EVANS, M. J. Adam Bede. Leipzig, 1859. 24°. 410.43

— Mill on the Floss. Leipzig, 1860. 24° . . 410.44

— Scenes of clerical life. Leipzig, 1859. 24°. 410.45

— Silas Marner. New York, 1861. 12° . . . 506.22

EVOLUTIONS of the line as practised by the Austrian infantry. Translated by Lieut. C. M. Wilcox. New York, 1860. 12° 205.17

EVOLUTIONS of field batteries of artillery. Tr. from the French by Maj. R. Anderson. New York, 1860. 24° 1199.18

FAIRBAIRN, W. Iron ; its history, properties, and processes of manufacture. Edinburgh, 1861. 8° 185.16

— Useful information for engineers. 2d series. London, 1860. 12° 185.5

FALCONER, W. Poetical works. Life by Rev. J. Mitford, Boston, 1854. 18° 1316.13

FAMOUS boys ; and how they became great men. New York, 1861. 16° 555.8

FARADAY, M. Chemical history of a candle. Ed. by Wm. Crookes. London, 1861. 12° . . 185.19

FARRAR, A. S. Science in theology ; Sermons. Philadelphia, 1860. 12° 1115.20

FARRAR, F. W. Essay on the origin of language. London, 1860. 16° 395.24 1159.5

FEIGE, E. Hebe, eine Sammlung von Erzähluungen, Gedichten, u. s. w. Berlin, n.d. sm.4°. 2026.2

FERGUSON, R. Swiss men and Swiss mountains. London, 1854. p.8° 1655.1

FEUGÈRE, L. J. Les femmes poëtes au XVIe siècle. Paris, 1860. 8° 2063.10

FIBRILIA. See Allen, S. M.

FIELD, T. W. Pear culture. N. York, 1858. 12°. 1176.1

FIELDING, H. Tom Jones. Leipz. 1844. 2v. 24°. 720.15

FIELDING, N. What to sketch with. London, n.d. 12° 1159.11

Shelf. No.

FIGUIER, G. L. L'année scientifique et industrielle. Paris, 1861. 12° 2065.29

FIRST patient (The) : a story, written in aid of the fair for the "Channing Home." Boston, 1859. 12° 2109.7

FISHER, S. W. The three great temptations of young men. Cincinnati, 1852. 12° 1115.7

FLETCHER, Mrs. The three historics. Philadelphia, 1834. 16° 450.35

FLINT, T. George Mason, the young backwoodsman. Boston, 1829. 12° 468.18

FORBES, C. S. Iceland : its volcanoes, geysers, and glaciers. London, 1860. p.8° 695.14

— The campaign of Garibaldi in the Two Sicilies. Edinburgh, 1861. 12° 917.11

FORESTER, T. Rambles in Norway. London, 1855. p.8° 1655.4

FORSTER, J. Daniel DeFoe and Charles Churchill. London, 1855. p.8° 1655.16

— Debates on the grand remonstrance, 1641, with an essay on freedom under the Plantagenets and Tudors. London, 1860. 12° . 113.11

— Oliver Cromwell ; Daniel De Foe ; Sir Richard Steele ; Charles Churchill ; Samuel Foote. Biographical essays. 3d ed. London, 1860. 12° 577.9

FOWLER, F. Texts for talkers. London, 1860. 12°. 395.25

FRAMPTON, L. C. Lives and martyrdom of the apostles, etc. London, 1860. 16° 1159.12

FRASER, J. Handy-book of patent and copyright law. London, 1860. 12° 133.20

FREER, M. W. Henry IV. and Marie de Medici. London, 1861. 2v. 12° 614.3

FREESE, J. H. Everybody's book. London, 1860. 8° 883.8

FRENCH and English phrase-book. Lond. 1861. 16°. 1169.10

FRENCH, G. J. The life and times of Samuel Crompton. 2d ed. Manchester, 1860. 12°. 587.22

FRENEAU, P. Poems. London, 1861. 12° . . . 1325.9

FRISI, P. Treatise on rivers and torrents, [and] an essay on canals. Tr. by J. Garstin. New ed. London, 1861. 16° 1169.54

FRISWELL, H. Footsteps to fame. Lond. 1861. 12°. 185.18

FROUDE, J. A. History of England. Vols. V.-VI. London, 1860. 2v. 8° 984.2

FULLERTON, Lady G. Ellen Middleton. Leipzig, 1846. 24° 410.46

— Grantley manor. Leipzig, 1847. 24° . . . 410.47

— Lady-bird. Leipzig, 1853. 24° 410.48

FYFE, J. H. The triumphs of invention and discovery. London, 1861. 12° 185.7

GALT, J. Annals of the parish. Phila. 1821. 12°. 477.6

GALTON, F. Vacation tourist and notes of travel in 1860. Cambridge, 1861. 8° 664.2

GAMES of skill, and conjuring. London, 1861. 16°. 185.13

GANOT, A. Cours de physique. Paris, 1859. 12°. 2065.17

— Natural philosophy, for schools and academies. Edited by W. G. Peck. New York, 1860. 12° 148.45

GARDINER, M. Country quarters. Leipzig, 1850. 24° 410.49

— Marmaduke Herbert ; or, the fatal error. Leipzig, 1847. 24° 410.50

— Memoirs of a femme de chambre. Leipzig, 1846. 24° 410.51

— Meredith. Leipzig, 1843. 24° 410.52

GARDNER, D. Institutes of international law. New York, 1860. 8° 132.16

GARDNER, J. Household medicine. London, 1861. 8° 162.8

GARRATT, A. C. Electro-physiology and electro-therapeutics. 2d ed. Boston, 1861. 8° . . 154.3

GARRATT, G. Marvels and mysteries of instinct. 2d ed. London, 1857. 16° 176.34

GASKELL, E. C. Life of Charlotte Brontë. 2d ed. Leipzig, 1859. 24° 410.53

— Lizzie Leigh ; and other tales. Leipzig, 1855. 24° 410.54

— Lois the witch. Leipzig, 1861. 24° 720.17

— Mary Barton. Leipzig, 1849. 24° 410.55

Shelf. No.

GASKELL, E. *continued.*
— North and South. Leipzig, 1855. 24° 410.56
— Ruth. Leipzig, 1853. 24° 410.57
GASPARIN, A. E. de. The uprising of a great people. The United States in 1861. New York, 1861. 12° 1133.3
GAUTIER, A. Introduction philosophique a l'étude de la géologie. Paris, 1853. 8° . . . 2063.20
GAVIN, A. The great red dragon; or, the masterkey to popery. [Appended, Blanco White's Preservative against popery.] Bost. 1854. 12° 1115.6
GAY, J. Poetical works. Life by Dr. Johnson. Boston, 1854. 2v. 18° 1317.1
    Contents. — Vol. I. Life, by Dr. Johnson; Fables; Rural sports; Trivia. II. The fan; The shepherd's week; Acis and Galatea; Epistles; Eclogues; Elegies; Tales; Miscellanies.
GENLIS, S. F. D. de St. A. B. de. Les petits émigrés. 4me éd. Berlin, 1824. 2v. 8°. . 2064.6
GEORGE Mason, the backwoodsman. *See* Flint, T.
GIBBON, J. Artillerist's manual. N. Y. 1860. 8° 204.13
GILBERT, J. *See* Ince, H.
GILHAM, W. Manual of instruction for the volunteers and militia of the United States. Philadelphia, 1861. 8° 205.16
GILLIES, J. Memoirs of the Rev. George Whitefield. Introduction by C. E. Stowe. Hartford, 1853. 8° 571.2
GIRARDIN, É. de. Civilisation de l'Algérie. Paris, 1860. 80 pp. 8° 2063.12
GLEIG, G. R. Chelsea hospital and its traditions. London, 1839. 12° 097.9
— The chronicles of Waltham. London, 1835. 3v. 8° 477.8
— The veterans of Chelsea hospital. London, 1842. 3v. 8° 477.7
— The Leipsic campaign. New ed. London, 1853. 8° 1655.14
GODET, T. L. Bermuda: its history, geology, climate, etc. London, 1860. 12° 265.5
GOLDSMITH, O. Poetical works. Life by T. B. Macaulay. Boston, 1859. 18° 1317.2
— Select works. Leipzig, 1842. 24° 410.58
GOODALE, S. L. The principles of breeding. Boston, 1861. 12° 1177.1
GOODWIN, T. Grammar of the Latin tongue. London, 1854. 16° 1169.18
— Latin-English [and] English-Latin dictionary. London, 1855. 16° 1169.3
GORDON, G., *earl of Aberdeen.* Principles of beauty in Grecian architecture. London, 1860. 16° 1169.34
GORE, C. F. Castles in the air. Leipzig, 1856. 24°. 410.59
— Cecil; or, the adventures of a coxcomb. New ed. London, 1860. 16° 477.5
— The dean's daughter. Leipzig, 1853. 24°. . 410.60
— Heckington. Leipzig, 1858. 24° 410.61
— A life's lesson. Leipzig, 1857. 24° 410.62
— Mammon. Leipzig, 1855. 24° 410.63
— Progress and prejudice. Leipzig, 1854. 24° . 410.64
— The two aristocracies. Leipzig, 1857. 24°. . 410.65
GORE, G. Theory and practice of electro-deposition. London, 1860. 12° 205.22
GOSSE, P. H. The romance of natural history. Boston, 1861. 12° 174.13-14
GOUGER, H. Personal narrative of two years' imprisonment in Burmah. London, 1860. 12° 695.13
GRAGG, W. F. A cruise to China and Japan, from 1857 to 1860. Boston, 1860. 8° 622.10
GRANT, J. Legends of the Black Watch, or 42d Highlanders. New ed. London, 1860. 16°. 468.19
GRAY, A. Structural and systematic botany. New York, 1860, 8° 164.24
GRAY, T. Poetical works. Life by Rev. J. Mitford. Boston, 1859. 18° 1317.3
GREAT BRITAIN. Limited liability act. Added, the joint stock companies acts. Notes by David Gibbons. London, 1858-9. 16° 1169.46
— Metropolis local management act. With notes and index. 3d ed. Lond. 1858-9. 16° 1169.47

Shelf. No.

GREAT BRITAIN, *continued.*
— Metropolitan building act. Notes, index, etc. by D. Gibbons and R. Hesketh. London, 1859. 16° 1159.4
— Nuisances removal, and diseases prevention amendment act. London, 1855. 64 pp. 16°. 1169.49
— Six legislative enactments for the guidance of contractors, merchants, and tradesmen. 2d ed. London, 1858-9. 16° 1169.57
GREAT Eastern's log (The). *See* Wallace, W. A.
GREENLEAF, S. Treatise on the law of evidence. 10th ed. Boston, 1860. 3v. 8° 132.17
GREGOROVIUS, F. Corsica, in its picturesque, social, and historical aspects. Transl. by R. Martineau. London, 1855. 8° 1655.2
— Siciliana: Wanderungen in Neapel und Sicilien. Leipzig, 1861. 12° 2025.19
GREGSON, A. W. The complete chest squarer, or chestmaker's reckoner. 3d ed. London, 1859. 16° 1159.15
GRENVILLE, R. P. T. N. B. C., *duke of Buckingham and Chandos.* Memoirs of the courts and cabinets of William IV. and Victoria. London, 1861. 2v. 8° 973.1
GRETTON, G. The Englishwoman in Italy. London, 1860. 2v. 12° 665.13
GRIMM, J. L. and W. C. Household stories. Boston, 1861. 2v. 12° 744.10-12
GROSS, S. D. Lives of American physicians and surgeons of the nineteenth century. Philadelphia, 1861. 8° 522.14
— Manual of military surgery. Phila. 1861. 18°. 1199.13
GUERRE (La) d'Orient, ses causes et ses consequences. Bruxelles, 1854. 8° 2063.19
GUILD, A. E. *See* Whitmarsh, C. S.
GUNDERODE, C. and Arnim, B. v. Correspondence. Boston, 1861. 12° 833.11
GUY Livingstone. Leipzig, 1860. 24° 410.66
HADDON, J. Book-keeping and commercial phraseology. 5th ed. London, 1861. 16° . . . 1169.50
HALDEMAN, S. S. Analytic orthography. Philadelphia, 1860. 4° 381.1
HALE, E. E. Ninety days' worth of Europe. Boston, 1861. 12° 656.2-4
HALE, L. P. Seven stormy Sundays. 3d ed. Boston, 1859. 12° 477.2
HALL, D. W. Arctic rovings; or, the adventures of a New Bedford boy on sea and land. Boston, 1861. 12° 747.15
HALL, W. W. Journal of health. Vol. VII. New York, 1860. 8° 154.1
— Sleep. New York, 1861. 12° 158.43
HALLAM, H. State of Europe during the middle ages. Boston, 1861. 3v. p.8° 946.12
HALLS, J. J. Two months in Arrah in 1857. 2d ed. London, 1860. 16° 1159.9
HALTRICH, J. Deutsche Volksmärchen aus dem Sachsenlande in Siebenbürgen. Berlin, 1856. 12° 2025.16
HAMILTON, H. C. Grammar of the Greek language. 2d ed. London, 1858. 16° 1169.23
HAMILTON, H. R. English-Greek lexicon. London, 1860. 16° 1169.6
— Lexicon of the Gr'k language. Lond. 1858. 16°. 1169.2
HAMILTON, N. E. S. A. Dictionary of the English, German, and French languages. London, 1853-55. 3v. 16° 1169.14
HANAFORD, L. B. and Payson, J. W. Book-keeping by single and double entry. Boston [1859]. obl.4° 133.21
HARDEE, W. J. Rifle and light infantry tactics. Philadelphia, 1861. 2v. 32° 187.31
HARDMAN, F. The Spanish campaign in Morocco. Edinb. 1860. 12° . . . . 917.13 and 928.14
HARRISSON, D. Jr. A voice from the Washingtonian home. Boston, 1860. 12° 1116.1
HASKELL, E. F. Housekeeper's encyclopedia. New York, 1861. 12° 185.12
HAYCOCK, W. The gentleman's stable manual. 2d ed. London, 1860. 12° 164.25

	Shelf. No.

HAYWARD, A. Lord Chesterfield and George Selwyn. London, 1854. p.8° 1655.17
HEADLAND, F. W. A medical handbook. London, 1861. 12° 157.39
HEATON, C. W. Threshold of chemistry. London, 1861. 16° 1148.1
HEBER, R. Poetical works. New ed. Boston, 1853. 18° 1317.4
HELPS, A. Spanish conquest in America. Vol. IV. London, 1861. 8° 254.2
HENDERSON, T. S. Memoir of the Rev. E. Henderson. London, [1859.] 12° 578.21
HERBERT, G. Poetical works. Memoir by the Rev. R. A. Willmott. Boston, 1855. 18° . 1317.5
HERBERT, H. H. M., 4th earl Carnarvon. Recollections of the Druses of the Lebanon. London, 1860. 12° 937.9
HERRICK, R. Hesperides. Boston, 1856. 2v. 18°. 1317.6
HERRING, R. Recollections of the late Rev. Geo. Croly. London, 1861. 18° 579.19
HERVEY-SAINT-DENYS, M. J. L. de. La Chine devant l'Europe. Paris, 1860. 12° 2063.13
HEUZÉ, L. G. L'année agricole. 2éme année. Paris, 1861. 12° 2065.30
HEWLETT, H. G. The heroes of Europe. Boston, 1861. 12° 555.3
HIND, H. Y. Narrative of the Canadian Red River exploring expedition of 1857, etc. London, 1860. 2v. 8° 622.9
HITCHCOCK, E. Religious lectures on phenomena in the four seasons. Boston, 1861. 12° . . 1115.16
HITOPADESA. The book of good counsels. From the Sanskrit, by E. Arnold. London, 1861. 12° 883.16
HOFF, G. A. Vie de Martin Luther. Paris, 1860. 12° 2065.31
HOLCROFT, T. Memoirs written by himself. London, 1852. p.8° 1655.17
HOLINSKI, A. L'Équateur, scènes de la vie Sud-Américaine. Paris, 1861. 12° 2065.21
HOLMES, O. W. Currents and counter-currents in medical science. Boston, 1861. 12° . . 158.45
— Elsie Venner. Boston, 1861. 2v. 12° 453.1
HOME-LIFE of English ladies in the XVII century. London, 1860. 12° 997.3
HOMERUS. New readings of Homer. London, 1860. 12° 394.10
HOOD, T. Poetical works. Boston, 1859. 4v. 18°. 1317.7
Contents, as on p.85 of the catalogue printed 1859. Shelf no. 318.1-5.
HOPE, I. Britanny and the Bible. London, 1852. p.8° 1655.7
— Britanny and the chase. London, 1853. p.8°. 1655.7
HOPKINS, T. On winds and storms. London, 1860. 8° 143.11
HOPKINSON, J. The steam engine explained. 3d ed. London, 1860. 8° 193.2
HOSKINS, T. H. What we eat. Boston, 1861. 12°. 185.11
HOWARD, G. W. F., 7th earl of Carlisle. Lectures in aid of popular education. New ed. London, 1857. p.8° 1655.25
HOWARD, H., earl of Surrey. Poetical works. With a memoir. Boston, 1854. 18° . . . 1317.8
HOWITT, M. Lillieslleaf: or lost and found. London, 1861. 12° 747.8
HUC, E. R. Journey through Tartary, Thibet, and China, 1844-46. Transl. by Mrs. P. Sinnett. London, 1859. p.8° 1655.8
HUGHES, S. Treatise on water-works for the supply of cities and towns. London, 1859. 16° 1169.24
HUGHES, T. Tom Brown's school days. Leipzig, 1858. 24° 410.67
— Tom Brown at Oxford. New York, 1860-61. 2v. 12° 433.1-6
HUGHES, W. The Australian colonies. New ed. London, 1853. p.8° 1655.13
HUGO, V. M. Ausgewählte Schriften. Teutsch bearbeitet von F. Seybold. Stuttgart, 1835. 4v. 32° 2019.11

	Shelf. No.

HUISH, R. Bees: their natural history and general management. New ed. London, 1844. 12° 1177.3
HUMPHREYS, E. R. Lessons on the liturgy of the Protestant Episcopal church in America. Boston, 1861. 16° 2109.1
HUMPHRY, G. M. The human foot and the human hand. Cambridge, 1861. 16° . . . 1158.16
HURLBUT, W. H. Pictures of Cuba. London, 1855. p.8° 1655.11
HUTCHINSON, T. J. Narrative of the Niger, Tshadda, and Binuë exploration. London, 1855. p.8° 1655.9
— Ten years' wanderings among the Ethiopians. London, 1861. 8° 684.12
HYMNS of the ages. See Whitmarsh, C. S.

INCE, H. and Gilbert, J. English history. London, 1860. 12° 997.5
INCIDENTS in the life of a slave girl. Edited by L. M. Child. Boston, 1861. 12° 537.28
IRMLER, J. G. F. Die Tafel-Eiche im Oderwalde und die Dragonaden in Schlesien. Eine Erzählung aus den Zeiten des 30 jährigen Krieges. 2e Aufl. Leipzig, 1846. 2v. in 1. 16° 2025.9
IRVING, J. T. The attorney. N. York, n.d. 12°. 486.16
— Harry Harson. New York, n.d. 12° 486.17

JACKSON, J. Another letter to a young physician. Boston, 1861. 12° 158.46
JAMES, G. P. R. Agincourt. Leipzig, 1844. 24°. 420.1
— Arabella Stuart. Leipzig, 1844. 24° 420.2
— Arrah Neil. Leipzig, 1844. 24° 720.18
— Attila. New York, 1860. 12° 464.24
— Beauchamp. Leipzig, 1846. 24° 420.3
— The castle of Ehrenstein. Leipzig, 1847. 24°. 420.4
— The club-book. New York, 1856. 12° 464.23
— The convict. Leipzig, 1847. 24° 420.5
— Darnley. New York, 1855. 12° 464.22
— Same. Leipzig, 1847. 24° 720.19
— De l'Orme. 6th ed. New York, 1855. 12° . 464.21
— The false heir. Leipzig, 1843. 24° 420.6
— Forest days. Leipzig, 1843. 24° 420.7
— The gentleman of the old school. New York, 1855. 12° 464.17
— The gipsy. Leipzig, 1847. 24° 420.8
— Heidelberg. Leipzig, 1846. 24° 420.9
— Henry of Guise. New York, 1855. 12° . . . 464.27
— The Huguenot. New York, 1855. 12° . . . 464.16
— The Jacquerie. New York, 1855. 12° 464.20
— The man-at-arms; or, Henry De Cerons. New York, 1855. 12° 464.15
— Morley Ernstein. Leipzig, 1842. 24° 420.10
— One in a thousand. New York, 1855. 12° . . 464.19
— Richelieu. New ed. New York, 1860. 12° . 464.25
— Rose D'Albret. Leipzig, 1844. 24° 420.11
— Russell. Leipzig, 1847. 24° 720.20
— Sir Theodore Broughton. Leipzig, 1848. 24°. 420.12
— The smuggler. Leipzig, 1845. 24° 420.13
— The step-mother. Leipzig, 1845. 2v. 24° . . 420.14
— The string of pearls. New York, 1856. 12°. 464.18
— A whim, and its consequences. Leipzig, 1847. 24° 430.71
JAMESON, A. Sketches in Canada. New ed. London, 1852. p.8° 1655.12
JANNEY, S. M. History of the religious society of Friends. 2d ed. Phila. 1860. 2v. 8°. 1084.18
JARVES, J. J. Art studies; the "old masters" of Italy; painting. New York, 1861. 8° . . . 202.12
JEFFREY, F. lord. Jonathan Swift. London, 1860. pp.92. p.8° 1655.16
— Samuel Richardson. Lond. 1860. pp.31. p.8°. 1655.16
JENNINGS, R. The horse and his diseases. Added. Rarey's method of taming. Phila. 1860. 12°. 1177.2
JERRMANN, E. Pictures from St. Petersburgh. Transl. by F. Hardman. New ed. London, 1857. p.8° 1655.6
JERROLD, B. The chronicles of the crutch. London, 1860. 12° 883.6

Shelf. No.

JERROLD, D. Men of character. Leipzig, 1852.
　24°. 720.21
— St. Giles and St. James. Leipzig, 1852. 24°. 420.15
JOHNS, M., and Nicolas, P. H. The naval and military heroes of Great Britain. London,
　1860. p.8°. 854.5
JOHNSON, S. The lives of English poets. Leipzig, 1858. 2v. 24°. 420.16
JOHNSTON, J. D. China and Japan. Philadelphia,
　1861. 12° 688.19
JONES, J. F. Egypt in its biblical relations and moral aspect. London, 1860. 12°. 946.11
JONES, P. History of the Ojibway Indians. London, 1861. 12° 2095.3

KAPP, F. Geschichte der Sklaverei in Amerika.
　Hamburg, 1861. 12° 2065.32
KAVANAGH, J. Adèle. Leipzig, 1858. 3v. 24°. 420.17
— Daisy Burns. Leipzig, 1853. 24° 420.18
— Grace Lee. Leipzig, 1855. 24° 420.19
— Madeleine. New ed. London, [1851.] 16°. 500.12
— Nathalie. Leipzig, 1851. 2v. 24° 420.20
— Rachel Gray. Leipzig, 1856. 24° 420.21
— Seven years. Leipzig, 1859. 24° 420.22
— Summer and winter in the Two Sicilies.
　Leipzig, 1858. 24° 420.23
KEATS, J. Poetical works. With a life. Boston,
　1859. 18° 1317.9
KELLOGG, E. A new monetary system. Ed. by
　M. K. Putnam. New York, 1861. 12° . . . 1138.2
KELTON, J. C. New manual of the bayonet. New
　York, 1861. 16° 205.23
KEMP, T. L. Indications of instinct. London,
　1854. p.8° 1655.24
— Natural history of creation. New ed. London, 1858. p.8° 1655.24
KIMBALL, R. B. Saint Leger, or, the threads of
　life. Leipzig, 1853. 24° 420.24
KING, W. H. Lessons on steam, the steam-engine, propellers, etc. Revised by J. W.
　King. 2d ed. New York, 1861. 8° 202.15
KINGLAKE, A. W. Eöthen. Leipzig, 1846. 24°. 420.25
— - Same. New ed. London, 1858. p.8° . . 1655.8
KINGSLEY, C. Alton Locke. Leipzig, 1857. 24°. 420.26
— Hypatia. Leipzig, 1857. 24° 420.27
— The limits of exact science as applied to history. Cambridge, 1860. 12° 883.12
— Two years ago. Leipzig, 1857. 2v. 24° . . 420.28
— Westward ho! Leipzig, 1855. 2v. 24° . . . 420.29
— Yeast. Leipzig, 1851. 24° 420.30
KIRK, E. N. Discourses, doctrinal and practical.
　Boston, 1860. 8° 113.15
KOHL, J. G. Travels in Canada, and through New
　York and Pennsylvania. Translated by
　Mrs. P. Sinnett. London, 1861. 2v. 12°. 634.6
KORMAK, an Icelandic romance of the tenth century. Boston, 1861. 12° 374.22

LA GIRONIÈRE, P. P. de. Twenty years in the
　Philippines. Abridged from the French by
　F. Hardman. London, 1858. p.8° 1655.8
LAING, S. Journal of a residence in Norway,
　1834-36. New ed. London, 1859. p.8°. . 1655.3
— Notes of a traveller on the state of France,
　Prussia, Switzerland, Italy, during the
　present century. 1st ser. Lond. 1854. p.8°. 1655.3
LAMARTINE, M. L. A. Prat de. Geneviève. Paris,
　1855. 12° 2065.15
LAMBORN, R. H. Rudimentary treatise on the
　metallurgy of copper. Lond. 1860. 16° . . 1169.30
LAMONT, J. Seasons with the sea-horses. London, 1861. 8° 704.22
LANG, J. D. Queensland, Australia. London,
　1861. 12° 695.16
LANGFORD, J. A. Prison books and their authors.
　London, 1861. 12° 883.14
LANKESTER, E. Half-hours with the microscope.
　2d ed. London, n.d. 16° 1158.14
LANMAN, C. Adventures in the wilds of North
　America. Edited by C. R. Weld. London,
　1854. p.8° 1655.12

Shelf. No.

LARCY, C. P. R. L. de. Des vicissitudes politiques
　de la France. Paris, 1860. 8° 2063.17
LASSALLE, F. Der italianische Krieg und die
　Aufgabe Preussens. 2e Aufl. Berlin, 1859.
　73 pp. 8° 2025.12
LAW of the territories. Philadelphia, 1859. 12°. 298.2
LECOMPTE, J. La Charité à Paris. Paris, 1861. 12°. 2065.19
LEE, E. Spain and its climates. Lond. 1860. 16°. 665.12
— The watering-places of England. 4th ed.
　London, 1859. 12° 645.21
LE-GAL, E. School of the guides. New York,
　1860. 24° . . . . 1208.4 and 1209.17
LEHNERT, J. H. Lehrreiche und Unterhaltende
　Märchen. Berlin, n.d. 12° 2019.6
LESLIE, E. Pencil sketches. Phila. 1852. 12°. 468.21
LEVER, C. Arthur O'Leary. Leipzig, 1847. 24°. 420.31
— Charles O'Malley. Leipzig, 1848. 3v. 24°. 420.32
— Confessions of Con Cregan. Leipz. 1860. 24°. 420.33
— The Daltons. Leipzig, 1852. 2v. 24° . . . 420.34
— Davenport Dunn. Leipzig, 1859. 2v. 24° . 420.35
— The Dodd family abroad. Leipz. 1854. 2v. 24°. 420.36
— The fortunes of Glencore. Leipzig, 1857. 24°. 420.37
— Harry Lorrequer. Leipzig, 1847. 24° . . . 720.23
— Jack Hinton, the guardsman. Phila. n.d. 8°. 502.14
— - Same. Leipzig, 1849. 24° 720.24
— The knights of Gwynne. Leipz. 1847. 2v. 24°. 420.38
— The Martins of Cro' Martin. Leipzig, 1856.
　2v. 24° 420.39
— The O'Donoghue. Leipzig, 1845. 24° 420.40
— One of them. Leipzig, 1860. 24° 720.25
— Roland Cashel. Leipzig, 1858. 2v. 24° . . . 420.41
— Tom Burke of "Ours." Leipz. 1848. 2v. 24°. 420.42
LEVIEN, E. Outlines of the history of Rome.
　London, 1855-56. 2v. in 1. 16° 1169.9
LEWES, G. H. Physiology of common life. Leipzig, 1860. 24° 720.26
— Ranthorpe. Leipzig, 1847. 24° 720.27
LINCOLN, A. A memoir. Appended, a sketch on
　slavery in the United States. Lond. 1861.
　16° 528.27
LIPPINCOTT, S. J. C. Bonnie Scotland, tales of
　her history, etc. Boston, 1861. 16° 997.4
LITTLE leaven, (A) and what it wrought at Mrs.
　Blake's school. New York, 1860. 16° . . . 450.37
LLORENTÉ, J. A. History of the Spanish inquisition. Abridged by L. Gallois. New York,
　1826. 12° 1115.22
LONGACRE, J. B. and Herring, J. National portrait gallery of distinguished Americans.
　Philadelphia, 1853, 54. 4v. l.8°. 521.1
LORD, E. The epoch of creation. Introd. by R.
　W. Dickinson. New York, 1851. 12° . . . 1115.23
LOSSING, B. J. Life of Philip Schuyler. Vol. I.
　New York, [1860.] 12° 514.4
LOSSIUS, C. F. Gumal und Lina. Eine Geschichte
　für Kinder. 7te Aufl. Gotha, 1827. 3v. 12°. 2026.5
— Moralische Bilderbibel. 2te Aufl. Umgearbeitet von C. F. Schulze. Gotha, 1821-24.
　5v. 8° 2026.1
LUCKEY, J. Life in Sing-Sing state prison. New
　York, 1860. 12° 1138.1
LYNDALL, J. Business: as it is, and as it may be.
　London, 1854. 12° 136.38
LYTTON, Sir E. G. E. L. B. Alice, or the mysteries. Leipzig, 1842. 24° 420.43
— Athens, its rise and fall. Leipzig, 1843. 24°. 420.44
— The Caxtons: a family picture. Leipzig, 1849,
　24° 420.45
— Devereux. Leipzig, 1842. 24° 420.46
— Dramatic works. Leipzig, 1860. 24° 420.48
— The disowned. Leipzig, 1842. 24° 420.47
— Ernest Maltravers. Leipzig, 1842. 24° . . . 420.49
— Eugene Aram. Leipzig, 1842. 24° 420.50
— Eva; and The pilgrims of the Rhine. Leipzig, 1842. 24° 420.51
— Godolphin. Roman, Aus dem Englische von
　G. N. Bärmann. Stuttgart, 1840. 2v.in 1. 16°. 2016.15
— Godolphin, and Falkland. Leipzig, 1842. 24°. 420.52
— Harold. Leipzig, 1848. 24° 420.53
— King Arthur. Leipzig, 1849. 24° 420.54
— The last days of Pompeii. Leipz. 1842. 24°. 420.55

	Shelf. No.

LYTTON, *Sir E. G. E. L. B. continued.*
— The last of the barons. Leipzig, 1843. 24°. 420.56
— Lucretia; or, the children of night. Leipzig, 1846. 24° 420.57
— My novel. Leipzig, 1851. 4v. 24° 420.58
— New Timon, and Lady of Lyons. Leipzig, 1849. 25° 720.28
— Paul Clifford. Leipzig, 1842. 24° 420.59
— Night and morning. Leipzig, 1843. 24° . . . 720.29
— Pelham. Leipzig, 1842. 24 . . . . 240.60
— Rienzi. Leipzig, 1842. 24° 420.61
— What will he do with it? Leipz. 1857, 58. 4v. in 3. 24° 420.62
— Zanoni. Leipzig, 1842. 24° 420.63
LYTTON, R. B. Serbski Pesme; or, national songs of Servia. London, 1861. 16° 1329.1
LUTFULLAH. (A Mohammedan) Autobiography. Ed. by E. B. Eastwick. Leipzig, 1857. 24°. 430.1

MACAULAY, T. B. Biographical essays. Leipzig, 1857. 24° 720.30
— Critical and historical essays. Leipzig, 1850. 5v. in 3. 24° 1966.3
— History of England. Vol. v. With index. New York, 1861. 12° 966.3–4
— ~ Same. Boston, 1861. 12° 966.2
— The history of England. Leipzig, 1849.–55. 8v. in 6. 24° 1966.1
— Lays of ancient Rome. Leipzig, 1851. 24°. 1966.2
— Speeches. Leipzig, 1853. 2v. in 1. 24° . . . 1966.4
— William Pitt [and] Atterbury. Leipz. 1860. 24°. 1966.5
— Selections from essays and speeches. London, 1852–59. 2v. p.8° 1655.19–20
  Contents. — Vol. 1. Horace Walpole; Life and writings of Addison; Lord Clive; Ranke's history of the Popes; Samuel Johnson; Gladstone on church and state; Warren Hastings; William Pitt, earl of Chatham. II. Comic dramatists of the restoration; Frederic the Great; Hallam's constitutional history; Lord Bacon; Lord Byron; Speeches on parliamentary reform in 1831 and 1832.

MACBRIAR, R. M. The Africans at home. London, 1861. 12° 688.20
McCULLOCH, J. R. London in 1850–51. London, 1851. p.8° 1655.25
— Russia and Turkey. London, 1854. p.8° . . 1655.6
MACKAY, A. Manual of modern geography. Edinburgh, 1861. 12° 945.5
McLEOD, L. Travels in Eastern Africa. London, 1860. 2v. 12° 688.18
MACMILLAN, H. Footnotes from the page of nature. London, 1861. 16° 175.21
McNICOLL, T. Essays on English literature. London, 1861. 12° 395.27
MAHAN, D. H. Treatise on advanced-guard, outpost, and detachment service of troops. New York, 1861. 18° 1209.18
— Treatise on field fortification. 3d ed. rev. New York, 1861. 18°. 1209.16
MAIDEN sisters. By the author of "Still waters." Leipzig, 1859. 24° 430.2
MANN, H. Lectures on various subjects. New York, 1859. 12° 1155.3
— Twelve sermons delivered at Antioch college. Boston, 1861. 12° 113.17
MANSFIELD, E. D. The political manual. New York, 1861. 12° 299.18
MANSFIELD, R. B. The log of the Water Lily. Leipzig, 1854. 24° 430.3
MARDON, E. R. Billiards: game, 500 up. 3d ed. Brighton, 1858. 8° 204.12
MAREY-MONGE, G. S. Memoir on swords. Tr. by H. H. Maxwell. London, 1860. 16°. . 1169.33
MARMONT, A. F. L. *duc de Raguse.* Voyage en Sicile. 2e éd. Paris, 1838. 8° 2063.4
MARRYAT, F. The children of the New Forest. Leipzig, 1848. 24° 430.4
— Jacob Faithful. Leipzig, 1842. 24° 720.31
— Japhet in search of a father. Leipz. 1843. 24°. 430.5
— The mission: or, scenes in Africa. Leipzig, 1845. 24° 430.6
— ~ Same. New ed. London, 1860. p.8° . . 854.8

	Shelf. No.

MARRYAT, F. *continued.*
— Percival Keene. Leipzig, 1842. 24° 430.7
— Peter Simple. Leipzig, 1842. 24° 430.8
— The privateer's-man. Leipzig, 1846. 24° . . 430.9
— ~ Same. London, 1860. p.8° 854.10
— The settlers in Canada. Leipzig, 1844. 24°. 430.10
— ~ Same. New ed. London, 1860. p.8° . . 854.9
— Travels of Monsieur Violet. Leipz. 1843. 24°. 430.11
— Valerie. Leipzig, 1849. 24° 430.12
MARRYAT, H. A residence in Jutland. London, 1860. 2v. 12° 665.15
MARSH, A. Aubrey. Leipzig, 1854. 24° 430.13
— Castle Avon. Leipzig, 1852. 24° 430.14
— Emilia Wyndham. Leipzig, 1852. 24° . . . 430.15
— Evelyn Marston. Leipzig, 1856. 24° 430.16
— The heiress of Haughton. Leipz. 1855. 24°. 430.17
— Ravenscliffe. Leipzig, 1851. 24° 430.18
— The rose of Ashurst. Leipz. 1857. 2v.in 1. 24°. 430.19
MARTIALIS, M. V. Epigrams. Translated into English prose. London, 1860. p.8° 854.6
MARTIN, W. C. L. Natural history. Tr. from 35th Germ. ed. by S. A. Myers. N. Y. 1861. 2v. 12° 176.30
MARTINEAU, H. Health, husbandry, and handicraft. London, 1861. 12° 166.34
MARVELL, A. Poetical works. With a memoir. Boston, 1857. 18° 1317.10
MASON, G. H. Life with the Zulus of Natal. London, 1855. p.8° 1655.9
MASSEY, G. Havelock's march and other poems. London, 1861. 12° 386.7
MATHER, C. *See* Calef, R.
MAYNE, F. Voyages and discoveries in the Arctic regions. London, 1855. p.8° 1655.7
MEIER, E. Deutsches Volksmährchen aus Schwaben. Stuttgart, 1852. 8° 2025.15
MELVILLE, G. J. W. Holmby House. Leipzig, 1860. 24° 430.20
MEMOIR of the Duke of Wellington, from The Times. London, 1852. p.8° 1655.14
MEREDITH, L. A. Over the straits; a visit to Victoria. London, 1861. 12° 695.15
MEREDITH, O. *Pseud. See* Lytton, R. B.
MICHELET, J. Historical view of the French revolution. New edition. Translated by C. Cocks. London, 1860. p.8° 854.7
MILES, P. Nordurfari: or, rambles in Iceland. London, 1854. p.8° 1655.4
MILMAN, H. H. History of Latin christianity. New York, 1860–61. 7v. 8° 1113.1
MILNER, T. Wonders of the earth and the heavens. Revised by C. Wright. 4th American edition. Boston, n.d. 2v. 8° 143.13
MILTON, J. Poetical works. Leipzig, 1850. 24°. 430.21
— Poetical works. Life by Rev. J. Mitford. Boston, 1859. 3v. 18° 1317.11
  Contents, as on p. 120 of the catalogue printed 1859, Shelf No. 329.6.
MOLESCHOTT, I. Physiologisches Skizzenbuch. Giessen, 1861. 12° 2025.20
MONTAGU, M. W. Letters and works. Ed. by Lord Wharncliffe. 3d ed. Vol. I. London, 1861. 8° 591.1
MONTGOMERY, J. Poetical works. With a memoir. Boston, 1860. 5v. 18° 1317.12
  Contents. — Vol. I. Memoir by R. Carruthers; The wanderer of Switzerland; Miscellaneous poems; The West Indies; Prison amusements. II. The world before the flood; Miscellaneous poems; Thoughts on wheels; The climbing boy's soliloquies; Songs of Zion. III. Greenland; Miscellaneous poems; Narratives; Translations from Dante. IV. The Pelican island; Miscellanies; Songs on the abolition of negro slavery in the British colonies; Verses to the memory of R. Reynolds; Sacred and scriptural subjects; Appendix. V. Original hymns; Posthumous poems.
MONTPENSIER, A. M. L. d'Orléans, &c. *Mlle.* La galerie des portraits. Nouv. éd. Par M. É. Barthélemy. Paris, 1860. 8° 2063.9
MOORE, A. W. Corpulency. Explaining his diet system. 4th ed. Lond. 1860. 73 pp. 8°. 1158.1
MOORE, F. Diary of the American revolution. New York, 1860. 2v. 8° 222.2

Shelf. No

MOORE, J. Edward, views of human nature. Mt. Pleasant, Westchester Co. 1799. 2v. 12°. 1479.1

MOORE, T. Poetical works. Lelpz. 1842. 5v. 24°. 394.8

Contents. — Vol. I. Odes of Anacreon; Odes; Epigrams from the Anthologia; Juvenile Poems; Poems relating to America. II. Corruption and Intolerance; The sceptic ; Twopenny post-bag; Intercepted letters, etc. ; Irish melodies ; National airs ; Sacred songs. III. Evenings in Greece; Legendary ballads; Set of glees; Songs from the Greek Anthology ; Unpublished songs; Lalla Rookh. IV. Lalla Rookh; Political and satirical poems; The Fudge family in Paris ; Fables for the holy alliance ; Rhymes on the road ; Miscellaneous poems; The loves of the angels ; Satirical and humorous poems ; The Fudges in England ; Songs from M. P., or the Blue stocking; Miscellaneous poems; The epicurean; Alciphron.

— — Same. With a memoir. Boston, 1856. 6v. 18°. 1317.13

Contents. — Vol. I. Memoir ; Odes of Anacreon; Epigrams from the Anthologia ; Juvenile poems. II. Poems relating to America; Corruption and Intolerance; The sceptic ; Twopenny post-bag; Satirical and humorous poems; The Fudge family in Paris; Fables for the Holy Alliance. III. Satirical and humorous poems; The Fudges in England. IV. Letter on music ; Irish melodies; National airs ; Sacred songs; Set of glees; Ballads, songs and miscellaneous poems. V. Evenings in Greece; Legendary ballads; Melologue upon national music; The summer fête; Songs from the M. P., or the blue stocking; Miscellaneous poems; Songs from the Greek anthology; Unpublished songs ; Rhymes on the road ; Alciphron ; Fragments from the epicurean ; Index of first lines. VI. Lalla Rookh; The loves of the angels.

MORMONISM : reprinted from the Edinburgh Review. London, 1854. p.8°. 1655.25

MOTHER'S (The) thorough resource-book. London, n.d. 12° 185.9

MOTLEY, J. L. History of the United Netherlands. New York, 1861. 2v. 8° 911.1–9

MÜLLER, G. The life of trust. Edited by H. L. Wayland. Boston, 1861. 12° 555.5

MULOCH, D. M. Agatha's husband. Leipzig, 1860. 24° 430.22

— The head of the family. Leipzig, 1858. 24°. 430.23

— John Halifax, gentleman. Lelpz. 1857. 24°. 430.24

— A life for a life. Leipzig, 1859. 24° 430.25

— Our year. New York, 1860. 12° 747.9–10

— Studies from life. New York, 1861. 12° 883.10

— A woman's thoughts about women. Leipzig, 1860. 24° 430.26

MURDOCH, D. The Dutch dominie of the Catskills. New York, 1861. 12° 485.23

MURRAY, J. Handbook for travellers in Berks, Bucks, and Oxfordshire. Lond. 1860. 12°. 645.20

NAPOLÉON I. Correspondance. Tome I. [1793–96.] Paris, 1858. 8° 2063.21

NEAR home. A poem. Boston, 1858. 52 pp. 12°. 1325.3

NEW, A. H. The history of Austria. London, n.d. 12° 927.16

NEW glories of the catholic church, transl. from the Italian. Baltimore, 1860. 12° 2107.1

NICHOLS, T. N. What's in a name? an explanation of ordinary christian names. London, 1859. 16° 1159.10

NISARD, M. E. C. Mémoires et correspondances inédits 1726 à 1816. Paris, 1858. 12° 2065.27

NOBLE, L. L. After icebergs with a painter. N. York, 1861. 8° 634.5

NOBLE traits of kingly men. London, n.d. 12°. 557.18

NORTHESK, *countess of.* See Carnegie, G. M.

NORTON, C. Stuart of Dunleath. Lelpz. 1851. 24°. 723.00

OESTERREICH keine Deutsche Grossmacht. Berlin, 1859. 32 pp. 12° 2025.14

ŒSTERREICHS Politik in Italien und die wahren Garantien seiner Macht und Einheit. Wien, 1859. 70 pp. 8° 2025.11

OGILVIE, G. Genetic cycle in organic nature. Edinburgh, 1861. 8° 174.15

OLIPHANT, M. The house on the moor. New York, 1861. 12° 495.16

ONCE a week. Vols. I.–II. Lond. 1859–60. 2v. 8°. 841.1

Shelf. No.

O'NEILL, C. Chemistry of calico printing, dyeing, and bleaching. Manchester, 1860. 8° 143.12

ORDRONAUX, J. Hints on the preservation of health in armies. New York, 1861. 8° 1199.16

OSBORN, S. Japanese fragments. Lond. 1861. 16°. 707.22

— My journal in Malayan waters. 2d ed. London, 1860. 12° 697.23

OSSIAN. Poems. Tr. by J. Macpherson. Dissertations by Dr. Blair, etc. Leipzig, 1847. 24°. 430.2

OUR coal and our coal-pits. London, 1859. p.8°. 1655.23

OWEN, O. F. Heroines of domestic life. London, 1861. 16° 599.16

PAGE, D. The past and present life of the globe. Edinburgh, 1861. 12° 1158.15

PAOLO Francesco Danei. Life of blessed Paul of the cross. Boston, 1860. 18° 2109.6

PAPE-CARPANTIER, M. Conseils sur la direction des salles d'asile. 2ème éd. Paris, 1856. 16°. 2068.1

— Enseignement pratique dans les salles d'asile. 3ème éd. Paris, 1859. 8° 2063.11

— Histoires et leçons de choses pour les enfants. Paris, 1858. 12° 2068.2

PARIS ; its historical buildings, and its revolutions. New ed. London, 1849. 16° 1819.1

PARLOR gardener (The). Tr. from the French by C. J. Randolph. Boston, n.d. 18° 169.39

PARNELL, T. Poetical works. Life by O. Goldsmith. Boston, 1854. 18° 1317.14

PARTON, J. Life of Andrew Jackson. Vol. III. New York, 1860. 8° 522.7–8

PATERSON, J. H. Wallace and his times. 3d ed. Edinburgh, 1860. 12° 589.20

PATMORE, C. Faithful forever. Boston, 1861. 12° 374.24, 376.8

PAUL FERROLL. Leipzig, 1856. 24° 430.28

PAULI, R. Pictures of old England. Tr. by E. C. Otté. London, 1861. 8° 997.8

PECK, G. Early methodism in the old Genesee conference, 1758–1827. New York, 1860. 12°. 1115.18

PELADAN, A. La Russie au ban de l'univers et du catholicisme. 2è éd. Paris, 1855. 8° 2063.18

PEPPER, C. The art of making wax flowers. London, n.d. 56 pp. 12° 1159.14

PEPPER, J. H. The playbook of metals. London, 1861. 12° 185.8

— Scientific amusements for young people. London, 1861. 16° 185.17

PERRY, B. C. Treatise on the human hair and its diseases. New Bedford, 1859. 12° 168.45

PETRUCCELLI de la Gattina, F. Préliminaires de la Question romaine de M. Ed. About. Londres, 1860. 8° 2063.6

PEYRAT, N. Les réformateurs de la France et de l'Italie au douzième siècle. Paris, 1860. 12°. 2065.22

PFEIFFER, I. R. A lady's voyage round the world. Tr. by Mrs. P. Sinnett. New ed. London, 1852. p.8° 1655.13

PHILIP Thaxter. A novel. New York, 1861. 12°. 504.2

PHILLIPS, J. Life on the earth. Camb. 1860. 12°. 158.42

PHILP, J. Washington described. Ed. by Wm. D. Haley. New York, 1861. 12° 228.18

PICHOT, A. Sir Charles Bell, — histoire de sa vie et de ses travaux. Paris, 1858. 12° 2065.26

PICTURES of Scottish life. *See* Wyse, G.

PIERRE, *L'Abbé.* Constantinople, Jerusalem, et Rome. Paris, 1860. 2v. 8° 2063.8

PIESSE, G. W. S. Laboratory of chemical wonders. London, 1860. 12° 185.6

PIOZZI, H. L. Anecdotes of Samuel Johnson. London, 1856. p.8° 1655.16

— Autobiography, letters, and literary remains. Ed. by A. Hayward. Lond. 1861. 2v. 12°. 595.15

PLAIN and easy account of the British ferns. [3d] ed. by Mrs. Lankester. London, n.d. 16°. 1158.13

POOLE, J. Comic sketches and recollections. 2d ed. London, 1843. 2v. 8° 735.17

POPE, A. Poetical works. Leipzig, 1848. 24°. 430.29

— — Same. Life by Rev. A. Dyce. Boston, 1859. 3v. 18° 1318.1

Contents, as on p. 142 of the catalogue printed 1859. Shelf No. 333.3.

Shelf. No.

PORTER, A. M. Narrative of Sir Edward Seaward's shipwreck, with events in his life. 1733–49. London, 1859. p.8° 1655.21

PRATT, L. J. Sheaves of love. A fireside story. Boston, 1861. 12° 486.14

PRIME, W. C. Coins, medals, and seals, ancient and modern. New York, 1861. sm.4° . . 204.15

PRINCIPLE and practice; or, the orphan family. Wellington (Salop.), 1827. 16° 479.14

PRIOR, M. Poetical works. Life by Rev. J. Mitford. Boston, 1853. 2v. 18° 1318.2
Contents, as on p. 144 of the catalogue printed 1859.

PROMISCUOUS examiner (The), containing questions on geography, history, natural science, etc. By M. F. London, 1858. 24° . . 1159.14

QUIET heart, (The.) From Blackwood's magazine. New York, 1860. 8° 803.14

RAE, J. Expedition to the Arctic sea in 1846 and '47. London, 1860. 8° 706.20

RAGGED homes and how to mend them. Philadelphia, n.d. 18° 2109.8

RAGONOT, L. C. Symbolisches Englisch-Deutsches Wörterbuch. Symbolic Anglo-German vocabulary. Edited by F. Lebahn. London, n.d. 8° 2025.18
— Vocabulaire symbolique anglo-française. Symbolic French and English vocabulary. 7th ed. London, n.d. 4° 1073.1

RAMSAY, E. B. Reminiscences of Scottish life and character. From 7th Edinburgh ed. Boston, 1861. 12° 1907.1
— - Same. 2d ser. Edinburgh, 1861. 12°.v.2 of 395.8

RAND, E. S. Life memories. Boston, 1859. 12°. 1325.2

RANKE, L. Ferdinand I. and Maximilian II. of Austria. Transl. by Lady Duff Gordon. London, 1856. p.8° 1655.15

RATHBONE, M. The day of small things. London, 1860. 12° 439.1
— The good old times. A tale of Auvergne. 2d ed. London, 1857. 12° 439.2
— The ladies of Bever Hollow. New ed. London, 1860. 12° 500.22
— Poplar house academy. London, 1859. 2v. 16°. 439.3
— Village belles. London, 1860. 12° . . . 500.19

RAU, H. Jean Paul. Leipzig, 1861. 4v. 12° . . 2026.6

RAUMER, F. L. G. v. Zur Politik des Tages. 2te Aufl. Leipzig, 1859. 54 pp. 12° 2025.13

READE, C. "It is never too late to mend." Leipzig, 1856. 2v. 24° 430.30
— "Love me little, love me long." Leipzig, 1859. 24° 430.31

REAL (The) and the beau ideal. Boston, 1861. 12°. 1907.2

REALITIES of Paris life. London, 1859. 3v. 12° 883.13

RÉCAMIER, J. F. J. A. B. *Mme.* Souvenirs et correspondance. Paris, 1860. 2v. 8° 2063.24

RECREATIONS of a country parson. Boyd, A. K. P.

REDPATH, J. Guide to Hayti. Boston, 1860. 12°. 266.13

REID, M. The boy-tar. Boston, 1860. 16° . . . 747.24
— Bruin: the grand bear hunt. Bost. 1861. 16°. 747.23

RENDU, E. De l'instruction primaire à Londres. 2de éd. Paris, 1853. 8° 2063.16

RICE, N. P. Trials of a benefactor. N.Y. 1859. 12° 158.47

RICHARDSON, T. A. Art of architectural modelling in paper. London, 1859. 16° 1159.3

RITA; an autobiography. New ed. Lond. 1860. 16°. 500.21
— - Same. Leipzig, 1859. 24° 720.33

RITCHIE, J. E. Modern statesmen. London, 1861. 12° 555.7

ROBERTS, J. Hand-book of artillery. 2d ed. New York, 1861. 18° 1199.17

ROBINSON, H. Sea drift. London, n.d. 16° . . 1158.12

ROBINSON, S. How to live. New York, 1860. 12°. 185.15

ROBISON, J. and Tredgold, T. Rudimentary treatise on carpentry and joinery. London, 1859. 16° 1169.44
— and Price. Rudimentary treatise on the construction of roofs. London, 1859. 16° . . 1169.25

ROGERS, C. Familiar illustrations of Scottish character. London, 1861. 16° 864.3

Shelf. No.

ROGERS, H. Life and genius of Thomas Fuller, with selections. London, 1856. p.8° . . . 1655.15

ROOS, R. Gedichte. Dresden, 1820. 12° . . . 2019.9

ROSCOE, W. C. Poems and essays. Ed. by R. H. Hutton. London, 1860. 2v. 12° 394.9
Contents.— Vol. I. Memoir; Minor poems; Eliduke, count of Yveloc, trag.; Violenzia, trag. II. Essays.

RUDIMENTARY chronology of history, art, literature, and civilization. [pp.195-412.] London, 1857. 16° 1169.16

RUFFINI, G. Lavinia. A novel. N. York, 1861. 12°. 495.13
— - Same. Leipzig, 1861. 24° 720.34

RUSSELL, J. R. History and heroes of the art of medicine. London, 1861. 8° 154.6

RUTLEDGE. New York, 1860. 12° 507.20

SAFFORD, A. E. A memoir of Daniel Safford. Boston, n.d. 12° 537.30

SANDEAU, L. S. J. Mademoiselle de La Seiglière. Comédie. 4 ème éd. Paris, 1854. 12° . . 2065-16

SANDERS, J. M. The crystal sphere. London, 1857. sq.12° 1158.11

SARGENT, E. Original dialogues. Bost. 1861. 12° 395.26

SARGENT, W. Life of Maj. John André. Boston, 1861. 12° 514.5

SCARTH, J. Twelve years in China. Edinburgh, 1860. 12° 938.18

SCENES and adventures in Spain from 1835-1840. Philadelphia, 1846. 18° 669.16

SCHILLER, J. C. F. v. Poems and ballads. Transl. by Sir E. B. Lytton. Leipzig, 1844. 24° . . 430.32
— Gedichte. Leipzig, 1818. 2v. in 1. sq.24° . . 2019.12

SCHOOLCRAFT, *Mrs.* H. R. The black gauntlet. Philadelphia, 1861. 12° 486.19

SCHOPPE, A. Erzähluugen für meine Töchter. Berlin, 1837. 16° 2019.7
— Feierstunden, oder Erzählungen und Mährchen. Leipzig, [1834]. 16° 2019.8
— Licht und Schatten. Berlin, n.d. 16° . . . 2019.5

SCOTT, H. L. Military dictionary. New York, 1861. 8° 202.16

SCOTT, *Sir* W. The abbot. Leipzig, 1860. 24° . 430.33
— The antiquary. Leipzig, 1845. 24° 430.34
— The black dwarf [and] A legend of Montrose. Leipzig, 1858. 24° 430.35
— Bride of Lammermoor. Leipzig, 1858. 24°. 720.35
— Fortunes of Nigel. Leipzig, 1846. 24° . . 720.36
— Guy Mannering. Leipzig, 1846. 24° . . . 720.37
— The heart of Mid-Lothian. Leipzig, 1858. 24°. 430.36
— Ivanhoe. Leipzig, 1845. 24° 430.37
— Kenilworth. Leipzig, 1845. 24° 430.38
— The monastery. Leipzig, 1859. 24° . . . 430.39
— Old mortality. Leipzig, 1846. 24° 720.38
— Peveril of the peak. Leipzig, 1860. 2v. 24°. 430.40
— The pirate. Leipzig, 1846. 24° 720.39
— Quentin Durward. Leipzig, 1845. 24° . . 430.41
— Rob Roy. Leipzig, 1846. 24° 430.42
— Waverley. Leipzig, 1845. 24° 430.43
— Poetical works. With a memoir. Boston, 1857. 9v. 18° 1318.3
Contents. — Vol. I. Memoir; Lay of the last minstrel. II. Marmion. III. Lady of the lake. IV. Rokeby; The vision of Don Roderic. V. The lord of the Isles. VI. Imitations of ancient ballads; Ballads, translated from the German; Songs. VII. The bridal of Triermain; Harold the dauntless; The field of Waterloo; Halidon Hill; Mac Duff's Cross. IX. The doom of Devorgoil; Auchindrane: or, the Ayrshire tragedy; The House of Aspen; Goetz of Berlichingen.

SCOTT, W. B. History and practice of the fine arts. London, 1861. 12° 205.15

SEABURY. S. American slavery justified. New York, 1861. 12° 299.19

SEALSFIELD, C. Adventures in Texas. Abridged by F. Hardman. Edinburgh, n.d. 16° . . 639.27

SEAWARD, E. Narrative of his shipwreck. *See* Porter, A. M.

SELECT tales from the Gesta Romanorum. New York, 1845. 12° 477.4

Shelf. No.

SEMI-ATTACHED couple (The). By the author of the semi-detached house. Boston, 1861. 12°. 495.15

SEMI-DETACHED house (The). Edited by Lady T. Lewis. New ed. London, 1860. 16°. . 560.20

SENIOR, N. W. Suggestions on popular education. London, 1861. 8° 122.24

SEWELL, E. M. Amy Herbert. Leipzig, 1857. 12°. 430.44

— Cleve Hall. New York, 1855. 12° 426.5

— Ursula. Leipzig, 1858. 24° 430.45

SEWELL, W. G. Ordeal of free labor in the British West Indies. New York, 1861. 12° . . 266.12

SHAKESPEARE, W. Plays and poems. Leipzig, 1843-4. 7v. 24° 394.7

> Contents. -- Vol. I. Measure for measure; The comedy of errors; Much ado about nothing; Love's labour's lost; Midsummer-night's dream; Merchant of Venice; As you like it. II. Taming of the shrew; All's well that ends well; Twelfth-night; or, what you will; The Winter's tale; King John; King Richard II. III. First part of king Henry IV.; Second part of king Henry IV.; King Henry V.; First part of king Henry VI.; Second part of king Henry VI. IV. Third part of king Henry VI.; King Richard III.; King Henry VIII.; Troilus and Cressida; Titus Andronicus. V. Coriolanus; Romeo and Juliet; Timon of Athens; Julius Cæsar; Macbeth. VI. Cymbeline; King Lear; Othello; Hamlet; Antony and Cleopatra. VII. Pericles; The tempest. The two gentlemen of Verona; Merry wives of Windsor; Venus and Adonis; Rape of Lucrece; Sonnets; Lover's complaint; Passionate Pilgrim; Glossary; Life.

— Poems. Memoir by Rev. A. Dyce. Boston, 1856. 18° 1318.4

SHARSWOOD, G. Essay on professional ethics. 2d ed. Philadelphia, 1860. 12° 1133.1

SHELDON, E. M. Early history of Michigan. New York, 1856. 8° 236.13

SHELLEY, P. B. Poetical works. Edited by Mrs. Shelley. Boston, 1857. 3v. in 1. 8° . . 1318.5

> Contents. -- Vol. I. Memoir; Queen Mab; Alastor; Revolt of Islam; Prometheus unbound. II. The Cenci; Hellas; Œdipus. III. Miscellaneous poems.

SHEPARD, maj. I. F. Household tales, by Job Puritan. Boston, 1861. 12° 486.12

SHEPPARD, J. G. The fall of Rome. London, 1861. 12° 917.16

SHERIDAN and his times. By an octogenarian. London, 1859. 2v. 12° 567.4

SIEGE of Bomarsund. Published by permission of the [French] minister of war, 1854. New York, 1856. 12° 206.19

SILENT woman (The). By the author of "King's cope." Boston, 1861. 8° 504.1

SIMONDS, W. Clinton; or, boy life in the country. Boston, 1859. 16° 747.18

— Ella; or, turning over a new leaf. Boston, 1861. 16° 747.19

— Marcus; or, the boy-tamer. Boston, 1859. 16° 747.21

— Oscar; or, the boy who had his own way. Boston, 1861. 16° 747.17

— Jessie; or, trying to be somebody. Boston, 1861. 16° 747.22

— Whistler; or, the manly boy. Boston, 1859. 16° 747.20

> Note. -- The six titles above belong to the series known as the "Aimwell stories."

SIMPSON, H. Lives of eminent Philadelphians. Philadelphia, 1859. 8° 521.2

"SINGLE blessedness." New York, 1852. 12° . . 2106.3

SKELTON, J. Poetical works. Bost. 1856. 3v. 18°. 1318.6

> Contents. -- Vol. I. Account of S. and his writings; Miscellaneous; The Bowge of Courte; Phyllyp Sparowe; The tunnyng of Elynour Rummyng; Poems against Garnesche; Miscellaneous; A replycacion agaynst certayn yong scolers abiured of late, &c. II. Magnyfycence, a goodly interlude and a mery; Colyn Cloute; Garlande of laurell; Speke, parrot; Why come ye nat to courte?; The douty duke of Albany; Poems attributed to S. III. Notes to volumes I and 2.

SLADE, D. D. Diphtheria; its nature and treatment. Philadelphia, 1861. 8° 162.6

SMITH, G. Ten weeks in Japan. Lond. 1861. 8°. 684.11

SMITH, J. Dictionary of arts, sciences, and manufactures. Boston, 1859. 8° 202.14

SMITH, S. Selections from [his] writings. London, 1854-59. 2v. in 1. p.8° 1655.18

— Wit and wisdom of Rev. S. Smith. London, 1860. 12° 883.7

SMITH, W. A first Latin course. 2d ed. London, 1860. 12° 1158.4

— A smaller history of Greece. New York, 1860. 16° 938.17

SMOLLETT, T. Humphry Clinker. Leipzig, 1846. 24° 430.46

— Roderick Random. Leipzig, 1845. 24° . . . 430.47

SOMERVILLE, T. My own life and times. 1741-1814. Edinburgh, n.d. 12° 588.20

SOULE, R. Jr. and Wheeler, W. A. Manual of English pronunciation and spelling. Boston, 1861. 12° 386.6

SOUTHEY, R. A love story: a fragment from "The Doctor." Edited by J. W. Warter. London, 1859. p.8° 1655.22

SOUTHEY, R. Poetical works. With a memoir of the author. Boston, 1860. 10v. 18°. . 1318.7

> Contents. -- Vol. I. Life, by H. T. Tuckerman; Joan of Arc; Vision of the Maid of Orleans. II. The triumph of woman; Poems concerning the slave-trade; Botany-bay eclogues; Sonnets; Monodramas; Amatory poems of Abel Shuffle-bottom; Lyric poems; Songs of the American Indians; Occasional pieces; The retrospect; Hymn to the Penates. III. English eclogues; Nondescripts; The Devil's Walk; Inscriptions; Carmen triumphale, for the commencement of the year 1814; Odes; Epistle to Allan Cunningham; Op Eene Verzameling van Mijne Afbeeldingen. IV. Thalaba the destroyer. V. Madoc. VI. Ballads and metrical tales. VII. A tale of Paraguay; All for love; The pilgrim to Compostella. VIII. The curse of Kehama. IX. Roderick, the last of the Goths. X. The poet's pilgrimage to Waterloo; The lay of the laureate; Funeral song for the princess Charlotte of Wales; A vision of judgment; Oliver Newman, a New England tale; Miscellaneous poems.

SOUVESTRE, E. An attic philosopher in Paris, or a peep from a garret. Lond. 1859. p.8°. 1655.21

— Confessions of a working man. Transl. from 3d ed. London, 1857. p.8° 1655.21

SPENCER, H. The principles of psychology. London, 1855. 8° 122.23

— Railway morals and railway policy. London, 1858. p.8° 1655.25

SPENSER, E. Poetical works. Notes by F. J. Child. Boston, 1855-1860. 5v. 18° 1319.1

> Contents, as on p. 170 of the catalogue printed 1859, shelf No. 329.10.

SPITTA, C. J. P. Lyra domestica. Transl. by R. Massie. Additional selections by Rev. F. D. Huntington. Boston, 1861. 16° 374.23

SPRAGUE, W. B. Annals of the American pulpit. Vols. V-VII. Episcopalian, Baptist, Methodist. New York, 1859. 3v. 8° 113.1

STAINED windows and painted glass by transfer process. London, n.d. pp.12. 13 pl. 12°. 1159.13

STANHOPE, P. H. earl. History of England from 1713-1783. Leipzig, 1853, 54. 7v. 24° . 1966.6

— Life of William Pitt [the younger]. London, 1861. 2v. p.8° 567.5

STARK, A. Printing; its antecedents, origin, history, and results. London, 1855. p.8° . . 1655.25

STARK, C. Memoir of Gen. John Stark. Also, a biography of Capt. P. Stevens, and of Col. Robt. Rogers. Concord, 1860. 8° 522.15

STEGGALL, J. H. History of a Suffolk man, narrated by himself. Enlarged edition, by R. Cobbold. London, 1859. 16° 580.21

STERNE, L. Tristram Shandy. Leipzig, 1849. 24°. 430.48

STEVENSON, D. Sketch of the civil engineering of North America. 2d ed. London, 1859. 16°. 1169.41

STILL waters. Leipzig, 1857. 24° 430.49

STIMSON, A. L. History of the express companies. New York, 1859. 8° 296.7

STORIES from Italian writers, with a literal interlinear transl. 1st Amer. ed. Philadelphia, 1832. 16° 1655.3

Shelf. No.

STORIES of boy-genius from the lives of great painters. Transl. from the French by Lady Jervis White Jervis. London, 1861. 16° . 555.9

STOW, B. Christian brotherhood. Bost. 1859. 16°. 2109.4

STOWE, H. E. B. Our Charley. Boston, [1858.] 16° 747.16

STRAUSS, G. L. German reader. New ed. London, 1859. 16° 1169.21

— Grammar of the French language. London, 1853. 16° 1169.22

— Grammar of the German language. 3d ed. corrected. London, 1861. 16° 1169.20

STRICKLAND, W. P. Life of Jacob Gruber. New York, 1860. 12° 577.11

SUMNER, C. The barbarism of slavery. Boston, 1860. 12° 299.17

SWIFT, J. Gulliver's travels. Leipzig, 1844. 24°. 430.50

— Poetical works. Life by Rev. J. Mitford. Boston, 1859. 3v. 8° 1319.2

    Contents. — Vol. I. Life; Odes; Miscellaneous poems. II. Miscellaneous poems; Verses for fruit-women; Epigrams on windows; Riddles by Swift and his friends; Poems made at Market Hill. III. Political poetry; Trifles; Verses to Swift and his memory.

SWORD and gown. Leipzig, 1860. 24° 720.40

SYMONDS, W. S. Old bones; or, notes for young naturalists. London, 1861. 18° 176.32

TALES from "Bentley." Lond. 1861. Vol. III. XV. 2v. in 1. 16° 479.15

    Contents. — Vol. III. Father Mathew; The double-bedded room; The handsome clear-starcher; The contrabandista; Marie de Villemare; Bononye the usurer; Pasquale, a tale of Italy; The man in the Spanish cloak; Les poissons d'Avril; Irish invention; Scenes in the life of a gambler; The deathbed confession; Mrs. Jennings. IV. Darby the swift; An excellent offer; The quarantine; The father; Richelieu, or, the conspiracy; Paddy Flynn, or, the miseries of dining out; The phantom funeral; The duel; The narrative of John Ward Gibson.

TALES from "Blackwood." Edinburgh, n.d. 11v. 16° 800.41

    Contents. — Vol. I. The Glenmutchkin railway, by Prof. Aytoun; Vanderdecken's message home; The floating beacon; Colonna the painter; Napoleon, by J. G. Lockhart; A legend of Gibraltar, by Col. E. B. Hamley; The iron shroud, by W. Mudford. II. Lazaro's legacy, by E. B. Hamley; A story without a tail; Faustus and Queen Elizabeth; How I became a yeoman, by Prof. Aytoun; Devereux hall, by Mrs. Southey; The metempsychosis, by R. Macnish; College theatricals. III. A reading party in the long vacation; Father Tom and the pope; La petite Madelaine, by Mrs. Southey; Bob Burke's duel with ensign Brady, by W. Maginn; The headsman, a tale of doom; The wearyful woman, by J. Galt. IV. How I stood for the Dreepdaily burghs, by Prof. Aytoun; First and last, by W. Mudford; The Duke's dilemma; The old gentleman's teetotum; "Woe to us when we lose the watery wall"; My college friends; Charles Russell; The magic lay of the one-horse chay, by J. Hughes. V. Adventures in Texas; How we got possession of the Tuileries, by Prof. Aytoun; Capt. Paton's lament, by J. G. Lockhart; The village doctor, by the late countess D'Arbouville; A singular letter from Southern Africa. VI. My friend the Dutchman, by F. Hardman; My college friends; Horace Leicester, W. W. Hurst; The emerald studs, by Prof. Aytoun; Christine, by F. Hardman; The man in the bell. VII. My English acquaintance, by F. Hardman; The murderer's last night, by F. Doubleday; Narration of H. Willis; The wags; The wet wooing, a narrative of '98; Ben-Na-Groich. VIII. The surveyor's tale, by Prof. Aytoun; The Forest-race romance; Di Vasari, a tale of Florence, by C. Edwards; Sigismund Fatello; The boxes. IX. Rosaura: a tale of Madrid; Adventure in the North-west territory; Harry Bolton's curacy; The Florida pirate; The pandour and his princes; The beauty draught. X. Antonio di Carrara; The fatal repast; The vision of Cagliostro; The first and last kiss; The smuggler's leap; The haunted and the haunt-ress; The duellists. XI. The Natolian story-teller; The first and last crime; John Rintoul; Major Moss; The premier and his wife.

TAUBERT, *Capt.* Use of field artillery on service. Transl. from the German by H. H. Maxwell. London, 1856. 16° 1169.56

TAUCHNITZ, C. B. v. Five centuries of the English language and literature. Leipzig, 1860. 24° 720.16

TAUTPHŒUS, *Baroness.* Cyrilla. Leipz. 1853. 24°. 720.41

— The initials. Leipzig, 1854. 24° 430.51

— Quits. Leipzig, 1858. 24° 430.52

— Same. New ed. London, 1860. 16° . . . 500.15

TAYLER, C. B. Not of the world; or, Lady Mary. London, 1860. 16° 500.13

TEFFT, B. F. Methodism successful. Introduction by bishop Janes. New York, 1860. 12°. 113.12

TEMPLETON, H. Diary and notes. Leipz. 1848. 24°. 430.53

TENNYSON, A. Poetical works. Leipzig, 1860. 3v. 24° 430.54

    Contents. — Vol. I. Idylls of the king; Maud. II. In memoriam; The princess. III. Miscellaneous poems.

THACKERAY, W. M. The English humourists. Leipzig, 1853. 24° 430.56

— Henry Esmond. Leipzig, 1852. 24° . . . 430.57

— Miscellanies. Leipzig, 1851-7. 8v. in 5. 24°. 720.42

    Contents. — Vol. I. The history of Samuel Titmarsh and the Great Hoggarty diamond; The book of snobs. II. The tremendous adventures of Major Gahagan; The fatal boots; Ballads; Love songs made easy; Four German ditties; Imitation of Horace; An old friend with a new face; Lyra Hybernica; The ballads of policeman x.

— The Newcomes. Leipzig, 1854. 2v. 24° . . 430.58

— Pendennis. Leipzig, 1849. 3v. 24° 430.59

— Vanity Fair. Leipzig, 1848. 2v. 24° 430.60

— The Virginians. Leipzig, 1858-9. 2v. 24° . . 720.43

THAYER, W. M. The printer boy; or, how Ben Franklin made his mark. Boston, 1861. 16°. 537.27

THOMPSON, J. P. Stray meditations. New York, 1852. 12° 1115.2

THOMSON, A. S. The story of New Zealand. London, 1859. 2v. 12° 935.1

THOMSON, *Mrs.* A. T. Life and times of George Villiers, duke of Buckingham. London, 1860. 3v. 12° 567.3

THOMSON, J. Poetical works. Leipzig, 1853. 24°. 430.55

— — Same. Boston, 1857. 2v. 18° 1319.3

    Contents. — Vol. I. Memoir by Sir H. Nicolas; Miscellaneous poems; Liberty; The prospect. II. The seasons; Castle of indolence.

THORNTON, J. W. The pulpit of the American revolution. Boston, 1860. 12° . . . 217.20

THREE barriers (The). Notes on Mr. Darwin's "Origin of species." Edinburgh, 1861. 12°. 175.20

TICKELL, T. Poetical works. Life, by Dr Johnson. Boston, 1854. 18° 1317.14

TILLEY, H. A. Japan, the Amoor, and the Pacific. London, 1861. 8° 695.17

TIMBS, J. Anecdote biography. Lond. 1860. 12°. 587.15

— Something for everybody. London, n.d. 12°. 185.22

TOMLINSON, C. The thunderstorm. London, n.d. 12° 1159.6

TOWLE, N. C. History and analysis of the constitution. 2d ed. Boston, 1861. 12° . . . 298.1

TRAVELLER's library, complete in 25 vols. London, Longman, v.d. p.8°.

    Contents. — Vol. I-XIII. Voyages and travels. XIV-XVII. Biography and history. XVIII-XX. Selections. XXI-XXII. Fiction. XXIII. Mines and mining. XXIV. Natural philosophy. XXV. Miscellanies. *As follow:*

Arago, F. D. J. History of my youth . . . 1655.17

Auldjo, J. Ascent of Mont Blanc 1655.1

Barrow, J. Tour on the Continent, 1852 . . 1655.2

Brooks, S. The Russians of the south . . . 1655.6

Cockayne, T. O. Life of marshal Turenne . . 1655.14

Cornwall: its mines and miners 1655.23

Custine, A. *marq.* de. Russia 1655.5

Dumas, A. Memoirs of a maitre d'armes . . 1655.22

Durrieu, X. The present state of Morocco . 1655.10

Ferguson, R. Swiss men and Swiss mountains 1655.1

Forester, T. Rambles in Norway 1655.4

Forster, J. Daniel De Foe and Charles Churchill 1655.16

Gleig, G. R. The Leipsic campaign 1655.14

Shelf. No.

TRAVELLER's library *continued.*

Gregorovius, F. Corsica 1655.2

Hayward, A. Lord Chesterfield and George
Selwyn 1655.17

Holcroft, T. Memoirs 1655.17

Hope, J. Britanny and the Bible 1655.7

— Britanny and the chase 1655.7

Howard, G. F. W. Lectures in aid of popular education 1655.25

Huc, E. R. Journey through Tartary, Thibet, and China 1655.8

Hughes, W. The Australian colonies . . . 1655.13

Hurlbut, W. H. Pictures of Cuba 1655.11

Hutchinson, T. J. Narrative of the Niger,
Tshadda, and Bluuë exploration 1655.9

Jameson, A. Sketches in Canada 1655.12

Jeffrey, F. Jonathan Swift 1655.16

— Samuel Richardson 1655.16

Jerrmann, E. Pictures from St. Petersburg. 1655.6

Kemp, T. L. Indications of instinct 1655.24

— Natural history of creation 1655.24

Kinglake, A. W. Eöthen 1655.8

La Gironière, P. P. de. Twenty years in the
Philippines 1655.8

Laing, S. Journal of a residence in Norway,
1834–6 . . . . 1655.3

— Notes on the state of France, Prussia,
Switzerland, and Italy 1655.3

Lanman, C. Adventures in the wilds of
North America 1655.12

Macaulay, T. B. Selections from essays and
speeches [14 titles, in 2 v.] 1655.19,20

McCulloch, J. R. London in 1850, '51 . . . . 1655.25

— Russia and Turkey 1655.6

Mason, G. H. Life with the Zulus of Natal. 1655.9

Mayne, F. Voyages and discoveries in the
Arctic regions 1655.7

Memoir of the duke of Wellington. From
the "Times." 1655.14

Miles, P. Nordurfari: or rambles in Iceland. 1655.4

Mormonism, from the Edinburgh review . . 1655.25

Our coal and coal pits 1655.23

Pfeiffer, I. R. Voyage round the world . . 1655.13

Piozzi, H. L. Anecdotes of S. Johnson . . 1655.16

Porter, A. M. Sir E. Seaward's shipwreck. 1655.21

Ranke, L. Ferdinand I. and Maximilian II. 1655.15

Rogers, H. Life and genius of T. Fuller . . 1655.15

Smith, S. Selections from his writings . . . 1655.18

Southey, R. A love story 1655.22

Souvestre, E. An attic philosopher in Paris. 1655.21

— Confessions of a working man 1655.21

Spencer, H. Railway morals and policy . . 1655.25

Stark, A. Printing, its origin, history, etc. 1655.25

Tschudi, F. v. Nature in the Alps 1655.1

Turkey and Christendom, from the Edinburgh review 1655.15

Wagner, F. and Bodenstedt, F. Schamyl . . 1655.14

Werne, F. African wanderings 1655.10

Wilberforce, E. Brazil viewed through a
naval glass 1655.11

Wilson, G. Electricity and electric telegraph 1655.24

TREDGOLD, T. *See* Robinson, J.

TRENCH, R. C. Sermons preached in Westminster Abbey. New York, 1860. 12° 113.16

TRISTRAM, H. B. The great Sahara. London,
1860. 8° 684.10

TROLLOPE, A. Barchester Towers. Leipzig,
1859. 24° 430.61

— The Bertrams. Leipzig, 1859. 24° 430.62

— Castle Richmond. Leipzig, 1860. 24° 430.63

— Doctor Thorne. Leipzig, 1858. 24° 430.64

— Framley parsonage. New York, 1861. 12° . 485.24

— The Macdermots of Ballycloran. New ed.
London, 1861. 12° 485.22

— The three clerks. New ed. London, 1860. 16° . 500.16

— The warden. Leipzig, 1859. 24° 430.65

— The West Indies and the Spanish main.
Leipzig, 1860. 24° 430.66

TROLLOPE, T. Social aspects of the Italian revolution. London, 1861. 12° 917.17

Shelf. No.

TRUTH answers best; or, Jean and Nicolette.
London, 1860. 16° 500.18

TUCKER, B. The partisan leader. A key to the
disunion conspiracy. Secretly printed in
1836, but suppressed. Vol. I. New York,
1861. 12° 298.3–4

TSCHUDI, F. v. Sketches of nature in the Alps.
London, 1858. p.8° 1655.1

TULLOCH, J. English puritanism and its leaders.
Edinburgh, 1861. 12° 997.7

TURGAN, J. Les grandes usines de France. Paris,
1860. 8° 1071.1

TURKEY and Christendom. From the Edinburgh
review. London, 1854. pp.94. p.8° . . . 1655.15

TURNER, G. Nineteen years in Polynesia. London, 1861. 8° 681.4

TYLOR, E. B. Anahuac, or Mexico and the Mex-
icans. London, 1861. 8° 255.3

TYNG, S. H. Forty years' experience in Sunday
schools. New York, 1860. 16° 2109.3

UNCLE Ralph. By the author of "Still waters."
Leipzig, 1858. 24° 430.67

UNION text book (The). Philadelphia, 1860. 12°. 299.15

UNITED States. Cavalry tactics. Philadelphia,
1861. 3v. 24° 1209.15

— Infantry tactics. Philadelphia, 1861. 24°. . 1199.1–12

— Regulations for the army, 1861. New York,
1861. 12° 185.20

VACHEROT, E. La democratie. 2ème éd. Bruxelles, 1860. 8° 2063.5

VALFONS, C. de Mathei de. Souvenirs, 1710–86.
Paris, 1860. 12° 2065.20

VAN EVERIE, J. H. Negroes and negro "slavery." New York, 1861. 12° 299.20

VARNHAGEN VON ENSE, C. A. Rahel. Ein Buch
des Andenkens für ihre Freunde. Berlin,
1833. 8° 2013.6

VAUGHAN, H. Sacred poems, Memoir by Rev.
H. F. Lyte. Boston, 1854. 18° 1319.4

VAUGHAN, R. A. Hours with the mystics. 2d
ed. London, 1860. 2v. 12° 115.23

VENN, H. Life and letters. Memorial by Rev. J.
Venn. Ed. by Rev. H. Venn. 7th edition.
London, 1853. 16° 2109.9

VIELE, E. L. Hand-book for active service. New
York, 1861. 12° 205.19

VISS. *See* Wyss, G.

VITET, L. La Ligue. Précédée des états d'Orléans. Nouv. éd. Paris, 1861. 2v. 12°. . 2065.23

VITRUVIUS Pollio, M. Architecture. Tr. by J.
Gwilt. New ed. London, 1860. 16° . . . 1169.45

VOLTAIRE, F. M. A. de. History of Charles XII.
of Sweden. Lansingburgh, 1822. 12° . . . 555.6

WAGNER, F., and Bodenstedt, F. Schamyl, the
sultan of the Caucasus Transl. by L. Wraxall. London, 1857. p.8° 1655.14

WALDEN, J. H. Soil culture. N. Y. 1860. 12°. 166.35

WALLACE, W. A. The Great Eastern's log. London, 1860. 12° 639.28

WARBURTON, E. The crescent and the cross.
Leipzig, 1852. 24° 430.68

— Darien; or, the merchant prince. Leipzig,
1853. 24° 430.69

WARD, J. H. Instruction in naval ordnance and
gunnery. New ed. New York, 1861. 8° . 204.18

— Naval tactics. New York, 1859. 8° 204.16

— Popular treatise on steam. New ed. New
York, 1860. 8° 204.17

WARREN, S. Diary of a late physician. Leipzig,
1844. 2v. 24° 720.44

— The lily and bee. Leipzig, 1851. 24° 430.70

— Now and then. Leipzig, 1848. 24° 430.70

— Ten thousand a year. Leipzig, 1845. 3v. 24° . 720.45

WASHINGTON, G. Diary from 1789 to 1791. Ed.
by B. J. Lossing. New York, 1860. 12° . . 518.18

WATSON, E. Men and times of the revolution.
Ed. by W. C. Watson. 2d ed. New York,
1857. 8° 514.6

Shelf. No.

WATT, A. Electro-metallurgy practically treated. London, 1860. 16° 1169.58

WATTS, I. Horæ lyricæ and divine songs. Memoir by R. Southey. Boston, 1854. 18° . . 1319.5

WEBB, *Mrs.* J. B. The martyrs of Carthage. New ed. London, n.d. 16° 500.14

WELBY, H. Mysteries of life, death, and futurity. London, 1861. 16° 1115.5

WELLS, D. A. Annual of scientific discovery for 1861. Boston, 1861. 12° . . . . . v.12 of 159.1

WERNE, F. African wanderings. Transl. by J. R. Johnson. London, 1852. p.8° 1655.10

WHATELY, R. Introductory lessons on mind. Boston, 1859. 12° 1115.21

— Miscellaneous lectures and reviews. London, 1861. 8° 882.5

— Rise, progress, and corruptions of Christianity. New York, 1860. 12° 2106.4

WHEELER, W. A. *See* Soule, R. J.

WHITE, E. S. The maltster's guide. London, 1860. 16° 1159.8

WHITE, H. K. Poetical works. Memoir by Sir H. Nicolas. Boston, 1859. 18° 1319.6

WHITMARSH, C. S. Hymns for mothers and children. Boston, 1861. sm.4° 373.2

— and Guild, A. E. Hymns of the ages. 2d ser. Boston, 1861. sm. 4° 373.1

WHY Paul Ferroll killed his wife. By the author of "Paul Ferroll." London, 1860. 8° . . 439.4

WIGHTMAN, J. B. Anuals of the rescued. New York, 1861. 12° 1115.15

WILBERFORCE, E. Brazil viewed through a naval glass. London, 1856. p.8° 1655.11

WILCOX, C. M. Rifles and rifle practice. New York, 1859. 12° 205.20

WILLIAMS, C. W. Combustion of coal, and the prevention of smoke. London, 1858. 16° 1169.28

WILMSEN, F. P. Der deutsche Kinderfreund. Ein Lesebuch. 113 Aufl. Reutlingen, 1833. 12° . . . 2025.8

— - Same. 2ter Theil. Berlin, 1810. 12° . . . 2026.4

— Hersiliens Lebensmorgen. Geschichte einer geläuterten Seele. 3te Aufl. Berlin, 1827. 16° 2026.3

WILSON, E. The Eastern or Turkish bath. London, 1861. 12° 1159.18

WILSON, G. Electricity and the electric telegraph. With the chemistry of the stars. New ed. London, 1859. p.8° 1655.24

WILSON, Jesse, A. Memoir of George Wilson. Edinburgh, 1860. 8° 577.7

Shelf. No.

WILSON, John. Lights and shadows of Scottish life. New York, 1860. 16° 477.3

WOLFF, J. Travels and adventures. London, 1861. 8° 683.15

WOOD, A. Class book of botany. N. Y. 1861. 8°. 164.23

WOOD, J. G. Athletic sports for boys. London, 1861. 18° 209.39

WOODWARD, S. P. Rudimentary manual of the mollusca. Part 3. London, 1856. 12° . . . 1169.61

WOOLHOUSE, W. S. B. Measures, weights, and moneys of all nations. 2d ed. London, 1859. 16° 1169.59

WORDSWORTH, W. Poetical works. Boston, 1859. 7v. 18° 1319.7

Contents of six vols. as on p. 198 of the catalogue printed 1859. Shelf No. 359.11. Vol. VII. contains the Prelude.

WRIGHT, E. An eye opener for the wide awakes. Boston, 1860. 12° 209.15

WYATT, *Sir* T. Poetical works. With a memoir. Boston, 1854. 18° 1319.8

WYNTER, A. Our social bees. London, 1861. 12°. 883.15

WYSE, G. Pictures of Scottish life. Edinburgh, 1847. 16° 1325.7

WYSS, J. R. de, and Montolieu, I. P. de B. Le Robinson Suisse. Nouv. éd. tr. de l'Allemand, et terminé. Paris, 1830. 5v. 18° . 2065.33

YEAR after year. By the author of "Paul Ferroll." Leipzig, 1858. 24° 430.72

YONGE, C. M. The daisy chain. Leipz. 1856. 24°. 720.46

— Dynevor Terrace. Leipzig, 1857. 24° 430.73

— Heartsease. Leipzig, 1855. 24° 430.74

— Heir of Redclyffe. Leipzig, 1855. 24° 430.75

— Hopes and fears. New York, 1861. 2v. 12°.784.9–12

— - Same. Leipzig, 1861. 24° 720.47–48

YOUNG, E. Poetical works. Bost. 1859. 2v. 18°. 1319.9

Contents, as on p. 199 of the catalogue printed 1859. Shelf No. 329.14.

YOUNG, J. R. Key and companion to the rudimentary algebra. London, 1856. 16° . . . 1169.55

— Navigation and nautical astronomy. London, 1858. 16° 1169.53

— Tables to facilitate navigation and nautical astronomy. London, 1859. 16° 1169.64

ZACHARIE, I. Diseases of the human foot. New York, 1860. 12° 168.24

ZAKRZEWSKA, M. E. A practical illustration of "Woman's right to labor." Ed. by C. H. Dall. Boston, 1860. 12° 1115.10

N O T E.

The following important works have been provided in numbers sufficient to meet a lage demand: Miss Nightingale's Notes on nursing; Bulfinch's Boy inventor; Northend's Teachers' assistant; Life of Amos Lawrence; Everett's Life of Washington. Additional copies of other books, as may be observed in the catalogues, have also been furnished in order to meet an increased demand for them.

FIFTH SUPPLEMENT TO THE INDEX.

CONTAINING A LIST OF THE BOOKS PLACED IN THE LOWER HALL, FROM DECEMBER 1, 1861,
TO OCTOBER 31, 1862.

Shelf. No.

ABBOTT, B., A, and L. Matthew Caraby, his adventures in 1858. By Benauly. New York, 1859. 12° 803.18

ABBOTT, J. S. C. Practical Christianity. For young men. New York, 1862. 16° 2109.17

ABERCROMBY, J., lord Dunfermline. Memoir of Sir Ralph Abercromby, 1793–1801, by his son. Edinburgh, 1861. 8° 577.12

ABOUT, E. F. V. Gaetana. Drame en cinq actes. 5ème éd. Paris, 1862. 16° 2076.3

— Lettres d'un bon jeune homme à sa cousine. Paris, 1861. 12° 2066.17

— L'homme à l'oreille cassée. Paris, 1862. 16° . 2075.31

ADAMS, H. C. Schoolboy honour. New ed. London, 1862. 16° 746.10

AGASSIZ, L. J. R. Contributions to the natural history of the United States. Vol. IV. Boston, 1862. 4° 170.2

AGUILAR, G. Home scenes and heart studies. New York, 1860. 12° 773.1

AIMARD, G. Balle-Franche. Paris, 1861. 12° . . . 2066.34

— Le Cœur-Loyal. Paris, 1861. 12° 2066.32

— Les Francs Tireurs. Paris, 1861. 16° 2066.33

— The Indian scout. Philadelphia, n.d. 8° . . . 792.5

— Les rôdeurs des frontières. Paris, 1861. 12° . 2075.12

AINSWORTH, W. H. The constable of the tower. Leipzig, 1861. sq.16° 730.6

— Guy Fawkes; or, the gunpowder treason. New York, 1848. 8° 802.50

ALCOTT, W. A. The young man's guide. 21st ed. Boston, 1858. 18° 1139.1

ALFIO Balzani; or, extracts from the diary of a proscribed Sicilian. New York, 1861. 12° . . 495.19

ALL the year round. Vol. V. London, 1861. 8° . 851.1

ALLEN, E. Sketches of Green Mountain life. Lowell, 1846. 18° 440.73

ALLEN, H. H. Compendium of Hardee's tactics. With manual of arms. New York, 1861. 18° . 1199.19

ALLINGHAM, W. Poems. First American ed. Boston, 1861. 32° 450.38

ALTMANN, J. Spiegelbilder der Sahara. Eine Sammlung arabischer Volkslieder übertragen. Leipzig, 1861. 12° 2015.7

AMALIE von Sachsen. Social life in Germany, illustrated in dramas. Tr. with an introd. by Mrs. Jameson. London, 1840. 2v. 12° . . . 352.1

AMMIANUS MARCELLINUS. Roman history during the reigns of Constantius, Julian, Jovianus, Valentinian, and Valens. Tr. by C. D. Yonge. London, 1862. p.8° 855.11

ANDERSEN, H. C. Danish fairy legends and tales. Tr., with a memoir, by C. Peachey. 3d ed., enlarged. London, 1861. p.8° 854.13

— The improvisatore. Tr. by M. Howitt. New York, 1861. 8° 792.2

ANDERSSON, C. J. The Okavango river. New York, 1861. 8° 683.16

APTHORP, H. O. A grammar of elocution. Philadelphia, 1858. 12° 393.6

ARTHUR, T. S. The three eras of a woman's life. Philadelphia, 1860. 3v. in 1. 12° 453.7

ASHTON, W. T. Hatchie, the guardian slave. Boston, 1853. 12° 487.25

Shelf. No.

ASPECTS of religion in the United States. London, 1859. 16° 2109.11

AUERBACH, B. Edelweiss. Stuttgart, 1861. 12° . 2016.18

AUREVILLY, J. B. d'. Les œuvres et les hommes. 1e partie. Paris, 1860. 12° 2066.20

AUTOBIOGRAPHY of a beggar boy. 4th ed. London, 1859. 18° 589.24

BALLANTYNE, R. M. The dog Crusoe. Boston, 1862. 12° 746.5

— The Red Eric. New ed. London, 1862. 16° . 746.9

BALLINGALL, G. Outlines of military surgery. 5th ed. Edinburgh, 1855. 8° 162.10

BALLOU, H. A treatise on the atonement. 6th ed. Utica, 1840. 12° 2106.18

BALZAC, H. de. Eugénie Grandet; or, the miser's daughter. Tr. by O. W. Wight and F. B. Goodrich. New York, 1861. 12° 495.18

BAND of hope review, and Children's friend. London, 1851–1860. f° 940.1

BARNARD, J. G. The C. S. A. and the battle of Bull Run. New York, 1862. 8° 293.2

BARRETT, B. F. Letters on the divine trinity, addressed to Henry Ward Beecher. 2d ed. New York, 1860. 12° 2095.8

BARTHET, A. Théâtre complet. Paris, 1861. 12° . 2076.4
 Contents. — Le moineau de Lesbie; Le chemin de Corinthe; L'heure du berger.

BASTEROT, le vicomte de. De Québec à Lima; journal d'un voyage dans les deux Amériques en 1858 et 1859. Paris, 1860. 12° 2066.37

BATTHYANY, J. Journal d'Ilma Szerendy. Paris, 1861. 16° 2066.28

BAYLY, Mrs. Workmen and their difficulties. London, 1861. p.8° 1138.7

BEECHER, C. E. Physiology and calisthenics. New York, 1860. 12° 159.3

BELGIOJOSO, C. T. di. Oriental harems and scenery. Tr. from the French. New York, 1862. 12° 697.24

BERQUIN, A. de. L'ami des enfans. Nouv. éd. Lyon, 1829. 7v. 24° 2069.6

— Bibliothèque des villages. Lyon, 1833. 2v. 24° . 2069.8

— Choix de lectures pour les enfans. Lyon, 1833. 2v. 24° 2069.7

— Historiettes et conversations à l'usage des enfans. Lyon, 1830. 24° 2069.12

— Historiettes et petits contes. Lyon, 1830. 24° . 2069.13

— Introduction à la connoissance de la nature, imitée de l'anglais. Lyon, 1833. 24° 2069.10

— Le livre de famille. Lyon, 1833. 24° 2069.11

— Le petit Grandisson, imité du Hollandais. Lyon, 1833. 24° 2069.9

— Lydie de Gersin, ou histoire d'une jeune Anglaise de huit ans. Lyon, 1832. 24° 2069.12

BERSOT, P. E. Littérature et morale. Paris, 1861. 12° 2066.12

BERTAULD, C. A. Philosophie politique de l'histoire de France. Paris, 1861. 8° 2063.27

BEST, M. C. Abroad: and how to live there. London, 1860. p.8° 669.17

BIBLE. A commentary on the New Testament. By L. R. Paige. Boston, 1860–61. 4v. 12° . . 2095.14

Shelf. No.

BIGELOW, T. Dream fulfilled; or, the trials and triumphs of the Moreland family. Boston, 1846. 18°ℰ 440.74

BLACKMAN, G. C., *see* TRIPLER, C. S.

BLACKMORE, J. The London by moonlight mission. Memoir of the author. London, 1861. 12° 2100.12

BOICHOT, J. B. Petit traité de connaissances. Bruxelles, 1862. 12° 2076.7

BÖLTE, A. Vittorio Alfieri und seine vierte Liebe, oder Turin und Florenz. Berlin, 1862. 2v. 12° 2075.5

BOMBONNEL le tueur de panthères. Paris, 1860. 12°. 2075.7

BONAR, A. A. Memoir of the brief ministry of Rev. David Sandeman. Lond., 1861. p.8°. . 579.20

BONER, C. Forest creatures. London, 1861. 8°. . 175.23

— Chamois hunting in the mountains of Bavaria and the Tyrol. New ed. Loud., 1860. p.8°. . 665.17

BOYD, A. K. H. Leisure hours in town. Boston, 1862. p.8° 903.22

BOY'S own book extended. N. Y., 1859. sq.12° . . 1198.1

BRAVE (The) old English confessors. London, 1861. p.8° 567.6

BRENTEN, J. H. The tragedy of life : records of remarkable phases of lunacy. London, 1861. 2v. p.8° 803.17

BRIGHTWELL, C. L. Difficulties overcome : scenes in the life of Alexander Wilson, the ornithologist. London, 1861. 16° 589.22

BRIMLEY, G. Essays. Introduction by R. H. Stoddard. New York, 1861. 12° 883.17

BRODIE, *Sir* B. C. Psychological inquiries. 2d part. London, 1862. 16° 129.18

BROOKS, C. S. The silver cord. N. Y., 1861. 8°. 502.16

— - Same. Leipzig, 1862. 3v. sq.16° 730.9

BROWN, C. F. Artemus Ward—his book. New York, 1862. 12° 803.21

BROWN, H. S. Lectures to the men of Liverpool. Liverpool, 1861. 4v. in 1. 12° 2106.8

BROWN, J. Health : five lay sermons to working people. New York, 1862. 90 pp. 16° 1157.4

— Spare hours. Boston, 1862. p.8° 883.21

BROWNING, E. B. Last poems. Memorial by T. Tilton. New York, 1862. 16° 373.7

BROWNLOW, W. G. Sketches of the rise, progress, and decline of secession. Phila., 1862. 12°. 634.10

BUNGENER, F. Rome et le cœur humain. Paris, 1861. p.8° 2066.36

BURDETT, C. Life and adventures of Christopher Carson. New York, 1860. 12° 1525.18–20

BURGESS, N. G. The photograph manual. New York, 1862. 16° 185.30

BURTON, R. F. The city of the saints. New York, 1862. 8° 622.11

CACCIA, A. Europa ed America, scene della vita. 1848–50. Monaco, 1850. 16° 2048.3

CADET life at West Point. By an officer of the United States army ; and, Descriptive sketch of West Point, by B. J. Lossing. Boston, 1862. 12° 494.4

CALKINS, N. A. Primary object lessons. 4th ed. New York, 1862. 12° 1133.7–18

CAMPBELL, J. John Angell James: his history, character, eloquence, and literary labours. London, 1860. p.8° 578.22

CAMPBELL, J. F. Popular tales of the West Highlands. Vols. III, IV. Edinburgh, 1862. 12°. 479.13

CAMPE, J. H. Robinson der Jüngere. 75e Auflage. Braunschweig, 1859. 2v. in 1. 16° 2019.14

CAMPIN, F. Hand-turning in wood, ivory, shell, etc. London, 1861. p.8° 185.23

CANTREL, É. Nouvelles à la main sur la comtesse Du Barry. Paris, 1861. 8° 2063.26

CAPEFIGUE, J. B. H. R. Anne d'Autriche. Paris, 1861. 12° 2075.17

— Le cardinal Dubois. Paris, 1861. 12° 2066.15

— Diane de Poitiers. Paris, 1860. 16° 2066.39

— La duchesse de Portsmouth et la cour galante des Stuarts. Paris, 1861. 12° 2075.20

— Marie de Médicis. Paris, 1861. 12° 2075.21

CAPENDU, E. Le chasseur de panthères. Paris, 1861. p.8° 2075.6

CARLYLE, T. History of Friedrich the second. Vol. III. New York, 1862. 12° 542.6

CASEY, S. Infantry tactics. New York, 1862. 3v. 32° 1208.21

CATLIN, G. Life amongst the Indians. A book for youth. London, 1861. 16° 746.1

CHAMBERS, R. Domestic annals of Scotland, from the revolution to the rebellion of 1745. Vol. III. Edinburgh, 1861. 8° 974.3

CHAPIN, E. H. The crown of thorns. Boston, 1860. p.8° 2106.17

CHEVALIER, H. É. Biographie de M. Eugène Godard. Montreal, 1856. 80pp. 24° 2069.15

CHORLEY, W. B. A handybook of social intercourse : political economy for the million. London, 1862. p.8° 1139.2

CLARK, R. W. Lectures on the formation of character. Boston, 1861. 12° 1126.8

CLARKE, L. and M. Narratives of the sufferings of Lewis and Milton Clarke among the slaveholders of Kentucky. Boston, 1846. 12°. 298.8

CLÉRY, J. B. C. H. Journal of what passed in the Temple prison during the captivity of Louis the XVI. Tr. by J. Bromfield. London, [1860]. p.8° 614.5

CLEVELAND, C. D. A compendium of classical literature. Philadelphia, 1861. 8° 393.2

CLOUGH, A. H. Poems. Memoir by C. E. Norton. Boston, 1862. 32° 440.75

COCKTON, H. Percy Effingham. Phila., n.d. 8°. 711.8

— The sisters ; or, the fatal marriages. Philadelphia, n.d. 8° 711.6

— The steward. Philadelphia, n.d. 8° 711.7

— Valentine Vox. Philadelphia, n.d. 8° 711.2

COGGESHALL, W. T. Stories of frontier adventure in the South and West. Columbus, 1861. p.8°. 745.19

COLLIER, W. F. A history of English literature in biographical sketches. London, 1861. p.8°. 945.7

COLLINS, C. A. A cruise upon wheels. London, 1862. 2v. p.8° 656.6

COLLINS, W. W. The stolen mask. Philadelphia, n.d. 64 pp. 8° 792.10

COLOMBEY, É. Histoire anecdotique du duel. Paris, n.d. 12° 2066.8

CONWAY, M. D. The golden hour. Bost., 1862. p.8°. 298.16

— Rejected stone, or insurrection *vs.* resurrection in America. Boston, 1861. 12° 298.5

COOKE, G. W. China and Lower Bengal : being the "Times" correspondence from China in 1857–58. 5th ed. London, 1861. p.8° 709.30

COOKE, P. St. G. Cavalry tactics. Philadelphia, 1862. 2v. 12° 1208.22

CORNE, H. M. A. Souvenirs d'un proscrit. Paris, 1861. 12° 2066.2

CORNWALLIS, K. Pilgrims of fashion. New York, 1862. 12° 494.5

COTTEN, E. R. Life of the Hon. Nathaniel Macon. Baltimore, 1840. 12° 528.29

COURCY, C. de. Les histoires du café de Paris. Paris, 1861. 12° 2066.19

CRAIGHILL, W. P. The army officer's pocket companion. New York, 1862. 24° 1208.25

CROMWELL, O. Letters and speeches, with elucidations by T. Carlyle. Leipzig, 1861. 4v. 24° 1579.2

CUMMING, J. Teach us to pray ; observations on the Lord's prayer. New York, 1862. 12° . . 2005.16

CZECHOWSKI, M. B. Thrilling developments : fifteen years as Roman Catholic clergyman and priest. Boston, 1862. 12° 2100.21

DALL, C. H. Woman's rights under the law. Boston, 1861. p.8° 1138.4

DALTON, J. C. A treatise on human physiology. 2d ed., revised. Philadelphia, 1861. 8° . . . 162.9

DANA, A. H. Ethical and physiological inquiries. New York, 1862. 12° 154.11

Shelf. No.

DARGAUD, J. M. Voyage en Danemark. Paris, 1861. 12° 2066.29
DAY, T. Sandford et Merton, imité [par A. de Berquin]. Lyon, 1829. 2v. 24° 2069.5
DEMOSTHENES. Orations. Tr. with notes, by C. R. Kennedy. London, 1861. p.8° . . . 833.1

Contents. — Orations against Timocrates, Aristogiton, Aphobus, Onitor, Zenothemis, Apaturius, Phormio, Lacritus, Pantænetus, Nausimachus, Bœotus, Spudias, Phœnippus, and for Phormio.

DENISON, M. A. The master. Boston, 1862. 12°. 477.19
DE QUINCEY, T. Beauties, selected from [his] writings. Boston, 1862. 12° 882.12
DESBAROLLES, A. Voyage d'un artiste en Suisse. Paris, n.d. 12° 2075.1
DICEY, E. Cavour, a memoir. Camb., 1861. p.8°. 555.10
DICK, T. Complete works. Cincinnati, 1857. 2v. 8° 1101.6

Contents. — Vol. I. Essay on the improvement of society; Philosophy of a future state; Philosophy of religion; Mental illumination and moral improvement of mankind; Essay on covetousness. Vol. II. Christian philosopher; Celestial scenery; Sidereal heavens, planets, etc.; Practical astronomer; Solar system; Atmosphere and atmospherical phenomena.

DICKENS, C. Great expectations. Leipzig, 1861. 2v. in 1. sq. 16° 720.50
— — Same. New York, 1861. 2v. p.8° 483.4
— Hard times. Leipzig, 1854. sq.16° 720.56
— Household words. Vols. 25, 33, 35, 36. Leipzig, 1854-6. 4v. sq.16° 1959.1
— Martin Chuzzlewit. New York, 1862. 4v. p.8° 483.6
— The old curiosity shop. N. Y., 1861. 3v. p.8° 483.5
DIXON, W. H. Personal history of Lord Bacon. Leipzig, 1861. sq.16° 1579.3
DODGE, M. A. Country living and country thinking. By Gail Hamilton. Boston, 1862. 12° 893.14
DRAYSON, A. W. The common sights in the heavens. London, 1862. 16° 1148.5
DREW, B. The refugee; or the narratives of fugitive slaves in Canada. Boston, 1846. 12° . 298.7
DUANE, J. C. Manual for engineer troops. New York, 1862. 12° 204.28
DUDEVANT, A. L. A. D. [George Sand.] Valvèdre. Paris, 1861. 12° 2075.15
DUFFIELD, W. W. School of the brigade, and evolutions of the line. Philadelphia, 1862. 24°. 1199.34
DUMAS, A. Amaury. New York, 1845. 8° 802.51
— Diana of Meridor. Tr. by H. W. Herbert. New York, 1846. 8° 802.53
— Geneviève, or the chevalier of Maison Rouge. Tr. by H. W. Herbert. New York, 1846. 8°. 802.52
— Louise La Vallière. Phila., n.d. 2v. in 1. 8° 711.5
— The three guardsmen. Philadelphia, n.d. 8°. 711.3
— Twenty years after. Philadelphia, n.d. 8°. 711.4
D'WOLF, J. Voyage to the North Pacific, and journey through Siberia, [1804-8.] Cambridge, [Mass.], 1861. 8° 682.7
EAMES, J. A. A budget of letters. Boston, 1846. 12° 1904.2
EARLY Egyptian history for the young. By the author of " Sidney Grey." Camb., 1861. p.8°. 937.10
EDDY, D. C. Europa. 50th ed. Rochester, 1862. 12° 644.3
ELEY, H. Geology in the garden; or, the fossils in the flint pebbles. London, 1859. sm.16°. 1148.4
ELLEN Mordaunt; or, the fruits of true religion. Philadelphia, n.d. 16° 2109.18
ELLICOTT, C. J. Historical lectures on the life of Christ. Boston, 1862. 12° 1092.11
ELLIOTT, G. D. Mémoires sur la révolution française. Tr. de l'Anglais par M. le comte de Baillon. Paris, 1861. 12° 2066.30
ELLISON, T. Slavery and secession in America. London, [1861]. p.8° 298.11
ELTON, C. A. Specimens of the classic poets. London, 1814. 3v. 8° 1395.19
ELY, A. Journal of a prisoner of war in Richmond. Ed. by C. Lanman. New York, 1862. 12° . . 298.13

Shelf. No.

EMERSON, G. B., and Flint, C. L. Manual of agriculture. Boston, 1862. 12° 1167.4
ERINNERUNGEN eines chemaligen Jesuitenzöglings. Leipzig, 1862. p.8° 2024.11
EVANS, M. J. Silas Marner. Leipzig, 1861. sq.16°. 720.54
EYMA, L. X. Excentricités américaines. Paris, n.d. 32° 2069.4
— La république américaine. Paris, 1861. 2v. 8°. 2063.25

FAIRHOLT, F. W. Up the Nile, and home again. London, 1862. p.8° 684.13
FETRIDGE, W. P. Handbook for travelers in Europe and the East. New York, 1862. 12° . 644.4
FINLAY, G. History of the Greek revolution. Edinburgh, 1861. 2v. 8° 924.5
FITZPATRICK, W. J. Lady Morgan; her career, literary and personal. London, 1860. 16° . 599.17
FITZWYGRAM, F. Notes on shoeing horses. London, 1861. 79 pp. 8° 202.18
FLINT, C. L. See Emerson, G. B.
FLORIAN, J. P. C. de. Gonzalvo; or, the fall of Grenada. [Tr.] by C. Hood. Bost., 1845. 16° 1326.2
FLOWER of the family. New York, 1861. 12° . . 453.8
FOR better, for worse. Boston, 1861. 8° 502.19
FRANCONI, V. Le cavalier; cours d'équitation pratique. 2e éd. Paris, 1861. 12° 2066.1
FREILIGRATH, F. Sämmtliche Werke. New York, 1858. 6v. 12° 2015.1

Contents. — Vol. I. Tagebuchblätter; Balladen und Romanzen; Terzinen; Alexandriner; Vermischte Gedichte; Gelegentliches; Zwischen den Gerben. II. Das Waldheiligthum, von F. Hemans; Der Sang von Hiawatha, von H. W. Longfellow. III. Venus und Adonis, von Shakespeare; Aus den englischen Sonnettisten; Aus neueren englischen Dichtern. IV. Aus neuern englischen Dichtern; Aus dem Italiänischen; Aus dem Französischen. V. Aus den Oden und vermischten Gedichten; Aus den Orientalen und Balladen; Aus den Dämmerungs-gesängen; Nachträgliches. VI. Ein Glaubensbekentniss, Zeitgedichte 1844; Ca ira; Neuere politische und soziale Gedichte.

FRISWELL, H. Footsteps to fame. Lond., 1861. p. 8° 589.23
FROEBEL, J. A travers l'Amérique. Trad. par E. Tandel. Paris, 1861. 3v. 12° 2075.36

GAIRDNER, W. T. Public health in relation to air and water. Edinburgh, 1862. p 8° 1157.7
GAME fish of the northern states of America, and British provinces. By Barnwell. New York, 1862. 12° 174.20
GARASSE, F. Mémoires publiés et avec une notice, par C. Nisard. Paris, 1860. 12° 2066.11
GARRATT, G. Marvels and mysteries of instinct. 3d ed. London, 1862. p.8° 174.19
GASKELL, E. C. Ruth, a novel. Leipzig, 1853. 2v. in 1. sq.16° 720.55
GASPARIN, A. É. de. America before Europe. Principles and interests. Tr. by M. L. Booth. New York, 1862. p.8° 634.9
— Des tables tournantes, du surnaturel en général, et des esprits. Paris, 1854. 2v. 12° 2066.35
— Les États-Unis en 1861: Un grand peuple qui se relève. Paris, 1861. 8° 2063.30
— Une parole de paix. Sur le différend entre l'Angleterre et les États-Unis. Paris, 1862. 31 pp. 8° 2064.7
GATTY, A. Aunt Judy's letters. London, 1862. 8°. 439.8
GENLIS, S. F. D. de St. A. de. De l'influence des femmes sur la littérature française. Paris, 1826. 2v. 12° 2066.38
GERSTÄCKER, F. Heimliche und unheimliche Geschichten. Leipzig, 1862. 2v. in 1. 12° . . 2024.5
GILFILLAN, G. The bards of the Bible. New York, 1851. 12° 2095.5
GODWIN, W. Fleetwood. N. Y., 1805. 2v. 18°. 458.9
GOGOL, N. Cossack tales. Tr. from the Russian by G. Tolstoy. London, n.d. p.8° 803.16
GOUGER, H. Narrative of two years' imprisonment in Burmah, 1824-26. Lond., 1860. 12°. 698.27
GOULD, E. S. John Doe and Richard Roe; or, life in New York. New York, 1862. 12° 453.9
GRANT, J. Jack Manly. London, 1861. 16° . . . 746.7

Shelf. No.

GRAY, D. The Luggie and other poems. With a memoir by J. Hedderwick. Cambridge, 1862. 16° 1325.16

GRENIER, É. Poèmes dramatiques. Paris, n.d. 12°. 2075.41

GREY, *Hon. Mrs.* The flirt. Phila., n.d. 8°. . 792.7

GRIMM, A. T. v. Die Fürstin der siebenten Werst. 2te Aufl. Leipzig, 1861. 2v. 16° 2017.1

GÜELL Y RENTÉ J. Traditions américaines. Paris, 1861. 16° 2075.14

— La vierge des lis, [et] Petite-fille de roi. Paris, 1862. 12° 2075.25

GUIZOT, F. G. P. Memoirs to illustrate the history of my time. Tr. by J. W. Cole. Vol. IV. London, 1861. 8° 1003.5

GUNN, T. B. The physiology of New York boarding-houses. New York, 1857. 12° 803.19

GUTHRIE, G. J. Commentaries on the surgery of the war, 1808-15, with additions relating to the Crimea, 1854-55. 6th ed. Phila., 1862. 12°. 154.10

GUTHRIE, T. Seed-time and harvest of ragged schools. Edinburgh, 1860. p.8° 1126.2

HABITS of good society. From the last London ed. New York, 1860. 12° 1126.1

HACKLÄNDER, F. W. Der Wechsel des Lebens. Stuttgart, 1861. 3v. in 1. 12°. 2024.10

HALL, A. M. Can wrong be right? Bost., 1862. 8° 502.21

— The St. James's magazine. Vols. I.-III. London, 1861-62. 3v. 8° 831.2

HAMILTON, F. H. Practical treatise on military surgery. New York, 1861. 8° 162.11

HAMILTON, W. Metaphysics. Collected by Francis Bowen. Cambridge, 1861. 12° 882.10

HANDY-book for the U. S. soldier. Philadelphia, 1861. 94 pp. 32° 1199.20

HARRIS, W. C. Prison-life in the tobacco warehouse at Richmond. Phila., 1862. 8° . . . 298.18

HART, J. S. Mistakes of educated men. An address. 2d ed. Philadelphia, 1862. 77 pp. 12°. 2106.11

HAURÉAU, J. B. Singularités historiques et littéraires. Paris, 1861. 12° 2066.10

HAUSSONVILLE, *Mme* d'. Robert Emmet. 2me éd. Paris, 1858. 12° 2066.42

HAY, E. History of the Irish insurrection of 1798. New ed. New York, n.d. 12° 997.11

HEADLEY, J. T. Sketches and rambles. New York, 1850. 12° 1666.4

HEINE, H. Briefe. Herausg. v. F. Steinmann. Amsterdam, 1861. 2v. 16°. 2026.7

— Poems. Tr. by E. A. Bowring. London, 1861. p.8° 843.11

HERBERT, L. Louis Napoleon. Roman und Geschichte, 1808-48. Leipzig, 1860-62. 10v. 12°. 2015.10

HÉRICAULT, C. d'. Les patriciens de Paris. Paris, 1861. 12° 2075.19

HESIODUS. Remains, including The shield of Hercules. Tr. with a diss. on his life and poems, by C. A. Elton. 2d ed. London, 1815. 8° . 1395.18

HEUZÉ, L. G. L'année agricole. 3me année. Paris, 1862. 12° 2065.30

HISLOP, A. The proverbs of Scotland, with notes and a glossary. Glasgow, 1862. 16° . . . 373.6

HITTELL, J. S. Mining in the Pacific states of North America. San Francisco, 1861. 16°. 187.32

HOEFER, E. Die Honoratiorentochter. Eine Erzählung. Stuttgart, 1861. sq. 16° 2017.2

HOGG, J. Elements of experimental and natural philosophy. [2d ed.] London, 1861. p.8°. 855.13

HOLLAND, J. G. Lessons in life. N. Y., 1861. 12°. 882.7

— Letters to young people single and married. 26th ed. New York, 1861. 12° 903.21

HOLMES, O. W. Songs in many keys. Boston, 1862. 12° 373.4

HOPKINS, S. The puritans. Vol. III. Boston, 1861. 8° 982.3

HORNE, R. H. Ballad romances. Lond., n.d. 16°. 364.5

HORNER, S. A century of despotism in Naples and Sicily. Edinburgh, 1860. 16° 918.18

HOUDETOT, C. F. A. d'. Galerie des chasseurs illustres. Nouv. éd. Paris, 1861. 12° . . . 2066.16

Shelf. No.

HOWARD, J. H. Athletic and gymnastic exercises. London, 1860. 95 pp. sq. 16° 1199.31

HOWITT, M. Lillieslea. London, 1861. 18° . . . 746.8

HOWSON, J. S. Deaconesses; or, the help of women in parochial work. London, 1862. 16°. 2107.4

HUGO, V. M. Châtiments. Genève, 1853. 32° . . 2069.14

— Les contemplations. 5me éd. Paris, 1858. 2v. 12° 2075.26

— Le Rhin. Paris, 1858. 2v. 16° 2075.29

— Les voix intérieures, [et] Les rayons et les ombres. Paris, 1859. 12° 2075.27

— Napoléon le petit. Londres, 1852. 18° . . . 2068.3

HUNT, J. Stammering and stuttering, their nature and treatment. London, 1861. 16° 1157.6

HUNT, J. H. Leigh. Correspondence. Ed. by his son. London, 1862. 2v. 8° 567.7

HUNTINGTON, J. V. Alban, a tale of the new world. New York, 1851. p.8° 477.17

IBBOTSON, H. W. The legal prompter; or, statute indicator. London, 1860. 16° 1138.6

ILLUSTRATED (The) boy's own treasury. London, 1860. sq.16° 185.25

IRISH abroad and at home. New York, 1856. 12°. 477.16

ISHERWOOD, B. F. Engineering precedents for steam machinery. New York, 1859. 2v. 8°. 193.4

JACKMAN, W. The Australian captive. Ed. by Rev. I. Chamberlayne. Auburn, 1852. 12°. 528.28

JACKSON, C. T. A manual of etherization. Boston, 1861. 12° 1157.2

JACQUES, D. H. Hints towards physical perfection. New York, 1861. 12° 154.8

JAL, A. Études sur la marine antique. Paris, 1861. 12° 2066.4

JAMES, J. A. Life and letters. Edited by R. W. Dale. New York, 1862. 8° 571.3

JANIN, A. Fulton, Georges, et Robert Stephenson. Paris, 1861. 12° 2066.22

JANIN, J. G. La fin d'un monde et du neveu de Rameau. Paris, 1861. 12° 2075.33

JENNER, W. Diphtheria: its symptoms and treatment. London, 1861. 16° 1157.3

JERVIS-WHITE-JERVIS, H. Our engines of war, and how we got to make them. London, 1859. p.8° 205.30

— The rifle-musket. 2d ed. London, 1859. viii+81 pp. p.8° 204.19

JOHNSON, A. C. Cottages of the Alps; or, life and manners in Switzerland. London, 1860. 2v. 12° 665.18

JOHNSTON, J. F. W. Elements of agricultural chemistry and geology. 7th ed. Edinburgh, 1856. 16° 1148.2

JUSTE, T. Vie de Marie de Hongrie. Nouv. éd. Bruxelles, 1861. 12° 2075.28

KARR, J. A. En fumant. Paris, 1861. 12° . . . 2075.2

KAVANAGH, J. French women of letters. Leipzig, 1862. 24° 1609.1

KELLY, W. Life in Victoria, or Victoria in 1853, and in 1858. London, 1859. 2v. p.8° . . . 696.18

KENNEDY, E. S. Peaks, passes, and glaciers. 2d series. London, 1862. 2v. 8° 664.5

KIMBALL, R. B. Romance of student life abroad. Leipzig, 1854. sq.16° 720.22

— Undercurrents of Wall-Street. New York, 1862. 12° 803.20

KINGSLEY, C. Town and country sermons. London, 1861. 16° 2109.15

KINGSLEY, H. Ravenshoe. Boston, 1862. 12°. 504.5

KINGSTON, W. H. G. The boy's own book of boats. London, 1861. sq.16° 185.24

— Old Jack. A tale for boys. London, 1861. 16°. 745.20

— Round the world. Boston, 1862. 16° 746.4

KIRBY, M. and E. Caterpillars, butterflies, and moths. London, 1860. 16° 1179.8

— Plants of the land and water. 2d ed. London, 1860. 24° 1179.10

KIRKE, E. Among the pines. New York, 1862. 12°. 298.15

	Shelf. No.
KLOSS, M. Die Turnschule des Soldaten. Leipzig, 1860. 16°	2025.24
KNOWLES, J. S. Fortescue. A novel. New York, 1855. 8°	792.8
KNOX, R. The races of men. 2d ed. London, 1862. p.8°	174.16
KOHL, J. G. Geschichte der Entdeckung Amerika's von Columbus bis Franklin. Bremen, 1861. 16°	2025.25
— History of the discovery of America from Columbus to Franklin. Tr. by R. R. Noel. London, 1862. 2v. p.8°	308.4
KÖNIG, T. Calvin ; culturhistorischer Roman. Leipzig, 1861. 3v. 16°	2024.8
KUNISCH, R. Bukarest und Stambul. Berlin, 1861. 16°	2075.10
KURTZ, J. H. Text-book of church history. Vol. II. Philadelphia, 1862. 8°	1104.16
LA LANDELLE, G. J. G. de. Le tableau de la mer, [et] La vie navale. Paris, 1862. 12°	2076.2
LA MADELÈNE, J. de. Brigitte ; [et] Le comte Alghiera. Paris, 1861. 16°	2075.4
LAMBERT, F. The handbook of needlework. New York, 1842. 8°	193.3
LAMBORN, R. H. Treatise on the metallurgy of silver and lead. London, 1861. 12°	1158.17
LAMÉ, É. Julien l'apostat. Paris, 1861. 16°	2066.3
LAMSON, A. Sermons. Boston, 1857. 12°	2095.13
LANDRETH, P. Studies and sketches in modern literature. London, 1861. p.8°	393.4
LANKESTER, E. Lectures on food, delivered at the South Kensington museum. London, 1861. p.8°	1167.2
— Uses of animals in relation to the industry of man. Lectures. London, n.d. p.8°	174.21
— - Same. First course. London, 1860. p.8°	1167.3
LAPRADE, P. M. V. R. de. Psyché : poëme ; odes et poëmes. 3e éd. Paris, 1860. 12°	2075.22
LAST of the cavaliers (The). Leipzig, 1862. 2v. 24°	730.15
LAVALLÉE, T. S. Jean Sans-Peur : scènes historiques, 1407-19. Paris, 1861. 12°	2066.14
LA VALLIÈRE, L. F. de. Confessions, écrites par elle-même, et corr. par Bossuet, avec un commentaire, par R. Cornut. 2d ed. Paris, 1857. 12°	2066.40
LAW and practice of the game of euchre. By a professor. Philadelphia, n.d. 18°	1197.2
LECOQ, H. La vie des fleurs. Paris, 1861. 12°	2075.11
LEFROY, J. H. Handbook for field service. 3d ed., revised. Woolwich, 1862. Obl. 18°	1199.33
LÉGER, E. Trois mois de séjour en Moldavie. Paris, 1861. 16°	2066.24
LE LOUTEREL, F. P. Field manual for battalion drill. Tr. and adapted by H. Coppée. Philadelphia, 1862. 32°	1208.26
— Field manual of evolutions of the line, in tabular form. Tr. with adaptation to U. S. service, by H. Coppée. Philadelphia, 1862. 32°.	1208.27
LÉOUZON LEDUC, L. A. Gustave III, roi de Suède, 1746-1792. Paris, 1861. 12°	2066.13
LESTRELIN, A. Les paysans russes et les droits des nobles. Paris, 1861. 12°	2075.32
LEVER, C. Maurice Tiernay, the soldier of fortune. Leipzig, 1861. 2v. in 1. sq. 16°	720.51
— Sir Jasper Carew. Leipzig, 1861. 2v. in 1. sq.16°	720.59
LEVY, U. P. Manual of internal rules and regulations for men-of-war. New York, 1861. 70 pp. 24°	1208.5
LEWES, G. H. Studies in animal life. London, 1862. p.8°	174.22
LIEBLER, P. A. Die deutsche Geschichte. 10te Aufl. Mannheim, 1843. 8°	2025.22
LIFE and adventure in the South Pacific. By a roving printer. New York, 1861. 12°	638.16
LIGHTHILL, A. D. and E. B. A popular treatise on deafness. Ed. by E. B. Lighthill. New York, 1862. 12°	154.12
LINTON, E. L. Witch stories. London, 1861. p.8°.	803.22

	Shelf. No.
LITTELL's Living age. Vols. 1-30, 32-40. Boston, 1844-54. 39v. 8°	1820.1 & 1821.1
LITTLE (A) tour in Ireland. By an Oxonian. London, 1859. sq.16°	645.22
LLOYD, G. T. Thirty-three years in Tasmania and Victoria. London, 1862. p.8°	704.23
LONGFELLOW, H. W. Poetical works. London, 1861. p.8°	843.8
LOVER, S. Barney O'Rierdon, [and other tales]. New York, 1862. 87 pp. 8°	711.12
— Handy Andy. New York, n.d. 8°	711.10
— Irish heirs. New York, 1862. 8°	711.11
— Legends and stories of Ireland. [Two] series. Philadelphia, 1846. 2v. in 1. 8°	477.14
— Rory O'More. New York, n.d. 8°	792.1
— Songs and ballads. 3d ed. N. Y., 1853. 12°.	1325.15
— Tom Crosbie and his friends. N. Y., n.d. 8°	711.9
LUDLOW, J. M. History of the United States from independence to secession. To which is added, The struggle for Kansas, by Thomas Hughes. Cambridge, [Eng.], 1862. 12°	305.7
LUTHER, M. Life, written by himself. Collected by M. Michelet. Tr. by Wm. Hazlitt. 2d ed. London, 1862. p.8°	855.12
LYON, Gen. N. Last political writings. With a sketch of his life. New York, 1861. 12°	527.24
LYRICS for freedom ; and other poems. New York, 1862. 12°	2106.22
LYTTON, E. G. E. L. Bulwer. A strange story. New York, 1862. 8°	502.23
MACAULAY, I. S. A treatise on field fortification. 5th ed. London, 1860. 8°	205.26
MCCLELLAN, G. B. Regulations and instructions for the field service of the U. S. cavalry in time of war, etc. Philadelphia, 1861. p.8°	205.31
M'COSH, J. The supernatural in relation to the natural. Cambridge, [Eng.], 1862. p.8°	123.6
MACDOUGALL, P. L. The theory of war. 3d ed. London, 1862. p.8°	204.26
MACKARNESS, M. The house on the rock. Boston, 1852. 16°	746.11
— Minnie's love. London, 1860. 12°	439.7
— Ray of light to brighten cottage homes. New York, 1857. 18°	746.12
MACKNIGHT, T. Thirty years of foreign policy : the secretaryships of Aberdeen and Palmerston. London, 1855. 8°	993.3
MACLEOD, G. H. B. Notes on the surgery of the war in the Crimea. Philadelphia, 1862. 12°.	154.9
MACLEOD, N. Good words. Vols. 1-II. Edinburgh, 1860-61. 2v. 8°	831.1
— The old lieutenant and his son. Boston, 1862. 8°	802.55
M'LEVY, J. Curiosities of crime in Edinburgh, during the last thirty years. Edinburgh, 1861. 16°	477.13
MAGOON, E. L. Proverbs for the people. Boston, 1849. 12°	2095.7
MAINE, H. S. Ancient law. London, 1861. 8°	132.19
MALING, E. A. Flowers and foliage for in-door plant cases. London, 1861. 16°	1158.25
— Flowers for ornament and decoration. London, 1862. 18°	1165.2
— In-door plants, and how to grow them. London, 1861. 16°	1179.6
MALLET, J. W. Cotton: the conditions of its successful cultivation. London, 1862. 8°	1165.3
MALTITZ, H. von. Der Herzog an der Leine. Berlin, 1862. 3v. 16°	2017.3
Contents.—Vol. I. Das Turnier zu Göttingen. II. Schloss Hardegsen. III. Der Vetter des Herzogs und die Göttinger Bürger.	
MANN, M. The flower people. Boston, 1862. sq.16°.	1165.4
MANNING, A. Town and forest, by the author of "Mary Powell." London, 1860. 12°	439.6
MANUAL for heavy artillery, for the use of volunteers. New York, 1862. 72 pp. 12°	1208.17
MARCOY, P. Scènes et paysages dans les Andes. Paris, 1861. 2v. 12°	2066.26

Shelf. No.

MARGARET Howth. A story of to-day. Boston, 1862. 12° 494.3
MARMONT, M., *duke of Ragusa*. The spirit of military institutions. Tr. by H. Coppée. Philadelphia, 1862. 12° 1208.29
MARRYAT, F. The pirate, and The three cutters. New ed. London, 1861. 16° 854.12
MARSH, C. English hearts and English hands. London, 1859. 12° 2109.16
MARSH-CALDWELL A. Adelaide Lindsay, a novel. London, 1850. 3v. p.8° 493.2
MARSHALL, E. C. History of the United States naval academy. New York, 1862. 12° . . . 298.12
MARTHA Brown, the heiress. Leipzig, 1861. sq. 16°. 730.7
MARTIN, L. A. Histoire de la femme. Antiquité, 1e partie. Paris, 1862. 12° 2076.1
MARTINEAU, H. Household education. New ed. London, 1861. 12° 123.4
MARTINEAU, J. Studies of Christianity. Ed. by W. R. Alger. Boston, 1858. 12° 2106.20
MARY-LAFON, J. B. Pasquin et Marforio, histoire satirique des papes. Paris, 1861. 12° 2075.5
MATTERS of taste among common things. London, 1862. 77 pp. 12° 1126.7
MAYHEW, H. Young Benjamin Franklin; or, the right road through life. London, 1861. 16°. 519.11
MELVILLE, G.J.W. Digby Grand. Leipz., 1862. 24°. 730.10
— Good for nothing. Leipzig, 1862. 2v. in 1. sq. 16°. 730.11
MENDELSSOHN BARTHOLDY, F. Reisebriefe, 1830-32. Leipzig, 1861. 8° 1032.11
MERLET, G. Le réalisme et la fantaisie dans la littérature. Paris, 1861. 12° 2066.5
MÉRY, J. Théatre de salon. Paris, 1861. 12° . . 2076.5
MEYER, H. Why the shoe pinches. A contribution to applied anatomy. Tr. from the German by J. S. Craig. Edinburgh, 1860. 55 pp. p.8°. 1158.18
MEYLAN, G. F. Geschichte des Handels der Europäer in Japan. Ins Deutsche übertragen von F. W. Diederich. Leipzig, 1861. p.8° . . . 2025.21
MEYR, M. Vier Deutsche. Stuttgart, 1861. 3v. p.8°. 2015.6
MIGNET, F. A. Histoire de la révolution française depuis 1789 jusqu' en 1814. Nouv. éd. Stuttgart, 1839. 24° 2069.3
MILES, G. H. Mohammed, the Arabian prophet. A tragedy. Boston, 1850. 12° 1395.13
MILTON, J. Poetical works. With memoir by J. Montgomery. New ed. With a selection of notes by H. G. Bohn. London, 1861. 2v. p.8° 843.9
MODERN domestic cookery. New ed. Based on Mrs. Rundell's. London, 1860. 12° 185.26
MÖLLHAUSEN, B. Der Flüchtling. Erzählung aus Neu-Mexico, u. s. w. Leipzig, 1862. 4v. in 2. 16° 2024.7
— Der Halbindianer. Erzählung aus dem westlichen Nord-Amerika. Leipzig, 1861. 4v. 16°. 2015.4
MONNIER, M. Garibaldi. Conquête des Deux Siciles; notes prises sur place au jour le jour. Paris, 1861. 12° 2066.7
MONTROSE, and other biographical sketches. Boston, 1861. 12° 555.12
MORE, H. Letters to Z. Macaulay. Ed. by A. Roberts. London, 1860. 16° 599.18
MOREL, A. L'ésprit des Grecs. Paris, n.d. 12°. 2066.6
MORELL, J. D. Introduction to mental philosophy, on the inductive method. London, 1862. 8°. 123.5
MORRIS, F. O. Records of animal sagacity and character. London, 1861. 16° 1179.11
MORROW, J. A voice from the newsboys. [New York], 1860. l. 12° 1126.4
MORSE, A. Further traces of the ancient Northmen in America. Boston, 1861. 16 pp. 12°. 299.21
MOSELEY, J. What is contraband of war, and what is not. London, 1861. 12° 298.6
MÜGGE, T. Der Prophet. Historischer Roman aus dem Bauernkriege. Leipz., 1860-61. 3v.8°. 2015.8
MÜLLER, O. Der Klosterhof. Ein Familienroman. 2te Ausg. Berlin, 1862. 3v. p.8° 2015.2
MÜLLNER, A. Theater. Wien, 1816-17. 4v. in 2. 32° 2019.13

Shelf. No.

MÜLLNER, A. *continued*.
Contents.—Vol. I. Der neun und zwanzigste Februar; Die Vertrauten; Der Angolische Kater; Die Zurückkunft aus Surinam. II. Die Schuld; Die Zweiflerinn; Die grossen Kinder.
MULOCH, D. M. Romantic tales. Leipz., 1861. sq. 16°. 730.4
MUNDT, C. Kaiserin Josephine. Ein Napoleonisches Lebensbild. Berlin, 1861. 3v. 12°. . 2015.9
— Neues Bilderbuch. Berlin, 1862. 2v. 12°. . . 2024.6
Contents.—Vol. I. Welt und der Natur. II. Gift und Bücker; Ein Liebesdienst; Der Sohn der Natur; Aurora Gräfin von Königsmark; Gold und Kohle.
MUNDT, T. Czar Paul. Berlin, 1861. 3v. 12°. . . 2016.17
— - Same. 2te Abtheilung. Berlin, 1861. 3v. 12°. 2016.20
MURET, T. C. Histoire de Jeanne D'Albret. Paris, 1862. 12° 2075.34
MURRAY, J. Handbook for travellers in North Wales. London, 1861. 16° 1656.2
— Handbook for travellers in South Wales and its borders. London, 1861. 16° 1656.1
MUSSET, L. C. A. de. Contes. Paris, 1861. 12°. . 2075.40
— La confession d'un enfant du siècle. Nouv. éd. Paris, 1861. 12° 2075.39
— Nouvelles. Paris, 1861. 12° 2075.38
— Poésies nouvelles, 1836-1852. Nouv. éd. Paris, 1860. 12° 2075.36
— Premières poésies, 1829-1835. Nouv. éd. Paris, 1861. 12° 2075.23
— Œuvres posthumes. Paris, 1860. 12° 2075.37
MUSSEY, R. D. Health: its friends and its foes. Boston, 1862. 12° 154.14
MUSTON, A. Histoire populaire des Vaudois. Paris, 1862. 12° 2075.35

NATION'S manhood (A), or, stories of Washington and the war of independence. Lond., 1861. 16°. 519.10
No church. Leipzig, 1861. 2v. in 1. sq.16° 720.57
NOLAN, L. E. Cavalry; its history and tactics. 3d ed. London, 1860. 12° 204.22, 205.33
— System for training cavalry horses. Ed. by K. Garrard. New York, 1862. 12° 204.27
NORIAC, C. A. J. C. Le 101e régiment, [et autres pièces]. 36e éd. Paris, 1861. 12° 2066.31
NOUVION, V. de. Histoire du règne de Louis-Philippe 1er. 2me éd. Paris, 1858-61. 4v. 8°. 2063.29
NUGÆ criticæ. Occasional papers written at the seaside. By Shirley. Edinburgh, 1862. 12°. 882.11

OBOLENSKI, E. Mon exil en Sibérie. Leipzig, 1862. 89 pp. 16° 2076.6
OGDEN, J. The science of education; and art of teaching. Cincinnati, 1859. 12° 1126.3
OLIPHANT, M. The last of the Mortimers. New York, 1862. 12° 752.17
— - Same. Leipzig, 1862. 2v. in 1. sq. 16° . . 730.13
— Lilliesleaf: a concluding series of passages in the life of Mrs. Margaret Maitland. Boston, 1862. 12° 494.2
OLMSTED, F. L. The cotton kingdom. New York, 1861. 2v. 12° 634.7
ONLY son (An). Boston, 1862. 8° 792.6
OPIE, A. Illustrations of lying. Boston, 1826. 12°. 477.11
ORPHEUS C. Kerr papers. New York, 1862. 12°. . 205.17
OSBORN, S. A cruise in Japanese waters. Edinburgh, 1859. p.8° 703.51
OWEN, F. Aden Power. Boston, 1862. 8° 502.25
OYSTER (The); where, how, and when to find, breed, cook and eat it. Lond., 1861. 96 pp. 16°. 1179.9

PALLESKE, E. Schiller's life and works, translated by Lady Wallace. London, 1860. 2v. p.8°. 543.16
PARKER, J. H. Introduction to the study of Gothic architecture. 2d ed. London, 1861. 16°. . . 205.32
PARKER, T. Prayers. Boston, 1862. 16°. . 2106.9 and 19
PARSONS, T. Essays. 3d ser. Boston, 1862. 16°. . . . . Vol. III. of 875.9
PASSAGES in the life of a young housekeeper. London, 1862. 16° 184.2
PATERSON, J. James the fifth; his poetry and adventures. Edinburgh, 1861. 16° 555.11

	Shelf. No.

PATIENCE of hope (The). By the author of " A present heaven." Introduction by J. G. Whittier. Boston, 1862. 16° 1116.12

PATRIOTIC and heroic eloquence. New York, 1861. 12° 393.3

PATTEN, G. Army manual: instruction for officers in the preparation of rolls, etc. New York, 1861. 12° 205.29

— Cavalry drill and sabre exercise. New York, 1861. 12° 1208.23

— Infantry tactics and bayonet exercise. New York, 1861. 12° 1208.24

PATTERSON, L. B. Twelve years in the mines of California. Cambridge, 1861. 12° 237.23

PAYN, J. Mellbœus in London. London, 1862. 16°. 494.6

PERCY, J. Metallurgy; fuel; fire-clays; copper, zinc; brass, etc. London, 1861. 8° 193.5

PERRAULT, C. Mémoires, contes, etc., précédé d'une notice sur l'auteur par P. L[acroix] et une dissertation par Walckenaer. Paris, 1842. 12° 2066.41

PETERSON, C. J. Cruising in the last war. Philadelphia, n.d. 8° 711.14

— Kate Aylesford. Philadelphia, n.d. 12° . . . 453.11

PFEIFFER, I. Last travels. With a memoir of the author. Tr. by H. W. Dulcken. New York, 1861. 12° 689.24

— Visit to the Holy Land, Egypt, and Italy. Tr. by H. W. Dulcken. 3d ed. Lond., 1857. 16°. 879.5

PHIN, J. Open air grape culture. New York, 1862. 12° 1165.1

PLUMPTRE, C. J. Principles and practice of elocution. Lectures at Oxford. Lond., 1861. 16°. 393.5

PONTMARTIN, A. A. ?. M. de. Les semaines littéraires. Paris, 1861. 12° 2066.18

POPULAR science review (The). Ed. by J. Samuelson. Vol. I. London, 1862. 8° 141.1

PROCTOR, A. A. A chaplet of verses. London, 1862. p.8° 1325.13

PROUDHON, P. J. La guerre et la paix. Paris, 1861. 2v. 12° 2075.8

PUTNAM, M. L. Record of an obscure man. Boston, 1861. 16° 495.17

— Tragedy of errors. Boston, 1862. 16° 373.5

— Tragedy of success. Boston, 1862. 16° . . . 1325.14

QUINCY, J. Memoir of the life of Josiah Quincy, Jr. Boston, 1825. 8° 524.20

RAIKES, R. His Sunday schools and his friends. Philadelphia, n.d. 24° 2109.10

RANDOLPH, J. T. The cabin and parlor; or, slaves and masters. Philadelphia, 1852. 12° . . . 803.15

RANKE, L. Englische Geschichte, im XVIten und XVIIten Jahrhundert. Berlin, 1859–60. 2v. 8°. 1022.1

RANKINE, W. J. M. A manual of civil engineering. London, 1862. p.8° 185.28

RAU, H. Hölderlin. Roman. Leipzig, 1862. 2v. p.8° 2024.2

RAVENSTEIN, E. G. The Russians on the Amur. London, 1861. 8° 924.6

RAWLINS, C. E. American dis-union: constitutional or unconstitutional? London, 1862. sq.16°. 208.14

READ, W. T. Popular and mathematical astronomy. London, 1862. 12° 1148.6

READE, C. The cloister and the hearth; or maid, wife, and widow. New York, 1861. 8° 412.1

RECREATIVE science; a record and remembrancer of intellectual observation. Vol. I. London, 1860. sm. 4to 205.28

REMINISCENCES of a Scottish gentleman, commencing in 1787. London, 1861. 12° 644.2

REPLIES to " Essays and Reviews." Preface by the bishop of Oxford. New York, 1862. 12°. 1102.1

Contents.—Education of the world, by E. M. Goulburn; Bunsen, the critical school, and Dr. Williams, by H. J. Rose; Miracles, by C. A. Heurtley; Idea of the national church, by W. J. Irons; Creative week, by G. Rorison; Rationalism, by A. W. Haddan; Interpretation of Scripture, by C. Wordsworth.

	Shelf. No.

REVILLON, T. Les bacheliers. Etudes. Paris, 1861. 12° 2075.24

REYNOLDS, E. W. The true story of the barons of the South. Boston, 1862. 12° 298.10

RILEY, H. H. The Puddleford papers, or humors of the West. New York, 1857. 12° 477.18

RIO, A. F. Léonard De Vinci et son école. Paris, 1855. 12° 2076.8

RISPART, E. [*Dr.* Frankolm.] Die Juden und die Kreuzführer in England. Leipzig, 1861. 12°. 2026.8

ROBERTS, B. H. E. History of the colonial empire of Great Britain. London, 1861. p.8° . . . 997.13

ROBERTSON, F. W. Sermons. Leipzig, 1861. 3v. sq.16° 2109.14

ROBIN Hood. Ballads and songs. From Ritson and others. London, 1862. 32° 1329.3

ROLLAND, A. La foire aux mariages. Paris, 1861. 12° 2075.16

RONGE, J. Ronge, the holy coat of Treves, and the new German Catholic Church. New York, 1845. 12° 2099.1

ROSSETTI, D. G. The early Italian poets from Ciullo D'Alcamo to Dante Alighieri. With the Vita nuova. London, 1861. p.8° 855.10

RUFFINI, G. Doctor Antonio. Leipzig, 1861. sq.16°. 730.3

— Lorenzo Benoni. Leipzig, 1861. sq.16° . . . 730.2

RUPPIUS, O. Ein Deutscher. Roman aus der amerikanischen Gesellschaft. Leipzig, 1862. sq.16° 2024.9

RUSH, C. E. Robert Morton, or the step-mother: Edmund and Ione, etc. Phila., 1850. 12° . . 487.23

RUSKIN, J. Selections from [his] writings. London, 1861. p.8° 204.23

— " Unto this last:" Essays ou political economy. London, 1862. 16° 1126.10

RYAN, G. Our heroes of the Crimea. London, 1855. 16° 589.25

SAAL, G. Ungarische Volksmärchen. Uebersetzt von G. Stier. Pesth, 1851. 16° 2016.19

SACY, S. U. de Silvestre de. Variétés, littéraires, morales, et historiques. Nouv. éd. Paris, 1861. 2v. 12° 2066.1

ST. JOHN, J. A. History of the four conquests of England. London, 1862. 2v. 8° 993.2

SAINTINE, J. X. B. La mythologie du Rhin. Illustrée par Doré. Paris, 1862. 1.8° 1072.2

SALA, G. A. Dutch pictures; with some sketches in the Flemish manner. London, 1861. p.8°. 883.19

— The seven sons of Mammon. Boston, 1862. 8°. 502.17

— The two prima donnas. Phila., n.d. 62 pp. 8°. 792.9

SAXBY, S. M. The study of steam and the marine engine. London, 1862. 8° 185.20

SCENES where the tempter has triumphed. By the author of " The jail chaplain." New York, 1849. 16° 466.20

SCHILLER, J. C. F. Song of the bell. Tr. by W. H. Furness. With other ballads, [tr.] by F. H. Hedge. Philadelphia, 1850. 48 pp. 12° . . . 373.8

SCHLEIDEN, M. J. Poetry of the vegetable world. 1st Am. ed. from Henfrey's London ed. Ed. by A. Wood. Cincinnati, 1853. p.8° 1167.1

SCHMITZ, L. History of the middle ages. Vol. I. London, 1859. p.8° 945.6

SCHWARTZ, M. S. Die Arbeit adelt. Aus dem Schwedischen, von A. Kretzschmar. Leipzig, 1862. 3v. in 1. 16° 2024.4

SCHWEGLER, A. A history of philosophy in epitome. Tr. from the German by J. H. Seelye. 3d ed. New York, 1860. 12° 1116.9

SCIENCE for the household. The earth, and its garment of water and air. London, n.d. 18°. 1179.7

SCOFFERN, J. A handy book of the chemistry of soils. London, 1862. p.8° 1167.5

SCOTT, M. Cruise of the Midge. Edinburgh, 1859. 12° 735.19

— Tom Cringle's log. New ed. Edinburgh, 1859. 12° 735.18

SCOTT, *Sir* W. Poetical works. Leipzig, 1861. 2v. sq. 16° 1329.2

Shelf. No.

SCOTT, *Sir W. continued.*

> *Contents.* — Vol. I. Lay of the last minstrel; Marmion; Lady of the lake. II. Vision of Don Roderick; Rokeby; Lord of the Isles; Songs, ballads, etc.

SCOTT, *Rev.* W. A. The church in the army; or the four centurions. New York, 1862. 12°. . . . 2095.15

SCRYMGEOUR, D. Poetry and poets of Britain from Chaucer to Tennyson. Edinb., 1860. p.8°   373.3

SEIFART, C. Altdeutsche Geschichten. Cassel, 1862. 2v. 12° 2017.4

SEWELL, E. M. Ancient history of Egypt, Assyria, and Babylonia. London, 1862. 16° 945.9

— Impressions of Rome, Florence, and Turin. London, 1862. p.8° 664.4

SHAKESPEARE, W. Dramatic works. Ed. by R. Carruthers and W. Chambers. London, 1861–62. 5v. sq. 16° 1326.1

> *Contents.* — Vol. I. Memoir of Shakespeare; The tempest; Two gentlemen of Verona; Comedy of errors; Merry wives of Windsor. II. Much ado about nothing; As you like it; Measure for measure; Taming of the shrew. III. All's well that ends well; Love's labor's lost; Midsummer night's dream; Twelfth night. IV. The winter's tale; King John; King Richard II.; Merchant of Venice. V. King Henry IV., part I., II.; King Henry V.; King Henry VI., part I.

— Sonette. In deutscher Nachbildung von F. Bodenstedt. Berlin, 1862. sq. 32° 2019.15

SHELLEY, P. B. Relics. Edited by R. Garnett. London, 1862. 16° 373.9

SHELTON, E. The historical finger-post. London, 1861. 16° 945.8

SHERMAN, H. Slavery in the United States of America. 2d ed. Hartford, 1860. 16° . . . 298.9

SHERWOOD, M. Works. New York, 1858. 16v. 12°.   452.1

> *Contents.* — Vol. I. Henry Milner. II. Fairchild family; Orphans of Normandy; The latter days. III. Little Henry and his bearer; Little Lucy and her dhaye; Memoirs of Sergeant Dale, his daughter, and the orphan Mary; History of Susan Gray; History of Lucy Clare; The hedge of thorns; The recaptured negro; Susannah, or the three guardians; Theophilus and Sophia. Abdallah, the merchant of Bagdad. IV. The Indian pilgrim; The broken hyacinth; The little woodman; The babes in the wood; Clara Stephens; The golden clew; Katharine Seward; Mary Anne; The iron cage; The little beggars. V. The infant's progress; The flowers of the forest; Juliana Oakley; Ermina; Emancipation. VI. The governess; The little Momiere; The stranger at home; Père La Chaise; English Mary; My uncle Timothy. VII. The nun; Intimate friends; My aunt Kate; Emmeline; Obedience; The gipsy babes; The basket-maker; The butterfly; Alone, or Le bächen Holzli; Procrastination, or the evil of delay; The mourning queen. VIII. Victoria; Arzoomund; The birthday present; The errand boy; The orphan boy; The two sisters; Julian Percival; Edward Mansfield; The Infirmary; Mrs. Catherine Crawley; Joan, or Trustworthy; The young forester; The bitter sweet; Common errors. IX.–XII. The lady of the manor. XIII. The mail coach; My three uncles; The old lady's complaint; The shepherd's fountain; The hours of infancy; Economy; "Hoe age"; Old things and new things; The Swiss cottage; Obstinacy punished; The infant's grave; The father's eye; The red book; Dudley castle; The happy grandmother; The blessed family; My godmother; The useful little girl; Caroline Mordaunt; Le Fevre; The penny tract; The potter's common; The china manufactory; Emily and her brothers. XIV. The monk of Cimiès; The rosary, or Rosée of Montreux; The Roman baths; Saint Hospice; The violet leaf; The couvent of St. Clair. XV. Henry Milner, pt. 4th; Sabbaths on the continent; The idler. XVI. John Marten, sequel to Henry Milner.

SIMMONDS, P. L. Waste products and undeveloped substances. London, 1862. 16° 1155.5

SIMMS, W. G. Egeria; or, voices of thought and counsel. Philadelphia, 1853. 12° 1116.11

SIMON, J. F. Recueil des pensées les plus sublimes, tirées des auteurs allemands. Bruxelles, 1853. 12° 2066.23

SIMON, J. F. S. S. L'ouvrière. 2me éd. Paris, 1861. 12° 2066.9

SIVERS, J. v. Ueber Madeira und die Antillen. Leipzig, 1861. 8° 1022.2

Shelf. No.

SMILES, S. Workmen's earnings, strikes, and savings. London, 1861. 16° 1138.8

SMITH, Albert. Mont Blanc. With a memoir of the author by Edmund Yates. London, n.d 16°.   669.18

SMITH, Alexander. City poems. Boston, 1858. 16°.   1395.14

SMITH, E. O. Bertha and Lily; or the parsonage of Beach Glen. New York, 1854. 12° 477.15

SMITH, J. O. The lawyer and his profession: a series of letters. London, 1860. 12° 1138.5

SMITH, J. T. Book for a rainy day; or, recollections, 1766–1833. 3d ed. London, 1861. 16°.   997.10

SMITH, W. Gravenhurst; or, thoughts on good and evil. Edinburgh, 1862. 8° 1102.2

SMYTH, C. P. Three cities in Russia. London, 1862. 2v. 8° 684.14

SOCIAL life and manners in Australia. By a resident. London, 1861. 8° 606.17

SOUTHEY, R. The life of Nelson. New ed. London, 1861. p.8° 843.10

SOUTHWORTH, E. D. E. N. The deserted wife. Philadelphia, n.d. 8° 453.3

— The discarded daughter. Phila., n.d. 12°. .   453.2

— The gipsey's prophecy. Phila., n.d. 12° . .   453.7

— India: the pearl of Pearl river. Philadelphia, n.d. 12° 443.4

— Love's labor won. Philadelphia, n.d. 12° . .   453.10

— The missing bride. Philadelphia, n.d 12° . .   453.5

SPENCER, H. Social statics. London, 1851. 8°.   123.7

STANHOPE, P. H. *earl.* Life of William Pitt. Vol. III, IV. London, 1862. 2v. 8° 567.5

STANLEY, A. P. The Bible in the Holy Land. London, 1862. 16° 2109.22

STERNBERG, A. v. Künstlerbilder. Leipzig, 1861. 3v. 16° 2015.3

STERNE, L. A sentimental journey through France and Italy. Leipzig, 1861. sq.16° . . 720.49

STODDARD, E. D. B. The Morgesons. New York, 1862. 12° 494.7

STORY, S. A., jr. Caste. Boston, 1856. 12° . .   458.8

STOWE, H. E. B. Agnes of Sorrento. Bost., 1862. 12°.   454.15

— The pearl of Orr's Island: a story of the coast of Maine. 3d ed. Boston, 1862. 12° 454.14

STREAKS of light; or, fifty-two facts from the Bible. By the author of "More about Jesus." New York, 1862. 16° 2109.13

STRICKLAND, A. Lives of the bachelor kings of England. London, 1861. p.8° 554.9

STRICKLAND, W. P. Old Mackinaw. Philadelphia, 1860. 12° 236.14

STUART, H. B. A history of infantry. London, 1862. 16° 1208.19

STUDENT'S France. A history. London, 1862. 12°.   1006.6

SUE, M. J. *dit* Eugène. The wandering Jew. Philadelphia, n.d. 8° 711.13

SUNLIGHT through the mist; or, practical lessons drawn from the lives of good men. London, 1860. 16° 743.3

SUTHERLANDS (The). By the author of "Rutledge." New York, 1862. 12° 494.1

SWISS family Robinson (The). New ed. London, 1861. 16° 746.6

TAILLANDIER, R. G. E. *dit* Saint René. Écrivains et poëtes modernes. Paris, 1861. p.8° . . .

> *Contents.* — Charles Sealsfield, Henri Heine, Henri Conscience, Frédéric Hebbel, Jérémie Gotthelf, Oscar de Redwitz, Leopold Kompert.

TALES of the day. Vol. I. Boston, 1861. 8° . . . 851.2

TAYLOR, H. St. Clement's eve. A play. London, 1862. 16° 364.6

TAYLOR, I. Saturday evening. Hingham, 1833. 12° 1116.10

TAYLOR, J. B. At home and abroad. 2d series. New York, 1862. 12° 688.14

TAYLOR, S. H. Method of classical study. Boston, 1861. 12° 393.7

TEGTMEYER, E. Die Kaiserbrüder. Historischer Roman. Lübeck, 1862. 4v. in 2. 16° 2024.3

TENNENT, J. E. Natural history of Ceylon, including the elephant. London, 1861. 16° . . 175.22

Shelf. No.

THACKERAY, T. J. The soldier's manual of rifle firing. 3d ed. London, 1861. 94 pp. 12° . 1208.18
THACKERAY, W. M. The adventures of Philip. New York, 1862. 8° 502.27
— The four Georges ; Lovel the widower. Leipzig, 1861. sq.16° 720.58
THAYER, T. B. The Bible class assistant. Boston, 1850. 24° 2109.19
— Christianity against infidelity. New ed. Cincinnati, 1849. 12° 2106.12
— Origin of the doctrine of endless punishment. Boston, [1855]. 12° 2106.10
THIENEN-ADLERFLYCHT, C. v. In das Land voll Sonnenschein. Bilder aus Spanien. Berlin, 1861. 16° 2024.12
THIERRY-MIEG, C. Six semaines en Afrique. Paris, 1861. 12° 2075.9
THOMAS, J. J. Rural affairs. Vol. II. Albany, 1860. 12° 164.26
THOMPSON, G. Thompson in Africa : an account of missionary labors. New York, 1852. 12° . 2095.6
THOMSON, W. Aids to faith ; a reply to " Essays and reviews," by several writers. New York, 1862. 12° 1113.2

Contents. — Miracles as evidences of Christianity, by H. L. Mansel; Study of the evidences of Christianity, by W. Fitzgerald; Prophecy, by A. McCaul; Ideology and subscription, by F. C. Cook; Mosaic record of creation, by A. McCaul; Genuineness and authenticity of the Pentateuch, by G. Rawlinson; Inspiration, by E. H. Browne; Death of Christ, by W. Thomson; Scripture and its interpretation, by C. J. Ellicott.

THORNBURY, W. Cross country. Lond., 1861. p.8°. 644.1
TIECK, L. The old man of the mountain ; The love charm ; and Pietro of Abano. From the German. 2d ed. London, 1860. 16° . . . 466.19
TIMBS, J. The year book of facts. London, 1862. 12° . . . . Vol. xxv. of 159.2
TOCQUEVILLE, A. C. H. C. de. Memoir, letters, and remains. Tr. from the French. With large additions. London, 1861. 2v. p.8° . . . 614.4
— - Same. Boston, 1862. 2v. p.8° 614.6
TONNA, C. E. Helen Fleetwood. 2d Am. ed. New York, 1844. 12° 477.10
TOTTEN, B. J. Naval text-book and dictionary. New ed. revised. New York, 1862. 12° . . 143.16
TOWNSEND, V. F. While it was morning. Philadelphia, 1860. 12° 453.6
TRACTS for priests and people. By various writers. Boston, 1862. 12° 1092.12

Contents. — Religio laici, by T. Hughes; The mote and the beam, by F. D. Maurice; The atonement as a fact and as a theory, by F. Garden; Signs of the kingdom of heaven, by J. L. Davies; Terms of communion, by J. N. Langley, etc.; Dialogue on doubt, by J. M. Ludlow; Morality and divinity, by F. D. Maurice; Laws of nature, by J. M. Ludlow; On positive philosophy, by J. M. Ludlow.

TRENCH, R. C. Commentary on the epistles to the seven churches in Asia. Revelation II, III. New York, 1861. 12° 2095.4
TRIPLER, C. S., and Blackman, G. C. Hand-book for the military surgeon. 2d ed. Cincinnati, 1861. 12° 154.7
TROLLOPE, A. Framley parsonage. Leipzig, 1861. 2v. in 1. 16° 720.53
— North America. New York, 1862. 12° . . 634.8
— Struggles of Brown, Jones, and Robinson. New York, 1862. 8° 792.11
— The warden. New York, 1862. sq.16° . . 730.5
TROLLOPE, F. The young countess, or, love and jealousy. London, 1848. 3v. p.8° 493.1
TROLLOPE, T. A. Paul the pope, and Paul the friar. Story of an interdict. London, 1861. p.8°. 917.18
TUCKER, B. The partisan leader. Vol. II. New York, 1861. 12° 298.3
TUCKER, St. G. Hansford : a tale of Bacon's rebellion. Richmond, Va., 1857. 12° . . . 487.24
TWO COSMOS (The). A tale. Leipzig, 1861. sq.16° 730.12
TYNDALL, J. Mountaineering in 1861. London, 1862. 8° 664.3

Shelf. No.

UCHARD, M. Raymon. Paris, 1862. 12° 2075.18
UNDERHILL, E. B. The West Indies, their social and religious condition. London, 1862. p.8°. 264.9
UNITED States. Instruction for field artillery. Philadelphia, 1861. 12° 205.27
— Ordnance manual for the officers of the United States army. 3d ed. Phila., 1862. 8° . . 204.25
— Revised regulations for the army, 1861. Philadelphia, 1861. 8° 296.8
URE, A. The cotton manufacture of Great Britain. Supplement by P. L. Simmonds. London, 1861. 2v. p.8° 855.15
— Philosophy of manufactures. 3d ed. Continued by P. L. Simmonds. London, 1861. p.8° . 855.14

VANDENHOFF, G. The clerical assistant : an elocutionary guide. London, 1862. 16° 393.9
— The lady's reader. London, 1862. 16° . . 393.8
VAN NESS, W. W. The national school for the soldier. New York, 1862. 75 pp. 18° . . . 1208.20
VASSAR, J. G. Twenty years around the world. 2d ed. New York, 1862. 8° 681.5
VECCHJ, C. A. Garibaldi at Caprera. Tr. from the Italian. Preface by Mrs. Gaskell. Cambridge, 1862. 18° 917.19
VEGA, L. F. de. Théâtre. Trad. avec une introd. par Damas Hinard. Paris, 1861-62. 2v. 12°. 2075.13

Contents. — Vol. I. Le moulin ; Le chien du jardinier ; Le meilleur alcalde est le roi ; La découverte du nouveau monde par Christophe Colomb ; L'enlèvement d'Hélène. II. L'Hameçon de Phénice ; Fontovéjune ; Les travaux de Jacob ; La belle aux yeux d'or ; Aimer sans savoir qui.

VENABLES, E., and others. Guide to the Isle of Wight. London, 1860. 16° 1656.3
VENEDEY, J. George Washington. Ein Lebensbild. Freiburg, 1861. 12° 2016.16
VICTOR, O. J. History of the southern rebellion and the war for the union. Vol. I. New York, 1862. 8° 293.1
VIGNY, A. V. de. Le More de Venise ; La maréchale D'Ancre. Bruxelles, 1834. 16° . . . 2068.6
— Théâtre complet. Nouv. éd. Paris, 1848. 12°. 2068.4

Contents. — Le More de Venise, [tr. de Shakespeare]; Le marchand de Venise, [tr. de Shakespeare]; La maréchale D'Ancre ; Quitte pour la peur, comédie ; Chatterton, drame.

— Vie militaire, [contes, etc.] Bruxelles, 1834. 2v. in 1. 16° 2068.5

WALDMÜLLER, R. Wander-Studien. Italien, Griechenland und daheim. Leipzig, 1861. 2v. p.8° 2025.23
WALKER, J. Sermons preached in the chapel of Harvard College. Boston, 1861. p.8° . . . 2100.5-7
WALTER, J. P. Altar at home. 2d series. Boston, 1862. 16° 2106.21
WALKER, W. M. Notes on screw propulsion. New York, 1861. 51 pp. 8° 202.17
WALL, A. H. A manual of artistic colouring as applied to photographs. London, 1861. p.8°. 185.27
WALTHER, F. H. The horse-owner's guide. Boston, 1861. 39 pp. 8° 173.7
WAR (The), or, voices from the ranks. London, 1855. 16° 997.12
WARNEFORD, R. Tales of the slave squadron. London, n.d. 16° 477.12
WARTER, J. W. The sea-board and the Down, or, my parish in the south. By an old vicar. London, 1860. 2v. sq. 16° 882.6
WATSON, H. C. Camp fires of the revolution. Philadelphia, 1860. 8° 733.5
WATSON's woods, or, Margaret Huntington's experiment. New York, 1860. 12° 746.2
WELBY, H. Predictions realized in modern times. London, 1862. 16° 1126.11
WELLS, D. A. Annual of scientific discovery, for 1862. Boston, 1862. 12° 159.1
WHITTEMORE, T. Life of Rev. Hosea Ballou, with accounts of his writings. Boston, 1854-55. 4v. 12° 2095.11

	Shelf. No.
WHITTEMORE, T., continued	
— Notes and illustrations of the parables of the New Testament. Rev. ed. Boston, 1855. 12°	2095.12
"WHO breaks—pays." Leipzig, 1861. sq. 16°	720.60
WHY Paul Ferroll killed his wife. Leipzig, 1861. sq. 16°	720.52
WIELAND, C. M. v. The republic of fools: the history of Abdera. Tr. by H. Christmas. London, 1861. 2v. 12°	883.20
WILKINSON, J. G. On colour; with remarks on geometrical gardens. London, 1858. 8°	204.24
WILLIAMS, H. W. Diseases of the eye. Boston, 1862. p.8°	154.13
WILLIAMSON, I. D. Exposition and defence of universalism. New York, 1840. 24°	2109.20
WILLS, A. "The Eagle's Nest" in the valley of Sixt; a summer home among the Alps. London, 1860. p.8°	665.16
WILLS, W. G. Notice to quit. N. Y. 1861. 8°	792.4
WINTHROP, T. Cecil Dreeme. Boston, 1861. 12°	504.3
— Edwin Brothertoft. 3d ed. Boston, 1862. 12°	504.6
— John Brent. Boston, 1862. 12°	504.4
WITT, C. de. Thomas Jefferson, étude historique sur la démocratie Américaine. Paris, 1861. 8°	2063.28
WOOD, E. Castle Wafer; or, the plain gold ring. New York, n.d. 8°	792.3
— The Channings. Philadelphia, n.d. 8°	502.22

	Shelf. No.
WOOD, E., continued	
— East Lynne; or, the earl's daughter. New York, n.d. 8°	502.18
— — Same. Leipzig, 1861. 3v. sq. 16°	730.1
— Heir to Ashley. New York, n.d. 8°	502.25
— A life's secret. Philadelphia, n.d 8°	502.24
WORTHEN, W. E. First lessons in mechanics. New York, 1862. 12°	184.1
WRAXALL, F. C. L. Wild oats. Leipzig, 1862. sq. 16°	730.14
WRIGHT, H. C. Human life: my individual experience. Boston, 1849. 12°	536.16
WRIGHT, H. G. Headaches, their causes and their cure. 3d. ed. London, 1860. 16°	1158.19
WRIGHT, T. History of France. Lon., n.d. 3v. 18°	991.1
WYTHES, J. H. Curiosities of the microscope. With colored illustrations. Philadelphia, 1852. sq. 12°	1148.3
YONGE, C. M. The young step-mother. Leipzig, 1861. 2v. in 1. sq. 16°	730.8
— — Same. New York, 1862. 2v. 12°	784.14
YVAN, M. Légendes et recits. Paris, 1861. 12°	2075.3
ZIMMERMANN, W. F. A. Der Vulcanismus, oder das Todesthal auf Java, ein Roman. 2te Aufl. Berlin, 1862. 8°	1032.12

PERIODICALS.

NOTE. — The following works, either Periodicals, or partaking of the character of Periodicals, are received regularly at the Library. The latest portions of most of them which may have come to hand, will be found, arranged upon the tables, in the large Reading Room, in alphabetical order, beginning at the northwest corner with the letter A, and ending with the letter Z, at the northeast corner. Those marked with an asterisk are not generally placed upon the table, but can be had on application at the desk.

The letters affixed to the titles signify respectively, m. monthly, ½m. twice a month, 2m. once in two months, d. daily, w. weekly, ½y. semi-annually tr. w. tri-weekly, q. quarterly, un. uncertain.

ALBION. New York	f° w.	ARTIZAN, The. London	8° m.
ALL the year round. London	8° w.	*ASTRONOMISCHE Nachrichten. Altona	4° w.
*ALLGEMEINE Zeitung. Augsburg	4° d.	ATHENÆUM. London	4° w.
AMERICAN Agriculturist. New York	4° m.	ATLANTIC Monthly. Boston	8° m.
AMERICAN Journal of Insanity. Utica	8° q.		
AMERICAN Journal of the Medical Sciences. Phila.	8° q.	BANKERS' Magazine. New York	8° m.
AMERICAN Journal of science and art. N. Haven.	8° 2m.	BANKERS' Magazine. London	8° m.
AMERICAN Medical Times. New York	8° w.	BENTLEY'S Miscellany. London	8° m.
AMERICAN Phrenological Journal. New York	4° m.	*BERLIN. Akademie der Wissenschaften. Abhandlungen.	4°
AMERICAN Publisher's Circular. New York	4° w.	*— Monatsberichte. Berlin	8° m.
AMERICAN Quarterly Church Review. N. Haven.	8° q.	BIBLICAL Repertory. Philadelphia	8° q.
AMERICAN Railroad Journal. New York	4° w.	*BIBLIOGRAFIA Italiana. Milan	8° m.
*AMI (L') de l'enfance. Paris	8° m.	BIBLIOGRAPHIE de la France. Paris	1.8° w.
*ANNALES Archéologiques. Paris	4° m.	BIBLIOTHECA Sacra. Andover	8° q.
ANNALES Médico-Psychologiques. Paris	8° q.	BIBLIOTHÈQUE de Genève. Genève	8° m.
ANNALES de Chimie. Paris	8° m.	BLACKWOOD'S Edinburgh Magazine. Edinburgh.	8° m.
ANNALES d'Hygiène publique. Paris	8° q.	BLÄTTER für literarische Unterhaltung. Leipzig.	4° w.
*ANNALES de la Marine. Paris	8° m.	BON Ton, (Les). New York	4° m.
*ANNALES de la Propagation de la Foi. Paris	8° m.	*BOOK, (The) and its missions. London	8° m.
*ANNALES des mines. Paris	8° m.	BOSTON Medical and Surgical Journal. Boston.	8° w.
ANNALES des Ponts et Chaussées. Paris	8° m.	BRAITHWAITE'S Retrospect of practical medicine. New York	8° ½y.
*ANNALES des Sciences Naturelles. Paris	8° m.	BRITISH Quarterly Review. London	8° q.
ANNALS and Magazine of Natural History. London	8° m.	BRITISH Workman. London	f° m.
*ARCHIV für Anatomie. Leipzig	8° q.	BRITISH and Foreign Medico-Chirurgical Review. London	8° q.
*ARCHIV für Naturgeschichte. Berlin	8° un.	BROWNSON'S Quarterly Review. New York	8° q.
ARCHIV für das Studium der neueren Sprachen und Literaturen. Braunschweig	8° un.	BUILDER (The). London	f° w.
*ARCHIVES Diplomatiques. Paris	8° m.	BULLETIN de Thérapeutique Medicale. Paris	8° ½m.
*ART Journal. London	4° m.		

*BULLETIN des Lois. Paris . . . .   8° *un.*
*BULLETIN des Lois. Pte. Supplementaire. Paris.   8° *un.*
*BULLETIN du Bibliophile. Paris . . . .   8° *m.*
*BULLETIN du Bibliophile belge. Bruxelles . . . .   8° *un.*

*CENDRILLON. Paris . . . .   8° *m.*
CHAMBERS' Journal. London and Edinburgh . .   8° *m.*
CHRISTIAN Examiner. Boston . . . .   8° 2*m.*
CHRISTIAN Observer. London . . . .   8° *m.*
CHRISTIAN Review. Baltimore . . . .   8° *q.*
CHURCH monthly. Boston . . . .   4° *m.*
CIVIL Engineer and Architect's Journal. London.   4° *m.*
COLBURN's New Monthly Magazine. London . .   8° *m.*
COLBURN's United Service Magazine. London . .   8° *m.*
CONTINENTAL Monthly. New York . . . .   8° *m.*
CORNHILL MAGAZINE. London . . . .   8° *m.*
*CORRESPONDANCE Littéraire. Paris . . . . . .   8° *m.*
COTTON Supply Reporter. Manchester . . . . .   *un.*
COURRIER des États Unis. New York . . . . . .   f° *w.*
CRITIC, The. London . . . .   f° *m.*

DEBOW's Review. New Orleans . . . .   f° *m.*
*DEUTSCHE Jugendblätter. Dresden . . . .   4° 2*m.*
DUBLIN Quarterly Journal of Medical Science. Dublin . . . .   8° *q.*
DUBLIN Review. London . . . .   8° *q.*
DUBLIN University Magazine. Dublin . . . . . .   8° *m.*
DWIGHT's Journal of Music. Boston . . . .   4° *w.*

ECLECTIC Magazine. New York . . . .   8° *m.*
ECLECTIC Review. London . . . .   8° *m.*
ECONOMIST. London . . . .   f° *w.*
EDINBURGH Medical Journal. Edinburgh . . . .   8° *m.*
EDINBURGH New Philosophical Journal. Edinburgh . . . .   8° *q.*
EDINBURGH Review. London . . . .   8° *q.*
*EUROPA. Leipzig . . . .   8° *un.*
EVENING Mail. London . . . .   f° *tr-w.*
EXAMINER. London . . . .   f° *w.*

*FLECKEISEN. Jahrbücher für classische Philologie. Leipzig . . . .   8° *un.*
*FRANK Leslie's Pictorial. New York . . . . . .   f° *w.*
FRAZER's Magazine. London . . . .   8° *m.*
FRIEND of the people. London . . . .   4° *w.*

*GAZETTE des Hopitaux. Paris . . . .   f° *tr-w.*
GENTLEMAN's Magazine. London . . . .   8° *m.*
GODEY's Lady's Book. Philadelphia . . . .   8° *m.*
GOOD words. Edinburgh. . . . .   8° *m.*
*GÖTTINGEN. Königl. Gesellschaft der Wissenschaften. Abhandlungen. Göttingen . . . .   4° *un.*
*— Gelehrte Anzeigen. Göttingen . . . . . .   8° *w.*
*— — Nachrichten. Göttingen . . . .   8° *un.*

HARPER's Monthly Magazine. New York . . . .   8° *m.*
HARPER's Weekly. New York . . . .   f° *w.*
HEIDELBERGER Jahrbücher der Literatur. Heidelberg . . . .   8° *m.*
HISTORICAL Magazine. New York . . . .   4° *m.*
HOME Journal. New York . . . .   f° *w.*
HORTICULTURIST, and Journal of rural art and taste. New York . . . .   8° *m.*
HUNT's Merchants' Magazine, and Commercial Review. New York . . . .   8° *m.*

ILLUSTRATED London News. London . . . . . .   f° *w.*
ILLUSTRATED News of the World. London . . .   f° *w.*
ILLUSTRATED Times. London . . . .   f° *w.*
ILLUSTRATION (L'). Paris . . . .   f° *w.*
*ILLUSTRIRTE Welt. Stuttgart . . . .   8° 2*m.*
*ILLUSTRIRTE Zeitung. Augsburg . . . .   f° *w.*
INTELLECTUAL Observer. London . . . .   8° *m.*
IRISH Quarterly Review. Dublin . . . .   8° *q.*

*JAHN. Jahrbücher für Philologie. Dresden . . .   8° *m.*
*JOURNAL asiatique. Paris . . . .   8° *m.*
*JOURNAL de la Physiologie. Brown-Séquard. Paris . . . .   8° *q.*
*JOURNAL de Mathématiques. Paris . . . .   4° *m.*
JOURNAL de Médicine. Paris . . . .   8° *m.*

JOURNAL des Débats. Paris . . . .   f° *d.*
JOURNAL of the Franklin Institute. Philadelphia.   8° *m.*
*JURISPRUDENCE Générale. Paris . . . .   4° *m.*

KNICKERBOCKER. New York . . . .   8° *m.*
KRITISCHE Vierteljahreschrift. München . . . .   8° *q.*

LABOURER's Friend. London . . . .   8° *m.*
LANCET. London . . . .   4° *w.*
LEISURE hour. London . . . .   8° *m.*
*LIEBIG. Annalen der Chemie. Leipzig . . . . .   8° *m.*
LITERARY Gazette. London . . . .   4° *w.*
LITTELL's living age. Boston. . . . .   8° *w.*
LONDON. Chemical Society. Quarterly journal. London. . . . .   8° *q.*
— Geological Society. Quarterly Journal. Lond.   8° *q.*
*— Microscopical Society. Quarterly journal . . .   8° *q.*
*— Royal Agricultural Society. Journal. London.   8° *un.*
*— Royal Geographical Society. Journal. Lond.   8° *un.*
*— Society of Arts. Journal. London . . . .
*— Statistical Society. Journal. London . . . .   8° *q.*
LONDON, Edinburgh, and Dublin Philosophical Magazine. London. . . . .   8° *m.*
LONDON Society. London . . . .   8° *m.*

MACMILLAN's Magazine. London . . . .   8° *m.*
MASSACHUSETTS Teacher. Boston . . . .   8° *m.*
MECHANICS' Magazine. London . . . .   8° *m.*
MEDICAL Critic. London . . . .   8° *m.*
MEDICAL Times and Gazette. London . . . . . .   4° *w.*
*MÉMORIAL du Commerce. Paris . . . .   8° *m.*
METHODIST Quarterly Review. New York . . . .   8° *q.*
MISSIONARY Herald. Boston. . . . .   8° *m.*
MONEY Market Review (The). London . . . . . .   8° *w.*
MONITEUR Universel. Paris . . . .   f° *d.*
MONTHLY Religious Magazine. Boston . . . . . .   8° *m.*
*MUNICH. Königl. bayerische Akademie. Historische Classe. Abhandlungen. München .   4° *un.*
*— — Mathemat. Physikalische Classe. München   4° *un.*
*— — Philosoph. Philologische Classe. München   4° *un.*
*— — — Sitzungsberichte. München . . . . . .   8° *un.*
*— — Gelehrte Anzeigen. München . . . .   8° *un.*

NATIONAL Review. London . . . .   8° *q.*
NAUTICAL Magazine. London . . . .   8° *m.*
NEW England Historical and Genealogical Register. Boston. . . . .   8° *q.*
NEW-ENGLANDER. New Haven . . . .   8° *q.*
NEW Jerusalem Magazine. Boston . . . .   8° *m.*
NEW Orleans Medical and Surgical Journal. New Orleans. . . . .   8° 2*m.*
NEWTON's London Journal of Arts and Sciences. London . . . .   8° *m.*
NORTH American Review. Boston. . . . .   8° *q.*
NORTH British Review. Edinburgh . . . .   8° *q.*
NOTES and Queries. London. . . . .   4° *w.*
NUMISMATIC Journal. London . . . .   8° *q.*

ONCE a week. London . . . .   sm.4° *w.*

PARIS. Académie Impériale de Medicine. Bulletin. Paris. . . . .   8° 2*m.*
*— — Mémoires . . . .   4° *un.*
*— École des chartes. Bibliothèque. Paris . . .   8° *m.*
*— École polytechnique. Journal. . . . .   4° *un.*
*— Institut de France. Académie française. Recueil de discours . . . .   4° *un.*
*— — Académie des Inscriptions. Mémoires . . .   4° *un.*
*— — Académie des Sciences. Mémoires . . . .   4° *un.*
*— — — Comptes Rendus des Séances. Paris . . .   4° *w.*
*— — — Mémoires par divers savants . . . . .
*— — Acad. d. sciences morales. Séances et Travaux. Paris . . . .   8° *m.*
— Journal des savants. Paris . . . .   4° *m.*
*— Société géologique de France. Bulletin. Paris.   8° *m.*
*— — Mémoires . . . .
*— Société zoologique d'acclimatation. Bulletin. Paris . . . .   8° *m.*
*— Société d'encouragement pour l'industrie nationale. Bulletin. Paris . . . .   4° *m.*
*— Société de géographie. Bulletin. Paris. . . .   8° *m.*

PARTHENON. London . . . . 4° w.
*PETERMANN. Mittheilungen aus Justus Perthes'
   Geographischer Anstalt. Gotha . . . . . . 4° m.
PETERSON'S Ladies' National Magazine. Phil-
   adelphia. . . . . 8° m.
*PETZHOLDT'S Anzeiger f. Bibliogr. Dresden . . 8° m.
PHARMACEUTICAL Journal. London . . . . 8° m.
PHILANTHROPIST. London . . . . 4° m.
*POGGENDORFF'S Annalen der Physik und Chemie.
   Leipzig . . . . 8° m.
*POLYTECHNISCHES Journal. Stuttgart . . . . . 8° 2m.
POPULAR Science Review. London . . . . 8° q.
PRACTICAL Mechanics' Journal. London . . . . 4° m.
PUBLISHERS' Circular. London . . . . 8° ½m.
PUNCH. London . . . . 4° w.

QUARTERLY Review. London . . . . 8° q.

RANKING'S Abstract of the Medical Sciences. Lon-
   don . . . . 8° ½y.
REBELLION Record. New York . . . . 8° m.
REVUE des Deux Mondes. Paris . . . . 8° ½m.
REVUE Médicale. Paris . . . . 8° ½m.

ST. JAMES'S Magazine. London . . . . 8° m.
*ST. PETERSBURG. Académie Impériale, Bulletin.
   St. Pétersbourg . . . . 4° un.
*— - Mémoires. St. Pétersbourg . . . . 4° un.

SATURDAY Review. London . . . . sm. f° w.
SCIENTIFIC American. New York . . . . 4° w.
*SERAPEUM. Zeitschrift für Bibliothekwissen-
   schaft. Naumann. Leipzig . . . . 8° ½m.
SHARPE'S London Magazine. London . . . . . . 8° m.
SOUTHERN Literary Messenger. Richmond . . . . 8° m.
SPECTATOR. London . . . . sm. f° w.

TAIT'S Edinburgh Magazine. Edinburgh . . . . . 8° m.
TEMPLE Bar. London . . . . 8° m.

UNIVERSALIST Quarterly. Boston . . . . 8° q.

VANITY Fair. New York . . . . 4° w.
VETERINARIAN. London . . . . 8° m.
*VIENNA. Kaiserliche Akad. d. Wissensch. Math-
   ematisch - Naturwissenschaftliche Classe.
   Denkschriften. Wien . . . . 4° un.
*— — - Sitzungsberichte. Wien . . . . 8° m.
*— — - Philosophisch-Historische Classe. Denk-
   schriften. Wien . . . . 4° un.
*— — - Sitzungsberichte. Wien . . . . 8° q.
*ZEITSCHRIFT für die Gesammten Naturwissen-
   schaften. Berlin . . . . 8° m.
ZEITSCHRIFT für Musik. Leipzig . . . . 4° w.

WESTMINSTER Review. London . . . . 8° q

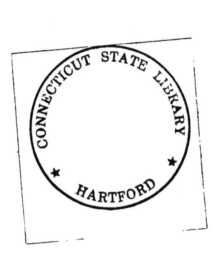

Lightning Source UK Ltd.
Milton Keynes UK
UKHW030708270620
365625UK00012B/1015